Power in the Isthmus

Power in the Isthmus

A Political History of Modern Central America

JAMES DUNKERLEY

VERSO

London · New York

First published by Verso 1988

Verso
UK: 6 Meard Street, London W1V 3HR
USA: 29 West 35th Street, New York, NY 10001-2291

Verso is the imprint of New Left Books

British Library Cataloguing in Publication Data

Dunkerley, James.
Power in the Isthmus: a political history
of Central America.
1. Central America, Political events
I. Title
972.8′053

ISBN 0 86091 912 9 pbk
0 86091 196 9 hbk

US Library of Congress Cataloging in Publication Data

Dunkerley, James.
Power in the Isthmus: a political history of Central America/
James Dunkerley.
p. cm.
Bibliography: p.
Includes index.
ISBN 0–86091–196–9. ISBN 0–86091–912–9 (pbk.)
1. Central America – Politics and government – 1821-1951.
2. Central America—Politics and government—1951– I. Title.
F1438.D86 1988
972.8—dc 19

Printed in Great Britain by Biddles Ltd., Guildford
Typeset by Falcon Graphic Art Ltd, Wallington, Surrey

To Barbara and the memory of Tony

Contents

List of Maps

La soberanía de un pueblo no se discute; se defiende con las armas en la mano.

Augusto César Sandino

Abbreviations

The following abbreviations have been adopted for reference to frequently used sources:

BIH	*Boletín Informativo Honduras* (Tegucigalpa)
CAR	*Central American Report* (Guatemala City)
ECA	*Estudios Centroamericanos* (San Salvador)
ESC	*Estudios Sociales Centroamericanos* (San José)
HAHR	*Hispanic American Historical Review*
JLAS	*Journal of Latin American Studies* (London)
LA	*Latin America* (London, 1967–76)
LAPR	*Latin American Political Report* (London, 1977–9)
LAWR	*Latin American Weekly Report* (London)
NYT	*New York Times*
RMS	*Revista Mexicana de Sociología* (Mexico City)
TW	*This Week* (Guatemala City)
WMR	*World Marxist Review* (Toronto edition)
WMRIB	*World Marxist Review Information Bulletin* (Toronto edition)

Where short titles for books and articles are used, please refer to the bibliography for full details.

Preface

There are many books in English on Central America. It is now possible to buy a review of Honduran politics, a study of Coca Cola workers in Guatemala or a survey of the peasantry of northern El Salvador in inexpensive paperback edition. This would have been inconceivable before 1979, when the Nicaraguan revolution ended decades of autocratic rule, challenged US hegemony in the Americas, and drove the isthmus into the international headlines. Less than a decade after the overthrow of the Somoza dictatorship Central America has become established as a prominent and permanent fixture in US foreign policy as well as an issue of some consequence to domestic political life. The interventionism and Cold War rhetoric of the Reagan administration naturally determined that the great bulk of the literature was concerned with US policy for and activity in the region, analysed from a multitude of perspectives and criticized from most.

One of the peculiarities of the present text is that it does not focus primarily on the role of the US. In part this is because I am not as qualified to dissect Washington's behaviour as I am incensed by it. In part it is because the critical political task of analysing and opposing US policy is widely recognized and has been shouldered by an increasing number of people. Perhaps most importantly, it is because however crucial and iniquitous the role of Washington in Central America, it is by no means the whole story. There is, indeed, some risk of the left throwing the baby out with the bathwater and losing sight of Central America itself. The five countries of the region – Panama and Belize are excluded from this account – are not simply victims or puppets of Washington. These countries are certainly very small, economically backward, and historically vulnerable to the mandate of the 'colossus to the north'. At the same time, they possess long and rich histories; they are societies more complex in their structure and political character than can be understood in terms of the vulgar designation 'banana republic'. The political crises and revolutionary upsurge of the late 1970s and early 1980s can only be comprehended in terms of the social systems that provoked them and within which they developed. For this reason an explanation of Central American politics in terms of US power and policy is necessary but still insufficient.

As the revolutionary advances of 1979–82 were stalled it became evident that much of the polemical and introductory literature published in the wake of the Nicaraguan revolution lacked the resource to explain a whole welter of issues. If the regional conflict could adequately be explained in terms of US imperialism, local autocracy and crushing poverty how was it that the revolutionary movement had succeeded only in Nicaragua? How and why had it been resisted in El Salvador and Guatemala, and to what effect? Why had it not taken place at all in Costa Rica and Honduras? These questions were not generally posed in solidarity circles that had a priority to denounce Washington's barbarities and defend revolutionary Nicaragua. Equally, they were seldom addressed in academic studies reluctant to engage with major new issues on the basis of rapid research and shallow analysis. And although they were considered in depth by Central Americans, very little of this local literature was translated and debated in the Anglo-Saxon world.

The idea for this book grew out of a concern with the critical gap between these parallel approaches. To test whether others shared this sense, that obvious but difficult questions were not being asked in the English-speaking milieu, it seemed better to try and answer them in a synthetic manner than simply to map out an agenda of desiderata. The approach adopted here is in no sense original and derives very heavily from the work of Central American intellectuals whose concerns predictably fuse the political with the academic in a much more profound manner than is readily achieved by a foreigner.

The text is organized as an orthodox historical narrative. The first part considers the region as a whole, chapters 1 to 4 covering general historical developments up to around 1950 whilst chapter 5 surveys the post-war economy. The second part consists of chapters dedicated to the modern politics of the separate countries, the exceptional case of Nicaragua being studied in two sections (pre- and post-1979). Given the fact that the history of five countries from the 1820s to the present is covered, it should be obvious that the level of detail is relatively low and attention to general phenomena correspondingly high. This is particularly true for the more distant history and although the focus narrows from 1950 onwards, restrictions of length and the deliberately broad compass mean that those seeking precise and detailed analysis of recent developments will have to look elsewhere.

Both physical and intellectual constraints have prompted a number of more questionable decisions. There is no discussion of the colonial period as such, the central legacies of the colony being briefly discussed in the first chapter. Since independence from Spain caused relatively slight social change this starting point will bemuse historians and those who hold persuasive theses that Central America can only be understood within the framework of colonial structures and mentalities. On the other hand, the nineteenth century retained enough of these for the broad character of the republican inheritance to be intelligible from a depiction of this period. Independence represents a cogent point of departure insofar as it moulded the states that exist today out of the societies that developed under Spanish rule from the terrible experience of the conquest. I have also chosen to avoid a general discussion of important contemporary phenomena, such as the radical Church, revolutionary theory, US economic and political strategy, concentrating instead upon their existence and effects in specific countries. This has entailed a particularly heavy reliance upon footnotes, which on occasions become a veritable subtext.

The effort to answer certain specific questions has not been developed into an attempt to respond to major interpretative issues such as the cause of revolutions, the nature of nationalism or the character of the peasantry. General theory and the construction of definitive models are beyond our scope. Apart from anything else, the pace of events in Central America in recent years has been too frantic to permit sober elaboration of any set of general definitions and principles other than those that are so abstract as to be of little direct value. Nevertheless, the text does possess two prominent themes, both of which withhold a tension if not an outright contradiction. The first – unity and diversity – is directed towards distinguishing the degree to which Central America constitutes a coherent whole and the extent to which its five constituent states and societies are distinct both from any general pattern and from each other. The second – continuity and rupture – is more directly historical in character and places emphasis upon the timing and pace of change. Clearly these two themes relate quite closely to each other and may be seen as little more than impressionistic devices. Still, they do provide some means for approaching key issues. The framework of unity and diversity, for example, offers an intelligible context for explaining why it was that five broadly comparable socio-economic systems in neighbouring countries produced three revolutionary crises and one successful assault on state power. Likewise, the exchange between continuity and rupture permits a more sensitive appreciation of the differing historical impetus of apparently similar phenomena. Perhaps most important in this regard is the identification of critical points of change in the past that have seeded a particular legacy, such as that of Sandino in Nicaragua or the 1944–54 'revolution' in Guatemala. For our purposes it allows one to retain the matrix of the contemporary crisis for viewing historical developments without endowing them with a linear logic and inevitability.

The manifest danger of a survey of this type is that it will fall between two stools. By depicting the existing English literature on Central America as formed by two broad currents – solidarity and academic – I am, of course, inflicting a gross injustice upon scores of authors who have written politically informed and committed work based upon painstaking research and of considerable intellectual value. Moreover, this account depends very heavily upon sources that belong to both these figurative groups. The imagery should, therefore, be seen as a mechanism convenient for an author who has a foot planted in both camps and is acutely aware of his vulnerability to charges of precious irrelevance on the one hand and massive oversimplification on the other. It is customary in such cases to protect one's flanks by espousing a desire to provoke debate and further work. Predictable, presumptuous and pious though it may be, this is certainly the case here. Perhaps the generous traditions of radical scholarship will beguile those infinitely better versed in Central American history and politics than I to pardon the inordinate liberties taken with profoundly complex issues. It is equally to be hoped that they might mollify comrades in Central America and abroad disturbed by an excessive and nervous complication of life.

My knowledge of Central America, like that of many students of the region, was negligible before 1979. The limits and fragility of subsequent progress are amply evident in the pages that follow but they would have been very much greater were it not for the advice, support and criticism of a number of individuals. I am grateful to my colleagues at the Kellogg Institute, University of Notre Dame, and the Department of Political Studies, Queen Mary College, University of London, for tolerating absences and what was at the very least distracted behaviour. While sketching the plan for the book at Kellogg I benefited considerably from the friendship and intellectual stimulus of Alex Wilde and Ian Roxborough, who is the maestro of unity and diversity. David Ruccio and Oscar Ugarteche tried with great energy to make the Nicaraguan economy intelligible to me whilst Carol Smith, James Painter and George Lovell have indulged my arriviste opinions on Guatemala with a generosity that is spectacular in view of the singular complexity of that country and the enormous time and care evidently required to make some sense of it. Nicky Miller kindly lent me her unpublished thesis on Soviet policy; Laurence Whitehead and Malcolm Deas gave me the benefit of their very different but equally stimulating and knowledgeable views. Both Zayda Ureña in San José and Raquel Caravia in London provided material with a diligence that is rare in others but not in them. Those who are familiar with the core debates in Central American historiography will appreciate how much this book owes to the work of Edelberto Torres Rivas and Rafael Menjívar. I must also thank both for supplying me with other material. As my original editor, Neil Belton trespassed well beyond the bounds of duty in steering the text through a number of rocky passages. Leslie Bethell and Perry Anderson commented upon a draft with impressive speed and a range of original suggestions, a few of which I have been sensible enough to adopt and thus improve important passages. The eccentricities and sheer bloody-mindedness born of three years' writing have been supported far from effortlessly by Penny, Jutta, Ana María and, most of all, Bill. They have finally convinced me that I should view the word processor more in the light of a labour-saving device than as furniture for witless yuppies too indolent to do the job with a pencil, and it is only through their love that I have managed this work with the latter instrument. The fact that a high percentage of this long list would not wish to be associated with many of the opinions I advance only goes to show how generous they have been and confirms that the customary exclusion of all collaborators from responsibility for the end result is both real and necessary.

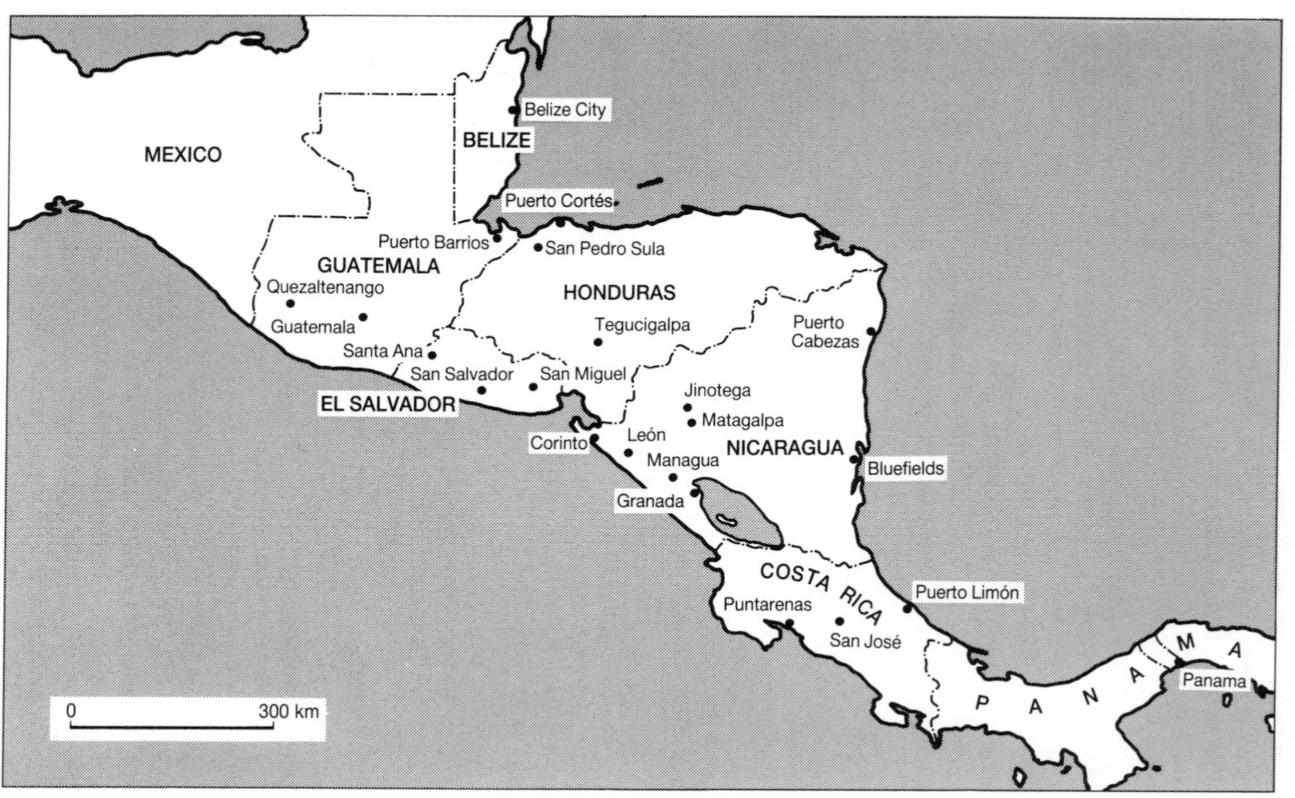

Central America

1

The Formation of a Liberal Regime, 1820–1910

[Central Americans] are, have been, and for ages will remain entirely unfit for any government under heaven but an unqualified despotism.

US Consul Charles Savage, 22 August 1832[1]

[We require] an ordinance for the fulfilment of the obligations of personal labour so that the authorities might, on such occasions as are necessary, compel those who make a commitment and then break it without just cause to meet their obligation . . . this is of the utmost importance . . . whilst in the more civilized countries the failure to fulfil a contract for personal labour leads only to an action for damages against the culprit, in those that are less civilized the matter cannot and should not be so restrained. It is essential that authority intervene in order to compel them to work . . . it is also necessary that there is efficient and zealous action on the part of the same authority to repress energetically the frequent infringements of contracts by our workers. The enforcement of work in a prudent fashion is the best means by which to repress vagrancy, drunkenness and other vices, and it is the best way to develop agriculture.

Submission of *La Sociedad Económica* to President Vicente Cerna, Guatemala City, 17 May 1866[2]

Although the crisis in contemporary Central America is 'modern' insofar as many of its causes and much of its character can be attributed to developments since 1945, its roots are to be found in the contradictions of a social structure established in the late nineteenth century. The endurance of the system of production and socio-political domination introduced by the Liberal free-trade regimes from the 1870s has kept twentieth-century Central America in a state of backwardness and thus, figuratively, closer to its history. There is no direct, linear descent in this history; the ruptures, permutations and piecemeal disappearances obtain just as much as they did between the colonial era and the early republican period. Yet nowhere has there been a qualitative eradication of the Liberal legacy and its own colonial inheritance such that these might now be accounted no more than a primitive background.

If this is true for the socio-economic aspects of the present crisis, it is equally so for the political features of the conflict since these have revolved as much around the issue of national sovereignty as they have around that of underdevelopment. The unexpected agreement of August 1987 by the five governments of the isthmus to attempt a local resolution of the crisis in the face of alternative proposals tabled by Washington indicates that a regional identity has not been entirely erased by 150 years of separate nationhood or the deep divisions of recent years. Central America is neither a collection of uniform 'banana republics' distinguishable solely by the degree of nuisance they cause the US nor a set of completely heterogeneous states with some ephemeral cultural ties. The tension between unity and diversity within the region is today as potent an element as is that between continuity and rupture. Again, it is to the last century that one must look to grasp the roots of the present pattern. Indeed, it would be perfectly plausible to regress further still into the colonial history of the Captaincy General of Guatemala, which incorporated the present states of Central America, but for the purposes of a predominantly 'political' perspective the rupture with Madrid provides a viable point of departure.

In September 1821 Central America declared formal independence from Spain, the provinces' future remaining uncertain for the next two decades, and particularly so until 1823, when they successfully resisted inclusion within the transitory Mexican 'empire' set up by General Iturbide. Defence of the colonial limits of the Captaincy General against Mexican expansionism was shared by the fluid camps of Liberals and Conservatives, but the subsequent formation of the Central American Federal Republic was primarily a Liberal initiative, reflecting the strength of this more radical political current in the immediate aftermath of independence. Liberal ascendancy soon proved to be as fragile as the Federal Republic, the forces of secularism and free trade being driven into full retreat by the mid 1830s and the Republic finally dismantled in July 1838, when full independence was devolved to the parts that could not make a whole. There followed three decades of Conservative hegemony marked by economic stasis and political instability. The failure to give life to the ideal of union and the distended chaos that accompanied the construction of individual states owed less to partisan antagonism than to the structural conditions which underpinned this process of factionalism within the dominant sectors. Pockets of commercial agriculture and allied mercantile circuits existed in a much more extensive economy dedicated to subsistence farming and petty commodity production within a semi-permeable provincialism, yielding very little revenue to a minuscule state apparatus controlled through the conduct of a largely pre-modern politics. This revolved around ad hoc military levees, a concept of public office derived from colonial tradition and the experience of owning land (and directing more or less unfree labour) along with minimal attention to matters beyond the retention of power, maintenance of 'public order', and a suitable distribution of the perquisites of office.

It was not until the late 1870s that, in the wake of the Mexican movement, a second generation of Liberals was able to consolidate its conquest of political power and introduce measures providing for the expansion of capitalist agriculture. The character and strength of this resurgent Liberalism varied quite widely, its ideas having already regained ground in Costa Rica by the 1840s whilst they continued to lack a viable socio-economic base in Honduras until the twentieth century. 'Modern' Liberalism possessed the vestiges of a democratic voice, pitched against the conservative 'oligarchy' as well as the Church, but in Central America it never acquired the popular momentum witnessed in Mexico or Colombia. Its central feature was the pursuit of free trade and expansion of commercial agriculture, both of which were prejudicial to the immediate interests of the mass of the population. Equally, the Liberals of the 1870s no longer placed the reformation of the Federal Republic at the top of their agenda, which was altogether less ambitious than that held by forebears as mesmerized by the ideals of the North American and French revolutions as they were exalted by the advent of independence from Spain. Instead, the second generation consolidated their republics under the mandate of the free market, which equated democracy with property and remained unchallenged for half a century, as evidenced by the longevity of the constitutions introduced by the new oligarchy: Guatemala, 1879–1945; El Salvador, 1886–1945; Nicaragua, 1893–1939; Costa Rica, 1871–1949; Honduras, 1894–1924.

At the time of independence the population of Central America probably did not exceed 1.25 million people, a third of whom lived in Guatemala and only 75,000 of whom populated the province of Costa Rica. By the outbreak of World War One the isthmus was inhabited by some five million people, as many of them living in Guatemala City as had populated all of Costa Rica in

1825. This was, of course, still a rural and widely dispersed population, but over the previous decades hundreds of thousands of its members had been drawn into a system of commercial agriculture that, first through coffee and then bananas, had multiplied revenues and produced critical alterations in the structure and dynamics of land, labour and capital. These developments in turn provided a basis for tangible nation states to replace the republicanized provinces that had existed under Conservative domination. In political as well as economic terms, therefore, the nineteenth century proved to be a period of considerable national change as well as of parochial vegetation. By the end of it significant portions of society still conducted their lives much the same as they had under colonial rule but many aspects of existence had taken on a form similar to that prevailing today.

The Colonial Inheritance

Neither the geographical nor the social distribution of wealth and power was significantly altered by the rupture of the old Captaincy General or 'Kingdom' of Guatemala from Spain. The termination of nigh-on three centuries of colonial administration, of the transfer of surplus through trade monopoly and taxes, statutory direction of the affairs of the Indian population, and disbursement of posts, land grants and *fueros* (the corporate privileges of Church and military establishments) entailed no profound social conflict. It was arrived at through a series of meetings between local merchants, landlords and dignitaries and a now woefully isolated and disorientated cluster of Spanish officials, denied any clear mandate by the reimposition in the metropolis of the Liberal 1812 Constitution. This charter effectively met many of the demands of local creoles in conceding more local government, freer trade and greater liberty of the press (which in this region might be more meaningfully construed as 'opinion') as well as undermining the *fueros*, which operated as a form of sinecurial conduit for social mobility and distribution of privilege.[3] Moreover, the claims of Mexico to the Captaincy General provided a further complication insofar as Iturbide's assumption of the title of emperor clashed with the emergent spirit of local republicanism although the Mexican regime itself derived from a series of insurrections against Spanish forces that effectively precluded uprisings in the isthmus itself. Although Iturbide's grandiose scheme collapsed within two years and left the provinces of the old Captaincy General to their own devices, it resulted in the secession of Chiapas and the first major deployment of troops in the region. Henceforth, the settlement of disputes between the landed and merchant groups of what were first termed 'provinces', then 'states' and finally – more than two decades after independence – 'republics' was principally by resort to military intervention.

In a very few cases, such as the Honduran Liberal crusader Morazán, this process threw up a posthumous heroic image that might serve to compensate for the absence of sacrifice on behalf of the nation against the colonial oppressor. Yet it did little, compared to other Latin American republics, to upset the internal balance of the creole elite, engender a distinct military caste, produce significant demographic shifts through attrition or propel the emergence of new political sectors.

The first step in 'national liberation' was essentially conservative – the *ayuntamientos* or *cortés*, in which clusters of provincial dignitaries debated the best course for their localities, were more consultative bodies produced by the late reforms of the Bourbon monarchy than organs of the third estate imposed by some waxing bourgeois democratic strain. They were also bereft of experience of struggle against Spain and its local allies – an absence that was to preserve much confusion and in-fighting for the post-independence era. This chaos was indeed critical in its political effects and often materially destructive, but it revolved about an internal distribution of power. Its long-term consequence was that the founding fathers of this gaggle of quasi-states were divided between the defeated upholders of federalism, for whom posterity was to provide no grateful nation, and the victorious proponents of provincial autonomy, whose legacy was less the conquest of alien power or forging of national consciousness than resistance to the ideal of union. The mythic qualities of original nationhood were thus quite depleted. Despite a lugubrious historiography persistently in pursuit of centuries of patriotic heritage – it was dug out of Indian resistance to the conquistadores, out of the truculence of these same conquistadores towards a crown less than even-handed in grants of lands and Indians, out of similar attitudes displayed by merchants hamstrung by the fleet system – these were nations that owed more to internecine strife than to anti-imperialist struggle. There was scarcely less confusion in the rest of Latin America during the post-independence period, and several states – Ecuador, Venezuela, Colombia, Argentina, Uruguay – emerged well after severance from Spain. Yet each had been the site of battles against the metropolitan power and could lay some form of claim to this as part of their patrimony, fixing it far more prominently than parochial disputes in the constellation of images that form what Benedict Anderson has termed the 'imagined community'.[4]

Such matters might appear rather rarefied, but they have purchase in as much as 'national liberation' struggles are taking place during the 1980s in states that acquired formal sovereignty two years after the Florida purchase and two decades before the incorporation of Texas and the entire western seaboard into the US. Clearly the capacity of the US to evacuate much of the substance from such sovereignty in the twentieth century is a critical element in this, but it is not solely an issue of subjugation. The marked insufficiency of material bases for the constitution of genuine nation states through most of the nineteenth century was paralleled by a lack of ideological ordnance for the local dominant blocs beyond that shipped in from Europe and North America or carried over from the colony. This historic absence of a genuinely indigenous component to what one can, without fear of embarrassment, term bourgeois democracy was to be overcome erratically and episodically, but rarely to such a degree that more modern rulers could draw upon a compelling native lineage of republican citizenship in order to forestall demands for a 'new' nation – one genuinely liberated and not simply cobbled together out of a colonial province.

Independence 'made a sovereign state of every village', and even fifty years later, on the cusp of the Liberal 'revolutions', Central America was a 'fragmented and feuding cluster of city states calling themselves republics'.[5] Insofar as a notion of collectivity existed beyond the constricted circles of landlords, merchants and clerics, it cannot have been of anything more than a *patria chica*, a community of neighbours. Certainly, for the Indian communities it was assessed, on those occasions when it took the form of state power, by the degree of intrusion and level of exaction that had to be resisted. These communities had been subjected to extraordinary exploitation and oppression, but they had also been afforded a measure of judicial protection by the crown. Many landlords also shunned a comprehensive overturning of the colonial system once the transfer of the surplus to Cadiz was halted. The recession in trade of rural produce and the absence of new dynamic crops provided little incentive to appropriate further tracts of land and antagonize the vast majority of the population who were subsistence agriculturalists. In this they were at one with the Church, which, like all sectors, lacked a completely uniform stance but was indisputably set against the rise of a secular republic and designs upon its own wealth. Although this was – sometimes quite consciously – an ill-fitted and sometimes contradictory alliance, it expressed a historical limitation on the ideals of Liberalism.

The Federation was also prejudiced by the imbalances between its constituent parts, most obviously in terms of concentration of population. Guatemala possessed over one-third of the total (595,000), the rest of the states, except El Salvador (248,000), being dwarfed by both this and the insufficiency of their own human stock to populate large areas of land and undertake more than scattered cultivation of foodstuffs with occasional participation in export agriculture that was seldom labour intensive. Although often hemmed into limited tracts of national territory, the inhabitants of Honduras (135,000), Nicaragua (186,000) and Costa Rica (75,000) could provide no alternative to Guatemalan hegemony and yet their provincial elites resisted submitting to it in exchange for fealty to Madrid.[6] As the seat of the Captaincy General, Guatemala was well endowed with officials and clerics; as the commercial nucleus of the isthmus its merchants continued to attract opprobium even after being deprived of administrative monopoly; as a state with a massive Indian population it possessed more troops than any other centre. It has been said that if they did not form part of this colonial administrative apparatus, creoles migrated as far as possible to escape its controls. Yet Guatemala also possessed a university that had weaned as many ardent Liberals as defenders of the old order. Its own internal divisions between the promulgation of the 1824 Constitution – a fusion of the Spanish charter of 1812 and the US Constitution – and the final collapse of the Federation in 1838 frequently mirrored those elsewhere. One distinction, which was to affect the local balance of power as well as to contribute to the defeat of the Federation, was the primacy of Guatemala City within the state (Quezaltenango being of marginal importance). In the other states political and commercial power was contested between various towns: León and Granada in Nicaragua; San José and Cartago in Costa Rica; Comayagua and Tegucigalpa in Honduras; San Salvador, San Vicente and Sonsonate in El Salvador.[7] Hence, the 'national' representations in the Federal Congress neither indicated a clear ideological affiliation nor guaranteed consistent regional policies. Moreover, the Congress had to contend with those of the various states that, whatever the dominant faction, contested its fiscal demands.

All these factors underwrote the demise of a Central American nation. Yet the process of dispersion was not without important political characteristics, and independence was not simply reducible to a regression into parochialism. Many in the Liberal vanguard were landlords of resource and authority, more still were resolutely anti-clerical. An appreciable constituency could perceive in the Liberal programme of free trade, modern civic codes and the concept of land as property to be disposed of on an open market the means by which to break free of colonial restrictions, which often elided with Guatemalan control and thereby bestowed on Liberalism its own appeal to localist interest. The challenge was, therefore, not lacking in weight at an ideological level; for a while it threatened to give substance to independence, and it was fifteen years before this possibility was definitively erased.

Shortly before independence the Church owned some 900 haciendas and sugar mills.[8] Many lay members of the elite viewed this property as under mortmain, an anachronistic and privileged possession exploited solely for corporate welfare. The Church's tithe constituted a considerable fiscal imposition, especially for peasant farmers, and was a major obstacle to the raising of secular taxes. The number of priests was relatively small, but both the wealth they controlled and the degree of influence they exercised were considerably greater than is readily appreciated today. Furthermore, the Church was a particularly appealing target since even before independence sections of it had come under attack: the Bourbon expulsion of the Jesuits in 1767 had preceded a phase of expropriation of lands of some pious communities early in the nineteenth century. (In Costa Rica sales of these holdings between 1805 and 1808 produced more than 23,000 pesos whereas expropriation between 1833 and 1842 yielded some 31,000.[9]) The Church was also divided regionally, San Salvador in particular evidencing sharp opposition to Guatemala's refusal to grant it a bishopric even though the Spanish monarchy had elevated San Salvador to the status of an intendancy in 1786. When the Salvadoreans unilaterally declared the moderate Liberal José Matías Delgado their bishop the Vatican denounced him as a schismatic and refused to recognize the see until 1842, when it included only twenty-four priests. (El Salvador had to wait until 1929 for its archbishopric.)

The struggle was fiercest in Guatemala, whence the archbishop and 289 friars were exiled to Cuba in 1829. Piecemeal expropriation of property preceded suppression of the tithe in 1832, the reduction of religious holidays, establishment of civil marriage, legalized divorce, and secular education.[10] Elsewhere the offensive was less zealous but still involved prohibition of tithes and persecution of anti-Liberal clerics in addition to the seizure of lands. By the mid 1830s the clergy had become a bastion of Conservative opposition to the new order; Costa Rican priests even attempted a rising in 1835. Although the alienation of much religious property was broadly accepted and became sufficiently incorporated into the public sphere (as private freehold) to ensure that the Liberal measures in this quarter were never fully reversed, the suppression of the tithe and religious responsibility for education were probably net losses for much of the population – the tithe was replaced by often more exigent taxes and education largely fell by the wayside. Disruption of familiar religious administration, the paternalist attractions of which should not be underestimated, was complemented by the attempt to refurbish the legal system in 1837 with the introduction of trial by jury and the 'Livingston Codes', initially drawn up for Louisiana (where they were never applied). This was seen as no less alien than the Liberals' European colonization plans that were designed to encompass nearly a half of Guatemala's territory, provoking an outburst of xenophobia. Trial by jury was perceived less as a democratic advance than as a centralist imposition; it was seen as an insult for literate creoles and *ladinos* faced with the possibility of judgement by illiterate Indians, and an attack on both formal and informal juridical traditions followed in the countryside. It was a completely impracticable and idealist piece of egalitarianism; some Conservatives were also adepts of Benthamite utilitarianism, but few of its designs, bar those for gaols, proved workable.[11]

Liberal endeavours to provide a free market in land were more restrained and do not appear to have fuelled widespread encroachment on either municipal commons (*ejidos*) or the lands of Indian communities (*tierras comunales*). Patterns varied, but even in Guatemala the distribution ordered in 1825 and 1829 was limited to unoccupied state-owned lands (*baldíos*).[12] However, economic policy was contradictory and eventually self-defeating. Having outlawed personal service as a form of rent in 1829 and thereby antagonized many landlords, the government backtracked and introduced first a vagrancy law and then the *mandamiento*, a colonial mechanism for forced labour which naturally produced discontent amongst the rural masses.[13] These fitful exchanges between laissez faire and colonial initiatives were most pronounced in Guatemala and underpinned the popularity of Conservative reaction there, but the failure to establish a viable source of revenue was generalized, reflecting a more extensive impediment to even superficial modernity.

For the Indian population of Spanish America tribute to the crown was a two-edged sword. On the one hand, it compelled participation in the market for labour and goods, generally reducing the communal surplus. On the other, it reaffirmed communal status and with it rights to inalienable lands and royal protection from both creole and *ladino* abuses. In many places after independence Liberal regimes abolished the tribute, incorporating into their new republican codes the essence of the 1812 constitution's stipulation that anyone born in a Spanish possession and not of African ancestry was a full citizen and therefore to be taxed according to their means. However, the fiscal requirements of the state and resistance of the communities frequently obliged reversion to the tax, often the principal source of revenue in republics with a large indigenous population.[14] This was the case in Central America, with over a third of the Federal government's income of $460,000 in 1825 being derived from the tribute.[15] Yet by no means all communities embraced this tax as the cost of guaranteeing corporate rights, especially when it was levied without any semblance of negotiation. In the spring of 1820 Indian leaders in the Guatemalan province of Totonicapán challenged the Spanish authorities in Guatemala City to halt collection on the grounds that under the restored constitution they were now citizens and not obliged to pay. This movement – led by the *cacique* Atanasio Tzul who had refused to levy the tribute in 1816 – proved very popular and posed a sharp threat of mass mobilization. It required the deployment of 400 troops, and even after the government climbed down tension was not fully dissipated until the leaders were given a full amnesty. The Totonicapán revolt has sometimes been depicted as an attempted restoration of the Quiché kingdom, threatening the outbreak of a caste war, and Tzul himself was (unreliably) reported to have dressed as the Spanish king. But the issue was more limited and soon deprived of its most dangerous elements when the Indian leadership was obliged to raise funds in order to pay for the costs of its petitions.[16] Although subsequent disturbances were directed against new taxes, Totonicapán proffered a sobering illustration of the dangers of misconceived exaction.

These dangers were persistently embraced by the Liberals, whose reduction of the sales tax (*alcabala*) on textiles in the name of free trade deprived the exchequer of important income that unaltered state monopolies on liquor, tobacco, playing cards and gunpowder could not replace. The result was the imposition in 1832 of a head tax of two pesos – a not inconsiderable sum for most peasants – on the entire population, as well as lesser charges on the sale of meat and certain crops. The head tax soon proved completely unenforceable in El Salvador and was a contributory factor in the 1833 rebellion in Los Nonualcos that dwarfed Totonicapán in its violence and challenge to creole authority. In Guatemala the tax was levied but, along with extraordinarily ill-advised imposts on Indian communal revenues, it undoubtedly stirred discontent and fortified the clerical/Conservative campaign against both the Federation and Liberalism. Subsequent concessions on the part of the Liberal regime to demands for protectionism failed to stave off political defeat, further emphasizing the strength of colonial tradition.

The scope of fiscal problems at independence was determined by the productive capacity of the isthmian states and hence diminished only marginally after the collapse of the Federation. It was certainly the case that the project of a regional government exacerbated difficulties, but in practice the Federal revenues were always less than, and constantly undermined by, those of the separate states.[17] In 1824 the minister of finance of the state of Guatemala confessed that matters were so chaotic that it was impossible to assess income; in all likelihood it barely exceeded $200,000 a year for the following decade.[18] The decline in local mining reduced access of local mints to bullion, and as early as 1825 debased coinage was being issued in Tegucigalpa. Ten years later new clipped coin was authorized in Honduras and El Salvador; the effects of this on both local and international commerce were compounded by a notable refusal by Indian communities to release their stocks of strong coin, probably upon clerical advice. Although the position improved upon the Liberal defeat, the tradition of hoarding coin continued well beyond the appearance of the first banks in the 1880s. Lack of local specie allowed the free circulation of British, US, Chilean, Bolivian and Peruvian coin (that of the latter two states at both full and debased value) which entered through the commercial circuit.[19] Whilst each republic necessarily respected the intrinsic value of its neighbours' currencies, it still proved necessary to conduct many transactions in cacao beans, in the case of Nicaragua until as late as 1900.[20] In 1870, following an improvement in acquisition of bullion, Guatemala's official monetary stock amounted to $4.2 million, $1.5 million of which was in foreign coin.[21] Under such circumstances, the direct booty available through control of the state was evidently quite limited, and the purchase of the state upon civil society as a whole was even more constrained. For fifty years after the Barclay loan of £1 million in 1827 there were very few sources of external finance that could be embezzled, there was not enough local bullion for a recurrent source of accumulation through direct appropriation, and the tax base could not sustain more than a handful of sinecures. Yet, by the same token, state power was relatively accessible.

At the beginning of the republican period professional military forces were very slight indeed; Guatemala City had a garrison of 250 men, and there were less than 600 in the rest of the province.[22] El Salvador possessed two battalions but depended upon frantic mobilization of civilian militias and the dispatch of regular troops from Guatemala in order to suppress Anastasio Aquino's 1833 revolt, a process which took an entire month to organize.[23] The normal yardstick for military establishment was the existence of Indians and Blacks under the colony. It was by virtue of their absence, or at least minimal presence, that Costa Rica reached statehood without a standing force, managed thereafter by occasionally raising a militia out of a population that could scarcely afford any depletion of its labour force, and never sustained more than a few hundred troops as a formal army up to the point of its abolition in 1948.[24] Nicaragua, on the other hand, maintained some regular forces through much of the nineteenth century, as she had done in the eighteenth, to establish at least nominal control of the San Juan river against any British incursion from the Miskito coast.[25] Through most of this period these forces bore little resemblance to modern armies. Even by the early twentieth century, when Europeans and Chileans were drafted in to instil some notion of professional conduct, they had not evolved a great deal: of the 195 cadets enrolled in the Honduran military academy between 1903 and 1906, sixty deserted and thirty were released as unfit or dismissed for bad conduct.[26]

Despite all this, military activity was extremely important. Armies were less professionalized than socialized; contenders for power pressganged peons in their localities (but preferably not off their own lands), sustained them on freelance foraging and forced loans, and frequently stood a good chance of besting an 'official' army little better trained or armed. Very few ever approached the size of the 13,000-strong Guatemalan force under General Barrios that invaded El Salvador in 1885, but a great many started out, as did Barrios in 1871, with fourteen officers and fourteen men.[27] These armies were, then, small, rapidly mustered and equally speedily disbanded, but they were persistently in action. Salvadorean troops engaged in forty battles even before the collapse of the Federation; by the time the Liberals took power in Honduras in 1876 that country had been ruled by more than fifty separate administrations, many of them installed by force, or at least the movement of armed men.[28] Outside Guatemala a turnover of this order was high but not abnormal; it generally rotated persons of the same class and minimal difference in ideology (upon which a high premium was not necessarily placed) through the offices of a state with little authority.[29]

However, recruitment did have a social impact that extended even to the very *Indios* whom the forces of order were supposed to vigilate. One of the causes of the 1833 revolt in Santiago Nonualco may well have been the news that Indians of that region who had been forced to serve in the garrison of San Miguel had been attacked and slaughtered by the *ladino* population of the town.[30] Conscription was evaded everywhere in much the same way as were the taxmen, and such evasion was often more damaging to production than was the passage of an army. It could be said of many an absentee landlord ensconced in his townhouse that, 'He had gone through several revolutions, securely locked in, eating and sleeping as usual', but crops on plantations as well as subsistence plots suffered as able-bodied peasants made themselves scarce.[31] This was particularly true of indigo, which required relatively little labour in sowing or cultivation, but needed to be picked at a precise time and then processed intensively.[32] The flight of peasants, Indians and *ladinos* alike, was sometimes prompted by fear of recruitment for the *corvée* or plantation, but until the arrival of coffee it was primarily in order to provide soldiers that new vagrancy laws were enacted. In Guatemala such a law remained on the statute book until 1945, but both there and in El Salvador the practice of the rural populace taking refuge from both conscription and passing armies remains as widespread in the late 1980s as it did a century ago.[33]

For Guatemalan Indians the culture of refuge spans all history since the Conquest and has led to their society being described as a scattering of closed corporate communities.[34] The ability to sustain resistance against creole/*ladino* state and society in physical or social form and by defensive or offensive means has varied considerably. At the end of the 1830s it took the shape of an aggressive social mobilization that cowed even its clerical and Conservative sponsors, effectively prolonging the epoch of paternalist colonial control for a further forty years. This should not be viewed solely as a response to provocative Liberal measures that lacked social backing or even to the coincidental outbreak of cholera in 1837, which ravaged the population of the highlands and compounded superstitions spread abroad two years before when the eruption of the volcano Cosigüina in Nicaragua blacked out the sun for a week.[35] Priests certainly played on this anguish and laid responsibility for the calamities upon the sin of Liberalism, yet their agency was but one figure in the resistance of communities that had to some appreciable degree recovered from both the initial demographic collapse of the Conquest and the disruptive, centrifugal dynamics of labour on indigo plantations, which had been in decline in Guatemala itself for several decades. Although its replacement, cochineal, was subject to a no less concentrated system of processing and marketing, it was generally cultivated on small *ladino* properties, and because it generated little demand for external labour has been described as a 'democratic' crop.[36] This might be the case in comparison with coffee, but it is plain that even a production that peaked in 1854 at 2.5 million lbs of the dyestuff cultivated over 510,000 acres exercised only low pressure on the lands and disposable labour power of the communities.[37] Despite being stricken in 1847 by a plague that affected the insects which feed off the *nopal* plant and from which the dye is extracted, severe storms in 1852 which destroyed the *nopales* themselves, and the progressive adoption of synthetic dyes in Europe from the mid 1850s that made the shift to coffee imperative, cochineal may be said to have provided the material basis for the Conservative republic.

Neither the *ejidos* nor the *tierras comunales* were ever entirely free of pressure upon their considerable holdings. Poor *ladinos* were excluded from the communities and often laboured under the status of 'strangers'; this was very disturbing for the Liberal concept of land and nationhood and yet integral to the preservation of Indian society.[38] When not employed on haciendas this sector frequently took to squatting on uncultivated land that was often within the bounds of the commons or, occasionally, to subleasing such land, thereby extending the circuit of emphyteusis under which perhaps 70 per cent of Guatemala's best land was still held, albeit seldom with title. Such a form of tenancy was legally permitted, in contrast to de facto appropriation through cattle grazing, a particularly efficacious means of establishing claims to land on the basis of precedent in an era when the precision of boundaries was not sanctioned by barbed wire.[39] Some creole landlords, like Barrios himself, extended the frontiers of private holdings in such a fashion, but as a rule they could not legally register it under Conservative governments.[40]

By the end of the 1850s discontent over the degree to which the indigenous subsistence lands were protected was growing: 'The Indians have always objected to seeing the land they do not cultivate given to others who do, and it is my wish . . . to develop a new source of wealth, such as coffee. . . . As far as the *ejidos* are concerned, these chief sources of wealth are quite extensive in many Indian villages, which only grow corn and beans and which today, and in the future, will only take up a very small part of that expanse.'[41] Nevertheless, communities frequently managed to stave off incursions by making recourse to arson, legal dispute or other means. The fear of provoking open rebellion remained strong: 'the Indians are not prepared to give up their lands and have suggested as much with words and deeds, and though it might seem appropriate to distribute the land so that agriculture might prosper, this ought to be done gradually, and coupled with the participation of the Indians. To proceed otherwise would encourage a series of complaints, protests and friction.'[42] Much of the rationale for the continued defence of the common lands stemmed from this fear; its effect was the maintenance of a level of rural subsistence that was certainly higher than that at the end of the century and very probably than that of today – a remarkable fact that is often ignored in contemporary debate.[43] Moreover, while the Conservative regime did not remove the vagrancy law from the statutes, it was not enforced with vigour. Equally, although the practice of advancing debts to Indians as a means of acquiring labour obligations was eventually reinstated, the system was not actively encouraged, giving rise to the complaints of the *Sociedad Económica*. In 1851 the government went so far as to revive the colonial *Leyes de las Indias* which restored the labour draft but also established the office of 'Protector of Indians' for a population that by dint of once again becoming 'wards of the state' was entitled to free legal representation.[44]

These measures were implemented under the 28-year rule of Rafael Carrera, a *ladino* swineherd who had taken the leadership of the peasant insurrectionary movement of 1837 and thereafter artfully exploited the military skills, political cunning and common touch typically ascribed to Latin American *caudillos* either to manipulate the Conservative gentlemen who held office or to occupy it himself. As a parochial firebrand egged on by the priests in an atmosphere of rural antipathy towards Liberalism that acquired almost messianic proportions, Carrera rose to prominence on an oppositional platform that could not fail to gather support: the eradication of the Livingston Codes, abolition of the head tax, prohibition of civil marriage and divorce ('*ley de perros*'), resumption of the traditional place of the Church and the social contracts of the colonial order.[45] His barefoot troopers outfought Liberal cavalry by chanting hymns, promising 'death to foreigners and heretics', and remaining sufficiently loyal to 'Our Lord' that none of his more worldly advocates – be they busy merchants of the *Consulado de Comercio*, concerned landlords or astute military officers – challenged his power for long. Carrera was the first of Guatemala's plebeian dictators but the only one to enjoy genuine popularity, not least because he promised nothing but the security of the past and was dead before the demands of the future found an audience. Guatemala entered a period of comprehensive reaction; the tithe was reinstated, the regular orders (including the Jesuits) encouraged to return, and the first concordat signed between a Latin American state and the Vatican (1852).[46] The *Consulado* retained its backward mercantile character, exploiting its longstanding dominance of regional markets but never transforming them. Apart from a brief flurry in cotton production during the US civil war, dependence on cochineal persisted; the process of capital accumulation was hampered by a refusal to accept land as collateral for credit.[47]

A Conservative Guatemala implied a Conservative Central America. But one of the inescapable consequences of the defeat of the Liberals and dismantling of the Federation was that it devolved full sovereignty to the individual states and left no ready mechanism through which to channel power from Guatemala City. Hence, Guatemala lost direct control even if it retained hegemony. It could invade or sponsor rebellions, but notwithstanding much success in these tactics and a general suppression of Liberal counter-attacks until the 1870s, the political pattern of the isthmus began to fan out somewhat. At one level it was of some consequence that all the other states except El Salvador (ever the maverick in matters ecclesiastical) made their peace with the Vicar of Christ and signed concordats. But nowhere beyond Guatemala did this carry great political weight since no state possessed a comparable clerical apparatus or indigenous population. Behind the unity of Conservatism there was both political pragmatism and a perceptible socio-economic diversity.

Even in the early nineteenth century the survival of indigenous culture in El Salvador had effectively been reduced to the zones of Izalco (Sonsonate) and Los Nonualcos (La Paz), heartlands of Pipil and Lenca society. The latter region, already affected by the resurgence of indigo after independence, was the site of the 1833 uprising which, with its origins in the head tax, military recruitment and the pressure of the indigo estates, derived from the oppression and exploitation of the natives as both Indians and peasants. Izalco, afforded greater protection at this stage by its dedication to the low intensity crops of cacao and balsam, was not to come under such pressure until the onset of coffee, but when this reached its peak in the early 1930s the response was no less fierce and manifested pronounced Indian as well as peasant features. Because the process of *ladinización* is one that bears on more than miscegenation and is characterized principally by acculturation – the adoption of Spanish (or at least bilingualism), distancing from autochthonous organization (the socio-religious *cofradías*, or Indian *alcaldías* that mirrored Spanish mayoralties) and dress – it is exceptionally hard to quantify with precision.[48] Hence, even the assessment that at the end of the eighteenth century one-third of El Salvador's inhabitants were *ladinos* and 10 per cent 'white' may be an underestimation, and the subsequent revival of indigo undoubtedly caused appreciable dislocation of Indian society.[49] One important consequence of this was a growing lack of distinction between the *ejidos* (municipal commons available to all inhabitants of a settlement) and the *tierras comunales* (lands belonging specifically to Indian communities).[50] As in Guatemala, both institutions were protected throughout this period (statutes of 1832, 1838 and 1853), perhaps more consciously as a means of ensuring a subsistence base in a state that was highly populated, particularly in the central highlands and their piedmont, and where the expansion of the hacienda had been quite marked. Indigo, like cochineal, was by no means a predominantly plantation crop; it could be picked wild or, more often, needed slash and burn clearance, broadcast sowing, and a six-month growing season with only light weeding.[51] It was, therefore, widely cultivated on small plots, particularly in the regions of San Miguel and Chalatenango (the sole zone of Central American production by the mid twentieth century). But El Salvador was the centre of regional production, its sales remaining as high as 2.6 million pesos in 1870.[52] Larger plantations and the processing of the vegetable dye (particularly unhealthy and thus the cause of many colonial ordinances) required a seasonal labour force of some size and fuelled a general migratory outflow from the north of the country, but this was never sufficiently large or voluntary to avoid recourse to vagrancy laws (1837, 1841, 1843). At this stage, then, the requirement of El Salvador's haciendas, perhaps 500 in number, was less directly land than labour and capital. Guatemalan control over both credit and markets had made ardent free-traders of most Salvadorean merchants and Liberal figureheads of several large landlords. El Salvador was the state most securely controlled by Guatemala but also that most positively resistant to such control; it is not surprising that the Liberal and Federalist hero Morazán, a Honduran executed in Costa Rica, desired to be buried there. Liberalism was stalled by both external Conservative tutelage and the buoyancy of indigo, the market for which held up longer than did that for cochineal; but when these impediments were removed the Salvadorean economy underwent the most rapid and all-encompassing transformation in Central America.

One notable feature of Liberal capitalism in El Salvador was the marginal role played by external capital right through to World War Two.[53] Less predictable in every sense was the comparably minimal role it played in Nicaragua, which from the first decade of independence had been identified as the most likely site for a trans-isthmian canal.[54] Early proposals to this end were given weight by the 'Gold Rush' to California from the end of the 1840s; over twenty years perhaps 130,000 migrants to the US Pacific seaboard traversed Nicaragua, often in the less than gentle hands of Cornelius Vanderbilt's Accessory Transit Company.[55] The British presence at San Juan del Norte and its maintenance of a farcical 'Miskito Kingdom' on the Caribbean coast made Nicaragua the first real test case for the Monroe Doctrine (1823) that rejected European rights of intervention in hemispheric affairs. However, at this stage Washington, which had only just terminated its two-year war with Mexico to secure Texas and the western territories, was in no position to enforce its ambitious and self-conferred mandate. The Clayton–Bulwer treaty of 1850, which provided for joint control over any trans-isthmian route, registered the strength of the position held by the British, who could operate out of Belize and Jamaica, and had in Frederick Chatfield a diplomat capable of exploiting such logistical advantages.[56] Chatfield is frequently presented in Central American histories as the imperialist agent behind the defeat of the Federation. This is to be doubted, but he did demonstrate a Palmerstonian commitment to establishing British hegemony in the region, particularly Guatemala. In the case of Nicaragua it is evident that, beyond the Miskito coast, the British role was marginal in terms of domestic politics, which centred on the competition between the towns of León (predominantly Liberal) and Granada (correspondingly Conservative). The productive basis for this conflict was not very strong. Although Granada was a more active commercial centre, tied into the cacao, tobacco and sugar zones, while León was linked with the Pacific port of Realejo (Corinto) and in the heart of cattle country, commercial agriculture remained at a low level until the end of the century.[57] Cacao was not exported heavily, indigo did not approach Salvadorean levels, and the sparse population effectively determined that ranching predominated, with cattle outnumbering human beings. Indeed, so substantial were the opportunities for subsistence farming that the *ejido* was consistently defended as a means of keeping the labour force near urban settlement and thus accessible at harvest time.[58] Production of gold and silver was too modest to exercise much impact except, perhaps, to make state power rather more attractive than would otherwise have been the case. The rush to California certainly bolstered the economies of Granada and Rivas, but it did not propel significant alteration of a national circuit in which a still important Indian population was unable to escape the reach of the manorial hacienda though still capable of bartering the terms of labour rent or share-cropping.[59]

The dispute between León and Granada had simmered for decades, breeding small-scale civil wars and attractive working conditions for bandits like Bernabé Somoza. The intervention in 1855 of the US mercenary William Walker on behalf of the beleaguered Liberals of León qualitatively transformed the conflict.[60] Walker's four-year effort to dominate Nicaragua might perhaps be seen as a filibustering extension of the somewhat less exotic adventurism taking place in the western reaches of the US in the same period.[61] It markedly increased the attrition of local struggles, exacerbated a xenophobia kept on the boil by the British presence, and its final, awful phase (which included the introduction of English as the republic's official language) provoked a campaign by forces from all Central American states that resulted in Walker's expulsion (followed understandably by execution) and perhaps a greater degree of regional unity than was ever achieved by the thirty-five formal initiatives essayed to this end between 1840 and 1930.[62] This conflict was known as the 'National War', but in the nation where it was fought its effect was to taint Liberalism so severely with the stain of '*anti-patria*' that Conservatism persisted far longer than elsewhere. Such longevity was no mere curiosity: it was to underlie a conflict that endured in substance until 1950 – in form until 1979 – and throughout engendered the conditions for further foreign intervention, no less bloody or shameful in effect but far more sober in preparation and serious in consequence.

The Honduran authorities could take pride in putting the wretched Walker before a firing squad, but he had been piously delivered up to them by a British navy that patrolled their Caribbean coast as actively as that of Nicaragua, protected the Bay Islands as colonial territory until 1859, and provided little-needed support for British lumber operations in the mahogany forests in the north of the country. Then as now Honduras was the most backward region of Central America. In the first phase of the colony it had promised mineral wealth, yielding some 12,000 marks of silver in the early 1580s, but within thirty years the shallow veins were exhausted.[63] Cacao production also fell off, leaving little large-scale activity beyond ranching, with perhaps half a million head of cattle grazing in 1800.[64] Until the establishment of Puerto Barrios in 1884, Omoa was Guatemala's principal Atlantic port, but it remained a conduit for other people's trade and not a focus for Honduran growth. Although the Copán region had some commercial links with the economies of Guatemala and El Salvador, its own growth was limited and not contagious. In all probability the population of Honduras did not recover its eighteenth-century levels until the last quarter of the nineteenth, at which point *ladinos* outnumbered Indians by 263,000 to 69,000.[65] The predominance of ranching within the orbit of commercial agriculture, the low level of mining, and the poor standard of much soil also had the effect of preserving the *ejido* and limiting the degree to which peasants were obliged to work on the basis of labour rent or wages. In 1887 there were 23,253 day-workers, most of whom would have had some access to land, against 30,369 small peasant farmers and 45,037 'artisans' (a remarkably high number that is probably the result of a fiscally determined census response by agriculturalists who also engaged in some petty commodity production). At this stage the Honduran state apparatus employed 1,684 civilians and 534 soldiers; 73 priests, many of them foreigners, attended to spiritual welfare albeit without the aid of the tithe or access to schools.[66] Common land necessarily provided the major productive resource for this human stock and, during a period when elsewhere it was simply being defended, in Honduras the *ejido* was expanding: between 1800 and 1899 375 new titles were issued, suggesting a very much higher de facto growth. Of course, private ownership was also on the increase, but it was in the nature of both nineteenth-century economic organization and the form of commercial agriculture implanted in the twentieth that the pressure on subsistence lands remained markedly lower than elsewhere until the 1950s.[67] This was to have important socio-political consequences, the country's very backwardness determining a distinct and less political form of *campesino* agitation.

For some time to come Honduras and, to a lesser degree, Nicaragua would lack an economic structure capable of engendering a decisive process of capital accumulation to override colonial barriers and propel a transformation of the relations of production. Nowhere did this process ever fully subordinate vestiges of a pre-capitalist economy and society, but increasingly such subordination was determined by the demands of production for an international market organized on the logic of capitalism. For countries like those of Central America undergoing this experience in the late nineteenth and early twentieth centuries, such a process amounted to what is called 'combined and uneven development' in that the capitalization of agriculture advanced without producing a comprehensive modernity throughout the economy as a whole (the absence of industry and generalized wage relations). What is often overlooked is the fact that, apart from obtaining between these national economies and those of the metropolitan states as well as inside each Central American economy, such combined and uneven development existed between the isthmian economies, producing within the unity that is captured in the vulgar expression 'banana republic' a diversity that conditions the pace and form in which these systems were established and, more importantly for our purposes, subsequently broke down.

The Rise of Capitalist Agriculture

The subordination of subsistence agriculture to that determined by the market was a distended process. It is usually identified as an integral part of the Liberal 'revolutions' that began in Guatemala in 1871 and eventually toppled the Nicaraguan Conservatives in 1893, but although that period undoubtedly witnessed unparalleled advances in the commercial production of coffee, cultivation of this crop had begun in Costa Rica in the 1830s. By 1860 the country was exporting nine million kilos, a figure not attained by Guatemala or El Salvador for a further decade.[68] Between 1838 and 1890 land in the *Meseta Central* given over to coffee rose from 345 to 20,000 hectares – over a third of the area in which 80 per cent of the population lived was dominated by the crop.[69] By that stage over 70 per cent of the rural population were landless labourers, a far higher proportion than elsewhere. Yet one of the central elements determining the peculiarity of Costa Rica's development was precisely the absence of large haciendas and the relatively even distribution of land not only at the onset of the coffee era but also well into it. The largest single farm (*finca*) established in Costa Rica was 604 hectares in size – a modest holding by Latin American standards – and the number over 100 hectares is today very limited.[70] In 1963 58.5 per cent of cultivated land was in units of less than thirty-five hectares, with an average farm size of forty-one hectares, compared to 7 per cent in El Salvador and 8.3 in Guatemala.[71] Thus, whilst it led to a high degree of proletarianization, coffee did not produce the polarities of land ownership witnessed in the rest of the region. This factor has encouraged explanations of the country's distinct political development on the basis of an egalitarianism sustained by a class of yeoman farmers formed in a colonial period characterized by isolation from the centres of Spanish power, the virtual absence of an Indian population and minerals, and the weakness of the Church.[72] On occasion these factors have been distilled into an image of a communitarian arcadia that was destroyed by the advent of coffee but bequeathed a legacy of innate democratic impulse in the *tico* character.[73] Such a comfortable teleology does not stand up for long when set against the historical evidence but it remains a fact that of all the Central American economies, that in Costa Rica approximated most closely to development in the 'small farmer' mode. This, in turn, undoubtedly derived from its colonial heritage and certainly exercised influence on the form of political domination, for such it was and remains, notwithstanding the progression of claims for an unambiguously consensual heritage.

As a colonial province Costa Rica was indeed exceptionally poor; so much so, in fact, that in the eighteenth century governors were obliged to work on the land as well as on their papers. An extremely low level of external trade placed a premium on local production of foodstuffs organized around nuclear village settlements in the *Meseta Central*. Access to land was general and necessary, but there was also differentiation in the extent of land-holding that abetted the colonial elite's control over tobacco, cattle and some silver production.[74] The challenge to the colonial centre of Cartago, which administered state monopolies, pre-dates independence and has been linked to the rise of a more open market, originating in the smuggling of cattle, in San José.[75] Thus, although less marked than elsewhere, direction of the colonial apparatus did both provide the basis of economic power and prompt the rise of a competitive and more dynamic free-trade faction of landlords and merchants. However, in a society as small as Costa Rica's – no more than 53,000 people in 1801 – accumulation of wealth was necessarily limited. Well into the coffee era one notes strong resonances of village society, with heads of state tending their shops, a premium placed on ties of kinship (not hindered by priestly proclivities for rearing families or a notable incidence of extramarital liaisons under what was a less than rigid moral code), politics and petty accumulation still focused on a round of lotteries, cock-fighting and card games.[76]

For such a society, which at independence had no doctors and in 1863 only seven, the historical timing of the adoption of coffee must be of some relevance; it took place in the context of an economy that was not fully autarkic but produced a very slight surplus and had not developed profound structures for the division of labour. Under such conditions the political aspects of political economy acquire unusual prominence, in this case as manifested by the power of a social elite – a 'pseudo-aristocracy' – descended from a small number of conquistador families.[77] It has been shown that by the mid 1970s thirty-three of the republic's forty-four presidents and over 300 deputies were descendants of two early Spanish settlers, Juan Vázquez de Coronado and Antonio de Acosta Arévalo.[78] Although it had not realized its power primarily through the mechanism of the hacienda, this dominant stratum undoubtedly exploited its political control in the early republican period to manipulate the first distribution of *baldíos* and obtain ownership of larger tracts of fertile land in a region ecologically perfect for coffee.[79] Revenues from a particularly high grade coffee bean facing little competition soon became substantial, in no small part due to the circumvention of the intermediary market of Valparaiso (Chile) but also as a result of overcoming some of the considerable difficulties of transport to the coast and the establishment of the port of Puntarenas.[80]

Given the quite broad pattern of land ownership within a geographically limited zone, early commercial success had the effect of inflating land prices, perhaps twentyfold in thirty years, to levels well above those in the rest of Central America.[81] The Costa Rican market in land was therefore established very early and, despite a degree of manipulation, it was essentially free. The preparedness of British merchants to advance favourable crop liens and the capacity to purchase land incrementally as well as through direct payment in coffee had two effects that exercised more than purely economic influence right through to the contemporary period. The first was that for a number of small-scale owners it made economic sense to sell first their plots and then their labour power to the new commercial estates. This option was made attractive by both the high price of land and the very low availability of labour, resulting in high wages, particularly but not exclusively at harvest time; as early as 1859 a day's work was valued at $1.[82] On the other hand, while such demand produced an expansion of wage relations, it also derived from a scarcity of labourers that was itself connected with the possibilities of modest coffee cultivation on land previously dedicated almost exclusively to subsistence crops. Hence, parallel with the consolidation of fully commercial estates there emerged another important market – that in coffee between small and large farmers. Here the nexus revolved around the capacity of the commercial concerns to advance some of their mercantile credit to the small growers. A part of this was disbursed early in the season, a further portion at harvest and another upon sale, but prior to delivery the loan never exceeded 40 per cent of the projected consignment. This system enabled the landlord-merchants to exercise control in the market and pass on any losses to the small farmers; it also gave this latter sector a margin of solvency in the cultivation of a crop that is slow and intermittent in yielding returns on capital.[83] Such a mechanism for credit persists to this day, sustaining inequitable but powerful bonds between small- and large-scale growers. It delayed the emergence of banks – the attempt to found one in 1858 led to a popularly backed coup – and served to retain a relatively extensive stratum of modest farmers alongside the new population of landless labourers. The decisive point of power in such a system lies not in direct control of land but rather in control over processing, through possession of a coffee *beneficio* (the machinery for extracting the coffee bean from the cherry and then removing its outer layers), access to which was vital to small growers and the determinant factor in securing credit.[84] In 1850 sixteen *beneficios* accounted for 85 per cent of coffee exports and, although the total number varied between 256 in 1887, 221 in 1940 and 114 in 1970, the pattern of ownership was always more concentrated.[85]

The distinctiveness of agrarian capitalism in Costa Rica lay in more than its early emergence; it may be characterized by a limited, and predominantly market-determined, direct control of land on the part of rural entrepreneurs, a small labour force possessing significant capacity to negotiate wage levels, and the importance of the *beneficio* as a mechanism for concentrating wealth. Nowhere else in the region did these factors obtain to such a pronounced degree even after the Liberal epoch. The effects of such a productive system can be traced in the realm of politics which was, if anything, more strictly oligarchic than in the rest of Central America; it was also susceptible more to patterns of patriarchal and commercial domination than to those of coercion. This was less a case of democratic yeoman pressure upon the landed gentry than one of the requirements of hegemony making coercive appropriation of land and labour unproductive. In other respects late nineteenth-century Costa Rica was less singular. The unqualified advance of coffee produced acute shortages in foodstuffs, to the degree that butter and cheese were imported from Britain.[86] Moreover, although Conservatism was relatively restrained in Costa Rica (the country furthest from Guatemala), it was not fully displaced until the dictatorship of Tomás Guardia (1870–82).

Despite building railways and implementing a bevy of free trade measures, Guardia still faced substantial opposition from sectors of the oligarchy. A good measure of this may be ascribed to his authoritarian rule, but it also had its origins in the persistence of a backward culture that was ambivalent with regard to restraints on the Church, against which Guardia did not pursue a vehement campaign. Even after traditional Liberal measures were implemented for the ecclesiastical domain (1884), the drive against obscurantism was prejudiced by the closure in 1888 of the country's sole university, Santo Tomás, which was not to reopen until 1940. Three or four generations of Costa Rican upper-class youth were obliged to pick up the tenets of positivism abroad, but this was not converted into political capital with any facility since government remained in the hands of a handful of gentlemen – 'the Olympians' – right through to 1940. It is perhaps no paradox that this group rejoiced in the title of 'the generation of '88'. Their rule was sometimes complicated by bursts of clerical politicking, which acquired an increasingly reformist tone,[87] but it was not substantially affected either by rising rates of literacy (11 per cent in 1889; 31 per cent in 1892; 76 per cent in 1927) or by a very slight expansion in suffrage that as late as 1919 produced a vote of 47,500 or 11.3 per cent of the population (in 1970 33.1 per cent of the populace cast votes).[88] The notion that after 1889 Costa Rica was governed democratically because in that year the opposition won the poll and was permitted to take office must be sharply tempered by recognition that this went no further than a refinement of the rules of competition between very small numbers of landlords – Cleto González Viquez and Ricardo Jimenez Oreamuno held power between themselves for twenty years between 1906 and 1936. Such a regime assuredly incorporated some of the consequences of a plebeian culture that by dint of both the market value of labour and a still limited process of dislocation from homestead – many day-labourers naturally belonged to families with land – was not essentially servile nor wholly submissive.[89] It rarely made recourse to military force – this was almost exclusively employed for the settlement of intra-oligarchic disputes – and rested on a state apparatus that in 1883 employed no more than 786 people.[90] Yet the regime of the *cafetaleros* proved sufficiently resourceful to contain latent conflict in the coffee heartland of the *Meseta* without major crisis until the 1940s. It was able to retain significant autonomy with respect to the foreign interests which from the last decades of the nineteenth century were extending the historic parameters of the country by developing the banana industry on the Caribbean coast.

Both geography and climate (along with the diseases it nurtured) isolated the lowland plantations of the region around Limón from the central valley, and for many years the Caribbean labourers employed in the coastal zone were prohibited from travelling beyond the hinterland. In 1884 the zone was divided into some 350 farms covering only 4,000 acres and producing a banana crop worth less than $50,000.[91] By the end of the decade the entrepreneur Minor Keith had completed a railway from the sea to San José and, on the basis of munificent concessions as well as his monopoly on transport (which provided control over wholesale purchasing), the forerunner of United Fruit had captured and transformed the region. Between 1883 and 1907 exports of bananas rose from 110,000 bunches to 10.2 million.[92] Although the trade was not to displace coffee from its leading role, the banana industry was central to Costa Rica's economy in the twentieth century. It was throughout controlled by foreign capital, and even if the coffee oligarchy was able to preserve its authority in the social nucleus of the nation, the emergence of an enclave on the Atlantic coast presented a new site for economic and political activity that was to be of great consequence.

In Costa Rica the second Liberal era may be said to have opened with the Guardia regime, but its impact beyond altering the language and (temporarily) the methods of government was quite slight. In both Guatemala and El Salvador the onset of Liberalism produced far more profound changes even though there were between these two countries differences in style and effect. It is perhaps unsurprising, given both the radical character of the ancien regime and the influence of resurgent Mexican Liberalism, that Guatemala should provide the core revolution, most emphatic in its political measures and capable – like the Conservative order it replaced – of making itself felt throughout the isthmus. Within five years of the Liberal victory in Guatemala only Nicaragua retained a Conservative regime, and even that was not averse to implementing a number of reforms. Everywhere, whether applied concertedly or not, the language and legislative devices of laissez faire, land as property, and order as progress imbricated with the old strain of secularism.

Even in Guatemala the new order only advanced by stages. Having gained state power in 1871, the longstanding Liberal leader Miguel García Granados endeavoured to direct a strictly modulated regime in which the traumatized circles of reaction were given a modicum of representation and spared the introduction of substantial changes, although the *Consulado* was disbanded. However, such a tempered approach did not meet the demands of both urban and rural middle sectors that had chafed under commercial and political restrictions for over thirty years. Hence, a second phase opened in 1873 when García Granados, unwilling to clash with this sector, submitted to and lost an election, in which only 10,000 votes were cast. The winner was the military architect of the Liberal victory, Justo Rufino Barrios. Barrios, clear leader of the most outspoken wing of Liberalism, ruled in the dictatorial and interventionist mould established by Carrera. His government lasted until he was killed in battle in 1885, but his political legacy endured until 1920, when the Liberal Party was ousted from power, and his economic measures until 1945, when the vagrancy laws were abolished. Yet the first four years of the now consolidated regime were notable less for major initiatives on behalf of commercial agriculture than for a resolute offensive against the Church. Inveighing against clerical privilege and its sustenance of poverty and superstition, Barrios expelled the orders (over seventy priests, mostly foreigners, left the country), secularized education and marriage, suppressed the tithe once more, obliged clerics to wear lay dress in public, and expropriated what remained of the institution's property beyond the churches themselves.[93] Although by this stage ecclesiastical holdings were not so extensive as to constitute a large market in cheap land, relations with the Pontiff were soured, and a basis laid for later Protestant advances as well as an unstable and fractious relationship between state and Roman Catholic Church that would by the 1970s combine affable coexistence between colonels and a supine, simpering hierarchy with extra-judicial execution of catechists and parish priests.

In the long term these measures were of less consequence than those less precise items in the Liberal economic programme, which, in its broad objective of emulating the Costa Rican experience, sought to expand coffee cultivation. This demanded a liberalization of commerce, only partially achieved by the abolition of the *Consulado*, whose erstwhile members still maintained an impressive hold over credit, as well as requiring a comprehensive clearing away of the colonial defences of indigenous agriculture.

Guarantees of access to labour lay at the heart of the Liberal measures, but although it eventually proved necessary to introduce new statutes and establish a 'modern' apparatus to implement them, little of this went beyond streamlining systems inherited from the colonial period and hitherto left largely dormant. The three devices employed to disaggregate the communal economy and drag its labour force into the commercial circuit were the traditional *mandamiento* (obligatory *corvée* service), vagrancy laws and, most importantly, debt peonage. This latter system was not strictly coercive but, like the others, it was enforced with rigour and fully sanctioned by a state that committed considerable resources to supporting individual landlords' claims. These, in turn, were manipulated extensively, exploiting widespread illiteracy and the extraordinarily onerous terms under which indebted peasants endeavoured to free themselves from what generally amounted to informal and temporary, but cyclical, slavery.

The means for prising labour from its communal refuge did not lead to a full-scale eradication of common cultivation in the 'cold lands' of the *altiplano* (which was anyway unsuitable for coffee), but they undoubtedly produced a substantial seasonal dispersion of the Indian population, a dislocation of indigenous culture centred on cultivation of family plots (*milpas*), and the loss of some – occasionally much – communal property, especially on the lower slopes.[94] Moreover, although debt peonage was a private contractual tie between landlord and worker, public authorities and sometimes the Indian hierarchies assisted in enforcement; this further encouraged what was rapidly to become an impressive system of control in which the contemporary military counter-subversion network has many of its origins. There was some aggressive resistance, but as a rule the Indian response combined the tactics of evasion and negotiation in its overall retreat.[95]

We can date the start of this third stage of the Liberal revolution from the instructions issued by Barrios to the *jefes políticos* (departmental administrators) on 3 November 1876 to render all assistance to landlords by providing drafts of Indian labour according to need.[96] This effective revival of forced labour was notable for its late appearance – over five years after the Liberals took power. By this stage Guatemalan coffee production stood at 20.5 million lbs with a gross value of $4.7 million.[97] The decision to accelerate both production and demands on labour may well have been connected with the erratically increasing price of coffee, which had moved from $0.13 per lb in 1871 (when production was 11.3 million lbs) to $0.23 in 1876, a peak that it was not to reach again for over thirty years.[98] It is equally likely that commercial production was approaching its limits on the basis of expansion through piecemeal expropriation and purchase of land (both *baldíos* and de facto possession of commons) as well as irregular harvest labour by landless *ladinos* and some indebted Indians. After 1876 the price of coffee started to fall but production rose, doubling by 1880 and increasing fivefold by the turn of the century, when it comprised over 80 per cent of all exports.[99] Such growth reflected a qualitative change in the structure of land, labour and, to a lesser degree, capital. It corresponded to a realization of the demands of those, like the Honduran Marco Aurelio Soto, who in 1870 had urged that all land be converted into property: 'Land which we should esteem as the most valuable of the country's riches, is among us almost without importance. It is necessary that national credit put into circulation this dead value, deliberately mobilizing property.'[100] At the same time, management of the coffee economy was in the hands of those who nurtured few illusions as to which sector of society provided the main obstacle to progress: 'The Indian is a pariah, stretched out in his hammock and drunk on chicha, his natural beverage. His house is a pig sty; a ragged wife and six or more children live beneath a ceiling grimy with the smoke of a fire, which burns night and day in the middle of the floor. . . . Yet, in this state the Indian is happy and desires nothing more.'[101] The paternalism of the Conservative years was not entirely liquidated, but it was now a strictly subordinate phenomenon.

Since 1835 some coffee had been grown in Escuintla and the department of Guatemala, traditional *ladino* zones. From the 1850s it was extending to the piedmont, both on the western slopes (San Marcos, Sololá, Quezaltenango, parts of Retalhuleu and Suchitepéquez) and, more vigorously, to the east in Alta Verapaz. Thus, it had already affected some *tierras comunales* in the foothills – lands that were for ever lost – but it had not encroached in more than a piecemeal fashion on most of the core area of indigenous settlement. (We may identify this as those seven departments where Indians constituted more than 70 per cent of a population of 450,000 – Totonicapán, Sololá, Alta Verapaz, Chimaltenango, Huehuetenango, Quiché and San Marcos – although Suchitepéquez, Quezaltenango and Chiquimula possessed a population that was more than 60 per cent Indian.[102]) Uncultivated and unclaimed land had been sufficiently available to meet much of the demand for coffee, but in January 1877 the Barrios government abolished emphyteusis, thereby making communal holdings accessible to claims for individual ownership. The general impact of this measure is hard to assess and the subject of debate.[103] Between 1871 and 1883 the state sold 970,522 acres of nominally unclaimed lands. Some of this land was undoubtedly considered by the municipalities and communities to belong to them, but such a figure cannot be taken as an accurate indication of nett loss for the additional reason that many private claims to title would not have been included in it.[104] Areas such as San Marcos, Sololá, Quezaltenango, Suchitepéquez and Alta Verapaz were particularly affected, but evidence of resistance elsewhere suggests that there was no clear pattern limited to the ecological reach of coffee.[105] One mechanism that was employed by the new *finqueros* (plantation owners) was the establishment of *fincas de mozo* in the highlands which, as an alternative to debt peonage, were let to peasants for a rent paid in harvest labour on the coffee farms in the piedmont. This never became a general system, but it did assist the formation of an impressive network of large estates, greater in average unit size than anywhere else in Central America and, even after the agrarian reform of 1952, controlling only a slightly smaller proportion of national land than the formidable *fincas* of El Salvador. In this respect and in the connected low level of wages Guatemala differed substantially from the model of Costa Rica on which the system was supposedly based.

It is clear that, even when combined with the labour measures, no uncomplicated process of proletarianization of the peasantry came into being overnight. Although this was their ideal, Barrios and his colleagues were far more diligent than their Liberal predecessors and constantly sought to evade a peasant backlash of the type witnessed in the 1830s. Resolute communal resistance was often enough to temper and sometimes even to reverse the process for fear of a complete breakdown in order.[106] Moreover, the principal labour requirement was specifically for the harvest, and levels of permanent workers for such tasks as weeding remained relatively modest. Since the coffee harvest of October to December did not coincide with the most critical moments in the cycle of attendance to food crops, the needs of seasonal and migratory labour on the plantation could be met without compelling direct destruction of the subsistence economy and communal society.[107] Indeed, insofar as this sector – still the overwhelming majority of the population – produced the bulk of Guatemala's food supply, it had to be preserved, however precariously.

Attendance to the labour needs of the *fincas* followed close on the heels of the formal abolition of communal ownership: on 3 April 1877 Barrios introduced Decree 177 which contained a new labour code. This fully revitalized the system of debt peonage by creating three classes of rural worker: the *colono*, whose tenancy of a subsistence plot was limited to four years and tied to year-round labour on the plantation, but who was not permitted to leave employment until all debts had been cancelled; the *jornalero habilitado*, whose obligation to repay debt through labour had no time limit; and the *jornalero no habilitado*, who was obliged, without the mechanism of debt, to work for one week per year on an estate in a variant of the *mandamiento*, which was itself officially retained until 1893.[108] Those peasants who were in debt or who owned enough land to pay tax were conveniently exempted from military service as well as the *corvée*.[109] The roots of this system lay within the confines of Indian society itself. Although some debt was incurred by purchase of commodities at shops – the storekeeper then auctioning the debt to plantation agents – a great deal of it derived from the cycle of religious obligations, such as the acquisition of candles and provisions for fiestas in honour of the saints. Labour contractors (*habilitadores*) toured the highland villages in July and August, when corn was scarce and expensive, as well as attending the religious festivals, dispensing cash.[110] The loan could be cancelled by direct repayment but this was rare outside of those few areas, such as Totonicapán, where there existed appreciable petty commodity production (which would anyway reduce the incidence of such prejudicial debt). The debt was, therefore, labour on account, the contractors receiving, as well as a wage, commissions for the number of workers they recruited. They were obliged to track down all debtors who absconded – a frequent occurrence – or, failing this, pay the *finquero* compensation. Hence their entrepreneurial activity included an important coercive element that put them in close collaboration with the local police and militia, which, although always stretched, could now require presentation of papers from an able-bodied Indian male as proof that he had cancelled his debts or had incurred none. Here again an obligatory but private economic relation dovetailed with an unprecedented system of state control, underwritten by the new Remington and Winchester repeating rifles that had such an impact on the conquest of the plains of Argentina and the US at the same time.

The principal beneficiaries of this system included a new layer of *finqueros*, often originating from the urban sector and now able to invest savings from commerce or raise credit on more attractive legal as well as economic terms. They bolstered those established landlords who had shifted from cochineal as well as a numerically small but very important group of foreign farmers. These immigrants were principally German and concentrated in the department of Alta Verapaz, where they remained somewhat distanced from the vagaries of local political life but exploited to the full the concessions made by the Liberal order as well as high levels of investment and good external contacts. By 1913 the Germans accounted for 35.8 million lbs of total coffee exports of 52.5 million although they farmed only 170 estates compared to 1,657 owned by Guatemalans.[111] This economic dominance – which did little to upset Liberal notions of racial superiority – was maintained until World War Two and played a part in complicating the consolidation of an oligarchic class, similar to that in Costa Rica, that had little need of dictatorial regimes to mediate its internal conflicts. In the case of Guatemala we can trace a lineage of authoritarian control from Carrera through Barrios to Estrada Cabrera (1898–1920) and Ubico (1931–44), whose regimes were certainly structured by the requirements of control in the countryside, particularly since it involved the supervision of first tens and then hundreds of thousands of migrant workers, but also reflected an insufficiency of landlord hegemony. There were no comfortable exchanges of power between members of the landed gentry; if there was a Guatemalan oligarchy then this was only in the most expansive, socio-economic sense of the term since the *finqueros* never established a civilian political system of their own. Their social power remained formidable, but long before it became the rule elsewhere the Guatemalan ruling class had transferred the task of direct political administration to an expanded dominant bloc in which the military played a central role. Parallel to this, the development of the state was more advanced, particularly in its mechanisms of control, than in the rest of the region even though it was still largely dependent upon external loans and contracts for the construction of telegraphs, railways and electricity plant which provided the rudiments of an infrastructure with which to deliver coffee to the pierhead as well as assure social control.

After an initial lottery of concessions to assorted gringo venture capitalists, the principal source of external capital outside the coffee economy was the United Fruit Company (UFCO), which two years after its establishment in 1899 signed its first contract for banana lands and the construction of railways. As in Costa Rica, this heralded the substantive as well as the calendar advent of the twentieth century. Yet more than twenty years later there were still Indians attempting to clear obligations – often inherited from their parents – incurred under statutes first introduced hundreds of years before by the Spanish. In the eyes of the banana company executives Guatemala might have been only marginally distinct from Costa Rica, but it was in fact very much so, the key mechanisms of its economy and polity being trapped in a social contradiction that corresponded only partially to that of modern capitalism.

If the central thrust of Guatemalan Liberalism was towards creating and regimenting labour supply, the emphasis on appropriating new land for coffee being complementary, that in El Salvador was without doubt towards expropriation of common land. This was undertaken in a much more comprehensive fashion than in Guatemala and was so concerted that it simultaneously met most of the requirements for labour; dispossessed peasants found themselves in or on the edges of newly created estates that occupied land previously exploited for subsistence. The productive relations and patterns of socio-political control were, therefore, also distinct from those in Guatemala.

The ousting in 1871 of President Dueñas, the last Conservative to rule in El Salvador courtesy of Carrera's fiat, had the effect of further loosening already flexible restraints on free trade rather than unleashing a pack of radical Liberal policies. Dueñ˜as himself had succeeded Gerardo Barrios (1860-63), an indigo farmer who had made efforts to encourage the cultivation of coffee; the Guatemalan mandate cut short this precipitate stab at reintroducing some Liberal measures yet Dueñ˜as was neither able nor willing fully to turn the clock back. The process of primary accumulation of capital realized in the coffee economy has been dated from 1864, although in that year coffee production was worth only 80,000 pesos (less than one per cent of export earnings), because communal land tenure was henceforth not defended whilst coffee cultivation expanded at an accelerating pace.[112] In fact, the indigo crop was not to fall precipitately until the late 1870s, being surpassed as an export by coffee only in 1876. This quite prolonged combination may have both delayed the implementation of new land laws and facilitated a gradual transfer of land and funds (through the availability of mortgages) to the commodity that was waxing from that on the wane; historians engaged in the debate over the initial configuration of the country's rural capitalist class dispute the degree to which this took place.[113] In all events, the replacement of indigo by coffee was no simple matter since the latter crop required greater extensions of land, a much larger workforce and more substantial investment. In the case of El Salvador it also needed considerably more careful and intensive cultivation since the potential land-base was closely circumscribed. Thus, whatever the degree of transfer undertaken by the established landlords, the decline of indigo posed a sharp question as to the future of the country's landed regime. The possibilities of responding to this through expropriation of ecclesiastical properties were minimal. Late in creation, small in establishment, its own holdings limited by the high proportion of land held in commons, the Church possessed more property in the towns than in the countryside. The extent of those lands it administered on behalf of religious associations (*cofradías*) amounted to some 1,207 hectares compared to at least 257,523 hectares in *ejidos* and *tierras comunales*.[114] These lands, many of which were situated in the central highland zone that is excellent coffee country, needed to be possessed for commercial cultivation if the crop was to expand.

It was the regime of Rafael Zaldívar (1876–83), a man very much in the mould of Justo Rufino Barrios, which undertook the major operation of alienating the commons. These lands had contained some 60 per cent of the labour force in 1806 and covered perhaps 40 per cent of national cultivated land in 1879.[115] The process varied from that in Guatemala insofar as El Salvador's historically higher degree of miscegenation had reduced the specifically indigenous and cultural character of the commons in many – but not all – areas, often confusing the municipal holdings with those of the Indian communities. This was perhaps of limited consequence since in both countries all common land was transferred to the private sphere, but in El

Salvador a higher proportion of *ladinos* undertook subsistence farming on the commons than was the case in Guatemala. Thus, alienation in itself not only went further to resolve the problem of labour shortages on the new *fincas* but also produced a more general pressure on peasant agriculture.

The Liberal offensive was launched very rapidly; its central measures were implemented between 1879 and 1882.[116] A preliminary step was taken late in 1878 when Zaldívar issued a decree guaranteeing property rights in general. This was followed in March 1879 by a new statute that introduced the right of private ownership for those who were cultivating the commons on the basis of usufruct. The measure went no further than a reform, albeit an important one, of the existing system, and by maintaining the payment of rent to the municipality preserved one of its central features as well as prompting a perhaps critical differentiation in the status of those who continued to work on *ejido*. A national survey of land in November 1879 was followed by outright abolition of communal ownership, indigenous lands being alienated in March 1881 and the *ejidos* in March 1882. As in Guatemala, the precise result of these measures is less easy to quantify than the extent of the communal holdings they abolished. In some areas – generally the less fertile north and the coastal strip dedicated to ranching – abolition was by no means always co-substantial with loss of direct access to land and certainly did not witness a generalized emergence of large new estates at this stage. In the densely populated central highlands, by contrast, it did, and in emphatic fashion. First the complex legal process and relatively high price needed to secure title impeded any general transfer by peasants of lands held in emphyteusis to private property. Then, after 1893, they lost even the formal defence of proof of previous possession as a requirement for title. This final measure reflected the advances made by a predominantly new class of *cafetaleros* now consolidating their estates on the basis of labour rent (*colonato*) or sharecropping (*aparcería*) by a peasantry increasingly concentrated in hacienda-owned villages.[117]

The limited possibilities for physical retreat from a system that had attacked the central zones of settlement exacerbated competition on the part of the *campesinos* for the scarce land made available for subsistence by the *fincas*. One result of this was the ability of the landlords to impose very onerous terms of tenantry, but another – scarcely less predictable – was the outbreak of violent resistance. Although this never reached the proportions of the 1833 revolt, the intermittent destruction of coffee groves, attacks on haciendas and assaults on rural judges charged with the removal of squatters amounted to a more directly belligerent reaction to alienation than that which occurred (in the context of a more limited assault on land) in Guatemala. Significant breakdowns in 'public order' both preceded and followed expropriation (1872, 1875, 1880, 1885, 1889) but a more residual opposition, often following the expulsion of '*intrusos*' by landlords, prompted the establishment of a rural police force (1889), then the national agrarian police (1907) and finally the National Guard (1911), which persists to this day with its particular reputation for brutality. These forces were successively charged with enforcing the 1889 vagrancy law which, in contrast to similar Guatemalan legislation, was concerned less with recruitment of those evading labour on the hacienda than with the expulsion and control of those who, lacking any ready alternative for refuge and space on which to grow maize, squatted on hacienda lands.[118]

The form of both settlement and labour made the Salvadorean coffee *finca* much more directly the locus of social control than elsewhere. Migratory seasonal labour was an integral factor in the coffee economy and continues to draw workers from outside the central highlands, but such movement was never so regimented as in Guatemala and thus did not require a comparable extension of the central state apparatus. Well into the twentieth century members of the police and National Guard received their orders from the local *finquero*, on whose premises they were often billeted, even if they were nominally answerable to headquarters in the capital. The Salvadorean landlords were, in a manner of speaking, in and amongst their workers; their regime was the most comprehensive in the region. This system was, to some degree, mirrored at the level of national politics, which continued to be competitive, with fluid intra-oligarchic exchanges of power based on coups until 1906. Thereafter both external and internal factors encouraged a more consensual model but without any surrender of state management to the military; the Meléndez–Quinóñez clan challenged the Costa Rican 'Olympians' for the record in easy monopoly of public office on behalf of the landed elite. With the partial exception of Carlos Ezeta (1890–94), who responded to popular discontent by increasing both rural and artisanal wages and consequently caused a rare crisis in the ruling class, none of these regimes acquired pronounced authoritarian characteristics of the Guatemalan type.[119] Although a national army was re-established in 1886, it was the paramilitary forces that were responsible for rural order (and effectively remained so until 1980), leading to something of a dual system whereby state power revolved around matters of fiscal policy and landed power ensured social order. This general tendency, which did absolutely nothing to relieve the burden of the peasantry, was reinforced rather than impeded by the inclusion of a significant number of foreign immigrants into the landlord class since, unlike the German community in Guatemala, they generally intermarried with local families and became integral members of the oligarchy. Some, such as the Bloom family, which had owned a commercial house in the country since 1835, played a central role in providing initial credit for coffee; others arrived later to combine cultivation with processing and commerce. By the 1920s seventeen of the country's twenty-four *beneficios* were owned by immigrants, and surnames such as Deininger, Duke, Goldtree-Liebes, Hill, Dalton and Llach still figure prominently in the roll-call of one of the world's most tightly-knit oligarchies.[120] The capital these entrepreneurs brought with them, together with the absence of fruit plantations, kept levels of new foreign investment in El Salvador extremely low until the 1960s. This, in turn, assisted the configuration of a particularly 'national' political trajectory and resistance to US intrusion even amongst the landlord class; it is less a paradox than it might appear that the contemporary figurehead of this tendency, Roberto d'Aubuissón, should be of immigrant stock and neo-Fascist persuasion.

Lacking a banana enclave, El Salvador was more dependent on coffee than either Costa Rica or Guatemala; in 1904 sales of 13.5 million pesos accounted for over 80 per cent of export earnings.[121] The crisis of 1897 demonstrated the effects a downturn in world demand and price could have but, lacking any ready alternative, the most compelling logic for the *cafetaleros* was to expand and increase production. This period laid the basis for the country's later reputation as 'the Ruhr of Central America', with high levels of return from intensively worked farms that covered much of the landscape and gave rise to an increasingly modern infrastructure. The emergence of an urban middle class can be discerned in the existence of 150 doctors, an equal number of lawyers and over 400 university students by the 1890s.[122] Members of the Salvadorean elite were judged to be 'more intellectual' than other Central Americans of similar station although celebration of this burgeoning liberal demi-monde should be treated with some circumspection: the national library was stocked with volumes purchased from the estate of a Roman cardinal, and in 1909 imports of porcelain were five times, and those of perfumery nearly three times as great as those of books.[123] Moreover, the formation of this small professional stratum was due to a redistribution of surplus value extracted on the basis of the most inequitable tenure of land and greatest concentration of capital in all of Central America. Neither differential rent nor foolish notions of 'industriousness' can exist without exploitation, and that in El Salvador was maintained at a markedly high pitch.

It is difficult to identify any real 'Liberal revolution' in Honduras. Although between 1876 and 1883 Marco Aurelio Soto and Ramón Rosa tabled a series of reforms – suppression of the tithe; public education; new civil codes and fiscal organization – few of these had much impact.[124] The subsequent regimes of Bográn (1883–93) and Policarpo Bonilla (1893–99) made little more headway, and if they were Liberal in devotion, they by no means represented a new landed capitalist class. The Honduran 'oligarchy' was limited to a sprinkling of merchants in San Pedro Sula and Tegucigalpa and a few hundred *hacendados* still dedicated to ranching, tobacco and lumber production; they possessed great authority in their own domains but lacked the means with which to realize a wider 'national project'. Coffee was not cultivated on anything but a very modest scale until the 1940s, thereby embalming many of the socio-political features of the nineteenth century: late in 1985 the general election in Honduras was won by the Liberal Party against National Party opposition. Although the passage of time had fractured the internal coherence of these two political organizations (the National being less Conservative than a Liberal break-away faction), it had not reduced the level of personalist competition or produced new vehicles for the political interests of any major social class. This distinguishes Honduras from Nicaragua, the only other country in which nineteenth-century currents still possess at least formal representation. However, in both cases this endurance reflects the absence of a decisive rupture with colonial economic patterns until after World War Two. In Nicaragua coffee was beginning to expand by the turn of the century but not to such a degree that it could erase intra-oligarchic disputes or forge a coherent dominant bloc. In Honduras, where the landlord class was weaker but less polarized, the foreign influence and intervention that was to persist through the twentieth century was engendered less directly by political motives than in the interests of new and rapidly growing US enterprises. Insofar as Liberalism amounted to the sale of crops on the world market, one might say that Honduran Liberalism owed as much to Standard and United Fruit as it did to Soto and Rosa. Although the image of an absolute and uniform subordination of the nation to Yankee enterprise is often exaggerated, obscuring the contradictions and conflicts caused by such tutelage, there can be little doubt that the development of Honduras from the early twentieth century was closely determined by the preponderance of foreign capital.

The banana era was prefigured by a modest resurgence in mining over the last quarter of the nineteenth century. For some time the production of gold and silver was believed by both local dignitaries and foreign speculators to be of great promise: between 1882 and 1915 276 concessions were granted and eighty-nine companies, some of them Honduran and very small, began operating.[125] Yet it soon became apparent that colonial excavation had exhausted most of the richest and most shallow veins, requiring considerable capital investment in addition to resolution of the perennial transportation difficulties presented by the broken Honduran landscape. A number of small local enterprises continued to extract sufficient quantities of ore to make a return and help sustain a very modest manufacturing base (hats, cigarettes, soap, textiles, shoes, and so on), but by 1900 only twenty-five firms were still in business and of these only one, the Rosario Mining Company, was an enterprise of any size. Rosario had begun working the deposits of San Juancito, north of Tegucigalpa, in 1880 and by 1892 had produced ore worth $3.6 million.[126] Although controlled by the capital of the Valentine family, the inclusion of Soto and other Honduran politicians and merchants amongst the stockholders served to foment some local accumulation as well as to ensure that the company was ceded full rights to water and lumber on the surrounding land, taxed very modestly, and given state assistance in acquiring labour.[127] This generated appreciable opposition since the company was soon trespassing the lands of local *ejidos* and attracting odium for the labour drafts undertaken, largely unsuccessfully, on its behalf. But the main source of discontent was Rosario's intervention in political life, most obviously in its support for Bográn's re-election in 1887 which provoked the circulation of early nationalist tracts attacking foreign capital.[128] The fears of Bográn's opponents that the company would dominate Honduras were, however, unfounded. The scale of its operations effectively precluded such a possibility – at its peak, in 1900, Rosario directly employed only 1,000 workers, many of whom continued to engage in subsistence agriculture, as did the carters and muleteers who serviced the mine.[129] Washington Valentine built a fifty-kilometre railhead from Puerto Cortés, but it still took mule-trains a week to reach it and the railway transformed neither Rosario's operation nor the economy as a whole. Most investment was in the plant at San Juancito itself or restricted by dividend payments made principally to foreign stockholders.[130] Moreover, in the 1890s the mine was producing fifty times more silver than gold, and although the price of both metals was falling from the latter part of the decade, that of silver was on a more pronounced and constant descent, in large part due to the ending of bi-metallism and the adoption of the gold standard in the US.[131] Rosario continued operations at San Juancito until the late 1940s (by which time it had extracted ore worth $100 million), but it could only sustain income by increased excavation of progressively poorer seams. Thus, although the real boom in banana production did not occur until the 1920s, exports overtook those of minerals in 1902 and, excepting the years of the Great War, the gap between them was to continue widening.[132]

Over the last third of the nineteenth century banana cultivation on the northern coast of Honduras was undertaken by local farmers whose plantations were generally small but in combination yielded over two million stems in 1900. By 1914 this figure had more than quadrupled, generating receipts of over $3 million; this was not in itself a particularly impressive sum but accounted for two-thirds of the modest national export revenue.[133] This growth was almost exclusively attributable to the arrival of three US banana concerns: the Vaccaro brothers (later to become Standard Fruit), Cuyamel Fruit Company (owned by Samuel Zemurray) and United Fruit (controlled by the railway entrepreneur Minor Keith, who later bought out Zemurray). These companies did not immediately displace the local farmers since the key point of control in the trading of a perishable commodity lay in distribution – the possession of refrigerated ships and railways – which obviated the need to expend large sums of initial capital in direct cultivation on a wide scale whilst retaining power to fix the wholesale price. This was ensured by the virtual monopoly of Caribbean fruit shipping by UFCO, its own 'Great White Fleet' being complemented by the company's investment in both the Vaccaro and Zemurray fleets.[134] Nonetheless, the economies of scale, high returns, and technical advances encouraged an increasing tendency towards ownership of plantations. This was facilitated by exceptionally generous land grants made in exchange for railway construction, thereby resolving two problems at once. In 1906 the Vaccaros received a concession for their operation at La Ceiba that was to last for fifty-five years and included a grant of 250 hectares for each kilometre of railway constructed. Over the ensuing decade both Zemurray and UFCO followed this lead, gaining concessions of ninety-nine years or even for an indefinite period, with land grants of up to 5,000 hectares per kilometre of railway being made to UFCO's Trujillo and Tela Railroad Companies.[135] (Significantly, no line reached the capital which to this day lacks a rail link with the rest of the country.) By 1914 these accords had delivered to the three enterprises nearly a million acres, 75 per cent of all banana land. They monopolized rail transport in the north of the country and manipulated their freight rates accordingly. Even before production accelerated in the 1920s their returns were very high and only a minuscule portion was recycled through tariffs to the state: in 1918 tax exemptions granted to the firms amounted to 4.9 million pesos when total fiscal revenue was only 4.8 million.[136]

Such a state of affairs did not correspond to a completely unproblematic subjugation of the republic to capitalist enterprise. Despite a degree of shared capital, these companies were in competition and established their local operations at different times, UFCO not engaging in cultivation until 1912. Each had a distinct set of clientelist relationships and allies inside the dominant bloc even if all sought a general stability within the class that managed the state. Just as Rosario before them, the banana firms patronized, cajoled and indulged first and foremost according to the needs of competition. Thus, when Zemurray's favoured president, Manuel Bonilla, was overthrown by Miguel Dávila in 1907 the balance of power and preferment shifted insufficiently to damage Cuyamel's operation but enough to prompt Zemurray's support for Bonilla's coup against Dávila in 1911. This particular incident also emphasized the importance of the Honduran state's financial weakness, a weakness that was maintained and even encouraged by the companies. The central factor in Dávila's fall was not the landing of Bonilla's force of adepts and mercenaries at La Ceiba but pressure on the regime from Washington. Both the State Department and the US banker J.P. Morgan insisted that the Dávila government sign a treaty passing control of the national customs to Morgan's agents. He, with his government's open support, required such a guarantee before advancing a loan of $10 million, almost all of which was to be used to cancel debts either inherited from the

Federation or incurred in the 1860s in an effort to build a railway.[137] It was a sign of the times that these loans had been raised in London and were now to be cancelled in New York. However, when the hesitant Dávila eventually capitulated to the US demands and signed the treaty, he was strenuously opposed by a Honduran congress resistant to such an unqualified surrender of state authority, especially as it was to yield virtually no tangible reward. In the end the US marines were landed 'to protect foreign interests', Washington arranged the protocols for Dávila's departure from office, Morgan withdrew from the loan, and Bonilla eventually repudiated the treaty himself.[138] The question of the Honduran debt did not, of course, disappear and was to underpin further direct financial intervention; both the landing of troops and the complicating opposition to official sepoy status were phenomena which remained very much alive in the 1980s. The power of the colossus to the north was irrefutable, and yet Honduras remained a nominally sovereign state to which at least the pretence of self-determination had to be conceded. The point at which the bluff bargaining of local state managers shifted from protection of privilege and remuneration to the adoption of nationalism was rarely reached but this possibility could never be entirely discounted. While the banana companies could exploit the weakness of Honduran regimes for profit, the US government was obliged to assess how far such exploitation could be taken before it liquidated its own basis in destroying even the vestiges of a state. This constant process of mediation was henceforth to form the stuff of Honduran politics.

Two years before they cleared La Ceiba of what Theodore Roosevelt called 'small bandit nests of a wicked and insufficient type', some 400 marines had landed at Bluefields, Nicaragua, in order to protect US and neutral interests (what else?). Far from coincidentally, they provided a rearguard for rebel Conservative troops led by Emiliano Chamorro and Juan Estrada, who subsequently forced the Liberal and anti-US president, José Santos Zelaya, from power. This intervention was of greater historical significance than that in Honduras, forming part of a tradition not just of occupying the country to assure Washington's preferred order but also of destabilization and invasion when Nicaragua was ruled by regimes that questioned the desirability of such an order. It was also distinct from the case of Honduras in that the direct interests of US capital played only a minor part in the affair. Offering few prospects for the banana companies after initial forays, Nicaragua never attracted appreciable US capital. In 1908 direct investment in the country amounted to only $3.4 million; after World War One this sum was to rise modestly, but it was always the lowest level of US investment in the region and as late as 1950 did not exceed $10 million.[139] The intervention of 1909 must therefore be viewed in a wider context: that of a palpable decline in British influence and its rapid replacement by the US, now openly dedicated not simply to strengthening its economic role in the region but also exercising close political supervision over it. Although direct British investment in Central America still outweighed that of the US in 1914 by $114.9 million to $86 million, the shift in the balance of power had been apparent for some time.[140] In 1894 London withdrew from the Miskito coast, and the following year President Cleveland intervened when British gunboats were sent to blockade the Nicaraguan port of Corinto. Of even greater importance was the ability of US forces to wrest control of Cuba, Puerto Rico and the Philippines from Spain in the space of twelve weeks in 1898. The appetite for and confidence in such interventionism lay behind the second Hay–Paunceforte treaty (1901) which substantially revised the terms of that between Clayton and Bulwer in 1850 and gave the green light for sole US control over any trans-isthmian route. This was, of course, to be constructed not in Nicaragua but in Panama, which was prompted to secede from Colombia in 1903, the US-owned canal opening in 1914. These developments had important ramifications for all the isthmian states: in 1905 Roosevelt's secretary of state, Elihu Root, declared, 'The inevitable effect of our building the Canal must be to require us to police the surrounding premises. In the nature of things, trade and control, and the obligation to keep order which go with them, must come our way.'[141]

This assessment formed the basis of Roosevelt's 'Corollary' to the Monroe Doctrine, asserting the right of the US to supervise the political regimes of the Caribbean Basin on the preposterously reasonable assumption that 'they cannot be happy and prosperous unless they maintain order within their boundaries and behave with just regard for their obligations towards outsiders.'[142] The assertion and implementation of this doctrine opened twentieth-century politics in Central America, and one of its early effects was to diminish the level of direct and independent intervention of the states in each others' affairs. This longstanding tendency reached its apogee in 1906 with a Nicaraguan invasion of Honduras in order to reduce the influence of Estrada Cabrera's Guatemalan regime in that country. Concerted US pressure, directed primarily against Zelaya, led to the establishment of the Central American Court of Justice, designed to be the arbiter of all regional disputes. The Court offered an eminently modern mechanism for superseding the pattern of conflict nurtured by the collapse of the Federation. Somewhat more tentatively, it held out some promise for the reactivation of that body which the combined Liberal regimes had failed to re-establish by their own efforts. Within nine years any expectations of this nature were shown to be hopelessly misplaced; the Court proved unable to impose its judgements on the US itself, whose refusal to recognize findings in favour of Nicaragua presaged the most important regional conflict of the following thirty years and provided a desultory antecedent for Washington's inability to stomach the decision of international jurisprudence, in the shape of the World Court, nearly eighty years later.

If Nicaragua can be compared with Honduras with regard to the degree of US intervention, it still related more closely to the other states in terms of economic structure. The last quarter of the nineteenth century witnessed an extension of coffee cultivation that was slower than elsewhere and coexisted with rather than replaced other exports. In 1871 some 150 *fincas* produced 1.2 million lbs of coffee (9 per cent of exports); by 1885 this had risen to 9.2 million lbs (when El Salvador exported 17.1 million; Guatemala 39.3 million; Costa Rica 24.5 million).[143] Even after the Liberals took power coffee did not eclipse other exports: in 1906 it earned 32.5 per cent of export revenues against 21 per cent for gold, 16 per cent for bananas and 9 per cent for rubber.[144] Even such relatively modest and gradual growth required the Conservatives to introduce measures that were Liberal in all but name; in 1877 the common lands were deprived of inalienable status and drawn into the market, vagrancy laws were introduced and the mechanisms for debt peonage were given legislative sanction.[145] The economic impact of this was certainly less than in El Salvador and Guatemala since the tendency of landlords to combine coffee with other crops and activities preserved both servile relations of production and space for subsistence. On the other hand, the process went further than in Honduras in eroding the peasant land-base, and the use of forced labour to develop a modern infrastructure of roads, railways, telegraph, and so on, did not go unchallenged.

In 1881 the activities of 'rural judges' created to assess land claims exacerbated discontent amongst the indigenous population caused by military conscription and labour drafts for the construction of a road from Matagalpa to León and a telegraph line from Matagalpa to Managua.[146] The resulting rebellion centred on Matagalpa was perhaps the most powerful in the isthmus between 1837 and 1932, mobilizing some 7,000 Indians who launched attacks over a wide area for seven months. The sentiments of one Captain Villalta, staring out at the massed host of Indians besieging Matagalpa early in August 1881, could not have been unique during this period in Central America (or, indeed, any part of the continent): 'by tomorrow afternoon we will all be dead because of that sonofabitch telegraph'.[147] But the technology of the telegraph was also that of the repeating rifle, over which the bows and arrows of the Indian communities could not prevail for long, and the rising petered out in generalized attrition, entering the annals of history as 'the forgotten war'. The Conservative Zavala regime blamed the rebellion on the machinations of Jesuits to whom it had given sanctuary after their expulsion from Guatemala. These supposedly turbulent priests were obliged to seek out fresher pastures, but the more general tide of the times could not be eternally resisted: as Liberal-style policies were applied, the political exponents of that order sought a definitive capture of state power. When this finally occurred, in 1893, it was significantly the result of an alliance between dissident Conservatives from Granada and moderate Liberals from León.[148] Their resolution of the regionalist impasse was to back for the presidency a compromise candidate from Managua, the French-educated José Santos Zelaya. Yet Zelaya was able neither to rule on the basis of such a superficial and tenuous accord nor to provide Liberalism with the initial dynamism of new banks, railways and social laws, all of which had already been introduced.[149] Thus, the main requirement of the new government was to improve upon existing progress, guarding against further prolongation of conflict through the maintenance of a strong, partisan regime.

The regular re-election of Zelaya during his sixteen-year rule has encouraged the description of this as dictatorial whereas, in fact, it was little more so than the regimes of his co-religionists elsewhere twenty years before. It is undoubtedly the case that the Liberals were obliged to deal with a rigorously political opposition that, even though it possessed a social base of traditional landlords and merchants, had incorporated more than a few of the motifs of modernization that in other countries were distinctly not part of the Conservative canon. The legacy of Walker and the regionalist question also persisted in a manner that gave greater primacy to party affiliation and thereby a more pronounced partisanship in government. Yet Zelaya was most zealously traduced by voices in the US – a matter of exceptional importance since, although a Liberal pursuing policies on behalf of a new landed class, the president had to contend with an international balance of power quite distinct from that of the 1870s. While his staging of the 1906 campaign in Honduras harked back to those years, the pursuit of stronger ties with British and German capital and resistance to US claims of control over the Gulf of Fonseca – in order to forestall any alternative canal route – solicited a response from Washington that corresponded to a new era. This was, no doubt, enhanced by factors such as the links between Conservative leaders working for the Luz and Los Angeles Mining Company and US Secretary of State Philander C. Knox, legal adviser to the same concern.[150] But the conflict was more general in origin and had the effect of making the last Liberal of the nineteenth century the first nationalist of the twentieth. Opposition to his efforts to diversify Nicaragua's trade and loan patterns at a time of acute great-power rivalry led Zelaya to describe the operation of US capital as 'impositions adorned with words of civilization and progress'.[151] The manner of his eventual removal and the use of Taft's marines to defeat and kill General Benjamín Zeledón along with several hundred of his troops after an attempted Liberal comeback in November 1912 served to consolidate a peculiarly robust sentiment of anti-Americanism that until 1934 would belong to the Liberal idiom if not to the organized party as a whole. Such a sentiment was nurtured on the consequences of what had rapidly become 'America's truly imperial conviction that the most trifling injury done to it matters far more than the worst injuries done by it'.[152]

Even by the time of World War One the differences between the political economies of the Central American nation states were significant. This diversity did, of course, obtain within a clearly recognizable unity derived from both the colonial era and the implantation of commercial agriculture. In a global context the configuration of landlord and peasant classes, agricultural methods, political and social systems that existed at that time might well appear unremarkably homogeneous. Yet by 1914 one can already discern specific national patterns that are important factors in determining the character of the contemporary conflict.

The case of Costa Rica stands out, in that coffee production consolidated an oligarchy that resorted neither to forced labour nor to expropriation of lands to achieve both economic and political domination. Its correspondingly slight dependence upon military methods underwrites a tradition of civilist politics that has been broken only once this century. At the other end of the spectrum, the case of Guatemala manifests a considerably more coercive, state-supported labour system, while the demands of subsistence and the formidable 'other' of the Indian placed some constraints upon appropriation of land. The new capitalist landlords in El Salvador were not confronted by the latter obstacle, but their unparalleled alienation of lands for coffee went beyond constituting a small and powerful oligarchy in creating a mass of peasant tenants for whom the possibilities of refuge were much more limited and the hacienda regime more all-encompassing than in Guatemala. Although the Salvadorean landlord class was similar to that in Costa Rica in terms of its confidence, cohesion and only relative dependence upon the apparatus of the central state for the maintenance of production, it was closer to that in Guatemala with respect to the degree of social conflict required for the profitable operation of its *fincas*. Yet, for some time to come the Salvadorean oligarchs could structure such conflict at the point of production – on the hacienda – and thereby stave off a general class concession to a partially autonomous state.

These particular variants of the political economy of coffee did not obtain in Honduras, where the crop was not grown, and only partially in Nicaragua, where it was combined with other agricultural and mining activity. The allied 'backwardness' of these two countries was itself varied. In Honduras the fiat of the banana companies generated a degree of US intervention that was as high as that in Nicaragua but distinct in that it did not mediate an expanding but politically divided landed elite so much as subordinate a less developed one wholesale. The absence of possibilities for independent accumulation and the scramble for largesse diminished the scope for any burgeoning nationalism. In Nicaragua, by contrast, this was encouraged by a much more directly political interventionism, which certainly did not lack its quota of financial exaction but could not wean a coherent dominant bloc out of the warring factions without antagonizing some of them.

Over the following forty years these structural differences were to acquire a much more pronounced political character, determining developments that are recognizable factors in the present conflict, not least in the minds of its principal actors.

Notes

1. Quoted in Robert S. Smith, 'Financing the Central American Federation, 1821–1838', HAHR, vol. 43, no. 4, 1963, p. 485.
2. Quoted in Manuel Rubio Sánchez, *Historia del Añil o Xiquilite en Centro América*, San Salvador 1976, vol. 2, pp. 433–6.
3. John Lynch, *The Spanish American Revolutions, 1808–1826*, London 1973; Mario Rodríguez, *The Cadiz Experiment in Central America, 1780–1826*, Berkeley 1978; Ralph Lee Woodward, *Central America. A Nation Divided*, New York 1976.
4. Benedict Anderson, *Imagined Communities. Reflections on the Origin and Spread of Nationalism*, London 1983; Tulio Halperín Donghi, *The Aftermath of Revolution in Latin America*, New York 1973.
5. David Browning, *El Salvador. Landscape and Society*, Oxford 1971, p. 140; Ralph Lee Woodward, 'Central America' in Leslie Bethell, ed., *The Cambridge History of Latin America*, vol. 3, Cambridge 1985, p. 471.
6. The population figures given here are taken from Woodward, 'Central America', p. 498. Since official censuses were not taken until the last twenty years of the century, and were anyway of questionable accuracy, particularly with respect to the racial composition of the population, these statistics are necessarily estimates, culled largely from late colonial reports and the accounts of travellers in the early republican period.
7. Carol A. Smith, 'El desarrollo de la primacía urbana, la dependencia en la exportación y la formación de clases en Guatemala', *Mesoamérica*, no. 8, December 1984.
8. Hazel Ingersoll, *The War of the Mountain. A Study of the Reactionary Peasant Insurgency in Guatemala, 1837–1873*, unpublished PhD, George Washington University 1972, p. 137.
9. Yamileth González García, 'Desintegración de bienes de confradías y de fondos pios en Costa Rica, 1805–1845', *Mesoamérica*, no. 8, December 1984; Lowell Gudmundson, 'La expropiación de los bienes de las obras pias en Costa Rica: un capítulo en la consolidación económica de una elite nacional', *Revista de Historia*, Heredia, no. 4, 1978.
10. J. Lloyd Mecham, *Church and State in Latin America. A History of Politico-Ecclestiastical Relations*, Chapel Hill 1966, p. 314; Mary P. Holleran, *Church and State in Guatemala*, New York 1949.
11. For a display of Bentham's lack of realism, see Miriam Williford, *Bentham on Spanish America*, Baton Rouge 1980.
12. Valentin Solórzano, *Evolución Económica de Guatemala*, Guatemala City 1963, p. 278.
13. Julio Castellanos Cambranes, *Coffee and Peasants in Guatemala, 1853–1897*, Stockholm 1985, p. 55.
14. In Bolivia the revenue from tribute consistently exceeded that from customs until the 1880s and yet its suppression was resisted by Indian communities. Erwin Grieshaber, *Survival of Indian Communities in Nineteenth Century Bolivia*, unpublished PhD, University of North Carolina 1977, pp. 291–3; Tristan Platt, 'Liberalism and Ethnocide in the Southern Andes', *History Workshop Journal*, no. 17, spring 1984.
15. Browning, *El Salvador*, p. 117.
16. Daniel Contreras, *Una Rebelión Indígena en el Partido de Totonicapán en 1820: el Indio y la Independencia*, Guatemala City 1968; Victoria Reifler Bricker, *The Indian Christ, the Indian King. The Histroical Substrate of Maya Myth and Ritual*, Austin 1981, pp. 79–84.
17. Robert S. Smith, 'Financing'; Solórzano, *Evolución*, pp. 286–7.
18. Solórzano, *Evolución*, pp. 284, 287. This may be compared with state revenues

of Venezuela, 1.6 million pesos; Colombia, 2 million; Ecuador, 580,000 in 1836/7. For an instructive survey of problems similar to those in Central America during this period and later, see Malcolm Deas, 'Fiscal Problems of Nineteenth-Century Colombia', JLAS, vol. 14, no. 2, London 1982.

19. Solórzano, *Evolución*, pp. 294–300.

20. In the early 1850s the US Chargé d'Affaires Ephraim Squier noted that in northern Honduras the debased republican coin was widely rejected whilst both the colonial 'macaco' and Federal coin circulated alongside that of Great Britain and the US. E.G. Squier, *Notes on Central America*, New York 1855, p. 230. In Costa Rica the exchange rate of cacao, established as an official medium of exchange in the early eighteenth century, was 100 beans to one *real*, or 800 beans to one peso. Samuel Stone, *La Dinastía de los Conquistadores*,San José 1982, p. 62. For Nicaragua, see Jaime Wheelock, *Imperialismo y Dictadura*, Mexico City 1975, pp. 60–1. For El Salvador, Alejandro Marroquín, *Panchimalco. Investigación Sociológica*, San Salvador 1955, pp. 140–1. El Salvador issued its first republican coin in 1892 while Honduras, which possessed an imperfect but operable mint in the 1820s, did not adopt the Lempira as its national currency until 1930.

21. Solórzano, *Evolución*, p. 335.

22. Miles L. Wortman, *Government and Society in Central America, 1680–1840*, New York 1982, p. 230.

23. Alastair White, *El Salvador*, London 1973, pp. 73–4.

24. In 1801 Costa Rica's population of 52,591 was judged to include just thirty Blacks and 8,281 Indians. Stone, *Dinastía*, p. 55.

25. The garrison at Castillo had been established for protection against pirates and had the dubious distinction of being attacked by a force under Horatio Nelson in 1780. When visited by Squier in 1849 it was deserted, and the fort upstream at San Carlos lacked ordnance, its small garrison apparently dedicating themselves to recreational pursuits, which was justified given the presence of no more than an asthmatic Scots administrator and half a dozen Jamaican policemen in San Juan del Norte but rather misguided at a time when the bandit chieftain Bernabé Somoza was stalking the area. The fort later fell to him without casualties. E.G. Squier, *Nicaragua: its People, Scenery, Monuments and the Proposed Inter–Oceanic Canal*, New York 1852, vol. 1, pp. 114–16.

26. Steven C. Ropp, 'The Honduran Army in the Sociopolitical Evolution of the Honduran State', *The Americas*, vol. 30, no. 4, April 1974, p. 508.

27. Paul Burgess, *Justo Rufino Barrios*, New York 1926, p. 72.

28. Romulo E. Durón, 'Gobernantes de Honduras en el Siglo XIX', *Economía Política*, Tegucigalpa, no. 2, 1972.

29. It was, for example, accepted by the government of Honduras that in the province of Olancho the Zelaya family constituted the local authority, no national officers being stationed or taxes raised in that department. Wortman, *Government and Society*, p.270. In the 1980s Olancho is little changed, since despite the presence of state officials, its landed families still exercise considerable power.

30. White, *El Salvador*, p. 73.

31. Squier, *Nicaragua*, p. 138. The author also notes the absence of labour to harvest cacao due to political instability, p. 159.

32. Rubio Sánchez, *Añil*, vol. 1, p. 196. It is perhaps no more than an irony of history that the Guatemalan Liberal Revolution of 1871 which was to replace the era of colorants with that of coffee took place in June and thus impeded the indigo harvest (p. 204).

33. 'Journalists who were taken in an army helicopter . . . saw a group of 73 people cowering against a stone wall near the hamlet of Mirandilla on the north west side of the hill. . . . Few had shoes and all were covered with dirt. They had been hiding in a ravine in the woods for some days.' *The Guardian*, London, 26 January 1986.

34. I have borrowed the notion of refuge from George Lovell, 'Surviving Conquest. The Guatemalan Indian in Historical Perspective', Paper to the Institute of British Geographers, Leeds, January 1985. Lovell respects but questions – in my view correctly – the full explanatory value of the concept of closed corporate communities at least on the basis of internal divisions. For the fullest presentation of this analysis, see Eric Wolf, 'Closed Corporate Communities in Mesoamerica and Central Java', *Southwestern Journal of Anthropology*, vol. 13, no. 1, 1957,

and Wolf's *Sons of the Shaking Earth*, Chicago 1959. For historical surveys of the Indian population, see W. George Lovell, *Conquest and Survival in Colonial Guatemala. A Historical Geography of the Cuchumatán Highlands, 1500–1821*, Montreal 1985; R.M. Carmack, J. Early and C. Lutz, eds, *The Historical Demography of Highland Guatemala*, Albany 1982; Linda A. Newson, *Indian Survival in Colonial Nicaragua*, Norman, Oklahoma 1987.

35. Jim Handy, *Gift of the Devil. A History of Guatemala*, Toronto 1984, p. 44.

36. Castellanos Cambranes, *Coffee and Peasants*, p. 28; Solórzano, *Evolución*, p. 311.

37. Solórzano, *Evolución*, pp. 310–11; Thomas R. Herrick, *Desarrollo Económico y Político de Guatemala, 1871–1885*, Guatemala City 1974, pp. 25–6.

38. Severo Martínez Peláez, *La Patria del Criollo*, Guatemala City 1973, p. 403.

39. Castellanos Cambranes, *Coffee and Peasants*, p. 68.

40. Ibid., p. 85.

41. Quoted in ibid., p. 69.

42. Corregidor of Suchitepéquez to Minister of the Interior, 23 October 1858, quoted in ibid., pp. 71–2.

43. The reversal of this state of affairs will be considered later, but the claim being made here is sufficiently large to merit some supportive comment. It might even be thought ridiculous given that in 1854 Guatemala generated an export revenue of some $2 million against $1.13 billion in 1983. Yet export revenues are quite distinct from levels of subsistence, and if we are unable to calculate per capita GDP for the 1850s, it stood at only $489 in 1983, the poorest 20 per cent of the population receiving only 5 per cent of national income. The claim is more immediately plausible in view of an increase of population from 1.2 million (*c.* 1880) to 7.3 million on roughly the same quantitive land-base, although by 1970 only 25.3 per cent of it was dedicated to food crops. Even between 1965 and 1975 per capita consumption of staples decreased. John Weeks, *The Economies of Central America*, New York 1985, pp. 41, 47, 102, 107. As early as 1883 Guatemala's wheat imports amounted to 35 per cent of national production. It should also be noted that daily wages on plantations expressed in terms of corn at current prices rose from 7.5 lbs in *c.* 1880 to 10 lbs in 1895 but fell thereafter to 4.5 lbs in the 1930s. David McCreery, *Development and the State in Reforma Guatemala*, 1871–1885, Athens, Ohio 1983, p. 54; and 'Debt Servitude in Rural Guatemala, 1876–1936', HAHR, vol. 63, no. 4, November 1983, p. 749. It is quite probable that this argument could be extended to all the countries over the last century, albeit on rather different bases, as suggested by Ralph Lee Woodward, 'The Rise and Decline of Liberalism in Central America: Historical Perspectives on the Contemporary Crisis', *Journal of Inter-American Studies*, vol. 26, no. 3, August 1984, p. 297. Mid-nineteenth-century travellers placed great emphasis on the abundance of food and the minimal incentives to labour for a wage anywhere except Costa Rica: Squier, *Nicaragua*, p. 274; E. Bradford Burns, 'The Modernization of Underdevelopment: El Salvador, 1858–1931', *The Journal of Developing Areas*, vol. 18, no. 3, April 1984, p. 293; R. Fernández Guardia, ed., *Costa Rica en el Siglo XIX. Antología de Viajeros*, San José 1985. The case of Costa Rica is somewhat distinct because of high wages.

44. Antonio Batres Jaúregui, *Los Indios. Su Historia y Civilización*, Guatemala City 1893; Robert M. Carmack, 'Spanish–Indian Relations in Highland Guatemala, 1800–1944', in Murdo J. MacLeod and Robert S. Wasserstrom, eds, *Spaniards and Indians in Southeastern Mesoamerica. Essays in the History of Ethnic Relations*, Lincoln, Nebraska 1983, p. 243. Carmack shows that Carrera enjoyed far from constant and uniform support in the countryside but was able to handle it with a deft combination of concession and repression.

45. Ingersoll, *War of the Mountain*; Keith L. Miceli, 'Rafael Carrera: Defender and Promoter of Peasant Interest in Guatemala, 1837–1848', *The Americas*, vol. 31, no. 1, July 1974.

46. Mecham, *Church and State*, p. 316.

47. Ralph Lee Woodward, *Privilegio de Clase y Desarrollo Económico. Guatemala 1793–1871*, San José 1981, gives a full account of the *Consulado*. See also his 'Guatemalan Cotton and the American Civil War', *Inter-American Economic Affairs*, vol. 18, no. 3, winter 1964. Solórzano, *Evolución*, p. 317, and David McCreery, 'Coffee and Class: the Structure of Development in Liberal Guatemala', HAHR, vol. 56, no. 3, August 1976, discuss the absence of credit. The Church was a source of some loans but these were rarely for productive purposes.

48. Rodolfo Barón Castro, *La Población de El Salvador*, Madrid 1942, p. 234. Martínez Peláez suggests, in his attack on 'fetishistic' approaches to Indian culture, that contemporary Indian dress is not pre-hispanic and very often European in origin, part of a culture of oppression (*La Patria*, pp. 596, 605, 612). It has been claimed that in 1830 most Salvadorean *ladinos* were dressed in British cloth (White, *El Salvador*, p. 75). It is likely that with or without Liberal trade policies this would have been the case by virtue of contraband. Of course, the international division of labour entailed that the losses of the Salvadorean textile industry corresponded to some degree to the gains made by its dyestuffs, but if it is the case that Levi denims 'are blue because indigo was so cheap in the nineteenth century', this historical element in an apparently unchanging sartorial landscape may not be entirely Salvadorean in character. Philip L. Russell, *El Salvador in Crisis*, Austin 1984, p. 7.

49. Mario Flores Macal, *Formas de Dominación en El Salvador*, San José 1983, pp. 25–6. Flores here refers to an earlier period, but since levels of production in the mid nineteenth century approximated to those of the boom years in the eighteenth it seems reasonable to assume that the effects were similar.

50. Rafael Menjívar, *Acumulación Originaria y Desarrollo del Capitalismo en El Salvador*, San José 1980, pp. 93–9.

51. Browning, *El Salvador*, p. 167.

52. For distribution of production, see Rubio Sánchez, *Añ~il*, p. 87; for serial data on exports, Menjívar, *Acumulación*, p. 35.

53. In 1940 US direct investment in El Salvador was $11 million out of a total of $149 million in the region as a whole. In 1939 British capital holdings amounted to $5.17 million against $87.3 million for all Central America. Unlike Guatemala and Costa Rica, German capital was unimportant in El Salvador. Menjívar, *Acumulación*, pp. 48, 59. I have converted sterling to dollars at an exchange rate of £1 to $4.68. For a full survey of British investment, see J. Fred Rippy, *British Investment in Latin America, 1922–1949*, Minneapolis 1949.

54. For a synoptic presentation of the canal issue, see Woodward, *Central America*, pp. 120–39. More detail is given in David Folkman, *The Nicaraguan Route*, Salt Lake City 1972.

55. Jaime Biderman, *Class Structure, the State and Capitalist Development in Nicaraguan Agriculture*, unpublished PhD, University of California at Berkeley 1982, p.40. Ephraim Squier arrived in Nicaragua on the heels of the first contingents, which appear to have parted with at least a portion of their savings through consorting with local women, to whose handsome physique, languid disposition and lack of clothing Squier returns with understandable but scarcely diplomatic insistence throughout his account.

56. Mario Rodríguez, *A Palmerstonian Diplomat in Central America. Frederick Chatfield Esq.*, Tucson 1964; R.A. Humphreys, 'Anglo–American Rivalries in Central America', in *Tradition and Revolt in Latin America*, London 1969.

57. Wheelock, *Imperialismo*, pp. 50–6.

58. Biderman, *Class Structure*, p. 42. Biderman suggests that only one-third of property was officially registered, which would indicate a high degree of common land.

59. Ibid., pp. 37–8. Sources for Nicaraguan agriculture are poor and give only impressionistic evidence of the relation between the high level of what Wheelock terms *'autoconsumo'* and servile labour on the hacienda.

60. The indefatigable Squier managed to evade an encounter with Somoza in 1849 but reported a meeting on Lake Nicaragua between a compatriot and the great-uncle of Anastasio Somoza that could be taken as a prophetic metaphor for relations between Washington and the family in the following century: Faced with a man 'with a feather in his hat, a red Spanish cloak hanging over one shoulder, a brace of pistols stuck in his belt, and a drawn sword in his hand', the bemused North American succumbs to an *abrazo* (hug), 'which made his back ache even to think of. This was repeated several times, until the pain overcoming all alarm, he cried, "No más, Señor, no más!" But this infliction only terminated to give place to another; for, taking both of our friend's hands in his own, with the grip of a vice, he shook them until his arms were on the point of leaving his shoulder; delivering, meantime, an energetic oration, perfectly unintelligible to his auditor, who could only ejaculate, in broken syllables, "Sí Señor, sí." . . . This finished, Somoza took a splendid ring from his finger and insisted on placing it on the hand of our friend, who, however, looking upon it in the double light of stolen property and a bribe, sturdily refused to accept it . . . .' (Squier, *Nicaragua*, p. 166).

61. For Walker, see Woodward, *Central America*, pp. 135–45; William O. Scroggs, *Filibusters and Financiers*, New York 1916.

62. Miguel Wionczek, 'The Central American Integration Experiment', *BOLSA Review*, March 1967.

63. Murdo J. MacLeod, *Spanish Central America. A Socioeconomic History, 1520–1720*, Berkeley 1973, pp. 149, 236–9.

64. Héctor Pérez Brignoli, 'Economía y Sociedad en Honduras durante el Siglo XIX. Las Estructuras Demográficas', ESC, No. 6, 1973, p. 52.

65. Ibid., p. 68.

66. Ibid., p. 75. It should be noted that the size of the central state apparatus was very much smaller than might be supposed from these figures, which include teachers, postal workers and municipal employees. In 1880 the Honduran government comprised the presidency and six ministries (Interior; Justice and Education; External Relations; Industry; War; Development), none of which possessed more than half a dozen civil servants. Posas and Del Cid, *Construcción*, p. 18.

67. Pérez Brignoli, 'Economía y Sociedad', p. 66. An account of land legislation, presented with rather touching faith in the efficacy of statutory devices but also rendering a clear view of how extensively these were employed, is given in William S. Stokes, 'The Land Laws of Honduras', *Agricultural History*, vol. 21, no. 3, July 1947.

68. José Luis Vega Carballo, 'El Nacimiento de un Régimen de Burguesía Dependiente: el Caso de Costa Rica', ESC, no. 6, 1973, p. 118.

69. Ciro F.S. Cardoso, 'La Formación de la Hacienda Cafetalera en Costa Rica (Siglo XIX)', ESC, no. 6, 1973, pp. 30–1.

70. Ibid.

71. CEPAL; FAO; OIT, *Tenencia de la Tierra y Desarrollo Rural en Centroamérica*, San José 1973.

72. The main themes of this historiography are presented in the introduction to Chester Zelaya, ed., *Democracia en Costa Rica?*, San José 1983.

73. The sources for such a perspective are given and subjected to sharp criticism in Lowell Gudmundson, 'Costa Rica before Coffee: Occupational Distribution, Wealth, Inequality and Elite Society in the Village Economy of the 1840s', JLAS, vol. 15, part 2, November 1983. This polemic is well supported but at times acquires a momentum of its own. Although serious authorities have generally postulated a very low level of class differentiation prior to coffee, this has usually been through stressing the high degree of 'self–sufficiency', which is clearly not reducible to agriculture but, by contrast, suggests a quite extensive system of petty commodity production, which Gudmundson himself demonstrates. His subsequent book, *Costa Rica Before Coffee*, Baton Rouge 1986, provides a fuller perspective.

74. There is some dispute between historians of Costa Rica over the importance of mining (largely silver in the zone of Los Montes de Aguacate) within the process of primary accumulation. The case is most strongly made by Carlos Araya Pochet, 'La Minería y sus Relaciones con la Acumulación de Capital y la Clase Dirigente de Costa Rica, 1821–1841', ESC, no. 5, 1972. Araya suggests that mineral exports to Britain during the 1830s of the order of 300,000 pesos a year, together with the fact that some twenty mine-owners subsequently cultivated coffee, indicates a strong link. Vega Carballo, supported by Cardoso and Stone, questions Araya's figures and emphasizes the ephemeral nature of the mining 'boom'. Although Araya may have overstated the case, the existence of small mines in Central America during the nineteenth century may represent a more important source of accumulation than is generally recognized. The case of Honduras is distinct since the renaissance of silver there is well documented, but it is worth noting that as late as 1913 the Salvadorean iron mines at Metapán (Santa Ana) accounted for 16 per cent of export earnings, and in 1907 revenue from gold constituted 22.4 per cent of Nicaragua's exports. Menjívar, *Acumulación*, p. 51; Oscar René Vargas, 'El Desarrollo del Capitalismo en Nicaragua', ESC, no. 20, 1978, p. 43.

75. Rodolfo Cerdas Cruz, *La Crisis de la Democracia Liberal en Costa Rica*, San José 1972, pp. 21–4.

76. Stone, *Dinastía*, p. 115.

77. Cerdas, *Crisis*, p. 21.

78. Stone, *Dinastía*, p. 40. Of the twenty-eight signatories of Costa Rica's independence

twenty-three were blood relatives. It is occasionally suggested that the origins of this formidable genealogical unity ina predominantly Sephardic Jewish stock from Andalucia combined with the absence of significant Indian and negro populations to confer upon the nucleus of Costa Rican society not simply an unusual 'whiteness' but also a penchant for equitable management in public affairs.

79. A dispute between Braulio Carillo and Juan Rafael Mora, both of whom served as president, over the partiality of land grants was probably only the most celebrated of many instances of such activity while the commercial market for land remained quite small until around 1840. Cardoso, 'Formación', p. 28.

80. In 1846 the cost of 100 lbs of coffee was $2.5 at the *beneficio*, $5 in San José, $7 at Puntarenas (to which transport costs from the capital were $1 per hundredweight), $13 at Valparaiso and $20 in Liverpool. Stone, *Dinastía*, p. 81. A railway connected Puntarenas with Esparta in 1854 but a dependable link with the capital was not established until the turn of the century, explaining why in 1886 there were 2,000 carters compared with 18,000 day-labourers and 7,000 farmers. Cardoso, 'Formación', p. 31. The question of transport remained important throughout this period, even after the completion in 1855 of the Panama railway which was inefficient and charged such high freight rates that much trade continued to be run via the Horn. One should also note the internal difficulties, even in a small country like El Salvador, which early in the nineteenth century possessed only three bridges, two of them built of wood.

81. In 1850 an acre of good coffee land in the *Meseta* cost $88 whilst an acre of good coffee land in Guatemala in 1877 cost $17. Stone, *Dinastía*, p. 96.

82. By 1872 a day-labourer's wage had risen to 1.5 pesos (6/ – or nearly $3). Vega Carballo, 'Nacimiento', p. 94. Such a precipitate rise was apparently caused not only by the residual scarcity of harvest hands – often leading to harvests that were due in November and December not being completed until April – but also by the effects of Walker's reign in Nicaragua and an outbreak of cholera in 1856 that killed around 9,000 people out of a population of less than 110,000. In the 1880s a piece rate of $1 per 25 lbs picked compared with $0.10 paid in Guatemala. Castellanos Cambranes, *Coffee and Peasants*, p. 143.

83. Stone, *Dinastía*, pp. 118–19. This system did not, of course, circumvent the initial difficulties incurred by coffee bushes yielding marketable bean only after three to five years' growth, but one may suppose that distribution of seed, early land grants and combined cultivation with subsistence crops reduced the impact of this for modestly sized farms whereas the transfer of funds from other activities plus graduated payment for land by large farmers made it a quite superable obstacle.

84. There are three types of coffee: robusta, arabica and Brazilian. Brazilian coffee is grown on arabica trees and often graded as mild, its distinction from other arabicas being determined by climate, altitude and method of cultivation (Brazil cherries tend to ripen more uniformly, thereby permitting the harvest of entire trees at once whereas arabica cherries are generally picked individually). Robusta is grown on a different type of tree which is more hardy, can flourish in tropical climates and provides a heavier yield but coarser fruit than arabicas. Robustas are cultivated in Africa and Asia, and like Brazils they are normally processed 'dry', the cherries being left in the sun, then 'hulled' in machines to remove the dried husk, the 'silver skin' and the 'parchment' covering the two beans inside each cherry. Outside Brazil Latin American coffee is mild arabica and best processed by a 'wet' method whereby the cherries are first washed to float off the stalks and 'light' or unripe cherries, then pulped to remove the flesh of the cherry. The beans are then fermented and washed again to remove the 'silver skin', dried, and then husked of their parchment by machines. In some countries, particularly Colombia, small farmers undertake processing up to the parchment-removing stage with hand-pulpers. This is very rare in Costa Rica and Central America. For full surveys of the coffee trade, see J.W.F. Rowe, *The World's Coffee*, London 1963; William H. Uckers, *All About Coffee*, New York 1922. Costa Rican imports of machinery were modest but constant and in line with technical advances. Carolyn Hall, *El Café y el Desarrollo Histórico-geográfico de Costa Rica*, San José 1976, pp. 49–51; Ciro F.S. Cardoso and Héctor Pérez Brignoli, *Centro América y la Economía Occidental (1520–1930)*, San José, 1977 pp. 247–8.

85. Mitchell A. Seligson, *Peasants of Costa Rica and the Development of Agrarian Capitalism*, Madison 1980, pp. 32, 50. In 1850 Juan Rafael Mora controlled 16 per cent of

all processed coffee exports. It was Mora's proposal to establish a bank that raised fears of monopoly and led to his removal as president and execution.

86. Vega Carballo, 'Nacimiento', p. 102.

87. For example, the Catholic Union Party, established in 1890 under the influence of Archbishop Thiel, who was opposed to the Liberal statutes of 1884 that secularized education and the cemeteries, permitted divorce and allowed work on feast days but also pronounced against 'social injustice' under the oligarchic regime. In this Thiel prefigured Jorge Volio's Reformist Party of the 1920s and the less organized but more decisive impact of Archbishop Víctor Sanabria in the 1930s and 1940s.

88. Stone, *Dinastía*, p. 236.

89. The relative lack of servility displayed by Costa Rican peasants towards landlords because of success in retaining a hold on their lands and thereby a sense of property/identity is the central theme of the analysis of Costa Rican history produced by the exiled political leader of the Dominican Republic Juan Bosch, (*Apuntes para la Interpretación de la Historia de Costa Rica*, San José 1963). As noted above, the high level of proletarianization did not necessarily entail loss of lands by entire families although this was probably greater than often implied in the historical literature. In all events, however proud the rural plebeian stock may have been, it enjoyed precious little participation in the formal political process: the 1847 Constitution restricted the vote to literate fathers over 25 years of age with property worth at least 1,000 pesos (£250). Edelberto Torres Ricas, 'Síntesis Histórica del Proceso Político', in *Centro América Hoy*, Mexico City 1976, p. 73.

90. Seligson, *Peasants*, p. 43.

91. Chester Lloyd Jones, *Costa Rica and Civilization in the Caribbean*, New York 1935, p.65.

92. Clarence F. Jones and Paul C. Martin, 'Evolution of the Banana Industry in Costa Rica', *Economic Geography*, vol. 28, no. 1, January 1952, p. 3.

93. 'For more than three hundred years [Guatemala] has been ruled by an oligarchic-theocratic regime. Government has been retrograde and despotic; the clergy has enjoyed the greatest pre-eminence and meddled in everything. It has been kept in opulence and luxury by the sweat of the people. And what have they been given in compensation for so much sacrifice? Nothing, absolutely nothing! Here are some 800,000 men, women and children who cannot read or write, who cannot understand the religion they profess and which is reduced to mere formulas of superstition. They go without shoes, almost naked, and work as beasts of burden' (Message to Congress, 11 September 1876). This and other central statements and edicts of the Liberal epoch are reproduced in J.M. García Laguardia, ed., *El Pensamiento Liberal en Guatemala*, San José 1977.

94. A. Dessaint, 'Effects of the Hacienda and Plantation Systems on Guatemala's Indians', *América Indígena*, vol. 22, 1962.

95. 'Not only are the Indians of Tecpán opposed to the idea of forced labour, but Indians from all the other villages of this department have also shown their discontent and I have to deal with this every day, since both the Indians and the landowners are abusive. The Indians run and hide, or register unfounded complaints and flee the *fincas*. The landowners request men without respite, ordering them to perform difficult tasks without paying them just wages. . . . It is true that the *fincas* . . . desperately need men to harvest their crops, but the Indians also need time to attend to their own grains' (*Jefe Político*, Chimaltenango, to Minister of Development, 30 October 1893, quoted in Castellanos Cambranes, *Coffee and Peasants*, p. 191).

96. 'If we abandon the farmers to their own resources and do not give them strong and energetic aid, they will be unable to make any progress for all their efforts will be doomed due to the deceit of the Indians. You should therefore see to it: First, that the Indian villages in your jurisdiction be forced to give the number of hands to the farmers that the latter ask for, even to the number of 50 or 100 to a single farmer if his enterprise warrants this number. Second: when one set of Indians has not been able to finish the work in hand in a period of two weeks, a second . . . should be sent to relieve the first, so that the work may not be delayed. Third: the two weeks should be paid for ahead of time through the mayor of the Indian town. . . . Fourth: above all else see to it that any Indian who seeks to evade his duty is punished to the full extent of the law, that the farmers are fully protected and that each Indian is forced to do a full day's work . . .' (quoted in Chester Lloyd Jones, *Guatemala Past*

and Present, Minneapolis 1940, p. 150).

97. McCreery, *Development and the State*, p. 43.

98. Ibid.

99. McCreery, 'Debt Servitude', p. 737. In quantum terms there was little increase in production between 1905 and 1936.

100. Quoted in Herrick, *Desarrollo*, p. 116.

101. *El Diario de Centro América*, 19 April 1892, quoted in McCreery, 'Debt Servitude', p. 737.

102. Ibid., p. 741, which gives the population of these departments in 1893, 1921 and 1950. According to the 1880 census Guatemala possessed 1,244,602 people, 379,828 of them *ladinos* and 844,774 Indians. Augusto Cazali Avila, 'El Desarrollo del Cultivo del Café y su Influencia en el Régimen del Trabajo Agricola. Epoca de la Reforma Liberal (1871–1885)', *Estudios Centroamericanos,* vol. 2, 1976, p. 81. For a racial disaggregation of the 1950 population, see Mario Monteforte Toledo, *Guatemala. Monografía Sociológica*, Mexico City 1959, p. 81. The early areas of coffee cultivation are identified by Castellanos Cambranes, *Coffee and Peasants*, p. 110.

103. For example, Robert A. Naylor challenges the belief that large amounts of Indian land were lost, 'Guatemala: Indian Attitudes towards Land Tenure', *Journal of Inter-American Studies*, vol. 9, no. 4, October 1967, p. 629. On the other hand, Antonio Goubaud Carrera suggests a figure of 100,000 acres lost. 'Indian Adjustments to Modern National Culture', in Sol Tax, ed., *Acculturation in the Americas*, Chicago 1952, p. 245. It should be stressed that *ejidos* and Indian community lands were not outlawed but simply lacked juridical defence of their collective character, which may or may not have prompted transfer of ownership.

104. Herrick, *Desarrollo*, pp. 232–3; Ricardo Falla, *Quiché Rebelde*, Guatemala City 1978, p. 227. Some communities purchased title to some if not all of their old lands. Castellanos Cambranes, *Coffee and Peasants*, p. 290.

105. For example San Juan Ixcoy and Momostenango, both in Quiché, which lost substantial lands, prompting both active resistance and efforts by the authorities to limit alienation. In the case of San Juan Ixcoy David McCreery notes the practice of the community leadership sending labourers to plantations in order to raise cash for the surveying of the *ejido*. David McCreery, 'Land and Labour in San Juan Ixcoy, 1846-1945', forthcoming. According to Robert Carmack, Momostenango lost 11,000 acres under Barrios. 'Spanish–Indian Relations', p. 242.

106. Momostenango Indians engaged in guerrilla warfare in 1876 and were attacking the Quiché army barracks in September 1877 with a heavy loss of lives. Barrios subsequently ordered a more cautious allocation of lands. Ibid., p.242. For other examples, see Castellanos Cambranes, *Coffee and Peasants*, pp. 269–72.

107. The cycles are not, however, fully complementary: the season for the first corn crop is from April to August and for the second from August to December; that for the first bean crop is from May to August, for the second from August to December. It is the second crop that is most prejudiced by seasonal labour for both coffee and cotton (harvested between December and February). Rodolfo Quirós Guardia, 'Agricultural Development in Central America: Its Origin and Nature', Research Paper no. 49, Land Tenure Center, University of Wisconsin, Madison, January 1973, p. 78.

108. Jones, *Guatemala*, p. 150; McCreery, 'Debt Servitude', p. 741. McCreery notes that the *mandamiento* was not fully erased until the 1920s, shortly before debt peonage was itself suppressed in favour of new vagrancy laws. Whilst Indians still possessed land direct forced labour was difficult to organize. The less coercive and more market-based character of debt peonage was a preferable method at this stage.

109. McCreery, 'Debt Servitude', p. 743.

110. Ibid., p. 744. For a view of more contemporary ritualistic obligations, and a rather questionable analysis that ties them to the guerrilla movement of the 1960s, see Paul Diener, 'The Tears of St Anthony: Ritual and Revolution in Eastern Guatemala', *Latin American Perspectives*, vol. 5, no. 3, summer 1978. The primary basis of such a comprehensive labour system in festival debt is so singular that it deserves further research, which may well reveal a parallel concentration in petty commodity production, creating a drain on cash beyond that determined by seasonal cycles (reduced second crops, etc.). Nonetheless, it does appear that commodities

such as candles continue to be produced predominantly by *ladinos*. Carol Smith suggests that peasant markets expanded in the Conservative period and demonstrates that petty commodity production was quite extensive in the department of Totonicapán by the end of the century: 'Local History in Global Context: Economic and Social Transitions in Western Guatemala', *Comparative Studies in Society and History*, vol. 26, no. 2, April 1984; 'Does a Commodity Economy Enrich the Few while Ruining the Masses? Differentiation among Petty Commodity Producers in Guatemala', *The Journal of Peasant Studies*, vol. 11, no. 3, April 1984.

111. Woodward, *Central America*, p. 165. By the end of the century the German colony had invested 200 million marks in 300,000 hectares of Guatemala's best land. Castellanos Cambranes, *Coffee and Peasants*, p. 145. For full details of one such enterprise, see Guillermo Nañez Falcón, *Paul Diesseldorff, German Entrepreneur in the Alta Verapaz: 1871–1937*, unpublished PhD, Tulane University 1970.

112. Menjívar, *Acumulación*, pp. 35, 87.

113. Menjívar, ibid., p. 131, suggests, on the basis of a lack of names of provincial indigo farmers figuring amongst those of coffee, that the main stock of new entrepreneurs had an urban background. Flores Macal, *Formas*, p. 58, questions this on the grounds that relatively high indigo sales must have permitted a quite intensive process of accumulation. Browning, *El Salvador*, p. 159, suggests that both mortgages and sale of equipment enabled indigo farmers to convert to coffee production. However, one is struck by how few obviously successful cases of this there are.

114. Menjívar, *Acumulación*, pp. 112–17.

115. Ibid., pp. 93–4; Browning suggests that land in *ejido* covered more than a quarter of the country. *El Salvador*, pp. 189–90.

116. The central and supplementary legislation is described in Menjívar, *Acumulación*, pp. 101–4; Browning, *El Salvador*, pp. 182–207.

117. This was true even in some parts of Chalatenango, not a region badly affected by alienation at this stage. Carlos Rafael Cabarrús P., *Génesis de una Revolución*, Mexico City 1983.

118. Menjívar, *Acumulación*, pp. 90, 150–1; Browning, *El Salvador*, pp. 217–18.

119. An interesting note of 'critical support' for Ezeta is given by the Communist leader Miguel Mármol, born early in the twentieth century when the memory of this maverick was still alive amongst both rural and urban poor. Roque Dalton, *Miguel Mármol*, San José 1977, pp. 55 ff.

120. The members and production of the leading landed families in the 1920s are given in Eduardo Colindres, *Fondements économiques de la Bourgeoisie Salvadorienne dans la Periode 1950 à 1970*, Paris 1975; Everett Alan Wilson, *The Crisis of National Integration in El Salvador, 1919–1935*, unpublished PhD, Stanford University 1970, pp. 63–4.

121. Menjívar, *Acumulación*, p. 50.

122. E. Bradford Burns, 'The Intellectual Infrastructure of Modernization in El Salvador, 1870–1900', *The Americas*, vol. 61, no. 3, January 1985, p. 63.

123. Percy F. Martin, *El Salvador of the XXth Century*, London 1911; Burns, 'Intellectual Infrastructure', p. 66; Menjívar, *Acumulación*, p. 30.

124. Durón, 'Gobernantes', pp. 16–17; Posas and Del Cid, *Construcción*, pp. 13–15; Kenneth V. Finney, 'Rosario and the Election of 1887: the Political Economy of Mining in Honduras', HAHR, vol. 59, no. 1, February 1979, p. 81.

125. Guillermo Molina Chocano, 'La Formación del Estado y el Origen Minero–mercantil de la Burguesía Hondureña', ESC, no. 25, 1980, pp. 65, 67–8.

126. Kenneth H. Matheson, 'History of Rosario Mine, Honduras, Central America', *The Mines Magazine*, vol. 51, nos 6 and 7, June and July 1961, p. 37.

127. Besides several members of the Soto and Bográn cabinets, stockholders included Santos Soto, who established the Banco de Honduras in 1889, and the leading landlord/merchants Ignacio Agurcia and José Esteban Lazo, who bought the lease to the national mint in 1886. Molina Chocano, 'Formación', pp. 73–5.

128. The anti-semitic vitriol directed at Valentine did not suffuse all the sentiments of the election slate drawn up for San Juancito by enemies of the company: 'We will no longer swallow the indignities of this individual, unfit to live in this Republic – Ruined, Miserable

Jew! We know how to administer justice. Honduras is very free and independent. We will no longer tolerate a "gringo", a "Yankee" and a foreign upstart that comes to insinuate himself into our political affairs and hand down laws as if he were king' (quoted in Finney, 'Rosario', p. 107). Bográn won the election by 28,394 votes to Policarpo Bonilla's 5,326. Bonilla finally took power through an invasion from Nicaragua in December 1893.

129. Matheson, 'Rosario', p. 27. Wage rates varied between $0.63 and $1.50 in Honduran mines in 1889/90; this was above average but not markedly so. Molina Chocano, 'Formación', p. 77. The state's efforts to provide Rosario with labour through the *enganche* produced only a high level of desertion.

130. Between 1887 and 1915 Rosario issued an average dividend of $139,000 a year. Molina Chocano, 'Formación', p. 70.

131. For the value of gold, see Pierre Vilar, *A History of Gold and Money 1450–1920*, London 1976, pp. 351–2. The average price of silver on the London market fell from over 48d per ounce in 1885 to 27d in 1898. Metallgesellschaft, *Statistical Compilation of Lead, Copper, Spelter, Tin, Silver, Nickel, Aluminium and Quicksilver*, Frankfurt 1899, p. 30.

132. In 1903/4 exports of minerals were 1.2 million pesos against 2.3 million of banana sales; in 1914/15 3.7 million and 3.9 million, but by 1918/19 2.1 million and 5.6 million. Vilma Lainez and Víctor Meza, 'El Enclave Bananero en la Historia de Honduras', ESC, no. 5, 1973, p. 145.

133. Ibid.; Molina Chocano, 'Formación', p. 80.

134. For histories of the fruit companies, see Thomas L. Karnes, *Tropical Enterprise: The Standard Fruit and Steamship Company*, Baton Rouge 1978; Thomas P. McCann, *An American Company. The Tragedy of United Fruit*, New York 1976; Charles D. Kepner and Jay H. Soothill, *The Banana Empire*, New York 1935; Charles D. Kepner, *Social Aspects of the Banana Industry*, New York 1936.

135. Mario Posas, *El Movimiento Obrero Hondureno*, unpublished thesis, San José n.d., p. 29.

136. Lainez and Meza, 'Enclave', p. 147. The level of exemptions in 1917/18 was significantly higher than those extended before the end of the war, although these still accounted for the equivalent of 50 per cent of fiscal revenue.

137. Dana G. Munro, *Intervention and Dollar Diplomacy in the Caribbean, 1900–1921*, Princeton 1964, pp. 217–25.

138. Ibid., pp. 228–30. In a typical incident during the invasion US naval officers refused to allow fighting in La Ceiba and insisted that the government garrison and rebel troops, led by 'General' Lee Christmas of Louisiana, stage their battle outside town instead. This would have lost the garrison its strategic advantage, and so it evacuated.

139. US Department of Commerce, cited in Menjívar, *Acumulacion*, pp. 58–9. There are some anomalies in these figures as a result of different means of calculation. However, the low level of foreign investment in Nicaragua is not in doubt: Rafael Menjívar, ed., *La Inversión Extranjera en Centroamérica*, San José 1974; Gert Rosenthal, 'El Papel de la Inversión Extranjera Directa en el Proceso de Integración', in *Centroamérica Hoy*.

140. Rippy, *British Investment*, Tables 25 and 26.

141. Quoted in Walter LaFeber, *Inevitable Revolutions. The United States in Central America*, New York 1984, p. 37.

142. Ibid. A detailed survey of the development of this policy is given in Munro, *Intervention*, pp. 65–159.

143. Biderman, *Class Structure*, p. 52.

144. Vargas, 'Desarrollo del Capitalismo', p. 43.

145. Wheelock, *Imperialismo*, p. 77.

146. Jaime Wheelock Roman, *Raices Indígenas de la Lucha Anticolonialista en Nicaragua*, Mexico City 1974, pp. 166–7; Enrique Miranda Casij, 'La Guerra Olvidada', *Revista de Pensamiento Centroamericano*, no. 144, September 1972.

147. Quoted in Miranda, 'Guerra Olvidada', p. 81.

148. Charles L. Stansifer, 'José Santos Zelaya: A New Look at Nicaragua's "Liberal" Dictator', *Revista Interamericana*, vol. 7, fall 1977.

149. According to Wheelock, Zelaya removed the forced labour and vagrancy laws, which were 'strictly Conservative', and provided the major impulse for coffee although extensive

expropriation of lands did not take place until after 1910. *Imperialismo*, pp. 71, 78. While it is the case that Nicaragua's financial problems did not become very acute until after Zelaya's fall and coffee production did accelerate in the late 1890s, to ascribe to him all the 'good' features of capitalist development – investment, immigration, modernization of infrastructure – and all the 'bad' ones to the Conservatives stretches even nationalist sympathies too far.

150. Gregorio Selser, *Sandino*, New York 1981, p. 27. The basis of local opposition to Zelaya is usually identified in commercial interests trading with the US and cattle ranchers. These sectors resented both what they saw as a 'mestizo' displacement of the aristocracy from power and what they suffered in the market by virtue of extensive foreign, usually German, ownership of new coffee *fincas*. By the turn of the century foreign-owned plantations were producing more coffee than those in the hands of Nicaraguans. John Booth, *The End and the Beginning. The Nicaraguan Revolution*, Boulder 1982, p. 23; Amaru Barahona Portocarrero, 'Breve Estudio sobre la Historia de Nicaragua', in Pablo González Casanova, ed., *América Latina: Historia de Medio Siglo*, Mexico City 1981, vol. 2, p. 379; Woodward, *Central America*, p. 157.

151. José Santos Zelaya, 'Refutación a las Afirmaciones del Presidente Taft', reprinted in *Revista Casa de las Américas*, no. 88, 1975, p. 108.

152. V.G. Kiernan, *America: The New Imperialism*, London 1980, p. iii.

2
The Oligarchy in Control, 1910–30

The Central American area down to and including the Isthmus of Panama constitutes a legitimate sphere of influence for the United States. . . . We do control the destinies of Central America and we do so for the simple reason that the national interest dictates such a course . . .

US Under-Secretary of State Robert Olds, 2 January 1927[1]

Bolshevism? It's drifting in. The working people hold meetings on Sundays and get very excited. They say, 'We dig the holes for the trees, we clean the weeds, we prune the trees, we pick the coffee. Who earns the money then?' . . . Yes, there will be trouble one of these days.

Coffee *finquero* James Hill, El Salvador, 1925[2]

It is distinctly worthy of note that the number of registrations amounts to 85,619 in the city of San Salvador alone . . . this would mean that practically every man, woman and child in the city would be voting.

US Ambassador Warren D. Robbins, El Salvador, 1931[3]

I remain your most obedient servant, who ardently desires to put you in a handsome tomb with beautiful bouquets of flowers.

Augusto César Sandino to USMC Captain G. Hatfield, 1927[4]

In the 1970s the military regimes that took power in a welter of South American countries uniformly abolished both the substance and the trappings of constitutional government. The ritual claims of the armed forces to be the 'highest expression of nationhood' fused easily with the requirements of campaigns against 'subversion' in making all political activity except that of the military inherently 'anti–national' and 'corrupt'. These motifs were equally common in Central America, but there some outward semblance of democratic procedure was preserved: elections were diligently held on the ordained date, congresses were frequently permitted to hold debates, and the division of powers was formally observed. As will be seen, all this amounted to very little more than a convenient device, devoid of any substance and in no sense prejudicial to the prosecution of repressive campaigns often as radical and brutal as those in the Southern Cone.

It is of some consequence that while the freedom to oppose was resolutely withheld, it was, in contrast to the South American regimes, rarely removed entirely from the statute books to be replaced by new 'organic' codes of a corporatist character. For Washington, the Central American regimes remained strongly anti-Communist and yet could still be defended as aspiring to democratic norms even if their practice in this regard sometimes gave lamentable cause for concern. Under Carter this meant that the observance of human rights could be required through adjustment of the existing system; under Reagan it facilitated the holding of 'better' (US-supervised) elections without intruding upon the structure of military control on which the entire apparatus of domination rested. The opposition quite naturally attacked the regimes as dictatorial because the civil liberties they proclaimed did not exist in practice. Yet when, in the early 1980s, some limited space had to be yielded to the forces of reform, all but the radical left found reason to avail themselves of such restricted opportunities and engage in open activity. This simultaneously fortified the system, by giving it a more robust semblance of ideological latitude, and placed pressure upon it, precisely through the participation of those who had heretofore been excluded.

Our concern at this point is less directly with this tension and the degree of authentic political competition – let alone genuine civil liberty – that has been permitted; rather it is to signal the existence of a specific mode of modern political domination which draws on the traditional forms of Liberal oligarchic rule of the late nineteenth and early twentieth centuries. It should, of course, be noted that the retention of democratic formalities derived from a certain weakness of the military relative to their counterparts in the Southern Cone, the Central American forces lacking the institutional resources to make a complete break with the existing political system. On the other hand, the form of government that prevailed in the region in the 1970s had a long pedigree and was not the result of some recent rupture. The fact that, with the exception of Costa Rica and to some degree Honduras, the military had already held political power for decades with only short and minor interruptions indicates that they possessed palpable strengths relative to the ruling classes of the region. The manner in which they have ruled in recent years is neither essentially new nor simply the product of 'backwardness', but it does reflect an enduring strain in the protocols of the Liberal oligarchic system well beyond the crisis this system encountered in the early 1930s and the modifications progressively undertaken thereafter.

Except in the case of Guatemala, the regimes of the Liberal oligarchy (1880–1930) were neither democratic nor wholly despotic. Once the principal requirements of primary accumulation had been met, the tasks of social control became more modulated and systematized. It should be recognized that, notwithstanding levels of exploitation and impoverishment that would today appear to compel peasant jacqueries and widespread violence, the Liberal order persisted for nearly half a century in conditions of relative stability. Although frequent changes of administration in both Nicaragua and Honduras betokened the absence of a fully consolidated ruling class, they interrupted the agricultural cycle much less than in the nineteenth century and never provoked substantial social unrest until the late 1920s. Elsewhere, the impact of World War One and the sharp recession that followed it disturbed the ascendant trend in trade and growth in commercial agriculture, but only for a short period. Hence, when the full impact of the 'Crash' of 1929 came to bear in 1930–31 it was on economies at an unprecedented level of expansion and with a correspondingly reduced subsistence base. Moreover, partially as a result of these conditions, political life, while very far from free, became more competitive than ever before; new parties complicated contests between comfortable *caudillos*, the rudiments of trade unions were beginning to win the right to exist (even if only to be persecuted above ground), and germs of 'alien ideologies' such as Socialism and Communism had started to infect the body politic. The rupture of 1930–32 was, therefore, no less pronounced in the field of politics than in that of the economy. Everywhere it either completely halted or considerably reduced a grudging and erratic expansion of the political nation and thereby simultaneously preserved the guts of the oligarchic system, by reversing the concessions it was perforce making, and laid the basis for its subsequent modification, by deepening its autocratic features and closing off the space for ideological exchange.

The general form of domination that followed the Crash is frequently viewed as a simple quantum increase in oppression, but it amounted to more than this. The new political autocracy suppressed many of the civic and specifically oligarchic characteristics of the Liberal system that, by virtue of providing a framework for political competition within the ruling class, made at least a passing nod to the notion of extending this to literate, *ladi-*

no and urban society as a whole. In this sense at least the period preceding the depression is by no means as unremarkable as it is sometimes depicted, and in some respects it offers similarities with political developments in the mid 1980s. The years up to 1930 are also important in terms of what had become an irreversible US involvement in Central American affairs, encouraging the emergence of nationalist and radical currents that were not permitted to exist for long but left an indelible mark on both the local political systems and Washington's relations with the region. The historical record does not bear out any putative 'golden age' in the radical tradition of the isthmus, but it was in these years that this was established. Its existence tarnishes what is certainly viewed by the Central American ruling class as an epoch of social order in which the ancien regime flourished on the basis of its own virtues, the most celebrated of which was a harmonious bonding of peon and landlord through the rigours of the seasonal cycle. Not even in the heyday of the mean suburban colonels, sporting dark glasses, trained in the US and advised by the Israelis, did this motif lose its pride of place in official odes to subordination. Whereas such mystifications had never cohered with reality, after 1930 they could no longer rest on automatic acceptance.

The Liberal Order

Between 1920 and 1924 Central American GDP was rising by 3 per cent a year; over the next five years it averaged 4.3 per cent.[5] In 1924 the world coffee price touched an unprecedented high of $0.25 per lb.[6] Salvadorean coffee exports worth $22.7 million in 1928 were three times those of 1915, the area under coffee in 1930 (106,000 hectares) being 50 per cent higher than that in 1919.[7] Costa Rican production doubled between 1915 and 1929, and that of Guatemala in 1927 was nearly seven times greater than at the beginning of the Liberal era.[8] Over the decade following World War One Honduran banana exports increased tenfold; the country maintained its place as the world's leading producer until 1945.[9] By the mid 1920s the banana companies were cultivating over 100,000 acres with a labour force of 22,000; UFCO had expanded its investment to $26 million (over four times its capital in Colombia) and was buying less than a quarter of its fruit from independent growers.[10] The size of the coffee labour force elsewhere is more difficult to determine, but it is evident from the scale of the expansion that it was generally on the increase. In El Salvador coffee accounted for over 90 per cent of export earnings in 1929, and escalating exploitation of land for its cultivation, in the west of the country particularly, was provoking concern about such an acute dependence upon one crop: 'where formerly there was yucca, tobacco, bananas and many other crops, today one sees only coffee, coffee, coffee.... People are not philanthropists but agriculturalists who work land in order to make as much money as possible.'[11] Even in Nicaragua, which by virtue of its ability to exploit modest quantities of wood, gold, bananas and sugar had the most diversified export structure of the region, coffee rose from 27 per cent of exports in 1920 to 62 per cent in 1926.[12] The growth in GDP increased correspondingly from 1.9 per cent (1920–24) to 6.4 per cent (1924–29).[13]

It is very tempting to view such impressive indices of both growth and increasing dependence on a single commodity solely in the light of the catastrophe that was to occur at the end of the decade. But one should not lose sight of the fact that this expansion formed part of both a consolidation of the Liberal landed regime and rising US interests in the region. Between 1913 and 1929 the increase in sales to the US was appreciably greater than that in the total level of exports for Guatemala (150 and 67 per cent), Honduras (800 and 600 per cent) and Nicaragua (100 and 37 per cent) whilst imports from the US doubled in every Central American country over the same period, quadrupling in the case of El Salvador.[14] As Table 1 demonstrates, US direct investment grew equally rapidly but was still far

Table 1: British and US Direct Investment in Central America ($million)[1]

	1913/14[2]		*1929*		*1939/40*[3]		*1949/50*[4]	
	GB	*US*	*GB*	*US*	*GB*	*US*	*GB*	*US*
Guatemala	50.5	35.8	57.7	58.8	50.3	68.0	39.4	106.0
El Salvador	10.9	6.6	9.5	24.8	5.2	11.0	6.7	17.0
Honduras	15.2	9.5	25.5	80.5	8.1	38.0	3.6	62.0
Nicaragua	6.0	7.3	4.0	17.3	2.0	8.0	–	9.0
Costa Rica	32.2	21.6	27.4	20.5	22.0	24.0	18.0	60.0
Total	114.8	80.8	99.1	201.9	87.6	149.0	67.7	254.0

Notes:

1. Since these figures are derived from different sources and investment can be calculated by various methods, they should be taken only as approximate levels and general trends.

2. 1913 for US; 1914 for Britain. Sources: Rippy, *British Investment*; US Department of Commerce, cited in Rafael Menjívar, *Acumulación, Originaria y Desarrollo del Capitalismo en El Salvador*, San José 1980, pp.58–9. Sterling converted at $4.83.

3. 1939 for Britain; 1940 for US. Sources: as above, with US figures already rounded. Sterling converted at $4.68.

4. 1949 for Britain; 1950 for US. Sources: as above, with US figures already rounded and sterling converted at the pre-September 1949 rate of $4.03, which further exaggerates the nominal value of British holdings.

from ubiquitous; even thirty years later when multinational corporations other than the banana enterprises began to set up operations in the region, aggregate levels remained relatively modest. All the same, by the end of the 1920s investment in strategic infrastructure, the gradual displacement of European capital, and much greater possibilities for loans all served to enhance the political interests that Washington unreservedly espoused and pursued in Central America. This, though, was no unproblematic imperialism. Although the US had emerged from the world war in incomparably better shape than the European powers and was now entering a new phase of industrial production – that of 'Fordism' and the assembly line science of Frederick Taylor – the passage from Roosevelt's 'Big Stick' through the 'Dollar Diplomacy' of the Taft and Wilson administrations to F.D.R.'s 'Good Neighbour' policy was strewn with problems. None of the landed bourgeoisies controlling the states of Central America possessed the capacity or collective will to resist the diplomatic arrogance and feigned propriety of incursions by loan sharks and contingents of marines. However, by the same token, none of them exercised such resolute control over the population that they could afford to adopt full sepoy status without courting major risks. When, in the case of Nicaragua, such risks were indeed run, they provoked a response – in the form of Sandino's guerrilla – that was containable (for forty-five years) but also the source of considerable embarrassment for both the metropolitan power and its local allies. Of course, the advantages gained by both parties outweighed such attendant setbacks but, as has become particularly evident in the post-Vietnam era, however great these advantages might be and whatever the violence employed to obtain them, the contradictory aspects of such control are never wholly absent and can at times acquire a critical importance.

In the 1920s, as in the 1980s, the case of Nicaragua proved to be distinct in terms of US policy towards Central America. Yet one can perceive a generalized grain of oligarchic recalcitrance caused by overbearing Yankee activity. This was the case in Guatemala, where such sentiments played a subordinate but visible part in accumulating opposition to the dictatorial regime of Manuel Estrada Cabrera (1898–1920). The length of Estrada's government – surpassed in the twentieth century only by that of the Somoza family – reflects a general acquiescence of the landlord class in a personalist regime that ensured social control but restricted political participation and competition even inside the ruling class itself. Whereas elsewhere the autocracy of the early Liberal era had been replaced either by easy concordats between civilian dignitaries (Costa Rica and El Salvador) or by more unsettling exchanges based on 'insurrections' (Honduras and Nicaragua), in Guatemala Estrada was regularly re-elected by virtue of his control of the military, both in a general sense and in terms of the specific mechanisms employed, as on polling day in 1916:

> Under the compulsory service law every citizen between twenty and sixty was a soldier. The bugle call was blown in the village as notice for all to appear the following day. At the convenient time the bugles were blown again, the roll called, and the voters lined up for the performance of their duties. Campaign buttons were then pinned on them and each was handed a ballot bearing the statement: 'I hereby give my vote for Licenciado Don Manuel Estrada Cabrera for President of the Republic for the term 1917–1923'. Voters then signed their ballots or made their marks . . .[15]

The length of the Estrada regime may also be attributed to his compliance with the requirements of UFCO, which received concessions of positively Honduran generosity. Since banana land did not trespass that fit for coffee, the establishment of company plantations was not in itself an item of dispute for local *finqueros*. However, the monopoly of bulk transport to the Caribbean coastal port of Puerto Barrios held by UFCO's subsidiary International Railroads of Central America (IRCA) was a persistent source of discontent. Estrada's concessions exempted both UFCO and IRCA from presenting their accounts to the state, taxed the shipment of bananas much more lightly than that of coffee (even in 1928 the rate was 1.9 per cent against 8.7 per cent), and permitted an open market in freight rates.[16] In line with the longstanding UFCO strategy of exploiting its transport system to control markets, IRCA not only charged differential rates that penalized coffee but also applied surcharges on cargo which did not enter Puerto Barrios or travel in company ships.[17] Such an open exploitation of monopoly was bound to excite opposition. Moreover, although during the world war Estrada had refused to impose restrictions on German planters to the degree demanded by the US (and confiscated lands were later returned), partly out of apprehension over losing local support, he succeeded in offending an even wider constituency by facilitating the forced sale of the European-owned *Empresa Eléctrica* to US capital at an extremely low price.[18] By this stage the impetus of a personalist regime was clearly on the wane and even an anxious US government was seeking out alternatives. But the ability of Estrada's opponents to make political capital of his concessions gave their movement a nationalist and populist edge, averting independent and more radical mobilization by a growing middle class and artisanate in the capital, which now had a population of over 100,000 and was rapidly becoming the site of a new urban politics.

The regime of Carlos Herrera, conservative but constitutionalist and momentarily pledged to the re-establishment of Central American union, betokened a shift in the character of oligarchic administration that was evident throughout the region as a whole. Although Herrera's commitment to both union and revising the terms of operation for foreign capital provoked his removal by a coup within eighteen months, the regime of General José María Orellano (1921–26) being recognized immediately by the US in contravention of several international agreements to boycott regimes founded on insurrection, there was no easy or immediate reversion to the pattern of absolutism. Both Orellano and his successor Lázaro Chacón (1926–30) were fulsome in their concessions to UFCO and other US interests, and Orellano's minister of war, General Jorge Ubico, repressed strikes and opposition with a vehemence that exceeded even that of Estrada. But throughout this period such policies were continually contested and constituencies canvassed on an unprecedented scale. The election of 1926 was not by any means open but neither was the result a completely foregone conclusion. The stern Ubico was obliged to form a political party (*Partido Progresista*) that courted popular support with a platform sufficiently buoyant in language to be considered reformist and shunned by the oligarchy, which put Chacón into office. Yet the new ruler still faced opposition to his policy of favouring UFCO both in congress and from the landlords' *Confederación de Asociaciones Agrícolas*, which produced a political stalemate within the ruling class.[19] In 1930 Chacón's illness finally permitted Ubico to assume power, but it is extremely unlikely that the resumption of the dictatorial tradition would have been so smooth had the recession not cut short the export boom, privileging defence of the landed regime as a whole over that of certain competitive interests within it.

The contrast between the oligarchic regime in Costa Rica with the likes of Estrada Cabrera and Ubico was so great that even contemporary writers in receipt of wages for the exercise of critical faculties are prone to go dewy-eyed: 'There was a kind of noblesse oblige about the Costa Rican oligarchy since it was neither oppressive nor venal and spent more money on education than on armaments. Facilitating this attitude was a friendly and hard-working population . . . [which] was egalitarian. . . . The oligarchy was content to conserve this tranquil scene.'[20] Such an image is undoubtedly encouraged by the hegemony of the 'Olympians' and in particular the hold on office of Cleto González (1906–10; 1928–32) and Ricardo Jiménez (1910–14; 1924–28; 1932–36). Such continuity was never simply 'conserved'; however cohesive the landlord class, it was obliged to manoeuvre to retain its control. This was fully evident during and immediately following the world war, when the disruption of trade forced the government of Alfredo González Flor (1914–17) to impose an income tax, intervene in the banking system, and even tax land in order to preserve fiscal order.[21] As a temporary abandonment of the full Liberal programme these initiatives presaged developments in the 1940s; but at the time they antagonized a majority of the oligarchy, which, in an action not unlike that taken against Mora in 1859 for attempting to establish a bank, patronized a coup by General Federico Tinoco in 1917. Tinoco gave the grandees a salutary lesson in realpolitik by refusing to give up power and reimposing the taxes, making the most of the possibilities open to an armed arriviste. He was, however, ill-served by concerted lobbying on the part of UFCO, currently out of favour in the Wilson White House and unusually misguided in its assessment of the political balance of forces. Tinoco further antagonized Washington by preferring the interests of a British oil company to those of a US competitor, and was unable to negotiate Wilson's refusal to grant recognition, a move praised by a now chastised oligarchy. The General fell in 1919, a rare example of US destabilization being directed against a dictator.[22] The subsequent cut in the military budget, which enabled the taxes to be lifted, and effective dismemberment of the army's organization to avoid any repetition of this militarist episode was probably a more significant contribution to the maintenance of civilist politics than the theatrics of disestablishment in 1948.

Tinoco's removal was not followed by a simple reversion to the status quo ante. Over the ensuing decade aggressive activity on the part of UFCO and US companies controlling electric power and communications interests gave rise to the first organized expressions of nationalism. These were still weak and subordinate currents, but in the case of Jorge Volio's short-lived *Partido Reformista* formed part of a recognizably modern ideology of reform, development and social justice. Volio's training for the priesthood at Louvain brought him into contact with the early social Christian movement, an influence that was fortified by Leo XIII's *Rerum Novarum*, which stipulated the social obligations of private property, as well as the example of Archbishop Thiel; but he eventually found his vocation less as a clerk in holy orders than as 'el tribuno de la plebe y guerrillero de la libertad'. Established early in 1923, Volio's party received the backing of the country's first trade union confederation, *Confederación General de Trabajadores*, for the 1924 election and proved sufficiently dynamic to oblige the wily Jiménez to propose an alliance. Despite persistent promises to reject this anticipated offer, the conditions for a resolutely independent petty-bourgeois politics were manifestly not given and the tyro Volio finally took the bait; he was rapidly outmanoeuvred and responded to the party's subsequent demise by staging an ill-judged and hopeless attempt at rebellion. Yet Jiménez was astute enough to embrace the reformists' proposed accident insurance bill, and henceforth Costa Rican politics were to bear the imprint of *reformista* influence as well as that of the wartime experiment in state intervention.[23] Volio's idealist programme for social betterment was by no means unique in this period, but it provided a singularly important precedent for ecclesiastical reformism over the coming decades and represented an early version of Christian Democracy, a movement which history has denied a voice in contemporary Costa Rica to anything approaching the degree that obtains elsewhere in the isthmus.

The landed class of El Salvador evaded the traumas of military and economic intervention, going further than any other regional oligarchy to broaden the scope of political activity in the period up to 1931. This phenomenon is seldom appreciated because of the small size and great economic power of the rural bourgeoisie as well as the extreme repression of 1932. However, the degree to which political life was opened up undoubtedly played a part in determining the severity with which it was subsequently closed down. Moreover, the temporary disaggregation of the liberal concordat may be seen as something of a precedent for the much more stable, structured and successful political concessions made by the oligarchy to the military after 1932.

It should be stressed that neither strategy involved a loss of economic power. As has been noted, expansion of coffee during the 1920s was unprecedented, and by the end of the decade the area under cultivation was 90 per cent of that farmed in 1960.[24] Control of this land has popularly been attributed to 'the fourteen families' of the oligarchy whereas in 1920 there were around sixty-five major commercial enterprises, almost all of them built on a family basis.[25] The 1930 census listed 640 people (0.2 per cent of the population) who were identifiably large landlords – there were 3,400 growers of coffee but only 350 owned more than 125 acres of land – or capitalists.[26] By the mid 1970s the country's economic structure had altered quite appreciably, most notably because of the expansion of cotton, but the physiognomy of this ruling class was little changed: twenty-five firms accounted for 84 per cent of all coffee exports while forty-nine families held estates over 1,000 hectares in size.[27] Almost all of these enterprises were linked directly to agriculture although there was from quite an early stage some degree of specialization between direct cultivation, trading, banking and general commerce.[28] This in itself has never prompted a strategic division in the ruling class, but it has on occasions enhanced the natural competition between capitals and spawned varied projects; it is not difficult to appreciate the potential tensions between planters, exporters and bankers in moments of duress. Such a set of secondary imbalances – of a type much less evident in Costa Rica and more extensive but less concentrated in Guatemala – can impede direct and consolidated political initiatives on the part of a ruling class. Hence, even a concentration of economic power so great as that in El Salvador is not necessarily reproduced in a specific form in the political terrain.[29]

The short-lived and popularly elected government of Arturo Araujo (1931) is frequently considered a complete anomaly within the framework of the Salvadorean oligarchic regime, stabilized from 1906 and effectively monopolized from 1911 by members of the Meléndez and Quinóñez families.[30] Araujo took office with his *Partido Laborista* – modelled on the British Labour Party, which he admired as the result of a stay in Liverpool – enjoying widespread popular support and subscribing to a heady programme of social egalitarianism and economic reform. Although the Depression ensured that Araujo's vague policies were never applied, the young Communist Party was permitted to operate in public. For a short while open political life was more extensive in ideological reference than at any time in the nation's history, except perhaps between October and December 1979 (again in the midst of an escalating campaign of repression). It is of some significance that when Araujo's chaotic regime was overthrown in December 1931, it was by junior military officers with no tangible evidence of direct landlord participation.[31]

The government was certainly subjected to singular tensions as a result of the collapse of the economy, but its distinction from more stable and identifiably conservative administrations was not as great as is sometimes claimed. Araujo's predecessor, Pio Romero Bosque (1927–31), had been directly placed in office by the Meléndez Quinóñez clique and yet was able to preside over a relatively open and competitive election in November 1930. In this Romero made a break with the old model of continuism: he had already opened a breach, in formal terms at least, by legalizing the eight-hour day, protecting artisanal interests, and removing a longstanding state of siege. This was quite compatible with continued attacks on the left, repression of attempts at rural unionization, and an aversion to increases in social expenditure, which remained more or less constant from 1911.[32] As early as 1917 Carlos Meléndez had created a popular political organization, adventurously dubbed *Liga Roja*, which professed some egalitarian ideals whilst physically combating the new trade unions and the growing middle-class urban opposition movement. The *Liga* was in no sense progressive, but it did represent a new form of landlord-sponsored political activity, complementing the services of the National Guard and the upper-class coteries gathered in the *Casa Salvadoreña* in securing public order. Addressing and organizing the plebian masses in more than an exclusively repressive manner was, therefore, not a complete innovation in 1930, and Romero had demonstrated that it could be undertaken without undue prejudice to the system. Thus, although Araujo was a dissident within the ranks of the landlord elite, and his regime a threat to continued hegemony, his dissidence derived from taking previous essays in co-optation to their ultimate expression rather than breaking with them. The threat he posed to the status quo lay less in his own opposition to it than in a reluctance to meet external challenges by dispensing with the artifice of democracy.

The alignment of the Honduran political class into the camps of Liberal and National Parties remained too strong throughout this period to give that popular mobilization which they dared to undertake a more than strictly partisan character. Moreover, the most potent constituency for such activity comprised the workers of banana companies that were certainly not averse to direct participation in political life but strenuously resisted all bar the most closely supervised 'agitation' of their employees. The very limited growth of the urban centres in the country's interior prompted little alteration in traditional forms of political conduct, which despite the expansion of the banana industry were only to be rectified at the end of the 1920s. Over the first thirty years of the century Hondurans were ruled by eighteen administrations, largely indistinguishable in terms of substantive policy. Although the interests of Zemurray's Cuyamel company have usually been identified with those of the Liberals whilst UFCO's links were with the National Party, both enterprises maintained wider lobbies.[33] This reduced neither political nor economic competition, but it did ensure generally favourable conditions for business; tax exemptions continued to be made, accumulating to $21 million between 1912 and 1955. If an incumbent regime endeavoured to develop some infrastructure outside the enclave at marginal expense to the corporations, its mandate was automatically put in doubt. When the veteran Francisco Bertrand (1916–19), no radical or nationalist by any stretch of the imagination, had the temerity to increase the tariff on bananas by one half of a US cent per stem in order to finance municipal works, the ever-present domestic opposition seeking access to the spoils of office was fortified by Washington's ambassador, one Thomas Sambola Jones, who promptly sent Bertrand a note urging him to resign. The president's declaration to the public upon bowing to this sage advice bears eloquent testimony to the fortunes of a political class that was doomed to nursing its fighting words until the battle was lost: 'not being able to withstand forces that are extremely superior for such a weak country, it was better to withdraw, giving way to the arrogant pretensions of a foreign power, whose right to intervene in the private affairs of a people which controls its own destiny I do not recognize in any way.'[34]

The conflict between Liberals and *nacionalistas* reached its peak in 1924, coinciding with Zemurray's sharpest challenge to the much larger but not omnipotent UFCO. In the presidential elections of 1923 UFCO had patronized the candidacy of the National Party's General Tiburcio Carías Andino, who had won the greatest number of votes against a Liberal opposition divided between two candidates. However, the Liberals as a party maintained their control of congress and reunified to block their opponent's assumption of office. Carías then no less characteristically declared himself in revolt, and for two months in the spring of 1924 scattered fighting took place, 400 US marines occupying Tegucigalpa while the young Honduran airforce undertook the first aerial bombardment to be witnessed in Central America.[35] Although he was supported by the belligerent *caudillo* Gregorio Ferrera and had the more than tacit backing of UFCO, Carías lacked the ability to take power, and eventually acquiesced in a truce organized by Coolidge's worried envoy Sumner Welles (Treaty of Amapala). This demonstrated sufficiently strong US concern for the maintenance of formal political procedure that when the Liberals, now united behind a single candidate, won the polls of late 1924 and 1928 Carías resisted joining the predictable 'revolutions' staged in the provinces by his co-religionists. Now content to accumulate authority by leading a parliamentary opposition pledged to constitutionalism, he even held back from joining the revolts of April and November 1931 in which the hand of UFCO, in dispute with the Liberal government over water rights and railway concessions, was quite visible.[36] The necessity of the parochial risings was open to some question since followers of Carías controlled the supreme court of a traditionally decentralized state apparatus, and UFCO's requirements were duly met, albeit after some delay. Furthermore, opposition to the company had by this stage been reduced to more radical elements of the Liberal Party and a small number of trade unionists and socialist activists. In December 1929 UFCO had finally bought out Zemurray for $32 million, thereby eliminating any commercial competition of consequence since Standard Fruit remained too small to stage a serious challenge. Zemurray, always a more resourceful lobbyist than the starchy gringo executives employed by UFCO, henceforth turned his talents to the service of his old competitor. This enhanced Carías's claims to office that were anyway difficult to resist given his longstanding and relatively sober leadership of the opposition to a Liberal regime now racked by personalist divisions and the impact of the recession. He won the poll of October 1932 with ease as an unusually powerful but still traditional politician favoured with an unambiguous imprimatur from Washington. Before very long it was clear that this background made him one of the most adept practitioners of the new regional autocracy.

The Nicaraguan Challenge

Washington's intervention in Nicaragua following the overthrow of Zelaya was different in both form and scale to that in Honduras. A year after the marine corps rushed into Tegucigalpa another contingent vacated Managua for the first time in thirteen years (1912–25), but within a few months troops had to be sent back, their number soon rising to 5,400, requiring the support of eleven warships. From the bloody defeat of Zeledón and his partisans to the 1925 withdrawal Washington had sustained the Conservative Party in office, ensuring that factions of the party led by Adolfo Díaz and Emiliano Chamorro kept the upper hand in persistent clashes both with the Liberals and between contending Conservative claimants to power.[37] The first years of this restoration were marked by an unrestrained auction of Nicaraguan public finances that rapidly increased the national debt and encouraged speculative buccaneering by US banks to such a degree that in 1917 the Wilson administration obliged them to devolve direct control of the customs and other revenues to the national government.[38] This curtailed the most shameless instances of pillage and reintroduced a semblance of order, but it was barely tantamount to restoring genuine sovereignty. Indeed, it was Secretary Bryan who both called a halt to the bankers' antics and negotiated a treaty with the pliant Chamorro (signed 1914, ratified 1916) that stated that, 'the Government of Nicaragua grants in perpetuity to the Government of the United States, forever free from all taxation or other public charge, the exclusive property rights necessary and convenient for the construction, operation and maintenance of an inter-oceanic canal.' For good measure Washington received a ninety-nine-year lease to the Caribbean Corn Islands and a naval base in the Gulf of Fonseca, to be administered exclusively under US law.[39] In return the US government made a payment of $3 million, all of which passed directly to US banks holding the Nicaraguan debt. Washington's reason for drawing up this treaty was simply to ensure that no canal other than that currently being completed in Panama would be constructed in the isthmus. This pre-emptive objective was easily met but at no little cost to Nicaragua and her neighbours. The agreement effectively destroyed the already debilitated Central American Court of Justice, which rejected it as a violation of the territorial rights of Honduras and Costa Rica. This prompted a US and Nicaraguan withdrawal that brought the Court's activities to an end (1918). Chamorro's reward for a contract that is infamous in Nicaraguan history and caused the first of several scandals in the US Congress was Wilson's support for the presidency, duly assumed without having to concern himself with the impertinence of an opposition campaign.[40]

Although they met the immediate needs of the US government and banks, neither the Bryan – Chamorro treaty nor the lottery of Nicaragua's finances constituted the basis for an enduring stabilization of the country. Nicaragua produced some bananas but there was no large company-dominated enclave as in Honduras and thus no permanent source of external political mediation. In 1923, when the elderly President Diego Manuel Chamorro died, over one-third of the country's export revenues came from the sale of coffee, the producers of which were generally committed to the Liberal cause. Clearly, employment of the 100-strong marine garrison to support the suppression of this party fell far short of a productive and ultimately reliable reconstitution of the ruling class. In 1910 Washington had rejected the option of a coalition, but by 1923 this seemed the best way out of the impasse, especially since the presence of the marines was now provoking much discontent. Accordingly, the Conservative hard-liners behind Chamorro were browbeaten into accepting a minority representation of moderate Liberals in a cabinet headed by the Conservative Carlos Solórzano, backed by Liberal Vice-President Juan Bautista Sacasa. The experiment did not work. In 1925, shortly after the marines departed, Chamorro, fearful of the new National Guard they had trained up to replace them, took direct control of the force and forced Solórzano to purge the Liberals from government. In January 1926 Chamorro assumed the presidency himself, although without the recognition of the US, which correctly viewed such a move as certain to provoke a Liberal revolution. When this broke out, Chamorro was initially able to suppress it with the very National Guard that Washington intended to be a 'non-partisan force'. But Sacasa had himself superseded the old rules of the game and obtained the backing of the Mexican government of General Calles, who duly armed the Liberal forces under the command of General José María Moncada. Faced with this unprecedentedly powerful challenge, Chamorro stepped down. However, the US, alarmed at the Liberals' links with the Mexican regime, which it viewed as 'bolshevik', now withdrew from the policy of rapprochement and replaced Chamorro with the ever-indulgent Adolfo Díaz. Since Díaz was one of the principal political architects of Zelaya's overthrow, his elevation to the presidency was guaranteed to harden positions and escalate the conflict. With the Conservatives themselves divided over tactics and confused by Washington's erratic dispensations of political patronage, now withdrawn from their leading military commander, Díaz obeyed his basic instincts and petitioned the US for direct military protection. According to one source, this was requested for a period of one hundred years in exchange for the inalienable right to intervene in national disputes, a ratification of the canal treaty and full control of the customs.[41] Such terms were no longer beguiling to the Coolidge administration, but it was apparent that some form of intervention was once again necessary.

From the autumn of 1926 until May 1927 Nicaragua was submerged in a civil war. In January 1927 the marines returned. Their increasing numbers guaranteed Díaz's formal tenure of office but were not committed to a direct encounter with Moncada's Liberal forces, which were now sizeable and could make a plausible claim to legitimacy because of the enforced removal of Sacasa from the vice-presidency in 1926. In recognition of this stalemate Coolidge sent a special envoy, Henry Stimson, to negotiate a truce built around guarantees for the completion of Díaz's term of office followed by free elections and the establishment of a new National Guard free from all partisan affiliation. For their part, Sacasa and Moncada accepted that Washington was able to block their rebellion but would accept an almost certain electoral victory in 1928; they therefore opted for the compromise. On 12 May 1927 Moncada signed for the Liberals an agreement with Stimson known as the Pact of Espino Negro. In 1928 he was duly voted to office in an election supervised by US forces, who also oversaw the poll of 1932, won in turn by Sacasa. Washington and the Nicaraguan Liberal party had finally resolved their longstanding conflict.

The details of this process would be of strictly marginal interest were it not for the fact that one of Moncada's commanders, 'General' Augusto César

Sandino, refused to sign the Espino Negro Pact. For the following six years he pursued a low-level guerrilla campaign against both the US forces and the National Guard, now controlled by the leaders of a party to which he claimed loyalty throughout. Sandino's adhesion to the cause of expelling the 'Yankee invader' soon became celebrated around the world, and for a while his 'mad little army' received support from the Communist International and the followers of Haya de la Torre's pan-American APRA. Yet even this unprecedented extension of the dissident qualities of Nicaraguan Liberalism would not have acquired great historical significance were it not for the resurrection of Sandino's example some thirty years later by the *Frente Sandinista de Liberación Nacional* (FSLN), which was built around a more modern but little less heterogeneous set of ideological influences. In view of the concerted celebration of Sandino after the overthrow of Somoza in July 1979 – a celebration that is at times so exalted as to become hagiography – it is important to set the principal hero of the Nicaraguan revolutionary lineage in sober context.

At the time of his assassination in 1934 Sandino had drawn away from some of the radical positions that attended his campaign. Once US troops had left the country in January 1933, he recognized Sacasa's presidency, accepted the authority of the National Guard, and pledged himself to maintain the constitution of 1893.[42] By this stage his links with Central American Communists were irrevocably broken, and he apparently sought little more than to withdraw to the Rio Coco and establish a farming cooperative along with the remnants of his guerrilla.[43] The plan for a cooperative rather than a traditional hacienda signals an important deviant element, but acceptance of the post–1927 order minus the marine corps by an undefeated leader highlights the fact that Sandino had a limited programme that could quite plausibly be construed as fulfilled within a reformulation of Nicaragua's dominant bloc and a resumption of legalist propriety. In all events, having secured what was an outstanding victory in the withdrawal of US troops, the rebel leader was not allowed to live long enough for the full substance of the rest of his programme to become clear.[44]

However heterogeneous his ideas, Sandino continued to be a major threat to a regime in transition. Those traditional elements, personified by Sacasa, that were now in retreat as a result of the economic crisis and the expansion of the National Guard made necessary by the campaign, feared a resurgent *caudillo* championing radical Liberalism; the burgeoning absolutist forces, in the shape of Anastasio Somoza García, combined this fear with that of a revival of the popular nationalism that had accompanied the guerrilla. Sandino's execution at the hands of Somoza's Guardsmen in February 1934 was not pre-ordained but logical in terms of both the political era that was passing and that which this act effectively permitted to open. It not only confirmed the mandate of Espino Negro but also petrified the legacy of its sole opponent at an optimum point for a future generation. Yet the heritage was tardy in realization; for decades Sandino represented a heroic but defeated cause, and even in the early 1960s when a survivor of the original guerrilla, Santos López, guided the student activists of the young FSLN through the northern mountains neither he nor they could lay claim to a ready constituency.

The details of Sandino's military campaign from 1927 to 1933 need not detain us here.[45] After a disastrous frontal engagement with the marines at Ocotal in July 1927 when the Sandinistas were subjected to an aerial attack – the first of a number of military innovations that precluded the customary strategy of political insurrection – the *Ejército Defensor de la Soberanía Nacional de Nicaragua* restricted itself to guerrilla tactics. Operating out of its base in 'El Chimbote' in the mountainous region of Las Segovias, this force never exceeded a thousand combatants and was often only a few hundred strong. Yet by cultivating the support of the local peasantry, maintaining an efficient intelligence network (in which, as in more contemporary struggles, the role of children was vital) and a formidable ability to manoeuvre, it tied down the marines and the less professional, more brutal National Guard for nearly six years. The scale of the campaign was not great – only 200 US and government troops were killed – and Sandino, true to his new profession, did not attempt to take urban centres, still less make a direct assault on state power; he wanted the marines out of Nicaragua, and for this purpose aggressive survival was sufficient. Yet in their endeavour to subdue the 'bandit' the marines were eventually obliged to clear the population from and destroy villages in large tracts of Jinotega and Nueva Segovia. This proved disastrous, creating thousands of refugees as well as greater local support for Sandino. In 1931, when it had become evident that Sandino was far from a mere bandit, the Japanese invaded Manchuria, drawing strong condemnation from the US as well as opposition from the nationalist Kuomintang, which had named a division of its army after the Nicaraguan rebel. The contradiction between its protests at the Japanese action – officially undertaken to protect their citizens and property in China – and the Nicaraguan operation was not lost either on the US government or on the growing number of domestic opponents to its Central American activities, concerned at their questionable morality, cost and loss of lives.[46] This, combined with the conviction that the reconstituted National Guard was now capable of maintaining internal order on a non-partisan basis, laid the ground for the withdrawal of the marines following the election of 1932.

The removal of US forces met Sandino's central demand and permitted the signing of a truce with the Sacasa regime, but it is clear that the political content of the campaign cannot be reduced to this sole objective. Although he consistently declared himself a Liberal, Sandino had come under other influences. His contact with Socialism, Communism and anarcho-syndicalism when working as a mechanic for a US oil company in Tampico, Mexico, evidently had considerable impact in consolidating a profound antipathy to imperialism, the Church, and – to a lesser but occasionally pronounced degree – authoritarianism. His devotion to freemasonry and theosophy was much more in keeping with the orientation of petty-bourgeois ideology in Latin America during this period. Although this sustained a persistent mysticism, it should not be interpreted as directly contradictory to the influence of secular political currents; Mexican freemasonry and spiritualism were at the time highly politicized and often very radical in character.[47] The incorporation of the Salvadorean Communist Agustín Farabundo Martí into the guerrilla as Sandino's secretary did undoubtedly fortify the social content of its policies for a while, but neither Martí nor the US–based Anti–Imperialist League, which acted as the conduit for the Communist movement's support, could broaden Sandino's platform into an unambiguous manifesto for socialism.[48] Sandino's insistence upon a broad multi-class front put him much closer to the politics of APRA, some of whose militants also participated directly in the campaign.[49] The very vague social content of APRA's anti-imperialism based on the concept of an 'Indoamerican' liberation – a term at times employed by Sandino – was altogether more comfortable to work with in a country that possessed only the germs of a working class.[50]

Apart from his prolonged stay in Mexico, which finally severed links with the Communists, Sandino formulated his strategy in the backlands of Las Segovias and the company of predominantly plebeian and parochial followers, many of whom were either dissident Liberals or local peasants. Reverence for a leader who was on occasion wont to give expression to spiritualist sentiments was also shared by a number of modest farmers as well as workers from the mine at San Albino whom Sandino first recruited on behalf of the Liberal revolution in 1926.[51] The guerrilla was, therefore, neither as 'proletarian' as is sometimes claimed nor simply a force of apolitical rural malcontents collected by an astute populist *caudillo*; socially as well as ideologically it offered a fairly comprehensive reflection of the lower orders of Nicaraguan society. If its radicalism proved to be mutable, this was as much a function of the structural conditions of the period as of Sandino's own agency, and it is no mere coincidence that his peculiar blend of radical ideas was closely mirrored in the programme of the only successful revolutionary party of post-war Central America – the FSLN.

Popular Organization

Sandino's campaign was given much sympathy but little substantive support by what was probably the weakest national trade-union movement in the region. Nicaraguan workers were physically more dispersed and politically more handicapped by the persistence of traditional rivalries than even their Honduran comrades. The civil war of 1926–27 effectively broke the momentum of the artisan-dominated organizations while the initial promise of an urban radical movement offered by the *Partido Trabajador Nicaragüense* (1931) was rapidly dissipated by a combination of repression and agile co-optation.[52] As a result, no genuinely Communist organization appeared until the *Partido Socialista Nicaragüense*, formed out of the ashes of the PTN in 1939. This historic delay can only be partially ascribed to the existence of Sandinismo, but, together with the PSN's ambiguous relations with the anti-Somoza movement in the mid 1940s, it contributed to the enduring weakness of an orthodox Communist tradition in offering an alternative to Sandino's heirs in the FSLN. Of the other states, only Guatemala lacked a Communist party by 1931, and in that case such an absence corresponded less to a lack of initiatives than to the efficacy of repression.[53] Everywhere else parties were established, and although they were organizationally weak, theoretically unsophisticated, and soon subjected to an untempered repression, their mere existence was of consequence both at the time and for the subsequent configuration of radical politics.

Whilst these organizations were almost exclusively led by people of bourgeois or, more commonly, petty-bourgeois origin, their emergence was largely the result of a radicalization of the trade unions throughout the 1920s. This process was undoubtedly connected with the downturn in the economy after the war followed by steady growth over the following decade, reflecting an erosion of the apolitical traditions of artisanal mutualism that was not attended by the emergence of a significant new industrial working class. The impetus for a political syndicalism was still largely given within the orbit of an artisanal labour force, albeit one growing in size and linked with a substantial plantation proletariat. The limits of the movement, always uneven in strength, are evident in the rapid halt of its advance in the early 1930s, this generally being achieved by recourse to state violence prompted by a 'great fear' that growing radical influence in the countryside would spark off an uncontrollable jacquerie. Such a fear, which was entirely justified in the case of El Salvador and not without some basis in Guatemala, was also informed by the example of the Bolshevik Revolution and, much more sharply, that in neighbouring Mexico, which had engendered massive social turbulence for over a decade and was now apparently mutating into an anti-Catholic state dictatorship little different in the eyes of Central American oligarchs to that established in Russia. Both the Soviet Union and Mexico played a part in encouraging the spread of local radicalism, but this still centred on the achievement of basic syndicalist objectives: the eight-hour day, rights of association, a living wage, and so on. Agitation over such demands, the winning of some of them, and the emergence of an embattled but vibrant culture of opposition marked a distinctive shift in the politics of the region in the years prior to the Depression.[54]

The growth of trade-union organization and syndicalist consciousness was, and remains, much more modest in practice than the formal establishment of national and international confederations suggests. Nonetheless, the increasing constitution of such bodies in the post-war period was clearly paralleled by rising mobilization. Although scattered mutualist organizations had existed since the last quarter of the nineteenth century and a congress of Central American workers was held in San Salvador in 1912, they formed part of a proud lineage of association that fortified craft identity rather than marking rising belligerence. The second congress of the *Confederación Obrera Centroamericana* (COCA) in 1921 was distinct in that it reflected a much more profound discontent and expanding unionization. In 1920 a general strike in Costa Rica had obtained state recognition of the eight-hour day.[55] The following year a stoppage by UFCO workers was cut short by repression but, like a number of wildcat strikes in the Honduran plantations, it formed part of a growing trend towards direct action.[56] The participation of Guatemala City's plebeian masses in the mobilization to overthrow Estrada Cabrera in 1920 and the subsequent relaxation of political control encouraged a strong movement for increased wages, a limited working day and the defence of national interests against those of US corporations. The strike wave of 1925 was of such proportion that it required both direct deployment of troops and the introduction of a new law prohibiting withdrawal of labour.[57] As in Guatemala, the craft guilds in El Salvador preserved much of their authority during this period and adopted an ambivalent attitude towards the pursuit of demands beyond the confines of their craft and the tradition of negotiation with paternalist *patrones*.[58] At the same time, the popular demonstrations in San Salvador against the devaluation of the currency in 1922 heralded a new and much broader pattern of mass activism which, following the initial repression, prompted a degree of oligarchic manoeuvre as well as the establishment of new unions. In 1925 May Day marches took place in every Central American capital, and by the end of the decade the eight-hour day was at least formally enshrined in the statutes of the republics, all of which now possessed a trade-union confederation.[59]

With the exception of Nicaragua, the leadership of these confederations was either in the hands of radicals or strongly challenged by them. Accelerated unionization had not in itself disturbed the mutualist traditions – in some senses it positively fortified them – but the concomitant commitment to active participation in politics represented a major threat. In the case of Central America, conflict between 'pure unionism' and the concept of political organization of workers upheld by Socialists and Communists rarely took the form of disputes between these latter currents and those attached to anarchism or anarcho-syndicalism, in part at least because of the low level of European immigration which provided the principal source of libertarianism elsewhere in the hemisphere.[60] This did not impede a series of demonstrations in support of Sacco and Vanzetti in 1927, but it did assist a close identification between the workers' movement and the nascent Communist groups, which were increasingly capable of winning unions away from an artisanal apoliticism that frequently, but by no means unerringly, entailed acquiescence in the status quo. The translation of formal declarations, agreements and positions into concrete action was, therefore, a highly tenuous but not completely hopeless endeavour. The recognition accorded to some federations by Moscow laid the basis for the first trips of young Central American activists to the Soviet Union and encouraged an increasing phobia on the part of the ruling class.[61] Although such a reaction might be expected to exceed the objective threat, it is of some importance that Communist parties appeared just prior to the full impact of the depression. On the one hand, this provided them with a widespread constituency of impoverished and recently laid-off workers and peasants often already engaged in independent mobilization. On the other, it encouraged the ruling class to ascribe all such activity to the bolshevik contagion, associating it integrally with economic collapse and social disturbance unprecedented in republican history. Such an identification underpinned an anti-communism that was henceforth based upon legal prohibition and violent repression.

In practice it was only in El Salvador that the Communist Party (PCS) attained any real momentum and became a national political force of consequence during this period. Founded in 1930 by Farabundo Martí, the PCS drew much strength from its identification with the leadership of the *Federación Regional de Trabajadores de El Salvador* (FRTS), which claimed to have some 75,000 members. This connection exercised considerable influence on the activities of the middle-class intellectuals who occupied the party's inner circles, and it permitted important links with the autonomous peasant leagues in the western coffee zone.[62] Contacts such as these could to some degree be manipulated by the PCS, but they never corresponded to direct control.[63] Moreover, while the party could exercise influence over the decisions of the FRTS leadership in San Salvador, it lacked a secure organizational base outside the capital and possessed virtually no presence in the east of the country. The series of strikes and popular demonstrations that took place in 1930 and 1931 cannot be attributed principally to the agency of the PCS although they undoubtedly assisted the party's growth.[64] Araujo's *Partido Laborista* possessed a much more proletarian leadership and enjoyed far greater support than did the Communists, who, despite having built up a following through broad-based organizations such as *Socorro Rojo* and the Anti-Imperialist League, maintained the 'class against class' strategy of the Comintern's third period and rejected any possibility of united front work.[65] Adhesion to this line was not the result of close organizational ties with the international movement; financial contributions from abroad were as slight as direct programmatic invigilation, permitting Martí to express sympathy for Trotsky after the leader of the Left Opposition had been transformed from reprobate into mortal enemy by Stalin and his apparatchiks.[66]

Within Central America itself links between revolutionaries were much greater, and to some degree compensated for national imbalances in organization. Although intra-regional migration was less intensive than today, it was still greater than that of the nineteenth century and often belied the image of an exclusively parochial rural society. Salvadoreans were already beginning to work in the plantations of Honduras, and Nicaraguans in those of Costa Rica, where they played an important role in the 1934 banana workers' strike. There was also seasonal movement from El Salvador to the coffee *fincas* of south-western Guatemala. In all events, national borders did not represent great impediments to economic, cultural and political movement; they were increasingly treated with scant regard by peripatetic activists for whom exile was a frequent but generally temporary experience.[67] Although the Costa Rican Communists remained rather isolated during this early period, Salvadorean revolutionaries such as Martí, Modesto Ramírez, Felipe Armando Amaya and Gabriela García were often to be found in Guatemala and Honduras, whilst Hondurans like Manuel Cálix Herrera and the eternally mobile Juan Pablo Wainwright contributed to the sense of rising internationalism with frequent proselytizing journeys outside their native land; this first generation considered itself above all Central American.[68]

Such an impressive voluntarism was made necessary by the overall weakness of Communist organization and the substantial obstacles it faced in consolidating a caucus of militants, let alone gaining mass support. If active sympathizers of the PCS could be numbered in hundreds, those of the Honduran party (PCH) scarcely exceeded double figures.[69] Although founded in 1929 on the basis of a Leninist study group as well as supporters of the *Federación Sindical Hondureña*, the PCH remained little more than a tight group of agitators for the three-year period during which some semblance of organized activity is discernible. Under the leadership of Cálix and Wainwright, this group was largely based in Tegucigalpa and San Pedro Sula, lacking an established presence in the banana zone. Only thirty-nine delegates attended the first congress in 1932, shortly prior to a repression of the party which would delay a second plenary meeting for over thirty years. Yet, supported by the irregular broadsheet *El Martillo*, Cálix opposed Carías in the presidential poll of that year in the name of the *Bloque Obrero Campesino*. Carías's predecessor evidently did not appreciate the threat that this posed to the national fabric: before the election he indulged himself in requesting the presence of the party leadership in the presidential palace, admonished them for attachment to exotic and wayward beliefs and offered remuneration for reversion to normal behaviour.[70] A not dissimilar response met the establishment of the Communist Party of Costa Rica (PCCR), set up in June 1931 by the nineteen-year-old Manuel Mora, who remained its leader until 1984. While the PCCR's initial campaign for the right to contest elections elicited little popular support, it fell more securely within the parameters of existing political protocols than elsewhere and generated heated parliamentary debate before being rejected.[71] The subsequent establishment of a 'front' organization – named, as in Honduras, *Bloque Obrero Campesino* – circumvented constitutional prohibitions of international ties and permitted participation in the municipal elections of 1932. In Honduras and El Salvador the decision to contest elections in 1932 was taken on essentially tactical grounds – it is, though, debatable how far these were consciously limited to the advantages of propaganda – but in Costa Rica the early adoption of electoralist methods was more significant. While it may have reflected the influence of the Chilean party, it was also related to the existence of a parliamentary regime altogether more substantial than elsewhere in the region.[72] Although the party was formally outlawed between 1949 and 1975 – under that very parliamentary regime which is so widely considered a paragon of democratic virtue – it continued throughout to conduct an electoralist strategy under a variety of guises.

By the 1960s this orientation was gaining some support within the resurrected parties elsewhere. Many of the founders of the movement had been laid in an early grave, and those who survived the pogroms of the 1930s to contribute to a resurgence of radical and democratic politics in the mid 1940s were soon confronted by yet another period of concerted counter-revolution. The accumulated effect of this experience, together with the longstanding petrification at the supposed hub of the world Communist movement, produced a second generation of Central American Communism that was upheld by many valiant, often heroic, militants yet weighed down by a programmatic torpor that both evacuated it of real radicalism and relegated the early years to a distant history that was constantly evoked but rarely explored with critical vigour.

Notes

1. Quoted in Richard Millett, *Guardians of the Dynasty. A History of the US–created Guardia Nacional de Nicaragua and the Somoza Family*, Maryknoll, New York 1977, p. 52.
2. Quoted in Arthur Ruhl, *The Central Americans*, New York 1927, p. 189.
3. Quoted in Kenneth J. Grieb, 'The United States and the Rise of General Maximiliano Hernández Martínez', JLAS, vol. 3, no. 2, 1970, p. 153.
4. Quoted in Neill Macaulay, *The Sandino Affair*, Durham, North Carolina 1985, p. 72.

5. Victor Bulmer-Thomas, 'Economic Development over the Long Run – Central America since 1920', JLAS, vol. 15, no. 2, 1983, p. 272.

6. Enrique Baloyra, 'Reactionary Despotism in Central America', JLAS, vol. 15, no. 2, 1983, p. 304.

7. Thomas Anderson, *Matanza. El Salvador's Communist Revolt of 1932*, Lincoln, Nebraska 1971, p. 8; Everett Alan Wilson, *The Crisis of National Integration in El Salvador, 1919–1935*, unpublished PhD, Stanford University 1970, p. 109.

8. Rodrigo Facio, *Estudio sobre la Economía Costarricense*, San José 1975, p. 41; McCreery, 'Debt Servitude', p. 737.

9. Lainez and Meza, 'Enclave', p. 145.

10. Posas and Del Cid, *Construcción*, p. 38; Kepner and Soothill, *Empire*, p. 123.

11. *La Patria*, San Salvador, 30 September 1929; 20 October 1928, quoted in Wilson, *Crisis*, pp. 123; 187.

12. Pedro Belli, 'Prolegómenos para una Historia Económica de Nicaragua de 1905 a 1966', *Revista de Pensamiento Centroamericano*, vol. 30, no. 146, January–March 1975.

13. Bulmer-Thomas, 'Economic Development', p. 272.

14. Panamerican Union, *The Foreign Trade of Latin America since 1913*, Washington 1952, quoted in LaFeber, *Inevitable Revolutions*, pp. 60–1.

15. Jones, *Guatemala*, p. 6. For a dated and less than concise but still suggestive biography of Estrada that throws some light on the political life of the era, see Rafael Arévalo Martínez, *Ecce Pericles. La Tiranía de Manuel Estrada Cabrera en Guatemala*, San José 1982.

16. Kepner and Soothill, *Empire*, p. 213.

17. The most exhaustive account of UFCO's operations and concessions in Guatemala is given in Alfonso Bauer Paiz, *Como Opera el Capital Yanqui en Centroamérica (El Caso de Guatemala)*, Mexico City 1956. For IRCA, see pp. 104–87; for UFCO, pp. 188–361.

18. Ibid., pp. 62–5.

19. In 1930 the president of the Confederation opined, 'The railroad company, the owners of the farms situated in the interior . . . and the United Fruit Steamship company are intimately bound together and everything which is conceded to them without stipulating anything in favour of the country is conducive to the strengthening of the monopoly of the exploitation of bananas.' Quoted in Kepner and Soothill, *Empire*, p. 159.

20. Charles D. Ameringer, *The Democratic Left in Exile. The Antidictatorial Struggle in the Caribbean, 1945–1959*, Coral Gables 1974, p. 39.

21. Jaime Darenblum, *Crisis Internacionales y Economía Nacional. Costa Rica ante dos Guerras Mundiales y la Gran Depresión*, Centro de Investigación y Adiestramiento Político Administrativo, San José, Serie Estudios, no. 6, January 1982, pp. 14–19.

22. George W. Baker Jnr, 'Woodrow Wilson's Use of the Non-Recognition Policy in Costa Rica', *The Americas*, vol. 22, July 1965; Munro, *Intervention*, pp. 426–48.

23. Despite his futile rebellion, Volio remained very popular, obliging Jiménez to send him back to Europe, where he ended up in a mental hospital. Marina Volio, *Jorge Volio y el Partido Reformista*, San José 1973.

24. Wilson, *Crisis*, p. 22.

25. Colindres, *Fondements Économiques*, pp. 43–4. The 'fourteen families' are: Dueñas, Regalado, Hill, Meza Ayau, De Sola, Guirola, Alvarez, Meléndez, Menéndez Castro, Deininger, Quinóñez, García Prieto, Vilanova, Sol Millet.

26. Alejandro Marroquín, 'Estudio sobre la Crisis de los Años Treinta en El Salvador', *Anuario de Estudios Centroamericanos*, vol. 3, 1977, p. 117; Wilson, *Crisis*, p. 40.

27. Colindres, *Fondements Économiques*, pp. 43–4.

28. Robert Aubey identifies three groups: those predominantly engaged in cultivation but with other interests (Alvarez, Battle, Dueñas, Escalón, Guirola, Magaña, Mathies, Meza Ayau Quinóñez, Regalado); those who possessed more extensive capital interests (Deininger, De Sola, Hill, Wright); and a predominantly commercial sector (Batarse, Bernheim, Borgonovo, Frenkel, Freund, Galada, Goldtree Liebes, Hasbún, Nasser, Poma, Safie, Schwartz, Simán, Sol Millet, Zablah). 'Entrepreneurial Formation in El Salvador', *Explorations in Entrepreneurial History*, second series, vol. 6, 1968/9, pp. 272–6. It should be noted that the last group contains several names of Arab and German origin not usually listed as members of the oligarchy. This survey omits a number of families identified by Colindres as possessing significant lands in

the mid 1970s. Care should also be taken in identification simply by surname as many families have intermarried, and property is exchanged laterally as well as vertically.

29. The thesis that the landed class was not so integrated – and thus pledged to a uniform politics – as is often believed, is advanced by Rafael Guidos Vejar, *Ascenso del Militarismo en El Salvador*, San José 1982, pp. 135–9, and supported by Rafael Menjívar, *Formación y Lucha del Proletariado Industrial Salvadoreño*, San Salvador 1979, p. 60.

30. Carlos Meléndez (1913–14); Alfonso Quinóñez (brother-in-law, 1914–15); Carlos Meléndez (1915–18); Alfonso Quinóñez (1918–19); Jorge Meléndez (brother of Carlos, 1919-23); Alfonso Quinóñez (1923–27); Pio Romero Bosque (1927–31).

31. Robert Elam, *Appeal to Arms. The Army and Politics in El Salvador, 1931–64*, unpublished PhD, University of New Mexico 1968, pp. 27–32.

32. Guidos Vejar, *Ascenso*, pp. 135–9.

33. The fullest account of these relationships is given in Edward Boatman Guillán, 'The Political Role of the United Fruit Company in Honduras', unpublished draft for PhD thesis, Johns Hopkins University, which will hopefully be published as soon as possible. Some extracts are given in Posas and Del Cid, *Construcción*, pp. 45–51. Zemurray maintained good relations with the father of the National Party, Manuel Bonilla, and the young Nationalist lawyer Juan Manuel Gálvez, who lacked great influence at this stage but was to serve as Carías's minister of war for fifteen years and later became president. According to Boatman, Cuyamel's attachment to the Liberals and dissident factions of the National Party in the 1920s was largely a function of antipathy to Carías himself, unequivocally a supporter of UFCO. In Zemurray's words, 'in Honduras a deputy costs less than a mule'.

34. Quoted in R. Oqueli, 'Gobiernos Hondureños durante el Presente Siglo', *Economía Política*, Tegucigalpa, May–October 1984, p. 35.

35. This was apparently the only time US forces entered the capital, where there were protests against their presence. The air corps had been established in 1922 under Italian supervision. Engagement in combat after only two years' existence was remarkable even by Latin American standards, but the Honduran state henceforth devoted far more attention to air power, and to aviation in general, than did its regional counterparts because of the very poor state of road and rail systems in a peculiarly mountainous terrain. By 1942 the airforce possessed twenty–two craft whilst the army's Basic Arms School was not established until 1946 and the Military Academy not re-established along professional lines until 1952. Ropp, 'The Honduran Army,' p. 509.

36. Posas and del Cid, *Construcción*, pp. 50–67.

37. Immediately following Zelaya's removal in 1909 the Nicaraguan congress appointed the León Liberal José Madriz as president, but US forces continued to support the Bluefields-based Conservative rebellion of Juan Estrada, who finally took power in 1910. In 1911 rivalries amongst Conservatives led to a challenge by General Luis Mena, but although he overthrew Estrada, Washington preferred its old ally Adolfo Díaz, who duly became president. It was Mena's second revolt, against Díaz in 1912, which sparked off Zeledón's separate Liberal rising and prompted new deployments of US troops. In 1916 Díaz was persuaded to drop his candidate for the succession in favour of General Emiliano Chamorro, the principal military leader of opposition to Zelaya. In 1921 Chamorro was succeeded by his aged uncle, Diego Manuel Chamorro, who held office but little power until he died in harness in 1923.

38. In 1913 Díaz, who surely set a hemispheric record in his propensity for surrendering to US interests, exchanged a debt of $711,000 to the bankers Brown Brothers and Seligman for control of national customs and the returns of the railway, rendering a profit to the bank of $1.5 million even according to the conservative estimate of Secretary of State Bryan. Those who require further details on a whole rash of such honourable deals, for which Díaz's enthusiasm manifestly perplexed an increasingly embarrassed State Department, should consult Munro, *Intervention*, pp. 392–417.

39. Booth, *End and Beginning*, p. 34.

40. The terms of the treaty were strongly contested in the US Senate and even by Elihu Root. According to Senator William Borah, 'I've never considered this a treaty with Nicaragua but rather between ourselves and a government that represents our interests.' For details, see Munro, *Intervention*, pp. 389–406.

41. Associated Press cable, 23 February 1926, quoted in Rodolfo Cerdas, *Sandino*,

el APRA y la Internacional Comunista. Antecedentes Históricos de la Nicaragua de Hoy, Centro de Investigación y Adiestramiento Político-Administrativo, San José, Serie Estudios, no. 4, November 1979, p. 20.

42. After he had signed a peace treaty with the Sacasa government, and when the National Guard was harassing members of his force, Sandino declared, 'It's not up to me whether there is a Guard or not, or who might direct it. I, as a citizen, am obliged to pay the taxes that maintain the army of the Guard, or whatever it is called. The only thing that I desire is that they give us constitutional guarantees and that the Guard is constitutionalized.' Quoted in Gregorio Selser, *Sandino, General de Hombres Libres*, Buenos Aires 1959, vol. 2, p. 297.

43. Although Sandino retained amicable relations with the Salvadorean Communist Agustín Farabundo Martí rather longer than with the movement as a whole, his ten-month stay in Mexico (1929–30) and attempts to establish an alliance with President Portes Gil at a time when relations with the Soviet Union were cooling and then broken (January 1930) led *Correspondence Internationale* (4 January 1930) to declare that, 'Sandino has passed over to the Imperialist camp', accusing him of accepting $60,000 from the Mexican regime. Although this position was contested by some contributors to the journal, Sandino's final treaty with Sacasa was described by J. Gómez of the Mexican Communist Party as treason, Sandino being, 'a typical *caudillo*, petty bourgeois . . . a little dictatorial chief . . . the fight against American imperialism was limited by him to a fight against the armed intervention of the US.' *Correspondence Internationale*, 22 March 1933, quoted in Cerdas, *Sandino*, pp. 78–80.

44. Sacasa named Sandino's confidant, the educationalist and labour leader Sinofonías Salvatierra, as minister of agriculture and labour early in 1933, but apart from facilitating the ending of the military campaign, this appointment had little impact upon a regime that was in retreat from the moment it entered office. Sandino's terms for laying down arms were: an end to foreign intervention; the creation of a department in the north of the country where his men could bear arms and appoint local officials; the destruction of all records that referred to him and his followers as 'bandits'; and the calling of a pan-American conference to revise the terms of the Bryan-Chamorro treaty. He rejected agrarian reform and the expropriation of land for redistribution to the peasantry, believing that the amount of virgin land in Nicaragua made all talk of unemployment risible. Millett, *Guardians*, p. 147; Cerdas, *Sandino*, pp. 45–6.

45. The most detailed treatment is in Selser, *Sandino* (edited English translation, New York 1981) and Macaulay, *The Sandino Affair*.

46. According to Henry Stimson, the dispatch of more US troops 'would put me in an absolute wrong in China, where Japan has done all this monstrous work . . .' Quoted in LaFeber, *Inevitable Revolutions*, p. 67. US congressional discontent, which had a potent precedent in opposition to the Bryan–Chamorro treaty, reached the point where Senator George Norris suggested that if marines were necessary to ensure fair elections they ought to be sent to Philadelphia and Pittsburgh. For details, see Bryce Wood, *The Making of the Good Neighbour Policy*, New York 1967, pp. 13–47; Thomas G. Paterson et al., *American Foreign Policy: A History*, New York 1977, pp. 355–7; Millett, *Guardians*, p. 117.

47. There were open 'bolshevik' and anarchist masonic lodges in Mexican towns at the time Sandino was working there. Adherence to spiritualism was common amongst anti-clerical Liberals during this period and, in the case of theosophy, did not necessarily entail a specific political orientation, as is evident from the commitment of Salvadorean dictator General Martínez to such a system. Sandino was particularly influenced by the Basque Joaquín Trincado's *Spiritism* and became head of the Nicaraguan branch of the Magnetic-Spiritualist School of the Universal Commune, which was based in Buenos Aires. According to Donald Hodges, who has studied this side of Sandino's thought in some depth, he kept expression of such beliefs to a minimum: 'if I was to say this openly people would take me for a screwball or a drunkard.' Hodges's thesis is that Sandino was not confused in his ideology but dissembled in order to uphold an essentially conspiratorial politics, a characteristic that, in Hodges's view, he shares with the FSLN. *The Intellectual Foundations of the Nicaraguan Revolution*, Austin 1987. Daniel Ortega notes the importance of freemasonry to the opposition movement in the 1950s and 1960s. Interview in *Playboy*, November 1987.

48. According to Sandino, 'On several occasions there have been attempts to deviate this movement from defence of the nation, converting it into a social struggle. I have opposed this with all my energy. This movement is national and anti-imperialist. We raise the standard of

liberty for Nicaragua and all Hispanoamerica. As for the rest, we recommend a progressive approach to social aspirations . . . Martí, the propagandist of Communism, saw that he could not prevail and left.' For his part, Martí is reported to have stated shortly before his execution in San Salvador in January 1932, 'I testify to the moral purity of General Sandino . . . my break [with him] did not stem, as is sometimes claimed, from differences over moral principles or opposing norms of conduct. I refused to return to Las Segovias with him because he did not want to embrace the Communist programme which I defended. His banner was that of independence, of emancipation, and he did not pursue a social rebellion.' Quoted in Cerdas, *Sandino*, pp. 76–7.

49. Established in 1924 by the Peruvian Víctor Raúl Haya de la Torre, APRA never developed into a regional movement and was soon reduced to an exclusively Peruvian party, eventually coming to power, albeit on a very distinct platform, in 1985. However, for a while APRA attracted widespread sympathy for its demands of united action against US imperialism; nationalization of lands and industry; and the internationalization of the Panama Canal. APRA supported Sandino from the start, working with his representative Froylán Turcios in Tegucigalpa as well as sending its own delegate, the Peruvian Estebán Pavletich, to El Chimbote. Although Haya himself visited Honduras, according to Cerdas he never entered Nicaragua. Ibid., p. 42.

50. For a while the *apristas* collaborated with the Communists in the Anti-Imperialist League and Haya attended the International's fifth congress as an observer, but relations were soon dropped when the Communists took complete control of the League and their concept of the dictatorship of the proletariat was shown to be at variance with APRA's much more flexible notion of the worker–peasant alliance. In 1929 Sandino registered his support for the APRA line: 'Neither extreme right nor extreme left but a United Front. That is our slogan. As a result, it is not illogical that we seek the cooperation of all social classes.' Ibid., p. 45.

51. According to Jaime Wheelock, the social composition of Sandino's force distinguished it politically from the rest of the Liberal army as early as 1926. *Imperialismo*, p. 114. At their first meeting Sandino appears to have antagonized Moncada with a few proudhonian ejaculations, which he subsequently suppressed, and displayed a black and red flag, a legacy of anarcho-syndicalist influence that remains, if only in this limited sense, alive in Nicaragua today. Yet it is to be doubted if the initial composition of the force indicated a clearly distinct politics. A number of landowners (Ortez, Randales, Colindres, Cockburn) can be identified alongside more modest agriculturalists. The miners of San Albino do constitute an exceptional case but were never a majority and in all probability were still close to their rural roots. There was a miners' strike in 1924, but this does not appear to have affected San Albino. Ibid., pp. 26–8; Gustavo Gutiérrez Mayorga, 'Historia del Movimiento Obrero de Nicaragua', in Pablo González Casanova, ed., *Historia del Movimiento Obrero en América Latina*, Mexico City 1985, vol. 2, pp. 213–14.

52. The *Federación Obrera Nicaragüense* (1918) was consistently mutualist in character whereas *Obrerismo Organizado* (1923) remained dominated by the intellectuals around Sinfonías Salvatierra and never established a secure rank-and-file organization. The founding programme of the PTN evidenced some influence of the Salvadorean Communist Party, which may also have been responsible for its resistance to supporting Sandino despite the predominantly nationalist character of its platform. Somoza was able to manipulate elements tied to the PTN in the 1936 strike, which enabled him to overthrow Sacasa, and the party finally disintegrated in 1939. Although the PSN emerged from the ashes of the PTN, its forebear cannot properly be described as a socialist formation, and was certainly distinct from the Communist Parties of that era. Gutiérrez, 'Movimiento Obrero', pp. 226–31.

53. In 1922 a short-lived attempt was made to establish both a Guatemalan and a Central American Communist Party on the basis of the *Unión Obrera Socialista* (1921), which the Comintern official responsible for Latin American affairs described in 1922 as 'stand[ing] near us and in connection with us'. Despite links with the Mexican party over the following years no party was ever established. In 1928 Luis Sánchez Obando and José Luis Chigüichon participated in the sixth congress of the International. The following year the *Federación Regional Obrera de Guatemala* was recognized by the Red Trade Union International, and in 1930 Guatemalan delegates attended its fifth congress in Moscow. A Communist Party is said to have been founded in 1929 but was never consolidated, and the contemporary party – *Partido*

Guatemalteco del Trabajo, formally established in December 1952 – dates its initial, clandestine foundation from 1949. Victor Manuel Gutiérrez, *Breve Historia del Movimiento Sindical de Guatemala*, Mexico City 1964; Huberto Alvarado Arellano, *Apuntes para la Historia del Partido Guatemalteco del Trabajo*, Guatemala City 1975; Robert Alexander, *Communism in Latin America*, New Brunswick 1957, pp. 350–8.

54. By 1930 the Salvadorean union movement could organize a May Day march of 80,000 people in a capital city of 125,000. According to the Communist leader Miguel Mármol, a cobbler by trade, this was an era when artisans were selling 'bolshevik shoes', 'bolshevik bread' and even 'bolshevik sweets'. Dalton, *Miguel Mármol*, pp. 113–39.

55. Manuel Rojas Bolaños, 'El Movimiento Obrero en Costa Rica (Reseña Histórica)', in González Casanova, *Movimiento Obrero*, vol. 2, pp. 257–8.

56. Ibid., p. 263. There were strikes on the Honduran plantations of the Cuyamel company (1916 and 1917), the Vacarro Brothers (1920) and on the Puerto Cortés railway (1924) as well as throughout the industry in 1925 in demand of recognition for the eight-hour day, introduced by statute the previous year. Victor Meza, *Historia del Movimiento Obrero Hondureño*, Tegucigalpa 1981, pp. 21–8; Posas, *Movimiento Obrero Hondureño*, pp. 119–21.

57. José Luis Balcárcel, 'El Movimiento Obrero en Guatemala', in González Casanova, *Movimento Obrero*, vol. 2, p. 24. The mobilization of the Guatemalan peasantry during the 1920s is badly understudied despite the existence of a number of local mutualist societies and quite extensive manifestations of discontent in 1922 and 1931. Brian Murphy, 'The Stunted Growth of Campesino Organisations', in Richard N. Adams, *Crucifixion by Power. Essays in Guatemalan Social Structure, 1944–1966*, Austin 1970, p. 441; Jones, *Guatemala*, p. 161.

58. The strength of the artisanal guilds should not be underestimated. of the forty-five identifiable organizations in El Salvador in 1917, one, 'La Concordia', possessed capital assets of $12,000. Menjívar, *Proletariado*, pp. 25–7.

59. *Federación Obrera Nicaragüense* (1918); *Federación Regional de Trabajadores de El Salvador* (1924); *Federación Regional Obrera de Guatemala* (1925); *Unión General de Trabajadores* (1928) in Costa Rica; *Federación Sindical Hondureña* (1929).

60. This is argued specifically for El Salvador by Rafael Menjívar, *Proletariado*, p. 48, but would seem to be the case everywhere.

61. Although the San Salvador newspaper *La Patria* was sufficiently prescient to identify Araujo's *laboristas* as no more than 'crackpots', its editor was disconcerted by the effects of the Romero government's scaremongering: ' "Communist" is today a facile expression that is used to condemn any act that is approved by persons who fear the laws of God and man. It is customary in the Republic to label Communist any demand for justice', 15 November 1930, quoted in Wilson, *Crisis*, p. 214. After 1932 such sentiments were very rarely espoused by the Salvadorean press. In 1930 Miguel Mármol and Modesto Ramírez travelled to Moscow to attend the Red Trade Union International Congress with Sánchez Obando and Chigüichon of Guatemala. Dalton, *Miguel Mármol*, pp. 179–225.

62. Although Martí was not formally a member of the PCS Central Committee and technically worked on behalf of the US-based *Socorro Rojo*, he undoubtedly played a leading role in its decisions. During this period the general secretary was Narciso Ruíz of the bakers' union but most of the committee were intellectuals. Ibid., p. 232.

63. This is fully evident from Mármol's memoirs, which show that the PCS was barely able to restrain *campesinos* in the Ahuachapán region over the last months of 1931 and early in 1932. Ibid., p. 252.

64. Following the large May Day march in the capital in 1930 discontent amongst *campesinos* around Sonsonate provoked extensive repression by the National Guard. Between November 1930 and February 1931 over 1,200 people, including Martí, Mármol, Ramírez and Juan Pablo Wainwright, were jailed for political activity. In 1931 there were short rural strikes in April and May, and a student demonstration in June led to the declaration of martial law.

65. Rafael Menjívar identifies one cause of the party's collapse in the rejection of work with the rank and file of the *Partido Laborista* on the basis of a schematic application of the Comintern's general policy. This made the lack of military preparations in January 1932 completely disastrous. *Proletariado*, pp. 69–70.

66. The *Socorro Rojo* office in New York dispatched very small sums ($50 in February

1931) for local work, and when the PCS requested advice over its plans for an insurrection in 1932 there was no response before the fateful decision was taken. Martí wore a red star with a portrait of Trotsky on his lapel, and was believed to be a Trotskyist by some in the New York office of the Anti-Imperialist League where he worked for a short while early in 1928. Anderson, *Matanza*, pp. 36–7; 68.

67. Martí, for instance, was exiled from El Salvador in 1920, from Guatemala in 1926, and from El Salvador again in 1927. In 1928 he was in the US, Cuba, Jamaica, Belize, Guatemala, Honduras and Nicaragua. Late in 1929 he left Nicaragua with Sandino for Mexico. Early in 1930 he returned to Guatemala, whence he travelled to El Salvador. Jorge Arias Gómez, *Farabundo Martí, Esbozo Biográfico*, San José 1972. Recourse to exile was not, however, always quite as simple as it might seem. In 1932 the US ambassador to Honduras noted that, having put pressure on Carías to do something about 'the communistic movement making very rapid headway. . . . The President explained that the main difficulty in ridding Honduras of all these agitators was that according to Honduran law any Central American could become a nationalized Honduran upon making a declaration, and that Hondurans could not be deported.' Quoted in Posas, *Movimiento Obrero*, p. 210.

68. Of these figures only Ramírez, a *campesino* from Soyapango, was of humble extraction. Martí (1898–1932) was the son of modest farmers. Manuel Cálix Herrera (1900–35) was a schoolteacher who, together with Zoroastro Montes de Oca, had been instrumental in organizing a banana workers' strike at La Ceiba in 1929, and in that year founded the FSH in opposition to the artisan-dominated *Federación Obrera Hondureña* (1921), He died of tuberculosis shortly after release from jail. Felipe Armando Amaya and Gabriela García were from an upper-class background in El Salvador but began their political work in the PCH. Amaya visited Moscow and died in Honduras in 1935; García was exiled to Mexico, playing an active role in the women's and Communist movements in both Guatemala and Honduras in the late 1940s. In 1981, at the age of 85, she published a brief and unsophisticated but moving memoir of her political life: *Páginas de Lucha*, Tegucigalpa 1981. In this text she records with special warmth the life of Juan Pablo Wainwright (1894–1932), born of an English father and Honduran mother, a worker in San Francisco, Alaska and Mexico, and a decorated sergeant in the Canadian forces during World War One. Gaoled for subversion in El Salvador in 1928, Wainwright was later exiled to Guatemala, where he is sometimes credited with establishing a Communist Party in 1929. Close to Martí, he worked as a salesman, which enabled him to travel widely. Captured by Ubico's police in Guatemala City, he was shot in February 1932, leaving the legend that he spat in the dictator's face and daubed 'Viva la Internacional Comunista' in his blood on the walls of his cell. Evidence of activity by militants from outside Central America is slight. Rómulo Betancourt, later president of Venezuela, was briefly a member of the Costa Rican party, and Estebán Pavletich, the Peruvian *aprista*, worked with Martí and the Cuban Communist leader Juan Antonio Mella in Mexico City after a period in Guatemala. The North American Russell Blackwell was arrested in Tegucigalpa in 1925 whilst endeavouring, in a far from efficacious manner, to establish a regional party.

69. According to Wainwright, the party had some sixty active militants. Posas, *Movimiento Obrero Hondureño*, p. 200.

70. García, *Páginas de Lucha*, pp. 47–8. García recounts a separate incident when the bus she was taking to visit her imprisoned brother at Puerto Cortés stopped at Zambrano, where Carías's wife Elena owned a restaurant; the general climbed aboard to debate with her while fellow travellers breakfasted. After Carías came to power Doña Elena continued to purvey tortillas on certain days from the presidential palace although she had by then acquired a monopoly on the supply to the military and was successfully speculating in real estate on the outskirts of Tegucigalpa. Ibid., pp. 44–5; William Krehm, *Democracies and Tyrannies in the Caribbean*, Westport 1984, pp. 92–3. The 1931 electoral programme of the *Bloque* is reproduced as an appendix to Anibal Delgado Fiallos, *Honduras. Elecciones 1985*, Tegucigalpa 1986.

71. Vladimir de la Cruz, 'El Primer Congreso del Partido Comunista de Costa Rica', ESC, no. 27, September–December 1980, pp. 28–32.

72. De la Cruz suggests that the Chilean party's electoral programme was used as a model for the PCCR's minimum platform but indicates no other link. Ibid., p. 37.

3

The Rise of Modern Politics: Autocratic Retrenchment

Communism is like a tree shaken by the wind. The moving tree causes the seeds to fall; the same wind carries the seed to other places. The seed falls on fertile soil. To be done with Communism it is necessary to make the ground sterile.

Colonel Marcelino Galdamez, El Salvador, 1932[1]

While I am President I will not grant liberty of the press nor of association because the people of Guatemala are not prepared for democracy and need a strong hand.

President Jorge Ubico, 1944[2]

There are no volcanos, no earthquakes, no Communists, no labor unions, no wage or social security laws, no income tax . . . [Honduras works on] a pay as you go basis . . . through old-fashioned orthodox virtues of hard work and frugality, without recourse to screwball economics.

John D. Erwin, US Ambassador to Honduras, 1937–47[3]

I cannot place great confidence in his promises.

US Ambassador Henry Bliss Lane on General Anastasio Somoza, 1934[4]

By 1950 the Liberal oligarchy no longer exercised direct political control in most of Central America. The effects of the Depression and World War Two had compelled shifts in the management of state power to forms of government that are recognizably modern and were to persist almost everywhere until 1979 and beyond. However, nowhere – not even in Guatamala after the agrarian reform of 1952 – did the bourgeoisie lose its control over either land or the commanding heights of the economy; it retained all the social power of a ruling class. What had altered since 1930 – and was in some respects predictable even before that date – was less the character of the landed regime than the manner in which it was upheld in the political sphere.

Liberal economic policy was progressively qualified, producing a number of secondary conflicts within the capitalist class as well as a collective recognition that a degree of state intervention was necessary for the maintenance of essential economic structures. The extent to which this took place varied, but everywhere it tended towards a displacement of direct oligarchic control into a wider hegemony. Such a progress did inevitably encompass some change in the physiognomy of the ruling class. The early 1930s witnessed a further concentration of estate ownership, usually at the expense of tenants and owners of medium-sized holdings. Equally, World War Two radically reduced the role played by German capital – although there is some evidence, particularly in the case of Costa Rica, that the affinities of class mitigated those of international political alliance through dummy purchases and informal wardship of lands. In general, however, it was less the 'ruling class' than the 'dominant bloc' that altered in configuration during this period. This bloc remained dependent upon landed power for its authority and the maintenance of the relations of production; in moments of crisis such a dependence became very clear and direct. Nevertheless, the governors of Central America ceased to be co-substantial with the landlord class. In the 1930s they generally came from the ranks of the military, bringing all the countries except Costa Rica into line with the Guatemalan model. In the following decade the army was joined by lawyers, administrators, technicians and professional politicians in directing the state apparatus. The mandate of the Liberal oligarchy was thus executed in a more distended fashion, the expanded political class lacking an independent social base from which to challenge the essentials of such a mandate but being able to negotiate some of its terms. This negotiation was henceforth to be the stuff of political activity within the dominant bloc.[5]

The piecemeal disaggregation of oligarchic Liberalism between 1930 and 1950 was far from coincidentally linked with developments at a global level, reflecting the expansion of export agriculture and progressive integration of the Central American economies into the world market over the preceding decades. The disruption of this market both in the early 1930s and between 1940 and 1945 issued challenges which the landed bourgeoisie weathered quite well compared to its counterparts in many other Latin American states, local politics during the Depression being singularly devoid of the populist motifs often adopted elsewhere, even by dictatorial regimes. In Central America the autocratic and largely military-based governments established in the early 1930s came to power and crushed opposition with relative ease, encountering only minor threats until the mid 1940s, when the emergence of democratic demands, renewed popular mobilization and even more novel strategies of 'development' combined to compel a diminution of coercive control, greater reliance on co-optation and, occasionally, an authentic democratic opening. There was a close relationship between these two phases that were less than a generation apart. The upsurge in demands for civic freedoms in the 1940s clearly emanated from the lived experience of dictatorship as well as from the impact of Allied commitment to the 'Four Freedoms' and the existence of a historical 'window of opportunity' for some three years before the onset of the Cold War. Washington's replacement of a most erratically applied 'Good Neighbour' policy with a gleeful and unencumbered anti-Communism excited a profusion of phantoms and paranoia. Yet, despite all the make-believe, gobbledegook, pseudo-science and atomic-age inquisition that was in attendance – and is today familiar through the Reagan school of historiography – this 'closure' was also the product of a clear political rationality. Authentic liberal democracy, which existed nowhere in Central America in 1947 yet remained on the agenda everywhere, was now an incubus since by its very nature it offered succour to political forces already or potentially opposed to US hegemony. Even in Central America, the outward manifestations of democratic procedure could not be readily discarded precisely because of their popularity in the wake of a war supposedly fought by Washington in their defence. There was, therefore, no simple reversion to the fully autocratic modes of the 1930s, but rather the re-investment of their essential features within a shell of formal democracy sustained by regimes that were for some time imbalanced by this marriage.

The rites of passage towards the post-war political systems under challenge today took a particularly distinct form in Guatemala and Costa Rica. In Guatemala the strength of popular mobilization against the Ubico regime opened a period of political and economic reform (1944–54) which eventually came to threaten a real shift in class power and had to be halted by open counter-revolution. It is significant that, like the heyday of Nicaraguan Liberalism under Zelaya, the Arbenz regime (1951–54) was 'out of time' with changes elsewhere, drawing its strength from a popular movement that began at the end of the war but which also held the forces of reaction at bay through most of the Cold War period. The consequent consolidation of political camps was appreciably less polarized than that which obtains today, but it was still sufficiently strong to make 'the revolution' the central reference point of national politics for the following thirty years. For the left it was a solitary instance of measured but authentic reform curtailed and held in abeyance by counter-revolution, and for the right a sobering and unrepeatable example of such reform acting as handmaiden to Communism.

In the case of Costa Rica the influence of developments in the 1940s upon contemporary political patterns is no less strong but quite different in nature. The civil war of 1948 is almost universally identified as opening the modern era of electoralist politics under the aegis of the *Partido de Liberación Nacional* (PLN) led by José Figueres, but the war did not itself introduce a period of popular and reformist government. On the contrary, such a government, supported by a hirsute coalition of Communists, Conservative populists and the Church, was ousted by the victorious forces headed by Figueres, then allied with the oligarchy under a resolutely anti-communist banner. However, this alliance never blossomed into a full counter-revolution, the reforms of the mid 1940s being too popular to be rescinded without engendering further conflict. At the same time, renewed state intervention in the economy and adhesion to the rules of electoralism were cushioned against decisive external meddling by a refusal to lower the anti-communist profile given to such initiatives.

This singular development in Costa Rica may be ascribed in part to the absence of a properly autocratic regime in the 1930s. In the case of El Salvador and Nicaragua such regimes were not only comparable to that in Guatemala but also persisted, with only moderate embellishments and temporary interruptions, until 1979. In El Salvador this longevity was in no small part due to the emphatic nature of the army's repression of the peasant rising of 1932 and the establishment of a militarist tradition that was capable of surviving the disturbances of 1944 and 1948 as well as retaining a fitful oligarchic acquiescence for nigh-on fifty years. The Somozas nearly matched such endurance, but in Nicaragua the survival up to the cusp of the 1980s of a regime founded in the 1930s was marked by a progressive loss of institutionalism contrary to the tendency elsewhere. The extraordinary partisanship and self-enrichment practised by the family ultimately made it peculiarly vulnerable, but these characteristics were not simply anachronistic residues of the pre-war epoch; indeed, they exhibit a certain forlorn modernism when taken together with the examples of the Pahlavi, Duvalier and Marcos regimes. The first years of Somoza rule were marked by a less remarkable species of bonapartism, with control of the National Guard the central figure in arbitrating the disputes of a still divided ruling class as well as containing popular unrest. It was Anastasio Somoza's ability to negotiate the challenges that confronted his government in the late 1940s that condemned the rivalry between Liberal and Conservative Parties to the status of a purely secondary and increasingly formalistic dispute.

In Honduras, by contrast, the relatively untroubled termination of the dictatorship of Tiburcio Carías (1932–48), through an electoral handover to a longstanding servant of the regime, breathed new life into traditional partisan politics and secured a much more modulated continuity. Although it formed part of a regional autocratic model, the *cariato* was not born in the midst of significant political turmoil and proved capable of overriding popular discontent to supervise its own transition. As a result, many of the developments witnessed in the rest of the isthmus during these twenty years took a less pronounced form in Honduras, and major alterations in the political model were delayed until the 1950s.

This chapter surveys the first, autocratic phase of this progressive dislocation of the Liberal political regime up to the onset of World War Two; chapter 4 studies developments throughout the 1940s, which, as a political phase, may be said to terminate with the Guatemalan counter-revolution in June 1954.

The New Autocracy

Between 1929 and 1933 the volume of world exports fell by 25 per cent and their average price by 30 per cent.[6] Although the general reduction in quantum exports from Latin America was less marked, the terms of trade were exceptionally bad, especially for commodities such as coffee and bananas that were not basic necessities and had a relatively high elasticity of demand. The effect of the Crash of 1929 on the economies of Central America was, therefore, little short of catastrophic. The average price of Salvadorean coffee fell from $0.25 per lb in 1925 to $0.09 in 1935 and did not reach $0.20 until after 1945; Guatemalan and Nicaraguan bean prices collapsed to a similar degree. Costa Rican coffee was only marginally protected by its higher quality, its price being cut by more than half between 1929 and 1935.[7] In November 1940 the US, which had by then replaced many of Central America's traditional European markets, effectively set a fixed price of 13.4 cents per lb through the Inter-American Coffee Agreement, and this level, equivalent to that prevailing in 1920, was maintained throughout the war.[8] Only in the late 1940s, after the Agreement's quotas had been removed, did demand begin to match supply and push the price of the region's staple export back to the levels of the mid 1920s. The price of bananas fell less precipitately, but still by some 30 per cent between 1924 and 1935. Although Tables 2a and 2b are incomplete and based on different sources, they give an adequate picture of the crisis in the export sector; Tables 3a and 3b clearly indicate the impact of this on the economies as a whole. Even these figures probably understate the immediate effects of the Crash. In Guatemala total receipts from exports fell by 40 per cent between 1929 and 1932, and state

Table 2a: Exports of Coffee, 1925–40

	1925	*1926*	*1927*	*1929*	*1930*	*1931*	*1932*	*1933*	*1935*[1]	*1939*[2]	*1940*[3]
Costa Rica											
Volume (kg mn)	18.2	18.3		19.7	23.5		18.5	27.8	24.2	18.7	
Value ($ mn)				9.8					4.9	4.6	4.0
El Salvador											
Volume	32.0	50.6	36.2	46.8	58.6	54.6	39.7	56.2	50.1		
Value	30.4	46.7	25.2	84.1	23.9	21.7	12.9	19.5	24.2		
Guatemala											
Value			34.0	25.0	23.6		9.3		12.5		
Nicaragua											
Volume		17.6		13.2		15.8		13.7	13.1	14.3	12.7
Value		8.1		5.9		3.3		2.2	2.1	2.0	2.6

Notes
1. Nicaragua: 1936
2. Nicaragua: 1938
3. Nicaragua: 1941

Sources:
Costa Rica – Rodrigo Facio, *Estudio sobre la Economía Costarricense*, p.41.
El Salvador – Rafael Guidos Vejar, *Acenso del Militarismo en El Salvador*, p.142.
Guatemala – Kenneth Grieb, *Guatemala Caudillo. The Regime of Jorge Ubico*, p.53.
Nicaragua – Jaime Wheelock, *Imperialismo y Dictadura*, p.201.

expenditure was cut by some 30 per cent between 1930 and 1932.[9] In El Salvador a fall of 62 per cent in the price of coffee between 1928 and 1932 required a somewhat less severe reduction in an already low budget but still drove many modest farmers to the wall, with 28 per cent of all coffee holdings changing hands during the Depression.[10] In both Costa Rica and Honduras the effects of the crisis were aggravated by outbreaks of sigatoka disease on the Atlantic banana plantations; together they caused abandonment, wage cuts and increased unemployment.[11] Nicaragua's reserves of gold could not be exploited rapidly enough to compensate for the collapse in the coffee market, and neither could a brief expansion in banana production halt a general fall in output that was so great that, notwithstanding steady recovery after 1935, it was twenty years before per capita GDP regained its 1929 level.[12] Everywhere the gold standard was abandoned, access to credit gravely restricted and loans called in, and payments on the foreign debt were officially or unofficially suspended. In the space of three years a contraction of the value of the export economy by one-third or more placed the future of the Liberal system in doubt.

Table 2b: Exports of Bananas, 1924-40 (millions of stems)

	1924	*1926*	*1927*	*1931*	*1935*	*1939*	*1940*
Honduras	14.7	16.2	17.0	29.0	15.8	12.5	4.6
Costa Rica	8.1			5.1	3.88		
Guatemala		2.6	3.1	2.9	3.7	5.1	4.0
Price ($/stem)	0.75			0.62	0.51		

Sources:
Honduras – Mario Posas, *El Movimiento Obrero Hondureño*, pp.33; 173.
Costa Rica – José Luis Vega Carballo, 'Costa Rica', in González Casanova, *América Latina*, vol.2, p.5.
Guatemala – Alfonso Bauer Paiz, *Como Opera el Capital Yanqui*, p.298.

Table 3a: Growth in GDP, 1920–54
(Annual average per cent at 1950 prices)

	C. Rica	*El Sal.*	*Guate.*	*Hon.*	*Nica.*	*C. America*
1920–24	3.0	4.3	5.4	0.5	1.9	3.0
1925–29	0.2	2.6	3.8	8.3	6.4	4.3
1930–34	0	−0.7	−0.6	−2.4	−4.9	−1.4
1935–39	8.0	3.3	12.5	0.2	2.4	5.3
1940–44	−2.7	3.5	−4.7	2.4	4.6	0.6
1945–49	10.9	6.8	6.9	5.3	6.9	7.3
1950–54	5.1	3.8	3.5	2.0	11.3	5.1

Source: Victor Bulmer-Thomas, 'Economic Development in the Long-Run', JLAS, 1983, p. 272.

Table 3b: GDP and Domestic Expenditure Per Capita (US$ 1950)

	Costa Rica		*El Salvador*		*Guatemala*		*Honduras*		*Nicaragua*	
	GDP	*Exp.*	*GDP*	*Exp.*	*GDP*	*Exp.*	*GDP*	*Exp.*	*GDP*	*Exp.*
1920	226	186	110	98	166	151	147	133	154	148
1929	212	199	128	119	184	182	184	155	185	153
1939	252	250	128	107	256	240	129	111	132	105
1949	286	271	185	168	220	223	152	133	182	189

Source: as above, p.276.

The lack of foreign exchange for imports did little to shield the artisanate from the crisis, and pressure for protectionism persisted throughout the decade. Moreover, the urban economy registered not only a fall in demand from the export sector but also the effects of large reductions in state budgets; wage cuts in the public sector were 30 per cent in Guatemala and El Salvador, 15 per cent in Costa Rica, and many of these were not restored, as in Honduras, until 1936 or even later.[13] Although there are no dependable statistics, urban unemployment rose significantly in both public and private sectors, the internal market contracting correspondingly. In Guatemala, where over half a million quintals had been imported to meet demand in 1928, the price of corn fell over the following three years from 4.33 to 0.95 quetzales; in El Salvador the price of maize dropped 35 per cent and that of beans 57 per cent between 1928 and 1935.[14] Such reductions enabled an urban populace with a depleted purchasing power to eat, but they compounded the difficulties of the peasantry, which at the onset of the Depression came under increased pressure from commercial landlords endeavouring to offset the fall in price of export crops. The most obvious means of achieving this was to increase the volume of production, but, as Tables 2a and 2b demonstrate, the general pattern of quantum production remained quite stable. In El Salvador and Costa Rica this was primarily due to the ecological limits to immediate expansion, in Nicaragua to diversification away from coffee; only in the case of Guatemala was there a significant, but not rapid, extension of land under coffee.[15] In the case of El Salvador it is frequently stated that the *finqueros* responded to the crisis by laying off seasonal labourers and failing to collect the harvest. There is some evidence for this in 1930, and the rebellion of 1932 occurred at the height of the harvest, undoubtedly reducing production, but the overall tendency was still to keep export levels as high as possible.[16] It seems probable that peasant discontent was most directly exacerbated by the obvious alternative – or complementary – strategy open to farmers, that of reducing wages. These were cut from 50–75 centavos per day to 15 in two years, precisely at a time when earnings from market produce were at their lowest and many small tenants were losing their leases. The wage cuts were certainly the cause of the 1931 rural strikes and most likely the determinate factor in pushing the peasantry of the west of the country into open rebellion in January 1932. In the case of Guatemala, the response to reduced cash income from seasonal labour was much less emphatic but seems to have increased evasion of the obligations caused by debt, contributing to the abolition of debt peonage in 1934 and its replacement by a more direct system of obligatory labour based upon vagrancy laws.[17]

The effects of the crisis in both El Salvador and Guatemala were marked less by an expansion of the frontier of the plantation economy as a whole than by a concentration of land ownership within these frontiers. In

Costa Rica such a tendency was constrained by intervention on the part of the *Instituto de Defensa del Café*, established in 1933 to control the price paid at the *beneficio*, thus preventing large merchants from deliberately bankrupting smallholders.[18] In 1940 there were still in Costa Rica some 19,400 holdings that possessed between one and 5,000 coffee bushes, compared with 1,832 with between 5,000 and 25,000, and 377 possessing over 25,000.[19] Yet even this singular form of intervention, in which the state played only a partial role, did little more than limit the damage.

The initial strategies of large landlords were demonstrably aggressive, but they could not prevent a prolonged and general stagnation in the regional economy. Thus, although the terms of plantation labour remained prejudicial for the peasant seasonal worker, the frontier of the plantation advanced very modestly, and over the period as a whole cultivation of food crops for the internal market was not subjected to continuously high pressure from the agro–export sector. In 1945 production for the domestic market accounted for 61 per cent of total agricultural output compared with 39 per cent for export crops, the extent of non-marketed subsistence production making the real difference greater still. Of course, not all locally consumed staples were grown on small peasant plots, and the ratio between domestic and export production varied between countries: in Guatemala export crop sales were little more than a third the value of those for the local market whereas in both El Salvador and Costa Rica they were some 25 per cent higher. But the very limited growth of export production strengthens the view that, in addition to bolstering a modicum of import-substituting commercial farming and allied trades, developments up to at least 1945 enabled peasant agriculture to hold its own, giving the rural masses a modicum of social and productive space.[20]

The character of the new dictatorial regimes reflected the stasis in the export economy. Prepared on occasion to sanction state intervention, they pursued essentially defensive and pre-emptive strategies in order to maintain the plantation economy. The suppression of social unrest and violence directed against political opponents was primarily to ensure the preservation of existing social relations rather than in support of an aggressive expansionism. Thus, after the initial successful onslaught made necessary by the Crash there was relatively little active opposition from either the rural or urban masses. At least in this respect the bases of the autocracy of the 1930s were different from those of the 1870s or the 1960s, and they bestowed a perceptible unity on the regimes of Jorge Ubico (Guatemala; 1931–44), Tiburcio Carías Andino (Honduras; 1932–48), Maximiliano Hernández Martínez (El Salvador; 1931–44) and Anastasio Somoza García (Nicaragua; 1936–56). There were also some, more limited, similarities between these governments and the final, austere phase of the Costa Rican 'Olympians' under Ricardo Jiménez (1932–36) and León Cortes Castro (1936–40). The formal niceties of democratic procedure were motioned at, but in a completely effortless fashion and, outside Costa Rica, by rulers whose authority derived from military strength. In the case of Guatemala there already existed a tradition of prolonged authoritarian rule that had been only partially unhinged in the 1920s. In Nicaragua Zelaya provided something of a distant example for Somoza, but in that country as elsewhere the new regime constituted an abrupt break with the political modes of the Liberal oligarchy. For the plebeian masses such a distinction might have been of a purely secondary order, but it was certainly far from irrelevant insofar as it terminated those vestiges of independent organization that had come into existence in the late 1920s. Equally, it would be misconceived to discount the fact that, while these regimes upheld the old social order with absolute discrimination against the lower classes, their forceful and partisan policies were also prejudicial to the interests of certain sectors of the dominant bloc, particularly members of those traditional parties now excluded from power. This quite natural consequence of the dictatorial mode of government was to colour the form in which it was eventually brought to an end, placing a premium upon the demand for authentic democratic liberties and giving those traditional sectors which had upheld such a demand, usually for narrow partisan objectives, more than a modicum of influence in the post-dictatorial era. Thus, José Angel Zuñiga, defeated Liberal Party candidate in the Honduran election of 1931, could sixteen years later still command a significant popular following through a not entirely spurious identification with the travails of the populace under Carías: 'I am assaulted by the doubt that twenty-one years of exile and all the setbacks encountered throughout a life that now approaches its natural end are due to the fact that I chose the road taken by Don Quixote instead of that followed by Sancho Panza, on which others have prospered so much, but no . . . I do not repent of my political romanticism.'[21]

Nowhere was the onset of dictatorial government so radical as in El Salvador, where repression of the uprising in the west of the country led to the death of no less than 10,000 people and possibly as many as 40,000 in the last week of January and throughout February 1932.[22] It should not be forgotten that this unparalleled pogrom, which laid the basis for over forty years of military rule, was as much the work of civilian viligantes as of regular military forces – a telling precedent for the death squads of the modern era.[23] Moreover, the rebellion itself was less a direct result of the military coup of December 1931 that finally overthrew the luckless Araujo than of a long-planned rural strike and the cancellation of the municipal elections of early January 1932 that the new government of General Martínez had originally permitted to go ahead. Indeed, at first even the PCS congratulated the military for ousting Araujo, and although such a sentiment was out of touch with the ex-president's extensive popularity, it reflected a quite widespread feeling that the army, which had rebelled because of lack of pay, would not overturn the existing political system.[24] Both the impact of the Depression and the effects of Araujo's populist campaign were too great to give substance to such an illusion.[25] On the one hand, the peasantry, only partially affected by the course of national politics but keenly interested in the municipal elections, was by the end of 1931 in a state of active mobilization, particularly in the west. On the other, Araujo's removal effectively made the conduct of radical politics in the capital the exclusive preserve of the PCS, which now reversed its anti-electoralist policy and contested the 1932 poll.

The true nature of the 1932 rebellion remains the subject of debate, it being frequently described as both 'Communist' and 'peasant' in character. For many, such a distinction was at the time and still remains of absolutely minimal importance, but it is clear that, although linked by both the general crisis and a number of tenuous organizational ties, the rural and urban movements possessed quite different characteristics. The latter took the form of a traditional insurrectionary operation, organized immediately after the cancellation of the poll, delayed for the purposes of gaining support from the troops garrisoned in the capital, and eventually revealed to the regime through an almost inevitable lack of precaution because of such hasty preparation.[26] Farabundo Martí was arrested together with two important aides on 18 January, when an attempted mutiny by conscripts was suppressed, but the party leadership decided to persist with the uprising planned for four days later. Both the regime's forewarning and the absence of any military support ensured a rapid and disastrous defeat in San Salvador, the leaders of the PCS being detained, executed or forced underground in a matter of hours.[27] The urban movement was effectively limited to the capital and the forces of the PCS; it generated no mass following and failed to spread further than Ilopango, a few kilometres east of San Salvador. Although dwarfed by the repression in the countryside, that in the capital was still exceptionally fierce; hundreds of people were killed and many more gaoled, most of them apparently supporters of Araujo.

In the western departments of Ahuachapán, Sonsonate and Santa Ana, which had been the site of constant agitation throughout January, the rebellion that broke out on the night of the 22nd and lasted for three days was almost exclusively directed and overwhelmingly backed by local peasants, whose leaders had been in contact with the PCS and were aware of the party's plans but also operated with significant independence.[28] The areas most affected by the uprising – Izalco, Juayúa, Tacuba, Ahuachapán – corresponded to intensively farmed coffee territory where the Indian communities had largely been dispossessed of their lands but still retained appreciable cultural and organizational autonomy. Leaders of the revolt such as Feliciano Ama and Felipe Neri were the most important local Indian *caciques*, and the insurrection took a resolutely peasant character in its ritualistic celebrations and humiliation – infrequently, execution – of local representatives of the state and landlord class.[29] The quite pronounced Indian aspect of the rising may have played a part in stemming wider support since the rebels did not manage to take any town of size and within a day their control of urban settlements had been reduced to Juayúa alone. Although there was a signal lack of mobilization in the other major centre of indigenous population, Santiago Nonualco, the rebellion was perceived by many *ladinos* as being one of '*naturales*', and the counter-revolutionary repression was conspicuous in its identification of '*indios con machetes*' as the principal targets.[30] By 25 January this repression was so emphatically under way that US and Canadian warships, hurriedly dispatched to assist in averting any Communist revolution, were requested by Martínez to re-embark their forward parties since 'calm was restored'.[31] Indeed, it is the all-encompassing nature of the counter-revolution rather than the scale of the rising, in itself quite localized and of less than forty-eight hours' duration, which made the events of 1932 so singular in Central American history. In unleashing the most rancorous racism it effectively suppressed Indian culture in El Salvador. The most obvious feature of this was the discarding of indigenous dress, undertaken initially as a simple strategy for survival, but it went deeper, throwing the traditional *cofradías* into crisis and depriving them of an authority that was never to be recovered.[32] Beyond this, the slaughter terminated general peasant unrest in a region where 75 per cent of El Salvador's coffee was cultivated, permitting landlords to consolidate their appropriation of communal lands and secure the terms for seasonal labour that had been so central in provoking the discontent of the previous years. The trauma suffered by rural labourers extended beyond a death toll so great that it was to have a significant demographic effect for several generations. The absence of any major outbreak of peasant rebellion in the west of the country in the 1970s or during the civil war of the 1980s, when the central and eastern zones of El Salvador witnessed an extensive guerrilla campaign, may in part at least be ascribed to the legacy of 1932. Similarly, the PCS itself, which effectively ceased to exist for the following twelve years, showed the scars of its defeat in a subsequent aversion to insurrectionary methods so profound that it only quit the 'peaceful road to socialism' with great reluctance in 1980, much later than the other forces that today comprise the guerrilla named after the party's principal hero, *Frente Farabundo Martí para la Liberación Nacional* (FMLN).[33]

Aside from his very odd personality, it is difficult to depict Martínez as a mere cypher of the oligarchy.[34] Whereas Araujo had trenchantly resisted a devaluation of the colón, Martínez now proceeded to meet this longstanding demand of the coffee *finqueros*. However, the strength of the regime after the repression of the January rising enabled it to undertake some initiatives that were not included in the oligarchic programme. Within a week of the revolt Martínez suspended payment of the debt to the US and, despite complaints from the bankers, Washington desisted from retaliation. A month later the government declared a moratorium and cut the interest rate by 40 per cent. In 1934 a central bank was established and private financial institutions lost their right to issue notes.[35] The following year a state credit bank was set up, but the majority of shares were held by the private *Asociación de Cafetaleros* (40 per cent) and *Asociación de Ganaderos* (20 per cent). This felicitous arrangement, which gave private capital an active interest in the very state initiatives it had previously resisted, was extended in 1942 to the reorganization of the *Asociación de Café* (1929) into the *Companía Salvadoreñ˜a de Café* as the principal national body for the marketing of coffee.[36] Equally, while the oligarchy was at first able to resist exchange controls, Martínez forced these through in 1935, and four years later established a number of tariffs to protect artisanal industry. None of these measures actively prejudiced oligarchic interests as a whole but some, such as the banking legislation, did curtail the advantages of specific sectors. Taken together, they indicate a realignment of politico-economic power. Landed and commercial capital acquiesced in a modest quotient of intervention along with military control of government while maintaining a veto on economic policy both directly, through holding economic portfolios in cabinet and participating in mixed regulatory bodies, and indirectly, through the capacity for non-compliance held by the formidable corporate associations. This system was to endure intact until 1979 and, after a collapse of its formal mechanisms, was effectively reinstated little more than a year later, albeit principally by virtue of the exercise of veto powers rather than through government policy.

As a man of modest background and indisputably eccentric character, Martínez incurred plenty of scorn from the landed gentry; but if he was a 'crazy Indian', he was also a more than adequate guarantor of order. From time to time his 'elections', sometimes followed by inauguration on the same day, excited poorly prepared coup attempts by ambitious colleagues, but none flourished. For over twelve years the military institution remained subordinate to a personal rule so confident that the existence of an officialist *Pro-Patria* party was little more than a vanity. Martínez was not greatly inconvenienced by the absence of US recognition for four years until, in 1936, Roosevelt reversed Washington's compliance with the 1923 agreement not to sustain full diplomatic relations with de facto regimes. 'Good Neighbour' status was conferred upon the Salvadorean dictator shortly after it had been extended to Somoza. This was little more than a fait accompli; with the absolute repression of worker organization, a cowed middle class, and an indebted oligarchy, Martínez lacked internal opposition of any consequence, and the US had less political interest in insisting upon democratic government than it had local investment with which to support any such insistence.

Jorge Ubico's assumption of power in Guatemala by a marginally more legal route than that taken by Martínez – 305,841 votes against no competition in 1931 – circumvented any problems with US recognition. There were some obvious similarities between these two tyrannical regimes formed by the ministers of war of their predecessors, not least the fact that they collapsed within weeks of each other in 1944. If Ubico was somewhat less exotic than Martínez in his beliefs, he was no less striking in his personal comportment over the dozen years in which he managed the most monolithic regime in Guatemalan history.[37] This issued from a crisis in the ruling class that never attained the political extremes evident in El Salvador and was not marked by a single 'moment' such as January 1932. Yet, just as Ubico remained within the traditions of Guatemalan government in distrusting his Salvadorean counterpart, so did he reaffirm the despotic heritage of his godfather Barrios. His belief that 'peace and order [are] the only conditions essential for human development' was realized principally through an unprecedented centralization of the state apparatus.[38] The radio and motorcycle gave Ubico more than pleasure, enabling him constantly to tour the country and to keep in daily contact with departmental *jefes políticos*. There are few written records of the inner workings of his regime, the cabinets of which scarcely ever met; ministers acted as simple functionaries, less important as servants of the dictator's fiat than the regional executive officers, who were unfailingly members of the military. Insofar as such a system required increased finance and a degree of professionalism it escaped the axe of fiscal conservatism, but while some elements of military organization were divested of the trappings of the nineteenth century through a US-directed training programme, it was in the nature of the regime that it did not permit 'modernization' to exceed the brief of enhanced tehnical skills in service of the established order. The junior officers who eventually overthrew Ubico were trained in the new *Escuela Politécnica*, but their adhesion to vague notions of development and democracy was greatly assisted by discontent with an institution in which there were eighty generals for 15,000 troops who built bridges of wood rather than stone or brick to save money.[39] Of necessity this army sustained a social order that had relied for fifty years upon direct support from the central state apparatus, but Ubico preserved his own rule more narrowly through a police force and espionage network as efficient and radical in method as those operating fifty years hence.

The suppression of popular mobilization and radical activists in the first years of the government set the seal of its character and was assisted by the Salvadorean rising, which encouraged Ubico to invoke the spectre of Communism and clear his own gaols of dissidents by executing them.[40] Opponents within the middle class and even the oligarchy were liberally persecuted; in 1934 perhaps 300 people were killed following the dictator's 'discovery' of an assassination plot against him. This particular clampdown enabled Ubico to call 'elections' for a constituent assembly, which duly proceeded with its sole task – that of amending article 66 of the constitution to permit the head of state to succeed himself. The consolidation of the regime that resulted was rather greater than is suggested by the increase from 306,000 votes cast for Ubico in his first victorious poll to 308,000 in the last one, since over the span of a decade electoral support for opposition candidates could not match even this modest increment and remained stable at zero votes.[41] In this Ubico conformed to the image of omnipotent patriarch depicted so vividly by his fellow countryman Miguel Angel Asturías as well as by Gabriel García Marquez.[42] It was less than coincidental that such works of literature should dwell upon the tractability of their 'heroes' with respect to the requirements of the banana companies; Ubico, who had gained US support for his campaign in 1930 by championing the interests of IRCA, was ever compliant in his dealings with UFCO.[43] Equally, while he encouraged some diversification of agriculture, suppressed the *Cámara de Comercio*, and enjoyed less than harmonious relations with the German planters of the Verapaces, Ubico gave resolute support to the coffee oligarchy.[44] Shortly after taking power he introduced a number of statutes that completely altered the mechanisms for recruiting rural labour and effectively terminated the longstanding tradition of debt peonage. It is difficult to reach a decisive conclusion as to how much this was founded upon increased problems faced by the *finqueros* in meeting the capital outlay involved in debt servitude and how much it derived from increased evasion, equally attributable to the effects of the Depression. In all probability the introduction of the vagrancy law of June 1934 corresponded to a combination of these factors since the seasonally concentrated outlay of credit to peasant labourers had become relatively more costly than before even if reduced wages permitted greater, but delayed, returns on such advances. At the same time, lower wages discouraged indebtedness and increased evasion. In all events, the new measures were far from the 'liberation of the Indian from slavery' that Ubico proclaimed them to be, and reflected the apprehension of the planters that a simple introduction of free labour would be construed by the population of the highlands as the freedom not to work.[45]

Whatever the degree to which the new statutes represented a reduction in quasi-feudal relations, they did very little to improve the lot of the Indian.[46] Preceded by a 1932 decree which exempted landlords from the legal consequences of any action, including homicide, taken in defence of their goods and lands, the law of 5 June 1934 replaced debtors with 'vagrants' as the primary source of plantation labour. Vagrants were deemed to be those without a profession or personally farming less than 2.76 hectares (four *manzanas*) of land; all such persons, a considerable proportion of the male population in the countryside, were henceforth required to work at least 100 and up to 150 days a year on commercial estates.[47] The overspill of the resulting supply of workers – greater than under debt peonage – was employed on public works, principally building roads. Management of the new system was assisted by the obligation of the rural population to carry a *libreta* or identity card that contained details of an individual's status; another factor was Ubico's replacement of Indian mayors by intendants appointed by and directly answerable to the presidential office, which exploited the filling of such posts with an eye on popular sentiment as well as the needs of political control.[48] The effect of these measures was to improve the position of the landlords and maintain order in the countryside; they contributed towards oligarchic acceptance of a regime that was not in the least timorous in prohibiting independent association, either of *finqueros* or of *campesinos*, and quite prepared to transgress longstanding political traditions, as, for instance, in its invitation to the Jesuits to return to the country. In this respect Ubico carved out as much, if not more, authority than did Martínez.

The Honduran regime of Tiburcio Carías was much more closely based upon the backing of UFCO, narrowly conservative in character, and generally made less resort to violence than other governments. Such a distinction mattered little to Hondurans, upon whom Carías imposed an extended dictatorship of unprecedented severity. It did, however, reflect a relatively lower level of conflict in a state where coffee was a very minor export and the contraction of the banana economy tended to throw workers back into the subsistence circuit, still based upon extensive *ejido* lands, rather than producing critical polarization within the plantation. The degree to which the popular economy in the countryside suffered the effects of a reduction of banana exports to one-fifth of their 1930 value by 1937 was, therefore, less severe than either in the towns or across the border in El Salvador.[49] This, nevertheless, did not occur without conflict. Although Standard Fruit workers were able to strike and gain some concessions in January 1932, the prolonged stoppage in UFCO's Trujillo Railroad Company between February and April was terminated by fierce repression once it became clear that it was about to spread to the rest of the plantation workforce.[50] Thereafter union activity was minimal, and Carías was quick to consolidate his electoral victory. Communists were imprisoned rather than executed, but the Liberal Party was persecuted as assiduously as were disparate radical activists. The introduction of internal passports in 1933 marked an extension of social control that eventually included the proscription of baseball clubs as potential foci of discontent. Lacking the patronage of a US company, the opposition was comprehensively subdued by such methods, and Carías faced even less trouble than Ubico in obtaining re–election through amendment of the constitution in 1936 and parliamentary ratification in 1939. To those who questioned such extensions through to 1948 of a mandate won in 1932 he remarked: 'God also is *continuista* . . .'[51]

Carías, a large man and every bit the warrior who won his first major engagement in 1907, deftly exploited his humble background and popular touch to sustain a rather broader political style than either Martínez or Ubico, although he was no more resistant to the vanities of office.[52] His fiscal conservatism, effective suppression of municipal autonomy – traditionally strong in Honduras – and aversion to cabinet government all cohered with the regional pattern, but rather than being manifestations of a qualititative erosion of the Liberal oligarchic model they corresponded more to its suspension. The absence of both economic change – beyond quantitive contraction – and new social and political forces led to a form of petrification in which the traditional structure of partisan politics was sustained but one side simply frozen. The army continued to be professionally backward and did not acquire an autonomous presence in the dominant bloc, which at the end of this period was still firmly mediated by UFCO. As Tables 3a and 3b (see p.92) demonstrate, economic recovery was the weakest in the region, reflecting in large part the absence of alternatives to the banana trade, which responded more slowly and erratically than did coffee to a gradual improvement in the market. Thus, both in itself and in its subsequent effects, the Honduran experience of autocracy was the most static in Central America.

If the eventual continuity of the pattern of partisan politics in Honduras may be attributed to nearly two decades of stasis during which no new form of domination emerged, the case of Costa Rica was distinct from both this experience and those elsewhere. Here, the oligarchic model survived largely intact throughout the Depression and provided the orbit within which were engendered many of the elements of post-war politics. The relative strength of the national economy, which was unique in avoiding negative growth in the first five years of the 1930s, combined with the weakness of the military apparatus to reduce both the need for an outright dictatorship and the capacity to impose one. Nonetheless, although the Communist Party was permitted to operate above ground during the last phase of 'Olympian' rule, its militants in the banana zone were persecuted with little less zeal than elsewhere in the isthmus. The relative success of the banana workers' strike in the Limón region in mid 1934 cannot be attributed solely to the organizational skills of the PCCR's Carlos Luis Fallas. In fact, from 1930 conditions on UFCO's Atlantic coast plantations had been the object of sharp criticism within the dominant bloc, enabling the government of Ricardo Jiménez to enforce arbitration on the US corporation without provoking a major crisis.[53] The popularity of the Communists in the enclave was secured by the strike, and the party's 5 per cent of the vote in the 1934 congressional elections may be almost exclusively attributed to support from banana workers, whose trade union was henceforth accorded full recognition. This was in itself a singular deviation from the rule in the other states but it was limited in its ramifications within the country. In neither the central coffee zone nor the main towns, which together encompassed the great bulk of the population, was there evidence of a comparable shift towards radical politics or even sustained popular mobilization.[54] In this regard the effort to mediate the impact of the crisis through initiatives such as the *Instituto de Defensa del Café* and some limited deficit financing to support a minimum wage proved sufficient to uphold the existing order. However, from 1937 Costa Rica's balance of payments went into the red, progressively eroding the basis for easy handovers of office from Jiménez to Cortes Castro and from him, through the National Republican Party, to Rafael Calderón Guardia in 1940.[55] This deterioration of the economy opened contradictions within the dominant bloc earlier than in the rest of Central America, prompting a redistributive populism under Calderón that retained a traditionalist form but lacked sufficient oligarchic support to endure in a systematic fashion.

If the Calderón administration was to leave a singular influence upon Costa Rican history, in no sense did this match the impact of a regime set up four years previously across the border in Nicaragua. In its longevity and monolithic character the Somoza dynasty stands out as possibly the most remarkable feature of Central American political life in the twentieth century. Yet, in 1940 it appeared to be, and indeed was, much less distinctive, despite the fact that Anastasio Somoza García had come to power significantly later than his potentate peers, reaping maximum benefit from the presence of foreign troops during Sandino's campaign and at the peak of unrest caused by the economic crisis. The result of this was an unusually weak and subordinated popular movement but also one antagonistic towards the Sacasa regime. This regime, in incurring most of the odium generated by policies attempting to deal with the recession, was also increasingly bereft of oligarchic support, further paving the way for Somoza, whose challenge would have been far more difficult to stage a few years earlier when the terms of Espino Negro dominated the political scene. Moreover, Somoza was 'the last marine', his control of the small but powerful National Guard conferring upon him the imprimatur of the US as well as a power-base without precedent in a country traditionally subdued by purely partisan forces. Washington's first ambassador in the post-occupation period, Matthew Hannah, was of the opinion that 'no one will labour as intelligently or as conscientiously to maintain the non-partisan character of the Guardia'.[56] In a sense he was correct. Although a lifelong Liberal, Somoza was building a force in the service of bonapartism rather than party affiliation, a fact quickly recognized by Hannah's apprehensive successor Arthur Bliss Lane.[57] Thus, Somoza manipulated both Liberals, divided by the increasingly listless Sacasa government, and Conservatives, opposed to the regime by tradition, lacking a strong candidate of their own, and impressed both by Somoza's management of the crisis caused by the

1931 earthquake and by his violent antipathy to Sandino and his followers, many of whom were wiped out by the Guard upon their leader's assassination. Still, this eclipse of longstanding political divisions was only temporary and insufficient for a stable realignment of the dominant bloc. The Liberal traditionalists headed by Sacasa, to whose niece Somoza was married, were less concerned by the fact that the commander of the Guard was a raucous arriviste than by the threat to party unity that had been growing since 1933 and took the form of an independent electoral campaign in 1935.[58] It was primarily on the basis of traditional rivalries and preoccupations that the president supported the opposition of party loyalists to Somoza within the officer corps and took care to maintain a Liberal militia in León.[59] On the other hand, Ambassador Lane sought to supervise the effective stalemate that this caused on the basis of a prescient perception that Somoza aimed to keep to the rules of the old political game only as long as they were of value to him. When Washington finally dropped its embargo on de facto regimes in 1936, Somoza forsook his electoral efforts and, in a typical manoeuvre, first supported the general strike of February 1936 against the government and then repressed the PTN when it tried to prolong the stoppage after he had arranged mediation. He thus combined a groundswell of popular support with military force for the final move, which was to remove Sacasa in an easy coup.

By this stage Somoza had obtained complete control of the Guard, which formed the basis of a regime that was militarized rather than belonging to either of the traditional camps.[60] It was the Guard that underwrote an impressive electoral victory over Leonardo Argüello of 107,201 to 169 votes following the coup although Somoza then had the backing of most of the Liberal Party and some Conservative factions. In 1939, when such support had largely disappeared, the Guard enabled Somoza to push through constitutional amendments and further extend his term. Such military control, which faced relatively little active opposition up to 1944, was comparable to that of Ubico and Martínez, but its peculiar organization around a network of corruption headed by the dictator should be viewed in the context of a young force lacking independent traditions or close political ties with the landlord class. Early US training made it an efficient repressive force, possibly more so than any other in the isthmus, yet this professionalism was almost from the birth of the institution subsumed by a political identification with a single ruler. Thus, independent initiatives within the Nicaraguan military were exceptions to the rule, this being one critical feature in Somoza's ability to survive the unrest of the 1940s. It was also to be a vital factor in the form of the final collapse of the dynasty, with the Guard's lack of autonomy effectively precluding any pre-emptive efforts at 'Somocismo without Somoza', thereby delivering power directly to the FSLN. In 1979 this issue greatly vexed a virtually impotent State Department that manoeuvred frantically to obtain a 'moderate' solution, but forty years previously the US had no qualms about a concentration of power which Washington had done a great deal to support. In 1939 Roosevelt organized a state visit by Somoza, and although this was employed by the White House as a dress rehearsal for the impending arrival of King George VI of England, it was rightly viewed in Nicaragua and Central America as an exceptional event, reaffirming both backing for Somoza and traditional US concern for the stability of the most vulnerable of the region's countries.

By 1940 Somoza had dominated Nicaraguan political life for a decade but ruled it directly for less than four years. The accumulation of personal and family wealth, which so often takes pride of place in depictions of the regime, was sufficiently advanced to complement matrimonial ties and bring the Somozas into the bosom of the oligarchy and not yet so extensive as to exceed the norms of the epoch. The particular pattern of plunder through the state and mediation of national rules of competition emerged during the world war and became systematic thereafter.[61] Distinct in the nature of its military support and degree of US backing, the first phase of Somocismo conformed in most other respects to the despotic standards of the day. However, it should be recognized that Somoza was more discerning than his counterparts in repressing the workers' movement and, following the example of 1936, took care to meet the demands of certain sectors, dividing the urban labour force rather than subjecting it to wholesale violence.[62] Difficult though it may be for those familiar with the vile character of the regime in its dying days to appreciate, this populist undercurrent was sufficiently strong to permit Somoza senior to negotiate the troubles of the 1940s, providing critical political space in which to muster his forces for the subsequent imposition of an unbending coercive control.

Notes

1. Quoted in Anderson, *Matanza*, p. 148.
2. Quoted in Carlos Samayoa Chinchilla, *El Dictador y Yo*, Guatemala City 1950, p. 176.
3. Quoted in Thomas M. Leonard, *The United States and Central America, 1944–49*, Birmingham, Alabama 1984, p. 110.
4. Quoted in LaFeber, *Inevitable Revolutions*, p. 85.
5. This is not the place to engage in an extended debate over the explanatory value of the terms 'dominant bloc' and 'ruling class', not least because I believe that although the former is much less familiar and altogether more precious in its connotive aspirations, both lack the precision of purely economic categories, such as 'capitalist class' or 'working class'. Insistence upon such an apparently obvious observation can easily be taken to the point of pedantry, but it should be made clear that I am not here postulating the existence of either a bureaucratic elite which is anything more than functionally distinct (as is encouraged by the norms of liberal sociology) or that of a fraction within the landed bourgeoisie (as might be encouraged by the concern for intra-class divisions in the work of Nicos Poulantzas). As should become evident below, the notion of a dominant bloc is felicitous insofar as it extends beyond the direct functions of government but incorporates both the agents and the holders of economic power. What is lost in terms of signalling the economic origins of political power is compensated for

– to an admittedly debatable degree – by reference to the broader nature of the realization of that power. My use of this term is, therefore, much more impressionistic and extensive than Poulantzas's 'power bloc' and relates to the politico-economic orbit within which specific alliances may take shape and exercise a more conjuncturally determined dominance. Although theoretical exercises such as this can rapidly decompose into taxonomic scholasticism, they often throw light on political conditions for which conflict between dominant and dominated social forces is a necessary but insufficient explanation. It is, for example, impossible to render a convincing explanation of the crises accumulating within the Somoza regime between 1972 and 1979 without reference to the contradictions between it and the 'ruling class' as a whole as well as between them and the popular movement, itself far from socially or politically homogeneous. Equally, little is gained for our comprehension of recent Salvadorean politics if the distinction between the strategies of Duarte and D'Aubuissón is restricted to one of relative disposition to employ violence against the opposition. This does not mean that class conflict loses its primacy in determining political activity, but that this obtains in a complex, mediated form which extends to all forces, however essential their objectives and brutal their means.

6. Celso Furtado, *Economic Development of Latin America*, Cambridge 1970, p. 39.

7. The highest prices paid for Salvadorean and Guatemalan coffees over this period were (US cents per lb): 1925 – 25; 1930 – 16; 1940 – 7; 1945 – 13.4. Average prices of Nicaraguan coffee were: 1930 – 10; 1935 – 7; 1940 – 9; 1945 – 13.4. Costa Rican coffee held its relative price advantage over other Central American beans but fell with respect to African bean. The price index of Costa Rican coffee (1945/6 = 100) fell from 136 in 1928/9 to 64 in 1932/3, 52 in 1939/40 and 81 in 1944/5. *Commodity Year Book 1939*, pp. 313; 318, quoted in Baloyra, 'Reactionary Despotism', p. 305; Instituto de Defensa del Café, Costa Rica, cited in José Luis Vega Carballo, 'Costa Rica: Coyunturas, Clases Sociales y Estado en su Desarrollo Reciente, 1930–1975', in Pablo González Casanova, ed., *América Latina*, vol. 2, p. 3; Reinaldo Carcanholo, *Desarrollo del Capitalismo en Costa Rica*, San José 1981, p. 103.

8. Rowe, *World's Coffee*, p. 14.

9. Grieb, *Ubico*, pp. 54–8.

10. Anderson, *Matanza*, p. 8.

11. UFCO's Trujillo Railroad Company cut its workforce from 6,416 in 1929 to 616 in 1937. In January the company cut the wages of its stevedores from 25 to 17 centavos per hour while Standard Fruit reduced those of all its workers at the same time. In 1935 sigatoka disease played a part in UFCO's decision to abandon its Trujillo division as well as ripping up 125 km of railway track, for which the Honduran state received compensation of just $150,000. In Costa Rica UFCO began reducing its Atlantic plantations in the 1920s (by 29,000 acres before 1926) and shifting back to contract buying, its efforts to cut costs provoking the strike of 1934. An outbreak of sigatoka disease in 1938 effectively terminated the company's banana operations on the Caribbean coast, which were replaced by new plantations on the Pacific at Golfito. Posas, *Movimiento Obrero*, p. 172; Meza, *Movimiento Obrero*, p. 51; Jones and Morrison, 'Banana Industry', pp. 7–10.

12. Edmundo Jarquín, 'Migraciones Rurales y Estructura Agraria en Nicaragua', ESC, no. 11, May – August 1975, p. 95; Biderman, *Class Structure*, p. 176.

13. Menjívar, *Proletariado*, p. 55; Grieb, *Ubico*, p. 58; Darenblum, 'Crisis', p. 47; Posas and Del Cid, *Construcción*, p. 69.

14. Jones, *Guatemala*, p. 189; McCreery, 'Debt Servitude', p. 751; Menjívar, *Proletariado*, p. 55. Production of basic foods in Guatemala remained quite constant in the 1930s. In El Salvador it fell radically in 1932 but recovered substantially in the middle of the decade, and after another sharp fall remained relatively high during the war years. For a detailed study of the relationship between population, food base and export agriculture in El Salvador and Honduras, see William H. Durham, *Scarcity and Survival in Central America*, Stanford 1979.

15. In Guatemala the area cultivated for coffee rose from 100,064 to 135,589 hectares between 1930 and 1942. In El Salvador the area in coffee in 1929 was already 90 per cent of that in the 1960s, but between 1931 and 1933 it rose from 93,000 to 95,000 hectares, in itself a modest increase but especially critical given the political turbulence of the time. Feliciano Ama, Indian *cacique* of Izalco and one of the principal figureheads of the 1932 revolt, justified his activity not in terms of political afilliation – he had, in fact, been opposed to Araujo's

reforms – but because the Regalado family had appropriated communal lands. Grieb, *Ubico*, p. 146; Guidos Vejar, *Ascenso*, p. 142; David Alejandro Luna, 'Un Heroico y Trágico Suceso de Nuestra Historia', in *El Procesco Político Centroamericano*, San Salvador 1964, p. 53.

16. According to the estimate of Alejandro Marroquín, adult male unemployment in El Salvador in 1930 was 40 per cent in the countryside and 15 per cent in the towns. 'Estudio sobre la Crisis de los Añ˜os Treinta en El Salvador', in Pablo González Casanova, ed., *América Latina en los Anos Treinta*, Mexico City 1978, p. 116. Rafael Menjívar states that such a figure must have risen to almost 100 per cent in the countryside because the oligarchy harvested no coffee between 1930 and 1933. *Proletariado*, p. 57. If this is indeed the case, the export levels registered for those years can only be attributed to a combination of existing stocks and smallholder production, which, given the comparatively high quantities, does not seem likely. The cut in wage rates, which is attested by all sources, would appear to be an altogether more logical course of action for the *finqueros*. According to British Consul Rodgers one plantation in the west had not paid its workforce of 1,500 for eleven weeks in 1931. Cited in Dermot Keogh, 'The Politics of Hunger, Peasant Revolt and Massacre in El Salvador', unpublished ms., quoted in Michael McClintock, *The American Connection. State Terror and Popular Resistance in El Salvador*, London 1985, p. 110. Although the attrition following the 1932 rebellion was of such an order that one might be inclined to feel that the landlords had little interest in keeping their workers alive, they were later obliged to recruit from the eastern regions where there had been no violence. Browning, *Landscape and Society*, p. 273. According to US military attaché Major A.J. Harris, 'All work is paralysed on the farms. Half the servants have fled. Commerce is ruined. Nobody dares trust anybody else.' Quoted in McClintock, *American Connection: El Salvador*, p. 103.

17. Details of the vagrancy laws will be discussed below, but it is worth noting here that in the 1930s plantation wages were half those prevalent in the 1890s, relative to the price of corn. Although pay varied according to region and the state of the coffee trade, even after the removal of debt peonage it was less than half the rates of the late 1940s, when labour was free of all coercive mechanisms. This is in itself predictable but also suggests that in economic terms at least peasants had less incentive to engage in harvest labour during the 1930s than either before or after. McCreery, 'Debt Servitude', p. 749; Neale J. Pearson, 'Guatemala: The Peasant Union Movement, 1944–1954', in Henry A. Landsberger, ed., *Latin American Peasant Movements*, Ithaca 1969, p. 336.

18. Vega Carballo, 'Costa Rica', p. 2; Rodolfo Cerdas Cruz, 'Costa Rica: Problemas Actuales de una Revolución Democrática', in Zelaya, ed., *Democracia?*, pp. 158-9. Cerdas identifies the Instituto, on the board of which the state had one representative, as an important precedent for the interventionism of both Calderón and Figueres. It should, however, be noted that Costa Rica was the only country where there was an important internal coffee market of this nature; elsewhere similar bodies were established to oversee prices and production levels in more direct connection with the external market.

19. Instituto de Defensa del Café, quoted in Schifter, *Fase*, p. 23.

20.

Agricultural Production, 1945 ($ millions)

	Internal Market[a]	*Export Market*[b]
Guatemala	133.3	55.7
El Salvador	44.7	54.8
Honduras	35.1	39.7
Nicaragua	53.4	17.3
Costa Rica	30.1	44.8

a: principally maize, beans, rice, wheat, sugar, cattle.
b: principally coffee, bananas, cacao, wood, oils.

Both these statistics and the general tenor of this passage with regard to the relative resilience of subsistence agriculture are drawn from Edelberto Torres Rivas, 'Centroamérica. Algunos Rasgos de la Socieded de Postguerra', Working Paper no. 25, Kellogg Institute for

International Studies, University of Notre Dame, August 1984. There are two qualifications to this interpretation. The first, and most obvious, is that it postulates a *relative* condition, and, moreover, one that obtains principally with respect to developments in the late 1940s and 1950s. It is less easy to argue that the peasantry improved its position relative to that of the previous decades although this is not unlikely since, for example, production of corn increased in Guatemala, Nicaragua and El Salvador from 1932 to 1938 whereas it had been quite extensively imported in the 1920s. Secondly, Torres Rivas calculates the size of production for the internal market including both cattle and the rubric of 'others', which, particularly in the case of sugar, tobacco and some cotton, clearly span small- and larger-scale agricultural enterprises more than subsistence plots. Thus, as he stipulates clearly, there is no direct correspondence between production for the domestic market and peasant agriculture, but rather a more general association within a rising tendency for foodstuff production to exceed the parameters of subsistence. For a full discussion of this period, see Victor Bulmer-Thomas, *The Political Economy of Central America*, London 1987. Torres Rivas calculates that for the period 1945–48 50.2 per cent of agricultural production was for the export market, 20 per cent for subsistence, and 29.8 per cent for the internal market. Ibid., p. 49. The figures given in the above table consolidate those in the original.

21. Quoted in Oqueli, 'Gobiernos Hondureñ̃os', p. 57.

22. According to Thomas Anderson, *Matanza*, pp. 135 and 145, there is no sure means of calculating the death toll, his own estimate of 10,000 being based on no more sound basis than those of up to 45,000 which are often cited in secondary texts. In all likelihood Anderson's total figure is conservative since according to eye-witnesses some 985 people were killed in one day in Nahuizalco as late as 13 February. There is little sensible purpose in haggling over such macabre statistics, but some notion of the sheer extent of the attrition is necessary in order to appreciate its wider consequences.

23.General José Tomás Calderón encouraged the formation of *Guardias Civicas*, which took the form of 'brotherhoods', directed lynch-mobs and assumed some of the features of Fascist organization. On 27 January *La Prensa Gráfica* issued a call for 'honourable labouring men of every centre of El Salvador to organize themselves . . . into militias patterned on the Italian fascio . . . for the defence at any time of our families and homes against the deadly and ferocious attacks of the gangs of villains that fill the ranks of the Red Army that hopes to drown in blood the free and generous nation left to us by our ancestors', Quoted in Elam, *Appeal to Arms*, p. 42.

24. The first issue of *Estrella Roja*, 12 December 1931, declared, 'First of all, let us congratulate you on your *golpe de estado*. In reality, the blunders of Araujo imposed on the military the moral obligation of overthrowing him . . . we agree that your act was heroic and necessary, but, and you must forgive the scepticism, I do not believe that you can solve the Salvadorean crisis which is indescribably more transcendent a problem than your government can handle . . . it is the inevitable result of the fact that there exists amongst us a capitalist class which . . . has dedicated itself to a monoculture: coffee . . .' Quoted in Anderson, *Matanza*, pp. 80–1. While Martínez was not publicly identified as a leader of the initial coup staged by the junior officers, he was appointed president within a day and so can validly be considered one of the intended recipients of this message. Within thirty days the PCS was circulating amongst rank-and-file troops manifestos stating, 'the discontent which the soldier feels in the barracks . . . is the result of the fact that a soldier, enduring all the lies of the chiefs and officers, feels that they are his enemies because [they] belong to the same class that exploited him in the factories, shops and fields.' Two days before the rising, which was by that stage known to the regime, PCS fliers declared, 'Comrade soldiers: Don't fire a single shot at the revolutionary workers and peasants, kill the chiefs and officers . . .' Quoted in Jorge Schlesinger, *Revolución Comunista*, Guatemala City 1946, p. 163. The initial stance clearly incorporates the longstanding antipathy towards Araujo on the part of the PCS as well as misconceptions about the role of the military that were rapidly revised. The later literature in fact circulated amongst an appreciable number of conscripts sympathetic to the party, many of whom were later executed by their officers.

25. The president combined the paternalism expected of his social station with strong maverick tendencies that extended beyond rebuffs to predictable oligarchic importuning to support for Alberto Masferrer's *vitalismo*, an almost algebraic system of minimum social

standards from housing to nutrition that, when fulfilled, would produce a perfectly equitable and thriving society. However rarefied the system, its promulgation excited much support and expectation. According to US military intelligence, 'Araujo, the candidate of the common people, is enormously popular in the western departments . . . [he] is nothing but a labor agitator and admitted anarchist.' G-2 reports, 4 December 1930; 20 January 1931, cited in McClintock, *The American Connection: El Salvador*, p. 105.

26. Details are given in Anderson, *Matanza*, pp. 83–93; Dalton, *Miguel Mármol*, pp. 227–306. The party leadership agreed upon an insurrection on the night of 7 January, following the cancellation of the municipal elections planned for 3–5 January in which PCS participation had been the subject of much debate but finally agreed upon in combination with plans for a general rural strike. The original date set for the rising was the 16th, but this was put back to the 19th and then to the 22nd, by which time Farabundo Martí had been in jail for four days.

27. In his memoirs Mármol, who led the argument for continuing with the plan, states that the rationale for this position was that to hold back spelt certain disaster whilst to proceed still offered the possibility of victory, especially since it was clear that the western peasantry was on the verge of insurrection anyway. Ibid., pp. 274–5. Mármol and Menjívar stress the general interpretation that the failure of the rebellion was principally due to the insufficiency of PCS policies and preparation. This perspective is partially shared by Abel Cuenca, PCS leader from Tacuba, but he also believed, along with Alejandro Marroquín, that the regime actively provoked the revolt in order to destroy the peasant movement. *El Salvador. Una Democracia Cafetalera*, Mexico City 1946. This latter explanation would seem to be fortified by Martínez's encouragement of the drawing up of the electoral register, which stipulated voters' party preferences and thus permitted the identification of 'subversives' before any poll need be held. Such an obvious move and the clear indication to the PCS leadership from military sympathizers that wholesale repression was being planned certainly prompt questions as to the party's tactics in the final weeks, but these should be treated as somewhat distinct from its general strategy.

28. Mármol, ibid., p. 252, describes the difficulties of restraining the peasant leadership. Although the PCS had for some two years organized night schools, proselytized and offered modest organizational support to the peasant communities around Izalco, this should be seen as conducive more to a clientelist relationship than to the incorporation of the rural masses into the files of the party. Anti-Communist propaganda made much of the 'clandestine' nocturnal congregations, but the *cofradías* always met after dark and it is clear that the Communist militants attended only some of the meetings. Aside from the Cuenca family from Tacuba, there were few local activists to provide more solid and enduring links. According to Segundo Montes, the Indians of Izalco 'were not Communists and did not understand what Communism was. They were, though, making social demands which the Communist Party took advantage of.' *El Compadrazgo. Una Estructura de Poder en El Salvador*, San Salvador 1979, p. 181.

29. Wealthy women were obliged to grind flour, and *ladinos* to participate in celebrations, sometimes including fireworks and musical accompaniment provided by local bands. Since great press attention was given to the 'barbarism' of the rebels it is possible to enumerate their victims with some accuracy, Anderson calculating a maximum possible figure of thirty civilians and fifty military personnel. *Matanza*, p. 136.

30. Montes, *Compadrazgo*, p. 181. Anderson denies that there was a severe racial division in Tacuba but accepts that this existed in the Izalco region. However questionable the identification of discontented peasant with savage Indian, it certainly prevailed in *ladino* perceptions of the time: 'the Indian has been, is and will be the enemy of the *ladino* . . . there was never an Indian who was not afflicted with devastating Communism.' *La Prensa*, 4 February 1932, quoted in Anderson, *Matanza*, p. 17. 'We would like this race of the plague to be exterminated. . . . They did it right in North America, having done with them by shooting them before they could impede the progress of the nation . . . ' Quoted in Joaquín Méndez, *Los Sucesos Comunistas en El Salvador*, San Salvador 1932, p. 105. The failure of the rural rebels to loot churches or harm religious artifacts was noted by foreign observers as indicative of their traditional peasant piety and lack of Communist beliefs. This extended to the subsequent *matanza*, Miguel Mármol recounting how, 'a lieutenant . . . recall[ed] that the peasants who were being executed in groups in the courtyard would sing "Corazón Santo, Tu Reinarás", and that in the pools of blood he and the soldiers of the firing squad had seen,

as clear as day, the image of Christ, and had refused to go on killing and protested to their superiors. The protest was made so forcefully that the commander of the garrison ordered a temporary halt to the massacre. [That is how] Modesto Ramirez was saved . . .' Dalton, *Miguel Mármol*, p. 345.

31. Three US and two Canadian warships were dispatched to Salvadorean waters upon news of the abortive mutinies by conscripts on 18 and 19 January. A platoon of Canadian marines landed at the request of the British vice consul at Acajutla, and one Canadian officer travelled as far inland as Armenia before the US and British diplomats were informed that Salvadorean forces would permit no intervention. These events were later, 'hushed up', not least because Washington refused to recognize the Martínez government until 1936. As a result, the landing does not appear in Anderson's text or in Kenneth J. Grieb, 'The United States and the Rise of General Maximiliano Hernandez Martínez', JLAS, vol. 3, part 2, November 1971, but is briefly described in White, *El Salvador*, pp. 113–14.

32. Montes, *Compadrazgo*, pp. 194 ff.

33. A 1979 document outlining the theses of the Seventh Congress of the PCS mentions 1932 in a two-line reference to the 'defeat'. *El PCS Celebró su Séptimo Congreso*, San Salvador 1979. The party collaborated with the military and social democrats in the junta of October to December 1979, finally allying itself with the rest of the left on the anniversary of the 1932 rebellion in January 1980. Up to that point it had undertaken no military activity, and subsequent to it the guerrilla forces it organized were smaller than those of most other groups, some of which had been engaged in the armed struggle for nearly ten years.

34. Martínez, like Ubico, had contested an election before taking power and had presented a platform that was confused but far from exclusively reactionary in its language. As a devout theosophist he was by no means so distanced from the petty-bourgeois milieu as might appear today. However, the experience of having a head of state who propounded theories on the transmigration of human souls, dispensed personally concocted medication, and, at the end of his rule, directed policy on the basis of his claimed ability to tune into the ether waves broadcasting the cerebral activity of Churchill and Roosevelt, must have sometimes been as unnerving for his oligarchic supporters as it was oppressively bizarre for those Salvadorean citizens from whom he had removed all rights. Nonetheless, one should not lose sight of the fact that, as with his contemporaries elsewhere, such peculiar characteristics positively assisted suppression of the old protocols of office.

35. For details of the principal measures of the Martinez era, see Guidos Vejar, *Ascenso*, pp. 19–24; Marroquín, 'Años Treinta'. The moratorium was essential to halt widespread foreclosures at a time when land prices had fallen by up to 50 per cent and nearly 85 per cent of all mortgages were held by three private banks.

36. The *Asociación* had been established as a private body to control the distribution of credit at a time when five owners of *beneficios* controlled 53 per cent of all coffee. Wilson, *Crisis*, p. 109. Anderson describes it as 'a second state' and, whatever the form taken by the coffee regulatory body, it has throughout modern Salvadorean history exercised considerable authority. However, it should be noted that from 1941 to 1945 the export price of coffee was effectively fixed in New York, making reorganization a somewhat less charged process. Equally, the nationalization of coffee exports under the Duarte regime in the 1980s should be viewed in the context of national quotas set by the International Coffee Organization, the margin for manoeuvre with respect to external prices being relatively restricted (until 1985/6) but still the object of private sector discontent.

37. Ubico, the son of a leading Liberal lawyer, lived in Europe and the US before embarking upon a military career. His service as *jefe político* in Retalhuleu from 1911 to 1919 was fierce enough to impress both local landlords and the US embassy, which was also taken by his campaign to stamp out yellow fever – a cooperative venture in preventative medicine similar to that later undertaken with François 'Papa Doc' Duvalier in Haiti in that it introduced a future dictator to Washington. Ubico was always considered a 'macho' ruler although he had been made impotent by a fall when riding. He was rumoured to dress up as a Dominican monk but was much more public in his emulation of Napoleon, whose portrait adorned the presidential office. The dictator's two greatest loves were motorcycles and the wireless, the former almost inevitably used in frequent tours of the provinces, the latter as a means of educating the nation on matters ranging from photography to cooking. The tours

are avidly described in the two-volume work *Viajes Presidenciales*, issued just prior to Ubico's fall. Despite the fact that the most sycophantic newspaper of the day was *Nuestro Diario*, edited by Ubico's frequent breakfast companion Federico Hernández de León, its competitor, the ill-named *El Imparcial*, sometimes directed its admirable standards of accuracy to the same end: 'President Ubico has returned after covering 2,018 kilometres and 67 metres. The 13th was the day of the greatest distance covered by automobile – 223 kilometres 33 metres in five hours and 18 minutes.' 24 January 1944, quoted in Krehm, *Democracies and Tyrannies*, p. 37. Such trips were in part necessary to inspect Ubico's private lands, which at some 150,000 acres not only supplemented his salary of $33,800 but also made him the country's third largest landholder. Prisoners held in the dungeons of the presidential palace might have been grateful for the exeats since Ubico possessed a set of drums which he liked to bash away at despite lacking any sense of rhythm.

38. Presidential Message 1937, quoted in Grieb, *Ubico*, p. 33.

39. Kenneth J. Grieb, 'The Guatemalan Military and the Revolution of 1944', *The Americas*, vol. 32, no. 1, July 1975, p. 526. Ubico never completed his own military training. An explanation of military involvement in the events of 1944 that also stresses 'generational' differences is given by Jerrold Buttrey in Adams, *Crucifixion by Power*. See also Jerry L. Weaver, 'The Political Style of the Guatemalan Military Elite', in Kenneth Fidel, ed., *Militarism in Developing Countries*, New Brunswick 1975.

40. It was at this time that Juan Pablo Wainwright and other Communists were shot. Their fate was shared by some activists of the FROG. After strikes in the coffee plantations in 1929 there were few instances of labour mobilization during this period. When, early in 1931, workers at a cement factory struck they were immediately gaoled and held for three months, being released on May Day in an act typical of Ubico. Only a few artisanal guilds survived the dictatorship.

41. The historical record should, nonetheless, record that a 1935 referendum on whether Ubico should continue in office logged 1,227 votes against and 834,168 in favour.

42. *El Señor Presidente* (1946) by Asturias was, in fact, based on Estrada Cabreta. García Marquez, who dislikes Asturias's novel, had the Venezuelan dictator Juan Vicente Gómez as his main reference for *El Otoño del Patriarca* (1975) but admits to attempting a synthetic depiction of Caribbean despots in which the eccentricities of Martínez are evoked as sharply as the traits of Ubico's rule. Plinio Mendoza and Gabriel García Marquez, *The Fragrance of Guava*, London 1982.

43. Garcia Marquez's opening passages of *Cien Años de Soledad* (1967) make reference to the 1928 strike on UFCO's Colombian plantations in which hundreds of workers were killed. Nothing of this order occurred in Guatemala, where the company's labour force was controlled more tightly than elsewhere in Central America. All the same, the images of corporate appropriation of national property painted in *El Otoño del Patriarca* ring true for UFCO's relations with Ubico, who not only forced the monopolistic contract of 1930 through congress but later amended it to remove the company's obligation to build a Pacific port, reaffirming IRCA's right to set freight rates completely free of state interference. In 1936 a new agreement was reached prolonging UFCO's concessions to 1981. Ubico also suggested that banana workers' wages be reduced from 70 to 30 cents a day, a piece of advice readily accepted by the enterprise. For details, see Bauer Paiz, *Capital Yanqui*.

44. As *jefe político* of Alta Verapaz between 1907 and 1909 Ubico had sometimes clashed with local German planters, which may have affected his subsequent attitude. While he admired Mussolini and was the first president to recognize Franco, Ubico considered Hitler 'a peasant'. Although German *finqueros* remained important throughout the 1930s, Guatemala's coffee exports to Germany fell from 60 per cent of the total in 1930 to 15 per cent in 1939, almost exactly reversing the proportion sold to the US.

45. McCreery, 'Debt Servitude', p. 757. According to Chester Lloyd Jones, the essence of the new law was 'to shift the basis of regulation of Indian labour from the obligation of the labourer to work to pay off his debt to an obligation to work whether he was in debt or not.' *Guatemala*, p. 162. It is by no means the case that the abolition of debt peonage as a legal mechanism for enforcing labour led to the eradication of debt itself. In the following decade there is quite extensive evidence of the *cofradías* losing some of their following because of the level of financial contribution they required. Ricardo Falla, 'Evolución Político-Religiosa

del Indígena Rural en Guatemala (1945–1965)', ESC, no. 1, January–April 1972. In the mid 1950s, after the counter-revolution, it was noted by Paul Kennedy, not a professional anthropologist but a keen-eyed journalist, that peasants on the *fincas* still noted their debts in a *libreta*: 'they are almost never out of debt . . . thus they are bound to their plantation almost as irrevocably as if they were indentured servants.' *The Middle Beat. A Correspondent's View of Mexico, Guatemala and El Salvador*, New York 1971, pp. 142–3.

46. Jim Handy suggests that the new system began a process of debilitation of feudal ties by virtue of *generalizing* labour obligation both at source and in its final realization. *Gift of the Devil*, pp. 98–9. Yet how much the identification of the state with the interests of specific landlords affected Indian perceptions remains unclear.

47. Decree 1996 classified as vagrants, '7. Those who, having taken out a labour or service contract, fail to fulfil without just cause the obligations assumed; 8. Those who have no known home; 9. Labourers [*jornaleros*] who have neither contracted their services in the *fincas* nor cultivate with their personal work at least three *manzanas* of coffee, sugar cane or tobacco in some zone; three *manzanas* of corn with two crops a year in a hot zone; four *manzanas* of corn in a cold zone; or four *manzanas* of wheat, potatoes, vegetables and other produce in any zone.' Cited in Jones, *Guatemala*, p. 163. (One *manzana* = 0.69 hectares.) The penalty for non-compliance was one month in gaol for each offence. In 1933 another decree had stipulated that those obliged to provide labour for public works should do so for not less than two weeks a year. It has been established that throughout the Liberal era (1880–1945) such obligations consumed some 16 per cent of the total work days of the community of Momostenango in Quiché. Carmack, 'Spanish–Indian Relations', p. 243.

48. In his biography of Ubico Kenneth Grieb suggests that the president enjoyed appreciable popularity in the countryside, but this assessment seems to be based on largely official sources, and it might be doubted whether any following extended beyond the natural response given to a powerful and peripatetic president. It certainly did not match Carrera's popularity, and Ubico himself conformed to traditional oligarchic views in describing the Indians as 'rude, brutish and with primitive origin'. Quoted in Handy, *Gift of the Devil*, p. 99.

49. Durham, *Scarcity and Survival*, p. 116.

50. After a three-week stoppage the Standard Fruit workers were able to gain all their demands bar an increase in wages. The Trujillo strike eventually succeeded in reversing a wage cut, but if troops had not been sent to control both movements it seems likely that the resistance of all banana workers to company cutbacks would have been quite extensive and fierce. Meza, *Movimiento Obrero*, pp. 49–51; Posas, *Movimiento Obrero*, pp. 216–225.

51. Quoted in Guillermo Molina Chocano, 'Honduras: de la Guerra Civil al Reformismo Militar', in González Casanova, *América Latina*, vol. 2, p. 241.

52. 'The Superior Man'; 'the Great Statesman'; 'the Maximum Arbiter of the Destiny of Honduras'; 'the Great Leader and Regenerator'; 'the Great Reformer'; 'Illustrious Governor'; 'Symbolic Man'; 'Benefactor and Protector of Progress and Peace' are but a sampling of the appellations conferred upon the man. Posas and Del Cid, *Construcción*, p. 70. Carías's birthday, 14 March, was declared 'day of Peace and Giving Thanks to God', only being removed from the state calendar as a holiday in 1958, which suggests that one should not treat these matters simply as grotesque frivolities. Such personalism is not reducible to an 'ephemeral', subjective history, but constitutes a significant political tradition, variable in its declension of patriarchy yet rarely so petty as to be accounted no more than a residue of the protocols of hispanic absolutism.

53. In 1930 a congressional commission had strongly criticized UFCO for the conditions in its Limón plantations, giving the 1934 strike more than normal resonance in the political heartland. Nevertheless, it required two stoppages in the space of two months to halt wage cuts and redundancies. The following year UFCO, which was already reducing direct cultivation on the Caribbean coast because of the depressed market, made the best of a bad situation and distributed 250,000 acres to small farmers. For details of the 1934 strike, see Rojas, 'Movimiento Obrero', in González Casanova, *Movimiento Obrero*, vol. 2, pp. 263–5.

54. Ibid., p. 262. Rojas indicates an unemployment rate of 6 per cent in 1932, a figure which he suggests is high, but in comparative terms was not so at all.

55. During the early 1930s substantial reductions in imports maintained a general balance of payments but damaged state revenues from tariffs. In the last years of the

decade stable exports were rapidly overtaken by renewed growth of imports, producing a balance of payments deficit of $10 million in 1940 when exports were valued at only $7 million. Schifter, *Fase*, p. 18.

56. Quoted in Millett, *Guardians*, p. 134. Millett identifies Hannah and his wife, with whom Somoza enjoyed a very close relationship, as his most forceful patrons for the post of Guard Commander.

57. 'The people who created the National Guard had no adequate understanding of the psychology of the people here. Otherwise they would not have bequeathed Nicaragua with an instrument to blast constitutional procedure off the map. Did it ever occur to the eminent statesmen who created the National Guard that personal ambition lurks in the human breast, even in Nicaragua? In my opinion, it is one of the sorriest examples on our part, of our inability to understand that we should not meddle in other people's affairs.' 27 July 1935 to Willard Beaulac, quoted in Bernard Diederich, *Somoza*, London 1982, p. 16.

58. Somoza came from a middle-class Liberal background and displayed little talent for conforming to the traditional standards expected by his wife's family, which was shocked by his rude behaviour, propensity for low-life pursuits and lack of financial sobriety. A string of temporary jobs in his youth included those of sanitary inspector, electricity meter reader and car dealer before he threw in his lot with Moncada's rebellion. His facility with English made him a valuable liaison officer with the marines and brought him to Ambassador Hannah's attention. By 1934 Somoza's relations with his uncle-in-law were so poor that he was obliged to stage an independent campaign for the 1936 elections.

59. Richard Millett's detailed survey of the National Guard makes it clear that while Somoza consistently gained ground, he was obliged to manoeuvre considerably and even in 1935 his rise to power was not assured. In November a political meeting he held signally failed to engender popular support, and by the following year leading elements of the traditional parties had become sufficiently aware of the threat he posed to consider a joint election campaign. *Guardians*, pp. 134–171.

60. Upon Somoza's assumption of power the National Guard took control of the health, tax and railway services as well as all communications and police functions. A separate secret police force – *Oficina de Seguridad* – was created and soon acquired a distinctive character from the 'regular' Guard, which it vigilated as tightly as the populace at large. Booth, *End and Beginning*, p. 55.

61. Perhaps one of the most important moves in the accumulation of the family fortune was Somoza's acquisition in 1943 of the Bahlke family holdings through the confiscation and auction of property belonging to German nationals. Such 'purchases' fell into a pattern of primitive accumulation through prostitution, contraband and the merchandising of bootleg liquor in addition to direct levies on exports of beef, at half a cent a pound, minerals, which produced upwards of $200,000 in the 1940s, and textiles. Contributions of 5 per cent of all public salaries were deducted at source in favour of the dictator's *Partido Liberal Nacionalista*. By 1944 Somoza allegedly possessed fifty-one ranches and forty-six coffee *fincas* as well as receiving income from a wide variety of sources, including $3,000 a month as director of the Pacific Railroad, which built special spurs and dock facilities to service his estates. Although evident throughout the regime, the 'taxation' of almost all state contracts, concessions and activities became commonplace during World War Two, at the end of which Somoza was worth at least $10 million and possibly five times that amount. Insofar as the dictator's imposition of tariff barriers in order to bolster his contraband operations damaged local commerce it prejudiced the merchant interests historically tied to the Conservative Party, but so ubiquitous was Somoza's *fiscalización* of the economy by the mid 1940s that it is improbable that only this sector of the oligarchy was affected. Wheelock, *Imperialismo*, pp. 197–8; Krehm, *Democracies and Tyrannies*, pp. 22–4; Diederich, *Somoza*, p.22; Millett, *Guardians*, p. 197; Barahona, 'Nicaragua', in González Casanova, *América Latina*, vol. 2, p. 393.

62. This aspect of the early years of Somoza's rule is often suppressed in accounts coloured by the later unambiguous character of his regime. While it was certainly subordinate, it should not be forgotten that Somoza manipulated the anti-oligarchic sentiments of the masses and backed some strikes, for example that of the taxi drivers in 1937. Moreover, while he generally repressed the PTN, in 1938 he sought an agreement with its leadership to facilitate his control of the Constituent Assembly. For this he promised a minimum wage, eight-hour

day, and respect of union rights. This split the left, those opposed to collaboration eventually forming the PSN, which in 1944 was itself to enter into a partial and temporary alliance with the regime. This populist strand to Somoza's early phase was quite distinct from the general regional pattern of paternalism and may be more readily compared with the example of Batista in Cuba. It is the subject of as yet unpublished research by Jeffrey Gould of Harvard University, from whose work I have drawn the substance of this comment.

4

The Rise of Modern Politics: Crisis and Intervention

I have no objection to Marxist philosophy . . . but I am not clumsy like Manuel Mora, who engages in open combat with the Yankee and capitalism . . . . I will befriend the capitalists and the Yankee State Department in order to win the battle from the inside, and it is of no consequence to me what I might be called in gaining their confidence.

José Figueres, Costa Rica, 1945[1]

[We will] transform our nation from a backward country and a predominantly feudal economy into a modern capitalist country . . . economically independent.

President Jacobo Arbenz, Guatemala, March 1951[2]

The fact is that the doctrine of non-intervention (under the Good Neighbour policy) never did proscribe the assumption by the organized community of a legitimate concern with any circumstances that threatened the common welfare. On the contrary, it made the possibility of such action imperative. Such a collective undertaking, far from representing intervention, is the alternative to intervention. It is the corollary to intervention.

Assistant Secretary of State Edward Miller, May 1950[3]

Well, Colonel, there is diplomacy and then there is reality. Our ambassador represents diplomacy. I represent reality. And the reality is that we don't want you.

CIA agent Enno Hobbing to Colonel Carlos Enrique Díaz, Guatemala, July 1954[4]

The general exhaustion of autocratic government visible everywhere in 1944 and indicative of terminal decline in Guatemala cannot be attributed to a single cause. The capacity of personalist dictatorship for endurance is directly constrained by human frailty as well as the relative ease with which hero transmogrifies into ogre. Both Ubico and Martínez were incapable of escaping this inevitable inversion of the salvation vested in their persons, but Carías remained in harness for a further four years before taking retirement rather than scurrying into retreat, and Somoza manipulated his Machiavellian skills to survive a dozen years more; when he was finally felled by the region's solitary act of tyrannicide the products of his seed, whether legal heirs or not, were ready to perpetuate the regime.[5] The individualist nature of these despotic governments undoubtedly made them vulnerable but did not in itself determine their collapse, erosion or reconstitution.

At the other end of the spectrum it is difficult to establish as close a correspondence between movements in the economy and political developments as had obtained in the early 1930s. The year 1944 was one of political agitation everywhere yet at that stage the price controls and market quotas established for coffee in 1940 remained in force, there being no general pattern either of accelerated growth or of pronounced recession. In the case of Guatemala the reversal of high levels of growth during the pre-war period certainly fuelled urban discontent as well as a gradual renaissance of the workers' movement. In Costa Rica, which suffered a comparable decline caused by the commandeering of banana transports by US forces and the low level of diversification to compensate for this loss of trade, political mobilization only approached critical levels in 1947–48, in the midst of the post-war rise in prices and export revenue.[6] The general economic boom that resulted from this was of great importance since it opened a phase of commercial innovation, adoption of new crops and some industrialization from the turn of the decade. By the time this shift towards revitalized export agriculture and a modicum of import-substitutionist manufacturing was underway the political turmoil that 'was not the end of oligarchical rule but rather the beginning of its (inevitable) modification' had already been subdued and the Cold War was exercising palpable effect everywhere.[7] Hence, in a sense the political impetus for realignment of the liberal oligarchic system preceded its economic basis, this impetus itself being far from wholly the product of internal factors and accumulating most rapidly in a period when the economic depression was prolonged by the same war that provided external support for political freedoms long derided by Washington's regional allies.[8]

By 1940 the flow of trade between Central America and the US had become so great that the loss of European markets caused by the war did not have a critical impact on the regional economy. Although the coffee agreement was far from generous, it provided a necessary safety net that did not exist for the banana industry. However, it also made it absolutely essential that the regimes rescind public displays of sympathy with the political systems of the Axis powers and then follow the US lead in declaring war upon them. Thus, Martínez, who in 1940 had made it a 'national crime' to express open support for the British and happily permitted demonstrations in San Salvador by the 'Blackshirts' of his *Pro-Patria* party as late as September 1941, was inevitably obliged to 'change sides' if for no other reason than that by 1943 96.4 per cent of Salvadorean coffee was sold to the US (compared with 14.9 per cent in 1930).[9] Similarly, Somoza had to dispense with the services of the *Camisas Azules* whilst Ubico cancelled joint German and Guatemalan citizenship as early as June 1940, having told the US ambassador after Munich that, 'Guatemala will follow the policy of the US as long as it is not communistic'.[10] Carías, who appears to have been less excited by the affinities between local forms of government and European Fascism, followed suit, the 150 Honduran sailors who died whilst serving in the Allied merchant fleet being virtually the only Central American victims of the conflict.

The influential German community suffered a lesser fate, and this was the subject of often charged debate both within the region and in relations with Washington. While 'enemy nationals' were everywhere deported to camps in the US regardless of their political views, there were differences over how to handle their property, which, after the US entered the war, was entered in the 'Proclaimed List' and subject to embargo. In Nicaragua state intervention amounted to little more than appropriation at a minimal price by Somoza; in Guatemala Ubico was prepared to 'intervene' but not to nationalize the extensive German holdings. For a period Washington acquiesced in this reluctance, which probably reflected the influence of the German community rather less than a broad oligarchic aversion to any example of expropriation as well as the fact that, so long as the US army purchased 'enemy coffee' included in Guatemala's market quota, the state earned some $1 million a year in emergency export taxes. It was only on the very eve of his overthrow that Ubico was harried into what he undoubtedly viewed as a 'communistic' measure and nationalized the bulk of German property.[11] At a stroke this apparently minor measure not only altered the configuration of the ruling class but also provided an example of state appropriation of private property that was to influence policy over the ensuing decade.[12] In Costa Rica Calderón exploited the sinking of a banana transport off Limón by a German submarine in 1942 to deport two hundred 'enemy aliens' and intervene their property. This provoked a sharp outcry in the region that may certainly be attributed to the fact that the Germans were a 'very respected' group in the community, but should also be seen in the light of oligarchic antipathy to Calderón's proposals for increased social expenditure, constitutional amendments on the nature of the inviolability of private property, and the support given to the regime's intervention by the *Bloque Obrero Campesino*. This, the sole surviving Communist organization above ground, was taking every advantage of the collapse of the Hitler–Stalin pact and pursuing an energetic campaign in support of the Allies.[13]

German interests were very limited in El Salvador, where the collapse of the Martínez regime during the spring of 1944 was only marginally affected by intra-oligarchic tension stemming from the introduction of a new coffee export tax at the end of 1943 to assist payment of the foreign debt. Despite a measure of recovery in working-class organization over the previous years – railway workers, for instance, had been able to revive their union in 1943 – this still remained very limited and tenuous. The union movement was to grow after Martínez's fall but it did not play a leading role in the anti-dictatorial movement. The major thrust of opposition came from the middle class, led by army officers dismayed at the privileges received by the paramilitary forces and responsive to discontent amongst civilian professional groups such as the employees of the National Mortgage Bank, to the fore in denouncing corruption and demanding technical efficiency as well as civil liberties.[14] Thus, when Martínez, who was fond of pronouncing that 'lower forms of democracy emphasize rights, higher forms emphasize duties', had a congress exclusively composed of *Pro-Patria* members amend the constitution to permit a further term of office from March 1944, he contrived to maximize antipathy towards his personal despotism amongst the officer corps as well as exciting a broader anti-dictatorial campaign. Although many military conspirators sought only an internal and more institutionalized realignment of political power, it was impossible to escape the logic of a situation in which both national and international factors compelled an embracing of democratic ideals: 'the people here drank their sedition directly from slogans of the United Nations. It was possible for the *Diario Latino* to conduct an anti-Martínez campaign for a whole year merely by featuring phrases of Roosevelt and Churchill on the Four Freedoms . . .'[15]

The military revolt finally broke out on 2 April 1944. Martínez was able to rally the paramilitary forces, and the rebels, refusing to distribute arms to civilians, were crushed with the loss of over two hundred lives. However, the dictator erred in compounding such impressive attrition for a predominantly internal feud by putting ten officers before a firing squad and sentencing a further forty to death.[16] This move – extraordinary by the standards of Latin American military traditions, let alone those of *ladino* political culture – provoked an immediate general strike headed by the students and doctors of San Salvador and supported by a traumatized middle class. The strike movement was signally devoid of peasant participation and did not last for long. On the other hand, the threat of a more radical resurgence effectively terminated Washington's backing for the regime, and within a month Martínez was obliged to step down, being replaced by a trusted colleague in General Andrés Ignacio Menéndez.[17] The appointment of Menéndez succeeded in achieving a degree of political relaxation whilst ensuring continuity in the structure of power. Nevertheless, it proved impossible to sustain this without announcing new elections, and, despite the heterogeneity of a political movement that had acted in an essentially defensive manner to support military opposition to Martínez, the initially cautious electoral campaign began to pick up impetus around the candidacy of Dr Arturo Romero, whose reformist *Unión Nacional Demócrata* was supported by the newly-established *Unión Nacional de Trabajadores.*[18]

Although Romero espoused a programme less radical than that of Araujo's Labour Party, his popularity clearly posed a threat to an oligarchy that retained a sharp memory of the chaos of 1931 as well as of the *matanza* that followed it. On 21 October, when a large crowd was gathered in the central plaza of San Salvador to celebrate the overthrow of Ubico in Guatemala, Menéndez finally bowed to landlord pressure and acquiesced in a pre-emptive coup led by Colonel Osmín Aguirre, one of the leaders of the repression in 1932. The massacre of scores of people in the city centre reflected an unambiguous regression to the methods of Martínez within twenty weeks of his removal, Aguirre being unrestrained in his crushing of efforts to stage another general strike as well as a disorganized student-led invasion from Guatemala in December.[19] These resolute actions imposed temporary unity on the military apparatus. No civilian candidates stood in the new elections held in January 1945, the 'overwhelming majority' of votes being cast in a manner quite distinct from that envisaged by the UN for an old Martínez ally, General Salvador Castaneda Castro, who headed the aptly-named *Partido Agrario*. Between them, Aguirre and Casteneda achieved a resumption of the *martinato* by ambushing the nascent civilian reform movement and repressing its popular constituency. By refusing to accept any of the demands of the anti-Martínez movement or sponsor any new measures itself, the Castaneda regime amounted to little more than a holding operation.

It was four lacklustre years before Castaneda was removed, again by a coup. This was not simply the result of his desultory attempt at re-election, which only excited a broader military opposition to personalist methods and encouraged an already advanced attachment to the idea of a fully institutionalist system for apportioning office. The 'Majors' coup' of 1948 represented a consolidation of the military apparatus around many of the objectives of the 1944 revolt; it also marked a clear shift towards modernizing the form of political control with the introduction of a quotient of state intervention, tolerance of a number of closely-vigilated trade unions and civic associations, acceptance of some political competition within the middle class as well as the oligarchy, provided it did not trespass the parameters of 'democracy', and a degree of support for those factions of the capitalist class seeking to invest in manufacturing and new agricultural methods.[20] The principal figurehead of this movement was Colonel Oscar Osorio, who manoeuvred diligently and forcefully for two years following the coup to establish the *Partido Revolucionario de Unificación Democrática* (PRUD) in 1949 as the military-backed official party of government that would in 1961 mutate into the *Partido de Conciliación Nacional* (PCN) and rule with only one short break until October 1979. The junta that held power until 1950 was young, middle-class, and technocratic in character, initially attracting widespread sympathy for the military in what was seen as a successful reprise of April 1944. But the *apertura* ('opening') that many expected was never granted. Anti-Communism remained resolutely at the centre of a system that replaced Martínez's narrow conservatism with a more dynamic mode of domination predicated upon the belief that, 'the only truly effective way to achieve [social and economic] equilibrium and avoid the evils of dangerous doctrines is to promote broad transformative doctrines within the framework of cooperation between government, the capitalists and the workers . . .'[21]

'Transformismo' was a much-used term in Central America at the start of the 1950s, yet despite the inclusion in the 1950 constitution of formal stipulations for agrarian reform and the 'social function' of property, the Salvadorean majors (who had now become colonels) desisted from any substantive challenge to the landed bourgeoisie and concentrated their reforms on the urban sector. The period 1948 to 1950 witnessed an anti-oligarchic movement only insofar as it confirmed Martínez's exclusion of civilians from political power and adjusted the terms of that exclusion to incorporate the statist and developmentalist currents that emerged in the post-war period within a pretence at democratic procedure that assuaged Washington and permitted the existence of some tame opposition parties. The absolute prohibition of organization in the countryside and tight control of unions through both repression and co-optation in the towns made such a system only marginally different to its forebears for the mass of Salvadoreans and, by the same token, confirmed the support of a bourgeoisie that had conceded only a modest reformulation of economic policy outside the rural sector, which remained its power-base, and still retained an effective veto on how far this would be realized in practice.

Although developments in both El Salvador and Guatemala increased the activity of Honduran exiles, neither they nor the opponents of Carías inside the country were able to exploit the shifting international balance of forces and cripple the regime. It is probable that the fall of Martínez played a part in encouraging a march by some three hundred women on 29 May 1944 to demand freedom for political prisoners; significantly the protestors carried the US flag as well as that of Honduras. On 4 and 6 July further demonstrations were held, being broken up in Tegucigalpa by customary police methods. By contrast, more than a hundred of the marchers were shot down by troops in San Pedro Sula under orders from the minister of war, Juan Manuel Gálvez.[22] Apart from the massacre of Salvadoreans on the border in the early 1980s this was the single most bloody incident in the country's twentieth-century political history and it provoked widespread repudiation. It did not, however, generate a new wave of organized opposition akin to that in El Salvador. The PCH was signally unable to revive itself during this period and Carías, while losing popularity and coming under pressure from Washington for the first time, maintained a tight hold on power. His response to the events of 1944 was to replace the *continuismo* vested in his person with one channelled through the National Party, represented at the elections of 1948 by Gálvez. This move required the legalization of the Liberal Party in order to present a plausible contest, but Zuñiga confronted such an efficient electoral machine that the opposition eventually decided to boycott the poll. Gálvez was untroubled by their subsequent attempt at a 'constitutionalist' revolt that was little more than an anachronistic act of desperation by *políticos* who had yet to come to terms with developments during their years of exile. Their defeat enabled Gálvez – who, it should be recalled, had been a legal adviser for UFCO for more than twenty years – to loosen control and adopt the status of constitutional ruler in more than name. Assisted by a revival in the economy, which prompted UFCO to increase its cultivation of bananas from 82,000 to 133,000 acres between 1946 and 1953, he began to develop the rudimentary state apparatus, establishing the basis for mediation in the economy beyond simply processing the requests of the fruit companies.

Somoza's unique capacity to survive the challenges of the 1940s was based on a combination of military power and a critical absence of labour support for the anti-dictatorial movement as a result of concessions made to the unions. Underlying this often ignored factor of the dynasty's endurance was a relatively buoyant economy during the war founded upon Nicaragua's reserves of gold, which earned half of national export receipts between 1940 and 1945. This permitted a modest expansion of industrial activity, increasing the waged labour force by perhaps 25,000 and membership of trade unions from a virtually insignificant figure of under 2,000 in 1940 to some 17,000 in 1945.[23] Parts of this working class – which, although still very small, now formed a sizeable portion of Managua's population of 83,500 – had already been co-opted by Somoza's discriminatory patronage, and all of it was vulnerable to the ubiquitous National Guard. All the same, the influence within a growing labour force of the illegal pro-Moscow PSN, established in 1939, threatened a regime that was by 1943 already confronted by opposition from Conservative and dissident Liberal sectors as well as a student movement attracted by the example of Sandino. In the face of this unprecedented alliance, Somoza built upon his early efforts to co-opt the PTN and reduced repression of both the Communist Party and the union movement as a whole. When, in the spring of 1944, oligarchic and middle-class opposition began to broaden into a mass movement fortified by events in El Salvador, the dictator moved from a strategy of variable repression to one of active populist overtures towards the working class. These were constructed around a revival of the promise made in 1938 to introduce a new labour code enshrining full union rights, limited social security provisions, and statutory defence of minimum conditions of employment. In April, just as the youthful Liberal dissidents founded the *Partido Liberal Independiente* (PLI), Somoza declared that, 'I have made a mistake' in attacking the left, which, he observed, contained some of 'Nicaragua's best sons'.[24] The tangible offer of meeting essential syndicalist demands was pitched by the country's largest capitalist in resolutely anti-oligarchic language at a time when both the PLI and the students were accepting the leadership of the Conservatives in the anti-dictatorial movement. Hence, while the PSN was legalized and its major constituency permitted to form unions and undertake collective bargaining, the wider democratic objectives of the party were complicated by the fact that the Conservatives persisted with a resolutely anti-communist and anti-union policy in their direction of the campaign against Somoza.[25] This impasse thwarted the anti-dictatorial movement by provoking the PSN's refusal to support a general strike against the regime in June 1944, which collapsed as a result. The party has subsequently been accused of absolute capitulation to a temporary pragmatic manoeuvre by Somoza, but both the PLI and the students refused to break from Conservative leadership and were only marginally interested in meeting the demands for labour unity which formed the basis of the left's strength. Moreover, the PSN retained sufficient autonomy to place pressure on Somoza's still weakened regime for a further year, sustaining illusions that it could obtain both socio-economic reform and democracy by traditional methods as well as strengthening the conviction that the oligarchic opposition would not concede the former and probably not the latter.[26] It was not until mid 1945 that the dictator had recouped enough authority to reduce his dependence on the patronage of the unions, the increased repression of the PSN from August of that year being provoked by the party's opposition to his plans for a further re-election.

This disaggregation of a potential popular bloc under oligarchic hegemony did not provide Somoza with enough space for manoeuvre during the critical months of 1944–45 to permit a full reimposition of the status quo ante. The issue of re-election superseded many of the divisions encountered in 1944 and propelled a campaign of such popularity that it even began to affect the rank and file of the Guard; the general was finally obliged to withdraw, supporting the candidature of his opponent in 1936, Leonardo Argüello, now an old and presumably pliable man. Argüello was duly installed in office but the 'puppet' transpired to be a great deal more than relatively autonomous, appointing a majority of anti-Somocistas to the cabinet, countermanding Somoza's orders and holding discussions with the opposition, both left- and right-wing. The impetus of anti-Somoza sentiment proved too great for intermediate measures, its target reverting to type and staging a full coup less than a month after Argüello's assumption of office. In so doing Somoza regained full authority over the Guard, which was beginning to manifest the effects of two years of instability by losing its political cohesion. Although the replacement of Argüello with a bona fide puppet in Benjamín Lacayo Sacasa produced both Conservative rebellion and a notable absence of US recognition, the easy defeat of Chamorro's disorganized revolts reduced Washington's options as the Cold War began to set in. The nomination as president of Somoza's uncle, Benjamín Román y Reyes, by a dutiful constituent assembly in 1948 provided a convenient moment for resumption of full diplomatic ties that was consolidated by the outlawing of the PSN and return to the repressive methods of the 1930s. At the same time, Somoza took advantage of his position to recognize the claims of the Conservatives for a quota of representation; the pacts of 1948 and 1950 signed with the party ensured the traditional opposition a minority share of congressional seats, thereby binding the oligarchy within a dominant bloc controlled by the dictator. This mechanism was comparable in substance to the new mode of rule introduced in El Salvador. It did not entirely suppress the dissident tendencies of Conservatism since the nature of its inclusion within the system required a degree of formal opposition, but it effectively terminated a historic rivalry, placated the coffee bourgeoisie, and sundered many young members of the Conservative Party from their leaders. Following generations were to remain bereft for the better part of three decades of any ready organization within which to realize their repudiation of the dynasty. The co-optation and repression of the major forces on both left and right in the mid 1940s left a strategic space on the map of Nicaraguan politics so that the apparently inevitable opposition to such a singular form of domination did not coalesce for an exceptionally long time. Moreover, the eventual form of this opposition was far from casually characterized by a revival of Sandino's anti-imperialism as well as by a programme for both political democracy and radical social reform which Sandino himself had failed to combine and the opposition of the 1940s could not reconcile. By 1979 this made little less than 'common sense', having a particular historical trajectory determined primarily, but not exclusively, by the Somoza dictatorship.

The Point of Rupture: Costa Rica

Developments in Costa Rica during the mid 1940s were comparable to those in Nicaragua only insofar as they produced a specific and enduring form of national political organization from the realignment of the dominant bloc. The strategy of the Communist Party was superficially similar to that in Nicaragua in that it allied itself with the incumbent regime against the oligarchy and the bulk of the middle class, which as a result adopted a trenchant anti-communism. But the line of Mora's party – renamed *Partido Vanguardia Popular* (PVP) after the dissolution of the Comintern in 1943 – was quite distinct from that of the PSN, since the government of Calderón enjoyed considerable popularity and actively pursued a programme of reforms despite its failure to break from the residual practices of petty corruption and electoral manipulation. This singular regime, which effectively allied the Communists, Church hierarchy, and elements of the established political class, forged a rudimentary populism based upon a modicum of state-mediated redistribution. In time its opponents and eventual conquerors were to revive a particularly static and vulnerable system based upon taxing a depressed wartime economy with a more profound state intervention in an economy dynamized by the post-war boom. One can, therefore, discern an essential complementarity between the projects pursued by the two political blocs although this was far from obvious even in the wake of the civil war of the spring of 1948, an exceptional event in Costa Rican history that was contested by alliances that have subsequently been dubbed *populismo no transformista* and *transformismo no populista*.[27] It is worth making a brief survey of this process, if only to demonstrate that the distinctiveness of the post–1950 political system in Costa Rica was the result of sharp political conflict that was resolved in hegemonic terms – rather than those of simple control and management – through significant displacement of the class objectives of all the forces involved.[28]

The Calderón government (1940–44) was elected into office by an overwhelming majority – 93,000 of 102,000 votes in a poll contested by ex-president Jiménez – but with a very vague programme of reform that neither impeded support for Calderón from his predecessor, the strongly anti-communist Cortes Castro, nor won backing from the Communists, who sided with Jiménez. It therefore seemed to be a traditional regime, assisted into office by the longstanding methods of electoral manipulation and patronage, promulgating sentiments as worthy as the new president was deemed to be in person whilst offering little challenge to the oligarchic system. Yet Calderón had been infected by the same Catholic reformism as had influenced Volio, with whom he maintained close relations, and sought to implement many features of the *reformista* platform from within the dominant bloc. What appeared to be merely the philanthropy of an earnest patriarch was in fact a more consequential commitment to social amelioration. Hence, the measures of 1940–44 were less the result of significant conflict than of a limited, pre-emptive strategy, in part compelled by economic depression but also consonant with the tradition of redistributive reformism that stretched back to the policies of Archbishop Thiel in the 1880s and possessed an agile contemporary advocate in Archbishop Víctor Sanabria.[29] Furthermore, although the fiscal measures during World War One had resulted in major dissension within the oligarchy, they constituted a precedent for state intervention in an economic depression appreciably less severe than that of the early 1940s. Thus, when Calderón moved in 1941 to table legislation for a social security system, this drew opposition from private doctors but excited relatively little controversy.[30] It was in 1942 that the scope of the president's campaign for 'social justice' became evident with the introduction of measures that froze rents, established housing cooperatives, and permitted uncultivated land to be worked until title was clearly established. The following year many of these reforms were consolidated in a comprehensive labour code that also gave statutory support for full rights of association and collective bargaining, the eight-hour day, and basic health and safety standards. At the same time, the government moved a constitutional amendment to stipulate the 'social function' of property, thereby providing a broad statutory basis for alienation under certain circumstances.[31]

It is certainly the case that the great bulk of these measures were 'petty-bourgeois and democratic' in character, being welcomed with the classic belief of that class that a little capital resolves all the world's problems.[32] Calderón's 'social guarantee' programme, however partially it was realized, also inflated the budget, imposed an extra cost on large capital, and provoked fears of expropriation – not dimmed by intervention of German property – in adverse economic circumstances without offering countervailing guarantees to the bourgeoisie or dynamizing production.[33] As a result, by 1942 the government had lost almost all its original supporters within the capitalist class, and, backed only by the Church, was obliged to make recourse to the Communists in order to stay in office. Mora, who had been alerted to the gravity of the situation by oligarchic overtures in support of a coup, seized this opportunity to subordinate the party's traditional invectives against electoral malpractice – charges now eagerly taken up by the oligarchy and middle class – and support a popular programme as well as benefiting from the increased unionization resulting from the labour code.[34] This volte face opened the government to charges of being Communist that were hardly distracted by alteration of the nomenclature of the party or the exchange of open letters between Mora and Sanabria that provided anxious Catholics with unequivocal ecclesiastical permission to support the new PVP.[35]

The introduction of a modest progressive income tax (2–20 per cent) by Calderón's successor Teodoro Picado (1944–48) in 1945 both heightened oligarchic fears of creeping socialism and gave the ruling class a potential ally against the popular bloc in the urban middle sectors affected by this measure.[36] The election of Picado, a member of Calderón's National Republican Party (PNR), had resulted from a boycott of the 1944 poll by a still divided opposition that in all probability would have lost anyway but could plausibly veil its lack of cohesion and popularity with accusations of malpractice by the PVP, police, followers of the PNR, and government employees. Over the following four years a profoundly ideological contest was partially obscured by an increasingly violent political conflict over formal democratic liberties. This was by no means an irrelevance since it is undoubtedly the case that the regime and its allies took full advantage of state power notwithstanding widespread support and the making of major concessions to the opposition in 1947. Thus, both the oligarchic organizations and those representing the opposition within the middle class could generate a following around both anti-communism and demands for authentic democracy that were elsewhere exciting support on a much more profound basis. Furthermore, although neither the *cafetaleros* nor the emergent middle-class political vanguard were at all consistent in their practice of the democratic ideals they espoused and, in fact, came to exceed supporters of the government in employing violence, they were saddled with the logic of their campaign once it had finally been won. After the civil war there existed minimal scope for extending the proscription of the PVP and major unions to the system as a whole; the locus of politics reverted to a reformed electoralist arena.

Oligarchic repudiation of the regime was, despite the respectability of Calderón and Sanabria, cause for little surprise. Headed first by an outraged Cortes Castro, it was led from 1944 by Utilio Ulate, owner of *Diario de Costa Rica* and head of the *Partido de Unión Nacional* (PUN), formed that year to contest the presidential poll. Ulate attacked Calderón and Picado principally for corruption and being crypto-Communists although it proved difficult to unearth much hard information on malfeasance – rather than sheer inefficiency – at the top; red-baiting yielded only modest returns until 1947 and the onset of the Cold War. On the one hand, Sanabria's support for the reforms was awkward to negotiate, and on the other, even the US embassy was disinclined to get very agitated about the PVP, describing Mora as 'moderate' and the party as 'an entirely national organization' with a programme that 'would be defined in most countries as liberal'.[37] Moreover, as late as 1946 this same embassy had described the government's middle-class opponents organized around the *Centro para el Estudio de los Problemas Nacionales* (1940) as 'a small bunch of hotheads without either popular appeal or political experience', their leader José Figueres being an 'aggressive opportunist'.[38]

While it could scarcely be denied that Figueres was an ambitious character, lacking scruples and prone to violence – his reputation stands a great deal higher today than it did in the early 1940s – it remains a fact that the young professionals and intellectuals gathered under the auspices of the *Centro* were by 1946 conducting a political campaign of considerable importance. Originally established in 1940 as a 'think-tank' to develop viable alternatives to the policies of the oligarchic regimes and declaring itself apolitical in character, the *Centro* incubated an anti-capitalist and anti-imperialist tendency that has been ascribed to the influence of APRA.[39] There were, furthermore, shades of corporatism in the group's early rejection of parliamentarianism, the oligarchy and Communism. Despite occasional usage of Marxist language, it had no difficulty in viewing the *vanguardistas* as 'the worst of bad Costa Ricans . . . who must be treated as totalitarians and not with reason or decency'. Indeed, not much later it transpired that 'the Communists are not Costa Ricans'.[40] The bilious nature of *Centro* attacks on both the PVP and the Calderón and Picado governments occluded the fact that many of its own policies were being implemented by these forces. The social security measures were criticized as 'unscientific' and denounced as a 'comedy', the income tax was opposed in congress, and housing cooperatives pilloried in the press, yet all these measures were included in the *Centro*'s own platform for modernization and reform.[41] Thus, although members of the *Centro* considered themselves 'socialists', from 1942 onwards, when the PVP allied with Calderón, they had little possibility of winning a popular following on the basis of their initial policies, and found themselves in an increasingly anomalous situation. This was temporarily resolved by a strengthening of links with the political forces of the oligarchy whereby more directly political issues, such as anti-Communism and electoral propriety, overshadowed the question of social reform. Before too long it became evident that the social programme had been suppressed for short-term pragmatic ends rather than entirely eradicated out of unmitigated opportunism.

Figueres personified this contradictory characteristic of the young technocrats. A wealthy landlord and entrepreneur who embraced cooperativism and yet could not resist the calling of a rural *caudillo*, he had been exiled by Calderón in 1942 for making a heated radio address in which he was supposed to have revealed military secrets about the national coastal defence system whereas, in fact, his attacks on the government's popular mobilization against the Axis powers had exceeded the limits of even Calderón's appreciable tolerance.[42] In exile Figueres began preparations for what he termed the 'second republic', manifesting an increasing attraction to conspiracy and insurrection as a result of his participation in the 'Caribbean Legion', an assortment of exiled groups dedicated to the overthrow of dictatorships in Venezuela, Cuba, the Dominican Republic and Nicaragua.[43] In 1944 Figueres was permitted to return from exile and formed the *Partido Social Demócrata* (PSD) as the political expression of the policies of the *Centro*. The following year members of the PSD joined *Acción Demócrata* (AD), a group that had split from Cortes Castro's *Partido Democrático* and was now provoked by the new income tax law to make amends with its old foes.[44] This fusion brought the Figueres group firmly into the oligarchic camp and further suppressed its reformist programme in favour of a single-minded campaign against the Picado regime and its PVP allies. In 1944 the Social Democrats had denounced Picado's election as a 'coup', which was tough but barely dangerous rhetoric; in 1946 they considerably sharpened their position under the slogan 'Elections No; Rebellion Yes!' despite the fact that the opposition won 44 per cent of the congressional poll and the PVP's support dropped from its modest 1942 level of 16,198 out of 100,296 votes.[45] The Picado regime was by no means the local equivalent of Somoza or Trujillo, dictator of the Dominican Republic, and neither was the PVP, from which Picado had attempted to break but for which he could find no substitute, in any sense the dominant force in the regime.[46] Thus, Figueres found minimal response to his calls for rebellion, and in February 1947 was easily beaten by Ulate for the opposition candidacy against Calderón in the 1948 presidential poll.

What was in effect a year–long campaign took place during the beginning of the Cold War, giving the PVP response to attacks by Figueres's vigilantes and the general anti-communist 'crusade' of the opposition an increasingly central place in the contest. This was, at root, fought out between two political blocs, in which 'the first, led by the middle sectors, was allied to the majority of the oligarchy [and] the second was led by the rural and urban proletariat in alliance with the progressive sectors of the state'.[47] The polarization between these two blocs was sharpened by a capitalist-led general strike in July and August 1947 against alleged government persecution of Ulate. But although the language of the campaign was extreme, the crisis building up beneath it appeared to slacken once Picado made a major concession to the opposition in agreeing to equal representation on the Electoral Tribunal, which had executive authority over the poll, and giving them the power to appoint the president of the Electoral Register, which drew up voting lists and supervised the elections. This apparently minor administrative step, which was disowned by the PVP, in fact surrendered the government's powers of electoral manipulation to its opponents, some of whom were already committed to an insurrectionary strategy, while the regime still retained control of the state apparatus and the support of the PVP's militias. As a result, the poll of 8 February 1948 was transformed from a contest that certainly encompassed unprecedented violence and ideological conflict but could still have been resolved outside the terms determined by the extremes of the two blocs (PVP and AD) into a civil war in which these minority factions were both politically and militarily dominant.

The details of the campaign and final poll are beyond our scope here. On the day after the election Picado denounced the election, over which he had no authority, as fraudulent. The number of votes cast was the lowest since 1936, and as detailed a survey as is possible on the basis of incomplete figures indicates a clear fraud in favour of Ulate.[48] On 28 February the Electoral Tribunal declared Ulate the winner by 54,931 votes to Calderón's 44, 438 although it had re-counted only one third of all the ballots cast and several thousand had been mysteriously incinerated. This increased charges of partiality which had scarcely been discouraged by the flight of the president of the Electoral Register, one Odio, to join Figueres's forces in the south well before the final announcement of the result. In San José Ulate was detained by the government and then released through Sanabria's intervention, but neither he nor forces pledged to the oligarchy participated in the fighting. By the time the congress, controlled by Calderón, threw out the result Figueres was well prepared for his 'war of liberation'. He had already established an alliance with the Arévalo regime in Guatemala which provided him with several plane-loads of weapons and munitions throughout the forty days of combat in which the *liberacionista* forces were directed by a Canadian mercenary, Alexander Murray, assisted by a group of foreigners affiliated to the Caribbean Legion.[49] Picado, on the other hand, was reluctant to commit the already weak and divided forces of the police and army, which had only 300 regulars, while the 1,500-strong PVP militia was largely held in reserve to protect the capital, where only two people died throughout the fighting. This was itself intermittent and generally took the form of guerrilla actions. It was still very bloody, and the level of casualties bore every indication of both the superiority of Figueres's forces and their reluctance to take prisoners; at El Tejar on 13 April 190 ill-organized supporters of the government were killed while the rebels lost only four men, their losses in the war as a whole amounting to less than 100 out of a total of some 2,000.[50]

El Tejar was the turning point in the conflict, enabling Figueres to take Cartago whilst Picado resigned the presidency and only the PVP militia in San José prevented a complete collapse of the government forces. On 17 April Figueres declared that although he intended to honour Ulate's election, he would allow no concessions to US anti-Communism or any reversion to nineteenth-century social policies, and on this basis he demanded an end to resistance. On the same day Somoza, who was threatened by both Figueres and his allies in the Caribbean legion, sent the National Guard across the border in a belated attempt to salvage the old regime (although the desire to exterminate the PVP is also often attributed to him). Simultaneously with this unforeseen development US forces in the Panama Canal Zone were preparing to intervene. This never came to pass since the threat alone was enough to prompt Somoza to withdraw his troops, and the PVP had already agreed to negotiations. On 18 April the 'Pact of the Mexican Embassy' between Mora and Figueres guaranteed the lives and property of all those in the pro-government forces, a general amnesty, the retention of the social legislation of the previous eight years, full trade-union rights, and the legality of the PVP.[51] Five days later Figueres formally took control of the capital as the leader of a new junta. Despite a level of attrition quite extraordinary by Costa Rican standards, it appeared as if an honourable peace had been secured, transferring power to the middle-class reformists but guaranteeing the gains made by the left.

This rapidly transpired not to be the case. Once the junta was installed, Figueres reneged on his agreement with the PVP. The party itself was outlawed, the *Confederación de Trabajadores Costarricenses* (CTCR) and all its affiliated unions were also made illegal, all state employees were removed from their posts, and the freedom to fire workers at will was restored to the capitalist class. Over the following year some 60 unions were disbanded, 7,000 people – almost one per cent of the population – sent into exile, 3,000 gaoled, and at least fourteen executed.[52] In short, the Communist and workers' movement was comprehensively repressed. On the other hand, Figueres had no intention of handing over power to Ulate and the oligarchy, insisting that the junta remain in office for at least eighteen months. Ulate had little choice but to accept this, giving Figueres and his *Movimiento de Liberación Nacional* a critical opportunity to exploit their military control in moving against the bourgeoisie as well as the left. In June the junta issued Decrees 70 and 71 that nationalized the banking system and levied a 10 per cent tax on incomes over 10,000 *colones* as well as freezing prices.[53] Moreover, although Calderón's labour code remained a dead letter, it was not formally rescinded and the other social reforms were also kept on the statute books. A disorganized rightist coup aimed at reversing this 'betrayal' collapsed almost immediately; together with the effective repression of a general strike on the Pacific coast in 1949, this defeat strengthened the position of the 'truly middle sectors, more developmentalist than social democratic in inspiration'.[54] According to Figueres, 'the idea which we are now pursuing is that, with the impulse of economic techniques, all social classes might merge into one great middle class'.[55]

Yet the forces behind Figueres were unable simply to dictate the course of events. Despite their military victory, they lacked the resources to sustain a coercive regime for any length of time and were constrained by the fact that, notwithstanding their own highly questionable commitment to democratic protocols, the war had been 'fought inside the democratic paradigm'.[56] The initial repression of the left was followed within two years by the formal disestablishment of the army. Equally, both its political background and the nature of its victory deprived the Figueres camp of popular support;

the retention of the central reforms and early economic measures of the junta did little in the short term to alter this, thereby preventing any further assault on the oligarchy. Although the *Partido de Liberación Nacional* (PLN) established by Figueres in October 1951 had its origins in the military defeat of the working class, it proved impossible to launch a political formation that aspired to be social democratic in nature without much broader support than it enjoyed in 1948–50. This was made amply evident in the resounding defeat of the Figueres group in the elections for a constituent assembly in December 1948, when it won only 6,411 votes against Ulate's 62,041. Although they gained some sympathy for accepting such a defeat and for the fact that the constitution of 1949 incorporated many of their proposals – most notably the establishment of autonomous state agencies – the 'social democrats' won only three seats to Ulate's thirty three in the congressional poll of October 1950. It was only with the formation of the PLN and after extensive campaigning that Figueres was finally able to assume office with a congressional majority in 1953. Moreover, a good proportion of his support came from the countryside and was mustered in a style far more resonant of the traditional *caudillo* than the technocratic social democrat.[57]

There was, therefore, no immediate exchange of power in 1948, still less a rapid transformation of the political system. The overthrow of the Picado government opened the latent conflict between the middle class and the oligarchy at the same time as it resulted in the subordination of the left and the working class by these forces. All the same, Ulate's desistence from reversing the junta's initial economic measures corresponded to more than a conjunctural balance of coercive power. Neither these nor the Calderón reforms amounted to more than a modest tax on capital, yet the decrees of 1948 were distinct in that they imposed such a tax not to redistribute income to the masses but to provide a basis for increased state regulation of the economy, particularly with respect to channelling investment into manufacturing. This certainly did not go unchallenged since it was a measure of considerable consequence, but neither was it at root anathema to all but a small sector of a capitalist class that had historically combined landed and commercial capital to a very high degree.[58] The upturn in the economy already underway at the time of the civil war helped to strengthen this limited shift towards interventionism. Ulate, therefore, was able to acquiesce in the key measures tabled by the junta and give them legal status without pursuing an interventionist course any further. It was evident that his assumption of the presidency was more strictly related to the lack of support for Figueres than to any popular mandate for a regression to the days of 'Olympian' rule.[59] When it became plain that Figueres was committed to a constitutionalist strategy, having appropriated many of the populist motifs of his old enemies for a campaign in support of economic modernization and expansion of the state sector, the PLN was able to win a stable constituency and consolidate as a system the policies it had begun to signal in 1948.

The erosion of the liberal oligarchic model in Costa Rica was distinct in more than the form of its replacement. Perhaps the most notable feature compared to developments elsewhere in the isthmus lies in the dispersion of its major components in different political projects, neither of which possessed a stable class character. Moreover, both blocs reflected the absence of an autocratic tradition, which enhanced a strategy of alliances whereas in the rest of Central America the essential elements of not dissimilar projects were generally channelled through the military. Although the initial conflict over the composition and terms of the dominant bloc was exceptionally violent, subsequent negotiation of political power was situated within the domain of civil society and that of economic mediation within the orbit of state much more emphatically than elsewhere. Whilst Figueres's pipe-dream of one vast middle class never approached the realm of reality, it continued to possess validity as a hegemonic device beyond reflecting the expansion of the petty bourgeoisie itself. More importantly than this, it represented an ideological intersection of the polar points of a social formation in which the political expression of both capitalist domination and proletarian interest was already more circumscribed than in other states. It was this history that provided the form of 'political centre' that is today so ardently sought in the rest of the region.

The Point of Rupture: Guatemala

Early in the 1986 the Guatemalan Christian Democratic Party (DCG) took office under the presidency of its youthful and athletic leader Vinicio Cerezo. Although within the country the response to Cerezo's electoral triumph was one of marked caution, elsewhere, and nowhere more readily than Washington, it was celebrated as a most significant extension of the regional process of 'redemocratization'. The importance of this resumption of a long suppressed constitutionalist politics was deemed to lie in the fact that for the first time since the counter-revolution of 1954 the military and extreme right accepted the transfer of office to civilians without a public and formal guarantee for the continued powers of the army outside its strictly professional sphere. Yet, as sceptics pointed out, such written agreements were hardly necessary because Cerezo had made a positive virtue of the moderation of his platform and, most critically, categorically rejected the option of an agrarian reform.[60] This notable absence from an otherwise nondescript programme of minor adjustments to the economy was peculiar even by the standards of Latin American Christian Democracy. The decision to omit any substantive measure for change in the countryside was an astute initiative on the part of the DCG since it was precisely such a reform, introduced in June 1952, that lay at the heart of the 'revolution' of 1944–54; its repudiation had formed the core of ruling-class politics for the ensuing thirty years and still lay deep in its political psyche. Even at such a distance, following the Alliance for Progress and the Salvadorean experience of a limited and coercive reform with exceptional guarantees for landlords, it was not possible to court the risks of a backlash on this issue. The spectre of 1952 had not lost its terror, condemning the country to a backwardness all the more grotesque in that it was now presided over by debonair young technocrats whose platitudes about democracy were as empty of substance for the millions of rural poor as they were pleasing for the orators themselves, the calculating colonels listening in their barracks, and a US government delighted at the public relations triumph of having ushered the soldiers out of the limelight yet preserved their formidable apparatus of control that over the previous decade had proved more comprehensive than that of any other military force in the region.

In view of the subsequent importance of the 'ten years of spring in a land of eternal tyranny', it is worthy of mention that we still lack a full scholarly study of the reformist decade.[61] Apart from the reform itself, the regime of Jacobo Arbenz (1951–54) is far better known for the manner in which it was overthrown by the Eisenhower administration than for what actually happened in Guatemala while the government was in power; still less is known about the regime of Arbenz's predecessor, Juan José Arévalo (1945–50).[62] It is evident that none of the measures introduced in this period, not even the agrarian reform itself, amounted to a decisive assault on the ancien regime of the order witnessed at the same time in Bolivia, let alone that of a few years later in Cuba. The overthrow of Ubico's transient heir General Federico Ponce in October 1944 opened a phase of pronounced but constrained political change that henceforth went by the title of '*revolución*', a term which distinguishes it from '*la reforma*' of the 1870s under Barrios, although there is a case for suggesting that the terms be reversed in view of the historical substance of the two periods. The 'revolution' has entered history as such to some extent because it was abruptly cut off, its possibilities and promise being suspended by outright defeat rather than eroded by its own insufficiencies. This, to be sure, has encouraged a less than subliminal sense of anticipation or apprehension that it will be 'picked up' again, the contemporary forces of the left struggling to realize the 'outstanding business' of a political agenda opened in 1944.[63]

It is frequently observed that the measures of 1944–54 were sufficiently modest in character that had they been introduced in the early 1960s, during the Alliance for Progress, instead of in the depths of the Cold War, they would have been entirely acceptable to Washington. Insofar as they might be compared with the policies of the Frei government in Chile, this observation is not without some validity. The limits of capitalist reproduction and control that obtained throughout Latin America even in the 1950s were not transgressed by the agrarian reform itself, the 1945 constitution, establishment of a rudimentary social security system, unrealized plans for a state-controlled power and road network, a degree of municipal autonomy, state credit for small enterprises or assistance for the manufacturing sector. These features indicate an essential similarity between the Guatemalan modification of the oligarchic system and that taking place elsewhere in Central America at the same time. There was, however, a crucial distinction in that this developmentalist project was undertaken in conditions of unprecedented political democracy that incorporated an increasingly prominent role by Communist activists and eventually permitted the legalization of their party (four years after the Costa Rican PVP was driven underground). At the time the State Department noted that the Communists were small in number and occupied only minor posts in the government apparatus, and it recognized that the prevalent sentiment of both the Arbenz government and the mass of its supporters was nationalist rather than socialist in character. Nevertheless, it was believed, not without justification but with increasing singularity of purpose, that precisely such an atmosphere provided the Communists with considerable potential for growth.[64] Thus, although a tank anti-Communism underwrote 'Operation Success' which overthrew Arbenz in the summer on 1954, the counter-revolution could not be a partial affair; it had of necessity to wipe away almost the entire fabric of reforms introduced over the prior decade. It is indeed possible to speculate that ten years later Washington might have baulked at such a comprehensively regressive strategy, but there is little indication that, in the aftermath of the Cuban revolution and on the evidence of the invasion of the Dominican Republic, the methods as well as the gut instincts of the US government would have been markedly different. Such speculation is anyway of minimal consequence when set against the real, and now historically embedded, ramifications of the counter-revolution.

Soon displaced from the pattern of developments at a regional level – by 1950 'order' had been firmly secured elsewhere in Central America with anti-Communism as a necessary but never absolutely central factor – the Guatemalan experiment persisted into a 'world time' in which ideological polarization dominated political activity to an unprecedented degree. This seeded a profound and enduring anti-Communism within a dominant bloc that, distinct from the Salvadorean oligarchy, was not just menaced by the pulsar threat of a distant peasant jacquerie in which all the villainies of bolshevism might be conjured up but had itself lived a tangible experience of political liberalism and social reform, which was equally strongly identified as Communist. This perception was no less real because it was false. It was the catalyst for the restoration of a local autocratic tradition that was in time to undergo important modifications but would never relinquish a rigorous rejection of structural reform as a permissible strategy. Elsewhere – even in El Salvador – there was always more space for at least formal adherence to this than was henceforth to exist in Guatemala. Ambushed by the petty bourgeoisie and increasingly threatened by the working class, the ruling class emerged from a decade of reform buoyed up by Washington's intervention but also deprived of a viable claim to the political heritage of 1944, which remained firmly associated with its popular and radical elements. This unusually early settling of accounts has now, of course, lost much of its effect, the majority of Guatemalans having been born after Colonel Castillo Armas and Ambassador Peurifoy flew into Guatemala City to reclaim the country for the free world. Yet that which has been historically won and lost exercises an influence on popular memory and political culture distinct from that which has always been pending. However misplaced they might be, the fears of the ruling class and the hopes of some of the radical left that the contemporary political agenda be reopened at its advanced point of closure in 1954 are products of a finite past.

The reform era may be divided into two phases. The first, which lasted from the anti-Ubico popular mobilization of June 1944 until the assassination of Colonel Arana in June 1949, was dominated by reforms in the political sphere that were generally controlled by the middle sectors although it proved increasingly difficult to contain growing pressure from the labour movement. The second phase, opened by the general strike in defence of the Arévalo regime against the abortive right-wing coup provoked by Arana's killing, was marked by a shift towards more substantial economic initiatives, for which plebeian support was more marked than that of the middle class.[65]

As in El Salvador, the anti-dictatorial movement was headed by the students, with the pupils of San Carlos advancing from the limited sectoral demand for the replacement of faculty deans early in June 1944 to the staging of a large demonstration for full institutional autonomy on the 24th.[66] This unprecedented event was transformed into a march for full political democracy, the United Nations charter being read out to the multitude while 311 leading professionals submitted to Ubico a petition almost entirely formulated in the language of the 'Four Freedoms'.[67] The solidity of middle-class support for this movement and a marked neutrality on the part of the US embassy convinced Ubico, after an initial bout of instinctive repression, that he should resign. On 1 July, having called the first full cabinet meeting of his regime, he handed power over to a junta of senior officers and made his way to the British legation. There then ensued three months of political indecision in which one can sense a momentary petrification of the popular movement caused by the sudden and relatively untaxing removal of the *caudillo*. Although the first moves towards unionization were already underway in both the city and UFCO plantations, the impetus of the campaign for constitutionalization was temporarily checked by the junta's lifting of Ubico's state of siege and the manipulation of the old hand-picked congress to appoint General Federico Ponce as provisional president and ratify his call for elections in October. However, the project of sustaining *ubiquismo* without Ubico himself stalled upon an overly ambitious effort to reverse the *apertura* without any incorporation of the newly emergent political forces. Ponce presented himself as the Liberal Party candidate in the poll, trucked Indians from the community of Patzicia into the city to cow the opposition, and duly 'won by a handsome, not to say fantastic, margin, garnering 48,530 votes out of a total of 44,571'.[68] Such a flagrant manoeuvre was unworkable. Four days after the election, on 20 October, junior officers broke into revolt. A fortuitous direct hit by the rebels' artillery on the capital's arsenal gave them a psychological and logistical advantage over Ponce's supporters, both the junta and the military hierarchy being subdued without great bloodshed. The password of the rising was '*Constitución y Democracia*' and it was backed by many students to whom weapons were distributed, but the military clearly dominated the new junta composed of Majors Arana and Arbenz and the lawyer Guillermo Toriello.[69] While this body immediately convened fresh elections for the presidency and a constituent assembly, the army established a strong administrative presence that it retained throughout the reform period. The 'October Revolution' was at no stage anti-militarist and it eventually collapsed less as a result of the military prowess of its opponents than because the army finally withdrew its support.[70] Even at the onset of the revolution this contradictory feature can be perceived in the slaughter of Ponce's wretchedly manipulated Indian followers by the military advocates of constitutionalism.

This bonapartist element, which re-emerged more strongly during Arbenz's presidency, was initially occluded by the concerted advance of constitutionalism, most immediately evident in the enormous popularity of the candidacy of Juan José Arévalo, who, as a mild-mannered schoolteacher, was seen to personify the civic virtues of democratic government. In December Arévalo categorically consolidated the insurrectionary work of his young military sponsors by winning 255,000 of 295,000 votes cast in the new, and generally fair, presidential poll. Such support owed little to party organization and although Arévalo was endorsed by the newly-formed political organizations of the middle class – most notably the *Frente Popular Libertador* (FPL) and *Renovación Nacional* (RN) – the Guatemalan revolution was notable for the weakness, constant division and dependence upon state patronage of the political parties. Under Arbenz the *Partido de Acción Revolucionaria* (PAR) came to act as an unofficial vehicle of the regime, but even with government support it failed to established a coherent organization and was interminably sundered by programmatic and personal disputes.[71] Efforts to replace the PAR with a single 'revolutionary' party on the Mexican model were stillborn, their failure as late as 1953 clearly corresponding both to a conjunctural crisis within the middle class over the degree to which economic nationalism and popular mobilization should be embraced and to a more structural weakness in national political culture bred of prolonged periods of authoritarian rule. In time this debility was to be made fully evident in the capacity of Communist militants to capture the leadership of the PAR and then, when they discarded 'entryism', to give their own organization a political importance out of all proportion to its numerical size and financial resources.

In 1944 and 1945, by contrast, the limits to an organized political expression of middle-class reformism were obscured by the expectations vested in Arévalo; his return from over a decade of exile in the provinces of Argentina was artfully stage-managed and enthralled an urban anti-dictatorial movement more inebriated with the symbolism of liberty than adjusted to ideological debate. Moreover, Arévalo's own politics gave full rein to the medley of currents that sprang up in the first flush of the democratic 'spring'. Indubitably pledged to the ideal of constitutional government, the new president viewed this in the same terms as his allies in the Caribbean Legion and was happy to supply Figueres with arms in order to overthrow Picado and the PVP. On the other hand, his commitment to Central American union led him to negotiate with a military ruler such as General Castaneda in El Salvador, whose regime was founded on the slaughter of crowds celebrating the very revolt that enabled Arévalo to take office. Such pragmatism was entirely in keeping with the espousal of a far from archaic salon socialism that resonated robustly in a young and energetic congress whilst in itself threatening little more than the sensibilities of the oligarchy and the US.[72] Consistently pitched in terms of modernization and self-consciously derived from Franklin Roosevelt's New Deal, this was a 'spiritual socialism' that fused recognizable motifs of secular mysticism with the less familiar cadences of a developmentalist vision:

> We are socialists because we live in the twentieth century. But we are not materialist socialists. We do not believe that man is primarily stomach. We believe that man is above all else a will for dignity. . . . Our socialism does not aim at an ingenious distribution of material goods or the stupid economic equalization of men who are economically different. Our socialism aims at liberating man psychologically and spiritually. . . . The materialist concept has become a tool in the hands of totalitarian forces. Communism, Fascism and Nazism have also been socialist. But theirs is a socialism which gives food with the left hand while the right mutilates the moral and civic values of man.[73]

In 1945 language such as this did not disturb the State Department unduly, and the first two years of the Arévalo regime produced few substantive measures that were perceived as threatening to US interests. The 1945 constituent assembly, comprised almost entirely of San Carlos graduates and with an average age of thirty-five, drafted a national charter that assigned a formal social character to property – this was now common practice in the hemisphere – and held back from extending the franchise to illiterate women, thereby restricting the new political nation much more sharply than parliamentary rhetoric suggested. In all probability the rural population benefited more directly from the 1946 municipal law that abolished Ubico's intendant system and introduced local elections. In some areas this certainly had the effect of bolstering Indian autonomy, but it should not be seen as promoting a consistent and universal resurgence of indigenous society. This is partly because the socio-economic power structure in the countryside was left largely intact, and partly because in those instances when it was disturbed the challenge was frequently organized around new clientelist links with the urban political sphere rather than an unqualified reconstitution of communal independence.[74] It should, though, be recognized that the early abolition of the vagrancy law and supplementary legislation had an impact that went beyond the economic realm and helped to increase a general temper of civil liberty even before rural organization was legally permitted.[75] Abolition was viewed as no less important than the new constitution in the overhauling of an anachronistic quasi-feudal juridical system. In the same vein, and in direct response to the 'vanguard' of the revolution, the university was given full autonomy and funded with 2 per cent of the national budget. Arévalo, the leader of a 'teachers' revolution', also considerably increased the general educational budget, nearly doubling the number of schools and teachers in the countryside from the levels of 1940.[76] It is said that more books were published between 1945 and 1950 than in the previous fifty years, reflecting a general vitality – it could scarcely be termed a renaissance – in urban culture. However, such advances soon reached the limits imposed by the meagre fiscal resources of a state that approached structural economic reform with great caution. At the end of the revolutionary period the level of education in Guatemala was still one of the lowest in the hemisphere; while a literacy campaign that was reported to have taught 23,500 people to read and write in 1947 constituted a far from insignificant phenomenon by the standards of the day, it could in no sense compare with later examples in Cuba and Nicaragua, and never approached the hopes for a generalized enlightenment nursed by its managers.[77] It did, all the same, correspond to a modest development of state infrastructure, which was based on stable growth in the economy as a whole rather than any major alteration of the fiscal system and expanded the civil service, now extended beyond the traditional spheres of central government and education to a central bank, social security system and statistical office.

These institutions provided only a rudimentary regulation of the economy but still symbolized the shift towards a degree of intervention and planning that many of the political generation of 1944 accepted as necessary for the modernization of Guatemalan capitalism.[78]

The constraints to any 'bourgeois democratic' revolution in Guatemala at the end of the 1940s were considerable. Progress towards the construction of a secular republic beyond mere legislative ordinance was certainly possible in Guatemala City itself, which by 1950 had a population of a quarter of a million and a concomitant urban culture. Yet even this was very limited since the capital was the sole city of any size, and less than 12 per cent of the population lived in settlements of more than 10,000 people. In 1953 there were in the country as a whole only 6,421 telephones and 16,704 motor vehicles.[79] The 'national bourgeoisie' that might form the social basis for an alternative to the agro-export capitalist sector, and was deemed by the Communists to be championed by Arévalo and Arbenz, could only plausibly be associated with a manufacturing circuit that in 1953 comprised 1,072 workshops employing a labour force of 16,759 workers, 12.7 per cent of the economically active population.[80] It would, therefore, be misconceived to construe the reforms of this period as a direct product of any burgeoning industrial capitalist class; small manufacturing interests were but one element in a realignment of the dominant bloc that produced a partial conflict with large landed capital. Under Arévalo these disputes stemmed primarily from an erratic extension of political democracy to the relations of production rather than from the introduction of a qualitatively new economic programme. Indeed, it is worth noting that in the first years of the revolution US investment in Guatemala rose – from $86.9 million in 1943 to $105.9 million in 1950 – and that the general climate for local entrepreneurs was significantly improved by the establishment of the National Institute for the Development of Production (INFOP), which channelled state credit to the private sector.[81] Even in the case of the controversial labour code of 1947 the complaints of landowners at an unprecedented legal sanction of rural organization were tempered by the fact that unionization was initially permitted only on estates with a labour force of over 500 where a minimum of 50 workers wished to form a union, of whose members 60 per cent had to be literate for registration to be extended.[82] This conservatism was reflected in the government's prohibition of rural organization until the code was finally ratified, so that by 1948 there were only eleven registered unions in the countryside.[83] In the urban sector such restrictions were implausible on both political and practical grounds, but the establishment of minimum working conditions in the constitution and the rights of association in the labour code did not extend to the freedom of the Communists to maintain evening schools for workers. Arévalo was able to close these with almost as much ease in 1950 as in 1946, and the government's insistence upon the constitutional clause which outlawed political parties with international links delayed the emergence of the PGT until 1952.

Objections to the labour code manifestly entailed a repudiation of the democratic ethos of the time, and it is notable that UFCO's strenuous resistance to the measure was based less upon a rejection of the rights of collective association per se than on the claim that the limitation of these to large enterprises in the rural sector constituted an act of discrimination against the company. On this basis UFCO succeeded in persuading the State Department to browbeat Arévalo into amending the statute so that all enterprises were treated equally, thereby extending the legal and real scope of worker organization in the countryside.[84] More general landlord discontent was provoked by what was perhaps Arévalo's most adventurous measure, the law of forced rental of December 1949, which realized the 'social property' clauses of the constitution in obliging the leasing of uncultivated estate lands at a rent of no more than 5 per cent of harvest value. Even in this case complaints reflected apprehension about a more permanent and comprehensive agrarian reform rather than any substantial loss of holdings since the law was not generally applied to large commercial estates held in freehold.[85] Nonetheless, landed capital had cause to be concerned. Following the state expropriation of German-owned properties, UFCO was the most obvious target for nationalist attacks; both its tax exemptions and efforts to reduce a labour force that was now largely unionized exacerbated discontent over the company's monopoly of the railway system and the Atlantic outlet at Puerto Barrios.[86] Equally, the coffee capitalists had to confront the consequences of a free market in labour, the most obvious and important of these being a rise in rural wage rates, which in some areas increased threefold over the decade.[87] There was, however, no contraction of either land under coffee or export levels, and the generally favourable market conditions cushioned some of the effects of increased labour costs that were still amongst the lowest in the region. Furthermore, the relative stability of production for the internal food market in the early 1950s suggests that following the abolition of forced labour no major alteration in the agricultural cycle of the Indian population took place, increased wages proving sufficient to attract a supply of seasonal labour.[88] It is significant that after the counter-revolution there was no attempt to re-establish a formal apparatus for debt peonage or vagrancy.

Studies of the reform period depict a generally passive rural population that benefited from improved conditions in the labour market, desisted from violence and was organized very loosely indeed.[89] Although there existed a clear difference between the rural proletarians working for UFCO, who were unionized even before the October revolution, and *campesinos* divided between production of food crops and temporary plantation labour, this latter sector was still far from being an inert mass.[90] Instances of anti-landlord violence were rare but not unknown, and once the labour code had been revised the initially slow pace of syndicalization picked up. In 1950 the *Confederación Nacional Campesina de Guatemala* (CNCG) was formally established, the number of local unions having grown over the previous three years from twenty-three to ninety-six. By May 1954 the CNCG had 345 affiliates, only twenty-six of which were comprised of small farmers as opposed to agricultural labourers, and it claimed a truly formidable total membership of 256,000.[91] Commentators less than sympathetic towards the movement accept the figure as at least broadly reflective of the scale of rural organization.[92] The national leadership of the CNCG was composed of middle-class activists rather than radicalized *campesinos*; at the local level this was less the case, and while the impressive scope of formal affiliation was undoubtedly not matched by active militancy, one can perceive in the early tension with the urban movement and subsequent internal disputes over the degree and speed of agrarian reform the characteristics of an organization that was a great deal more than a paper body.[93] In addition, organization on a communal rather than workplace basis – through *uniones* as opposed to *sindicatos* – accelerated in the last phase of the Arévalo government and under Arbenz, with some 315 bodies being recognized by the state between 1950 and 1953.[94] Thus, however distinct from the urban working class in the nature of its politicization, the organization of the rural masses during this period was advancing to a point that was manifestly threatening to landed capital. The agrarian reform certainly enhanced this threat, and it should be borne in mind that while oligarchic support for the counter-revolution was necessarily predicated upon a full restitution of alienated lands, the need to liquidate *campesino* organization was equally central.

The CNCG was never controlled by the 'bolsheviks' denounced by the landlords; the ties of its leadership with the more cautious factions of the PAR and Arbenz government were strong enough to arouse a bitter dispute with an urban union leadership that had developed much earlier and was by 1950 under the control of the left.[95] The establishment of the *Confederación de Trabajadores de Guatemala* (CTG) in September 1944 marked the revival of a labour movement that had lacked all vestige of organization for fifteen years, leaving many sectoral and political conflicts suppressed. Within a year of the revolution these had emerged strongly enough to cause a sharp division, the teachers championing a more radical and political line against the railway workers, within whose organization the pull of mutualism remained strong.[96] However, the rise in urban wages by some 80 per cent in the first five years of the revolution and the gains made through the constitution and labour code generally benefited the forces of radicalism. Arévalo's suppression of open Communist activity failed to dislodge militants such as Víctor Manuel Gutiérrez from the leadership of the confederation or to provide enough support for the breakaway FSG to expand beyond its original core.[97] In October 1951 this balance of forces was sealed with the establishment of the *Confederación General de Trabajadores de Guatemala* (CGTG), which within a year won back the forces of the FSG and became the sole national confederation, incorporating some 500 affiliated unions and a rank and file in excess of 100,000 workers by 1954. Under Gutiérrez's diligent direction both the syndicalist leadership and that of the Communist movement reached a rapprochement with the CNCG, founded upon recognition of its independence and the central importance of an agrarian reform. This convergence of the workers' movement responded in part to the resolution of strategic disputes inside the nascent Communist Party but should also be seen as reflecting a natural organizational consolidation following the measures of 1945–49 as well as a more conjunctural response to rising reactionary opposition to the post-1944 system.

The shift to a more resolutely reformist programme is usually associated with Arbenz's assumption of the presidency in 1951. This itself was largely made possible by the failure of a conservative challenge for power eighteen months earlier centred on Arbenz's fellow conspirator from 1944, Colonel Arana. As chief-of-staff of the army Arana held greater effective military authority than Arbenz, who was minister of defence under Arévalo, and he was largely responsible for defending the government against persistent plotting. Most of this opposition was poorly planned, but the regime was confronted by over thirty coup attempts in five years, indicating a general instability that required continuous military neutrality if not active political support. One of the quite predictable consequences of this was that both Arana and Arbenz developed acute political ambitions of their own, and when Arana failed to gain FPL backing for a presidential bid in 1948 he himself began to move towards a *golpista* position. This was clearly intended to halt further radical organization and threatened the popular movement since Arana had already attempted on several occasions to repress strikes, only to be held back by Arévalo. In July 1949 Arana increased his pressure on the government by seizing an arms cache to be used by the president's colleagues in the Caribbean Legion seeking to overthrow General Trujillo of the Dominican Republic. It was whilst returning from inspecting these weapons that Arana was ambushed and killed by individuals identified as close to Arbenz; he was subsequently attacked by the right as responsible for the crime but no conclusive evidence of his implication was produced.[98] The assassination of the strongest candidate of the right within the post–1944 order immediately provoked a reactionary uprising that attracted enough military support to oblige Arbenz to distribute arms to civilians whilst the unions staged a full general strike. The failure of the coup, in which scores of people were killed, marked a significant turning point, with the political confidence of the left and unions greatly enhanced. The right, by contrast, lost much initiative, its commemorative 'minute of silence' for Arana in July 1950 being but a pale echo of the prior challenge and the cause of sufficient mobilization by the unions to oblige Arévalo to stand down temporarily as president while the army took direct control in order to prevent further escalation of conflict. Thus, although Arbenz won the election of November 1950 by 267,000 votes against 74,000 for the conservative General Ydígoras, and despite the fact that he continued to enjoy the confidence of the military until the counter-revolution was fully under way, the new president's most vocal supporters at the peak of the Cold War were on the left of the political spectrum and lodged in the popular movement. This helped to transform what was a limited, statist economic policy typical of a nationalist army officer into a burgeoning bolshevism when viewed by the political managers in Washington.

The details of the anti-communist campaign directed by the US government against the Arbenz regime are now well studied and need not occupy us here.[99] It should, however, be noted that under Truman the State Department was reluctant either to identify Arbenz as a Communist or the Communists themselves as controlling the country.[100] Although from 1948 onwards – that is, when Arévalo was still in office – arms shipments were cut off, aid radically reduced and the possibilities of a boycott of coffee explored (and rejected), the rising diplomatic pressure on the Guatemalan government was handled with a modicum of dexterity until Arbenz had been in power for a year. For some time it proved possible to tolerate more theatrical provocations, such as the welcoming of a Puerto Rican sports team with the flying of the nationalist flag instead of the 'Stars and Stripes' or the formal mourning of Stalin's death, on the basis of an absence of nationalizations and diplomatic relations with the Soviet union, a general pattern of voting in the UN favourable to the US, and the very limited public gains of the Communists, who won only four of fifty-six congressional seats in 1953.[101] Indeed, given the eventual nature and outcome of the counter-revolution, it is remarkable how late it was prepared and how extensive were the political and diplomatic problems encountered by the Eisenhower administration in ensuring its success. Such qualifications are necessary to what has subsequently become an overly simplistic and conspiratorial perspective on US interventionism, but it remains the case that they eventually proved to be of secondary importance, being overridden by a renewed commitment to military action in support of a foreign policy predominantly pitched in terms of anti-Communism. This required a further adjustment of the Monroe doctrine not just to elevate hemispheric security above respect for national sovereignty but to do so in terms of the internal politics of a single state. Such a step was made necessary by the fact that the Guatemalan Communists made very few forays outside their own country and could not plausibly be accused of directly destabilizing any government, least of all that of Guatemala. As a result, a completely unprecedented situation had to be cast in much wider terms of reference, both the Monroe Doctrine and the pan–American treaty of 1947 being reinterpreted to cover 'intervention' by a creed that, notwithstanding its dissemination by nationals within their own country and without transgressing its laws, was alien and inimical to the hemispheric order. The adoption of this stance amounted to a great deal more than a reprise of the interventionism of the early decades of the century in both political form and diplomatic scope. While great efforts were made to assure pan-American support – or, at least, acquiescence – the new policy inevitably entailed a suspension of many of the features of the 'Good Neighbour' era and a growing tendency to distinguish between 'authoritarian' and 'totalitarian' rule that suppressed brave talk about democracy for a decade and provided a clear precedent for Jeane Kirkpatrick's nasty realpolitik of the 1980s.[102]

With respect to Guatemala the problem revolved around about two finite issues more familiar today than thirty years ago: how to deal with a popular nationalist regime that was boisterous in language, modest in substantive policy but committed to reducing the dominance of US economic interests, and how to liquidate a small but influential Communist organization. Under Acheson the general policy was to encourage marginalization of the radicals through placing increased pressure on the centre. However, events inside Guatemala had already made the government appreciably more accessible to left-wing support before Foster Dulles took over the direction of foreign policy and assiduously combined the two issues as one integral problem. Thus, the distinction between US Ambassadors Richard C. Patterson, who is usually depicted as a 'moderate', and John Peurifoy, who oversaw the invasion and is justifiably viewed as little more than an executioner, was in practice quite small; the former had his simpleton's 'duck test' for identifying Commies while the latter was content to opine after his first meeting with Arbenz that, 'if [he] is not a Communist he will certainly do until one comes along . . . normal approaches will not work in Guatemala'.[103] Such easy attribution of guilt by association was, of course, underpinned by the logic of the Cold War but it cannot be brushed aside as a purely grotesque rationalization since an organized Communist presence had clearly been established in Guatemala and no less manifestly contributed to the challenge posed to US interests in that country.

The Guatemalan Communists never numbered more than several hundred and probably possessed less than two thousand active sympathizers.[104] At no stage did openly declared members of the party or even closet supporters serve in the cabinet; no more than eight members of the party held senior administrative posts in public administration; and the movement only acquired a public and legally recognized organization in December 1952 with the registration of the *Partido Guatemalteco de Trabajo* (PGT).

Its leading cadre were young, predominantly middle-class, and generally radicalized by the early campaign against Ubico. This probably accounted for much of their initial popularity, the late appearance of a Marxist political formation betokening a lack of experience that, despite the advice of an important contingent of Communist refugees in the country, the Mexican party and Moscow, served to delay the constitution of an open and united party for a number of years after figures such as Gutiérrez and José Manuel Fortuny had achieved a national prominence.[105] Of these two Gutiérrez was the more popular, instinctively radical, and adept practitioner of open politics, his leadership of the CGT and CGTG being the most obvious source of Communist influence throughout the entire period. Fortuny, on the other hand, was more of a back-room strategist, and soon became the driving force behind the entry of the militants grouped around *Vanguardia Democrática* into the PAR in 1947. This entry tactic was in large part determined by the constitution's proscription of parties with international links, but it also reflected the accessibility of a significant sector of the government's followers to the limited anti-imperialist and reformist strategy proposed by the Marxists. Fortuny became general secretary of the PAR, within which a clandestine (and illegal) *Partido Comunista Guatemalteco* (PCG) was brought into existence as the first genuinely Communist organization in Guatemalan history and the last to make an appearance in the isthmus as a whole. Gutiérrez and a nucleus of predominantly working-class activists split in November 1949, discontented above all else with the absence of a 'mass orientation' and a more combative approach following the July 1949 general strike. Gutiérrez was only later to develop a sharper position on the agrarian question notwithstanding the fact that he had his own significant differences over this with the leadership of the *campesino* movement.[106] Shortly after this break Fortuny's group also left the PAR (which, as a result, split into three factions without great support) and operated in public through the newspaper *Octubre*. Although by October 1950 this paper was permitted to circulate legally, and by the spring of 1951 Fortuny was openly defending its editorial line as that of the PCG, the division of the movement was manifestly impeding further progress.[107] This was not resolved until February 1952, when Gutiérrez returned from a visit to the Soviet Union and dissolved his short-lived *Partido Revolucionario Obrero de Guatemala* (PROG) in order to re-enter the PCG, accepting Fortuny's leadership but also receiving a greater commitment to agrarian reform at the party's fifth plenum in March.[108] This laid the basis for the second congress in December at which an unremarkable set of programmatic positions was adopted, committing the party to support Arbenz's 'nationalist bourgeois' regime, deepen the anti-imperialist struggle, and work for a 'bourgeois-*campesino*' agrarian reform to establish the capitalist relations in the countryside necessary for a subsequent collectivization of agriculture.[109] At the same time the change in name from PCG to PGT allowed the party to enter the public domain completely.

The successes of the Guatemalan Communists were always less profound than those ascribed to them by the US government. They were at root based upon the occupation of key positions in the leadership of the urban union movement and the collapse of the parties of the petty bourgeoisie rather than on the construction of a mass following either through or independently of these organizations; the absence of a popular membership was particularly apparent in the countryside. Moreover, there was little or no presence inside the military, which after 1949 clearly constituted a key element in the regime.[110] Equally, there is little evidence that the central policies of the Arbenz government were either drawn from or revised under advice from the PGT; they remained firmly within the parameters of a programme for national capitalism that had a momentum independent of, although discernibly mirrored by, the PGT's unremarkable strategy of revolution by stages. The limitations imposed upon the party by the small size of the manufacturing working class were inescapable. Its doctrinaire belief in a 'national bourgeoisie' and its failure to develop policies on the 'colonial question' other than those borrowed from the Indian and Chinese parties reflected a deeper political weakness camouflaged for a while by the agrarian reform but eventually laid bare by an incapacity to stage any concerted defence of the revolution once Arbenz capitulated. The PGT was born and flourished on the left flank of a reformist regime but the logic of dependence was, in fact, the reverse of that proclaimed by the Cold War warriors of the right.

The Arbenz government exhibited much more pronounced features of petty-bourgeois radicalism than had that of Arévalo, permitting more extensive mass organization as well as legalizing the Communist Party. However, the regime never exceeded the bounds of an economic programme which may be described as nationalist but was in essence drawn from recommendations made by a World Bank mission that visited the country in 1950. The Bank had suggested that the government 'seek by negotiation to modify the existing agreement between the IRCA and the government' so that UFCO would concede both its rail monopoly to the Atlantic coast and total control of the pierheads at Puerto Barrios.[111] In pursuit of this end Arbenz drew up plans for the construction of a public road to the port. At the same time the government proposed to establish a state-owned electricity plant, also suggested by the Bank although this too would prejudice US corporate interests. These projected measures undoubtedly raised the hackles of UFCO but were of much less importance than the agrarian reform that the 1950 mission proposed as a limited, technical means of rationalizing and increasing agricultural production.[112] Even before the establishment of the CNCG there had existed a constituency for some form of land redistribution both as part of the general democratic agenda opened in 1944 and as a means of enhancing economic efficiency; such a measure fell just as squarely within the orbit of a developmentalist model as it did within that of the left. At no stage did the Communists, still less the government, seek anything more than a rationalization along capitalist lines of the grossly imbalanced pattern of land tenure indicated by the 1950 census. Arbenz himself was scrupulously clear on this point: 'It is not our purpose to break up all the rural property of the country that could be judged large or fallow and distribute the land to those who work it. This will be done to *latifundia*, but we will not do it to agricultural economic entities of the capitalist type.'[113] In line with this general brief the government's specialists made studies of reforms not only in the eastern bloc but also in Italy and Mexico, which conformed much more closely to a model that should have been acceptable to Washington.[114] Nonetheless, this was the first substantial proposal for an agrarian reform in all Central America since the Liberal era; whatever its fundamental objectives, it was perceived by the oligarchy as an unprecedented challenge to its economic base and a major assault upon the entire political culture erected upon the hacienda. Although it never matched the landed bourgeoisie's forebodings, the reform was an issue of considerable controversy, and Arbenz was not merely resorting to rhetoric when, in 1953, he declared, 'the question of the agrarian reform law has drawn the classical line in the sand: those who are definitely with the revolution are on one side; and those definitely opposed to the revolution are on the other.'[115]

The 1950 census demonstrated why support for an agrarian reform extended well beyond the ranks of the radical left: some 2 per cent of the population controlled 74 per cent of Guatemala's arable land while 76 per cent of all agricultural units had access to only 9 per cent; 84 per cent of all farms possessed under seventeen acres and 21.3 per cent less than two acres at a time when nine acres was considered the minimum plot for the sustenance of a family.[116] So great was the imbalance of land tenure that when Decree 900 was introduced on 27 June 1952 even its limited stipulations for direct expropriation offered appreciable gains for the *campesinado*. The decree exempted all farms under 90 hectares (219 acres) and those of up to 300 hectares (488 acres) of which two-thirds was cultivated; all communal lands; all properties of whatever size completely cultivated; and forests. Altogether, a total of 917,659 acres were expropriated and distributed to 87,569 families over a period of two years,[117] but the impact of the reform on the landed bourgeoisie as a whole was less sharp than these figures might suggest. A significant portion of the reform – 365,561 acres distributed to 39,737 recipients – was centred on the *fincas nacionales* and other state and municipal lands.[118] Furthermore, the total area affected amounted to only 3.9 per cent of all privately-owned land outside that held by UFCO, and in this respect the reform manifestly fell well short of a major reorganization of national agriculture, however great the benefits it yielded to those who received lifetime leases or complete title.[119] It is probable that the rise in plantation wages following the measure in the 1953 season engendered landlord antipathy more than is generally recognized, but only 15 per cent of the 19,000 *fincas* located in Indian departments were touched by the law and there is little evidence of the seasonal labour force being significantly reduced as a result of it.[120]

The fact that 653,197 acres of land marked for expropriation were owned by UFCO – which kept 85 per cent of its total holdings uncultivated – considerably increased the political conflict engendered by the measure. This was further heightened by the decree's stipulation that compensation was to be paid to owners in the form of government bonds and to be assessed on the basis of tax declarations made for the fiscal year 1950. In the case of UFCO this amounted to $627,527, at $2.99 per hectare, whereas the company rapidly filed a claim and gained US government support for a sum of $15.8 million, at $75 per hectare.[121] As a result, while the oligarchy refused any cooperation with what was a long and highly bureaucratized process of surveying, filing of claims, allocation and issuing of deeds, an altogether more dangerous opposition was put up by UFCO and Washington, which now began to talk of a reform with the broad approval of the World Bank as 'persecuting' and 'victimizing' private enterprise.[122] Parallel with this, accusations of Communist manipulation of the reform started to multiply despite only isolated instances of direct appropriation by *campesinos*, very few of which could be persuasively attributed to the direct agency of PGT militants, who occupied no more than twenty-six of the 350 posts created to administer the measure in the *Departamento Agrario Nacional* (DAN).[123]

The agrarian reform had the effect of escalating the US offensive by virtue of both its impact on UFCO and its polarization of political camps within Guatemala itself. The degree to which direct involvement of senior figures in the Eisenhower administration – particularly the Dulles brothers – in UFCO's affairs determined the policy of direct intervention remains open to debate, although it can scarcely be accounted of minimal importance and manifestly helped to encourage anti-Arbenz press coverage in the US.[124] Moreover, whatever the precise terms of expropriation, the effects of the reform upon UFCO were sufficiently proximate to nationalization to be depicted as 'socialistic' and to permit a much sharper identification of the government with the PGT than had hitherto been possible. Hence, both in public propaganda, which had reached impressive proportions by the spring of 1954, and in internal discussions US policy towards Guatemala increasingly focused on the 'Communist threat'.

In June 1954, almost exactly two years after the agrarian reform was introduced, a motley band of insurgents – most, but not all, Guatemalan nationals – crossed the Honduran border under the leadership of Colonel Carlos Castillo Armas and precipitated an internal coup by Arbenz's high command that terminated the entire reformist enterprise. 'Operation Success' was, of course, an almost exclusively US-directed campaign, dependent upon considerable diplomatic and logistical support for its triumph. The importance of this cannot be overemphasized, in terms of both its immediate impact upon the balance of power in the isthmus and its effect on subsequent US policy and operations in the region. The principal characteristics of the campaign have become familiar to later generations precisely because its success encouraged repetition in 1961, in the Bay of Pigs invasion of Cuba, and, from 1982, in the siege of Sandinista Nicaragua. There have, naturally, been modifications, but there is a remarkable consistency in the rationale and methods employed, ranging from the interdiction of arms – real or imagined – from the Soviet bloc; funding of counter-revolutionary forces operating across borders; a concerted campaign of diplomatic isolation in both regional and global fora; condemnation of basic social reforms as Communist in character; economic boycott; manipulation of the relative liberty permitted to local media as well as use of clandestine broadcasts; aerial and maritime sabotage; assertion of an underlying Soviet 'imperialistic' conspiracy and mortal danger to the hemispheric order; and agitation of the religious question. In all this the Dulles brothers laid an impressive blueprint for the Reagan administration that is now so widely recognized that it merits little elaboration.

There are, nevertheless, differences between 1954 and the counter-revolutionary offensive of the 1980s that deserve mention. The most obvious is that the global conditions in which the Arbenz government strove to survive gave it very limited possibilities of success. The concentration of US political and economic power in the 1950s effectively reduced the defence of national sovereignty and condemnation of foreign intervention to a worthy complaint that had some echo but could not harness active international support. Guatemala was isolated with relative ease inside the Organization of American States (OAS), within which US hegemony was too strong to permit more than expressions of disquiet even by governments – Mexico, Bolivia and Argentina – that still pursued foreign policies at least partially out of temper with Washington's requirements.[125] In the UN the Soviet bloc opposed the US campaign and invasion but patently lacked the local interests attributed to it whereas the European states were still debilitated by the war, indebted to Marshall aid, and compliant with Washington's dictates as to its own sphere of influence. There was, of course, no forum of independent 'Third World' states within which to lobby and through which a single imperialist intervention could be exploited into a global issue of contention that might have affected US strategy. Both Guatemala and Latin America as a whole were far more isolated than they are today.

Notwithstanding this considerable advantage, it is notable that 'Operation Success' was in tactical terms very nearly a failure; this was due only in part to military incompetence, an equal if not more important factor being the remarkable weakness of the counter-revolutionary forces inside the country before the invasion. The sheer military inefficiency of Castillo Armas's force, which was initially halted by military resistance and for a while in danger of collapsing altogether, owed much to Washington's decision not to commit its own forces and to rely upon the psychological impact of bombing of towns by CIA planes. This was part of a clear policy of presenting the entire operation as the result of both national and regional efforts, full advantage being taken of Somoza's eagerness to participate and Gálvez's inability to avoid involvement. As in the 1980s, the depiction of an autonomous Central American initiative was viewed abroad as a transparent invention born of a reluctance to court both the domestic risks and international embarrassment of direct employment of US troops, giving Washington what is now called 'a basis for deniability' – the latest euphemism of the US political class for lying. In contrast to the contemporary case of Nicaragua, the Guatemalan revolution collapsed almost immediately such a strategy was put into effect. The root cause of this lay in the fact that the regime had throughout been sustained by the neutrality of a traditional and largely unreformed military apparatus. Once this came under direct threat from outside, the colonels staged their own coup. This avoided a prolonged military campaign but in no sense protected the left and popular movement from subsequent repression or reduced Peurifoy's role as king-maker, which assured Castillo Armas the presidency within a matter of weeks and ushered in a comprehensive reversal of the major reforms.

The fact that it took a direct invasion and untempered US threats to prompt the military to bring down Arbenz strengthens the view that his government had disturbed the Guatemalan social structure rather less than it had antagonized Washington. It is certainly the case that the landed oligarchy was sharply provoked by the reforms and that under Archbishop Rossell the Church had embarked upon a forthright anti-Communist 'crusade', but neither possessed sufficient political force to oust the government.[126] Despite the fact that significant sections of the middle class that backed the initial political reforms had become disenchanted with the consequences of Arbenz's economic programme, they too lacked the ability to shift the balance of forces decisively against it even within urban, *ladino* society. This may largely be attributed to the level of popular support expressed through the unions, although the regime was at no point exclusively reliant upon such backing. Very few of the gains made by the popular movement emanated from campaigns independent of the government or were unambiguously foisted upon it; even in 1949 it was the army that took the leadership in suppressing the rightist revolt.

By the spring of 1954 the PGT still remained very small. It had signally failed to capitalize on the popularity of the agrarian reform by building an anti-imperialist front independent of the government or developing plans for the defence of the revolution beyond recourse to the still unfamiliar tactic of strike action and the expectation of distribution of arms on the part of the military, an expectation that was never fulfilled.[127] Equally, while the Church proved incapable of arousing its rural constituency to oppose a reform that had provided it with limited but unprecedented benefits, organized political support for the regime in the countryside was far more limited than in the towns and encompassed only a minority of rural unionists. In sum, even the restricted programme of the Arbenz government had produced a stalemate for which the internal balance of forces provided no ready solution. Given the fact that the traditional state apparatus remained almost completely intact, it is quite possible that if Washington had not moved to intervene some form of gradual ossification would have taken place along the lines of the contemporaneous revolution in Bolivia, where the initial offensive on the oligarchy had been considerably more emphatic.[128]

The intervention itself eradicated this possibility, enhancing a manichaean vision of the decade-long *apertura*. 'Operation Success' lived up to its title in almost every sense, but while it did not fully turn the clock back to the pre-1944 era, its trenchantly reactionary character gravely reduced strategic possibilities for the ruling class. The political instincts of both the landed oligarchy and a stratum of entrepreneurs emerging in the 1950s and 1960s became more attuned to the rejection of political reform tout court than did those of any of their regional counterparts, even in El Salvador. This vitalized the extreme right, which established its own political and paramilitary organizations for the first time, but provided little option beyond military rule of a most narrow type. The decisive defeat of the left and the fact that the rural labour force could now be locked into the plantation circuit largely through economic mechanisms, qualified the coercive character of such rule for a period and permitted space for intra-class and institutional competition. Yet within a decade a military challenge by new radical forces, to which the post-1954 dominant bloc would not and could not concede the most minimal space, required a sharp tightening of the system and increase in violent control. By the late 1970s the need for a comprehensive dictatorship was consolidated by mobilization in the countryside of such an order that it was inconceivable that the military could respond in the manner it had adopted thirty years previously. As will be seen, these phenomena bore the stamp of broader and more conjunctural influences as well as corresponding to more enduring structures that neither Arévalo nor Arbenz succeeded in altering, yet they were also moulded by the logic of 1954.

Notes

1. Quoted in Jacobo Schifter, *La Fase Oculta de la Guerra Civil en Costa Rica*, San José 1981, p. 71.

2. Quoted in Carlos Sarti Castaneda, 'La Revolución Guatemalteca de 1944–54 y su Proyección Actual', ESC, no. 27, September–December 1980, p. 73.

3. Quoted in LaFeber, *Inevitable Revolutions*, p. 94.

4. Quoted in Stephen Schlesinger and Stephen Kinzer, *Bitter Fruit. The Untold Story of the American Coup in Guatemala*, London 1982, p. 207.

5. José Somoza Rodríguez ('Papa Chepe'), Anastasio's illegitimate heir, became a general in the National Guard and loyal backer of recognized heirs Luis and Anastasio junior ('Tachito'). The patriarch was gunned down by the young poet Rigoberto López Pérez in León on 21 September 1956. Ubico died in New Orleans in 1946, Carías in Comayaguela at the age of ninety-three in 1969, and Martínez at the age of eighty-eight in 1966, also in Honduras, killed with a machete by his farm steward.

6. The price of 'Santos 4' bean, which sets the level of the arabica market as a whole (with Central American coffees generally obtaining a slightly higher price) averaged $0.187 in 1946 (the first year of free trading), $0.265 in 1947/8 and $0.505 in 1950. The price of Costa Rican coffee (1945/6 harvest = 100) rose to 163 in 1948/9 and 295 in 1950/1.

Central American Exports ($ millions)

	1940	*1950*
Guatemala	12.0	79.8
El Salvador	12.2	68.9
Honduras	9.6	56.8
Nicaragua	9.4	27.7
Costa Rica	7.4	56.9
Total	50.9	290.0

Source: Torres Rivas, 'Industrialización', p.16.

7. Ibid., p. 7. 'Had such political changes not taken place at the level of the constellation of interests represented by the State, the economic changes would have been different or difficult.' Torres's comment should be taken in the context of his view that, 'the commodity-producing sector is in the long-term the only source of economic activity. In this sense, it is not true that Central America was a backward society because its agriculture was such; on the contrary, it was the entire society, i.e. the state and the dominant ideologies, that conditioned the nature of the primary sector.' Ibid., p. 11.

8. The State Department was very aware of this dilemma, which arose earlier in Central America than elsewhere in Latin America. The problem is lucidly depicted in a dispatch from Acting Director of the Office of American Republic Affairs Norman Armour to US Ambassador to Guatemala Boaz Long in October 1944: '. . . a number of us in the Department are deeply concerned at political developments in Guatemala and elsewhere in Latin America. This problem of support for democratic process is not an easy one and was discussed at some length at a staff meeting this morning. The idea was advanced that we might have President Roosevelt or the Secretary include in an early address a statement more or less along the following lines: "We wish to cultivate friendly relations with every government in the world and do not feel ourselves entitled to dictate to any country what form of government best suits its national aspirations. We nevertheless must naturally feel a greater affinity, a deeper sympathy and a warmer friendship for governments which effectively represent the practical application of democratic processes." This would take quite some drafting in order to fit into a speech on high policy without hurting the sensibilities of countries outside the hemisphere. It might also present certain problems within the hemisphere.' Armour to Long, US National Archives (USNA), Diplomatic Records, 814.00/9–2644. Within four years such difficulties in present-

ing policy had effectively been resolved by the Cold War although then, as under Reagan, the State Department laboured to introduce a certain finesse and malleability into the effusion of anti-Communism by its political superiors that inevitably entailed support for dictators.

9. Although Martínez was slower than Ubico in recognizing the Franco regime, he did so before either Germany or Italy. Moreover, he openly courted US disapproval in being the first ruler to extend recognition to the Japanese puppet government in Manchuria. Until 1940 officers were sent to both Italy and Germany for training and a member of the Wehrmacht was appointed Director of the Escuela Militar in San Salvador. Weapons were bought from both Axis powers. Elam, *Appeal to Arms*, pp. 48–9.

10. Grieb, *Ubico*, p. 252. The dictator admired Franco and Mussolini but considered Hitler 'a peasant', which may have been something to do with his sometimes fractious relations with the German landlords when *jefe político* in Alta Verapaz in 1909–11.

11. By early 1944 the issue of nationalization was the subject of sharp exchanges between Washington and Guatemala City, with Ambassador Long resisting pressure from the State Department and urging restraint, which earned him a lightly veiled rebuke from Cordell Hull. By this stage Washington was confining its attacks to 'principal axis spearheads', such as the large properties of the Nottebohm family, within its policy of general nationalization. It is possible that Ubico had some room in which to manoeuvre on this issue because, unlike the other Central American republics, Guatemala had no loan agreements with the US Export-Import Bank, although by 1942 this had lent out only $15.3 million to finance coffee production.

12. The German business community was effectively broken by the world war and never regained its authority after 1945. Some entrepreneurs, such as Enrique Weissenburg and Carlos Kong, acquired citizenship before the war whilst others, such as the Skinner-Klee family, were already sufficiently intermarried and locally established to evade proscription. However, the failure to regain property – as had occurred in 1918 – destroyed the coherent ethnic class faction based in Alta Verapaz. For details of the oligarchy at the end of the 1960s, see NACLA, *Guatemala*, New York 1974. Most, but not all, of German property was run by state managers from 1941, the farms becoming *fincas nacionales* after nationalization. In 1948 109 of these enterprises, covering 313,046 hectares, had previously been owned by German nationals and another ten had belonged to Ubico, most of whose lands were expropriated after his fall. In total these properties provided between one-fifth and one-third of the national coffee crop, employed 21,378 workers, and defrayed more than 15 per cent of the national budget. Leo A. Suslow, *Aspects of Social Reform in Guatemala, 1944–1949*, Hamilton, New York 1949, p. 66; Mario Monteforte Toledo, *Guatemala. Monografía Sociológica*, Mexico City 1959, p. 427.

13. John Patrick Bell, *Crisis in Costa Rica. The 1948 Revolution*, Austin 1971, p. 110.

14. Elam, *Appeal to Arms*, p. 60; McClintock, *American Connection: El Salvador*, pp. 127–9; Krehm, *Democracies and Tyrannies*, pp. 12–13.

15. Krehm, *Democracies and Tyrannies*, p. 19, quoting his contemporaneous dispatch in *Time*.

16. Elam, *Appeal to Arms*, pp. 60–6. Some executed officers, such as Colonel Tito Tomás Calvo, were renowned for their role in the *matanza* and were scarcely radical figures.

17. Although the strike gained mass support and paralysed the major towns, the initial propaganda for the stoppage had all the character of a broad civic campaign rather than a plebeian movement: 'We decree a general strike which will include hospitals, public works etc. Strikers will employ passive resistance and will not cooperate with the government. Mourning dress should be worn. All social classes must be united, and fiestas are prohibited. By showing the tyrant the abyss which exists between him and the people, by isolating him completely, we will cause him to fall. Boycott movies, newspapers and the national lottery! Don't pay taxes, quit your government jobs. Even the Archbishop has been humiliated!' Quoted in Ricardo Gallardo, *Estudios de Derecho Constitucional Americano Comparado*, Madrid 1961, p. 137, and cited in Russell, *El Salvador*, p. 41. Peasant participation seems to have been limited to Martínez's dispatching of some 800 *campesinos* to the capital, apparently in an effort to stir memories of 1932. Washington rejected opposition requests to boycott Martínez on the grounds of non-intervention and because the 1923 treaty withdrawing recognition from de facto regimes had been abrogated, although one can surmise that the real reason was to avoid creating a highly dangerous precedent. Nonetheless, Cordell Hull's statement that the US 'feels

itself bound not to express either approach or disapproval' of Martínez effectively doomed his regime. Leonard, *US and Central America*, pp. 51–2.

18. By October 1944 the UNT had some 50,000 members and was effectively led by supporters of the still outlawed PCS who, according to Mármol, were uncertain whether they were forming a party front organization or a genuinely syndicalist body. It is possible that the decision to support Romero reflected the Communists' anxiety not to divorce themselves from a popular reformist candidate as they had done in 1930–31. A leader of the Costa Rican party, Arnoldo Ferreto, visited San Salvador at this time and advised UNT leader Marroquín to follow the PCCR policy of alliances with bourgeois forces. Menjívar views such a decision as delivering up the leadership of the popular movement to the advocates of bourgeois democracy precisely at a time when the forces of the right were preparing to suppress it. Dalton, *Miguel Mármol*, p. 488; Leonard, *US and Central America*, p. 54; Menjívar, *Proletariado*, p. 79.

19. On 28 November, four days after a university strike had been declared and spread to the press and banks, Aguirre issued a statement: 'Employees who do not report to work in twenty-four hours will be dismissed. There are unemployed who are ready to take the good positions that others have left for *romerista* fanaticism. This time the strike cannot triumph because it lacks a banner, not having the Communist banner as in May.' Quoted in Elam, *Appeal to Arms*, p. 99. The desperate invasion of 12 December was wiped out with the loss of some 600 lives, a level of casualties which may have been affected by the fact that the rebels were engaged in Ahuachapán, principal site of the 1932 revolt.

20. Abel Cuenca, *Democracia Cafetalera*, pp. 100–1, interprets the 'revolution of '48' as reflective of the interests of a nascent industrial bourgeoisie challenging the landed oligarchy. Rafael Menjívar, *Proletariado*, pp. 84–5, disputes this but accepts that the coup formed part of a hemispheric tendency towards developmentalist projects as well as corresponding to a degree of variegation within the local capitalist class. In 1949 there were in San Salvador a total of 1,017 manufacturing enterprises with a labour force of 11,241, but only thirty-two firms employed more than fifty workers and investment in manufacturing was not to accelerate until the early 1950s. Ibid., pp. 86–7. The 1950 constitution formally allowed for state intervention in the economy, 'in order to assure all the inhabitants of the country an existence worthy of a human being', and upheld regulations on working hours, minimum wages, rights of association and collective contracts. While few of such objectives were ever met or significantly pursued, it is not unimportant that they were for the first time included in the political discourse of the dominant bloc.

21. Colonel José María Lemus, later president, quoted in Elam, *Appeal to Arms*, p. 146. Although the Salvadorean military were influenced by some features of the economic policy adopted by their colleagues in Guatemala, they exploited the growing radicalism and independence of the Guatemalan workers' movement to cajole their own capitalist class into accepting state sponsorship of minimum wages and legal urban unions as infinitely preferable to clandestine organization and wildcat strikes by workers who were no less aware of developments across the border.

22. The fact that almost all those killed were unarmed women on a peaceful march did much to harm the regime's image, but official spokesmen were nothing if not resilient in their counter-attack: 'Women of today are not the same as those of yesteryear and are nothing more than a clutch of unrestrained firebrands, wanting to intervene in politics while understanding absolutely nothing of it.' Quoted in Oqueli, *Gobernantes*, p. 55.

23. These figures, together with much of the substance of the following paragraph, have been drawn from an unpublished manuscript by Jeffrey Gould.

24. *La Nueva Prensa*, 28 May 1944, cited by Gould. The date of the PSN's foundation is often given as 1944 rather than 1939, encouraging the depiction of a political party that capitulated entirely upon its inception, a prominent motif in later FSLN propaganda.

25. Student supporters of the opposition by no means mirrored the positions of its traditionalist leadership but proved unable to change them. PSN students cooperated with young Conservatives and dissident Liberals, this latter group forming the *Frente Juvenil Democrático*, in which several members of the abortive guerrilla campaign of the late 1950s militated. Rigoberto López Pérez, Somoza's assassin, was a member of the FJD while figureheads of bourgeois opposition to the regime in the 1960s and 1970s, such as Pedro Joaquín

Chamorro and Rafael Córdova Rivas, belonged to the Conservative youth movement that was subsequently sold out by the party leadership.

26. There are clear parallels between the strategy adopted by the PSN and that of its Costa Rican sister party in allying with Calderón against the oligarcho-middle-class axis on the basis of limited social reform. However, both these examples can be contrasted with those of Argentina and Bolivia, where Perón and Villarroel won working-class support away from the pro-Moscow parties, which soon joined the opposition bloc led by the oligarchy only to be comprehensively defeated within it during the Cold War years. It should be noted that, notwithstanding his earlier dalliances with Fascism and economic links with Japanese-controlled Manchuria, Somoza had no option other than to be a fervent supporter of the Allies (which in itself distinguished his regime from those in Bolivia and Argentina). Hence, the PSN, like the Costa Rican PVP, could rationalize its line in terms of support for the anti-fascist cause as well as more local and immediate gains.

27. Jacobo Schifter, 'La Democracia en Costa Rica como Producto de Neutralización de Clases', in Zelaya, *Democracia?*, p. 185. Despite the title of his essay, Schifter provides a far more persuasive depiction of the fallacies of claims that the PLN was born of a democratic and populist movement than of any eradication of class conflict in 1948 or thereafter.

28. 'They do not like unpleasantness and shun extremes and fanaticism. Disputes are resolved *a la tica* – that is, the *tico* way: with civility and without rancor. It is their idiosyncrasy, their manner of being, and everything is adjusted to it. *Ticos* are essentially conservative, exhibiting a healthy skepticism and preferring, when confronted with change, to "think about it". They are indeed a decent people, and that may explain why their country is a democracy.' Charles D. Ameringer, *Democracy in Costa Rica*, New York 1982. p. 1.

29. Santiago Arrieta Quesada, *El Pensamiento Político-Social de Monseñ˜or Sanabria*, San José 1982. Calderón had studied at Louvain, headquarters of the Catholic social reform movement. Sanabria, on the other hand, had been educated at the Gregorian University and had acquired a reputation for historical scholarship rather than social doctrine. He was, however, of a very humble background and ethnically far from 'white', which may have helped to spark some sympathy from the *reformistas*, many of whom were his contemporaries. He was made archbishop at the age of forty-one in 1940 and retained this post, despite apparent efforts to remove him in 1949, until his death in 1952.

30. Mark B. Rosenberg, 'Social Reform in Costa Rica: Social Security and the Presidency of Rafael Angel Calderón, HAHR, vol. 61, no. 2, May 1981.

31. Bell, *Crisis*, pp. 24–30.

32. Cerdas, *Crisis*, p. 73.

33. Export levels stayed stagnant from 1941 to 1946 while imports continued to rise, producing a balance of trade deficit in 1945 of $15 million – larger than total exports. Between 1940 and 1943 the budget deficit rose from C2.3 million to C30 million. Calderón attempted both to win some entrepreneurial support and reduce state expenditure by privatizing the electricity and oil refining industries, a contradictory aspect of his administration that helped to delay PVP backing. Darenblum, *Crisis*, p. 55; Schifter, *Fase*, pp. 16, 68.

34. In the two years after the code was introduced 125 unions affiliated to the *Confederación de Trabajadores Costarricenses* (CTCR), established in October 1943. Rojas, 'Movimiento Obrero', p. 271.

35. In these epistles Mora drew Sanabria's notice not only to the change in the party's name but also to its stated policy of support for the measures 'based on papal encyclicals' being implemented by the Calderón government. For the correspondence and an interview of Sanabria in *La Tribuna* that has overtones of contemporary Christian radicalism, see Arrieta, *Sanabria*, pp. 236–47. The PVP did not enter the government and under its new 'minimum programme' made every effort to keep an independent platform. This produced only a modest increase in direct support for the party, but even twenty-five years later North American academics could opine with blithe confidence the PVP backing gave Calderón's regime 'left-wing and extremist tendencies which were not conducive to stable democracy'. James L. Busey, *Notes on Costa Rican Democracy*, Boulder 1967, p. 9.

36. The income tax was primarily intended to compensate for the loss of state revenue caused by exemptions from payments of coffee export taxes during the war. The economic reverse suffered by the coffee bourgeoisie was, therefore, only relative, and its opposition may

be considered primarily political in character.

37. Quoted in Leonard, *US and Central America*, p. 24.

38. Quoted in ibid., pp. 28, 31.

39. *Surco*, the journal of the *Centro*, was unambiguous on these matters in the early 1940s: 'the country is a victim of foreign capital represented by United Fruit, the electricity company, and Standard Oil, which distribute the majority of their great profits between foreign shareholders.' Quoted in Schifter, 'Neutralización', p. 213. The attitude towards local capitalists was more muted and reformist in character than directly aggressive. Rodolfo Cerdas identifies the influence of APRA, which his work generally characterizes as no less important than that of the Communist movement as an exogenous factor and, implicitly, possessed of a more viable political strategy. 'Problemas Actuales', p. 153. Leading members of the *Centro* included Rodrigo Facio, Daniel Oduber, Carlos Monje Alfaro, Alberto Cañ˜as and Jorge Rossi.

40. *Acción Democrática*, 5 August 1944; *El Social Demócrata*, 2 February 1948, quoted in Bell, *Crisis*, p. 53.

41. For details, see ibid., pp. 38, 77, 86.

42. Figueres was born in 1906 of first-generation settlers from Cataluñ˜a. He may have been impressed by the possibilities of technical progress from an early age since his father was one of the few members of the national medical establishment to specialize in electrotherapy. If so, such a conviction must have been deepened by two marriages to North American women and, prior to these, a four-year stay in the US, although the rigours of studying electrical engineering at MIT were rapidly forsaken in favour of general literary exploration in the Boston City Library. By 1942 Figueres was a rich man thanks to the expansion of his estate 'Lucha sin Fin' and a larger agricultural enterprise run in partnership with Francisco Orlich (president, 1962–66). Figueres was strongly opposed to the intervention of German properties by Calderón, but his complaints must have been sharpened by the fact that his own property was damaged during the government-orchestrated campaign. For a sympathetic biography, see Charles D. Ameringer, *Don Pepe. A Political Biography of José Figueres of Costa Rica*, Albuquerque 1978.

43. For details of this loose but momentarily influential grouping, see Ameringer, *Democratic Left in Exile*.

44. *Acción Democrática* declared itself to favour 'an honourable and progressive capitalism that works to create riches and social welfare . . .' Quoted in Bell, *Crisis*, p. 84.

45. Ibid., pp. 95–6, 110, 116.

46. As late as May 1947 the State Department considered that, 'Communism in Costa Rica is not now a force which ought to greatly concern this government.' Quoted in Leonard, *US and Central America*, p. 34. A detailed survey of US policy towards the country during this period is given in Jacobo Schifter, *Costa Rica 1948*, San José 1982.

47. Schifter, *Fase*, p. 84.

48. Jacobo Schifter shows a fall of 75,000 votes compared to the poll of 1944, this reduction being most marked in areas that had previously shown support for Calderón – Puntatenas, Limón – whereas it was minimal or non-existent in zones of oligarchic support – Alajuela, Cartago, Heredia. For full details, see ibid., pp. 80–2. It is clearly unusual to encounter instances of decisive electoral malpractice on the part of an opposition, but this should be viewed as the logical result of Picado's capitulation, and as such both more predictable and verifiable than, for instance, suggestions of simple fraud by Mrs Aquino's supporters in the Filipino elections of 1986 made by that eminent psephologist Ronald Reagan.

49. Figueres had signed a 'Pact of the Caribbean' with Arévalo and groups linked to the Caribbean Legion on 16 December 1947. For details of these ties and the course of the fighting, see Ameringer, *Democratic Left in Exile*, and Bell, *Crisis*, pp. 131–51.

50. Bell, *Crisis*, pp. 148, 182. The political ramifications of such great attrition were soon to become manifest and should be seen as a key factor in Figueres's failure to establish a popular political base for some years after the war.

51. Ibid., p. 181; Rojas, 'Movimiento Obrero', p. 273. Prior to the poll the US embassy reported that, in contrast to Ulate, Calderón and Mora were 'definitely not averse to compromise'. Yet by this stage Mora and the PVP had become victims of Washington's Cold War vision so that despite being 'level-headed, intelligent' and 'dedicated to a liberal and

unobjectionable social legislation programme', Mora was operating by 'the well-known means of international Communism' and Costa Rica 'may be of continually greater interest to Moscow'. Quoted in Leonard, *US and Central America*, pp. 36, 39. For details of US preparations for direct military intervention, see Schifter, *Costa Rica 1948*.

52. Schifter, *Fase*, pp. 112, 114; Rojas, 'Movimiento Obrero', p. 274.

53. Schifter, *Fase*, p. 115. In 'Neutralización', p. 218, Schifter quotes Figueres as stating upon his victorious entry into San José that he would not hand power over to Ulate.

54. Cerdas, *Crisis*, p. 73.

55. Quoted in ibid., p. 74.

56. Vega Carballo, 'Costa Rica', p. 16.

57. The pattern of voting between 1950 and 1966 is surveyed in Schifter, *Fase*, pp. 89–109. For a less scientific but more evocative depiction of Figueres's methods on the stump, see Ameringer, *Don Pepe*.

58. Schifter appears to concur with Cerdas's general view that it was precisely the high degree of integration of commercial and landed capital that held the Costa Rican capitalist class back from investment in industrial enterprises. Cerdas holds that Ulate's ability to defeat Figueres in the 1949 poll indicates that the agro-export and commercial sectors retained their strength although the middle class was now 'present' in politics and its adhesion to the strategy of import substitution had gained resonance by virtue of the fact that for most of the years between 1939 and 1947 exports did not reach even 50 per cent of imports. He also perceives a more historical feature of the state's subsequent role as economic agent lying in the colonial and early republican monopolies. *Crisis*, pp. 74–5; 'Problemas Actuales', pp. 152, 155–7.

59. It should be noted that in 1949 a total of 82,148 votes were cast, compared with the artificially reduced figure of 101,060 in 1948. This suggests that a considerable proportion of the electorate was either disenfranchised or abstained from voting in a contest in which the left was not permitted to participate.

60. Cerezo agreed with his opponents on the extreme right as early as July 1984 that there would be no banking or agrarian reform. For a critical survey of the background to 'redemocratization', see James Painter, 'The Return to Civilian Rule in Guatemala', *Third World Quarterly*, vol. 8, no. 3, 1986.

61. The phrase belongs to Luis Cardoza y Aragón, whose *La Revolución Guatemalteca*, Guatemala City 1955, is one of the better studies of the period. Other important sources include: Manuel Galich, *Por Que Lucha Guatemala. Arévalo y Arbenz: Dos Hombres contra un Imperio*, Buenos Aires 1956; Guillermo Toriello, *La Batalla de Guatemala*, Mexico City 1955; Archer C. Bush, *Organized Labor in Guatemala*, Hamilton, New York 1950; Suslow, *Aspects of Social Reform*; Tomás Herrera, *Guatemala: Revolución de Octobre*, San José 1986. The literature of those fervently opposed to the 'red menace' in Guatemala is not without some value both in empirical terms and as an illustration of the ideological temper of the day. Foremost among such works are: Ronald Schneider, *Communism in Guatemala, 1944–1954*, New York 1958, and Daniel James, *Red Design for the Americas*, New York 1954. Schneider makes extensive use of captured documents currently housed in the Library of Congress. Although these have just as strong a claim as the Elgin marbles to be returned by their pillagers to their place of origin, the unlikelihood of this occurring should act as a spur for further research by those able to gain access to an unusually rich archive. Some work has already been done by Jim Handy, *Gift of the Devil*, to support a lucid narrative and critique of the 'Cold War warriors' who burrowed amongst the papers before him. Now that the State Department documents up to the end of 1954 have been made accessible to the public, the documentary basis for a complete study of 1944–54 is readily available. A good résumé is given in NACLA, *Guatemala*, and in the texts mentioned below that are principally occupied with the US operation to overthrow Arbenz. Suffice it to say that the narrative given here reflects the absence of a full scholarly account. I am preparing a short study based partly on US diplomatic records as a contribution to a critical collection on Latin America in the Cold War edited by Leslie Bethell and Ian Roxborough.

62. The most readable survey is Schlesinger and Kinzer, *Bitter Fruit*. Another survey which stresses the role of UFCO in the overthrow of Arbenz is José M. Aybar de Soto, *Dependency and Intervention: The Case of Guatemala in 1954*, Boulder 1978. The work of Richard Immerman presents the UFCO campaign as generally subordinate to wider US political interests

in the Cold War: 'Guatemala as Cold War History', *Political Science Quarterly*, vol. 95, no. 4, Winter 1980/81; *The CIA in Guatemala. The Foreign Policy of Intervention*, Austin 1982.

63. At one level this is construed as moving beyond the 'bourgeois democratic' stage of a socialist revolution: 'the entire revolutionary process of 1944–54 is nothing less than the transfer of political power from the landlords to the bourgeoisie . . . we can affirm that the bourgeois or bourgeois democratic revolution in Guatemala has terminated because there no longer exists, inside the logic of power, any fraction of the bourgeoisie which might attempt to foster the development of capitalism by a route distinct from that of the landlord strategy, re-established upon the defeat of the Revolution of October.' Sarti, 'La Revolución Guatemalteca', p. 76. On the other hand, even before it was obliged to confront the supporters of permanent revolution lodged in the guerrilla movement of the 1960s, the pro-Moscow PGT viewed the defeat of 1954 in terms of the collapse of the 'national bourgeoisie' and a resulting need to rebuild a 'revolutionary democratic opposition', first against the big landlords and then 'the monopoly bourgeoisie which . . . replaced them.' There was, therefore, a need to 'go back' and rebuild a 'democratic, anti-imperialist and agrarian revolution'. PGT, *La Intervención Norteamericana en Guatemala y el Derrocamiento del Régimen Democrático*, 1955; Hugo Barrios Klee, 'The Revolutionary Situation and the Liberation Struggle of the People of Guatemala', WMR, vol. 7, no. 3, March 1964, p. 19; 'Guatemala – A Step toward Unity', WMR, vol. 24, no. 3, March 1981. Neither of the two most important contemporary revolutionary organizations – *Organización del Pueblo en Armas* (ORPA) and *Ejército Guerrillero de los Pobres* (EGP) – publicly characterizes the Arévalo–Arbenz period in orthodox terms of Leninism. For ORPA, it was 'an attempt at capitalist "reform" with a modernizing and nationalist content', whereas for the EGP leadership it was 'a democratic government', the defeat of which remains fresh in the memory of Guatemalans 'because it gave rise to a period of repression that persists until this day'. Despite these differences of perspective, the entire left is dedicated to defeating a system which it sees as rooted in the counter–revolution of 1954. ORPA, *Erupción Internacional*, Guatemala 1982, p. 4; Rolando Morán, interviewed in EGP, *Compañero*, no. 7, November 1983; Unión Revolucionaria Nacional Guatemalteca, *Proclama Unitaria*, January 1982.

64. 'Communist political success derives in general from the ability of individual Communists and fellow travellers to identify themselves with the nationalist and social aspirations of the Revolution of 1944 . . . the extension of their influence has been facilitated by the applicability of Marxist clichés to the "anti-colonial" and social aims of the Guatemalan Revolution.' National Intelligence Estimate, 11 March 1952, reprinted in *Foreign Relations of the United States, 1952–1954*, Washington DC 1984, vol. 4, pp. 1031, 1034. Hence the difficulty, expressed so engagingly by Ronald Schneider, in formulating any remotely persuasive and popular anti-Communism: 'It was useless to tell the people that they would lose their freedom and basic liberties under Communism since they felt they had none to lose'. *Communism*, p. 47.

65. According to Carlos Guzmán Böckler, the petty bourgeoisie had its first experience of political power in 1944, an experience which opened up the internal contradictions of the class, not least that between desiring a quantum increase in production whilst supporting redistribution. Although Arbenz's policies tended far more towards developing the forces of production than any egalitarianism, Guzmán would seem to be correct in noting a 'sense of relief' amongst the middle class when the regime was overthrown, only a minority staying pledged to the reformist strategy. 'La Enseñanza de Sociología en las Universidades de los Países Subdesarrollados. El Caso de Guatemala', *Revista Mexicana de Sociología*, vol. 29, no. 4, October–December 1967, pp. 618–9. By 1952 the State Department assessed the bulk of the student movement to be opposed to Arbenz. National Intelligence Estimate, 11 March 1952, *Foreign Relations*, vol. 4, p. 1035.

66. Although there were only 681 students at San Carlos in 1943–4 and a school of economics had only been founded in 1934 (that of humanities was not set up until 1945, some 269 years after the institution was established), it should be noted that most of these were enrolled on a part-time basis and had daytime jobs, which gave them much greater contact and influence with the middle-class population at large.

67. The famed '*Memorial de los 311*' declared, 'Guatemala cannot remove itself from the democratic imperatives of the era. It is impossible to frustrate with coercive means the

uncontainable impulses of that generous ideology which is being reaffirmed in the world's conscience by means of the bloodiest of struggles between oppression and liberty.' The full text is given in Galich, *Por Que Lucha Guatemala*, pp. 334–6.

68. Affeld to Washington, 17 October 1944, USNA, 814.00 10–1744.

69. Details of the revolt are given in Grieb, 'Military', and *Ubico*; Galich, *Por Que Lucha Guatemala*; Aybar, *Dependency and Intervention*; Handy, *Gift of the Devil*.

70. Although, after an initial spending spree, the military's portion of the national budget fell from 16.5 per cent in 1943 to 9.4 per cent in 1954, virtually all *jefes políticos* during this period were army officers. Jim Handy discusses the question of a 'generational' division within the institution, tending away from Grieb's emphasis on this as a key political factor. *Gift of the Devil*, p. 134. It is certainly the case that the Guatemalan army lacked the central role and resources given to its counterpart in Argentina by Perón, its backwardness being enhanced by the US arms boycott after 1948. Nonetheless, one should not underestimate the influence of nationalist ideas as a complement to continued participation in public administration and an impediment to untempered reaction. If, as claimed by Mario Monteforte Toledo, the officer corps was unambiguously opposed to the revolution by 1954, one still has to account for the remarkable fact that, contrary to every other example of bonapartist rule in Latin America in this period, it acquiesced in the legalization of the Communist Party and even accepted the congressional impeachment of one of its leaders for suppressing the PGT's paper. Nor should it be forgotten that in 1954 the officer corps was reluctant to move against Arbenz.

71. Although in the early stages of the revolution both the FPL and RN were dominated by the middle class, the FPL had a wider mass following. The PAR developed as a more radical alternative but despite being colonized by the Communists never advanced beyond the limits of a nationalist reformism. In the congressional poll of 1949 – the first to be contested by a field of clearly distinguishable parties – the right won 15 seats, FPL 30, RN 5, PAR 10, and independents 3. When the Communists quit the PAR in May 1950 it divided into three bickering factions.

72. Even the most trenchant anti-Communist propaganda tended to distinguish Arévalo from Arbenz, depicting the former as a misguided idealist rather than a fellow traveller. The State Department came to view him as less a dupe than an increasingly powerless individual, unable to contain the rise of the left. In 1945 there were still fears that he might be a convinced radical but a dispatch from the US embassy on Buenos Aires soon put them right: '. . . it is my considered opinion that anyone reasonably well informed about his teachings, writings and general activities would be inclined to pass over such suspicions as being so utterly without foundation as to call for no response.' USNA, 814.00/1–1345.

73. Juan José Arévalo, *Escritos Políticos*, Guatemala City 1945, p. 199.

74. We still lack a consolidated treatment of the response of the rural population to this partial devolution of power, but the synoptic survey given by Ricardo Falla, 'Evolución Político-Religiosa', suggests a complex pattern of adjustment.

75. Handy, *Gift of the Devil*, p. 125.

76. Arévalo more than tripled rural teachers' wages, the education budget rising from \$1.6 million in 1944 to \$4.2 million in 1947. Yet the total number of registered pupils only rose from 130,802 to 174,890 during this period. Suslow, *Social Reform*, pp. 15, 24–5.

77. The modernizing zeal of the middle-class reformists should not be underemphasized but, as evidence of the activity of one 'Misión Ambulante de Cultura Inicial' suggests, it possessed very limited resources with which to contend with formidable structures of backwardness: 'For the concerts given on Saturday afternoons, the Mission played records of a guitar and the town pharmacist sang with the medical student into a microphone attached to a portable loudspeaker situated in the town square. Schoolgirls sang songs or recited poems through the microphone. Only ten or twelve of the townspeople usually gathered around the goings-on but the loudspeaker carried the voices of the participants throughout the village . . . Lieutenant Galich read excerpts from the new Constitution during the concerts in order to make the people aware of a national loyalty with its corresponding rights and duties. At the bingo games about eight *ladinos* played with numbered cards, instead of the pictures used by most professional bingo games in Guatemala which hope to attract a large population of Indian customers. One third of the winnings of the games is collected as tax in order to provide meals for visiting soccer teams.' Ibid., p. 35. A more deadly threat to western

civilization could scarcely be imagined.

78. By 1950 the number of state employees had risen to 15,500, and by 1954 to 22,300, more than the country's manufacturing labour force. Adams, *Crucifixion by Power*, p. 149. The revenue for this expansion was raised through traditional means, over three-quarters of state receipts in 1949 deriving from import and consumption taxes and income from government enterprises, less than 6 per cent from export taxes and less than 2 per cent from levies on property. The absence of an income tax, which might be thought to be essential in forging a capitalist democracy, is unsurprising given the vulnerability of the middle class to such a measure. This largely accounted for the absence of such a tax in the Second Spanish Republic and lay behind the ability of the Guatemalan congress to evacuate Arbenz's proposal for such a levy of any real force. Although more than a fifth of the 1949 budget was allocated to 'development', total domestic expenditure per capita was still lower than in 1939 and the budget deficit kept to less than 3 per cent of income by completely conventional means of fiscal management. J. Antonio Palacios, 'Formas de Redistribución del Ingreso en Guatemala', *El Trimestre Económico*, vol. 19, no. 3, July–September 1952, pp. 423, 441–2; International Bank for Reconstruction and Development (World Bank), *The Economic Development of Guatemala*, Baltimore 1951, pp. 20–1. One of the most important immediate results of the expansion of the central state apparatus was the holding of the 1950 census, which provided the statistical basis for the 1952 agrarian reform, and in its zealous itemization of computable indices of national life logged 68 per cent of couples as joined in common-law unions, 63 per cent of the population as barefoot, 12.4 per cent wearing sandals, and only 24.3 per cent wearing shoes – an example of progress revealing its own limits. Nathan L. Whetten, *Guatemala. The Land and the People*, New Haven 1961, pp. 186, 242.

79. Torres Rivas, 'La Sociedad de Postguerra', p. 22.

80. Torres Rivas, 'Industrialization', p. 17. The revolutionary epoch witnessed the establishment of a number of commercial and manufacturing entrepreneurial associations as well as the revitalization of landlord organization. Table 6.1 in Adams, *Crucifixion by Power*.

81. INFOP was capitalized with Q6.5 million and provided loans of Q7 million a year. J.H. Adler et al., *Public Finance and Economic Development in Guatemala*, Los Angeles 1952, p. 266.

82. For details of the code, see Balcárcel, 'Movimiento Obrero', pp. 31–2; Brian Murphy, 'The Stunted Growth of *Campesino* Organizations', in Adams, *Crucifixion by Power*, pp. 443–4.

83. Murphy, '*Campesino* Organizations', p. 444. Two of these were on UFCO estates, three on the '*fincas nacionales*' created from the expropriated German properties, and six on private plantations.

84. In June 1948 the stipulations of the code for the countryside were brought into line with those for the urban sector. The US embassy's campaign on behalf of UFCO on this matter can be seen as the first major step in what was soon to be a forthright opposition to economic policy. It should be noted that the State Department's own labour section counselled against open attacks on the code, and the World Bank developed and publicly favoured much more substantial limitations to UFCO's power. The irony of UFCO's campaign against the code, which in its initial form would have affected twenty-nine other agricultural enterprises, was that it led to much wider rural unionization.

85. The law was in part a response to hurricane damage, but it still represented a significant alteration of productive relations in the rented sector, particularly in the *ladino* zones of the east of the country where tenant farming was more common. Murphy, *Campesino* Organizations', p. 445; Whetten, *Guatemala*, p. 153.

86. Although Arévalo's government intervened to end strikes by IRCA and Tiquisate workers in 1946 and 1948–49, UFCO came under heavy pressure on both economic and political fronts. Tax concessions granted by Ubico lost the Guatemalan treasury some Q356,000 in 1948 but under the US Western Hemisphere Trade Act the company was still liable to an overall 24 per cent US tax on its locally untaxed income; thus the local exemption was quite rightly viewed as a Guatemalan subsidization of the US state. Production and investment levels were only substantially reduced after 1950, by which time it is estimated that the company was making a loss on its Guatemalan operation despite a reduction in the labour force from 15,697 in 1946 to 9,795 in 1954. Increased labour costs cannot be advanced as the central

cause for this slump, which seems to be more closely linked to a constant divestment from 1951. This may well have been politically inspired, but it should be borne in mind that UFCO was simultaneously running down its Honduran operation. Richard Allen LaBarge, 'Impact of the United Fruit Company on the Economic Development of Guatemala, 1946–1954', in *Studies in Middle American Economics*, New Orleans 1968; Frederick B. Pike, 'Guatemala, the United States, and Communism in the Americas', *The Review of Politics*, vol. 17, no. 2, April 1955, pp. 238–9.

87. While there is general agreement that rural wages rose appreciably, regional and seasonal differences make it difficult to identify an overall rate. Moreover, even the new minimum wage was not always paid entirely in cash. Pearson, 'Peasant Union Movement', p. 336; Mario Monteforte Toledo, 'La Reforma Agraria en Guatemala', *El Trimestre Económico*, vol. 19, no. 3, July–September 1952, p. 393.

88. The figures for production, import and export of beans and corn given by Aybar, *Dependency and Intervention*, p. 212, show stable production levels but much reduced imports, which could well indicate an increase in peasant consumption outside the market.

89. Reference is often made to an article in *New Republic*, 20 June 1951, in which a US journalist reports being told, 'Now we are free. We are equal to *ladinos*. . . . No one can force us to work on a coffee plantation far away against our will. We will only go if we want to.' Quoted in Handy, *Gift of the DEvil*, p. 124; Immerman, *CIA in Guatemala*, pp. 56–7. Handy stresses the late formation and limited power of the rural unions. Frederick Pike's interpretation of this is typical of the ideological mode of the day and close to the perception of the State Department: 'Fortunately, the Indian peasants, denied since time immemorial the right of political articulateness, were psychologically incapable of assuming the fanatical devotion to the Communist Party aspired for by Mexican agents. Political interest has never been part of the docile . . . Indian's outlook.' 'Guatemala, US, Communism', p. 243.

90. For details of the unions at the Tiquisate plantation (STEG), Puerto Barrios (SETUFCO) and on the IRCA, see Murphy, '*Campesino* Organizations', p. 443; Balcárcel, 'Movimiento Obrero', pp. 30 ff; Schneider, *Communism*, p. 27. Although wages at both Tiquisate and Puerto Barrios were higher than the national average, working conditions were very poor, and efforts to lay off workers produced disputes throughout the decade. Outside the banana industry there was much less open conflict, but outbursts of violence, such as that at El Tumbador, San Marcos, in 1948, and more general discontent, such as that in 1949 which played a part in prompting the Law of Forced Rental, contributed to rising apprehension on the part of landlords whose notions of *campesino* 'passivity' were rather more restricted than those of rural sociologists.

91. Pearson, 'Peasant Union Movement', p. 350; Murphy, '*Campesino* Organizations', p. 445.

92. Pearson presents a figure of 1,500 unions on 1,408 large plantations (those with either a population of more than one hundred or an annual production of over two hundred quintals). Estates of this size were concentrated in Alta Verapaz, Escuintla, San Marcos, Santa Rosa, Suchitepéquez and Quezaltenango, but there is no direct correspndence with the number of unions on a regional basis. 'Peasant Union Movement', p. 351. For union recognition, see Murphy, '*Campesino* Organisations', p. 447.

93. The figurehead of the CNCG was Leonardo Castillo Flores, a schoolteacher in his twenties, and although the union's popular organizer, Amor Velasco de León, was an agricultural worker from Huehuetenango, the bulk of the national leadership were from the middle class. For short biographies, see ibid., pp. 347–50. It is noteworthy that many of these people had previously worked with the CTG, with which relations deteriorated in 1950 over the CTG's reluctance to organize non-plantation rural workers and its subsequent holding of a '*campesino* congress' in an effort to pre-empt Castillo's initiative.

94. Murphy, '*Campesino* Organizations', pp. 446–8.

95. For details of the dispute, see Pearson, 'Peasant Union Movement', pp. 346–8.

96. Balcárcel, 'Movimiento Obrero', pp. 34–40; Handy, *Gift of the Devil*, p. 118. The railway workers' union, SAMF, withdrew with nine others to form the *Federación Sindical de Guatemala* (FSG) in 1946, rejoining the rest of the movement in 1952.

97. Gutiérrez, a schoolteacher born in Santa Rosa in 1922, headed a CTG leadership that was almost entirely under thirty years of age and middle-class in origin. Its establishment

of a quasi-party, *Vanguardia Democrática*, gave the radicals a caucus inside the PAR that was eventually transformed into the PGT. For details of this and background to the principal figures, see Schneider, *Communism*, pp. 40, 90–5; Balcárcel, 'Movimiento Obrero', pp. 35–41.

98. Even US military intelligence was reluctant to make a direct arraignment out of the implications of its internal investigation. Immerman suggests the possibility of a right-wing plot to implicate Arbenz, *CIA in Guatemala*, p. 60.

99. See, in particular, Schlesinger and Kinzer, *Bitter Fruit;* Aybar de Soto, *Dependency and Intervention*; Immerman, *CIA in Guatemala*. Synoptic surveys are given in NACLA, *Guatemala* and Handy, *Gift of the Devil*.

100. 'It would appear our ultimate objective should be to reduce or destroy the influence of pro-Communists by bringing about their political separation and isolation from non-Communist elements which they are now using and which supply principal source of their strength. To accomplish this Department believes we should carefully avoid actions or statements which tend lump pro-Communists and non-Communists together and give them reason to make common cause. We should also avoid providing . . . alleged foreign pressure which moderates would have to join in opposing or be left in untenable position of appearing unpatriotic.' Acheson telegram to US embassy, Guatemala, 5 May 1950. USNA 611.14/5–550. 'President Arbenz himself is essentially an opportunist whose politics are largely a matter of historical accident.' National Intelligence Estimate, 11 March 1952, *Foreign Relations*, p. 1033.

101. As late as June 1951 Deputy Assistant Secretary of State Thomas Mann was reported as telling a departmental meeting that economic pressure should be undertaken cautiously: 'He emphasized that we should proceed quietly since this proposed policy is, in effect, a violation of the Non-Intervention Agreement [of Rio, 1947] to which we are a party.' USNA, Under-Secretary's Meetings, Lot 53, D 250. Although in August 1953 a State Department draft policy paper noted that, 'in Guatemala Communism has achieved its strongest position in Latin America, and is now well advanced on a program which threatens important American commercial enterprises . . . [and would] ultimately endanger the unity of the Western Hemisphere against Soviet aggression', its authors also noted that, 'the use of direct military or economic sanctions on Guatemala would violate solemn US commitments and under present circumstances would endanger the entire fund of goodwill the US has built up in other American republics through its policies of non-intervention, respect for judicial equality, and abnegation of a position of privilege. Loss of this goodwill would be a disaster for the US far outweighing the advantage of any success gained in Guatemala.' The paper went on to support a policy of 'firm persuasion' based on regional diplomatic pressure. This, however, was already a minority position inside the US government and effectively over-ruled by Foster Dulles, Draft Policy Paper, NSC Guatemala, 19 August 1953, *Foreign Relations*, pp. 1083–4.

102. A consolidated depiction of this process is given in LaFeber, *Inevitable Revolutions*, pp. 85–126. The businessman Francis Adams Truslow prefigured Kirkpatrick's 'double standards' at a meeting of the New York Council on Foreign Relations early in 1949 when he defended Somoza's dictatorship as acceptable in that although it 'involves autocratic rule', it was not totalitarian, which would be objectionable because it was 'autocratic rule, plus total, absolute control of economic life'. Quoted in ibid., p. 104. While there is no need to insist upon the moral bankruptcy, internal inconsistency and cynical exploitation of such a position, it should be emphasized that it has continued to have purchase since the late 1940s, albeit in a suppressed form under the Alliance for Progress in the 1960s and, briefly, during Carter's human rights phase of 1977–79. Late in the 1950s a respected US political scientist could opine without fear of shame that, 'under the retarded circumstances of Central American life, dictatorship – if competently administered and genuinely concerned with national progress – has an important role to play.' John D. Martz, *Central America. The Crisis and the Challenge*, Chapel Hill 1959, p. 19.

103. Peurifoy to Washington, 17 December 1953. USNA 611.14/12–1753. A week later Peurifoy telegrammed the State Department: 'I am convinced Communists will continue gain strength here as long as [Arbenz] remains in office.' 611.14/12–2353. Peurifoy, who as ambassador in Athens had directed the liquidation of the Communist partisans in Greece, was assigned to Guatemala as a 'trouble-shooter', his lack of Spanish and knowledge of the region being secondary to his skill in organizing anti-Communist operations. However, it was a sign

of the times that he still fell under Joseph McCarthy's gaze as a suspiciously 'un-American' character. Would that this were the case! Yet even if the junior senator from Wisconsin had proceeded further against Peurifoy there would have been no lack of replacements at a time when a supposedly sober career officer diplomat such as his predecessor Patterson could enchant a rotary club meeting with his methodology for identifying the enemy: 'Many times it is impossible to prove legally that a certain individual is a Communist; but for cases of this sort I recommend a practical method of detection – the "duck test". The duck test works this way: suppose you see a bird walking around in a farm yard. This bird wears no label that says "duck". But the bird certainly looks like a duck. Also he goes to the pond and you notice he swims like a duck. Then he opens his beak and quacks. Well, by this time you have probably reached the conclusion that the bird is a duck, whether he's wearing a label or not.' Quoted in Immerman, 'Cold War History', p. 637. It was advances such as this in the theories of cognition and amateur ornithology that underpinned the establishment of a regime under which some 100,000 Guatemalans were killed over thirty years. It should, though, be noted that in the early 1950s the 'duck test' was not limited to Guatemala, it being employed by the Catholic bishop of Nairobi at the time of the Mau Mau rebellion. *Memoirs of Lord Chandos*, London 1964, pp. 400–1. My thanks to Cliff Barnes for drawing my attention to this fact.

104. Estimates of the size of the Communist Party vary. In 1952 the State Department assessed its strength at no more than 500, and in 1953 at less than 1,000 members, of whom half were active. Mario Monteforte Toledo, who had a much closer knowledge, puts its size at around 1,300. There is no immediate evidence from the papers available in the US National Archives that the CIA maintained agents inside the PGT, but if this were the case it is unlikely that documentary proof would have been 'declassified'. National Intelligence Estimate, 11 March 1952; 19 May 1953, *Foreign Relations*, pp. 1033, 1065. Monteforte Toledo, *Guatemala*, p. 316.

105. In addition to some 250 Spanish émigrés, the youthful Guatemalan movement drew on the experience of Salvadorean veterans of 1932 (Abel and Max Cuenca and Pedro Rivas), Gabriela García from Honduras, Lombardo Toledano from Mexico, and visits from Pablo Neruda and several other Chilean Communists with whom Arbenz's wife, María Cristina Vilanova, had close contacts although not herself a militant. The appearance in Guatemala City of the young Argentine Ernesto Guevara was of more importance to subsequent developments of the Latin American revolutionary heritage than to the fortification of Guatemalan Marxism. -Guevara stayed in the country until the counter–revolution and was profoundly affected by it. Visits of local Communists to Moscow were, as logged by the CIA, not particularly frequent. There is no obvious indication that the PGT drew on the works of the early Peruvian Communist Mariátegui, whose writings on the peasant question would have been of far greater value than the schemas emanating from Moscow.

106. Gutiérrez disliked Fortuny as much as he was suspicious of his political leanings. His departure from the PAR was both in solidarity with militants expelled for rejecting entryism and, even as early as November 1949 when he himself was battling with the burgeoning peasant union leadership, over Fortuny's supposed obstruction of agrarian work and failure to stress the political independence of the working class. There can be little doubt that Gutiérrez's departure obliged Fortuny to take the party out of the PAR. At this stage Fortuny had just returned from a trip to Moscow and argued that the CPSU's position on agrarian reform was not applicable to 'colonial states' and that the central thrust of political work should be along the lines laid down by Zhdanov at the establishment of the Cominform in 1947: 'the struggle against imperialism; against war and for national sovereignty and peace'. Schneider, *Communism*, p. 58–9.

107. The attempt of Minister of Interior Colonel Monzón to suppress *Octubre* led to his interpellation in congress and resignation. While Fortuny was able to draw on such support from a parliament in which his comrades had no representation, Gutiérrez had succeeded in healing the divisions in the union movement, and won key leaders of the FSG to the PROG, which declared that the revolution had to 'enter a second era in which the economic power of the imperialists and reactionaries would be curbed'. This much more aggressive line had the support of the majority of the leadership of the urban workers' movement and clearly compelled a rapprochement on the part of the PCG.

108. This trip followed the failure of an attempt at mediation by Lombardo Toledano in 1951. The fifth plenum rejected a collectivist agrarian reform and the 'democratic' model of

Eastern Europe, on the grounds that no assault on private property was possible 'until power is in the hands of the alliance of workers and peasants, that is to say, the establishment of a popular-democratic regime or a socialist regime.' Schneider, *Communism*, p. 75. It should be noted that Gutiérrez's group in the CTG still held to classic formulations of the historical balance between the working class and the peasantry and was far from Maoist in orientation: 'the working class . . . is the only one that can instantly direct the battle of the peasants for the conquest of their goals: bread and land. Because of this, the peasants ought to align themselves with the working class and be the great ally and reserve of the proletariat.' *Materiales del Congreso General de la CTG*, May 1950. When, two weeks later, the CNCG was established, it stated that, 'the CNCG recognizes that as a class organ it is a functional ally of the proletariat in the struggle for economic liberation.' Quoted in Pearson, 'Peasant Union Movement', p. 348.

109. At the sixth plenum in June 1952 Fortuny argued that the case of Guatemala with respect to agrarian reform was most closely paralleled by that of the US prior to the civil war, and that it was necessary to create a stratum of small peasant farmers. For details of the second congress, at which Fortuny claimed that 13 per cent of the PGT's membership were peasants, see Schneider, *Communism*, pp. 79–80.

110. This particular point was raised in the PGT's self-criticism of 1955 that identified the general line as having been correct but held that the party had not been sufficiently independent of the 'national bourgeoisie' and overestimated the capacity of that sector to resist imperialism; that united front work had been directed at the leadership rather than the rank and file of allied political forces; that peasant work had been under-played (although this is not projected as a central shortcoming); and – perhaps unsurprisingly, given that the Twentieth Congress of the CPSU had yet to occur and unhinge at least some of the catechisms of the world movement – that bourgeois revisionism had infected the party. PGT, *La Intervención Norteamericana en Guatemala y el Derrocamiento del Régimen Democrático*, 1955. For a Trotskyist critique of the PGT prior to the counter-revolution, see Ismael Frías, 'La Révolution Guatemaltèque', *Quatrième Internationale*, vol. 12, nos. 2/3, March–May 1954. Fortuny was ousted as general secretary in May 1954 and replaced by Bernardo Alvarado Monzón, who presided over a more collective form of leadership which the following year removed Fortuny from all positions (but not the party itself), a move that was no doubt facilitated by his proclivity for 'bourgeois weaknesses' as well as his opposition to an 'excessively radical' orientation. By the late 1960s Fortuny was back in favour, without having altered his views significantly. 'Guatemala: The Political Situation and Revolutionary Tactics', WMR, vol. 10, no. 2, Feb. 1967. Gutiérrez was killed by the military in 1966, Alvarado Monzón in 1972.

111. World Bank, *Economic Development of Guatemala*, p. 144. The chief of the mission, Canadian economist G.E. Britnell, wrote, 'the monopoly possessed by UFCO and IRCA, of both rail transportation and pier facilities at the country's principal port, to which the rest of the Republic has no access by road, inevitably gives rise to charges of discrimination of all kinds. . . . It would be a mistake . . . to neglect the fact that nationalism, inflamed by the arrogance of North American capitalism and fanned by a well-entrenched Communist movement, is probably the most important factor in the economic development of the country today.' 'Underdeveloped Countries: The Theory and Practice of Technical Assistance: Factors in the Economic Development of Guatemala', *American Economic Review*, vol. 43, no. 2, May 1953, pp. 110, 112.

112. Ibid.

113. Quoted in Aybar, *Dependency and Intervention*, p. 168. The PAR declared the reform to be 'the fundamental prerequisite of all the economic, political and social reforms of the October Revolution. No democratic conquest will be stable or permanent without the previous achievement of agrarian reform.' Quoted in Handy, *Gift of the Devil*, p. 124. It should be stressed that Article 1 of the law declared that its primary objective was 'to develop a capitalist economy amongst the peasantry and in agriculture generally'.

114. For details of the background to the reform, see Monteforte Toledo, 'Reforma Agraria'; Pearson, 'Peasant Union Movement'.

115. Quoted in Handy, *Gift of the Devil*, p. 124.

116. Ibid., p. 127. For further details of the 1950 census, see Monteforte Toledo, 'Reforma Agraria'; NACLA *Guatemala*.

117. Whetten, *Guatemala*, p. 163; Pearson, 'Peasant Union Movement', p. 343.

118. Pearson, 'Peasant Union Movement', p. 343, gives details of the forms of land affected by the reform. It should be noted that while there is some dispute over the exact scope, it is agreed that this was less than allowed for in the statute.

119. Ibid. Recipients of land from the state sector received lifetime leases only; a mere 14 per cent of all recipients received full freehold title to land.

120. Wasserstrom, 'Peasants and Politics under Arbenz', p. 475.

121. For details of the UFCO campaign, see Schlesinger and Kinzer, *Bitter Fruit*. The high proportion of uncultivated land cannot be explained solely by the traditional practice of keeping fallow as a guarantee against sigatoka and Panama disease, and probably corresponds to a greater degree of UFCO's general policy of pre-empting competition by purchasing the best potential banana lands.

122. See, for example, National Intelligence Estimate, 19 May 1953.

123. Pearson, 'Peasant Union Movement', p. 341, where he rebuts Schneider's claims of an extensive PGT presence in the reform. The PGT was most active in the Pacific departments, where figures such as Carlos Pellecer certainly attracted attention with their activities but failed to build a mass following.

124. Schlesinger and Kinzer, both working journalists, pay great attention to the manipulation of the press, particularly by Edward Bernays, who was employed by UFCO largely on the basis of having been the pioneer of mass-marketing techniques in the 1920s and 1930s. The Guatemalans were themselves sharply aware of this campaign but their complaints to the US embassy received an indulgent rejoinder to the effect that in an advanced democratic state no single corporation could determine press content. Peurifoy to Washington, 17 December 1953. USNA 611.14/12–1753. It should be remarked that a figure such as Herbert Matthews, who did so much to project Fidel Castro's campaign against Batista to the US public, was resolutely anti-Communist in his coverage of Guatemala. A sense of the hysteria built upon a truly remarkable patchwork of downright lies and tendentious comment can be gleaned from Professor Martz's scholarly comments five years later: 'Veteran newsmen who visited Buchenwald and Dachau in the last days of Hitler's Reich testified to the brutality of the Guatemalan security forces. . . . Many families retain the memory of loved ones tortured or executed by the Red regime. . . . It is superfluous to repeat the innumerable proofs that Guatemala under Arbenz was Communist, undemocratic and almost totally cynical.' *Central America*, pp. 27, 57, 59. Following the counter-revolution a number of lurid publications appeared depicting cadavers alleged to be victims of the Arbenz government. While there was undoubtedly a degree of bloodletting in July 1954, the great bulk of it was at the hands of the invaders, the 'innumerable proofs' cited by Professor Martz putting one in mind of similar concoctions produced by the US administration in the 1980s and shown by a press community hardened by the experience of Vietnam to be less than nimble falsifications by a government never backward in peddling falsehoods.

125. Details of the international campaign undertaken by the US are given in LaFeber, *Inevitable Revolutions*, pp. 111–25; Frank Parkinson, *Latin America, the Cold War, and the World Powers*, Beverly Hills 1974; Cole Blasier, *The Hovering Giant*, Pittsburgh 1976, in addition to the sources cited for the intervention itself.

126. For the role of the Church, the establishment of which still remained weak and was recognized by the State Department as such, see the chapter by Bruce Calder in Adams, *Crucifixion by Power*. Falla, 'Evolución Político-Religiosa', notes a proclivity for the now quite substantial Protestant community in the countryside to favour the regime, a position which was subsequently reversed into a staunch conservatism.

127. There was some scattered resistance in Guatemala City, but elsewhere supporters of the regime were rapidly subdued in a disorderly repression in which many extra-political scores were settled. For local examples, see John Gillin and K.H. Silvert, 'Ambiguities in Guatemala', *Foreign Affairs*, vol. 34, no. 3, April 1956, and Falla, 'Evolución Político-Religiosa'. Some light is thrown on the repression by Richard Adams who, arriving in Guatemala City shortly after Castillo Armas, set about applying the scientific norms of North American sociology to the population of overcrowded gaols to discern levels of Communist influence amongst the peasantry. An instructive piece of literature for those who believe that detailed mathematical analysis of questionnaire responses provides the future for social science, Adams's essay fell foul of the obvious 'strategy' of his interlocutors in saying the safest thing that entered their heads –

although 'only' 17 per cent were 'hostile' – and the less predictable inconvenience of his sample being reduced by the release of prisoners against whom no firm charge could be sustained. In fairness to the author, it should be said that both his politics and his methodology were far from unique at the time. Nonetheless, the article appeared under the pseudonym of Stokes Newbold: 'Receptivity to Communist Fomented Agitation in Rural Guatemala', *Economic Development and Cultural Change*, vol. 5, no. 2, January 1957.

128. This is not the place to engage in a comparative analysis although a more profound survey along such lines would be of great interest. The MNR regime in Bolivia was broadly supportive of Arbenz, but by 1954 was already reversing the initial radical thrust of the Revolution of April 1952. James Dunkerley, *Rebellion in the Veins. Political Struggle in Bolivia, 1952–1982*, London 1984.

5

Uneven Development, 1950–80

It's back-breaking work, and you couldn't get a single person in California to do it, especially for $2.80 a day. . . . If you can pay a worker thirty-five cents an hour, why buy a tractor?

Del Monte executive, Guatemala[1]

One cannot destroy the entrepreneurial spirit without creating greater poverty. . . . Used as a political instrument, agrarian reform only makes any sense within a class struggle wherein it is intended to destroy the power of one class in order to transfer it to another.

Asociación Nacional de la Empresa Privada, El Salvador, July 1976[2]

El Salvador's greatest advantage lies in the character of the working people, who are industrious, adapt willingly to new methods and demand lower wages than those prevailing in the developed world. It is said that if you tell Salvadorans to plant rocks and harvest more rocks, they'll do it . . .

Rand Corporation Report to the US Department of Commerce, 1981[3]

With the launching of the Alliance for Progress in 1961, the role of the United States in Central American development underwent a major transformation. This was a bold and unprecedented effort to encourage comprehensive national planning and to promote a wide array of social, political, tax and land reforms. . . . The goals of the Alliance were three: economic growth, structural change in societies, and political democratization. But . . . it was only in the first area that significant progress was made.

Kissinger Report, January 1984[4]

Nobody in their right mind could plausibly refute the view that the Central American conflict is rooted in the economic structure of the region. Even the 'interpretation' of the present crisis which holds that it is the product of a Russo–Cuban conspiracy accepts that inequitable distribution of wealth and the progressive impoverishment of the great mass of the isthmian populace provided propitious terrain for the Reds' first substantial sortie into mainland America since Guatemala. Knowledge that social conditions prevailing in San Miguel, El Salvador, are profoundly distinct from those in Muncie, Indiana, is too widespread within the US public to have permitted Washington's 'great communicator' much success in peddling a Disneyland picture of plump peasants affably awaiting the arrival of the man from Del Monte, only to be ambushed by bearded aliens whose antipathy for the boss excites nothing but fear and contempt. It is, though, rather too easy to respond to the more asinine variations of the domino theory issuing from the White House with the assertion that the people of the region have rebelled simply because they are poor.

There is, of course, a common acceptance in theories of revolution ranging from the contradictions of the Marxist canon to the rationalist calculus of North American social science that people do not rebel solely on the basis of poverty, not even when they are very poor and getting poorer. Nevertheless, it is one thing to stipulate an inexorable logic between increasing immiseration and popular revolt and quite another to see that the accelerating tendency of the Central American political economy over the post-war period has been to deepen both the social and political contradictions at the heart of the productive system, it seeming far from illogical to many people affected by this process to resort to extreme activity in order to defend their basic interests.

As Table 4a shows very clearly, between 1950 and 1980 the economy of Central America grew considerably; the population more than doubled and production rose more than fourfold. Even if we leave aside the basis, character and effects of this growth, it is evident that any notion that the contemporary political struggles have been exacerbated by a prolonged and uniform experience of stagnation is misplaced. In none of the countries is the rise of production or population significantly out of balance with the regional pattern of expansion. Moreover, it is only in Nicaragua during the 1970s that population growth overtakes that of GDP (Table 4b), suggesting that the figurative race between production and people was won by the forces of production, although by a markedly less wide margin in the 1970s than in the prior decade.

This progress would also seem to be confirmed by expansion in the region's infrastructure, which, although unevenly distributed and manifestly modest by global standards, reflects both increased production and the consolidation of some allied characteristics of modernization (Table 4c).

Table 4a: Size of the Economy, 1950–80

	Population[1] *(thousands)*	*Urban Population (total)*	*Urban Pop. (%)*	*GDP*[2] *($ million)*
Central America				
1950	8,082	1,300	16	1,955.1
1980	20,696	8,904	43	8,260.0
Costa Rica				
1950	801	208	26	257.3
1980	2,213	1,015	46	1,592.0
El Salvador				
1950	1,856	334	18	376.9
1980	4,797	2,130	44	1,526.0
Guatemala				
1950	3,006	421	14	767.1
1980	7,262	2,791	38	3,067.0
Honduras				
1950	1,369	137	10	320,2
1980	3,691	1,484	40	1,011.0
Nicaragua				
1950	1,050	200	19	233.6
1980	2,733	1,484	54	1,064.0

Notes:

1. 1980 – estimates.
2. Millions of 1970 dollars; 1950 and 1978.

Source: Román Mayorga Quirós, *El Crecimiento Desigual en Centroamérica*, Mexico 1983, pp.11, 12.

Indeed, even when the statistical focus is narrowed somewhat in terms of GDP and income per capita, it can be seen that whether calculated in terms of the value of the dollar at the beginning of the period or that at the end of it, the general balance between people and total wealth follows a very modestly progressive pattern until the end of the 1970s (Tables 5a and 5b).[5] Although by the standards of the advanced capitalist states these figures are impressively low even before allowance for grossly inequitable distribution of income, they represent an overall advance in quantum terms from all previous indices of wealth per head in the isthmus. The statistics in Table 5a show that growth in the Honduran economy over some thirty-five years of unparalleled technological and material progress on a world scale amounted to an astounding $25 per head per annum and that in El Salvador to no more than $11 (a figure that, like that for Nicaragua in 1979, is somewhat anomalous in that it reflects the impact of political turmoil and civil war).

Table 4b: Growth of the Economy, 1950–79

	Annual Average GDP[1] *(%; 1970 prices)*	*Annual Average*[2] *Population (%)*
Central America		
1950–9	4.9	3.3
1960–9	6.2	3.3
1970–9	4.5	3.1
Costa Rica		
1950–9	6.8	4.2
1960–9	6.8	3.3
1970–9	5.8	2.5
El Salvador		
1950–9	4.8	3.0
1960–9	6.1	4.0
1970–9	4.7	3.0
Guatemala		
1950–9	4.0	3.3
1960–9	5.4	3.1
1970–9	5.8	3.1
Honduras		
1950–9	3.3	3.2
1960–9	5.3	3.3
1970–9	3.6	3.4
Nicaragua		
1950–9	5.6	3.2
1960–9	7.5	3.3
1970–9	2.5	2.6

Notes:

1. Versions vary appreciably; for an alternative table, see Victor Bulmer-Thomas, 'Economic Development over the Long Run', JLAS, vol.15, November 1983, p.272.
2. Population – 1950–60; 1960–70; 1970–80.

Sources: Statistical Abstract of Latin America, Berkeley 1974; John Weeks, *The Economies of Central America*, New York 1985, p.41; Héctor Pérez Brignoli, 'Growth and Crisis in the Central American Economies, 1950–1980', JLAS, vol.15, November 1983, p.366.

Table 4c: Growth of Infrastructure, c.1950–c.1975

		Region	*C.Rica*	*El Sal.*	*Guate.*	*Hon.*	*Nica.*
Paved road (km)	1953	1,263	497	373	205		188
	1975	8,909	1,939	1,408	2,638	1,327	1,597
Automobiles	1953	57,816	10,585	15,704	16,704	7,074	8,200
	1976	236,000	59,800	41,000	82,700	20,500	32,000
Electricity	1950	50	130	39	26	29	29
(kilowatt per cap.)	1976	391	791	291	200	201	475
Port capacity	1950	3,754	625	542	1,246	867	474
(mm tons)	1977	10,811	2,644	1,771	2,075	2,319	2,002
Railways	1945	4,646	1,276	612	1,150	1,259	347
(km)	1970	4,243	1,042	696	1,109	1,018	378
Aviation	1960	14,445	3,766	3,100	2,082	3,121	946
(000 km flown)	1970	34,538	5,978	5,900	4,850	10,530	2,240
Telephones	1953	42,358	10,589	15,012	6,421	7,017	3,487
	1978	356,897	145,069	70,400	70,614	14,984	55,830
Radios	1953	22	35	22	24	12	20
(sets per 1,000)	1976	156	75	333	43	49	280
Newspapers	1952	35	84	35	19	19	49
(per 1,000)	1975		88	39	51		26
Television stations (1967/8)		21	8	3	3	5	2
Sets per 1,000			42	14	13	4	14

Sources: Torres Rivas, 'Sociedad de Postguerra', pp.19; 22; Mayorga, *Crecimiento Desigual*, p.56; *Statistical Abstract*, pp.414; 416.

Table 5a: GDP per capita, 1949–82 (1950 dollars)

	Costa Rica	*El Salvador*	*Guatemala*	*Honduras*	*Nicaragua*
1949	286	185	220	152	182
1959	309	192	243	158	262
1969	390	256	300	175	363
1979	558	289	377	193	251
1982	493	196	353	177	263

Source: Bulmer-Thomas, 'Economic Development', p.276.

Table 5a: GDP per capita, 1949–82 (1950 dollars)

	Costa Rica	*El Salvador*	*Guatemala*	*Honduras*	*Nicaragua*
1949	286	185	220	152	182
1959	309	192	243	158	262
1969	390	256	300	175	363
1979	558	289	377	193	251
1982	493	196	353	177	263

Source: Bulmer-Thomas, 'Economic Development', p.276.

However, these figures can also be employed to demonstrate that until the onset of the current world recession there was at least no general downturn in production per head.

Table 6 vividly illustrates the insufficiencies of a ratio of production to population as a reflection of the real distribution of wealth. It is at this point that we gain a sharp sense of the structure of poverty within poor economies. Once one progresses from a simple subdivision of production by the number of humans to the depiction of real possession of wealth the numbers begin to lose some of their mystique. Even if one allows a generous margin of error for these estimates, they reveal that approximately half the population of the isthmus exists at a level of poverty comparable to that attributed to the entire society thirty five years ago, with an income only one quarter the size of the miserly average calculated per capita today. Both the sums involved and the enormous disparities between them confirm the existence of a mass of some ten million people in conditions of absolute penury. On this basis, the argument that the current turmoil in Central America stems from a human condition submerged in despair must quite manifestly be accepted.

The gap between the 'realities' presented in Tables 5a, 5b and 6 is more than that achieved by greater analytical specification. There is a quantum jump between the calculus of averages and concrete distribution of wealth. Tables 5a and 5b give a vivid depiction of the poverty of the regional and national economies as a whole but it is only a map of their parameters; it reflects the scope of the forces of production rather than the effects of the relations of production. Such an obvious fact is worthy of mention less as pedestrian guidance on a statistical tour than to register the limitations of analysis based primarily upon quantum forces. This is especially pertinent because a persistently popular feature of US policy towards both Central America and Latin America as a whole has been a preoccupation with the balance between aggregate resources and total human stock – the 'race'

Table 6: Income Distribution

Estimates for 1970 (% and Central American pesos of 1960 per head)

	lowest 50%		*middle 30%*		*high 15%*		*op 5%*		*average*
	%	*$*	*%*	*$*	*%*	*$*	*%*	*$*	*$*
C. America	13	74	26	246	30	568	31	1,760	284
Costa Rica	18	152	26	366	32	750	29	2,478	422
El Salvador	16	81	24	213	33	568	27	1,442	261
Guatemala	13	73	24	228	28	543	35	2,023	287
Honduras	13	52	24	164	30	401	33	1,349	202
Nicaragua	15	91	25	248	32	627	28	1,643	295

Source: Centroamérica Hoy, p.244.

Estimates for 1978 (% and 1970 dollars)

	% total income	*GDP per cap.*	*Population*
20% poorest	3.1	65.8	3,894,400
30% below median	12.9	182.4	5,841,600
30% above median	27.7	391.7	5,841,600
20% richest	56.3	1,194.1	3,894,400
of which 5% richest	27.9	2,367.0	973,600
average income		424.2	
total population			19,472,000

Source: Mayorga, *Crecimiento Desigual*, p.20.

mentioned above. It goes without saying that the productive capacity of all economies is of crucial importance, any diminution corresponding to increased poverty whatever the distribution of wealth. Nonetheless, it is possible to 'read' the relative health of an economy in a myriad of ways, and it has been an enduring characteristic of US government policy prescriptions for Central America's poverty that it be ameliorated through improvements in the ratio of production to population (Tables 5a and 5b) prior to those in distribution of income within that population (Table 6). The most familiar feature of this policy is its attachment to export-led growth as the key to success, but it should be noted that in this zone of the world such a prescription has over the last thirty years been supported by a Malthusian belief that it is not just the inadequacy of production but also an excessive human stock that underlies the problem.

Since the Alliance for Progress began in the early 1960s US planners have provided a remarkably persistent technocratic imprimatur to the popular prejudice that the root problem is 'too many people'. Even if this moral economy based its extraordinary presumptions solely on the mathematical averages in Tables 5a and 5b it would be perverse enough. However, its aversion to confronting the real imbalances of wealth within those nominal averages demonstrates that it is, in fact, less a crass and negligent diagnosis of the problem than a regressive form of social engineering. It is not the case that policy in this sphere has descended to the obnoxious lowest common denominator that is sometimes sloganistically attributed to it – cut people rather than increase wealth – but it has retained an active predilection for often coercive and deceitful birth-control programmes.[6] El Salvador, with a population density of 170 people per square kilometre – a level five times the regional average – has been a particular target for birth-control programmes.[7] These – it should be made scrupulously clear – are not by any means intrinsically objectionable and can be a nett gain for those who participate willingly, but any notion that curbs on the country's overall population growth will improve the general lot of the poor has to contend with the fact that since the war their share of national income has been progressively eroded in favour of the top 20 per cent rather than being reduced by a failure of production to keep pace with the number of heads (Tables 5a and 7).

When set in the context of economic growth as a whole, the failure to redistribute the fruits of this expansion to the mass of the population would seem to indicate without a shadow of doubt that the essential cause of social unrest lies within the countries themselves and revolves about the capacity of the landed bourgeoisie to impede any substantial reform of the liberal oligarchic model. However, we do not need to enter into a detailed discussion of the issues of 'underdevelopment', 'dependency' or 'combined and uneven development' – themselves the subject of a rich and prolonged debate largely generated in Latin America – to appreciate that the failure to achieve a comprehensive economic modernity is not exclusively attributable either to the internal configuration of productive forces and relations or to a monolithic determinism of the world market. It can, for instance, be seen that the adverse terms of trade for the region's agricultural exports preclude the development of an internal market by keeping wages low in the agro-export sector. Even, as in the case of Nicaragua, when the political power of the rural bourgeoisie is significantly reduced and the traditional dilemma between growth and redistribution is confronted on a resolute basis, the resulting 'transformation' in the agrarian sector has been partial and tenuous, revealing the structural confines of an impoverished economy still dependent upon a few staples for its foreign exchange earnings. On the other hand, the existence of this 'outer rationality' cannot alone account

Table 7: Distribution of Income in El Salvador

1976/7

Income bracket (colones/month)	*% of total income*	*% of total families*	*average income (family; colones/month)*
0–100	2.3	12.4	67.5
100–199	12.0	29.4	146.8
200–299	14.4	21.1	244.8
300–599	25.8	22.7	406.7
600–999	17.2	8.6	746.3
1,000–	28.3	6.2	1,621.8
average			358.0

Source: Ministerio de Planificación, 'Distribución del Ingreso y Gasto por deciles de Hogares, 1976–7', San Salvador 1981.

1946–71

Income group	*% of total income*		
	1946	*1961*	*1971*
lowest 60%	32.2	20.8	19.8
middle 20%	14.8	17.8	19.0
high 15%	17.4	28.4	30.4
top 5%	35.5	33.0	30.8

Source: CEPAL.

for local phenomena that correspond to related but distinct social struggles within the limits it establishes. The reduction of the contemporary political conflict to a simple function of an inequitable global economy captures more of its character than the poor versus rich equation in that it gives this a clear dynamic. It suffers, though, from related insufficiencies in that there is little scope within it for explaining either the chronological and geographical variation of social unrest between states of comparable economies or the specific character that it has acquired.

Acceptance of the fact that the present crisis is underpinned by a withering immiseration of millions of people and that this regressive human condition is ultimately determined by Central America's exceptionally vulnerable position in the world market, the local terms of which are imposed by the landlord class, should not obscure the efforts on the part of the ruling class to overhaul the system of production. Indeed, it is very largely this endeavour both to maximize the efficiency of the agro-export sector and to reduce overall dependence upon it through some industrialization that has produced both growth and impoverishment. This contradiction has produced more than a failure to break the cycle of backwardness; it has resulted in particular forms of dispossession and immiseration that correspond both to the traditional liberal oligarchic model and to new social forces. Thus the present struggles relate to historic antipathies between peasant and landlord, and may in many respects be compared with pre-war patterns. On the other hand, the wave of popular discontent and political mobilization witnessed since the mid 1970s represents more than a linear and 'natural' exhaustion of the liberal system since it stems from appreciable transformation of its structures both on the plantation itself and in the development of a sizeable urban economy.

Agriculture

Although the post-war period saw a rise in manufacturing industry and an even greater growth of the urban sector as a whole (Table 4a), Central America has remained a predominantly rural economy and society. Between 1950 and 1975 the proportion of the economically active population in agriculture fell from 67 to 52 per cent; over the same period the region's dependence upon the two traditional staples of coffee and bananas dropped from 80 to 61 per cent, but almost all this fall was due to the introduction of new rural exports, particularly cotton, sugar and cattle.[8] Although the configuration of both economy and settlement has altered significantly, it has not amounted to a qualitative erosion of the isthmus's historic role in the world market or traditional internal structure; the countryside remains the key factor in the political economy of the region.

The figures in Table 8a present the state of the rural economy roughly halfway through the post-war period. They reproduce most of the features of the historical trajectory that has already been outlined in terms of distribution of land and patterns of income. While it does reflect some of the effects of the first phase of the cotton boom, this table does not show the full impact of that expansion or the wider developments in the agro-export economy after the early 1960s; it should, therefore, be taken as something of a median point. Absolutely precise comparisons of land tenure patterns

Table 8a: Rural Sector, 1963

	Costa Rica	*El Salvador*	*Guatemala*	*Honduras*	*Nicaragua*	*Region*
Land use (%)	52.4	77.6	31.6	21.5	32.5	33.9
Land Tenure[1]						
% units:						
micro	43.2	91.4	87.4	67.5	50.8	76.8
small	35.1	6.7	10.5	26.4	27.4	17.0
medium	20.1	1.5	2.0	5.7	20.3	5.8
large	1.6	0.4	0.1	0.4	1.5	0.4
% total land farmed in:						
micro	2.9	21.9	18.6	12.4	3.5	10.8
small	14.3	20.6	18.9	27.5	11.1	19.1
medium	41.3	19.8	36.6	32.6	44.1	37.0
large	41.5	37.7	25.9	27.5	41.2	33.1
Average farm size (hectares):						
overall	41.3	7.0	8.3	13.6	37.4	14.5
micro/small	2.8	1.7	1.8	2.5	2.6	2.5
medium	16.8	21.4	14.9	14.1	15.4	16.3
large	158.2	208.2	244.9	134.2	146.3	164.4
Average family income ($):						
overall	1,199.0	581.0	453.0	na	902.0	
landless	727.0	229.0	340.0	na	370.0	
micro		302.0		na	380.0	
small	908.0	420.0	220.0	na	445.0	
medium	1,084.0	1,408.0	1,300.0	na	717.0	
large	2,117.0	7,106.0	8,000.0	na	2,248.0	
hacienda	20,473.0	25,748.0	40,000.0	na	18,226.0	
% families without land	42.4	15.6	16.5	26.1	31.4	22.7
Rural density (pop. per ha.)	6.1	13.5	13.8	4.4	5.3	8.1

Tenure categories, by hectares:

micro	to 0.7	to 1.0	to 0.7	to 1.0	to 0.7
small	0.7–6.9	1.0–9.9	0.7–6.9	1.0–9.9	0.7–6.9
medium	7.0–34.9	10.0–49.9	7.0–44.9	10.0–44.9	7.0–34.9
large	35.0–349.9	50.0–199.9	45.0–895.9	45.0–499.0	35.0–349.0
hacienda	350+	200+	896+	500+	350+

between countries is complicated by the different means of measurement employed, but the general picture is clear enough. In all countries there is a large number of very small plots, up to one hectare in size, that are unable to provide subsistence for the average *campesino* family. In the region as a whole these tiny units comprise over 76 per cent of all 'farms' yet cover just 11 per cent of cultivated land, this pattern being particularly pronounced in El Salvador and Guatemala. It is worthy of note that in 1963 there existed a significant stratum of medium-sized farms that, at an extension of around five hectares of reasonably fertile soil, began to match basic subsistence needs and offer the possibility of a marketable surplus. Although many of those *campesinos* cultivating 'small' units were undeniably extremely poor and unable to depend entirely upon the yield of their plots, they were in an incomparably better position than those without any land whatsoever. In this respect the very high figure for landlessness in Costa Rica ought to be distinguished from the rest of the region since, as can be seen from the size of the average family income, landless rural labourers in that country were still receiving the higher wages that were already evident by the mid nineteenth century. At the same time, it is evident that while the number and general share of land of middle-level farms in Costa Rica was not greatly out of proportion to those elsewhere (except El Salvador) these farms yielded a significantly higher income – more than double the figure for Nicaragua, which has the closest pattern of tenure but also a very high number of landless workers even at this stage. It is, of course, true that patterns of land tenure do not alone give a comprehensive picture of the rural economy. Yet it is entirely legitimate, given the inclusion of income figures, to confirm from these statistics the traditional image of a largely polarized system wherein a small number of large commercial estates covering huge swathes of land coexisted with tens of thousands of minuscule peasant plots pressed into a very much smaller area. Even with the presence at this stage of an appreciable number of modest farms, whose existence should be fully recognized to have important political and economic effects, the inequities in access to land and income are most striking.

It is difficult to obtain dependable statistics for the most recent period because the organization of censuses in Central America has been impeded over the last decade by both economic crisis and political violence. Still, on the basis of discrete indicators it is possible to trace a process of increased imbalance in patterns of land ownership and, more critically still, expulsion of large numbers of *campesinos* from their lands. Table 8b includes the general distribution of farm size in Guatemala and Nicaragua but, it should be noted, excludes the landless and, in the case of Nicaragua, aggregates all units up to seven hectares, thereby reducing the profile of both absolute and relative land poverty within what is the critical span between one and seven hectares. When compared to the figures for 1963 it can be seen that in the

Nicaraguan case there has not been a notable increase in the proportion of micro and small units within the total number of farms; however, the area they occupy has diminished greatly, from 14.6 to 3.8 per cent of the total. This suggests that pressure from the *fincas* has led less to subdivision of already tiny plots than to direct expulsion and loss of land. The picture in Guatemala is one of a somewhat less polarized distribution despite the fact that here also subsistence farmers lost a very substantial amount of land over twenty-five years, the share of cultivated land held in units of less than seven hectares falling from 37.5 to 16 per cent.

In the cases of El Salvador and Honduras the most remarkable feature is the increase in landlessness among rural families, from 15.6 to 41 per cent and 26.1 to 36 per cent respectively over a ten-year period. At the same time, there was sufficient increase in the number of plots less than one hectare in size to suggest a high level of subdivision; in El Salvador the number of these plots grew by 25 per cent between 1961 and 1971 whilst in Honduras they more than doubled between 1952 and 1974. Although we have no figures for the level of dispossession during the first phase of coffee, it is debatable whether, even in El Salvador, its effects were as extensive or profound as during this period. The figures for Honduras are in some respects more impressive because of the historically low levels of landlessness and general accessibility of land, albeit frequently of very low fertility. Moreover, as already suggested, while the possession of at least some land never ceases to be a critical barrier against absolute destitution, the difference between one and several hectares is of the utmost importance, making the high level of families, particularly in El Salvador, with use of less than one hectare an item of note. Between 1961 and 1975 the income of the rural population in that country that was either landless or held less than one hectare fell in real terms by 20 per cent whereas that of those farming between two and ten hectares increased by 30 per cent.[9] Similarly, in Guatemala during the 1960s the average income of migrant labourers from the eight 'Indian' departments that provide the bulk of the plantation seasonal workforce stood at $28.64 a year against $43.34 for non-migrant *campesinos* who may broadly be associated with those whose plots are large enough to enable subsistence.[10] The income estimates given for the region in Table 9 broadly confirm this picture although by aggregating all families with less than four hectares they obscure the condition of the very poorest strata of the *campesinado*.

In contrast to the assessment of the dynamics behind the figures for GDP, the statistics for real rural poverty and land distribution have been presented before the formal ratio of rural population to cultivable land area. In this sector a Malthusian perspective would seem to hold rather greater weight since, notwithstanding the important factors of yields and the balance between food and export crops, land may be seen as significantly less flexible than production as a whole. Indeed, although Table 8a

Table 8b: Land Property

Honduras and El Salvador, 1974/75

	Honduras 1974 rural families		*El Salvador 1975 rural families*	
	no.	*%*	*no.*	*%*
landless	108,621	36	166,922	41
less than 1 hectare	33,771	11	138,838	34
1–2	38,650	13	62,385	15
2–5	52,360	17	24,400	6
5–10	28,264	9	7,545	2
over 10	42,296	14	7,197	2

Source: Censos Agropecuarios, cited in J. Mark Ruhl, 'Agrarian Structure and Political Stability in Honduras', *Journal of Inter-American Studies*, vol.26, no.1, February 1984, p.47.

Distribution by farm size, Nicaragua, 1976[1]

	Farms		*Area*	
	no.	*%*	*000 hectares*	*%*
less than 7 hectares	99,766	60.8	194.0	3.8
7–35	36,181	22.1	541.7	10.6
35–350	26,649	16.2	2,440.0	47.6
over 350	1,454	0.9	1,951.5	38.0

Note:
1. Excludes Atlantic coast.

Source: Biderman, *Class Structure*, p.195.

Distribution by farm size, Guatemala, 1979

	Farms		*Area*	
	no.	*%*	*000 hectares*	*%*
less than 0.7 hectares	166,732	31	55.4	1
0.7–1.4	121,351	23	115.1	3
1.5–6.9	180,385	34	508.0	12
7.0–44.9	49,409	9	781.0	19
45–900	13,177	2	1,817.5	43
Over 900	482	–	903.2	22

Source: Censo Agropecunario 1979.

Table 9: Estimated Distribution of Rural Income, 1970

	% population	*% income*
landless and less than 4 hectares	83.3	34.8
4–7 hectares	6.8	10.1
7–35	7.3	11.7
35–350	1.4	23.5
over 350	0.4	17.2
administrators	0.8	2.7

Source: Centroamérica Hoy, p.245.

shows less than a third of the entire region in agricultural use in 1963 and Table 10 indicates an appreciable expansion in this overall frontier between 1950 and 1975, the land/labour ratio has decreased over the same period. A glimpse at the contrast between Tables 8a and 8b shows that the pattern of real dispossession over the period 1963–74/5 is far greater than that suggested by a division of acreage by people. In short, while the general land/labour ratio has indeed reduced, demographic expansion is not the principal cause of land poverty and cannot account for its exceptional acceleration over the last two decades. This is the result of a geographically uneven but general tendency for commercial farms to expand at the direct expense of the subsistence sector.

One central characteristic of the development of the early coffee hacienda was the need to supply itself with harvest workers. The form of ensuring labour supply varied to a marked degree but almost always encompassed an element of labour rent whereby peasants had usufruct of some *finca* lands in return for seasonal work. In Guatemala, where more directly coercive labour systems predominated, the highland *fincas de mozos* were established primarily for this purpose; neither was it entirely absent in Costa Rica despite the early proletarianization of the rural labour force. On the other hand, even at the start of the coffee economy demand for labour outstripped that which could be met through this mechanism, which also constrained the amount of land that could be employed for export crops. Removal of freehold permitted a greater purchase on labour but complete dispossession provided both directly cultivable land and a reserve labour army. Nevertheless, the modern phase of expansion and expulsion has not in general corresponded to a greater need for labour supply and control. As early as the 1960s there is evidence of widespread rural un- and underemployment,

Table 10: Extent and Form of Land Tenure, 1950–75

Agricultural frontier and land/labour ratios

	Frontier (millions hectares)		*Land/labour ratio*[1] *(hectares per worker)*	
	1950	*1975*	*1950*	*1975*
Central America	11.9	14.5	1.791	1.204
Costa Rica	1.8	2.7	0.893	1.328
El Salvador	1.5	1.6	0.961	0.553
Guatemala	3.7	3.8	1.701	1.102
Honduras	2.5	2.5	2.076	1.133
Nicaragua	2.4	3.9	3.327	1.908

Note:
1. Arable land and permanent crop area divided by rural labour force.

Sources: frontier – Mayorga, *Crecimiento Desigual*, p.50; land/labour ratio – Bulmer-Thomas, 'Economic Development', p.290.

Forms of land tenure, c.1970 (% of units)[1]

	C. America	*C. Rica*	*El Sal.*	*Guate.*	*Hon.*	*Nica.*
freehold	44.8	76	40	56	22	39
rented, incl. *ejido*	25.1	2	19	17	59	21
mixed	6.4	16	13	–	3	14
labour rent/ squatting	17.9	4	25	22	2	23
others	5.8	1	3	5	13	4

Note:
1. National percentages are rounded and do not necessarily equal 100.

Source: Tenencia de la Tierra y Desarrollo Rural en Centroamérica, San José 1973, p.84.

albeit of strictly modest proportions in Costa Rica. In El Salvador supply exceeded demand by a full 57.7 per cent in 1963 (484,044 labourer-years offered against 209,339 required) when the level of rural landlessness was 16.5 per cent. Although increased area and production has since broadly maintained the demand for harvest labour, this has been overtaken to an enormous degree by the supply created by loss of lands. Between 1961 and

1971 total temporary waged labour in the countryside actually declined by 0.06 per cent but landless temporary workers rose from 6.2 to 17.2 of the total labour force.[11] In less densely populated and more generally representative Nicaragua supply exceeded demand in 1963 by 29.6 per cent (274,934 labourer-years offered against 197,034 required) and, whereas total labour demand in the strategic cotton sector increased throughout most of the 1960s, the number of landless temporary workers in 1978 accounted for 32.1 per cent of the economically active rural population while permanent plantation workers formed only 7.5 per cent.[12]

The cause of this recent phase of dispossession is most comparable to that witnessed in the 1920s: the need to control more land for the purpose of production for export. This growth of the plantation frontier is more difficult to trace in terms of its form than in those of scale and effects. While the potential for alienating communal lands was appreciably lower than in the nineteenth century, except in Honduras, it is clear that this took place in Guatemala and Nicaragua, largely by direct expropriation of lands to which *campesinos* held no title or which title they could not defend. In many cases expulsion was no less violent than in the 1880s. Equally, in those countries where the general level of 'squatting' was already low, particularly El Salvador (for which the figure in Table 10 is of only marginal use since it combines labour rent with squatting), there was a shift from labour to money rent, frequently subjected to an inflation that subsequently uprooted tenants.[13] The overall result extended beyond the formidable increase in landlessness that has already been noted; it often included subdivision of plots and was generally marked by a retreat of the peasantry towards the agricultural frontier, away from both traditional areas of settlement and the most fertile zones. In some instances, most particularly Nicaragua, this process had the effect of opening up a new frontier rather than consolidating the periphery. In El Salvador there was minimal physical potential for this, whereas in Guatemala the site for 'refuge' became further circumscribed, there being negligible displacement of people to the sparsely populated and underdeveloped northern department of Petén.[14] In any event, simple movement proved to be an inadequate response to the pincer-effect of dispossession and either absolute or relative reduction of opportunities for labour on the plantation. This process was certainly incremental and subject to a plethora of strategies on both sides, but if not tantamount to the total, overnight dislocation of the rural masses that is sometimes extrapolated from the worst case of El Salvador, it was indubitably dynamic, extensive, frequently violent in form and overwhelmingly regressive in terms of the human condition in the countryside. In this respect the character of contemporary rural unrest may quite feasibly be compared with that in the Liberal era and at the end of the 1920s.

Tables 11a and 11b reveal the scale of growth in the agro–export sector

Table 11a: Growth of Traditional Agro-Export Sector, c.1950–c.1975

	Coffee				*Bananas*		
	Area[1]	*Production*[2]	*Yield*[3]		*Area*[1]	*Production*[2]	*Yield*[3]
Region 1950[4]	444	187.9	405	Region 1950	91	1,434	162
1977	714	525.0	781	1974	189	3,213	162
Costa Rica 1950	51	23.2	454	C. Rica 1950	16	434	271
1977	87	79.0	971	1974	33	1,100	333
El Salvador 1950	112	74.5	655	El S. 1950	–	–	–
1977	147	180.0	1,224	1974	9	53	57
Guatemala 1950	162	57.6	355	Guate. 1950	17	185	109
1977	270	147.0	544	1974	59	450	76
Honduras 1950	63	13.1	207	Hon. 1950	57	802	140
1977	122	57.0	467	1974	48	1,360	283
Nicaragua 1950	56	19.5	348	Nica. 1950	1	13	128
1977	88	62.0	700	1974	40	250	63

Notes:

1. Area = thousand hectares.
2. Production = thousand metric tonnes.
3. Yield = hundred kilos per hectare.
4. Average of 1949–52.

Source: Torres Rivas, 'Industrialization', p.17.

that prompted this pressure. In the case of the traditional crops of coffee and bananas (Table 11a) it should be noted that increased banana production was at a regional level entirely attributable to the greater area under cultivation rather than improvements in yield, but since such plantations are not in the zones of high *campesino* settlement this expansion cannot be considered critical in terms of direct pressure on subsistence lands. Higher coffee production, on the other hand, corresponded to increases in both yield and area and undoubtedly contributed to land pressure. Although the rise in average yield is generally more impressive than that in area – most particularly in El Salvador, where ecological constraints made greater efficiency imperative – coffee is mainly cultivated in core settlement areas so that almost all spatial expansion between 1950 and 1977 was at the expense of *campesino* plots established on the edges of the pre-war plantations. At the same time, the increase in yield was far greater than was the demand for labour that might be attributed to it. Acreage rose by 81 per cent and output by 128 per cent in Guatemala between 1950 and 1960 whereas the labour force increased by only 27 per cent; in Costa Rica the size of coffee deliveries to the *beneficio* indicates that smallholders held on to their share of production up to the 1970s although improvements in technology – for example, the use of chemicals instead of weeding by hand – meant that only 17 per cent of the increase in the labour force between 1950 and 1964 was employed on the coffee *fincas*.[15] Nonetheless, Central American coffee has always been harvested manually, and while labour demand lagged behind increased yields, it was maintained in absolute terms in this sector.[16]

The general rise in the coffee price on the international market until 1957 underlay this phase of growth while both increased world production and changes in consumption habits – the discovery by North Americans that stimulation had its price prompted a reduction of per capita consumption from 20.1 lbs per year in 1946 to 14.8 in 1965 – depressed the market through the 1960s and early 1970s. Although this downturn was subjected to a modicum of international regulation through quota agreements, it produced a general deterioration of the regional balance of payments precisely at the time of the Cuban revolution and contributed to a flurry of political unrest, notably in El Salvador and Guatemala. An analysis of the costs of production and returns of Salvadorean coffee *fincas* suggests that while the period 1950–57 produced exceptionally high profits, the general level never became remotely critical thereafter, with wages remaining consistently low.[17]

Mechanization had a far greater impact in the banana industry, the introduction of packing plants and aerial crop-spraying reducing the labour force substantially. Following the great strike of 1954 in Honduras, UFCO cut the number of its workers from 26,000 to 13,000 in three years; together with Standard Fruit's cutbacks this diminished the total banana proletariat

Table 11b: Growth of Non-Traditional Agro-Export Sector, 1948–77

	Cotton					*Sugar*			
	1948/52		*1967*		*1979*	*1961/65*		*1977*	
	area[1]	*prod.*[2]	*area*	*prod.*	*prod.*	*area*	*prod.*	*area*	*prod.*
Central America	73	28	307.6	229	339	135	5,869	257	16,498
Costa Rica	–	–	8.5	4	4	24	1,082	37	2,160
El Salvador	21	8	52.7	35	72	25	1,060	38	3,300
Guatemala	5	2	89.5	78	146	32	1,960	85	6,800
Honduras	–	–	11.2	10	8	33	796	55	1,660
Nicaragua	47	18	145.7	102	109	21	971	42	2,578

	Cattle (thousand head)		
	1947/52	*1972*	*1974*
Central America	4,325	8,665	8,953
Costa Rica	601	1,655	1,767
El Salvador	795	1,000	1,009
Guatemala	977	1,740	1,916
Honduras	884	1,600	1,661
Nicaragua	1,068	2,670	2,600

Notes:

1. area = thousands of hectares
2. production = thousands of tons.

Sources: Torres Rivas, 'Industrializatin', p.18; Roodolfo Quirós Guardia, *Agricultural Development in Central America. Its Origin and Nature*, Research Paper no.49, Land Tenure Center, University of Wisconsin, Madison, 1973, p.50.

by 19,000 before the end of the decade. Although both production and productivity rose initially, there was a subsequent fall in productivity, particularly when the corporations reverted to contract buying as the market became less favourable.[18] The epoch of fabulous concessions was over, and the major companies entered a period of corporate turbulence. After the Cuban revolution UFCO began to divest itself of many of its Latin American plantations, and from 1970 traded under the name of United Brands, selling its Guatemalan holdings to Del Monte in 1973, these passing in turn to the tobacco company R.J. Reynolds in 1979. Yet despite a series of law suits over business practices in the US and the unprecedented challenges posed by the decision in 1974 of the Central American states to join the Union of Banana Exporting Countries and levy an export tax of $1 per box, both United and Castle and Cook – which between 1964 and 1968 bought up Standard and put its 'Dole' brand-name into competition with United's 'Chiquita' – maintained a stranglehold over the trade.[19]

At root this struggle was over relative shares of a trade apparently in uncontainable decline: between 1950 and 1974 the real retail price of bananas fell by 44 per cent, with producing states receiving a total of only 17 cents for each $1 of the retail price at the end of this period.[20] Costa Rica's victory in maintaining relatively high fiscal pressure on the companies after 1975 was pyrrhic in character since by the mid 1980s United Brands had stopped all forms of fruit production on the Pacific coast, having previously increased its interests in palm oil (used to make margarine) both there and in Honduras, where bananas fell from 70 to 25 per cent of export revenue between 1950 and 1977.[21] Reduced in terms of overall importance, the Honduran fruit trade still continued at its historic levels of volume and the enterprises retained an extensive network of subsidiaries outside the enclave in food processing, light manufacturing, banking, transport and communications that mirrored the diversification of their interests in Costa Rica.[22] The 'banana war' of 1977 was in some respects the last traditional confrontation over the terms of fruit company ascendancy; thereafter disputes increasingly took on the character of preserving relative advantage in the context of recession. This neither diminished the importance of the multinationals nor improved the overall bargaining position of the states, but the general shift from aggressive expansionism to defensive divestment altered the traditional relationship in political terms, depriving both corporate managers and their local allies of many of the stock arguments as to why foreign investment invariably led to national prosperity.

In Honduras and Costa Rica, the two countries most directly affected by these shifts in the banana trade, rural unrest over the last decade has increased notably. The fact that it has not manifested the violence witnessed elsewhere may in part be attributed to the fact that rural labourers in the banana enclave have been proletarianized and unionized to a markedly greater degree than the largely seasonal labour force in the coffee sector, but it also corresponds to the relatively low level to which cotton – the most dynamic of the new export crops – was developed in these two countries. As Table 11b shows, it is unlikely that this economic factor was solely or even predominantly responsible for such disparities in rural unrest since the expansion of cattle ranching, with a significantly higher need for land and lower requirement for labour, occurred everywhere in the region. Nonetheless, the dramatic growth of cotton over the post-war period has had a considerable impact upon social relations in the countryside, augmenting the pressure on the subsistence sector from the growth of traditional coffee *fincas*. This expansion occurred earliest and had the greatest effect in Nicaragua, where cotton rose from 5 to 44 per cent of total exports between 1950 and 1965, establishing such a central role in the national economy that even in the early 1980s, when the price was exceptionally low, the crop accounted for 27 per cent of export revenue and Nicaragua remained one of the world's leading producers. Overall growth in Guatemala, particularly during the 1970s, was barely less impressive, but this took place in the context of a much larger economy, and by 1985 cotton constituted only 7 per cent of exports against coffee's 29 per cent. In El Salvador a broadly similar pattern occurred – cotton with 9 per cent and coffee with 50 per cent of 1985 export earnings. To an even greater degree than in Guatemala expansion of the new crop led not to the extension of the agricultural frontier as a whole – as Table 10 shows, this grew almost imperceptibly between 1950 and 1975 – but to the growth of export farmland within that frontier. Even in the case of Nicaragua, where the potential for spatial expansion of cultivated land in the interior remains considerable, the growth of cotton had this effect since its cultivation is dependent upon low-lying flat land and requires a high level of infrastructural support. In general, cotton was developed on established but under-exploited haciendas and their surrounding lands which had been progressively occupied by *campesinos* often previously displaced from the coffee heartland. It has been suggested that the fact that this second wave of expulsion was from lands generally held in some form of tenantry and not communal ownership resulted in a relatively low level of direct agitation against it. [23] Although this would appear to be the case, it should not obscure the fact that in some regions, particularly the north-western Pacific zones of Nicaragua, the structural shift in both land usage and population was considerable and progressively accumulated new generations of rural workers dependent upon harvest labour in order to supplement subsistence cultivation on the marginal lands in the central region to which they had been pushed.

The advent of cotton cannot be viewed simply in terms of expropriation of *campesino* holdings. Just as with coffee, the crop demanded a large seasonal labour force. In Nicaragua this reached its peak in the 1973/4 harvest with a total of over 202,000 workers, compared with a permanent labour force of 26,000.[24] Although the average time spent by seasonal labourers on the cotton harvest is less than that for coffee – an average of seventy-four against ninety-nine days in a survey of Guatemalan migrant workers – the wages paid are generally higher: $1.31 against $0.58 per day, excluding rations, in the same survey.[25] Nonetheless, cotton, both intrinsically and by virtue of its more recent introduction, is more mechanized and less labour intensive a crop than is coffee. In the case of Nicaragua the difference is most marked, with cotton requiring seventy-four labourer days per year for each *manzana* (0.69 hectares) while coffee needs 160.[26] This reflects the relatively higher degree of modernization of that country's cotton industry – imports of agricultural machinery rose from C4.3 million in 1960 to C72.1 million in 1975; those of insecticides and pesticides from C32.4 million to C208.1 million – but even on a regional basis the disparity is most marked, coffee needing sixty-nine labourer-days per acre each year in contrast to cotton's requirement of just thirty-one.[27] Thus, despite its relatively efficient production, cotton generated neither a permanent nor a seasonal labour demand sufficient to provide the peasant economy with some form of generalized balance for the loss of land. Moreover, it should be borne in mind that this productive efficiency was obtained largely by intensive use of agro-chemicals, at a regional level greater than that used on US cotton farms, and in Nicaragua accounting for a full 72 per cent of all chemicals used in agriculture.[28] Such usage remained strictly sectoral and was mainly restricted to the largest farms; only 2.8 per cent of all Nicaraguan units up to five *manzanas* in size used fertilizer and 14.5 per cent employed insecticides in 1971.[29]

In Guatemala agricultural practices retained an even more backward character despite certain areas of modernization: in 1964 less than a half of all farms between 45 and 900 hectares – that is, non-subsistence concerns – used chemical fertilizers, deriving 60 per cent of their energy from human labour, 26 per cent from animals and only 14 per cent from machinery.[30] Even within the cotton sector the relative advances in technical methods were distinctly double-edged in effect: intensive use of chemicals produces such a high level of general toxification and immediate discomfort for workers that there is evidence of an aversion, on eminently sensible grounds, to working on cotton plantations rather than those of other crops despite the higher wages to be found in cotton.[31] It is the chronic inability to make such a choice that lies behind the fact that levels of DDT in breast milk in Guatemala and Nicaragua are amongst the highest in the world, greatly exceeding international safety limits.[32]

The expansion of sugar, very largely as a result of the market opportunities opened by the US embargo on Cuban production in the early 1960s, contributed to pressure on the peasant economy. As can be seen from Table 11b, the total area in sugar nearly doubled between 1961/5 and 1977. This growth was relatively evenly distributed between the countries and only tended to encroach substantially on subsistence lands when, as in the case of El Salvador, the general level of displacement had reached the point where there had been resettlement on hotter coastal territory. Outside of Costa Rica and Honduras the area dedicated to sugar is less than that for cotton, and the crop's demand for labour is somewhat higher (thirty-eight labourer-days per acre per year); yet it is much lower than that for coffee, and the growth in production between 1950 and 1980 has derived much more from increases in area rather than in yields.[33] Indeed, the disparity between the two is sufficiently large to deprive the typical arguments for the relative efficiency of commercial agriculture of much of their force.

The rise in cattle ranching is perhaps the most emphatic feature of the new phase of agro-export growth. Central American cattle are predominantly grass- not grain-fed and need extensive pastures while requiring a very low labour input – some five labourer–days per acre per year. This has given a highly conflictive character to the expansion of grazing land to 43.2 per cent of the total area in agricultural use in 1970 (when food crops accounted for 16.2 per cent; export crops 9.9 per cent; and land in fallow 29.6 per cent) as well as causing considerable ecological damage.[34] The development of the regional cattle trade in the modern era follows the typical pattern of ranching in that it is only commercially viable on extensive estates: in 1970 farms over forty-five hectares held 82 per cent of all pasture and 60 per cent of stock, whilst units of less than seven hectares occupied only 3 per cent of grazing land and raised 17 per cent of all cattle.[35] It is less easy to give a precise numerical illustration for the other general attribute of ranching: that it develops at the expense of smallholdings. Nonetheless, it is clear that the overall increase of both the cattle herd – the figures for which cover only marketed stock – and land in pasture was overwhelmingly concentrated on large ranches and occurred at the same time as levels of land poverty were rising. In the case of Nicaragua the growth of cattle land was remarkable, more than doubling between 1960 and 1979, when ranches over 500 *manzanas* (2 per cent of total farms) held 27 per cent of the national herd and a significantly greater share in the key Pacific provinces already affected by cotton.[36] The twofold increase of the Honduran cattle herd between 1952 and 1974 was almost exclusively attributable to that on farms of over fifty hectares, the proportion of animals held on units of less than fifty hectares falling from 61.6 to 43.7 per cent while the number of such farms tripled.[37] Even in El Salvador, where the increase in herd was comparatively modest, ranching led to an overall reduction in the total area cultivated in all types of crop at the same time as access to that area became ever more restricted (Tables 8a and 8b).

On the understanding that the domestic market for livestock should be more active than those for coffee, cotton and sugar, it might be expected that a significant proportion of the increased regional herd was directed to higher local consumption and an improved dietary regime. However, between 1960 and 1974 per capita consumption of beef fell in every Central American country to an impressive degree, ranging from 50 per cent in Guatemala to 37.5 per cent in El Salvador. In 1978, when US consumption stood at 123 lbs per year, the highest local level was in Costa Rica, at 35 lbs; that in Honduras, for centuries a cattle-raising zone, had dropped to 13 lbs.[38] This reflects the increasing export-orientation of the industry which, despite being overwhelmingly based on grass-fed animals – and therefore with reduced scope for increasing yield in terms of weight per head, still less quantity of lean beef – found an expanding market in the appetite of North Americans for the hamburger and other 'junk-food' concoctions in which lower-quality meat may be used. Central American beef, which already had a price advantage of between 10 and 20 per cent over other beef imported into the US, was thereby assured a ready basis for expansion once local abattoirs and facilities for refrigerated transport were established at the end of the 1950s.[39] Without great need to match increased demand with better quality, ranchers naturally adopted the strategy of more extensive cattle-raising and a degree of cross-breeding rather than concentrating on improving pasture quality or shifting to grain feeds. Over the same period in which total acreage in pasture doubled in Nicaragua, the average live weight of cattle only rose from 351 to 379 kilos per head.[40] This tendency inevitably accelerated encroachment on peasant lands.

As was the case in the nineteenth century, cattle provide a particularly efficacious means of expulsion of the *campesinado* since they consume its crops at the same time as establishing 'right of precedence'. From the 1960s this process was especially marked because pasture requires less fertile terrain than do coffee and cotton; it was, as a consequence, carved out of land hitherto not employed for export crops but occupied by subsistence farmers. Since this expansion frequently took place outside the borders of established *fincas* and allowed minimal scope for negotiation of leases or temporary labour, it provoked a more concerted resistance by *campesinos*. In the 1960s the growth of ranching in the Zacapa and Matagalpa regions of Guatemala and Nicaragua was far from unconnected with outbreaks of guerrilla activity in those zones. Although this was suppressed quite quickly, the high incidence of land disputes connected with the expansion of commercial livestock raising in Olancho, Honduras, the Pacific coastlands of Nicaragua, and the 'Northern Transverse Strip' of Guatemala in the 1970s led to profound unrest and unprecedented deployment of troops. The massacre of over a hundred Kekchi Indians in the town square of Panzós, Alta Verapaz, Guatemala, on 29 May 1978 is now widely accepted as marking the onset of the contemporary *campesino* opposition movement. Those killed had gathered to hear a government response to their claims to title of land, much of which was disputed by ranchers in possession of recent land-grants from the government and supporting them with the use of hired gunmen, who a week before the massacre had killed and beaten several Indians resisting expulsion from their *milpas*.[41] Panzós is distinguished by the scale rather than the nature of the response to resistance; similar experiences in Nicaragua, both on the coastal plains and in the wake of clearance of virgin land undertaken by displaced *campesinos*, undoubtedly provided the FSLN with a social base in the central and north-western regions in its operations against Somoza's National Guard from 1977 onwards.

The tendency of cattle ranches to produce unqualified expulsion of peasants from land and thereby provoke direct conflict should be seen as an extreme feature of the agro-export sector's expansion rather than as a reflection of its general character. As Table 12 shows, domestic market agriculture, which may be broadly associated rather than directly linked with peasant production, generally grew in area cultivated, yield and overall production from 1950. This, together with the fact that in 1970 food crops still occupied 60 per cent more land than did export crops, provides something of a qualification to the image of absolute decline that can so easily be distilled from evidence of relative retreat. The qualification is, however, strictly limited in scope. Growth in domestic staples had been much less than for export crops and, as is evident from Table 13, was by the early 1960s insufficient to sustain the population in basic foods. Even with imports of most basic grains rising from the early 1960s, overall per capita consumption of corn and beans decreased everywhere between 1964/6 and 1974/6 except in El Salvador, where imports were particularly high.[42] Between 1969 and 1980, when production of both export and food crops rose, imports of basic grains could barely compensate for the fall of food crop production on a per capita basis to maintain average calorie intake and failed to do so with respect to proteins; for the poorest third of the population the level of nutrition was falling even before the recession of the early 1980s took hold. It is quite arguable that, with the possible exception of Costa Rica, Central American rural labourers were less well fed in 1980 than a century earlier. The specifically political effects of this may be debated, but it is highly likely that the general image of an era of relative plenty recalled by grandparents and passed down through oral tradition has been contrasted with much more tangible and immediate evidence of increased hardship. In those areas where ethnic and communal structures have been retained such a reverse in material terms reinforces a more extensive sense of embattlement.

The loss of land and opportunities for waged harvest labour produced increasing movement in the rural population, both structurally and seasonally. The peasant economy was already much more extensive than the limits of the village with which it is most obviously associated, the advent of coffee increasing levels of labour mobility required by supply of markets and dispersion of communal lands as well as mule-trains and cattle-drives. Post-war developments in the rural economy expanded the numbers engaged in seasonal work but since the cotton harvest (November to February) overlaps with that of coffee (October to January) the extent of the slack season on the plantations was not greatly reduced and underemployment became more chronic. Between 1945/50 and 1964 the number of short-term interdepartmental migrants in Guatemala – movements which may be linked to harvest labour – rose from 122,169 to 578,236.[43] The principal source of this seasonal workforce remained the eight 'Indian' departments although the increased proportion coming from Huehuetenango, Quiché and San Marcos, followed at some distance by Chimaltenango, suggests that differentiation within this core area of indigenous settlement had become important.[44] It is, in all events, of some consequence that the areas providing the greatest number of migrant workers have been the principal sites of guerrilla activity in recent years whereas those, such as Totonicapán, providing a much more modest level of migrant labour have witnessed a significantly less severe incidence of unrest and open political activity. Between 1961 and 1971 the total size of the seasonal labour force in El Salvador changed little, around 250,000 migrant workers being employed at harvest-time during this period, the general zones of attraction continuing to be Santa Ana, Ahuachapán, Usulután and San Miguel, to which workers were generally drawn from the central and north-eastern regions of the country. Some 182,300 workers – 30 per cent of the economically active rural population – were employed for two months or less in 1975, a further 115,400 (19 per cent) for between two and six months, so that nearly half the total labour force may be considered to be not only underemployed but also migratory in character.[45] In the case of Nicaragua harvest-based movement nearly tripled between 1960 and 1975 in the cotton sector, with up to 200,000 workers, one third of the economically active rural population, being engaged in seasonal labour for a maximum of three months per year.[46] The north-western Pacific departments drew this influx from the north-central region, which had become a major zone of settlement for a peasantry largely displaced from the area to which it now returned for only a few weeks a year.[47]

In these three countries it is primarily those sections of the *campesinado* settled outside the central agro-export zones but travelling to them at harvest-time that provided the social base for political opposition and guerrilla movements in the late 1970s. In the cases of Costa Rica and Honduras the pattern is notably less marked. In part this may be attributed to the low level of cotton production, but it is also the case that banana plantations depend upon an almost exclusively permanent labour force.

Table 12: Growth of Domestic Market Agriculture, c.1950–78

	Maize						*Rice*					
	1948/52			*1978*			*1948/52*			*1978*		
	Area[1]	*Prod.*[2]	*Yield*[3]	*Area*	*Prod.*	*Yield*	*Area*	*Prod.*	*Yield*	*Area*	*Prod.*	*Yield*
Central America	1,172	1,025	980	1,377	1,947	1,410	81	119	1,460	134	384	2,860
Costa Rica	58	77	1,320	50	98	1,960	25	35	1,420	73	195	2,660
El Salvador	182	191	1,050	252	540	2,150	15	26	1,960	17	60	3,510
Guatemala	538	437	810	522	760	1,450	8	9	1,180	11	26	2,360
Honduras	283	205	730	325	340	1,050	11	18	1,640	15	21	1,390
Nicaragua	111	115	1,030	228	209	930	22	31	1,390	28	82	2,920

	Beans					
	1948/52			*1978*		
	Area	*Prod.*	*Yield*	*Area*	*Prod.*	*Yield*
Central America	209	113	5,580	375	240	7,720
Costa Rica	27	11	4,100	30	15	5,300
El Salvador	36	29	8,100	53	43	8,200
Guatemala	63	30	4,700	135	80	5,900
Honduras	50	22	4,400	90	50	5,500
Nicaragua	33	21	6,600	67	51	7,700

Notes:

1. Area = thousands of hectares.
2. Production = thousands of tons.
3. Yield = kilos per hectare.

Source: Torres Rivas, 'Industrialization', p.17.

Table 13: Grain Imports and Consumption

A. Central America: Nett Imports of Grains from Rest of World (tons)

	Corn	*Rice*	*Beans*	*Sorghum*	*Total*
1950–54	−60,630	−45,568	−18,649	−4,305	−129,152
1955–59	44,003	45,243	−17,687	−5,034	66,525
1960–64	53,045	35,567	7,548	12	96,172
1965–68	101,458	51,409	388	6,373	159,632

B. Index of Per Capital Grain Consumption 1975/6 (1964/6 = 100)

	C. America	*C. Rica*	*El S.*	*Guate.*	*Hon.*	*Nica.*
Corn	87	81	111	77	90	77
Beans	81	60	105	79	84	72
Rice	108	135	107	108	117	75
Calories	89	111	107	80	95	76

C. Central America and Guatemala: Daily Calorie and Protein Intake (grams)

		1966–8	*1969–71*	*1975–7*	*1978–80*	*1969–80 (% change)*
C.America	calories	2,141	2,178	2,223	2,263	3.9
	proteins	57.4	58.3	57.3	58.0	−0.5
Guatemala	calories	1,971	2,049	2,035	2,064	0.7
	proteins	54.4	56.6	53.7	55.9	−1.2

Sources:
A. Quirós, *Agricultural Development*, p.96.
B. Weeks, *Economies*, p. 107
C. Charles D. Brockett, 'Malnutrition, Public Policy and Agrarian Change in Guatemala', *Journal of Inter-American Studies*, vol.26, no.4, November 1984, p.478.

The large numbers of Honduran workers made redundant in the late 1950s were initially obliged less to enter into a peripatetic search for seasonal work than to return to a predominantly subsistence existence, for which there was at the time still some space. They took with them the experience of workers accustomed to a distinct labour regime and the syndicalist methods employed to ameliorate it. By the late 1960s conditions in the Honduran countryside were beginning to mirror those elsewhere, as the levels of landlessness for the mid 1970s clearly indicate, but the peasant response to this was in general more modulated than in neighbouring countries. This reflected the strength of corporate forms of organization designed for negotiation and defensive resistance as well as the comparatively low level of exposure to seasonal work in the limited coffee sector and the fact that between 1972 and 1975 the military regime sought with partial success to implement an agrarian reform and revive some of the advantages historically given by the extent of land in *ejido*. In those areas, such as Olancho, where ranching had expanded, the pattern of social relations and conflict cohered much more directly with that elsewhere. Yet, while it remained the most impoverished sector of the Central American population, the Honduran *campesinado* was not as a rule subjected to such high levels of dislocation on a temporary basis as were rural people in the rest of the region. When, as increasingly occurred, it came under pressure to cede part or all of its traditional lands, there was relatively greater scope for permanent resettlement despite the fact that this was diminishing both spatially and in terms of soil fertility. The differences are of scale not type, but they have patently affected the character of *campesino* politics.

In Costa Rica the extent of landlessness and waged harvest labour was historically the highest in the isthmus but had developed within the context of a distinct agrarian system. Although from the 1960s the capacity of the coffee sector to provide employment for seasonal workers increasingly failed to match the rise in their number, its inability to do so was at a markedly lower level than in the other countries. Generally higher wages and smaller *fincas* further reduced the extremities in a system in which pressure on subsistence land did not result in such a dynamic dislocation of established patterns of rural society. In that sector where pronounced change did take place – the banana enclave – many of the features exhibited in Honduras are evident. The banana proletariat is quite distinct from that not only in the central meseta but also in the cattle and hacienda regions of Guanacaste and Nicoya, and this cannot be attributed solely to differences in ethnic background, which have become progressively less pronounced after the movement of the plantations from the Atlantic to Pacific coast. In recent years the crisis in the banana economy has generated unrest and mobilization on a scale not seen since the strike of 1934, but while this has progressively eroded collective and trade-union methods and outlook, it has not provoked major crisis in a rural order less dependent upon subsistence agriculture and migratory labour than elsewhere.

The mobility of rural labour is in itself secondary to the socio-economic conditions prevailing at the points between which it takes place. Nevertheless, movement of hundreds of thousands of workers has important effects both objectively and in terms of the consciousness of those who are uprooted. This is most evident with regard to seasonal movement, but perhaps the single most critical example of the phenomenon on a more permanent basis was the displacement of large numbers of Salvadoreans to Honduras, between the Depression and the 'Football War' of 1969. Total emigration from El Salvador is estimated to have been in the order of 347,000 people between 1930 and 1950, 187,000 between 1950 and 1961, and 23,150 between 1961 and 1971, the bulk crossing the border into Honduras.[48] An outflow of this magnitude obviously represented a valuable safety-valve for the Salvadorean oligarchy in terms of reducing pressure on land and facilitating general social control in the countryside. Its reversal – not total but appreciable in that some 100,000 people returned in late 1968 and early 1969 – was an important element in the deterioration of the popular economy in the early 1970s. At the same time, these returned migrants amounted to more than extra demographic pressure. Their experiences, both in Honduras, where they had generally improved their condition even when working in the banana enclave, as well as that upon return to their country of origin, engendered a proclivity for collective organization and political mobilization that was to spread on an unprecedented scale throughout the countryside over the following decade. The influx of refugees was only a contributory factor in this, but it was still important; both the number of people involved and the fact that their experience was at heart a highly acute version of the structural rites of passage involved in harvest migration gave this singular phenomenon an especially dynamic character.

It is evident that despite differences in formation, size and importance within the agricultural labour force as a whole, a stratum of rural proletarians grew over the post-war period to comprise at least one third of workers in the countryside. Yet only a minor proportion of waged labourers was employed beyond two or three months a year, and although dependence upon wages became more acute from 1950, the wage relation was in itself no innovation for large numbers of these labourers. Equally, while the vulnerability of the worker in transient employment is increased by the predominance of piece-work systems, these also tend to reduce the degree to which the characteristics normally associated with 'proletarianization' may be said to be in play.[49] Many of the attributes of such a formal transition from one system of production to another are highly distorted precisely because the real transition has been very partial, tending to disturb traditional *campesino* strategies based upon cultivation for family subsistence but scarcely ever entirely to suppress or displace them. The alterations in commercial agriculture over the last forty years have not required a fully waged labour force whilst they have compelled a reduction in the scope of traditional systems of cultivation when these impede expansion. Sometimes this has resulted in alterations in the type of economic relation between landlord and peasant, sometimes in a complete severance of that relation.

Insofar as this eroded the influence of a manorial universe it may be said to represent a diminution of typically feudal conditions; yet in that it prompted more precarious conditions for subsistence through squatting on more marginal lands it cannot properly be considered within any linear logic of modernization. Whatever the theoretical perspective into which it is placed, the concrete effect of this process has been less to draw a section of the rural population out of its condition as a peasantry than to subject that condition to a stress that has necessarily fused traditional with newer strategies for survival in a combination that includes defence of historic rights and customs; negotiation of the terms of tenantry; subdivision of plots; migration; harvest labour; consolidation of communal forms of association and adoption of newer organizational bonds, often with extra-parochial links and influences. It is not necessary to pursue discussion of these factors at this point to perceive that they reflect the intrinsically uneven nature of the developments to which they are a response, both mitigating the traditional characteristics of peasant existence by providing it with a general, supra-local expression, and yet reaffirming the primacy of local conditions and identity within such an expression.

The Urban Sector

Between 1950 and the Nicaraguan revolution inhabitants of Central America's towns increased from one-sixth to nearly one half of the total population (Table 4a, p.172). Although this calculation is made on the basis of settlements of 2,000 persons or more and cannot therefore be considered an index of integral urbanization or definitive departure from the rural milieu, it reflects a growth in urban settlement far higher than that of the population as a whole. Whether by step migration – movement to the cities by stages, usually starting in smaller towns – or by direct relocation, increasing numbers of *campesinos* sought the means of survival within the urban orbit, or at least partly within it. One effect of this was to break down the colonial and early republican pattern of relative balance between towns, the capital cities now expanding very much faster than other centres and becoming the focus of both economic and political activity. By the end of the 1970s these disparities were, with the exception of Honduras, very marked and had given rise to metropolitan centres still modest in global terms but of unprecedented influence within each country.[50]

This increased urbanization is clearly related both to pressure on the popular economy in the countryside and to the strategy of developing a manufacturing base and decreasing dependence on agro-exports by import substitution. This project was shared by the reformulated dominant bloc that emerged in the decade after 1945 and CEPAL, which in 1958 began to

Table 14: Growth of Manufacturing Industry, 1950–78

A. Share of Manufacturing in GDP (% at 1970 prices)

	Region	*Costa Rica*	*El Salvador*	*Guatemala*	*Honduras*	*Nicaragua*
1950	11.1	11.5	12.9	11.1	9.1	10.8
1960	12.1	11.1	13.9	11.7	11.4	12.6
1978	17.5	18.4	18.7	15.1	14.3	20.2[1]

B. Growth of Manufacturing (%)

	Region	*Costa Rica*	*El Salvador*	*Guatemala*	*Honduras*	*Nicaragua*
1950–60	6.1	8.0	5.5	4.6	7.0	7.3
1960–70	8.4	8.8	8.2	7.7	6.8	11.1
1970–77	6.2	6.9	5.4	6.6	7.1	5.0

C. Value Added in Manufacturing (millions of 1970 dollars)

	Region	*Costa Rica*	*El Salvador*	*Guatemala*	*Honduras*	*Nicaragua*
1950	254.0	34.3	66.0	98.0	29.9	25.8
1960	432.0	65.8	112.2	150.5	53.4	50.1
1978	1,630.7	341.5	391.6	531.7	152.8	213.1

D. National Share of Regional Manufacturing Production (%)

	Costa Rica	*El Salvador*	*Guatemala*	*Honduras*	*Nicaragua*
1950	15.9	22.6	39.6	9.5	12.4
1960	19.2	21.6	34.8	10.4	14.0
1970	19.9	21.0	32.2	9.0	17.9
1977	19.8	19.0	34.5	11.6	15.1

Notes:

1. Statistics for the years 1978 and 1979 are notably suspect in the case of Nicaragua as a result of political turmoil; some figures put the manufacturing share of GDP at over 30 per cent in 1978.

Sources:
A and C. Pérez Brignoli, 'Growth and Crisis', p. 373.
B and D. Mayorga, *Crecimiento Desigual*, p. 58.

realize plans for an integrated regional market so that industrial production in certain sectors could acquire a viable scale. While the US government also sought a modernization of these economies through both improved agriculture and an expansion of the manufacturing sector, it was never prepared to countenance this at the cost of depriving its own industrial interests either of markets or of optimum terms for production. Washington opposed and was eventually able to sabotage the CEPAL project that sought to constrain the operation of foreign capital, replacing it with patronage of a Central American Common Market (CACM) that positively favoured the role of US investment in keeping with the general policy of the Alliance for Progress, founded under the Punta del Este Charter early in 1961.[51] At the time, this spoiling operation appeared to many outside CEPAL and the left as almost inevitable and a piece of technocratic politicking of only limited importance; the ambitions of the Alliance were sufficiently impressive to offer a real opportunity for a manufacturing 'take-off', for which local capital resources were very limited. The failure of the Alliance to meet the targets for overall growth, redistribution of income, diversification of trade, and improvements in health and education that were proclaimed in the wake of the Cuban revolution has proved to be abject in the extreme but it should not obscure the fact that the strategy had an appreciable impact.[52] This was by far the most ambitious and concerted US plan for Latin American development within the framework of export-led and foreign-capital-based growth, and while the projected US commitments in terms of aid and investment were never reached, those that were forthcoming significantly altered the character of the Central American economy.

As Table 14 shows, the overall growth of manufacturing industry was modest, and by 1978 provided less than one-fifth of total GDP. At the same time, the sectoral growth rate through the 1960s was high, producing a significant increase in value added. Moreover, while Guatemala accounted for a third of total production, only Honduras lagged badly behind in terms of regional distribution. Both the general rise in foreign investment and its increasing concentration on the manufacturing sector over the 1960s is reflected in Table 15. It should, however, be noted that by the time the Alliance for Progress had effectively disintegrated, less than a third of all foreign investment in the region was in manufacturing; this was despite the fact that 60 per cent of the increase over the decade had been in that sector. US corporations dominated this process, controlling 72 per cent of the 572 foreign operations in 1969 although the US share of total foreign investment had dipped slightly from 90 to 80 per cent over the previous ten years.[53] In 1980 US control of more than 1,000 businesses in the region rested on a total investment barely in excess of $1 billion – less than 3 per cent of US direct investment in Latin America as a whole when Central America accounted for 6 per cent of the population, over 4 per cent of

Table 15: Foreign Investment, 1959–69

	1959			*1969*		
	total (\$000)	*manufacturing (\$000)*	*%*	*total (\$000)*	*manufacturing (\$000)*	*%*
Central America	388.2	14.6	3.8	755.3	232.8	30.8
Costa Rica	73.2	0.6	0.8	173.3	36.7	21.1
El Salvador	43.0	0.7	01.6	114.6	43.7	38.1
Guatemala	137.6	1.1	0.8	207.0	90.3	43.6
Honduras	115.5	6.9	6.0	184.1	20.6	11.2
Nicaragua	18.9	5.3	27.8	76.3	41.5	54.4

Source: Centroamérica Hoy, p.125.

GDP and over 9 per cent of trade south of the Rio Grande. The total sum is, therefore, very modest in both absolute and relative terms, and is not in itself a central feature of increased US political interest in the region. This is particularly evident in the case of Nicaragua, where US capital investment shortly prior to the revolution stood at only \$100 million. Nevertheless, even very limited capital holdings provided North American corporations with great purchase over such small and backward economies. By the end of the 1960s the regional markets in animal feeds, cigarettes, petroleum, margarine, paper, steel, and tyres were either completely monopolized or overwhelmingly controlled by US businesses; thereafter it was only in oil that this control was significantly eroded.[54] At the end of the 1970s all bar eight of the top sixty-five US corporations in the fields of paper, chemicals, drugs, food processing and oil possessed operations in the isthmus.[55] From the mid 1960s the constant nett outflow of capital from Central America reflects general profitability, in most cases stemming less from local market control than from highly favourable conditions for production.[56]

Increased foreign investment in manufacturing did not alter the general character of production very greatly, and neither did it result in a rise in locally produced consumer durables and capital goods sufficient to approach the degree of import substitution envisaged by the CEPAL planners (Table 16a). The constraints imposed upon this by the character of the region's natural resources and infrastructure were in any event formidable in the extreme. This cannot be said for much of the light industry that was established from the 1960s onwards, and the generally high level of external inputs even for some traditional sectors of manufacturing registered in Table

Table 16a: Structure of Manufacturing Production, 1960–78 (%)

	Perishable goods		*Intermediate goods*		*Durable/capital goods*	
	1960	*1978*	*1960*	*1978*	*1960*	*1978*
Central America	86.3	70.1	9.0	21.2	4.7	8.7
Costa Rica	84.0	65.0	10.4	24.4	5.6	10.6
El Salvador	82.1	64.7	10.4	26.7	7.5	8.6
Guatemala	88.8	71.6	8.3	18.4	2.9	10.0
Honduras	84.8	80.0	8.6	16.0	6.6	4.0
Nicaragua	90.0	72.9	7.2	20.2	1.9	6.9

Source: Mayorga, *Crecimiento Desigual*, p.60.

Table 16b: Manufacturing Input Origin, by sector, 1975 (%)

	Costa Rica			*El Salvador*			*Guatemala*		
	nat.	*C.Am.*	*world*	*nat.*	*C.Am.*	*world*	*nat.*	*C.Am.*	*world*
foods, drink, tobacco	59.0	3.0	26.0	70.5	3.2	26.3	84.7	2.7	12.6
textiles, tannery	20.0	11.0	35.0	55.7	4.2	40.1	59.3	7.6	33.1
wood	43.0	1.0	19.0	40.5	23.3	28.2	91.5	0.4	8.1
paper, print	13.0	2.0	67.0	12.6	12.8	74.6	27.1	2.6	70.3
chemicals	12.0	6.0	65.0	7.1	4.2	88.7	8.0	4.6	87.4
non-metallic minerals	–	–	–	79.1	13.4	7.5	54.0	0.9	45.1
base metals	–	–	–	34.8	0.1	65.1	–	–	–
engineering	14.0	3.0	63.0	26.1	4.3	69.6	14.9	3.2	81.9
others	–	–	–	21.2	0.6	78.2	25.7	9.4	64.9

Note:
1. Guatemala – 1976.

Source: Mayorga, *Crecimiento Desigual*, p.63.

16b reflects less the absence of local raw materials than a distinct strategy on the part of foreign capital to develop enterprises dedicated primarily to finishing or assembly. Such a form of production – typically known as *maquiladora* – had its corporate rationality in low labour costs and high tax concessions rather than exploitation of local primary materials. As a consequence it severely limited the 'trickle-down effect' of new investment through to other areas of the local economy. The chronic limitations of this form of completing semi-finished imports for re-export – incarnated by Kimberly Clark's reduction of rolls of paper to lavatorially manipulable proportions – not only yielded a low level of value added and fiscal gain for the state but also failed to exercise much impact upon the regional import bill. Thus, a significant proportion of new industrial investment under the Alliance pertained more closely to enclave operations than to any autonomous process of manufacturing sufficiency.

The new phase of industrialization, critically flawed though it was as a strategy for integrated growth, did increase intra-regional trade; manufacturing products accounted for nearly 90 per cent of registered commerce within the CACM that rose from less than one per cent to over 5 per cent of GDP between 1950 and 1980.[57] This undoubtedly produced greater commercial ties between the states than at any time in their history (even allowing for historically high levels of contraband, which still continues), the links proving remarkably durable even in the current climate of border wars. However, the initial external tariffs established under the CACM were soon rendered inefficient by lack of modification, and the fact that they unduly favoured traditional manufacturing interests. Moreover, even the protectionist structure that was set up was not coordinated with any regional plan for the siting of strategic production, local specialization being largely determined by the relative advantages obtaining in the 1960s and thereby prejudicing the position of Nicaragua and Honduras in particular. The outbreak of the 1969 war between Honduras and El Salvador may be attributed in no small degree to the fact that over the previous eight years Salvadorean exports to Honduras had increased fivefold while those in the opposite direction had merely doubled; at the time of the conflict El Salvador contributed 24 per cent of the regional value added whilst Honduras accounted for only 7.7 per cent.[58] Much of this local trade was in goods produced in the traditional sector in which local capital was well represented, but its imbalances reflected the state of competition rather than coordination in national strategies to attract foreign investment, leading to inefficient duplication of resources in the more favoured countries while the controls upon foreign capital remained absolutely minimal everywhere.[59]

The new industries were rarely labour-intensive, the very much lower labour costs in Central America than in the US or even Mexico being only one of a series of attractions for foreign capital usually based upon modern plant and techniques. While the industrial proletariat did grow between 1962 and 1975 (Table 17), it did so at a markedly slower rate than either investment or production; its share of the total labour force rose only minimally at a regional level, falling in Costa Rica and El Salvador, and increasing most in Nicaragua at less than two percentage points. Further-

Table 17: Industrial Workforce 1962–75

		Economically Active Pop. (thousands)	*Industrial Workforce (thousands)*	*Proletariat as % of Total Labour Force*
Central America				
	1962	3,664	351.9	9.6
	1968	4,398	441.7	10.0
	1975	5,569	572.6	10.3
Costa Rica				
	1962	400	40.9	10.2
	1968	496	54.1	10.9
	1975	654	65.0	9.9
El Salvador				
	1962	858	87.3	10.2
	1968	1,017	101.8	10.0
	1975	1,271	118.8	9.3
Guatemala				
	1962	1,288	128.5	10.0
	1968	1,524	162.7	10.7
	1975	1,912	219.5	11.5
Honduras				
	1962	604	44.9	7.4
	1968	743	57.3	7.7
	1975	948	78.7	8.3
Nicaragua				
	1962	514	50.3	9.8
	1968	618	65.8	10.6
	1975	784	90.6	11.6

Source: Mayorga, *Crecimiento Desigual*, p.66.

more, an elementary disaggregation of the manufacturing sector by size of workplace (Table 18) shows that even when calculated on the basis of five or more workers, the 'factory' sector failed to match small workshops in terms of overall employment although almost everywhere workers engaged in this sector doubled during the period. Indeed, Table 18 understates the degree to which a general artisanal culture has survived since this frequently prevails in workplaces of many more than five labourers. All the same, it is clear that foreign companies generally employed larger labour forces, a survey of Guatemala, Honduras and Costa Rica revealing that in the early 1970s 83 per cent of local firms employed less than fifty workers while 38 per cent of foreign enterprises had a labour force of this size; 37.6 per cent of foreign firms employed more than 100 workers against 7.3 per cent of local companies.[60] Hence, while manufacturing remained remarkably traditional in form, with food products, textiles and clothing only falling from 79.5 to 62.6 per cent of gross output between 1960 and 1978, increased foreign investment in these sectors and chemical and mineral production (up from 8.1 to 18 per cent) tended to produce a more concerted pattern of proletarianization within a working class that continued to be generally dispersed.[61] This internal tendency assisted the consolidation of a working-class culture in the urban centres through a more extensive experience of assembly-line discipline, the congregation of larger numbers of workers, and the establishment of new plant and sectoral unions, within which a greater incidence of negotiation with foreign enterprises – much less frequently foreign management – enhanced the more political features of syndicalism. On the other hand, this sector was often marked by the 'newness' of workers – in terms of age, the high number of women workers, and lack of specific craft traditions – as well as their greater vulnerability to replacement in unskilled jobs. The objective conditions of the expansion of the working class from the early 1960s do not allow for an easy identification of a 'vanguard', and there is equally little evidence from trade union and political activity of a clearly distinct leadership within a specific group of the working class; however, at times certain elements, such as the Coca Cola workers in Guatemala City or the power workers in El Salvador, have played this role.

Most importantly, in no country did the manufacturing working class constitute a majority of the urban labour force. In 1974 artisans, workers and apprentices amounted to only 33 per cent of Managua's working population; in 1975 industrial workers comprised 27 per cent of all employees in San Salvador and 35 per cent in Guatemala City.[62] Of the total non-agricultural labour force in Costa Rica in 1976 22.4 per cent were employed in industry and mining, the numbers engaged in commerce and services growing more rapidly than those in manufacturing throughout the decade.[63] This was a general pattern, nurturing a proletariat that had grown by 61 per cent between 1962 and 1973 within a much wider popular urban culture of artisans and employees. In practice the social weight of the industrial working class was still more limited since even in the early 1970s the number of 'self-employed' workers in the service and commercial sectors was much greater than that formally registered in censuses and employment statistics. According to official sources the self-employed grew at the same pace as the economically active population as a whole, comprising 27 per cent of all workers in 1950 and in 1973.[64] However, the incapacity of the urban economy to provide wage labour for an escalating population increasingly bolstered the number of those for whom there was no alternative but to engage in petty trading of goods and services on their own account as a means of survival. This population, often described as 'marginalized' or engaged in the 'informal economy', is itself heterogeneous

Table 18: Factory and Workshop Production and Employment, 1962–75

	Gross Industrial Production (millions of 1970 C.Am pesos)			*Industrial Employment (thousands)*		
	Total	*Factory*[1]	*Workshop*	*Total*	*Factory*	*Workshop*
Central America						
1962	502.9	331.2	171.7	351.9	127.9	224.3
1968	851.4	610.0	241.4	441.7	169.7	272.6
1975	1,236.6	1,014.7	221.9	572.6	256.8	315.8
Costa Rica						
1962	89.8	71.8	18.0	40.9	22.1	18.0
1968	150.3	123.2	27.1	54.1	27.2	26.9
1975	240.7	209.4	31.3	65.0	35.0	30.0
El Salvador						
1962	112.1	78.2	33.9	87.3	38.4	48.9
1968	189.4	138.3	51.1	101.8	46.9	54.9
1975	247.2	197.8	49.4	118.8	66.7	52.1
Guatemala						
1962	170.3	105.1	65.2	128.5	31.4	97.1
1968	283.7	179.0	104.7	162.7	44.5	118.2
1975	406.1	317.6	88.5	219.5	69.4	150.1
Honduras						
1962	57.5	34.4	23.1	44.9	15.3	29.6
1968	92.3	65.6	26.7	57.3	20.9	36.4
1975	133.3	112.0	21.3	78.7	36.8	41.9
Nicaragua						
1962	73.2	41.7	31.5	50.3	20.4	29.9
1968	135.7	103.9	31.8	65.8	29.6	36.2
1975	209.3	177.9	31.4	90.6	48.9	41.7

Note:
1. Factory – workplace with labour force of over five persons.

Source: Mayorga, *Crecimiento Desigual*, p.67.

and does not simply constitute a disguised pool of unemployed since even after the reversal of growth in formal employment and real wages in the mid 1970s a significant proportion was employed in established economic activity with earnings comparable to and sometimes superior to those of waged workers.[65] It would, though, be more erroneous to depict it as typically petty-bourgeois and based upon a stratum of shopkeepers and affluent market vendors. Between 1971 and 1975 the number of 'self-employed' in El Salvador rose from 47,000 to 131,000, an increase far exceeding any potential for successful entrepreneurial activity even of the most limited nature. This remarkably high figure may certainly be explained by the impact of the

'Football War', but if the scale of urban underemployment elsewhere was more modest, it also began to exhibit chronic tendencies. It is not possible to identify a clearly differentiated 'informal' working class since many of those engaged in petty commerce do so as part of a wider household strategy that may well also include a more or less regular wage income. Moreover, this sector is by its very nature resistant to measurement by all but the most global indices of economic activity. Yet it is evident that by the end of the 1970s recourse to non-waged marginal work had become necessary for a larger proportion of urban dwellers than that registered in very conservative figures for open unemployment (derived almost exclusively from the urban sphere in 1980): Costa Rica 6.0%; El Salvador 16.2%; Guatemala 28%; Honduras 14.4%; Nicaragua 16.2%.[66] Subsequent figures reflect the impact of the world recession and political instability, which have maintained levels everywhere except in Costa Rica above 20 per cent for more than six years; in addition to being a potent factor in the generation of social tension prior to 1979, the fall in regular paid work thereafter has clearly played a part in fuelling political conflict.

This burgeoning urban 'under-class' exchanges too dynamically with the formal sectors in both the towns and countryside to be denoted as a lumpenproletariat. Both increased dependence upon seasonal wages in the rural economy and the limited size of the manufacturing working class have reduced the social distinctiveness of underemployment and marginalized petty trading, generalizing the experience of partial or temporary wage labour to such an extent that it has become far more common over the last thirty years than that of a 'pure' worker or peasant. This has created a complex of alignments and contradictions that frequently resist categorization in classic economic terms. The urban environment has tended to enhance those features of a general 'popular economy' that unite the poor whatever their status as labourers. The communality engendered by the appalling conditions and absence of services in sprawling suburban shanty-towns that attended the soaring and unplanned influx into the primary cities defies a simple occupational explanation. It is in this sphere that one encounters the most fluid interaction between, on the one hand, a strategy of negotiation and cautious, incrementalist defence of livelihood and domestic terrain characteristic of the squatter predicament and, on the other, that of pugnacious civic mobilization and direct conflict with the local and national agencies of the state when individualist remedies have been exhausted. The *tugurios* of Central American cities are only partially comparable to the Palestinian refugee camps in terms of a communal retention of the culture of original settlement and the centrality of a politics of displacement, and they generally lack the bipolar character of the South African 'townships' and illegal squatter-camps, such as Soweto and Crossroads, where such elements are sustained by state policy in both economic and racial fields.

However, throughout the 1970s the *barrios* of Managua, San Salvador and Guatemala City in particular became the site of a robust and extensive politics beyond that of a plebeian mass goaded by the absence of bread. In each case accumulating settlement on the urban periphery was affected by natural disasters – the earthquakes of 1965 and 1986 in San Salvador, 1972 in Managua, and 1976 in Guatemala – that severely prejudiced minimal advances in town planning. However, it was the more enduring structures and insufficiencies of the urban economy that lay behind the extraordinary series of popular mobilizations in San Salvador in 1979 and 1980, the effective *levée en masse* of Managua's *barrios* against the National Guard in 1979, and the lightning riots that shook an unprepared military dictatorship in Guatemala in 1978 and 1985.

However great the pressure on the popular economy from the early 1950s onwards, it was only from the mid 1970s that the regional economy as a whole entered into major difficulties. The scale of this recession (Table 19) is fully comparable with that in the rest of Latin America. The 'oil shocks' of 1973/4 and 1979 hit the balance of payments – only Guatemala possesses reserves of petroleum – and encouraged greater borrowing of surplus Euro-dollars from the banks, particularly in the case of Costa Rica, which subsequently acquired a debt profile very close to that of the larger Latin American states.[67] In 1973/4 the impact of the oil price rise was appreciably softened by increases in the price of coffee, but from 1979 the prices of Central America's principal exports did not follow this pattern and the general terms of trade became more adverse (Table 20).[68] The region's historically low levels of inflation increased, and although price rises did not approach the hyperinflationary rates of the Southern Cone countries (except in Nicaragua after 1984), they began to erode wages everywhere.[69] (The figures in Table 19 do not follow a 'purely economic' pattern: the great drop in Guatemalan wages in 1977 was caused by the earthquake of the previous year, and the rise in 1981 belatedly registers the results of plantation strikes; the Nicaraguan figures for 1979 and 1980 reflect the impact of the civil war.) The high rates of growth that had characterized the isthmian economy since 1945 were first slowed and then, from 1980, sent into reverse. Together with this termination of a thirty-five-year cycle there emerged the familiar financial features of recession ranging from reduced export earnings and cutbacks in imports to depletion of foreign exchange reserves, a growing tendency to devaluation and capital flight, reduced social expenditure and accelerated indebtedness.[70] With the exception of Nicaragua, effectively boycotted by Washington from 1981, the response of the regimes was to acquiesce in pressure from the North for neo-liberal policies of stabilization even though these increased the political crisis considerably. This naturally prompted dissident voices within the dominant blocs, but the states lacked the resources of even the smaller Southern American countries to support

Table 19: Principal Economic Indicators, 1977–83

	1977	*1978*	*1979*	*1980*	*1981*	*1982*	*1983*
1. GDP per capita growth (%)							
region	4.6	1.0	−3.0	−2.4	−3.8	−7.1	−2.5
Costa Rica	6.4	3.7	2.1	−2.3	−4.8	−11.1	−1.6
El Salvador	3.4	2.6	−4.3	−11.5	−11.1	−7.3	−0.6
Guatemala	4.2	1.7	1.2	1.0	−1.5	−5.8	−5.2
Honduras	7.4	3.9	2.9	−0.6	−3.4	−4.7	−3.6
Nicaragua	2.8	−10.0	−27.8	6.5	5.0	−3.9	2.6
2. Balance of Payments deficit ($ millions)							
region	−572	−1,131	−833	−1,681	−2,144	−1,688	−1,547
Costa Rica	−226	−364	−554	−658	−408	−249	−383
El Salvador	+22	−292	+16	−2	−265	−265	−239
Guatemala	−37	−271	−180	−178	−565	−405	−195
Honduras	−139	−170	−205	−331	−321	−249	−209
Nicaragua	−192	−34	+90	−512	−585	−520	−521
3. Growth of real wages (%)							
Costa Rica	9.4	8.8	4.5	0.8	−11.8	−19.7	−6.2
El Salvador	–	−5.9	1.7	−6.1	−12.9	−10.5	−11.7
Guatemala	−14.9	4.8	0.1	0.1	17.6	6.0	−6.4
Honduras	−7.8	−5.4	11.5	8.3	5.1	−1.0	−8.2
Nicaragua	−1.6	–	−13.6	−14.9	1.4	−12.9	−25.4
4. External debt ($ millions)							
region	2,984	3,590	4,396	6,322	7,927	9,779	11,062
Costa Rica	812	1,112	1,463	2,140	2,413	2,860	3,096
El Salvador	458	517	511	947	1,254	1,487	1,658
Guatemala	302	304	427	549	809	1,119	1,187
Honduras	538	696	864	1,107	1,288	1,516	1,736
Nicaragua	874	961	1,131	1,579	2,163	2,797	3,385
5. Debt service as % of exports							
Costa Rica	12.6	21.1	20.8	25.1	31.0	32.3	66.6
El Salvador	6.0	3.5	2.4	3.3	4.1	5.6	6.7
Guatemala	1.9	2.9	2.5	2.6	4.1	6.8	11.0
Honduras	16.7	17.2	22.6	20.2	27.5	34.2	18.2
Nicaragua	13.6	14.3	8.9	11.9	31.4	43.7	20.0

Source: CEPAL, *Notas Económicas de 1984.*

any qualification of IMF rationality.

This severe contraction of the economy at the turn of the decade fuelled political conflict but did not cause it. Even if a breakdown in social order of the scale witnessed in Central America were to correspond to short-term economic performance, it can be seen that the recession took hold properly in 1980–81, two to three years after the first phase of popular mobilization in Nicaragua, Guatemala and El Salvador. This, as should now be clear, derived its impetus from much longer-term dynamics within the social and economic structure (reflected in Table 21). These dynamics, in turn, cannot be divorced from the social and political controls that they engendered. Most evidently in the case of Nicaragua but to a significant degree elsewhere, it was at this level – that of political domination – that the system was subjected to most forceful challenge. It should, however, be borne in mind that as political confrontation broke into guerrilla warfare and the threat of governmental collapse in El Salvador and Guatemala, markedly increased the level of social unrest in Honduras and Costa Rica, and embattled the new Sandinista government in Nicaragua, the economic climate was at its worst since the early 1930s. This inevitably aggravated the conflict, consolidated the opposing blocs, and gravely reduced the possibilities for tactical solutions.

Table 20: Prices of Principal Regional Exports, 1975–82 (1980 dollars)

	1975	*1976*	*1977*	*1978*	*1979*	*1980*	*1982*[1]
Coffee (cents per kg)	241	519	804	468	428	343	306
Bananas ($ per ton)	413	423	417	367	364	379	398
Sugar ($ per ton)	751	419	271	220	238	632	311
Beef (cents per kg)	103	119	115	111	189	194	170
Cotton (cents per kg)	206	288	247	206	191	207	193

Note:

1. 1982 – estimate.

Source: World Bank, *Year-End Updating of Commodity Price Forecasts*, Washington 1981.

Table 21: Basic Social Indicators, 1980

	%GDP spent on:			*Infant*	*Life*	*Pop. per*	*% pop. under*	*School*	*Literacy*[4]
	health	*educ.*	*milit.*	*mort.*[1]	*expect.*[2]	*doctor*	*15 years*	*attendance*[3]	
Costa Rica	1.3	6.2	0.4	30	71	1.198	36.6	60	90
El Salvador	1.5	3.4	3.9	85	62	3,163	44.3	23	70
Guatemala	1.4	1.6	1.9	79	56	8,600	42.7	18	56
Honduras	1.6	3.5	4.6	95	59	2,529	46.9	32	60
Nicaragua	1.7	4.3	7.0	58	57	1,484	46.5	43	88

Notes:
1. Infant mortality – deaths per 1,000 live births.
2. Life expectancy – in years at one year of age.
3. School attendance – percentage of secondary age group.
4. Literacy – percentage of adults functionally literate.

Sources: Inter-American Development Bank; World Bank; CEPAL.

Notes

1. Quoted in Roger Burbach and Patricia Flynn, *Agribusiness in the Americas*, New York 1980, p. 214.

2. Quoted in ECA, no. 335/36, September–October 1976, pp. 611–13.

3. Quoted in Tom Barry, Beth Wood and Deb Preusch, *Dollars and Dictators. A Guide to Central America*, London 1983, p. 3.

4. *The Report of the President's National Bipartisan Commission on Central America*, New York 1984, p. 43.

5. Tables 5a and 5b do not, of course, purport to demonstrate exactly the same phenomena, but they will suffice for general comparative objectives here. It should be stressed that statistics originating in Central America are subject to greater qualifications with respect to accuracy than those from industrialized states. Moreover, although efforts have been made to employ sources drawn from CEPAL (*Comisión Económica para América Latina*), this has not always been possible either directly or indirectly. The three main sources of data in this chapter are the special issue of the *Journal of Latin American Studies* (JLAS) of November 1983 (which should be consulted particularly for Bulmer-Thomas's explanation of his methodology); John Weeks, *The Economies of Central America*, New York 1985; and Román Mayorga Quirós, *El Crecimiento Desigual en Centroamérica*, Mexico 1983. Professional economists may dispute such a cavalier entwining of secondary sources but until we possess a comprehensive collection of serial data for the post-war period based on a uniform methodology there is little alternative to promiscuity.

6. For a general account, see Bonnie Mass, *Population Target. The Political Economy of Population Control in Latin America*, Toronto 1976, which contains a case study of Guatemala.

7. Critical surveys of the cases of El Salvador and Honduras that refute simplistic Malthusianism on the basis of income distribution, the changing food-base and access to subsistence resources may be found in G.E. Karush, 'Plantations, Population, and Poverty: The Roots of the Demographic Crisis in El Salvador', *Studies in Comparative International Development*, vol. 13, no. 3, 1978, and, more extensively, in the innovative study by William H. Durham, *Scarcity and Survival in Central America*, Stanford 1979. For the consequences for health of a demographic crisis that has only become such as a result of the structure of wealth, see Roberto Badia, 'Consideraciones Básicas para una Política de Población en El Salvador; Aspectos de Salud', ECA, no. 329, March 1976.

8. Mayorga, *Crecimiento Desigual*, p. 33.

9. Carlos Samaniego, 'Movimiento Campesino o Lucha del Proletariado Rural en El Salvador?', *Revista Mexicana de Sociología*, vol. 42, no. 2, April–June 1980, p. 663.

10. Adams, *Crucifixion by Power*, p. 390.

11. *Tenencia de la Tierra y Desarrollo Rural en Centroamérica*, San José 1973, p.42; T.J. Downing, 'Agricultural Modernization in El Salvador, Central America', Occasional Paper no. 32, Centre for Latin American Studies, University of Cambridge, 1978, p. 40.

12. Biderman, *Class Structure*, p. 196; *Tenencia de la Tierra*, p. 42. In the mid 1960s the most complete available survey reveals regional surplus agricultural labour to be high but also very variable between states:

	Surplus labour power (labourer-years)	*Farms*	*Surplus labour power per farm (labourer-years)*
Central America	1,059,490	59,049	17.9
Costa Rica	105,953	13,987	7.6
El Salvador	320,060	4,362	73.4
Guatemala	249,637	7,580	32.9
Honduras	183,000	10,831	16.9
Nicaragua	200,840	22,289	9.0

Source: Tenencia de la Tierra, pp.39, 83.

13. Downing, 'Agricultural Modernization', p. 40. Between 1961 and 1971 the area in *colonato* fell from 10 to 7 per cent while that farmed by tenants paying a money rent rose from 13 to 16 per cent. When the proportions are taken by size of unit they suggest that this shift was the result of a 'knock-on effect' through the system, with 'middle peasants' passing on the pressure to tenants of the smallest plots: the rise in money rent of plots of less than one hectare was from 31 to 53 per cent of total land held in units of this size (the fall in *colonato* being from 43 to 22 per cent).

14. Nancy Peckenham, 'Land Settlement in the Petén', *Latin American Perspectives*, vol. 7, nos 2/3, 1980.

15. Carcanholo, *Desarrollo del Capitalismo*, p. 132; Quirós Guardia, 'Agricultural Development', pp. 98–9.

16. Héctor Pérez Brignoli goes as far as to argue, albeit without statistical support, that improved techniques introduced in the 1950s 'meant the intensive use of manual labour'. 'Reckoning with the Central American Past: Economic Growth and Political Issues', Working Paper no. 160, The Wilson Center, Washington, p. 4.

17. Daniel and Esther Slutzky, 'El Salvador: Estructura de la Explotación Cafetalera', ESC, no. 6, September–December 1973.

18. Daniel Slutzky and Esther Alonso, *Empresas Transnacionales y Agricultura: El Caso del Enclave Bananero en Honduras*, Tegucigalpa 1980, cuadro A.

19. Barry et al., *Dollars and Dictators*, p. 19.

20. *Food Monitor*, September–October 1979, p. 11.

21. Slutzky and Alonso, *Empresas Transnacionales*, cuadro 6.

22. Barry et al., *Dollars and Dictators*, give comprehensive lists of the subsidiaries of US corporations in each country.

23. Robert G. Williams, 'Land and the Crisis in Central America', mimeo, Greensboro, North Carolina, 1985, p. 27. This paper contains some of the central arguments of the author's *Export Agriculture and the Crisis in Central America*, Chapel Hill 1986, which was not available when this chapter was drafted. I am grateful to Robert Williams for permitting me to draw on his important work prior to publication.

24. Biderman, *Class Structure*, p. 180.

25. Lester Schmid, 'The Role of Migratory Labor in the Economic Development of Guatemala', Research Paper no. 22, Land Tenure Center, University of Wisconsin, Madison, July 1967, p. 26.

26. *Tenencia de la Tierra*, p. 173.

27. Biderman, *Class Structure*, p. 183; Williams, 'Land and the Crisis', p. 30.

28. Biderman, *Class Structure*, p. 184.

29. Ibid.

30. L.B. Fletcher, Eric Graber, William C. Merrill, Erick Thorbecke, *Guatemala's Economic Development: The Role of Agriculture*, Ames 1970, p. 75.

31. Schmid, 'Migratory Labor', p. 20.

32. In the case of Guatemalan mothers' milk the Central American Nutritional Institute found the level to be eighteen times the medically safe limit. NYT, 27 March 1978. For Nicaragua, see Biderman, *Class Structure*, p. 105.

33. Increase in Area and Yield of Cane Sugar, 1950–80 (per cent):

	Costa Rica	*El Salvador*	*Guatemala*	*Honduras*	*Nicaragua*
Area	130	154	392	279	131
Yield	36	25	83	35	81

Source: Victor Bulmer-Thomas, 'Economic Development in the Long Run', JLAS, vol.15, no.2, 1983, p.288.

34. Weeks, *Economies*, p. 102; Bernard Roux, 'Expansión del Capitalismo y Desarrollo del Subdesarrollo. La Integración de América Latina en el Mercado Mundial de la Carne de Vacuno', ESC, no. 19, January–April 1978, p. 23. Between 1960 and 1980 the Central American rainforest was reduced from 400,000 square kilometres to 200,000 square kilometres. According to the FAO half of the existing Honduran rainforest will be destroyed by the year

2000. In Costa Rica only 15,900 square kilometres are left, 11,300 of them in national parks. James J. Parsons, 'Forest to Pasture; Development or Destruction?' *Revista de Biología Tropical*, no. 24, Supplement 1, 1976; Billie DeWalt, 'The Cattle are Eating the Forest', *Bulletin of the Atomic Scientists*, vol. 39, no. 1, January 1982; Joseph Skinner, 'Big Mac and the Tropical Forests', *Monthly Review*, December 1985.

35. Roux, 'Expansión', p. 23.

36. Biderman, *Class Structure*, pp. 114–16.

37. Daniel Slutzky, *El Caso de la Agroindustria de la Carne en Honduras*, Quito, p. 42.

38. Barry et al., *Dollars and Dictators*, p. 25; *Multinational Monitor*, October 1981, p. 17; Carcanholo, *Desarrollo del Capitalismo*, pp. 186–8.

39. Slutzky, *Carne en Honduras*, pp. 77, 87.

40. Biderman, *Class Structure*, p. 183. Slutzky, *Carne en Honduras*, p. 37, illustrates the relative rates of productivity in 1970.

41. A detailed account of this important incident in the heart of the *Franja Transversal del Norte* is given in *Panzós: Testimonio*, Guatemala City 1979.

42. Indeed, according to Durham's statistics for per capita food production in El Salvador, *Scarcity and Survival*, p. 25, the level was significantly worse than that suggested by Table 13, being consistently less than 3.5 quintals per capita from 1952 onwards. Imports of food crops rise and the amount of land in basic grains falls from the mid 1950s, suggesting a close correspondence with the expansion of cotton. Although Durham does not present directly comparable figures for Honduras, where cattle rather than cotton produced the pressure on peasant holdings, he indicates a somewhat more modest pattern. Durham's thesis is at heart a radical neo-Malthusianism, but although based upon resource abundance, his study is distinguished by its concern with the dynamics behind the progressive 'difficulty of subsistence', carefully disaggregating the type of crop and patterns of tenure to demonstrate the importance of allocation of resources rather than simply their gross levels.

43. *Estructura Demográfica y Migraciones Internas en Centroamérica*, San José 1978, pp. 32, 37. Alternative figures are given in *Tenencia de la Tierra*, p. 120, and Claude Bataillon and Ivon LeBot, 'Migración Interna y Empleo Agrícola Temporal en Guatemala', ESC, no. 13, January–April 1976, that broadly conform with this picture despite different methods of calculation.

44. Bataillon and LeBot, 'Migración Interna', p. 51. For a detailed development of this theme, concentrated largely on the case of Totonicapán, see Carol A. Smith, 'Beyond Dependency Theory: National and Regional Patterns of Underdevelopment in Guatemala', *American Ethnologist*, vol. 5, no. 3, August 1978.

45. Ministerio de Agricultura y Ganadería, *Diagnóstico del Sistema Agropecuario, 1960–75*, San Salvador 1976, vol. 1, cited in Federación de Trabajadores del Campo, *Los Trabajadores del Campo y la Reforma Agraria en El Salvador*, Chipalcingo 1982, p. 9.

46. Biderman, *Class Structure*, pp. 94–5.

47. *Estructura Demográfica*, p. 356, gives the figures for 1970.

48. Ibid., p. 328.

49. Cabarrús, *Genesis de una Revolución*, pp. 121–9, goes to some lengths to reject the notion of the migratory labour force of Chalatenango, El Salvador, being 'proletarianized' in any formal sense, but if this process is viewed in a more expansive sense it is less than clear that such a wholehearted rejection can be upheld, even for Chalatenango, which cannot be described as a 'typical' region of the country. For an analysis that postulates an unqualified process of proletarianization, see M. Flores Alvarado, *La Proletarización del Campesino en Guatemala*, Guatemala City 1970. A theoretical response to this work is given in Edelberto Torres Rivas in ESC, no. 2, May–August 1972.

50.

Country	*Total Pop.*	*Largest City*	*Second City*
Guatemala	7.7 mn	Guatemala: 1.18 mn	Quezaltenango: 92,000
El Salvador	5.2 mn	San Salvador: 500,000	Santa Ana: 100,000
Honduras	4.3 mn	Tegucigalpa: 533,000	San Pedro Sula: 397,000
Nicaragua	3.1 mn	Managua: 650,000	León: 95,000
Costa Rica	2.5 mn	San José: 500,000	Cartago: 50,000

51. For a detailed survey of the origins of the market and the economic and political debate that attended it, see Susanne Jonas Bodenheimer, 'El Mercomún y la Ayuda Norteamericana', in *La Inversión Extranjera en Centroamérica*, San José 1974.

52. At Punta del Este, Uruguay, Kennedy aimed to achieve an overall hemispheric growth rate of 2.5 per cent per capita per year by 1970. This level was first reached in 1968, but over the decade only Chile registered any significant shift in the pattern of income distribution, also being virtually the only country to introduce an agrarian reform, which was central to the Alliance's strategy. The objectives of eradicating adult illiteracy, adding five years to the average life expectancy, and building up local savings to provide 80 per cent of investment all proved wildly unrealistic. Jerome Levinson and Juan de Onis, *The Alliance that Lost its Way. A Critical Report on the Alliance for Progress*, Chicago 1970.

53. For details, see *La Inversión Extranjera* and Gert Rosenthal, 'El Papel de la Inversión Extranjera Directa en el Proceso de Integración', in *Centroamérica Hoy*.

54. David Tobis, 'La Falacia de las Inversiones Norteamericanas en Centroamérica', in *La Inversión Extranjera*.

55. For details, see Barry et al., *Dollars and Dictators*.

56. For slightly different calculations of direct investment and remittances of profits that nonetheless concur in identifying a nett outflow from 1956/6, see Weeks, *Economies*, p. 93; Guillermo Molina Chocano, 'Estado y Proceso de Acumulación en Centroamérica', ESC, no. 37, 1984, p. 95.

57. Mayorga, *Crecimiento Desigual*, pp. 90–4; Pérez Brignoli, 'Growth and Crisis', p. 368.

58. Comprehensive analysis of the commercial and other aspects of the conflict is undertaken in *La Guerra Inutil*, San José 1971; *Análisis sobre el Conflicto entre Honduras y El Salvador*, Tegucigalpa 1969; Thomas Anderson, *The War of the Dispossessed*, Lincoln, Nebraska 1981.

59. It is difficult accurately to assess the relative weight of foreign and national investment by sector for the region as a whole. However, with the exception of food processing, there is little evidence that foreign capital deviated greatly from the predictable pattern of concentration in more advanced areas of production. In the case of Costa Rica between 1960 and 1970 foreign investment dominated food and drink processing, auto parts, chemical and pharmaceutical products, office equipment and paper, fertilizers and furniture; local capital remained preponderant in clothing and textiles, construction, cosmetics and agricultural machinery. Jose Luis Vega, 'Inversiones Industriales en Costa Rica', *Revista de Ciencias Sociales*, San José, no. 7, April 1973, cited in Helio Fallas, *Crisis Económica en Costa Rica*, San José 1981, p. 43.

60. *Centroamérica Hoy*, pp. 126–7.

61. Weeks, *Economies*, p. 136.

62. James Dunkerley, *The Long War. Dictatorship and Revolution in El Salvador*, London 1985, p. 55; Carlos Vilas, *The Sandinista Revolution. National Liberation and Social Transformation in Central America*, New York 1986, p. 102; M. Soto, C. Sevilla and E. Frank, *Guatemala: Desempleo y Subempleo*, San José 1982, p. 17.

63. Fallas, *Crisis Económica*, pp. 53, 135.

64. Pérez Brignoli, 'Growth and Crisis', p. 386.

65. The work of Leo Despres on the Brazilian city of Manaus – one of the few detailed anthropological surveys of the modern 'informal sector' – shows that it is erroneous to assume that the standard of living of workers in the modern industrial sector is either greater or more stable than those in the informal sector, even than those who are very modest pedlars. In the case of Manaus many poor workers reject inducements such as transport and creches provided by the new industrial park, favouring autonomy over assembly-line discipline and the regular but poor remuneration that accompanied it. Few Central American zones have exhibited the rates of growth of the Amazon region and although sharply limited by the absence of labour protection, the relatively greater stability of labour in the formal circuit than in the self-employed sphere would seem to exercise a rather different effect to that noted for Manaus. For a pioneering study of the urban poor in Guatemala, see Brian Roberts, *Organizing Strangers*, Austin 1973.

66. Inter-American Development Bank, 1983. By 1983 only Costa Rica had averted a critical deterioration while the level in Nicaragua had risen only slightly over the war-affected figure for 1980: Costa Rica – 8.6%; El Salvador – 40%; Guatemala – 33.7%; Honduras – 21.2%; Nicaragua – 17.5%.

67. A detailed survey of the Central American debt is given in Jorge F. Pérez–López, 'Central America's External Debt in the 1970s and Prospects for the 1980s', Occasional Paper no. 6, Florida International University, Miami, fall 1983. For the adjustment process: Victor Bulmer-Thomas, 'The Balance of Payments Crisis and Adjustment Programmes in Central America', Paper to the Twelfth Congress of the Latin American Studies Association, Albuquerque, April 1985.

68. Terms of Trade (1877 = 100):

	1979	*1981*	*1983*
Costa Rica	80.2	66.1	56.8
El Salvador	67.7	50.4	49.9
Guatemala	81.6	61.0	57.1
Honduras	90.9	76.9	78.6
Nicaragua	81.3	75.3	60.0

Source: CEPAL, *Notas Económicas*, 1983.

69. Inflation (per cent):

	1978	*1980*	*1982*	*1984*
Costa Rica	5.9	18.2	90.1	8.6
El Salvador	12.9	17.4	11.7	14.3
Guatemala	7.9	10.7	0.2	5.0
Honduras	5.7	18.1	9.4	5.2
Nicaragua	4.5	35.3	24.8	60.0

Source: Bulmer-Thomas, 'Balance of Payments', p. 14. The impact of a severe adjustment programme can be seen in the case of Costa Rica between 1982 and 1984. After 1984 prices in Nicaragua entered a hyperinflationary spiral, the government responding with increasingly severe methods of adjustment.

70. With the exception of Costa Rica total current expenditure rose in every Central American state between 1978 and 1983 faster than did revenue. Outside of Nicaragua direct tax income stagnated while that from trade generally fell. Ibid., p. 13. In real terms taxes fell everywhere except Costa Rica and Nicaragua, the level in Guatemala, which has the lowest rate of direct taxation in the western hemisphere, becoming an issue of political controversy.

6

The Nicaraguan Revolution – Origins

I believe that the Nicaraguan revolutionary should embrace a doctrine which can lead the Nicaraguan people victoriously to liberation. In my own thought I welcome the popular substance of different ideologies: Marxism, Liberalism and Christian Socialism.

Carlos Fonseca Amador, 1964[1]

'Yeah, how about those jerks', replied the dictator. 'First they send me this', and he took a small envelope from a drawer and tossed it across to the Voice of America correspondent. It was President Carter's 1977 letter to Somoza praising the suspension of the state of siege. 'And then they send an ambassador down here to tell me I have to resign!'[2]

The issue isn't Somoza but Nicaragua and the security interests of the US. This Sandinista uprising is a Cuban, Panamanian, Costa Rican operation. It's another Vietnam and it's in this hemisphere.

Congressman John Murphy (D-NY), June 1979[3]

The FSLN Directorate is the head of the Revolution. The Vanguard.

Alfonso Robelo, MDN leader and member of Junta, 1979[4]

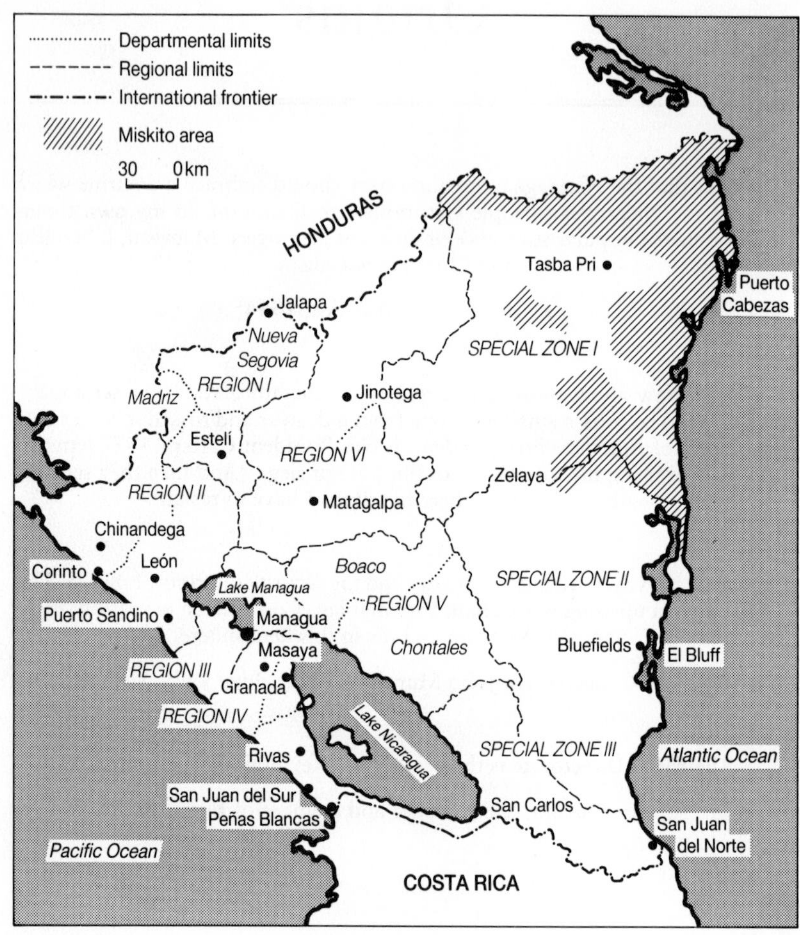

Departmental limits
Regional limits
International frontier
Miskito area
30 0 km
HONDURAS
Tasba Pri
Puerto Cabezas
Jalapa
Nueva Segovia
SPECIAL ZONE I
Madriz
REGION I
Jinotega
Estelí
REGION VI
Zelaya
REGION II
Matagalpa
Chinandega
Corinto
León
Boaco
SPECIAL ZONE II
Lake Managua
Puerto Sandino
Managua
REGION V
Masaya
Chontales
Bluefields
El Bluff
REGION III
Granada
REGION IV
Lake Nicaragua
Rivas
SPECIAL ZONE III
Atlantic Ocean
San Juan del Sur
Peñas Blancas
San Carlos
San Juan del Norte
Pacific Ocean
COSTA RICA

Nicaragua

The historical importance of the overthrow of the Somoza regime and establishment of a revolutionary government under the leadership of the *Frente Sandinista de Liberación Nacional* (FSLN) in July 1979 is beyond serious dispute. The highly destructive civil war of 1978–79 opened a revolution that not only terminated forty-five years of dynastic rule but also decisively shifted the balance of power within Central America as a whole. Inside eighteen months it was apparent that the new regime in Managua was presiding over a process of political and social transformation comparable to or surpassing that witnessed in previous Latin American revolutionary movements: Mexico (1910–40); Bolivia (1952–64); Cuba (1959–); and Chile (1970–73). The example of Nicaragua was widely celebrated in South America as a somewhat distinct instance of national liberation rather than as a directly imitable model since most countries were ruled by either liberal democratic regimes or institutional dictatorships established after the failure of the very guerrilla strategy that proved successful in ousting Somoza. Moreover, by 1982 the South American states as well as Mexico were entering a severe economic depression that, despite imposing extraordinary hardship on the labouring masses, was not immediately conducive to the eminently political and military forms of struggle that characterized the Nicaraguan revolution.

Within Central America, by contrast, the victory of July appeared to be fulfilling all the fears of the domino theorists as social conflict escalated in El Salvador and Guatemala. Even before the Carter administration trooped out of office it was clear that events in Nicaragua had transformed US policy towards the isthmus; with the inauguration of Ronald Reagan early in 1981 the rapid reversal from an ignored and unimportant backwater into a zone of transcendent strategic importance for Washington was fully confirmed. Henceforth Central American affairs were so directly influenced by US intervention that it became implausible to treat this as simply one variable amongst many. Debate over US government activity rapidly dominated analysis of the region and began to acquire the characteristics of a North American domestic issue. As a result, many people living outside Central America came to engage with its affairs principally through the perspective of Washington's policy. In view of the form and degree of intervention this was fully understandable, yet it has tended to restrict debate to the parameters of the prevailing US political discourse. Nowhere is this more evident than in the case of Nicaragua, the depiction of which has become sufficiently stereotyped to require a brief remark upon the reception of the revolution in the US before moving on to an appraisal of its origins and course.

The public vision of Nicaragua in North America has naturally revolved around the claims made by the Reagan administration that the FSLN has suppressed western liberal democracy and established a totalitarian state on the basis of the Marxist–Leninist beliefs and in the service of a Russo–Cuban conspiracy in the western hemisphere. According to the US government the Sandinistas betrayed the original broad-based and purely anti-dictatorial revolution of July 1979, subverted constitutional regimes in the rest of the isthmus, and are well underway in their project of eradicating capitalism in emulation of Cuba. As a result, by the end of 1981 Reagan secretly approved the funding of a counter-revolutionary campaign organized by the CIA. Over the following six years the possibility of direct US military intervention was never formally disavowed; it was kept alive by particularly pugnacious rhetoric as well as by constant manoeuvres in Honduras and, for a time, congressional approval for the policy of supporting the contras. The Irangate scandal that broke late in 1986 effectively ruled out an invasion of the type witnessed in the Dominican Republic (1965) and Grenada (1983), whilst the revelations that followed the scandal confirmed that the administration had concentrated its energies on a 'strategy of tension' dedicated to destabilizing the economy and forcing the Sandinista state into an expensive and unpopular policy of militarization. Although aspects of this policy were illegal under international and US law, Reagan steadfastly refused to withdraw his charges against the FSLN or alter his approach to revolutionary Nicaragua. We need not concern ourselves with the detailed debate over this policy, which is extensively covered in many studies. The debate was for a long time taken up with the veracity of the evidence presented to support the administration's charges against the FSLN (the supply of weaponry to the Salvadorean guerrilla; the establishment of bases for advanced fighter aircraft; the mass slaughter of Miskito Indians) as well as the acceptability in terms of both law and realpolitik of Washington's own activities (the mining of harbours; training and funding of terrorists; economic sabotage) against a government and nation with which it continued to maintain diplomatic relations, albeit largely to sustain the pretence of seeking a solution through formal treaties. Much of this activity dismayed Washington's allies and fortified the US public's aversion to prolonged and costly foreign adventures. A press made more curious and critical by Vietnam and Watergate hampered the manipulation of North American popular anti-communism less in terms of whether or not the government of Nicaragua deserved to be overthrown – even the *New York Times* agonized over the merits of this – than in terms of the desirability and consequences of this for its readers and their children. The administration tended to excite open derision in liberal circles by its clumsy inventions, enthusiasm for skulduggery that made a mockery of the term 'covert operation', and matinée projections of an 'Evil Empire' against which were ranged the forces of democracy and civilization. However, if one concurs with the liberal appraisal that the US government was and is fully intent upon breaking international law if necessary, fostering terrorism and warmongering, it should be made clear that this is not primarily because of incompetence, misguided perceptions or moribund stratagems. On the contrary, such a response derives from a cogent policy based upon the understanding that whether or not the Sandinistas were aiding the Salvadorean guerrillas, preparing invasions of Honduras and Costa Rica, or in receipt of protective guarantees from the Soviet Union and Cuba – in each case all the available evidence confirms that they were not – the Nicaraguan revolution remained a direct challenge to US hegemony and must be comprehensively defeated along with the rest of the Central American radical bloc.

Such a policy could only be enunciated in code. It was, for instance, impossible openly to declare that the US will not respect Nicaraguan rights as a sovereign state. Liberal opponents to Reagan's policy have drawn much rhetorical strength and been able to tap domestic democratic idealism in invoking the formal equivalence of Washington and Managua in national and international law. How can it possibly be, they argue, that a state as small and poor as Nicaragua might pose a threat to the security of the world's greatest power? In seeking national self-determination the Nicaraguan government is not only within its rights but also in pursuit of ideals realized in the US in the late eighteenth century and still enshrined in its constitution. Moreover, this government presents no danger to North American society since it has repeatedly declared that it will not exploit its natural right to extend logistical facilities to Washington's recognized and powerful enemies.[5] The Sandinistas have sensibly and understandably laid great stress on this position, encouraging the broadest defence of their revolution at home and abroad around the motif of national sovereignty that did so much to ensure its success in the first place and remains a critical feature of its subsequent consolidation. However, the Sandinista Comandantes appreciate as well as does the Reagan administration that while they are the wronged and innocent party in terms of the formal and juridical conception of relations between nation-states as equals, they constitute an acute danger to the US insofar as it is an imperialist power that cannot afford to countenance authentic national sovereignty in its own 'sphere of influence'. This is because what is irreducibly specific in form – the revolution's patriotism – is also contagious in that it is engendered as much by a repudiation of US hegemony as by unique historical experiences within the frontiers of Nicaragua. The defence of Nicaraguan national sovereignty is, therefore, most efficaciously sustained by campaigns in support of the rule of law but it cannot be fully understood in such terms.

Unable publicly to repudiate Managua's claims to national independence, Washington turned its attentions to the domestic policy of the FSLN government.[6] In this quarter the liberal critique was noticeably less secure: despite a series of flagrant propagandist concoctions by Washington, it was evident from early on that the Nicaraguan regime was not engaged upon a complete adoption of the norms of bourgeois or liberal democracy. Although it eventually held presidential and parliamentary elections by secret ballot in November 1984, the FSLN remained pledged to a form of 'popular democracy' which, while preserving space for organized political opposition not dedicated to subversion, was clearly distinct from the type of pluralism practised in advanced capitalist states and partially comparable to the *form* of mass organization practised within the Soviet bloc. Increasingly convinced that this hybrid system of government served to enhance one-party domination – regardless of whether or not it was encouraged by the Reagan offensive – many of those who previously opposed Washington's approach tout court began to launder their views, criticizing the FSLN for either tactical ineptitude or residual bad faith.[7] The liberal critique thus decomposed into a plethora of discrete positions, losing in the process much of its purchase inside a sceptical congress, with the result that by mid 1986 the administration was able to win support for public funding of counter-revolutionary activity.

Although the US government's version of Nicaragua dominated the electronic media and that of the liberal doubters and pragmatists filled the up-market magazines and op-ed pages, supporters of the internal political regime and socio-economic policies of the Nicaraguan revolution succeeded in retaining a significant following in academic and religious circles. Extending well beyond the compass of the orthodox left and entirely excluded from debate at governmental level, this current took on the characteristics of a broad activist and solidarity movement in which the need for unity in order to oppose Washington's policies naturally tended to subordinate discussion of the complex and critical features of the revolution not readily attributable to these policies. Hence, although sympathizers of the revolution have produced by far the most incisive analysis of it, the inevitable logic of their public campaign has been to denounce Washington 'from the other side' and embrace the Sandinistas' version of their own history. This is far closer to reality than the self-serving belligerence of the Burbank school of historiography dished out from the White House, but it has tended to support a rather narrow and teleological perspective that dispenses with the awkwardnesses of politics as well as those of history. Thus, just as the insurrection of July 1979 is perceived to result from an entirely logical combination of contradictions in social structure and the agency of the FSLN, so also are the constituent features of the contemporary political economy characterized by an immanent coherence and necessity.[8] This does not, of course, preclude debate over the extraordinary difficulties encountered at all levels in post-revolutionary Nicaragua. On the other hand, it does militate against a more profound interrogation of the nature of Sandinismo since doubts over its immutable specificity both challenge one of its central canons and open the door to right- and left-wing interpretations and criticism considered prejudicial to a revolution that is most felicitously defended in terms of its individuality and distance from orthodox ideological currents.

If the denunciation or celebration of all or part of the Nicaraguan revolution in the US does not provide us with the best starting point for discussion by virtue of the intrusion of factors beyond our scope here, the intellectual debate has certainly been focused on issues of central importance. The first of these relates to the origins and character of the 1979 insurrection itself. Clearly, such factors as the exceptionalism of the Somocista state, the critical divisions within the dominant bloc, the strategy of the FSLN, the peculiarities of Nicaraguan social structure, and the peculiarly bleary policy of the Carter administration are of direct consequence for an understanding not only of subsequent developments but also of why it was in Nicaragua and not elsewhere in Central America that a popular revolution triumphed. Not surprisingly, the FSLN possesses a far more developed explanation of its success in its own terms than in those of the conditions and limitations of fraternal organizations elsewhere in the isthmus. Yet it is of more than marginal interest to assess the peculiarity of Nicaraguan conditions in the context of Central America as a whole. Whilst Washington's view that the revolution was simply 'ambushed' by Marxist–Leninists resists sober historical analysis, the opposing view that the FSLN's leadership of the movement derived from a constant and optimum expression of the popular will needs to be reviewed in the light of the organization's longstanding isolation and major shifts in strategy. In each case the balance in explanation between the structural condition of the country in the post-war period and the role of socio-political agency within it deserves reconsideration.

The contesting claims that Sandinista Nicaragua is an unpopular totalitarian Marxist state pursuing the destruction of capitalism or a new form of popular democracy in which both opposition and private enterprise are permitted evidently derive in good measure from differing interpretations as to what occurred in 1979. At the same time, the heated debate over the character of the regime reflects the fact that even eight years after the revolution it has not yet settled into a stable and necessary pattern of development, its many contradictory tendencies encouraging different views as to a probable future course. Given the continued US offensive, an exceptionally grave economic crisis, and the difficult logistical situation of the country, it is less easy to hazard a detailed view on what this might be than it is to demonstrate that the revolution remains in transition to a far higher degree than most comparable regimes after a similar period in power. Nicaragua is not a workers' state since a considerable portion of the economy remains in the hands of large capitalist enterprise, although state control over finance and foreign trade has tended to reduce the incentives for private companies to reinvest and reproduce themselves. The political system is no less complex since the FSLN is patently more than the party in government, its victory in the polls of 1984 confirming a hegemony won in 1979 and subsequently consolidated through the state, the military and the popular organizations. On the other hand, both formal and informal opposition is tolerated to a far greater degree than in the Soviet bloc, to a point comparable with most liberal democracies in Latin America and certainly beyond anything permissible in El Salvador or Guatemala, Washington's local showcase regimes. The social policy of the government is redistributionist, statist and egalitarian but notably dedicated to furthering the interests of 'the people' rather than those of any specific social class. Here, as in so many other aspects, Sandinista political discourse is as clear to those on the right, who perceive a process of Leninism by stealth, as it is to adepts of absolutist Marxist orthodoxy, who anticipate a comprehensive capitulation to capitalist forces. It is only in terms of the national question that Sandinismo has insisted from the start upon an entirely clear and unnegotiable position, reflecting a national history in which the mode of domination was tied with peculiar strength to US hegemony.

The Peculiarities of the Somocista State

Very few governments, let alone forty-five-year regimes, can properly be characterized by their terminal state. Insofar as it is not a truism, the argument that the Somoza regime was an exceptionally vulnerable target for popular opposition is only partially persuasive. During its final months the Somocista state was revealed to lack control over not only the masses but also a significant sector of the ruling class, becoming exclusively dependent upon the backing of a distinctly brutal and surprisingly incompetent military machine that had no institutional identity separate from the dynasty. Finally subjected to historic justice at the hands of both the heirs of its ancestral enemy, Sandino, and its traditional ally, Washington, the government of Anastasio Somoza Debayle collapsed with its weaknesses and contradictions laid bare and fully exploited. Yet for all its anachronism, brutality, personalism and dedication to the political economy of plunder, this regime had not only subsisted for nearly half a century but had also been able to do so with relative facility. The subsequent debility of bourgeois political forces reflected more than the momentum given to the FSLN by the final battle for power; it underscored the central importance of the Somozas to the unity of a dominant bloc that had been upheld by much more than state violence. Thus, while in one sense it is entirely apposite that Somocismo remain in the popular memory as a beastly enterprise doomed to extinction through blind self-interest, this is an insufficient history.

The Somoza state cannot be characterized exclusively by its personalism; three members of the family held office with discernibly different styles and without lodging claims to either supernatural prowess (their preference was for prowess in the carnal realm) or supra-institutional powers (they manipulated the apparatus of liberal democracy at will but, like their regional peers, never dispensed with it). This regime did not lack political acumen, being as successful in imposing alliances as in harrying those who would not make them, and it did not neglect the systematization of co-optation and control that simultaneously generated income. Perhaps most important of all, it was the most favoured US ally in the isthmus until two years before its collapse, exploiting more than the legacy of the 1930s in maintaining this role. Nonetheless, the circumstances and conditions that attended the establishment of the Somocista state exercised an enduring influence, the dominant bloc continuing to revolve around the Somozas' arbitration within a ruling class lacking a firm base in the traditional hacienda (together with its customary social control through peonage) and unable to secure hegemony through continued attachment to nineteenth-century political ideologies and organization.

Following the pact of 1950, which confirmed the participation of most of the Conservative party in the Somocista system, political divisions in the ruling class acquired an increasingly formalist character. This was partly because the conflicts of the 1940s had greatly depleted the potential of traditional Conservatism and badly ruptured Liberalism – Somoza expropriated much of the party's apparatus and ideology through his *PL-Nacionalista* (PLN) – and partly because the expansion of cotton placed a premium upon commercial activity and subordinated the importance of partisan disputes. The cotton boom did not, however, promote the consolidation of the ruling class that a late and partial adoption of coffee had failed to endow. A significant proportion of the new cotton estates were of a modest size (a position reflected in Table 8a, p.180), which shows the average extent of Nicaraguan farms as far higher than the regional median, with 44 per cent of units being between seven and thirty-five hectares) and a great many were not operated directly by landlords but rented out – in the 1970s 50–60 per cent of cotton production was from rented lands, ground rent becoming a central feature in economic relations from the early 1960s. This organization of what was to become Nicaragua's strategic export corresponded to both the logic of production, whereby control was most readily exercised through credit, processing and merchandising, and to the absence of a traditional *system* of large-scale non-pastoral agriculture. It therefore tended to reproduce, albeit at a higher level of activity, longstanding divisions within the capitalist class. The *Banco de América* (1952) generally represented the interests of sugar, cattle and traditional commercial sectors tied to the Conservative oligarchy (and now linked to the Wells Fargo bank) while the *Banco de Nicaragua* (1953) concentrated upon extending credit for cotton and adopted a more dynamic policy of diversification from the 1960s. However, BANIC remained both dependent upon international capital – its ties were primarily with Chase Manhattan – and representative less of direct producers than of mercantile interests in an economy where credit amounted to 62 per cent of the value of agricultural production (Costa Rica – 64%; El Salvador – 25%; Honduras – 31%; Guatemala – 10%) with farmers controlling less than 25 per cent of the sales of raw cotton and 10 per cent of the ginned product.[9] Thus, although their share of the market was comparable to that of the Somoza clan, neither of these two groups represented a distinctively new and progressive sector of capital that might be associated with a 'national bourgeoisie'. It was not until the mid 1970s that they began to protest the clan's practice of 'disloyal competition', and even then they were markedly more reluctant to dispute the terms of this than was COSIP (*Consejo Superior de la Iniciativa Privada*), which represented a wider group, including small businesses dependent upon BANIC or BANAMERICA loans.

Despite being concentrated in the strategically important financial and commercial sector, foreign capital maintained its historically low levels, failed to sustain enclave operations for any length of time, and was equally associated with the three large entrepreneurial groups. Anastasio Somoza's speculative dalliances with the likes of Howard Hughes and Bebe Rebozo, and the higher profile given to his commercial ventures in the US, resulted less in stronger business ties with North American capital than in a closer public association with it than was the case for his competitors. The Somozas' interests continued to be bolstered by their control of the state apparatus which facilitated the funding of the PLN from civil servants' salaries, generation of liquid funds through sinecures (more petty in form than reward), the siphoning off of external loans and aid, and equally remunerative manipulation of government contracts. At the same time, the family was able to move beyond the realm of pure plunder with the cotton boom, in which it shared a leading role with BANIC and through which it became fully established as a strategic faction of the capitalist class. This shift from absolute parasitism was consolidated in the late 1950s, when the clan also confirmed its dominance in the cattle trade through the control of abattoirs and transport. Here it both competed with Conservative interests and provided the basis for expansion of the industry as a whole. Moreover, since in the late 1960s over half the national herd was still raised on farms of less than 85 acres, family control of the market was no less conducive to friction with smallholders than with traditional livestock enterprises.[10] As will be seen from the scale of expropriation after July 1979, even by global standards the family accumulated quite extraordinary wealth, which was extracted from virtually every quarter of a small and impoverished economy as well as from ventures further afield. Yet the extent of the Somozas' holdings did not match claims made at the time of the revolution that they controlled half of the economy, and neither was their importance restricted to the reaping of fabulous private reward. This certainly engendered critical political effects, but it was only the most tangible and repugnant form of an enterprise that served for many years to bond rather than to factionalize the local capitalist circuit. Indeed, class unity was long preserved precisely by the uneven terms of competition. It was given a historical logic in the absence of foreign investment and the need for forceful arbitration caused by both this and the particular form of development that had denied the Nicaraguan bourgeoisie a productive basis for control and hegemony to the degree reached elsewhere in Central America (except Honduras, which, of course, possessed a dominant enclave).

This contradictory aspect of the Somozas' economic interests was mirrored in their relations with the bourgeois political parties. Although competition in this sphere necessarily took a more explicit character, it was also curbed by the logic of participation in a system that was more transparently continuist than any other in the region. The basic methods whereby compliance and control were obtained remained constant throughout the period between the death of the patriarch and the revolution. With short interruptions family power was exercised through the offices of the PLN, which continued to win elections less by complex fraud than by the mechanism of issuing an identity card – the *magnífica* – only to those who cast a readily identifiable ballot for the Somozas and their supporters; without this card employment in the public sector was effectively closed and encounters between the individual and all agencies of the state made complicated and generally antagonistic. Although it was always possible simply to 'cook' the count, elections were exploited in a more systematic fashion to extend PLN control. Opposition in the formal political sphere necessarily revolved around gaining minority representation and some space for debate although the public presumption of possibilities to take office was unavoidable. The official Conservatives ('*Zancudos*') were,by virtue of being the largest and most historically rooted opposition party, most directly affected by this system, but with only short interruptions they complied with it from 1950 until the eve of the revolution. In return for guaranteed minority representation in congress Conservatism accepted Somocista control and was permitted to lead the formal opposition to it, thus sustaining the fiction of a liberal democracy. In practice, more telling and substantive oligarchic opposition was expressed in the columns of *La Prensa*, the daily newspaper owned by the Chamorro family that for decades had nurtured a deep personal and only loosely Conservative political enmity for the Somozas. This channel for dissent and competition with the officialist *Novedades* was permitted in order to evade charges of authoritarianism at a relatively low cost, since *La Prensa* had a limited circulation in a largely illiterate country and its leaden prose was very far from radical in tone.

The general lack of turbulence through the 1950s and most of the following decade must certainly be linked to the expansion of the economy and the influence of the Alliance for Progress, which encouraged an acquiescent attitude on the part of the bourgeoisie. It can also be related to the disposition of Luis Somoza (1957–63) and the puppet president René Schick, who held office from 1963 to 1967 under the close supervision of Luis and Anastasio junior, to avoid violence in the regime's relations with the oligarchy, preferring to strike bargains on the understanding that coercion remained an omnipresent option. Although this was a distinctly imbalanced exchange between regime and opposition, the fact that it was manipulated with some flexibility is often overlooked in the light of the increasing reliance upon direct antagonism and violence on the part of Anastasio junior, president from 1967 to 1971, de facto ruler from 1972 to 1974, and re-elected president in 1974.[11] Since the regime was from 1972 progressively more personalist in character, it is natural that such a policy reflected in good measure the proclivities of the man himself, who had been commander of the National Guard from 1956 onwards. At the same time, greater dependence on the National Guard corresponded to rising social conflict and was in line with developments in the other states.

As in Guatemala and El Salvador, the military was at the centre of the system long before it came to dominate it. In marked contrast to the pattern in those countries, the Nicaraguan National Guard (GN) did not operate with institutional autonomy, being commanded throughout its history by members of the Somoza family (during the insurrection Anastasio III was directing many operations) and dedicated as much to furthering their economic and political interests as to fulfilling less narrowly partisan tasks of state control. Since the great majority of the Guard's 3,000 men were employed as policemen, and only the elite EEBI (*Escuela de Entrenimiento Básico de Infantería*) and BECAT (*Brigadas Especiales Contra Actos del Terrorismo*) given full military training, the force was less an army than a paramilitary body, best suited to enforcing local control, overseeing graft and undertaking surveillance. Subjected by Somoza to tight internal control through dispensation of favours, frequent rotation of postings, and the occasional expulsion of ambitious officers, it was large enough to seem ubiquitous in a small country and yet too small to develop an institutional ethic beyond loyalty to its commander. Eventually the Guard's overwhelming dedication to police duties and the practice of corruption at all levels undermined its military capacity to resist the FSLN as much as did Somoza's persistent reluctance to expand its numbers and provide it with greater logistical capacity, which he perceived as a potential threat to the regime. Such organizational traits enhanced the private character of the force, making it dependent upon the administration of an informal economy, pitting it against a society that it both taxed and harassed as well as binding it irredeemably to a state that could not be dissociated from a political cause.[12]

Despite being the ultimate guarantor of Somocismo, the Guard was more than a purely partisan force. It upheld a state of a combined and contradictory character, simultaneously dedicated to the interests of a specific sector of capital and to maintaining the rule of the bourgeoisie as a whole. When in the late 1970s Somoza lost the support of much of the bourgeoisie and the state came under challenge from the masses, the Guard was doubly stretched. In operational terms it could no longer rely upon the coordination of the rural *jueces de mesta* (provincial magistrates and executive officers) or discrete acts of dissuasive repression; instead it was obliged to adopt a strategy of extensive terror that was both politically counterproductive and logistically unsustainable for any period of time. Furthermore, whilst its role as defender of the capitalist state instilled in the bourgeois opposition considerable reluctance to demand its abolition and led Washington to insist upon both its retention and incorporation into a post-Somoza government, the Guard's brutality in defence of Somoza and its inability to divorce itself from him made such a position completely untenable. Unable to escape from this impasse, the National Guard was more comprehensively defeated than the praetorian forces of other personalist regimes destroyed in the same period (Trujillo; Pahlavi; Marcos; Duvalier).

Until the late 1970s there was little evidence that such demands would be placed upon the force. The flurry of disorganized invasions by dissident Conservatives in the late 1950s was contained without difficulty and the early guerrilla operations of the FSLN in the central zones of the country had been brought to a halt with the disastrous Pancasán campaign of 1967. However, in that year control though the formal political system began to break down when the Conservatives, the PLI and the *Partido Socialcristiano Nicaragüense* (PSCN; founded in 1957) combined to form the *Unión Nacional de la Oposición* (UNO) and challenge the candidacy of Anastasio II to succeed the puppet Schick. This resumption of the demand for democratic propriety was backed by the pro-Moscow PSN and encouraged by the relatively free rein given to the bourgeois opposition by Luis Somoza, who thereby unwittingly enticed the Conservatives to mobilize their still appreciable popular following. Late in January 1967 UNO staged a demonstration of some 60,000 people in support of the candidacy of Dr Fernando Aguero and to protest the attacks upon the opposition by government forces taken unawares by the strength of its challenge. Belief in the potential of this campaign was shown to be tragically misconceived when Anastasio Somoza ordered the National Guard to attack the march; over 500 people were killed in a massacre that effectively terminated popular commitment to an anti-dictatorial electoralist strategy earlier than elsewhere in the isthmus. Somoza allowed himself to win 70 per cent of the subsequent vote, but he had been made aware of the dangers of so tightly circumscribing the formal opposition. As a consequence, at the end of his term in 1971 he signed the 'Kupia-Kumi Pact' with Aguero whereby the *Zancudo* Conservatives had their congressional quota increased to 40 per cent, a constituent assembly was established, and a triumvirate comprised of Aguero and two Somocistas designated to rule until the end of 1974, when fresh elections were to be held. Throughout this period Somoza would retain his post as Guard commander, just as his father had done in the late 1940s, to ensure no loss of real power. This pact confirmed and legalized the Conservatives' preference for minority participation in the system to leading a sustained challenge on it, and as such it broke the historic constituency of the party. Neither the PLI nor the PSCN possessed sufficient popularity to replace it, and over the ensuing decade the legal opposition parties proved incapable of forming a coherent alliance against Somoza, their lassitude prompting internal divisions and further weakening the appeal of electoralism.

This state of affairs owed little or nothing to the FSLN, which lacked popular backing for its guerrilla strategy until at least 1974, possessing only a few dozen militants at the beginning of the decade. It should also be noted that one central consequence of the dynasty's prolonged rule was that the Nicaraguan people had the least reason of all the electorates in Central America to place faith in change through the ballot box. In Guatemala the polls of 1944, 1950 and even to some extent 1966 had produced a reasonably faithful expression of popular choice between the options on offer; the system in El Salvador provided at least some scope for registering dissent, the opposition winning important local elections and possessing a presence in parliament that sustained illusions about the possibility of forming an administration. In Costa Rica the electoral system formed the basis of political activity, and even in Honduras competition between the Liberal and National Parties was sharp enough to give elections some value even if they yielded minimal changes in government policy. In short, even where it was comprehensively manipulated and periodically suspended, the apparatus of liberal democracy was elsewhere a far more resilient mechanism for the maintenance of the dominant bloc than was the case in Nicaragua. Here, the last poll arguably deserving serious psephological attention was that of 1932, which, as agreed under US mediation in 1927, raised the listless Sacasa to office. The consequence of this electoral history was that while democratic demands were naturally at the centre of the anti-dictatorial movement, they lacked a powerful point of reference to the liberal system. The delay of five years in holding a national poll after the revolution should, therefore, be seen as just as much a function of popular lack of interest as it was the result of FSLN policy.

The irony of the pact of 1971 was that it greatly diminished the efficacy of control through co-optation. This aspect of the Somocista system was to be reduced a great deal further when, just after 12.30 a.m. on 23 January 1972, an earthquake struck the country and demolished the city of Managua, which is situated on a major geological fault-line. According to official statistics 10,000 people died, 20,000 were injured and 300,000 made homeless; the real figures were certainly higher still. Some 75 per cent of the capital's buildings were destroyed and 90 per cent of commerce brought to a halt, the damage being estimated by the UN at $772 million. As in all catastrophes, the real nature and capacity of government and state was rapidly revealed. Somoza retreated to his home and the National Guard all but disintegrated as officers and troops alike engaged in unhampered pillaging or simply deserted. So chaotic and ineffectual was the regime's immediate response that for several days what vestige of public order existed in the capital was provided by troops from CONDECA and the US flown in once the scale of the disaster and the precarious condition of the government became apparent. The awful destruction and trauma caused by the earthquake were to persist for a very long time – sixteen years later Managua remains a city bereft of an urban aspect, with few buildings of more than two storeys and large areas of wasteland. Yet it was the nature of the regime's 'reconstruction' programme that unhinged Somocismo. Declaring the earthquake to have offered 'a revolution of possibilities', Somoza grasped this unparalleled opportunity to extend the family's economic operations without any concern about the effects of resorting to plunder. While the population was most immediately and directly affected by the Guard's theft of emergency supplies – soon offered for resale – more substantial gains were made in appropriation of relief grants and channelling of contracts for demolition and reconstruction of infrastructure into the hands of family concerns. Somoza's speculation in real estate reached proportions that scandalized those interests not offered a cut in the considerable profits, and the extent of his grip over reconstruction contracts may still be seen in the ubiquitous paving-stones of the capital's streets, rebuilt not with asphalt but materials monopolized by family concerns. Such unqualified exploitation of the disaster effectively eroded Somocista hegemony within the bourgeoisie as a whole, which was henceforth obliged to contend with methods of primitive accumulation that gravely prejudiced the position of small and medium enterprises and disturbed the confidence of large capital. The subsequent disaggregation of class unity and damage to the regime's image abroad were so marked that when Guatemala was hit by an earthquake in 1976 the Laugerud regime went to some lengths to avoid repeating Somoza's example.

The declaration of a state of emergency as a result of the earthquake and Somoza's simultaneous adoption of de facto executive powers put paid to any lingering expectations that the 1971 pact would yield a change in government. Because of the formal interregnum, Somoza was free to stand in the poll of 1974. He won 743,985 out of 815,758 votes cast, the Conservatives picked up their allocation of 40 per cent of the seats for fulfilling the tryst, and an equal proportion of the electorate abstained. The very predictability of this result provoked a growing number of dissidents from the Conservative and Liberal Parties to join with the PLI, PSCN, PSN and a number of trade unions in forming the *Unión Democrática de Liberación* (UDEL). This alliance, as might be expected from its constituent parts and as readily admitted by its leader Pedro Joaquín Chamorro (owner and editor of *La Prensa*), possessed no coherent plan as an alternative to Somoza yet under the conditions prevailing in 1974 could draw substantial support simply by opposing him. Critical declarations at the COSIP conference of March 1974 had fired warning shots across the government's bow but to no avail, and when UDEL, which was very much the political vehicle for COSIP, called a boycott of the September poll Somoza proffered no bargain and gaoled two dozen of its leaders.

UDEL did not represent large capital as a whole, but its strong ties with medium enterprises and sections of the petty bourgeoisie, together with its ability to gain support from elements of the left seeking to realize a popular front, made its withdrawal from the system a matter of some importance. When faced with such a response the regime's claims to have democratic status appeared distinctly threadbare, increasing the incentive for Somoza to cut his losses and declare a completely authoritarian government at a time when these were proliferating in South America. In real terms such a step would have produced little change and required minimal preparation. Although it would not have been encouraged by Washington, it is unlikely that Somoza would have encountered great difficulties in that quarter; he had long enjoyed close relations with the US, built not solely upon ideological affinity and the maintenance of social stability but also upon the direct and important logistical assistance for the invasion of Guatemala and the Bay of Pigs. Such support had added extra charm to the historic 'special relationship' between Managua and Washington established in the 1920s and 1930s and sealed at a diplomatic level between a president whose guttersnipe English was more fluent than his Spanish and enchanted envoys such as the amenable and long-serving Thomas Whelan (1951–61) and the equally non-Spanish-speaking Turner Shelton, appointed by Nixon in 1970 and capable of little beyond adulation of his host. This won the fawning diplomat his portrait on the twenty-cordoba note but scarcely provided the State Department with an accurate picture of the condition of its leading regional ally. The appointment of characters like Whelan and Shelton was, of course, largely a manifestation of Washington's desire to disturb incumbent regimes as little as possible with requests for social and political reform prior to and following the failure of the Alliance for Progress. Nowhere was the propensity to follow such a policy more pronounced than in the case of Nicaragua, for which the attitude captured in Roosevelt's description of Somoza senior as a 'son of a bitch' but one on the right side, continued to prevail, as was disastrously evident in the failure to rein in the dictator after the earthquake. It was, then, quite unremarkable that the State Department raised no objections to the declaration of siege on 28 December 1974. However, the fact that this move was provoked, not by UDEL's truculent boycott of the polls, but by an audacious guerrilla kidnap of leading members of the regime that very nearly resulted in the capture of Ambassador Shelton, should have sounded the alarm that new and dangerous forces were afield.

The Rise of Sandinismo

The raid on the house of Agriculture Minister 'Chema' Castillo in December 1974 was a magnificent propaganda coup for the FSLN. Once it became clear to Somoza that the distinguished hostages could not be released by force, he was obliged to pay $2 million in ransom, broadcast guerrilla communiqués that were not timid in their analysis and denunciation of his person and government, and concede the pay rises they had demanded even for the enlisted men of the National Guard. According to the Sandinistas the raid marked a watershed in breaking the regime's image of invulnerability and linking popular economic demands to a radical political programme. Yet, as is common in operations of this type, it was staged with very much greater logistical flair and individual courage than mass support, and while its demands proved both popular and successful in themselves, they also presaged rising repression under a state of siege that was to last for nearly three years. Over this period the FSLN contrived to establish a limited organized following and to generate wider sympathy whilst it suffered from fierce internal divisions and failed to make much military headway against the Guard. Hence, what is now seen as a critical landmark in Sandinista history was by no means simply a point in a consistent linear ascent of the organization to leadership of the popular bloc. Although this image can be readily derived from the eventual success of the revolution, it corresponds only with the last eighteen months of the FSLN's pre-revolutionary existence and does little justice to the skill and resource of the organization in confronting its many difficulties and setbacks as well as exploiting subsequent conjunctural opportunities. The heroic vision of the FSLN's past is justified by the fact that it sets equal store by defeats as by victories, venerating the entirety of a struggle that was ultimately triumphant. Yet however honourable, historically determined and ultimately uncontainable, this was not the product of a natural and logical process nor purely the result of the agency of the FSLN itself.

Established in Tegucigalpa in 1961, the FSLN only acquired the critical 'Sandinista' element of its title after internal debate, the immediate political origins of the young radicals who formed it being in dissident Conservatism and the PSN. The three founders – Carlos Fonseca Amador, Tomás Borge and Silvio Mayorga – belonged to a generation that had been rudely disappointed by the dictatorship's ability to survive the death of the patriarch – for which Fonseca and Borge, together with Pedro Joaquin Chamorro, were held for some time as suspects – and exasperated at the lack of combativity of the Conservative leadership as well as the cautious organizational and anti-insurrectionist approach of the PSN. They therefore made their voyage from student oppositionism (for which Fonseca's home-town of Matagalpa had been an important centre) to a still multifaceted but coherently radical national liberation strategy not only at the time of the Cuban revolution, the Algerian war and the resurgence of the Vietnamese revolution but also via repudiation of the two 'natural' foci of domestic opposition.[13] Over the better part of two decades the internal emphasis of FSLN policy would oscillate between the ideal poles of authentic democracy and economic transformation, but these were always combined with a third predominant motif in authentic national independence and sovereignty, which was far more directly drawn from Sandino's example. Since the FSLN was for almost all of its pre-revolutionary history a military organization and only infrequently engaged in semi-clandestine popular organization, these constituent features of its politics were generally mediated and often dominated by the idea of armed struggle and debate over the most adequate means by which to pursue it. Guerrilla strategy definitively separated the FSLN from both orthodox socialism and the rest of the anti-dictatorial opposition from the start and was a critical factor in giving the Sandinistas the leadership of the popular bloc.

If Sandino provided a powerful precedent for opposition through a guerrilla army and not a political party as such, it should be recalled that Nicaragua did not lack an erratic history of 'revolutions' and petty insurrection right up to the early 1960s. Mostly undertaken by dissident Conservatives, but sometimes by survivors of the campaign of the early 1930s such as Ramón Raudales, these ill-organized ventures amounted to little more than isolated and desperate efforts to revive nineteenth-century methods, being sustained less by domestic support than by readily crossable frontiers and accessible havens in Costa Rica and Honduras. A participant of one such 'revolt' in 1959 recalled,

> About three weeks passed, and I was still waiting. The Hondurans stole the weapons whilst one of them, Selva, director of the *Gran Diario*, went to Costa Rica, dressed up as a general and made his way to the studios of *Radio Reloj*. There he got hold of the microphone and began to shout, 'At this moment a second front is being opened in the north of Nicaragua,' and it was me with one .38 pistol and a double-barrelled shotgun.[14]

Such enterprises generally began with the air of an *opéra bouffe* about them but they almost invariably collapsed without a shadow of comedy. The exigencies of operating in very difficult terrain, lack of support from a peasantry naturally inclined to a survivalist suspicion and under the tight vigilance of the *jueces de mesta*, and the efficient brutality of the National Guard finally reduced them to little more than a needless loss of lives. The first ten years of the FSLN's sporadic operations in the north and central zones of the country were characterized by significantly greater seriousness of political purpose and logistical preparation, yet they were still severely hampered first by the illusions traditionally bred by 'invading' the country and then by the allied but distinct problems of the *foco* strategy. The 1963 campaign in the Bocay region was, like all the organization's early intromissions, beset with basic difficulties of survival, being most directly doomed by the fact that the zone was one inhabited primarily by Miskitos, more than usually unlikely to support the 'Spanish' youth who threatened to attract the attentions of the Guard to their isolated communities. Greater tactical skill was evident in 1967 with the campaign around Pancasán, where a poor peasantry prejudiced by commercial farming proved to be supportive to a point at which the small vanguard force could subsist for several weeks before its operations were halted by a few ambushes in which thirteen fighters, including Silvio Mayorga, were killed. Again in 1970, operations in Zinica collapsed for lack of sufficient political and military infrastructure, but if this defeat terminated the first rural phase of the guerrilla, it also saw the survival of most of the small FSLN column. Rural *foquismo* had proved a failure and the Sandinistas had been incapable of generating a challenge to the state which matched that posed by the FAR and MR-13 in Guatemala. At the same time the leading cadre had undergone an extended baptism by fire, learning their lessons by bitter experience as much as by theoretical debate. (It should not be forgotten that the FSLN was fourteen years old when it underwent its first major experience of programmatic dispute and factionalization.) Both Fonseca and Borge survived this first period to oversee the development of a new generation of recruits – most of the current leadership joined in the late 1960s – won to the strategy of armed struggle less by the tangible achievements of the FSLN than by its endurance as a combative alternative to traditional opposition currents increasingly bereft of potential for overthrowing a regime possessed of all the characteristics of a dictatorship.

The survival of the FSLN through a period in which the Guatemalan guerrilla was comprehensively defeated and none was in existence elsewhere in the isthmus was a matter of no little consequence. It reflected impressive individual courage and provided appreciable political capital, if only by virtue of the fact that the population knew that somewhere out there people were seeking to overthrow Somoza. It is, however, in the nature of guerrilla warfare that it is, at least until the onset of widespread conflict, precisely 'out there', separate from the great bulk of its existing and potential supporters. The intrinsic qualities of such a strategy are conducive to both elitism and militarism even if it should succeed in mobilizing mass support and develop into a movement dependent on more than those who are young, fit and so completely identified with the cause that they are permanently prepared to lay down their lives for it. The resolution of this dilemma cannot be found within a purely military logic, the conversion of a guerrilla vanguard into a people's army requiring the pursuit of political activity amongst the masses as well as the existence of conditions that make them accessible to it.[15]

At the start of the 1970s the FSLN was directly confronted with such a challenge and subsequently encountered considerable problems in overcoming it. In the countryside the *Comité Evangélica de Promoción Agraria* (CEPA), created by the Jesuits in 1969, increasingly acted as a vehicle for peasant organization and radicalization – particularly in the north-western region – and was an important factor in the outbreak of rural strikes and land seizures in 1973–74. The increasing repression by state and landlords drove a significant number of CEPA activists into the ranks of the FSLN yet also had the effect of equating all organizational activity with subversion. The resulting shift to semi-clandestine work reduced the scale and pace of peasant organization to a level below the potential created in good measure by the repression itself. It was not until 1977 that the agricultural proletariat began to break through the impasse with strike action and this was largely autonomous of the FSLN, which was confronted with major difficulties in operating in the densely populated, open terrain of the Pacific coast cotton estates. Whilst conditions for direct political work in the north-central uplands were much better, not least because this had been Sandino's main zone of operations, the harsh treatment meted out by the Guard and the *jueces de mesta* to a largely subsistence peasantry instilled as much caution and fear as it provoked anger and resistance. As a result, the FSLN was able to maintain and gradually augment its presence but unable to undertake major offensive operations until the crisis of late 1977, when the *campesinado* began to sense the possibilities of direct action. Before this the most obvious potential for the Sandinistas lay in patiently building confidence and support amongst the population and harassing the agents of the state – a process that was only partially underway in early 1978 when Somocismo began to collapse.

Prior to the 1974 raid the FSLN had increased its work in the towns, recruiting from disenchanted PSN militants and students. It was, however, very slow to cultivate support amongst the urban labour force, the 1973 construction workers' strike – particularly important in the wake of the earthquake – being largely the work of the PSN, while the rest of a small and divided union movement remained under the influence of the bourgeois parties.[16] Although this position altered somewhat in later years, the FSLN never established an *organizational* presence within the working class before the revolution and tended to build contacts with workers at home rather than in their place of work. With its leading cadre predominantly from the middle class, the Frente found itself in the wake of the defeated *foquista* operations particularly weak in the traditional sphere for building a socialist movement. Thus, despite the fact that the 1974 raid raised the profile of Sandinismo amongst the working class, it also demonstrated the FSLN's distance from it.

As a result of this and differences over military strategy, the FSLN split into factions at the end of 1975. The *Tendencia Proletaria* (TP; headed by Jaime Wheelock, Luis Carrión and Carlos Núñez) argued for the establishment of an orthodox Marxist–Leninist party and greater concentration on organizational work amongst the urban masses whilst the *Guerra Popular Prolongada* tendency (GPP; led by Tomás Borge, Henry Ruiz and Bayardo Arce) insisted upon the continuation of a rural campaign of attrition against the Guard on the model of Vietnam. Carlos Fonseca was killed by Somoza's troops in November 1976 when he returned to Nicaragua in order to settle this dispute; his death impeded any speedy rapprochement and, in the context of a fierce sectarian struggle, encouraged those at odds with both strategic conceptions not only to seek mediation but also to defend a further alternative. The *Tendencia Tercerista* or *Insurrecional*, led by Daniel and Humberto Ortega and Víctor Tirado, shared with its competitors both an element of traditional Sandinismo – in this case emphasis upon broad, multi-class alliances, over which they opposed the *Proletarios* – and a deviation from it – insistence upon the potential for insurrectionary politics, over which they were in disagreement with the GPP.

This division continued in substance until the autumn of 1978, in form until March 1979, and in spirit for some time after the final insurrection. It not only reinforced the sociological tendency to sectarianism in small political groups and sundered the open and semi-clandestine support structure, but also critically debilitated the possibilities of the FSLN, which in 1977 possessed less than 200 active militants, posing a serious military challenge to the Guard.[17] No less importantly, the dispute raised questions as to the real political character of Sandinismo, within which the varying politico-military projects of Leninists, Castroists and Social Democrats were identified by commentators and occasionally employed internally to characterize opposing lines.[18] As a consequence, the organization's remarkable success in moving from a state of isolation and military retreat in 1976 to a full offensive in the vanguard of the mass movement two years later was frequently perceived as a predominantly logistical development with major political questions still pending and liable to engender further internal disputes. The fact that these did not occur to anything approaching the degree that might have been expected from the heated exchanges of 1975–77 may be explained in good measure by the demands of waging campaigns both against the military and within the opposition bloc. In the public domain broad populist language and slogans quite naturally predominated in a fierce anti-dictatorial struggle in much the same fashion as the Bolsheviks called simply for 'bread and peace' in 1917, notwithstanding complex and charged internal debate over tactics and strategy. At certain moments political crisis become so compacted that the slogan is the programme.

The retrieval of Sandinista unity cannot be attributed solely to the accumulating logic of the political conjuncture; it also corresponded to a pattern of historical development and an objective social structure for which none of the three factions had an adequate programmatic response. Their recombination was both a tactical necessity for the purpose of winning the military campaign and the product of recognition that the success of the revolution could not be assured on the basis of support from a single social class or simply by means of tactical alliances and military adventurism. The result was that the discourse and policy of the FSLN became more distinctly populist or, in the words of Sergio Ramirez, based upon a 'conception of the people as a class'.[19] What Carlos Vilas calls 'the popular subject' of the revolution was not identified with the interests of any particular class so that, aside from the tactical requirements of the moment, it appeared as if Sandinismo had completely jettisoned a class-based strategy in favour of a purely political and democratic revolution in which the social project of the *Proletario* and GPP factions had been subordinated by *Tercerismo*.[20] In fact, Sandinismo was properly *created* in the period 1977–79 on the basis of a much wider political exchange in which the policies of each of the tendencies was rearticulated without any of them being subjected to a major defeat. Hence, while the insurrectionary period appeared to manifest *Tercerista* hegemony, subsequent developments confirmed that the strategic concerns of its erstwhile opponents remained at the heart of FSLN policy, albeit no longer expressed in an explicitly partisan fashion.

As has already been suggested, the most obvious and intractable feature of Sandinismo is its patriotism, which intrinsically supersedes class and was not the subject of dispute in 1975–78; then, all the wings of the movement maintained their claims to its name and gave prominence to the objective of national liberation. In this regard the differing social projects and military strategies within the FSLN shared a strong supra-class component throughout, as was also the case with basic democratic demands, which tend to acquire an openly class character only when they are amalgamated into a full legal system. Here the potential pitfalls of the *Tercerista* strategy were of a clear and historically familiar nature: a broad alliance including the opposition bourgeoisie stood in danger of simply harnessing popular mobilization to the achievement of a liberal democratic system with Somoza expelled from the dominant bloc but the class structure unchanged. What was less evident was the fact that neither the *Proletario* nor the GPP tendency possessed a viable policy for both maintaining the necessary national and democratic character of the opposition movement and simultaneously ensuring that either the proletariat or the peasantry would supervise the liberation of the oppressed nation. The absence of such a policy was less the result of inadequate political skills or poor theory than the fact that the peculiarities of Nicaragua's class structure confounded the sociological coherence, let alone the conscious self-identification, of the proletariat and the peasantry and enhanced the role of the petty bourgeoisie.

The difficulty of assigning primacy to the traditional working class was most evident since this comprised less than 20 per cent of the labour force (29 per cent if all non-agricultural productive labourers are included). As can be seen from Table 22, even within the capital's labour force the manufacturing factory proletariat was dwarfed by artisans, employees and the commercial petty bourgeoisie. Moreover, this small size was not offset by the strategic importance to the economy of the areas of production in which the proletariat was engaged, as for example in mining enclaves; the working class was simply one sector of a labour force in an economy where agro-exports were the central source of foreign exchange. The general phenomenon of the urban proletariat being numerically swamped by the petty bourgeoisie and 'marginalized' sectors has already been noted in chapter 5. It should be noted that within a popular culture less of workers than of 'tradespeople' the instability of urban industrial labour increased the permeability of 'proletarian' status and tended to throw greater weight on more extensive, less class-based factors.[21] Thus, the traditional working class could not provide the social base of a revolutionary movement, as was readily accepted by most *Proletarios*, and even its capacity to provide political leadership remained severely prejudiced by its fluidity, internal disaggregation and youth, which further strengthened the logic of a political campaign based more on the general conditions of existence than on those of production. Here, then, the advantages of championing the 'people' rather than the class were manifest. The direct application of formal Marxist categories was additionally complicated by the fact that the bulk of Nicaragua's 'proletarians' were waged rural labourers, generally employed on a temporary basis. There is some debate over the extent of dispossession of lands and the salarization of the rural labour force, and the degree to which these factors conferred upon it the characteristics of a proletariat.[22] However, there can be no doubt that, especially in cotton farming, there existed a large number of itinerant labourers in receipt of a wage for quite extended periods, still possessed of many characteristics of the *campesino* and yet also dependent upon complementary employment in the informal urban sector.

These workers accounted for perhaps one-third of the economically

Table 22: Structure of Employment, Managua, 1975 (%)

Professionals, Technicians	10.7
Managers, Administrators	4.0
Office employees	15.8
Commercial farmers	1.1
Traders and Vendors	15.4
Transport workers	6.3
Artisans (spinners, dressmakers, carpenters, bricklayers, mechanics	22.2
Workers and apprentices	6.8
Service employees	17.6

Source: Vilas, *Sandinista Revolution*, p.103.

active population in the countryside, their loss of lands generally being the result of the extension of agro-export enterprises over the post-war period. Yet, as already noted, although this expansion of large commercial farms produced appreciable direct expulsion, it provoked less subdivision of plots than elsewhere in Central America and did not significantly diminish the historical importance of medium-sized farms (Table 8a, p.180). The result of this was that the 'poor peasantry' dependent upon waged labour to supplement production from its subsistence plots and generally concentrated in the regions of northern Segovia, Madriz, Estelí and south eastern Matagalpa tended not to expand as such, constituting perhaps 40 per cent of the rural labour force on the eve of the revolution, whilst 'middle peasants', defined by their general capacity to market a surplus from their lands, accounted for some 22 per cent. The size of units given in Table 23 does not correspond directly to these groups, but the figures do indicate that a good portion of small-scale agriculture was dedicated to production for the export market as well as of food crops. One important consequence of this was that the medium peasantry was frequently in conflict with the large agrarian entrepreneurs, who controlled its

Table 23: Distribution of Agricultural Production by Unit Size, 1971 (%)[23]

*Unit (mas.)**	*Cotton*	*Coffee*	*Sugar*	*Rice*	*Sorghum*	*Corn*	*Beans*	*Total*
–50	6	22	4	9	34	32	59	25
51–500	52	58	18	18	28	57	38	45
501+	42	20	78	73	38	11	3	30

* One *manzana* = 1.72 acres or 0.69 hectares.

credit and the prices of its unfinished produce as well as competing with it for land.

Opposition to the rural bourgeoisie over the questions of land, fair prices and better credit united the medium and poor peasantry and the landless proletariat. At the same time, significant numbers of small farmers and richer peasants who disputed these issues with the bourgeoisie employed poor peasants and proletarians for harvest labour and occasionally on a permanent basis, putting them in an antagonistic position with respect to the question of wages. As a result, the establishment of a revolutionary strategy in the countryside was no less complicated than that in the towns since it had to encompass powerful anti-oligarchic forces that were in partial contradiction with each other. On the one hand, the extreme condition of the landless proletariat and poor peasantry provided the principal impetus for opposition since these sectors were subjected to the highest levels of exploitation and impoverishment. On the other, it was impossible to ignore and highly dangerous to antagonize the middle peasantry, whose numbers and scarcely less sharp antipathy for large capital made it critical to the bonding of the popular bloc.

These factors compelled a rearticulation of strategies based explicitly upon the working class or the poorest rural workers as well as the objectives of socialism, of which the petty bourgeoisie was for all its radicalism as suspicious as a peasantry far from instinctively dedicated to collectivism. Hence, whilst the Sandinista catechism insisted that only the workers and peasants would 'go all the way' (by implication, to socialism), socialism appeared only twice in the FSLN reunification agreement of March 1979, and its public use after the revolution was largely limited to urban working-class circles, where it was a traditional motif of syndicalism. The key organizations from which the FSLN drew support and recruits within the student population (*Federación Estudiantil Revolucionaria*; *Movimiento Estudiantil de Secundarios*), youth (FMJBM; *Juventud Revolucionaria Nicaragüense*), and the radicalized Christian groups (*Movimiento Cristiano Revolucionario*) were directly engaged in the debate over programme and divided either formally or informally by it. However, in the longer term the nature of their membership and type of activity encouraged the concentration of the revolutionary platform on those features – popular, democratic and anti-imperialist – that suppressed the effects of the heterogeneity of the class structure and highlighted the common experience of poverty and oppression. As a result, both the form of Nicaraguan society and the agency of the FSLN maximized membership of the popular bloc and militated against its domination by any one class.

A partial but vivid portrait of this is given in Carlos Vilas's study of the background of a sample of fallen rebel combatants, amongst whom students and artisans outnumbered workers whilst office employees exceeded peasants. (It should be noted, though, that this pattern is affected by the fact that much of the fighting of 1978–79 took place in and around towns as well as by the youth of the rebel troops, whose parents tended to be self-employed, followed at some distance by peasants and small entrepreneurs.[24]) Little less eloquent is the high incidence of illegitimate children (54 per cent) and those raised by a single parent (47 per cent), almost always the mother. This pattern is a typical outcome of systems of itinerant labour with single women obliged to support families largely through work in the service sector or market vending. It may also be plausibly interpreted as conducive to lower levels of domestic authoritarianism and earlier socialization than might be expected in a nuclear family with the mother more likely to be restricted to the domestic terrain. Whatever the case, the high representation of children of those working in the informal sector ('self-employed') and living in the urban *barrios* signals one of the critical points of social tension created by the economy under Somoza in which school and street matched factory and field as the sites of conflict. Largely outside the compass of trade unions, taxed and harassed by a state system that had developed few mechanisms for its co-optation, and of little attraction to the bourgeois opposition parties – the logical candidates, the Christian Democrats, were significantly weaker than in Guatemala and El Salvador – this important social stratum was both heavily influenced by radicalized schoolteachers and priests and inherently inclined to direct action. Its symbiosis with the traditional petty bourgeoisie, the peasantry (within which it had its recent origins), the rural proletariat (amongst whom its members often figured), the urban artisanate and the working class underscores the multiplicity of contradictions and complex social structure engendered by Nicaraguan capitalism in the post-war period.

This structure was neither markedly atypical for Central America nor the principal factor in provoking the revolutionary crisis from late 1977. It has already been seen that the short-run performance of the economy from the mid 1970s was not so poor as to provoke a breakdown of the Somocista system, and while the social antagonisms accumulated over previous decades were undeniably sharp, they were discernibly less so than in either Guatemala or El Salvador. There was, then, no overbearing and inescapable economic logic to the Nicaraguan revolution. It was generated far more directly by a crisis of a *political* nature in which the determinants of oppression prevailed over those of exploitation. In this regard the peculiarities of state and polity under the Somozas were of critical importance since they disaggregated the dominant bloc in such a fashion as to weaken its class character whilst reducing the political effects of the heterogeneity of the dominated classes to such a point that domination alone could cohere the popular bloc.[25] Nowhere else in Central America did this position obtain in such a sharp form in the late 1970s. It was not the sole 'cause' of either the success or the peculiarities of a revolution that was equally determined by critical confusion in Washington and remarkable exploitation of the possibilities by the FSLN. Nevertheless, it did contribute to the relatively short duration of the insurrectionary campaign and the extremely broad nature of the socio-economic issues left outstanding when military victory was achieved.

The Overthrow of Somoza

From the end of 1977 Nicaragua was dominated by political activity to a degree unprecedented in its history. Although the socio-economic structure of the country continued to underpin and condition the course and character of national life, this was increasingly determined by subjective and conjunctural factors; politics was 'in command'.[26] An exhaustive analysis of those phenomena – tactical initiatives, shifts in the balance of forces, movements in popular sentiment, even the role of chance – that acquire an enhanced importance under such conditions is beyond our scope here. The chronological outline given in Table 24

Table 24: The Overthrow of Somoza – A Chronology

Year	Month	Day	Event
1977	Aug.		Somoza suffers heart-attack.
	Sept.		State of Siege lifted.
	Oct.		*Terceristas* attack GN in Ocotal, Masaya, San Carlos.
	Nov.		*La Prensa* publishes manifesto of '*Los Doce*' supporting FSLN.
1978	Jan.	10	Pedro Joaquín Chamorro assassinated.
		13	50,000 demonstrate at Chamorro funeral; Chamber of Commerce and UDEL call 'civil stoppage' (24th); sporadic rioting.
	Feb.	2	FSLN attack Rivas and Granada garrisons.
		5	UDEL and COSEP call off strike, losing popular support.
		21	Popular uprising in Masaya *barrio* of Monimbó, lasts four days.
	Mar.	3	Popular uprising in Subtiava *barrio* of León follows spontaneous revolt in Diriamba.
			Alfonso Robelo's MDN formed; ATC holds founding congress.
	May		FAO established (includes UDEL; *Los Doce*; MDN and CUS), its call for Somoza's resignation backed by Bishop Obando y Bravo; FSLN tendencies discuss reunification.

Jun. Strikes by municipal and health workers, students.

20 Carter congratulates Somoza on improvement in human rights.

Jul. *Los Doce* return to country; Aguero Conservatives join FAO; establishment of MPU under FSLN leadership (includes PSN, 20 popular organizations and trade unions).

19 One-day general strike called by FAO; land seizures continue in Chinandega.

20 *Terceristas* attack Intercontinental Hotel and Somoza's bunker.

Aug. 22 *Terceristas* capture National Palace; Somoza forced to concede to demands.

27 85 GN members arrested for conspiracy.

28 Three-day popular uprising in Matagalpa and Jinotepe (300 killed); FAO calls general strike, endorsed by MPU, 75% businesses close; US blocks IMF loan.

Sept. 9 Columns from all FSLN factions attack major garrisons throughout country; martial law declared.

20 FSLN withdraws; some 3,000 lives lost in offensive; general strike ends.

Oct. OAS mediation begins; through *Los Doce*, FSLN insists that FAO not talk directly with Somoza and demand his resignation; FAO agrees.

26 *Los Doce* leave FAO over concessions to US plan for GN and PLN participation in a new provisional regime; FSLN resumes combat, numbers grow to 2,500.

Nov. Somoza rejects resignation; FAO halts talks; Costa Rica cuts diplomatic relations.

Dec. 10 FAO accepts direct talks with Somoza which collapse; PLI, PPSC leave FAO.

UN condemns regime's violation of human rights.

1979 Jan. Large demonstrations mark anniversary of Chamorro death; strikes.

19 Somoza announces continuation of government until 1981 elections.

Feb. US suspends military aid.

1 Establishment under FSLN leadership of FPN (includes MPU, *Los Doce*, PPSC, PLI and unions).

Mar. Currency devalued by 43%, basic prices rise to same degree; economic crisis accelerates; FSLN tendencies reunite formally.

Apr. FSLN offensive in north and west; Estelí occupied for five days.

May 14 IMF $66 million loan granted with US support.

20 Mexico breaks diplomatic relations; OAS calls for Somoza's resignation.

30 FSLN declares 'final offensive' and invades from Costa Rica; southern front (Benjamin Zeledón) attacks Rivas; northern (Carlos Fonseca) Estelí and Jinotega; north-western (Rigoberto López Pérez) Chinandega and León; central (Camilo Ortega) Managua and Masaya; eastern forces based in Nueva Guinea and the northern mining zones advance on Managua and Matagalpa; GN badly stretched, with numerical superiority of only 2.5:1.

Jun. 2 FSLN enters León.

4 General strike declared, backed by both FPN and FAO.

9 Insurrection in Managua; FSLN hard-pressed in south but controls 25 northern towns; Episcopal Conference declares 'legitimate right of popular insurrection'.

16 Provisional Junta of National Reconstruction formed in Costa Rica (includes Violeta Chamorro [UDEL], Alfonso Robelo [MDN], Moisés Hassan [MPU], Sergio Ramirez [Los Doce], Daniel Ortega [FSLN]).

21 US TV reporter Bill Stewart killed on camera by GN.

22 US Secretary of State Vance proposal for OAS peacekeeping force rejected.

27 FSLN and supporters begin strategic retreat from Managua towards Masaya; GN continues to hold out in Rivas; FAO and COSEP endorse provisional junta.

28 US envoy William Bowdler meets junta in Costa Rica; Conservative rump finally boycotts congress.

Jul. 2 Matagalpa falls.

5 Estelí largely controlled by FSLN, which makes Masaya base for offensive on Managua; US continues to insist upon PLN and GN representation in new regime; Bowdler's proposed expansion of junta rejected; Somoza declares call-up of all reservists.

8 Somoza offers Washington his resignation conditional upon guarantees for PLN and GN in future regime.

9 Costa Rica demands removal of recently deployed US helicopters from its territory.

10 Managua completely encircled.

15 Washington drops demand for PLN and GN representation in new regime.

16 Estelí barracks fall.
17 Somoza resigns and flies to Miami; congress names Francisco Urcuyo interim president; FSLN resumes final thrust on capital's centre.
18 GN disintegrates; Junta flies into León.
19 GN formally surrenders; FSLN forces occupy Managua.

---

includes only the most critical developments of the period 1977–79, and since these are now fully studied and widely known no more than a brief discussion of their context and consequences need be made.

One of the notable features of the Nicaraguan revolution was the speed with which it developed. Prior to Somoza's heart-attack in August 1977 the level of popular mobilization was low, strikes still infrequent, and none of the popular organizations (as opposed to trade unions) that came to dominate post-revolutionary society was yet in existence (the women's organization AMPRONAC was established in September 1977; the rural workers' *sindicato* ATC in March 1978).[27] In El Salvador the principal plebeian organizations were formed in the period 1974–76, the political crisis of the autumn of 1979 in that country being the result of an extended and entrenched process of social conflict. The Nicaraguan revolution, by contrast, was of a truly 'insurrectionary' character. Less than two years separated the dictator's illness from his overthrow, the most important political developments taking place in the twelve months between the assassination of Pedro Joaquín Chamorro in January 1978 and the organizational consolidation of the popular bloc under FSLN hegemony in the *Frente Patriótico Nacional* (FPN) in February 1979. Thereafter activity was largely restricted to the military-diplomatic sphere, the final Sandinista offensive from the end of May 1979 acquiring such an impetus that Washington was obliged to treat with an opposition that it could no longer cajole into division along ideological lines.

Nicaragua was not completely quiescent in mid 1977. Workers at the large San Antonio sugar estate and mill were engaged in unprecedented agitation for better conditions – their strike would propel the formation of the ATC – and urban strikes had increased in frequency over the previous years, demands for the release of political prisoners becoming commonplace. Nevertheless, open economic and political challenges to the status quo were at a lower level than in the period prior to December 1974. This undoubtedly encouraged the Carter administration to press the convalescing dictator to lift the state of siege. Equally, Somoza himself evidently did not anticipate that this measure would greatly increase the uncertainty that his illness had caused within the ruling class and the expectations it had sparked amongst his opponents. Within a month this mood was heightened further still by *Tercerista* attacks on provincial garrisons and a declaration supporting the FSLN issued in San José by a group of twelve prominent individuals, *Los Doce*. These figures had been brought together by the *Terceristas* but henceforth maintained a publicly independent campaign for the removal of Somoza, serving as a critical bridge for the formation of an alliance between the bourgeois opposition and the Sandinistas.[28] Lacking a background in politics, largely of upper- and middle-class origin, and drawn from a range of professions as well as private enterprise, the group was able to give a non-partisan authority to its endorsement of the FSLN's role in the anti-dictatorial struggle. At a stroke it reduced the image of extremism that had restricted popular support, enabled UDEL to reject collaboration with the FSLN, and encouraged the wider bourgeois opposition to pursue its policy of negotiation with the regime without major challenge. *Los Doce* brought the FSLN to the centre of the political stage and acted as its broker within the liberal opposition through most of 1978.

In November 1977 *La Prensa* had published the declaration of *Los Doce* and early in the new year it had been pursuing a story on the sale of blood to the US by Somoza associates. Although this had raised widespread interest and seriously embarrassed the government, it scarcely amounted to a reason for killing Chamorro, whose shooting on 10 January was quite possibly not ordered by Somoza himself, although it was undertaken by his underlings. Despite his proclivity for violence, Somoza was a sufficiently astute politician to recognize that the liquidation of the individual most closely identified with opposition to his rule would provoke a fierce reaction well beyond the ranks of the bourgeoisie. If he did indeed seek an immediate and terminal solution to Chamorro's invectives he miscalculated very badly since the assassination opened a crisis from which Somocismo never escaped. The spontaneous rioting that followed the killing and the extraordinarily large demonstration at Chamorro's funeral compelled the bourgeois opposition to take some action in protest at the assassination of a man who was, after all, one of their own. The 'civic stoppage' of 24 January therefore began at the behest and under the leadership of the Chamber of Commerce and UDEL, being assured initial support not only by the strength of popular feeling but also because many strikers continued to receive their wages. However, when the FSLN launched attacks on the garrisons at Rivas and Granada and pressure was applied by an alarmed Washington, the liberal opposition obeyed its instincts and called an end to a measure that was in any case highly unfamiliar and worrying. (The strike was, indeed, unparalleled in modern Nicaraguan history, its scale outstripping the mobilizations of 1944 and 1967, themselves singular occurrences in a country that had the weakest syndicalist tradition in Central America.) UDEL's retreat may well have been necessary in any case – rank-and-file attempts to prolong the strike soon foundered – but it was profoundly at odds with popular sentiment, which had been transformed in the space of three weeks and sought a decisive settling of accounts with the regime. Hence, whilst UDEL lost appreciable sympathy for back-pedalling in early February, it had also laid the basis for the independent insurrections in Masaya, León and Diriamba at the end of the month and in early March. These spontaneous ghetto risings were suppressed by the Guard with unrestrained bloodletting, their subjugation marking the end of the opening phase of popular mobilization. Nonetheless, they reflected an unprecedented preparedness of the urban poor directly to attack the forces of the state with minimal guerrilla support. Such instinctive insurrectionism altered the whole character of the conflict in its demonstration of the depth of popular antipathy towards the dictatorship and the urgent need for the opposition forces to harness it to their various causes before it was extinguished in a series of uncontrolled revolts and widespread slaughter.

The repression meted out in February and March succeeded temporarily in halting popular rebellion, but this had already acquired such a momentum that the opposition was obliged to take further initiatives. In March the entrepreneur Alfonso Robelo, who was linked with the BANIC group, set up the *Movimiento Democrático Nicaragüense* (MDN), which represented those sections of capital – particularly cotton growers and medium-sized firms – that sought to provide the liberal opposition with a more modern and flexible leadership, adopting some social democratic motifs in a prescient effort to draw middle-class support away from the periphery of the FSLN. Whilst the MDN failed to generate a significant popular following, it did fill an important political gap between the Sandinistas and the traditional parties, thereby expanding the potential for some form of alliance. This became a reality when, in May, both the MDN and *Los Doce*, who effectively represented the minimum programme of the *Terceristas*, joined with UDEL to form the *Frente Amplio Opositor* (FAO), which called for general social reforms and Somoza's resignation and received guarded but influential backing from Bishop Obando y Bravo of Managua.[29]

The formation of FAO presented the regime with a political opposition that was still heterogeneous but united in organization to a degree greater even than that in 1944. In recognition of the predominance of bourgeois currents within it Somoza responded with a modicum of moderation, especially since such a body possessed obvious potential to win US backing. Thus, the dictator's decision in June to lift the state of siege and readmit the exiled members of *Los Doce* was directed principally at Washington, which responded by easing its pressure, Carter even congratulating Somoza for the move – a signal that was interpreted as poorly as it was designed. The return of *Los Doce* was the occasion of much popular celebration and had the effect of fortifying both the FAO and the Sandinistas' indirect participation within it. Yet dependence upon a handful of sympathizers, however committed some of them (Ramirez, D'Escoto, Cardenal) were to its cause, was plainly an insufficient basis for the FSLN's political activity, which was still under debate between the tendencies. While the *Terceristas* had achieved tactical progress in both military and political fields by mid 1978, it was evident to the movement as a whole that the liberal opposition had to be challenged in a more concerted fashion if mass support was to be secured and the political leadership of the anti-dictatorial bloc ensured. The potential for this had been made clear not only in the spring risings but also in the June strikes that had been largely outside the orbit of FAO and UDEL. As a result, in July the FSLN built on the foundations laid by *Los Doce* in creating the *Movimiento Popular Unido* (MPU), which, comprising the recently formed mass organizations, several important unions (teachers; public employees) and confederations as well as all the parties of the left, was of a resolutely popular nature. Remaining outside the FAO, the MPU issued a detailed platform that was in essence the FSLN's own manifesto and henceforth constituted the political expression of the popular bloc within the opposition. The MPU called for the broadest opposition alliance, preserving the independence of its component parts, which would form a 'government of national unity'. This call, together with the MPU's demand for a full programme of civil liberties, the establishment of a constituent assembly, and judicial and agrarian reforms, could not plausibly be rejected by the majority of the forces in the FAO and was firmly within the sphere of liberal democracy. However, the programme's inclusion of the abolition of the National Guard, a non-aligned foreign policy, confiscation of Somoza's property, price controls, nationalization of all natural resources and public transport, a new labour code, equal pay and an end to sexual discrimination, rent controls and a national economic plan represented a direct challenge to the bourgeois opposition and succeeded in consolidating almost all popular organizations of any influence within an alliance under FSLN leadership. Indeed, the only substantive difference between the MPU platform and the FSLN's own public programme was that the latter clearly characterized as Sandinista the military force that would replace the National Guard.[30] Thus, between January and July 1978 the FSLN had covered much ground, gaining a presence in the liberal opposition front (FAO), establishing a plebeian front (MPU) under Sandinista leadership, and reaching informal agreement on its own reunification.

This last issue was greatly advanced by the most audacious operation staged by the *Terceristas* in pursuit of their insurrectionary strategy: the capture late in August of the National Palace together with the entire congress, several ministers and over 1,500 public employees. Led by the mercurial Edén Pastora and the restrained Dora Tellez, this remarkable event was in effect a repetition of the 1974 raid on a grand scale. The kidnapping of almost the entire political apparatus of the state mesmerized both Nicaragua and the wider world, and Pastora, whom Borge would later attack as a 'film star', took full advantage of the theatrical possibilities of the event. The inability of the increasingly aggravated Guard commanders of stage a counter-attack and the eventual capitulation of Somoza to the FSLN's demands (publication of its manifesto, the release of leading militants, including Borge, and sixty other political prisoners, $500,000 in ransom, and free passage out of the country) increased the sense of the regime's weakness and drove popular opposition to an even higher level than that of February. One of the FSLN's aims had been to forestall a National Guard coup against Somoza that would have greatly complicated the political situation and at least temporarily defused the anti-dictatorial movement, but while they succeeded in this, they also provoked a level of mass mobilization that they were not in a position either to lead or logistically to support.

Within a matter of days the *barrios* of Matagalpa and Jinotepe broke into open revolt, the first rising lasting for three days before a thousand troops suppressed it with some 200 casualties. At the same time wildcat strikes by health and construction workers encouraged the FAO to call a general strike for 28 August, the MPU making its first public appearance in backing this call. The regime, now deeply apprehensive at the turn of events, responded by arresting the leadership of the FAO, forcing the liberal opposition into a harder stance and narrowing the possibilities for a resolution of the crisis within the ranks of the bourgeoisie. Several days later, all three FSLN tendencies, impressed by the scale of the popular urban uprisings and the need of the Guard to concentrate large numbers of troops to subdue them, launched attacks throughout the country with relatively small contingents. However, it was only in León that the FSLN obtained a firm foothold for any length of time, an operation on this scale being beyond its existing resources and requiring a strategic withdrawal after eleven days. Whilst its losses were comparatively light, those of the civilian population subjected to blanket aerial bombing, artillery fire and indiscriminate killing in 'mopping-up operations' through October were very high. The Sandinistas had failed to sustain a hastily prepared offensive on a national scale, but the Guard had suffered high casualties and a clear loss of morale. The FSLN now began to recruit at a much faster rate, and the level of violence attracted international pressure for negotiations. Somoza's reimposition of martial law merely confirmed that the conflict had escalated beyond the reach of the mediation sought by the FAO, which was insufficiently supported by Washington in this respect, to the verge of civil war.

The first phase of external mediation began in October under the auspices of the OAS. By this stage the fierceness of the struggle obliged the FAO – representing the opposition in these negotiations – to share with the FSLN a rejection of any direct talks with Somoza himself as well as the demand that he resign and go into exile. In response to the dictator's insistence that he finish his official term of office (until 1981) the OAS mediators proposed, under transparent prompting from Washington, an interim three-year regime that would include the National Guard and the PLN. This suggestion met many of the requirements of the traditional bourgeois parties, which were essentially concerned with removing Somoza and retaining the existing party system together with a reformed National Guard. But *Los Doce* refused to consider any deal involving the authors of such extensive carnage or upholding 'Somocismo without Somoza'. They therefore left the FAO, whose position was further weakened by the dictator's own refusal to entertain the OAS proposal. Although Robelo's MDN and the PSCN remained, the Christian Democrat trade-union confederation (CTN) followed *Los Doce* out of the FAO, which was itself obliged to withdraw from talks in which it was seen to have made major concessions to supporters of the regime. Nonetheless, both the Sandinistas' immediate resumption of combat and intense pressure from Washington spurred the reduced opposition front to return to negotiation since it possessed no military force of its own and its very existence had no logic if it could not reach an accord through mediation.

This second effort at a negotiated agreement compounded the political setbacks caused by the first since the FAO now accepted direct talks with Somoza while he continued to maintain his position. As a result, the bourgeois opposition was widely perceived to have capitulated on the central democratic demands of its own programme over which there had been no dispute with the FSLN and the forces of the popular bloc and which the liberal opposition needed to champion most zealously if it was to retain popular support. Although the FAO was once more forced to break off talks, it had effectively eliminated its claims to the leadership of the anti-dictatorial movement. The decisive element in this regard was not the latent dispute with the MPU and the FSLN over the class character and social policy of any new regime but the fact that the liberal opposition had become attached to the proposition of a compromise and prejudiced its democratic bona fides. This led to a rupture in the unity of the bourgeois alliance, the PLI and PPSC (a reformist schism from the PSCN established in 1976) leaving the FAO in the wake of the failure of the second round of talks. Since at least September 1978 the FSLN had possessed a considerable advantage in the political field simply by virtue of the fact that it was the only organized military force in the anti-dictatorial movement; the bourgeois opposition necessarily depended upon its operations in order to force concessions from Somoza. In December the balance of forces underwent a crucial change in that the Sandinistas now represented the logical political as well as military focus for the maintenance of the democratic programme of the opposition; whereas before the liberal opponents to Somoza could present the FSLN as a threat and seek to find a 'third way', they were henceforth obliged to search for such a compromise within the broad Sandinista bloc. The organizational form of this new balance of forces emerged in February 1979 with the formation of the *Frente Patriótico Nacional* (FPN), which included the MPU, *Los Doce*, the PPSC, the small pro-Albanian *Frente Obrero*, the CTN, and the PLI. (The adhesion of this last party restituted the unity of a Liberalism that had been sundered since the Pact of Espino Negro in 1927 and was now reconvened in its most radical voice.) The FPN platform was somewhat less precise than that of the MPU, but it still reflected a significant movement by elements of the liberal opposition towards the popular-democratic motifs of Sandinismo in its explicit rejection of 'Somocismo without Somoza', condemnation of external interference, and its proposals for the creation of a new military 'of a national character', confiscation of Somoza's property, state control of natural resources and economic planning as well as democratic freedoms and general social reforms.[31]

The logic of opposition determined the acceptance by subordinate but still important bourgeois parties of the amalgamation of their liberal democratic programme into one that, being based upon the overthrow of the regime in its entirety, necessarily promulgated structural social reform. This process was completely sealed in January 1979 when Somoza declared that he would serve out his full presidential term. As a result, the FAO, now effectively reduced to the MDN and the Conservative Party led by Rafael Córdova, was without a viable strategy, lacked the independent means by which to realize an already superseded programme, and was no longer properly a front at all. Its continued existence rested less on any internal basis of support than on the possibility of US patronage, permanently nestled in the historical psyche of the Nicaraguan bourgeoisie. In the event, even on this score the FSLN was able to outmanoeuvre the remarkably disorientated and clumsy State Department, exploiting its leadership of the anti-dictatorial movement to reincorporate the FAO within it during the final stages of the insurrection.

Following the establishment of the FPN, the conflict was dominated by military and diplomatic activity. On the military front the operational collaboration of the FSLN tendencies in the autumn of 1978 was consolidated with formal reunification in March 1979. This signalled not only programmatic agreement on the basis of the existing 'popular democratic' platform rather than the previous 'socialist' manifestos of the GPP and *Proletario* tendencies but also a much enhanced strategic coordination. In very broad terms it enabled the FSLN to maximize pressure on the Guard by orchestrating offensives from the north (primarily GPP forces) with those in the central zones (predominantly *Proletario*) and thrusts from the south-west made by the *Terceristas* operating out of Costa Rica and Nueva

Guinea. A series of attacks in the north during April succeeded in displacing the Guard from Estelí, but while fighting became constant throughout the spring, it was clear that the regime could at least impose a stalemate in terms of control of garrison towns so long as the Guard was not attacked simultaneously throughout the country. Preparations for such an offensive were highly demanding, and since the FSLN lacked by a very wide margin the numerical superiority required in purely logistical terms to guarantee success for an attacking force, it was obliged to plan its campaign with a view to wider political factors. These took on a decidedly favourable character when Somoza was forced to accept the consequences of his decision to stay in office and confront the acute economic crisis caused by the conflict. In meeting the demands of the IMF for orthodox readjustment in return for vital loans, devaluing the currency and thereby greatly increasing the prices of basic necessities, the dictator succeeded in eliminating any lingering vestiges of popular acquiescence in his government. By supporting the IMF loan the Carter administration only compounded its own problems although these, like those of the Nicaraguan bourgeoisie, were just as much the product of history as of tactical miscalculation. On the one hand, Washington's failure to veto the IMF package was seen as an important decision not to boycott Somoza, and given the campaign around the issue this amounted to little less than an identification of the US with the Nicaraguan regime. On the other, the terms of the loan obliged Somoza further to increase his unpopularity, weakening a government that it was designed to fortify.

Matters came to a head a week after the IMF made its announcement, with Mexico following Costa Rica in breaking diplomatic relations and the OAS calling for Somoza's resignation. Ten days later the FSLN launched its 'final offensive', with the principal thrust being directed from Costa Rica towards the town of Rivas. The deployment of elite Guard units to contain this attack weakened the regime's capacity to resist in the north, where small towns fell to the FSLN with relative rapidity. However, it was not until the general strike declared on 4 June was transformed into a full insurrection in the capital on the 9th that the situation became qualitatively different from previous crises and plainly amounted to a final battle for power. In Managua the Guard's resort to indiscriminate bombing of popular *barrios* produced thousands of casualties and finally compelled the Church hierarchy to reduce the ambiguities of its many proclamations to the point at which it effectively sanctioned the revolt. After a week of exceptionally fierce fighting in which the Guard was forced into slow tactical retreats yet maintained control of most of the major towns, the FSLN confirmed the decisive character of the offensive by announcing the formation of an adroitly titled Provisional Junta of National Reconstruction in which the *Tercerista* leader Daniel Ortega was the only open FSLN representative. Of the other members Sergio Ramirez *(Los Doce)* and Moisés Hassan

(MPU) were both entirely in accord with the Sandinista programme whilst the inclusion of Chamorro's widow Violeta and Alfonso Robelo provided representation for the opposition bourgeoisie. In taking the initiative to include members of FAO within the junta the FSLN made only a formal political concession since it retained a working majority. On the other hand, the incorporation of leading figureheads of local capital in the provisional government gave it a non-partisan, 'national' character that optimized popular backing.

In view of the subsequent preponderance of interpretations that depict this composition of the junta as little more than a 'trick' on the bourgeoisie, it is worth noting that both Robelo and Chamorro were fully aware of the sympathies of their colleagues and scarcely ignorant of the character of the FSLN, with which Robelo in particular had profound ideological differences. It is certain that once the offer of inclusion was made they had little choice other than to accept both the balance of forces within the opposition and the responsibility of supporting a programme that did not openly contradict their own even if it exceeded it. Their decision also corresponded to a correct identification of political possibilities within the terms of the alliances supported by the Sandinistas since mid 1978. The fact that these possibilities were subsequently greatly diminished does not confer upon the alliance in the junta the character of a mere deceit. On the contrary, for some time it was only marginally less crucial for the FSLN than for the bourgeois parties since Sandinista hegemony depended centrally upon the existence of political competition as well as on the FSLN's capacity to control the terms of that competition. At no stage was this balance more fragile than over the summer of 1979 when the ideological breadth of the alliance was critical to the defeat of Somoza, the avoidance of US intervention, and the establishment of a new state.

Such an underlying tendency does not, of course, signify any lack of carefully crafted tactics on the part of the FSLN, merely that these had to be developed in an objective situation that was only partly of its making.[32] This became very clear in the third week of June when Washington finally registered the scale of the crisis and began to manoeuvre frantically in order to avert an FSLN victory. Although immediate US public interest in the war had been greatly affected by the sight on its TV screens of a North American cameraman being executed in cold blood by a member of Somoza's National Guard, Washington's central proposal for mediation continued to be the inclusion of both the Guard and the PLN in a post-Somoza government. Outside these organizations themselves there was absolutely no support within Nicaragua for such a 'solution', the Guard being the object of much more hatred than at the end of 1978, when the FAO had been wrecked by considering this solution. Having accepted the consequences of this and finally pledged itself to the cause of the eradication of the odious military machine, the FAO leadership was fully aware that any further change of its position could only lead to a rapid and irreversible disappearance into history. Similarly, the efforts by US envoy William Bowdler to expand the junta were rejected by all the forces represented in it since any greater 'representativity' could only entail inclusion of elements of the Somocista apparatus. Such proposals by the US assuredly amounted to a grave miscalculation, but they also resulted from a prior lack of resolution in supporting the democratic bourgeoisie and ditching Somoza so that the Guard might retain sufficient autonomy to be plausibly included in a tame liberal concordat. It is clear that from mid 1978 the FSLN was deeply apprehensive about such a possibility with many (not all) in the bourgeois opposition and even some Guard commanders perceiving it as infinitely more desirable and less risky than did Washington. (Carter's nervous reluctance to intervene decisively was, of course, later reversed by Reagan, who made much political capital out of the failures of his predecessor's policy. What is often missed in this is the fact that the Reagan administration subsequently directed much of its intervention towards precisely the institutional disaggregation of the dominant bloc that Carter failed to promote in Nicaragua. Thus, military apparatuses were separated from government and the bourgeoisie encouraged – nay, obliged – to engage in electoral competition, thereby reducing its superficial homogeneity and impeding a corresponding consolidation of the popular bloc. It need hardly be added that this policy both left the repressive capacity of the military intact and bestowed a veneer of democracy upon a system that excluded radical forces and largely satisfied the bourgeois opposition. Thus, although Reagan himself remained sublimely unaware of the fact, the lesson of Nicaragua for Washington was not just that intervention was necessary but also that it should take the form of maximizing competition within the dominant bloc.)

That attempt at direct intervention which was staged by the Carter administration came far too late to have more than a remote chance of impeding a Sandinista victory. Secretary of State Vance's proposal for an OAS peacekeeping force made on 22 June not only served to harden nationalist sentiment within Nicaragua but also received an unprecedented rebuff within the OAS itself, the Andean Pact states already being aligned with the junta, Mexico and Costa Rica openly supporting the destruction of Somocismo tout court, and those dictatorial regimes in sympathy with it more anxious to avoid creating a precedent for their own demise than to salvage an already lost cause.[33] Hence, while Washington felt obliged to stage a show of military force outside Nicaraguan territory during the last days of the war, it could generate no diplomatic support for collective intervention. Not even the prospect of halting the huge loss of life persuaded the major Latin American states into such a course, which was broadly perceived as obstructing the triumph of a popular cause. Clearly, the timing of Vance's proposal deepened this conviction but it is highly likely that many members of the OAS – even the Central American states – would have resisted such a move in any event, the particular history of US involvement in Nicaragua enhancing an already profound reluctance to engage in initiatives beyond the sphere of diplomacy. In the summer of 1979 such a position was neither particularly surprising nor of critical importance. Somoza was an unpopular autocrat on the verge of defeat and the US government lacked the political commitment, logistical preparation or domestic political support for any major intervention, which would have been completely at odds with the pattern of Carter's policy. Over the following years the position of the Latin American states changed very much less than did that of the US, and while many governments tempered their initial enthusiasm for the revolution, they remained notably reluctant, especially after the Falklands/Malvinas War of 1982, to countenance attacks on Nicaraguan sovereignty as such. As US–Nicaraguan relations became increasingly poor such a stance obviously reflected wider considerations in a different international context, but it was conditioned to no small degree by the widespread acceptance in 1979 of the revolution as authentically national in character. This was facilitated by both the breadth of the revolutionary alliance and the resonance of Sandinista patriotism within a shared political culture strongly projected through the struggle for independence from Spain, with which the Nicaraguan revolution had sufficient parallels to evoke the sense of presiding over the birth, or at least the entry into adulthood, of a sister nation. Elusive and emotional though it may seem, this wider 'imagined community' was henceforth to present Washington with considerable problems since few state managers proved to be as tractable as those of Honduras in prejudicing their nationalist credentials in the service of the US regardless of ideological affinity.

Once Vance had failed to browbeat the OAS into intervention the fall of Somoza became simply a matter of time although continued resistance by the Guard in the south and Managua, from which the FSLN was obliged to retreat at the end of June, placed the prospects of a rapid victory in some doubt. In the event these proved to be superable tactical problems, the level of military exhaustion, international repudiation and domestic isolation being too great for Somoza to withstand. As the encirclement of Managua tightened and succour from either Washington or his regional peers was refused, he made his parting shot in having the Guard destroy industrial plant that had escaped the blanket bombing of the popular neighbourhoods. The pretence at democracy was sustained until the bitter end, Somoza's resignation being followed by the congressional appointment of a sidekick, Francisco Urcuyo, as provisional president until 1981. The risible Urcuyo lasted barely 24 hours, during which time the National Guard disintegrated, relieving the FSLN of the need to negotiate the articles of its surrender.

Notes

1. *Desde la Carcel Yo Acuso a la Dictadura*, Managua 1964, quoted in George Black, *Triumph of the People. The Sandinista Revolution in Nicaragua*, London 1981, p. 90.

2. Bernard Diederich, *Somoza and the Legacy of U.S. Involvement in Central America*, London 1982, p. 231.

3. Quoted in ibid., p. 289.

4. Quoted in Booth, *End and Beginning*, 2nd edition, p. 187.

5. Perhaps the best example of a critique of Washington's policy towards Central America on the basis of its denial of liberties enshrined in the US constitution is Walter LaFeber, *Inevitable Revolutions*. It could be added that when, in September 1986, Neil Kinnock, the leader of the British Labour Party, was informed of direct criticism of his defence policy by US Secretary for Defence Weinberger, 'he said he could not believe that any US administration would be so foolish as to interfere with a sovereign government's right to implement the policy on which it was elected . . .' *The Guardian*, 24 September 1986.

6. For the Reagan administration's view, see Department of State: *The Soviet–Cuban Connection in Central America and the Caribbean*, March 1985; *Broken Promises: Sandinista Repression of Human Rights in Nicaragua*, October 1984; *Misconceptions about U.S. Policy toward Nicaragua*, March 1985.

7. A good example of criticism of FSLN tactics from a previously fervent supporter is given in George Black's review of political activity prior to the 1984 elections, *New York Times*, 3 November 1984. Black's article, which advised caution as the best means of dealing with the US, prompted much heated debate in the columns of the North American radical journal *The Nation* over the following months. This debate is perhaps the most useful for understanding the approaches of the broad left inside the US to the Nicaraguan question. The nominally 'liberal' attack on the Sandinistas has been headed by the ex-Maoist Robert S. Leiken, whose invectives are a good deal less innocent than they appear and have been fully exploited by the State Department: 'The Nicaraguan Tangle', *New York Review of Books*, vol. XXXII, no. 19, 5 December 1985.

8. Even Carlos Vilas, who has written the best interpretive study of the revolution, tends to reconfirm the Sandinistas' exalted version of their own history with occasional statements like 'as the masses moved ever closer to the FSLN', although it should be said that his book concentrates on structural conditions rather than political agency. *The Sandinista Revolution. National Liberation and Social Transformation in Central America*, New York 1986.

9. Ibid., p. 78. For full details on these two groups, see Wheelock, *Imperialismo y Dictadura*, pp. 143 ff. and appendices.

10. E. Valdivia, 'Estructura de la Producción Agropecuaria, 1960–71', mimeo, Managua 1974, quoted in Eduardo Baumeister, 'The Structure of Nicaraguan Agriculture and the Sandinista Agrarian Reform', in Richard Harris and Carlos M. Vilas, eds, *Nicaragua. A Revolution under Siege*, London 1985.

11. Diederich gives good journalistic portraits of the two sons. Anastasio junior ('Tacho') has naturally come to dominate the image of the dynasty since he presided over its last dozen years in power. The importance of Luis's management of the political system for a decade after his father's death should not be underestimated since he succeeded in negotiating not just the disappearance of the patriarch and consequences of economic growth but also those of the Cuban revolution and the Alliance for Progress, which shared a motif of modernity that was especially challenging for a dominant bloc that more than any other in Central America lacked a distinctly post-war political style. The failure of Tacho to maintain the veneer of modernism adopted by Luis was, of course, determined by the nature of Somocismo as well as the political economy of Nicaragua (which distinguishes it from the case of Iran, where the Shah was able to forge his autocracy in the culture of high growth and modernity, winning the support of a sizeable portion of the middle class). One of the great residual strengths of the FSLN rested in its simultaneous promise of modernity – incarnated in its youthfulness and that of most of its followers – and invocation of history, where it could call on traditions that both pre-dated Somocismo and contradicted it. Exploitation of this bond between old and new is not in itself unusual and indeed was not very forcefully managed until quite late in the organization's

history, but its cultural impact was important in a notoriously poetic nation.

12. For a detailed history, see Richard Millett, *Guardians of the Dynasty*. Between 1950 and 1975 4,897 Guardsmen attended US military training programmes only to apply the lessons as a police force, contrary to the letter of US statutes. It should not be forgotten that the Guard was created by the US and, distinct from other Central American military forces, could not incorporate into its institutional mythology the struggles of the nineteenth and early twentieth centuries that revolved about national independence. This was partly because it post-dated these and partly because the political consequences were too dangerous: William Walker had been allied with the Liberals whereas Zelaya, a Liberal, had challenged the US. Thus, the force was tied to the history of Somocismo in more than a purely institutional manner.

13. For surveys of the FSLN's background and history see Black, *Triumph of the People*; John Booth, *End and Beginning*; Claribel Alegría and D.J. Flakoll, *Nicaragua: La Revolución Sandinista. Una Cronología Política, 1855–1979*, Mexico 1982.

14. Quoted in Alegría and Flakoll, *Nicaragua*, p. 152.

15. I am here endeavouring to circumvent the voluminous literature and charged debates on guerrilla warfare by means of an exceedingly brief comment on its generic qualities. These perhaps require restating if only because one can lose sight of the obvious when it is subjected to complex extrapolation in many different political discourses. The distinction between social banditry and guerrilla warfare as a political strategy is important even if the two occasionally elide, which is very infrequently the case in twentieth-century Central America. Here, as has already been mentioned, the modern movements draw on local traditions of the last century as well as the examples of the Cuban and Vietnamese revolutions as strategic models. The failure of *foquismo* derived from the Cuban experience led to the rejection of the Cartesian postulates (more complex than their high-handed presentation suggested) expressed by Régis Debray, particularly in *Revolution in the Revolution*, London 1967, and *Strategy for Revolution*, London 1973, both subjected to revision and partially criticized in the two volumes of *Critique of Arms*, London 1975. However, the repudiation of a narrow model for averting both the subjective and objective contradictions of guerrilla warfare as a strategy does not itself resolve the latter and may affect the former to only a limited degree. Of course, when a culture of social banditry exists – as in pre-revolutionary China, parts of South-East Asia and Spain in the nineteenth century – the distinction disappears, and it is partly suppressed when, as in Mexico between 1910 and 1930, similar conditions are engendered by prolonged civil war. In Central America the rural population has generally been socialized into conditions of repression rather than warfare, and where the latter is the case, as in El Salvador from 1980, there is very little evidence of non-political banditry. For social banditry, see Eric Hobsbawm, *Primitive Rebels*, Manchester 1959; *Bandits*, London 1971. The longstanding rejection of *vanguardist* guerrillaism by orthodox western Marxism as essentially petty-bourgeois and ultra-leftist in nature can frequently be sociologically as well as politically correct, but besides resting upon alternatives of decidedly questionable superiority outside the northern political culture whence this critique derives, it fails to grant the necessary social importance to the different class structure in the backward capitalist economies or historical importance to the fact that even the 'classical' proletarian revolutions were forged in a profoundly military context. Struggles for national liberation are by virtue of their very character likely to possess a strong military component since they are not waged primarily in factories or parliaments but against systematic subordination, whether by a local or a foreign army. As this type of struggle has predominated as the *form* of revolution in the post-war epoch, regardless of whether it incubates a more profound social revolution or not, it is evident that some revision of traditional Marxist doctrine on both the political culture of warfare and the contradictions of nationalism is required. In practice, instances of revolutionary mobilization that fit the Bolshevik model are very few and far between – in the case of Latin America only Bolivia in 1952 would seem to be readily comparable. As a result, Communist Parties have frequently been obliged to accept a suspension of orthodoxy when confronted with the success of 'direct action', and even when orthodoxy has been given full rein in the many instances of failure it has often exhibited a vacuous dogmatic nature rather than going to the heart of the concrete situation.

16. The government-controlled *Confederación General de Trabajo* (CGT) split in 1963 with the CGT–*Independiente* (CGTI) passing into the control of the PSN. The *Central de Trabajadores de Nicaragua* (CTN) was formed in 1972 with the support of the PSCN and

backing from the regional Christian Democratic confederation, CLAT. The *Confederación de Unificación Sindical* (CUS) was established in 1964 and affiliated to the International Confederation of Free Trade Unions (ICFTU), dominated by the US AFL–CIO.

17. The position of the *Proletarios*, who declared their existence to demonstrate 'the failure of messianic voluntarism of petty-bourgeois hegemony within the FSLN', may be found in FSLN *Proletario, Documentos Básicos*, November 1978. That of the GPP, generally less aggressive in tone, was reproduced in *Lucha Sandinista* whilst the *Tercerista* perspective is contained in Julio López C. et al., *La Caida del Somocismo y la Lucha Sandinista en Nicaragua*, San José 1980.

18. For examples of the debate on the left, see James Petras, 'Whither the Nicaraguan Revolution?' *Monthly Review*, vol. 31, no. 5, October 1979, and the rebuttal of his view that the *Terceristas* were social democrats in Henri Weber, *Nicaragua. The Sandinist Revolution*, London 1981, p. 55. In 1982 I rejected Weber's criticism of Petras on the grounds that it is perfectly possible for proponents of social democratic policies to stage insurrectionary general strikes against a dictatorship, and that what mattered was less the form of struggle than the policies behind it. James Dunkerley, *The Long War. Dictatorship and Revolution in El Salvador*, 2nd edn, London 1985, note 7, p. 272. I still believe this to be correct in itself but it was clearly an insufficient response to Weber's overly voluntarist criticism of Petras's excessively orthodox depiction. The following paragraphs represent an interim effort to disentangle some of the strands of this discussion. Despite the generally starry-eyed approach adopted by Black in *Triumph of the People*, his description of the different tendencies, pp. 91–7, has the merit of factual detail.

19. Sergio Ramirez, *El Alba de Oro*, Mexico 1983, p. 126.

20. 'By regarding the *popular* subject as a politico-ideological process which has a class base but is not reducible to it, we can look at how the non-proletarianized – or not fully proletarianized – working masses are subordinated to the dominant classes and how they get incorporated into the popular camp.' Vilas, *Sandinista Revolution*, p. 22.

21. 'Tradespeople' is a term borrowed from Vilas and at the centre of his thesis, which stresses the importance rather than the marginality of petty industry and commerce. Ibid., pp. 74, 119. A similar situation obtains elsewhere in Central America but in the cases of El Salvador and Guatemala the weight of the working class and peasantry is relatively greater.

22. Ibid., pp. 60 ff. Vilas argues that the rural proletariat is much greater than generally assumed, questioning the depiction given in Carmen Diana Deere and Peter Marchetti, 'The Worker-Peasant Alliance in the First Year of the Nicaraguan Agrarian Reform', *Latin American Perspectives*, no. 29, spring 1981. He presents persuasive statistical evidence to show a relatively constant pattern of work throughout the year and properly emphasizes that, 'what is seasonal is employment, not the class or fraction that fills this employment', describing this labour force as *itinerant* rather than seasonal. It is, however, open to question as to what proportion of the seasonal rural labour force is comprised of poor peasants and what proportion moves on the complementary temporary labour in the urban sphere. By stressing this latter group Vilas may be overestimating the degree to which the rural proletariat is dislocated from the poor peasantry and is conditioned by dispossession as well as salarization.

23. The source for this table is Eduardo Baumeister, *Notas para la Discusión del Problema Agrario en Nicaragua*, mimeo 1982, cited in ibid., p. 66.

24. Ibid., pp. 112–17, which also gives a breakdown by department of origin that partially rectifies the natural urban bias of the sample. This survey, based on 542 cases identified through the payment of state pensions, is evidently open to a number of statistical objections as to precise accuracy but its impressionistic value is unlikely to be affected. The figures below are given in ibid., pp. 112, 115.

Occupation of Participants and Parents

Participants	%	*Parents*	%
Students	29.0	Self-employed	39.0
Tradespeople*	22.0	Peasants, farmers	19.0
Workers	16.0	Tradespeople	17.0
Office employees	16.0	Employees	9.5
Professionals	7.0	Professionals	9.5
Peasants	4.5	Workers	5.0

* = includes artisans, workshop owners, petty vendors.

25. The identification of the secondary importance of economic factors in the revolution is by no means novel and is most cogently expressed by Vilas: 'I would argue that in mid 1978 a true *revolutionary* crisis opened up in Nicaragua, of which the economic crisis unleashed in 1978 – and *not before* – is but one dimension', ibid., p. 99. However, Vilas's rebuttal of the view that 'Somoza was some sort of "ideal enemy" ' as 'trivial' (p. 125) runs the risk of throwing the baby out with the bathwater for despite the fact that many North American academics have 'explained' the revolution on such a facile basis, the singularity of Somocismo is not sensibly disputable and cannot be divorced from an interpretation of the revolution's success and form.

26. Again, I am evading a laboured disquisition on structure and agency in the explanation of social phenomena. The most muscular and suggestive exchange at this level within the Marxist canon is between E.P. Thompson, *The Poverty of Theory*, London 1978, and Perry Anderson, *Arguments within English Marxism*, London 1980. Something of the tenor as well as the organization of the present study derives from a reaction to what may be described as the 'overly-Thompsonian' or excessively subjectivist perspective of Anglo-Saxon writing on Central America from the left.

27. AMPRONAC – *Asociación de Mujeres Ante la Problemática Nacional*, which was converted into the *Asociación de Mujeres Nicaragüenses Luisa Amanda Espinoza* (AMNLAE) after the revolution. ATC – *Asociación de Trabajadores del Campo*.

28. *Los Doce* were: Ernesto Castillo and Joaquín Cuadra (lawyers); Emilio Baltodamo and Felipe Mantica (entrepreneurs); Fernando Cardenal and Miguel D'Escoto (priests); Carlos Tunnerman and Sergio Ramirez (academics); Casimiro Sotelo (architect); Arturo Cruz (banker); Carlos Gutiérrez (dentist).

29. FAO comprised: UDEL; MDN; *Los Doce*; three wings of the Conservative Party (*Auténtico; Agüerista; Oficial*) and the PSCN. Its programme called for the establishment of a 'national army . . . at the service of the liberty and interests of the people' together with a new organic military law and an end to military justice being applied to civilians (at the centre of many nineteenth-century Liberal programmes in Latin America); full human rights; full democratic liberties; an agrarian reform; better educational, health and transport services; judicial reform; municipal autonomy and 'the inauguration of a new political order that guarantees a genuinely free electoral process . . .' López et al., *La Caida del Somocismo*, pp. 357-9.

30. The MPU was comprised of: PCN; PSN; *Centro de Acción y Unidad Sindical* (CAUS) dominated by the PCN; *Movimiento Sindical Pueblo Trabajador*; CGT; CLT; *Movimiento Obrero Revolucionario*; ATC; *Unión Nacional de Empleados*; *Asociación Nacional de Ecuadores Nicaragüenses* (ANDEN); AMPRONAC; FER; FER–*Marxista Leninista*; *Centro de Estudiantes de la Universidad Privada*; *Movimiento Estudiantil de la Secundaria; Asociación de Estudiantes de Secundaria*; *Juventud Revolucionaria Nicaragüense; Juventud Revolucionaria Sandinista*; *Juventud Sandinista Nicaragüense*; *Federación de Movimientos Juveniles de Managua*; FSLN. The full MPU platform is reprinted in ibid., pp. 360–72. The FSLN programme called for: nationalization of the property of the Somoza family and their principal allies; an agrarian revolution; improved working conditions and pay in both town and countryside; free unionization; price controls for basic necessities (food, clothing, medicines);

expansion of public services, including social security; rent controls and a housing construction programme; expansion of education and a literacy campaign; nationalization of natural resources, including the mines; development and integration of the Atlantic coast; elimination of organized crime and police corruption; abolition of torture and political killings; full democratic liberties (speech, organization, religion); equality for women; a non-aligned foreign policy and an end to foreign interference; formation of a new popular, democratic army under FSLN leadership. See José Fajado et al., *Los Sandinistas*, Bogotá 1979, pp. 245–57.

31. López et al., *Caida del Somocismo*, pp. 372–8.

32. If a document purporting to be the minutes of an internal FSLN meeting in October 1979 and later circulated by the State Department as 'The 72-Hour Document' is in fact authentic, the leadership itself described its strategy in 1978–79 as an 'ambush' of imperialism and the local bourgeoisie (p. 5). Yet – apart from the fact that the FSLN has a penchant for military vocabulary – it is evident that this is not an 'admission' of any discrete deceit but merely a figurative depiction of their capacity to maintain the abolition of the National Guard at the centre of the opposition campaign and thereby evade the dangers of 'duality' between the Guard and the bourgeois opposition similar to that which obtained between Sacasa and the Guard, identified as being instrumental in Sandino's defeat. The 'revelation' of such a perspective does little but confirm the tactical resourcefulness of the FSLN.

33. This contradictory unanimity inside the OAS is emphasized by Petras, 'Whither the Nicaraguan Revolution?' See also Weber, *Nicaragua*, p. 52.

7

The Nicaraguan Revolution – Sandinismo in Power

We cannot be Marxist–Leninists without Sandinismo. Without Marxism–Leninism Sandinismo cannot be revolutionary. Thus, they are indissolubly linked. . . . Our political strength is Sandinismo and our doctrine is Marxism–Leninism.

Comandante Humberto Ortega, August 1981[1]

The government of Nicaragua has imposed a new dictatorship; it has refused to hold the elections it promised; it has seized control of most media . . . it denied the bishops . . . the right to say mass on radio during Holy Week; it insulted and mocked the Pope; it has driven the Miskito Indians from their homelands . . . it has moved against the private sector and free labor unions. . . . The Sandinista Revolution in Nicaragua turned out to be just an exchange of one set of autocratic rulers for another, and the people have no freedom, no democratic rights and more poverty. Even worse than its predecessors, it is helping Cuba and the Soviets to destabilize our hemisphere.

Ronald Reagan, 27 April 1983[2]

Many foreign observers assume that it is a socialist revolution . . . this is not so. . . . The Sandinista revolution can most accurately be characterized as a revolution of national liberation . . . the revolution seeks primarily to transform Nicaragua into a modern nation-state that is politically, economically and culturally independent of foreign domination.

Richard Harris and Carlos Vilas[3]

If the Americans invaded Nicaragua, what would we do? What could we do? Nothing.

Soviet Foreign Ministry, February 1981[4]

Since July 1979 the Nicaraguan state has retained the traditional sky-blue and white flag as the national standard. Because this flag is derived from the original banner of the Central American confederation – the model for the insignia of all the isthmian states – its removal would signal a rupture with the heritage of a regional patriotism that is a vital component of Nicaraguan nationalism. The real emblem of the revolution is the red and black anarcho-syndicalist standard inherited from Sandino by the FSLN as one of the few devices of Sandinismo that denotes its partisan character and is not interchangeable with the motifs of nationalism or the nation as a whole. The title of the state – *República de Nicaragua* – has been left unadorned by adjectives (popular, democratic, socialist, cooperative, etc.) often employed by regimes seeking a complete codification of their radical bona fides. This, though, is not a Latin American tradition, and even the Cuban state lacks an official designation similar to that of the 'Peoples' Democracies'.[5] It is clear that the declaration of a 'Sandinista Republic of Nicaragua' would create immediate difficulties for the maintenance of political competition. But perhaps the central reason for resisting this particular and most obvious appellation is simply that it is deemed unnecessary since the term 'Sandinista' has become virtually co-substantial with 'national'.

The revolution itself was from the start 'Sandinista', and since Somoza's defeat the army, police and a whole range of state entities and social organizations have been entitled in like manner. The term is so ubiquitous that it has spurred constant opposition invectives against the subsumption of state to party by what is seen as an unambiguously Marxist force, but although 'Sandinismo' evidently has a strong hegemonic signature, it should not be viewed as an exclusively organizational appropriation. The nomenclature of Sandinismo is far more extensive than is the presence of the FSLN as a political party. The first 500 militants did not receive their cards until January 1981, and since then membership has been very tightly controlled, corresponding to only a small number of those who belong to one 'Sandinista' organization or another. Thus, whilst the FSLN itself is undoubtedly of a vanguardist nature, it is also a great deal more than simply the party in government. The open identification of most of the state and much of society with its cause goes beyond a nominal imposition, representing a fusion of the discrete and partisan with the general and national that simultaneously maintains the party's formal and political dominance and seeks to provide it with a general, social and supra-sectarian aura.

This expansion of Sandinismo has compounded the problems of defining its principal characteristics since it not only shares with Somocismo that peculiarly Nicaraguan tendency to elide the party with the state (in a manner distinct from Cuba, just as Somoza's system was different from those of Stroessner, Pinochet or Perón). This has further dissolved an already vague and sometimes contradictory political ideology into the condition of society as a whole; agency and structure become infernally entwined. There are a number of prominent features here. First, the intrinsically corporate nature of nationalism, the leadership of which may be claimed in specifically partisan terms but must be exercised largely outside them. Secondly, the FSLN's vocal espousal of a mixed economy, which necessarily entails sustenance of private capital in a system where its relations with the state sector are unstable, with the result that the regime is identified through objective conditions as well as by its own ambiguous pronouncements with both the defence of capitalist enterprise and its progressive eradication. Thirdly, the nurturing of political competition essential to the pluralism advocated by Sandinismo whilst its hegemony is directly dependent upon determining the terms of that competition, resulting in a position where the FSLN must simultaneously champion and deny its domination.

Of course, none of these factors is at all unique to Nicaragua. Partisan claims on nationalism have been a central feature of twentieth-century politics throughout the world. The dynamics of 'mixed economies' engender tension between state and private enterprise even in advanced industrialized societies where such a division of labour is often vital to the stable reproduction of capital. Equally, it is not difficult to encounter systems of political domination that depend upon the existence of opposition and yet would be qualitatively transformed should the opposition come to power. Nevertheless, all these tensions obtain in a particularly sharp manner in Nicaragua and are presented as positively characteristic of the revolution rather than as an impediment to it or simply transitory phenomena. The FSLN has fully embraced such a fluidity and lack of definition, maintaining and tactically exploiting rather than seeking a complete and rapid resolution of the underlying anomalies of the political regime, economy and class content of the revolution. On the other hand, these anomalies have not persisted simply as a result of strategy; they depend no less upon internal and external objective conditions that have increasingly limited the Sandinistas' scope for flexibility. It can, therefore, be said that neither the FSLN's policies nor objective conditions have determined a necessary course of future development but that they have established important tendencies and a pattern of limits and possibilities.

Consolidating Leadership

Following the victory of July 1979 the latent conflicts between the FSLN and the bourgeois opposition to Somoza were soon brought into the open. While these were no longer suppressed by the requirements of the anti-dictatorial alliance, they still remained constrained by the need of both sides to extract maximum advantage from their alliance and the broad support given to a Government of National Reconstruction rather than one of an openly partisan nature. There was, therefore, no immediate post-insurrectionary struggle either for the exclusion of certain individuals and currents from the regime or for the adoption of a fully socialist or even markedly radical social programme. Nonetheless, if much of the logic of the anti-Somoza alliance persisted beyond his defeat, the first fifteen months of the revolution witnessed a series of sharp encounters over the key issues of elections and confiscation of property in which the leading figures of the bourgeoisie were increasingly outmanoeuvred by the FSLN and effectively defeated in political terms by November 1980. A detailed narrative of this process is beyond our scope, but it is sufficiently important to warrant a brief itemization and assessment of the central events (Table 25).

One critical feature of this period was precisely the fact that the proponents of liberal democracy withdrew and were not expelled from government. This had the effect of presenting the bourgeois politicians as opponents of the alliance despite the fact that they had been forced by the FSLN into untenable positions. In adopting this course of action the Sandinista leadership alternated between pressure and concession in such a manner as to divide the bourgeois bloc. The withdrawal of Decree 38, confiscating the property of all those 'related to Somocismo', reduced apprehension over widespread expropriations whilst the Fundamental Statute issued a fortnight later liquidated the Somocista state when the bourgeoisie was simply seeking piecemeal institutional reform and a change in personnel (which hardly took place at all at administrative levels). Similarly, the decision to delay the establishment of the Council of State until May 1980, thereby giving the FSLN time to consolidate the popular organizations so that the new body could incorporate bodies beyond the pre-revolutionary parties, was matched by a further relaxation in the impetus of nationalization, which was in any case proving difficult to administer. This also provided support for the December cabinet change in which the Sandinistas strengthened their hold on the strategic portfolios, providing a more secure basis from which to launch the measures of spring 1980.

The establishment of popular tribunals, the militia and the literacy crusade took place in a period when the FSLN was moving most concertedly against the far left, which – it is often forgotten – was suppressed earlier and more decisively than the right, not least because it did possess some capacity to challenge the Sandinista monopoly over military organization.[6] However, it was the bourgeoisie that suffered from these measures since even in the case of the literacy crusade – the ideological content of which was firmly Sandinista and the subject of much dispute – the whole impetus was away from reconstituting the traditional organs of the state and liberal democracy

Table 25: The Political Consolidation of the FSLN, 1979–80

1979	Aug.	8	Suspension of Decree 38, ordering confiscation of property of all those 'related to Somocismo', to placate capitalist fears of total expropriation.
		22	Proclamation of Fundamental Statute of the Republic, abolishing old constitution, congress, judiciary and 'remaining structures of Somocista power'.
			CST established.
	Sept.	19	Minister of Defence, ex-Guard Colonel Bernardo Larrios, arrested.
	Nov.		FSLN Directorate declares new Council of State will include popular organizations and not meet before May 1980; MDN and COSEP call for poll in 1982.
		22	Decree 3, nationalizing Somoza family property, suspended, some bank accounts unblocked; relations with bourgeoisie eased.
	Dec.	4	Cabinet reshuffle strengthens FSLN presence in government; Wheelock becomes minister of agriculture; Humberto Ortega defence minister.
		19	Rents reduced 40–50%.
			War crimes tribunals open.
1980	Jan.		FSLN suppresses Maoist-backed MILPAS militia and *Frente Obrero* paper *El Pueblo*; land rent reduced; foreign debt accepted.
	Mar.		Formal establishment of Sandinista militia.
		2	Decree penalizing decapitalization and 'economic sabotage'.
		3	Lands squatted by *campesinos* nationalized.
		15	Literacy crusade begins.
	Apr.		Chamorro resigns from junta for 'health reasons'.
		21	FSLN announces membership of Council of State, giving majority of seats (2447) to Sandinista bloc; Robelo resigns from junta; COSEP demands guarantees of freedom of press, lifting of July 1979 state of emergency, separation of party and state, clear reaffirmation of property rights, date for full elections.
			FSLN agrees to lift state of emergency, introduce bill of rights, guarantee private radio stations, and announce election date on 19 July.
	May		Conflict inside *La Prensa* over criticism of regime leads to dissident journalists forming pro-Sandinista *Nuevo Diario*.

	4	COSEP attends inaugural meeting of Council of state (MDN and PCD enter later).
	18	Rafael Córdova Rivas (PCD) and Arturo Cruz (*Los Doce*) replace Robelo and Chamorro on junta.
Jul.	19	Daniel Ortega announces law for expropriation of uncultivated *latifundia* but no date for elections; bourgeois criticisms increase.
Aug.	23	Humberto Ortega announces elections to be held in 1985.
Oct.		Borge asks Robelo to cancel MDN demonstration protesting drift to 'totalitarianism'.
Nov.	8-9	MDN demonstration leads to sacking of its offices by Sandinista crowds.
	10	Junta reaffirms pluralism but warns against 'lack of understanding'.
	12	MDN, PCD, COSEP and opposition unions CNT and CUS boycott council of state.
	17	COSEP vice-chairman Jorge Salazar killed by police in shoot-out; bourgeois parties allege cold-blooded execution.
	22	FSLN publishes proof of Salazar involvement in conspiracy.

---

and towards popular mobilization and participation. The decree against decapitalization was introduced on the clear rationale of maintaining production yet simultaneously posed a major challenge to the capitalist class by reopening the option of nationalization. This was done, moreover, in terms that were difficult to oppose politically and economically most threatening since progressive decapitalization was in many senses a more logical response to the uncertain conditions than either total closedown or maximization of output in the short term. However, the central points of conflict were in the political sphere, and the first substantial crisis occurrred in April 1980 over the FSLN's arrangement of representation in the Council of State so that the Sandinista bloc had a one-vote majority.[7] This led Robelo to quit the junta (Chamorro already having left on ostensibly non-political grounds) and provoked COSEP to demand a number of guarantees upon which the continued collaboration of the bourgeoisie would depend. The FSLN once again made concessions, but in no case did these amount to surrendering its hold on real power despite some hesitation as to the question of elections, over which there was a change of tactics in July and August. The eventual announcement of a poll five years hence was not in itself a decision of overbearing consequence to the Sandinistas since although it amounted to a pledge to retain a liberal electoral system, the date was sufficiently distant to permit the prior consolidation of the regime on a more extensive basis and through direct methods of popular participation. (In this respect one should note the general subordination of electoralism – if not always elections – in post-insurrectionary conditions; the delay of nearly two decades in holding a poll after the US revolution was continually raised in the FSLN's defence of its policy of establishing socio-economic and administrative stability prior to engaging in full political competition.)

The MDN and several other bourgeois parties had been campaigning for a series of polls over the period 1981–83 and viewed the promise of the later date as one of highly questionable value as well as being most advantageous to Sandinismo. This interpretation was also shared by the US, which from 1981 began to focus much of its invective against the Sandinistas around the absence of a poll, Washington's belief in its own propaganda handing the FSLN a public relations gift of exceptional value when the election was held (ahead of time). All the same, the concessions of April 1980 – excluding a firm date for elections – proved to be enough to retain the participation of the bourgeoisie, and this was not altered in August when the date of the poll was finally announced. The Sandinistas continued to resist the traditional demand of the far left for an end to bourgeois representation in government whilst the appointment to the junta of Córdova and Cruz – representatives of precisely those forces considering a rupture with the regime – had the effect of reducing the April crisis from one of principle to one of tactics, in which the MDN's challenge was successfully isolated from the majority of the opposition bloc.[8] Cruz, of course, was later to leave government and enter the opposition in April 1982, moving into the counter-revolutionary camp early in 1985. It is, however, a reflection of the critical uncertainty bred by the FSLN's policy of incorporation that he only withdrew from the November 1984 elections at the last moment. Córdova, on the other hand, remained within the system beyond the poll along with a section of the Democratic Conservatives.

This first critical phase of the revolution was brought to an end in November 1980 when Robelo attempted to challenge the government on the streets as well as in the apparatus of government. In this he signalled a refusal to accept the growing division between 'popular' and liberal democracy, effectively proving the preponderance of the former when the MDN demonstration was broken up by the pro-Sandinista '*turbas divinas*' ('divine mobs'). The actions of these were presented by the opposition, for such it had now become, as confirming the 'drift to totalitarianism' over which there had been appreciable tactical discord within the Liberal parties prior to the march. At this juncture the FSLN clearly broke from organizational manoeuvre and permitted its popular support to be reaffirmed in a direct manner. There can be no doubt that the government acquiesced in the actions against the MDN and that these, as befits the activities of a crowd, were of a physically aggressive nature. Nevertheless, Robelo's initiative – against which Borge had publicly warned him on a number of occasions – was widely seen as a deliberate provocation, and it is of no little importance that his supporters were routed in the street since they were greatly outnumbered by Sandinista followers. It was – to draw an analogy with Marx's *Eighteenth Brumaire* – the 'mob' not the Guarde Mobile that settled the issue, and whilst accusations of manipulation may satisfy liberal objections to the FSLN stance, they fail to register the important fact that no such manipulation was necessary.[9] In late 1980 popular support for Sandinismo was as great as at any time since the insurrection, and its expression in this manner was entirely in keeping with the mood of the majority as well as the nature of extra-parliamentary politics. Thus, just as it suited Robelo to increase the stakes of competition, so also did it suit the FSLN to reveal the basis and strength of its support. This inevitably caused greater bourgeois dissidence but it also underscored the risks of any repudiation of 'popular democracy' and insistence upon an exclusively liberal system. By holding its rally in protest at 'totalitarianism' the MDN had crossed an important line – it not only rejected the claims of the mass organizations to political participation but did so in their own terrain. The predictable response to this succeeded in provoking another withdrawal of the main opposition parties from the Council of State, propelling them into a political impasse that was rapidly turned into a decisive trap less by the FSLN itself than by sections of the right convinced that matters had already gone beyond the point of negotiation and required conspiracy. Hence, when, less than a week after the walk-out, COSEP vice-chairman Jorge Salazar was shot by police in what appeared to be nothing less than a gratuitous act of state violence to complement mob rule, the opposition invested considerable political capital in its condemnations and swung fully behind Robelo. Returning to its policy of tactical engagement, the FSLN let this campaign run for a number of days before publishing documentary proof of Salazar's involvement in plans for a putsch and possession of arms with which to stage it. These revelations completely neutered the impact of the opposition's offensive and forced it much closer to a choice between, on the one hand, accepting the terms of Sandinista hegemony and negotiating them from within and, on the other, committing itself wholeheartedly to the overthrow of the system. In no immediate condition either politically or logistically to take the latter course, the bulk of the parties opted for the former. But they did so in an unprecedented state of division and without the capacity to stage a coherent defence of liberalism against the FSLN, which continued to accept their claims to a quota of representation and institutionalization but refused to countenance the suppression of the corporate participation of the mass organizations.

It is notable that from 1981 the defence of bourgeois liberalism was upheld less effectively by the political parties that subscribed to it than by the Church, which, despite itself entering into increasing conflict with the regime, possessed a number of distinct organizational and ideological advantages as a vehicle for political opposition. The divisions in the Church ran largely along hierarchical lines so that the bishops were able to maintain a high degree of unity – occasionally near unanimity – to bolster the righteousness of their invectives against the temporal order. This was most marked in the case of the introduction of obligatory military service in 1983 but also obtained in attacks on the state of emergency that was declared in March 1982 and only temporarily suspended on the eve of the 1984 poll; by this time Obando y Bravo was engaged in denunciations of the government markedly more virulent in tone than those of the opposition parties in the Council of State. These reflected more than Obando's palpable loathing for the FSLN since the opposition had now divided into counter-revolutionary and legalist camps, requiring the cleric to assume pastoral responsibility for the former as well as the latter despite the fact that he stopped short of openly sanctioning rebellion and simply called for negotiations with the Contra.

Once the political defeat of the bourgeoisie was effected at the end of 1980 its division proceeded apace. In July 1981 the right-wing opposition in the Council of State allied as the *Coordinadora Democrática Nicaragüense* (CDN) whilst Robelo refused all negotiations with the regime, finally leaving the country in June 1982. (In April 1982 Alfredo César left as director of the Banco Central and in May Arturo Cruz resigned as ambassador to Washington – the timing is not coincidental; all these figures had close links with the State Department and would, eventually and by different routes, unite in the Contra.) In September 1981 the rump of Somocismo, principally ex-Guardsmen, established a counter-revolutionary military force in the *Fuerzas Democráticas Nicaragüenses* (FDN), which was soon joined by most of the ultramontane spirits in the PCD led by Adolfo Calero (Table 26). The legalist wing of the party continued to act as the focal point of the CDN first in the Council of State and then in the National Assembly under the leadership of Rafael Córdova. In September 1982 a second armed Contra group – *Alianza Revolucionaria Democrática* (ARDE) – was established by Robelo and the now disgraced Sandinista commander Edén Pastora, whose personalism and pique greatly exceeded his political prowess. Pastora's *Frente Revolucionario Sandinista* (FRS) persisted in repudiating both Somocismo and US threats to Nicaraguan sovereignty, claiming to champion a social democratic Sandinismo against the Leninist variant entrenched in Managua. However, both Pastora's poorly funded and ill-organized campaign in the south and the incongruous nature of his political programme eventually obliged the more Machiavellian Robelo to shift his allegiance to the CIA-backed FDN, which, following

Table 26: Principal Political Forces

PRO-GOVERNMENT

Frente Patriótico para la Revolución (FPR: 23/vii/80)

FSLN
PLI (–ii/84)
PPSC
PSN
PCN
MAP-ML[1]

LEGAL OPPOSITION

Coordinadora Democrática Nicaragüense (CDN; vii/81)

1981:	1985:
PCD	PCD-Córdova
PSD[2]	PSD
PSCN	PSCN
PLC[3]	(CUS)
COSEP	(CTN)
CUS	
CTN	

COUNTER-REVOLUTIONARY

Fuerzas Democráticas Nicaragüenses (FDN; ix/81)

Somocistas
PCD-Calero
Misura-Fagoth (viii/84–)
MDN (viii/85–)

Alianza Revolucionaria Democrática (ARDE; ix/82–viii/85)

PRS (Pastora)
MDN
Misurata-Brooklyn Rivera (1982–84)

Unión Nicaragüense de la Oposición (UNO; vi/85)

FDN; Arturo Cruz (until iii/87)

Notes:
1. *Movimiento Acción Popular – Marxista-Leninista.*
2. Split from PSCN, ix/79; boycotted 1984 poll.
3. Centrist wing of Somocista PLN; majority boycotted 1984 poll.

the 1984 elections, also acquired the support of the fretful pilgrim Cruz. These figures gave the FDN some elemental political literacy and plausibility that remained beyond the gift of either the ranking thugs of Somoza's National Guard or the conspiratorial technicians and Cuban mercenaries loaned by the CIA.

Over the next three years the counter-revolutionary alliance between the Conservative 'democrats' headed by Cruz and Robelo and the Somocista military leadership under the political control of Adolfo Calero hung together in a very tenuous and largely formal fashion, the latter exploiting the former as the 'human face' of the Contra. On the ground the counter-revolutionary soldiers, who grew in number from some 500 in late 1981 to perhaps 15,000 in 1986, proved to be much better terrorists than freedom fighters, failing to hold any territory for a significant period and provoking no popular revolts. By 1983 the US government accepted that this force could not defeat the FSLN despite the enormous damage it caused to the economy both through direct destruction and by obliging the Sandinistas to maintain a massive military apparatus. This, in fact, was of only secondary importance to the CIA, which had planned a prolonged war of attrition and even in closed Senate hearings disavowed any intention of overthrowing the regime in Managua. On the other hand, tensions and disputes rose inside the counter-revolutionary bloc as it became increasingly identified with the violation of human rights and a fruitless campaign of attrition based on the politics of plunder rather than popular support. Those figures seeking a defeat of Sandinismo in the political as well as military field proved unable to win US patronage away from Calero and his brutal Somocista *condottieri* headed by Colonel Enriqué Bermudez, whose ex-National Guard comrades controlled forty-six of the forty-eight Contra commands. As a result, when the Irangate scandal broke late in 1986 the Cruz–Robelo axis was completely isolated; Cruz underwent one of his customary crises of decision before quitting UNO in March 1987 whilst Robelo endeavoured to establish some distance from Calero without severing all organizational links. As over the previous five years, there was plenty of fighting talk but the confusion and parasitism was plain for all to see.[10]

The precise activities of the reactionary and counter-revolutionary organizations are of less interest to us here than the fact that they allied an important faction of the original anti-dictatorial alliance with erstwhile servants of the dictatorship and yet still did not include the majority of the bourgeois parties. This meant, amongst other things, that Washington was subjected to concerted lobbying both for and against economic boycott, increased sabotage and direct intervention on openly capitalist grounds by forces that were themselves required to enter into competition with each other for external political patronage.[11] One faction reverted to historical type in dependence on the US and the tradition of pacts with Somocismo, unambiguously in military control of the Contra once Pastora, having suffered a decisive defeat at San Juan del Norte in April 1984, shaved off his beard and regressed to the traditions of *caudillismo* in waging a campaign against all and sundry in the foreign media. The other bloc responded to the alternative logic of the past in accepting minority representation within a heavily qualified liberal system, for which attachment to popular patriotism served to qualify at least some of the loss of US patronage. As can be seen from the results of the 1984 poll (Table 27), the holding of which was vital to this second group as well as to its external sponsors, the rewards of such a strategy were less substantial than under Somoza, but they were far from derisory and signalled that even after five years of Sandinismo the traditional bourgeois currents of Conservatism, Liberalism and Christian Democracy had retained appreciable support. (This was despite considerable confusion in the weeks before the poll over whether the CDN's demands for FSLN negotiations with the Contra should be taken to the point of boycott, as demanded by Cruz.) Furthermore, the very fact that the election was held and on terms infinitely more fair than under Somoza or anywhere else in

Table 27: The Election of 4 November 1984

Registered	1,560,580	
Voted	1,170,142	
Turnout	75%	
Null	6%	
Presidency	*Votes*	*% Votes*
FSLN: Ortega/Ramírez	735,967	67
PCD: Guido/Rodríguez	154,327	14
PLI: Godoy/Pereira	105,560	10
National Assembly	*Seats*	*% Seats*
FSLN	61	64
PCD	14	15
PLI	9	9
PPSC	6	6
PSN	2	2
PCN	2	2
MAP-ML	2	2

Central America other than Costa Rica amounted to a justification of their strategy for important elements inside the CDN and something of a shock for those forces (PSD; the majority of the PLC; a faction of the PLI) preparing to claim fraud as a pretext for changing camps.[12] One important factor in the assessment of the opposition parties that entered the Assembly was that despite the FSLN's overwhelming victory, the poll terminated a period of institutionalized corporatism through the Council of State, which was the formal sphere for 'popular democracy'. Hence, while the practical activity of the mass organizations did not alter after the elections and they continued to be the principal channels of FSLN organization amongst the population, this linkage now lacked a formal character and could be construed as no longer impinging upon the constitutional realm. In this respect the FSLN's acceptance of the *form* of liberal democracy and its own participation as a party in government at least dimmed the early fears of a possible Soviet-style regime and provided the opposition with a familiar forum for its activity.

Popular Democracy

With the inauguration of the Assembly the trade unions, interest groups and principal popular organizations lost official corporate representation at a national level, their members now occupying congressional positions as members of political parties. However, it is apparent that 'popular democracy' lost none of its importance for Sandinismo and remained an important prop of the revolution. Until 1985 it was through the major organizations – the *Comités de Defensa Sandinista* (CDS); the *Juventud Sandinista* (JS-19); CST and AMNLAE – that the FSLN not only built popular support but also channelled important state and social tasks ranging from distribution of food to health and literacy campaigns. Participation in such activities at the heart of daily life and the social programmes of the regime cannot be divorced from politics even though it involved tens of thousands of citizens who were not militants of the FSLN and despite the fact that it tended to concentrate organizational activity around specific and local socio-economic matters in a predominantly instrumentalist fashion. Perhaps the best depiction of the objectives of the system was given by Sergio Ramirez in July 1983:

> Effective democracy . . . consists of . . . a permanent dynamic on the people's participation in a variety of political and social tasks; the people who give their opinions and are listened to; the people who suggest, construct and direct, organize themselves, who attend to community, neighbourhood and national problems; a people who are active in the sovereignty and the defence of that sovereignty and also teach and give vaccinations; a daily democracy and not one

> that takes place every four years . . . when formal elections take place; the people don't go as a minority but in their totality, and they consciously elect the best candidate and not one chosen like a soap or detergent . . . for us democracy is not merely a formal model, but a continual process capable of giving the people that elect and participate in it the real possibility of transforming their living conditions, a democracy which establishes justice and ends exploitation.[13]

'Popular democracy', which in reality only approximates to such ideals in uneven fashion, clearly need not, and in practice does not, enter into direct conflict with the parliamentary model alongside which it exists. The FSLN, which views the development of popular participation as an evolutionary process from the socio-economic to the political sphere, has purposefully preserved this parallelism, presenting it as a necessary complementarity rather than a temporary prelude to collectivist government.[14] It is certainly the case that the CDSs have not become transformed into bodies in the mould of soviets or workers' councils that the right initially feared and sections of the left hoped for.[15] This is a result less of the span of activities that the CDSs undertake than of restricted deliberative and executive authority, which is generally accepted to reside with the FSLN as the vanguard party. As a consequence, there is little debate along partisan lines over national policy, and while the leadership of the CDSs was from 1983 fully elected and technically subjected to immediate recall, in practice these bodies discuss and occasionally dispute the '*orientaciones*' they receive from the government largely in terms of local applicability and administrative detail rather than those of general character and acceptability. There have been important exceptions to this pattern – in 1980 the ATC obliged the regime to accelerate land distribution against the wishes of some of the cabinet; also in that year the unions objected to the designation of beer, rum and cigarettes as luxury rather than basic goods and thus subject to taxation (they were over-ruled); and in 1983 AMNLAE crossed swords with the FSLN over the exclusion of women from the obligatory military service bill, winning only tactical concessions. Nonetheless, the popular organizations have not developed into distinct arenas for political debate and remain firmly within the orbit of Sandinismo; since the growth of the counter-revolutionary campaign from 1983 this became even more firmly the case.

The opposition and US government present 'popular democracy' as little more than the mass expression of the FSLN and thus not democratic in the slightest, but it cannot be understood purely in terms of instrumentalism. It is clear that the major organizations were formed immediately before, during or straight after the insurrection and were firmly allied to the FSLN through the MPU, which was dissolved after the victory. They therefore lacked prior traditions independent of Sandinismo and developed under its political leadership; the youth movement, in particular, was a body that came into being primarily as a party front. Moreover, recalling earlier observations depicting Sandinismo as a simultaneously narrow partisan and extensive cultural form of politics, it is implausible to deny that a similar ambiguity exists within the popular organizations, most of which, after all, carry Sandinista titles. Nonetheless, these bodies have their being in civil society; by virtue of this and their very corporate nature they must elevate the general attributes of Sandinismo above its more restricted political identity. Since they are participatory and include thousands of people they cannot preserve a rationale for their existence – still less authentic popularity – if they are seen as mere artifacts of the party. Thus, the FSLN stresses the importance of the space between them and the apparatus of government:

> Should the mass organizations resort to their own force, means of expression and mobilization when their demands are not heeded, when the doors are closed on all sides? We believe that they must. The mass organizations must collect and make their own the demands of their members, they must struggle to see them realized through the mechanisms that the revolution has established.[16]

Such a depiction stresses autonomy not independence, and it is in these terms that the relationship with the party is most generally described. According to one CDS secretary, 'If the Frente has a task for us we talk with them and decide whether we can do it or not. We negotiate with them to see whether it is possible. We are an autonomous organization. We don't have a vertical relationship with them.'[17] If in general terms the whole operation of 'popular democracy' remains under the hegemony of the FSLN, in local, practical and administrative affairs it is frequently the site of exchanges with the party that are far from automatically compliant; most critically, it endows the expression of popular views on everyday matters with a consequence that is palpably greater and more immediate than under the possibilities offered by the liberal system of representation. In sum, 'popular democracy' is not a system of full and independent political activity on the part of the masses and it does not correspond to the source of political initiative and leadership in Nicaragua, but it is equally not a sphere of pure manipulation and administration; it has exercised critical effects on the population at large in its own terms, retaining some sense of practical identity with the revolution even when, as from 1984/5, popular enthusiasm was considerably diminished by economic crisis and the stalling of social change.

Opposition and US attacks on the lack of independence of the mass organizations are combined with invectives against the burgeoning collectivism that they are seen to be building. Here the assault on 'popular democracy' is markedly discriminatory since it is exceptionally difficult to inveigh against mass participation in the provision of health and educational programmes, which initially depended heavily upon local administration and support from the mass organizations. (This did not, however, hold the opposition back from attacking the literacy crusade – a major enterprise involving over 100,000 volunteers – as an exercise in mass brainwashing.) Such a 'parastatal' role was reduced after the first couple of years of the revolution but remained partially intact in the CDSs, which administered the rationing and distribution of basic necessities (rice, beans, eggs, salt, sugar, oil, soap) in the towns until 1985 and have continued to have responsibility for the supervision of public order in their neighbourhood ('*vigilancia revolucionaria*'), the allocation of claims to housing lots, and general coordination of government programmes in the locality as well as the representation of corporate interests to the central state. They are, then, a form of municipal or local power with all citizens eligible for election to the leadership and able to attend meetings.

In the early stages of the revolution the frequently ad hoc nature of the CDSs was tolerated largely because the weakness of the state apparatus and the level of destruction caused by the war placed a premium upon action and relegated the importance, in the eyes of the FSLN, of procedural matters. As a result, the obvious potential for petty tyranny, corruption, favouritism, personalism and general excesses of control began to be realized to a perceptible degree. Since the CDSs included over half a million people these may be seen as largely social rather than political traits, but they nonetheless had the effect of reducing the popularity, efficiency and authority of many bodies, and this in turn prejudiced the position of the FSLN. Thus, in October 1982 the party called for a 'restructuring', attacked abuses and ordered the full institution of democratic procedure.[18] This clearly had some impact and diminished the incidence of flagrantly arbitrary behaviour. All the same, it did not lead to the withdrawal from the CDSs of their general supervisory role – the voluntary and unarmed *vigilancia* – presented by the opposition as a structural violation of individual liberty and a key feature of the 'totalitarian' character of a regime that monitors all citizens, imposes a rigid model of social comportment and persecutes those who deviate from it. The similarity of the CDSs to the *Comités de Defensa de la Revolución* set up in Cuba in September 1960 (a time when there was a grave threat of US intervention) sharpened accusations of party dictatorship and encouraged projections of the Orwellian nightmare that suffuses the liberal vision of collective activity. Yet despite evidence of more than discrete partiality in the activities of some CDSs, the notion that they incarnate a comprehensive system of social control, fully bureaucratized and subject to suffocative political supervision is untenable, if only because Nicaraguan public life continues to be of a distinctly ramshackle nature. The coercive powers of the communitarianism enshrined in the CDS are themselves limited, being a great deal less than those possessed by Somoza's infinitely more arbitrary and unpopular *jeuces de mesta* and no more than those held by the elders of most Latin American villages. But they are organized in a collective form and represent the incorporation of some traditional state tasks into civil society; they challenge the bourgeois conception of the distance between state and individual – a conception that has never obtained in reality for the mass of Nicaraguan citizens. Here invectives against the CDSs are informed as much by a fear of 'the mob' as by its political sympathies. Moreover, limited to observation and information though they may be, the supervisory tasks of the CDS do constitute precisely a 'defence' of the revolution that is of importance and justified by the scale of counter-revolutionary activity. If this were not perceived to be the case by a significant proportion of the population the FSLN would face far greater problems than it has encountered hitherto in maintaining support for and acquiescence in the system since the CDS, by virtue of the geographical and non-sectoral character of its organization, tends to reflect more directly than other popular bodies fluctuations in public opinion and commitment to the regime.

The relative lack of institutionalism in 'popular democracy' makes it much more erratic than claimed by many of its supporters and less monolithic than presented by its enemies; it also makes it only partially intelligible in terms of western political models. The weight of indigenous and conjunctural factors is especially great because of the predominantly social character of this movement. Thus, the localism that marks the CDS should be seen as corresponding as much to the traditions of the *cabildo abierto* as to the constraints imposed by FSLN vanguardism. Equally, both cultural and political factors inform the activities of AMNLAE, for which dedication to women's emancipation is in some respects counterposed to the forms prevalent in Europe and North America: 'In Nicaragua we cannot conduct a struggle of a western feminist kind. This is alien to our reality. It doesn't make sense to separate the women's struggle from that of overcoming poverty, exploitation and reaction. We want to promote women's interests within the context of that wider struggle.'[19]

In terms of military power the Nicaraguan revolution conforms much more closely to general patterns. The FSLN confronts its opponents' attacks on the politicization of the regular army – *Ejército Popular Sandinista* (EPS) – and the large militia set up in 1981 in unambiguous fashion: 'There is no apolitical army in the world. This is a sophism . . . there are no apolitical armies; every one serves some determinate political purpose. In the case of Nicaragua, the EPS is a Popular and Sandinista Army. It is not by accident that we call it such.'[20] Nicaraguan experience of this general law was, of course, particularly sharp, the absence of a 'national' army – that is, one at least autonomous from political parties – being marked throughout its history. However, the Sandinista military is not simply a radical variant of the National Guard since it conforms to the western tradition of a 'nation in arms' in which norms of professionalism and institutionalization are temporarily suspended by those of an 'armed citizenry'.[21] It need scarcely be recalled that the great bourgeois revolutions in England, France and the US derived much of their ideology as well as their capacity to overthrow the state from precisely such a '*levée en masse*' of common folk. Reagan might have compared the Contras to the likes of Francis Marion but it is the Sandinista forces that have won the claim to this tradition. Nevertheless, while the militia has naturally continued to retain a more civic character, the EPS has increasingly developed into a very large and progressively professionalized force, its internal regime becoming more hierarchical at the expense of many of the features of the guerrilla out of which it was born. In this it is following a pattern typical from Vietnam to Cuba – one of bureaucratization of the forces of national liberation that echoes the earlier consolidation of the forces of bourgeois insurrection. It also proceeds from the profoundly military character of the FSLN's history – still evident in its political language – that has enhanced the latent tendency not only to fortify the state but also to politicize the nation's youth through the army. Increased potential for a progressive militarization of politics is the natural corollary to the politicization of the military, and this is only partly qualified by the voluntary nature of the militia, which was from its inception the product of party organization rather than the independent expression of worker or peasant mobilization. Perhaps most important of all, the fierce counter-revolutionary campaign supported by Washington has demanded the diversion of an enormous proportion of the state's depleted budget to defence (over 40 per cent) and ensured that the military question remains at the centre of politics. This was dominated by the undeclared war waged by the US through its proxies and the conflict between the FSLN and the opposition over the politicization of the army and militia. The effect of both the FSLN's vanguard role and the counter-revolutionary campaign has been to fortify an erratic but residual proclivity for more dirigiste leadership. Here both objective and subjective factors accentuate the dangers of a creeping bonapartism in which the impetus of 'popular democracy' shifts from '*orientaciones*' to diktat whilst the increasingly severe economic crisis that necessarily places popular compliance under great strain is confronted with policies of a more pronounced coercive character, just as desired by Washington. Occasional instances of this – most particularly the treatment of the Miskito 'problem' – have naturally been subjected to feverish exploitation by the right, but they do possess a logic inside Sandinismo and are not merely discrete 'errors' of judgement. Neither the effects of US aggression, nor the experience of other victorious national liberation movements, nor indeed the limited existing powers of 'popular democracy' ensure that continued concentration of power in the FSLN leadership will necessarily militate only to the detriment of the bourgeoisie, imperialism and the right.[22]

The invectives of the opposition and counter-revolutionary forces against the regime have undoubtedly been weakened by its lack of personalism. Insofar as the revolution has a personalist character it is posthumous, the martyred figure of Carlos Fonseca reducing the scope for any of the existing nine *Comandantes de la Revolución* to be projected as the natural generational heir to Sandino. Although by dint of his age, experience and fluid populist style Tomás Borge appears the most obvious candidate for this role, the FSLN National Directorate has evidently established a collective model of leadership that is practical, not unpopular, and little prejudiced by the existence of presidential office insofar as this is held by the resolutely uncharismatic Daniel Ortega. Furthermore, despite the occasional lapse, the lifestyle of the leadership is sufficiently parsimonious to deprive predictable opposition claims of personal enrichment of much credibility, the contrast with Somoza continuing to have political value.[23] Largely resistant to comparisons with the boisterous personalism of Fidel Castro or the leaden anonymity of the Soviet bloc bureaucracies, difficult to attack as acquisitive arrivistes, including enough priests and Christian radicals to be unwholesomely pious even by Nicaraguan standards, and leavening its general youth with a scattering of sages, the FSLN government has proved uncommonly difficult to impugn outside its substantive policies. Even Mario Vargas Llosa, that most indefatigable flayer of left-wing 'tyrannies', found himself as disarmed by the candour of political leaders who are writers and poets as did the interviewers from *Playboy*, ambushed by easy discussion of Trappism, Marlon Brando and *Ripley's Believe it or Not* in their conversations with members of the cabinet.[24] Although anecdotal and superficial, these are also manifestations of a political style that is markedly modern and agile – much more so than that of Gorbachev, whose minimalist innovations have spectacularly flummoxed those in Washington who believed that skill with the autocue and off-the-peg sincerity were their private preserve and almost an article of the US constitution. Sandinista style is not just the product of an adolescent regime, and if it relates to external influences, these are assuredly much less the vacuous and fashionable shibboleths embraced by a redundant Eurocommunism than the product of US attention to and influence in Nicaragua. One ironical legacy of the US Marines' sojourn in the country is that anti-imperialist meetings are held in a Managua stadium sporting a scoreboard registering 'strikes', 'bolas' and 'outs'. In the same vein, Vice-President Bush's gleeful presentation of a postage stamp bearing Karl Marx's profile as proof positive of Nicaragua's accredited membership of the 'evil empire' floundered somewhat upon publication the next day in the US press of a rather more engaging depiction of Babe Ruth, also available to users of the country's appalling mail service.

None of this, however, has enabled the FSLN leadership to evade a series of sharp conflicts with the Church hierarchy, which has become its principal political enemy inside the country despite the presence of several priests and a number of devout Catholics in the government. Tensions between the two reflected the declining stock of the bourgeois opposition parties and had reached a point of complete antipathy well before the debacle of the Pope's visit in March 1983. This conflict is often understood to be anomalous insofar as the position of the religious hierarchy is contrasted with that of Archbishop Romero in El Salvador and with its own initial support for the insurrection against Somoza. However, Romero must be seen as both something of a maverick inside the Salvadorean hierarchy and as acting under very distinct circumstances at the time of his death in March 1980, when the representatives of the popular forces had been fully excluded from government in a phase of exceptional repression by a right wing evidently prepared to provoke a full civil war. Although Romero was an altogether more inquisitive and intelligent man than is Obando – regarded even by many of his allies as a witless and inflexible creature – and despite the fact that he had been converted from conservative to progressive views by a markedly more violent government campaign against radical priests than took place in Nicaragua, his stand against the military and the right was not qualitatively different in its underlying objective of securing a social pact from the Nicaraguan bishops' tardy imprimatur for rebellion in June 1979.[25] This itself should be seen within the logic of the anti-dictatorial alliance and not as backing for Sandinismo, with which only a part of the clergy was prepared to align itself. The position of Obando and the majority of bishops is less a retreat from that of June 1979 than from the 1950 pronouncement of Archbishop González y Roberto in support of subjugation to the temporal order, citing Gregory XVI's encyclical *Mirari Vos*: 'All authority comes from God and all things are ordered by that same God. Therefore he who resists authority resists God.'[26] Little chance of any Sandinista being declared a 'Prince of the Church' as was Somoza senior after his death.

Yet Obando has not declared that the FSLN 'is capable of anything' or offered his first communion in the guise of cardinal to Contras in Miami because the new state is atheist but because it embraces a radical Christianity that is even more dangerous to the hierarchy. Thus, Comandante Víctor Tirado can proclaim, 'The Gospel, Sandinismo and Marxism coincide in their central goals. They are in agreement as to the need for upgrading the condition of the poor, of the marginalized classes.'[27] Similarly, Sergio Ramírez can depict the combination of these currents in a basic 'human solidarity' as integral to the revolution and manifested in the government's prohibition of the commercial exploitation of Christmas.[28] This coincidence has led the FSLN to deny the religious nature of the hierarchy's attacks on it, thereby challenging the claims of the Church leadership to both a non-partisan position and a monopoly over doctrinal interpretation. The vehemence of these exchanges is vividly portrayed in a speech by Comandante Jaime Wheelock on May Day 1984 in the town of Chinandega, where he characterized the differences between Church and government as political:

> They are political because . . . what contradictions are there between the principles of religion and everything we have been doing all these years? [Shouts of 'Between Christianity and revolution there is no contradiction!'] But why is there no contradiction? Do you know why? For a few simple reasons. Is this a government of the rich or the poor? ['The poor!'] Who were those who could not enter the Kingdom of Heaven? ['The rich!'] In fact, it seems that first a camel had to pass through the eye of a needle. So who does the revolution defend? The poor. Whatever the right wing says, is it true or false that we defend the poor? ['True!'] Who said, 'Blessed be the poor for they shall inherit the earth'? ['Jesus Christ!'] And who is giving land to the poor here? Who took land away from the Somocistas and the rich to give it to the poor? . . . Teach those who do not understand. Who here is teaching those who do not understand? Who here loves his neighbour? Who here is fulfilling most consistently the principles of Christianity? ['The revolution!'] And the Sandinistas ['The vanguard!'][29]

No genteel disquisition on biblical exegesis, for sure. Nonetheless, Wheelock's tub-thumping oratory amounts to more than an opportunist appropriation of social doctrine. It is the polemical expression of a progressive Catholicism which manifests the broad tenets of 'liberation theology' and has coexisted in uneasy terms with the hierarchy for over two decades. Since 1965, 'Ecclesiastical Base Communities' (CEBs) had been engaging in evangelical practice along these lines, simplifying the liturgy and adopting popular motifs in their work. By 1979, when Nicaragua had 120 priests, there were over 300 CEBs and more than 5,000 attached *delegados de la palabra* (catechists), whose activities extended beyond bible study to coordinate Church educational, health and agricultural projects that provided a wider organizational base amongst both the urban and rural poor. Involvement in the CEBs and related organizations sometimes led to direct engagement in radical politics (*Movimiento Cristiano Revolucionario*; *Juventud Obrera Católica*; *Movimiento de Jóvenes Cristianos*; *Movimiento Estudiantil Cristiano*), but more generally established popular familiarity with and frequent sympathy for an activist and social Catholicism that, despite its accessibility, was not without the 'mystique' of the indulgence-peddling variety upheld by the hierarchy. Although not a fully consolidated political bloc within the Church, subject to the discipline of both the bishops and the orders, and generally reluctant to engage in open conflict with the hierarchy instead of raising coded disagreements, this current has continued to challenge reactionary biblical interpretation. The 'battle of the quotations' conducted through *La Prensa* and the pro-FSLN *Nuevo Diario* displays an exegetical ingenuity and combativity quite the equal of that manifested by the divided constituents of Marxism–Leninism. When, in 1983, Obando effectively denounced 'patriotic military service' as the pressganging of the nation's youth in the interests of a political sect he received appreciable support for his stance since it coincided formally with the general anti-militarist position of the Latin American Church and, more immediately, gave voice to the unpopularity of the draft at a time of war. Yet he came under challenge from within the Church as well as from the state: 'A true Christian will defend his home and does not think only of himself, because if one sees that they come to kill children, as do the Contras, the Christian must fight.'[30] Despite receiving sterling support from Rome and general backing from the Latin American bishops' conference (CELAM) in its opposition to government measures, the hierarchy has been unable to impose unity on the clergy, the majority of which is still of foreign birth and education and more inclined to independence than native priests. It has, furthermore, encountered considerable problems in pursuing the general shift of the Latin American Church to a doctrinal and pastoral defence of 'the weak' since it confronts a government that, as Jaime Wheelock is not hesitant to point out, defends the poor precisely by making the economically and socially strong bourgeoisie weak in the political arena.

It has, then, proved difficult for Obando and the bishops to paint the FSLN as anti-clerical and anti-Christ despite the restriction on the broadcasting of his homilies, the heckling of a Pope who refused to pray for victims of the Contra, occasional expulsions of foreign priests opposed to the regime, or even the celebrated incident in 1983 when a diocesan official, Father Bismark Caballo, was paraded naked in front of TV cameras suspiciously rapidly on hand when the police detained him allegedly for his own protection against the irate husband of a woman with whom he had been fornicating.[31] The withdrawal of the rights of priests in the cabinet to offer the eucharist, the removal of several radical clerics from their parishes, and strenuous denunciation of the treatment meted out to the Holy Father himself have, though, all succeeded in impairing the social authority of the government and explain much of the vigour in responses such as that made by Wheelock.

It is not only the religious question but the role of the Church in the revolution as a whole that distinguishes Nicaragua so clearly from the case of Cuba, where this was strictly secondary. In addition to the controversies already mentioned, Obando confirmed his importance as a political leader in heading the campaigns against the censorship of *La Prensa*, the treatment of the Miskito Indians, and the state of siege with impressive persistence. In these cases the inconsistency, highhandedness and occasional violence of the government was denounced in formal terms but with telling reference not only to a burgeoning Communist dictatorship but also back to that of Somoza. The impact of this has been marked, not least because these particular issues engendered controversy well beyond the Church and were not settled by government claims that *La Prensa* was printing objectively subversive material, that the Miskito question was affecting both the unity of the country and the safety of the revolution, or that the state of siege was necessary for national defence. Each case presented real conflicts with the liberal view of pluralism and sometimes within 'popular democracy' itself. It mattered little that *La Prensa* was pledged to destabilizing the government, highly tendentious in its coverage and manifestly favourable to the counter-revolutionary forces (still less that it was of execrable quality and much more limited circulation than is generally depicted abroad); the government's violation of the paper's right to free expression was much more finite in form than the paper's exploitation of this freedom to attack its extension beyond the boundaries of liberal democracy. Unduly zealous in controlling *La Prensa*, the FSLN suffered in terms of external image at least from the paper's closure in June 1986 in response to the approval of $100 million in aid to the Contras by the US Congress. The longstanding dispute was not at root over the paper itself but rather a propaganda battle in which *La Prensa* represented private capital and, once it was clear that it would not itself be nationalized, sought to goad the Sandinistas beyond tactical restrictions into complete suppression as emblematic of their general policy. Revelations of foreign funding for *La Prensa* and the notable lack of US complaint about the earlier suppression of the left-wing papers deprived the protest campaign of the moral force it sought.[32] Moreover, since the paper's commitment to negotiations with the Contra was identical to Obando's own position, his condemnation appeared partisan as well as lacking great domestic popularity. All the same, the closure was a significant setback for the Sandinista policy of 'coexistence without conciliation' less because it signalled the incompatibility of unrestricted universal rights under conditions of acute social conflict than because it limited the space in which such incompatibility was permitted outside institutionalized politics. Somoza, after all, had tolerated the paper; here, for once, the pluralist claims of the FSLN looked somewhat threadbare by the usual yardstick of comparison with the dictatorship.

The importance of this affair rested in the curbing of the rights of the bourgeoisie in particular rather than citizens in general. In the cases of the Atlantic coast and the state of siege, the liberties of a far more extensive section of the population or all of it were subject to restraint under the same rationale of national security. Here, paradoxically, the religious dignitaries found themselves on weaker ground. With respect to the Miskito question (addressed briefly below) they were quick to condemn the FSLN's policy of enforced relocation but lacked a substantial following within the communities concerned, largely members of the Moravian Church, with which Obando did not deign to consult before denouncing the government and which was itself discernibly less vitriolic in its protests. Escapades such as Bishop Schaeffer's 'exodus' to Honduras in the company of Miskito refugees late in 1983 were celebrated as a blessed deliverance, and although upon closer inspection of the circumstances this incident transpired to substantiate FSLN claims of coercion by Contra forces, Obando maintained a positively papal rectitude in his reluctance to castigate the counter-revolutionaries to the same degree as the regime, if at all. (Reagan, of course, simply revelled in growing pronouncements of genocide that had now become more plausible than when Alexander Haig had presented photos of rebel corpses being burnt during the insurrection as those of Miskitos executed by the Sandinistas. The key point here is less the US government's persistent lying – in this instance it was unusually misled by a third party – but the fact that for once a concrete charge levelled by Washington against Managua had some distant relation to reality.)

With respect to the state of siege, the opposition (this time left- as well as right-wing), the Church and Washington could not denounce partiality by the government, the marked increase in Contra attacks from late 1982 onwards combined with open US threats and military operations in Honduras lending considerable credibility to Sandinista declarations that the state as a whole was under attack. Here the reactionary opposition was confronted with a dilemma largely of its own making: it could not feasibly expect the maintenance of liberal democracy in conditions of virtual civil war and yet large sections of it privately supported the Contra precisely to force political concessions from the FSLN. Both Sandinista intransigence on the question of national sovereignty and the Contra's failure to make significant military advances deprived this equation of much value, increasingly obliging the bourgeoisie to choose between acquiescence and outright counter-revolution. The Church hierarchy, by virtue of its specific institutionality, was alone in being able to resist this logic. For the capitalist class as a whole the political dilemma had become even more acute than that facing it in terms of economic strategy – the formal guarantees for activity were sufficient to ensure continued existence but precluded the possibility of control. Poised between subordination, extinction, and flight into the arms of the US in expectation of some future restoration, the bourgeoisie was presented with alternatives of historic proportion; it had to choose between flight and armed resistance predicated exclusively on the eventual success of a counter-revolution or acceptance of restricted powers for which the future remained uncertain. Much of the distinctiveness of the

Nicaraguan revolution derives from the distended nature of this process; it thus contrasts with revolutionary movements where the capitalist class surrendered and fled immediately, as in Cuba. Yet while the FSLN has skilfully forced the bourgeoisie into responding to its terms rather than imposing them by direct fiat, the scope for this in the economic field is more limited than in terms of political power since complete non-compliance by private enterprise would leave the Sandinistas presiding over an even more devastating collapse of production than that provoked by US aggression. This prospect together with the FSLN's monopoly of political power has entailed a much more graduated exploitation of the contradictions of the mixed economy than of those between liberal and 'popular' democracy.

Class Interests and the Economy

It is not necessary to engage in a detailed analysis of the economy and FSLN policy in order to grasp that the pattern of production and ownership since 1979 corresponds to neither a simple 'mixed economy' with a judicious and stable balance between public and private sectors nor a relentless advance of collectivization.[33] Although the regime immediately nationalized the financial system and foreign trade and thereby gained control of the commanding heights of the economy, it was subsequently reluctant to extend expropriation beyond Somoza's holdings and those enterprises that were structurally inefficient (primarily in the countryside) or deliberately undercapitalized. As can be seen from Table 28, by 1982 the public sector (*Area de Propriedad Popular*; APP) controlled less than 40 per cent of GDP although the share of large and medium private capital had fallen to 31 from 67 per cent, a large proportion of this loss taking place in the first year of the revolution with the nationalization of the ex-dictator's interests.

On a purely statistical basis the case for a balanced mixed economy would, then, appear to be plausible, the state controlling key infrastrucure but private enterprise clearly accounting for the bulk of production. (These proportions did not alter significantly between 1982 and 1987.) The FSLN has extended credit and sought to guarantee the conditions for reproduction of capital not only for small enterprises but also for large concerns so long as they maintain production; in the critical agricultural and manufacturing sectors over half of all output is controlled by large and medium capitalist concerns. However, although the stated policy of the FSLN is not 'socialist', it is explicitly founded upon the removal of political power from the bourgeoisie and dedicated to maintaining the conditions for profitability only insofar as these correspond to continued investment and production. Both these factors have engendered a loss of confidence within the bourgeoisie and encouraged a widespread conviction that its existence is

Table 28: Production by Property Sector (% GDP)

	1977	*1980*	*1982*	*1984*
Agriculture	(22)	(22)	(24)	
APP	–	14	21	24
Private (large/med.)	77	63	54	
Private (small)	23	23	25	
Manufacturing	(22)	(25)	(24)	
APP	–	25	31	37
Private (large/med.)	85	60	54	
Private (small)	15	15	15	
Construction and Mining	(9)	(7)	(9)	
APP (1977: state)	10	80	90	92
Private (large/med.)	75	5	5	
Private (small)	15	15	5	
Government	(5)	(10)	(9)	
Commerce and Services	(42)	(36)	(40)	
APP (1977: state)	10	25	38	32
Private (large/med.)	60	25	12	
Private (small)	30	50	50	
Total GDP				
APP (1977: state)	11	34	39	43
Private (large/med.)	67	38	31	
Private (small)	22	28	30	

Sources: Harris and Vilas, *Nicaragua*, p. 42; David Ruccio, 'The State and Planning in Nicaragua', in Rose Spalding, ed., *The Political Economy of Revolutionary Nicaragua*, Boston 1987, p.65.

highly precarious and determined largely by the imperative of sustaining output in a period of acute crisis rather than by any genuine commitment on the part of the FSLN to a mixed economy. It is, then, impossible to derive from the existing balance of economic forces a necessary logic for the progressive liquidation of large private enterprise just as it is far from clear whether the regime will be able to avoid improving the conditions for capitalist concerns as the crisis deepens.

Much of the uncertainty can be attributed to the ambiguous nature of Sandinista pronouncements on the economy. For Tomás Borge Nicaragua has 'a mixed economy at the service of the workers . . . in other countries it is a mixed economy at the service of the bourgeoisie'.[34] According to Jaime Wheelock the basis of this peculiarity can be found not in a unique mode of production but specifically in the loss of the bourgeoisie's hegemony and its historic lack of political power. All the same, it remains far from clear whether its reduction to the status of a managerial stratum can be assured:

> Is it possible for the bourgeoisie as such, or a system moulded along bourgeois lines, to exist alongside revolutionary power? I don't think it's possible. The fundamental, characteristic element of capitalist society is the power of the bourgeoisie, the military power of the bourgeoisie. . . . Here what has to be posed theoretically is whether it is possible that the bourgeoisie simply produce, without power, that they limit themselves as a class to a productive role. That is, that they limit themselves to exploiting their means of production and use these means of production to live, not as an instrument of power, or imposition. I think it is possible in Nicaragua. We inherited a country in which neither capitalism nor the capitalist class was fully formed and, on top of that, did not directly hold political power. . . . I believe that in these conditions it is possible to find ways in which a social organization under revolutionary hegemony can maintain forms of production, groups of capitalist production relations, that are not dominant but subordinate.[35]

Such an explicit differentiation between the economic and political spheres raises a plethora of theoretical issues beyond our scope here, but it is notable that FSLN policy in general towards the bourgeoisie is predicated upon this basic condition of political subordination:

> As long as they produce, they can continue . . . [But] politically in this country they have no future. They will have to fit in with the economic plans of the state.
>
> As long as they don't question the authority of the Revolution they will continue. There is no political project to do away with the private sector. It depends entirely on their willingness to participate.[36]

Of course, for many capitalists the 'economic plans of the state' constitute precisely 'the political project to do away with the private sector' that is being disowned, the guarantees derived from maintenance of production being of marginal value when free movement of capital and the full gamut of managerial strategies for profit are withheld. The capacity of the FSLN to impose such restrictions has led Borge to declare the class moribund: 'There are some workers who believe that the main enemy of the working class is the bourgeoisie. But the bourgeoisie as a class has been mortally wounded in this country, and the dying have never been dangerous enemies.'[37] On the other hand, Wheelock's perception of its defeat being essentially political in character prompts him to resist the central implication in Borge's declaration:

> It is important to understand that the socialist model is a solution for contradictions that only exist in developed capitalist countries. . . . Even though we have socialist principles, we cannot effect the transformation of our society by socializing all the means of production. This would not lead to socialism. On the contrary, it could lead to the destruction and disarticulation of our society.[38]

The problems in decoding Sandinista declarations derive at least in part from the very free use of the term 'bourgeoisie', but at root they emanate from the actual and latent contradictions of excluding the capitalist class from political power and yet encouraging it to continue producing. Thus, at the same time as Borge vilifies the bourgeoisie in his speeches and pronounces it all but dead, he is obliged to insist that, 'it is necessary to maintain national unity with wide sectors of society, including those sectors of the bourgeoisie who are ready to work in a common cause with the workers, in production and the defence of the sovereignty of our *patria*.'[39] As has already been seen, such a call for national unity above class interests is at the heart of Sandinista policy. Just as in the immediately post-insurrectionary period of 'national reconstruction' so, under increased pressure from counter-revolutionary invasions and the US boycott, production is presented as an integral component of that unity. Indeed Borge, persistently the most mobile of FSLN leaders in rhetoric, even calls the productive bourgeoisie an 'ally against imperialism'.[40] Such a position clearly entails a desistence from the expropriation of the bourgeoisie as a class rather than certain of its members as individual anti-patriots, although the bourgeoisie is identified as the class liable to produce most anti-patriots. Ironically, perhaps, patriotism is conferred upon capitalists precisely by their continued exploitation of the means of production, including labour. Correspondingly, although the FSLN does publicly attach itself to the cause of socialism, it makes the familiar expressions of socialism 'by stages' with demonstrable caution:

> The Nicaraguan working class – we believe its big majority – sees socialism as the radical long-term solution (and some see it as the short-term solution) to its problems. Ideas about what socialism will be or should be in Nicaragua are still diffuse, not very clear, and it is natural that they be that way. At the right moment we will embark upon socialism, but before travelling this path it is essential, necessary, indispensable to have a very clear idea of the steps that we are going to take.[41]

There can be little doubt that the caveats and qualifications in declarations such as this carry little weight with most major entrepreneurs, for whom all talk of socialism is anathema. Nevertheless, the marked post-revolutionary diminution of private investment shown in Table 29 cannot be ascribed primarily to the effects of fierce Sandinista talk since despite the fact that both this and that expropriation which has taken place have been a preoccupation for the bourgeoisie, its activities have been far more directly affected by the world recession and the crisis of the Nicaraguan economy provoked by the Contra war and US boycott.

Table 29: Investment, 1977–83 (1980 C mn)

	1977	*1978*	*1979*	*1980*	*1981*	*1982*	*1983*
Total	7,008	2,875	−304	3,500	4,967	3,392	4,460
Fixed	6,186	3,436	1,404	3,032	4,473	2,894	3,955
Private	3,139	1,895	726	622	1,093	797	712
Public	3,047	1,541	678	2,410	3,380	2,097	3,243
Stock Exchange	822	−561	−1,752	468	493	487	505
Percentage:							
Private	51	55	52	21	24	27	18
Public	49	45	48	79	76	73	82

Note: Figures are rounded and thus do not tally exactly.

Source: Vilas, *Sandinista Revolution,* p.160.

Although opponents of Sandinismo constantly cite parallels between it and the Cuban revolution, the distinctions with respect to economic policy are marked. Apart from the fact that the FSLN from the start directed its strategy towards obtaining basic food security and has not engaged in a project of industrialization, it is worth noting that in the case of Cuba Washington imposed a total trade embargo in October 1960 (less than two years after Castro came to power) whereas it took six years to realize this policy for Nicaragua. Equally, although the FSLN immediately expropriated Somoza's holdings and redistributed significant amounts of land in 1980 and 1981, the Cuban government had already seized the great majority of private estates by the time of the US boycott and nationalized most large concerns and all US property when it was declared, effectively liquidating private enterprise in the country. The ability of the Cuban regime to survive such a rapid and thorough expropriation of private property as well as the repudiation of the external debt was eventually assured by the Soviet Union's acceptance of the role of principal trading partner and economic sponsor. However, both the Cuban experience and the international conditions prevailing in the early 1980s helped to broaden the possibilities for Nicaragua, which besides having had a different trajectory to political victory and retaining a higher proportion of the capitalist class following it, could take some advantage from the greater potential for diversification of external trade and aid than had existed in the early 1960s. This position is reflected in Tables 30 and 31. Faced with a reluctance on the part of Moscow either to acquire heavy economic losses through subsidization of a rapidly nationalized economy or to provoke US hostility with full patronage of a radical regime in its 'backyard', the FSLN was able to fortify its pluralist bona fides and reduce dependence on commerce with the US by selling to Europe and Japan and buying from the newly industrialized Latin American states. (Although Moscow replaced Mexico as Nicaragua's principal supplier of oil in 1984, in mid 1987 the Soviets declared that they were halting supply – a surprising move that caused the major Latin American states to seek a regional arrangement for providing an essential commodity for which Managua lacked hard cash.) The scale of trade with COMECON states has certainly increased – commerce with the Soviet Union rose from 4 million rubles in 1981 to 212 million in 1985 – but it remains less than that with capitalist countries, as have the levels of financial assistance and debt. The lack of comprehensive economic linkages with the Soviet bloc has not, of course, freed the Sandinistas from political pressures despite reducing the force of accusations that they have become pawns of Moscow.

The costs of retaining an 'open economy' were perhaps highest in terms of the external debt, the FSLN accepting Somoza's debts in January 1980

Table 30: Major Trading Partners, 1977–83 (%)

	1977		*1981*		*1983*	
	Exps	*Imps*	*Exps*	*Imps*	*Exps*	*Imps*
CACM	21.0	21.6	13.9	21.1	7.8	15.3
Mexico and Venezuela	2.6	14.7	2.2	26.0	2.1	23.5
EEC	28.4	12.6	19.4	11.5	25.7	9.7
US	22.8	28.8	25.8	26.3	18.1	19.4
Japan	11.0	10.1	11.2	2.8	15.3	2.4
COMECON	1.0	0.3	7.3	3.3	12.7	16.6

Source: CEPAL, *Notas Económicas.*

after much discussion as to the viability of keeping western sources of finance available. Recognition of the dictatorship's debts was a difficult policy to uphold within the country, and although it permitted an early renegotiation with the banks on favourable terms, both the acceptance of responsibility for the large sums loaned to Somoza and Washington's ability to sabotage Nicaragua's dealings with the international finance community have resulted in the country possessing the highest debt ($4.37 billion) and the second largest debt per capita ($1,355) in Central America by 1985.[42] Both the diversification of trading links and the continued ties with the banks have helped to uphold the position of domestic private capital although it does not export itself. This position is likely to endure since both Cuba and the Soviet Union have stated unequivocally that if Nicaragua were to be invaded they could not rally to its military defence, confirming that while they will continue to support the country, they will desist from deepening economic relations to such a point that provokes Washington into a direct intervention.[43] Of course, under Reagan the US government's singularity of purpose in liquidating Sandinismo has greatly limited the opportunities for negotiation in this quarter, but it remains a fact that the commercial ties beyond the US and COMECON have provided conditions whereby both greater internal collectivization and direct external intervention have been made more problematic. Finally in this regard, the fact that Cuba is an island and Nicaragua has two highly permeable land frontiers has economic as well as logistical ramifications. The construction of 'socialism in one country' in Nicaragua would be exceptionally difficult to maintain in simple market terms, even in the highly unlikely case of underwriting from COMECON, since any planned economy would be just as vulnerable to destabilization through contraband with neighbouring states as to a blockade.

Falling export prices meant that between 1980 and 1983 the proportion of imports funded by liquid foreign exchange tumbled from 81 to 33 per cent.[44] (In 1980 exports for 1985 at current prices were projected to be $1,093 million whereas they actually amounted to a mere $297 million, imports remaining relatively constant at around $800 million.) Aside from external aggression, a weak manufacturing base, limited energy resources that can be tapped in the short term (Nicaragua's thermal electricity plant has just one turbine and one empirically qualified engineer to run it), a minimal domestic base for investment, and a high import component to popular consumption, the need to generate foreign exchange is critical. Wheelock's identification of the perils of any abrupt acceleration of collectivization is clearly correct in that this would compel an autarky that Nicaragua could not survive for more than a few weeks. On the other hand, even before it took power the FSLN had identified one of its core economic policies in a delinkage of as much of the economy as possible from foreign

Table 31: External Assistance by Source, 1979–83 (US$ mn and %)

		1979	*1980*	*1981*	*1982*	*1983*	*1979-83*
Total	$ mn	272	528	687	541	415	2,443
Multilateral	$ mn	213	171	86	94	65	629
	%	87	32	13	17	16	26
Bilateral	$ mn	59	357	601	448	350	1,815
	%	22	68	88	83	84	74
US	$ mn	0	73	0	0	0	73
	%	0	14	0	0	0	3
EEC	$ mn	15	63	60	39	87	263
	%	6	12	9	7	20	11
Africa/Asia	$ mn	0	0	103	3	34	140
	%	0	0	15	1	8	6
Latin America	$ mn	44	119	333	154	84	733
	%	16	23	48	28	20	30
COMECON	$ mn	0	102	105	253	146	607
	%	0	19	15	47	35	25

Note: Figures do not tally exactly due to rounding.

Source: Michael Conroy, 'External Dependence, External Assistance and Economic Aggression against Nicaragua', Working Paper, Kellogg Institute, University of Notre Dame, 1984.

exchange constraints and the establishment of basic food security; in these areas there has been appreciable progress. Following the insurrection, the essence of these strategies was to avoid redistribution through a simple increase in the monetary income of the labouring poor (identified from the experience of Chile in 1970–73 as excessively inflationary in effect and hence of ephemeral value to the masses) and to concentrate upon a more extended system in which most basic needs would be either removed entirely from market forces at the point of consumption or significantly distanced from them by state intervention. This system of a 'social wage' has been erratic as a whole and with respect to subsidized foodstuffs came to an end in May 1985. Nonetheless, it has remained a central feature of the Sandinista conception of a remodelled economy, and despite the fact that it only acquires an easily quantifiable and 'hard' economic aspect at the level of state finances, it cannot be excluded from an assessment of the popular standard of living in the towns, which, as Table 32 vividly illustrates, had undergone a sharp fall in strict pecuniary terms well before the decisive shift away from redistributionism signalled by the May 1985 measures. It should also be borne in mind that with nearly two-thirds of GDP in the hands of the private sector, and 30 per cent in those of small-scale businesses that are notoriously difficult to subject to fiscal and administrative controls, redistribution through a global increase in nominal wages was an effectively impossible proposition.

The social provision, particularly in health and education, introduced under the FSLN is widely accepted as one of its main achievements and a permanent challenge to its enemies. Although Nicaragua has yet to match Cuba in confronting problems of child obesity rather than malnutrition, its rate of functional literacy and provision of free medical services are higher than those of the US. While the disposable income of the Nicaraguan masses has contracted severely, urban unemployment remained static at around 20 per cent, and the fiscal resources for maintaining the 'social wage' have themselves come under extraordinary pressure, it is evident that the impact of all this has been critically qualified in terms of popular support by the accessibility of services that were previously poorly provided or rendered completely unavailable by their high price in the market. Between 1978 and 1981 the proportion of GDP spent on education doubled, which even

Table 32: Real Wages and Unemployment, 1977–83

		1977	*1978*	*1979*	*1980*	*1981*	*1982*	*1983*
Wages								
1980 C:	Average	2,829	2,752	2,370	2,001	1,859	1,782	1,618
	Min. Indust.	1,276	1,293	1,103	973	879	725	586
Index:	Average	140.5	136.8	80.9	117.8	100	92.4	88.5
	Min. Indust.	131.0	132.8	60.1	113.3	100	90.3	74.4
Inflation (%)		10.2	4.3	70.3	24.8	23.2	22.2	32.9
Urban Unemployment (%)			14.5	32.9	22.4	19.0	22.2	18.9

Sources: CEPAL, *Notas Económicas;* Vilas, *Sandinista Revolution*, p.244.

despite the recession meant a budget increase from $18 to $50 million, funding a rise in the stock of teachers from 12,975 to 41,422 (of which 20,000 are 'popular teachers' in the adult education programme) and a qualitative jump in secondary school enrolment, which in 1980 stood at 43 per cent compared to 7 per cent in 1960.[45] This level is still far below those of most industrialized states, and, of course, the Sandinista elements of a curriculum modelled on the theories of Paulo Freire have excited the ire of conservatives, but it has proved very difficult for the opposition to impugn advances in the educational sphere that are especially important in a country where 47 per cent of the population is less than fifteen years old. Improvements in health provision have been similarly impressive, with a fall in the rate of infant mortality from 121 per thousand live births in 1977 to 58 in 1983 reflecting the success of new oral rehydration centres and national vaccination programmes. Some 85 per cent of the health budget is still directed to curative medicine and the level of health education in the countryside is much lower than in the towns, yet Nicaragua spends a higher percentage of GDP on health than any other Central American state and has improved its ratio of doctors per head of population to a level close to that in Costa Rica and twice as high as the regional average. The extension of family-planning facilities to one-eighth of women of childbearing age, the eradication of polio and diphtheria and a major reduction in the incidence of malaria must all be directly ascribed to government policies, although further progress has been halted, and in some cases reversed, by the war.[46] More modest advances in the provision of housing have been made through state clearance of lots, opening of streets and laying-in of water and electricity ('site and services') while construction itself is undertaken by the local community.[47] Equally, although the total number of workers registered for social security remains low, between July 1979 and September 1983 the figure doubled, as did that of people receiving pensions.

In the opening years of the revolution the key element of this sytem of a 'social wage' was state distribution of basic foodstuffs, undertaken by ENABAS and the national food programme PAN, established in March 1981 following the cancellation of US wheat shipments. Despite poor climatic conditions, particularly in 1982 and 1986, and restrictions imposed by the war, basic food supply has been maintained to a much higher level than other necessities. Prices for the urban consumer have soared, but the objective of the agrarian reform to provide a defence of the means of subsistence was sufficiently successful to avert the state of widespread hunger and popular discontent typically associated with post-revolutionary 'situations' (Table 33). The greater success in reactivating domestic market crops than those for export corresponds in part to the priority given to this sector by the FSLN, but it also reflects problems of adjustment within the reformed agricultural system established in 1980–81.

Table 33: Agricultural Production 1977/78–1981/82

		1977/8	*1981/82*
Export Crops	Cotton	100	55
	Coffee	100	112
	Sugar cane	100	106
	Bananas	100	73
	Cattle	100	70
Domestic	Corn	100	104
	Beans	100	119
	Rice	100	182
	Pigs	100	158
	Chickens	100	268
	Eggs	100	348
	Cooking Oil	100	143
	Pasteurized Milk	100	187

Source: MIDINRA, 1983.

Since 1979 change in the rural economy has outstripped that in the urban sector, the agrarian reform rapidly becoming a central feature of the revolution and vital to the maintenance of support for Sandinismo from the majority of the labouring population. The impact of the two basic phases of expropriation (1979–81) upon the pattern of tenure can be seen in Table 34, the average size of expropriated *fincas* being 1,364 *manzanas* (2,186 acres). In the first phase the rural properties of leading Somocistas were transferred to the state sector (APP) and formed the basis of new state farms, although some of these lands were distributed to peasants in production cooperatives or CASs (Decrees 3 and 38, 1979); lease prices were radically reduced from $200 to $40 per hectare for cotton lands and from $80 to $14 for basic grain lands (Decrees 230 and 263, 5 and 41 January 1980); and access to credit was greatly expanded. The impact of these measures was substantial: 21 per cent of all Nicaraguan *fincas* and 42 per cent of all estates over 500 *manzanas* were confiscated.[48] In the second phase, announced on 19 July 1981, expropriation was extended under pressure from the organized peasantry and rural proletariat in the ATC and at some risk to continued 'coexistence' with the rural bourgeoisie. Properties marked for confiscation now included poorly exploited land; enterprises decapitalizing or extracting ground rent through leases or sharecropping; those with less than 75 per cent of total area in use; cattle ranches with a low density of herd; and large rented estates. As a result of this extension of the reform, by December 1983 a total of some 421,000 *manzanas* had been redistributed. It should, though, be stressed that commercial farmers owning or working less than 500 *manzanas* (864 acres) in the Pacific zones or 1,000 *manzanas* (1,728 acres) in the interior were left unaffected, accounting for the relatively stable pattern of tenure of units between 50 and 500 *manzanas* between 1978 and 1983 shown in Table 34.

The reform produced four discernible types of rural enterprise: the APP state farms founded principally on the initial expropriations; the cooperative sector, including production (CAS), service and credit (CCS) and – primarily in the north – some production and defence cooperatives; the

Table 34: Land Tenure, 1978–84 (*manzanas*/%)

Property Sector	*1978* Area	%	*1984* Area	%
1. *Private*				
Over 500 *manzanas*	2,920.0	41.2	932.5	11.0
200–500	1,311.0	13.8	1,021.0	12.0
50–200	2,431.0	30.0	2,463.0	28.9
10–50	1,241.0	13.0	710.5	8.3
less than 10	170.0	2.0	219.8	2.6
2. *Credit and Service Cooperatives*				
50–200	–	–	107.5	1.3
10–50	–	–	464.6	5.5
less than 10	–	–	332.2	3.9
3. *Production Cooperatives*	–	–	699.3	8.2
4. *State farms*	–	–	1,557.4	18.3
TOTAL	8,073.0	100	8,507.8	100

Source: MIDINRA, *Agricultural Sector: Results of 1983; Work Plan 1984*, Managua 1984, pp. 55–6, cited in *Envío*, no. 37, July 1984.
Source: CEPAL, *Notas para el Estudio Econòmico de América Latina y el Caribe, 1984:*

independent peasant sector; and the commercial farmers. According to MIDINRA in 1982 the objective of the reform was to restrict the APP to 20–25 per cent of lands (a figure already reached at that time) and to expand cooperative agriculture to 40 per cent of land.[49] Only 17 per cent of redistributed land was given to the independent peasantry, the great bulk being allocated to the cooperative sector, which by late 1982 numbered 3,200 units and over 70,000 shareholders. The most notable feature in this regard was the predominance of service and credit co-ops, which included 65 per cent of cooperative producers and provided a vital bridge between the peasantry's attachment to individual property and autonomy in production and the state financing and distribution systems; in 1980 70 per cent of the 57,000 new clients of the National Development Bank were members of cooperatives.

The relative strength of the CCS and the gains made by independent peasants through the abolition of *colonato* and sharecropping and the reduction of rents fortified small-scale agriculture. As can be seen from Table 35, this sector not only continued to control production of food crops but also expanded its cultivation of cotton to over half the level of the large estates in 1984/5 and, together with medium farmers, it accounted for a significant proportion of all production outside of agro-industry. The size and importance of what might be termed a Kulak class has already been noted, it being quite predictable that its relative distance from the central demands of the ATC – land, employment and increased wages – should prompt the emergence of a separate corporate body – the *Unión Nacional de Agricultores y Ganaderos* (UNAG), established in April 1981. UNAG effectively bonded independent peasants with modest farmers, differing from the ATC in that it did not demand more land.[50] Nevertheless, the membership of UNAG, although susceptible in some regards to overtures from UPANIC (the association of the rural bourgeoisie), remained firmly within the popular bloc and concentrated its campaigns precisely upon an extension and improvement of financial, technical and infrastructural facilities provided under the reform. Although budgetary restraints have greatly diminished the capacity of the state to respond to these demands, the increase of total land under cultivation from 831,000 *manzanas* in 1980/2 (1970–77 = 898,000) to 932,000 in 1983/4 and that in domestic crops from 482,000 (1970–77 = 490,000) to 549,000 strongly suggests that even with such constraints smallholders are prepared to expand production. Their virtual monopoly over food production, appreciable share of agro-exports and general support for a reform that has benefited them no less and possibly more than the members of the ATC – overwhelmingly concentrated in the APP and large private sector – makes this 'middle peasantry' a key component of the FSLN's constituency. By 1986 UNAG could lay claim to being the most active and viable mass organization in the country. Given

Table 35

a) *Agricultural Production by Sector, 1982/83 (%)*

	State Farms	*Private Farms*		
		Small	*Medium*	*Large*
Export crops	24.0	17.0	21.7	37.3
Internal market crops	15.7	61.5	8.1	14.7
Cattle	24.7	33.0	30.4	11.0
Agro-industry	28.0	2.4	5.7	63.9

Source: Barricada, 28/11/83, cited in Walker, *First Five Years*, p.311.

b) *Area Sown in Cotton in Sector, 1980/81–1984/85*

	1980/1		*1984/5*	
	000 ma.	*%*	*000 ma.*	*%*
Small producers and co-ops	12.5	9	44.5	27
Large private estates	99.4	74	76.0	46
APP	22.8	17	44.5	27

Source: Vilas, *Sandinista Revolution*, p.173.

c) *APP Share of Agricultural Production, 1981/2 (%)*

Crop	*APP Share*
Export crops	19
Raw cotton	22
Coffee	16
Sugar cane	31
Sesame	4
Havana tobacco	100
Domestic market crops	13
Corn	6
Beans	5
Sugar	32
Sorghum	14
Light tobacco	10
Total	16

Source: Vilas, *Sandinista Revolution*, p. 156.

that it does not press for further distribution of land, and in view of the enhanced importance of the large estates for generating foreign exchange, it is unlikely that the rate of expropriation will be accelerated beyond that established under the 1981 law unless the condition of the rural proletariat and poor peasantry undergoes major deterioration and those sectors of the rural bourgeoisie still producing embark upon a concerted strategy of decapitalization. This would be more likely to follow developments in the political field than in economic policy since there is little apparent pressure on them, and some sectors, particularly the rice-growers, have been able to expand their operations.

If it is hard to fit the Nicaraguan case into a model of revolution founded on the leading role of the poor peasantry or rural proletariat, it is even more difficult to characterize it as being in the specific interests of the working class. The introduction of the 'social wage' favoured no particular sector of the poor and was properly 'popular' in its range whilst, as has been noted, the direct income of the urban labour force has declined sharply. At the same time, the organized working class did not establish a distinct political force or role outside the general parameters of the 'popular democracy'. This provided it with the capacity to monitor and denounce decapitalization and sabotage in the private sector but gave it little direct involvement in management outside the APP, which covers less than a third of manufacturing industry.

The structural weakness of the urban proletariat needs no further discussion although it clearly underpins the relatively low incidence of open conflicts counterposing the basic interests of the class (collective management, better conditions and wages, and so on) with those of the nation (continued production and improved efficiency). Since 1979 unionization of workers in general has expanded considerably, from a total of 133 organizations with 27,000 members (161 collective contracts) to 1,099 unions with 227,931 members (1,000 collective contracts) in 1984.[51] These figures include all workers – rural and urban, manual and white collar – and, as can be seen from Table 36, their political affiliation is overwhelmingly with the FSLN. This has led to the existence in the field of syndicalism of the same sort of ambiguous autonomy prevailing inside 'popular democracy' although the prohibition of the right to strike under the state of emergency is a particular restriction for this section of the popular movement.

Under the leadership of the CST, the Second Assembly for Worker Unity produced an unremarkable declaration of proletarian radicalism, emphasizing 'the class independence of the proletariat in the light of revolutionary doctrine . . . the hegemonic role of the working class in our revolutionary process . . . to sustain categorically the revolutionary alliance of the workers and the poor peasants . . . the unity of all forces around the theory of the proletarian revolution'.[52] While these general objectives remain an integral part of syndicalist discourse, they should be seen in the light of the declarations made by the CST in April 1980 in which the revolution was identified as giving a new character to the trade union and transforming its 'methods, style and habits' from the previous methods of struggle.[53] Here the immediate independence of the working class is subordinated to the requirements of the revolution as a whole, the interests of the class being distinguishable from but not in contradiction with those of the nation. In practice the tension in this relationship has proved far less easy to negotiate, the period up to December 1981 in particular witnessing marked mobilization for improved conditions and drawing a rising number of attacks on labour 'indiscipline' from the FSLN leadership.[54] Moreover, it is not just the fact that the state is the employer within the APP that has raised questions as to the independence of the CST and its ability to avoid becoming an officialist body. This is the only area of 'popular democracy' in which FSLN hegemony is subject to organized political competition from both right and left, which despite their weakness can draw on the motifs of working-class independence to campaign for simple economistic demands or the deepening of 'workers' power', principally through further nationalization. The FSLN has not desisted from direct attacks on these tendencies – the early offensive against CAUS as well as the suspension of the right to strike – and there is clear evidence of a tendency to use strong-arm tactics in recruiting workers to CST-affiliated unions. However, the bourgeois opposition has enjoyed very little success in expanding its tiny union base through manipulation of economistic demands and although the non-Sandinista left

Table 36: Trade Unions in Post-revolutionary Nicaragua

Central Organization	*No. unions*	*Membership*	*Party links*
Central Sandinista de Trabajadores (CST)	504	111,498	FSLN
Asociación de Trabajadores del Campo (ATC)	480	42,000	FSLN
Federación de Trabajadores de la Salud (FETSALUD)	39	15,613	FSLN
Confederación General de Trabajo – Independiente (CGT-I)	19	17,177	PSN
Central de Acción y Unidad Sindical (CAUS)	15	1,939	PCN
Frente Obero (FO)	?	2,000	MAP-ML
Consejo de Unificación Sindical (CUS)	17	1,670	CDN
Central de Trabajadores de Nicaragua (CTN)	21	2,734	PSCN

Source: Barricada, 7/ii/85, reproduced in Harris and Vilas, *Nicaragua*, p.121.

still disputes many aspects of government policy, the wider political crisis has drawn it into a greater acceptance of the party's vanguard role and the priority of defence of the revolution in its entirety. What for some of these groups was the pursuit of genuine working-class independence and for the FSLN unadulterated 'ultra-leftism' has diminished considerably since 1982.

According to Carlos Vilas, the 'current reality is too fluid and complex, and the participants in it too active, to draw definitive conclusions about the relationship between the state, the FSLN and the mass organizations', the identification of an 'authoritarian position (on the part of the FSLN) that prefers to tranquillize the union organizations' capacity for criticism and autonomy' being tendentious.[55] Yet it remains a fact that the pattern of developments since 1980–81 has generally consolidated those vanguardist features evident at the overthrow of Somoza. Such a position is by no means wholly the product of FSLN policies and conforms both to the lack of deep syndicalist traditions before 1979 and to the growing external challenge, but there is very little evidence to suggest that the 'dynamic and dialectical' relation between party and unions will readily break its existing tight limits.

As should already be evident, the issues discussed above were from 1982 increasingly subjected to pressures exerted by both the world recession and the military and economic aggression of the US. Within a year these external forces had greatly slowed the pace of social change and administrative reorganization, first stalling and then reversing the economic progress made in the first years of the revolution. Indeed, by late 1985 some observers believed the scale of economic contraction heralded a collapse of the Sandinista order in its entirety, which was certainly the aim of the Reagan White House. If such prognostications proved to be excessively pessimistic (or optimistic), it was undeniably the case that a year after the election government policy was organized almost totally around ensuring economic survival and the defence of the revolutionary state. Henceforth the central objective in almost all fields was less further transformation than how to hold on to what had already been achieved. Private businesses were largely relieved of their fears of creeping collectivism yet confronted by increasingly exigent conditions for the reproduction of capital in what was little more than a war economy. Agricultural enterprises of all types, but particularly the cooperatives, were subjected to Contra raids in which crops and plant were destroyed and workers slaughtered or kidnapped. The urban populace was less vulnerable to direct physical attacks but it was progressively compelled to seek subsistence in an informal economy dominated by scarcity, scavenging and inflation.

Tables 37–39 indicate the scale of this crisis, which struck an economy still reeling from the impact of the 1978–79 war that, according to CEPAL, resulted in $480 million being lost through physical destruction and $700 million through capital flight. As a result the level of GDP in 1986 was the

Table 37: Nicaragua: General Economic Indicators, 1978–84

	1978	*1979*	*1980*	*1981*	*1982*	*1983*	*1984*
GDP growth (%)	−7.8	−26.4	10.0	5.3	−1.2	4.7	−1.4
GDP per cap. growth (%)	−10.7	−28.4	6.7	2.0	−4.4	1.2	−4.7
GDP per cap. ($ 1970)	442	316	337	344	329	333	316
Total imports ($ mn)	762		887	993	776	819	775
Total exports ($ mn)	637		450	508	406	429	393
Quantum exports (1970=100)		163.7	103.8	127.3	108.2	126.3	105.6
Purchasing power of exports (1970=100)		133.5	81.7	88.5	67.4	68.7	62.1
Foreign debt ($ mn)	961	1,136	1,588	2,200	2,730	3,324	4,003
Debt service (% exports)	9.3			22.2	32.2	14.3	11.7

Source: CEPAL *Notas para el Estudio Económico de América Latina y el Caribe, 1984: Nicaragua.*

same as that in 1979, the real standard of living of the bulk of the populace being worse than in the immediate pre-revolutionary period. The collapse of state finances was made vividly clear in the government's continual problems in ensuring a supply of oil, lack of money as much as politics underlying the difficulties with Mexico (1984–85) and the Soviet Union (1987). The popular economy was most directly afflicted by the contraction in wages caused by hyperinflation, which by 1987 was estimated to be in excess of 750 per cent. In the spring of 1985 the government attempted to minister to the crisis by resorting to a largely orthodox stabilization plan including a devaluation and reduction of price subsidies as well as an extension of rationing. This effectively brought a halt to the direct redistributionism of the early years but signally failed to limit a burgeoning black market or stem the wider economic collapse upon which it was founded and in which Washington and the Contras invested considerable energy. Indeed, while economists of every technical and ideological stripe proffered more or less judicious advice to the FSLN, there was only so much scope for internal adjustment to a recession and campaign of sabotage emanating from powerful external forces. Moscow was patently unprepared to cover more than a very modest proportion of the costs incurred as a result of Washington's offensive; this was fully evident in the cold shoulder given to Managua by erstwhile sympathizers such as France and Venezuela, whilst no Latin American state was in a position to subsidize Nicaraguan recovery.

The post-1983 experience underscored in increasingly severe fashion the fragility of radical change in a small and backward economy. Since this was

Table 38: Sandinista Nicaragua: Selected Economic Indicators

a) *Official and Black Market Price Indices of Various Basic Goods (1981=100)*

	1982		*1983*		*1984*		*1985*	
	Off.	*Mkt*	*Off.*	*Mkt*	*Off.*	*Mkt*	*Off.*	*Mkt*
Beans	100	137	100	139	140	245	561	1083
Eggs	104	120	104	152	169	235	357	1207
Cheese	100	142	100	204	100	255	635	894
Meat	108	112	126	158	138	181	471	633
Soap	100	100	100	267	100	222	400	2116

Source: Peter Utting, 'Domestic Supply and Food Shortages', in Rose Spalding, ed., *The Political Economy of Revolutionary Nicaragua*, Boston 1987, p.146.

b) *Exchange Rate of the Cordoba to the US Dollar: Official and Black Markets*

	Official	*Black*
1980	10	21
1981	10	28
1982	10	45
1983	10	78
1984	10	212
1985 (Apr.)	28	700

Source: Roberto Pizarro, 'The New Economic Policy', in ibid., p.222.

c) *The Nigaraguan Debt in Comparative Perspective (per cent of GDP)*

	1978	*1979*	*1980*	*1981*	*1982*	*1983*	*1984*	*1985*
Nicaragua	51	74	86	99	123	143	170	196
Honduras	49	56	59	60	61	68	74	79
Costa Rica	54	59	73	73	78	84	85	87
Mexico	26	25	27	33	34	37	38	37
Latin America	30	31	33	37	39	43	44	44

Source: Richard Stahler-Sholk, 'Foreign Debt and Economic Stabilization', in ibid., p.156.

Table 39: Nicaragua: Economic Costs of Aggression (US$ mn)

a) *Direct Economic Damage of Contra Campaign*

	Raw Material and Capital Damage	*Production Losses*	*Total*
1980	0.5	0.9	1.4
1981	2.7	4.3	7.0
1982	9.0	22.3	31.3
1983	41.1	102.4	143.5
1984	16.1	171.4	187.5
	69.4	301.3	370.7

Source: V. Fitzgerald, 'Economic Costs of US Aggression', in Spalding, *Political Economy of Revolutionary Nicaragua*, p.197.

b) *Estimated Cost of Financial Aggression*

	1981	*1982*	*1983*	*1984*
Loss of Bilateral and Multilateral Aid	8.2	38.3	61.3	91.8
Damage to Trade Balance	2.8	1.7	78.8	83.8
Damage to Balance of Payments	2.8	1.7	81.2	62.4

Source: derived from ibid., p.200.

kept relatively 'open' after 1979 Washington experienced little difficulty in making it 'scream' just as it had destabilized the Chilean economy under *Unidad Popular*. The Sandinistas and their advisers had studied that experience very carefully but it was beyond their power to do anything more than mitigate the effects of an assault that eroded the socio-economic reforms of 1979–82 and reduced the popular goodwill they had established. It was not the case, however, that these changes simply disappeared from the scene. On the contrary, the impressive resistance to the politico-economic crisis can only be understood in terms of widespread identification with them, whether they remained underway or had been brought to a halt. Equally, Sandinismo rested on far more than its socio-economic record and programme. As the siege tightened and conditions of life became ever more onerous the resilience of FSLN nationalism became correspondingly more evident. On the one hand, this consolidated an appreciable core constituency for which the travails of the economy were a necessary price to be paid in the defence against US imperialism. On the other, and of greater significance, it superseded purely partisan politics, stood in stark contrast to the Contras, and prevented the inevitable rise in popular discontent from escalating into a mass opposition movement.

Birth of a Nation?

Since 1981 the survival of Sandinista Nicaragua has been threatened most sharply by a US government that charges the FSLN with supporting the Soviet bloc and being dedicated to joining it. However, at almost exactly the same time as Reagan came to office the Sandinistas found themselves challenged internally by a large section of the population of the Atlantic coast. This was much less dangerous than Washington's opposition but still of importance since it impeded the FSLN's central objective of consolidating national unity. Indeed, what has become known as the 'Miskito question' generated quite extensive subversive activity against the government in Managua, complicated control of the Honduran border and provided Washington with a powerful propaganda weapon as well as practical means with which to attack the FSLN. The initial failure of the Sandinista leadership either to comprehend or sensitively to handle the distinct ethnic character and socio-economic condition of the communities of the Atlantic region was in part attributable to a simple lack of experience of what had long been an isolated zone of the country successfully marginalized by Somoza from the hispanic-mestizo political circuit and culture centred on the Pacific coast. It is also clear, though, that the opposition and major setbacks experienced by the FSLN in the eastern departments were not simply the result of lack of awareness and tactical ineptitude, which were recognized and partially rectified at a relatively early stage.

This issue must be seen in the broader context of strong centralist, statist and republican traits that Sandinismo inherited from the Liberal and Marxist political traditions and which it tended to exaggerate through its military background and defence of national sovereignty against an external foe. Elsewhere in the country such a militant mestizo republicanism fortified anti-imperialist sentiment and assisted the strategy of forging Nicaragua into a coherent nation-state; on the Caribbean seaboard it generated widespread popular repudiation. The most important consequence of this was the incorporation of large numbers of Miskito Indians into the Contra, but the fact that Nicaragua's ethnic minorities seemed to be paying a much higher cost than the rest of the population for the consolidation of the revolution also posed sharp questions as to the FSLN's general priorities. At a time when in many parts of Latin American the non-hispanic oppressed communities were emerging as a critical force in opposition to the dominant bloc, the failure of Sandinismo to establish a firm alliance with this sector of society was viewed as a major anomaly and seen by many *indigenista* groups as reflective of an autocracy and hispanicist hegemony little different from that under which they had existed for centuries.

Although mestizos comprise nearly two-thirds of the inhabitants of Nicaragua's eastern departments, the population of the northern Atlantic coast is dominated by 67,000 Miskitos and the central and southern regions by blacks (25,723), these zones also containing small settlements of pre-colonial ethnic groups: Sumo (4,851); Carib/Garifono (1,287); Rama (649).[56] Following the revolution the Sandinistas set up for these communities a mass organization with the name of MISURATA (*Miskito, Sumo, Rama, Sandinista Asla Takanka* – Miskito, Sumo, Rama, Sandinista All Together). MISURATA came into being with sharper internal contradictions than any other organ of 'popular democracy' since the Sandinistas had a very weak representation within a population that had few economic ties with the rest of the country, exhibited marked anti-Communist sentiments (despite the relatively greater historical presence of US enterprises in the region than elsewhere), and resisted the establishment of the other mass organizations in their area. Furthermore, the Miskitos' almost millenarian attachment to the tradition of a kingdom independent of the government of the interior, begun in 1687 with the 'proclamation' of King Jeremy I by the British authorities in Jamaica, could not simply be dismissed as the legacy of imperialist manipulation since it was a powerful representation of communal autonomy. Equally, the Miskitos maintained historic claims to large swathes of territory that had been nationalized after July 1979 as forest, and while they and the smaller groups spoke their own languages, the blacks had English as their mother tongue. This provoked problems with the FSLN's initial use of Spanish as the principal idiom in the literacy crusade – an effort at integration that was widely seen as the imposition of an alien culture. These tensions rapidly spilled into a more profound political dispute over whether the local leaders of MISURATA were pursuing a secessionist course in their demands or merely campaigning for greater autonomy. By the spring of 1981 the FSLN leadership was convinced that some Miskito leaders grouped around Steadman Fagoth were pledged to separatism, and in February 1981 thirty-three members of MISURATA were arrested on this charge. It remains highly questionable whether Fagoth was either at that point or since genuinely attached to the cause of Miskito 'independence', but he was undoubtedly deeply opposed to Sandinismo, and when released he immediately made common cause with the Contra. Late in 1981 he was joined by Brooklyn Rivera, a less mercurial Miskito leader. By mid 1982 the great majority of the local leaders had regrouped in the anti-Sandinista MISURA.

If Fagoth made little substantial effort to negotiate with Managua and demonstrated all the qualities of an ambitious *cacique*, his example was made much more compelling by the declaration in August 1981 of the 'Principles of Nicaraguan Territorial Unity' by Managua and what became known as 'Red Christmas', when, in response to the rising number of armed clashes in the Rio Coco region from October of that year, the EPS forcibly evacuated some 8,500 Miskitos from thirty-nine communities to a new settlement at Tasba Pri in mid January 1982. Tasba Pri was allocated over 53,000 hectares of land and progressively provided with infrastructure, but this was minimal compensation for those whose original villages, churches and crops had been razed. The trauma caused by this destruction and dislocation from traditional lands provoked a further 10,000 people to flee to Honduras so that over a quarter of the Miskito population was uprooted in the space of a few weeks. The degree to which the flow of refugees to Honduras was sustained by coercion on the part of the MISURA Contra is disputed, but it remains a fact that for the following two years the FSLN remained bitterly unpopular in the region, and the general level of violence strongly suggests that the local population was far from an unwilling pawn of Fagoth and his new allies in the FDN. Whilst this situation was aggravated by several instances of ill-judged and sometimes brutal behaviour by Sandinista troops in the latter half of 1982 – for which some forty-four soldiers were brought to trial – at root it corresponded to the FSLN's mechanistic pursuit of its political objectives, thus placing the EPS in an untenable position.

From the end of 1982 the balance of forces that simply counterposed the bulk of the local populace and its leaders against Managua began to shift. On the one hand, the FSLN embarked upon some rectification of its position, admitting 'errors', introducing more modulated policies, and recruiting greater numbers of local people to the militia (by 1984 70 per cent of Sandinista forces in the area were of local origin). At the end of 1983 a general amnesty was granted and 307 Miskito rebels were released. This slow and uneven process coincided with a series of ruptures in the opposition forces that centred on Fagoth's increasing dictatorial tendencies, dependence upon forced conscription, and conformity with the general Contra practice of according minimal importance to human rights or the interests of the local population in its campaign. Elsewhere on the northern border this often confirmed the absence of active support for the FDN forces and encouraged the continued employment of terrorist tactics. Within the Miskito community it similarly diminished enthusiasm for the war and sharpened existing political differences. As a result of these Rivera split with Fagoth late in 1982 and led his faction of MISURA into Pastora's ARDE. For a number of months this increased the scale of Miskito Contra activity but Pastora's forces were concentrated in the south of the country where the Miskito population was sparse and discontent with Managua at a lower level. Already geographically separated from his ally, Rivera's position became even more embattled after April 1984 when Pastora's efforts to hold the southern coastal town of San Juan del Norte collapsed in a major military defeat. Following this collapse Rivera entered into negotiations with the FSLN, but these produced no immediate resolution of the question of autonomy since the rebel leader insisted upon the maintenance of an independent military force for the Atlantic zone – a demand to which the Sandinistas could not extend the flexibility they displayed over other issues.

Both the Fagoth–Rivera split and the preparedness of the FSLN to distinguish the latter from the rest of the Contra by entering into discussions constitute an important development in the Miskito conflict. On the one hand, it is evident that despite the maintenance of at least 3,000 MISURA troops in Honduras and the department of Zelaya, communal support for the counter-revolution waned as a result of the travails it imposed, the absence of any major strategic success, and the most dubious support from the Contra leadership as a whole for specifically Miskito interests. While this has not greatly lessened suspicion about Sandinismo, it has contributed to a modest yet steady return of refugees from Honduras, some reduction in antipathy reigning in the principal towns, and the ability of Rivera to reject the Contra, presenting himself as a mediator between the Miskito people and Managua. On the other hand, the retreat of the FSLN from its initial pugnacious and inflexible attitude to ethnic resistance can be seen as only a partial change in course forced upon it by the strength of opposition. Managua is unable to concede full Miskito demands for autonomy, cannot promote markedly greater development for a badly depressed local economy, and is obliged by the continuing Contra campaign to resist any reversion to traditional patterns of settlement. Despite the establishment in July 1984 of a new pro-FSLN regional organization (MISATAN) the medium-term prospects for improved relations remain limited and are unlikely to exceed a resigned neutrality. In view of the threat of a complete loss of control that prevailed in 1981–84 this is in itself an achievement and, should the FSLN continue to resist the US–Contra siege and the economy recover, it could presage a gradual expansion of support beyond the caucus of urban black youth where it has hitherto been concentrated. However, this will depend on a disposition on the part of the Sandinista leadership to interrogate the cultural suppositions and political bases of its activity to a far higher degree than permitted by the general strategic position at the end of 1987 and will almost certainly require continued popular pressure from outside the established Sandinista community.

The Miskito question was one of the few issues that Washington was able to exploit to the Sandinistas' detriment in terms of national unity. In virtually every other area the US offensive tended to deepen Nicaraguan nationalism at the same time as it wrecked the economy, thereby complicating the objective of forcing the FSLN into dictatorial measures and destroying its social base. For our purposes the development of US policy under Reagan towards Nicaragua can be distilled into a few paragraphs.[57] The year 1981, which opened with Reagan's inauguration, witnessed a sharp turn from the attitude of suspicious caution adopted by the Carter administration. It is certainly the case that on the eve of the presidential handover the FMLN offensive prompted Carter to increase aid to the Salvadorean military and allege Nicaraguan complicity in the campaign, but the 'White Paper' of February which made much more extensive charges of Soviet and Cuban involvement was exclusively a product of the Reagan team and marked the beginning of what was henceforth to be a consistent presentation of Central American conflicts as fundamentally engendered by Communist conspiracy and an integral part of Moscow's strategy to subvert the western hemisphere. At the same time, and contrary to the pleas of the legal bourgeois opposition in Nicaragua, Reagan cancelled the outstanding credits of the $75 million that had been advanced to Managua by Carter on the understanding that with such loans Nicaragua would be 'kept tied to the West's political economy'.[58] In April Washington cut all bilateral aid on the pretext of the FSLN's 'exaggerated militarization' and its assistance to the Salvadorean guerrilla. Henceforth US government officials exercised much effort and enjoyed significant success in impeding Nicaragua's receipt of loans and aid from multilateral financial institutions.[59]

At this stage reports that exiles were receiving military training in Florida appeared in the US press, the response of Secretary of State Haig clearly indicating a favourable attitude to such activity on the part of the government. In December Reagan authorized under his executive powers a budget of $19 million for CIA operations in Nicaragua, this sum effectively serving as a down-payment for the organization of the Contra although military offensive did not get fully underway in the border zones until mid 1982. In October 1981 Washington initiated a complementary programme of escalating military assistance and collaboration with Honduras that also provided support for the Contra and circumvented a number of statutory restrictions upon activity of this type. US military aid to Honduras rose from $8.9 million in 1981 to over $90 million in 1986, this increase being paralleled by the construction of new military facilities (including seven air bases) and the holding of virtually continuous joint manoeuvres almost all close to the Nicaraguan border.[60] From the spring of 1983 joint US–Honduran military activity was constant, sometimes congregating 30,000 troops in manoeuvres. In addition to common Contra intrusions, the EPS logged a total of 1,259 aerial violations of airspace from Costa Rica, 1,381 from Honduras, 775 US intelligence flights, and 160 violations of Nicaraguan waters between 1981 and 1984.[61]

This policy of military support to Nicaragua's unsympathetic neighbours together with funding and operational assistance for the Contra was to continue and expand over the following years, but in 1982 Washington made major efforts to back it up with diplomatic activity. In January of that year the State Department patronized the *Comunidad Democrática Centroamericana*, comprised of all the regional states except Nicaragua. However, both this alliance and an attemped successor – the 'Forum for Peace and Democracy' announced in October – failed to take off, largely because they were so transparently devices for US policy rather than initiatives of the countries involved. Furthermore, a February 1982 plan for an inter-American force of 2,000 troops from Argentina, Chile, Colombia and Paraguay to combat Central American guerrillas was rendered a dead letter in April with the outbreak of the Falklands/Malvinas War between Britain and Argentina (although the fact that all bar one of the countries were ruled by military dictatorships would anyway have severely limited the potential for presenting such an intervention as genuinely hemispheric and pro-democratic in character). The Falklands War created further problems. In the first place it obliged Buenos Aires – hitherto the Latin American power giving greatest military support to the regional dominant bloc – to withdraw several dozen advisers and halt major logistical assistance. More importantly, it terminated any real possibility of direct Latin American involvement in the military campaign against Nicaragua since US aid for Britain in the Malvinas had hardened general nationalist sentiment whilst support for Argentina from Cuba and Nicaragua drew them more than momentarily closer to the rest of the Latin states.

The inability of Reagan to reverse this process or to mesmerize the southern nations to the same degree as he could his own countrymen during his tour of Latin America in November 1982 – when he contrived to address the citizens of Brazil as those of Bolivia – further encouraged an independent Latin American diplomatic initiative to resolve the Central American conflict. This took shape in January 1983 with the formation of the Contadora group, which comprised the most affected local states – Mexico, Venezuela, Colombia and Panama – and later received the support of the civilian governments of Brazil, Argentina, Uruguay and Peru. Over the following four years Contadora presented a series of draft treaties and established a diplomatic influence that the US was unable to repudiate but which it constantly sought to impede, since beneath the complex terms of negotiations the general thrust of all its proposals was the security of the sovereign rights of Nicaragua no less than those of its neighbours.[62] Thus, when in October 1984 Managua declared that it was ready to sign a treaty that had already received the assent of the rest of the Central American states, Washington – completely ambushed by this adroitly staged reversal of prior objections – was forced to embark upon a frantic spoiling operation with open cajoling of Costa Rica and Honduras in particular to insist on extra terms that would be unacceptable to Managua. The essence of all Contadora proposals throughout this period lay in mutual demilitarization and reduction of the numbers of foreign advisers as well as agreement to desist from supporting insurgent groups in other states. This certainly represented a challenge for Nicaragua, which would be obliged to diminish the number of Soviet bloc advisers even if it no longer backed the Salvadorean FMLN in material terms. But the corresponding reduction required of El Salvador, Honduras and even Costa Rica represented a far greater threat to Washington's strategy in terms of both formal military aid and support for the Contra. Hence, from late 1984 Contadora was treated by the US as a decided hindrance if not an outright danger, the group maintaining its existence but with markedly reduced chances of success in conditions of escalating tension. This was especially the case between Washington and Mexico, which traditionally follows a foreign policy more radical in tone than its domestic regime, and which from August 1982 was submerged in a debt crisis that scarcely improved relations with a conservative US government reluctant to permit more than short-term and absolutely necessary renegotiation by the international financial organizations it effectively controlled. The exceptionally aggressive character of US diplomacy in Mexico, particularly over the drugs question, did little to improve the situation.

The need for diplomatic intervention predicated upon the understanding that the US was a major protagonist in Central American affairs and not an external onlooker was underscored in April 1983 with Reagan's 'Star Wars' speech in which the 'threats to hemispheric security' were presented in language of unprecedented force and lack of sophistication. The publication of aerial photographs of Nicaraguan military installations to demonstrate Soviet involvement in planned aggression was not considered persuasive by the US press or public but, together with Reagan's extraordinary description of the Somocista leaders of the Contra as 'freedom fighters', the importance the administration gave to the charges was quite reasonably considered as marking a distinct move towards direct intervention. The FSLN's introduction of the military draft in August reflected such apprehension, and this was deemed a very wise precautionary move when, in late October, Reagan ordered the invasion of Grenada. The success of that rapid intervention, prompted by the assassination of Maurice Bishop and the establishment of military rule on the island, undoubtedly bolstered the advocates of a similar operation against Nicaragua, as well as undermining suppositions that the established 'rules of the game' would be adhered to in the international arena as a veil for 'covert operations'. Although there was, of course, no immediate attempt to repeat the Grenadan operation for the infinitely more taxing case of Nicaragua, Washington's preparedness openly to respect international law and standards of conduct was placed in considerable doubt. This was highlighted in April 1984, when the mining of Nicaraguan harbours and the damage to international vessels the previous October was demonstrated to be the work of the CIA and taken by Managua to the International Court at The Hague as an act of direct hostility. Both this affair and the revelation that the CIA was responsible for a terrorist manual distributed to Contra forces did much to tarnish the administration's policy at home, but in 1985 the White House rejected the Court's ruling against it without the slightest show of contrition and continued to demand congressional support for funding the Contra. A major step towards this had already been taken in January 1984 with the publication of the report of the 'bi-partisan' commission on Central America under Henry Kissinger. Yet while many Democrats were prepared to accept Kissinger's artful translation of Reagan's sabre-rattling into measured trilateralist language, they continued to be profoundly sceptical as to the domestic and international consequences of public funding for the overthrow of a sovereign government with which Washington, like the bulk of the international community, retained diplomatic relations and common responsibilities under the UN Charter. This aversion – often more pragmatic than high-minded – was strengthened by the transparent contradictions in government policy that trumpeted the values of constitutionalism for those states ruled by regimes of favourable ideology.

The upshot of this balance of forces was that between 1981 and 1985 the Democrats in Congress reluctantly approved the CIA–Contra operation in closed committee on the condition that the objective of the campaign was limited to wringing 'concessions' out of the Sandinistas and not extended to overthrowing them – a position enshrined in the so-called Boland Amendment (December 1982). Reagan and Casey were more than content to accept this since the distinction made no difference to the conduct of a campaign that had little or no chance of producing a direct offensive on state power and was anyway being undertaken with minimal oversight on the part of the legislature. From the viewpoint of the administration the 'semi-covert' character of the operation following the revelations of *Newsweek* late in 1982 was also a two-edged sword. The minor embarrassments on the global stage were qualified by the ability to sop up criticism from the extreme right at home for more radical remedies as well as by the pressure placed upon Congress to ratify the executive's initiative properly or court the risks of 'capitulating to Communism' in the backyard.

Minutely studied and ardently disputed, US policy to Nicaragua over this period continued to follow the shifting pattern of advantage both between the White House and Congress and within the administration itself, where the 'cowboy element' did not always reign supreme. The early failure of

Ambassador Lawrence Pezzullo to broker the State Department view and secure support for continuation of the Carter approach of 'pressure through contact and conditionality' was entirely predictable. Somewhat less foredoomed were the efforts of Assistant Secretary of State Thomas Enders to reach a negotiated solution without recourse to military hostilities. However, once he failed to cow the FSLN leadership with a characteristically candid depiction of the consequences of its stance during a visit to Managua in mid 1981 the adoption of direct action was inevitable. This policy received a vital boost with Reagan's re-election in November 1984, enabling the president to win congressional approval for a full economic boycott in May 1985; support for Contra aid was undoubtedly also affected by Daniel Ortega's much publicized trip to Moscow that April in order to secure emergency supplies of oil. In June 1986 Congress narrowly voted to back the administration's request for $100 million for the Contras without imposing the previous restrictions. This was widely seen as a major shift towards the White House position, which was in turn apparently vindicated by the closure of *La Prensa*, whose owners had advocated aid for the counter-revolution.

However, in the mid-term elections of November 1986 the Republicans lost control of the Senate, and within a month it was revealed that funds derived from the secret and illicit sale of arms to the Khomeini regime in Iran had been passed on to the Contras. The scandal caused by this revelation dealt a critical blow to the fortunes of the Reagan government and proved to be particularly prejudicial to the Nicaraguan rebels, who were in the public mind now tied both to the abhorrent regime in Tehran and to the clandestine antics of Colonel Oliver North. Despite having been blessed with the considerable public support of Ronald Reagan, the Contras had experienced inordinate difficulty in shrugging off the reputation of being brutal parasites. Now their efforts to gain political respectability were further hampered by the stigma of attachment to an irresponsible and illegal foreign policy run out of the nether regions of the White House.

Even before the breaking of the Irangate scandal Washington's offensive was subjected to significant restraint by international as well as domestic factors. It can be said that Nicaragua has benefited from greater Latin American neutrality than did Guatemala, Cuba and the Dominican Republic. Although the Sandinistas were brought under sharp pressure by the failure of all the Central American states, with the partial exception of Guatemala, to resist US influence, both the paucity of hard evidence of FSLN intervention in their affairs and the open use of Honduras and Costa Rica for attacks on Nicaragua substantially weakened the US diplomatic campaign. It was clear and openly admitted that the FSLN relied upon the services of Soviet bloc military advisers, but their numbers were very much fewer than the 3,000 claimed by Washington, most probably no more than

450. Equally, while Nicaragua received appreciable Soviet materiel, most of this was old and of a defensive nature, with particular emphasis on anti-aircraft weapons systems. Managua trained a new generation of pilots to fly MiG fighters in Bulgaria, but it received only a few aged models that were no match for the advanced craft delivered in large numbers to the Honduran airforce by the US; the Sandinista airforce is accepted by protagonists on both sides to be no match at all for its Honduran counterpart, the strongest in the isthmus. Moreover, in the terrain on the borders with both Honduras and Costa Rica the decrepit Soviet tanks possessed by the EPS were of minimal value and could not possibly spearhead any invasion, as Pentagon analysts freely admitted when not in the glare of TV lights. The Contra was most sorely taxed by new helicopter gunships used on sorties on, and sometimes across, the border, but while these might be more plausibly categorized as 'offensive' weapons, they were manifestly of a tactical nature and could not support any strategic salient into territory defended by fighter aircraft of the capacity possessed by the Hondurans.[63] In short, Washington suffered from a broad consensus abroad that Nicaragua lacked ready means by which to transform its undeniably formidable defensive armoury into a threat to its neighbours. Moreover, Managua continually renounced any intention of establishing or permitting foreign military bases on its soil, and while some Sandinista disclaimers as to Soviet ties and influence were open to a grain of scepticism, this policy appeared sufficiently firm and sensible to have engendered broad international acceptance.

All revolutions lose their spark and initial purchase on the imagination as the new order acquires a routine character and memories of what it has replaced begin to fade. In many respects this has been true of Nicaragua.But the US campaign against Sandinismo succeeded in maintaining the impetus of nationalism to a far higher degree than would otherwise have been the case. By late 1986 positive support for the FSLN stood below that registered in the 1984 election. On the other hand, opposition to the Contra extends well beyond affection for the Sandinistas. Many economic problems were identified as stemming directly from US and counter-revolutionary activity, and the Contra itself was widely recognized to be both a creature of the CIA and overwhelmingly staffed by Somocistas. The practice of terrorism against civilians in the north was assiduously documented by the local press, and although it certainly inflicted enormous damage on the economy and obliged the EPS to undertake unpopular measures – the evacuation of areas of Jinotega as well as of Zelaya – it also hardened conviction that any counter-revolutionary victory would mean a return to the old regime, not some benign social democracy.[64] This view was strengthened by the collapse of Edén Pastora's campaign and with it the defeat of the only Contra figure with some plausible claim to popularity. Significantly, despite being routed by EPS troops, Pastora was more decisively taken out by Washington, which refused to finance him because of his independent turn of mind. In the same vein, domestic support for Arturo Cruz's withdrawal from the 1984 poll because it was insufficiently democratic was greatly diminished by his subsequent dedication to a completely undemocratic military campaign and well publicized acceptance of CIA funds.[65]

Although the US government could scarcely be accused of possessing an exaggerated sense of its own importance in the Caribbean basin, it would by no means be an idle comment to suggest that the very greatness of its power cultivated a profound myopia in terms of registering the importance of popular sentiment and the need to incorporate this into its strategy. This has not been consistent – the holding of elections in El Salvador, in particular, reflected recognition of a constituency for such a policy as well as its necessity on wider logistical and diplomatic grounds. Nor, quite naturally, need such an appreciation of public opinion amount to a subordination of US interests to it. However, in the case of Nicaragua there was a marked recidivism in dependence upon force and poorly veiled techniques of destabilization. These intrinsically cast doubt on claims to champion 'democracy' and 'freedom' – threadbare but not entirely unworkable in the other countries – as well as rekindling memories of Washington's role in opposing Sandino and supporting the Somozas. The Nicaraguan populace was offered nothing new and the US is clearly associated with the prospect of further violence. This trait was frequently cited by liberal opponents to Reagan's policies who compared them unfavourably with the opportunities for a gradualist diplomatic and economic campaign against the Sandinistas in order to oblige them to negotiate a reduction in their political power. The Reagan policy assuredly corresponded in good measure to tactical incompetence and an inability to comprehend the indigenous qualities of Sandinismo by virtue of a besotted belief in the primacy of the Cold War elements of the conflict. It was impossible fully to exclude the possibility that such a strategy was part of a much more ambitious objective of securing complete military victory over the revolution for which the cultivation of local sympathy was a consideration of strictly secondary importance.

Such a possibility had preoccupied the FSLN since 1982, and within the US it prompted debate and conjecture to such a degree that by 1984 estimates of probable US troop commitments and casualties in the event of a direct intervention were appearing in the press. (One such 'guestimate' had the figures at 125,000 and 15–20,000 respectively; another projected the cost of a military occupation of Nicaragua from 1984 to 1989 at $10.6 billion.[66]) At a more immediate level discussion as to the military value as well as the moral acceptability of supporting the Contra became a familiar item on the US evening news as Congress eternally debated executive budget submissions of a more or less candid nature. Although opinion polls revealed popular opposition to Washington's backing of the rebels and direct military involvement in Central America, a large proportion of the US public expressed extraordinary ignorance of the issue, suggesting that while Reagan was unable to excite support to anything approaching the scale won for his projection of 'Star Wars', so also was the opposition to his Central American policies failing to generate apprehension over a possible 'Vietnam syndrome'.[67]

Insofar as Washington was conducting a campaign against a political movement holding state power, the extenuation of its offensive over a period of more than five years may be contrasted with those against Cuba (where the attempted invasion at the Bay of Pigs in April 1961 occurred only twenty-seven months after Castro took power, the 'missile crisis' of October 1962 ending with Washington's pledge to desist from such operations); Guatemala (where the invasion of July 1954 was prepared in a matter of months and preceded by diplomatic and economic pressure rather than any military campaign); the Dominican Republic (where the invasion of April 1965 by the marines was essentially an emergency response); Chile (where destabilization was directed principally at ending popular support for the Allende government and assisting the autonomous decision of the native military to stage a coup); and Grenada (where the weakness and divisions of the New Jewel Movement government permitted an immediate seaborne landing in the style of nineteenth-century imperialism without prolonged preparations beyond residual harassment and low-level CIA activity). Nicaragua is distinct from these cases in that it possesses land frontiers and a domestic military apparatus that is united and fully pledged to supporting the regime. Further abroad, there are evident similarities with the policies pursued either directly or at one remove in the cases of Angola, Mozambique, Ethiopia, Afghanistan and Cambodia/Kampuchea, where long-term guerrilla campaigns against radical governments have been directly or indirectly supported. In each instance the stability of the incumbent regime was not put at immediate risk despite considerable economic damage and high loss of life. Yet none of these cases shared Nicaragua's great vulnerability to direct US invasion.

The stress on parallels with Vietnam made by US liberals derived in the main from fear of such an unencumbered intervention, and so long as Washington proved capable of upholding its campaign through proxy forces in the region the administration seemed secure in its rebuttals of the comparison and rejection of any accumulating logic towards a final strike. The matter necessarily remained in the realm of second-guessing and conjunctural shifts in the balance of forces as well as long-term strategy. However, the parallel with South-East Asia until 1975 is valid in the broader sense of a varied US campaign in which one state of the region – North Vietnam – retained independent statehood under direct siege and constant attack but no outright effort at invasion. Moreover, the nationalist resolve of the northern population was strongly reaffirmed under such duress. This appears to be a consistent absence in the lessons that the US right, in its turn, has drawn from the experience of South-East Asia. These do not lack a certain belligerent critique of missed opportunities to win a winnable war but they tend to focus on the strategy of the enemy and the logic of dominos falling rather than their original arrangement. The most obvious parallel in domino terms is, of course, the linkage between the Sandinistas and the Salvadorean FMLN although this invariably has a 'run back' via Havana to Moscow.[68] The fact that Central America is far less ethnically divided and more superficially balkanized than South-East Asia lends some superficial plausibility to such claims for a potential 'knock-on effect', yet Washington's undervaluation of the importance of nationalism has led it to confuse the nature of the challenge it faces. The threat posed by the FSLN never resided in the modest logistical support it extended to the FMLN up to 1981, still less in any backing for the Guatemalan guerrilla, to which only 'moral support' was proffered, thereby permitting relatively harmonious relations between Managua and Guatemala City.[69] By contrast, the Sandinistas' full retreat to the defence of their *patria chica* following the failure of the Salvadoreans' 'final offensive' of January 1981 signalled not only recognition of their very limited ability to assist regional comrades in material terms but also a decision to consolidate the specifically national basis of liberation as their contribution to the Central American movement as a whole. In one sense Reagan's quotation of Borge's declaration of July 1981 that the revolution 'transcends national boundaries' may be viewed as a piece of unremarkable black propaganda since it studiously omitted the Sandinista's following remarks that, 'this does not mean that we export our revolution. It is enough – and we couldn't do otherwise – for us to export our example.'[70] On the other hand, it is tempting to see this as another instance of North American failure to appreciate the value of a statement that called into question the value of the prolonged siege of Nicaragua should it not terminate in a successful invasion.

The US debate over this issue recalled not only the experience of South-East Asia but also the differing interpretations of the Cuban revolution that boiled down, at least at the popular level, into the contentions that 'she was pushed' and 'she jumped' into the Soviet bloc. In the case of Nicaragua the Reagan policy manifested almost from the start the public assertion that the FSLN was actively moving towards Moscow combined with the application of pressure to encourage such a move. Yet despite the evidence of stronger ties with Moscow and Havana, Washington was hamstrung by the resistance of both Managua and the Soviets to sealing a comprehensive alliance as well as by domestic and international charges that such links as existed were very much the product of US pressure. This political quandary was further compounded by the fact that while the US public was largely unconcerned by, and the Pentagon happy to acquiesce in a low-cost siege by proxy forces, the human cost of a direct intervention was patently unacceptable to the former and its strategic merits seriously questioned by the latter.

On the Nicaraguan side the impact of US aggression was enormous. Apart from the economic damage, over 31,000 people had been killed between August 1979 and the end of 1986 (17,000 of them Contras), 100,000 people placed under arms, and over a quarter of a million displaced from the war zones. The need to secure some respite from the offensive had thus become critical by the time Irangate broke and provided a 'window of opportunity' of vital importance. This fact was reflected in the flexibility displayed by the Sandinista leadership in 1987 as the impetus for a negotiated solution to the regional conflict accelerated both in Central America and the US.

The openness of the FSLN to an isthmian pact was not as anomalous as many in the US claimed. In 1984 Managua had accepted the Contadora proposals rejected by the governments of the other regional states, and the FSLN leadership subsequently held a series of meetings with the US in Mexico in an effort to halt the Contra war. It thus approached the February 1987 proposals tabled by Costa Rican President Oscar Arias with cautious approval, accepting the provisions for a cessation of aid to insurgents in other countries and the opening of domestic rapprochement based upon a ceasefire and re-establishment of constitutional mechanisms. Arias's plan did not require the FSLN to break its existing foreign ties nor to alter the existing constitutional order. In effect this meant that whatever the cost of permitting open political opposition, Managua was offered recognition of Sandinista legitimacy and a continued lifeline to its international friends. At the same time, it was not specifically required to drop its political and military guard before the Contras although, of course, President Arias was in no position whatsoever to guarantee an end to Contra funding and covert operations on the part of Washington. These terms were deemed sufficiently generous to Managua to prompt the White House into a desperate effort to sabotage the Arias plan. It therefore moved swiftly back to the diplomatic arena, presenting an alternative set of proposals early in August 1987. These required Managua to negotiate with the Contras, break its links with the Soviet bloc, and initiate an immediate and comprehensive electoral programme. In short, Washington simply repeated its traditional demands for a complete capitulation, withholding all recognition of the existing order other than as a signatory to the articles of surrender. The weakness of this position was not so much that it was bound to be rejected by the FSLN but that it was seen as completely unviable by the rest of the Central American governments.

The US effort to ambush the Central American summit convened to discuss amendments to the original Arias plan provoked the local governments into an unexpected display of autonomy since they were offered nothing new by proposals that explicitly rejected their authority to determine isthmian affairs. As will be seen, each of the regional regimes had specific cause to embrace the risks of a local settlement and seek negotiations with the opposition. All, however, were drawn to this position by the impact of Irangate and the manifest dangers of making their tenuous political futures dependent upon the markedly belligerent policies of a 'lame duck' administration. The Arias initiative was, therefore, approved as both a more viable piece of diplomacy and a proposal that could be celebrated as authentically Central American. In spite of the enormous difficulties it faced, the 'fatal flaws' widely trumpeted by the White House proffered a less daunting prospect than the further years of fighting and unrelieved social conflict that were promised by a continued siege of Sandinista Nicaragua and the insurgencies in El Salvador and Guatemala.

The August 1987 agreement represented a form of Brest Litovsk for the FSLN in which the primary objective was to protect the revolution from further and perhaps mortal external attacks; however, in this case such an aim could only be met by making concessions with respect to the internal regime. These were not regarded as tantamount to a fundamental retreat since the restitution of civil liberties required by the Arias plan fell within the compass of the existing constitutional order even if it meant suspending the exceptional powers declared under the State of Emergency and deemed essential to the defence of the country. Consequently, Managua moved with some speed and to appreciable diplomatic effect by nominating Obando y Bravo as president of the commission to oversee compliance with the treaty. This adroit and unexpected challenge thrown down to the legal opposition was followed by the lifting of the ban on *La Prensa* and the right-wing *Radio Católica*, the declaration of unilateral ceasefires in key combat zones, and the extension of entry visas to exiled priests, including the celebrated Bismark Caballero; this stole much of the clerics' thunder although it was to be expected that they would issue pious perorations as to the insufficiency of such moves. Local and North American declarations along these lines took on a more buoyant tone as the FSLN continued to resist direct negotiations with the Contra and insisted upon talks with the US as the party responsible for the counter-revolution. Similarly, continued subjection of press copy to state censorship in the name of national security and the refusal of the government to extend the amnesty to the Contra leadership encouraged denunciations that Sandinismo was inherently untrustworthy. The attention paid to these issues in what was evidently a tense waiting game of tactical exchanges reflected the fact that the FSLN's enemies could extract little political capital from charges of Managua's intervention in the affairs of neighbouring states since it was now accepted that aid to the Salvadorean guerrilla had been cut.

The obstacles faced by the 1987 accord were recognized by all parties to be legion. It did, however, mark a major watershed in the regional conflict, in which the future of the Sandinista revolution was no less central than it had been on the morrow of Somoza's overthrow. Eight years later many of the options that had remained on the agenda between 1979 and 1982 had been either erased or markedly reduced by Washington's offensive and the internal limits of Sandinismo. Perhaps most important of all, it was no longer plausible to hold any expectation in the foreseeable future for a regional revolt based upon the Nicaraguan model. Since 1982 the national, regional and international balance of forces had undergone major shifts, the most notable of which derived from US intervention. The failure of the revolutionary movements in El Salvador and Guatemala to stage a decisive assault on state power in 1979–81 was the most outstanding result of this. Yet the inability of the radical forces in those countries to follow the FSLN's example also corresponded to important local factors, underscoring the fact that Central American politics continued to be characterized by diversity as well as the unity imposed from without.

Notes

1. Quoted in Theodore Schwab and Harold Sims, 'Relations with the Communist States', in Thomas W. Walker, ed., *Nicaragua. The First Five Years*, New York 1985, pp.463–4.
2. Presidential Address to Joint Session of Congress, excerpts reprinted in Peter Rosset and John Vandermeer, eds, *The Nicaragua Reader. Documents of a Revolution under Fire*, New York 1983, p.19.
3. Richard Harris and Carlos M. Vilas, eds, *Nicaragua. A Revolution under Siege*, London 1985, p.19.
4. *The Guardian*, London, 3 March 1981.
5. As 'Federal' and 'United' states, Brazil and Mexico invoke their origins rather than trumpet the nature of their present polity. Uruguay's denomination as the 'Oriental republic' displays a certain pride in distinction from its overbearing trans-Platine neighbour but is still a residue of nineteenth-century parochialism. Otherwise, Guyana, designated a 'cooperative' republic, is the only other South American state to advertise the nature of its republicanism, but the country cannot properly be considered part of Latin America and belongs to the English-speaking Caribbean.
6. Shortly after the revolution the FSLN expelled from the country foreign members of the 'Simon Bolivar Brigade' which had organized independent demonstrations in Managua and Bluefields demanding an immediate radicalization of the regime. Largely comprised of supporters of the Colombian PST, a Trotskyist organization attached to the current led by Nahuel Moreno, the Brigade did not participate directly in the fighting and had little time in which to establish a popular following. However, the unqualified response of the FSLN did betoken an exceptionally sharp attitude to 'ultra-leftism' that, in a style reminiscent of Stalinism, was often depicted as at the service of imperialism. Nonetheless, CAUS, the PCN's labour front, proved too entrenched to permit a simple administrative liquidation, and while the leader of the party, Eli Altamirano, was briefly gaoled and the PCN banned from attending the Council of State, it was allowed to continue in existence and took two seats in the Assembly after the 1984 elections. It would appear that the existence of an independent militia was the

principal reason for the early bout of repression. Once the force was dissolved criticism from the left was tolerated, not least because it attracted little popular support but also perhaps because it reflected aspects of debate inside the FSLN.

7. Following some minor adjustments in 1981, the composition of the Council of State was:

Political parties:	
FSLN*	6
PLI	1
PSN*	1
PPSC*	1
MDN	1
PCD	1
PSCN	1
PLC	1
Popular Organizations:	
CDS*	9
JS–19*	1
AMNLAE*	1
Labour Organizations:	
CST*	3
ATC*	2
CGTI	2
CTN	1
CUS	1
CAUS	2
FETSALUD*	1
Corporate Organizations:	
Armed Forces*	1
Clergy (ACLEN)	1
Higher Education*	1
ANDEN*	1
Journalists*	1
MISURATA	1
Professionals*	1
UNAG*	2
Ecumenical Axis	1
Private Sector:	
Development Institute	1
Chamber of Industry	1
Chamber of Commerce	1
Chamber of Construction	1
Large farmers (UPANIC)	1
TOTAL	51

* indicates general pro-Sandinista vote.
Source: Booth, *End and Beginning*, 2nd edn, p. 193.

8. The call for the immediate expulsion of the bourgeoisie went beyond the confines of Trotskyism although the orthodox elements of this current upheld it most vigorously, less in tactical terms than as an essential precondition for establishing a workers' and peasants' government and proceeding to the construction of socialism. This view, not shared by the leadership of the United Secretariat of the Fourth International, was highly formalistic although its basis in a scepticism as to the character and strategy of the FSLN was somewhat less so and hardly surprising. Weber's belief that the FSLN is a 'revolutionary organization of the Nicaraguan proletariat' represents the alternative view within the European radical left. *Nicaragua*, p.59. It is difficult to accept such a characterization insofar as the organization is both sociologically and ideologically far more extensive than this formulation implies and, as we shall argue, the FSLN is not dedicated to the interests of the working class above all else. Nevertheless, this does not entail, as is often claimed by orthodox Trotskyism, that the Sandinista leadership will necessarily fail to realize those interests. Debate over these matters was at a peak in 1979–82, the subsequent US offensive tending to concentrate attention on defence of the revolution. In terms of bourgeois participation in government it is clear that the FSLN showed greater appreciation of the tactical state of play than did many of their radical critics, as Adolfo Gilly correctly identified (from a revolutionary standpoint) at the time: 'If the composition of the government involves a latent conflict, this stems not from a "tendency to conciliation" on the part of the Sandinistas, but from the fact that such a conflict is present in reality and cannot be settled at the level of institutions before it is resolved in the relation of social forces. . . . We consider futile those discussions and slogans that seek to universalize and codify every specific feature of the Russian revolution: for example, "All Power to the FSLN!" or "Out with the Bourgeois Ministers!" Such scholastic exercises do not take into account, *inter alia*, the fact that the Tsarist army survived in Russia between February and October 1917, whereas the National Guard was destroyed by the insurrection in Nicaragua.' *La Nueva Nicaragua*, Mexico 1980, p.113.

9. Attacks on mass mobilization as entirely manipulated are ingenuous and generally reflect a derision for 'the crowd' that sits very uneasily with the critics' claims to popular representation. Indeed, the FSLN's exploitation of its popular following against its opponents has been markedly restrained and devoid of violence compared to other revolutions. The absence of the death penalty and a very low level of revenge and assassination after the victory were central rather than incidental to Sandinista policy. The importance of this should not be underestimated and extends well beyond the realm of public relations, just as in Uganda the strategic desistence of the forces of Yoweri Museveni from exacting traditional revenge on their enemies constituted a decisive feature of their claims to government and the establishment of a new order.

10. Details on the Contra are given in William Robinson and Kent Norsworthy, *David and Goliath. Washington's War against Nicaragua*, London 1987; Bob Woodward, *Veil. The Secret Wars of the CIA 1981–1987*, London 1987; Peter Kornbluh, *The Price of Intervention*, Washington 1987.

11. Vilas, *Sandinista Revolution*, p.152, stresses the importance of this division of the bourgeoisie.

12. The fairness of the elections was, of course, hotly disputed by Washington but without much impact. For full details of the poll, see Latin American Studies Association (LASA), 'The Electoral Process in Nicaragua: Domestic and International Influences', *LASA Forum*, vol. 15, no. 4, winter 1985, part of which is reprinted in Walker, *First Five Years*, pp.523–32; International Human Rights Group and Washington Office on Latin America (WOLA), *A Political Opening in Nicaragua. Report on the Nicaraguan Election of 4 November 1984*, Washington 1984; *Envío*, Managua, ano 4, no. 46, April 1985.

13. Quoted in Gary Ruchwarger, 'The Sandinista Mass Organizations and the Revolutionary Process', in Harris and Vilas, *Nicaragua*, p.89.

14. 'Sandinista democracy so far is more developed in the socio-economic than the politico-institutional sphere. The FSLN characterization of popular democracy – as popular participation that begins in the socio-economic sphere and progressively advances to the politico-institutional terrain – expresses the current stage of development of this process.' Vilas, *Sandinista Revolution*, p.252.

15. Henri Weber places excessive expectations in the capacity of the mass organizations to develop into genuine organs of popular power although he is at pains to resist a narrow model based on the Soviet experience in Russia. Even by mid 1980 the mass organizations manifested clear signs of lacking powers of decision necessary for this *whether or not they were in agreement with the FSLN.*

16. Carlos Nuñez, 20 April 1980, quoted in Carlos Vilas, 'The Workers' Movement', in Harris and Vilas, *Nicaragua*, p.128.

17. Quoted in ibid., p.96.

18. See the list of complaints presented by Comandante Bayardo Arce in a letter to the CDSs of 7 October 1982, reprinted in *Nicaragua. The Sandinista People's Revolution*, New York 1985, p.62.

19. Nora Astorga, quoted in Maxine Molyneux, 'Women', in Walker, *First Five Years*, p.147.

20. Tomas Borge, quoted in Stephen Gorman and Thomas Walker, 'The Armed Forces', in Walker, *First Five Years*, p.100.

21. This point is stressed by Vilas, *Sandinista Revolution*, fn.23, p.292, and is correctly counterposed to the self-serving demands made by Washington that the revolution effectively disarm itself. The need for the defence of the revolution is so obvious that I have not insisted on it at great length, the following passage being dedicated to an observation that is far less frequently made by its supporters.

22. This is not a comment of a spurious or deliberately provocative character. At the very least the suppression of *El Pueblo* provides a precedent. Moreover, aversion to addressing the problem of militarization – resulting either from the objective conditions of war or from FSLN policies – on the understanding that this debilitates the defence of the revolution is indicative of a familiar and threadbare realpolitik. The undeniable need for a strong military defence in no sense precludes discussion either of its political character or of its wider consequences. The silence of much of the left on this point is, however, not simply the result of nervous

pragmatism. It is notable that the orthodox Communist currents which subjected *foquismo* to such severe criticism tend to reverse their position on militarism when the popular forces hold power, this being in no small measure due to the continuing influence of the Stalinist fetishization of the state. Equally, many Sandinista fellow travellers, particularly in North America, are distinguished by their reluctance to demonstrate equal enthusiasm for regimes such as those in Cuba and Vietnam, and celebrate exclusively the divergences of the Nicaraguan experience from these in preference to confronting the more taxing points of similarity. The divergences are real and important, and emphasis upon them is natural in the context of domestic US politics, where the tasks of anti-imperialism are central and dependent upon tactical campaigns. However, it is entirely misconceived to evade this question on the grounds that it fortifies the counter-revolution and is intrinsically anti-Sandinista. The dangers of suppressing debate are fully evident from the tragic case of Grenada and – to a less disastrous degree – the internecine struggles within the Salvadorean revolutionary forces. In both cases external support predicated upon blanket and uncritical acceptance of the positions of the local left may well not have altered the internal conditions of crisis one iota – the degree at least is debatable – but it left the anti-imperialist movement badly weakened in responding to them and brought into question the credibility of those who suddenly became wise after the event. For further discussion of these two cases, see Dunkerley, *The Long War*, 2nd edn; and James Dunkerley and Fitzroy Ambursely, *Grenada: Whose Freedom?*, London 1984. By 1984 the EPS numbered 40,000 troops and the militia at least 60,000 and possibly as many as 90,000. These are substantial numbers for a population of 3.1 million, the ratio of soldiers to population being the highest in Central America.

23. In April 1985 the *New York Times* reported that on a visit to that city Daniel Ortega spent $3,500 at an optician's although this was for six pairs of spectacles made of a supposedly bullet-proof material. *New York Times*, 25 April 1985. The president's subsequent explanation that he had not paid for them personally did not do a great deal to remedy the effect. *Playboy*, November 1987; Salman Rushdie, *The Jaguar Smile*, London 1987.

24. 'Five and a half years after the fall of the dictator . . . Somoza . . . a pluralist society still exists even though it is under stringent state control . . . Nicaragua is far from being a satellite of the Soviet Union.' *New York Times*, colour supplement, 28 April 1985. For the interview of Borge, Ernesto Cardenal and Sergio Ramirez as well as Daniel Ortega by Claudia Dreifus, see *Playboy*, September 1983.

25. Of the several biographies, the best is James R. Brockman, *The Word Remains: A Life of Oscar Romero*, New York 1982.

26. Quoted by Luis Serra, 'Ideology, Religion and Class Struggle in the Nicaraguan Revolution', in Harris and Vilas, *Nicaragua*, p.159.

27. Ibid., p.160.

28. Ramirez, *Alba de Oro*, p.163.

29. Quoted in *Sandinista People's Revolution*, p.286.

30. Quoted in Harris and Vilas, *Nicaragua*, p.156. For the contemporary progressive currents, see also Michael Dodson and Laura Nuzzi, 'Religion and Politics', in Walker, *First Five Years*. A full background is given in Berryman, *Religious Roots*, and Hodges presents useful discussion of the links with Sandino's religious views.

31. These matters are discussed in both the above texts as well as Booth, *End and Beginning*, 2nd edn.

32. The case of *La Prensa*, always more of a cause célèbre abroad than in Nicaragua, is succinctly discussed in John Spicer Nichols, 'The Media', in Walker, *First Five Years*.

33. In addition to the surveys in Vilas, *Sandinista Revolution*; Vilas and Harris, *Nicaragua*; and Walker, *First Five Years*, see in particular George Irvin and Xabier Gorostiaga, *Towards an Alternative for Central America and the Caribbean*, London 1984; Michael Conroy, 'False Polarization? Alternative Perspectives in the Economic Strategies of Post-Revolutionary Nicaragua', Working Paper no.26, Helen Kellogg Institute, University of Notre Dame, July 1984; E.V.K. Fitzgerald, 'Stabilization and Economic Justice: The Case of Nicaragua', Working Paper no.34, Helen Kellogg Institute, University of Notre Dame, September 1984; Richard Sholk, 'The National Bourgeoisie in Post-Revolutionary Nicaragua', Working Paper no.123, Latin American Program, The Wilson Center, Washington 1982; David Ruccio, 'The State and Planning in Nicaragua', Working Paper no.53, Helen Kellogg

Institute, University of Notre Dame, December 1985; George Irvin, 'Nicaragua: Establishing the State as the Centre of Accumulation', *Cambridge Journal of Economics*, vol.7, 1983; CEPAL, *Nicaragua*, mimeo, Santiago de Chile, July 1985; Rose Spalding, ed., *The Political Economy of Revolutionary Nicaragua*, London 1987.

34. Speech, June 1983, quoted in *Sandinista People's Revolution*, p.178.

35. Wheelock in conversation with Marta Harnecker, 'El Gran Desafío', May–July 1983, reprinted in ibid., pp.134–5.

36. Interview with Sandinista officials by Denis Gilbert, 'The Bourgeoisie', in Walker, *First Five Years*, p.179.

37. Quoted in *Sandinista People's Revolution*, p.30.

38. Wheelock, 'El Gran Desafío'.

39. Ibid.

40. Borge, quoted in *Nuevo Diario*, 14 May 1982, cited in Walker, *First Five Years*, p.180.

41. Víctor Tirado, speech to CST, 26 February 1983, quoted in *Sandinista People's Revolution*, p.99.

42. Discussion of the Nicaraguan debt is hampered by the great unreliability of government statistics caused by the lack of professionals in the state sector and the very high turnover of personnel. According to Oscar Ugarteche, adviser to the government under the supervision of the 'proto-Contras' (Cruz, Robelo, etc.) as well as after their departure, the lack of coherent policy to replace efforts at 'coexistence' with the western banks up to 1982 can be ascribed in more than incidental terms to the very low level of technical skill and the enormous pressure on the few qualified staff, obliged constantly to travel the world in order to drum up cash. In 1986 President Ortega was personally vetting all claims for dollar expenditure over $1,000. On the other hand, the pressures on this small and superexploited staff were undoubtedly the main cause of difficulties in economic management; Ugarteche himself visited 300 banks in 18 months in search of loans but received only four favourable responses, suggesting that the policy of rapprochement was of very limited value after the first renegotiation. It is of some interest that, like Nicaragua, Mozambique, Angola and Vietnam also recognized all or a good part of their external debt whereas Cuba, following the example of the Soviet Union and China, did not. Oscar Ugarteche, 'Rescheduling Nicaragua's Debt', Paper to St Antony's College, Oxford, 18 November 1986. For other sources, and somewhat varying data, see CEPAL, *Nicaragua*; Conroy, 'External Dependence'. Details of US sabotage of Nicaragua's relations with the Inter-American Development Bank reported by the British representative were leaked and published in the *New Statesman*, 9 August 1985. Details of the attitude of the IMF and the World Bank may be found in Richard Swedborg, ed., 'Confidential IMF and World Bank Reports on El Salvador and Nicaragua', CAMINO, Boston, 1982. The 1985 figures for the debt of the other Central American states were: Costa Rica – $4.24 billion ($1,696 per capita); Guatemala – $2.45 billion ($327); Honduras – $2.44 billion ($567); El Salvador – $2.10 billion ($404). Between 1978 and 1981 the Nicaraguan debt jumped from $961 million to $2.2 billion with debt service at 22 per cent of exports; by 1985 debt service had fallen to 17 per cent of exports, in line with the level for the rest of the region except Costa Rica (28 per cent).

43. The fullest survey of Nicaraguan–Soviet bloc economic relations available at the time of writing was Rubén Berrios, 'Economic Relations between Nicaragua and the Socialist Countries', Working Paper no.166, Latin American Program, Wilson Center, Washington 1985, which provides full and persuasive empirical data to back the view that the Soviet Union pursued a limited and pragmatic approach. See also Nicky Miller, *The Soviet Union and Latin America*, unpublished D.Phil., University of Oxford 1986; Cole Blasier, 'The Soviet Union', in Morris J. Blackman, William M. Leogrande and Kenneth Sharpe, eds, *Confronting Revolution*, New York 1986; Marc Edelman, 'The Other Superpower: The USSR and Latin America'. NACLA, vol.xxi, no.1, January 1987.

44. Sylvia Maxfield and Richard Stahler-Sholk, 'External Constraints', in Walker, *First Five Years*, p.260.

45. For a succinct survey, see Deborah Brandt, 'Education', in ibid.

46. Thomas John Bossert, 'Health Policy: The Dilemma of Success', in ibid.

47. 10,162 housing units were completed in 1981–83. For fuller figures, see Harvey Williams, 'Housing Policy', in ibid.

48. This schematic account relies heavily on Eduardo Baumeister, 'Nicaraguan Agriculture and the Agrarian Reform', in Harris and Vilas, *Nicaragua*. For other surveys, see Joseph Thone and David Kaimowitz, 'Agrarian Reform', in Walker, *First Five Years*, and Vilas, *Sandinista Revolution*.

49. Jaime Wheelock, quoted in Vilas, *Sandinista Revolution*, p.165.

50. See, for example, UNAG, *Asamblea Nacional Constitutiva*, Managua, 25–26 April 1982, discussed in ibid., p.171.

51. Harris and Vilas, *Nicaragua*, p.121.

52. Quoted in ibid., p.131.

53. CST, *El Papel de los Sindicatos en la Revolución*, Managua, April 1980, p.7.

54. See, for example, the declarations of Luis Carrión, quoted in Harris and Vilas, *Nicaragua*, p.132.

55. Vilas, *Sandinista Revolution*, p.205.

56. 1983 population figures are from the Centro de Investigaciones y Documentación de la Costa Atlántica (CIDCA), cited in Gillian Brown, 'Miskito Revindication: Between Revolution and Resistance', in Harris and Vilas, *Nicaragua*, pp.176–8. Further sources on this issue include Philippe Bourgois, 'Ethnic Minorities', in Walker, *First Five Years*; and Roxanne Dunbar Ortiz, *Indians of the Americas*, London 1984, especially part iv, which is the fullest general survey published in English.

57. The following comments make no pretence at a proper review of US policy, which has been extensively described and analysed in both popular and academic texts. For a detailed Nicaraguan view, see the monthly *Envío*, published by the Instituto Histórico Centroamericano. A broader Latin American critique is given in Luis Maira, ed., *La Política de Reagan y la Crisis en Centramérica*, San José 1982. Critical Anglo-Saxon analysis can be found in: LaFeber, *Inevitable Revolutions*; Pearce, *Under the Eagle*; PACCA, *Changing Course: Blueprint for Peace in Central America*, Washington 1984; Richard Newfarmer, ed., *From Gunboats to Diplomacy: New US Policies for Latin America*, Baltimore 1984; Martin Diskin, ed., *Trouble in Our Backyard. Central America and the United States in the Eighties*, New York 1983; Philip Berryman, *Inside Central America*, New York 1985; Richard Allen White, *The Morass: United States Intervention in Central America*, New York 1984; Noam Chomsky, *Turning the Tide. US Intervention in Central America and the Struggle for Peace*, London 1986. For a calm consideration of the institutional context of the US debate, see Laurence Whitehead, 'Explaining Washington's Central American Policies', JLAS, vol.15, part 2, November 1983. A particularly lucid and suggestive appraisal of Washington's general strategy is given in Fred Halliday, 'Beyond Irangate: The Reagan Doctrine and the Third World', Transnational Institute, 1987.

58. Viron Vaky, 'Hemispheric Relations: "Everything is Part of Everything Else" ', *Foreign Affairs*, vol.59, no.3, 1981, p.622.

59. See Conroy, 'External Dependence'; Swedborg, *Confidential IMF Documents*.

60. For a summary, see Painter and Lapper, *Honduras: State for Sale*, pp.124–7.

61. Tables are given in Marlene Dixon, ed., *On Trial. Reagan's War against Nicaragua*, London 1985, pp.50–1.

62. For a selection of Contadora proposals and other related documents, see Bruce Bagley, Robert Alvarez and Katherine Hagedorn, eds, *Contadora and the Central American Peace Process*, SAIS Papers in International Affairs no.8, Johns Hopkins University, 1985.

63. According to the Sandinista defector Miguel Bolaños, there were in 1983 70 Soviet military advisers, 400 Cubans, 40–50 East Germans, 20–25 Bulgarians. Published surveys of Central American relations with the Soviet bloc include: Morris Rothenberg, 'The Soviets and Central America', in Leiken, *Anatomy of Conflict*; Theodore Schwab and Harold Sims, 'Relations with the Communist States', in Walker, *First Five Years*; Robert S. Leiken, 'Soviet and Cuban Policy in the Caribbean Basin', in D. Schulz and D. Graham, eds, *Revolution and Counter-revolution*.

64. For details of US and Contra aggression, see Rosset and Vandemeer, *Nicaragua Reader*; Marlene Dixon, ed., *On Trial; Envío*, which carries details every month.

65. *Wall Street Journal*, 23 March 1985; *New York Times*, 25 August 1985. I cite precise sources here because the evidence is disputed with particular vigour but in general press references have been avoided in this text because any consistent usage would entail excessive citation.

66. The figures for troops belong to Colonel John Buchanan, interview, 15 October 1984, cited in Berryman, *Inside Central America*, p.155. Those for financial cost are calculated by Theodore Moran, 'The Cost of Alternative US Policies towards El Salvador: 1984–1989', in Leiken, *Anatomy of Conflict*, p.169. Perhaps the most fluent and suggestive assessment of US strategy in the region at this time was Allen Nairn, 'Endgame: A Special Report on US Military Strategy in Central America', NACLA, vol.XVIII, no.3, May–June 1984.

67. A *New York Times*–CBS poll conducted in June 1985 showed 53 per cent opposed to aid to the Contra, 32 per cent in favour and 15 per cent undecided. (In 1984 the figures were 55%, 27%, and 18% respectively.) However, only 26 per cent of the respondents were aware of which side the US government supported in Nicaragua (19% in 1984). *New York Times*, 5 June 1985. It should, though, be noted that in 1982 a *Newsweek* poll found that 74 per cent of those questioned believed that US involvement in El Salvador 'could turn that country into the Vietnam of the 1980s' and 89 per cent were opposed to the sending of US troops. At the time US policy was more heavily concentrated on El Salvador than Nicaragua and the level of fighting in the civil war was particularly fierce. However, ignorance in the US as to events in Central America was still impressive: at that time a *New York Times*–CBS poll discovered that 50 per cent of respondents thought that Soviet and Cuban troops were fighting in El Salvador. *Newsweek*, 1 March 1982; *New York Times*, 21 March 1982.

68. For details of early US allegations of arms flow into El Salvador, see US Department of State, 'Communist Interference in El Salvador', Washington, 23 February 1981. Discussion of the veracity of these claims can be found in James Petras, 'White Paper on the White Paper', *The Nation*, March 1981; Raymond Bonner, *Weakness and Deceit: US Policy and El Salvador*, New York 1984, pp.267–9; Nairn, 'Endgame', p.33. In 1984 the CIA analyst David MacMichael, assigned in 1981 to produce evidence of logistical support, publicly concluded that none could be found after early 1981. Interview, *Sojourner*, August 1984, and a synthesis of his findings given in Walker, *First Five Years*, p.463.

69. According to Jaime Wheelock, 'With the government of Guatemala we really haven't any problem.' *Sandinista People's Revolution*, p.148. This statement was made in late 1983 when Guatemala was ruled by a right-wing military dictatorship. The peculiarities of Guatemalan foreign policy are suggestively discussed in Gustavo Porras Castejón, 'Guatemala: Un Proyecto de Recomposición bajo el Signo de la Contrainsurgencia', mimeo 1984. These will be considered later.

70. The fabrication and deliberate misuse of quotes by the US administration is outlined in COHA, 'Washington Report on the Hemisphere', 16 October 1985, and discussed in Chomsky, *Turning the Tide*, pp.269–70.

8

El Salvador: The Long War

The North Americans preach democracy to us while everywhere they support dictatorships.

José Napoleón Duarte, 1969[1]

There is no mistaking that the decisive battle for Central America is underway in El Salvador. If, after Nicaragua, El Salvador is captured by a violent minority, who in Central America would not live in fear? How long would it be before major US strategic interests – the canal, sealanes, oil supplies – were at risk?

Assistant Secretary of State Thomas Enders, February 1982[2]

You've really got two choices when you get into a nasty human rights situation. You can say, 'Oh Jesus, these guys are real pricks, we can't have anything to do with these kind of people. We're going home.' Or you can say, 'All right, it's terrible, it's lousy, it's horrendous, what are we going to do about it?' You've just got to decide who your pricks are and go with them.

US Foreign Service Officer[3]

What happened in El Salvador is this: Aid and pressure to reform, exerted by the government of the United States, offered the military an alternative to its traditional role as the murderers of the Old Right. It gave reformist officers like General Vides Casanova a chance to create a professional and genuinely patriotic force, representing not a single interest group but the nation as a whole. It is a policy that's worked.

Notre Dame Magazine, summer 1985[4]

Colonel García is the man from whom we take orders, not the junta. We have put you in the position where you are, and for the things that are needed here we don't need you. We have been running this country for fifty years and we are quite prepared to keep on running it.

General Vides Casanova to the cabinet, December 1979[5]

I believe in compassion, tolerance and love. That's why I'm trying to be tolerant with everyone.

José Napoleón Duarte, November 1984[6]

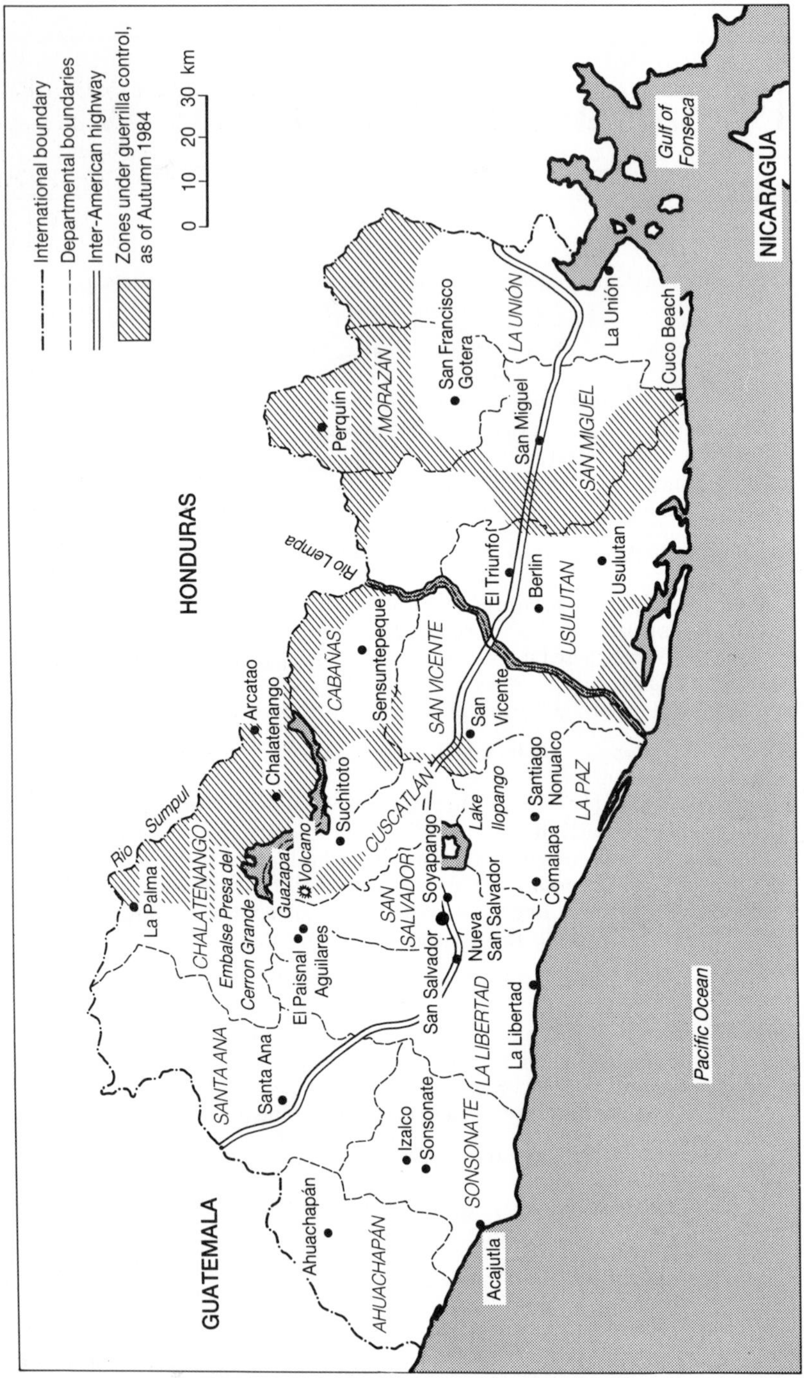

International boundary
Departmental boundaries
Inter-American highway
Zones under guerrilla control, as of Autumn 1984
0 10 20 30 km
GUATEMALA
HONDURAS
NICARAGUA
Rio Sumpul
Rio Lempa
Pacific Ocean
Gulf of Fonseca
AHUACHAPÁN
SANTA ANA
SONSONATE
CHALATENANGO
LA LIBERTAD
SAN SALVADOR
CUSCATLÁN
CABAÑAS
SAN VICENTE
LA PAZ
USULUTAN
SAN MIGUEL
MORAZÁN
LA UNIÓN
La Palma
Embalse Presa del Cerron Grande
Arcatao
Chalatenango
Santa Ana
Ahuachapán
El Paisnal
Aguilares
Guazapa Volcano
Suchitoto
Sensuntepeque
Izalco
Sonsonate
San Salvador
Soyapango
Acajutla
Nueva San Salvador
Lake Ilopango
San Vicente
El Triunfo
La Libertad
Comalapa
Santiago Nonualco
Berlin
Usulutan
Perquín
San Francisco Gotera
San Miguel
La Unión
Cuco Beach

El Salvador

In turning from Nicaragua we should be mindful of a change in narrative voice from that which explains the success of revolutions to that which discusses their failure, absence or prospects. Even outside partisan debate there is a notable shift in temper between, on the one hand, the study of events that are important because they can cogently be argued to be consummated and thus – regardless of chronology and consequence – in a real sense historical and, on the other hand, that of developments which may be no less contemporaneous or even momentous but lack any clear and decisive outcome. The difference is largely one of perspective and style and should not be invested with methodological pomp and circumstance. Yet it can be of particular importance in a context such as Central America where one finds not only one successful political revolution, one (El Salvador) that has been seriously essayed for the better part of a decade and another (Guatemala) that has a far more erratic history, but also two countries (Honduras and Costa Rica) for which it is not possible to talk of any radical movement threatening the state in the near future. Clearly, it would be misconceived constantly to measure these other countries by the yardstick established by the FSLN. Yet equally obviously the impact of Nicaragua has affected their particular development since 1979 and produced a distinct regional condition in which it is plausible to imagine a Central American revolution, however distant and variegated that might be. The issue at stake here is less the viability of more or less sophisticated domino theories than the way Nicaragua colours our understanding of events elsewhere in the isthmus, and the need to maintain some clarity as to the underlying assumptions and approaches this encourages in terms of the other nations.

Such a notion may seem to be unduly pedantic but it is particularly germane to the case of El Salvador, which since the autumn of 1979 has been viewed by right and left alike very much in the light of Nicaragua and as a failed/imminent revolution largely comparable to and directly influenced by the Sandinista example. For over eight years El Salvador has been either the next domino or the most obvious extension of a regional revolution. Of course, after such a length of time these fears or expectations are less sharp than they were in October 1979 when, a mere twelve weeks after the defeat of Somoza, the military regime in San Salvador was overthrown in an apparently reformist coup leading to a rapid escalation of mass mobilization and, within the space of a year, civil war. In January 1981 the guerrillas of the *Frente Farabundo Martí para la Liberación Nacional* (FMLN) staged what they called a 'final offensive'. It soon turned out to be badly mistitled, but indicated that they, just as much as the Carter and Reagan administrations, believed that the crisis might be resolved in short order by insurrectionary manoeuvre. Even when this belief was shown to be unfounded it was some time before it became fully apparent that US military force and political supervision could uphold the dominant bloc and resist any immediate threat from the radical movement.

This course of events has not unjustifiably encouraged the view that a Salvadorean revolution would have quickly followed that in Nicaragua were it not for US intervention. Indeed, the Salvadorean left may be said to have paid a high price for the Nicaraguan revolution although they have received much support from it. They were, figuratively, doomed by being second in line. Yet before the Sandinistas cut back their logistical aid to the FMLN early in 1981 the Salvadorean guerrilla received exceptionally modest quantities of materiel from Nicaragua and was leading a mass movement that was, even in the eyes of the most recalcitrant hawks in Washington, resolutely national in social origin and political character.[7] In fact, if one judges the incidence of revolt purely by indices of exploitation and social deprivation the probability of a popular uprising was far higher in El Salvador than in Nicaragua during the 1970s.

The course of events in El Salvador cannot properly be explained through comparison with Nicaragua since it corresponds above all else to a national history with its own logic and only limited relevance to any successful 'model' established by the FSLN. Nonetheless, some of the contrasts between the two countries during this period are instructive if only because they challenge the more base and unthinking formulations of domino theory and its radical equivalent which understand all but the ephemera of politics to flow from conscious, organized agency.

Perhaps the most obvious difference between the two cases derives directly from the failure of the FMLN to secure military victory in 1980–81: the speed of the revolutionary movement. Following the collapse of the 'final offensive' the political wing of the opposition, the *Frente Democrático Revolucionario* (FDR), and the guerrillas of the FMLN accepted – with varying degrees of conviction – that they would henceforth be embarked upon a *guerra popular prolongada* in which the possibilities for political manoeuvre and alliances of the type witnessed in Nicaragua in 1978–79 and in El Salvador itself in 1979–80 would be greatly reduced and the potential for outflanking Washington outside the military sphere very limited indeed. Moreover, the extenuated nature of the conflict not only diminished the immediate decisiveness of programme and specific political demands but also provided the US with time in which to reorchestrate a dominant bloc that had been plunged into turmoil. This was not itself easily achieved: it was nearly five years before Washington could secure an elected government of the Christian Democratic Party (PDC), employing a combination of blackmail and enticement with the officer corps and oligarchy, whose political instincts resisted any concessions to this nominally reformist force. The recomposition of the dominant bloc was a decidedly erratic and risky enterprise and succeeded in mediating only the most prominent contradictions thrown up by the crisis of 1979–80, but it did stand in marked contrast to the Nicaraguan experience where the local equivalents of the PDC were won over to the cause of the popular bloc because unreconstructed Somocismo resisted any extension of the regime. Moreover, although the establishment in El Salvador of a pro-US government that inveighed against the landed oligarchy and yet did nothing to alter the bases of its power or restrain the brutality of the military was very largely due to Washington's intervention, it also corresponded in some respects to the pattern of post-war political life. Since 1932 the landlord class had accepted restrictions on its claims to political power and acquiesced in military rule; this gave it experience in tolerating regimes that were not drawn directly from the oligarchy, always provided these remained subject to its veto over key economic policies. There were, of course, important differences between the PDC and its military forebears in terms of public policy and style, but while these generated much heat in the early 1980s, the ability of Washington, the army and the bourgeoisie to impede any substantial independent initiative on the part of the Christian Democrats made their elevation to office at least sufferable if not exactly palatable. Additionally, the increased aid and institutional autonomy that the US guaranteed for the military made this rearrangement of the protocols of control less of a rupture with the post-1932 system than might appear to be the case.

A second element of continuum in the system – again notably absent in Nicaragua because of the character of the Somoza regime and the speed with which it was brought down – was the fact that despite its wholehearted obeisance to Washington and its failure to curb the power of large capital and the military, the PDC retained significant popularity at least in the first phase of its shift from opposition to government, during 1980–84. The support for the party in the 1970s was not entirely based upon its opposition to the military regime, stemming in part from its confessional nature and its administration of many towns, including the capital. It cannot, therefore, be easily compared with any Nicaraguan party of the time, and its resistance to joining the popular bloc in a period of acute conflict was an appreciably greater loss to the FDR-FMLN than would have been that of, say, the Conservative Party to the Sandinistas. Again, this state of affairs owed as much to the pattern of politics prior to 1979 as it did to manoeuvres thereafter. Its most critical consequence was to deprive the opposition of a clear target comparable to Somoza and to distance the government from the interests of the oligarchy. This problem for the FDR-FMLN was undoubtedly complicated by the holding of three elections between 1982 and 1985 since although these excluded the left, took place amidst extreme violence and were marked by malpractice, they could be contrasted with those of previous decades insofar as the outcome of the contest (between the PDC and the extreme right) was not entirely preordained. They were only a pretence at democracy but a pretence distinct from that of the pre-1979 period, assisting the disaggregation of the political and military features of the dominant bloc and impeding its depiction as a consolidated dictatorship. In this regard the very weakness of President Duarte and the PDC was an essential prerequisite for the operation since Duarte's vacuous and impotent complaints about the army and the right could be presented as a genuine 'second front' and the real stuff of politics. The man himself obviously believed this, but it was at the end of the day little more than political theatre, albeit a production of considerable value to Washington in its international and domestic presentation of the regime.

If the experience of the Salvadorean left was distinct from that of the FSLN in terms of its political enemy, its own development was no less so. The radical forces in El Salvador had been far more sharply divided over programme and strategy throughout the 1970s than had been the tendencies of the FSLN; these differences, which on occasion reached the point of bloodletting, were only erratically overcome even after formal unification was achieved in 1980. This division was due in part to the more advanced radical culture in El Salvador and the more prominent role of the orthodox pro-Moscow party (PCS), in part to the greater challenge presented by electoralism, and in part to a higher degree of mass mobilization prior to 1979. In contrast to Nicaragua, the working class in El Salvador was comparatively large by Central American standards and was the most politicized of the isthmus. Equally, the peasantry, not to the fore of insurrectionary mobilization in Nicaragua, was joining unions and radical organizations a number of years before the onset of full-scale political crisis. As has already been mentioned, the formation of broad plebeian fronts in El Salvador took place before the possibility of any insurrection, and mass organization was far more advanced than at a comparable point of political conflict in Nicaragua. Thus, even in the charged events of 1979–80 the Salvadorean crisis had a greater sense of a war of position than one of manoeuvre. In this respect it should not be forgotten that despite the very varied political and military projects that existed within the orbit of the popular bloc, the collective memory of 1932 provided a sobering illustration of the costs of insurrection that was unique in Central America and certainly had no parallel in Nicaragua. Here the superficial similarities between the figures of Farabundo Martí and Sandino begin to break down, for while the former was also a victim of the dictatorships of the 1930s, he was a Communist before a nationalist (this being the issue over which the two broke relations) and identified with a mass movement rather than being a solitary hero and herald. One can, of course, make too much of the emblematic importance of these father-martyrs. It is, however, plain that the Salvadorean revolutionary movement could never be Martista in a sense comparable to Sandinismo both because Farabundo Martí was a militant of the PCS – which exists today as only one of several components of a politically varied popular bloc – and because although he more than any other figure evokes the experience of 1932, that experience cannot be reduced to his individual example. Farabundo Martí was a resolute internationalist and could not be moulded into a figurehead for a specifically Salvadorean nationalism, not least because he opposed US hegemony in general and fought against a national regime that had no historic need of support from Washington's troops.

Finally, it is worth noting that at the same time as it has to contend with the consequences of a more entrenched social conflict than did the Sandinistas, the FMLN is also confronted with a more exacting logistical position. The Salvadorean civil war has lasted much longer than that in Nicaragua and is being fought in terrain far from advantageous to a guerrilla force. The country is very small (21,000 square kilometres against Nicaragua's 148,000), is not mountainous, does not contain large tracts of densely wooded and lightly populated territory, and its two borders are less permeable than those of Nicaragua in both physical and political terms. The FMLN lacks any easily accessible rearguard and, as a number of massacres in which the Honduran military participated vividly illustrate, the possibilities of refuge for its supporters are greatly restricted by 'free-fire' zones that do not stop at the border. These factors have compelled a more profound socialization of the guerrilla in its operational areas than that which obtained in Nicaragua, but they have also determined shifts in the opposition's campaign between town and countryside that both respond to the level of attrition and reflect a social support that cannot be described as predominantly rural or urban.[8] In this regard there is a clear similarity with Nicaragua although the socio-geographical poles of activity have tended to be more extreme and class conscious.

These contrasts – to which many more could be added – signal the need for great caution in approaching any specific model for revolution derived from Nicaragua, notwithstanding the comparable pace of polarization up to 1979. Thereafter, of course, the direct similarities terminate, and El Salvador begins to mirror the bitter experience of Guatemala.

Class Domination and Military Power

In recent years the high profile of US intervention in El Salvador, the guerrilla war, extensive violation of human rights, and a flurry of noisy elections have tended to reduce attention to the importance of economic power in the country and the extraordinary concentration of wealth in a small capitalist class still based on the cultivation and export of coffee. On the one hand, reference to the oligarchy of 'fourteen families' is often treated as a very loose image deployed more as a convenient slogan drawn from the past than a carefully considered and empirically substantiated piece of class analysis. On the other, the fact that the landlord class did not appear as the principal *political* protagonist between 1932 and 1982 is taken as an indication that it was not in reality such a dominant force. This latter interpretation is often encouraged by the introduction of an agrarian reform in 1980 and the eventual acceptance of a PDC administration of middle-class technocrats in 1984. We will consider the real substance and dynamics of the reform and the political role of the bourgeoisie later, but it is worth dwelling momentarily on the character of the capitalist class in the modern period.

The nature of the Salvadorean bourgeoisie is of particular importance not just because of its small size and concentration of wealth but also because during the 1960s and 1970s there was a fierce debate on the left as to whether there existed a 'national bourgeoisie' distinct from and in conflict with the traditional landed oligarchy. Perhaps one of the most adventurous theses produced by the left in that period was that landed capital could reproduce itself on the basis of differential rent and had little need to reinvest any of its surplus. This, of course, would entail any faction that did plough back funds into production being seen as distinct and probably progressive; but in practice the levels of investment made by the landed oligarchy were uniformly high, and the theory owed more to wishful abstraction than empirical rigour.[9] A more contentious – or at least contended – analysis was proposed by the PCS, which, in line with orthodox doctrine as to the stages of capitalist development, held that both agricultural diversification in the 1950s, particularly into cotton, and the growth of light industry in the 1960s had spawned a new generation of entrepreneurs whose interests lay in the expansion of the domestic market and thus redistribution of wealth, which would in part be secured by an agrarian reform.[10] The importance of this perspective lay in its political connotations since it clearly opened the possibility of a class alliance with a sector of the bourgeoisie that would be prepared to challenge the stranglehold of the landed oligarchy, support democratic reforms and promote economic modernization, even at the cost of partial conflict with the US.

As has already been seen, there was an appreciable boom in cotton in the 1950s (although, contrary to the case in Nicaragua, this waned from the mid 1960s), and industry certainly expanded during the following decade under the CACM. The effect of this was to expand the profile of the local capitalist class beyond the traditional roles of landlord, merchant and banker that had obtained since the turn of the century. Although a great deal of new industrial capital was foreign, some local entrepreneurs diversified their holdings, and it is possible to identify secondary contradictions based not only on different commercial sectors but also within the production and distribution process of single commodities. Tensions of this latter type were nothing new and corresponded to a division of commercial labour that had prevailed since the onset of the coffee economy. Thus, for example, one might expect somewhat varied strategies and policies between the De Sola family, which sold far more coffee than it produced, and the Regalados, who were much less prominent as exporters than growers. Nonetheless, the existence of a clearly distinct faction of local capital based on manufacturing industry and divorced from agro-export is far less evident than the fact that many landed capitalists diversified their holdings while remaining centrally dependent upon commercial farming and the existing agrarian structure. As a brief perusal of Tables 40–42 should demonstrate,

Table 40: The Salvadorean Oligarchy I

A. *Agro-Export Production, 1970/71*

	Coffee[a]	*Cotton*[a]	*Cane*[b]
Regalado	85	–	105
Guirola	72	67	9
Llach-Schonenberg	50	27	–
Hill-Llach Hill	49	77	–
Dueñas	46	124	44
Alvarez Lemus	42	–	–
Meza Ayau	41	–	–
Sol Millet	37	–	–
Daglio	39	18	–
Alvarez	33	–	–
Salaverría	32	31	–
Deininger	22	–	–
Alfaro	22	–	48
Dalton	22	35	–
Lima	20	–	–
García Prieto	20	92	–
Avila Meardi	19	18	–
Liebes	18	–	–
Battle	18	–	–
Alvarez Drews	16	–	22
Quiñónez	15	–	45
De Sola	14	–	22
Kriete	13	100	–
Cristiani Burkard	13	79	51
Salaverría (Eduardo)	12	10	–
Bonilla	10	–	–

a. Thousands of quintals (46 kg).
b. Thousands of metric tonnes.

B. *Exports of Coffee, 1974 (% total sales)*

De Sola	14.37
Cia. Salvadoreña de Café	8.16
Liebes	7.03
Daglio	6.66
Prieto	5.92
Borgonovo	5.76
Cafeco S.A.	4.15
Battle	3.93
Dueñas	2.88
Llach	2.87
Salaverría-Durán	2.80
Cristiani Burkard	1.80
Homberger	1.79
Salaverría (José Antonio)	1.64
Salmar	1.59
Herrera Corneio	1.55
Castro Liebes	1.46
Industrias de Café S.A.	1.41
Bonilla	1.32
Renjifo Nuñez	1.15
Regalado	1.10
Monedero	1.09
Hill	1.07
Sol Millet	1.02

Source: Colindres, 'Tenencia de la Tierra', ECA, nos 335/6, p.471.

by the 1970s the oligarchy numbered rather more than fourteen families, and over a hundred large capitalist enterprises can be distinguished. Many of these – particularly those owned by immigrants – were primarily engaged in commerce, but it is significant that none of the largest thirty concerns had emerged after the 1920s or was engaged solely in coffee cultivation. The recurrence of the same surnames in the lists for production, export, land ownership and capital investment is far from coincidental. In 1971 the country's thirty-six largest landlords controlled 66 per cent of the capital of the 1,429 largest firms (that is, virtually all non-artisanal enterprises). Moreover, the great oligarchic families retained control over El Salvador's leading banks: *Banco Salvadoreño* (Guirola); *Banco de Comercio* (Dueñas, Regalado, Alvarez); *Banco Agrícola Comercial* (Escalante-Arce, Sol Millet); *Banco Capitalizador* (Alvarez, Borja, Natán, Alfaro). The control of this small class over the economy was not only very tight indeed – the 116 groups listed in Table 42 received 60 per cent of all accounted commercial income in 1979 – but also remained firmly based upon agro-exports.[11]

One can certainly locate mavericks such as the De Solas, who were prepared to countenance some reform and maintained links with the PDC, or Enrique Alvarez, who first questioned and then broke entirely with the traditions of his class, turning his dairy farm into a cooperative, attempting to introduce a land reform as minister of agriculture in the 1970s, and eventually becoming general secretary of the FDR, in which capacity he was executed by the right in November 1980. Equally, it would be incorrect to label the entire non-artisanal capitalist class as oligarchic; in 1978/9 medium-sized enterprises controlled 26 per cent of commerce and nearly a third of production in the service and construction sectors even if their share of the strategic coffee (8.9 per cent of cultivation; 15.2 per cent of processing), sugar (15.3 per cent) and cotton (14.6 per cent) sectors was very modest.[12] A good portion of the 3,350 firms that in terms of size at least may be labelled non-oligarchic might be expected to look favourably upon expansionary reforms and even explicitly anti-oligarchic policies insofar as they guaranteed property relations in general, which those of the PDC did, and strenuously. Nevertheless, just as occasional deviance from

Table 41: The Salvadorean Oligarchy II

*Families Possessing over 1,000 Hectares of Land, 1971**

Family	*Hectares*
Aguilar	1,488.2
Alfaro	6,138.8
Alvarez	4,602.7
Alvergue Gomez	2,048.5
Barrientos Sarmiento	1,530.6
Baum	3,034.4
Benecke	1,038.6
Borja	5,905.0
Bustamante	6,816.8
Carranza Martínez	1,545.8
Daglio	1,869.8
Dalton	1,480.4
Deininger	3,295.9

Family	*Hectares*
De Sola	2,581.2
Dueñas	5,713.0
Regaldo Dueñas	6,424.7
Gallardo	1,484.8
Giammattei	5,490.2
Guirola	13,682.6
Gutiérrez Diaz	2,464.5
Hernández	1,140.6
Langeneger de Bendix	1,452.5
Letona de Trigueros	1,152.0
Magana	13,778.1
Martínez	1,234.7
Meléndez	1,306.6
Mendoza de Cross	1,477.6
Menéndez Castro	1,176.8
Menéndez Lorenzo	1,546.5
Menéndez Salazar	1,968.6
Meza	4,247.1
Milla Sandoval	1,349.6
Orellana	2,717.9
Padilla y Velasco	1,626.5
Palomo	1,316.0
Parker	1,893.3
Peña Arce de Espinoza	1,054.8
Romero Bosque	1,831.1
Saca	2,072.0
Salaverría	7,808.0
Salguero Gross	1,091.0
Sandoval Lengeneger	1,175.8
Schmidt	1,054.1
Schonenberg	1,018.2
Sol Castellanos	2,864.8
Sol Millet	2,146.9
Urrutia Fantolli	1,555.3
Venutulo	3,005.8
Vilanova Kreitz	2,407.0

* Refers only to departments of Santa Ana; Sonsonate; Chalatenango; La Libertad; San Salvador; Cuscatlán.

Source: Colindres, 'Tenencia de la Tierra'.

Table 42: The Salvadorean Oligarchy III

Family Investment in Companies (number and capital) 1979

Family	*Firms*	*Capital (C mn)*
García Prieto	46	73.0
De Sola	69	145.0
Daglio	21	48.5
Guirola	52	122.5
Dueñas	44	80.1
Alvarez	95	167.3
Schwartz	19	47.5
Am Thor Daglio	9	49.2
Cohen Henríquez	23	42.7
Borgonovo	16	19.9
Alfaro Gastillo	22	37.9
Quinóñez	45	90.1
Sol Meza	11	22.0
Meza Hill	12	24.0
Henríquez	12	24.0
Paini	3	6.0
Llach-Schonenberg	6	12.0
Alfaro Morán	15	14.3
Alfaro Durán	12	2.5
Baldochi-Dueñas	22	72.7
Cristiani-Burkard	8	6.0
Borja-Nathan	33	33.3
Meza Ayau	104	239.0
Liebes	41	101.9
Salaverría	85	161.7
Jorge Mena Ariz	24	26.4
Schmidt	21	23.0
Regalado	135	440.2
González Guerrero	49	118.6
Ortiz Mancia	33	94.1
Aviles	6	12.0
Belismelis	5	10.0
López Harrison	10	20.0
Cartagena	4	8.0
Dalton	2	4.0
Escalón Nuñez	4	8.0
Soler	18	36.1
Nottebohn	8	16.0

Family	*Firms*	*Capital (C mn)*
Kriete	9	18.0
Duke	4	8.0
Palomo Sol	19	12.1
Pacas Trujillo	6	15.1
Avila Magaña	2	2.6
Aguilar Bustamante	4	5.1
Santi	5	52.6
Zabhatt Katan	4	3.1
Zelaya Castro	25	18.3
Bonilla	9	7.5
Tinoco Guirola	3	2.1
Von Hondeshausen	7	26.0
Vilanova Castro	7	18.4
Martínez Martínez	9	14.0
Barahona Munguía	4	6.6
Bustamante	8	27.4
Suvillaga Zaldivar	10	23.8
Vidri Miro	5	1.1
Funes	11	5.9
Meléndez	3	3.7
Panamá	4	1.5
Battle	6	8.1
Bollat Inffantossi	3	1.6
Wright	61	83.5
Homberger	21	14.2
Baum	19	44.0
Palomo	29	73.5
Schildknecht	15	9.0
McEntee	19	58.0
Sol Millet	26	90.0
Noltenius Velázquez	36	20.2
Sol (Hernández)	6	10.2
Keilhauer	9	24.3
Orellana	14	28.4
Avila Meardi	5	10.0
Araujo Esersky	14	13.3
Dutriz	11	4.3
Freund	47	227.3
Frenkel	21	29.4
Guerrero	23	16.6
Gadala María (Bartse)	21	7.8
Hasbún Payes	6	11.6
Membreno Baires	8	1.3

Family	*Firms*	*Capital (C mn)*
Mungía Rubio	5	2.9
Molins Payes	5	4.4
Nieto Costa	12	6.7
Ortiz López	7	1.4
Pascual Portet	6	2.2
Boet Rodríguez	11	6.4
Poma	18	35.4
Cuellar	5	3.5
Rivas Gallont	17	16.6
Bloch	4	2.1
Bahía	2	1.5
Miguel	9	6.9
Safie	13	24.1
Sagrera	13	21.9
Saca	5	3.8
Silhy	17	8.7
Simán	52	135.2
Vairo Riccio	8	5.4
Yarhi	23	42.1
Zamora Babich	4	1.6
Novoa	10	33.7
Stubig	12	6.6
Alfaro Morán	11	2.1
Giammattei	6	6.7
Duke López	3	5.1
Lima	3	3.1
Lassaly	4	19.5
Magaña	4	3.4
Schonenberg	3	4.3
Alfaro Vilanova	6	5.2
Hill (Arguello, Llach)	86	213.8
Jaspersen	29	40.4
Funes Hartman	10	24.6
Alfaro	23	26.0
Guttfreund	27	70.8

Exchange rate with US$ in 1979 = C2.50.

Source: Manuel Sevilla, 'El Salvador: La Concentración Económica y los Grupos de Poder', Cuaderno de Trabajo no.3, Centro de Investigación y Acción Social, Mexico, December 1984, p.37.

absolutely hidebound attitudes within the great bourgeoisie did not signal any major rupture in its unity, so also did medium capital lack the characteristics of a new, dynamic sector founded on manufacturing industry, in which its share of production was less than 18 per cent at the end of the 1970s.[13] Hence, although there was significant differentiation within the local capitalist class and this was echoed to some degree in the political field, it did not amount to a strategic intra-class challenge to the oligarchy. The PCS theorists failed to grasp that the diversification and expansion of the post-war epoch was based precisely on the agro-export sector and the concentration of landed wealth.

The unity of large capital persisted not only throughout the 1970s but also into the 1980s, when the banks were nationalized and a land reform tabled with compensation payable in industrial bonds. This contrasts with the case of Nicaragua, where the ruling class was historically ruptured, albeit not along the lines of a split between 'national' and 'oligarchic' factions. The challenge facing the Salvadorean bourgeoisie did not derive from internal differentiation but from class conflict generated by levels of exploitation and immiseration of the labouring masses more acute than anywhere else in the isthmus. At the same time, though, much of this conflict was channelled through the system of political domination over which the oligarchy possessed only indirect control.

The most obvious rebuttal of the PCS line on the 'national bourgeoisie' was to describe all large capital as oligarchic and to see it as strategically dependent upon the US. However, the latter characteristic does not flow naturally from the former, and it is of particular relevance to political developments in the late 1970s and early 1980s that the Salvadorean bourgeoisie was not only high unified but also depended less heavily on direct US investment than any other Central American ruling class, even including that of Nicaragua in the 1970s. It is tempting to overemphasize this factor and paint the oligarchy as primordially resistant to collaboration in modern ventures. That this was not the case can be seen in the appreciable rise in foreign investment in manufacturing in the 1960s (Table 15, p.204) and the fact that at the end of the 1970s only three of the fourteen firms operating in the San Bartolo free trade zone were Salvadorean, the nine US companies holding the great bulk of investment and employing all bar 400 of the 3,774 workers.[14] Nevertheless, the historically low profile of the US in El Salvador compared to that elsewhere was matched by strictly modest levels of investment (Table 1, p.60). Up to 1950 these generally exceeded those in Nicaragua in absolute terms but their relative weight was significantly less inside the larger Salvadorean economy. By 1977, when the Salvadorean economy was half as large again as that of Nicaragua, direct US investment in it stood at only $79 million against $108 million. Even after a 30 per cent increase over the following three years, US investment in El Salvador was only marginally greater than that in Nicaragua ($103 million against $89 million) and amounted to just over 10 per cent of the total for the region as a whole.[15] Thus, despite its high concentration of wealth and resistance to the most limited reforms, the entire local capitalist class could in a certain sense be labelled 'national'. Notwithstanding its longstanding orientation to the external market and the appreciable advantages reaped under the Alliance for Progress and CACM, it was completely unprepared for the scale of US intervention in economic as well as political terms following the crisis of 1979. The truculence with which it responded to this intromission was, then, not quite so extraordinary as has sometimes been thought.

After 1979 the oligarchy was able to exploit both its influence over the military and growing US acquiescence to sabotage many of the reforms that the latter insisted and the former gradually accepted should at least be kept on the statute book and given prominence in public relations. However, the scale of the crisis following the coup of October 1979 pushed the landed bourgeoisie into involvement in party politics for the first time in nearly fifty years. The *Alianza Republicana Nacionalista* (ARENA), established by Roberto D'Aubuissón in September 1981, can be viewed as the first serious and openly partisan political vehicle of the oligarchy since the early 1930s despite the fact that small rightist organizations challenged the officialist party of the military in elections from the 1940s onwards. In this sense we can talk of a major reorganization of the dominant bloc that had been forged in the crisis of 1932 although, as has been seen, this was subjected to important alterations in 1944, when the personalist regime was suppressed, and in 1948–50, when institutionalist rule was secured along with a commitment to statist and developmentalist motifs in political discourse and the introduction of limited flexibility in the mode of social control of the towns.

There is very little disagreement about the importance of 1932 and 1979 in Salvadorean politics although on occasions the military regime that collapsed in October 1979 is dated from September 1961 and the foundation of the *Partido de Conciliación Nacional* (PCN) as the officialist successor to the PRUD, set up by Colonel Osorio in 1950. While the democratic junta that held office for a few weeks in 1960–61 did represent a break of some importance in the system of control and it was only after 1963 that reformist parties were permitted to win some congressional seats through proportional representation, there was little profound difference between the PRUD and the PCN. The form of political domination between 1950 and 1979 may, therefore, be seen as essentially consistent even if marked by shifts in style and interrupted by periodic crises. It reserved control of government for the army, honoured the oligarchic veto over economic policy, preferred the forms of electoralism over those of dictatorship, and to this end allowed a modicum of opposition activity, although serious challenges to the regime were repressed without quarter and independent organization in the countryside remained outlawed. By the mid 1970s this system had become gravely debilitated not just by the social polarization that it failed to mediate but also by the sharp contradictions between appearance (rights of association and political opposition; free elections; government commitment to reform) and reality (proscription of the left and harassment of centrist forces; fraudulent elections; failure to implement any reform embargoed by the landed bourgeoisie). Yet, as in the case of the Somocista state, the general character of the regime should not be reduced to the state of atrophy and extreme violence that marked its final phase. This certainly represented a development of tendencies innate to it as well as a reprise of features of the 1932 crisis that had been suppressed rather than eradicated, but in many senses the government of El Salvador between 1950 and at least 1972 may be seen as more efficacious, stable and consistent than that of any other regional state except Costa Rica. By virtue of the rapid and institutional resolution of the political crises of the mid 1940s, the Salvadorean military evaded the traumas of the reform period in Guatemala, an unqualified counter-revolution, and the subsequent need for outright dictatorship and extreme violence. It provided a more stable basis for political administration than was achieved by the combination of Liberal and National parties and the army in Honduras, and it was able to sustain much greater institutional autonomy of the military and incorporation of opposition forces than was possible under the Somocista state. Although many of these distinctive characteristics had been liquidated by 1977, some elements were to persist through the crisis and assist the reconstruction of the dominant bloc in the midst of civil war during the 1980s.

The regimes of Colonels Oscar Osorio (1950–56) and José María Lemus (1956–60) benefited greatly from the buoyancy of the coffee market until 1957, when the value of exports was over five times that in 1945.[16] Together with the growth of cotton this permitted the state to expand its fiscal base, and government revenue increased fivefold between 1946 and 1954 with export taxes rising from 12.3 to 29.7 per cent of the total.[17] Under Osorio the policy of appropriating a greater proportion of the oligarchy's surplus was matched by a clampdown on renewed working-class activism under the *Ley de Defensa del Orden Democrático*, which provided a convenient counterbalance to the freedoms of the 1950 constitution and was applied with particular fierceness in 1952–53 when worker mobilization in San Salvador registered the influence of that in Guatemala. Moreover, the president, who was perhaps the most bonapartist of all the military leaders to follow Martinez, did not hold back from purging those elements of the officer corps who showed some sympathy for the experiment being undertaken by Arbenz (in whose overthrow Osorio played an auxiliary part) and neither did he baulk from imposing Lemus on both the oligarchy and those factions of the army which laboured under the illusion that the presidency was open to all rather than in the gift of the conclave of colonels favoured by the incumbent. Accordingly, Lemus won the 1956 poll with 93 per cent of the votes and the PRUD took all fifty-four seats in congress. Henceforth the nomination of the official candidate was the subject of tough bargaining within the high command but once he was confirmed the only means by which assumption of office could be impeded was by a coup.

The success of this first institutional handover in 1956 combined with continued economic growth to encourage Lemus to relax Osorio's restrictions; he dropped the *Ley de Defensa* and permitted greater union activity in the towns. In 1957 the *Confederación General de Trabajadores de El Salvador* (CGTS) was established with government support, but when its leadership demanded a new labour code, freedom to organize in the countryside and the realization of the reforms on the statute book, the regime joined with the US-controlled pan-American labour organization ORIT to set up the tame and predominantly mutualist *Confederación General de Sindicatos de El Salvador* (CGSS). This had a very limited following in the capital and remained loyal to the government for the next two decades.[18] Between 1951 and 1961 employment in the industrial sector rose from 51,700 to 85,000, and this expansion evidently required some form of vigilation other than repression, but the real period of growth was over the following decade when, according to some sources, the working class nearly doubled to 150,000.[19] In all events, when the Lemus regime came under pressure as the price of coffee fell after 1957 – the value of exports in 1960 dropping by 30 per cent to their 1951 level – it was less from the working class and the CGTS, obliged to operate in semi-clandestine manner within months of its birth, than from the middle class and the students. These sectors were not only aggravated by the government's failure to sustain the limited liberalization begun in 1956 but also enthused by the example of the Cuban revolution, which in 1959 appeared to be very much in the vein of the Salvadorean and Guatemalan movements of 1944. As with the working class, the real boom in university education came in the 1960s, during which student numbers rose from 3,000 to 30,000 and the number of courses from twenty-one to forty, although by 1972 more than half the student population was enrolled in the 'subversive' faculties of humanities and social science. This process took place under the aegis of the progessive rectorships of Fabio Castillo and Rafael Menjívar and provided a vital source of support for the left in the 1970s. Yet it was the movement of 1959–60 that brought the students to the centre of the political stage, realized the potential given by the winning of university autonomy in 1950 and, as in 1944, upset comfortable notions of the irrelevance of puerile idealism to adult affairs of state.[20]

Initially the students, organized in their union AGEUS, were protected to some degree by their middle-class status. However, when they started taking to the streets in support of the Cuban revolutionaries Lemus did not hesitate to crack down, the repression leading to riots in San Salvador on the eleventh anniversary of the 'revolution' of 1948. It was, though, to 1944 that the students and middle-class reformists harked back in their formation of the *Partido Revolucionario de Abril y Mayo* (PRAM), which became part of the *Frente Nacional de Orientación Cívica* (FNOC), established to contest the congressional and municipal elections of 1960. Despite the fact that FNOC was based on a very loose platform of democratic and social reforms, the regime constantly denounced it as 'Communist', 'Cuban-backed' and 'a threat to democracy'. Possibly as a result of attracting such appellations the Front won six mayoralties – including that of San Salvador – from the PRUD and had clearly generated much popular support when, in August 1960, the regime, lacking experience in handling reformist opposition and fearful of the influence of Cuba, declared martial law, arrested the university authorities and occupied the campus. Such a precipitate exclusion of a less than radical middle-class challenge and the reversion to dictatorial methods proved to be misjudged even in a political climate overshadowed by Cuba. Late in October a group of officers dismayed at the discontent caused by the repression and Lemus's increasingly erratic behaviour staged a bloodless coup and established a junta in which were included civilian reformists associated with or sympathetic to the students' campaign and FNOC.

Military coups are by their very nature decisive actions but their objective in removing the regime in power is frequently much more coherent than are their plans for what is to replace it. This was the case in October 1960, Lemus's overthrow being supported by many conservative officers grouped around Osorio who had become disenchanted with his successor's lack of consistency. All the same, it was the more liberal elements in the army, who believed that they were staging a repetition of 1944, that gained the initial advantage through popular support and were thus able to accept the demands of the civilian members of the junta for the holding of free elections. This, in effect, remained the sole stable policy of the fledgling government, which permitted the PCS to operate although the party was not formally legalized.[21] Once it became apparent to the officer corps as a whole that the restrictions imposed by Lemus were to be fully reversed rather than simply readjusted in a piecemeal manner, the bulk of the army swung behind a counter-coup organized by Colonel Julio Rivera, who succeeded with great ease in overthrowing the disorganized junta just twelve weeks after it had taken office. The collapse of this short democratic interlude mirrored the experience of 1944 and was to be echoed in a similarly abortive endeavour between October and December 1979, albeit under very different circumstances. Its lessons were registered more clearly by the military leadership than by those who had fleetingly held office. While Rivera and his colleagues henceforth accepted the need to grant the opposition a quota of elected representatives and some space for manoeuvre, this opposition went beyond exploiting the undoubted advantages proffered by such flexibility to believe that it included a genuine opportunity to take office. In encouraging such a presumption the PCN was certainly distinct from the PRUD, yet in ensuring that it would win all parliamentary and presidential elections it remained faithful to the example set by its forebear.

Like Osorio, Colonel Rivera proved to be a particularly prescient and powerful officer capable of harnessing both the military and the bourgeoisie to a political project which combined the requirements of social control with a number of finite concessions that appeared to many in the dominant bloc to be neither desirable nor immediately necessary. Rivera's leadership of the 1961 coup, resolute arbitration of differences within the officer corps, and establishment of the PCN in September laid the basis for the conversion of his presidency to 'constitutional' status in the election of March 1962. This, in turn, began a series of successful elections of senior officers to the presidency on the PCN ticket: Colonel Fidel Sánchez Hernández (Rivera's minister of interior) 1965–72; Colonel Arturo Molina (Sanchez's secretary) 1972–77; and General Carlos Humberto Romero (Molina's defence minister) 1977–79. Such continuism quite naturally proved reassuring to the landlords and the high command only over time, and if Rivera set in train a system that ten years later was described as 'repression with reforms', it started off under his leadership as one of 'reforms with repression' and proved decidedly uncomfortable for some elements of the ruling class. This was in good measure due to the influence of the Alliance for Progress, which prompted the new president to discard a fully counter-revolutionary strategy, describing his government as anti-Communist and anti-Cuba but 'not reactionary' since 'if we do not make the reforms the Communists will make them for us'.[22] It was the case that much of the reform programme remained a dead letter and none of the measures altered the basic structure of production. Yet the bourgeoisie was sufficiently harassed by the pronouncements of the new regime that in its first year, during which 325 decrees were passed, capital flight reached $30 million. There was minimal sympathy on the part of the oligarchy for the reduction of urban rents, introduction of a compulsory rest day for rural labourers and the establishment (after much debate) of an income tax law and exchange controls. Most of the measures related to the urban sector and could be evaded or compensated for without undue difficulty, but they did amount to a further increase of pressure from the state and some limitation on the oligarchy's economic mandate. This was gradually and grudgingly recognized as necessary, and while the regime was insulted and threatened, it was never actively destabilized. The shadow of Cuba and worries caused by the 1960 junta convinced sufficient numbers of the coffee aristocracy that, as one of its members put it, 'if Rivera goes down we all go down'.[23] The colonel tested the terms of the historic entente between army and landlords whilst sensibly desisting from pushing it to the limit in the tabling of an agrarian reform. He thereby secured his own survival but also left little room for manoeuvre to his successors.

In the wake of the 1961 coup and with the example of Cuba very much alive, the PCS turned momentarily to the tactic of guerrilla warfare in a poorly organized effort that was suppressed by the army without great difficulty. The principal shift in the pattern of politics during the 1960s – soon accepted and adhered to with remarkable persistence by the PCS – was not to guerrillaism, as in Guatemala and to a lesser degree in Nicaragua, but to a negotiation of the possibilities opened by the Alliance for Progress and Rivera's reversal of Lemus's excessive restriction of legal opposition. This conflicted with the heritage of 1932 but much less so with that of the prolonged oligarchic rule in the first decades of the century or with that of 1944. Moreover, although Lemus had rejected opposition claims to parliamentary representation, he had permitted it to win municipal polls in 1958 as well as 1960. The principal party to take advantage of that experiment was the *Partido de Acción Renovadora* (PAR), a middle-class reformist organization established in the 1940s that had accepted the restrictions of the post-1944 order and thus been allowed to continue as a vehicle for non-oligarchic civilist opinion. The events of 1960 created divisions within the party between those inclined to uphold tame objections to the status quo and those, led by Fabio Castillo (a prominent member of the 1960 junta), who sought more radical policies and structural reform. Moreover, in the wake of the coup against Lemus the PAR was presented with unprecedented competition in the formation of the PDC (November 1960), which was firmly anti-Communist, pledged to a temporal application of Catholic social doctrine and soon showed singular skill in orchestrating a largely urban and petty-bourgeois following around its programme for evolutionary social reform and authentic liberal democracy. It is a mark of the PDC's acceptability to the regime that in 1961 it placed agrarian reform only fifth on its list of seven priorities for the peasantry whilst concentrating upon the same programmes for urban improvement and support for the Alliance for Progress as did the PCN. Indeed, although it made fully free elections a central issue, the PDC was not without some support within the officer corps and, like many of its co-religionists elsewhere in Latin America, the party would retain at least a modest constituency within the military through the rest of its history. Whilst in the elections of 1961 the

PCN retained all congressional seats for itself, in those of 1964 it permitted the PDC fourteen and the PAR six (PCN – thirty-two). In the poll of 1966 it ceded twenty-one of the fifty-two seats to the opposition (PDC – fifteen; PAR – four; PPS – one; PREN – one); and in 1968 it respected the wishes of the electorate to an even greater degree in reducing its parliamentary majority to only two: PCN – twenty-seven; PDC – nineteen; PDS – four; MNR – two.[24] In 1967 the radical wing of the PAR was banned following a sharp rise in support in the presidential poll after the adoption of agrarian reform as a central demand and the split with the party's Conservative elements, now ensconced in the PPS. However, in 1968 the regime allowed the PAR's Social Democratic successor, the *Movimiento Nacional Revolucionario* (MNR), to take two seats and present a reformist programme discernibly more muscular and precise than that of the PDC.

The notion that these electoral contests were either fairly conducted or constituted a process of authentic political development must be subjected to sharp qualification.[25] Yet it is easy to throw the baby out with the bathwater and miss the fact that they not only served to reduce the image of a dictatorial regime but also engendered an expectation within the urban populace that electoral support for the opposition was a viable means of altering the social condition of the country and securing genuine political change. This sense was particularly prevalent in the capital, where the PDC leader José Napoleón Duarte won the mayoralty in 1964 and cultivated a strong constituency with a robust populist style that did full justice to his prominent position in the Latin American boy-scout movement. Allied with programmes for the reduction of pot-holes, construction of markets and provision of street lighting, Duarte's skills on the stump returned him to office for three consecutive terms and provided the Christian Democrats with a formidable political machine in San Salvador.[26] In 1966 the party won control of a third of the country's towns and did not lose that of the capital until 1976. As was soon to become very clear, such a quota of administrative responsibility was only conceded by the PCN on sufferance and was not permitted to exceed the limits of local authority or congressional opposition. Furthermore, it did little or nothing to impede the accelerating social deprivation and polarization outlined in chapter 5; even before the end of the 1960s this was propelling significant elements of the population well beyond the tepid recipes proffered by the PDC. Nonetheless, the presence of the party within the system gave some significance to the electoralist road absent in Nicaragua and Guatemala, and this was to continue even up to 1977, by which time the dominant bloc was relying heavily upon formal and informal repression in order to maintain public order and social control.

Renewed popular mobilization was even a contributory factor in the difficulties experienced by Rivera in obtaining the presidency for his dauphin Sánchez Hernández against the claims of officers who urged a more consistent commitment to either populism or repression in response to the expectations and discontent engendered by 'controlled democrary'.[27] In April 1967 the metal-workers of the Zacatecoluca-based Acero SA company, owned by the prominent Borgonovo family, went on strike for a wage rise, collective contract and improved medical facilities despite the fact that their union was linked to the officialist CGSS. Already worried by a series of stoppages in February and now threatened by solidarity strikes promised by the independent *Federación Unitaria Sindical Salvadoreña* (FUSS), set up in October 1965, the CGSS was obliged to follow the lead of its competitor. Although this sympathy action fell short of a general strike, 35,000 workers were supporting it by the time the Acero dispute was resolved, and it clearly signalled a resurgence of the labour movement. This was confirmed in 1968 with a national stoppage by the independent teachers' union ANDES against government educational 'reforms' supported by the official union. The strike was soon broken but the opposition union remained intact, received considerable popular support for a further strike in 1971, and was henceforth an important element of the popular bloc, rural teachers playing a particularly prominent part in the growing radicalism of the 1970s.

It is arguable that the Honduran regime of Colonel López Arellano had greater cause to stoke up the nationalist sentiment that led to the 'Football War' of 1969 than did that of Sánchez Hernández. As has been seen (chapter 5), the CACM had accelerated rather than curbed the disparities in commerce between the two states, Honduras's trade deficit with its more advanced neighbour reaching $5 million in the first six months of 1969 alone. Moreover, while the migration over previous decades of more than 150,000 Salvadoreans to Honduras was a major safety valve for the Salvadorean economy and a valuable source of labour and production for that of Honduras, these immigrants presented a vulnerable and not unpopular target for a hard-pressed government in Tegucigalpa. It is unlikely that even up to the last minute either regime sought to push matters as far as armed conflict, but in 1968–69 both evidently saw some incentive to increase nationalist propaganda and engage in chauvinist brinkmanship in order to reduce domestic political pressure. The eventual escalation of this into a hundred hours of fighting across a disputed border in the summer of 1969 was certainly a singular occurrence in modern Central American history and marked an important watershed in the politics of both states.

The June 1969 soccer matches in the heats for the 1970 World Cup exacerbated effusions of chauvinism by the military governments but these games were merely the final theatrical manifestations of a conflict that had been subjected to constant manipulation since mid 1968 when the Honduran regime had revived agrarian reform. In April 1969 letters were sent to Salvadorean settlers giving them thirty days in which to 'return' their lands to the state for distribution to its citizens. This deliberately provocative act greatly sharpened a longstanding diplomatic dispute over sections of the border between the two countries and was compounded by instances of persecution of the immigrant community by groups linked to the Honduran regime and military. By the spring of 1969 this harassment had succeeded in driving tens of thousands of Salvadoreans back to their country of origin as dispossessed refugees.[28] As incidents, both real and imagined, during the football competition excited widespread jingoism, neither government made any move to restrain extravagant rumours and Sánchez Hernández even filed a complaint of 'genocide' with the Inter-American Human Rights Commission in late June. The reluctance of the military regimes to back off in such a situation is perfectly understandable, but what was remarkable about the campaign was the degree to which the opposition supported it. In El Salvador this enabled Sánchez to form an all-party bloc, the *Frente de Unidad Nacional*, and exploit the conflict to reduce internal discontent. On 24 June the PDC called for military action and Duarte made use of his government of the capital to organize civilian patrols and release troops for action. Even the illegal PCS capitulated before the predictable wave of popular belligerence caused by the expulsions, and despite initially opposing the warmongering, the party eventually encouraged its student militants to enlist. Significantly, the Honduran party took a similar stance, both organizations coming to perceive the conflict as one representing the interests of the 'national bourgeoisie' and the 'genuine patriotism of the armed forces' on either side.[29] In the event, the Salvadorean military crossed the border on 14 July and encountered little serious resistance from the smaller and poorly prepared Honduran land forces. However, after three days' fighting – during which well over 1,000 Hondurans and 100 Salvadoreans were killed – the invading force found itself operating with over-extended lines whilst Salvadorean installations had suffered from a number of efficient bombing raids by the superior enemy airforce. Resolute diplomatic intervention by Guatemala, alarmed at such a major crisis in the regional dominant bloc at a time when it was still facing a guerrilla threat, laid the basis for an OAS-controlled ceasefire that both sides eagerly accepted.

The strategic setbacks suffered by the Salvadorean government as a result of the war were considerable. The country lost trade worth $23 million in addition to $20 million spent on the war and a further $11 million over the next two years in replenishing its arsenal. Less directly, both the military and the bourgeoisie had to adjust to the withdrawal by Honduras from both the CACM and CONDECA, which as a result went into effective abeyance. Perhaps most important of all, the regime was confronted with the political and economic consequences of a rapidly accumulated refugee population in excess of 100,000 that understandably harboured high expectations of resettlement and economic opportunity after its travails and the fact that a war had ostensibly been fought on their behalf. The complete insufficiency of government programmes, sharply deteriorating conditions for the rural labour force, and the absence of employment possibilities in an industrial sector no longer in expansion hit the refugees with particular force. Already politicized by their experience in Honduras, which frequently included work on the unionized banana plantations, as well as that of dislocation, many returned émigrés settled in the *tugurios* (shanty-towns) on the outskirts of San Salvador, bolstering the army of impoverished labourers in the 'informal sector' who were to the fore of popular mobilization over the following years. Thus, despite the fact that the Sánchez Hernández regime was able to take full advantage of the wave of nationalism excited by the war, the political effects of this over the longer term were at least comparable to those of the earthquakes elsewhere in the region.

The war caused a political hiatus that was not purely superficial, insofar as Sánchez felt confident enough to put a limited agrarian reform bill on the government agenda and even offered the PDC a subordinate role in the administration. However, the oligarchy, which was in particularly bullish mood and expanding its estates as a result of the high coffee price, moved speedily to obstruct the government's effort at emulating the (very much easier) reformist policies of its Honduran counterpart. Equally, the PDC rejected the coalition overtures out of confidence that it could win the poll of March 1972. This prospect did indeed appear reasonable to the extent that the party had both increased its popularity and agreed upon the formation of an electoral front with the MNR, which despite losing its congressional seats in 1970 still had an important following within the professional middle class, and the *Unión Democrática Nacionalista* (UDN). Formed in 1969, the UDN stood clearly to the left of the other two organizations and while it incorporated some leaders of the old PAR, it was at root a front for the PCS that circumvented the party's continued outlaw status and Duarte's much proclaimed refusal to collaborate with Communists. The UDN's appeal to the labour movement was broader than that of the PCS since it operated on the basis of a minimum programme in which basic democratic demands were given prominence and Marxist discourse kept distinctly sparse. Thus, it both avoided the impedimenta of open Communist affiliation and contributed towards unprecedentedly broad support for the new electoral alliance, the *Unión Nacional Opositora* (UNO), which fielded Duarte and MNR leader Guillermo Ungo as candidates against Colonel Arturo Molina for the PCN. The formation of such an alliance was little less than obligatory for a reformist opposition that could no longer afford the luxury of internal sectarian competition if it was to keep the electoralist strategy alive and retain the initiative against the more radical forces that were beginning to emerge at the turn of the 1960s.

Although Molina was also challenged from the right, in the shape of General José Alberto Medrano, patronized by some of the most reactionary elements of the landed bourgeoisie, the UNO campaign compelled the PCN apparatus to go to exceptional lengths to ensure the victory of its candidate.[30] Having failed to cow Duarte's exuberant meetings with a series of physical attacks, the official party resorted to prohibiting media coverage of the count once early returns showed the opposition to have a 62,000 vote lead in the capital and some 54 per cent of the poll at the national level. The next public announcement to be made was that Molina had won by 9,844 votes or just 1.3 per cent of the total. Aware of the risk that he was courting, the president-elect made the ingenuous offer of a recount, but the UNO leaders insisted upon completely fresh elections and threatened a general strike should it not be conceded. Caught off balance once again, the PCN cut its losses and convened a special session of congress to have Molina ratified ten days before the appointed time in a ceremony boycotted by all other parties. Several days later UNO called for the casting of spoilt ballots in the congressional and municipal elections, which were also predictably won by the PCN. Yet despite rising incidents of violence, the UNO leadership signally failed to act upon its strike threat and seemed at a loss as to how to react once outmanoeuvred in the electoral sphere, in which it had invested all its political capital.[31]

It was in such conditions of paralysis on the part of the legal opposition and disconcerting indications of guerrilla activity in the capital that a faction of the army's officer corps staged a coup on 25 March. The rebels, led by Colonels Benjamín Mejía and Manuel Antonio Nuñez and Major Pedro Guardardo, were largely backed by junior officers stationed in the capital and had no obvious ties with UNO despite attacking the electoral fraud and urging the political opposition to rally to their cause. Once he was convinced that it was not a rightist rising led by the mercurial Medrano, Duarte agreed to offer his support. However, the rebels had no organized following outside San Salvador, refused to distribute arms to civilians, and were rapidly confronted with a counter-attack by superior forces that succeeded in suppressing the rising within a matter of hours and after the loss of a hundred lives. This counter-offensive was based on the paramilitary forces, particularly the National Guard, which was not equipped with such heavy weaponry as the army but included many veterans and, by dint of its much more direct role in maintaining social control, was unambiguously reactionary in political disposition. No less than in the 1930s and 1940s, the National Guard, supplemented by the *Policía de Hacienda* and smaller units, provided the oligarchy with something of a safeguard against the political excesses of the institutionalist ethic within the army, and this was to be a factor of secondary but consistent importance over the following decade.[32] In 1972 it contributed directly to the suppression not only of military dissidence but also of many popular expectations vested in legal opposition and the strategy of electoralism. As a badly beaten Duarte was put on a plane into exile it became evident that the rules of the game established by the PCN and the military high command in the early 1960s had not so much been altered as clarified: elections could be contested but not won by the opposition. As in 1961, the restorationist counter-coup did not presage an immediate round of restrictions and general repression. Indeed, it even prompted Molina to engage in a policy of graduated rapprochement with the opposition. But the failure of UNO proved to be critical in advancing the radical left, which rejected the stance of the legal opposition as 'parliamentary cretinism', as well as the independent mass organizations, for which the parties of reform offered little more in terms of finite resources and much less in terms of combativity than the burgeoning revolutionary currents. For the PDC, by contrast, the traumatic experience of 1972 was taken to show the importance of cooperating as far as possible with the military in order to preserve a quota of power.

The System under Challenge

The fraud of 1972 weakened the strategy of electoralism more than it did the institutional autonomy of the PCN from the landed bourgeoisie; the following four years witnessed appreciable conflict within the oligarcho-military axis. Nevertheless, from the mid 1970s – and in particular from 1977 – the distinctive features of Salvadorean government were rapidly reduced so that by the end of the decade it had become an unqualified dictatorship fully comparable to those in Nicaragua and Guatemala. In view of the degree of immiseration and social polarization that prevailed in the country this development can scarcely be deemed remarkable. The indices for the deterioration of the human condition further than that anywhere else in Central America have already been seen. This statistical evidence has not been seriously contested by right-wing commentators, and it is significant that in the 1980s even a government as reactionary as that of Ronald Reagan felt constrained to pay at least lip-service to economic reforms in El Salvador that it regarded as anathema in general. Indeed, the remarkable feature of the Salvadorean experience is less the emergence of dictatorship, widespread social violence and civil war than the fact that they took so long to develop. This was undoubtedly due in part to the flexibility of the dominant bloc, but it also corresponded to the legacy of 1932 and the efficiency of the system of coercive control in the countryside that, in the hands of the National Guard and its vigilante network, remained largely unaffected by the vagaries of national politics. In this regard, the escalation of class conflict and consolidation of a political challenge on the part of the popular forces from the mid 1970s was part of a process in which electoral contests played only a secondary role, tending intermittently to accelerate a movement dynamized by oppression and exploitation.

The combination of these factors meant that when popular organization did develop it took a particularly profound form. It challenged not only the oligarchy and the repressive state apparatus but also much of the reformist politics that had been permitted greater scope to establish and make good its claims than in either Guatemala or Nicaragua. Thus, in a sense, the pattern of Salvadorean politics may be said to have encompassed a broader set of options prior to the outbreak of guerrilla war than either of the other two states, at least over the period since 1954. This fact did not preclude subsequent moments of feverish manoeuvre – especially between October 1979 and August 1980 and within the dominant bloc between 1982 and 1984 – yet it ensured that these took place within a wider war of position in which fundamental class issues were directly at stake and which was contested by protagonists for whom the real scope for negotiated alliances was much smaller than that which existed in Nicaragua between 1978 and 1980.

The development of independent organizations and radical currents within the labour movement was already underway before 1972, but in the countryside and *tugurios* it accelerated in the years following the election so that by the time of the 1977 poll and the subsequent descent into dictatorship one can talk of an organizationally coherent popular movement, albeit one still riven by sharp programmatic differences. The earliest signs of a shift away from both the pro-government bodies and those attached to the PCS appeared inside the manufacturing working class, within which the number of unions grew from 80 in 1966 (24,124 members) to 127 in 1975 (64,186 members). Although these numbers are not in themselves very large, such an increase in less than a decade was most impressive. Furthermore, it should be borne in mind that by 1975 the organized Salvadorean working class was nearly three times the size of that in pre-revolutionary Nicaragua and possessed far fewer individual, plant-based unions. This should not be interpreted as signifying a qualitatively different class structure, and indeed the percentage of the Salvadorean labour force engaged in independent commerce was much higher than that in Nicaragua (14.1 against 7.1 per cent). Nonetheless, the higher profile of manufacturing workers (26.4 against 20 per cent) and the lower dependence upon employment in the service sector (8.1 against 10.9 per cent) combined with the fact that the Salvadorean urban labour force was nearly twice the size of that in Nicaragua gave the working class an appreciably stronger profile in both society and political life.[33]

Initially much of the union growth was due to the activity of the PCS-dominated FUSS, which pushed the *oficialista* CGSS into competitive recruitment. Some also resulted from the small PDC-sponsored *Unión de Obreros Católicos* (UNOC), the urban vanguard of a Catholic syndicalism that was to have greater purchase in the countryside. In 1968 the 'yellow' confederation lost the support of the important transport and construction workers' federation FESINCONTRANS, which by 1975 was the largest national union with a membership of 20,000. Between 1971 and 1976 the membership of the CGSS fell from fifty-three to forty unions (19,470 to 12,592 members), its share of the organized labour force dropping from 42 to 19 per cent.[34] Yet the Communists were also placed under pressure, FESINCONTRANS rejecting their overtures and the important FENASTRAS federation, based upon the power workers (STECEL), passing into the control of the radical left. The PCS held on to its base in the textile and food industries (FESTIAVETCES) but it could depend upon the allegiance of only a part of one of the new anti-government confederations spawned in the 1970s, the *Confederación Unificada de Trabajadores Salvadoreños* (CUTS), which included FUSS and FESTIAVETCES. Moreover, the party had no following inside the *Comité Coordinador Sindical* (CCS), set up in 1975 by radicals centred on ANDES and the resurgent *campesino* movement, of which the Communist union ATACES soon proved to be only a minor component. Thus, by 1976 the government had lost any significant support amongst the organized working class and the PCS had been effectively surpassed as the main political force of proletarian opposition. This latter phenomenon owed much to the Communists' continued membership of UNO through the UDN and their reluctance to adopt a combative line precisely when real wages in the industrial sector were falling for the first time in ten years.[35]

In many respects the growth of independent organization and radicalism amongst the *campesinado* from the early 1970s was more remarkable than such developments in the urban sphere since it brought to an end forty years of quietude and undermined the prohibition of rural unions that had been enforced since 1932 and codified in the 1950 constitution. The effective collapse of this historic bulwark of the oligarchic order led the Salvadorean rural masses to take a much more prominent part in political struggle than was the case in Nicaragua, encouraging the view that the revolution in El Salvador was primarily a peasant movement. The general economic position of the Salvadorean peasantry was worse than that in Nicaragua for although in 1963 nearly one-third of rural families in Nicaragua were landless against 15 per cent in El Salvador, their average wages were significantly higher and by the mid 1970s the level of landlessness in El Salvador had surpassed that in Nicaragua. It should also be noted that the average farm size in El Salvador was much smaller even in 1963 (7 hectares against 37.4) and average rural family income barely 60 per cent of that in Nicaragua; the profile of a 'middle peasantry' was markedly more modest (farms up to 35 hectares accounting for 20 against 44 per cent of cultivated land). Just as in the case of the urban sector, these differences were important in determining the more 'social' or class-based character of the Salvadorean popular movement. It is, all the same, difficult to identify a determinate 'peasant revolution' in El Salvador, and the attribution of a predominantly peasant character to the revolutionary movement as a whole should be treated with great caution.

It is certain that at no point between 1970 and 1987 was there a consolidated rural insurrection combining strikes, occupation of *fincas* and attacks on state institutions as in 1932. Moreover, in the western zones of the country there were relatively few instances of any of these phenomena even after the outbreak of civil war. On the other hand, it would be entirely erroneous to derive from this the conclusion that there existed simply a state of generalized discontent in the countryside open to manipulation by the guerrillas. By 1978 at least, it is possible to perceive a revolutionary movement that manifested appreciable political and social autonomy from that in the towns and provided critical support for urban mobilization. Furthermore, while this movement did not engage in a strategy of coordinated insurrectionism – to which both the example of 1932 and the condition of the rural masses provided major obstacles – it certainly challenged in direct and often violent fashion the economic power of the landed bourgeoisie and the state apparatus. A great many of the troops of the FMLN were peasants radicalized in the 1970s, and it is a salient feature of the Salvadorean revolutionary movement that for most of the period after 1980 it has been able to sustain guerrilla warfare in a countryside which from a purely logistical perspective is badly suited to such a campaign. The waxing and waning of military fortunes in this war have tended to produce overly precipitate and inflexible assessments of the social nature of the struggle just as the erosion of the 1932 order in the countryside during the 1970s has sometimes been mistakenly interpreted as a uniform rupture of control and adoption of radical politics. Nevertheless, uneven though it was, this rupture was undeniably critical, nurturing the growth of a powerful radical current within the rural masses that altered the national balance of political forces and subsequently provided the basis for localized peasant 'revolutions', particularly in the north and east of the country.

From the mid 1960s the economic condition of the rural population as a whole was patently entering a state of crisis, principally through the rate of dispossession of subsistence lands. It was particularly in the central zones (San Salvador; Cuscatlán; Chalatenango; Cabañas; San Vicente), where many migrant seasonal workers were settled, that this economic pressure developed into a political struggle. The vanguard of a resurgent peasant unionism appears to have been the 'semi-proletariat' which still had some access to land – now largely on the basis of money rather than labour rent –

but was increasingly obliged to rely upon harvest waged labour in order to survive. Inevitably, the profile of landless labourers was also high, but in that area for which more than impressionistic evidence is available (northern San Salvador; Cuscatlán and Chalatenango) it is apparent that a 'middle peasantry' with few tight links to the labour circuit on the commercial *fincas* was not a major force in the radical movement.[36] At a national level it is difficult to identify precise socio-economic characteristics behind peasant activism since this was very low in the coffee heartland of the west, uneven and relatively late to emerge in the departments of Usulután and San Miguel, and yet little less advanced in the backward eastern provinces of Morazán and La Unión than in the central region. Evidently regional variation as well as political conditions had an important influence even if one may confidently identify a general economic dynamic in the combination of pressure on subsistence plots, lack of opportunities for seasonal employment, and the highly exploitative conditions in which this was undertaken.

As in Nicaragua, the organizational impetus for rural unionization was closely tied to the pastoral work of the Catholic Church, which can be said to have had a more profound impact in the countryside of El Salvador than in that of any other Central American nation during the 1970s. The Church was by no means alone in fostering some form of limited communal and cooperative organization in the 1960s; the *Unión Comunal Salvadoreña* (UCS) was funded and directed by the US labour agency AIFLD and incorporated some 70,000 nominal members in its network of closely regulated and apolitical mutualist cooperatives by 1975.[37] However, it was through the *Federación Cristiana de Campesinos Salvadoreños* (FECCAS) that the germs of independent organization were established, the influence of the progressive clergy and then the radical left converting what began in 1965 as a largely confessional body of mutualist character into a vehicle for both economic and political militancy by the mid 1970s. The initial scope of this movement can easily be overemphasized; in 1976 FECCAS had only 66 *bases* and 3,500 affiliates, and it still lacked a fully national organization by the end of the decade although it had by then reduced dependency upon the kinship ties and extra-political factors that marked its early years. Yet once it had laid firm roots and entered into an alliance with the *Unión de Trabajadores del Campo* (UTC) based in San Vicente and Chalatenango, it expanded its influence very rapidly, repudiated the politics of the PDC (around which it had initially been organized) and rejected those of the PCS (with which it had a fleeting alliance, through ATACES, in the early 1970s). By 1978 the combined forces of FECCAS and the UTC were still less than the predominantly passive membership of the UCS but the new united organization – *Federación de Trabajadores del Campo* (FTC) – was indisputably a leading force in the popular movement with an influence well beyond its direct affiliates.

The original driving force behind much of this movement was the new evangelism, and this would retain a very strong resonance in both organizational and ideological terms even as the union adopted the motifs of secular radicalism. Although El Salvador possessed far less clergy per head of population than did Nicaragua (one per 7,600 in 1960 against one per 4,200), the orders, and especially the Jesuits, were quick to respond to the innovations of Vatican II so that by the mid 1970s there were at least 15,000 lay catechists, many of whom lived in those areas most affected by the economic crisis.[38] It is clear that in 1973–74 progressive priests played a direct role in assisting the organization of peasant strikes in the Aguilares-Suchitoto region. This, however, was less important than their pedagogical and evangelical work, which raised the general level of education and inquiry amongst a congregation much expanded through the activity of the *delegados de la palabra* and the repudiation of those elements of individualism and spiritual resignation at the core of traditional Catholicism. To the secular eye this might appear as merely a partial demystification but it destabilized the deep-seated proclivity of the peasantry for a highly cautious vision of the world based upon expectations of 'limited good'. It was, then, far from inconsequential that in the 1970s thousands of impoverished rural workers in Cabañas, Cuscatlán and Chalatenango were reciting a credo that marginalized adoration and invested spirituality with a combative vision of the material world: 'I believe in a God of justice, love and peace and not in a God who is in the clouds, in the hearts of the exploiters, a God of exploitation, a God converted into cash, a God turned into propaganda. Nor do I believe in a God celebrated with fireworks nor with traditional ceremonies.'[39]

Unsurprisingly, the practice of pastoralism forged on such liturgies both encouraged disputes within the ranks of the clergy and engendered first suspicion about certain priests and then outright hostility towards progressive evangelism as a whole on the part of the landlords and security forces. In the late 1970s this was to take the form of singular persecution, but long before this the burgeoning peasant movement faced a more profound impediment in the existence of ORDEN, a formidable popular organization in the countryside that defended the oligarchic order under the direction of the National Guard and the semi-official auspices of the state. Established in the early 1960s and a significant force in the rural areas by the end of the decade, ORDEN was largely based upon ex-conscripts organized, in the words of its longstanding commander General Medrano, 'to disseminate democratic ideology to the peasants and workers of the countryside, to make a barrier against the attempts of the Communists to provoke subversion amongst the rural populace'.[40] While perhaps as many as 100,000 peasants were drawn into a loose affiliation determined by petty favours, distribution of cash and foodstuffs and protection against repression, many such 'members' played only a marginal role, making periodic reports on persons of dubious loyalty in their villages, attending PCN meetings and generally supporting the apparatus of national government and local landlord power. A much more modest number was actively enlisted in the 'cantonal patrols' and engaged in the vigilante activity that first emerged in attacks on the PAR in 1966, became prominent in the suppression of the 1968 teachers' strike, and was a permanent feature of conflict in the countryside through the 1970s. ORDEN was openly patronized by Sánchez Hernández, who was proclaimed its 'Supreme Chief', and it was fully integrated into the military intelligence system. As violent conflict grew in the late 1970s its goons were drawn into the penumbra of the death squads, but the mass character of the organization should not be minimized on this count, and some elements of the left viewed it with some justification as the cornerstone of a movement with marked fascist characteristics.[41] This perspective underrated the degree of superficial survivalist compliance with a particularly coercive form of clientelism on the part of the peasantry, yet it was undoubtedly the case that the existence of ORDEN increased the violence within rural communities – by no means consistently along class lines – and deepened the civil character of the war of the 1980s. No comparable organization existed in Nicaragua, where the *jueces de mesta* lacked a stable social base, or even in Guatemala, where the military patronized similar bodies only in certain regions during the 1960s and where the 'civilian patrols' of the 1980s possessed a more artificial and regimented character.

The emergence of new political forces on the radical left was associated with rather than directly linked to the expansion of popular organization in the first years of the 1970s. Well before the end of the decade these revolutionary groups had established close organizational and programmatic affiliation with a series of plebeian fronts, blocs and leagues drawn largely from the new union formations and mass associations. Like the FSLN, very few of the radical groups took the form of political parties, retaining the structure and nomenclature of military organization up to and beyond the formation of the FMLN in late 1980.[42] This in no sense reduced their various claims to a vanguard role and neither did it preclude sharp clashes over political as well as military questions. Indeed, conservative analysts consistently emphasize the sectarian nature of the Salvadorean left, generally ignoring the scope of the organization of ordinary working and poor people in which it was involved well before the outbreak of fighting.[43] A pattern of factionalism is indubitably evident even after the establishment of the FMLN, which should be seen as the equivalent of the reunification of the FSLN in 1978–79 rather than its initial foundation in 1961. However, the depiction of such sectarianism as primarily, if not exclusively, determined by the innate need of small radical groups to scrap over esoteric points of doctrine is self-serving and misses, either wilfully or otherwise, the importance of its wider historical context. The fractiousness of the Salvadorean left derived principally from the need to compete in a wider political arena than anywhere else in Central America and certainly than in Nicaragua. Although the Salvadoreans resolved the question of popular organization much more comprehensively than did the Sandinistas, they engaged in similar disputes over the forms of military strategy and the class nature of the struggle. Indeed, many of these issues preoccupied the radical movement throughout Latin America and were reproduced in a generally unremarkable form in El Salvador. It is, though, important that the revolutionary left had to contend with a Communist party that was unusually influential in Central American terms as well as competing with the advocates of electoralism which, until 1977 at least, represented a more substantial challenge to the policy of armed struggle than in the other isthmian countries where any such strategic competition obtained. When combined with the analytical and tactical difficulties presented by the partial yet real divergences between the oligarchic economy and the management of the state, these factors necessarily produced a variety of views that went beyond the differing political origins of the groups on the left. Thus, the eventual unity forged inside the FMLN and FDR may be seen as a major achievement of political initiative.

The radical left had its political origins in dissidence within both the PCS and the PDC during the late 1960s. The PCS was the first to undergo internal crisis with a revolt against the 'bourgeois democratic path' and the class analysis that underpinned it. Opposition to both claims for the existence of a 'national bourgeoisie' and the trend towards electoralism (which had yet to be fully consolidated through membership of UNO) took outward form in the party's fourth congress in 1970. This discontent was sharpened by the ambiguous position adopted by the PCS over the war with Honduras and its support for the Soviet invasion of Czechoslovakia in 1968. Yet at root the division may be ascribed to the party's effective repudiation of armed struggle, a repudiation that was not only conditioned by the scars of 1932, the debacle of the early 1960s and the scope for legal opposition, but also the tendency to associate all guerrilla warfare with *foquismo*. In this PCS support for Moscow in the Sino–Soviet split may well have played a part by marginalizing the importance of 'Asiatic' traditions of revolutionary warfare.[44] Although it is hard to identify more than very occasional flourishes of Maoism within the revolutionary left over the subsequent period, during which international issues did not have a high profile, it is the case that pro-Soviet sentiment was very thin on the ground outside the ranks of the PCS.[45] The challenge of the party line in 1969–70 was defeated without great difficulty, and it was only after a decade under the leadership of the new secretary general, Jorge Shafik Handal, that the PCS began to shift towards the positions of the rest of the left, finally embracing the armed struggle in 1980. As late as the spring of 1979, after two years of dictatorship and with popular mobilization at an unprecedented pitch, its seventh congress reaffirmed the centrality of the 'bourgeois democratic path' in a document that made a two-line reference to 'the defeat' of 1932.[46] The result of such fidelity to electoralism was that in the 1980s the PCS contingents in the FMLN were dwarfed in terms of numbers, military skill, and a popular base in the countryside by those of the rest of the left.

The split from the party in 1970 was led by its former secretary general, the veteran union leader Salvador Cayetano Carpio, who along with other prominent cadres set up the *Fuerzas Populares de Liberación – Farabundo Martí* (FPL), publicly established late in 1972. The central policies of the FPL revolved around a rejection of electoralism and the existence of a national bourgeoisie, and a commitment to an unambiguously class-based politics founded on the strategy of 'prolonged people's war' for which the example of Vietnam was central.[47] While the FPL's programme was clearly based on a repudiation of most of the positions of the PCS and gave much greater prominence to the role of the poor peasantry, it shared with the Communist perspective a highly critical view of the 'petty-bourgeois *foquismo*' and 'ultra-leftism' of the other new armed organization, the *Ejército Revolucionario del Pueblo* (ERP), established in 1972 by radical dissidents from the PDC. In line with many youthful renegades from the regional Christian Democratic movement in this period, the founders of the ERP were largely of middle-class and student background, greatly influenced by the example of Cuba and, lacking significant experience of work inside the popular movement, drawn to the more adventurist aspects of guerrillaism. Unlike the FPL, which was formed on the basis of an already developed critique of the PCS and suffered few major internal disputes in its early years, the initial period of the ERP's existence was marked by an erraticism in policy and organization. Although the most unrefined variants of insurrectionism were rejected within a couple of years and dalliance with a species of Maoism rapidly discarded, the ERP only stabilized its strategy after undergoing a major crisis early in 1975.[48] This was provoked by the emergence of backing for a less adventurist and militarist policy and demands for greater attention to be paid to building mass support and tactical alliances. It was perhaps significant that the leader of this tendency, the historian and poet Roque Dalton, was not only older than many of his comrades, but also a maverick – he had previously been a militant of the PCS and shared some strategic positions with the FPL (although this did not apply to the principal policy at issue, that of 'national resistance' built upon a broad front against Fascism). Accused by the ERP leadership of 'right-wing revisionism' and being a CIA agent, Dalton was submitted to a most cursory and cynical pretence of 'revolutionary justice' and summarily executed.[49]

The outrage caused within the movement by the assassination of a distinguished and internationally renowned revolutionary intellectual forced the FPL to intervene in order to avert a bloodbath whilst a sizeable faction of the organization left to establish *Resistencia Nacional* (RN; sometimes known as *Fuerzas Armadas de Resistencia Nacional* or FARN). The cost of this 'incident' for the ERP was high; it could not be accounted an aberrance committed by callow youths deranged by militarism since it had been formally sanctioned by the leadership and provided with a complete, if bizarre, political rationale. Some purges followed and a sop was offered to the demands for broader organizational work in the formation of the *Partido Revolucionario Salvadoreño* (PRS), but this never developed beyond existence on paper and the ERP retained its insurrectionist maximalism, giving a lower priority than the other groups to the political tasks of building the opposition movement.[50] Such an orientation, which was to result in the ERP developing into the most powerful of the guerrilla groups, had only a superficial similarity with that of the *Terceristas* in Nicaragua. It certainly incubated appreciable pragmatism in terms of social policy, but the relatively low profile given to the tenets of orthodox Marxism was matched by a fierce sectarianism on the military question that greatly limited potential for the type of alliances at the heart of *Tercerista* strategy.

Resistencia Nacional not only responded to the ERP with predictably sharp attacks on *foquismo* but also criticized the FPL for its 'proletarian purism' and 'divisionism' although the RN clearly aligned itself with the Marxist–Leninist tradition and disparaged the PCS as right-wing and opportunist.[51] Less resolutely attached to class politics than the FPL or to military vanguardism than the ERP, RN identified the PCN regime as quasi-Fascist and held that the formation of a broad anti-fascist front was a central requirement for the popular movement. Its predominantly tactical and defensive orientation clearly begged many questions of a guerrilla organization with the objective of taking state power. On the other hand, this more graduated approach was a key element in RN's ability to break the traditional division between armed vanguard and mass organization through the establishment of an alliance with the *Frente de Acción Popular Unificada* (FAPU), set up in 1974. FAPU's incorporation of ANDES (teachers), FECCAS (*campesinos*), FUSS and FENASTRAS made it a body of considerable influence within the labour movement. Nevertheless, its informal alliance with RN soon exacted a high organizational price since adherence to the positions of the ex-*erpistas* produced a split within the space of a year.[52] Rejecting the thesis that the principal danger was a distant fascist faction of the dominant bloc and insisting that the ruling class possessed a united and coherent position that required an aggressive class-based response, first FECCAS and then ANDES left FAPU, forming the nucleus of the new *Bloque Popular Revolucionario* (BPR). The BPR soon established links with the FPL similar to those between FAPU and RN, echoing the positions of its politico-military ally in fierce attacks on the PCS, UNO, FAPU and the ERP for variously misleading the masses with their illusions in electoralism, false characterization of the bourgeoisie, and dangerous insurrectionism.[53] Experiencing particular success in recruiting within a student movement radicalized by the 1975 military occupation of San Salvador's main campus (in response to demonstrations against expensive government patronage of the 'Miss Universe' contest), the BPR also attracted numbers of equally active secondary school students with its sharp radical line. Within a comparatively short period of time affiliated membership had reached 60,000, making the *Bloque* the largest and most socially representative left-wing organization in the country until unification of all the radical groups in 1980.[54]

These precedents eventually obliged the ERP, which like its guerrilla counterparts was at this stage capable of only very minor operations such as kidnapping, bank raids and economic sabotage, to follow their example. In 1977 it duly patronized the *Ligas Populares – 28 de Febrero* (LP–28), named after the popular mobilization against the fraud of that day.[55] On a much more minor scale, the small *Partido Revolucionario de Trabajadores Centroamericanos* (PRTC), founded in Costa Rica in 1975 and openly active in El Salvador only from 1979, attracted a cluster of organizations around its attachment to a regional struggle with a strategy that was similar to that of the FPL but notably more flexible in terms of political fronts.[56] Neither the PRTC nor the small *Movimiento de Liberación Popular* (MLP) that it set up in 1979 had much impact prior to the onset of civil war. Both were subsequently represented in the FDR-FMLN but lacked much independent authority, the importance of the PRTC often lying in its mediation between the larger radical groups and the PCS, towards which it progressively gravitated.[57]

By the end of the 1970s the left had established a clear set of linkages between politico-military bodies and mass organizations, which possessed a combined membership of at least 250,000 and had carved out a major role in public life even if their adherence to the programmes of their 'vanguard' organizations was more coherent on paper than in practice:

PCS (1930) – UDN (1969)

FPL (1972) – BPR (1975)

ERP (1972) – LP–28 (1977)

RN (1975) – FAPU (1974)

PRTC (1979) – MLP (1979)

In many respects the programmatic divergences between these groups appeared no less incomprehensible to ordinary workers and peasants than they did to a bourgeoisie quite disposed to let the radical ideologues slog it out between themselves. All the same, the process of competition was rapidly overtaken by one of organizational consolidation and expansion as social conflict deepened in the second half of the decade.

The differences of perspective and strategy within the left during this period of growth did not simply represent the residues of past disputes or the inner logic of some indigenous sectarian strain. They must be seen in the context of a rare and particularly pronounced crisis within the dominant bloc that came to a head in 1975–76. At first this seemed to vindicate the view that the bourgeoisie was deeply divided over political strategy, then it appeared to confirm the capacity of the oligarchy to impede any major reform. Although the clash between the Molina regime and the landlords over proposals for a limited agrarian reform had few immediate consequences for the debate between electoralism and armed struggle, it raised key questions as to the nature of the PCN regime, the balance of forces within the dominant bloc, and the broader strategy necessary for securing social and political change. Very often accounts of this period jump from the electoral fraud of 1972 to that of 1977 as if little occurred in between bar an almost automatic rise in repression. In reality the scale of the fraud in 1977, the character of General Romero's regime that emerged from it, and the conflict of the last years of the 1970s were closely related to the failure of Molina's project of tentative redistribution in order to slow the pace of polarization.

The decision in 1973 to establish a ministry of planning (CONAPLAN) charged with overseeing an expansionary economic programme was not in itself markedly innovative, similar projects having been undertaken by Osorio and Rivera in their day. Furthermore, while some of the proposed measures bore the influence of policies followed by the Peruvian military under General Velasco (1968–75), they never acquired such an extensive or radical character and amounted to little more than an effort to bolster exports and experiment with tariffs to protect small enterprises in a manner similar to that advocated by the PDC.[58] Indeed, the entire project may be seen as an attempt by the Molina government to both co-opt and outflank the Christian Democrats in the wake of the debacle of the 1972 elections. However, under the supervision of Agriculture Minister Enrique Alvarez, proposals for the rural sector were pursued with unexpected vigour, leading to the establishment in June 1975 of the *Instituto Salvadoreño de Transformación Agraria* (ISTA) with the formal objective of securing 'structural change in the tenure of land'. This was in itself a highly disturbing development for the landed bourgeoisie, and when the following year ISTA published a plan to transfer to 12,000 peasant families some 60,000 hectares belonging to 250 landlords in Usulután and San Miguel, glowering suspicion rapidly mutated into a pugnacious anti-government campaign.[59] Led by the *Asociación Nacional de Empresas Privadas* (ANEP) and the *Frente de Agricultores de la Región Oriental* (FARO), the landlords accused the PCN regime of circumventing parliamentary procedure, introducing centralized planning, attacking private enterprise and importing false foreign doctrines that would destroy the fabric of national society.[60] The press overflowed with protests from newly-created 'civic' associations; officers were assiduously lobbied; the government lost much of its authority over ORDEN; capital flight prompted a run on the *colón*; and ISTA was prevented, on occasion by physical force, from realizing its programme. With advocates of expansionary redistribution comprehensively defeated inside ANEP and the officer corps, Molina was obliged to back down four months after the measure was announced. The president subsequently endorsed as PCN candidate for the 1977 poll General Carlos Humberto Romero, a leading sympathizer of the 'agrarian' lobby, this nomination signalling the end of any significant autonomy held by the PCN and the 'regency state' over which it had presided.[61] Between 1975 and 1980 ISTA succeeded in purchasing and distributing a mere 14,000 hectares of land.

If this conflict may be described as secondary insofar as it occurred within the dominant bloc and not directly between social classes or the leading forces of right and left, it was scarcely less critical for all that. Landlord hegemony was more strenuously reaffirmed than in 1948–50 or 1961 and at a time when the space for political manoeuvre was much more limited than on those occasions. Molina's inability to support the modernizing technocrats who had purposefully designed a moderate measure demonstrated that the strategy of those political forces seeking to gain ground within the system was exceptionally vulnerable. On the other hand, despite the variety of interpretations it drew from this affair, the entire radical left understood its outcome to vindicate the need for greater popular mobilization and preparation for armed struggle.

The elections of February 1977 fully confirmed the shift in forces that had taken place the previous autumn and seriously damaged the credibility of the electoralist opposition. Responding to the new circumstances, UNO replaced Duarte and Ungo with Colonel Ernesto Claramount, a respected retired officer, and Antonio Morales Erlich, a conservative Christian Democrat, as its candidates. This move, which was similar to that taken by the Guatemalan Christian Democrats in the elections of 1974, gained the support of reform-minded junior officers organized in the *Movimiento de la Juventud Militar* (MJM) and attracted the sympathy of the new US administration led by Jimmy Carter. But this was to little avail. Expectations of decisive pressure from Washington proved ill-founded whilst Claramount's careful lobbying of the military to the cause of constitutional rectitude was emphatically undone by the removal of some 200 officers from the active list.[62] In the event, the PCN improved upon its 1972 performance, creating 150,000 'phantom' voters, situating all San Salvador's 400 voting booths on the outskirts of the city far away from the working-class *barrios*, and exploiting the outbreak of a number of industrial disputes to flood the capital with troops. At the poll UNO was frequently denied observer's rights, ballot boxes were stuffed, intimidation freely employed, and state radio coordination used to ensure Romero's victory by 812,281 votes to Claramount's 394,661. When questioned about this, Molina, who was above all else a party man, deigned to comment that 'only God is perfect'.[63]

Faced with such blatant malpractice, UNO finally resorted to direct action. The redoubtable Claramount declared that the legal path was exhausted and led some 40,000 supporters in occupying the capital's main plaza. This protest, which lasted three days and was ended only by a violent paramilitary attack, coincided with spontaneous demonstrations and strikes that reflected a level of popular exasperation notably higher than that of 1972. With no sign of a coup d'état from the MJM and no call for a general strike from UNO, crowds of protestors simply assaulted official buildings and burnt cars. The military exercised even less restraint, killing some 200 people the day after Claramount's protest was suppressed and he followed Duarte into exile. A state of siege was declared and constitutional liberties formally suspended; over the next decade they would be officially recognized for a period of no more than a few months. The events of February 1977 were assessed at the time as amounting to a 'pre-revolutionary situation' by RN, later recognized by the PCS as signalling the need for armed struggle, and certainly constituted a critical watershed in Salvadorean politics.[64] UNO stumbled on, with PCS support, for two more years, but popular expectations of change through the ballot box had all but disappeared.[65]

It could be argued that the 1977 fraud was the most decisive in modern Central American history. Whilst it was neither unprecedented nor out of keeping with the general conditions of political control prevailing at the time, such unabashed manipulation and wholehearted recourse to violence had a particularly sharp effect in the context of high popular expectation, sharp social conflict, the battle over agrarian reform, the disputes within the opposition, and pressure from Washington over violation of human rights. This latter factor had not existed in 1972 – when the Nixon administration was seeking ways to overthrow the constitutional government of Chile – and the others had been less pronounced. Perhaps the nature of the election had already been determined by the oligarchy's victory over Molina's proposed reforms, but even if it was only a formal confirmation of the new balance of power, the poll was still of sufficient importance in itself to cripple the post-war political system and provoke levels of violence not witnessed in the country for forty years.

From 1977 the activity of the reactionary death squads became much more pronounced. Such bodies had been in existence for some time, the FALANGE (*Fuerzas Armadas de Liberación Nacional – Guerra de Exterminación*) accepting responsibility for thirty-eight killings during one week in October 1975. The following year FALANGE mutated into the *Unión Guerrera Blanca* (UGB; White Warriors' Union), which similarly undertook operations that could not be formally sanctioned by the high command; it drew many of its faceless assassins from the ranks of the military and ORDEN as well as collaborating closely with the intelligence units of the armed forces.[66] Over the following years a plethora of such organizations emerged with more or less stable titles and although their victims multiplied enormously from 1980, the basic pattern of activity varied little from that of the mid 1970s. Opponents of the government were usually issued with threats – often in the press – or simply identified as 'subversive', seized and executed, their bodies generally being found in a dismembered state and carrying some macabre message of warning. In this respect at least the executioners of the Salvadorean right differed from their peers in Chile and Argentina, who were content simply to abduct their victims and eschew the deterrent effect of mutilated corpses for the arguably greater psychological impact and apparent forensic protection of complete 'disappearance'. Of course, El Salvador is an altogether less sophisticated society and it is clear that the example of 1932 loomed large in this new phase of vigilante violence – one squad even naming itself after General Martinez – but there can be little doubt that the example of the Southern Cone dictatorships spurred the right to engage in an unqualified 'crusade against Communism', which, as in South America, was expanded to include virtually any person opposed to the ruling order.

This 'dirty war' was publicly justified and to some degree aggravated by the activities of the left-wing guerrillas, although until 1980 these remained very few and perpetrated relatively few acts of terrorism against individuals, usually prominent members of the ruling class or the military hierarchy.[67] The death squads first acquired international renown for their attacks on the Church, and in particular the Jesuit order, which ran the Catholic university and was identified by the right as a source of subversion. The government fully subscribed to this view, expelling seventeen foreign priests of the Jesuit, Maryknoll and Benedictine orders in the three months after the election. In the same period the death squads assassinated a further six clerics, and in May the army invaded the town of Aguilares in an especially bloody operation against the local Christian community, closely linked to FECCAS. By June the UGB was proclaiming the slogan 'Be Patriotic – Kill a Priest', and at the end of the month it presented to the press 'War Bulletin

No. 6' in which it accused forty-six Jesuits of 'terrorism' and gave them a month in which to leave the country, failing which their execution would be 'immediate and systematic'.[68] President Romero showed every sign of sympathizing with such an attitude, but these declarations prompted Oscar Arnulfo Romero, the new archbishop of San Salvador and no relation, to boycott his inauguration and they also threatened a damaging split with the US. The president therefore warned the UGB off such excessively provocative tactics.

The new regime went to some lengths to assure the US that it was different to Molina's outgoing team, on which the unfortunate occurrences of early 1977 could be conveniently blamed. Nevertheless, the character of the governments in Washington and San Salvador almost inevitably entailed conflict between them. Romero lacked the socio-political resources of the dictatorship in Guatemala, let alone those of Argentina and Chile, fully to repudiate Carter's human rights policy as 'interventionist' and court the risks of complete diplomatic rupture. At the same time, his truculence in negotiation was assisted by a landlord class in particularly bullish temper as well as by the absence of a tradition of direct political dependence on the US such as that which obtained in Honduras and Nicaragua. Thus, although Romero bowed to Washington's requests in suspending martial law once he took office (in return for which important loans were released), the campaign launched by ANEP and the coffee exporters (ABECAFE) for unrestricted imposition of order soon pulled the president back into line.[69]

This new political offensive by the oligarchy was no less vehement than that against the agrarian reform and whilst it incorporated denunciations of 'the mania for freedom' together with the UN Charter and US intervention, it is evident that the call for 'peace, security and order' was directly affected by the mobilization led by FECCAS-UTC for an increase in harvest wages.[70] Undeterred by a marked rise in activity by ORDEN and the National Guard throughout the autumn, this popular campaign reached its peak in November with the staging of sympathy strikes and demonstrations in the capital and the occupation of the ministry of labour. Romero immediately responded by introducing the 'Law of the Defence and Guarantee of Public Order', which was directly modelled on the security codes of the Southern Cone regimes and outlawed every manifestation of opposition in a manner more comprehensive than even Somoza's dictatorship.[71] This draconian law remained in force from December 1977 to March 1979, providing legal cover for increased government violence. This in turn accelerated guerrilla activity so that a year after the statute was introduced rebel raids were taking place every week.[72] Although the Church only began issuing detailed information on the victims of political violence on a monthly basis from 1979 – sad statistics that were soon recognized as one of the clearest indicators of shifts in government policy – it is evident that the average numbers were rising from dozens in 1977 to scores in 1978 and hundreds by mid 1979. In responding to this violence and the suspension of constitutional guarantees the Carter administration was stymied not only by the entrenched attitude of the oligarchy but also by its own lack of resolution, increasingly determined by a fear on the part of elements in the State Department as well as the Pentagon that any rupture with the regime in San Salvador would simply open the field to the left.[73] By mid 1978 such apprehension was very clearly conditioned by the course of events in Nicaragua, where a sharper crisis elicited even more confused signals from an administration firmly impaled on the horns of a politico-moral dilemma it had itself played no small part in creating.

In the event, relatively few risks were run in persuading Romero to reinstate at least the formalities of the constitution. Throughout 1978 his authoritarian law had diminished neither guerrilla activity nor popular mobilization, the coercive climate in the country already being so pervasive that any statutory confirmation of this state appeared almost unnecessary. Moreover, the level of capital flight and a loss of nerve within the dominant bloc caused by the tension with Washington, the crisis in Nicaragua and the absence of any new political initiatives at home prompted Romero to grasp at straws.[74] For the first time in nearly ten years the extreme right was rumoured to be planning a coup while the De Sola family and the PDC were visibly engaged in talks with Washington that unnerved the regime. Equally, the junior officers – unreliable not so much because of their youth but because of their direct command of troops – had for over a year witnessed the travails of the Nicaraguan National Guard, which even by March 1979 seemed doomed to institutional calamity through the absence of any alternative to incremental repression. Only a minority of such officers supported a turn to authentically reformist policies but a great many perceived that as a politician Romero was substantially inferior to Somoza and even his own PCN predecessors; this leaden cypher of conservative coffee barons who had met all their needs in 1975–77 had now become a distinct liability. With the exception of the critical days of the 1977 election, the army had not yet been required to deploy its troops in repressive operations with great frequency, yet continual reliance upon the careless brutality of the paramilitary forces and ORDEN as well as the effects of death-squad activity brought such a prospect ever closer and caused some apprehension within the officer corps.

The official restitution of constitutional guarantees in March 1979 had no effect on the incidence of violence; in March and April 130 people fell into the hands of the death squads never to reappear alive, and at least fifty militants of the BPR were killed in more open fashion by ORDEN. However, in that area where legal ordinances were still of some consequence – the right to strike – there was an immediate response. Within days of the lifting of the authoritarian law workers occupied two bottling plants in San Salvador owned by the Quinoñez family. The immediate dispatch of troops, killing of eight workers and wounding of another twenty was par for the course in Salvadorean industrial relations, but an urban working class that was organized to an unprecedented degree and greatly impressed by events in Nicaragua was now prepared to face down such coercion. Although the sympathy stoppages of late March amounted to neither a general strike nor an insurrectionary mobilization, they involved more than 150,000 workers across the country and posed a threat even greater than the 1967 strike.[75] Romero rapidly forced the Quinoñez clan to concede the day in order to avert a complete collapse of production and public order, but the strikes opened a phase of agitation which, like that of January 1978 in Nicaragua, could no longer be contained by tactical moves. In early May militants of the BPR occupied the metropolitan cathedral, several other churches, and some embassies and schools to demand the release of eight *Bloque* leaders arrested by the regime. Romero again responded in the preferred manner of his fraternity by reimposing martial law and authorizing the troops to fire on demonstrators outside the cathedral. Twenty-five people died in the mad scramble to reach the precarious safety of the church. Unlike similar events in 1977 the foreign media were now on hand. Pictures of what was to become the familiar sight of Salvadoreans being slaughtered on the steps of their metropolitan church were beamed into the living rooms of Europe and North America, the effect being infinitely more powerful than short notices in the serious press laconically noting the death of equal or greater numbers of anonymous peasants in the distant backlands. In May the death toll stood at 188 and by July Japan, Switzerland, West Germany, Britain and Costa Rica had closed down their embassies because of the violence. Romero was badly isolated and even the belligerent grandees of ANEP momentarily lost their collective nerve, calling for 'peace . . . to correct errors that have been committed'.

It was no longer sufficient for the Carter government to issue pious injunctions and chat with the PDC. Aside from the fact that Nicaragua was now under Sandinista control, the scale of conflict in El Salvador clearly required action if either an extreme right-wing coup in the style of 1932 or a radical insurrection were to be avoided.[76] Yet even at this stage Romero was able to resist demands for rescheduled elections made in secret visits by the eternally peripatetic State Department duo Viron Vaky and William Bowdler. Washington was apparently too traumatized by the experience of Nicaragua to increase the pressure any further or undertake adventurous initiatives. Moreover, the Brzezinski faction was winning the upper hand inside the administration, urging a retreat from all but the rhetoric of human rights along with a retrieval of hard-nosed realpolitik. Central American affairs were increasingly depicted in terms of the radical threat, and although this was still modulated with acceptance of the need for democratic and social renewal, many of the motifs that would be so closely associated with the Reagan policy began to make an appearance.[77]

By early September the momentum of demonstrations, strikes, occupations, guerrilla attacks and almost ritual burning of buses – a favoured tactic of the Salvadorean left – had plainly brought the regime to the verge of collapse. Romero's brother was killed by guerrillas and even the sacrosanct independence day parade was cancelled for fear of provoking a revolt. More than a hundred people lost their lives in the first three weeks of the month as had nearly 800 in the preceding seven months; it was not yet civil war but public order had dissolved completely. Washington's requests for Romero to resign met with no more response than had those directed at Somoza. At the same time important forces of the left and centre took a leaf out of the FSLN's book and complicated the political scene further still in setting up a new alliance. The *Foro Popular* was in many respects similar to UNO, but in addition to the PDC and the MNR, it included the LP–28 and FENASTRAS as well as independent unions and professional associations in supporting a minimum programme for free elections, political pluralism, respect for human rights and economic reform. The BPR, however, did not join, declaring 1980 'the year of liberation'.[78] Representing a wide section of the political opposition and popular movement, the *Foro* constituted a critically important new initiative since Washington, the military dissidents and even sections of the right could now deal with a force on the left that was above ground, stood short of rebellion and was prepared to negotiate. Although it only had a fleeting existence, the *Foro* represented a timely resuscitation of the electoralist forces familiar to the right whilst possessing sufficient popular support through the unions to speak with authority for the wider opposition movement. Thus, at the same time as Carter's team was retreating to the exploitation of Cold War phobias in 'discovering' 3,000 Soviet troops in Cuba and establishing a new 'Caribbean Task Force' to combat 'possible Communist domination', it was presented in El Salvador with the opportunity to treat for a political solution distanced from both dictatorship and revolution.

In the event, Washington played little direct part in the overthrow of Romero, who was ousted early on 15 October by a coup planned and largely directed by officers identified with the reformist cause and in contact with the *Foro*. These men were rapidly joined and soon to be outmanoeuvred by hardliners anxious to obstruct any significant concessions to the popular movement. However, in its initial phase the coup appeared to be a resolutely progressive enterprise on the part of the army, the 'proclamation of the Armed Forces of El Salvador' issued on 15 October condemning the Romero regime for widespread violation of human rights and corruption as well as the 'inadequate economic, social and political structures that have traditionally prevailed in the country'. Electoral fraud and inadequate development were ascribed to 'the ancestral privileges of the dominant class' whilst promises were made to dissolve ORDEN, guarantee human rights, hold fair elections, introduce an amnesty and permit political activity across the ideological spectrum.[79]

It seemed very much like the movements of 1944 and 1960, and henceforth both the Carter and Reagan administrations would insist that the post-1979 regimes in El Salvador stood by and were realizing all these commendable aspirations. The proclamation manifested a 'centrism' that could be presented as anathema equally to right and left, terminating reactionary dictatorship and yet designed to halt Communist subversion. In reality the proclamation was a dead letter almost from the day it hit the world's telexes. Within twelve weeks its most assiduous supporters had been removed from office and in just over a year many of those who had championed it were executed by the right. The fact that over the following seven years members of all the political parties represented in the new revolutionary junta, including a number of prominent Christian Democrats, joined forces with the left in a civil war that took the lives of over 60,000 people demonstrated Washington's presentation of subsequent governments as a natural continuation of this short-lived administration to be empty propaganda. On the other hand, the fact that the PDC's conservative leadership refused to follow its erstwhile allies in UNO into opposition and received Washington's patronage in return for this gave a veneer of plausibility to the deceit. However bitter the conflict of the subsequent years, it was certain that the unrealized programme of the junta and the resistance of the PDC to joining the popular bloc prevented the rapid political manoeuvres and crises of 1980 from developing into the total polarization witnessed in Nicaragua in 1978–79. It thereby both salvaged the existing order and ensured that El Salvador would suffer a protracted civil war.

Polarization and Rupture

Between the coup of October 1979 and the FMLN's 'final offensive' of January 1981 Salvadorean political life was unusually dynamic, a confusion of events altering the balance and pattern of forces. These shifts in political allegiances and strategies were directly related to the generalization of violence, but it would be mistaken to view this period as simply one of incremental attrition and a natural consolidation of the belligerent forces. Although it was during 1980 that the political 'centre' was effectively liquidated and its constituent parties obliged to side with the military forces of either the left or the right, the new alignments fully or partially forged by the end of the year were by no means predestined or lacking contradictions that would continue to surface over the subsequent period.

In the case of the popular bloc this process took place remarkably rapidly. The PCS, MNR and dissident Christian Democrats allied themselves with the radical left within a matter of weeks of the collapse of the junta established in October 1979. The recomposition of the dominant bloc was much more extenuated and more manifestly problematic, the Conservative majority of the PDC needing all of Washington's support over the space of five years to gain grudging acceptance by the military high command of its claims to office and through this the capacity to survive attacks from the oligarchic right. As a result, the form of the dominant bloc shifted from the post-1950 'dual system' of military government and oligarchic economic control to a fitful tripartite arrangement whereby the military retired from office but was assured full operational independence and US backing, the PDC was permitted to assume office and parade its reformist policies, and the landlords were deprived of the advantages of electoral fraud but also protected from any major realization of the reforms upheld by its newly privileged political competitor. Such an arrangement entailed the holding of elections in 1982, 1984 and 1985 and even thereafter it remained subject to sharp challenges. However, the basis of the new division of power was clearly laid in 1979–80, when the oligarchic mandate was brought under US discipline if not absolute control, the PDC enticed away from its old centrist allies, and the military persuaded to accept formal collaboration with its erstwhile opponents. The principal events in this process are included in Table 43.[80]

It could be said that the fate of what became known as the 'October junta' was prefigured by the events immediately following the coup against

Table 43: El Salvador: The Descent into Civil War, 1979–81

Year	Month	Day	Event
1979	Mar.		Widespread strikes and US pressure force General Romero to lift 'Public Order Law'.
	May		Romero imposes martial law.
		8	BPR occupies embassies and metropolitan cathedral; 25 shot by military.
	Jul.	19	FSLN overthrows Somoza in Nicaragua.
	Aug.		Vaky and Bowdler urge Romero to relax control and advance elections or resign.
	Sept.	20	Establishment of *Foro Popular* grouping PDC; MNR; UDN; LP–28 and many unions.

Oct. 13 Romero visits US.

15 Romero ousted in coup; military attacks occupied factories.

16 Abortive ERP uprising in San Salvador *barrios*.

19 Colonels accept *Foro* terms for joining government; economic and social reforms publicly declared.

24 Popular demonstrations repressed with high casualties; LP–28 and FENASTRAS quit *Foro*.

BPR occupies ministries demanding immediate economic reforms, end to repression and dissolution of paramilitary forces.

Nov. 6 BPR occupations lifted upon declaration of 30-day truce.

Carter administration sends 'non-lethal' military equipment worth $205,000.

Dec. US sends military advisory team.

BPR–Junta truce ends, occupations, strikes and repression increase; 700 people killed in final 12 weeks of 1979. Major economic reforms blocked by military and courts.

27 Civilians in regime demand military end repression and accept authority of junta.

1980 Jan. 1 Civilian members of junta and cabinet resign after military reject ultimatum.

9 PDC joins military in new junta.

10 FPL, FARN, PCS declare coordination of guerrilla activity.

11 Popular organizations (BPR; FAPU; LP–28; UDN) unite to form CRM.

22 San Salvador demonstration of at least 100,000 to mark anniversary of 1932 revolt and celebrate formation of CRM; many marchers killed by military.

Feb. CRM issues Programmatic Platform; LP–28 occupies PDC offices peacefully – military executes leading protesters.

D'Aubuissón/Medrano coup plan halted by US diplomats.

Attorney General Mario Zamora assassinated by death squad after D'Aubuissón accuses him of 'subversion'; archdiocesan radio station YSAX and library of University of Central America (UCA) bombed by right.

Repression increases – 600 killed in first two months of year.

Mar. 3 Héctor Dada (PDC) resigns from junta denouncing repression.

5 José Napoleón Duarte enters junta.

6 Agrarian reform introduced and state of siege declared.

10 PDC splits; dissidents form MPSC.

17 CRM calls general strike.
24 Archbishop Romero assassinated.
26 Further PDC resignations from cabinet.
30 General strike; some 100,000 attend Romero's funeral, which is attacked by military.
Apr. 1 US Congress approves $5.7 million in military aid.
4 Establishment of FDS.
18 FDS joins with CRM to form FDR.
May 7 D'Aubuissón arrested and expelled for further rightist coup plot.
9 Salvadorean high command meets Guatemalan and Honduran military chiefs to discuss regional strategy.
10 Colonel Majano removed as joint commander of military; Gutiérrez retains post.
Guerrilla groups, including ERP, form DRU.
14 Agrarian reform partially halted.
Some 600 people killed by Salvadorean and Honduran troops at Sumpul River on border.
Jun. FDR recognized by Social Democratic International.
24 One-day general strike called by FDR.
27 Army occupies National University, which is closed for four years.
Aug. 13 3-day general strike called by FDR fails to prompt urban insurrection; heavy repression cows labour movement.
21 Power workers (STECEL) strike blacks out country but results in arrest of leadership and militarization of major public service unions.
FARN quits DRU in dispute over strike tactics.
Sept. Majano loses battle over military postings; army reformists removed from major troop commands.
FARN leader Ernesto Jovel dies.
Oct. 4 El Salvador and Honduras sign peace treaty.
10 FARN rejoins DRU; FMLN established.
29 Félix Ulloa, rector of National University, killed by death squad.
Nov. 4 State Department 'Dissent Paper' criticizes US policy; Reagan wins US elections.
27 Leadership of FDR assassinated by death squad.
Dec. 3 Three US nuns and one lay-worker killed by troops; US cuts aid.
Bowdler and William Rogers visit San Salvador.
13 Majano ousted from junta; Duarte named president of junta, Gutiérrez vice-president.

			PRTC joins FMLN, which increases attacks in Chalatenango and Morazán. 14,173 people killed in 1980 according to archbishopric of San Salvador.
1981	Jan.	3	US labour advisers Hammer and Pearlman and agrarian reform director Viera assassinated by death squad.
		10	FMLN launches 'final offensive'.
		13	General strike called by FMLN fails to take root.
		14	US restores military aid after Ambassador Robert White claims Managua is assisting FMLN offensive; small arms worth $5 million and 20 advisers are sent immediately.
		16	Guerrilla offensive is brought to a halt.
		20	Reagan inaugurated.
	Feb.	2	White fired as ambassador.
		23	State Department alleges major logistical support for FMLN from Cuba and Nicaragua in 'White Paper'.
	Mar.		US sends military aid worth $25 million; number of advisers increased to 54; Duarte freezes reform programme. Major military operations in north and east.
	Apr.		Military counter-offensive loses momentum.
	May	3	Major Washington demonstration against US intervention.
	Jun.		'White Paper' assertions discredited in US press; guerrilla activity increases.
	Jul.		FMLN stages campaign against economic targets.
	Aug.		ERP seizes town of Perquín, Morazán.
		28	France and Mexico grant belligerent status to FMLN-FDR.
	Sept.		Duarte tours US. ARENA established.
		24	US Congress approves new aid conditional upon executive certification of improvements in human rights.
	Oct.	15	FMLN destroys strategic Puente de Oro bridge.
	Nov.		Secretary of State Haig issues strong threats against Cuba and Nicaragua, refuses to discount possibility of US troops being sent to region. According to *Washington Post* FMLN has effective control over a third of national territory.
		10	Over 600 peasants massacred by army's Atlacatl brigade at Mozote, Morazán; Washington disparages reports of massacre.
	Dec.	18	Junta calls elections for constituent assembly in March 1982. FMLN withstands offensives in Chalatenango, Morazán and Guazapa. 17,303 people killed in 1981.

Romero when the ERP attempted an uprising in the *barrios* of San Salvador and the military abandoned all restraint in attacking factories occupied by workers during the rising. However, the ERP's action was out of line not only with the attitude of the rest of the left but also with that of its own popular organization, the *Ligas*, which had just joined the *Foro* in the search for a negotiated social pact. The anomalous nature of the army's actions is much more debatable although it was clear that divergences existed within the officer corps and that neither the 'pragmatists' nor the 'reformists' yet held sufficient advantage to impose policies on the other faction. The figurehead of the progressive current, Colonel Adolfo Majano, entered the new junta but US influence and adroit manoeuvring by those traditionalists who had backed the coup as a lesser evil once it became a fait accompli impeded the elevation of Colonel René Guerra y Guerra, a more decisive organizer and politically adept figure.[81] This initial resistance to a takeover of the military leadership by the 'Young Turks' was soon extended to the winning of control over the *Consejo Permanente de las Fuerzas Armadas* (COPEFA) by pro-US hardliners such as Colonel Jaime Abdul Gutiérrez, who replaced Guerra y Guerra on the junta, and Colonel José Guillermo García, who was to serve as minister of defence for the next four years and safeguard many ultra-right officers due to be purged or reassigned immediately after the coup. Nonetheless, neither the old hierarchy nor 'tradition' could be fully reimposed within the officer corps overnight, and even after December 1979 Gutiérrez, García and their minions were obliged to recognize the 'alternative' institutional caucus in COPEFA and publicly to support Majano's policies of rapprochement even while they were constantly seeking to inflict a decisive defeat on the left.

At the same time, the composition of the government appeared to offer some scope for a new initiative since in addition to Majano and Gutiérrez, the junta included Guillermo Ungo (MNR), the much respected university rector Román Mayorga, and a representative of large capital in Mario Andino, local manager of Philips Dodge. The cabinet contained four soldiers, four members of the 'progressive bourgeoisie', ten members of the *Foro* and a further five ministers proposed by it and accepted with minimal opposition by the officers and businessmen. The PDC was compensated for the lack of a full member of the junta with Héctor Dada receiving the foreign ministry and Rubén Zamora the ministry of the presidency. José Napoleón Duarte, the civilian who was to dominate political life over the next seven years, held no post, and it was perhaps a key factor in his subsequent comportment that both he and almost all the ministers in later PDC governments did not share the miserable experience of the civilians in the October junta. The balance of party representation in the government was, though, far from uneven; the PDC held five portfolios, the UDN-PCS five (including the ministry of labour) and the MNR four. It would have been very hard to contrive a more equitable distribution of posts across such a broad political spectrum; it ranged from deeply reactionary colonels and entrepreneurs to militants of the Communist Party, enabling the former to retain their customary authority and the latter to deny that they were in alliance with the bourgeoisie or had capitulated to the right.[82]

If on paper the regime assembled in the last weeks of October seemed to have all the trappings of a major new social pact, in practice it soon proved to be an unworkable confection. This was less because it was, as Washington would persistently claim, besieged from right and left alike than because its rightist members refused to allow the government's founding programme to be put into effect, thus setting it on an inevitable collision course with the popular movement. The state of siege was maintained at the insistence of the officer corps, and the earnest Majano was unable to persuade his colleagues either to release political prisoners or to account for the 'disappeared', amongst whom, it was soon realized, most of the political prisoners now had to be numbered. The formal dissolution of ORDEN merely prompted its reincarnation under the title of the *Frente Democrático Nacional*, and the much publicized commitment to purge the paramilitary forces, which the left wanted totally disbanded, extended to the trial of twelve members of the National Guard. Proposals for an agrarian reform and new social policies were accepted but stalled by legal objections and dilatory administration at the hands of ministers who belonged to ANEP. All of these factors deepened popular distrust and disenchantment, but none was so decisive in ending the experiment in coalition government as the violence employed against the popular organizations when they attempted to force the regime into honouring its promises.

Before the end of October the military had repressed not only the ERP revolt and the factory occupations but also a funeral march for slain FAPU militants, a demonstration of all the mass fronts for the release of political prisoners, and the traditional student *bufonada* parade. Over 100 people were killed and 250 wounded in these events in San Salvador within the space of a fortnight, the civilian ministers refusing to condemn their new military allies and even stressing the right of the army to 'legitimate self-defence'.[83] As a result of this posture both the *Ligas* and FENASTRAS quit the *Foro*, bringing them closer to the BPR, which on 24 October embarked upon a major campaign of direct action, occupying a number of ministries (including those controlled by the PCS) and taking hostages to back demands that were little different from those of the *Foro* itself or indeed the FSLN in 1978–79: a 100 per cent wage rise; reduction of prices of basic necessities; dissolution of all the paramilitary bodies; and the removal of all foreign military advisers.[84] The *Foro* organized counter-demonstrations and denounced the 'adventurism' of the left, but popular support for the occupations reflected the diminishing stock of those who urged forbearance over matters of such gravity. The collapse of the *Foro* was only slightly delayed by the eventual agreement to a thirty-day truce during which the *Bloque* economic demands would be met, it being more generally determined by the fact that the centrist parties were in alliance with a soldiery that had killed more people in the last twelve weeks of 1979 than in the rest of the year and showed no sign of changing its conduct.

As the guerrillas resumed retaliatory action and the death squads conducted their grisly mission undisturbed by the government, Duarte returned to the country to a great fanfare and immediately began to put space between the PDC and the other *Foro* parties, now in a state of open crisis and disinclined to enter into competitive politicking amongst themselves. The failure of the government throughout December to curtail the military's repressive activities combined with the revelation that ministers had not been informed of a highly sensitive visit by a US military mission finally spurred the civilians in the regime to present the army with an ultimatum: either the officer corps recognized the junta's authority to give it orders or both the junta and the cabinet would resign. On 1 January 1980 this ultimatum was unambiguously rejected by COPEFA and over the next few days Ungo and Mayorga resigned from the junta (followed a little later by Andino) and thirty-seven ministers quit office, leaving only two colonels to represent the brave new democracy. In line with its traditions since 1932, the military rejected all restrictions placed by civilians upon its operational independence, and this rejection was especially decisive when these controls were seen as directly prejudicial to the mission of liquidating the left. Significantly, it was over this rather than the hastily tabled socio-economic reforms that the officer corps refused to compromise and was prepared to neuter the experiment in centrist government.

The fall of the 'first junta' – several more were to hold office before the constituent assembly elections of 1982 – was distinct from that of the reformist administrations of 1944 and 1960 in that the military had no need to stage a fully fledged coup. Although the effect of refusing to accept orders was not dissimilar, the form in which the junta and cabinet were obliged to leave office permitted Washington and the high command to project an image of continuity and greatly facilitated overtures to the PDC, the bulk of which was still prepared to collaborate with the army. Accordingly, in mid January the party entered government on condition that no representatives of private capital served in the administration, the banks were nationalized, an agrarian reform introduced, foreign trade in key agro-exports controlled by the state, organization of the peasantry permitted, and dialogue opened with the popular organizations.[85] These terms were very close to those made by the *Foro* in October and would have seemed in light of developments in the interim to be completely unacceptable to the colonels. However, as with the *Foro*'s demands, they were accepted almost immediately by a high command that was well aware of the need to have civilian partners beyond the ranks of the extreme right. Moreover, by insisting that such an agreement would be binding and dependable, despite the army's conduct over the autumn, the PDC was clearly signalling the distance between it and the rest of the centrist parties, which no longer placed any faith in formal military commitments. Henceforth the Christian Democratic resistance to making repression an issue of principle was to be a central factor in bonding it to the dominant bloc. Its tiresome complaints and public wringing of hands over the violence was never taken to the point of rupture, and so long as it held to such a position the army did not repudiate its socio-economic policies, despite the conflict this caused with the oligarchy. There can be little doubt that until at least 1982 such a concession by the officer corps was primarily pragmatic and designed to secure support from Washington, which even under Reagan insisted upon continued attachment to the cause of reform. Moreover, it proved relatively easy to stall, circumvent or sabotage the most threatening policies. Yet over time the exchange of operational freedom and US largesse for acceptance of secondary alterations in social policy acquired a momentum of its own and increasingly qualified military subordination to the oligarchic mandate. Such a state of affairs did not obtain in full prior to 1984, by which time the exigencies of war dominated military decisions, but it is notable that as early as January 1980 the high command was prepared to countenance a formal entente along these lines despite landlord fury.

The need to retain US support and some form of mixed administration that could be presented as democratic and progressive was made particularly sharp by the rapid unification of the left in January. This process was directly related to the experience of the popular movement over the autumn, when the radical left reached greater uniformity through its analysis of the regime and collaboration in confronting it.[86] A key element in this delayed rapprochement was the historic recognition by the PCS that it had now to engage in armed struggle and ally itself with those forces that had fiercely criticized it over the previous decade. On 10 January RN, the FPL and the PCS agreed to coordinate guerrilla activity and combine their mass organizations in the new *Coordinadora Revolucionaria de Masas* (CRM). On 22 January the left as a whole held a march to celebrate the anniversary of the 1932 rebellion, estimates of the number who demonstrated through the streets of San Salvador varying between 100,000 and 250,000. It is likely that by virtue of its unprecedented size this event would have constituted an important moment in national political life in any event, but the decision of the military to open fire upon the marchers as they passed through the centre of the capital transformed it into a peculiarly bitter occasion which for many wiped out the possibility of reaching a truce with the military and conducting opposition through 'open' politics.

The 'Programmatic Platform of the Revolutionary Democratic Government' published by the CRM the following day provided the left's response to this state of affairs and served as its manifesto until the end of 1983. This document – which received the support of the ERP and *Ligas* in March once difficulties with RN had been overcome – broadly mirrored the programmes issued by the FSLN-sponsored MPU and FPN in Nicaragua in 1978–79; it eschewed the language of class for that of radical populism which had a broad appeal and could be accepted by the entire left as at least a minimum programme. Built around democratic, anti-dictatorial, anti-imperialist and reformist motifs, the Platform spoke of a 'new society' and 'social progress', combining the demands of October with a call for 'the dissolution of the existing state powers', including the paramilitary and intelligence services but not all of the army. The 'healthy, patriotic and worthy elements that belong to the current army' would be merged with the guerrilla forces to form a new institution whilst guarantees were offered to 'medium-sized industrialists, merchants, artisans and farmers' by a future government that would 'put an end to the political, economic and social power of the great lords of land and capital'. Nationalization would be extended to banks, foreign trade, electricity and petrol refining, but would apply only to 'monopolistic' enterprises and large estates with the objective of liquidating 'once and for all . . . the dependence of our country upon Yanqui imperialism'. The popular democratic regime would enter the Non-Aligned Movement, maintain friendly relations with Sandinista Nicaragua, respect human rights and establish 'organs of revolutionary people's power', for which no precise format was outlined.[87]

The similarity between this charter and the Sandinista programme was not coincidental but neither was the CRM merely borrowing from the FSLN model. The Platform was formulated in conditions similar to those in Nicaragua in 1978–79 insofar as the left needed to provide both the mass movement and its liberal competitors with a coherent set of objectives that would maximize unity against a dictatorship. Yet the Salvadorean dictatorship was quite distinct from Somoza's; there was absolutely no possibility of co-opting important sectors of the capitalist class to the popular bloc, even on a temporary basis. On the other hand, the potential for splitting the military was greater than in the case of the Nicaraguan National Guard. Moreover, the CRM was confronted with more taxing demands in terms of unifying radical forces bitterly divided for nearly a decade; these forces possessed a common denominator not in a nationalist heritage open to pluralist interpretation but in the discourse of class struggle – more directly conducive to disputes and a more formidable barrier to collaboration with reformist or liberal forces. In its suppression of such language and avoidance of reference to socialism the CRM's Platform constituted a more emphatic reworking of the positions of the left than had taken place in

Nicaragua over the two years before the insurrection. This was necessary because the popular movement was not so much seeking fresh radical demands as unity between those organizations making them; a mass constituency of the left already existed and could no longer expand unless it was first consolidated. Equally, the form in which radical policies were condensed in the Platform made them accessible to the centrist refugees from the October junta precisely because the suppression of issues of contention within the left entailed the suppression of the very Marxist canon in which these had been framed. There is no doubt that the reformists continued to nurture a profound suspicion of the left, yet events no longer permitted them any other choice than to take up the challenge offered by the Platform and risk an alliance.

Following the demonstration of January and entry of the PDC into government, the extreme right expanded its campaign of violence to include all proponents of reform and not just the radical left. From the reactionary viewpoint the incorporation of the PDC into government and the level of popular mobilization seemed very similar to the position that prevailed in 1930–31 under Araujo and was extremely threatening. The resignation of the first junta had not led to a repudiation of its economic policies and there was still no unanimity within the officer corps as to how to respond to the crisis. US patronage of both reform and the PDC was deeply resented as malicious meddling akin to that over human rights in 1977–79. Thus, whilst in the eyes of the centre and left officers like García and Gutiérrez were sabotaging any possibility of peace and change, for the far right seeking a decisive and 'national' solution (that is, along the lines of 1932), these men were far from ideal leaders simply because of their public support for US policies. Thus, in February Washington was obliged to intervene with unusual celerity and force to avert a coup attempt by Major Roberto D'Aubuissón and General Medrano. It was, though, much more difficult to control the right's complementary strategy of pre-emptive terror against the PDC, a move that was designed to forestall the party's push for complete control of government. This campaign was undertaken with relative ease by the death squads, and despite being predicated on the perception of Christian Democracy as 'the enemy within' rather than a malleable partner, it required no major political initiative or risk in order to be put into practice. The preparedness of the 'ultras' to assassinate Mario Zamora, the attorney general of the republic, demonstrated that they were in earnest. The bombing of the university and the archdiocesan radio station and the killing of some 600 people in eight weeks inevitably had an impact upon the PDC. Junta member Héctor Dada resigned in protest at the lack of military action over such violence, and he was replaced by the party leader Duarte, who finally entered the political stage from the wings. Amidst a major crisis within the ranks of Christian Democracy caused by the extraordinary situation in which it was both the target of reactionary violence and directly associated with government repression, Duarte was able to oversee the introduction of a measure that was henceforth presented by him, his party and the US government as the principal justification for the PDC's continuation in office and a confirmation of its reformist and anti-oligarchic bona fides: agrarian reform.

Decree 153, the 'Basic Agrarian Reform Law', was issued on 6 March 1980 with impressive speed, a minimum of political and technical preparation and the redeclaration of the state of siege. Modelled by US experts on programmes introduced in South Vietnam in the 1960s, the reform proved to be a remarkably incompetent measure. It failed to strike at the heart of oligarchic economic power, was easily circumvented by practical and sometimes legal means, and it escalated violence in the countryside rather than reducing it. (This supposed palliative for the country's ills prompted an increase in killings from 234 in February to 487 in March and nigh-on 1,000 in June.) Of the reform's three phases, the first – put into effect immediately – covered estates of over 500 hectares; the second extended to farms of between 150 and 499 hectares, which accounted for 60 per cent of coffee production; and the third, or the 'Land to the Tiller' programme, gave freehold rights to all tenants of small plots through aggregate payment of rents.[88] The 65 per cent of the rural population who were landless labourers rather than *colonos*, sharecroppers or permanent estate employees received nothing. Compensation for expropriated land was to be paid 25 per cent in cash and 75 per cent in government bonds to increase investment in industry. Land distributed under the first two phases was to be administered by new cooperatives.

From the start the reform fell far short of the extravagant claims made by its local and foreign supporters. Although the introduction of Phase One led to the immediate expropriation of 30 of the 238 estates that came under its terms of reference, owners possessed the 'right of reserve' whereby they could claim back 150 hectares plus 20 per cent if improvements were made. This stipulation alone reduced the scope of the measure to less than 10 per cent of the country's cultivable land. With such a major buffer, widespread evidence of military collaboration in returning expropriated lands, attacks on members of the new co-ops and officials of the speedily reactivated ISTA, the landlords were determined and able to bring the reform to a precipitate halt. This was achieved by slaughtering cattle as well as *campesinos*, exporting essential machinery, altering deeds, and extracting large quantities of capital from the country.[89] Confronted with a further coup attempt and in danger of losing all cooperation from the army's historic patron, Colonel Gutiérrez ordered an end to all expropriations under Phase One and indefinitely suspended Phase Two on 14 May. He thus took the guts out of the reform and safeguarded the principal coffee estates less than nine weeks after the law had been introduced. The measure remained on the statute book as a necessary sop to Washington but the landlords had proved fully capable of imposing their traditional veto by means of an open political campaign, resort to conspiracy, and a concise demonstration of the economic cost of any offensive on rural capital.

The PDC was powerless and Washington given a vivid illustration of the enduring authority of the landlord class and the severe consequences of meddling with its economic base. Sobered up by such an efficacious response and the possibility of a complete breakdown in the fragile concordat reached in January, the US henceforth acted with great wariness and concentrated its efforts in the political sphere on the understanding that no recomposition of the dominant bloc could be viable without the acquiescence of the most powerful sector of El Salvador's capitalist class. This was possible in terms of the nationalization of the banking system and foreign trade since the deepening economic crisis gave these measures a certain capitalist and managerial rationality and directly prejudiced the position of relatively few entrepreneurs despite ANEP's constant invectives against such 'collectivism'. However, the agrarian reform was effectively reduced to the 'Land to the Tiller' programme and the reorganization of tenure within the subsistence circuit. This was at the heart of the propaganda campaign behind the reform, the designers of which fondly believed despite the lamentable experience of Vietnam that they were going to 'breed capitalists like rabbits' in granting freehold to thousands of peasants. Nevertheless, in its restriction to plots of less than seven hectares the measure primarily affected lands on the agricultural margin – particularly in the north and east – that required frequent periods in fallow historically facilitated precisely by cycles of intermittent leasing. In halting this system the reform did provide some families with much desired title to ownership, but it also bonded them to land incapable of maintaining subsistence for any length of time, thus failing to give any secure protection against the wider crisis in the rural economy or to obviate the need to undertake harvest labour on the commercial *fincas*. Moreover, the attempt to substitute reallocation of marginal plots amongst the peasantry for distribution of the large *fincas* that covered most of the country's fertile farmland was deprived of even propaganda value by the inertia of administration: a year after Phase Three was introduced only 1,000 titles had been issued whereas 150,000 had been envisaged upon its promulgation.[90]

The considerable disparity between the original objectives and concrete results of the agrarian reform after five years is shown in Tables 44 and 45. Radical claims that the measure exercised minimal impact upon the structure of rural society, left the landed bourgeoisie largely unscathed, and improved the lot of only a tiny proportion of the peasantry were completely justified. Yet it would be mistaken to view the reform purely as a formality or piece of propaganda. Its retention on the statute book irked and threatened the oligarchy to such a point that it felt obliged to engage directly in party politics for the first time in nearly fifty years. Equally, while the number of rural poor to benefit was only a tiny fraction of those eligible for and in great need of land, the reform was perceived by a proportion of those excluded from it as indicative of at least some disposition to change the historic structure of land tenure. Both past and recent experience meant that such an assessment was profoundly sceptical, and the PDC was signally unable to generate enthusiasm for its capital policy in the countryside. Nevertheless, even that flawed and crippled measure which was introduced had some impact upon the classic peasant vision of limited good and strategies for survival under the conditions of disruption and violence reigning after 1980. This was reflected in the results of elections from 1982 in which the PDC competed with parties on the extreme right that unreservedly repudiated change in the rural sector. When faced with such a restricted choice and obliged to cast a vote, the reform gave the rural electorate some basis for distinguishing between forces that for all their vehement disputes were of a piece when it came to anti-Communism, determination to rout the guerrillas and support for the army's unpopular and destructive operations. In this respect the PDC's achievement was to establish itself as the 'lesser evil' within the dominant bloc.

In the spring of 1980 the position of both party and reform was highly precarious, being threatened above all else by the wave of rightist violence that neither Washington nor the junta was able to curb.[91] Just four days

Table 44: Land Reform in El Salvador: Official 1980 Targets

	Phase 1	*Phase 2*	*Phase 3*	*Total*
Property size affected (has.)	500+	100–500	rented–7	
No. properties affected	328	1,839	30,000	
Area affected (has.)	224,326	342,877	200,000	767,203
% total farming land	15	24	14	53
Area after reserve (has.)	209,000	82,027	200,000	491,027
% land available	14	6	14	34
No. farmers to benefit	60,000	n.a.	150,000	210,000
Av. size per beneficiary	3.5		0.75	

Sources: US State Department, March 1983; Checchi and Co., *Agrarian Reform in El Salvador*, Washington 1981 and 1983; *Boletín de Ciencias Económicas y Sociales*, January–February 1984, cited in Pearce, *Promised Land*, p.294.

Table 45: Land Reform in El Salvador, 1980–85

	Phase 1	*Phase 3*[1]	*Total*
Land formally redistributed (has.)	213,791	96,750	310,541
% total farming land	15	7	22
No. claimants	31,359	63,633	95,022
Claimants as % rural poor[2]	8	16	24
No. titles issued	22	5,456	5,478
% rural poor entitled	1.0	1.4	2.4

Notes:

1. Phase 2 was not introduced
2. Rural poor includes the landless and those with less than one hectare, not including those dispossessed by the civil war.

Source: Pearce, *Promised Land*, p.295.

after the reform was introduced PDC dissidents split to form the *Movimiento Popular Social Cristiano* (MPSC), led by Rubén Zamora (brother of the slain attorney general) and Héctor Dada and supported by perhaps a quarter of the active militants of the PDC. On 17 March the CRM called a one-day general strike as a 'rehearsal for the people' and this received the backing of three-quarters of the country's labour force. However, the CRM was in no position to defend its supporters and fifty-four people were killed on the day of the stoppage. The only institution that now stood between the two polarized camps was the Church, although by this stage Archbishop Romero no longer felt able to modulate his frequent political statements and condemnations of violence. He was, as a result, seen by the right as a partisan of the radical cause and an especially dangerous figure. Having written a widely publicized letter to President Carter in February denouncing US military aid to the junta as prejudicial to the cause of social peace, he now attacked a government largely staffed by a Catholic party just as unpopular and utterly dependent upon foreign support.[92] In a sermon on 24 March this position was sharpened further still as a consequence of the evasive response from Washington to his letter and Romero's justified fear that matters were moving towards a repetition of 1932. By stating that 'No soldier is obliged to obey an order to kill if it runs contrary to his conscience', the archbishop issued both an unremarkable restatement of basic doctrine and an explosive political challenge; in effect, he had sanctioned mutiny.[93] A day later he was assassinated when celebrating mass. Whilst Duarte resorted to what can only be described as weasel words in suggesting that the left might be responsible for this extraordinary crime, there was from the start little doubt that the prelate had been executed by a death squad of the extreme right against which he had inveighed so constantly. His successor, Archbishop Rivera y Damas, maintained Romero's general policies and upheld the interventionist role of the Church. But although Rivera y Damas had long been identified with the progressive wing of the hierarchy (Romero had been a conservative when he became archbishop), he necessarily conducted a more circumspect mission than his predecessor. This was in part simply because of the physical danger faced by priests, Rivera y Damas being obliged to have bodyguards, and in part because a campaign as acute as that upheld by Romero threatened to destroy the Church's entire moral mission and basic pastoral responsibilities by identifying it entirely with the political opposition. Additionally, Rivera y Damas could rely upon only a modest section of the bishops and clergy for more than reactive condemnations of government violence and policy, and he enjoyed pitifully little support from Rome in this regard.

Romero's assassination had much the same effect as did that of Chamorro in Nicaragua. The killing during the eucharist of an exceptionally popular head of the national Church in a country noted by more than its name for religiosity was widely viewed as less a political execution than an act of brutal sacrilege. The archibishop's martyrdom bestowed upon him the unofficial status of saint and was taken to indicate that the extreme right would stop at nothing. Indeed, the leadership of the left interpreted it as a deliberate effort to provoke the popular bloc into an uprising as in January 1932. Apprehension was in no sense alleviated when in the midst of a further, week-long strike called by the CRM, the military attacked the archbishop's funeral procession and killed 40 of the 80,000 mourners in front of foreign dignitaries and TV cameras. Expectations that the exposure of a foreign audience to such carnage would inhibit Washington from pursuing its policies proved unfounded; even international opinion was becoming accustomed to the bloodletting in El Salvador. The day after Romero was shot the Carter administration duly declared that it would give $55 million in economic aid, and early in April Congress authorized the disbursement of $5.7 million in military assistance. Washington was determined not to repeat the mistakes made in Nicaragua, being convinced that the junta was beset equally by right and left, was not itself responsible for the violence, and should be given consistent support.[94] The most that can be said for this policy is that it was indeed stable.

In El Salvador the execution of Romero and the events surrounding it convinced precisely those groups who had previously striven to uphold such a doctrine of 'equidistance' that they now possessed no option but to ally with the left. On 4 April the MNR combined with the MPSC and a number of unions and professional associations to form the *Frente Democrático Salvadoreño* (FDS) as a fleeting preamble to complete fusion with the CRM and acceptance of its Platform in the new *Frente Democrático Revolucionario* (FDR) a fortnight later. This move expanded the political reach of the opposition and undoubtedly required both the radical left and the Social Democrats to make the most flexible interpretation of the CRM's manifesto in order to secure an operable entente. The endurance of this broad front of heterogeneous forces over the following years with only one major policy crisis reflects the fact that it did not simply correspond to the exceptional right-wing offensive of mid 1980. The 'minimal' character of what was now the FDR platform certainly allowed for wide divergences over long-term strategy but it did so in such a way as to subordinate these to the pressing and henceforth undisputed tasks of political and armed struggle in order to defeat the dominant bloc and establish an entirely new regime. The nature of such a regime was indeed unclear in terms of the traditional models built upon social class and international alignment, yet this was of secondary importance to the popular demand for a united opposition movement that both supported reform and fought against the repressive bodies of the state and the oligarchy. Compared to the FSLN the FDR lacked the advantages of holding socio-economic policies that were markedly distinct from those proclaimed by the government (and over time the erosion of popular belief in the PDC's programme would be offset to some degree by a concerted tempering of the FDR's proposals). But like the Sandinistas, the FDR derived much support simply from its opposition to an exceptionally violent regime within which Christian Democratic espousals of social peace counted for very little. Furthermore, the FDR represented an ideologically more focused and organizationally more coherent force than did the erratic and fragile pacts between the dissident Nicaraguan bourgeoisie and the FSLN. This was, of course, in part because the Salvadorean dominant bloc was politically more extensive and tactically more flexible than Somocismo, and it certainly did not preclude the emergence of important tactical differences and difficulties aside from the formidable task of confronting a US government chastened by the Nicaraguan experience. All the same, the FDR's high degree of stability and coherence over the better part of ten years of fighting is in itself remarkable and must be attributed in good measure to its capacity to fuse and uphold the distinct but related democratic and popular radical traditions over which its constituent forces had battled during the 1970s. In the sense that events had brought these two currents together the FDR may be described as a natural alliance. The absence of the pronounced nationalist element that obtained in Nicaragua was to a large extent compensated for by the higher level of class consciousness and the more comprehensive exhaustion of the possibilities of liberal democracy under the supervision of the army.

The centrists' recognition that a 'middle way' was no longer possible was vividly confirmed by the sequence of events following the establishment of the FDR. Although a further 'ultra' putsch concocted by the debonair psychopath D'Aubuissón was avoided in early May, the conspiracy achieved one of its main objectives: it prompted the high command to remove the 'softliner' Colonel Majano as joint commander of the military, thus clearing the way for a full purge of reformists in the officer corps. A few days later the army leadership signalled its own determination to inflict a physical defeat upon the left at any price when some 600 *campesinos* fleeing a 'search and destroy' operation in Chalatenango were killed on the banks of the Río Sumpul in an appalling bloodbath of innocents facilitated by the Honduran army, with which agreements over collaboration had been made by the high command several days earlier.[95] The first of a number of such massacres, this event signalled the military's establishment of 'free-fire zones' in areas of popular support for the guerrilla, compelling a significant reappraisal by the peasantry of how best to ensure survival. Henceforth the rural population in certain regions – Chalatenango, Cabañas, Cuscatlán and Morazán in particular – was presented with little option but to take up arms or actively cooperate with the army since abstention from the struggle no longer guaranteed physical safety. Yet the possibilities of involvement in the opposition's military activities still remained limited since the guerrillas were unprepared for a major campaign, lacked weaponry, and had only achieved a formal state of coordination with the establishment of the *Dirección Revolucionaria Unificada* (DRU) in mid May.[96]

Both this inability to stage a military insurrection and continuing difficulties over tactics within the left gave the initiative to proponents of urban mass mobilization. In calling a forty-eight-hour general strike on 24 June and desisting from any guerrilla activity the FDR aimed not only to fortify its popular support and weaken the regime but also to demonstrate that it was not responsible for the violence.[97] Backing for the strike was sufficiently strong to encourage a further such approach despite the high level of casualties and the army's occupation of the university (where it would stay for four years). On 13 August the FDR called another stoppage, this time for three days and with the (undeclared) objective of provoking a major political crisis and popular uprising. However, the declaration of a specific time limit militated against the aim of overthrowing the government, and the level of repression against a vulnerable and insufficiently protected movement rapidly thwarted any potential assault on state power. Disputes over the tactics adopted in the August strike led FAPU and RN to hold back their support, the affiliated power workers' union STECEL striking separately, belatedly, and to little avail. In fact, these groups were pledged more forcefully to an insurrectionary line than were many on the left, but their criticisms reflected the state of confusion and exhaustion that prevailed within a working class that had undertaken a series of general strikes at exceptionally high cost and with minimal gain beyond some improvement in clandestine organisation.[98] The attempt to bring down the regime through strike action may be interpreted as a misjudged application of the Sandinistas' tactics in June 1979, a continuing failure to register the superiority of the military in the towns, or an effort by the reformists in the FDR to avoid a prolonged struggle and the radicalization that would probably ensue. Whatever the case, the setbacks suffered by the urban movement amounted to a significant defeat, marginalizing the working class as an active political force until 1984. The immediate result was that RN temporarily left the DRU and was only reincorporated into the movement after fierce debate and the transformation of the DRU into the FMLN in October. This was on the basis of strategic agreement that provided the guerrilla with a more prominent role but still gave precedence to the insurrectionism favoured by RN and the ERP over the 'prolonged people's war' that was at the heart of the FPL's strategy.[99]

On the right the failure of the summer strikes gave García and Gutiérrez the resolve to settle accounts with the military reformists who were still seeking some settlement short of the annihilation of the left. A set of institutional assignments issued in September transferred Majano's allies from positions of authority, the reformists' attempts to resist coming too late and lacking the disposition to use force that was now necessary for settling any institutional conflict.[100] Deprived of its power base, Majano's position on the junta lost its significance; being himself a target for the death squads, the colonel was removed from all office in December. There was some irony but not a little political logic in the fact that Majano's defeat permitted the elevation of Duarte to the presidency of the junta (not yet the republic). Still, the preparedness of the Christian Democrat leader to cling to office was less remarkable for this than for the fact that it remained unaltered by the capture and murder of all bar one of the FDR leadership in November and the rape and killing of three US nuns and one lay-worker in December by government forces.[101] In both cases the victims were unarmed, the murder of US citizens proving to be of greater immediate consequence since it created such a domestic outcry that the defeated Carter administration was obliged to cut aid to the regime. Although the Reagan transition team was already engaged in discussions with the military and publicly committed to expand support, the immediate severance of aid was unavoidable, especially when the right killed two US employees of AIFLD working on the agrarian reform early in January.[102] This created a critical hiatus over the month prior to Reagan's inauguration, encouraging the FMLN to make a decisive drive for power and present the new administration in Washington with a fait accompli before it could intervene decisively to shore up the army and the right.

The 'final offensive' opened on 10 January 1981 produced a number of rapid gains for the guerrilla. FMLN troops threatened to capture Ilopango, just fifteen miles from San Salvador, made some incursions into the city, took the western town of Santa Ana, and engaged the military in fierce fighting in Chalatenango, Morazán, Sonsonate and Usulután. Within the first forty-eight hours some 500 people died in the fighting, but the rebels failed to make a major breakthrough. The re-establishment of US military aid by Ambassador Robert White, duped by the high command and his own advisers into believing that there had been major Nicaraguan involvement in the campaign, had little effect on the immediate balance of forces; within six days the FMLN was forced to embark upon a measured retreat.[103] When Reagan assumed office in Washington Duarte was still in place as his Salvadorean counterpart and although very badly pressed, the military remained in control of all major urban centres and most of the countryside in the south and west of the country. By the end of the month the prospect of a 'Nicaraguan scenario' had waned considerably. It would, however, require strong US intervention to keep it at bay.

Civil War and Elections

The months following the collapse of the FMLN offensive established the general pattern of military conflict for the next seven years. Within the rebel camp the FPL's strategy of prolonged war necessarily regained prominence as a series of clumsy government 'encirclement' operations under García's direction and against the counsel of US advisers failed to dislodge the guerrillas from their rural strongholds in Chalatenango (primarily the FPL), the Guazapa volcano north of San Salvador (all groups) and Morazán (primarily the ERP). Even after García's eventual removal from command in April 1983 and the adoption of more adroit counter-insurgency tactics by younger officers it was evident that the FMLN could not be categorically defeated in the foreseeable future. Military casualties remained unacceptably high whilst the guerrillas' general adherence to the policy of returning prisoners of war through the Red Cross encouraged surrender by troops of a government army massively expanded to 50,000 men by 1985 and composed of many more pressganged youths than US-trained veterans of the elite units deployed in the north and east.[104] After its early setback the FMLN proved to be disconcertingly efficient at fighting a tactical war of manoeuvre within a strategic war of position over adverse terrain, keeping a force of some 8,000 fighters in the field, constantly harrying remote towns, building a presence in the provinces of San Miguel and Usulután, and occasionally inflicting sharp reverses on the enemy (the Ilopango airbase, January 1982; Usulután, February 1982; El Paraiso, Chalatenango, December 1983; Cerrón Grande hydroelectric plant, June 1984; the training camp at La Unión, October 1985; El Paraiso, March 1987). On the other hand, at no stage between 1980 and 1987 did the guerrilla army appear close to staging a consolidated assault on state power and defeating the government forces. This was in large measure due to the huge rise in US military aid – from $5.9 million in 1980 to $136.5 million in 1984 – and the progressive improvement in the army's logistical skills under Washington's supervision. Perhaps the single most important element in this was increased use of the airforce and in particular helicopters, greatly improving the military's capacity for surveillance and mobility as well as facilitating the bombing raids that from 1984 accounted for a large proportion of civilian casualties.[105] Gradual adoption by the military of 'civic action' programmes in areas of contention was only partially successful in swaying the allegiance of the local population and by no means replaced 'free-fire zones' as the principal method of subduing rebel supporters. The involvement of US-trained troops in the massacres at Mozote (1981) and Tamarindo (1984) strongly suggests that the acquisition of new hardware and the adoption of more sophisticated strategies that were enthusiastically explained to the international press had not, in fact, changed the military's methods as much as was often claimed and reported.

From the outside the picture appeared very much as one of stalemate, with US support cancelling out the effects of the army's incompetence and counterproductive brutality while the FMLN's military skills and core of popular support ensured survival in an extended war of attrition. Such an image was encouraged by the fact that this was a 'low-intensity conflict' fought primarily in the countryside and without set-piece battles or the consolidated offensives seen in Nicaragua. The stalemate was, though, more apparent than real since the terms of the war now revolved less around the balance of purely military forces than the ability of the FMLN to withstand the effects of accumulating war-weariness amongst the population and the capacity of the regime to bear huge economic losses and the political costs of a campaign in which the vast majority of the 60,000 people who lost their lives were civilians killed by the army or its friends on the extreme right. The US military advisers – technically limited in number to fifty-five but in practice many more, and supported by a sizeable permanent garrison now established in Honduras – dropped the optimistic predictions of complete victory that had been the order of the day in 1981 and 1982 and instead celebrated the gains made in containing the FMLN.[106]

This was, in fact, the only viable objective in the medium term and it was undoubtedly achieved, despite the continuing inefficiency of a military apparatus that possessed more materiel than it could handle and failed to eliminate its traditions of rigid hierarchy, internal squabbling and corruption. In effect, it was US intervention that halted the advance of the Salvadorean revolution. Despite the political importance of the war to Washington and to the entire balance of forces in the region, its appalling human cost in terms of tens of thousands of deaths and hundreds of thousands of refugees (by 1985 possibly one-sixth of the population), the introduction of gunships by the army and the use of videos by the guerrilla, the conflict remained very Salvadorean in character.[107] Certain social protocols incomprehensible to the US advisers were respected partly out of tactical design and partly in order to preserve some semblance of order amidst the chaos and violence. The FMLN frequently permitted small contingents of government troops to withdraw unmolested from untenable positions whilst the army regularly allowed the transport of supplies to areas under guerrilla control. There was in this a strong echo of the etiquette of the nineteenth-century civil wars, the conflict being fought on a daily basis less between faceless protagonists of communist or fascist dictatorship than between youths of similarly humble origins. For these youths political commitment or orders from on high by no means compelled the killing of their opposite number or superseded the logic of survival, either in itself or to the end of fighting another day.[108] Although these features can easily be overemphasized, they do signal a certain socialization of the conflict often obscured by the more manifest brutality of peasant warfare as well as the effects of ideological polarization and the unprecedented deployment of modern machines of destruction.

The military advances made by government forces with the help of US equipment and advice were not pyrrhic. In the countryside both supporters of the FMLN and those who remained 'neutral' reacted to the growing death toll and the improvements in the army's operations by adopting a more cautious pattern of activity. This inevitably weakened the guerrillas' political base, but even after seven years it had not brought about a qualitative reduction in rebel activity or eradicated the government's apprehension about some surprise, Tet-like assault. In this respect the comfort of having Washington as a guarantor of last resort only partially alleviated the psychological and political pressure bred by a war in which the enemy had adapted to strategic containment and even when under extreme duress possessed an advantage of initiative in terms of launching a rapid offensive. However much the resources for this were whittled down, the government army could not afford to discount the threat of a strategic ambush or avoid the corresponding commitment of much of its activity to defensive tasks and predictable manoeuvres. Despite the formidable deterrent value of Washington's support the balance of nervous energy in this waiting game was finer than is often recognized. This was, of course, a largely intangible element but when, from mid 1984, the economic crisis began to bite very deeply and the popular movement in the towns retrieved some of the militancy of 1979–80 it could no longer be considered a mere formality in a zero-sum game.

From Washington's perspective it was necessary to alternate encouragement of such a fear with assurances that the large sums disbursed to its Salvadorean allies were paying dividends in a gradual defeat of the FMLN. As with the Contra campaign, this policy required a certain 'finesse' in presenting the local balance of forces as well as a cavalier – at times downright deceitful – response to objections about the conduct of the Salvadorean military. These were most marked with regard to the violation of human rights, which Reagan constantly 'certified' as diminishing, but also extended to matters such as the resale of munitions by local forces.[109] From the very first days of its term the administration devoted most of its energies to presenting the conflict in terms of domino theory, Ambassador White's erroneous claims of Nicaraguan involvement in the January 1981 offensive providing a convenient precedent upon which to build a much more extensive policy. Within a month of assuming office the government issued what became known as the 'White Paper', the first of an uninterrupted series of administration allegations of Soviet, Cuban and Nicaraguan intervention in El Salvador.[110] Since it came on the heels of the January offensive this outspoken document was initially treated with some gravity in press and political circles, but upon closer inspection the voluminous empirical evidence presented to support its claims appeared at best extremely flimsy and at worst clumsy concoction by an over-hurried CIA.[111] The Paper was rapidly discredited, and indeed over the following four years CIA specialists charged with 'proving' the existence of material support for the FMLN from the Sandinistas signally failed to turn up one shred of persuasive evidence.[112] In the short term, revelations that the White Paper was based upon wishful thinking rather than any concrete intelligence embarrassed the administration, but this was treated as a secondary inconvenience and not allowed to stand in the way of a Cold War logic in which the 'linkage' from Moscow to Morazán via Managua compelled intervention and 'holding the line' in El Salvador.

The fact that such a policy could be sustained by the government and supported by Congress despite the absence or inadmissibility of specific evidence to justify it and doubts as to its wider applicability must be attributed primarily to Reagan's insistence and rhetorical skill in propounding it. This factor was less irrational than is often claimed for although it incorporated a thoroughly asinine view of the world, it also provided a coherent rationale for pursuing a policy that many Democrats as well as Republicans favoured, regardless of whether the hand of the Kremlin was in evidence or not. Failure to support the Salvadorean military would very probably entail an FMLN victory and the entirely undesirable establishment in the region of another independent regime based upon insurrection. The president's simpleton explanations as to how and why this threat had come about were less important than his commitment to the cause of counter-revolution and the domestic support he was able to muster for it. All the same, Reagan could not depend upon bi-partisan and still less international support simply by opposing the guerrilla. Even in the fervent anti-Communist atmosphere his administration had generated, domestic political considerations required such an opposition to take the form of a defence of a regime that was at least superficially democratic and certainly distinguishable from that of Somoza. Counter-revolutionary intervention was no longer permissible solely on the grounds of Jeane Kirkpatrick's preference for right-wing 'authoritarianism' over left-wing 'totalitarianism'. Such callow realpolitik abdicated any claim to moral superiority and was recognized by more curious and critical politicians and commentators to be counterproductive in practical terms however acceptable they might find its murky ethics.[113] In fact, the Reagan government consistently sought to avoid falling back upon Kirkpatrick's rational but unpalatable blueprint. The lesson of Nicaragua had made it sharply aware of the diplomatic and practical merits of disaggregating local dominant blocs and cajoling them to adopt democratic forms of government, thereby justifying greater US military support as well as removing at least the form of dictatorship as an element in political polarization at the local level. This policy was finally fulfilled on a regional basis early in 1986 with the assumption of the presidency of Guatemala by Vinicio Cerezo. Yet if it took a full five years to organize the Guatemalan military's retreat from office, the supposed 'redemocratization' of El Salvador was in many respects a more erratic and taxing process.

This project was simultanously facilitated and threatened by the decision of the landlord class and extreme right to augment the power of economic veto and unofficial terror with the creation of a formal political party in the shape of the *Alianza Republicana Nacionalista* (ARENA), founded in 1981 under the leadership of Roberto D'Aubuissón. The emergence of ARENA as the first authentically oligarchic party to make a serious challenge for office since 1932 certainly permitted the contest within the dominant bloc to take the form of public competition and the allocation of office to be decided by poll rather than putsch and economic blackmail. On the other hand, ARENA's programme and D'Aubuissón's untempered pronouncements made it clear that if the party were to win power it would bundle the reforms off even the legislative record, to which most had already been restricted, and pursue a counter-insurgency policy virtually identical to that undertaken by General Martinez. Free talk about napalm and 'extermination' together with the denunciation of the PDC as crypto-Communist embarrassed Washington no less than did D'Aubuissón's unsavoury past.

However, the US had to run the risk of ARENA winning in order to maintain any semblance of democratic process.[114]

The election for a constituent assembly held in March 1982 did produce a genuine if far from clean contest between the right (PDC) and the extreme right (ARENA; PCN; POP; PPS; AD). This fact relieved Washington of much of the burden of explaining the notable absence of parties to the left of the PDC, all of which boycotted the poll on the grounds that participation could only lead to the killing of their supporters and candidates.[115] Moreover, the fierce campaign staged by the three serious contenders – the PDC, ARENA and a revived PCN – tended to distract attention from the embarrassing question of the poll's organization, which did not extend to the preparation of an electoral register but made voting mandatory and backed this obligation to reject the FDR-FMLN's boycott by requiring every citizen to obtain certification of having voted on their identity papers. Failure to do this was popularly seen as little less than courting death at the hands of the paramilitary which regularly inspect these documents. This fear combined with the general conditions of violence and the absence of any progressive representation to undermine the democratic pretensions of an election which few expected to be distinct from its fraudulent predecessors. Yet if the rebels' denunciation of the poll as a farce was accepted by a domestic and international opinion far wider than that which sympathized with the opposition, there was little that the FMLN could do to disrupt the election.[116] Although the guerrillas staged offensives in Usulután, Morazán, Chalatenango and San Vicente immediately prior to the voting, and fighting impeded many thousands from casting a ballot, it soon became evident that the population was more fearful of the consequences of not voting than of doing so. Furthermore, it proved difficult to attack polling stations around which large numbers of people were collected. Thus, even though the figures for participation presented by Washington were subsequently shown to be grossly inflated and the conditions in which the poll was conducted were in no sense free or fair, the US government viewed the election as an unqualified public relations success.[117]

The result was less acceptable to the Reagan administration since the PCN managed to revive its clientelist network of the previous decades and muster fourteen seats to form a bloc with the nineteen which ARENA had won on the basis of heavy spending on a carnival campaign that offered clear and emphatic solutions to the middle class as well as benefiting from open military collaboration and widespread coercion by sympathetic employers. Against this the PDC won only twenty-four seats. This gave the extreme right control of the new assembly although the PCN's success obliged ARENA to restrain its conduct and retreat from a number of its boisterous campaign promises.[118] When, after much manoeuvring inside the reactionary alliance, D'Aubuissón himself was elected president of the assembly Washington's gamble appeared to have backfired and the PDC even boycotted proceedings. The US had no option but to make the most of the situation and the Christian Democrats had to participate or disclaim their entire strategy and lose Washington's patronage. The party thus sat sullenly by as the assembly appointed the indulgent oligarch Alvaro Magaña as a provisional president of the republic completely beholden to the majority and the high command, suspended the last active phase of the agrarian reform for the coming season, and amended the already suspended phase to increase the size of farms exempted from any possible expropriation. Unable to split the 'ultra' front sufficiently to gain a decisive voice in the drafting of an unremarkably traditionalist constitution, bereft of what little power of patronage it had previously possessed, and having lost much of the political capital provided by the agrarian reform, the PDC could not even guarantee the physical safety of its militants. Although it managed to hold on to a good part of its provincial organization and municipal control of San Salvador, the party became critically dependent upon US backing in order to survive two years in formal as well as substantive opposition.

Neither ARENA nor the rest of the extreme right proved capable of converting its surprising electoral success into an emphatic and enduring triumph. Apart from the fact that its control of parliament depended upon a fractious coalition, there was in practice little scope for escalating the campaign against the FMLN, and Washington's control of the purse-strings limited the degree to which informal violence could be employed. More importantly, both the war itself and the record of the extreme right over the previous years restricted the potential for expanding support for the reactionary cause. Although many in the middle class saw D'Aubuissón as a decisive and charismatic anti-Communist leader, no less a number recognized that he lacked Washington's blessing and was therefore a liability for any stable conservative project. Moreover, for every ten followers of ARENA given government jobs there existed a thousand workers or peasants whose interests were prejudiced by the decisions they made and who were unalterably opposed to the reactionary policies and belligerent activity of 'Major Bob's' partisans. Both at home and abroad this suave proto-fascist remained stigmatized by his association with the death squads, and the party's agile exploitation of US campaigning methods to supplement traditional coercion failed to generate a mass corporatist movement. The socio-political impediments to this were too deeply rooted for ARENA, like ORDEN before it, to augment its natural constituency with more than a modest following of desperate petty bourgeois and those mesmerized by D'Aubuissón's macho style. ARENA even failed to displace the authority of the supposedly disgraced PCN, which was highly practised in securing votes and had exploited the new balance of forces within the dominant bloc to engage in a form of brokerage, curb ARENA's most primeval antics, and gain a modicum of support from a grateful Washington in return.

Both the holding of the 1982 elections and the right's victory produced fewer immediate changes than had been feared or expected. The bulk of the reforms of 1979–80 were already neutered. Little could be done in real terms to transform the prosecution of the war against a left that had long since been forced out of the formal political arena, and the loss of office by the Christian Democrats had more impact upon the style of government and Duarte's personal ambitions than it had on the substance of policy. This relative continuity allowed Washington to tolerate 'ultra' domination of the regime and, more importantly, to proceed with its plans for further elections and the complete restitution of constitutional form.

Within the FDR-FMLN the exigencies of both a prolonged war and the holding of elections exacerbated differences over strategy similar to those that had prevailed up to 1980. This conflict is often attributed to the impact of the 1982 poll and the rebels' inability to halt or severely disrupt it. However, the issues at stake were much wider and reflected a recognition shared by all the groups that the period following the January 1981 offensive had produced a new balance of forces both internally and externally. The dispute over how to confront this in programmatic and organizational terms came to a head during the first months of 1983 when a rift developed inside the FPL, with Salvador Cayetano Carpio opposing the establishment of a single party of the left and a strategy more centrally based on negotiations against which he defended the primacy of class politics, armed struggle and an explicitly radical socio-economic programme. Carpio's position was defeated inside the FPL, the majority led by Mélida Anaya Montes ('Ana María') accepting further modifications of the organization's radical policies towards the more pragmatic political line of the rest of the FDR-FMLN.[119] In a series of confused events, the substance and consequence of which was bitterly disputed, Ana María was murdered in Managua early in April 1983 by militants closely associated with Carpio. Several days later the veteran leader returned from a trip abroad and apparently committed suicide.[120] The apportioning of blame and strength of sentiment caused by these deaths and the conflict that preceded them threatened a major rupture inside the FPL, and several factions did indeed reject the new leadership to establish more or less stable independent groups.[121] However, there was no division comparable to that of 1975 inside the ERP caused by the killing of Roque Dalton, and while a significant sector of the FPL and its sympathizers was deeply dismayed at the new developments, the broader circumstances precluded either exodus from the FDR-FMLN or open repudiation of its policies.

The resolution of conflict inside the FPL permitted the FDR-FMLN to replace the old CRM Programmatic Platform of 1980 with a new strategic document aimed at establishing a *Gobierno de Amplia Participación* (GAP;

Government of Broad Participation). Made public in January 1984, this manifesto was appreciably less radical and more concerned with tactics than its predecessor. At its core was the proposal for a new coalition government 'in which no single force predominates' and which would uphold national sovereignty, respect human rights, meet immediate socio-economic needs, bring the war to an end, and prepare elections after a suitable period of time. Many of the specific objectives of the 1980 Platform, such as nationalization and economic planning, were dropped whilst others, such as agrarian reform, were substantially moderated in tone. Much space was devoted to the mechanisms for a ceasefire and truce.[122] In sum, the GAP no longer assumed the defeat of the government army but was based upon acceptance of military equivalence that obliged both sides to make concessions. Above all else, it offered a basis for negotiation.

The GAP's flexibility and proposals for peace revived the opposition's challenge to the US and the regime in San Salvador. While many guerrillas remained highly sceptical about ceasefire terms that would make them distinctly vulnerable to the undefeated army despite the proposed retention of arms, there was broad agreement within the FMLN that a new initiative was required prior to the elections of March 1984. In some quarters the proposal was seen as merely propagandistic and designed to be rejected despite the move towards the political centre. The FDR certainly possessed impressive diplomatic skills and was unafraid to exploit them, but the GAP did also represent a genuine shift in strategy within which emphasis upon concrete socio-economic objectives was diminished and that on political power and recapturing the political support of a war-weary population was enhanced. At one level this change reflected the rising stock within the FDR-FMLN of the PCS, which drew from the experience of Nicaragua less the imperative of categorical defeat of the military than the advantages of alliances and the potential of gaining a quota of power through which subsequently to consolidate the radical position.[123] In more general terms the GAP registered the need to make the objectives of an extremely taxing war more tangible and to challenge the claims made by the US and local dominant bloc that their own electoral competition constituted a genuine democratic process and was the only chance for peace. By declaring that it would not disrupt the impending presidential poll despite its fraudulent nature the FDR-FMLN accepted the limits of its position and also placed pressure on the PDC in particular to respond to the GAP's initiative and thus justify Christian Democratic claims to be the natural party of peace and social harmony. Conditions in El Salvador in 1984 were very different to those in Nicaragua in 1978–79, but in the sense that the opposition challenged a faction of the dominant bloc dependent upon popular support to honour its own programme and risk an alliance in order to terminate repression, the GAP may be seen as similar to the Sandinista overtures to the liberal bourgeoisie.

The rebel leadership was far too experienced to see the chances of such an outcome as more than minimal since the PDC both depended upon the backing of a US government unalterably opposed to negotiations with the FDR and had invested a great deal of its political capital in repudiation of the radical alliance. Moreover, Duarte's ambition to be president far exceeded that of most scoutmasters and he was scarcely likely to agree to terms that could deprive him of this prize. The opposition proposals cannot be discounted as a factor in the poll of 1984 since a large proportion of the electorate was seeking an end to the war, and over the last two years the claims of D'Aubuissón and ARENA in this regard had been shown to be threadbare. There was, however, little evidence that hopes for a PDC–FDR entente increased the popularity of the poll; indeed, the turnout in March 1984 was lower than that in 1982, and in areas of FMLN support markedly so.[124] The PDC's failure to capitalize upon the extreme right's control of the constituent assembly and conduct of the war was reflected in the result, which gave Christian Democracy a clear majority in the main war zones but only 43 per cent of the national vote against 28.3 per cent for ARENA and 19.3 per cent for the PCN.[125] This plurality necessitated the holding of a second round in May between Duarte and D'Aubuissón – a straight match in which the critical votes of the PCN were not promised to ARENA and the US made no secret about which candidate it favoured. Duarte's victory in the run-off may be ascribed to the influence of his external sponsor with the floating vote, and to acceptance by important sections of the far right and military that the PDC was now essential for continued US support. Yet his triumph by 53.6 per cent to 46.4 per cent was less than overwhelming, the PDC's control of only twenty-four of the legislature's sixty seats compelling the new president to include members of the reactionary opposition in the cabinet and to pursue policies that were little different from those of previous years. The dissolution of the paramilitary's intelligence units, creation of a new vice-ministry of defence, and the firing of one senior officer (Colonel Carranza) had minimal effect upon repression and fell far short of meeting Duarte's campaign promises and ushering in a new epoch of social transformation.

Duarte's election did all the same produce a hiatus in the pattern of politics and he exploited what could only be a momentary advantage to hold a meeting with the leaders of the FDR-FMLN. Although this encounter, held in the northern village of La Palma in October 1984, was projected by the US press in particular as the result of the new president's own initiative, it arose from his need to respond to the popular demand for a ceasefire that had been given extra impetus by the GAP. Moreover, despite the fact that Duarte seemed to risk a rupture with Washington, which remained studiously silent about this surprise outing by its protégé, and a more immediate threat from the officer corps, which indicated from the outset that it would brook no alteration in the political and military status quo, he skilfully used the opportunity to reject accusations that he was a mere puppet and then to inform the rebel leaders that his only condition for a ceasefire would be their surrender, thus ensuring the collapse of negotiations and a return to the status quo ante.[126] Over the next three years the possibility of further talks was never entirely ruled out and the FDR-FMLN continued to make Duarte the target of their offers, but the president's successful handling of the 1984 negotiations and Washington's capacity to sabotage the regional proposals of the Contadora group precluded the need for the military to veto any agreement.[127] (The negotiations of November 1985 that exchanged Duarte's kidnapped daughter Inés and a number of captured PDC mayors for FMLN prisoners aggravated the army but did not include any political accords.)

In the congressional and municipal elections of March 1985 the PDC won a working majority in parliament and seemed finally to have secured a decisive advantage over ARENA, D'Aubuissón being removed from the leadership of a party now in some disarray.[128] However, the turnout of less than 40 per cent reflected a distinct lack of popular enthusiasm for seemingly incessant elections held while the civil war continued unabated and the economic crisis deepened. Between 1978 and 1984 GDP had fallen by nearly a quarter, the production of basic grains by 15 per cent, the government budget by 15.5 per cent (the military budget had risen by 133.5 per cent), and the cost of living had more than doubled.[129] Real wages in the urban sector had fallen by over 40 per cent since 1980. Under such conditions the working class was prepared to face the threat of repression and challenge Christian Democracy to realize the promises it had made over a long period of partisan competition without administrative responsibility.

The opening of this new political front dealt a severe blow to the PDC. Accustomed to negotiating with the military, exchanging insults with the ultra-right, and disparaging the 'subversives', the party now found itself confronted by popular pressure of a type not witnessed for five years and which threatened its credibility as an alternative to the oligarchy and the left. In the month of Duarte's election there were more strikes than in all of 1983, and by the end of 1984 some 350,000 workers had engaged in industrial action for basic economic rather than political demands.[130] The leading force in this movement was MUSYGES (*Movimiento Unificado de Sindicatos y Gremios de El Salvador*), established on May Day 1983 and including many unions that supported the FDR.[131] By 1986 the process of regroupment had reached the point at which the newly founded *Union Nacional de Trabajadores Salvadoreños* (UNTS) included 150 unions and 400,000 members. At the same time, the failure of the government to detain the contraction of the economy or fulfil its promises of redistribution had led to the splintering of the PDC's own union confederation, *Unidad Popular Democrática* (UPD), and the threat of its leadership to join with the left.[132] The revival of urban militancy was seen by the US as directly threatening the re-emergence of military conflict in the towns, but while the FMLN did increase its activity in San Salvador from 1984 and was closely linked to sections of the new union movement, it did not attempt either to capture its leadership or to force it into precipitate political initiatives. The FDR's capacity to do this was in any case limited, and it suited the left that discontent was palpably the result of PDC failure to meet popular demands and not readily attributable to radical subversion. The FMLN's longstanding campaign of economic sabotage in the east of the country had done much to weaken the regime, but the guerrillas recognized that the disruption it caused prejudiced their popularity and, as with the occasional enforced conscription practised by the ERP in particular, threatened to make their activities indistinguishable from those of the government in the eyes of that significant sector of the population that held no strong partisan views.

For many ordinary Salvadoreans the gradual lessening of repression from the awful levels of 1980–82 was perceptible before the PDC came to office and only partially the result of government policies. (Although political deaths and 'disappearances' fell to 3,361 in 1984, they had already declined from 13,794 in 1982 to 6,352 in 1983 as the military shifted from the strategy of massacre towards that of 'civic action' and 'psychological operations' founded upon the early wave of terror.) Moreover, the relative loss of fear that this encouraged heightened discontent with government inability to deal with the economy and the severe refugee crisis as well as its refusal to pursue the initial effort to halt the war.[133] Nominally in control of the military, which notably desisted from staging the coups that were continually rumoured to be under preparation, and now in possession of a working majority in the legislature, the PDC could no longer plausibly cast blame for its inefficiency and inactivity on the extreme right. Doing this would mean recognizing the continuing power of the economic veto and thus admitting to the futility of the party's activities over the last five years and vindicating the decision of its old UNO allies to ally with the left. The government was not, of course, deprived of the luxury of blaming 'Communist subversion' for the country's ills, but this too was a two-edged sword whilst it refused to negotiate with the FMLN and failed to liquidate it.

The Duarte regime had already become widely discredited by October 1986, when a major earthquake struck San Salvador killing at least 12,000 people and making 150,000 homeless. Despite the fact that similar disasters in Nicaragua (1972), Guatemala (1976) and Mexico (1985) offered clear political and administrative lessons to the regime, its response to the calamity was remarkably inept. Indeed, Duarte himself appeared to abdicate political as well as personal responsibility by passing administration of all foreign aid to the very private sector he was pledged to curb. In January 1987, when the capital was still recovering from the disaster, the president announced the introduction of a new tax to raise $27 million towards the war effort. This ill-judged move provoked the private sector to stage a one-day strike that was fully supported by the unions. Once again the expected coup failed to materialize, but under the new rules of the game the extreme right saw no overbearing need to push the military into rebellion and run the risk of conflict with Washington. The prospects for the 'ultras' in the 1989 election already appeared increasingly bright and it was highly doubtful whether the government could collect a tax resisted by all sectors of the population. The much vaunted 'centrist' option for resolving El Salvador's structural crisis appeared no less impotent and a great deal more tarnished than it had late in 1980.

On the face of things, then, it might be expected that Duarte would welcome the regional peace accord in 1987. He, after all, was the only Central American leader to have attempted negotiations with the armed opposition. He retained a formal commitment to bring about peace, needed to revive a much reduced constituency, and might possibly find a way of diminishing the dependency on the military that had denied him a coveted position amongst the region's democratic reformists. Yet Duarte proved to be the most resistant of all the Central American presidents to the Arias plan, and he willingly complied with Washington's urging to withdraw from the summit scheduled for June 1987, thereby sabotaging it. This was assuredly because Duarte could not hope to survive without the support of the US, which at that stage believed that it could easily thwart the peace initiative before it got off the ground. In all likelihood it also reflected apprehension that the FDR-FMLN would lead him into a diplomatic trap. Recognizing this dilemma, the far right adroitly began to call for talks with the guerrillas, the army keeping disturbingly silent.

The 'shame factor' behind the initial impetus of the Arias proposals was most evident in Duarte's case, the general support for the plan casting his solitary opposition in a very poor light. Faced with the alternative of being labelled a Yanqui puppet and warmonger, he bowed to pressure and, having reiterated his customary charges that Nicaragua continued to aid the FMLN, sullenly signed the agreement. The left blew equally hot and cold, Rubén Zamora quickly declaring that he would return to open political activity whilst the guerrillas signalled extreme reluctance to negotiate with an individual who persisted in demanding total surrender as a precondition. Under the terms of the accord the GAP was rendered irrelevant but there still existed space for manoeuvre. The left used this skilfully, and in a quite remarkable event staged a mass political meeting addressed by all its leaders and defended by guerrillas in the capital itself whilst the army command deemed it wise to quit the area. For four years the FMLN had proposed a ceasefire, and it was little threatened by the prospect of losing external assistance. At the same time, however, it saw no reason to change its opinion of the value of Duarte's word and the army's adhesion to written agreements. There certainly existed some threat of a rupture in the 1980 alliance, but with the death squads still active and patently seeking to impede any negotiated progress, the future did not appear auspicious for the likes of Zamora who wished to jump the gun in more ways than one. Neither the population at large nor the major political and military protagonists held high hopes of the Guatemala agreement. Washington continued to stress the difficulties of making it work in Nicaragua because of Sandinista intractability, but if anything the problems in El Salvador were greater still.

Notes

1. *Diario de Hoy*, San Salvador, 9 June 1969, quoted in Stephen Webre, *José Napoleón Duarte and the Christian Democratic Party in Salvadoran Politics, 1960–78*, Baton Rouge 1979, p.57.

2. Statement to House Sub-Committee on Inter-American Affairs, 2 February 1982, quoted in Raymond Bonner, *Weakness and Deceit. US Policy in El Salvador*, New York 1984, p.233.

3. Quoted in ibid., p.231.

4. Georgie Anne Geyer, 'A Small Place in the Sun', *Notre Dame Magazine*, vol.14, no.2, summer 1985. José Napoleón Duarte graduated from Notre Dame in 1948 with a degree in civil engineering.

5. Quoted in Bonner, *Weakness and Deceit*, p.162. At that time Vides Casanova was Commander of the National Guard, the force widely accepted to be responsible for the greatest number of civilian deaths. He later became minister of defence.

6. Interview in *Playboy*, November 1984, p.75.

7. Even Jeane Kirkpatrick, who was the closest thing to a theorist of inter-American affairs on the staff of the Reagan administration and an uncompromising supporter of domino theory, was obliged to confess that 'the Soviets don't have very much popular support in El Salvador'. Quoted in Bonner, *Weakness and Deceit*, p.92.

8. In my 1982 text *The Long War* I tended to the view that the role of the urban masses and struggle was more pronounced. This was in part due to the fact that the bulk of the book was written in 1981 when the shift from town to countryside did not yet appear as important as it later transpired to be, at least until mid 1984. Some revision of this view was made in the postscript to the second edition (1985) but this failed to register the full importance of peasant mobilization in the pre-1979 period that the book underplayed. I think most of the objections and criticisms in this regard fair and correct but would still desist from embracing the wholeheartedly ruralist theories of the Salvadorean revolution that tended to gain popularity after 1981 largely on the basis of the concentration of the FMLN in the departments of Chalatenango and Morazán. The subsequent war of attrition, necessity of the peasantry to engage in survivalist strategies and recuperation of the mass movement in the towns, all indicate the need for caution in extrapolating general theses from conjunctural shifts. Although the present chapter incorporates a number of revisions and changes in emphasis, it is essentially a condensation of the arguments presented in *The Long War*. If anything, the literature on contemporary El Salvador is more voluminous than that on Nicaragua, perhaps because US intervention began earlier and was more direct. Aside from Bonner's *Weakness and Deceit*, which is the fullest account of the US role but rather thin and disjointed on Salvadorean

politics, general surveys of the recent period include Robert Armstrong and Janet Shenk, *El Salvador. The Face of Revolution*, London 1982; Tommy Sue Montgomery, *Revolution in El Salvador: Origins and Evolution*, Boulder 1982; Michael McClintock, *The American Connection. State Terror and Popular Resistance in El Salvador*, London 1985; Enrique Baloyra, *El Salvador in Transition*, Chapel Hill 1982; Lisa North, *Bitter Grounds. Roots of Revolt in El Salvador*, Toronto 1981; Cynthia Arnson, *El Salvador. A Revolution Confronts the United States*, Washington 1982; Philip L. Russell, *El Salvador in Crisis*, Austin 1984. The publication of many of these texts in 1982 is not coincidental and reflects the impact of the crisis in the US in particular over the previous eighteen months. Most were based upon personal experience and secondary documentation rather than prolonged study. They are, however, richly detailed and very useful for the reader concerned primarily with a narrative. Further, more specific sources are cited in the notes below.

9. This position was held for some time by the *Ejército Revolucionario del Pueblo* (ERP), which deduced from it the imminence of a revolutionary situation as early as 1972. Cabarrús, *Génesis de una Revolucion*, p.295.

10. See, for instance, Jorge Shafik Handal, 'El Salvador: A Precarious Balance', WMR, vol.6, no.6, June 1973, p.15.

11. Manuel Sevilla, 'El Salvador: La Concentración Económica y los Grupos de Poder', Cuaderno de Trabajo, no.3, Centro de Investigación y Acción Social, Mexico, December 1984, p.11; Mauricio Domenech et al., 'The Basis of Wealth and Reaction in El Salvador', mimeo, San Salvador 1976. The best consolidated source on landed wealth is Eduardo Colindres, 'Tenencia de la Tierra', ECA, nos 335/6, September–October 1976. I owe much of my knowledge of the Salvadorean bourgeoisie to conversations with Carlos De Sola, a member of one of its most prominent families who died before witnessing the catastrophe that he believed could be averted by redistributionist reform.

12. Sevilla, 'Concentración Económica', p.20. The identification of 'oligarchic' entrepreneurs solely on the basis of size is obviously not fully convincing although it seems logical to accept a general correspondence. Sevilla's own criterion is shareholding, 'oligarchic' families being those in possession of more than 50 per cent of investment in any given enterprise. I am here following his divisions of firm by size, those dubbed 'medium' producing between C1 million and C5 million per annum in manufacturing, between C500,000 and C5 million in services and commerce, and holding between 50 and 100 hectares in agriculture. For a full table of his criteria, see ibid., p.15.

13. Ibid., p.20.

14. Rafael Menjívar, *Formación y Lucha del Proletariado Industrial Salvadoreño*, San José 1979, p.151. Most of the US firms were in the electronics industry and assembled manufactured imports.

15. *US Direct Investment in Central America, 1977 and 1980 ($mn)*

	1977	*1980*	*% change*
Costa Rica	178	303	70
El Salvador	79	103	30
Guatemala	155	226	46
Honduras	157	288	83
Nicaragua	108	89	−18
Total	677	1,009	67

Source: US Department of Commerce, cited in Barry et al., *Dollars and Dictators*, p.40. While the scale of the increase during this period of acute political conflict is notable, the relatively modest fall of investment in Nicaragua is barely less so.

16. Héctor Dada, *La Economía de El Salvador y la Integración Centroamericana, 1954–1960*, San José 1983, p.38.

17. Ibid., p.48.

18. For a synoptic survey of the union movement, see Menjívar, *Formación y Lucha*, a version of which appears in González Casanova, *Historia del Movimiento Obrero en América Latina*, vol.2. An evocative memoir of the harsh repression of labour organizations in the early

1950s is given in Salvador Cayetano Carpio, *Secuestro y Capucha en un País del 'Mundo Libre'*, 1980.

19. F. Chavarría, cited in Menjívar, *Formación y Lucha*, p.134.

20. It was perhaps because his book was published in 1959, before widespread recognition of the importance of the generational features of post-war politics, rather than as a result of post-adolescent vanity, that John Martz could include the following passage on students in his survey on Central America: 'Many are quite sincere. However, they look around and see the social and political inequities of their country. The automatic response is to rectify all wrongs at once. And so the students take it upon themselves to be the conscience and guide of the nation. In their misguided enthusiasm they become involved in political rallies, defy government troops from the sanctuary of university walls . . . and only rarely do positive good. Nonetheless, they do at least have a strong nuisance value . . .' *Central America. The Crisis and the Challenge*, p.16. It should be reiterated that many Central American students are obliged to hold full- or part-time jobs during their stay at university so that although their age profile may not be markedly higher than that of their metropolitan peers (and certainly not compared with that of the 'professional' students who hang out in some European countries), they frequently possess a broader and harsher experience of the world.

21. A suggestive journalistic portrait of the junta that stresses its lack of coherence is given in the memoirs of the *New York Times* Central American correspondent Paul P. Kennedy, *The Middle Beat. A Correspondent's View of Mexico, Guatemala and El Salvador*, New York 1971.

22. *Diario de Hoy*, San Salvador, 20 June 1961, quoted in Webre, *Duarte and the Christian Democratic Party*, p.39.

23. Quoted in Kennedy, *The Middle Beat*, pp.190–1.

24. PPS: *Partido Popular Salvadoreño*, formed from the right wing of the PAR. Henceforth the PPS would remain a very minor element of the dominant bloc, absent from the political scene save on the occasion of a poll. Revived for the presidential election of 1984, it won 0.8 per cent of the votes. The PREN was the vehicle for the personal aspirations of Colonel Luis Roberto Flores and, like most such bodies, disappeared once the officer in question had availed himself of the opportunity of presenting a principled opposition to the PCN.

25. A good example of profound methodological misconceptions as well as entirely misplaced optimism in the assessment of the Salvadorean electoral system at this time may be found in Ronald H. McDonald, 'Electoral Behaviour and Political Development in El Salvador', *The Journal of Politics*, vol.31, no.2, May 1969. This piece does, however, have the merit of containing quite full results of the polls of 1964, 1966 and 1968.

26. Even with control over the electoral machinery, support for the PCN in San Salvador never rose above 41 per cent in the polls of the 1960s, the capital being the only department in which the government party received a lower percentage of the vote than its national score. The notably weak areas of support for the PDC were Usulután, Sonsonate, Ahuachapán and Cabañas (ibid., p.414). It should, though, be borne in mind that in none of these polls did more than 41 per cent of the eligible electorate register to vote and that average participation was 33 per cent, a level that might be thought to cast some doubt on McDonald's thesis of 'an increase in national awareness within the political culture, broadening perceptions of a relation between the individual in society and the central government; an increase in individual involvement with national government and an identification of personal interests, goals and attitudes with national government and political institutions'.

27. The existence of a progressive and populist sector in the army – as opposed to the military as a whole – should not be overlooked despite its distinctly minority status and the unremitting violence of the armed forces from the late 1970s. In 1966 13 of the 49 delegates at the PCN congress voted for the popular and liberal Colonel Mauricio Rivas, nine for the right-winger Colonel Mario Guerrero, 26 for Sánchez, and one deluded soul opted for a civilian candidate. This reformist current may be identified in the events of 1944, 1948 and 1960 and would later emerge in the coup of 1972, many of whose backers subsequently supported the rebellion of October 1979 against the PCN president General Romero.

28. The only consolidated English language source on the conflict is Thomas Anderson, *The War of the Dispossessed. Honduras and El Salvador, 1969*, Lincoln, Nebraska 1981.

Other valuable studies, which place greater stress on the socio-economic features of the conflict, include Mario Carías and Daniel Slutsky, eds, *La Guerra Inutil. Análisis del Conflicto entre Honduras y El Salvador*, San José 1971, which reproduces some parts of Universidad Autónoma de Honduras, *Análisis del Conflicto entre Honduras y El Salvador*, Tegucigalpa 1969; Eddy Jimenez, *La Guerra no Fue de Futbol*, Havana 1974; Vincent Cable, 'The "Football War" and the Central American Common Market', *International Affairs*, vol.XLV, 1969.

29. There was a notable silence on the part of both parties in the organs of the international Communist movement. Jimenez, representing the Cuban position, cites an earlier PCS text on tension with Honduras that stated that both populations 'ought to realize that armed conflict between them does not conform to their fundamental interests' (p.11). However, in 1969 PCS student militants were instructed by *La Opinión Estudiantil* to 'close ranks around the army to defend national sovereignty', and it is evident that the party believed that the most reactionary elements of the oligarchy would resist any conflict because they had no interest in an inter-state feud for its own sake. Yet the landlord class did in general support the war, not least in an effort to maintain its historic option on greater *lebensraum*, while the more prescient elements, such as the De Sola family, opposed it, apparently failing to perceive any fundamental class interest that could be furthered in a conflict of this nature.

30. General 'Chele' Medrano was an ex-commander of the National Guard and became established as a prominent right-wing figure by virtue of his leadership of the reactionary rural organization ORDEN, discussed below. His opposition to Sánchez Hernández's 1970 'irrigation law', which affected some property rights, reached the point of provoking his removal from office. However, close attachment with the oligarchy of the western departments, particularly the Salaverría family, made him a formidable force. He remained a key figure in the organization of paramilitary violence until executed by the FMLN in the civil war.

31. Details of the 1972 campaign are given in Webre, *Duarte and the Christian Democratic Party*.

32. Details of the army and paramilitary forces are provided in the richly illustrated study by Michael McClintock, *The American Connection*. It should be stressed that the National Guard was commanded by army officers, and that differences between the various arms of the coercive bodies were generally of secondary importance. The Guard, distinguished by its leather gaiters and machetes, was less a conscript than an NCO-based force and principally concerned with control of the rural areas. Its reputation for violence was matched by that of the *Policía de Hacienda* (treasury police), technically assigned to the control of contraband and traditionally active in the countryside in its task of suppressing illegal liquor production. The less militarized *Policía Nacional* was largely urban, charged with what might pass for normal policing duties in a civilized state and had an image rather less tarnished by mindless killing. In the 1980s the differences between these forces could often be identified by the forms of torture they employed. In 1981 the regular army numbered 13,000 troops; the National Guard 4,300; the Treasury Police 1,500; the National Police 4,300. In 1985 the army had 39,000 troops and the paramilitary forces 9,500. Prior to the civil war El Salvador had a very small airforce and a 'navy' that lacked any significant establishment and barely amounted to a coastguard; in 1985 these forces had 2,350 and 300 troops respectively. Such detail might appear unduly esoteric and even perverse in the context of this study but it is of some consequence, not least in comparison with Nicaragua, where the repressive apparatus of the Somocista state was both politically and organizationally much more limited. In many respects the Salvadorean National Guard was similar to its Nicaraguan namesake, being the main instrument of residual repression and, as often noted by US advisers, not very reliable in combat (although it is said to have been more impressive than the regular army in the 1969 war). After 1981 the US attempted to cut back the size and activities of the Guard and devoted most of its aid to the army. Colonel Mejía, leader of the 1972 coup, was executed by a right-wing death squad shortly after his return to the country in 1979.

33. Menjívar, *Formación y Lucha*, p.137; Vilas, *Sandinista Revolution*, p.176; FLACSO, *Centroamérica. La Crisis en Cifras*, San José 1986.

34. *Union Federations, 1971–6*

	1971		*1975*		*1976*	
Federation	*unions*	*members*	*unions*	*members*	*unions*	*members*
Total	121	47,000	125	63,545	127	64,986
CGS	53	19,470	38	10,988	40	12,592
FESITRIVESA			14	3,910	14	5,113
FESINTEXSIN			7	3,012	6	2,979
FESINTRABS			17	4,066	20	4,500
FUSS	24	9,526	19	7,754	19	7,587
FESTIAVETCES	15	3,840	16	3,533	16	3,466
FESINCONSTRANS	13	4,602	10	19,773	15	20,681
Independents	16	9,592	13	5,244	8	4,421
FENASTRAS			19	14,580	19	14,983
USTRAS			10	1,673	6	442
FESTRAS					4	814

Source: Menjívar, *Formación y Lucha*, p.156. Note that this table excludes the important components of the CCS as well as all rural unions.

35. Real urban wages increased after the recovery of the coffee price in the early 1960s and maintained a modest but steady growth until 1971, when they fell by 5.5 per cent. Over the next three years they dropped by a further 10 per cent. Downing, 'Agricultural Modernization', p.51.

36. These conclusions are mainly drawn from the pioneering work on the area around Aguilares, in the north of the department of San Salvador, by Carlos Cabarrús: *Génesis de una Revolución*. Cabarrús indicates that by the early 1970s the economic crisis had severely restricted local religious *cofradías*, the operation of which depended upon a rotating system of conspicuous consumption, usually by *campesinos* of some standing in the community. However, he clearly identifies what he calls the 'semi-proletariat' as the main revolutionary force (p.366). His survey of the economic position of those with some political affiliation suggests that this stratum was in general more politically orientated than the middle peasantry, which had greater representation in the right-wing pro-government organization ORDEN than in the left-wing FECCAS union (pp.183–4):

		Per Cent	
	Middle Peasantry	*'Semi-proletariat'*	*Day Labourers*
Apolitical	29	27	44
FECCAS/ORDEN	25	42	34
FECCAS	19	52	29
ORDEN	31	31	38

For an oral history of the somewhat distinct Chalatenango region, see Jenny Pearce, *Promised Land. Peasant Rebellion in Chalatenango, El Salvador*, London 1986, which concentrates more directly on the lived experience of the late 1970s and 1980s. Details on US involvement in rural unionization are given in Carolyn Forche and Philip Wheaton, *The Role of AIFLD in the Agrarian Reform Process, 1970–1980*, EPICA, Washington 1980.

37. Pearce, *Promised Land*, pp.94–7.

38. Ibid., p.113.

39. Cited in Cabarrús, *Génesis de una Revolución*, p.149. In the 1980s a peasant in Chalatenango would recount, 'What made me first realize the path of our farmworkers' union was when I compared the conditions we were living in with those that I saw in the scriptures; the situation of the Israelites for example . . . where Moses had to struggle to take them out of Egypt to the Promised Land . . . then I compared it with the situation of slavery in which we were living. For example, when we asked for changes in the work rates on the plantations, instead of reducing them for us, the following day they increased them, just like the Pharaoh did with the Hebrew people making bricks, right? Our struggle is the same; Moses and his people had to cross the desert, as we are crossing one now; and for me, I find that we are crossing a desert full of a thousand hardships, of hunger, misery and exploitation' (Pearce,

Promised Land, p.118). Although the activity of progressive priests and religious workers is evident in other areas of peasant mobilization, notably Morazán, progressive Catholicism had a stronger political impact in the north-central zone than anywhere else in the country.

40. Cited in McClintock, *The American Connection*, p.207, which gives a portrait of the organizational development of ORDEN.

41. The thesis that ORDEN was of a proto-fascist character was suggested, but not fully developed, by Roque Dalton, 'Lo que el pueblo debe saber sobre ORDEN', *Polémica Internacional*, no.1, Feburary 1980. This piece was written in the early 1970s when Dalton was a leader of the ERP but it corresponded to the perspective of those who, following Dalton's death in 1975, left the ERP to form *Resistencia Nacional.*

42. The exceptions are the *Partido Revolucionario Salvadoreño* (PRS) and the *Partido Revolucionario de Trabajadores Centroamericanos* (PRTC). The PRS may, to all intents and purposes, be seen as indistinct from the ERP and never established a presence in its own terms beyond some propaganda work, principally in Europe.

43. The most pronounced example of denigration of the Salvadorean left as pathologically factional is Gabriel Zaid, 'Enemy Colleagues: A Reading of the Salvadoran Tragedy', *Dissent*, winter 1982.

44. In the early 1970s the PCS held the slogan 'Democratic Government, reform and progress', general secretary Shafik Handal defending participation in UNO's election campaign because it 'revealed a favourable alignment of forces . . . demonstrated the vitality of the broad front policy . . . made for the people's political awakening and helped them to realize their potential'. WMR, vol.6, no.6, June 1973, p.16. For unambiguous PCS criticism of the Chinese party see the statements published in WMRIB, no.88, 1967, pp.50–2; no.93, 1967, pp.34–5. For a dissident perspective on the PCS during this period, see Salvador Cayetano Carpio, *La Lucha de Clases*, Mexico 1982.

45. Leiken, 'Salvadoran Left', identifies both the ERP and RN as suspicious of the Cuban presence in Sandinista Nicaragua. By the early 1980s the intractability of Salvador Cayetano Carpio had increased tension between Havana and the leadership of the FPL, traditionally the force closest to the Cubans. In general the radical Christian element of the opposition has been most reluctant to accept close association with the Soviet bloc, particularly since the invasion of Afghanistan (1979) and the suppression of Solidarity in Poland (1981). Yet Havana's consistent support for the FMLN after 1980 has complicated the picture, the ERP in particular shifting to closer relations with Cuba. By contrast, prior to 1979–80 only the PCS had formal ties and the FPL effective links with Havana.

46. 'El PCS Celebró su Séptimo Congreso', San Salvador 1979, p.3; PCS, *Fundamentos y Perspectivas*, San Salvador 1979, p.21.

47. For the positions of the FPL, see *El Salvador: The Development of the People's Struggle*, London 1980, and *Revolutionary Strategy in El Salvador*, London 1981.

48. Resistencia Nacional, *Por la Causa Proletaria*, San José 1977.

49. Ibid., pp.18–22; Manlio Tirado, *La Crisis Política en El Salvador*, Mexico 1980, pp.46–60; Zaid, 'Enemy Colleagues'.

50. PRS, *El Salvador: Une Perspective Révolutionnaire*, Algiers 1977.

51. *Por la Causa Proletaria*, pp.29, 71, 89.

52. FAPU's general positions are outlined in the journal *Polémica Internacional*, particularly no.3, July 1979.

53. The positions of the BPR are included in *El Salvador: The Development of the People's Struggle* and *Revolutionary Strategy in El Salvador*, being diffused within the country in the periodical *Combate Popular*.

54. In 1980 the major organizations belonging to the BPR were: ANDES; FECCAS; UTC; MERS (secondary school students); FUR–30 (university students); UR–19 (university students); *Central Coordinador de Sindicatos José Guillermo Rivas* (CCS); *Movimiento de Cultura Popular*. By that stage FAPU no longer included either FENASTRAS or FUSS although the leaderships of these federations generally followed its line. Its affiliates were: *Movimiento Revolucionario Campesino* (MRC); FUERSA (university students); ARDES (secondary students); *Vanguardia Proletaria*; OMR (teachers).

55. The *Ligas Populares* comprised sympathizers of the ERP from a variety of sectors although students and inhabitants of San Salvador's poorest *barrios* were strongly represented.

The only independent union to join was ASUTRAMES, formed by dissident workers in the capital's markets.

56. The Salvadorean origins of the PRTC can be located in the work of those, like Fabio Castillo, who collaborated with the PCS until the 1969 war but rejected the line of the FPL and ERP; exiles, particularly in Honduras and Costa Rica; and a number of early opponents to RN's strategy.

57. It should be stressed that the size of the different guerrilla groups in the 1980s is a poor guide to their broader political support in the 1970s. From the start of open civil war in late 1980 the ERP was clearly the most powerful military force (40 per cent of all rebel troops) and yet arguably that with the smallest organized popular following aside from the PRTC. Equally, the PCS which, according to a reasonable assessment by Robert Leiken, had the support of 10 per cent of the FMLN's combatants, is a far more substantial political force than the PRTC, which has the loyalty of an equal proportion of the guerrilla army. The military strength of RN (15 per cent of the FMLN numbers) may be taken as broadly indicative of its wider influence but the FPL's 20 per cent under-represents its popularity. Leiken, 'Salvadoran Left', p.121. As will be seen, the strategic tensions in achieving a balance between political and military organization proved to be relatively minor for the ERP, which was consistently militarist, and very serious for the FPL, which resisted throwing all its human resources into guerrilla activity.

58. Sara Gordon, 'La Transformación Agraria en El Salvador: Un Conflicto Interburgués', ESC, no.36.

59. Oscar Menjívar and Santiago Ruiz, 'La Transformación Agraria en el Marco de la Transformación Nacional', ECA, vol.XXXI, nos 335/6.

60. Gordon, 'Transformación Agraria', contains a selection of public statements, a large number of which are reprinted more fully in ECA, vol.XXXI, nos 335/6.

61. Francisco Javier Hernández, 'Estado y Sociedad. Crisis Hegemónica y Lucha Ideológica en la Coyunctura de la Transformación Agraria en El Salvador, 1975–6', RMS, vol.XLI, no.1, Mexico City, January–March 1979; Rafael Guidos Vejar, 'La Crisis Política en El Salvador, 1976–79', RMS, vol.XLII, no.1, January–March 1980.

62. *Inforpress*, Guatemala, no.220, 2 December 1976; no.226, 20 January 1977; Rafael Menjívar, *El Salvador. El Eslabón Mas Pequeño*, San José 1981, p.18.

63. Facts on File, *Latin America 1977*, p.139. Details of the 1977 poll are given in Latin America Bureau, *Violence and Fraud in El Salvador*, London 1977.

64. *Por la Causa Proletaria*, p.57; Mario Menéndez, *El Salvador: Una Auténtica Guerra Civil*, San José 1980, pp.124,154.

65. Despite the fact that their only other strategic option was military, both the PDC and the MNR seem to have given up hope in UNO before the PCS/UDN, which was formally pledged to an insurrectionary line. Italo López Vallecillos and Víctor Antonio Orellana, 'La Unidad Popular y el Surgimiento del Frente Democrático Revolucionario', ECA, vol.XXXV, March–April 1980, p.187.

66. In the early 1980s much detailed information on the death squads came to light, directly implicating members of both the military hierarchy and the parties of the extreme right. For discussion of these matters, which will not be pursued further here, see McClintock, *American Connection*; Bonner, *Weakness and Deceit*; Washington Office on Latin America, 'An El Salvador Chronology: Death Squads as a Political Tool', February 1984, which draws on some exemplary investigative reporting by Laurie Becklund and Craig Pyles in a series published in the *Albuquerque Journal* and the *Los Angeles Times* from 18 December 1983.

67. Guerrilla kidnapping and occasional execution of leading members of the oligarchy in 1976–79 often provoked 'tit-for-tat' assassinations by the right, but the left claimed responsibility for no more than a score or so of such killings in this period. Its priority was the raising of cash through ransom, as in the much publicized seizure of six foreign businessmen by RN in 1978. *Inforpress*, Guatemala, carried details of this activity.

68. Claribel Alegría and D.J. Flakoll, *La Encrucijada Salvadoreña*, Barcelona 1980, p.33; *Latin American Political Report*, 29 July 1977.

69. ABECAFE did not hesitate to evoke the example of 1932 in its public declarations: 'it is time we realized that internal security against whatever may eventually prejudice the destiny of our homeland is the first priority . . . many years ago one of our rulers understood this very well when he made the Republic's internal security, peace and order a primary and

indispensable condition for the development and prosperity of our country.' *El Diario Latino*, 24 November 1977, quoted in Latin America Bureau, *El Salvador under General Romero*, London 1979, p.100. The UN Charter was denounced as 'a Russian salad . . . with every sort of aspiration and sophistry' that made it impossible to treat 'political offenders', and it was bemoaned that 'today in Central America the armies are lacking the counter-revolutionary tradition . . .' Ibid., pp.74, 195.

70. In October FECCAS-UTC and ATACES demanded that the daily wage for the coffee, cotton and sugar harvests be raised to C11 from C8, C6 and C5 respectively in 1976/7. This demand was based on the government's own figures for the 1978–82 development plan that identified a fall in rural wages from an average of C530 a year in 1971 to C429 in 1975 whilst labour costs accounted for only 12 per cent of coffee production costs compared to 41.5 per cent in Guatemala. Ibid., pp.40–1.

71. For a detailed analysis of the law, see ibid., pp.115 ff.

72. For example, in the first fortnight of November 1978 the FPL killed six policemen, attacked the US embassy, destroyed the Bayer pharmaceutical plant in San Miguel, and blew up an electricity station; the ERP planted forty bombs in San Salvador and destroyed PCN offices in three towns; and RN kidnapped six foreign businessmen, netting at least $1 million and having its manifesto published in thirty-nine newspapers around the world.

73. In November 1977 Assistant Secretary of State Terence Todman told FARO's women's affiliate, 'Let me assure you that your government can continue to count on our active collaboration and support in promoting economic and social development while combating the cruel and unforgiveable challenge of terrorism within the framework of our shared standards for the protection of human rights.' Ibid., p.27. Such statements undid much of the work of Ambassador Lozano and Patricia Derian, appointed to the State Department by Carter to oversee human rights issues, who had lobbied persistently for a much more forceful approach.

74. During 1977–78 the important Japanese business community fell from 2,400 to 200. In 1979 private investment barely reached $5 million compared with $32 million in 1978, which was itself a bad year. *Latin American Political Report*, 9 March 1979; *Latin American Economic Report*, 26 October 1979.

75. It is significant that a detailed report of the strike was published in the London Sunday paper *The Observer*, 23 April 1979, reflecting the level of international interest. See also *El Pueblo*, no.3, July 1979; Menjívar, *Eslabón*, p.54.

76. General Medrano, Colonel Eduardo 'Chivo' Iraheta (deputy defence minister), General Ramón Alvarenga (Commander of the National Guard) and Major Roberto D'Aubuissón (assistant director of military intelligence) were widely identified as planning an extreme right-wing coup during this period. Full details of military politicking over the months prior to the October coup are contained in Dermot Keogh, 'The United States and the coup d'état in El Salvador, 15 October 1979: a case study in American foreign policy perceptions and decision-making', in Dermot Keogh, ed., *Central America. Human Rights and US Foreign Policy*, Cork 1985.

77. On 11 September Viron Vaky told the House Foreign Relations Committee, 'A great part of Central America . . . is subjected to strong pressures of change, terrorism and potential radicalization. . . . Even without Nicaragua the situation would be explosive . . . the geographical proximity of Central America means that the US has a special interest in the fact that the region enjoys peace, prosperity and cooperation.' Tomás Guerra, *El Salvador: Octubre Sangriento*, San José 1979, pp.9–11. By June 1980 Brzezinski was himself stating that 'the United States could never permit another Nicaragua, even if preventing it meant employing the most reprehensible means.'

78. For details of the *Foro* programme, see López Vallecillos and Orellana, 'La Unidad Popular', pp.189–90.

79. The full document is reprinted in Menjívar, *Eslabón*, pp.143–7.

80. A more detailed account of this period is given in Dunkerley, *The Long War*.

81. Keogh, 'Coup of October 1979'.

82. The PCS was, nonetheless, sorely taxed to explain its increasingly anomalous position, blaming repression on 'Fascists infiltrated into the government' and seeking to overthrow an administration that was not homogeneous and could still form the basis of an anti-Fascist front. *El Salvador: Alianzas Políticas y Proceso Revolucionario*, Mexico 1980, pp.26–30, 64

ff.; Guerra, *Octubre Sangriento*, p.72. Justice Minister Nelson Segovia and Economy Minister Manuel Enrique Hinds, both closely linked with ANEP, were prominent in stalling or sabotaging economic policy.

83. This was the response made by Ungo when challenged by foreign journalists over military killings of unarmed demonstrators in October. Guerra, *Octubre Sangriento*, pp.52–7.

84. Ibid., pp.119–24.

85. 'El Salvador en la Hora de Decisión, mimeo, Mexico, p.20.

86. Not all the left was as prescient as Rafael Menjívar, leading theorist of the BPR, who within days of the October coup identified US strategy as having the primary objectives of repressing the popular organizations and securing the election of the PDC to government. Yet FAPU recognized that distinct currents existed within the regime and that the PDC had become the most significant conservative force within it. The *Ligas* referred to the junta as '*romerismo* without Romero' and saw it as entirely at the beck and call of Washington, but increasingly this organization swung towards the positions of the BPR and FAPU following the disastrous confusion in its own line seen in October. The positions of all the main groups, including the PCS, are presented in *El Salvador: Alianzas Políticas y Proceso Revolucionario*. Interviews with the leaders of the different revolutionary groups may be found in Mario Menéndez Rodríguez, *Voices from El Salvador*, San Francisco 1983.

87. A full English translation of the Platform is given in 'El Salvador – a Revolution Brews', NACLA, vol.XIV, no.4, July–August 1980.

88. Pearce, *Promised Land*; Laurence R. Simon and James C. Stephens, *El Salvador: Land Reform, 1980–81*, Boston 1981; Philip Wheaton, *Agrarian Reform in El Salvador: a Program of Rural Pacification*, Washington 1980, provide highly critical assessments of the reform. A more favourable view is given in David Browning, 'Agrarian Reform in El Salvador', JLAS, vol.15, part 2, London, November 1983.

89. In addition to the sources mentioned above, Bonner, *Weakness and Deceit*, pp.187 ff., provides a number of concrete examples of sabotage, as did Leonel Gómez, formerly assistant director of ISTA, to the House Sub-Committee on Inter-American Affairs, 11 March 1981. Gómez narrowly escaped death at the hands of the extreme right: his boss, Rodolfo Viera, was not so lucky.

90. Simon and Stephens, *Land Reform*, pp.55–7.

91. The appointment as US ambassador of Robert White, formerly posted in Asunción to oversee the truculent General Stroessner and quite disposed to issue the Salvadorean entrepreneurial class with sharp warnings as to the consequences of its behaviour, greatly aggravated the right but produced little change in its political methods. Throughout 1980 White was constantly attacked in the local conservative press for his 'interventionism'.

92. Brockman, *The Word Remains*, pp.205–6.

93. Ibid., p.217.

94. In June 1980 John Bushnell of the State Department told Congress, 'The principal obstacle to the [agrarian] reform . . . is that extremists from both the left and right are intent on dividing the Government and preventing the consolidation of a powerful moderate coalition which it will attract to its program if it is allowed to prosper . . . I want to emphasize that contrary to a common misconception, our proposals for security assistance are not disconnected nor contrary to our support for reform in El Salvador. The redistribution of land would not be possible if it wasn't for the protection and security provided by the Salvadoran army to the new property owners.' Quoted in Wheaton, *Agrarian Reform*, p.17.

95. The Río Sumpul massacre was sufficiently horrendous to attract the attention of the European press: *Le Monde Diplomatique*, January 1981; *Sunday Times*, London, 22 February 1981. For a detailed survey of the violation of human rights in 1980–81, see Americas Watch Committee and the American Civil Liberties Union, *Report on Human Rights in El Salvador*, Washington 1982.

96. Examples of the relative lack of preparation in the case of the FPL in Chalatenango are given in Pearce, *Promised Land*. Having dedicated more energy to military organization in Morazán, the ERP was better prepared but still unready to wage a major campaign, as tacitly admitted by its commander Joaquin Villalobos, 'El Estado Actual de la Guerra y sus Perspectivas', ECA, no.449, March 1986.

97. *El Salvador: Un Pueblo en Lucha*, New York 1980, p.17.

98. Debate within the FDR over the lessons of the summer strikes was understandably not made public. However, it should be stressed that the image of a total failure encouraged by the junta was widely and uncritically accepted by an international press corps that expected nothing short of an uprising and had still to appreciate the particular pace of the Salvadorean conflict. For the DRU the tactical and logistical lessons of the strike were undoubtedly valuable if also less than encouraging. An incisive contemporary assessment by Adolfo Gilly is given in his *Guerra y Política en El Salvador*, Mexico 1981, pp.111–19.

99. For details of this rather confusing period, see the articles by Robert Armstrong in *The Guardian*, New York, 24 September and 1 October 1980. Upon its establishment the commanders of the FMLN were Salvador Cayetano Carpio (FPL); Fermán Cienfuegos (RN); Jorge Shafik Handal (PCS); Joaquin Villalobos (ERP); and Roberto Roco (PRTC). With the exception of the replacement of Carpio, who died in April 1983, by Leonel González, this leadership remained stable for the following six years.

100. Francisco Quinoñez, 'Informe sobre la insubordinación de las FF.AA. de El Salvador', mimeo, Mexico 1980.

101. Although it was an exceptionally angry Robert White who cut off aid following the killing of the Maryknoll missionaries, domestic interest and agitation over the issue obliged his successors under the Reagan administration to maintain some semblance of pressure on the regime in San Salvador to bring their killers to justice. In the event, several troopers involved were arraigned and gaoled but no officer was ever punished despite the fact that the soldiers had clearly implicated a number of their superiors. This event greatly influenced the decision of the US Congress to insist upon a presidential certification of improvement in the human rights situation prior to release of any aid. Three days after the killings William Bowdler and William Rogers visited the country in an emergency attempt to reorganize the government that ended up with the appointment of Duarte as president of the junta.

102. It later transpired that at least one of these advisers was connected with the CIA although both men may have died simply because they were meeting with ISTA director Rodolfo Viera, the assassins' main target.

103. The claims made by White at the time, and subsequently accepted by him to have been made on the basis of false information, was that canoes had been discovered on a beach opposite Nicaraguan waters and that these craft had been used for the transport of men and weapons. A vivid fictional representation of the manner in which White's decision was made is given in Oliver Stone's film *Salvador*.

104. According to the FMLN it took 1,825 prisoners between 1980 and 1983. Government figures for its own casualties were 3,000 in 1981 and 1982; 1,055 dead and 1,780 wounded in 1983–84. Guerrilla losses are not reliably reported but certainly much lower than those of the military. *Inforpress*, 9 August 1984.

105. By the end of 1984 the airforce and army had 49 helicopters, and US OV-1 Mohawk reconnaissance planes were making regular flights out of bases in Honduras. The relatively small number of US advisers formally permitted by Congress to be stationed in the country proved to be a minor problem for the Pentagon when both officer and basic training programmes could be provided in the US and, for a while, Honduras. Accounts of the effects of bombing raids in the countryside are given in Pearce, *Promised Land*; Charles Clements, *Witness to War*, New York 1984.

106. In July 1982 Colonel John Waghelstein, the pugnacious head of the US military mission, claimed that the guerrillas would be 'reduced to banditry in two years'. Bonner, *Weakness and Deceit*, p.137.

107. Much of the burgeoning literature on the war understandably fails to go beyond the level of brutality and US involvement. For some sense of its wider character, see Pearce, *Promised Land*; Clements, *Witness to War*; Gilberto Lopes, *Reportaje en El Salvador*, San José 1984.

108. It might also be added that opposing commanders sometimes treated the war as a personal contest, this being particularly true in Morazán, where Joaquin Villalobos eventually bested his longstanding enemy Colonel Domingo Monterrosa. Other army officers such as Colonel Sigifredo Ochoa, operating in Cabañas and Chalatenango, adopted a resolutely personalist profile and proved very difficult for the high command to control.

109. In late January 1982 Reagan made his first 'certification' that the regime had made a

'concerted and significant effort' to respect human rights; in the previous year 17,303 people had died as a result of political violence, 600 of them in the village of Mozote less than two months earlier. In July, when the next presidential confirmation was due, the death squads were compliant enough to reduce their activity for a number of weeks, only to increase it with a vengeance immediately new funds had been approved. In November 1983 Reagan finally vetoed the congressional requirement of his certification. A synopsis of the violation of human rights during this period based upon statistics provided by the Socorro Jurídico and Tutela Legal offices of the Archbishopric of San Salvador is given in *Human Rights in El Salvador*, Geneva 1984.

110. United States Department of State, Bureau of Public Affairs, 'Communist Interference in El Salvador', 23 February 1981.

111. Details of the questionable evidence and its political manipulation are given in James Petras, 'White Paper on the White Paper', *The Nation*, New York, March 1981 (reprinted in *Le Monde Diplomatique*, April 1981); Konrad Ege, 'El Salvador: White Paper?' *Counterspy*, May–July 1981; Bonner, *Weakness and Deceit.*

112. See the statements of the CIA officer engaged in this task, David MacMichael, in *Sojourner*, August 1984, a synthesis of which is provided in Walker, *First Five Years*, p.463. Duarte later said of MacMichael, 'The man is clearly a Marxist', *Playboy*, November 1984.

113. Jeane Kirkpatrick, 'Dictatorships and Double Standards', *Commentary*, vol.68, no.5, November 1979.

114. Mario Redaelli, ARENA's secretary, told the press, 'We don't believe the army needs controlling. We are fighting a war, and civilians will be killed. They always have been. It's got to be that way.' Another party spokesman opined that 'napalm will, of course, be indispensable' in order to 'exterminate' the guerrillas in a war 'without limit'. *Newsweek*, 22 February; 29 March 1982.

115. POP – *Partido de Orientación Popular*, headed by General Medrano; AD – *Acción Democratica*, headed by Alvaro Magaña. Between them, the PPS, POP and AD won 10 per cent of the vote. US Ambassador Hinton kindly suggested that if the FDR was really 'scared' of campaigning in person then it should use videos. Bonner, *Weakness and Deceit*, p.298.

116. Mexico and France had already recognized the belligerent status of the FDR-FMLN but Ambassador Hinton's declaration that this would be 'the first free election in fifty years' failed to convince forty of the sixty states invited to send observers. Of the EEC countries, only Thatcher's Britain was represented, the rest of the community concurring with the description of the poll by Labour politician Denis Healey as a 'macabre farce'.

117. Washington claimed 1.5 million people voted but subsequent analysis by the Catholic University in San Salvador produced a figure of between 750 and 900,000, the wide margin of error being due to the extraordinary lack of precise and dependable documentation despite the much-trumpeted donation of computers by Washington. ECA, May–June 1982. Charges of gross irregularities, fraud, and deliberately misleading statements by the US government did, however, appear in the US press, for example, NYT, 4, 5, 14 June 1982. For a discussion of both the poll and the disputes between the embassy and press, see Bonner, *Weakness and Deceit*, pp.290–7.

118. The eventual result (per cent of vote) was: PDC – 35.3; ARENA – 25.7; PCN – 16.7; AD – 6.6; PPS – 2.6; POP – 0.8. There was, of course, no figure for abstentions; 12.3 per cent of the votes were null. *Centroamérica. La Crisis en Cifras*, p.231.

119. For details of this controversial episode, see Dunkerley, *The Long War*, 2nd edn, pp.250–6; Adolfo Gilly, 'El Suicidio de Marcial', *Nexos*, Mexico, no.76, April 1984, and the retort by Gilberto Rincón Gallardo, 'El Asesinato de Ana María', *Nexos*, no.78, June 1984. The full text of Carpio's speech to the FPL outlining his position is reprinted in *Punto Crítico*, Mexico, July 1983. It should be noted that some effort at negotiation had already been undertaken, meetings between the FDR and representatives of the regime or the US taking place on five occasions prior to the La Palma talks of November 1984.

120. *Por Esto*, Mexico, 28 July 1983. By the end of 1983 the formal position of the FPL and FMLN was that Carpio was directly linked with Ana María's murder.

121. For some time after the 1983 events a section of the FPL operated in San Salvador as the *Frente Metropolitano Clara Elizabeth Ramos* whilst supporters of Carpio in the labour movement operated for a while in the shape of the *Movimiento Obrero Revolucionario*

(MOR). In *The Long War*, written when this conflict was still very much alive, I attributed too great an importance to these groups, but I still maintain the general thrust of the comments made about this issue in that book.

122. The full document is reprinted in *El Salvador Informativo*, San José, no.35, 15 February 1984.

123. The PCS position is clearly presented in Shafik Handal, 'El Poder, Caracter y Vía de la Revolucion y la Unidad de la Izquierda', *Pensamiento Crítico*, no.34, July–August 1984.

124. In 1982 28 municipalities held no poll; in 1984 Washington accepted that 40 and the FMLN claimed that 90 had failed to do so. According to the questionable official statistics, the turnout in 1982 was 1,308,505 (68.9 per cent) and that in 1984 1,266,276 (43.4 per cent), 11.4 per cent of whom cast invalid votes. *La Crisis en Cifras*, pp.231–2.

125. The final result was (per cent of votes): PDC – 43.3; ARENA – 29; PCN – 19.3; AD – 3.5; PPS – 1.9; *Partido Auténtico Institucional Salvadoreño* (PAIS) – 1.2; Merecen – 0.5; POP – 0.3. In the run-off the turnout rose to 1,404,366 (51.6 per cent). Ibid.

126. The FDR-FMLN accepted that Duarte was not simply a puppet and that his election had produced some alteration of the balance of forces within the country, *Analysis of the New Salvadoran Government in an International Context*, mimeo, June 1984. At La Palma the rebels presented Duarte with twenty-nine demands, listed in *The Long War*, pp.282–3, of which only that requiring the cessation of US military aid would have directly prejudiced his own programme and position as publicly avowed.

127. A second meeting between representatives of the FDR-FMLN and the regime at Ayaguelo on 30 November 1984 broke up when the government reiterated its insistence upon a complete surrender by the opposition. The right and the high command had already made it very plain that anything else would provoke a revolt against Duarte. See, for example, statements reported in the *New York Times*, 23 and 24 November 1984. Meetings planned in 1985, following the congressional elections, and in 1986 came to nought.

128. The result of the election of 31 March 1985 was:

Party	*Votes for Congress*	*Seats*	*Votes for Mayors*	*Mayors*
PDC	505,338	33	517,635	156
ARENA	286,665	13		
ARENA–PCN			334,244	105
PCN	80,730	12		
PAISA	36,101	1	31,995	1
AD	35,565	1	31,900	
PPS–POP–PAR	20,832		17,612	
Null	74,007			
Abstentions	57,690			

Source: Inforpress, 7 June 1985.

129. *La Crisis en Cifras*, passim.

130. *El Movimiento Sindical Salvadoreño, 1979–1984*, CIAS, Mexico, June 1985, pp.23–4.

131. MUSYGES included the FSR (unions backing the FDR through the *Bloque*); FENASTRAS; FUSS; FESTIAVETCES. Ibid., p.29.

132. The UPD included the CTS; CGS and factions of FESINCONSTRANS. Already divided in response to the assassination of its principal leader Felipe Saldivar by a death squad, the UPD decomposed further still in the wake of the earthquake of October 1986, when there was widespread discontent with the inactivity of the government. For details of the political situation at the end of 1986, see Michael Stuhrenberg and Eric Venturini, 'Ni Paix ni Guerre au Salvador', *Le Monde Diplomatique*, December 1986.

133. It is estimated that by 1983 there were more than 700,000 Salvadorean refugees, 468,000 of whom remained in the country and less than 13 per cent of whom were under UN supervision. *La Crisis en Cifras*, pp.240–1. This position was significantly worsened by the 1986 earthquake.

9

Guatemala: Garrison State

They are makers of enemies, users of owls, they are inciters of wrongs and violence, they are masters of hidden intentions as well, they are black and white, masters of stupidity, masters of perplexity.

Popol Vuh[1]

This is the first instance in history where a Communist government has been replaced by a free one. The whole world is watching to see which does the better job.

Vice President Richard Nixon, August 1955[2]

It seemed to the *campesino* . . . that the thin young man . . . with green eyes sitting on the ground and covered with mud might be a leader of the FAR . . . but refusing to credit his fears, he asked, 'Is it true that Turcios Lima is around here?' 'Yes, this is the *Comandante*', we replied. The shock was palpable but eventually he spoke up: '*Caramba*, the name is much bigger than its owner.'

Orlando Fernández[3]

If it is necessary to turn the country into a cemetery in order to pacify it, I will not hesitate to do so.

President Carlos Arana, 1971[4]

We will execute by firing squad whoever goes against the law. But no more murder.

President Efrain Ríos Montt, April 1982[5]

The soldiers then gathered all the villagers together, forcing the women and children into a chapel and a nearby house and the men into the town hall. The soldiers first began shooting all of the women and children in the house. They then turned to the remaining women and children in the chapel, hacking them with machetes and ripping out the stomachs of some with their knives. Finally, the soldiers turned on the men in the town hall, shooting some of them with their guns and killing the rest with their grenades and bombs.

Finca San Francisco, Huehuetenango, 17 July 1982[6]

[Ríos Montt] is totally dedicated to democracy in Guatemala . . . they've been getting a bum rap.

President Ronald Reagan, 4 December 1982[7]

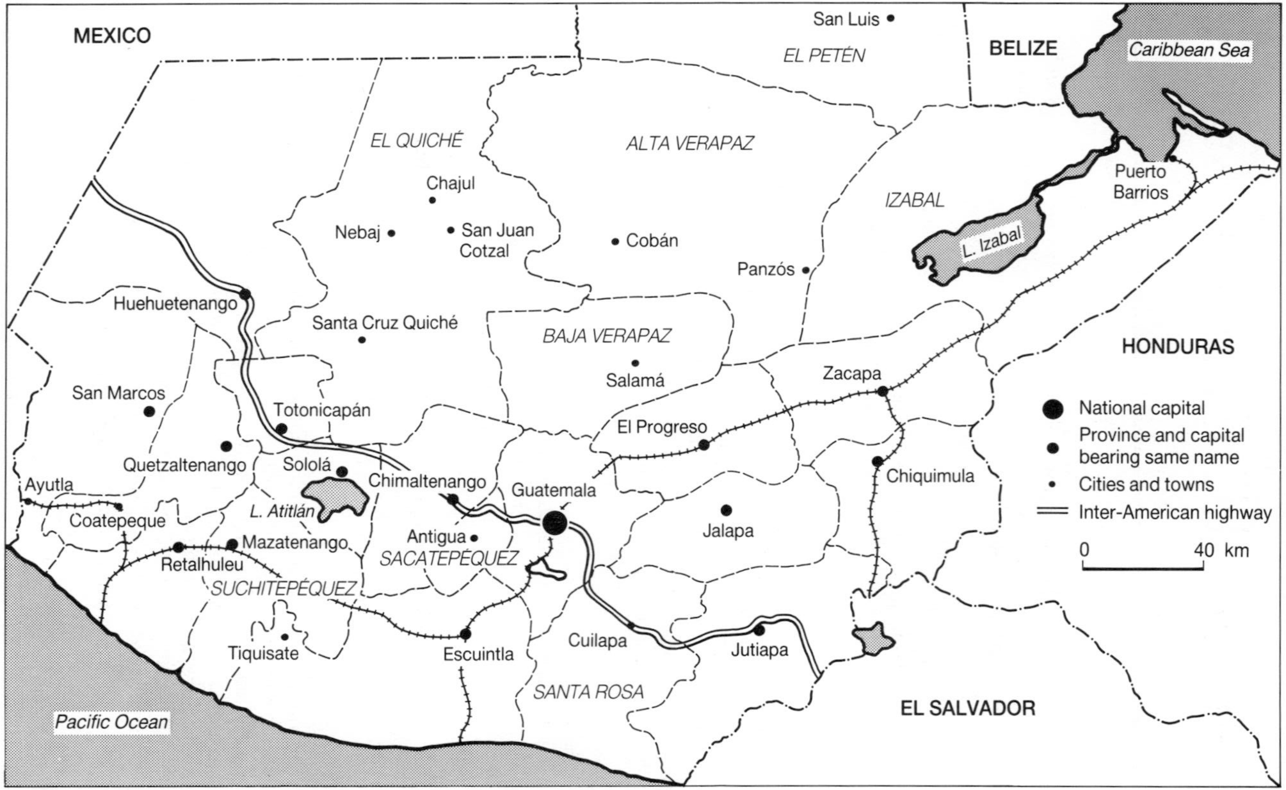

Guatemala

The CIA's intervention of June 1954, the overthrow of Arbenz and imposition of the fiercely anti-Communist regime of Colonel Carlos Castillo Armas are now distant events that took place well before the majority of Guatemalans were born. Yet the memory of both the decade of reform under Arévalo and Arbenz and the counter-revolution, or 'liberation', is still a remarkably vital factor in contemporary politics. In January 1986 a few insisted, some thought and more hoped that the assumption of the presidency by the Christian Democrat Vinicio Cerezo had terminated a 'long wave' of national history, bringing to an end the autocracy begun by Castillo Armas and upheld thereafter by a series of governments that in effect constituted a single regime despite significant variations in style and method. The claim that Cerezo and his party (*Democracia Cristiana Guatemalteca*; DCG) had taken a major step towards the 'redemocratization' of Central America – for Washington the penultimate step, to be followed by the liberation of Nicaragua – was supported by their emphatic victory in the clean if hardly free or fair polls of late 1985 as well as by a marked downturn in the horrendous levels of political killing that had obtained for twenty years. Although the establishment of civilian rule for the first time in sixteen years and only the second time since 1954 had been strongly advocated by the US, it also corresponded to important developments within the country, the most notable of which were a widespread desire for an end to the violence and a discontent with military rule even amongst powerful sections of the bourgeoisie. In short, it seemed entirely feasible to identify the legacy of 1954 as exhausted, the ancien regime passing into history not as a result of revolutionary rupture, as in Nicaragua, nor through prolonged negotiation and piecemeal concession, as in El Salvador, but rather as part of a more modulated process in which the military, having staved off a revolutionary assault in 1978–82 and now confronted with a severe economic crisis, was prepared to reduce its public responsibilities.

A more sober assessment of Cerezo's rise to office must concede greater strength both to the traditions of 1954 and to that autocratic lineage that encompasses most of republican history. In 1985–86 the Guatemalan military was unbowed and undefeated; it had, indeed, scored a major victory over the guerrillas, and its devolution of public office to civilians entailed no return to barracks. On the contrary, as vigorously demanded by the high command prior to the polls, the new president permitted an unprecedented operation of occupation and coercive restructuring of the Indian communities in the central and north-west highlands (*altiplano*) that had been the scene of the guerrilla campaign of previous years. The slaughter of 1978–84 made further widespread killing unnecessary, but the degree to which the army was engaged in the enforced relocation of scores of communities, the pressganging of all able-bodied males into 'civil patrols', the disruption of traditional patterns of cultivation, commerce and labour, and the extent to which it controlled not only the basic supplies of this region but also the daily life of many of its inhabitants cast considerable doubt on the notion that any new era of democracy had arrived.

This military strategy was both old and new. Far more intensive and efficacious than the simultaneous efforts of the Salvadorean military, it registered lessons learnt from Vietnam, the counter-insurgency campaigns of the French in Algeria and the British in Malaya as well as the influence of the Argentine and Israeli armed forces, to which the Guatemalans turned for aid and advice when their barbarism obliged President Carter to cut support in 1977. At the same time, the subjugation of the Indian heartland was but a continuation of a colonialism in which the period 1944–54 constituted only a fleeting and partial interruption. Hence, if the army was prepared to yield all the rigours and some of the rewards of political office, it was not willing to countenance any change in its central 'institutional mission' inherited from the Spanish system of 'reductions'. Nowhere else in Latin America – except El Salvador and Honduras – was a putative reversion to constitutional order matched by such a massive intervention by the military in the public sphere.

Even within a more formal interpretation of what constitutes politics, Cerezo's new order, so bright, modern and flexible on the surface, was in substance soon shown to be tightly constrained by the past. This was most evident with respect to agrarian reform – anathema to the bourgeoisie following the traumas of 1952 and yet a central demand of the popular movement largely responsible for voting the DCG into government. Whereas 1954 was for Washington a uniquely successful foray against international Communism, for most Guatemalans its central feature was the suppression of agrarian reform, and yet in his campaign Cerezo consistently disowned intentions to revive this question. Once in office he responded with nervous ambiguity to the mounting pressure for restoration of a policy that both pre-dated and denied the politics of the counter-revolution. The president's reactions and tactics must be understood in terms of the very fragile balance of forces prevailing when he came to office, but beneath these lay a deeper set of structural antagonisms that had certainly shifted in form during the 1960s and 1970s yet could still be identified with the nodal event in the country's modern history.

As such a critical watershed, the intervention of 1954 might feasibly be compared with the events of January 1932 in El Salvador or Somoza's rather more graduated rise to power in Nicaragua. On the other hand, the counter-revolution can be contrasted with these cases in that it did not repress an inchoate movement or liquidate an unclear challenge; it was not pre-emptive nor based upon fear of imminent danger. Instead, its decisive characteristic lay in the fact that it halted and turned back a ten-year experience of innovation that had already become codified and deeply embedded in the popular consciousness. In sum, it positively *reversed* history. As a result, it is often held – and not exclusively by the left – that this history is in a sense consumed and cannot be repeated, whereas in El Salvador and Nicaragua the precipitate suppression of nascent or unfinished movements preserved some scope for a subsequent development of their potential. Such an interpretation may be deemed excessively fatalistic and determinist, and it is indeed patently unsustainable when postulated as a schematic 'necessary logic' for all events. Nevertheless, a brief appraisal of the historical record shows that any reconstitution of the historical project which may be clearly identified by the time Arbenz was removed from power has been steadfastly resisted by both the leaders and the social sponsors of the post-1954 regime.[8] As in the mid 1960s, when the embattled civilian government of Julio César Méndez Montenegro (1966–70) endeavoured uselessly to retrieve a number of subordinate features of the reform era, the political and historiographical debate on this issue is likely to be rekindled by the experience of Cerezo's negotiation of some alteration of the edifice of reaction built upon foundations laid by Washington in June 1954. It is, however, clear that these foundations remain very firm indeed and are unlikely to be destabilized by anything short of a major challenge, which Cerezo himself has avidly disavowed and which the radical left failed to sustain in the wake of the Nicaraguan revolution.

The singularity of the counter-revolution has been diminished by the fact that it provided a model for US destabilization and intervention in the region, being followed by other instances – the Bay of Pigs (1961); invasion of the Dominican Republic (1965); Chile (1973); Grenada (1983); and the campaign against Sandinista Nicaragua – which made it part of a longer and wider pattern. Furthermore, while most of the motifs and methods of the overthrow of Arbenz can be situated in a particular 'moment of world time' determined by the Cold War, many of these were resuscitated in the early 1980s and appeared very familiar to a generation not yet born in 1954. What should not be lost is the fact that the Guatemalan intervention shaped the attitudes and strategems of an older generation of radicals, for whom this experience signalled the necessity of armed struggle and an end to illusions about peaceful, legal and reformist methods. The example of the Cuban revolution is generally evoked as a critical demonstration of the possibilities of guerrilla warfare which – with the exception of an apparently ineradicable tradition in Colombia – had been marginalized as a political phenomenon in Latin America since the 1920s. However, the Cuban rebels were themselves greatly impressed by the events in Guatemala, and one of their leaders, Ché Guevara, had witnessed the intervention, repeatedly referring to it in his later political career. Thus, if Cuba provided a positive vindication of the guerrilla *foco*, Guatemala stood (at least until the Chilean coup of 1973) as the cautionary illustration of a failure to match imperialist violence with force of arms.[9]

The lessons drawn by the Latin American left as a whole were, unsurprisingly, mirrored within the country itself. Guatemala was the only country in Central America to experience a protracted guerrilla struggle in the 1960s, and whatever the shortcomings of the FAR and MR-13, their influence on national political life at the time was much greater than that of the FSLN in Nicaragua. This thwarted essay in *foquismo* related more closely to the trajectory of South American countries (Venezuela; Colombia; Peru; Bolivia) than to that of the rest of the isthmus, where sustained armed insurgency did not emerge until the mid 1970s, and then in decidedly different national and international circumstances. It could be argued that this is a matter of strictly secondary importance since El Salvador and Nicaragua were ruled by barely less autocratic regimes throughout the same period and by 1979 all three countries possessed guerrilla movements of a broadly comparable character and challenge to the state. Yet the Guatemalan guerrilla of the 1960s was not merely an isolated and vanquished endeavour out of which a further chastened revolutionary generation would emerge with new political and logistical strategies. The erratic campaign that opened in 1962 with an attack on UFCO property and collapsed in 1971 in desperate acts of urban terrorism provoked the military into a response with few parallels in the modern history of the subcontinent. Still deeply scarred by the experience of the reformist years, emboldened by the liberation, determined to liquidate any possibility of 'another Cuba', and generally bolstered by US advice and equipment, the high command embarked upon the first real 'scorched earth' policy of the modern era, killing thousands in a counter-insurgency campaign that reflected the methods of the simultaneous war in Vietnam.

From the autumn of 1966, when the campaign was first fully implemented, the people of Guatemala were subjected to a policy of systematic state violence. This has certainly evidenced fluctuations, acquiring particular ferocity in 1966–68, 1970–73 and 1978–84, but it has been far more prolonged than in either El Salvador or Nicaragua and cannot simply be treated as the reaction of a regime in extremis. It is estimated that since 1954 no less than 100,000 people have died as a result of political violence, and whilst perhaps a half of this number have been killed since 1978, the political culture of assassination and massacre was established much earlier. By 1967 Guatemalans were already familiar with the phenomenon of 'disappearance' and in that year a committee of relatives of the disappeared was established – a full decade before the formation of the *Madres de la Plaza del Mayo* in Argentina. Significantly, in 1984, when Argentina was once again under civilian rule and army officers being arraigned for murders committed in their 'dirty war', members of the Guatemalan *Grupo de*

Apoyo Mutuo (GAM) seeking information and action on their disappeared relatives were still being assassinated by death squads that pre-dated their Southern Cone counterparts.[10]

In the early 1970s Régis Debray, the original ideologue of *foquismo*, was moved to comment upon terror that, 'administered in large enough doses over a long period, it has an anaesthetic effect . . . the obscene becomes commonplace, the abnormal normal'.[11] The risk of either the writer or reader of commentary upon such a state of affairs becoming anaesthetized by it is naturally of minimal importance when set against the abominable reality endured by the mass of Guatemalans, but this is, nonetheless, a danger that should be clearly signalled. It is, paradoxically, easy to lose sight of the enormity of terror when it is reduced to numerical tabulation of deaths, refugees, orphans and disappearances. Equally, one is enticed into seeking sanctuary from the image and evidence of barbarism in the laconic language of realpolitik since to engage constantly with the experience whether at an individual or a collective level courts a form of insanity as well as outrage or numb resignation. This solitary caveat is made here since it is beyond our scope to explore the psychological origins and ramifications of political violence or describe and denounce its recurrent incidence in Guatemala, and yet – ethical considerations aside – no proper understanding of the broader socio-political context and impact of terror can be gained without recognition of the subjective qualities of fear and their influence on strategies for survival.[12]

If, as Carlos Fuentes says, 'Western amnesia is selective', it proves highly resilient with respect to the victims of what passes for 'western civilization' when these are not, so to speak, of the west. Perhaps for this reason the extraordinary scope of political violence in Guatemala never attracted the international attention devoted to Argentina or Chile. For in Guatemala the great majority of those killed were not caucasian, middle-class and European in culture; they were 'Indian', indigenous Americans who if they speak Spanish at all do so only as a second or third language, adhere resolutely to their autochthonous culture and appear both physically and in their tangible 'otherness' to be oriental. Of course, their travails are not simply forgotten or ignored but very frequently they are seen – as in Biafra, the Congo, Indonesia and even Vietnam – as a lamentable consequence of some despotism identified with Latin 'temperament' but possessed of almost telluric qualities in Black and Asian society. It is not so strange that such an attitude often combines with a philanthropic sentiment – nowhere more evident than in recent western responses to famine in the horn of Africa – that privileges the plight of anonymous alien people afflicted by apparently natural causes for which they cannot somehow be held responsible. Maybe there is a general need to look again at the deconstruction of liberal racism made by Frantz Fanon and accepted by Sartre despite the fact that this is now deemed part of a bygone era in its unflinching precepts and attachment to theatrical guilt.[13] One does not have to go so far to register that the Indians of Guatemala, like the Blacks and 'Coloureds' of South Africa, are persecuted by a regime that is not the product of some alien culture but draws precisely on white, western and 'Christian' traditions to sanction its iniquities. Today this can no longer be forgotten or ignored; perhaps the only relief to hand lies in the continuing anonymity of the victims.

If embittered, this little excursus is not entirely idle since those who dominate Guatemala are still prone to describe the Indians who comprise over half the population as 'animals' and more generally view them as a primitive people, eternally resistant to progress, indigenous to the land and yet inhabitants of a world alien to the hispanic culture and polity that constitute state and nation. 'Indian' is, in fact, the term employed by *ladinos* (technically, those of mixed race) to describe the collectivity of some twenty-two ethnic groups whose origins can be traced to a Maya-Quiché root. The diverse settlement, culture and languages – a dozen distinct tongues with a variety of dialects – of these peoples combine into a unique otherness for Guatemala's 'whites'. For the indigenous population they cohere as one only in terms of *ladino* oppression and are both deeply and finely differentiated as Quiché, Kekchí, Cakchiquel, Mam, Ixil etc., self-identification as Indian being essentially determined by the outer, *ladino* world. A proper appreciation of the constituent features of this ethnicity is beyond our skills and scope, not least because it would require engaging in a sharp and complex intellectual debate as to the qualities of 'Indianness', of its relation to *ladino* culture, together with the allied question of how this relates to the definition of the peasantry and the even broader category of *campesino*.[14]

The importance of such issues reflects the peculiarity of Guatemala's social structure within a region whose Indian presence was elsewhere much smaller at the time of the Spanish conquest and subsequently eroded or suppressed more emphatically. In this sense, then, Guatemalan society stands far closer to those of the core Andean states (Ecuador, Peru and Bolivia) and parts of Mexico than to those of the rest of the isthmus. As a result, it is misleading to view the pattern of government in the country as simply a variant of that prevalent elsewhere with the Indian population comprising an extra community subjected to autocratic domination. The bulk of the indigenous peoples are subsistence farmers and seasonal labourers, and as such exploited and controlled in much the same manner as the hundreds of thousands of poor *ladino* peasants. By the same token, in recent years large numbers have rallied to the revolutionary movement in terms comparable to those in Nicaragua or El Salvador. However, their specific oppression as Indians underlies a singularity in the form of domination and the radical challenge to the state with regard to the rest of Central America.

For the *ladino*, and the ruling class in particular, the 'Indian question' is profoundly contradictory. On the one hand, the existence of the indigenous population establishes the distinctiveness of being *ladino* (or – better still – 'white') and the whole assemblage of cultural superiority that goes with this. Equally, although the intersection between race and class is extremely complex, there exists a clear identification between the Indian economy and the provision of basic foodstuffs and labour power and thus the maintenance of the Liberal agro-export system. On the other hand, the impulse to 'civilize' the indigenous community – whether through a socio-cultural process of '*ladinoization*' preferred by the new mandarins or by the more brutal ethnocidal remedies administered by the military – is intrinsic to the pathology of the *ladino* ruling class, promising not only Indian 'integration' within the nation but also some supposed liberation of the market economy (whereas, in fact, Indian commerce has always been very buoyant).[15] In its most base form this imaginary discourse oscillates between the fear of a race war and the imperative to assimilate. In practice the two are frequently conjoined, thus sustaining a residual discrimination and disparagement, and in recent years both physical violence and an offensive on the material bases of Indian culture.[16] For the high command of an army stocked largely with Indian troops the campaign in the highlands has not just been against 'reds' but against a doubly alien and obnoxious force of – the term is used advisedly – 'red Indians'.

What it generally terms 'the national question' presents the radical left with a challenge of a different nature. For those more orthodox currents, most particularly the PGT, social class has continued to enjoy primacy; the indigenous population is largely subsumed by the peasantry, and the need to eradicate ethnic oppression formally recognized rather than vigorously acted upon. Such a position corresponds not only to the historic base of the party in the capital and the fact that its activism in the countryside in the early 1950s was primarily in *ladino* regions, but also to an enduring scepticism about rural revolutionary strategies nurtured by the abortive *focos* of the 1960s. The setbacks suffered by the guerrillas in 1981–82 combined with remarkable outbursts of mobilization by a large and intensely repressed urban population in 1978 and 1985 have done little to modify this perspective and indeed even drawn some elements of what might be termed the 'new left' down from the highlands to the town with a related shift in political outlook. On the other hand, the second generation of guerrillas that emerged in the mid 1970s and identified the defeat of the 1960s in both misguided strategy and a failure to appreciate the importance of the Indian population has foundered more than momentarily and with very severe consequences less upon the problems of building a political base in the *altiplano* and *boca costa* (piedmont) than on those of defending that base when under concerted attack. The overvaluation of its capacity to do this is not intrinsically linked to the ethnic composition of these regions but neither should it be viewed from a purely politico-logistical perspective since one of its central results was the regeneration of distrust of outsiders and retreat into defensive corporatism by large sections of the indigenous population.

Both the *Ejército Guerrillero de los Pobres* (EGP) and the *Organización Revolucionaria del Pueblo en Armas* (ORPA) continue to include significant numbers of Indians, enjoy popular support in key zones and had established much more than an operational presence in the highlands by 1980. Furthermore, following the defeat of 1982, they demonstrated a capacity to expand political and military activity consistently if modestly, inculcating many of the lessons of the army's offensive. They have, however, never been Indian armies as such; both the differentiation between ethnic groups and the rising proclivity to work politically with poor *ladinos* have fortified the guerrilla's general objective of national liberation rather than caste supremacy. This would seem to be in every respect a progressive phenomenon. Yet it does not fully answer the question of what form of 'nation' the revolution is seeking to liberate and whether such a process can attract decisive support from the indigenous peoples on the basis of an end to oppression and establishment of national sovereignty for the republic of Guatemala in the broader world. After all, these peoples do not in themselves constitute either a single or several nations, identifying themselves far more closely with their ethnic community than with any notion of being 'Guatemalans'. The issue here is not so much one of the administrative mechanisms for any post-liberation autonomy or the pursuit of basic objectives essential for a humane existence (end to repression; agrarian reform; full democratic liberties; cultural freedom, and so on) as one of capturing that concatenation of affinities which, as in Nicaragua, endows the future with something more than the negation of the existing order. The need for such a negation is in Guatemala as strong as, if not stronger than, that in any other country in the region yet both the legacy of 1954 and the ethnic composition of the country present unparalleled enigmas as to how it might be achieved and surpassed.

The Old New Order

The 'liberation' of Guatemala in June 1954 and eventual establishment of Colonel Carlos Castillo Armas as president after brusque US disposal of contesting claims from within a militarily undefeated army changed the face of national politics. The new rules were essentially prohibitive rather than prescriptive, and despite a high degree of unity within the bourgeoisie, considerable US economic support, and the decisive subordination of the popular movement, the counter-revolution proved for the better part of a decade to be markedly disorganized. This might seem surprising in view of the scale of US political investment in the operation and the suppression of the changes wrought over the previous ten years. But the new government was a creature of its time and not some pioneer of the 'organic' dictatorial regime witnessed in Latin America in the 1970s; it looked determinedly backwards and sought little more than to restore the status quo ante once the vestiges of a putative bolshevism had been eradicated. Eisenhower's Washington possessed no alternative model beyond the restoration of unbridled free enterprise and, insofar as it sought to have this efficiently administered, it was stymied by the consequences of presenting the intervention as a national affair and patronizing one of Ubico's lieutenants to head it. As one of the organizers of the CIA's operation later declared, 'Our job was simply to get rid of Arbenz. We did that successfully. It was a success at one point of history, but this does not assure a happy ultimate outcome.'[17]

The Castillo Armas regime (1954–57) may have proved disconcertingly erratic and unreliable in its reversion to the *caudillo* style of Estrada Cabrera and Ubico but it undoubtedly succeeded in its essential task of subjugating the popular movement and reversing the apparatus of the reform era. In the first weeks some 17,000 prisoners were taken, an unknown but large number of people fled into exile, and perhaps 250 were summarily executed, mostly as a result of the settling of old scores in areas affected by the agrarian reform but on occasion at the hands of the vigilante groups that entered the country as part of Castillo Armas's invasion force or sprang up to support it.[18] Since Arbenz had already refused to arm the unions and the army remained intact, demoralization was widespread and resistance absolutely minimal. There was, therefore, no extensive bloodbath as might have been expected from the passions aroused and interests at stake or even the example of El Salvador just over twenty years earlier. While the bulk of the middle class was relieved by the halting of popular mobilization, external pressure and the atmosphere of uncertainty, the peasantry and working class had little choice but to submit and engage in both collective and individual strategies of self-preservation.[19]

The social gains made by these sectors were rapidly eliminated and their organizations dismembered. The Law of Forced Rental and the agrarian reform were immediately cancelled; both the state and private owners retrieved their lands with the result that by 1956 only 0.4 per cent of the beneficiaries of the reform still held title to redistributed property. At the same time, the practice of *colonato* was re-established and the registration of 533 rural *sindicatos* and *uniones* cancelled (85 per cent of those established under Arévalo and Arbenz), those left intact being resolutely apolitical organizations often dominated by the Church, local landlords or conservative Indian hierarchs.[20] The labour code of 1947 was not entirely suppressed and urban trade unions still remained technically legal, but the statute's most important measures with regard to basic rights and social provision were thrown out and many worker organizations were broken up either by executive order or at the hands of *liberacionista* forces acting at the behest of employers. Within a year of the coup union membership had dropped from 100,000 to 27,000; by 1961 only 54 plant unions were recognized by the state, the long-term effect of this being a fall in the unionized labour force from an already very modest 10 per cent in 1953 to less than 3 per cent in 1976, comparable with the level in Nicaragua.[21] Although Castillo Armas made some effort to identify himself with the original movement of October 1944, it was not just the PGT that was outlawed and persecuted. Many figures attached more closely to Arévalo than to Arbenz fell foul of the retribution meted out by the National Committee for Defence against Communism, an organization which was controlled by the president but reflected the more aggressively right-wing beliefs of his political lieutenant Mario Sandoval Alarcón, effective leader of the *Movimiento Democrático Nacional* (MDN; later to mutate into the *Movimiento de Liberación Nacional*, MLN), a man who happily proclaimed himself a Fascist. While Castillo Armas repaid his debt to Archbishop Rossell's tirades against Arbenz by restating the Church's rights to own land, employ foreign priests, and supervise religious education in schools – thereby contradicting core policies of the Liberal revolution of the 1870s – the National Committee regressed further still in its crusade by including Stendhal in the extensive list of authors whose work was banned and to be destroyed.

The only significant disturbance of this offensive was created by the army, which, already traumatized by its phantom defeat in the intervention, baulked at the sway of the *liberacionista* irregulars. When Castillo Armas endeavoured to introduce these unkempt militiamen into the military academy the cadets rebelled in protest. This revolt was easily quelled and followed by a purge, but the president was obliged to recognize the claims of the institution and limit his 'house-cleaning' of the army to firm supporters of Arbenz and leading figures who aspired to his own position. Although the military subsequently collaborated closely with both the vigilantes and the political leadership of the MLN, this early bad blood between it and the party's forebear stemmed from a wound that never properly healed and would reopen in the mid 1970s. The intervention both immunized the military against any serious reformist tendencies and engendered a form of shame that periodically rose to the surface in a belligerent institutionalism directed against the civilian right, and a reactionary nationalism that occasionally soured relations with Washington.

Castillo Armas's economic policy did not immediately reimburse the US for the cost of the CIA operation – estimated at between $80 and $90 million – but it did emphatically restore the position of foreign capital and reverse the statist economic tendencies of the previous years. Proclaiming 'private initiative and enterprise are the principal forces of progress', the president returned to UFCO all its expropriated lands and in return secured acceptance of a 30 per cent tax on profits that would undoubtedly have been ajudged 'socialist' had it been levied the year before.[22] The greater irony is that in 1958 the company, having already been in dispute with the US authorities over its manipulation of fiscal concessions, lost a domestic lawsuit over monopolistic practices in the banana trade, the US courts accepting in general terms the argument presented specifically for Guatemala by the Arbenz government. Within a few months those Guatemalans who reflected bitterly upon UFCO's role in the intervention had cause to discern what might be seen as historical justice: the company's extensive Cuban holdings were expropriated in toto and without compensation by a revolution that learnt so much from the Guatemalan experience. In December 1972 UFCO eventually sold its Guatemalan operation to Del Monte (owned by the tobacco company R. J. Reynolds) for $20.5 million.

If Castillo Armas was obliged to extract some modest price for the devolution of UFCO lands by virtue of the fact that the enterprise had attracted controversy for decades before Arbenz came to power, he charged virtually none at all in his general policy for foreign capital. Generous tax 'holidays' were declared, legislation limiting rights and concessions in the underdeveloped but strategically critical oil industry were repealed and replaced by an 'open door' approach, and the state hydroelectric project turned over to the very US interests against which it had been intended to compete. In return for such measures Washington rewarded the government with aid to the value of nearly $100 million at a time when total US assistance to all Latin America averaged less than $60 million a year.[23] Some of this largesse was immediately necessary – the destruction of the agrarian reform markedly reduced corn production, requiring imports from the US to make up a shortfall that did not reflect well on the new enterprise culture. Other aspects of the new policy, such as the lifting of Washington's embargo on World Bank loans for the building of the Atlantic highway, constituted little more than a reversal of measures that had been adopted for purely political reasons. Still others, such as the tenfold increase in military aid between 1956 (when it was apparent that the army was politically dependable and Castillo Armas far from stable) and 1963 (when the army began to demonstrate a certain nationalist truculence), reflected a prescient concern with safeguarding a system for which the merits of capitalist enterprise and anti-Communist government appeared strangely insufficient defences.

Together with Vice President Nixon's much fêted congratulatory visit of 1955 – a jaunt that was to provide singularly poor preparation for his later tour of Latin America – such support was intended both to consolidate the 1954 coup and to be a 'showcase' for the region. It was, though, the original intervention rather than the regime it spawned that impressed the rest of Latin America; it was there seen less as a reassuring defence of the free world than as a sobering deterrent against nationalist adventures. Although the Bolivian revolution of April 1952 escaped a similar offensive (largely by dint of the fact that the enterprises it expropriated were locally owned), the overthrow of Perón's Argentine government in September 1955 should be seen in this context since it was still broadly identified as progressive and anti-US in character despite having dropped the nationalist and redistributionist policies of the immediate post-war period. Perón's removal was at the hands of the national army, but it took place barely a year after Arbenz's fall and seemed to confirm a general Cold War regime that Argentina, Guatemala and (for part of the time) Bolivia had alone contrived to resist from the mid 1940s. It was not until the overthrow of Batista in Cuba that the terms of US hegemony were once again shown to be vulnerable to challenge.

In such circumstances it was less than surprising that the Castillo Armas regime 'is almost universally believed in Guatemala and the rest of the world outside the US to be the creation of the Department of State'.[24] All the same, the president soon transpired to be a disconcertingly erratic creature, and the Department was forced to swallow hard in the face of the antics of a man chosen first and foremost for his supposed qualities as a soldier (which had not themselves amounted to a great deal, as Somoza was quick to point out). In the McCarthy era and with Guatemalan affairs still treated with remarkably uncritical coverage by the press it was not difficult to dismiss the importance of those features of the new order that appeared rather unsavoury. However, Castillo Armas's democratic bona fides were not enhanced when, arguing that a secret ballot would be too costly, he instead held a public plebiscite by oral vote to confirm his position as president. Just as with those staged by Estrada Cabrera and Ubico, the result of this 'election' was a foregone conclusion; according to one estimate, 485,531 people voted for Castillo Armas, 393 against, and 655 voices remained mysteriously unheard.[25]

If such a charade was possible within a few weeks of the coup it failed to provide an enduring legitimation of the Castillo Armas regime, still less its bar-room 'New Life' philosophy cobbled together to replace Arévalo's 'Spiritual Socialism'.[26] The tension between the military and the MDN was only one factor impeding the consolidation of a stable government. Perhaps more important than this was the politically heterogeneous character of the *liberacionista* bloc itself, which ranged from traditional Conservatives through the newly founded Christian Democratic movement to Sandoval Alarcón's devotees of falangism and a substantial representation of that current which adhered to no philosophy other than lucrative self-advancement in a state apparatus enjoying unprecedented US patronage. (Castillo Armas himself might indeed be numbered in this latter contingent since his reputation was badly tarnished in 1955 by the revelation of a payment of $25,000 apparently received to enable a contract for the import of corn.[27]) Allied by little more than opposition to a phantom Communism, this bloc soon disintegrated into a cluster of feuding cliques revolving around the person of a president whose heroic status was demonstrably on the wane. In a climate made propitious for *golpismo* by unwarranted states of siege and expulsions, Castillo Armas was gunned down in his palace in July 1957 by an army guard said by the police to be a Communist but widely believed to have been in the pay either of one of several contenders for the presidency or of the dictator of the Dominican Republic, Generalíssimo Rafael Trujillo, who had fallen out with Castillo Armas after supporting the intervention.[28]

The vacuum created by the *caudillo*'s assassination gave the MDN the opportunity to call a quick election in which Minister of the Interior Miguel Ortiz Passarrelli was presented as the official candidate. This effort at *continuismo* came unstuck with the declaration of the candidacy of General Miguel Ydígoras Fuentes, ambassador in Bogotá, opponent of Arbenz in the 1950 poll, and an exuberant reactionary possessed of unpredictable character and more populist flair than his defunct competitor for the leadership of the counter-revolution. Once it failed to prevent Ydígoras from returning to the country and duly winning a plurality in the October election, the MDN machine simply took charge of the electoral tribunal and declared Ortiz the victor. Ydígoras, though, could lay claim to a sizeable faction of the reactionary bloc and the officer corps, and the combination of his coup threats with street demonstrations forced the interim junta to accept US arbitration, after which a fresh poll was called for January 1958. Despite the fact that the CIA funded the new MDN candidate, Colonel José Luis Cruz Salazar, to the tune of $97,000 in order to counter the disturbing calls for an end to persecution and a new period of reconciliation – as well as the demands made by Ydígoras's new *Redención* party for a greater distance from the US – the challenger again won a plurality and was eventually elected president by forty votes to eighteen in congress.

Over sixty when he came to office, Ydígoras was just as much as Castillo Armas a product of *ubiquismo*, and for all his talk of reunifying the nation he proved no less aggressive and notably more corrupt than his predecessor. In the style of the dictators of the 1930s he awarded himself a salary of $150,000 a year, appointed his daughter ambassador in Paris, and auctioned off the *fincas nacionales* in a spree of malfeasance that even Ubico and Castillo Armas had not entertained.[29] In a deteriorating economic climate caused by a 26 per cent fall in coffee prices in 1957 and 1958, the regime retained the catch-all *Ley de Defensa Contra el Comunismo*, persecuted the *Federación Autónoma Sindical de Guatemala* (FASGUA) that had been established in 1955 with government recognition, and cracked down on student demonstrations encouraged by the Cuban revolution. The effects of this were mitigated by neither the tabling of a new agrarian reform law nor the resuscitation of claims on Belize. Although the right, and particularly the army, possessed an ample reservoir of chauvinist ambition with respect to Belize and enjoyed some success in purveying this to the populace at large (since Guatemala's historic claim was reasonably founded on Britain's non-compliance with the 1850 treaty), the British colony was largely inhabited by people of Afro-Caribbean and Carib stock, and its 'reintegration' into Guatemala possessed little direct interest for the mass of citizens except as a pretext for venting a more generally determined exasperation. Furthermore, while the Belize issue gave a certain frisson to sabre-rattling, the escalation of stentorian claims and intermittent incursions over the border into a full-scale invasion and combat with British troops was not a compelling proposition for any but the wilder elements of the officer corps who believed that they should act as boldly as they talked. (The idea became, of course, markedly less enticing after the British military victory in the 1982 Falklands/Malvinas War against Argentine forces vastly superior to those of Guatemala. By that stage Belize had obtained independence (1981), a fact which fortified the Guatemalan left in its traditional recognition of Belizean self-determination and also enabled the Cerezo government to investigate the possibilities of reaching a diplomatic solution and resumption of full relations with London.[30]) If Belize was primarily a distraction, the issue of agrarian reform transpired to be little less illusory for the poor, Ydígoras's 1961 *Ley de Transformación Agraria* being entirely distinct from Arbenz's law in its aims of populating new 'development areas' (frequently tracts of inhospitable jungle territory), stipulating the terms of tenantry, and devolving a number of state farms either to their previous owners – sixteen of the seventy-eight returned were given to the pre-1944 German proprietors – or to state agencies. Of the 160,000 hectares distributed in eight years under this statute and a previous similar measure enacted by Castillo Armas, only a minuscule proportion was handed to landless peasants.[31] The new law responded to the vague precepts of the Alliance for Progress and enabled Ydígoras to employ some extravagant rhetoric but it necessarily left private land untouched and unthreatened.

Unable to sustain a genuinely populist project or cultivate a significant working-class and peasant following, repudiated by the progressive sectors of the middle class for its refusal to modify the counter-revolution, and yet outflanked on the extreme right by the MLN, which advocated a more consistent and resolute anti-Communist programme, the Ydígoras government came increasingly to depend upon corruption and political malpractice. In the 1961 congressional elections outright fraud gave *Redención* thirty of the thirty-three parliamentary seats, and just as in 1957, this attempt to maximize partisan advantage only succeeded in deepening fissures within the dominant bloc as a whole. Within a year twenty-one deputies dropped their support for the government, obliging Ydígoras to rely upon the backing of the military, representatives of which by now held all cabinet posts bar that of foreign relations. Even reliance upon the armed forces was fraught with factionalism and graft, Ydígoras first indulging the airforce with a welter of budget rises, promotions, and corporate advantages, and then, when the airforce demonstrated its gratitude by attempting a coup, resorting to similar tactics in favour of the army.[32] Such manoeuvres and the instability that underpinned them certainly reflected Ydígoras's personal insufficiencies as a leader, but more important than this was the fact that both the origins of the system and the limits of its natural constituency precluded any stable political competition either within the counter-revolutionary bloc or between it and the reconstituted reformist tendencies that were emerging. On the one hand, there was too little scope for ideological dispute within the right to suppress the conspiratorial subculture nurtured by the rewards of office. On the other, the system was increasingly subjected to the familiar dilemma of permitting some non-Communist opposition in order to substantiate claims to constitutionality yet resisting any significant concessions to forces that were seen as upholding precisely the kind of liberalism which had opened the floodgates of radicalism in the late 1940s and which formed an even sharper threat in the wake of Cuba.

The impact of the Cuban revolution on national politics took an immediate and unforeseen form when Ydígoras was requested by Washington in 1960 to repay part of the debt incurred in the counter-revolution by supporting the military training of Cuban exiles by the CIA in Guatemala. Although the president had originally campaigned on a nationalist platform and continued to harbour resentment over the fact that the US had preferred Castillo Armas to him as leader of the liberation, he owed the reversal of the 1957 fraud to Washington's intervention and could not escape the consequences of US economic and political aid to the regime. Both his profound anti-Communism and the opportunity to improve relations with Washington that had deteriorated badly because of his regime's corruption and unpopularity encouraged Ydígoras to extend direct assistance for the preparations of the Bay of Pigs operation. However, the provision of a large camp at the La Helvetia estate in Retalhuleu was made to the CIA without consultation with the high command and when, in the autumn of 1960, its existence was revealed there was widespread discontent within the officer corps.[33] According to one dissident officer, this was a 'shameful violation of our national sovereignty . . . our government is a puppet.'[34] Opposition to a CIA operation on Guatemalan soil together with anger at the extent of official corruption provoked a coup attempt on 13 November 1960 by troops stationed at Fort Matamoros, Guatemala City, and the garrison of Zacapa. However, only the conspirators at Zacapa rallied fully to the cause, and these units were soon isolated and forced to disperse under bombardment by the very CIA pilots against whose presence they were protesting. Forthright US political and military backing for Ydígoras kept the rest of the armed forces in line and the failed *cuartelazo* appeared to be different from others in this period only insofar as Washington had intervened rather more forcefully in order to protect its Cuban operation. A number of rebel leaders, most prominent amongst whom were Lieutenants Luis Turcios Lima and Marco Antonio Yon Sosa, refused to accept their defeat in traditional institutional terms and subsequently returned from exile to deploy their professional skills in a guerrilla campaign that soon acquired a political character very distinct from that of the abortive *golpe* in its radicalism and opposition not just to the government of the day but to the entire counter-revolutionary system.

The first real indication of such subversive activity came in March 1962, when the Ydígoras government encountered unprecedented opposition on the streets. United by the 1961 fraud and encouraged by the regime's precipitate loss of support in congress, the MLN, DCG and *Partido Revolucionario* (PR; established in 1957 out of the remnants of the FPL with a modestly reformist programme) staged a public campaign for the removal of the president from office. This demand was most forcefully supported by the students who on 16 and 17 March engaged with the police in clashes reminiscent of the events of June 1944, 20 people dying and over 200 being injured in the fighting. Fearful of an alliance between political parties so divided in their relation to 1954 and alarmed by indications of armed subversion for which the parallels with Cuba were immediate, Ydígoras now resorted to the appointment of a military cabinet and accepted US support for counter-insurgency operations. Applying a repression in the capital not seen since the immediate aftermath of the intervention and ostensibly crushing the nascent guerrilla over the following months, the president appeared to have weathered the storm and to be in a position to see out his term until the elections of 1963. These, indeed, seemed to offer both Washington and the high command, with which it now had close contact as a result of the guerrilla threat, the best means by which to see off the calamitous Ydígoras and secure a more coherent administration.

In the event, this reassuring scenario was spoiled by the re-emergence of the 1954 factor. As a consequence of divisions within the right and the extreme unpopularity of the government even with the bourgeoisie – from which Ydígoras had the temerity to levy the country's first income tax – neither *Redención* nor the MLN appeared likely to win the poll, whilst the PR had lost support through its gravitation away from a clear reformist stance and towards membership of the official political community of the dominant bloc. The resurgence of popular discontent under Ydígoras had given impetus to calls for a much more concerted retrieval of the policies of the reform era, and although the middle-class forces that led this social democratic movement – particularly the PR dissidents headed by Francisco Villagrán Kramer in *Unidad Revolucionaria Democrática* (URD) – themselves enjoyed little organized support, they posed a major and unexpected threat by backing the candidacy of the exiled Arévalo. Whilst the ex-president's positions had become even more moderate than twenty years before and were patently in keeping with the objectives of the Alliance for Progress, Arévalo personified the revolutionary decade just as much as, and in some senses more than, Arbenz. He was, therefore, entirely unacceptable to the military, the bourgeoisie, and even President Kennedy. Ydígoras, though, proved unpredictable to the last, and having failed to prevent Arévalo from legally returning from his Mexican exile, the president washed his hands of the matter by paying uncommon respect to the division of powers and requesting the Supreme Court to assess the acceptability of the candidacy. The resulting judgement in favour of Arévalo's claim both infuriated the office corps and convinced Washington that a military coup was now necessary. Kennedy finally gave 'the green light' for Ydígoras's removal in a swift and efficient revolt led by Defence Minister Colonel Enrique Peralta on 30 March 1963.[35]

The Foquista Challenge

It was not until ten years after the overthrow of Ydígoras that the military consolidated a pattern of institutional rule, and this itself was to last barely a dozen years before external pressure and internal divisions forced a return to a more arbitrational and veto-based political control. The populace at large was subjected to a consistently autocratic and generally violent regime from the spring of 1962 until January 1986 (for some sectors beyond). Such coercion did not in itself amount to an internally coherent political system of the type witnessed in the first half of the century or indeed in both El Salvador and Nicaragua between 1945 and 1979. The post-1954 proscriptions remained firmly in place without a clear demarcation of competition within the dominant bloc, producing unease in relations between the army and the formidable civilian right as well as enhancing the destabilizing effects of electoral manipulation similar to those that have already been seen in the case of El Salvador. In the long term both the substantial resources of the armed forces – always stronger than those in El Salvador and institutionally more coherent than the Nicaraguan National Guard – and the failure fully to halt the impetus of civilian party politics provided the dominant bloc with more strategic space than its counterparts in the other countries, where any substantial variation in the traditional division of power threatened a more profound crisis if only because there was no precedent in the post-war period.

This is not to postulate the existence of a coherent pluralism within the dominant bloc, but it is clear that the terms of control had constantly to be defended against efforts to revive the democratic heritage of 1944–54, efforts that were anathema more in substance than in form and thus produced an erratic response from the army. In the first place this took the shape of what might be called a 'parallelism' whereby, between 1966 and 1970, a civilian administration was permitted to hold office but denied the power to implement independent policy. Thereafter military control fell into a more predictable pattern of direct power recycled through fraudulent elections (1970; 1974; 1978; 1982).[36] This mode was subjected to greater pressure than in El Salvador because it came under challenge from both right and left as well as encouraging a much more marked intervention in the economy by the army. As a result, this institution entered into conflict with sections of the bourgeoisie in a manner not dissimilar to that witnessed under the Somocista state. In a third 'transitional' phase (1982–85) military autonomy was guaranteed by the need to defeat the guerrilla while progressive concessions were made to the civilian parties, as required by US pressure, the economic crisis, and internal divisions resulting from the partisanship built up over the previous decade. In these years an initial effort to sustain institutional government was soon supplanted by the commitment to restore electoral competition, albeit with the immovable proviso that the army maintain both complete freedom in its counter-insurgency campaign and a general supervisory role comparable to that of the late 1960s. Evidently, such a trajectory was far from free of contradictions and crises, and it proffered little or nothing for those who endeavoured to secure real change in social policy by acquiring a quota of authority within the system. This option was forestalled no less resolutely than in Nicaragua and El Salvador even if the opportunities for it were more varied in form (office without power as well as elections without office) before the crisis of the late 1970s. The variations in the pattern of domination were not great, but they did at least ensure that by the mid 1980s the ruling class and the military were able to reach some form of entente that met the essential requirements of both without in itself prejudicing the post-liberation order.

Even though organized by fraud and around the rewards of office, the maintenance of competition within the civilian right under Castillo Armas and Ydígoras established the claims of this sector to a quota of power and nurtured the regeneration of non-Communist forces dedicated to a partial recomposition of the reformist project. Henceforth the existence of these forces had to be tolerated even if they were repressed or denied the legal status of parties and rights to contest elections. The coup of March 1963 was decisive in this respect, for while hitherto the military had reacted to events in the political realm, it now sought to determine its inner workings as well as to limit its outer reaches. Relatively short, marked by some nationalist tendencies, and not exceptionally violent outside those zones affected by insurgent activity, the regime of Colonel Peralta Azurdia oversaw a critical transition not – as appeared to many at the time – to a new period of modern democratic administration shorn of the doleful corruption and placemanship of the immediate post-intervention years, but rather to a positive and systematic arbitration of public affairs by the military. In its initial phase the institutionalist character of the regime was particularly marked, Peralta taking office not as president in a personal capacity but as 'Chief of State' on behalf of the armed forces as a whole. The constitution was suspended and all political parties banned. Moreover, although deeply reactionary, the regime seemed to be charting a distinct course in Peralta's divergence from the supplicant attitude taken towards Washington by his predecessors. US military advisers alarmed by escalation of guerrilla activity complained of a lack of collaboration – even of positive opposition – from a government that appeared not to appreciate the severity of the threat and persisted in responding to it in traditional style. As a result, military aid, which had risen greatly under Ydígoras, was progressively cut back from $2.6 million in 1963 to $1.3 million in 1966 despite the increase of guerrilla raids over this period.[37] Peralta's high command undoubtedly did not perceive the insurgency in the same light as their North American colleagues but the president's response to it was not as slipshod as is depicted. He revived the system of military *comisionados* or temporary civilian militiamen formed of ex-soldiers and charged with supervising public order as well as organizing conscription in the villages. This system – not unlike Somoza's *jueces de mesta* or the core of ORDEN in El Salvador – henceforth acquired a central place in the control of the countryside, being greatly expanded in the eastern departments in the late 1960s to provide a framework for the vigilante organizations and death squads in which members of the MLN played a central role. Moreover, the *comisionado* system prefigured the 'civil patrols' established to regiment perhaps a quarter of the country's male population in the 1980s. It may initially have appeared a parochial and anachronistic form of rural control but it soon proved essential to the US-sponsored civic action programmes and was increasingly armed by a government that compensated for reduced military aid by buying more weapons. At the same time Peralta reformed the *Policía*

Militar Ambulante (PMA), which, despite numbering only 1,000 men, was henceforth to be a critical component of the state repressive apparatus. The articles of the PMA's organic law echoed with the language of the Liberal order of the late nineteenth century but they were applied in an unambiguously modern manner:

> The PMA [shall] lend assistance, in cases of emergency, to the owners or administrators of estates, haciendas, agricultural lands, forests and all rural properties. . . . Observe all activity that tends to inflame passions among the peasant masses or in the rural communities and, when necessary, repress through legitimate means any disorder that should occur.[38]

This refurbishing and extension of the apparatus of control was to have enduring consequences, but even before it had been properly begun it was clear that the Peralta government would be a corrective regime and not attempt a comprehensively institutional form of administration. The military itself was neither sufficiently free of partisan divisions nor logistically adjusted to undertake such a project. More important still, the broader circumstances did not favour it. Recovery from the slump of the late 1950s, rapid growth prompted by Guatemala's dominant commercial position within the new CACM, and high levels of US investment in both agro-industry and manufacturing all militated for civilian direction of economic policy and favoured a generally expansionist programme. Both Washington and the bourgeoisie accepted the need to reorchestrate the rules of competition. Hence, when Peralta signalled a return to parliamentary norms and convened elections for a constituent assembly, not only the MLN but also the PR participated in a manoeuvre to 'safeguard' the poll whereby the parties nominated the same candidates for twenty seats and the government those for the remaining sixty, leaving the electorate with no choice but to abstain or endorse this prearranged allocation of power.[39] The constitution of 1965 produced by the assembly was not quite so forthright in its manipulation of democratic procedures in that while it continued to outlaw Communism, and thus disposed of any open activity by the radical left, it limited participation in elections to those parties that could present a list of 50,000 supporters that satisfied the electoral tribunal controlled by the government of the day. This mechanism for the exclusion of threatening reformist forces subsequently became as important as simple ballot-stuffing to the practice of fixing polls.

What the authors of the 1965 constitution failed to appreciate was that the strategem of selective exclusion functioned efficiently only if supported by ballot-rigging since it naturally encouraged tactical voting by supporters of disenfranchised parties, thus uniting rather than dividing the opposition. Such a phenomenon may be deemed of purely marginal importance within a system that depended so centrally upon violence and fraud, but in the poll of March 1966 it contributed directly to the failure of the right to gain power. Perhaps the most important victim of the new conditions for participation was the DCG, which, under the leadership of René De León Schlotter, had mutated appreciably from the trenchantly *liberacionista* stance adopted at its birth in August 1955. Having presented its own candidate in the 1957 poll to no avail, the DCG closed ranks with the MDN in 1958 behind Colonel Cruz and propagated policies little distinct from those of Sandoval Alarcón beyond direct clerical patronage and aversion to violence. However, by the early 1960s the party was registering the influence of both the Alliance for Progress and the new pastoral tendencies in the Catholic Church, becoming closely linked with Archbishop Rossell's Catholic Action movement and establishing ties with small confessional trade-union and peasant bodies orientated towards cooperativism and thus largely spared from persecution. Such activity, funded in part by USAID, encouraged the burgeoning progressive tendencies of the party's youth and student followers. This group was resistant to the vestiges of orthodox radicalism still entrenched in the autonomous University of San Carlos and yet also increasingly divorced from traditional conservatism by the corruption of Castillo Armas and Ydígoras and the bellicosity of the MLN. Such a development was fully in keeping with that of Christian Democracy in El Salvador, Nicaragua and elsewhere in Latin America. It was also peculiarly vulnerable in the sense that the DCG was born directly out of the very counter-revolutionary experience that it subsequently sought to qualify, leaving it open to charges of betrayal from the extreme right and yet outflanked by other reformist parties which could uphold a much more substantial claim to leadership of the bourgeois democratic current because of their association with the reform era. This ambiguity was persistently to dog the DCG, which never came to pose a challenge to the military and ultra-right as programmatically sharp and independent as that of the Salvadorean PDC in the 1970s, the party tending always to accept offers of subordinate collaboration even in times of acute repression.[40] The Peralta coup had the effect of dividing the DCG; the diehard anti-Communists, distinguished from the rest of the *liberacionista* fold by no more than their confessional style, rallied to the new regime whilst the majority of the party adopted a clearly dissident stance in campaigning for a reduction in the size of the officer corps and an increase in Guatemala's exceptionally low direct taxes in order to fund a social welfare programme. With such a platform the DCG was a natural target for exclusion and subjected to harassment. Similarly, Villagrán Kramer's social democratic URD failed to gain recognition although it probably lacked the following as well as the politics to meet the requisites for registration.

Following their removal from the contest, these parties joined the outlawed PGT, which possessed a small but disciplined organization in the capital, to support the candidacy of Mario Méndez Montenegro, a leading figure in the overthrow of Ubico, and the PR. As a result, the PR ticket enjoyed unexpected popularity and became more clearly identified with the movement of 1944, the 1945 constitution, and the party's origins in the FPL than had been suggested by its acceptance of the post-intervention order in general and the right-wing domination of the constituent assembly in particular. This had won it official recognition that could not now be readily withdrawn without depriving the new electoral system of all legitimacy. This was despite the PR's formal retention of tax and agrarian reforms and a truce with the guerrilla on its platform. If the extreme right was in this sense ambushed from within the dominant bloc, it accepted what initially appeared only a minor setback by dint of its commitment to the project of 'controlled' elections, for which the Salvadorean PCN and, more directly, the Mexican PRI served as models. The Guatemalan equivalent of these officialist parties was the *Partido Institucional Democrático* (PID), founded for the 1966 poll by Peralta and stocked with émigrés from the right of the DCG and from the effectively moribund MDN and *Redención*. The PID was primarily designed as a political vehicle for the military and would field candidates selected by and from the high command from the elections of 1966 until that of November 1985, when, badly discredited even within the bourgeoisie, it was forced to support Sandoval. In 1966, by contrast, the party expected to exploit its control of the state and military support to force Sandoval's MLN into a secondary position and inherit its role as standard-bearer of the liberation.

The 1966 campaign was effectively opened by the shooting in mysterious circumstances of Mario Méndez Montenegro, who was replaced by his brother Julio César, dean of the USAC law school and a popular figure of more pronounced progressive views than his sibling. Benefiting from both popular sympathy and the 'bandwagon' effect caused by the exclusion of the rest of the bourgeois democratic parties, Méndez Montenegro polled an unforeseen 44.4 per cent of the vote whilst the right was badly divided between the PID (31.7 per cent) and the MLN (23.9 per cent).[41] Unprepared for such a result and the exigencies of organizing a substantial fraud, the PID and the army stalled congressional ratification of Méndez Montenegro's victory until guarantees of future conduct were formally agreed. Spurred by his victory, Méndez Montenegro threatened mobilization of the type sponsored by the PR against Ydígoras in 1962 as well as subjecting the PID to fierce rhetorical attacks. Yet neither he nor his party was in a position to challenge a system which they had supported against the left and which had by its idiosyncrasies proffered the only possibility for this minority party to take office. As a consequence, after a week of manoeuvres Méndez Montenegro finally put his signature to an accord that had already been required of the parties by the army and under which, 'the fight against subversive groups and factions will continue. In no case and under no pretext will the new government enter into any understandings or pacts with such groups, and it will give the army all the collaboration necessary to eliminate them.' In addition, Méndez Montenegro accepted the complete autonomy of the minister of defence and the continuation of general anti-Communist policies.[42] Having made much political capital out of publishing and criticizing this agreement prior to the poll, the new president now began his term disgraced by having to accede to its dangerously vague demands. In doing so he surrendered any possibility of instituting a reformist programme, laid the basis for the militarization of politics for the following two decades, and severely prejudiced the claims of electoral reformism to popular support.

Perhaps the greatest irony of Méndez Montenegro's acceptance of this forlorn concordat with the military was that the guerrilla against which it was directed had at least formally recognized the PR's claims to open a new democratic era. Albeit after sharp internal debate and in a tacit and critical fashion, supporters of the insurgent campaign born of the abortive 1960 coup and properly established in 1962 had rallied to the reformist candidate and thus held out some hope of his victory presaging a truce and the re-establishment of radical politics above ground. Such a possibility was eliminated a few days before the poll when the army captured twenty-eight leading members of the PGT and the union movement and summarily executed them. The new president's agreement to continued military operations of this type free of any political control merely confirmed that repression would continue; the guerrilla rejected Méndez Montenegro's offer of a truce as ingenuous and returned to its military campaign as the only viable means of opposition to the counter-revolutionary order. Within a year the campaign had been stalled, and by the time the PR left office it had to all intents and purposes been defeated. As a result, the 1970s opened with both revolutionary and reformist currents in a state of absolute disarray. This situation was quite distinct from that in El Salvador, where the radical left was only just embarking upon its challenge to a reformist electoralism that still enjoyed widespread support. It was also partially different to that in Nicaragua, where the consequences of the repression of 1967 for the formal opposition did not become fully apparent until 1972 whilst the FSLN survived the setbacks to its *foco* of 1967 in little better military shape than the Guatemalan guerrilla but with a much less extensive loss of political influence (largely due to the fact that it lacked this in the first place).

Table 46 charts some of the principal events of the guerrilla of the 1960s, the full political and military details of which cannot be explored here.[43] In military terms the rebels never posed a critical threat to the state and failed

Table 46: The Guatemalan Guerrilla in the 1960s

1960	Jun.	PGT 3rd Congress reflects discontent with traditional strategy and enthusiasm for the Cuban revolution but no fundamentally new policy.
	Nov.	Military revolt at Zacapa barracks quashed by Ydígoras regime with US assistance.
1961	Apr.	PGT formally identifies guerrilla warfare as principal strategy; defeated rebels of Nov. 1960 rising Alejandro de León, Marco Antonio Yon Sosa and Luis Turcios Lima return from exile.
	Jul.	Alejandro de León captured by police chief Ranulfo González and killed.
1962	Jan.	González shot; state of siege declared.
	Feb.	MR-13 (Yon Sosa and Turcios Lima) attacks UFCO offices at Bananera and clashes with troops in Izabal.
	Mar.	Large anti-government demonstrations in Guatemala City; army invests the capital and military cabinet appointed; PGT-sponsored guerrilla 'Movimiento 20 de Octubre' established under leadership of ex-*arbencista* officers in region around capital; rapidly suppressed.
	Dec.	Formation of FAR in unification of MR-13; student-based 'Movimiento 12 de Abril' and remnants of '20 de Octubre'; guerrilla leadership excluded from political control, given to PGT.
1963	Spring	Outbreak of combat in east; Ydígoras overthrown by Colonel Peralta.
	Jul.	Major FAR *foco* in Izabal destroyed.
1964	May	Yon Sosa negotiations for alliance with Villagrán Kramer's URD fail.
	Jun.	Establishment of distinct FAR fronts: MR-13 (Yon Sosa, primarily in Izabal) and Frente Guerrillero Edgar Ibarra (FGEI; Turcios Lima, primarily in Zacapa).
	Oct.	'Letter from FGEI' signals political distance from both MR-13 and PGT.
	Dec.	MR-13 draws up 'First Declaration of the Sierra de las Minas' under Trotskyist influence (published in *Revolución Socialista*, no.1, Feb. 1965).

1965 Feb. Assassination of Colonel Harold Hauser, head of US military mission, by MR-13; declaration of state of siege by Peralta regime.

Mar. FGEI convenes conference of rebel groups; MR-13 refuses to attend; new FAR established out of FGEI and PGT.

May Execution of Minister of Defence Colonel Ernesto Molina.

Sept. New constitution declares Communism to be illegal.

Oct. PR candidate for 1966 poll Mario Méndez Montenegro killed in suspicious circumstances.

1966 Jan. At Trincontinental Conference in Havana Fidel Castro launches fierce attack on Trotskyism and Turcios Lima rejects support for PR in poll; in Guatemala PGT leadership endorses support for PR; Turcios accepts this position; MR-13 begins to abandon Trotskyist programme.

Mar. 28 union and radical leaders, including Víctor Manuel Gutiérrez of PGT and *campesino* leader Leonardo Castillo Flores, captured and executed by military; elections won by PR.

May Julio César Méndez Montenegro elected president by congress; military forced to reconsider counter-insurgency strategy by Battle of Zunzapote with FAR; kidnap of leading figures in regime leads to new state of siege; guerrilla *focos* active in Zacapa, Izabal and Alta Verapaz.

Jul. Yon Sosa and Turcios Lima reject government proposal of truce favoured by PGT.

Sept. Turcios Lima calls for reunification of guerrilla.

Oct. Turcios Lima killed in car crash; replaced by César Montes (FAR) and Camilo Sánchez (military operations of FGEI); troops occupy Sierra de las Minas and destroy MR-13's *Frente Alejandro de León*; FGEI activity severely reduced.

Nov. Yon Sosa re-establishes contact with FAR; César Montes removed from influence by Camilo Sánchez; informal MR–13–FAR alliance.

1967 Feb. 'Plan Piloto' military civic action programme established in main guerrilla zones; popular support for rebels further reduced.

Aug. At OLAS meeting in Havana other Latin American guerrillas criticize FAR for links with PGT.

Oct. FAR and MR-13 operations in Izabal and Zacapa effectively halted; small fronts in south and west persist.

1968	Jan.	FAR leadership strongly criticizes PGT for ambivalent attitude to armed struggle and lack of material support.
	Mar.	FAR formally breaks relations with PGT; internal purges follow; MR-13 returns to independent operations; PGT loses many militants, particularly from youth wing, to FAR.
	Aug.	Camilo Sánchez captured by military; FAR responds by kidnapping US Ambassador J. Gordon Mein, who dies in the attempt; Sánchez executed; replaced in leadership of FAR by Pablo Monsanto.
1970	Jun.	Yon Sosa killed by Mexican forces when crossing border.
	Jul.	Colonel Arana takes power.
	Nov.	State of siege declared.
1971	Jan.	Military seal off Guatemala City in massive two-day counter-insurgency operation.
	Jul.	German Ambassador Count Von Spreti executed by FAR; FAR attempts to establish *foco* in Petén, re-establishes relations with PGT.
1972	Sept.	Eight members of FAR leadership executed by military, effectively liquidating the organization.

to build their campaign beyond the first stages of the *foco* strategy. Indeed, both the FAR and the MR-13 engaged in combat without possessing the degree of popular support necessary to resist the army's counter-attacks in their operational areas, let alone to develop a more extensive campaign of large formations. This in itself corresponded to one of the central insufficiencies of the *foco* theory elaborated by both Ché Guevara and Régis Debray out of the Cuban experience since the tactic of armed propaganda generally privileged contact with the enemy over organizational work amongst the local population.[44] The allied notion that exemplary executions of local landlords and agents of the state together with success in low-level combat with the police and army would necessarily generate a dynamic process of political support and military involvement sufficient to meet the predictable counter-offensive was also fraught with danger. It was, though, only over time that this risk intrinsic to guerrilla warfare was shown to be excessively high. Although the guerrillas of the 1970s and even the original FAR itself identified the overly adventurous and voluntarist features of a rigid *foquismo*, it was not until the autumn of 1966 that these became fully apparent as the army adopted US counter-insurgency tactics on a major scale. Until at least the spring of 1967 the military skills of Yon

Sosa and Turcios Lima, trained in 'special warfare' by the US army, and the fact that at their peak the FAR and MR-13 could muster perhaps 500 combatants, presented the military with significant problems and encouraged the Pentagon to believe that the guerrilla was a major regional threat. If in retrospect it appears very much less than this, it might be recalled that Guevara's Bolivian campaign was staged with a force one-tenth the size of the Guatemalan guerrilla and rapidly came to depend upon imported Cuban fighters. Equally, despite the fact that the second generation of insurgents – core members of which had survived the defeat of the late 1960s – also correctly identified a central flaw of their predecessors as being their resolutely *ladino* character and peripheral interest in developing a campaign amongst the Indian population, it is easy to overlook the political potential that did exist in Izabal and Zacapa – areas where a primarily *ladino* poor peasantry was subjected to increasing pressure from cattle ranchers and where the presence of foreign companies was of some consequence. The fact that in October 1964 the FAR staged a raid on the town of Panzós across the border in Alta Verapaz indicates that the guerrilla was not pursued in complete isolation from areas of potential popular support according to the criteria of the radicals of the following decade since the Panzós massacre of May 1978 is generally taken to mark the beginning of Indian rebellion in the highlands.

What was intended to be a rural guerrilla began and ended with a focus on urban operations, starting with support for the spring 1962 popular mobilization and terminating in the lost battle of kidnappings and executions fought out with the death squads of the right. All the same, it was less the rebels' military methods than their political strategy which proved to be erratic, differences in perspectives and tactics during the 1966 poll being only part of a succession of disputes. A good deal of this political inconsistency may be explained by the fact that the founders of the guerrilla were young military officers for whom the experience of Ydígoras and the 1960 revolt had provided a gut radicalism and antipathy towards their old institution but no clear political programme. Recognizing this and concerned principally to lead military operations, both Yon Sosa and Turcios initially sought not just allies but links with forces that would take complete responsibility for political work. The most obvious candidate in this respect was the PGT, the leadership of which had responded to enthusiasm for the Cuban revolution within its youth movement by making formal moves towards a strategy of armed struggle in 1960 and 1961, even going so far as to launch an ill-organized guerrilla of its own following the popular upsurge of March 1962. The failure of this effort combined with the existence of new groups of radicalized students prompted the PGT to accept the proposal of an alliance made by Yon Sosa and Turcios Lima's *Movimiento Revolucionario 13 de Noviembre* (MR-13) in December 1962. Under the terms of this agreement, which established the *Fuerzas Armadas Rebeldes* (FAR), the guerrilla leadership was excluded from political decision-making. In itself this extraordinary arrangement engendered acute problems of coordination. More importantly, it subordinated the guerrilla fronts being established in the east of the country to the political control of a party that, while formally impressed by the Cuban experience, remained very much an orthodox, urban Communist Party that perceived armed struggle to be only part of a general strategy designed less to destroy the state than to win back the gains of the reform era. Although the guerrillas themselves frequently explained their objectives to the *campesinos* of Izabal and Zacapa in a similar light, they increasingly came to attack expectations in the 'national bourgeoisie', presented by the PGT ideologues as integral to the reconstitution of liberal democracy and the renewal of socio-economic reform.[45] Furthermore, the daily experience of the insurgents instilled in them a far more sober view of the democratic vocation of the military, over which even the PGT leadership began to differ after Peralta's coup.[46] As a result, Yon Sosa first investigated an alliance with Villagrán's URD and, when this foundered on the Social Democrats' dedication to electoralism, displayed his inexperience rather than any deep Machiavellian traits in taking a jump right across the political spectrum to collaborate with members of the Posadas current of the Trotskyist movement.[47] This shift completely ruptured relations with the PGT as well as producing a split with Turcios Lima's section of the FAR, now commonly identified as the *Frente Guerrillero Edgar Ibarra* (FGEI) whilst Yon Sosa's group retained the MR-13 title.

Whilst the FGEI was itself at odds with the PGT's orthodox Stalinism and lack of commitment to armed struggle, it shared the party's critique of Trotskyism that was strongly backed by Havana, to which the FGEI was increasingly attached. Yon Sosa's Trotskyist alliance – made public late in 1964 and palpably in crisis by early 1966 – has subsequently been subjected to denigration on the typical grounds that it sought 'socialism tomorrow' and was in every respect an ultra-left enterprise.[48] It is evident that the adoption in Izabal of the tactic of 'armed defence' for supporters of the MR-13 was deeply flawed and left the guerrilla's peasant following disastrously vulnerable to military counter-attack.[49] Nonetheless, the experience of working with the Trotskyists radicalized Yon Sosa in a manner entirely distinct from the parody presented by their enemies and in practical terms quite similar to the path being taken by the FGEI. The Trotskyists' eventual departure from the guerrilla derived much less from any failure to secure instantaneous socialism than from the impossibility of collaboration between the Posadists, the PGT and Havana, which controlled much greater resources.[50] The rupture with Yon Sosa threw Turcios and the FGEI back into fitful collaboration with the PGT to form a renewed FAR early in 1965.

Unresolved differences, however, rose to the surface within a year, when the party leadership declared itself in favour of supporting Méndez Montenegro's candidacy whereas Turcios, visiting Havana, adopted a far more combative (and Castroist) stance by rejecting PR claims and the lures of electoralism.[51] His subsequent acceptance of the PGT's line was fully in keeping with organizational discipline but, as has been seen, his original assessment proved to be the correct one.

The effect of the 1966 election was once again to shift the balance of forces within the guerrilla camp, the MR-13 and FGEI increasingly coinciding in Castroist positions although maintaining operational autonomy from each other. After Turcios Lima's death in October 1966 and the successful counter-insurgency campaign led by Colonel Carlos Arana Osorio in Zacapa, political oscillations within the left took place in a context of declining popular influence. By early 1968 the MR-13 had been reduced to very sporadic activity whilst the FAR had effectively lost its base in Zacapa and split with the PGT, from which it recruited many dissidents on the basis of a critique that attacked the party's undervaluation of the role of the poor peasantry and the 'national' or Indian question – both central aspects of the guerrilla strategy of the following decade.[52] The FAR was obliged by its embattled circumstances to criticize the abstractions of *foquismo* and draw closer to a strategy of prolonged war in the Vietnam mould.[53] It was, though, impossible to build such a strategy upon the defeat of the *foco*, the military being entirely on the offensive and the guerrilla increasingly forced to retreat to the city for cover. The execution of Camilo Sánchez in August 1968 and that of Yon Sosa in June 1970 were symptomatic of the guerrilla's decline and hastened its demise. At the time of Yon Sosa's death the MR-13 had been inactive for a long period and although the FAR persisted in occasional urban operations for several years after Sánchez's death, these were more of a desperate response to the wave of repression accompanying the 1970 election and Arana's rise to power than the result of regrouped forces and fresh strategic initiatives.

Under the leadership of Pablo Monsanto the FAR continued to survive in skeletal form into the 1970s and eventually established a base in the remote department of Petén – entirely different in geopolitical characteristics to Zacapa – from where it gradually built up low-level activity over the latter part of the decade. It was, however, a dissident group of FAR survivors led by Mario Payeras (Comandante Benedicto) which re-entered Guatemala in 1972 to initiate a campaign in the Ixcán region of El Quiché as the *Ejército Guerrillero de los Pobres* (EGP) that succeeded in applying the strategy of prolonged popular war in the heartland of Indian society. Begun barely weeks after the last signs of rebel activity in the capital, the EGP's guerrilla might be viewed as a continuation of that of the 1960s. Yet it was a mark of the organization's rejection of *foquismo* that it did not undertake any offensive operations for a further three years and held back from frequent combat until 1978.[54]

The Counter-Insurgency State

The 1966 elections were a tactical setback for the extreme right and the high command but in the months following Méndez Montenegro's victory these forces acquired unprecedented organizational cohesion, launching an offensive on both military and political fronts that neither the PR nor the left could resist. Having failed to exploit a fundamentalist anti-Communist platform in the context of electoral competition, the ultra bloc took full advantage of the military's operational independence in deploying its power of veto and prosecuting a campaign that corresponded more directly to its economic and coercive strengths. Such was the momentum of this offensive that well before Méndez Montenegro left office it was evident that he would be succeeded by a fully autocratic regime.

The immediate origins of the military governments of the 1970s may be located in the intensive repression of 1966–68. One of the central features of these regimes was their reliance upon death squads, the informal nature of which may be at least partly explained by the fact that they first emerged under a civilian government opposed to extra-judicial assassination. The Guatemalan military would anyway have patronized and organized these bodies in the same general fashion as its Salvadorean counterpart, but they were from early on distinctive in more than their high level of activity. Well before the mid 1970s the death squads were operating against leading figures of the legal opposition as well as radicals and members of the labour movement. This pre-emptive approach stemmed in part from an earlier recognition of the limits of manipulating elections than occurred in El Salvador (where the killing of bourgeois dissidents was not adopted until 1980) and in part from the fact that the death squads were the expression of extremist partisanship as well as institutional strategy. This more narrowly political character was made fully evident within weeks of Méndez Montenegro's election when, following the appearance in the capital of leaflets announcing the formation of *Mano Blanca* ('the hand that will eradicate national renegades and traitors to the Patria'), the MLN publicly warned the government of 'impending vigilante action . . . the MLN cannot prevent the people from acting in self-defence . . . or [taking] justice into their own hands'.[55] *Mano Blanca* was soon followed by other groups, the most notable of which were NOA (*Nueva Organización Anti-Comunista*) and CADEG (*Consejo Anti-Comunista de Guatemala*), and within eighteen months some twenty such bodies had announced their supposedly separate existence in a spate of assassinations. There is, of course, no sure means of knowing the precise background and operational organization of the death squads, but it was fully apparent from the MLN's unqualified pronouncements that this party was deeply involved. In the countryside the system of *comisionados*, who numbered 9,000 by 1966 and were closely identified with the MLN as well as with the military, provided a ready organizational framework for identifying potential victims. It later became clear that the principal centre of information and operations coordination was the Regional Telecommunications Centre, which had been removed from the presidential palace prior to its occupation by Méndez Montenegro and placed under the control of the ministry of defence. Operating under various bureaucratic guises, this office continued to be the hub of military intelligence and 'deniable' acts of repression for the next twenty years, during most of which period it was once again located in an annexe to the palace.[56]

The climate of fear generated by the death squads and MLN threats was only made possible by the open military offensive undertaken without political constraint from the declaration of a state of siege in November 1966. This both curtailed the constitutional rights recently reinstated by the PR administration and enabled an intensive counter-insurgency campaign based on 'scorched earth' methods in Izabal and Zacapa under the direction of Colonel Arana. Unlike the campaigns of the 1970s, this operation was conducted along the lines of US strategy and with the advice of Green Beret forces. According to later statements by Vice-President Clemente Marroquín it involved the use of napalm, but whatever the precise ordnance deployed, the human cost of attacking the population in general was exceptionally high. It is estimated that between November 1966 and March 1967 some 8,000 people were killed in a comprehensive assault upon the guerrillas' social base.[57] Subsequently the intensity of the violence diminished as the army engaged in a civic action programme that provided basic supplies and infrastructural support to those communities clearly opposed to the rebels, but a 'free-fire' policy in areas deemed to be either neutral or sympathetic to the radical cause maintained a residual attrition and atmosphere of terror for several years in the south-east.

The staging of such a campaign fortified the army as a whole and led to greater levels of US military support under the Méndez Montenegro government than under its military predecessor.[58] In financial and training terms this assistance remained below that rendered to Somoza's National Guard and at a level average for Latin America at the time.[59] Moreover, with some 10,000 personnel at the end of the 1960s the Guatemalan armed forces were not markedly greater in per capita terms than those of the rest of the isthmian states bar Costa Rica. Nonetheless, such an absolute size gave the military an institutional character comparable to that of several South American armies and made it a significant circuit within both the state and civil society. With an officer corps of 2,500 the army was still highly prone to the influence of personalism and clique-based activity, but it supported an administrative apparatus that was in itself sizeable and significantly more independent from the political bureaucracy of the state than any other Central American force. It should be recalled that even between 1944 and 1954 the parameters of the institutional mission had remained very flexible and included participation in civil administration not greatly distinct in terms of scale from that of the Liberal epoch. By the late 1960s, augmented by some 3,000 police and paramilitary personnel and a network of 9,000 *comisionados*, the high command could feasibly countenance the logistical challenge of taking direct control of the state. Strengthened by the modernization begun by Peralta and continued under Méndez Montenegro (perhaps most tellingly in the formation of an elite counter-insurgency unit, the *Kaibiles* – 'tigers' in the Ixil language), bolstered by success against the guerrilla, directly supported by the MLN, PID and Washington, and emboldened by the impotence of the PR government, the army was able to overcome many of the direct and indirect restrictions imposed upon it by the 1954 intervention. It could not, though, transgress certain limits. The civilian right remained very powerful, and while the PID amounted to little more than an extension of the high command, the MLN could stake a serious claim to a quota of power that complicated any notion of an 'apolitical' government on the part of the colonels. Furthermore, the 1965 constitution provided an adequate means of securing direct political control so long as a supplementary combination of unofficial violence and manipulation of the vote was applied. In addition to preserving the democratic form of government, continued adherence to this system offered some scope for arbitrating between various personalist claims to high office; these claims were encouraged rather than diminished by the army's ascendancy and would revolve for the next decade around the person of Carlos Arana, the principal architect of the counter-insurgency state.

The fragile balance between old and new forms of political conduct was nowhere more evident than in Arana's activities. Deeply committed to the project of destabilizing the PR administration, the colonel was implicated in the 1968 kidnapping of Archbishop Casariego, a profoundly reactionary prelate whose undisturbed sequestration in the centre of the capital was designed to be attributed to the still active FAR. As a result of this excessively adventurous piece of 'black propaganda' and Arana's untempered public pronouncements, Méndez Montenegro was able momentarily to grasp the initiative and have the officer sent to Nicaragua, where his ambitions were diligently fostered by Somoza. Yet if Arana proved to be an exceptionally provocative figurehead of reaction, this only commended him to the extreme right as a potential leader of the new order. In a sense such a choice was unnecessary. The PR's vapid programme of reforms had been rendered inoperable early in Méndez Montenegro's term: constitutional liberties were suppressed in November 1966 and never fully restored; the property tax bill of 1966 was halted in its tracks by the MLN; and the 1967 sales tax was withdrawn because of fears of a coup shortly after it had passed with difficulty through congress. The author of this statute and bête noie of the right, Alberto Fuentes Mohr, accurately depicted the dilemma of the regime from which he was forced to resign by ultra pressure:

> We are confronted by a situation in which political conditions impede the adoption of policies that we recognize as necessary to create political stability. One could conclude that we are trapped by a form of vicious cycle; it is impossible to promulgate policies that assure political stability because there is no political stability; and by not making these policies we cannot hope to achieve political stability.[60]

This was no dilemma for the extreme right or the majority of the officer corps, for whom only a return to fully autocratic government and a decisive settling of accounts with the left could guarantee stability.

Chastened by the experience of 1966, the reactionary bloc staged a unified and violent campaign in the 1970 elections. Notwithstanding the fact that Arana's outspoken views and close ties with Somoza made him an ideal candidate for the MLN and thus promised further schisms, his following within the military obliged the latter to drop a separate PID candidacy and pledge support for the colonel's 'law and order' platform. The left as a whole urged a boycott, the FAR vainly tried to disrupt the poll with a number of kidnappings and executions, and the reformist centre was both split and cowed. Although the DCG finally obtained registration and campaigned for an agrarian reform, it fielded an officer (Colonel Lucas Caballero) as its candidate and failed to maintain an alliance with the Social Democratic parties (*Frente Nacional*). As a result, the DCG fell behind the PR, itself now divided and discredited, and shortly to crawl into the ranks of the right. Well served by official and unofficial coercion, efficient control over the vote and a weakling opposition, Arana and the MLN gained a comfortable victory although 46 per cent of registered voters abstained and only 21 per cent supported the winning ticket.[61]

In November 1970 Arana reminded a congress controlled by the MLN–PID alliance that, 'You elected me and you gave me this mandate: to pacify the country and put an end to the crime wave. You did not place any conditions on me . . . the government you elected made a promise, no matter who may not like it, even if it must make recourse to very dramatic measures in order to save the country.'[62] The state of siege that this peroration preceded was formally directed at the FAR but it went very much wider, applying the methods used in Izabal and Zacapa throughout the country and in Guatemala City in particular. By the turn of the year it was estimated that a casualty rate of three to four deaths a day stood in the government's favour by a ratio of 15:1.[63] After mid 1971, by which time some 2,000 people had died, virtually all the violence may confidently be attributed to the right. The real human cost is not sensibly reduced to statistics, but according to the Committee of Relatives of the Disappeared some 15,325 people were killed between 1970 and 1973, leaving 27,733 orphans.[64] Unsurprisingly, this phenomenon remained the single most important feature of Arana's presidency, during which a macabre kind of 'peace' did indeed come to prevail.

In 1973, when there were few signs of insurgency, a senior officer could confidently opine that, 'in the present conditions of chaos and violence the Army is the only force which is capable, morally and materially, of governing'.[65] Such was the balance of forces in the country at that stage that a declaration of this type was aimed less against the reformist parties than the MLN, which Sandoval Alarcón had himself declared to be 'the party of organized violence' and which thus retained uneasy relations with the military despite the 1970 alliance. Sandoval had long chafed at being unable to free himself from the semi-permanent status of bellicose amanuensis to the general of the day, but both his splenetic oratory and formidable political machine were regarded warily by the high command. Even under Arana a number of rogue MLN militants had been shot by the army as a warning against excessive ambition, and in the run-up to the 1974 poll the president acceded to the military's requirement that the official candidate stand in the name of the PID. The man chosen was General Kjell Laugerud, chief of staff, whom Arana promised to support 'with all the might that goes with holding power'.[66] As a sop Sandoval was given the vice-presidential candidacy, thereby retaining the ultra alliance but excluding the MLN from real power.

The 1974 poll was in some aspects the most decisive of the post-1954 era since there existed no tangible guerrilla challenge as in 1966 and 1970, the hope of the democratic opposition being that under such conditions the military might deem those polls to have been held under exceptional circumstances and thus return to a more flexible attitude. There is little evidence that the electorate as a whole saw matters this way – abstentionism rose from 46 per cent in 1970 to 58 per cent in 1974 – but it was in this poll that the constitutionalist right and reformist forces finally contrived to establish a united campaign in the *Frente Nacional Opositor* (FNO). The focus of this front was the DCG, which had responded to the militarist atmosphere of the day – the coup in Chile had occurred only a few months before – by nominating General Efrain Ríos Montt as the FNO candidate. Although Ríos Montt had been chief of staff at the height of the repression, he subsequently fell out with Arana, had a reputation for honesty, and might be expected to drum up some support – or at least deter fraud –

amongst the officer corps. He was not a member of the DCG but neither was the DCG particularly happy fighting elections without a military candidate. (In 1978 it would once again field an officer and in 1982 a civilian from another party with strong military ties; between 1957 and 1985 the party failed to offer the electorate a civilian member as a candidate.) The DCG managed to attract the support of a dissident wing of the PR led by Fuentes Mohr – one of the few figures to emerge from the Méndez Montenegro administration with his reputation enhanced – Villagrán Kramer's URD and the *Frente Unido de la Revolución* (FUR), led by Manuel Colóm Argueta, a man not dissimilar to José Napoleón Duarte in that he was a popular mayor of the capital in a period of autocratic government at national level. Colóm Argueta's robust style – he was impertinent enough to dub Sandoval 'a buffoon straight out of the middle ages' – and clear social democratic vocation ensured the FUR's failure to gain registration but by the same token consolidated the opposition challenge.

Determined not to repeat the experience of 1966, the regime responded to this threat by staging a fraud so manifest and clumsy that even the officer corps dithered and disputed over whether to recognize putative victory whilst Ríos Montt felt sufficiently agitated to promise the very demonstrations that five years earlier he would have ordered dispersed by gunfire.[67] Eventually a greatly indisposed Arana persuaded Ríos Montt to concede the day and take a diplomatic post in Spain in order to preserve institutional unity (and – allegedly – the buoyancy of the loser's bank account). Nevertheless, it was clear that some officers were unhappy with the machinations of the hierarchy and particularly so since these were conducted in league with the MLN. The DCG did not identify itself with the subsequent call of its exasperated general secretary Danilo Barillas for a coup, responding instead to the political domination of the army by seeking space for a collaborative role that might displace the influence of the MLN.[68] If this response was not unlike that of the Salvadorean PDC under Molina's regime then so too was the reaction of the populace very similar to that of the Salvadorean masses to the 1972 poll in its loss of belief in the possibility of obtaining change through the ballot box. What made the 1974 poll distinct in this respect was less the level of abstention than the fact that it was followed by a re-emergence of trade-union activity and mass organization that had been firmly suppressed since at least 1962.

Sharing the Surplus

It was under the Laugerud regime (1974–78) that divergences began to emerge within the dominant bloc, although these did not acquire political importance until the 1980s and never reached the level witnessed in Nicaragua. A more powerful and united Guatemalan bourgeoisie was able at least to contain the economic ambitions of the military largely because, although launched from an institutional base and possessing certain interventionist features, these were most firmly rooted in the opportunities for personal accumulation by senior officers. There was, as a result, an important separation between individual advancement *through* the state and corporate management *of* the state; the former was a predictable if disagreeable cost of military government whilst the latter was curbed by both the capacity of the bourgeoisie to uphold the historic terms of competition re-established in 1954 and the failure of the military to agree upon a coherent project in a time of deepening economic crisis. The position of the Guatemalan capitalist class in the 1980s may equally be distinguished from that in El Salvador in that although little less oligarchic in both structure and outlook, it was not directly threatened by a consolidated reformist programme patronized by Washington but by internally generated pressure for a greater transfer of the surplus to the state by fiscal means. Here the post-war pattern of development is of some significance for whilst the 1954 counter-revolution reimposed an almost completely free market model in Guatemala, the more graduated reorchestration of the dominant bloc in El Salvador had incorporated some concessions to the state by the landed oligarchy. These fell far short of permitting any major interventionist project and yet did allow a space for negotiation within the dominant bloc that was simply not required in Guatemala after Castillo Armas came to power. In this respect at least the Guatemalan ruling class may be seen as even more oligarchic than that in El Salvador.

The general form in which class interests were given political expression in Guatemala was closer to that in El Salvador than Nicaragua insofar as the bourgeoisie did not greatly depend upon direct representation through political parties. The MLN may be considered a partial exception since it purveyed a belligerent economic liberalism and inveighed with tongue and bullet against all manifestations of reform. However, although the MLN certainly possessed a diehard following in both the capitalist class and the petty bourgeoisie, particularly in the south and east, the party was never able to command the support of the bourgeoisie as a whole. The MLN's anti-Communism was much more than vestigial yet insufficient for the promulgation and arbitration of policy within the outer limits it so assiduously guaranteed. These tasks fell largely to the corporate associations of capital, amongst which the traditional organizations, such as the *Asociación de Agricultura* (AGA; 1920) and the *Cámara de Comercio* (1894, re-established in 1944), were gradually overtaken by the post-intervention bodies, such as the *Comité Coordinador de Asociaciones Agrícolas, Comerciales, Industriales y Financieras* (CACIF; 1957), the

Asociación Nacional de Café (ANACAFE; 1960) and the American Chamber of Commerce. This latter entity voiced the interests of US capital in the banana industry, a sector that had exercised a decisive influence over the economy for most of the twentieth century and was, of course, signally absent from El Salvador. The increased authority of both the American Chamber of Commerce and CACIF from the 1960s reflected a marked expansion of US capital beyond its historical redoubt in the plantation enclave and into the manufacturing commercial sectors.

Although the Cold War prompted the 1954 invasion as much as did the interests of UFCO, the company emerged from the counter-revolution with its position fully consolidated. In Guatemala banana exports were less important in both absolute terms and relative to the economy as a whole than in either Honduras or Costa Rica, and US investment in this sector was correspondingly lower than in the other states. Moreover, in the late 1960s UFCO responded to continued pressure over its monopolistic position by selling IRCA to the state; this transaction, together with the sale of the *Empresa Eléctrica*, represented a transfer of some 36 per cent of US capital in the country. Yet neither this reduction in the corporation's local profile nor its subsequent purchase by Del Monte greatly altered the terms of production and competition. The Guatemalan banana industry continued to be unique in its domination by a single foreign enterprise and the levying of exceptionally low export taxes by a regime born and bred under company patronage.[69]

The overthrow of Arbenz had in itself led to an increase in the number of US firms operating in the country from eight in 1954 to thirty-two in 1959. Investment rose more sharply still after the establishment of the CACM and the consolidation of Guatemala's superior position in regional commerce (CA$105.7 million of a CACM total of CA$297.4 million in 1970; CA$347.6 million of CA$811.1 million in 1983).[70] Between 1963 and 1970 the proportion of foreign investment in agriculture fell from 27.2 to 23.2 per cent whilst that in manufacturing rose from 10.4 to 36.3 per cent, commercial capital rising more modestly from 13.9 to 16.9 per cent.[71] This was similar to the pattern elsewhere and gross US investment (86 per cent of foreign capital) was not significantly higher than in Honduras and Costa Rica. Yet US interests in manufacturing were more than double those in any other country in dollar terms, and of the 1,043 US-controlled or owned companies operating in Central America at the end of the 1970s, 324 were located in Guatemala (95 in El Salvador and 82 in Nicaragua).[72] The greater part of this new capital took the form of transnational corporation purchases of local firms or establishment of subsidiaries, 90 of the top 500 US companies controlling some 480 branches or affiliates by 1980.[73] At the same time, the 1960s witnessed a strong tendency towards joint ventures with Guatemalan capital; in 1971 nearly half the US firms in manufacturing, 40 per cent of those in services and 21 per cent of those in commerce operated in this manner.[74]

A further feature of rising North American involvement lay in the relatively high profile of US companies of second rank, frequently associated with capital based in the 'sunbelt' states and sometimes depicted as politically more aggressive than the large corporations.[75] Such a difference may largely be attributed to managerial style, but it was by no means irrelevant that major industrial disputes took place in these enterprises – most notably the Coca Cola plant under the control of Houston lawyer John Trotter – or that the 'settler' entrepreneurs of the American Chamber of Commerce maintained a vehement campaign against all obstacles to profitability from Communism to tax reform.[76] These unalloyed redneck attitudes were struck in defence of a major US investment in the Guatemalan economy: by the end of the 1970s national capital in industry was outstripped by North American investment, which as a whole accounted for 27 per cent of all investment in the country.[77] The fact that a broad section of the local bourgeoisie was strongly and directly tied to US capital tended to militate against the type of autonomy shown by the Salvadorean oligarchy and impeded the development of some industrially-based modernizing 'national bourgeoisie' that PGT orthodoxy held would sponsor reform and compete with metropolitan capital.

The scale of US interests in the economy, the central role of Washington in the counter-revolution, and increasing domination of politics by the armed forces have all tended to reduce the perception of Guatemala as an 'oligarchic' state of the type so widely identified in El Salvador. A much larger capitalist class historically dependent upon regimes of a personalist or institutional character that steadfastly upheld its interests but were more immediately associated with their autocratic methods obscured the degree to which Guatemala remained a traditional agricultural society dominated by large landlords no less rooted in the Liberal order than their Salvadorean peers. The continued concentration of economic power in this class is clearly shown in Table 47. The key coffee sector is still based upon the oligarchic family enterprises established in the late nineteenth century and remains under the effective control of thirty-two private exporting houses that finance 65 per cent of national production.[78] The greatly expanded opportunities in cotton and sugar in the 1960s and 1970s attracted a combination of established and newer concerns, but direct control over production of these crops is even more concentrated than for coffee.[79] In 1977 forty-seven families controlled 70 per cent of cotton production (fifteen families accounted for nearly half) whereas in 1983 84 per cent of sugar production was processed by ten mills owned by a mixture of traditional oligarchic and German immigrant clans.[80] As elsewhere in the region, a significant proportion of small and medium farmers engage in

Table 47: Agro-Export Production by Farm Size, 1979

Commodity	*Value ($mn, 1980)*	*Total Farms*	*% Production on units › 92 has.*	*No. Farms*	*% Production on units › 1840 has.*	*No. Farms*
Coffee	464	97,679	83	3,651	19	188
Cotton	166	331	100	331	38	49
Sugar	69	16,854	95	1,250	41	91
Cardamon	56	12,267	68	645	13	82
Bananas	45	23,133	83	1,900	3	31
Beef	29	117,595	70	8,166	22	337

Source: Censo Agropecuario 1979, cited in Painter, *False Hope*, p.31.

cattle raising as well as coffee production, but large ranches account for the great bulk of the national herd and their owners retain still greater control over processing and export. The consolidation of these estates from Zacapa to the Petén during the 1960s and 1970s disrupted subsistence agriculture and provoked popular discontent to a degree equal to if not greater than that in Nicaragua.[81]

The pattern of diversification over the post-war period continued in the late 1970s with the adoption of non-traditional exports – by 1985 15 per cent of the total – frequently by third-generation members of traditional families (Botrán, Lamport, Castillo, Plocharsky). However, neither the investment of large amounts of capital in crops such as cardamon and carnations nor expansion of light industry and the pursuit of new markets beyond the US and CACM produced a significant conflict of interests with the established concerns from which this more modern group derived and upon which it continued to depend. More innovative in its approach to markets, the 'generational' faction was palpably uninterested in developing internal growth through import-substituting industrialization and adhered closely to the tenets of neo-Liberalism. Equally, it shared the strong opposition of the traditional sector to state intervention and any alteration to low tax rates, whether to finance infrastructural development or to fund anything but the most minimal level of residual expenditure. The political importance of this issue was evident in the downfall of Ydígoras and the boycott of Méndez Montenegro's measures, the result of entrepreneurial resistance being that in the mid 1980s Guatemala continued to have the lowest proportion of tax income to GDP (5.3 per cent) and direct tax to state revenue (15 per cent) of any Central American state.[82]

Insofar as it accepted the fiscal limits imposed by the private sector and encouraged the expansion of commercial agriculture, the Laugerud regime was entirely unremarkable. Indeed, the 'rush for growth' based upon the discovery of oil in the north and east in the early 1970s was highly beneficial to local and foreign enterprises. Buoyant prices for oil, minerals and beef promised a veritable bonanza from what soon became known as the *Franja Transversal del Norte* (FTN; Northern Transverse Strip) that ran from Izabal in the east along the Mexican border to Huehuetenango in the west. The 1973 concession of a large area of Izabal and Alta Verapaz to the Canadian-controlled EXMIBAL nickel company, followed by the first production of oil in the Rubelsanto field in 1977 and extensive prospecting by seven international firms consolidated a commercial frontier already forged over the previous decade by cattle ranching. Between 1964 and 1973 ranches in Huehuetenango and El Quiché had quadrupled their holdings and increased stock by 190,000 head whilst those in Petén, Alta Verapaz and Izabal had expanded their lands threefold and their herd by 135,000 steers.[83] From the mid 1970s both land prices and the rate of dispossession of subsistence farmers rose further still, the military exploiting its control of the state to accumulate considerable property. This was by no means a wholly institutional phenomenon and senior officers sometimes engaged in partnerships with established members of the landed bourgeoisie. However, the acquisition of estates by leading figures in the Laugerud and Lucas García regimes marked a new and conspicuous extraction of material reward from political office; four members of these governments owned an estimated 285,000 hectares in the FTN whilst 60 per cent of the department of Alta Verapaz was reckoned to be military property in 1983.[84]

If it was disturbed by this upsurge of 'disloyal competition' in land speculation, the civilian oligarchy was more generally apprehensive about the army's enthusiasm for the infrastructural development of the FTN through public investment and foreign loans. The need for a new highway – built by military engineers and the oil companies – could scarcely be denied, but the army's patronage of the Chixoy hydroelectric complex – from 1974 the country's largest public investment project (and reminiscent of Arbenz's scheme twenty years earlier) – was perceived less as a safeguard against high oil prices than as a source of chronic indebtedness and a dangerous extension of state enterprise in general, and military economic ambition in particular. Private sector concern was fully justified on all these counts. The Chixoy system was delayed long beyond the fall in oil prices in the 1980s and proved to be a major drain on the public purse through both corruption and inefficiency, and by the time the project had lost its initial lustre the armed forces were able to enforce their claims to continued political power and economic intervention on the basis of the anti-guerrilla war. As voiced by the once dependable and still powerful Arana, 'If the military are to combat subversion, they don't have to be the employees of the rich, but their partners.'[85] This status was obtained partly through simple increases in the defence budget and the control of some forty semi-autonomous state enterprises and partly from broadening the activity of the *Banco del Ejército* and the *Institución de Previsión Militar* into real estate, construction, insurance and manufacturing. As a result, by 1985 the bank was the seventh largest in Guatemala and the military had consolidated economic and managerial control over AVIATECA (the national airline), La Aurora international airport, Guatel (public telecommunications system), INDE (state electricity corporation), Channel 5 TV, two armaments factories and the country's major ports.[86]

This network of interests was neither exclusively a source for enrichment nor as extensive as the Somocista circuit, which dominated a smaller economy to a greater degree. It did, however, yield sufficient profit and authority over policy for the new left to identify a distinct 'bureaucratic bourgeoisie' nurtured through the state and mafia-like use of corruption and violence.[87] The high political profile and aggressive methods of this faction encouraged the view that it had come to dominate the class as a whole whereas in fact it had only been able to *enter* the bourgeoisie by such means. Compared to Somoza the Guatemalan military were arrivistes whose accumulation of capital was prevented by both time and the weight of established US and oligarchic interests from bestowing upon them a stable and enduring hegemony within the capitalist class.

Military confidence bred of the repression of 1966–72 and the economic growth under its rule led to some relaxation of the curbs upon urban labour, which had expanded in size over the previous decade but – in contrast to the experience in El Salvador – had been completely unable to translate greater numerical and economic strength into a regenerated trade-union movement. The violence of the 1960s impeded recovery from the 1954 defeat so that twenty years after the counter-revolution only 27,486 workers (1.6 per cent of the economically active population) were formally unionized.[88] Moreover, a large proportion of these workers belonged to the conservative and US-affiliated *Central de Trabajadores Federados* (CTF; formed in 1970 through a combination of the *Confederación de Trabajadores* and the *Confederación Sindical de Guatemala*). Lesser numbers belonged to the *Central Nacional de Trabajadores* (CNT), established in 1968, linked to the Christian Democratic regional labour organization CLAT, and if not so trenchantly *oficialista* as the CTF then certainly far from radical in its early years. Still fewer labourers declared their membership of FASGUA, closely linked with the PGT, subjected to consistent persecution from 1956 and unable to transform widespread sympathy into organized support until the mid 1970s. Indeed, the initial impetus for a revival of the labour movement came not from the manual working class but from the teachers, whose exclusion from government agreements to negotiate pay increases in the public sector led to a strike in mid 1973 that attracted enough open support to oblige the Arana regime to beat a hasty retreat.

Industrial action in 1974 by railroad, electricity and tobacco workers signalled a broader recuperation, weakening the pro-government leadership of the CTF and providing a constituency for organizational unity proposed by FASGUA and a CNT leadership moved by its rank and file to an increasingly combative stance that would lead it to sever links with CLAT in 1978. The product of this convergence was the *Consejo Nacional de Unidad Sindical* (CNUS), established in March 1976 on the basis of the CNT, FASGUA and some of the most important independent unions (teachers, municipal and state employees, transport workers, journalists and the students' AEU).[89] The constitution of CNUS represented an important challenge for the military since even the modest level of activism out of which it grew exceeded any seen since 1954 and promised to rise further still in the wake of the earthquake that had struck Guatemala just a few weeks before.

Natural and Unnatural Disaster

The earthquake early on 4 February 1976 was the worst natural catastrophe to afflict the isthmus in the twentieth century; 22,000 people were killed, 77,000 injured and over one million made homeless. Unlike the 1972 disaster in Nicaragua, the Guatemalan earthquake extended well beyond the capital and affected sixteen of the country's twenty-two departments. In Guatemala City itself the major residential, commercial and industrial zones escaped major damage since constant seismic activity along the fault-line on which the city is sited had prompted the construction of fortified buildings. By contrast, the shanty dwellings of settlements such as La Trinidad and El Gallito, located in ravines opened by the earthquake of 1917, were devastated, the high loss of life and shelter being compounded by destruction of the materials and workplaces of the city's artisanate. The plantation zones of the coast and south-east were not affected and production did not even suffer the momentary setback caused by electricity cuts and absence of labour experienced in the capital. Highland areas by contrast were badly hit. This was to have a delayed impact upon seasonal labour over the next few years as many migrant workers from the *altiplano* resisted the lure of harvest wages and dedicated themselves to restoring the fabric and production of their communities.

The political impact of the earthquake was sharp if not – in the short term at least – quite the same in form as that in Nicaragua four years earlier. Squatting on unoccupied land was met by rapid and often violent expulsion by the police whilst those political groups which attempted to organize relief independently of the official Committee for National Reconstruction (CRN) were threatened and attacked by the revived death squads; the FUR leader Rolando Andrade Ponce was killed, Manuel Colóm Argueta wounded, and the offices of the DCG assaulted. At the same time, the military occupied the Quiché township of Chajul as a pre-emptive move against exploitation of the disorder by the guerrillas of the EGP, known to be active in the north of the department for a number of months. Since the 'disappearance' of thirty peasants in Xalbal de Ixcán Grande in July 1975, formal and informal repression in this zone had been on the increase; henceforth it was to be permanent. On the other hand, Laugerud had registered the lessons of Somoza's debacle, adopting the pose of a concerned patriarch, keeping most coercive action out of the official sphere, and firmly resisting the efforts of his erstwhile patron and Somoza's understudy, Arana, to capture control of the CRN. In taking this course the president sought to impose institutional discipline on distribution of the large amounts of foreign aid entering the country and avoid the risks of unrestrained competition over the spoils. The outcome was a fierce feud in which the army attacked associates of Arana and even members of the death squads his party controlled. However, the *caudillo*'s personal power was considerable, and once organized as the *Central Aranista Organizada* (CAO) proved to be a persistent thorn in the flesh of this and following regimes both in and out of congress. Abetted by the residual distrust of the MLN by the military, the scramble for easy pickings set off by the FTN, personal animosities, the abundance of armed vigilantes and the omnipresent option of blaming the left, the extreme right increasingly resorted to violence to settle its internal disputes. Although the victims amounted to a few dozen compared to the tens of thousands of ordinary people killed as 'subversives', this internecine brutality corroded the already tenuous internal protocols of the dominant bloc. It thus progressively drove debates on policy and negotiations over distribution of power to a momentarily decisive but ultimately unsustainable cut-throat calculus. This was, of course, only a subculture determined by the wider terms of social conflict and military rule, but it accentuated the disaggregation of a dominant bloc which by early 1982 had become bereft of the political means by which to re-establish unity and sustain government outside of a coup d'état, a mechanism not employed since 1963.

By permitting somewhat greater space for popular organization Laugerud was primarily conducting a manoeuvre within the dominant bloc to establish the independence of his government, identify himself with a more efficient mode of social control, and marginalize both his predecessor and the MLN, foisted on him by Arana. He achieved some success in this latter case, conscripting the PR and DCG to exclude Sandoval Alarcón's acolytes from control of congress. This provoked a split in the MLN in 1977, by which time it had become clear that the high command would not honour its historic obligation to the vanguard of extremist reaction if more malleable and presentable allies were to hand. In this respect Laugerud strengthened military dominance through the PID by encouraging reactionary partisanship around it. On the other hand, he was quickly forced to reverse his limited concessions to the mass movement once it became apparent that these had opened not a new phase of stable co-optation but one of burgeoning militancy. As a result, the years following the earthquake witnessed a retreat to the strategy of wholesale violence against a popular upsurge that was erratic in both form and momentum but threatened a decisive convergence of the Indian jacquerie perpetually feared by the *ladino* ruling class, an urban syndicalism identified with the excesses of the reform era, and radical guerrillaism similar to that of the 1960s in that it raised the spectre of Cuba. By the end of 1978 this dreadful and unprecedented concatenation was clearly perceptible, and well before the final stages of the Nicaraguan revolution the army's response to it was of such an order that the Carter administration was given no option but to cut military aid.

The pattern of urban conflict was determined much less by guerrillaism or an openly political radicalism of the type that had provoked the defeat of 1966–70 than by economic struggle and a defence of syndicalism. According to CNUS leader Miguel Angel Albizures, the level of unionization rose 5 per cent in 1976; and the incidence of industrial disputes between 1975 and 1977 was markedly greater than in previous years as the manufacturing labour force attempted to halt the reduction of real wages by over 30 per cent since 1970.[90] Nonetheless, the industrial working class as a whole remained highly cautious and dependent upon the initiatives of key sectors. Perhaps the most prominent of these were the workers of the capital's Coca Cola bottling plant (EGSA) who, despite the successive assassination of their leaders, continued to demand union recognition following a dispute in 1975. Although temporarily resolved by the transfer of the franchise in 1980, the issue of union rights at EGSA attracted international attention for a further five years during which neither the death squads nor the new managers could reduce the resistance of a workforce that had become the effective standard-bearer of Guatemalan syndicalism and maintained a year-long occupation of their factory while people were being shot in their thousands around them.[91]

By June 1977 the strength of support for union rights was such that the funeral of labour lawyer Mario López Larrave, shot by the right to halt his efficacious campaign in a court system still prone to judge cases on their legal merits, was attended by 15,000 people and turned into an impromptu demonstration of singular resonance against the regime. In November seventy workers from the tungsten and antimony mine at Ixtahuacán (Huehuetenango) adopted the tactic of a march to the capital to draw attention to their four-year demand for union rights. This unusual initiative caught the popular imagination and drew such support that the miners continued the 250-mile walk even after their demands had hurriedly been met; the crowd of 100,000 people that received them in Guatemala City was the largest congregation seen for decades. The momentum created by the demonstration and a similar protest made in the same month by sugar workers was continued in February 1978 when 85,000 public sector workers staged a nine-day strike for a 50 per cent wage rise. This stoppage caused considerable disruption, and with the imminent election under threat the government eventually conceded the central demands although the state employees' union (CETE) was technically illegal.

Notwithstanding the inability of vigilante violence to halt the alarming resurgence of syndicalist organization, the military regime failed to register its importance and in June 1978 approved price rises for a string of basic necessities. Although this provoked popular discontent no less than the continuing killing of union activists, it was not until October that the mass movement was stung into major action when Lucas García's government approved the bus companies' demand for a fare rise of 100 per cent. This issue had been smouldering for a number of months as the companies refused to concede wage increases without higher fares, which were resisted by a conservative municipal government that feared the impact of an urban population whose transport costs amounted to some 15 per cent of average wages because the system of routes generally compelled payment of several fares. The mayor's apprehension was fully justified, the increase widely repudiated, and an adventurous call for a general strike made by CNUS, which received the backing of CETE and other major unions. Discontent extended well beyond the unionized working class, and organizations such as the slum-dwellers' *Movimiento Nacional de Pobladores* (MONAP) and the *Comité de Defensa del Consumidor* that had developed rapidly since the earthquake were to the fore of the popular campaign. The strike halted more than half the capital's industrial and commercial activity and was accompanied by rioting that lasted for a week and bore the influence of the Sandinistas' simultaneous 'Autumn Offensive' as youths sporting FSLN handkerchiefs built barricades, occupied public buildings and engaged in running street-battles with the police. The trade union leadership had minimal control over these protests, which were disorganized expressions of popular anger rather than coordinated actions designed to obtain limited objectives. As a consequence, this momentarily explosive movement was soon curtailed by a combination of military force – some 40 people killed and 800 arrested, including much of the union leadership – and the reversal of the fare rises by payment of a subsidy that cost the state $38 million.[92]

Lacking any strategy for maintaining the impetus of this remarkable but unexpected upsurge, CNUS was obliged to call off the general strike and attempt to reconsolidate an organization that had become dramatically over-extended. The right, on the other hand, proceeded immediately to ensure that no repetition of the quasi-insurrectionist movement would occur. Within days of the rioting a new organization, the *Ejército Secreto Anti-Comunista* (ESA), published a death list of forty names, promptly and calmly executing the student leader Oliverio Castaneda de León in the city centre before a group of impassive police officers. Castaneda was but an early member of an interminable line of activists whose assassination or 'disappearance' served to force popular organization underground once again. The selective nature of these killings did not liquidate all vestiges of opposition at a stroke – the Coca Cola dispute continued; USAC persisted in defending university autonomy despite the killing of seventy-seven faculty and students between March and September 1980; and in that year a May Day rally was held. However, the union movement was thrown fully on to the defensive in 1979, all but decapitated in 1980, and did not again resort to protest in the streets until late 1985. Lacking the depth of organization established in El Salvador throughout the 1970s or the breadth of political support achieved in Nicaragua, the Guatemalan working class was repulsed both earlier and more emphatically. It had, though, shown military control of the city to be vulnerable, and from October 1978 the regime could no longer depend upon the quietude of a capital that was increasingly viewed as its rearguard in a mounting struggle against the rural guerrilla.

The perception of town and country as two entirely separate spheres of social and political activity is no less misguided in the case of Guatemala than for the rest of the isthmus despite the fact that the capital dominates the urban system to a much higher degree than elsewhere and is the only proper 'city' in Central America. Albeit the fount of *ladino* culture and tangential to the powerful socio-economic nexus between *altiplano* and the piedmont plantations, Guatemala City remains the primary commercial centre and a strong pole of economic attraction for dispossessed sectors of the rural labour force. Furthermore, for centuries the site of unique administrative and political authority, the city necessarily draws the *campo* to it at the same time as it exists in a contradictory symbiosis with it. The importance of this exchange should not be underestimated, even as the political conflict of the late 1970s enhanced the distinctiveness of the two spheres, not least in terms of logistical conditions. Indeed, one of the largest popular demonstrations in the capital during 1978 was the June march called to celebrate the anniversary of López Larrave's death and to protest the Panzós massacre of the previous month, a large number of Kekchí *campesinos* travelling to the city precisely because it was the source of both oppression and support. Nevertheless, over the following years this exchange was to diminish in outward form with the countryside dominating political activity and the city remaining in a state of petrification. A reflection of the balance of forces following the precipitate *jornadas* of October 1978, this corresponded more generally to the simultaneous development of a profound crisis within a rural society where the radical left had established a strong presence.

The breakdown of order in the countryside during the late 1970s may be traced, as in Nicaragua and El Salvador, to the severe disruption of subsistence agriculture caused by expanded agro-export estates. As has been seen, the growth of cotton and particularly cattle provoked progressive division of plots and dispossession from the mid 1970s (Table 8b, p. 183). The acceleration of ranching in the 1960s, establishment of the FTN, and the earthquake combined to sharpen the pressure considerably so that at the end of the 1970s USAID established that 90 per cent of the population of the *altiplano* lacked sufficient land to meet basic needs whilst the number of landless labourers had risen to 420,000.[93] Subsistence grain production rose at a rate much below that of agro-exports and insufficient to avoid increasing imports of foodstuffs, from $56 million in 1970 to $313 million in 1980.[94] It is notable that cultivable land per capita in the three highland departments most affected by the guerrilla – San Marcos, El Quiché and

Huehuetenango – fell by 50 per cent between 1950 and 1980.[95] For a decade or more after 1954 popular organization in the countryside was either non-existent or too weak and cowed to respond to this creeping pressure; however, from the late 1960s the state accepted and even encouraged a steady growth in cooperatives since these were largely sponsored by the Church or US development schemes. By the time of the earthquake 132,000 people belonged to 510 such bodies, over half of which were located in the *altiplano*.[96] In the wake of the disaster these organizations and the clerics closely associated with them began to manifest greater independence, and as a result of their attachment to the progressive pastoralist currents and catechist network that had emerged over the previous period they were increasingly viewed by the military as a threat to the state. Well before the earthquake the MANO death squad had denounced the cooperative movement as a veil for Communism, and at least thirty-five cooperativists from Chajul, El Quiché, had been 'disappeared' in June 1975.[97] In the first year after the catastrophe some seventy leading activists from the Ixcán region were executed whilst over a hundred died in the Ixil triangle as the army consolidated its occupation of this zone around the towns of Nebaj, Chajul and San Juan Cotzal.[98]

There is perhaps some historical irony in the fact that the indigenous population of the area had been converted to Catholicism largely at the hands of Spanish priests, no longer the companions of *conquistadores* but proponents of popular liturgy and a robust catechist movement that fused elements of traditional paganism with liberation theology.[99] Indeed, the fact that foreign priests comprised four-fifths of Guatemala's clergy and were particularly prominent in challenging the established norms of spiritual resignation undoubtedly made it easier for the army and the right to launch both physical and political attacks on them and their predominantly Indian congregations.[100] This campaign, comparable with that prosecuted in El Salvador at the same time, was further facilitated by the deeply reactionary posture of Archbishop Mario Casariego, himself a Spaniard but determined that 'the poor should be grateful for being poor just as was the infant Christ'.[101]

Casariego had been one of the few Latin American prelates who refused to attend the 1968 Medellín conference which upheld heterodox ideas scarcely compatible with his 'love [of] military life. And I love it when it is based upon discipline, such as I believe is the case in our army . . .'[102] Casariego had few problems in securing the expulsion of US Maryknoll missionaries in 1967, at the height of the Zacapa counter-insurgency campaign, neither was he unduly troubled by the fact that he alone of the country's bishops did not sign the fifty-eight-page document issued in July 1976 attacking the seizure of peasant lands and rise in state violence since he possessed no administrative authority over the rest of Guatemala's prelates.[103] However, the cardinal's failure to respond to the killing of sixteen priests between 1976 and 1981 and his refusal to take a stand over human rights even as ambiguous as that adopted by Obando y Bravo isolated him not only from the rank and file of the clergy but also from the majority of the hierarchy; in 1979 seven bishops resigned in protest at his inactivity, and in July 1983 the Guatemalan-born Bishop Juan Gerardi of El Quiché formally closed his diocese and removed all clergy from the department after six clerics and hundreds of catechists had been killed and he himself threatened with death. By this stage it was clear that the great bulk of the largest Roman Catholic Church in Central America was at odds with the military regime, and some elements of this Church were prepared to support active resistance by the Indian population against the violence of the state and the ultra-right.[104] If the army possessed a precedent for its anti-clericalism in the Liberal order of the nineteenth century, the position of the clergy was itself no less historically informed and looked back well beyond Vatican II to the trenchant defence of the rights of the indigenous peoples sustained by Bartolomé de Las Casas, bishop of the neighbouring province of Chiapas in the mid sixteenth century.[105]

The religious campaign, elements of which resonated with colonial paternalism, was given particular impetus by the Panzós massacre of May 1978. This provoked a rupture with the pattern of generally passive resistance on the part of the Indian population, which henceforth proved increasingly open to guerrilla overtures and the possibilities of autonomous *campesino* organization. The EGP had already established a presence in and around the Cuchumatán mountains in the north, and discontent was rife in the communities affected by the FTN; Panzós had the effect of accelerating this process in part simply because of the number of people killed but also because the massacre was symptomatic of developments elsewhere in the FTN. Free of insurgent activity since the brief incursion of the FAR in 1964, the Polochic valley had not been greatly affected by the rise of ranching elsewhere in Alta Verapaz and Izabal until the construction of a road from the nickel centre of El Estor, on Lake Izabal, through Panzós and the village of Cahaboncito to Cobán and the highlands. This road made the region far more accessible and increased the value of local land with the result that the FIASA group, which linked the powerful Castillo family with US government and private capital, had established a ranch by 1971.[106] However, it was only early in 1978 with an end-of-term spate of new land titles made by the Laugerud regime that the issue of property rights became critical. The peasant farmers of Cahaboncito and surrounding villages who had cultivated corn on this land for decades appealed to the agrarian reform institute INTA for formalization of their longstanding usufruct. Since this appeal showed that they, like so many *campesinos*, lacked freehold title and would not receive it, the new landlords were encouraged in their use of vigilantes to

Table 48: Polarization in Guatemala, February 1976–March 1982

1976	Feb. 4	Earthquake leaves 22,000 dead, 77,000 injured, one million homeless.
	Mar.	Formation of CNUS.
1977		Carter administration cuts military aid.
	Nov.	Miners' march from Ixtahuacán met by large crowds in capital; sugar workers march to capital.
1978	Feb.	Public sector strike partially successful; military mobilization in Guatemala City.
	Mar.	General Romeo Lucas García (PID) wins fraudulent elections.
	Apr.	Formation of *Comité de Unidad Campesina* (CUC).
	May	Massacre at Panzós, Alta Verapaz.
	Oct.	Rise in bus fares provokes urban general strike and demonstrations; government concedes popular demands.
1979	Jan.	Assassination of Alberto Fuentes Mohr (PSD).
	Feb.	Formation of the *Frente Democrático Contra la Represión* (FDCR).
	Mar.	Assassination of Manuel Colóm Argueta (FUR).
	Sept.	ORPA announces its existence.
1980	Jan.	Massacre of Quiché Indians at Spanish embassy.
	Feb.–Mar.	Plantation workers' strike wins wage rise.
	May	Labour Day march attracts 40,000 supporters.
	Jun.	Assassination of 27 leaders of CNT.
	Jul.	Diocese of El Quiché closed by rightist violence against clergy.
	Aug.	Military kills 60 people at San Juan Cotzal, El Quiché; 17 CNT leaders assassinated in Escuintla; 5-year dispute at Coca Cola plant temporarily resolved.
	Oct.	ORPA joins EGP, FAR and PGT (Nucleo de Dirección) in coordinated guerrilla activity.
1981	Jan.	Formation of *Frente Popular – 31 de Enero* (FP-31)
	Feb.	Repressive operations intensify in Chimaltenango, some 1,500 people killed in two months.

	Apr.	Repressive operations intensify in Huehuetenango and El Quiché.
	Jun.	Reagan administration approves sale of military equipment worth $3.2 million.
	Aug.	Military attack on Coya, Huehuetenango, and death of some 200 people opens new counter-insurgency offensive under Chief-of-Staff General Benedicto Lucas García; 500 guerrillas occupy Chichicastenango, El Quiché, to celebrate anniversary of Nicaraguan Revolution.
1981	Aug. 12	Massacre of some 1,000 peasants around San Sebastián Lemoa, El Quiché.
	Sept.	Massacre of some 700 people at San Miguel Chicaj and Rabinal, Alta Verapaz.
	Oct. 10–20	Guerrillas launch attacks in Guatemala City.
	Dec. 2	Guerrilla force of *c.* 500 attacks garrison of Santa Cruz del Quiché.
1982	Jan.	Military renew offensives in El Quiché, Chimaltenango, Huehuetenango and San Marcos.
	19	Guerrillas attack military base of San Juan Cotzal, El Quiché.
	Feb. 7	EGP, ORPA, FAR and PGT (ND) establish *Union Revolucionaria Nacional Guatemalteca* (URNG).
	Mar. 7	General Aníbal Guevara (PID) wins plurality in fraudulent poll; demonstrations by opposition.
	23	Bloodless palace coup headed by General Efrain Ríos Montt.

oust the Kekchís on whose lands cattle were to be raised. Following a number of clashes, the peasants were called by the army to a meeting at Panzós to resolve the issue only to be shot down upon their arrival in the town square by troops already in firing positions. According to later military reports a major clash with 'subversives' took place, which explained neither the immediate burial of the dead in a single mass grave – alleged to have been dug by tractors two days earlier – nor the fact that only one soldier was hurt, with a slight wound to the leg. Well before the Church issued its detailed version of a premeditated mass execution the regime's clumsy rendition of events had been undermined by eye-witness accounts that coursed through countryside and city in both laconic and exaggerated form, exciting ire and fear on a considerable scale.[107]

Militant reaction to Panzós did not come out of the blue. A groundswell of discontent had been accumulating in the countryside since at least the earthquake. Only three weeks before the massacre it took organized shape in the *Comité de Unidad Campesina* (CUC), formally established on May Day 1978 as a broad rural workers' union that sought no recognition from the state and possessed no formal leadership structure. Organized largely underground and through local meetings, the CUC effectively became a popular extension of the guerrilla, and with a declared commitment to prolonged people's war it stood particularly close to the EGP. This affiliation was mirrored in the organization's initial base of support in El Quiché and Chimaltenango although until 1981–82 the CUC's following expanded to Huehuetenango and San Marcos – areas where ORPA was active – and the plantations of the south coast, where highland Indians merged with *ladino campesinos* in the harvest labour force. In geographical, racial and political terms the CUC had no precedent and the first four years of its existence witnessed a signal advance in rural radicalism. This was of necessity counterposed to racial sectarianism, and there can be little doubt that the initial dynamism to establish CUC came primarily from the Indian *campesino* movement of the *altiplano*. Although not universally poorer or more heavily exploited than the *ladino* peasantry, it did incorporate the most impoverished sectors of the rural population, and was larger in number, more concentrated in settlement, and subjected to a particular oppression that had sharp economic as well as socio-cultural consequences. Thus, if there could be no enduring radical movement in the countryside without the active support of the *ladino* peasantry, both the past practice of the left and the dominant racist culture led important sections of the new revolutionary leadership to lay more stress on the complementary assertion that there could be 'no revolution without the Indian'.[108]

The core element of Guatemala's indigenous population – some three million people and approximately 40 per cent of the total population – is formed by the Quiché, Mam, Kakchiquel and Kekchí peoples, largely concentrated in the north-west and central highlands (see map). By dint of both their size and areas of settlement these communities have traditionally provided the bulk of seasonal labour and in recent years suffered the harshest repression. There is, nonetheless, no general distinction on these grounds from the rest of the indigenous groups, which together number some 650,000 (10 per cent of the population): Kanjobal, Chuj, Jacalteco, Aguateco, Uspanteco, Ixil, Achí, Pocomochí, central and eastern Pocomam, Chorti, Tzutuhuil, Lacandon, Mopán, Itza, Araguaco, and Yucateco. As can be seen from the map, several of these ethnic groups also live in the heart of the FTN and areas of conflict. At the same time, it must be recognized that an appreciable degree of cultural differentiation exists between peoples that are not themselves economically homogeneous. It has

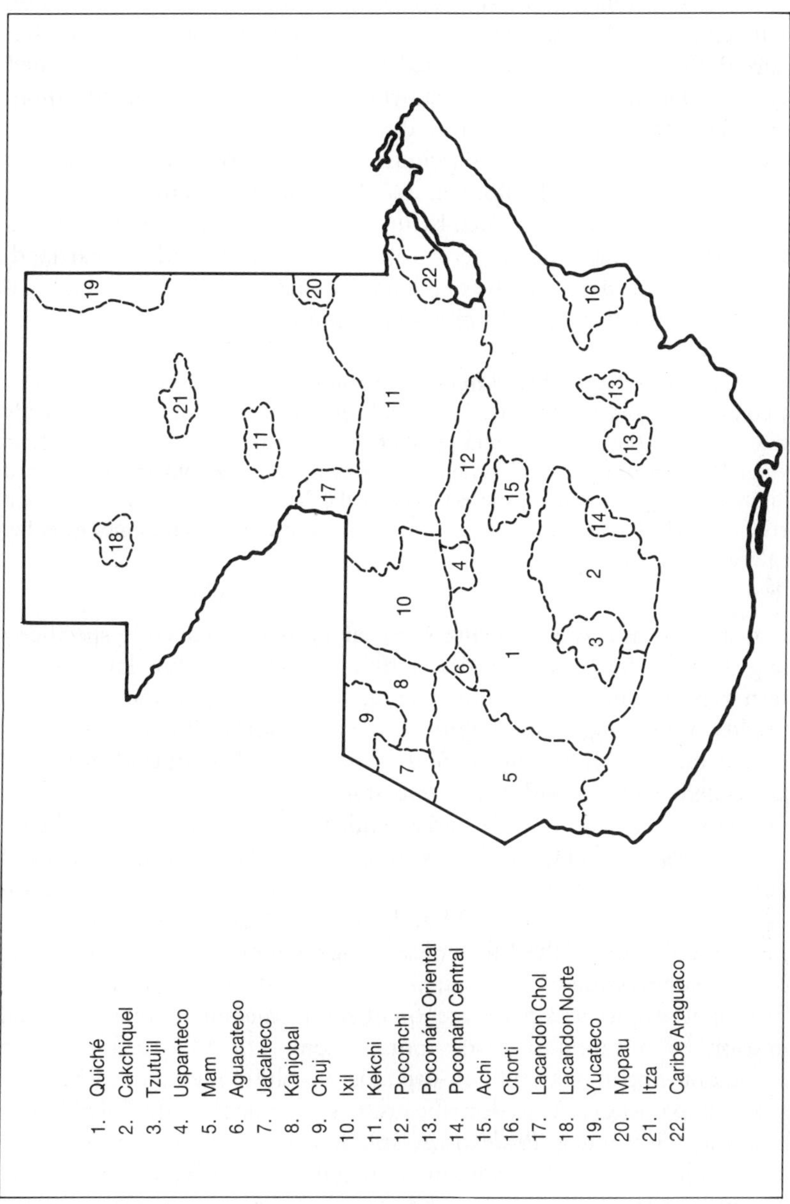

The Indigenous Population of Guatemala

been suggestively argued that a specifically *Indian* consciousness that subsumes and supersedes inter-ethnic identity was only consolidated by the economic and military offensive of the 1970s. This effective invasion outstripped that of the late nineteenth century and was of such an order that it realized the general and politicized qualities of 'Indianness' that had always been latent in the varied socio-cultural forms of self-identification. Despite the obvious terminological difficulties, such an awareness may plausibly be termed 'class consciousness' and arguably be deemed revolutionary.[109] The difficulties in ascribing distinct features to such a consciousness are clearly signalled by the manner in which the EGP, which has more than fifteen years' experience of activity in the Indian heartland, strives to present the constituent characteristics of the 'ethnic-national Indian groups [that] do not form a single nationality':

> . . . a particular being and hard-to-describe sense of ethnic-cultural identity. This can only be defined as the particular way of being and feeling of a collective body linked through the definitory and peculiar thought patterns produced in human beings by such complex and varied factors as the mother tongue, the place of childhood, life experiences, the relation to the land and to the basic foods it produces, habits, customs, traditions, in a place and time which cannot be either replaced or repeated.[110]

Such a passage leaves a strong sense of infinitely reducible specificity eluding any coherent general description in the orthodox language of western rationalism. On the other hand, it does indicate the scope and profundity of an indigenous experience which, if not itself readily quantifiable, may indubitably be understood as one side of a contradictory and deeply violent relation with the *ladino* state.

For the EGP, which by 1978 had extended well beyond its original base in the Ixcán region of El Quiché, 'this ethnic-national contradiction is one of the fundamental factors in . . . revolutionary change'.[111] Yet the organization's political origins in the FGEI and the radical Christian movement as well as the influence of the Vietnamese struggle upon its strategy militated against the suppression of a class analysis. It thus identified the domination of the Indian peoples as a phenomenon of complementary exploitation and oppression by a capitalist agro-export system. The EGP called for an agrarian, anti-imperialist and anti-capitalist revolution, employed Marxist language, and if less ready to describe itself as socialist than the Salvadorean FPL or the Nicaraguan *Proletarios*, still formed part of a recognizable regional radicalism in its criticism of social democracy, repudiation of electoralism, identification of Cuba as the 'socialist vanguard in the hemisphere', and its objective of capturing state power by force of arms.[112] Characterized primarily by adhesion to the strategy of prolonged people's war in the countryside, the EGP built upon its initial military activity in El Quiché with greater emphasis on popular organization in the department between 1976 and 1980; it extended its presence to Huehuetenango and Chimaltennago, and later and more tentatively to the Verapaces and the western plantation provinces. Although weak in the capital and absent from the entire east of the country, the EGP had by 1981 achieved an appreciable network and become the largest guerrilla force.

The EGP was not the only heir to the guerrilla of the 1960s. The experience and programmatic disputes of this period that had disposed of the claims of *foquismo* (together with a more general insurrectionist tendency of the type associated with the Nicaraguan *Terceristas*) did not by any means lead to a mending of deep divisions within the radical left. The Guatemalan revolutionary was less publicly and profoundly sundered along strategic and ideological lines than that in El Salvador, but it was also much weaker and reliant upon reorganization around the dispersed survivors of Arana's repression. For most of the 1970s it existed in an organizationally disaggregated manner that at times reflected substantial political differences and at times simply reflected the exigencies of maintaining some form of operable apparatus. Even after the establishment of informal coordination in 1979 followed by official unity in the *Unión Revolucionaria Nacional Guatemalteca* (URNG) in January 1982, internal divisions continued to prevail at a much higher level than in the FSLN and in a more pronounced fashion with regard to military questions (if not political strategy) than in the FMLN. This failure to maintain an authentic unity must be attributed in large measure to the adverse military situation in which the left was placed within a few months of the URNG's formation although it cannot be divorced from the distinct background of its component organizations.

The widest gap was clearly with the PGT, which had at its fourth congress in December 1969 produced self-criticism of 'reformist and rightist opportunist sentiments . . . a tendency towards economism and a one-sided approach to legal forms of mass work' but also strongly criticized the guerrilla as divorced from the population and – conveniently for the party apparatchiks – damned by the 'provocative, adventurist activity of Mexican Trotskyists in the service of the CIA'.[113] Although the excrescence of Trotskyism was not to re-emerge, the PGT leadership was at pains throughout most of the 1970s to distance itself from the guerrilla forces, attacking the newly independent FAR (which split completely with the PGT in 1971) as 'ultra-left', 'militaristic' and 'anarchistic'.[114] In short, while the PGT could not entirely reject the option of armed struggle, it retained a fundamental aversion to this 'petty-bourgeois' form of political activism, continued to harbour suspicion of movements based on a peasantry with which it possessed no influence, and was most reluctant to repeat the traumatic experience of collaboration of the 1960s. Even in the city the PGT found itself outstripped by the new left from the mid 1970s, the remnants of the FAR under Pablo Monsanto holding on to a limited urban base, and then recruiting radicalized Christian Democrats to gain some influence first in the CNT and then CNUS at least until the end of 1978. These links with the union movement gave the FAR an orientation not dissimilar to that of the Salvadorean FPL and the *Proletarios* of the FSLN in its objective of forming an armed and radical working-class party counterposed to the reformist caution of orthodox Communism. The headlong retreat of the unions after October 1978 hit the guerrilla badly, and the FAR later redirected much of its activity to the Petén, where it established a modest but telling presence, and the coastal plantations, where more marked initial advances were stalled by the army, whilst managing to undertake minor operations in the capital and Chimaltenango. With the broadest political and operational experience of the left in the 1970s the FAR adopted a modulated approach to the strategic dichotomies of town and country, race and class, military and organizational. The guerrilla did, however, champion socialism in its primary slogan, an attribute it shared with PGT dissidents who broke from the party in 1978 on the pretext that their leaders had failed to fulfil the commitment made at the 1969 congress to sustain some form of armed struggle.[115]

Distinguishing itself from the Central Committee by the title *Nucleo de Dirección*, this sector of the PGT attempted to establish an urban campaign and meet the challenge of the radical left by adopting its methods. Despite the fact that it received support from the party's youth, the group managed to sustain only very sporadic activity and soon transpired to be more a symptom of crisis inside the PGT than a distinctly new force. A further schism in 1980 compounded the PGT's lack of direction without producing either a viable Communist guerrilla or the unity of the left that all factions of the PGT now proclaimed a major objective. By 1981 the party's central committee declared itself open to discussion with its radical critics, and the following year it openly accepted that the absence of unity was in part due to its own rejection of armed struggle; it studiously avoided pretensions to a vanguard role, and announced that 'the whole party must join in the revolutionary war'.[116] The confusion caused by this erraticism effectively paralysed the PGT during the period of most acute political and military crisis in 1981–82 and eventually provoked the election of a new central committee in January 1984, this duly petitioning for membership of the URNG. In a sense this move was a political victory for a radical left which was largely led by ex-members of the PGT or people who had previously collaborated with the party. On the other hand, by 1984 no faction of the PGT was capable of undertaking coordinated military activity, the position of the party being markedly weaker than that of the PCS in 1980–81 or even that of the PSN in 1978–79 since its failure to take a military role was matched by a presence in an urban mass movement in full retreat. The absence of the PGT from the URNG was much less a function of sectarianism on the part of the guerrilla than might appear to be the case. All the same, the ability of the armed groups to deny any political role, let alone leadership, to the party stood in stark contrast to the state of play in the 1960s.

Of all the guerrilla organizations it was perhaps ORPA that responded to the experience of the 1960s most emphatically in operational terms. This force did not openly declare its existence until 1979, despite the fact that it had slowly built up an infrastructure in San Marcos, Sololá, Quezaltenango and Huehuetenango over the preceding eight years. With its origins in the small *Occidente* group that emerged from the division of the guerrilla alliance in March 1968 and – in contrast to the majority of the FAR – resisted any further collaboration with the PGT, ORPA became an entirely new organization during its prolonged gestation. Smaller but more resourceful in military terms, it shared the EGP's strong *indigenista* orientation and established particularly strong roots in the western Indian departments. It also placed greater emphasis on developing an autonomous military structure, and the greater flexibility of its political style gave it a broader constituency than the EGP, which lacked ORPA's following amongst middle-class intellectuals, or the FAR, which upheld a less populist programme. It is possible that ORPA's more expansive platform reflected lessons drawn from the experience of the FSLN in 1978–79 when the organization was preparing to launch its campaign. ORPA possessed some of the political pragmatism of the *Terceristas*, lacked the depth of popular organization required by the strategy of prolonged popular war, and generally resisted the lure of insurrectionism. Less ambitious than the EGP in terms of geographical expansion after 1980 and with a stronger presence in the plantation regions, it emerged from the army's counter-offensive of 1981–82 in better shape than its ally and in a manner not unlike that of the Salvadorean ERP.[117]

At the time of the Panzós massacre ORPA's existence was not broadly known about; the FAR appeared to have grown only very modestly if at all; the PGT was riven with enervating dispute; and only the EGP was widely recognized to be operating in the far north. Within four years this combined guerrilla force was active in all but eight of the country's departments, numbered perhaps 6,000 fighters, possessed a strong social base in the highlands, and had launched a strategic offensive that even the army high command admitted posed an exceptionally serious threat to the existing political order. The rebel challenge was out of all proportion to that of the 1960s and appeared to be on the verge of capturing state power. Precipitate and founded upon misplaced estimations of the guerrillas' military strength and popular support though it may have been, this offensive was only defeated by desperate recourse on the part of the military to the strategy of attrition, the human cost of which outstripped even that of 1932 in El Salvador.

The State Besieged

The March 1978 poll was momentarily put in jeopardy by the decision of the employees of the electoral commission to join the February public sector strike, but the high command was eventually able to secure victory for the PID candidate General Romeo Lucas García and perpetuate the system of fraud begun by Arana. Relations with Washington were already too bad to merit concern over any adverse US reaction; the Social Democratic parties led by Fuentes Mohr (PSD) and Colóm Argueta (FUR) were denied registration; and the DCG's popularity was at a particularly low level as a result of its decision to *coquetear* (as ORPA put it) with Laugerud. The desultory experience of 1974 led 69 per cent of registered voters to abstain whilst 20 per cent of those who did comply with the legal obligation to vote chose to cast spoilt ballots as requested by the FUR. The system was patently corrupt. Yet not all fraudulent elections are the same, and that of 1978 was distinct inasmuch as the fraud was directed principally against the MLN rather than the parties of reform.

Moving sharply back to full repressive control after 1976–77, the Laugerud regime continued to marginalize the MLN, first conscripting DCG support in congress and then forming an electoral alliance with the PR and CAO. To signal this rupture and demonstrate its confidence the PID deftly lured the old Social Democratic firebrand Francisco Villagrán Kramer into rejoining his erstwhile colleagues in the PR and serving as vice president. Villagrán was later to repent of his high-profile entryism in an attempt to civilize the regime from within, but at the time the move was not entirely inconsequential, persuading the excluded FUR to lobby for Lucas against the MLN and angle for registration. The party of 1954 still posed a major threat since the PID regime was deeply unpopular and the DCG possessed only a limited conservative constituency to compensate for its flagging reformist appeal even once it had enlisted as its candidate Colonel Ricardo Peralta, who headed the earthquake relief programme. Recognizing that running Sandoval would be excessively provocative, the MLN dragged ex-dictator Enrique Peralta out of his retirement in Miami and waged an aggressive campaign that most observers agreed produced the highest number of votes. The high command duly pronounced Lucas the victor and incinerated the ballots. With sharp exchanges in a congress where the government had only a three-vote majority, Sandoval's threats to flood the capital with peasant supporters, and those of Enrique Peralta to stage a coup, it was clear that the dominant bloc was in some danger of returning to the disunity of the early 1960s.[118] This did indeed prove to be the case at the next cycle of the electoral calendar in 1982, when the PID's system of control broke down completely. In 1978 a major crisis was averted because bourgeois sectarianism and military entrepreneurship had not yet exhausted their potential within the existing order whilst the resurgence of popular mobilization momentarily closed the ranks of the dominant bloc and drove its squabble over the spoils underground.

By the start of 1979 state violence against both the rural and the urban labour movement was widespread and of a type with that undertaken in the same period by the Somoza and Romero regimes. The Lucas government was easily the most entrenched of this unsavoury troika, but in the wake of the October riots and with guerrilla activity on the rise the regime sought to cauterize the popular movement before it acquired the alarming proportions already reached to the south. The death squads continued to be the principal mechanism, particularly in the towns, as was confirmed by the National Police when reporting the death of 1,224 'criminals' at the hands of the *Escuadrón de la Muerte* between January and June 1979 and the killing of 3,252 'subversives' by the ESA between January and November of the same year.[119] One distinctive feature of this campaign was its inclusion of reformist opponents as victims. The Lucas regime recognized the decisive role that the political 'centre' was playing wittingly or otherwise in the anti-Somoza movement, and this, combined with the Guatemalan right's deep aversion to the contagion of reform (aroused by Arévalo and Arbenz and not cured by the experience of Méndez Montenegro), prompted a pre-emptive strike against the democratic parties. Even the endlessly pliable DCG was not spared – Vinicio Cerezo survived several attacks whilst at least 300 of his co-religionists died at the hands of the death squads over five years.[120] The university was also identified as a key target, forty-one members of the USAC faculty being killed in eight months during 1980.[121] Perhaps the most politically decisive executions were at the beginning of 1979 – the assassination of Alberto Fuentes Mohr in January and that of Manuel Colóm Argueta in March, shortly after the FUR finally obtained official registration as part of the regime's programme of sustaining the veneer of democratic procedure.[122] Lucas naturally blamed unknown criminal elements for these killings, which conveniently removed the two most popular opposition politicians from the scene and from the 1982 election.

Without Fuentes Mohr and Colóm Argueta neither the PSD nor the FUR would represent a major electoral threat either as official winners, in the style of Méndez Montenegro, or as a defrauded force that, like UNO in El Salvador, might provoke popular protest and completely discredit the electoral system. (This was, of course, already the case, but it is of some consequence that no popular civilian reformist had been defrauded of victory in Guatemala, largely as a result of the DCG's reluctance to conduct its campaigns in its own name.) It was the right itself which finally managed to destroy the system of fraudulent polls and in the longer term it was the DCG that benefited from these assassinations, since Cerezo was untroubled in the 1985 poll by a Social Democratic challenge headed by figures with a more consistent record of opposition and clear policies of reform. This outcome lay some way in the future, but even at the time the DCG firmly signalled its sympathies and priorities by rejecting and attacking the *Frente Democrático Contra la Represión* (FDCR) established following Fuentes Mohr's death in February 1979. The platform of the FDCR was much more limited than that of UNO in El Salvador or even the Nicaraguan FAO since it stood simply for 'the commitment to fight permanently against repression and for the achievement of the democratic rights of the people . . . respect for the integrity and independence in matters of organization, ideology or philosophy, politics and religion of the participant organizations'.[123] The DCG was formally pledged to oppose repression and itself continued to be a victim of state and rightist terror yet it was not prepared to join forces with the left even on this elementary democratic platform. The FDCR was identified as a vehicle for the left since it included not only the PSD and FUR but also CNUS, CETE, CUC, MONAP and scores of lesser organizations in which radical currents were active.[124]

In both name and practice the FDCR was a defensive response to the military regime, and its existence as an open organization was shown to be exceptionally precarious as its leadership was decimated by the death squads. This attrition accelerated after the front, recognizing the limits of a vague and largely negative platform, resorted to the call for a 'revolutionary, popular and democratic government', for which it was in no state to campaign. Whilst supporting this call, the radical and popular organizations were badly hit by the losses resulting from the FDCR's public profile; the CNT, for example, lost almost all its national leadership in the summer of 1980. As a consequence, the CUC and a number of other bodies broke away to establish the *Frente Popular 31 de Enero* (FP-31) in January 1981, adopting clandestine methods and closer links with the guerrilla. By this stage the FDCR had been reduced to little more than a paper organization, and the FP-31 fared little better since any form of mass work was exceptionally difficult under such violent conditions. Although the process of pursuing a broad political alliance continued with the endorsement by the FDCR, the FP-31 and the armed groups of the *Comité Guatemalteco de Unidad Popular* (CGUP), formed in February 1982, this too lacked the organizational stability and political legitimacy of either the FDR in El Salvador or the successive fronts of the insurrectionary phase in Nicaragua. It was, instead, an umbrella group loosely linking organizations that were unable to support the guerrilla with a coordinated mass campaign and subscribed to a radical programme that could only be publicly upheld in exile, where the CGUP leadership was based.

In a sense the FP-31 incarnated this position of profound adversity in its name, being founded on the first anniversary of the killing of thirty-nine Quiché and Ixil *campesinos* at the Spanish embassy which they had peacefully occupied as a last resort to protest military repression in the Ixil triangle. Having drawn considerable public attention to their remonstrations and received an understanding reception from Madrid's envoy, the delegation represented an acute embarrassment for the government, which duly ordered the police to attack the embassy despite the ambassador's demand that they hold off and respect foreign territory. All the occupants except the ambassador and one peasant – taken from his hospital bed and killed the next day – were either burnt or shot to death. The assault caused the immediate rupture of relations with Spain, brought to the attention of the international community the unqualified brutality employed by the security forces against the rural and Indian population, and greatly increased sympathy for it from the urban movement. The embassy massacre would henceforth stand alongside Panzós as a signal event in the protracted calvary of the indigenous community. It provoked anger and deepened resolve to resist. At a personal level this can be seen in the subsequent radical activity of Rigoberta Menchú, daughter of Vicente Menchú, one of the moving forces of the CUC in San Miguel Uspantán who was killed in the embassy. Rigoberta's activism following her father's death was not, however, as exceptional in substance as it was in form. Her engagement in direct resistance was mirrored in many highland communities that were fostering and joining the armed opposition: 'In our indigenous languages . . . at first we called them a word that means foreigner; then we called them "gentlemen of the trees"; and now when the guerrilla arrives at a community, now they tell us that "the brothers" have arrived.'[125] For the next two years this relationship was to strengthen and benefit from the narrowing options for survival in the highlands. However, the most immediate manifestation of rural radicalism following the embassy massacre took the form of a widespread strike on the coastal estates.

The plantation strike of February and March 1980 was undoubtedly encouraged by a generalized discontent with political violence on the part of the seasonal labour force, and it is no coincidence that the stoppage was followed by a sharp increase in guerrilla activity in the sugar and cotton zones. Yet if the political radicals of the CUC rapidly took the leadership of the strike movement, this began with rank-and-file mobilization and was directly provoked by the fall in the real wage, which had lost half its value between 1970 and 1980.[126] The earthquake had enhanced the tendency of the highland *campesinos* to forgo seasonal labour, creating a shortfall in harvest hands that could not be made fully good by increasing numbers of migrants from El Salvador; it thus introduced an element of weakness into the intransigent position of the *finqueros*.[127] The strike began on a modest scale when 2,000 Indian and *ladino* workers stopped working on 18 February at six sugar and cotton estates in Santa Lucía Cotzumalguapa, Escuintla, in demand for a wage rise from Q1.14 to Q5.00 and provision of better transport for those travelling from the *altiplano*.[128] Within ten days this movement had spread along the coast at the peak of the harvest and drawn in a further 50,000 workers on eighty estates and in over twenty mills and gins. The harvest came to a halt with the workers occupying mills and administrative offices in a series of clashes with the police. Prompted by this remarkable mobilization, CNUS demanded an increase in the urban minimum wage to Q7.00; this demand together with the threat of a national general strike sufficed to convince the Lucas government that rapid concessions should be made – despite strong resistance by AGA that did nothing to improve relations between the regime and the agro-export bourgeoisie. Following the tactics employed in October 1978, the government made a partial concession by increasing the rural wage to Q3.20 whilst providing no means of enforcement and refusing to improve transport. CUC rejected this but CNUS, arguing that a partial victory had been won and further action would only provoke massive repression and a loss of all gains, managed to secure acceptance of the offer. In the following weeks the *finqueros* took their revenge, generally holding back the wage rise and firing at least 2,000 workers.[129] Moreover, as in the autumn of 1978, the aftermath of the strike was marked by a sharp clampdown by the police and military, halting the momentum of the unions.

For some fifteen months following the plantation strike the guerrilla made steady political and military advances in a manner that contrasted with the insurrectionist stop–go tendency of the Sandinistas. The strong presence of ORPA in Sololá made the important tourist centre of Lake Atitlán vulnerable to attack and contributed to a 25 per cent fall in tourist revenue – the country's second most important source of foreign exchange. With the rebels operating over at least half the country and effectively controlling large areas of the *altiplano*, business confidence slumped and capital flight increased. Between January 1979 and January 1981 foreign reserves fell from $744 million to $363 million, and by October 1981 they were reported to be as low as $81 million, intense rebel activity in September having prompted the export of $119 million in five days.[130] If the bourgeoisie had taken fright, the military was barely more confident in the face of this creeping guerrilla advance that avoided major battles, put the highland garrisons in constant threat and, with extensive rebel activity in Chimaltenango, even placed the western approaches to the capital in a precarious position. Despite this, the high command resisted any major alteration of strategy until the summer of 1981, and continued to rely upon residual repression; this led to perhaps 11,000 people dying during the course of the year but did little to stall the guerrilla. By July angry junior officers obliged to bear the brunt of the disorganized campaign claimed that between January and March 23 officers and 250 troops had been killed; throughout 1981 some 57 officers and 1,000 conscripts died.[131] Losses of this order were unacceptably high for a force of less than 20,000 troops. Significantly, the field commanders who took the unusual step of informing the foreign press of the absence of any coherent response to the rebellion also expressed their outrage at the corruption of the high command and stressed the need for US assistance.

In July 1981 the US Congress debated President Reagan's decision to lift Carter's ban on military sales and aid that had remained in force since 1977. Recognizing the particularly bad reputation of the Guatemalan military, the administration attempted only to send jeeps and trucks ('non-lethal' equipment), which, in the words of Assistant Secretary of State Stephen Bosworth, would increase government 'self-confidence' and enable it to contain the far right as well as to defeat the left. The feelings of the House were captured by Gerry Studs's blunt retort that this was 'like saying in 1939 that you would aid Adolf Hitler to get control of the Gestapo'.[132] In short, regardless of the scale of the crisis and the manoeuvres of the White House, Congress was not prepared to countenance for Guatemala the policy that it had willingly endorsed for El Salvador. As a result, Washington continued neither to finance nor to train or arm the Guatemalan army at an official level until 1985, when, after the constituent assembly elections, a mere $300,000, or 0.1 per cent of total military assistance to Central America, was disbursed.[133] It is clear that modest channels of unofficial support were maintained by the administration, particularly with respect to aviation parts but also in terms of intelligence collaboration, in which, as became fully evident after the Irangate scandal, the executive possessed much greater freedom from legislative control than was either recognized or lawful.[134]

The complaints of junior officers in 1981 did not arise from an absence of either materiel or external strategic support. Indeed, the Guatemalan commanders had proved quite successful in justifying their refusal to bow to US pressure by obtaining alternative supplies and advisers. The most important source of both was Israel, which had begun to supply Arava counter-insurgency aircraft, small arms and artillery in 1975 and consolidated its position as the country's principal source of weapons in 1980, when the M-1 was replaced by the Galil as the army's standard infantry rifle. Israeli experts provided advice and training in intelligence operations whilst Laugerud's temporary enthusiasm for cooperatives was not unconnected with the example of the kibbutz and burgeoning Israeli economic presence in the country.[135] At least until 1981 the Israeli connection represented a clear alternative to US military aid; thereafter it tended to become more of a surrogate although still providing the Guatemalan military with an appreciably wider margin of independence from Washington than was possessed by their regional counterparts. To some degree the same may be said of support from the Argentine armed forces, which had been to the fore in resisting Carter and were more broadly employed by Reagan as a proxy force in Central America until the Falklands/Malvinas War in April 1982. Argentine expertise in urban counter-insurgency operations gained during the 'dirty war' in Buenos Aires resulted in the effective destruction of ORPA's network in the capital in 1981.[136] Discontent amongst the officer corps was not directed against this support nor based upon a belief in the superiority of North American methods, which were, in fact, held in rather low esteem. It was, rather, aimed at a high command content to rely upon limited foreign assistance to hold matters in check instead of building it into the comprehensive overhaul of strategy that was manifestly required by the guerrilla advance. For the officer corps this issue was more immediate than the general desirability of improved political relations with Washington after Reagan's assumption of office.

The major shift in the army's campaign is generally dated from March 1982 and associated with General Ríos Montt, who came to power in that month. Ríos Montt certainly oversaw a significant defeat for the guerrilla in the *Victoria 82* operation, consolidating this with *Firmeza 83* – which involved less extensive fighting and greater attention to subjugating the rebels' social base in the highlands. Attended by atrocious violence and extensive social disorganization, this campaign was as successful as it was infamous. There is, nonetheless, good reason to identify the initial and decisive shift of the military balance of forces in the offensive directed by Chief of Staff General Benedicto Lucas García from June 1981. Although Lucas Garciá was closely associated with his brother's corrupt cabal, his experience with the French army in Algeria and clear views on counter-insurgency strategy distinguished him from his political allies and were to provide the succeeding military regimes with a firm basis upon which to drive home the advantage. Lucas García did not defeat the guerrilla, and by the time his brother was ousted from office the rebel forces – now formally united as the URNG – were still on the attack. However, the general did succeed in drawing the guerrilla into a strategic counter-offensive that it could not sustain in either military or political terms. The true balance of forces was not immediately apparent because the high level of fighting appeared to justify the rebels' overly optimistic assessment of their resources and consequent taking of the initiative. This new phase of the war began in June 1981 with concerted military attacks in Huehuetenango, El Quiché, Chimaltenango and the Verapaces. Rejecting a defensive strategy based on retention of urban centres, employing mobile tactical units and concerned primarily with contact and attrition rather than the possession of territory, Lucas García provoked a marked increase in combat, the EGP alone claiming to have carried out 153 major operations and 803 minor actions in the last twelve weeks of 1981.[137] In tactical terms the army suffered heavily and was greatly stretched; there is no doubt that Lucas took a risk. On the other hand, the guerrilla mirrored some of the mistaken assumptions made by the FMLN leadership in January 1981, the EGP in particular believing the moment propitious for a major assault on the state. This decision was marked by a further expansion, nearly 1,000 operations taking place in all but five of the country's departments between January and March 1982.[138] This seemed ominous for the regime but it required the guerrilla both to operate in areas where its popular base was poorly developed and fully to mobilize that support which it had diligently built up on the understanding that its followers would be provided with physical defence and would soon benefit from a decisive settling of accounts with the army. The inability of the URNG to sustain military operations outside its core areas of support and, more importantly still, its failure to provide protection where it possessed a longstanding base, proved to be disastrous. Less immediate than that of January 1981 in El Salvador, this strategic failure manifested several similar features, the most pronounced of which was the vulnerability of the civilian population to retribution from the army. Although the rebel combatants conducted a measured retreat in reasonable military order, all of the groups later recognized that the precipitate offensive of September 1981 to May 1982 permitted the army to separate them from a large sector of their support. This was especially so in the case of the EGP, within which a dissident faction began to emerge.[139]

The political platform announced by the new URNG in January 1982, when the offensive was at its peak, was similar to those of the FDR and the Sandinistas. Condensed into five main parts, it stipulated an end to repression; a solution to 'the problems of the majority' and an end to the economic and political domination of the '*grandes ricos*', including an agrarian reform under which large property would be expropriated but small and medium enterprises guaranteed; an end to the cultural oppression of the Indian and full equality with the *ladino* population; a 'new society' with political representation for all 'patriotic, popular and democratic sectors', freedom of expression, a new 'popular revolutionary army' and recognition of the key role of Christianity; a non-aligned foreign policy.[140] Less precise than the central manifestos of Nicaraguan and Salvadorean radicalism, the URNG document was patently not a blueprint for socialism and could be said to differ from the (unwritten) programme of the Arbenz government only in its stipulation about the army, positive attitude to the (progressive) Church, and more pronounced adhesion to the cause of Indian integration. Unlike the FSLN and FDR, the URNG lacked an organized political constituency beyond its own ranks for which such a platform could act as a focus for unification in a broad front. Hence, the rebels' *Proclama Unitaria* prompted no major reorganization of the popular bloc or shift in the general balance of political forces, the support of the CGUP being a phenomenon of purely marginal importance compared to the conflicts inside the dominant bloc that had been sharpened by the military campaign and were brought to a head by the elections of 7 March 1982.

Changing the Guard

Despite flagging business confidence and sharp in-fighting amongst the bourgeoisie, the failure to restore full relations with Washington under Reagan, and growing discontent within the military over strategy and corruption, the Lucas García regime took no initiative to unite the dominant bloc. Instead, driven by short-term cabalistic logic, the senior commanders resurrected the PID, chose Defence Minister Aníbal Guevara as its candidate, and proceeded to call and conduct the elections of 1982 in the same fashion as those of 1974 and 1978. Given the pattern of developments since Lucas's election this poll was predictably contested only by parties of the right, enhancing bourgeois sectarianism. The MLN staged an independent challenge led by Sandoval, unencumbered by his past attachment to the PID and bolstering the party's historic platform with the novel demand for electoral honesty.[141] Arana's followers – now known as the *Central Auténtica Nacionalista* (CAN) – had likewise divorced themselves from the officialist bloc and under the candidacy of Gustavo Anzueta Vielman, a leading figure of CACIF and the right-wing lobby *Los Amigos del País*, demanded an unqualified monetarist policy including the abolition of fifty of the fifty-six taxes currently on the books. Finally, the DCG once again demurred from staging an independent campaign, instead allying with the *Partido Nacional Renovador* (PNR), founded in 1977 after the MLN split conjured by Laugerud with DCG backing. This coalition, known as UNO, was headed by Alejandro Maldonado Aguirre of the PNR. Presenting itself as the 'voice of the silent and silenced majority' and with some support in the urban middle class, it proposed no major alteration of the political system, championed exceptionally modest economic reforms designed primarily to assist manufacturing capital, and stood no chance of victory under the established rules, which predictably produced a victory for Guevara.

As in 1974 and 1978, the combined opposition took to the streets in protest, the regime repressing demonstrations by elegant supporters of the MLN with little less vigour than that reserved for the popular movement.

Lucas García displayed a remarkable lack of political acumen in refusing to countenance any negotiation and arresting a cluster of leading rightist politicians; meanwhile Guevara scurried off to Washington to put the gringos in the proper frame of mind. The dominant bloc appeared to be hoist by its own petard; those forces that had traditionally supported and exploited electoral fraud were now its despondent victims and bereft of any further option. However, on 23 March an efficient and poorly resisted coup by field commanders ousted Lucas and appeared to have solved the problem, even though it meant resorting to an unseemly method not used for nigh-on twenty years. The junta set up by the rebels was led by Ríos Montt. Now a 'born-again' Christian and prone to decidedly peculiar rhetorical flourishes, he was recognized to be fervently opposed to the Lucas cabal, personally honest and committed to the counter-revolutionary war. The fact that Ríos Montt was still associated with his 1974 candidacy for the DCG did him little harm in the existing political climate since it identified him with electoral propriety and he was expected merely to hold the fort until the new elections formally promised by the government. Furthermore, Ríos Montt was joined on the junta by two officers – General Horacio Maldonado Shaad and Colonel Fernando Gordillo – connected with the MLN and CAN and linked to the death squads. As a result, the interests of the extreme right and particularly the MLN were seen to be in safe hands. The junta's initial manifesto sustained the belief that real change would be limited to the removal of the leaders of the high command and a cluster of scapegoats from the police. In the language of authoritarian populism that clearly distinguished it from the proclamation of the Salvadorean rebel officers of October 1979, the new regime promised to eradicate corruption, dynamize the counter-insurgency campaign, encourage free enterprise, reorganize public administration and restore constitutional government after an undetermined period.[142] Widespread anticipation that the coup would simply restore open competition within the dominant bloc proved to be misguided, and well before Ríos Montt's traditionalist colleagues on the junta had been sent packing by a combination of dollars and force, the regime had manifested an erratic bonapartism that was to persist throughout the fifteen unstable months during which it held power.[143]

The president's eccentric personality, extravagant public statements and religious fundamentalism attracted much international attention and were often seen as characterizing his regime more fully than was the case. It is true that Ríos Montt's wayward style aggravated discontent within the ruling class. His statement that, 'I am a true political leader . . . because I am here without your votes', was effectively true of all Guatemalan presidents since 1970, but it ran right against the protocols of fixed electoralism, which existed precisely in order to conceal such a reality.[144] In the same vein, Ríos

Montt's establishment of special military tribunals following the removal of the 1965 constitution was important less for upsetting the traditional judicial system – cowed but left intact under previous regimes – than for the fact that these courts martial brought the logic and process of the death squad into the public domain. Few on the right shed tears as members of the guerrilla were placed before firing squads since this had been customary practice for nearly twenty years; but when Ríos Montt explained that, 'We declared a state of siege so that we could kill legally', he reversed the entire rationale of the unofficial apparatus of terror and openly embraced a system that the dominant bloc had disowned in its efforts to maintain some semblance of democratic procedure.[145]

The diplomatic fall-out from this was at no time more calamitous than when the president ignored the Pope's appeal for clemency on behalf of condemned prisoners during his 1983 visit. This deviation from the political artifice of the 1970s towards an institutionalist regime similar to those of the Southern Cone was signalled from the start with the declaration that 'political parties in Guatemala are electoral machines and inoperative. For this reason the army must now protect itself politically.'[146] Although CACIF was given some cabinet posts, Ríos Montt continued to resist the announcement of a date for elections, refused to rule in direct collaboration with the parties of the right, and established a powerless and quasi-corporatist council of state as a forum for negotiation over policy. The MLN was most directly prejudiced by the new pattern of government, and within weeks of the coup its leadership was accused of subversion and subjected to harassment much more severe than that experienced in the 1970s. The right as a whole shunned the council of state and continued to press for elections and a return to open party politics. The president had gone some way to meet their objections to corruption but he seemed set on consolidating military control of government, albeit in a fashion distinct from that of Lucas García and his cronies.

Ríos Montt's membership of the fundamentalist sect *Del Verbo*, linked to the US organization Gospel Outreach, gave the president's public pronouncements a fantastic air which undoubtedly embarrassed a bourgeoisie that preferred orthodox Catholicism to Protestantism and was prone to blench at messianic homilies ominously evocative of Ubico in their personalism. Nonetheless, the *caudillo*'s faith was not in itself a major problem. By the early 1980s the popularity of the progressive currents within the Catholic Church was sufficiently great that the bourgeoisie was inclined to concur with senior officers who saw 'no difference between the Catholics and the Communist subversives'.[147] Moreover, the Protestant churches claimed to have 1.3 million members, or 18 per cent of the total population – a figure that was not greatly exaggerated and resulted from several decades of missionary work.[148] With only 1,000 members *Verbo* formed no more than a minuscule part of a substantial collection of fundamentalist sects and more established churches that were in general deeply opposed to political radicalism, considered valuable allies of the military, and often harnessed to its civic action programmes. Gospel Outreach's 1983 'Operation Lovelift' project of assistance for displaced *campesinos* was but one much-publicized element of a far more extensive network that provided a modicum of material and psychological support in conditions of unparalleled turmoil that were highly conducive to millenarianism.[149]

Bombastic piety and militant anti-Communism commended Ríos Montt to the Reagan White House, itself greatly indebted to the primitive millionaire theologians of the 'sunbelt' states and deeply anxious to secure a stable regime in Guatemala that would permit a restoration of military aid. Although there is little evidence that Washington orchestrated the March 1982 coup or had the local resources directly to influence events, it was clearly well informed in advance and Ambassador Frederick Chapin issued an unambiguous message of support for the junta less than twenty-four hours after it took power. Even after five months of dictatorship and firing squads the State Department was in no mood to retract its imprimatur: 'it is quite clear that in contrast to the previous regime this regime has adopted as one of its primary objectives the improvement of the human rights situation.'[150] Senator Jesse Helms was predictably closer to the point: 'Guatemala has not only done a notable job in cleaning up its government, but it also has the best record in Latin America for supporting the United States in the UN.'[151] Reagan was himself prepared publicly to endorse Ríos Montt even after the Guatemalan president had rejected Chapin's formal objections to the judicial murders of the special tribunals and the killing of US citizens, issues that eventually required the ambassador to be withdrawn. Ríos Montt's staunch defence of the tribunals in the name of '*Guatemalidad*' created a problem of presentation that was not easily resolved – in many senses it was compounded – by specious panegyrics emanating from Washington. As an impediment to the full restoration of relations, however, this matter paled in comparison to the wave of killing by the army in the highlands precisely at the time when the president was being lauded as a paragon of personal rectitude if no longer a man of unsullied democratic vocation.

It is difficult to quantify with precision the human cost of the military campaign that from March 1982 turned the tide against the guerrilla under the direction first of Ríos Montt and then his successor Oscar Mejía Victores. A count of separate army massacres of fifty people or more yields a minimum death toll of 2,500 people between 23 March and 31 July 1982.[152] Government officials put the number of orphans left by the counter-insurgency operation over the next three years at 100,000 and admitted to the destruction of 440 highland villages.[153] Opposition sources estimate the cost of the war between 1980 and 1985 to be 50,000 dead, 200,000 children losing at least one parent, and the true figure of those who were driven to take refuge in Mexico to be three times the official number of 46,000.[154] The number of people displaced inside the country is no less difficult to assess, but it must be accounted in hundreds of thousands. Although the migrant harvest labour force fell by 200,000 in 1985–86 because of enforced conscription into the civil patrols and the more general fear of being perceived as 'fleeing' (and thus a rebel supporter), at least 100,000 terrorized *campesinos* remained in the plantation zone after 1982–83 rather than return to their communities in the *altiplano*. One result of this dislocated reserve labour army was that agro-export production levels were little affected by the war and the *finqueros* untroubled by wage demands of the type made in 1980.

Through 1982 and most of 1983 the war was dominated by the army's adhesion to 'scorched earth' tactics and the establishment of 'free-fire' zones in which entire communities were liable to be eliminated. Even at the start of this slaughter the high command was assembling a long-term strategy by which the villages of the core Indian departments would not simply be eradicated or driven from political sympathy with the guerrilla but also rendered structurally dependent upon the military by enforced relocation in strategic hamlets, obligatory conscription into the civil patrols, and economic reliance upon the army's provision of supplies. This programme began under Ríos Montt as a modest if assiduously pursued civic action project known as *fusiles y frijoles* (guns and beans), later mutating from 'the two f's' into 'the three t's' (*techo, trabajo y tortillas*). The *Victoria 82* campaign under which this traditional 'carrot and stick' approach was realized envisaged a far more comprehensive policy of 'security and development' based upon prolonged military occupation and economic reorganization.[155] Over the next two years the army consolidated a system of 'Inter-Institutional Coordinators' (CICs) who managed conflict zones in a style not dissimilar to that of the old *jefes políticos* and who were subsequently to remain independent of local national civilian authorities. Operating in close liaison with the reorganized high command, these officers possessed total control over the six 'development poles' comprising fifty 'model villages' in Quiché and Huehuetenango.

The army exercised far greater influence over rural life in general through the system of civil patrols that obliged all able-bodied men to serve in local militias, which at their peak included some 900,000 people.[156] This unprecedented regimentation of the rural population was of limited military value since only a very modest proportion of patrol members could be relied upon and few were provided with modern weaponry capable of resisting a guerrilla attack. But the primary purpose of the patrols was less military than to ensure individual registration, control of movement, and dissemination of propaganda. The ambitious long-term objective was a coercive state-based 'incorporation' of the *campesino* and particularly the Indian into the 'nation'. The more immediate result was extensive disorganization of patterns of cultivation, trade and movement of labour as peasants either adhered to the requirements of service (which generally included participation on Sundays, the traditional day of rural markets) or suffered the consequences of evasion, which effectively entailed outlaw status.[157] Historically, conscription into military service of any type elicited opposition from landlords and could not be sustained for long without affecting agricultural production. In this case the agro-export interests remained well supplied with labour and were not disposed to object to a system that was seen as essential to defeating Communism and prejudiced peasant rather than commercial agriculture.

Within six months the army's offensive drove the guerrilla back to its core zones of support – northern Huehuetenango and Quiché (EGP), San Marcos (ORPA) and the Petén (FAR) – but it failed to eliminate the URNG as a military force. The rebels had clearly suffered a major political defeat and could not retrieve the level of activity reached in 1981–82 within the foreseeable future, this setback opening up internal divisions.[158] Nonetheless, the URNG claimed to have staged 173 actions in the first five months of 1985, a year in which it became evident that the guerrilla was expanding tactical operations once again with perhaps as many as 3,000 troops.[159] With the military inalterably opposed to any negotiation and no civilian party prepared to risk such an adventure it seemed that fighting in the countryside would continue interminably.

Ríos Montt's critical leadership of the counter-revolutionary offensive failed to resolve the major antagonisms inside the dominant bloc or stabilize his regime. Indeed, many senior commanders were disturbed by the high profile taken by the junior officers who had staged the coup, retained considerable influence with the president, and were prominent in both anti-guerrilla operations and public administration. A number of these figures appeared to be pursuing a form of generational bonapartism disturbing to the military hierarchy and civilian parties in that although unreservedly authoritarian, it possessed certain populist features that summoned the shade of Arbenz. Ríos Montt's handling of the economic crisis also alienated most of the bourgeoisie. The right applauded his cuts in expenditure, but it was divided over proposals for special tax concessions to the agro-export sector and completely opposed to the levy of a special war tax.[160] If CACIF came close to a split over the issue of privileged concessions to the landlords, it was at one in resisting Ríos Montt's introduction of a value added tax of 10 per cent; this tax had long been demanded by the IMF (in a rather notable variation from its normal prescriptions) but antagonized a bourgeoisie for which any increase in taxes was heretical.[161] Unable to quell discontent on all these issues and threatened by a series of conspiracies, Ríos Montt was forced into an erratic retreat. In June 1983 under pressure from the US and all the major parties he finally presented an election timetable with a poll for a constituent assembly marked for mid 1984. At the same time the high command managed to secure a promise to withdraw members of the military from positions in civil administration and thus marginalized the 'young Turks' as well as reducing the army's provocative high profile. These moves signalled a gradual recomposition of the concordat that had been under stress since 1978 and virtually inoperative since the previous year. Yet despite his grudging concessions Ríos Montt continued to be an obstacle to the reconsolidation of the dominant bloc, a fact vividly illustrated by his decision in July to sponsor a scheme for the purchase and distribution of land through a new state bank. Coming on the heels of the new tax, this measure that smacked of agrarian reform proved too much for the oligarchs and generals; the nerveless president was ousted on 8 August 1983 with minimal disruption by his Defence Minister Mejía Victores, who had, perhaps not coincidentally, paid a fleeting visit to the US aircraft carrier 'Ranger' the previous day.[162]

The two and a half years between Mejía's coup and the election of Cerezo and the DCG may be seen as a transitional period in which the military rectified the excesses stemming from Ríos Montt's government and engaged in a graduated retreat from public administration. This scenario had already been completed in Honduras and begun in El Salvador under US patronage; it had the support of all the leading bourgeois parties, promised a number of advantages on the diplomatic front, and posed little danger to a dominant bloc accustomed to the forms of competition and capable of adjusting to its idiosyncrasies. The military made a virtue of necessity and projected the return to constitutionalism as integral to its counter-insurgency programme enshrined in *Reencuentro 84* and *Estabilidad 85*. The time taken for the transfer of power was determined both by the organizational requirements of electing a constituent assembly, drafting a constitution, and holding presidental elections and by the army's need to maintain strict control over this process, ensuring that it terminated with institutional authority and independence fully guaranteed. With little option but to follow this course, the army keenly defended its interests throughout, withholding all legislative powers from the constituent assembly and retaining executive power during the assembly's deliberations although this aggravated relations with the parties. While there is little indication that candidates for the 1985 poll were required to put their pen to a formal agreement to respect the operational and administrative independence of the armed forces (as in 1966), members of the high command demanded this with sufficient vigour in public to suggest that at the very least a verbal entente was reached in private.[163] An interim administration of a few months could not have ensured a coherent return to civilian government, let alone a handover in which military interests were fully protected. In addition, the continuation of the guerrilla war encouraged the army to reinforce its authority in an extenuated transition.

Cerezo's eventual election and the pronounced 'moderation' of DCG policy in 1986 and 1987 may be described as successes for the military, but the Mejía regime was far from a smooth interregnum. One consequence of its purposefully protracted timetable was the need to engage with an economic crisis in which agro-exports fell from $880 million in 1980 to $580 million in 1985; half the growth of the previous thirty years was lost; per capita GDP fell to its 1971 level; un- and underemployment rose to 45 per cent and inflation to 35 per cent; and capital flight to the US alone amounted to $1.1 billion – half the foreign debt – in the space of four years.[164] Like Ríos Montt, Mejía accepted the demands of CACIF and the IMF for reduced state expenditure, which fell consistently from its peak in 1981 and represented only 10 per cent of GDP in 1984. The limits to this were not, however, restricted by the requirements of an expensive counter-insurgency war (the military had nearly quadrupled in size since US aid had been cut, the defence budget rising from 5.9 to 10.8 per cent of expenditure between 1981 and 1983). With a fall in tax collection from 9.0 to 5.3 per cent of GDP between 1979 and 1984, and the weakest fiscal regime in the region (producing less revenue in 1985 than in 1980), the government was determined to increase income. It therefore attempted to expand Ríos Montt's tax regime – 83 per cent of which was indirect and thus hit the consumer hardest – as well as limiting capital flight through variable exchange rates.[165] This provoked a running battle with CACIF, whose free-market leadership eventually won major concessions after the direct confrontations of April and May 1985. In itself the conflict reconfirmed the bourgeoisie's time-honoured resistance to fiscal pressure and demonstrated that management of the state had appreciably eroded military complicity in this. However, the clashes of Ríos Montt and Mejía with the capitalist class over the tax issue may be seen as providing Cerezo with greater political space for increasing fiscal revenue – income nearly doubled in 1986, albeit largely through more efficient collection – by virtue of both military acquiescence (never extended to Méndez Montenegro) and the fact that CACIF had to some extent shot its bolt in 1983 and 1985.[166]

It is enticing to view the Mejía regime as a product of Washington's design for the region, but the Guatemalan military was determined to maintain the nationalist stance adopted after the 1977 rupture even though it now had an ideological ally in the White House. This was especially the case because the transition to constitutionalism was conducive to accusations of capitulation to external influence and analogies with the Honduran experience. The persistent refusal of the armed forces to collaborate with Reagan's regional strategy must also be understood as part of a longer pattern of deviant right-wing nationalism derived in part from the historic strength of the country within Central America and in part from the contradictory heritage of 1954. Mejía was not backward in condemning the Sandinistas but he maintained diplomatic relations with them and blocked US attempts to revive CONDECA as a military means by which to besiege the Nicaraguan revolution.[167] In the same vein, the high command refused to participate in manoeuvres in Honduras for reasons beyond the cost of the counter-insurgency campaign at home – although this assuredly underpinned desistence from foreign adventures as much as did scepticism about US strategy.[168] This was not a conjuncturally determined phenomenon; Mejía's Foreign Minister Fernando Andrade Díaz Durán – later to gravitate towards the DCG – was doing little more than following Lucas García's example of sending a team to the 1980 Moscow Olympics (not mentioned by Senator Helms) when he criticized the invasion of Grenada, supported Contadora, reaffirmed Guatemala's 'neutralist' stance, and pointedly ruled out requests for US military aid.[169] It is possible that the bourgeoisie's desire to keep its markets in Nicaragua affected some of these decisions.[170] This was not, though, a major factor in a political tendency inherited without difficulty and to appreciable international advantage by Cerezo, who was instrumental in obliging President Arias of Costa Rica to reduce the anti-Sandinista clauses of his 1987 regional peace plan and thus give it at least some possibility of success.

The contrast between the DCG's continuation of established policy towards the US and the rupture in El Salvador between the PDC and the oligarchy over relations with Washington was mirrored in the differences in domestic policy between the two Christian Democratic parties. Whilst Duarte upheld a formally extensive reform programme and depended almost completely upon Washington's patronage in order to gain and keep office, Cerezo eschewed any significant plan for socio-economic change, made strenuous efforts to circumvent an oligarchic veto by reassuring CACIF of his caution and conservatism, and as a result came to office without requiring direct US intervention. This approach was consistent with the DCG's past record, in which the ructions of 1974 may be explained as largely a product of Ríos Montt's leadership and were exceptional for a party markedly less enterprising than its Salvadorean counterpart in pursuing either a bourgeois democratic alliance or authentic electoralism. More fully incorporated into a dominant bloc that was itself more politically competitive – if not more ideologically diverse – than that in El Salvador, the DCG was able to come to government on the basis of internal negotiation and without major crisis. However, the corollary to this was a weaker popular mandate and less expectation of real alteration in the conditions of daily life. In 1984 Cerezo declared that his party, 'would not embark on banking or agrarian reforms nor the nationalization of companies or property in the private sphere' since this would be 'disastrous for the economy and provoke capital flight'. Indeed, he went so far as to assert that, 'there cannot be an agrarian reform in a democratic country because that bankrupts or destabilizes a country's economy'.[171] With an entirely different approach to Duarte on these crucial matters, Cerezo assiduously lobbied both the agro-export and manufacturing sectors in CACIF, establishing enough rapport to secure some direct support on the basis of the opportunities for foreign investment and new markets as well as agreement on enhanced production and the undesirability of destabilization.[172] The remarkably popular campaign for agrarian reform led by the errant priest Padre Girón from 1986 raised the spectre of mass mobilization in support of this demand which was anathema to the oligarchy. Cerezo refused to sanction the repression of the movement, but his government adhered to the understandings that had enabled him to take office by withholding official support for expropriation even when this was urged by many DCG activists as both desirable in itself and necessary to retain popular support. Equally, the DCG introduced and enforced highly orthodox deflationary policies that rapidly drew opposition from the unions, including the small confederation set up in 1986 under the party's aegis, the *Coordinadora General de Trabajadores Guatemaltecos* (CGTG).

The party's release from a veto by the military and support for it from elements of the officer corps stood in less contrast to the Salvadorean experience although neither factor was based on any quid pro quo for US funds and weaponry. They rested instead upon recognition that the DCG would not intervene in the military's affairs, that it possessed the ability to improve Guatemala's international image and could bleed off at least some popular discontent at low political cost. In contrast to Méndez Montenegro, Cerezo evidently had no illusions as to the conditions for taking office, and he explicitly set himself the limited task of clinging on to the presidency and 'acclimatizing' the ruling class to civilian administration.[173] This was no less agreeable to the Reagan administration than to the high command or CACIF since by 1986 Washington had learnt the lessons of El Salvador. Despite the case made for land reform by USAID and that for tax increases presented by the IMF, the US neither needed to adopt a reformist posture to secure a presentable civilian government nor desired to upset its regional strategy of 'redemocratization'. Furthermore, the Salvadorean experience had given Washington a sobering illustration of the pitfalls of investing all its capital in one political party, and with a broad field of candidates from the right in Guatemala the US extended much less preferential treatment to the DCG than it had done to the PDC.

The absence of deep ideological differences between the parties deprived the elections of June 1984 for the constituent assembly and those of November 1985 for congress, municipal government and the presidency of much of the sense of decisiveness that attended the Salvadorean polls of 1982 and 1984. On the other hand, the absence of an officialist party reduced abstentionism – only 22 per cent in 1984 although 23 per cent of votes cast were spoiled and abstention rose to 35 per cent in 1985 – and produced relatively close contests. In 1984 the DCG gained the highest number of votes (16.3 per cent) but because of the imbalanced allocation of seats it received only twenty of the eighty-eight places in the assembly. This was against twenty-three won by the MLN–CAN alliance and twenty-one by the recently-formed *Unión del Centro Nacional* (UCN), a party that was led by Jorge Carpio Nicolle and fused standard neo-liberal economic policies with a modern style and less social belligerence than the MLN.[174] With such an outcome, the existence of a bevy of lesser parties ranging from the PID to the PR open to offers of alliance, and the assembly itself deprived of legislative power, the political field remained fluid and a plethora of coalition projects were made and collapsed over the following eighteen months. The result was that the November 1985 elections were contested by eight candidates, the DCG being on the 'left' simply by virtue of the fact that all bar one of its opponents deemed it so. The exception was a faction of the PSD led by Mario Solórzano which alone of the reformist parties submitted to Mejía's urgent invitations to return from exile and provide the poll with a semblance of ideological latitude and authenticity.

The lacklustre campaign over the autumn of 1985 reflected the absence of significant difference between candidates who could manage little more than trading 'accusations' of homosexuality in their efforts to entice an electorate singularly unmoved by proceedings. The notion – clearly popular amongst the parties – that this competition amounted to a genuine expression of popular sentiment was rudely upset by a renewed upsurge of mass mobilization that underscored the limits of 'redemocratization' and highlighted the level of support for radical options that were not exclusively represented by the guerrilla. In a manner remarkably similar to that of October 1978, the strike and protest movement of September 1985 was provoked by the extraordinary decision of the regime to sanction a 50 per cent increase in bus fares. The mobilization was started by secondary school students at the end of August and, as in 1978, it received wide support from the shanty-town population and the petty bourgeoisie in the capital and other towns. The initial demonstrations and wildcat stoppages were greatly exacerbated when an overly confident government announced a 100 per cent rise in the price of bread and a 38 per cent increase for milk. This led to the declaration of a general strike by the new radical union front UNSITRA-GUA, formed around the Coca Cola and state workers' unions, and perforce supported by the AIFLD-funded CUSG, set up in 1983 as a quasi-official confederation. Tempered by the experience of 1978 and the repression of 1979–80, UNSITRAGUA called for peaceful demonstrations, but the regime's violent response provoked rioting on the scale witnessed eight years before and deepened the strike. With the poll in jeopardy, Mejía took fright and overruled CACIF's protests to freeze the price rises.[175] This did not meet the unions' demands, and although free of the killing of 1978, army repression succeeded in halting further mobilization within four days. Yet, as in El Salvador in 1984, the urban population had demonstrated that its quiescence could not be guaranteed in conditions of economic crisis even after years of violent control. With the URNG recently reorganized and increasing its operations, the wider consequences of this development were more sober than was recognized by politicians unchallenged by parties of the left long since driven from official activity by the death squads.[176]

In the presidential poll of 3 November the voice of reform, in the shape of the rump of the PSD, received 2 per cent of the vote, which reflected recognition of the purely token character of Solórzano's challenge. There was no decisive tactical voting by supporters of the disenfranchised left, and the DCG failed to gain a clear victory with 38.6 per cent of the ballot against the UCN's 20 per cent and 12.6 per cent for the MLN–PID alliance.[177] The MLN predictably cried foul without presenting plausible evidence of fraud in a poll that showed a clear preference for parties more distanced from violence and the regimes of the 1970s. Once the field had been weeded out for a second round in December between Cerezo and Carpio, the DCG's large existing lead yielded greater benefit from the bandwagon effect. Cerezo gained 68 per cent in the presidential run-off to complement the party's tenure of 51 of the 100 congressional seats and 73 per cent of the country's mayors. This result gave Cerezo a claim to a clear popular mandate and the ability to extract better conditions for his new administration. In immediate terms such a claim appeared decidedly threadbare in view of the chronic sectarianism that had demolished the right in an election that was not fixed but also not free since the left could not stand. If the poll was distinct from those that preceded it, this did not mean that it heralded the end of a political system of thirty years' standing. The replacement of a gruff and plump general demanding order by a debonair young civilian pleading for *concertación* produced a change of style at the top and was accompanied by a continuing reduction in political killing, but the change was quite arguably of less consequence than Duarte's election in 1984.

Cerezo's regional 'neutralism' and early support for the Arias peace proposals were certainly vital to the agreement of 1987 and placed El Salvador and Honduras in a minority. Yet autonomy from Washington was already established as a figure in Guatemalan foreign policy, and although talks were held with the embattled URNG in Madrid, there was very little evidence that the army would permit anything more than superficial refinements in the system of domination.

Notes

1. *Popol Vuh. The Mayan Book of the Dawn of Life and the Glories of Gods and Kings*, edited and translated by Dennis Tedlock, New York 1985, p. 158.

2. Quoted in *This Week*, 7 August 1955, cited in NACLA, *Guatemala*, p. 74.

3. Orlando Fernández, *Turcios Lima*, Havana 1968, p. 11.

4. Quoted in NYT, 8 May 1971, cited in Jim Handy, *Gift of the Devil*, p. 167.

5. Quoted in *Time*, 5 April 1982.

6. The account of this massacre is given by the Maryknoll missionary Ron Hennessy and was reported in NYT, 12 Oct. 1982. Some 300 people died. For further details, see *Cultural Survival Quarterly*, vol. 7, no. 1, spring 1983.

7. *Weekly Compilation of Presidential Statements*, 13 December 1982, quoted in Central American Historical Institute, *On the Road to Democracy? A Chronology of Human and US–Guatemalan Relations*, Washington 1985, p. 33.

8. For the thesis that the Guatemalan bourgeoisie can no longer adopt the path of 1944–45, see Sarti, 'La Revolución Guatemalteca', p. 76, quoted in chapter 4, note 69, above.

9. 'The history of the guerrilla movements of Latin America itself cannot be understood without reference to this cardinal event. For the overthrow of Arbenz seemed to show – at least to a later generation of revolutionaries – that no government in Latin America which attempted to put through even the mildest economic and social reforms could survive the hostility of the United States.' Richard Gott, *Rural Guerrillas in Latin America*, London 1970, p. 61. 'The fall of Arbenz's national democratic regime in 1954 was decisive for the Latin American revolutionary movements of our time – in a negative sense it was their matrix. Its terrible warning haunted the Cuban leaders and taught them the most basic lesson of revolutionary Marxism as updated and demonstrated on American soil: the only way to secure the revolution is to destroy the bourgeois state apparatus, mobilize and arm the people, and disarm the enemy.' Régis Debray, *The Revolution on Trial*, London 1977, pp. 270–2.

10. It would be incorrect and invidious to establish a ranking of Latin American countries in terms of human rights violations. This comparison is used here because the Argentine case is particularly well known in Europe and North America and, together with the equally dreadful experience of Chile, has done much to establish a popular notion abroad as to when 'scientific terror' began in Latin America. Guatemala, by contrast, is frequently viewed simply as part of a Central American autocratic tradition aided and abetted by the Reagan administration from the early 1980s, its earlier history being forgotten or remaining unknown. Alfredo Stroessner came to power in Paraguay in May 1954 – before the Guatemalan intervention – and was still in office in 1987, thus sustaining the longest personal autocratic regime in the world outside North Korea. But Stroessner's rule has never relied on massacres and the use of selective terror has always been less intensive than in Guatemala. Perhaps the closest cases to Guatemala are Chile and Haiti, the former for the sheer extent of the attrition wrought by Pinochet (and the fact that he remained in power well into the period of 'redemocratization' in Latin America) and the latter because the Duvalier dynasty (1957–86) never hesitated to slaughter the peasantry. Both Stroessner and the Duvaliers represent a patrimonial autocracy now considered anachronistic whereas this tradition was never properly revived in Guatemala after Ubico. Finally, it should be noted that although the Brazilian military established the hemisphere's first 'organic' institutional regime in 1964, the use of death squads and reliance upon systematic terror was always less than in Chile and Argentina.

11. Debray, *Revolution on Trial*, p. 360.

12. The literature on human rights violations in Guatemala is voluminous and will not be regularly cited below. For the most detailed study of the organization and ideology of the

repressive state apparatus in its various incarnations, see McClintock, *The American Connection. State Terror and Popular Resistance in Guatemala.* For representative studies of its horrendous work, see Amnesty International, *Guatemala. A Government Program of Political Murder*, London 1981; Comité Pro Justicia y Paz de Guatemala, *Human Rights in Guatemala*, Geneva 1984; Comisión de Derechos Humanos de Guatemala, *Informe Preliminar a la ONU*, Mexico 1983; Survival International, *Witness to Genocide. The Present Situation of the Indians of Guatemala*, London 1983; *Cultural Survival Quarterly*, vol. 7, no. 1. The wider political and international context is covered by Lars Schoultz, *Human Rights and United States Toward Latin America*, Princeton 1981.

13. Frantz Fanon, *The Wretched of the Earth*, London 1965; *Black Skin. White Masks*, London 1970.

14. Severo Martínez Peláez, *La Patria del Criollo*; Carlos Guzmán-Böckler and Jean-Loup Herbert, *Guatemala: Una Interpretación Histórico-Social*, Mexico 1970; Carol A. Smith, 'Indian Class and Class Consciousness in Prerevolutionary Guatemala', Working Paper no. 162, Latin American Program, The Wilson Center, Washington 1984. Those wishing to investigate this debate are cautioned that these three sources are pioneering interpretations that occupy the high ground in terms of suggestion. It would not be excessively schematic to state that at various points Martínez Peláez denies an innate 'Indianness', Guzmán-Böckler and Herbert assert the 'fictitious' qualities of being *ladino*, and Smith throws doubt on the standard definition of the peasantry. As a result, it is possible to come away from these texts with the (mistaken) impression that Guatemala is bereft of Indians, *ladinos* and peasants.

15. The degree to which Guatemalan is 'Indian' is the subject of much dispute for the simple reason that *ladino* status does not derive simply from miscegenation and is often conferred by adoption of European dress and customs together with the use of Spanish (although not necessarily as the first language). Variations in this pattern are naturally myriad. Moreover, census returns are notoriously unreliable. For the thesis that 'ladinoization' advanced rapidly in the post-war period, the Indian population supposedly falling from 55.7 to 43.7 per cent of the total between 1940 and 1973, see John D. Early, 'The Changing Proportion of Maya Indian and Ladino in the Population of Guatemala, 1945–69', *American Ethnologist*, vol. 2, no. 2, May 1975. For the degree and variation in commerce in predominantly Indian regions, see the comments in chapter 3 above and Carol A. Smith, 'Beyond Dependency Theory: National and Regional Patterns of Underdevelopment in Guatemala', *American Ethnologist*, vol. 5, no. 3, August 1978; 'Does a Commodity Economy Enrich the Few while Ruining the Masses? Differentiation among Petty Commodity Producers in Guatemala', *The Journal of Peasant Studies*, vol. 11, no. 3, April 1984.

16. I have borrowed this final turn of phrase from Carol Smith's study of the economic effects of political disruption in Totonicapán, an area not heavily involved in the fighting: 'Destruction of the Material Bases for Indian Culture: Economic Change in Totonicapán, 1980–1984', mimeo 1985.

17. Richard Bissell of the CIA quoted in Schlesinger and Kinzer, *Bitter Fruit*, p. 225.

18. The figure for executions is given in John Gillin and K.H. Silvert, 'Ambiguities in Guatemala', *Foreign Affairs*, vol. 34, no. 3, April 1965, p. 47, which also contains some observations on the post-invasion repression in Jalapa. The sense of extreme caution adopted by religious groups that had previously demonstrated sympathy for the reform is noted in Falla, 'Evolución Político-Religiosa'.

19. Carlos Guzmán-Böckler, 'La Enseñanza de la Sociología en las Universidades de los Paises Subdesarrollados. El Caso de Guatemala' RMS, vol. XXIX, no. 4, Mexico City 1967, which attempts to comprehend the general class content of the political changes of this period.

20. Brian Murphy, 'The Stunted Growth of Campesino Organization', in Richard N. Adams, *Crucifixion by Power. Essays on Guatemalan Social Structure, 1944–1966*, Austin 1970.

21. Roger Plant, *Guatemala. Unnatural Disaster*, London 1978, p. 38; Mario López Larrave, *Breve Historia del Movimiento Sindical Guatemalteco*, Mexico 1976.

22. Quoted in Susanne Jonas Bodenheimer, *Guatemala: Plan Piloto para el Continente*, San José 1981, p. 219, cited in Handy, *Gift of the Devil*, p. 188.

23. NACLA, *Guatemala*, p. 81. This text contains considerable material on US economic interests in the country and aid to it in the post-intervention period.

24. Gillin and Silvert, 'Ambiguities', p. 469.

25. Marta Cehelsky, *Guatemala's Frustrated Revolution*, unpublished MA thesis, Columbia University 1967, pp. 78–9, cited in Schlesinger and Kinzer, *Bitter Fruit*, p. 224. According to Kenneth F. Johnson, the results were never officially published and numbers given here are only estimates of the local press (which apparently prided itself on its low margins of error): *The Guatemalan Presidential Election of March 6, 1966. An Analysis*, Institute for the Comparative Study of Politics, Washington 1967, p. 3. For further details on this period, see Julio Vielman, 'Stabilization of the Post-revolutionary Government in Guatemala', *Journal of Inter-American Studies*, April 1955.

26. According to 'New Life', 'No human being is free . . . while he is a victim of misery, illness or ignorance', this state requiring 'a dynamic attitude . . . of the nation toward the conquest of its own happiness'. Quoted in Handy, *Gift of the Devil*, p. 151.

27. NACLA, *Guatemala*, p. 81, citing *Time*, 22 August 1955; 27 October 1955.

28. Mario Rosenthal, *Guatemala: The Story of an Emergent Latin American Democracy*, New York 1962, pp. 265–6; Robert D. Crassweller, *Trujillo: The Life and Times of a Caribbean Dictator*, New York 1966, pp. 334–8. For an informative study of the general character and regional importance of the Trujillo regime written by an author almost certainly killed by the dictator the year before Castillo Armas died, see Jesús de Galindez, *The Era of Trujillo*, Tucson 1973.

29. John W. Sloan, *The Electoral Game in Guatemala*, unpublished PhD thesis, University of Texas 1963, p. 93, cited in Handy, *Gift of the Devil*, p. 153. For a brief but evocative opposition appraisal of the state of the country at this time, see Luis Cardoza y Aragón, 'Guatemala en 1960', *Cuadernos Americanos*, vol. CXIII, no. 6, 1960.

30. For a typical statement of the left's position up to 1981 that saw 'Belizean independence as part of our struggle', see the lengthy EGP manifesto published in *The Guardian*, London; NYT; *Le Monde*, 26 October 1979 in return for the release of the guerrilla's hostage Jorge García Granados. Talks between London and Guatemala City began under the Mejía Victores regime but only gained momentum after Cerezo came to power. In early 1987 the UK government made a small grant. The Special Air Services (SAS) elite unit of the British army retained a training base at Orange Walk whilst a squadron of Harrier fighters, so effective in the Malvinas campaign, provided the main deterrent against any serious Guatemalan incursion. The question of Belize's territorial limits is briefly surveyed in Anne Zammit, *The Belize Issue*, London 1978.

31. Plant, *Unnatural Disaster*, p. 74; Ross Pearson, 'Land Reform, Guatemalan Style', *The American Journal of Economics and Sociology*, vol. 22, no. 2, April 1963.

32. It appears that Ydígoras also made recourse to Ubico's practice of promotion as a means of securing loyalty; by the early 1960s some 500 of the 900 members of the officer corps held the rank of Lieutenant Colonel or above. Mario Monteforte Toledo, *Centroamérica. Subdesarrollo y Dependencia*, Mexico 1972, vol. 2, p. 172.

33. McClintock, *American Connection*, p. 49; Peter Wyden, *Bay of Pigs*, London 1979, pp. 53 ff.; William Blum, *The CIA. A Forgotten History*, London 1986, pp. 163–4.

34. Luis Turcios Lima, interviewed by Alan Howard, NYT, 26 June 1966, quoted in Gott, *Rural Guerrillas*, p. 70.

35. There now appears to be compelling evidence that President Kennedy personally approved the removal of Ydígoras. This claim was originally made in the US press late in 1966 and repeated by Thomas and Margorie Melville, *Guatemala: The Politics of Land Ownership*, New York 1971, pp. 148–50, and Jonas, *Plan Piloto*, p. 295. Confirmation by participants in White House discussions is given in Schlesinger and Kinzer, *Bitter Fruit*, pp. 243–4; 291.

36. Handy, *Gift of the Devil*, and Black, *Garrison Guatemala*, provide lucid surveys of this system.

37. NACLA, *Guatemala*, pp. 117, 195–6.

38. Quoted in McClintock, *American Connection*, pp. 64–5.

39. John W. Sloan, 'Electoral Frauds and Social Change: The Guatemalan Example', *Science and Society*, vol. XXXIV, no. 1, 1970, p. 86.

40. For a succinct appraisal of the DCG, see James Painter, *Guatemala: False Hope. False Freedom*, London 1987.

41. Johnson, *Presidential Election*, p. 19. According to Johnson, 'the presidential election

of March 6 offered convincing evidence of the Guatemalan body politic's capacity for peaceful change'.

42. McClintock, *American Connection*, p. 78.

43. The fullest accounts of the Guatemalan guerrilla are Gott, *Rural Guerrillas*; Debray, *Revolution on Trial*; Ricardo Ramírez, *Lettres du Front Guatemaltèque*, Paris 1970; Adolfo Gilly, 'The Guerrilla Movement in Guatemala', *Monthly Review*, May and June 1965. Since general texts fequently cite Debray as an authority it should be noted that the co-author of his chapter on Guatemala is no less partisan than the maestro himself – Ricardo Ramírez (aka Arnoldo Cardona Fratti, aka Rolando Morán), currently leader of the EGP.

44. Régis Debray, *Revolution in the Revolution?*, London 1967; Ernesto Ché Guevara, *Guerrilla Warfare*, London 1969.

45. According to the FAR leader César Montes, 'in all the peasant areas we have visited we easily explain ourselves by saying that the FAR struggle is merely the prolongation by other means of the 1944 revolution. The CIA won and Guatemala lost because that revolution was led by the national bourgeoisie.' Quoted in Eduardo Galeano, *Guatemala: Occupied Country*, New York 1969, p. 17. '[The PGT leaders'] mentality was formed by a dependence on the national bourgeoisie, which constituted the traditional line, leaving them unable to assume the position corresponding to them . . . taking the leadership of a Communist party, the vanguard of the proletariat and the people; thus, they did not succeed in the revolutionary, popular form of violence – armed struggle.' Arnoldo Cardona Fratti, 'Dogma y Revolución', *Tricontinental*, no. 8, September–October 1968, quoted in John Gerassi, ed., *Towards Revolution. The Americas*, London 1971, p. 577. A good if unsympathetic résumé of the political disputes and strategy of the left in this period is given in David Crain, 'Guatemalan Revolutionaries and Havana's Ideological Offensive of 1966–68', *Journal of Inter-American Studies*, vol. 17, no. 2, May 1975.

46. 'It would be a mistake to regard the armed forces as being entirely reactionary, immune to democratic influence and permanently hostile to the revolution.' Hugo Barrios Klee, 'The Revolutionary Situation and Liberation Struggle of the People of Guatemala', WMR, vol. 7, no. 3, March 1964, p. 21. '[The counter-revolutionary] coup of 30 March 1963 was staged by *all* the army leaders supported by the *entire bloc of the ruling classes*.' A. Guerra Borges, 'The Experience of Guatemala: Some Problems for the Revolutionary Struggle Today', WMR, vol. 7, no. 6, June 1964.

47. See Gott, *Rural Guerrillas*, who criticizes the alliance but at least takes an interest in it. Gilly, 'Guerrilla Movement in Guatemala', presents the perspective of a Trotskyist activist who participated. Debray, *Revolution on Trial*, attacks the Trotskyists with characteristic bravado.

48. The easy latter-day disparagement in Black, *Garrison Guatemala*, p. 74, is typical.

49. Debray, *Revolution on Trial*, p. 39.

50. Debray and others make much of the Trotskyists' expulsion for financial misdemeanours, a charge that is less readily proved than levelled but was taken up with alacrity by the PGT and the FAR, which had some difficulty in handling the MR-13's earlier and essentially correct critique of the PGT and its domination of the FAR's operations. For a rebuttal of Debray's general perspective, see Adolfo Gilly, 'Guerrilla, Programa y Partido en Guatemala', *Coyoacán*, no. 3, April–June 1978.

51. 'There will be elections. But let it be clear that when we are strong enough, and when the awareness of our people has better grasped the hollowness of elections with a reactionary government in power, we shall forcibly prevent this vile deceit of the people from continuing.' Quoted in Gott, *Rural Guerrillas*, p. 117. Five months after Méndez Montenegro came to power the PGT's leading ideologue, J.M. Fortuny, declared, 'it would be an oversimplification to qualify, as some people do, the new administration as "the fourth government of the counter-revolution" . . . whether the government can tip the scales in its own favour depends on its political dexterity . . . it wished to give the people a respite . . . an atmosphere conducive to organizing and rallying the masses set in.' Fortuny saw the state of siege of November as prejudicing the constitutional impetus of the regime but rejected any characterization of it as right-wing or reactionary. 'Guatemala: The Political Situation and Revolutionary Tactics', WMR, vol. 10, no. 2, February 1967, pp. 55–60.

52. The full FAR declaration of 21 January 1968 signed by César Montes is reprinted in Galeano, *Occupied Country*, pp. 133–44. Gerassi, *Towards Revolution*, pp. 577 ff., reprints

Cardona's similar critique. Fernández, *Turcios Lima*, pp. 42, 45, carries equally direct attacks on the PGT's attitude to the national question, contrasted with quotes from Mao on the importance of the poor peasantry. The PGT's position was remarkably clear and orthodox: 'Indian peasants in some areas of Guatemala . . . have the worst standard of living in the country; but their cultural backwardness, the downtrodden state in which they have been living since the times of Spanish colonial rule, their relative isolation from the economic and political life of the country. . . . have resulted in a situation in which these people are, by and large, not politically active. . . . Nor . . . will they be the main support of the democratic national liberation revolution maturing in the country. . . . The main forces of the revolution, and the most active, are concentrated in the south and eastern areas of the country and in those areas of the highlands where political and economic development are at a higher level' (WMR, 1964, p. 15). For the FAR (and MR-13) such a clear repudiation of basic Maoist tenets was compounded by the PGT's rejection of armed struggle as a strategy rather than a tactic, a position adopted without ambiguity by Fortuny (some of whose essay is reprinted in Gott, *Rural Guerrillas*, pp. 137–8). Interestingly, the FAR saw no political mileage in the religious question, identifying the Maryknoll order (shortly to be expelled from the country) as 'incarnating the religious counter-revolution' whilst César Montes is reported to have held up a copy of Paul VI's *Populorum Progressio* and declared, 'the Pope is more intelligent than the Guatemalan right. Read this and you'll see exactly how he nails down the causes of violence'. Fernández, *Turcios Lima*, p. 141; Galeano, *Occupied Country*, p. 34.

53. Galeano, *Occupied Country*, p. 31; Fernández, *Turcios Lima*, pp. 91–110, reproduces the FGEI letter of March 1965 to the MR-13 in which the importance of Vietnam and necessity of a prolonged struggle are already emphasized. By 1968, when Morán wrote 'Dogma y Revolución', these features had become central.

54. The first period of the EGP's operations in the Ixcan region is described in Mario Payeras, 'Days of the Jungle', *Monthly Review*, vol. 35, no. 3, July–August 1983.

55. Quoted in McClintock, *American Connection*, pp. 85–6.

56. Ibid., pp. 72 ff.

57. Ibid., p. 84.

58. Between 1950 and 1963 military aid totalled $6.4 million. Under Méndez Montenegro it averaged $2 million a year. The US Public Safety Program (police and paramilitary aid and training) averaged $188,000 a year between 1957 and 1965 and $380,000 a year between 1966 and 1970. It should, however, be added that the greatest increase was in 1971, the first year of Arana's regime, when military aid rose from $907,000 to $1.5 million, Public Safety aid having already been increased from $411,000 to $1.2 million. Arms purchases rose from $1.9 million in 1970 to $9.8 million in 1971. Ibid., p. 108; NACLA, *Guatemala*, p. 196.

59. Between 1962 and 1970 annual average US military aid to the Central American states was:

	US$ per capita	*US$ per soldier*
Costa Rica	–	–
El Salvador	1,050.00	1.83
Guatemala	1,822.22	3.17
Honduras	1,420.00	2.75
Nicaragua	1,700.00	5.33

Defence Department sales of arms – as distinct from free transfers of weaponry – between 1950 and 1970 was: Costa Rica – $900,000; El Salvador – $1.5 million; Guatemala – $2.7 million; Honduras – $1.1 million; Nicaragua – $2.3 million. Between 1950 and 1970 the number of personnel trained by US forces was: Costa Rica – 529; El Salvador – 1,071; Guatemala – 2,280; Honduras – 1,578; Nicaragua – 3,994. Military expenditure as a percentage of total budget in 1960 stood at: Costa Rica – 0.53; El Salvador – 1.58; Guatemala – 1.52; Honduras – 1.30; Nicaragua – 2.80. Philippe C. Schmitter, ed., *Military Rule in Latin America*, Berkeley 1973, p. 144; NACLA, *The US Military Apparatus*, Berkeley 1972, pp. 49, 67.

60. Quoted in Handy, *Gift of the Devil*, p. 194.

61. This result fell into a clear pattern, the levels of abstention since 1950 being: 1950 – 31.1%; 1958 – 33.1%; 1966 – 43.7%. The proportion of votes won by the victor was: 1950 – 45.7%; 1958 – 25.9%; 1966 – 22.2%. Although many commentators note the general apathy

of the Guatemalan electorate in the post-1954 era, this was not markedly out of line with the tendency elsewhere except Costa Rica.

62. LA, 29 May 1971.

63. Ibid., 29 January 1971.

64. Ibid., 16 May 1975; NACLA, *Guatemala*, p. 202. According to Amnesty International at least 20,000 people died between 1966 and 1976: 'Guatemala', December 1976, p. 16.

65. NACLA, *Guatemala*, p. 118.

66. LA, 2 November 1973.

67. When Ríos Montt gained 78,000 votes against Laugerud's 38,000 in the capital the government halted the count for a day and linked all radio stations to the state system. According to the FNO it scored between 45 and 49 per cent of the total vote whereas the official result was: FNO – 207,704; PID–MLN – 242,631; PR – 126,249. Congress subsequently elected Laugerud by 39 votes to 2 with 14 abstentions. LA, 8 March; 15 March 1974.

68. D. Barrillas, *Democracia Cristiana y su Posición ante el Ejército de Guatemala Hoy*, Guatemala City 1974, sections of which are reproduced in Painter, *False Hope*. In July 1974 collaboration with the regime in congress produced a split in the DCG. But by mid-1975 the Christian Democrats were formally working with PR and PID deputies to oppose the MLN, and early in 1976 an official policy of DCG collaboration with the PID to isolate the MLN had been clearly established.

69. Between 1975 and 1983 Guatemala charged an export tax of 35 cents per box whilst Costa Rica and Panama adhered to the Union of Banana Exporting Countries' standard tariff of $1. Honduras initially charged at this agreed rate but then, as a result of United Brands' (UFCO) bribery later to be revealed in the 'Bananagate' scandal, reduced it to 25 cents. From July 1983 the Honduran rate rose to 40 cents, broadly in line with those in Costa Rica and Panama, whereas the Guatemalan tax was reduced to 25 cents (1983), then 12.5 (1984) and then zero (1985). During the 1970s the three corporations exporting Central American bananas – United Brands, Standard Fruit and Del Monte – controlled 60 per cent of the world market between them. The approximate levels of market share by country in this period were: Del Monte: Guatemala – 100% and Costa Rica – 30%; United Brands: Costa Rica – 32%, Honduras – 54%, and Panama – 95%; Standard Fruit: Costa Rica – 38%, Honduras – 44%, and Nicaragua – 100%. José Roberto López, *La Economía del Banano en Centroamérica*, San José 1986, pp. 53, 94.

70. *Crisis en Cifras*, p. 103.

71. NACLA, *Guatemala*, p. 133.

72. *Centroamérica Hoy*, p. 125 (reproduced in Table 15 above); *Dollars and Dictators*, p. 232. Note that these statistics are subject to the caveat made above as to the different methods of calculating investment.

73. NACLA, *Guatemala*, p. 134, itemizes 37 cases of US transnational corporation acquisition of local firms beween 1960 and 1970. A table of the 77 largest US firms operating in the country is given on pp. 170–4.

74. Ibid., p. 135.

75. Ibid., pp. 65, 82; Black, *Garrison Guatemala*, pp. 24, 155.

76. In 1980 Fred Sherwood, ex-president of the American Chamber of Commerce, told the journalist Alan Nairn, 'Why should we do anything about the death squads? They're bumping off the commies, our enemies. I'd give them more power. Hell, I'd give them more cartridges if I could, and everyone else would, too . . . these peasants, they don't know how to run something. . . . They're dumb, damn savages.' Quoted in Jonathan Fried et al., eds, *Guatemala in Rebellion*, New York 1983, pp. 90–91.

77. Painter, *False Hope*, p. 45.

78. Amongst the leading clans in ANACAFE are the Mombielas, Campollos, Flores, Aragón Quinoñez, Pivaral and Plochansky in San Marcos and Quezaltenango, the Brols in El Quiché, the Peyres in Escuintla, and the Fallas in Sacatepéquez. After Castillo Armas's return of the national farms a number of German families recuperated their estates and continue to figure amongst the oligarchy. Ibid., pp. 35–6.

79. Cotton families include Molina, García Granados (the 'original' Liberal clan of the 1870s), Alejos, Herrera, Ponciano and Aycinena (a leading pre-Liberal oligarchic clan).

Perhaps the most pugnacious sector of the landlord class in the 1960s and 1970s, the cotton entrepreneurs were badly hit by the collapse of the market in the 1980s and despite some diversification built upon singular profits in the preceding period; their campaign for extra tax concessions produced some tension with the rest of a capitalist class effectively required by the state to cover the consequent shortfall.

80. These mills in Escuintla were fully owned or controlled by the following families: Herrera Ibarguen, Witman, Botrán, Molina Calderón, González Bauer, Compollo López, Weissenber Campollo, Alejos, García Granados, and Herrera. A further ten mills accounted for all the remaining production. Ibid., p. 42.

81. Ibid., pp. 45–7.

82. Ibid., pp. 32–3.

83. Williams, *Export Agriculture*, p. 140.

84. Black, *Garrison Guatemala*, p. 58. Perhaps the most celebrated case was the acquisition of the *finca* Yalpemech by General Romeo Lucas García and Raul García Granados, purchased from the Diesseldorff family in 1975 for $175,000, revalued a year later at $300,000, and used as collateral for a loan of $750,000 from the Bank of America. One of fourteen farms owned by Lucas García in the FTN, Yalpemech's enhanced value must be linked to its proximity to the new highway built by the army and the Shenandoah Oil Company. Ibid., p. 59.

85. Quoted in McClintock, *American Connection*, p. 225.

86. Painter, *False Hope*, p. 49.

87. The EGP drew a direct comparison with the Somocista state. *Compañero*, no. 4, 1982, p. 8; Comandante Benedicto in *Listen Compañero*, San Francisco 1983, p. 51.

88. López Larrave, *Movimiento Sindical*, p. 76; Miguel Angel Albizures, 'Struggles and Experiences of the Guatemalan Trade Union Movement', *Latin American Perspectives*, vol. 7, nos 2 and 3, 1980, p. 146. This official figure is very probably conservative, the well-informed journal *Inforpress* estimating membership of unions at 85,000, or some 6 per cent of the labour force. Plant, *Unnatural Disaster*, p. 46. In any event, the union movement remained exceptionally small.

89. Albizures, 'Struggles and Experiences', and López Larrave, *Movimiento Sindical*, provide surveys of this process.

90. Albizures, 'Struggles and Experiences', p. 145; Plant, *Unnatural Disaster*, pp. 46–63; *Crisis en Cifras*, pp. 168–9.

91. Mike Gatehouse and Miguel Angel Reyes, *Soft Drink. Hard Labour. Guatemalan Workers Take on Coca Cola*, London 1987.

92. LAPR, 6, 13, 20 October 1978.

93. USAID, 'Tierra y Trabajo en Guatemala', Guatemala City 1982; Painter, *False Hope*, p. 19.

94. Ibid., p. 17; Rolando Eliseo Ortiz Rosales, 'Guatemala. Generalidades sobre el Sector Agrícola', *Comercio Exterior*, vol. 34, no. 11, p. 1121.

95. *Cultivable Land Per Capita (hectares)*

	1950	*1964*	*1973*	*1980*
Huehuetenango	0.69	0.48	0.38	0.32
San Marcos	0.33	0.23	0.20	0.16
El Quiché	1.04	0.73	0.60	0.56

Source: USAID, 'Tierra y Trabajo en Guatemala', Guatemala City 1982, Table 3; Miguel Angel Castillo, 'Algunos Determinantes y Principales Transformaciones Recientes de la Migración Guatemalteca a la Frontera Sur de México', ESC, no. 40, San José January–April 1986.

96. Plant, *Unnatural Disaster*, p. 87.

97. 'We know of your pro-Communist attitude. . . . We know by experience that all labour organizations and cooperatives always eventually fall into the power Communist leaders infiltrated into them. We have the organization and the force to prevent this from occurring again. . . . As evidence that we speak the truth: there are thirty thousand clandestine peasant graves to bear witness.' Quoted in McClintock, *American Connection*, p. 134.

98. Shelton Davis and Julie Hodson, *Witness to Political Violence in Guatemala: The Suppression of a Rural Development Movement*, Boston 1982, p. 47.

99. The fullest study of this process is Ricardo Falla, *Quiché Rebelde*, Guatemala City 1978. For a remarkable personal account of the life of a radical Catholic woman from Quiché, see Elizabeth Burgos Debray, ed., *I . . . Rigoberta Menchú*, London 1984. The *Declaration of Iximche*, made on 14 February 1980, following the Spanish embassy massacre, provides the clearest political manifesto of the indigenous movement in this period.

100. In 1966 434 of 531 priests were foreigners, as were 705 of Guatemala's 805 nuns and all the religious brothers. Adams, *Crucifixion by Power*, p. 84.

101. *El Imparcial*, 24 February 1967, quoted in *Cultural Survival Quarterly*, 'Death and Disorder', p. 24.

102. Quoted in *Guatemala in Rebellion*, p. 221. Then the sole Cardinal in Central America, Casariego was the only Latin American cleric of this rank not to be invited to the 1979 Puebla bishops' conference. He died in harness in June 1983 and was replaced by the liberal Próspero Penados del Barrio.

103. *Mensaje del Episcopado Guatemalteco: Unidos en la Esperanza*, Guatemala City 1976, parts of which are reproduced in Berryman, *Religious Roots*, pp. 182–3.

104. In their pastoral letter of May 1981 even the bishops were prepared to countenance an implicit understanding of armed struggle: 'One more time, we repeat that violence, except in the case of legitimate self-defence, is anti-Christian.'

105. José Alcina Franch, ed., *Bartolomé de Las Casas. Obra Indigenista*, Madrid 1985.

106. FIASA was established in 1969 with seed money from USAID and capital from General Mills, Goodyear, Pillsbury, Lloyds Bank, Deutsche Sudamerikanische Bank and Bank of America in collaboration with the formidable Castillo clan, which was based on the brewing industry but diversified considerably into manufacturing and commerce in the post-war period. NACLA, *Guatemala*, pp. 143 ff.; Painter, *False Hope*, pp. 54–5.

107. The leading landlords involved in the Panzós area, some of them being directly implicated in the massacre itself, were Enrique Edwin Bics, Manuel Moco Sánchez, Joaquín González, and Flavio Monsón, a prominent member of the MLN who later told a member of the local community that the army's action had been previously authorized by the regime. Gabriel Aguilera et al., *Dialéctica del Terror en Guatemala*, San José 1981, p. 195. This text and the Church-sponsored *Panzós. Testimonio*, Guatemala City 1979, provide a very detailed reconstruction of the massacre and its background.

108. EGP, *Compañero*, no. 4, p. 7.

109. Carol Smith, 'Indian Class Consciousness', pp. 33–5.

110. EGP, *Compañero*, English edn, no. 1, p. 20.

111. Ibid., p. 24.

112. The fullest presentation of the EGP's positions prior to the crisis of 1981/2 may be found in their manifesto published in the western press in late October 1979, for example *The Guardian*, London, 26 October 1979.

113. Miguel Rodríguez, Secretary General of the PGT, 'Twenty Five Trying Years', WMR, vol. 17, no. 9, September 1974, pp. 27–8.

114. Pedro González Torres, 'Dictatorship versus People's War', WMR, vol. 16, no. 4, Apil 1973, p. 71.

115. The slogan of the FAR is: 'A Vencer o Morir por Guatemala, la Revolución y el Socialismo'; PGT (ND) – 'Por Guatemala, la Revolución y el Socialismo'; EGP – 'Hasta la Victoria Siempre' (a clear legacy from Cuba); ORPA – 'Vivimos para Luchar, Luchamos para Triunfar'.

116. WMRIB, December 1982, p. 26. A fraternal exchange between Antonio Castro of the PGT and Guillermo Toriello representing the guerrilla forces is given in WMR, vol. 24, no. 3, March 1981.

117. *Historia de ORPA*, Mexico 1982. Although both ORPA and the EGP have issued a number of publications abroad, the FAR is less well represented, and all the guerrilla organizations tend to present their views indirectly through journals and information bulletins sympathetic to them. The best consistent source of open discussion of policy is the Canadian-based newsletter ALAI, which frequently contains articles and interviews.

118. The official result was: Lucas García (PID; PR; CAO) – 262,960; E. Peralta (MLN) –

221,223; R. Peralta (DCG) – 167,073. The MLN won 20 congressional seats, PID 17, PR 14, DCG 7 and CAO 3. According to Colóm Argueta the dominant bloc was divided between importing interests (Ricardo Peralta), agro-export (PR and PID) and industrial concerns (E. Peralta). LAPR, 6 April 1979.

119. Amnesty International, *Government Program*, p. 5.

120. Painter, *False Hope*, p. 68.

121. NYT, 24 August 1980, cited in *Road to Democracy?*, p. 15.

122. Colóm Argueta was under no illusions as to the government's methods; in an interview shortly before his death he warned that the regime's registration of the FUR was purely a cosmetic act and 'in exchange they may want my head', just as Fuentes Mohr had been killed a fortnight before the registration of the PSD. LAPR, 6 April 1979.

123. FDRCR Bulletin, January 1980, quoted in McClintock, *American Connection*, p. 152.

124. A brief description of the FDCR and assessment of its role is given in ICADIS, *Los Hechos que Formaron la Crisis*, San José 1986, pp. 11–14.

125. This and other statements by Indian women who had joined the guerrilla were made in interviews with Tereza Gurza, *El Día*, Mexico, 13 January 1981, quoted in McClintock, *American Connection*, pp. 184–5.

126. The real rural minimum wage fell from Q35.1 per month in 1970 to Q15.1 in 1979 despite nominal increases from Q0.95 to Q1.14 per day between 1972 and 1976. Ortiz Rosales, 'Generalidades', p. 1124; *Crisis en Cifras*, p. 172.

127. Jude Pasini, 'Indian Seasonal Plantation Labor in Guatemala', *Cultural Survival Quarterly*, vol. 7, no. 1, p. 17.

128. A detailed description of two distinct plantations that shows the importance of apparently secondary conditions of employment is given in Laurel Bossen, 'Plantations and Labor Force Discrimination in Guatemala', *Peasant Studies*, vol VIII, no. 3, Summer 1979.

129. ALAI, 12 February 1982; *Los Hechos*, pp. 14–18.

130. LAWR, 6 November 1981. According to the EGP capital flight between 1979 and October 1981 amounted to $500 million. *Compañero*, English edn, no. 2, p. 8.

131. LAWR, 31 July; 6 November; 11 December 1981.

132. Ibid., 7 August 1981.

133. *Crisis en Cifras*, p. 244. US funds contracted in 1977 were disbursed the following year and a number of deliveries of arms purchased earlier were made in 1979 and 1980. McClintock, *American Connection*, p. 108.

134. Black, *Garrison Guatemala*, pp. 160–2, lists a number of links.

135. Ibid., pp. 164 ff.; McClintock, *American Connection*, pp. 192 ff., NACLA, 'The Israeli Connection', vol. XXI, no. 2, March–April 1987 provide succinct surveys of the Israeli connection.

136. In a chilling but instructive instance of combined and uneven development, the computerized assessment of telephone and electricity bills in the capital of this peasant country led Argentine intelligence officers to identify a key ORPA 'safe house' where bombs were being made. LAWR, 6 November 1981.

137. *Compañero*, English edn, no. 1, p. 7. The difficulties of the army in this period were evident in the loss of many convoys, a dramatic fall in public transport in the *altiplano*, vulnerability of helicopters, and particular pressure placed on the garrisons in Sololá and Escuintla, inadequately prepared for attacks. According to LAWR, 11 December 1981, the officer corps was still divided over whether to maintain a defensive strategy based on the towns or whether to pursue a rural 'scorched earth' offensive.

138. *Compañero*, English edn, no. 2, p. 17.

139. In mid 1983 Rolando Morán, commander of the EGP, accepted that the guerrilla had underestimated the enemy and committed significant errors in 1981–82 with the result that there would be no return to conventional forms of warfare for some time. *Compañero*, no. 7, November 1983, pp. 8–10. In November 1982 the EGP drew up a formal self-criticism of its 'triumphalist' approach, but this failed to meet the objections of a sector led by Mario Payeras (Comandante Benedicto) which split in January 1984 and criticized the leadership for harbouring illusions of a quick victory from a searly as the autumn of 1980, explaining this by an overly emotional response to the Nicaraguan revolution, excessive expectations of popular

mobilization in Honduras, and a failure to appreciate the limits to bourgeois divisions and differences with Washington. *Opinión Política*, nos 2 and 3, 1985. This assessment appears far more persuasive than that offered by George Black, who stresses the immediate strengths of the left in 1981–82 and presents the subsequent success of the military almost exclusively in terms of its improved methods and violence. *Garrison Guatemala*, pp. 128 ff.

140. URNG, *Proclama Unitaria*, January 1982.

141. The style of the MLN in 1982 was little different from that of 1954. According to one of its leaders, Leonel Sisniega, 'I admit that the MLN is the party of organized violence. Organized violence is vigour, like organized colour is scenery or organized sound is harmony. There is nothing wrong with organized violence . . .' Quoted in *Road to Democracy?*, p. 17.

142. *Los Hechos*, pp. 22–3. A succinct survey of the Ríos Montt government is provided in Black, *Garrison Guatemala*, pp. 121–52.

143. The payment of bribes of $50,000 to Maldonado and Gordillo was reported in LAWR, 18 June; 30 July 1982.

144. Black, *Garrison Guatemala*, p. 121.

145. Quoted in NYT, 12 September 1982. This was not a solitary aberration. In June Ríos Montt declared, 'Whoever is against the instituted government, whoever doesn't surrender I'm going to shoot. It is preferable that it be known that 20 people were shot, and not just that 20 bodies have appeared beside the road.' *Miami Herald*, 6 June 1982.

146. LAWR, 2 April 1982.

147. Quoted in Black, *Garrison Guatemala*, p. 141.

148. LAWR, 7 January 1983. Official figures put the Protestant community at 426,000 or 6 per cent of the population. *Crisis en Cifras*, p. 39. According to the *Wall Street Journal*, 7 December 1982, 22 per cent of the population was Protestant in 1982 with 6,767 congregations and 110 different sects. For detailed socio-economic surveys of protestantism in the late 1960s and early 1970s, see Gunter Golde, *Catholics and Protestants: Agricultural Modernization in Two Guatemalan Villages*, New York 1975; James D. Sexton, 'Protestantism and Modernization in Two Guatemalan Towns', *American Ethnologist*, vol. 5, no. 2, May 1978.

149. For 'Operation Lovelift', see LAWR, 7 January; 4 February 1983.

150. Assistant Secretary of State Stephen Bosworth to House Subcommittee on International Development Institutes and Finance, 5 August 1982, quoted in *Road to Democracy?*, p. 29.

151. Quoted in ibid., p. 39.

152. In view of frequent conservative rejections of assertions as to the degree of state violence because these are 'leftist inspired', it is worth listing these massacres with some precision:

Date	*Village*	*Dept*	*Approx. No. killed*
23 March	Parraxtut, El Pajarito, Pichiquil	Quiché/ Huehue'o	500+
24–7 March	Las Pacayas Chisirán, El Rancho	A. Verapaz	100
28 March–10 April	Estancia de la Virgen, Choatalun	Chimaltenango	250
30 March–2 April	Chinique	Quiché	55
3–5 April	El Mangal, Chajul	Quiché	100+
15 April	Río Negro	A. Verapaz	173
18 April	Macalbaj	Quiché	54
20 April	Josefinas	Petén	100
29 April	Palestina	Petén(?)	100+
17–22 April	Xesic, Choacamán, Chitatul, Chajbal	Quiché	67
29 April	Cuarto Pueblo	Quiché	200
21 May	Sajquiya	Quiché	110
June	Pampach, Tactic	A. Verapaz	100
June	Chisec	A. Verapaz	160 families
14 July	Xepocol	Quiché	52
20 July	San Miguel, Acatán	Huehue'o	200

20 July	Santa Teresa	Huehue'o	60
24 July	Lacaná II	Quiché	65
31 July	Lacaná I and II	Quiché	61

Source: Ricardo Falla, 'The Massacre at the Rural Estate of San Francisco, July 1982', *Cultural Survival Quarterly*, vol. 7, no. 1, 1983, p. 43.

153. *CAR*, 22 February 1985.

154. Painter, *False Hope*, p. xiv; *Crisis en Cifras*, pp. 240–1.

155. Extracts from the principal strategic documents of the Ríos Montt regime are reproduced in Black, *Garrison Guatemala*, pp. 189–92. The counter-insurgency campaign is described in ibid., pp. 147 ff.

156. For details, see McClintock, *American Connection*, pp. 249 ff.

157. A detailed appraisal of the impact of the military's strategy is given in Chris Krueger and Kjell Enge, 'Without Security or Development: Guatemala Militarized'. *WOLA*, 1985. The effects of this on a department not at the heart of the military conflict are assessed in Carol Smith, 'Destruction of the Material Bases'.

158. For the dissidents' assessment of the military's counter-offensive and their criticism of the EGP leadership, see *Opinión Política*, no. 2, which suggests a reorientation towards the urban sphere.

159. CAR, 30 August; 20 October 1985; LAWR, 16 March 1984.

160. LAWR, 10 and 24 December 1982; 4 March 1983; Painter, *False Hope*, p. 76.

161. LAWR, 5 August 1983; Painter, *False Hope*, p. 76.

162. LAWR, 19 August 1983.

163 Cerezo insisted that he would never emulate Méndez Montenegro's concessions to the army. However, the message from the commanders was very clear; a month before the elections Colonel Edgar Hernández declared, 'the new civilian government must maintain and respect the army's hierarchical order and the enabling legislation that governs all movements of the armed institution. The army also expects that the civilian government will respect the military's plans to combat the subversives.' CAR, 11 October 1985. Over the following eighteen months Cerezo scrupulously met all these demands.

164. *Crisis en Cifras*; Painter, *False Hope*, pp. 20, 28.

165. CAR, 19 April 1985; *Crisis en Cifras*, p. 144; Painter, *False Hope*, p. 33.

166. Painter, *False Hope*, p. 33; *Los Hechos*, pp. 38–42; CAR, 3 May 1985.

167. LAWR, 19 August 1983 for intervention in Nicaragua; *Road to Democracy?* p. 52, for CONDECA.

168. The army explicitly refused to join the manoeuvres because it lacked the resources to do both this and fight the guerrilla at home. *Prensa Libre*, 21 March 1984.

169. Ibid., 27 October 1983; 5 January 1984; NYT, 7 July 1984. Gustavo Porras views the stance as indicative of a far greater interest in foreign affairs under Mejía than his predecessors but also of a fundamentally pragmatic approach. 'Guatemala: Un Proyecto de Recomposición', mimeo 1984, pp. 29–32.

170. The interpretation of pressure to keep the Nicaraguan market open may derive from the fact that in 1980 Guatemalan exports to Nicaragua rose to $103 million from $36 million the previous year (afflicted by the civil war but still an average level for the decade). However, this rise was only moderately greater than that in trade to other states of the region in this boom year, and by 1984 exports had slumped to $34 million in line with a general fall in intra-CACM trade from 1981. *Crisis en Cifras*, pp. 103–7. The significant slump in commerce with Nicaragua can easily be interpreted on political grounds but in practice had far more to do with the foreign exchange crisis, and from 1982 there was a modest but constant rise in inter-state barter agreements, particularly with politically hostile Costa Rica. Rafael Menjívar and José Roberto López, eds, *Intercambio Compensado y Crisis del Comercio Regional*, San José 1986.

171. Quoted in G. Gaspar, *La Estrategia de la Democracia Cristiana en Centroamérica*, Mexico 1985, p. 15, cited in Painter, *False Hope*, p. 76.

172. Ibid.

173. Ibid.; NYT, 10 December 1985.

174. As the leading organization of authentic 'leftism' in Guatemala, the URNG

denounced the poll as a farce and part of the military's counter-revolutionary strategy. However, while the URNG as a whole saw the election as indicative of the weakness of the Mejía regime, the FAR recognized that it had, in fact, strengthened the government and that significant sectors of the population were confused by a poll that was not simply a product of Reagan's policy. Porras, 'Proyecto de Recomposición', pp. 37–38. The final result was:

	% Vote	*Seats*
DCG	16.3	20
UCN	13.7	21
MLN–CAN	12.5	23
PR	7.3	10
PNR	6.7	5
PID	5.3	5
PUA	3.1	1
FUN	2.3	1
AD	2.1	1
FCD	2.0	1

175. For the September mobilization, see *Los Hechos*, pp. 44–8; CAR, 13 September; 4 October 1985.

176. Details of increased guerrilla activity throughout 1985 are given in CAR. After the constituent assembly elections the URNG, now minus the PGT, sought to resolve internal divisions over strategy and political perspective. Although it is unclear how profound this process of reunification went, open disagreement and lack of coordination did reduce markedly in 1985. *Los Hechos*, pp. 42–4.

177. The URNG declared that the poll would result in a 'repressive, anti-popular, anti-democratic puppet government' regardless of who won. The PGT announced that the elections provided no solution to the structural crisis and called for popular support for the URNG. CAR, 11 October 1985. The increased level of abstention from that of 1984 suggests that these views were far from unpopular, especially in the wake of the September strike and riots. The percentage of votes in the first round of the election was: DCG – 38.6; UCN – 20.3; PR–PDCN – 13.8; MLN–PID – 12.5; CAN – 6.3; PSD – 3.4; PNR – 3.2; PUA–FUN – 1.9.

10
Honduras: The Limits of Sovereignty

It is the good fortune of the Patria that the two new active forces in Honduran life – the Armed Forces of the Republic and the free, democratic trade unions – are in essential agreement in their approach to the great problems of the Nation.

Colonel Oswaldo López Arellano, October 1963[1]

We are called arrogant, those of us who speak frankly of the pathetic reality of Honduras. Yet if it is arrogant to identify those responsible for the past and present ills that afflict us then there are many thousands of arrogant people in this country because we will not tolerate the possibility of continuing to be underdeveloped, children of a nation that inspires international compassion, inhabitants of a republic whose precarious existence has to depend upon those who are not our countrymen.

Colonel Mario Maldonado, April 1975[2]

Here they are frightened of the word revolution . . . but what do we want? A peaceful revolution or a violent one?

General López Arellano, November 1972[3]

This dump is the centre of the world now.

Captain Michael Sheehan, US Special Forces, 1981[4]

I can't ever envision a time when the military will not need to have to do exercises of various kinds [in Honduras].

Caspar Weinberger, 1985[5]

There might be some counter-revolutionary groups but it's really difficult to control them. Moreover, we can't make the effort to protect the Nicaraguan border when [the Sandinistas] are sowing subversion here.

General Gustavo Alvárez, August 1982[6]

The US has put its eyes on Nicaragua, its hands on El Salvador, and its feet in Honduras, flattening us.

Jorge Arturo Reina, MOLIDER, July 1985[7]

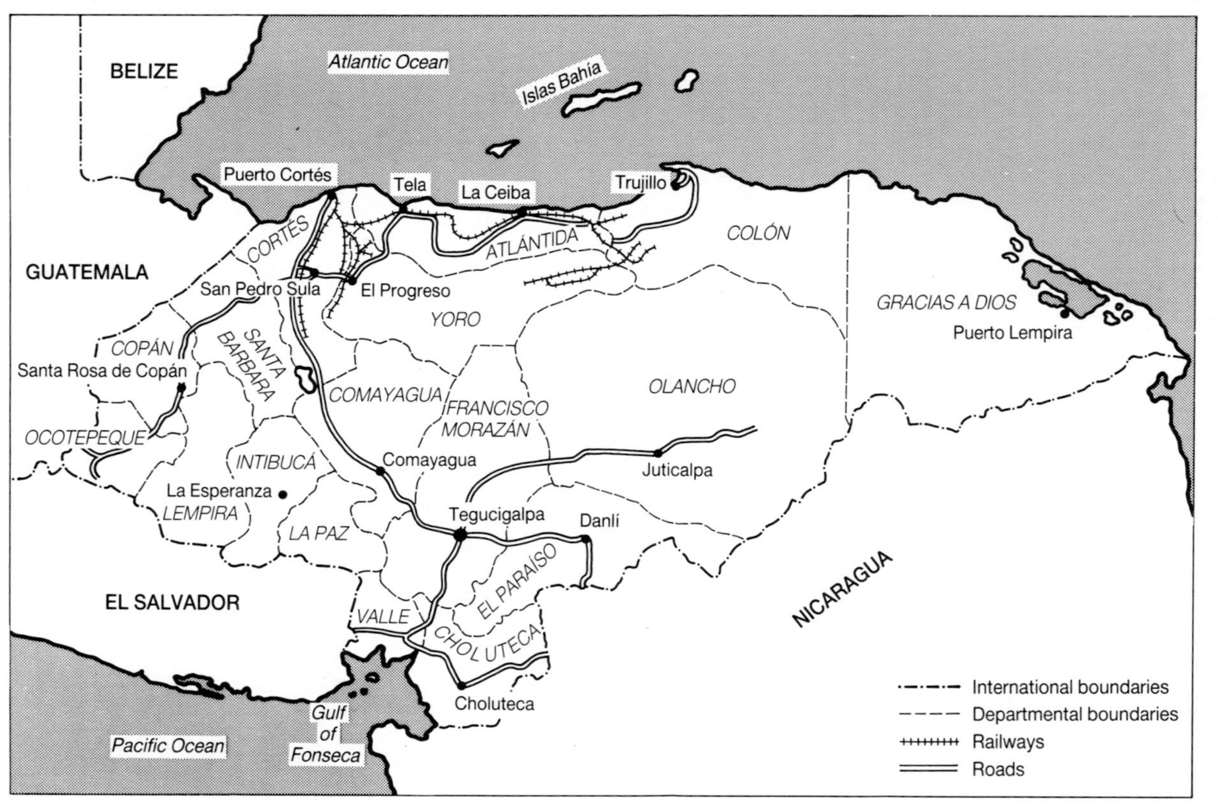

BELIZE
Atlantic Ocean
Islas Bahía
GUATEMALA
Puerto Cortés
Tela
La Ceiba
Trujillo
CORTÉS
ATLÁNTIDA
COLÓN
GRACIAS A DIOS
Puerto Lempira
San Pedro Sula
El Progreso
YORO
COPÁN
SANTA BARBARA
Santa Rosa de Copán
OLANCHO
COMAYAGUA
FRANCISCO MORAZÁN
OCOTEPEQUE
INTIBUCÁ
Comayagua
Juticalpa
La Esperanza
LEMPIRA
Tegucigalpa
Danlí
LA PAZ
EL PARAÍSO
EL SALVADOR
VALLE
CHOLUTECA
NICARAGUA
Choluteca
Gulf of Fonseca
Pacific Ocean
International boundaries
Departmental boundaries
Railways
Roads

Honduras

Since 1982 the presence of large numbers of US troops in Honduras and the decisive political influence of Washington in Tegucigalpa have led a country traditionally deemed to be the epitome of a banana republic to be dubbed a 'state for sale', 'republic for rent', 'Pentagon republic', 'captive nation' and – somewhat more bluntly – a 'US aircraft carrier'.[8] In a sense Honduras has come to be important by virtue of its very unimportance, a focus of regional interest not because of violent political crisis – as in Nicaragua, El Salvador and Guatemala – nor for the exceptionalism of a stable constitutional order – as in Costa Rica – but because a historically weak state bordering all three of the countries in conflict has proved incapable of upholding genuine sovereignty and resisting virtual colonization by Washington.

This operation is frequently viewed as it has been undertaken – with slight concern about Honduras itself and much greater attention to the salients driven from the country into Nicaragua and El Salvador. As demonstrated by the Irangate hearings, liberal critics of Reagan's Central American policies are far from united in opposition to the Contra campaign as such, but they are less at odds with Washington's general strategy in Honduras since they accept the need for containment of the left in the region and are relieved that at least part of this can be achieved at low economic and diplomatic cost through formal (if sometimes secret) agreements with a subservient foreign government. Radical opponents of Washington's presence have failed to sustain a telling campaign against it largely because, with only 147 deaths and disappearances attributable to political persecution between 1979 and 1986 compared to the tens of thousands elsewhere, Honduras appeared to be a tranquil and unproblematic ally. In the absence of armed opposition to the US presence, even the deployment of contingents of the US National Guard aroused little concern back in the states from which they had been sent despite the dubious legal status of their assignment. From a North American perspective the rearticulation of manifest destiny in the language of Cold War geopolitics has been less controversial and more efficiently realized in Honduras than in any other country of Central America. For the great majority of Hondurans the position appears distinctly different. When the president of the businessmen's association bitterly observes that his country is occupied by seven armies, including the unemployed, and the leading daily of San Pedro Sula declares, 'We have lost everything including our honour', it is evident that the US presence and its consequences have sown sufficient dismay to put the nerve and authority of the political class under threat.[9]

Outside the country the debate over US activity in Honduras has displayed a kind of parallax vision in which there is a confused elision between national and regional factors. On the left Washington's operation was attacked both because it violated Honduran independence and because it was the hub of the regional counter-revolutionary offensive. Radical critics overestimated the degree to which such an unabashed exercise of great power neo-colonialism might provoke a backlash and deepen local radicalism. Few would disagree with the diplomat who remarked in 1982 that, 'this place is too vulnerable and disorganized to play the role that it is being assigned by Washington. You're pushing Honduras into the line of fire. You can't destabilize Nicaragua any more from here without also destabilizing Honduras.'[10] Yet over the following five years that destabilization remained within tolerable limits and was viewed by Washington as an acceptable cost – 'collateral damage' – for the successes scored against the left in El Salvador and Nicaragua. Moreover, the failure of the Cinchonero guerrilla in 1981–82 and that of the PRTC in 1983 provided sober illustrations of the weakness of the strategy of armed struggle in Honduras no less than did the high turnout in the elections of 1980, 1981 and 1985. There can be no doubt that under Reagan's policies Honduran social and political life experienced unprecedented polarization and confusion, but the country has not suffered a crisis of the order witnessed elsewhere. The model of inexorable collapse based primarily upon external factors was not borne out.

On the other hand, supporters and practitioners of Washington's operation based excessively optimistic expectations on the legacy of fruit company hegemony and failed to appreciate that their own very different intervention drew other conflicts across the border as well as acting as a source of discontent and destabilization in itself. If the left failed to establish a guerrilla campaign in 1981–83, popular disturbance did not wane, mobilization through strikes, land occupations and mass protests being higher in the 1980s than in any other Central American state. Although the Liberal and National Parties retained their monopoly over the formal political sphere, they also entered a possibly irreversible phase of organizational decomposition and ideological confusion as economic crisis, the foreign presence and military arbitration eroded the traditional structures of *caudillismo* and patronage as well as subverting pretensions to representative democracy and an authentic division of powers. Whether it be the destructive marauding of Contra troops in the border zones, sanctioned incursions by Salvadorean forces, the epidemic of prostitution and venereal disease in the ghastly penumbra of the US base at Comayagua, the disingenuous disclaimers of the proconsul who is Washington's ambassador, or the futile trips to the US capital by presidents and generals to squeeze more aid out of their Faustian bargain with the North Americans, the constant demonstrations of national powerlessness did not simply confirm Honduran subjugation. They also exercised critical effects within the country that complicate that subjugation, albeit not to the degree or with the rapidity expected by the left. Despite the fact that its political projections are ostensibly more modest, the model of passivity based upon local traditions is no less flawed than that of polarization drawn from regional trends. It underestimates the degree of autonomy required by the political class to maintain a tenuous grip on legitimacy and it assumes that the degree of alien intromission is infinitely flexible so long as its outward form remains distinct from that taken in the period of regional dictatorships; nationalist sentiment is erroneously identified with the conditions of political violence.

Whether viewed primarily in terms of its impact upon the regional balance of forces or in those of domestic politics, the occupation of Honduras as Washington's forward military base has been the central feature of national life in the 1980s. This, together with the absence of a structural crisis of the order registered in the neighbouring states, has encouraged depiction of the country in terms of what it is not rather than what it is. The severe restraints upon national sovereignty and absence of a revolutionary movement are certainly coherent objects of study, yet neither can be properly understood in negative terms or without an appreciation of the domestic factors that underpin them as well as the exogenous factors that make them meaningful. Identification of the country as weak and poor is a necessary but insufficient task and tends to be made in relative and quantitative rather than intrinsic and qualitative terms. (Indeed, sometimes these features receive such insistent emphasis that one almost feels compelled to protest that Hondurans are taller and better players of sport than their neighbours.) There is a danger in emphasizing the debility of the state without presenting the strength of civil society; stressing the absence of modern political parties whilst ignoring the importance of corporate representation; itemizing the inadequacies of road and rail communications yet passing over a relatively advanced aviation system. None of these corollaries is a mere compensation but rather an integral part of the equation; each indicates a singular experience of combined and uneven development. Honduras may not be modern but she lives in the present; she may be backward but is less petrified in the past than expressive of her history. The problem with the standard radical and reactionary perspectives outlined above is that they share the notion that the country is subject to a chronological delay, somehow 'behind in time'. Accordingly, while many on the left place misguided hopes upon a 'great leap forward' (shades of Stalin as well as Mao, but no party), the forces of reaction fail to recognize the peculiar tensions and contradictions of traditional structures that exist in a contemporary environment.

The stock explanation as to why, unlike in the surrounding states, these tensions have not yet snapped is that the greater availability of land for subsistence in Honduras ensured a 'passivity' on the part of the peasantry. This argument is not without some validity, public land being more extensive than elsewhere and particularly so compared to El Salvador (see

Table 50, p. 559). However, as has already been seen in chapter 5, much of this land is of very poor quality and was not simply 'available' for redistribution without major struggles; pressure on the subsistence circuit rose considerably in the 1960s with the result that the rural population continues to be the poorest in all mainland Latin America except Bolivia.[11] This state of affairs did not so much provoke an insurrectionary movement – the peasant 'rebels' of 1965 were engaged in a decidedly defensive endeavour – as encourage collective organization and a growing tendency to direct occupation of both state and private lands in mobilization that forced the agrarian reforms of 1962, 1972 and 1975. The *campesino* movement has pursued a syndicalist and corporate rather than political and ideological course but it has been very far from passive and, as renewed *tomas* (land occupations) in 1987 indicated, it has been neither placated by the modest distribution of the 1970s nor cowed by the intermittent repression of the 1980s.

The origins of this distinctive pattern lie no less in the organization of agriculture than in the availability of land. In the first place, the existence of a powerful banana enclave on the Caribbean coast helped to delay the development of an agro-export landlord class in the interior and provided thousands of peasants with experience of waged labour, a sense of collectivism and – up to 1933 and after 1954 – trade-union organization. The natural exchange of labour between enclave and interior, on occasion abetted by large numbers of redundancies compelled by market fluctuations or technological change, carried the influence of syndicalism beyond the plantation despite the fact that the level of waged labour in the domestic agricultural system was not especially high. (The use of imported Afro-Caribbean labour had been formally prohibited in 1929.) This level rose from the 1940s along with expansion of the commercial *finca* as first coffee then, to a very limited degree, cotton were developed. The lateness and weakness of the new phase of export agriculture meant that although it combined with growth in ranching to place pressure on the subsistence circuit, it was incapable of enforcing a decisive and general shift from the patrimonialist culture and high level of reciprocity with the *ejido* that previously prevailed. As a result, the peasantry of the interior retained more of its communal strength than elsewhere, bolstering this from the 1960s with the campaign for devolution of public lands. This trajectory is emblematic of broader developments from 1950, the old and the new combining rather than existing in a parallel relationship. On the one hand, the threat of *campesino* unions to occupy the haciendas of candidates in the 1985 elections was in essence little different to the customs of militancy in the early republic or even the colonial period. On the other, the capacity of the Standard Fruit Company union to force the enterprise to fly an injured worker to the US for treatment through an overtime ban was firmly fixed in the conditions of the late twentieth century.[12]

Over the last three decades actions such as these have contributed to the establishment of a system of government based upon negotiation and co-optation allied with intermittent repression rather than one organized around constant persecution. Even under the prolonged dictatorship of López Arellano between 1963 and 1971, both urban and rural unions were dominated primarily through manipulation and division, as the colonel's first proclamation to the country indicates. After the 1969 war with El Salvador the tarnished reputation of the military made it even more reliant upon the support of the union bureaucracy, which took much of the initiative for establishing the 'National' government of 1971, was crucial to its overthrow in 1972, and, under considerable rank-and-file pressure, obliged the officer corps to undertake the reforms of 1972–75. The strength of the unions should not, however, be overemphasized. They have always remained subordinate political actors and only the 'moderate' AIFLD-backed barons of the biggest organizations – some of whom declared presidential ambitions – can properly be viewed as ex officio members of the dominant bloc. While the unusually high profile of organized labour in formal political life can be interpreted as a sign of the relative strength of the system, it is not indicative of a corresponding modernity, deriving as it does from the weakness of the state and the failure of the political parties to absorb or adequately represent the major corporate interests in civil society.

In 1987 Honduras was ruled by the same (Liberal) party that held office at the turn of the century. Although the opposition National Party may be more closely identified with the interests of landed capital, it is barely less divided than the Liberals. Both parties are still strongly attached to the localism and *caudillismo* associated with regional politics in the oligarchic era even though the manorial writ has never matched company patronage as a source of authority. The persistence of pre-modern dependence upon distribution of the posts and contracts of a state treated no less as a source of booty than as an instrument of class strategy is reflected by nondescript tussles over ideology and constant factionalism. Since the restitution of civilian administration in 1981 these attributes have become even more marked, the political class conducting a giddy pirouette as it endeavours simultaneously to sustain the old rules of competition and partisanship, hold on to some legitimacy in the face of overbearing US presence and military invigilation, and undertake the inescapable tasks of government with a quotient of gravitas now that it is subjected to unaccustomed international scrutiny. The least autonomous and truculent of the regional dominant blocs, it has enjoyed something of a new lease of life under Washington's patronage, but this sponsorship has not entailed any genuine renovation or reorganization, simply guaranteeing a system that shows a strong tendency to internal disaggregation and exhaustion.

The transfer from military to civilian rule in 1980–81 was in itself largely unproblematic and owed less to Washington's agency than did similar exchanges elsewhere. Whilst the political parties held office for only two years in the previous seventeen, the military had failed to establish a stable and systematic form of institutional rule, generally preferring to rely upon the counsel and support of the National Party than to adopt the obvious alternative of setting up an independent organization, as occurred in Guatemala and El Salvador. First entering government in 1956, logistically very weak, and lacking the long coercive traditions of its regional peers, the army was neither required nor able to impose a dictatorial regime sharply differentiated from the civilian administrations of the 1950s and early 1960s. Indeed, while it occasionally dispensed with the services of the legislature, the military's preparedness to recognize corporate representation may be said to have facilitated a degree of popular representation at least comparable to that afforded by the constitutional regime. By the same token, although the army intervened in 1963 to thwart the possibility of reform, it returned to power in 1972 with the precise aim of introducing and enforcing reformist measures resisted by the political parties. Between 1972 and 1975 it undertook a series of progressive measures not witnessed north of Panama since 1954, causing considerable consternation amongst its neighbours and giving rise to the expectation that the era of traditional partisan competition had passed. Just as the earlier effort at forging an anti-Communist regime through dictatorship failed to suppress the established norms of political exchange, so also did the project of progressive bonapartism founder upon interests that were vested deep in civil society and more predictably defended by powerful forces.The newfound collectivism and populism of the officer corps was shown to be exceptionally fragile, and as the military beat a retreat along the path of conservative personalism it became increasingly apparent that it could not feasibly aspire to a role beyond that of arbitrating between the National and Liberal Parties, with which it shared many characteristics.

These broad features would appear to confirm the argument that Honduras is safely ensconced in its 'political culture' with a series of socio-institutional checks and balances providing a safeguard against critical disequilibrium even if also preserving abject poverty and extreme weakness in relation to the outside world. However, that conservation of social order which has been achieved over recent decades has been tenuous, riven with confusion and frantic manoeuvre, and far more dynamic in character than any comfortable teleology can comprehend.

Change and Negotiation, 1950–63

The post-war political transitions resulting elsewhere from the crises of 1944–50 were delayed in Honduras. The anti-dictatorial movement was the weakest in the region and Carías comfortably able to secure the victory of the National Party and his Minister of Defence Juan Manuel Gálvez in the elections of October 1948, boycotted by the Liberals because of the lack of guarantees. Indeed, of all the autocrats of the 1930s Carías alone survived both physically and politically into the modern era; at seventy-eight years of age he orchestrated the 1963 election campaign of a party which he had founded forty years before. The poll was never held, being prevented by a military coup which finally brought the political role of the army into line with that of its counterparts insofar as it opened a long period of institutional government. Although the armed forces had already taken power in 1956–57, their action on that occasion had been directed primarily towards arbitrating competition between the civilian parties and establishing the conditions for elections, which, if not precisely free, at least provided the formal opposition with a chance of victory. It can, therefore, be said that the emergence of the military as a consolidated member of the dominant bloc occurred at least fifteen years later than elsewhere. Furthermore, its conduct reflected the different political climate of the period since the new wave of anti-Communism was less dependent upon blanket repression and more inclined to co-optation than was that of the late 1940s. By the time López Arellano took power in 1963 governments of both the political parties had achieved some modest success in developing the state apparatus, establishing a degree of autonomy from the fruit companies, and moving tentatively away from the torpor and rigidity of the sixteen-year *cariato*.

The material constraints upon such progress were enormous. With a very small and young coffee industry, Honduras was unable fully to exploit the post-war buoyancy in price despite the generous quotas it had been allocated under the Pan-American coffee agreement. The growth of the country's principal export – bananas – was negative between 1945 and 1953 whilst the expansion of cotton was of significance only relative to its previous level, having little effect upon overall receipts from trade. Manufacturing industry continued to be the most backward in Central America, its growth critically impaired by the tax-free imports sold in fruit company stores as well as by the absence of local surplus capital for reinvestment. In 1948 per capita GDP was still less than its pre-war peak; in 1950 only 10 per cent of a population of 1.4 million lived in communities of over 10,000 people, Tegucigalpa (72,400) being no more than a modest provincial town and San Pedro Sula (21,200) barely even that.[13] Even by 1957 the capital possessed only 6,000 vehicles and lacked a railway or a landing strip that could accommodate jet aircraft.[14] Nonetheless, both the effects of the war and those limited advances registered in production and trade from the mid 1940s permitted some escape from the stagnation of the Carías years. Faced with the loss of agricultural imports from Asia after 1942, the US government had sought an alternative source of supply in Latin America, Washington encouraging the banana companies to transfer some of their plantations to the cultivation of rubber, abacá and African palm, which accounted for a significant portion of Honduran export revenue at the close of the war. Equally, the country had been eligible for support for road construction, and US military engineers completed the highway around Lake Yojoa that finally connected Tegucigalpa with the northern rail network. In a different sphere, the excoriating criticism of backward and corrupt administration of national finances levelled by the 1943 Bernstein Commission laid the basis for the comprehensive reorganization of economic management of the state proposed by the IMF after its 1949 visit. As a result of these initiatives the Gálvez administration established in 1950 both a central bank, which permitted adequate circulation of the lempira for the first time since its introduction in 1931, and a development bank (BANAFOM), which provided a modicum of credit for agriculture and infrastructural support (warehousing and market outlets) that had long been ignored by the private banks. These modest measures gave central government at least a rudimentary apparatus through which to regulate that sector of the economy that operated upon the basis of official transactions in the domestic market; in 1951 an overwhelmingly agricultural country was finally provided with a ministry of agriculture.

The weakness of this incipient state structure can be grasped from the fact that in 1950 its total budget stood at 50 million lempiras whilst the local operations of UFCO and Standard Fruit (SF) produced a turnover of L48.6 million.[15] In 1951 the companies accounted for 91 per cent of all tax revenue from income and profits.[16] On the other hand, the stagnation of the banana trade and the expansion of the state did result in some diminution of the extraordinary degree of dependence that had hitherto prevailed. The last direct company loan to the government – $1 million from UFCO's subsidiary the Tela Railroad Company (TRRC) – was made in 1949, the same year in which the Gálvez regime introduced an income tax law that underwrote the increase in government expenditure from L24.8 million in 1949 to L60.8 million in 1954 ($1 = L2) and reduced the companies' share of income and profits tax to 12 per cent.[17] The corporations' acceptance of this long delayed tax was only secured, it might be noted, once the government agreed to grant major fiscal concessions to their non-banana operations, which, with bananas falling to less than half of exports in 1954, amounted to a more significant compromise on the part of the state than it might appear in retrospect. There was, then, no decisive shift in the balance of power, the effects of the measures of the late 1940s and early 1950s being less to curb corporate dominion than to augment the resources of a still supplicant state.

Nonetheless, the era of absolute corporate hegemony was on the wane with company influence being progressively replaced by that of the US government. This was evident in the economic missions of the 1940s and most vividly illustrated by the bilateral agreement on military aid signed in May 1954, just prior to the Guatemalan intervention and at the peak of the great plantation strike in Honduras. Under this treaty Honduras agreed to guarantee a supply of basic goods at favourable prices in the event of US shortages. It also committed itself to the defence of the US through the provision of troops, whose upkeep would be borne by the impecunious Central American state. In return Washington offered military aid and training but refused to reciprocate the extraordinary terms of Honduran military support on the grounds that this issue was already allowed for under the Rio treaties of 1947. The failure of the US to meet these obligations in 1969 during the war with El Salvador (which had no comparable treaty) made the 1954 accord infamous long before it was employed as the legal framework for Washington's intervention in the 1980s.[18]

At the time the military treaty appeared to be an unremarkable document fully in keeping with the political temper of the day and no more leonine than previous agreements made by the fruit companies. It provided the basis upon which the armed forces would be modernized to meet the challenge of both reformist Guatemala and El Salvador (the border with which was contested), and it bolstered the so-called '*ley fernanda*', a catch-all anti-communist statute of 1946 dubbed after its congressional sponsor, Fernando Zepeda Durón. It was not Gálvez but his vice president, Julio Lozano Díaz, who ratified and was identified with the 1954 agreement. In fact, despite his longstanding links with the companies, Carías and the PN, Gálvez oversaw a markedly conciliatory regime, breaking with the old dictator to form an independent party bloc that would later mutate into the *Movimiento Nacional Reformista* (MNR), adopting a populist style, and permitting the Liberals freedom of press and organization that they had not enjoyed for over twenty years. This effort at restoring the competitive element to partisanship came too late for the Liberal *caudillo* Angel Zúñiga Huete – trounced in the 1948 poll as he had been in that of 1932 – but it offered some space for a new generation that sought under the leadership of Ramón Villeda Morales to suppress the traditions of insurrection and attach itself to the current of constitutionalism and reform visible in the surrounding countries from 1944. Gálvez's rupture of the National bloc was directed principally against the personal influence of Carías and fell well short of liquidating established affiliations while restraining Liberal conspiracy and providing a 'third force' at a time when the army was still incapable of so doing.[19] There was a price to be paid for such mediation taking the form of intra-party dispute and reorganization since its natural effect was precisely to enhance partisan manoeuvre and thus the instability of a system built upon the spoils of office and lacking any precedent for yielding these to the opposition without external intervention. (Carías's initial electoral victory could be argued to be an exception, but it was forcefully underwritten by UFCO.) The limits of Gálvez's attempt to inject some equilibrium into this equation were fully demonstrated in the presidential elections of October 1954, from which the president, arguing ill health, had already divorced himself by handing office over to Lozano and leaving the country. Fortified by the division in the National bloc between Carías (79,648 votes) and the MNR's Abraham Williams Calderón (53,241), and receiving great popular support in the north for its discernibly more progressive attitude to the sixty-nine-day plantation strike of the early summer, the PL won the single largest number of votes (122,312) for the candidacy of Villeda Morales. Yet if the poll itself had been generally free of fraudulent practices – these being particularly difficult to orchestrate in a three-way contest – neither the PN nor the MNR was prepared to ratify Villeda Morales's victory in congress, thereby allowing Lozano to exploit Carías's *continuista* constitution of 1936, declare himself 'Chief of State' and rule through an advisory council in a manner akin to that witnessed in 1902 and 1923 (on each occasion the cause of further, increased conflict) and barely conducive to either stability or legitimacy.[20]

In one sense Lozano's regime was little different to that of Gálvez since it originated from undemocratic procedure and lacked a decisive partisan bias. (Carías was moved to comment, 'I don't know how it is possible that Julio Lozano has fallen so much in love with power. It is true that I was president of Honduras for sixteen years, but that was because they made me.'[21]) On the other hand, the Lozano government was significantly more anti-communist and repressive than that of Gálvez and throughout its two-year term never escaped the influence of the 1954 strike. This was to a great degree responsible for the boycott of the Liberal victory, viewed by the PN and MNR as tantamount to one of the radical forces thrown up by the dispute. The importance of constitutional manipulation, haggling over the separation of powers and retention of office for its own sake should not be underestimated. Even though formal government was infrequently co-substantial with real power, the rewards of administration itself had greater purchase in Honduran politics than elsewhere and were to be an important factor in the crises of 1971–72 and 1985. All the same, the manoeuvres of 1954–57 were most directly determined by the entry of the plantation proletariat on to the political scene.

The strike of May to July 1954 is sometimes presented as an essentially political phenomenon, the rank-and-file committees centred on the company town of El Progreso being identified as the core of a 'commune of the north' and agents of an independent political authority in the enclave that established a virtual state of dual power. Both the long-term and immediate political impact of the mobilization was indeed appreciable. Not only did the strike directly engender the modern trade-union movement but it also owed much to earlier agitation by the radical *Partido Democrático Revolucionario Hondureño* (PDRH), founded in 1944 under Guatemalan influence and with Communist affinities; the PCH itself was formally re-established with PDRH support in April 1954, shortly prior to the onset of the conflict. Moreover, the strike occurred just as the CIA and Castillo Armas were launching their coup against Arbenz, accusations of Guatemalan promotion of worker discontent providing Tegucigalpa with a convenient excuse for permitting the invasion to be staged from Honduran territory in a telling precedent for the Contra campaign thirty years later. Yet, while both Guatemalan influence and PCH involvement are evident, the strike originated from widespread rank-and-file discontent and it maintained a resolutely syndicalist form throughout its course. This explains its length, the relative absence of repression on the part of a government unwilling entirely to alienate the northern population, and the subsequent emergence of new trade-union organization that far outstripped the influence of the left.[22]

The original stoppage by stevedores of the TRRC stemmed from the company's failure to comply with Gálvez's Decree 96 of March 1949 that required payment of double time on public holidays. The strike at Tela on 10 April 1954 spread first to Puerto Cortés and then, when the leaders of the movement were fired, to the entire labour force at El Progreso. By the first week of May some 25,000 workers had stopped work, UFCO refusing to negotiate on the grounds that the strike was a subversive plot. Over the following days 10,000 Standard Fruit workers also walked out in demand for a 50 per cent wage claim, but the SF union leadership was weaker and less politically organized than that of the TRRC workers, agreeing to a disadvantageous return to work just as the TRRC lead was being taken up by factory workers in San Pedro Sula and the miners at Rosario's new El Mochito camp (opened in 1948 to replace San Juancito) as well as receiving the support of the town's small commerce and white-collar sectors. By the middle of May the strength of the movement had brought the north of the country to a complete halt and clearly precluded resolution through state coercion; meanwhile its demands had predictably mutated from those for specific terms of employment to that for the right to organize legally recognized unions. Although UFCO was obliged to succumb to a number of the original demands, the government bolstered its anti-communist propaganda by encouraging the establishment of non-radical worker committees, to which the promise of union recognition was immediately extended. The intransigence of the company initially thwarted this approach, and the *Comité Central de Huelga* advised by José Pineda Gómez of the PDRH retained its popular authority, but by early June government-backed forces led by the teacher Manuel Valencia succeeded in dividing the leadership, expelling the left and agreeing to negotiation. In mid June, by which time the economic pressure on the strikers was considerable and many of the radical leaders, such as César Augusto Coto, were in gaol, the new CCH agreed to a wage rise of 10–15 per cent (as opposed to the 50 per cent originally demanded) without any guarantees against reprisals in return for the promise of trade union rights.

The concession of these rights owed much to the intervention of George Meany, president of the US AFL, who had forcefully indicated to UFCO's executive vice president Joseph Montgomery the desirability of recognizing the anti-communist CCH so as to avoid giving the 'totalitarian communists' uncontested claim to worker organization and a monopoly of popular sympathy. UFCO's senior adviser Thomas Corcoran was eventually won round to this view, the invasion of Guatemala no doubt underlying his observation that it was 'only a matter of time before international and anti-communist trade-union organization comes to control Honduras and the rest of the region'.[23] As a result, it was under the auspices of the AFL–CIO and ORIT (now speedily recognized by Honduras) that a ministry of labour was set up (October 1954) and the workers of the TRRC were organized into SITRATERCO whilst those of SF formed SITRASFRUCO, both unions receiving official recognition in 1955. Over the next five years a further seventy-seven unions were recognized, and although the officially unionized labour force amounted to about one per cent of the total economically active population, the fact that corporate worker organization was permitted for the first time in thirty years was in itself a signal development.[24]

The new unions emerged under profoundly ambiguous conditions since a strike that had been unprecedented in its manifestation of collective organization and radical mobilization also ended in defeat. In the first place, the original rank-and-file leadership of the movement was displaced by a new bureaucracy co-opted by the government from its inception and subsequently schooled in the responsible etiquette of 'free and democratic' syndicalism by the AFL–CIO (after 1962 through AIFLD) and ORIT, which under the leadership of Luis Alberto Monge (subsequently president of Costa Rica) had given full backing to the Guatemalan intervention and would later support the reactionary coups in Brazil and the Dominican Republic. The control of this new leadership over the most advanced sector of the country's working class was supported by US funds and training and reinforced by the 1959 labour code, which prohibited the existence of more than one union in each enterprise and thus stymied efforts at independent organization by the left. As a result, the strongly pro-US Oscar Gale Varela dominated SITRATERCO from 1957 to 1974 whilst SITRASFRUCO enjoyed only slightly more autonomy under the prolonged rule of Víctor Artiles and Saúl Martínez Guzmán, both ORIT apparatchiks. This domination was by no means unchallenged. Having rejected informal parallel organization and recaptured the leadership of SITRASFRUCO, the PCH temporarily gained control of the federation of all the northern unions, FESITRANH, in the early 1960s. But the left was decisively ousted from both bodies by the coup of October 1963, and with the exception of progressive control of SITRATERCO from 1975 to 1981, all the major unions remained under the direction of a bureaucracy which, if not constantly pro-government, was resolutely anti-communist.[25] The difficulties experienced by this leadership in retaining its authority in the early 1960s derived largely from the fact that, having failed to insist upon guarantees against victimization and redundancies in the negotiations of June 1954, it presided over a headlong retreat of the labour movement throughout the rest of the decade as the companies mechanized and cut back their workforce. Between 1953 and 1957 TRRC reduced its payroll from 26,000 to 13,000, firing 10,000 people in the year that SITRATERCO was founded.[26] The loss of a third of SF's 9,000 workers over two years with only minor instances of agitation also demonstrated the weak organization of a banana proletariat that in 1952 comprised 20 per cent of the waged labour force. In the space of four years approximately half the plantation labour force was made redundant, the majority of workers returning to subsistence agriculture where average income was roughly one third of that in the enclave.[27] This faction of the rural proletariat had been radicalized by the strike and poorly defended by the new union leadership, from whose clutches it was perforce freed with the result that the *campesinado* of both the north and the interior began to manifest alarming signs of independence by the late 1950s.

The fruit companies' counter-offensive is sometimes depicted as a purely anti-union move yet the increase in productivity (from 552 boxes per worker in 1950–54 to 1,030 in 1960–64) was not solely the result of enhanced exploitation. It derived equally from recovery from disease, greater use of aerial spraying, and mechanization, which, together with improved market conditions, produced a rise in production per hectare from 849 boxes in 1950–54 to 1,154 in 1960–64.[28] While the enclave labour force did not regain its numerical strength of the early 1950s for thirty years and was progressively reduced in proportion to the workforce as a whole by accelerated population growth, the post-strike redundancies proved to be exceptional and from the early 1960s plantation employment began to rise once more. One of the prime reasons for this was the shift in cultivation from the 'Cavendish' banana to the 'Gros Michel' variety, more popular with metropolitan consumers and more resistant to disease but also an easily bruised fruit that required greater protection in shipment; it thereby compensated to some degree for the reduction in field labour by increasing that dedicated to packing. By the mid 1960s between a quarter and a third of the companies' labour force was engaged in packing, the total number of TRRC and SF workers rising from the historical low of 15,500 in 1960 to an average of 20,500 in 1971–75 and 32,800 in 1981–83.[29] Hence, despite the fall in company cultivated lands from 230,000 hectares in 1960 to 122,000 in 1975, enclave labour conserved more of its strength than appeared likely in the late 1950s. The economic gains it made were undeniably modest – SITRATERCO obtained a rise of 5 per cent in real wages between 1965 and 1973 – but the plantation unions continued to head the national labour movement and exercise pressure on the companies, both official and wildcat strikes being commonplace through to the present day.[30]

The change in political climate caused by both the strike and the overthrow of Arbenz saw a replacement of Gálvez's policy of refusing either to recognize unions or vigorously suppress them by Lozano's strategy of simultaneously extending official recognition, imposing tight controls, and repressing both the radical and Liberal opposition. Within six months of the formation of SITRASFRUCO renewed agitation amongst SF workers was met with decisive police action that succeeded in weeding out left-wing activists where the union leadership had failed. A month later Lozano issued Decree 206, the *Ley de Defensa del Régimen Democrático*, which was similar to the anti-communist statutes in force elsewhere (including Costa Rica) in its prohibition of 'the existence or organization of the Communist Party and any association, entity or movement, whatever title it may adopt, that by the spoken or written word aspires to implant in the nation a regime opposed to democracy'.[31] In practice the PCH was too young and weak to constitute a major threat and its activities were not greatly affected by the formal declaration of outlaw status; erratic publication of broadsheets and more constant organization of radical union caucuses continued much as before. The Liberals, by contrast, were highly vulnerable to any measure that restricted the rights of opposition since activists in the north had supported the strike and the party had generally closer ties with the labour movement than did the National bloc; the latter was too closely identified with the landlord interest and had been in power for too long to expand the instrumentalist recognition of a few unions into systematic co-optation. Neither Lozano's 1955 Charter of Labour Guarantees (which the Liberal 1959 labour code would consolidate rather than replace) nor his increase of the tax on banana company profits to 30 per cent from the 15 per cent imposed by Gálvez in 1949, nor even the granting of female suffrage succeeded in altering party loyalties despite popular support for these important measures. Lozano was too zealously dedicated to the causes of anti-Communism and *continuismo* to imbue necessary moves towards modernity with a wider sense of virtue.

Increased repression of Liberal opposition from early 1956 together with well-founded expectations that the regime would fix the constituent assembly elections planned for October of that year provoked a group of Liberal activists to resort to an old-style insurrection, taking temporary control of the capital's San Francisco barracks in August. The unusually bloody suppression of this ill-organized revolt – at least ninety people were killed – not only confirmed Carías's elimination of partisan rebellion as a viable strategem but also threatened the onset of that systematic violence which Honduras alone had managed to avoid in the post-war period. Yet Lozano was not moved to temper his policies; the PL was both formally permitted to fight the October poll and harassed at every turn by the *Partido de Unidad Nacional* (PUN) coalition formed by the president in 1955 on the basis of the MNR and anti-Carías factions of the PN. Following a turnout that was suspiciously high even allowing for the enfranchisement of women, the PUN received a formidable 89.4 per cent of the vote (370,318 votes) against the Liberals' 10.1 per cent (41,724) and a desultory 0.5 per cent (2,003) for the rump of the PN. The fraud was transparent. With both traditional parties denouncing Lozano's already illegal and increasingly unpopular regime and the prospect of further violence quite manifest, the army was obliged to intervene. On 21 October General Roque Rodríguez, commander of the military academy, took power at the head of a junta whose only declared objective was the return of constitutional government through new elections. In this spirit political prisoners were released and exiles allowed to return. The anti-communist law was retained but the armed forces had entered the political arena for the first time on a plainly constitutionalist platform, with the support of the traditional parties, and in opposition to what was broadly deemed to be an excessively authoritarian and personalist regime. As a consequence, the coup was highly popular and, unlike the comparable intervention of 1944 in El Salvador, its aims were fulfilled in short order and without violence. Limited and corrective in character, this initial political foray by the military was quite different in form to that witnessed in the other states.

There has been a tendency to attribute to the coup of 1956 and the junta of 1956–57 a greater political and institutional consistency than was the case. The 'professionalism' of the military was still germinal despite the establishment of the basic infantry school in 1946 and the foundation of the Francisco Morazán military academy in 1952, both under US supervision. The academy did not provide the rudiments of a civilian curriculum until 1956, had to be entirely reorganized the following year, and did not regularly send its cadets to the Canal Zone for some time thereafter.[32] Training for the airforce had a longer and more stable history but this was primarily due to the greater technical skills required, and in the 1950s the force possessed less than 300 personnel and 50 pilots. At the end of his rule Lozano was reported to have personally appointed the majority of the military's 271 majors, many of whom occupied profitable public positions and upheld a system of personalist local government that had become the norm under Carías and was most marked in the parochial despotism exercised by Carlos Sanabria in Colón.[33] This system has never been fully suppressed – in mid 1987 Honduran Miskitos threatened to rebel against the administration of Gracias a Díos as a personal fiefdom by Colonel Eric Sánchez, commander of the Fifth Infantry battalion – and it was only from the late 1950s that it was subjected to a modicum of institutional oversight and regulation.[34] Indeed, the leader of the 1956 coup, General Rodríguez, firmly belonged to the old school of *caudillismo*, this eventually leading to his removal from the junta for 'playing politics'. However, he was still able to create quite a stir with threats of rebellion scantily veiled beneath heated invectives against the 'dishonour' and 'mediocrity' of those upstarts who had ousted him. The ability of dissident senior officers to stage a challenge in their own name was not entirely eroded; under the succeeding Liberal government Colonel Armando Velázquez was perpetually engaged in conspiracy and his *golpe* of July 1959 was a sufficiently dangerous effort to cast doubt upon the depth of institutional unity and modern professionalism.

Those important steps made towards these objectives by the junta of 1956–57 were very largely the responsibility of Colonel Oswaldo López Arellano, who was instrumental in removing Rodríguez and later entered the junta to replace the populist Major Roberto Gálvez Barnes, son of the former president and representative of the airforce. Major Gálvez had displayed a disconcerting independence in clashing with SF during a strike at La Ceiba in March 1957, personally mediating the dispute in a manner not unfavourable to the workers; his flexible attitude allowed other sectors, such as the sugar workers, to make gains perfectly in line with Lozano's labour legislation but scarcely in keeping with the spirit of the anti-communist decree.[35] Fifteen years later López Arellano would himself adopt positions very similar to those of Gálvez junior, but at this juncture he intervened decisively to consolidate the disorganized forces of conservatism, curb populist outbursts, and, most importantly, confirm the institutional authority of the armed forces. Hitherto the senior commands and major military postings had been firmly in the gift of the presidency and openly manipulated for political ends; under the new organic law drafted by López Arellano and subsequently incorporated into the 1957 constitution the officer corps was given the right to nominate the commander-in-chief through the *Consejo Superior de Defensa Nacional* whilst the general staff received total independence in filling all other positions. The power of the executive was further limited by the requirement (Article 319 of the constitution) that any dispute over its decisions with respect to the military – decisions that were, significantly, to be 'respected' rather than obeyed – should be submitted to congress and resolved by majority vote. The full consequences of this loss of civilian authority over the military were not made clear until 1963, but the move was consistent with the army's role in 1956–57 and subsequently provided the means by which the military retained its independence in a political system that hovered uneasily between dictatorship (which required no responsibility to civilian authority but taxed a weak institutional structure) and constitutional government (which entailed a formal division of powers and yet could no longer safely subsist without privileged guarantees for the armed forces). The 1957 measures were, therefore, more than mere statutory devices. They firmly incorporated the military into the political system without surrendering civilian control over governmental office, as in El Salvador, or leaving it open to intermittent negotiation and crisis, as in Guatemala. The insufficiencies of this mechanism for meeting the demands of control were reflected in the fact that the army governed Honduras directly for much of the next three decades and López Arellano exercised a dominant personal influence over national political life for far longer than his ten years as president.

Although the Liberal Party possessed a strong anti-militarist contingent, the Villeda Morales leadership was prepared to accept the new terms of military organization, which worried it a good deal less than did the traditionally partisan police force of the regional *comandantes*. In the event, regular troops replaced these units in overseeing the September 1957 poll for a new constituent assembly, allowing relatively unhampered expression of support for a party that had been out of office for twenty-five years and promised a series of major socio-economic reforms. The National bloc could make some plausible claims for its record of economic regeneration and innovative legislation but its popularity was critically impaired by its authoritarianism, and even support from the bourgeoisie was diminished by the conservatives' reluctance to embrace economic integration with the rest of Central America, seen at the time as a project of enormous potential. Unchallenged to the left, the PL took 62 per cent of the ballot (209,109 votes), making the division of its opponents (PN – 30 per cent; MNR – 8 per cent) purely academic. Even with a fourteen-seat majority in the fifty-eight-seat assembly the Liberal deputies needed López Arellano's good offices to permit the indirect election of Villeda Morales as president and thus avoid three polls in as many years. In more precarious circumstances such a technically illegal move would undoubtedly have excited a crisis but the army had no cause to seek further complications, the PN was in disarray and some danger of complete marginalization, and Eisenhower's White House saw no need for two elections when one would clearly suffice.

The Villeda Morales administration (1957–63) has been likened to the original Liberal reform governments because of its ambitious legislative programme and attachment to the cause of modernization. In practice it went little further than extending the measures already taken by its Nationalist and military predecessors, albeit with a more open political style and in an international atmosphere more conducive to innovation; Villeda Morales was in many respects the perfect junior partner envisaged by Kennedy's Alliance for Progress. The 1959 labour code, a new social security law, and even the economic legislation of 1958 encouraged the right to attack Villeda as a closet Communist despite the fact that the first measure consolidated Lozano's statutes and yielded few new gains to the unions, the second taxed the banana companies harder than the domestic employers, and the third provided tax relief and investment guarantees. The government did, however, deepen state intervention in the economy, increase the external debt fivefold to fund the road construction programme begun by the junta, and adopt a conciliatory approach to both continued industrial disputes in the enclave and the worrying emergence of land occupations.[36] The PCH characterized the administration led by a man nicknamed '*pajarito*' (little bird) as 'puny', more progressive in word than deed, and constantly at the beck and call of the State Department. It also recognized that the PL did not defend the *latifundista* interest as faithfully as did the PN and was split in its attitude to the labour movement.[37] Villeda Morales himself was strongly anti-communist and became more so in the wake of the Cuban revolution: 'Central America is just a pistol shot from communized Cuba . . . we are supporters of peace but the cancer represented by the regime imposed upon Cuba must be eradicated, whatever the cost.'[38] Well before the nature of the Cuban regime had become clear the president confirmed the limits of his new liberalism by issuing Decree 183 (July 1959), which emulated the repressive statutes of 1946 and 1956 in prohibiting 'the publication and circulation of destructive doctrines that undermine the basis of the Democratic State' and imposing a rigorous censorship.[39] The Liberal government made more extensive use than its predecessors of the internal and external controls provided by 'free and democratic' trade unionism, which was greatly assisted by the creation of AIFLD in 1962. The fact that these controls failed to check the recovery of the left in SITRASFRUCO and were thoroughly inadequate for the containment of rising discontent amongst the *campesinado* compelled Villeda Morales to move towards the promulgation of an agrarian reform, this pre-emptive measure paradoxically but predictably ensuring the president's 'Communist' reputation amongst the right.

In the late 1950s and early 1960s the focus of peasant unrest was largely in the north of the country although the expansion of cotton had produced occasional agitation in the departments of Choluteca and Valle in the south. At first the regime welcomed the formation of local rural unions, primarily in the department of Yoro, supposing them to be little more than an extension of the enclave organizations to ex-workers settled on unused company property or lands bordering it. However, the influence of the PCH in the *Federación Nacional de Campesinos Hondureños* (FENACH), established by the local bodies at El Progreso in August 1962, reflected a much less stable position in which many redundant plantation workers were facing expulsion from lands leased to them upon dismissal and now required as pasture for the companies' expanding cattle interests. Neither beef nor cotton production underwent rapid acceleration until the mid 1960s but cattle exports to the US began in 1958 and the initial impact of the shift to grazing was borne by a peasantry both familiar with collective organization and highly vulnerable by virtue of the informal terms of its tenancy or squatter status (in 1952 133,561 hectares, or 5.3 per cent of cultivated land, was occupied without any legal form of tenure).[40] The government had perceived the dangers of this situation well before the emergence of FENACH, presenting its reform bill in April 1962. Even at the start of the Alliance for Progress this was an adventurous move. Nevertheless, with between a third and a half of national land formally in the public domain and a very modest but relatively successful precedent for state-sponsored cooperativization – begun with the 1949 Guanchías association for redundant enclave workers in 1949 and consolidated in the *Dirección de Fomento Cooperativo* (1955) – Honduras possessed greater scope for redistribution than her neighbours. Villeda Morales still faced the problem that his bill enabling the new *Instituto Nacional Agraria* (INA; 1961) to retrieve *ejido* lands and oblige landlords to improve production or face expropriation posed a direct threat to the fruit companies whose longstanding concessions included much common land to which they possessed no legally defensible title. Furthermore, the fact that the proposed legislation identified low exploitation of land as the principal criterion for expropriation and set no upper limit for property subject to alienation struck directly at the interests of foreign enterprises that habitually maintained tens of thousands of hectares in fallow well beyond the needs of safeguarding against disease or storm damage. Thus, although appreciably milder than Arbenz's 1952 measure, the legislation excited a sharp opposition campaign by UFCO in particular, prompting the intervention of US Ambassador Charles Burrows, who pointedly advised Villeda that the reform should not be ratified until the State Department gave its imprimatur. Despite strong lobbying by company supporters in both parties the president attempted to force his original bill through, but when the TRRC began to wind down its operations in earnest Villeda was obliged to travel to Miami and negotiate amendments with UFCO so that the final version of the reform ratified in September 1962 made it effectively impossible to expropriate land that was currently held in private hands. As a consequence, the great popular expectations of the bill were disappointed and an insignificant amount of property changed ownership (see Table 49, p. 559).[41]

The Liberal government was from the outset determined that redistribution should not result from independent organization in the countryside. Unable to co-opt the small but pugnacious FENACH, the regime encouraged AFL plans to set up a pro-government alternative, the *Asociación Nacional de Campesinos Hondureños* (ANACH). This was constituted in La Lima (Cortés) under the auspices of SITRATERCO in September 1962, which arrangement far from coincidentally enabled the president to travel north and sign the final reform decree in the union offices and deliver it ceremoniously to ANACH's first general secretary. This unambiguous signal of government patronage was a major boon and attracted support from a *campesinado* anxious for land and increasingly won away from FENACH by the repression now visited upon its radical activists. The initial strength of ANACH lay almost exclusively in its promise as a broker for land, bureaucratic *caudillos* such as Reyes Rodríguez being able to hold a significant sector of the rural population in check on this basis throughout the 1960s. All the same, before the end of the decade the minimal level of redistribution and very limited favours within ANACH's gift had generated internal dissent and a welter of competing unions that could not be controlled as readily as opposition in the plantations.

Despite its consolidation of the apparatus of corporate co-optation, encouragement of manufacturing, infrastructural development and regional integration, its fulsome support for the Alliance for Progress and unimpeachable anti-communist bona fides, Liberalism remained a vulnerable force. Although it held the sympathies of the urban petty bourgeoisie, this was too small and the manufacturing bourgeoisie still too weak to provide a hegemonic base. Equally, the PL's support in the northern and central departments depended upon the pursuit of more adventurous policies than did the maintenance of PN strongholds in the west and south, founded upon traditional landlord clientelism. Notwithstanding its own share of landlord support, customary reliance upon placemanship and the allegiance of provincial bosses, the PL was unable to overcome the antipathy of either the rural chieftains, alarmed at the organization of the peasantry and heady reformist rhetoric, or important sectors of the army and police, aggravated by the party's longstanding anti-militarist tendencies and jealously protective of their *fueros*.

The importance of this latter factor had been enhanced by Colonel Velázquez's precipitate uprising of July 1959, supported by elements of the army and the National Police, and defeated by a combination of the presidential guard and Liberal volunteers. As a result of this coup attempt Villeda Morales had been able to qualify the loss of coercive power under the 1957 constitution by abolishing the police force, traditionally controlled by the ministry of defence, and establishing a Civil Guard, placed under the ministry of government and rapidly expanded to a 2,000-strong force of Liberal sympathizers. By 1963 clashes between the Guard and the regular army had become commonplace, the existence of the paramilitary force, which effectively replaced a Nationalist police with a Liberal constabulary (but better armed and autonomous of the military hierarchy), being an issue of pre-eminent importance for the officer corps. Moreover, in the context of continued agitation in the countryside the Liberals' choice of Modesto Rodas Alvarado as their candidate for the October 1963 election amounted to a direct challenge to the military since Rodas was a protégé of the old *caudillo* Zúñiga Huete, fiercely critical of the army's powers under Article 319 of the constitution and not backward in berating the armed forces for repressive actions. An accomplished populist, Rodas was easily able to circumvent the impediments to his candidacy organized by a worried Villeda, and his campaign was sufficiently raucous to suggest that the Liberals were returning to their militant traditions.

Confronted with a belligerent *rodismo*, which was far less radical than it sounded but would dominate the PL until the *caudillo*'s death in 1979, the National Party looked a decidedly poor electoral prospect. The 1957 result suggested that even the reunited party might be permanently excluded from office in an open electoral system; this handicap was not reduced in the slightest by the fact that Carías remained a powerful force, championing the candidacy of his son Gonzalo against the supporters of Gálvez, who would certainly have run Rodas a close race. The upshot of this dispute, which mirrored that inside the PL by pitting backward partisanship against managerialism, was a compromise in the completely lacklustre Nationalist judge Ramón Ernesto Cruz. The more prescient Nationalist politicians, most notably Ricardo Zúñiga Augustinius, whose control of the PN would henceforth match that of Rodas over the PL, recognized that this outcome could only lead to a Liberal victory, which, with Rodas at the helm, would in turn provoke a military veto. Accordingly, when López Arellano duly staged his coup ten days before the poll and with heavy casualties amongst the Civil Guard, it was the Liberals rather than the civilian parties as a whole who were the victims. Under Zúñiga the Nationalists proffered a ready alliance for the conservative colonel and would remain fastened to the army's coat-tails up until 1981.

The 1963 coup may be viewed in the same light as the other reactionary revolts of this period even though it occurred before Kennedy's assassination and the more friendly attitude taken towards military regimes by the

Johnson administration. Yet if López Arellano's rebellion reflected the impact of Cuba and the limits of developmentalist reform in the wake of the Cold War, it was most directly caused by the cul-de-sac into which the political parties had driven themselves. On the one hand, the Liberals could not simultaneously secure a popular mandate and accept military arbitration. On the other, the Nationalists, who assiduously favoured the army, were unable to win a free election. In the space of one administration the arbitration of the armed forces in 1956–57 had shown itself to be insufficient and the new division of powers enshrined in the 1957 constitution inadequate for securing both equilibrium and continuity. By opposing this arrangement the Liberals, who now represented the only viable option for an openly elected party government, obliged the military to step up its intervention and overcome the unpopularity of the Nationalists by taking them under its wing and ruling directly.

From Autocracy to Populism

With one short break in 1971–72 the armed forces ruled Honduras from 1963 to 1981. This protracted control of government suggests that the political system was little different from those in the surrounding states and that the transition back to constitutional rule in 1980–81 was a development of comparable importance. But this was not the case since from a relatively early stage the military explored and exhausted a greater number of political options than its regional counterparts. As a result, when an elected Liberal government came to office late in 1981 it was in no position to pick up where Villeda Morales left off seventeen years before or to preside over a major reorganization of the dominant bloc based upon a marked contrast between military and civilian administration. The return to constitutionalism had been on the agenda since at least 1977, less because of mass mobilization for democratic rights than because the military found itself bereft of any viable initiative after the collapse of its reformist experiment of 1972–75. Unable fully to restore the alliance with the PN that underpinned the conservative autocracy of 1963–69 and incapable of eradicating the legacy of corporatist collaboration established during the war with El Salvador, the high command was left with little option but to beat a guarded and reluctant retreat to an arbitrational role of the type it had played in 1956–57, albeit this time with a much higher profile and greater external support.

This trajectory was interrupted by a number of important crises – the 1969 war; the abortive 'government of national unity' of 1971–72; the major shift in policy and rise in popular mobilization in the reform period of 1972–75; and the predictably taxing negotiation of 'redemocratization' at the end of the decade. It is, however, possible to discern two 'long waves' of political relations that do not correspond directly to either changes in administration or government policy. The first, which runs from 1963 to 1975, can be characterized as a period in which the military endeavoured to 'break the mould' of the established political structure, seeking through a variety of policies and subordinate allies to retain its domination over the system as a whole. This it failed to do, whether through traditional party alliance (1963–69), collaboration with the corporate bodies of manufacturing industry and labour (1969–75), presiding over party coalition government (1971–72) or pursuing a populist course under its own colours (1972–75). The second phase opened with the crisis of reformism and continues today despite the very different form of government, economic circumstances and external balance of forces. Its determinant feature is the prevalence of control through veto rather than positive initiative on the part of the military, adherence to defensive positional tactics as opposed to an offensive strategy of manoeuvre. Here again one finds crises and temporary exceptions, of which the most marked was General Alvárez's attempt to establish an institutionalized autocracy or 'security state' regime between 1982 and 1984. Nevertheless, the general logic of this period is less directly that of domination than of arbitration, undeniably exercised through forceful intervention but under constraints imposed by the established domestic political actors – including the labour movement – as well as the US.

The identification of these two phases helps to explain the distinctive tempo of Honduran politics, particularly from the late 1970s when developments apparently similar to those in the rest of the region reflect a quite different balance of forces. The particular socio-economic structure of the country is evidently the determinate feature in this, yet the absence of a crisis comparable to that elsewhere should be understood in dynamic and chronological as well as structural terms. Put figuratively, Honduran political life was both 'slower' and 'faster' than that in the rest of Central America, retaining many of its pre-modern facets but also incorporating instances of unparalleled innovation. It was this combination that produced a singular pattern of lower polarization being treated with reform at an earlier stage.

On the morrow of López Arellano's 1963 coup there was no sense whatsoever of the army having effected some corrective adjustment. Perhaps the single bloodiest episode in the country's modern history, the insurrection was intended to 'abolish the political army' (Civil Guard) and, as its authors announced immediately, 'to put an end to Communist infiltration'.[42] The high command simultaneously promised a 'regime of national unity' and free elections, thereby casting doubt on the second commitment since the Liberals were the immediate target of the coup, López

Arellano depicting Villeda's regime as 'leading the country to chaos, the verge of civil war, the dominion of most base passions, institutional collapse and perhaps even the disappearance of democracy'.[43] For many officers the party undoubtedly contained a strong crypto-communist element and although it was not formally outlawed, much of the leadership was forced into exile and activists were harassed on a routine basis. López Arellano sought a return not so much to the *cariato* as to Lozano's mixture of repression with co-optation, for which the formal existence of the Liberals was necessary if only because the anti-communist union leadership remained attached to the party. On the day of the coup the new regime made clear 'its decision fully to guarantee the operation of the Labour Code, other labour legislation and the Agrarian Reform as well as to protect free and democratic trade unionism so that the mass of workers and peasants may, with the assistance of the state, gradually resolve their problems and become a natural dam against the onslaught of Communism.'[44] It is indicative of the changes of the previous decade that even at the outset the army felt constrained formally to endorse agrarian reform although in practice redistribution was brought to a halt and the staff of INA were left to twiddle their thumbs for several years. The question of labour organization could not be resolved so easily, particularly because the left had managed to recover from the setbacks of the late 1950s. López Arellano therefore combined a major offensive against the radical currents with offers of continued patronage to the bureaucracy, which was disorientated by the coup, suspicious of military intentions, and unwilling to drop its demand for elections. With the assistance of the *Mancha Brava* goon-squad, staffed by PN militants and military elements, the left was expelled from the leadership of SITRASFRUCO and the union reorganized as SUTRASFCO under an ORIT–AIFLD leadership headed by Víctor Artiles, a man who was to be a dominant figure in the union movement for the next two decades. This move was consolidated at an organizational level by the establishment of the *Federación Central de Sindicatos Libres de Honduras* (FECESITLIH), which united all the bodies under pro-US leadership.

Control of the labour movement was not easily assured, even with witch-hunts against the left and general collaboration from the 'free and democratic' bureaucracy. The problem was most acute in the countryside and particularly in the department of Yoro where FENACH continued to be active under a leadership supported by the PCH. Refusing to treat with the organization, López Arellano eventually sent in his troops to kill FENACH leader Lorenzo Zelaya and the militants who had occupied unused land and established a rudimentary system of self-defence sometimes referred to as a guerrilla (Massacre of El Jute, 30 April 1965). Although this action eliminated a number of PCH cadres and wiped out FENACH for good, it was before long shown to be insufficient for containing a peasantry formally promised but effectively denied an agrarian reform. Furthermore, within weeks of this repression the military government was confronted with the consequences of allowing unions to exist when FECESITLIH, established precisely as a collaborationist body only months earlier, called a general strike in support of the demand for a collective contract at the *Empresa Hilados y Tejidos Rio Lindo*, owned by the powerful right-wing Facusse family. The plantation unions that controlled FESITRANH dutifully refused to support this action, but economic stagnation and increased discontent amongst an expanded proletariat obliged the urban leadership to respond to rank-and-file pressure. The strike was only called off once López Arellano declared a state of siege and paramilitary forces had occupied the factory, forcing the unprepared federation into negotiations.[45] The fact that twenty-nine out of FECESITLIH's thirty-three member unions had backed the strike ruled out any simple purge of the type conducted in the wake of the coup, the regime opting for the strategy of setting up yet another confederation, the *Central de Trabajadores Hondureños* (CTH), which included ANACH in addition to FESITRANH and FECESITLIH and was thus given a powerful safeguard against dissidence on the part of urban workers.

The confidence with which López Arellano employed force against popular organization in 1965 may be attributed in part at least to his 'election' in February of that year. This poll – for a constituent assembly, like those of 1956 and 1957 – was flagrantly fraudulent despite the ability of the Liberals to field candidates and be allocated 44 per cent of the vote. Military support and their control of the electoral apparatus, which resulted in the number of votes nearly doubling from the 1957 level, gave the Nationalists a suitably modest victory and allowed the 'blues' to enter into full collaboration with López Arellano under the direction of Ricardo Zúñiga, now minister of the presidency. The failure of the Liberals to boycott the poll bestowed a more than spurious legitimacy upon the exercise and appeared to justify the view that the army had no need to set up a new party of its own or discard an easily dominated constitutional system. Indeed, despite the continual machinations of the exiled Rodas, the Liberals would not henceforth raise a serious challenge to the army, and by the end of the 1970s, when the boss was dead, none of the several factions that subsequently emerged was either willing or able to resist the lure of collaboration with the officer corps. Animosity both real and supposed was to prevail for at least a decade after the 1965 poll but the failure of this election to establish a stable system of domination owed far less to traditional partisanship than to economic crisis and the necessity of extending political activity beyond the historic parties.

Honduras has always had the weakest manufacturing sector in Central America. In 1960 the country accounted for just 10 per cent of regional manufacturing output and one-eighth of value added. Over the next decade Honduran industry fell well behind that of El Salvador, production dropping from 51 per cent of the Salvadorean level in 1960 to 32.5 per cent in 1969. Moreover, what expansion did take place was very largely due to increased US investment, which doubled between 1963 and 1967, reaching $200 million in 1969 when total GDP was in the region of $800 million.[46] Much of the new investment resulted from diversification by the banana companies, particularly SF, which used the *Cervecería de Honduras* as its central holding company through which to establish joint operations with local capital and control some twenty subsidiaries. Yet North American interests ranged wider than this, First National City Bank taking over the Banco de Honduras in 1965 and Chase Manhattan acquiring the Banco de Atlántida in 1967; by the end of the 1960s control of the country's top five companies and 82 per cent of the top fifty was in US hands.[47] This impressive foreign domination precluded the emergence of a powerful entrepreneurial class of the type witnessed in El Salvador or even Guatemala; Honduran capitalism remained pathologically dependent upon North American leadership. On the other hand, the high manufacturing growth rate – approximately 7 per cent per annum from 1950 to 1978 – and an average yearly increase in public investment of 29 per cent during the 1960s (11 per cent in the private sector) assisted the development of a local business sector that by 1968 contained 498 manufacturing enterprises, 52 per cent of which were classified as 'small' with an average labour force of eleven workers whilst only 10 per cent were 'large' (averaging 209 workers each).[48] Hence, although exceptionally weak in regional terms, almost artisanal in character, and overshadowed by the US corporations, domestic capital was still stronger than before and able by the mid 1960s to register a distinct sectoral interest within national politics. The entrepreneurial core continued to be formed by the landlords, strengthened and to some degree 'modernized' by the expansion of cotton, which underwent a mini-boom in the early 1960s (area planted rising from 6,700 hectares in 1962/3 to 14,300 in 1965/6) and ranching, which experienced more modest growth from a higher point (the national herd increasing from 431,000 to 720,000 head betwen 1952 and 1965, land in pasture rising by 300,000 hectares).[49] This sector, traditionally represented by the PN, formed the *Federación Nacional de Agricultores y Ganaderos de Honduras* (FENAGH) in 1966 with the central objective of stalling further distribution of land by a regime seen as susceptible to popular pressure notwithstanding its conservative character. For the stockbreeders' corporate association was not just a reflection of the growth and cohesion conferred by new markets in the US but also provided support for the Nationalists' subordinate position in a government that could not sensibly be guaranteed to defer to PN counsel forever.

In 1967 FENAGH became an affiliate of the new *Consejo Hondureño de Empresa Privada* (COHEP), the character of which was far less rigid than that of FENAGH since it had been set up on the initiative of the northern chambers of commerce (Cortés and Atlántida) representing the interests of small-scale manufacturing and commerce in San Pedro Sula and the company towns which were frequently out of harmony with the large ranchers, banks and US corporations. Although these latter forces were well represented on COHEP's directorate, the umbrella body was by no means a simple vehicle for monopoly interests, and the numerical strength of minor local enterprises in the local chambers of commerce, particularly in the interior, gave them an audible voice. For many in this group COHEP replaced the Liberal Party as a political forum where they could oppose the free-tradism of big business and negotiate with the longstanding Syrian and Lebanese merchant community headed by the Adonie, Kafie, Larach and Facusse families, some of which had invested heavily in manufacturing and could not afford to pursue a purely mercantilist strategy. COHEP was, therefore, itself the site of important policy disputes – on occasion to the point of schism – but from the late 1960s until the clear adoption of reformist policies by the military the deterioration of Honduras's position in the CACM gave a clear advantage to domestic manufacturing interests. Indeed, by the turn of the decade the position had become so grave that FENAGH and the big corporations were placed firmly on the defensive.

As early as 1965 it was evident that Honduras's poor position within the CACM could not be improved without a substantial revision of the terms of regional commerce. With the bulk of its exports being agricultural commodities sold at prices near the international level and the majority of its imports from the CACM comprising manufactured goods bought at a price that reflected the high common external tariff, the country's trade deficit with its neighbours at the creation of the market rose every year thereafter. This position was at least tolerable whilst extra-regional exports earned sufficient dollars to cover the shortfall. However, from the mid 1960s international export revenue began to decrease, cotton sales dropping with the fall of price in 1965 and banana exports declining from a peak reached in 1967. The impetus to establish COHEP had stemmed from this increasingly prejudicial state of affairs for the manufacturing bourgeoisie of San Pedro Sula, the complaints of which had elicited scant sympathy from a government closely tied to agro-export interests that did not rely heavily upon imported inputs and were less concerned by the regional terms of trade. The political dimensions of this burgeoning dispute were already evident in April 1968 when the Chamber of Commerce and Industry of Cortés, the department that includes San Pedro Sula, joined the campaign of protest led by SITRATERCO and backed by FESITRANH against the fraud that had given the Nationalists victory in all but thirty-five of the country's 260 municipalities in the March local elections. Even some prominent Nationalists, such as César Batres, president of the *Asociación Nacional de Industrias*, felt constrained to call for rapprochement with the Liberals because of the breadth of discontent caused by the poll and the unpopularity of the regime. However, Zúñiga resisted all concessions and López Arellano remained indifferent to a campaign that he failed to recognize betokened not just traditional union support for outcast Liberalism but also a convergence of the urban bourgeoisie and labour. Accordingly, later in the year the government unhesitatingly endorsed the 'San José Protocol' under which the CACM imposed a common 30 per cent tariff on all imports from outside the region and introduced taxes of 10–20 per cent on consumer durables. This agreement provoked immediate protest from both the unions, whose members now faced price rises on a wide range of basic goods for which there was no ready substitute for imports, and the manufacturing bourgeoisie, which instead of celebrating the measure as protectionist condemned it for increasing the cost of its inputs and penalizing its pattern of consumption little less than that of the working class.

On 18 September twenty-two of the twenty-eight member unions of FESITRANH agreed to call an indefinite general strike from the next day if the government did not reverse the tax, whilst the Cortés chamber of commerce threatened to halt business activity from the 24th. However, FESITRANH was reluctant to call its supporters out into the streets and the entrepreneurs more naturally took little public action beyond issuing complaints through the *sampedrano* papers, *La Prensa* and *El Pueblo*, which the regime promptly closed down under a new state of siege. Once again, López Arellano responded with force, sending in the army, employing *Mancha Brava* to intimidate activists, and gaoling some forty-five FESITRANH leaders, including such normally dependable figures as Oscar Gale Varela of SITRATERCO. The strike lasted rather longer than that of 1965, largely because it was supported by the enclave labour force, but by 25 September the repression had obliged the unions to accept negotiations in the capital. Here the regime made only nominal concessions and even insisted upon the exile of FESITRANH leader Céleo González. In the short term, therefore, the action was an unqualified failure. But it had drawn the bourgeoisie of San Pedro Sula firmly into the political arena and demonstrated the possibilities of forging a more extensive alliance with the trade unions, to which prospect the increasingly embattled López Arellano now directed more of his attention.

It is possible that the government could have continued to keep the northern challenge at bay without a change in policy even though the protest campaign had gained cross-class support and acquired a nationalist tint that was particularly difficult for the military to ignore or repudiate. However, López Arellano's position was weakened by renewed pressure from the *campesino* movement, in particular the Church-sponsored ACASH (*Asociación Campesina Social Cristiana de Honduras*), which had been set up in 1964. This alliance of local peasant leagues and supporters of community development projects was responsible for organizing sporadic *tomas* in the southern cotton-growing departments of Choluteca and Valle; these had prompted the establishment of FENAGH and were occurring with disturbing regularity by 1968. Furthermore, the suppression of FENACH had prompted many of its former members to enter and attempt to radicalize ANACH, which continued to express discontent at the lack of land distribution.[50] The threat of a mass hunger march to Tegucigalpa by ANACH early in 1967 together with the increased incidence of *tomas* led López Arellano first to negotiate and then to concede to the reactivation of INA with an expanded budget under the directorship of the energetic and talented reformist Rigoberto Sandoval Corea. Sandoval was an enthusiastic proponent of cooperatives and responsible for the economically successful and largely uncontroversial restoration of the Las Guanchías association on land formerly used by TRRC in 1965. This example encouraged the president and elements of the high command to reopen the option of reform, which was violently denounced by FENAGH but could no longer be evaded without risking a serious collapse of public order in the countryside.

The problem faced by the regime was that the Las Guanchías model of cooperativization of ex-plantation lands was dependent upon company collaboration and available only to a limited section of the landless rural population. Hence, while this pattern was followed from the turn of the decade in the Aguán valley in Yoro under the auspices of the *Federación de Cooperativas de la Reforma Agraria de Honduras* (FECORAH), it was already evident by the time of the 1968 strike that distribution would have to take a wider compass and higher political profile. From the viewpoint of the government and FENAGH, which was quick to strike a strongly xenophobic pose, the most felicitous resolution to this problem lay in a transfer of land from immigrant Salvadorean *campesinos* to Honduran nationals of the same class. The landlords had long condemned *tomas* by the '*guanacos*' of properties in the border departments of Ocotopeque, Lempira, Intibucá and La Paz, certain areas of which were predominantly Salvadorean in population. Even if INA's declaration in 1969 that 216,619 undocumented Salvadoreans occupied 205,100 hectares may be treated with some scepticism, immigrant settlement certainly extended well beyond these zones and FENAGH enjoyed some success in cultivating popular jingoism in Yoro and Olancho despite the absence of incursions by Salvadorean forces or cross-border rustling.[51] Residual tension at a local level was forcefully abetted by a general anti-Salvadorean sentiment championed by the *rodista* Liberals and backed by the *sampedrano* bourgeoisie because of the overwhelming presence of Salvadorean goods in its national market.

It was in such a context directly determined by economic interest – some of it spurious, some very real – that historic claims and petty incidents could be blown up into major crises. The most obvious of these was the dispute over half a dozen stretches of the frontier, none of which was very great or affected major economic interests. However, the de facto border near Nueva Ocotopeque required Honduran aircraft to pass into Salvadorean airspace in order to reach the town whilst the lack of clear delineation between the departments of La Unión (El Salvador) and Valle (Honduras) provided a convenient corridor for cattle rustling. The potential for trouble in these spots was shown as early as 1967 when a certain 'Colonel' Martínez Argueta, a friend of López Arellano, prominent landlord and infamous rustler, was arrested by the Salvadorean *Policía de Hacienda* and gaoled for twenty years for murdering the mayor of the village of Polorós; this was done on the grounds that, despite his claims to the contrary, Martínez's hacienda was in El Salvador and he was a Salvadorean citizen. Several weeks later four Salvadorean army trucks arrived unannounced in the town square of Nueva Ocotopeque, their occupants being bravely arrested by the town's constabulary. According to the two lieutenants commanding the convoy, they had fallen asleep and missed the (unguarded) border; for this they were subsequently dubbed 'the sleeping beauties' although the high command in Tegucigalpa plausibly suspected a rather less innocent reason for the incursion.[52] In all events, these and similar incidents kept nationalist antipathy on the boil for several years before López Arellano forced a more substantial issue to the point of confrontation in April 1969 by approving INA's dispatch of notices to quit to Salvadorean settlers in Yoro, Santa Barbara, Copán and Choluteca on the grounds that only persons of Honduran birth were eligible for land under the 1962 reform, making the immigrants illegal squatters. This move, accompanied by often brutal official harassment, attacks by *Mancha Brava*, and frequent settling of old scores on both sides, provoked the flight of thousands of Salvadoreans prior to the outbreak of hostilities. The subsequent clashes at soccer matches were not unimportant in that they served to stoke up popular fervour and limit the flexibility of governments that had much to gain from nationalist distractions but also a great deal at risk in an open military conflict. The propaganda campaign was marked by the most extravagant claims and clumsy manipulation in both countries. In Honduras it also produced a level of popular support that took the military unawares and was an important factor in its political strategy following defeat in the hundred hours' war of July.

There can be no doubt that despite the success of the airforce in controlling the skies and bombing the Acajutla oil refinery, the Hondurans lost the military campaign.[53] Many of the casualties were civilian and the land forces failed to sustain an effective defence against the two main Salvadorean thrusts on Ocotopeque and Langue, which largely failed due to lack of logistical preparation and tactical ineptitude on the part of the much stronger invading army. On the other hand, the military 'defeat' did not produce a corresponding political collapse of an army that had been shown to be professionally incompetent and within which there was no lack of post-bellum recrimination. This did not apply to the airforce, which subsequently enhanced its institutional profile and acquired political influence disproportionate to its size. (It should, though, be noted that because of the very small size of the military as a whole competition between its various arms was relatively low and certainly much less than, for instance, in Argentina, where traditional inter-service rivalry was sharpened by the Malvinas War, in which the fleet air arm displayed an efficiency markedly greater than the rest of the military. The mystique of flying may have waned considerably in metropolitan society over the last decade with 'deregulation' of air services in the US and price wars on trans-Atlantic routes introducing millions to the questionable pleasures of air travel, but it should not be forgotten that in a backward country like Honduras the enormous technological gap between the flying of an aircraft and cultivation of the *milpa* continues to lend considerable prestige to aviation and obscures the more directly coercive character of the airforce.)

Still, celebration of its pilots' 'heroism' was but a minor part of the military's capacity to escape popular denigration. In the first place, rapid intervention by the OAS led to a Salvadorean retreat from all undisputed Honduran territory and supervision of the contested areas ('*bolsones*') by an inter-American force; in territorial terms the Honduran commanders could claim that they had emerged from the war in no worse a state than that in which they had entered it. Moreover, by closing the border and stopping all trade with El Salvador Tegucigalpa increased the diplomatic advantages of being the nominally wronged party since this move greatly impeded trade by land between El Salvador and Nicaragua and Costa Rica, threatening the unity of the CACM and placing regional pressure on San Salvador to make concessions. (In the event, a full peace treaty was not signed until 1980 and this failed to produce a settlement of territorial claims, which were transferred to the World Court in 1986.) Equally, a very disorganized battle of less than five days in the countryside resulted in relatively slight damage, more anger than fear in the towns, and the exodus of a further 60,000 Salvadoreans by the end of the year, allowing the regime to distribute more land than at any time since the reform was introduced (the 1969 grants account for most of the distribution of 1967–71 listed in Table 49, p. 559).

The trade unions were fully pledged to 'national defence' – FECESITLIH demanded a day's wage from each of its members to aid the war effort and the CTH organized a large pro-government demonstration after the fighting. The Liberals and the urban bourgeoisie stood to the fore in orchestrating the anti-Salvadorean campaign; FENAGH was stymied by its opportunist xenophobia; and the PN was confounded by its parasitism. In short, the army faced no direct challenge for power in the wake of the war. It could not, however, sensibly hope to rule on the same terms as before. Popular mobilization and support prior to and during the conflict both precluded and rendered unnecessary a retreat to the conservative authoritarianism of 1963–68 and although the military by no means halted its repressive activity, sections of the officer corps began to appreciate the virtues of the tenuously regenerated agrarian reform as well as the possibilities of closer collaboration with the unions. Nonetheless, three years were to pass before the army was prepared fully to embrace a populist and reformist strategy of the type forged by Torrijos in Panama and Velasco in Peru, and, as might be expected, this course was only adopted following considerable popular pressure.

The first major step in this regard was made before the war, in March 1969, when the second assembly of the CTH called for a political pact '*a la Colombiana*' whereby the PL and PN would suspend their partisan instincts and form a coalition government. (This, in fact, was rather different from the Colombian system, which provided for rights of opposition and minority representation.) The demand was naturally backed by the Liberals and received support from the students, who were beginning to find a political voice rather later than elsewhere. It was also championed by the *Comité Cívico Pro-Defensa Nacional*, a loose alliance dominated by Miguel Adonie Fernández, who subsequently formed the *Partido de Inovación y Unidad* (PINU) on timidly social democratic lines with the backing of urban professionals and a number of unaligned labour leaders. Although the CTH proposal threatened to be most damaging for the Nationalists, it posed a challenge to the entire bi-polar tradition and signalled the emergence of a fourth force in the political sphere. Moreover, the assembly's demand for 'the regulation of foreign investment and promotion of greater participation by Hondurans in its management' took on a much sharper dimension in the wake of the war, receiving the endorsement of the urban entrepreneurs, who were more sensitive to foreign competition than to restrictions on the free market, and teasing the statist nerve of the officers, who were anxious to avoid any suspicion of capitulating to foreign interests. These two broad themes – a government of national unity and greater economic nationalism – were reaffirmed in October 1969 at the third meeting of the *Fuerzas Vivas* headed by the CTH and COHEP, organizations which were now to all intents and purposes operating in tandem.

López Arellano initially resisted and then tried to hijack the proposal for a government of 'national unity' that threatened his personal position more than it did that of the military as a whole. The general was forced to give ground in July 1970, when the two political parties entered into a private agreement to collaborate, thus forming a formidable bloc in opposition to the *caudillo*'s obvious *continuista* pretensions. In December the president finally accepted formal talks with COHEP and the CTH, and on 7 January 1971 he declared that the two legally recognized parties had agreed to a pact for national unity based largely on the CTH's 1969 platform. However, the parties still possessed enough authority to reject the CTH plans for the nomination of a single presidential candidate and regulation of major policy by the country's principal corporate bodies. Having swung the balance against López and met the basic requirements for coalitionism, the parties were able to insist upon a restoration of the forms of competition and parliamentary democracy, obtaining the first direct presidential election since 1954. Just a day before the poll of 28 March 1971 they retrieved yet more ground by announcing their own '*pactito*' under which the winner of the election would receive a one-seat majority in congress and state posts would be divided equally by political affiliation – a direct contravention of the original terms of the pact, which stipulated that public appointments should be on the basis of merit not partisan preferment. The success of these manoeuvres may be attributed to López Arellano's unpopularity and the confusion of COHEP and the CTH in the face of a revived constitutionalism that they could scarcely repudiate without a cogent non-dictatorial alternative. On the other hand, the parties could not afford to upset a very fragile entente by fielding their leading and most controversial figures, Rodas and Zúñiga standing aside in a contest that reflected the colourless character of the two candidates: Dr Cruz for the Nationalists and the banker Jorge Bueso Arias for the Liberals. Given that the electorate was offered a choice between little more than party livery, the turnout of barely 50 per cent was unsurprising and Cruz's victory with the same percentage of the vote as in 1965 less of an upset than would have been the case had fully competitive conditions prevailed.

The Cruz administration lasted barely eighteen months and there is scant reason to suppose that even if it had been less hidebound and upheld the letter of the parties' *pactito* the government could have endured for much longer. Neither the PN nor the PL was happy with the January 1971 pact, which was formally 'guaranteed' by the military, the CTH and COHEP in a much more strenuous manner than had been proposed in 1969. López Arellano may have suffered a loss of prestige but he surrendered no real power, pointedly withdrawing the 1,000-strong presidential guard upon his departure from office, securing his election as commander-in-chief for six years, and appointing his ally, the popular airforce colonel Enrique Soto Cano, as defence minister. Zúñiga, now occupying the ministry of government, was little daunted and soon compelled his cypher Cruz to ignore the spirit of the broad pact as well as the letter of the bi-partisan *pactito*. The clearest instance of this was in the replacement of Sandoval Corea by the conservative Horacio Moya Posas as director of INA, an appointment that led to the prompt termination of new land grants. In response the peasantry reverted to staging occupations, one of which, organized by the *Unión Nacional de Campesinos* (UNC; formed out of ACASCH in 1970), resulted in the killing of six *campesinos* at La Talanquera, Olancho, in February 1972. At the same time, Zúñiga secured the dismissal of the Liberal minister of labour without PL agreement and against the terms of the 1970 accord. This was less an isolated incident than the most controversial of a series of partisan moves conducted by Zúñiga, who first allocated the Liberals ministries with a total budget of L49 million while the PN controlled portfolios worth L150 million and then fired two PL ministers with the sole apparent aim of gaining control of the central state lottery – traditionally a source of rich and quick pickings in Latin American countries. Rodas and his colleagues were left with little option but to break ranks, and they joined the CTH within the year to demand a revision of the 1971 pact by its 'guarantors'.

No immediate action resulted from the spring 1972 meeting to review the political position, but the Olancho deaths had heightened tension, and it was far from coincidental that López Arellano should address the large May Day rally shortly thereafter, criticizing 'economic stagnation', identifying an unresolved social crisis, and declaring, 'the unionized workers of our country are the forgers and creators of our collective wealth; unions have become the school of experience . . . the Armed Forces are not enemies of the workers and peasants'.[54] In a context where Zúñiga was breaking major political accords simply to extend his control of the spoils system, COHEP describing the agrarian reform as 'an indispensable tool for the incorporation of the peasantry into the country', and the CTH demanding that business, labour and the military take direct control of government, López Arellano's statements signalled a major threat to a regime that had frittered away its few claims to legitimacy.[55] In June 1972 the CTH insisted upon adhesion to the policies of reform agreed the previous year, increasing pressure on the army. In December, when ANACH prepared to stage another mass hunger march on the capital, López Arellano was finally forced to act, ousting Cruz on the 4th with the explicit support of the 'guarantors' of the long redundant pact and without a word of protest from the left.[56]

In the space of six weeks, the second López Arellano regime introduced a string of measures that indicated a radical change in direction. Decree 3 of 6 December 1972 ended the system of 'voluntary' contributions of 5 per cent of civil servants' wages to the governing party; since there were now more than 30,000 state employees this move commended the new regime to a significant constituency. Decree 8 of 26 December introduced the obligation to lease uncultivated lands and temporarily protected the tenure of rural squatters as an interim measure pending a completely new agrarian reform, the design of which was put in the hands of the University of Wisconsin. This decree fell well short of the demands made by ANACH and the more militant UNC but within a year it had trebled the amount of land distributed (Table 49, p. 559) and it temporarily stalled the accumulating political challenge presented by the *campesinado*. Decree 9 of 28 December cancelled the unpopular sales tax, and Decree 10 of the same day established the *Instituto de Formación Profesional* (INFOP), intended to improve technical and managerial efficiency for an era in which it was fondly hoped placemanship would be replaced by meritocracy. Decree 12 of 6 January 1973 met the longstanding complaints of the manufacturing members of COHEP by abolishing import taxes on items essential to national industry and penalizing unfair and monopolistic commercial practices. Decree 14 of 9 January altered the labour code to require all workers who did not belong to a union yet benefited from the terms of collective contracts to pay union dues – a modest overture to the CTH. This last measure and Decree 8 proved to be the most immediately controversial issues, but the right had been thrown into complete disarray and lost much influence with a military leadership that, as illustrated by López Arellano's statement to the nation in the new year, clearly relished its newfound bonapartist role: '[The military] has proved that it can no longer simply be characterized as "the armed force of the people" but that it also constitutes an instrument of irreplaceable efficiency for resolving the political, economic and social problems of the Honduran people, who once again have extended to it their unlimited support and confidence.'[57]

The new regime's flurry of decrees produced a 24.8 per cent increase in public expenditure within a year in stark contrast to the reduction of 4.4 per cent under Cruz – a fall that would have been greater still had it not been for the expansion of the military budget, which rose from $7 million to $15 million between 1969 and 1972.[58] Nevertheless, the government's initial measures amounted to a number of discrete developmentalist overtures designed to reduce political tension rather than a coherent and institutionalized programme of state-based modernization. It was only with the declaration of the fifteen-year *Plan Nacional de Desarrollo* (PND) in January 1974 that the regime consolidated its reformist character and showed itself to be in earnest. Although the agrarian reform continued to exist only on paper, the first six months of 1974 saw the establishment of the *Corporación Nacional de Inversiones* (CONADI) as a state industrial investment bank; the *Corporación Hondureña de Desarrollo Forestal* (COHDEFOR), charged with developing the country's considerable potential in forestry and bringing woodland back into public ownership; and the

Banco Nacional de Fomento para el Suministro de Productos Básicos (BANASUPRO), formed to subsidize and market basic grains. Before too long these institutions were revealed to be inadequately capitalized, inefficiently managed, and no less immune to graft than the traditional public entities, CONADI in particular disbursing millions of dollars on questionable grounds and with scant productive return. Still, the new semi-autonomous bodies provided the state with an unprecedented interventionist apparatus. When allied with the imposition of a minimum wage and the government's increase of the banana export tax to fifty cents a crate in line with the level fixed by the newly-established *Unión de Paises Exportadores del Banano* (UPEB), this seemed to herald a major assault on the economic power of large capital. López Arellano declared, 'We shall seize the banners of the left and make the revolution ourselves, although peacefully', whilst the president of the supreme court and FENAGH leader Roberto Ramírez was moved to announce the perpetually delayed agrarian reform 'Communist-inspired', threatening 'an end to private property'.[59]

Preoccupation on the part of landed capital was understandable even though the professors at Wisconsin's Land Tenure Center had produced an eminently modest and capitalist reform fully in keeping with their state's small-farmer heritage. (Some measure of this may be seen in the fact that by 1980, five years after the reform was introduced, land in basic grains was 33 per cent below its 1960 level whilst land in pasture was 16 per cent higher. This pattern was not, of course, wholly attributable to the reform and more often than not reflected the low level of redistribution, but even if it had been applied as extensively as was originally planned, the reform would never have prejudiced the position of commercial farming, still less extinguished private property in the countryside.[60]) All the same, landlords, foreign enterprises and merchants all faced new restrictions and reaped little short-term benefit from state intervention whereas the manufacturing bourgeoisie received direct support and rallied to the regime. The division of interest had been apparent before the coup, COHEP sending two separate delegations to the discussions of the political pact in March 1972 and existing in a most uneasy truce once the landlords recaptured control of the body in 1973. Whilst the conflict over agrarian reform in 1974–75 and the retreat of the progressive faction in the military over the next two years confirmed the restoration of the right, it is clear that the manufacturing sector of the capitalist class had been bolstered by the removal of Salvadorean competition and Honduras's withdrawal from the CACM in 1970. This move, which saw the replacement of the common external tariff with bilateral trade agreements with Guatemala, Costa Rica and Nicaragua, considerably reduced the level of imports from the region (whereas everywhere else this was increasing) and lowered the proportion of Honduran exports to the CACM countries to less than half the level registered elsewhere.[61]

In the short term the strategy appeared to have been disastrous with the economy registering the lowest growth rate of the region in 1970–75 (GDP: 2.3 per cent; GDP per capita: – 0.8 per cent) although this was partly the result of natural catastrophe. In the second half of the decade, by contrast, Honduras experienced the highest regional growth rate (GDP: 7.3 per cent; GDP per capita: 3.5 per cent) and over the 1970s as a whole value added in manufacturing doubled, its growth exceeded only by Guatemala and Costa Rica, the total level in 1980 being 65 per cent of that in El Salvador against 49 per cent in 1970.[62] The view that the regime of 1972–75 directly represented the interests of manufacturing capital must be qualified by recognition that these had been advanced no less by the absence of Salvadorean competition after the war, often merged with those of the merchant class, and were only in partial conflict with those of the landlords. Moreover, the proportion of GDP attributable to manufacturing rose very modestly during the 1970s, never exceeding 22 per cent or the regional average. The PCH was correct in identifying the *sampedrano* entrepreneurs as key supporters of López Arellano's second coming, but they could never act as patrons, being beneficiaries of a statist project rather than the vanguard of a new economic order.[63]

Of all the natural catastrophes to strike Central America in the 1970s Hurricane Fifi, which hit the north of Honduras on 18 September 1974, is perhaps the least known. At least 2,000 and possibly 5,000 people died in the storm and floods that followed it; the northern road system was badly disrupted, the damage to infrastructure and production amounting to $500 million at the very least; only the coffee crop escaped relatively unscathed, banana production being particularly hard hit. The response of the fruit companies was rather less aggressive than might have been expected from the conflict opened by the regime's imposition of the fifty-cent tax in March since López Arellano had suddenly and mysteriously reduced this to twenty-five cents on 23 August. Furthermore, storm damage provided the corporations with an excuse to lay off some 4,000 workers and reduce landholding during a period of general recession in the trade. Equally, the government's response to the emergency was more inefficient than corrupt and engendered little popular opposition. In contrast to the Nicaraguan earthquake two years earlier, US aid was parsimonious to the point of hostility, the provision of half a dozen aircraft and fifty-three troops being overshadowed by British military assistance dispatched from Belize and a Cuban medical team that soon outshone the gringos in its activities and raised questions in both Washington and the salons of the local gentry as to the president's real political agenda. The manifest antipathy of the Nixon administration towards the regime's policies did little harm to its reputation at home but there is no clear evidence of any coherent plan of destabilization, which may well have been deemed unnecessary after the reduction of the banana tax and would scarcely have constituted a foreign policy priority in any event, still less in the wake of the Watergate scandal.

Yet if the US was content to observe events coolly, members of FENAGH, whose herd had been decimated by the hurricane, were able to exploit the disaster by staging a campaign against the regime in general and the agrarian reform in particular. Right-wing attacks on López Arellano's handling of the emergency were rewarded with the appointment of Colonel Eduardo Andino, a protégé of the conservative interior minister Colonel Alberto Melgar Castro, as head of the national relief organization, COPEN. Further advances were made by the coalescing group of traditionalist officers headed by Melgar at the end of the year when they succeeded in having the Cuban medical team expelled for 'subversion', and conjured up a similarly spurious scandal about the Chilean refugees given asylum after Pinochet's coup of September 1973. (The Honduran embassy in Santiago was a favoured haven for persecuted radicals despite the country's military government.) On the other hand, the landlords' pressure for a rapid settlement of the border dispute with El Salvador was distinctly misguided and helped to rally the reformist current inside the officer corps led by the sixth and seventh promotions from the academy trained in the immediate post-1957 era, flush with expectations of modernity, unaccustomed to party rule, and blooded in the Salvadorean war. Distrustful of the personalism of both López Arellano and Melgar, this group of majors and junior colonels was less at odds with the former, who had, after all, been responsible for the modern military system and was now wily enough to grasp a new lease on life by forcing the full agrarian reform statute on to the agenda of the *Consejo Superior de Defensa*. He thus obliged his senior colleagues to make a clear stand on the issue and, when they bowed to his trump and appended their signatures, identified the institution as a whole with the measure. Decree 170 extended the provisions of the 1972 reform by increasing the size of farms liable to expropriation to 500 hectares, clearly exposing large landlords to the threat of official dispossession of idle or inefficient land. The populist Colonel Mario Maldonado was put in charge of INA and Melgar was transferred from his post whilst FENAGH greatly increased the virulence of its campaign, now given official backing by the new COHEP leadership as well as the traditional parties, which declared the reform illegal and demanded a return to constitutional government. This balance of powers forced López Arellano to hold back from authorizing the expropriation of private lands, but it was evident that such a stalemate could not hold for long and might well be resolved by battles inside the military.

The first break in the impasse came in March 1975 when, following the suicide of Eli Black, chairman of United Brands (formerly UFCO), the previous month, it was revealed in the US that the company had paid at least $1.25 million to a senior Honduran official as a bribe for the lowering of the export tax in August 1974. Suspicion naturally fell upon the president, who was now seen by the colonels as a distinct liability. López Arellano was removed from the position of commander-in-chief (held by him for nineteen years) by the new *Consejo Superior de las Fuerzas Armadas* (COSUFA) that had been constituted whilst he was visiting the US as a forum for collective decision-making and a safeguard against personalist exploitation of hierarchy. In an effort to secure some balance in a crisis felt as deeply within the officer corps as it was without, COSUFA appointed Melgar commander-in-chief and confirmed López Arellano as president. The investigation into 'Bananagate' clearly implicated the minister of economy Abraham Bennaton, who was subsequently gaoled for receiving the bribe, but when in April the president refused to reveal details of his Swiss bank accounts COSUFA immediately replaced him with Melgar. This substantially strengthened the position of the right although Melgar owed his position to *reformista* compliance with a collective decision that had not addressed ideological issues and simply passed an inevitable judgement insofar as the suspicion of López's malfeasance was too great to permit the normally generous presumptions of innocence. Equally, agitation in the countryside for realization of the reform was now so widespread that any withdrawal of the decree was unthinkable, threatening to provoke not only peasant revolt but also a return to civilian government, as much an anathema to Melgar as it had been to his predecessor.

The scale of rural conflict was vividly illustrated on 19 May, when the UNC staged a mass *toma* of 108 haciendas in ten departments to protest INA's inactivity. On this occasion Colonel Maldonado held back from a repressive response, ANACH's support for the invasions limiting the army's action to the temporary detention of a number of leaders of the UNC, which continued with its preparations for a series of marches on the capital. It was in an attempt to halt one of these that the especially belligerent landlords of Olancho prevailed upon the garrison commander at Juticalpa to attack the local *campesino* training centre on 25 June. Five people were killed in this attack and the bodies of another nine, including priests from Colombia and the US, were later discovered buried in the well of a local ranch. These assassinations, which had clearly been perpetrated in cold blood and accompanied by torture, caused such an outcry that the officer responsible, Major José Enrique Chinchilla, was detained and gaoled after legal proceedings that would have been completely unimaginable in either Guatemala or El Salvador. On the other hand, the Olancho massacre scarified a weak Church and the small Christian Democratic party – formed in 1968 and still not officially recognized – which now withdrew support from the combative leadership of the UNC. This encouraged the emergence of a more cautious current that moved closer to the conservative leaders of ANACH (Reyes Rodríguez) and FECORAH (Efraín Díaz Galeas) in threatening rather than actively organizing mass mobilization to force through the expropriation of private land.[64]

In the face of these events, the twenty-two-man COSUFA underwent further factionalization. However, the split between officers who wished to pursue 'the Peruvian path' with continued radicalism and greater popular participation and those who argued for a consolidation of the existing measures could not be exploited fully by the conservative wing, in part because this was still a minority and in part because it was hampered by Zúñiga's attacks on 'military immaturity' and the bipartisan campaign for civilian government.[65] Hence, Melgar agreed to the demand of the entire pro-reform group for the retirement of twenty-nine senior officers, not least because this disposed of figures who coveted his own position as well as those favouring a return to the barracks. The repression of a joint Liberal-Nationalist demonstration for a return to constitutionalism in Choluteca reinforced the shift inside the officer corps towards the middle ground, and in October Melgar finally approved the first expropriations under the reform to avert a further spate of *tomas* that the union bureaucracies were unwilling to detain in view of the impending *postrera* (autumn sowing season).

The belated implementation of Decree 107 seemed to presage a renewed radical offensive. Although the bulk of the 80,000 acres immediately tabled for redistribution comprised two large properties owned by SF and United Brands, lands belonging to Rodas and Roberto Ramírez (and even López Arellano) were expropriated, landlord fears being further excited by government declarations that another eighty notices were in the pipeline. Yet, as can be seen from Table 49, the rate of distribution was actually lower in 1975 than in 1974, and despite the replacement of the demagogic Maldonado by Sandoval as INA director early in 1976 the level of entitlement continued to fall. In fact, the realization of the reform marked the peak of mass mobilization rather than the onset of a major shift in ownership; it represented the outer limit of a political enterprise that had tarried nigh-on three years in bringing its central policy to fruition and was worn out by the conflict this had caused. By early 1977, when Sandoval was hounded out of his post, it was estimated that at the existing pace of distribution it would take seventy years before the original fifteen-year target envisaged under the PND would be met.[66] A substantial proportion of the reform sector was comprised of ex-plantation land, fruit company holdings falling to 122,000 hectares in 1975 from 230,000 in 1960. This process was, though, very largely the result of the corporations' own initiative in generally disadvantageous economic conditions that had reduced bananas' share of exports from 77 per cent in 1960 to 60 per cent in

Table 49: Land Distribution, 1962–81*

Year	*No. Peasant Groups*	*%*	*No. Families*	*%*	*Land Distributed (hectares)*	*%*
1962–66	12	1	453	1	1,357	1
Average (p.a.)	2		91		271	
1957–71	63	5	5,292	10	24,019	10
Average (p.a.)	13		1,058		4,404	
1972	72		3,331		10,585	
1973	224		8,674		32,454	
1974	287		9,828		47,098	
1975	186		6,751		37,252	
1976	182		6,274		26,913	
Subtotal	951	73	34,858	65	154,302	67
1977	106		3,381		15,985	
1978	42		1,745		5,415	
1979	43		1,161		6,355	
1980	63		2,935		9,648	
1981	30		3,981		13,958	
Subtotal	284	22	13,203	25	51,361	22
TOTAL	1,310	101	53,806	101	231,039	100

* Percentages are rounded up.

Source: Painter and Lapper, *State for Sale*, p. 64.

Table 50: Forms of Land Tenure in Honduras and El Salvador, 1970s

	Honduras 1974		*El Salvador 1971*	
	farms	*%*	*farms*	*%*
Private freehold	65,518	34	108,014	40
Ejido/state lands	63,804	33	–	–
Rented from private	44,054	23	88,495	33
Mixed rent/private	19,449	10	36,345	13
Colonato	–	–	17,018	6
Other	2,516	1	20,996	8

Source: Censos Agropecuarios, corresponding years, cited in Ruhl, 'Agrarian Structure', p.40.

1977. The single most important transfer of property under the entire reform – the cooperativization of SF's 22,000-hectare Las Isletas plantation in the Bajo Aguán valley in April 1975 – was not opposed by the enterprise, which had abandoned the lands after the hurricane and was quite prepared for the state to subsidize cooperative production that it could purchase on favourable terms. Las Isletas was championed by the military as the model for new reformist enterprises as the cooperative increased its production from 43,000 crates in 1975 to four million in 1977, trebling wages and establishing basic health and educational facilities. Such success encouraged SF to veto a transfer of sales to the state's banana development board (COHBANA), this embargo opening a battle for managerial control of Las Isletas that was only resolved when a government unwilling to court company ill-will first patronized a pliable and corrupt cooperative leadership and then, when this was strenuously opposed, sent in troops to ensure its 'election'.[67] By the mid 1980s much of the Bajo Aguán was organized in cooperatives yet these were consistently prevented from developing by both company and state control, normally channelled through FECORAH, which was the smallest and most malleable of the three rural unions that continued to organize the majority of the *campesinado* despite a dizzying array of minor organizations and umbrella bodies emerging from 1975 onwards.[68] The cooperative sector accounted for the bulk of the increase in unionized workers from 31,000 in 1970 to 131,000 in 1975.[69] As both the conflict inside the Bajo Aguán organizations and the fierce contest for the leadership of SITRATERCO demonstrated, this much expanded popular organization was never easily dominated, but from early 1976 onwards the general level of mass mobilization fell in the face of a concerted recovery by the right. The real gains of the rural labour force were soon shown to be much less impressive than they appeared; those of urban workers remained even more modest.

The Retreat to Reactionary Civilism

The Melgar regime was less transitional than restorative of conservative confidence. Although the president announced in March 1976 and May 1977 that new electoral legislation would be tabled, neither he, who wished to be a candidate, nor the civilian parties, who were expected to support a military nomination, were in any rush to re-establish constitutional rule before the reformist impetus had been fully checked. In December 1976 FENAGH and COHEP launched a new tirade against 'Communist infiltration' in INA, and by May 1977 the rural union leadership had been cajoled into accepting the establishment of the Agrarian Reform Committee. This was staffed by FENAGH sympathizers and soon marginalized INA, from which Sandoval departed to be replaced by the wealthy coffee *finquero* Fabio Salgado; henceforth distribution diminished considerably and there was negligible expropriation of private lands. These moves had been prefigured in February, when troops of the Fourth Battalion led by Colonel Gustavo Alvárez, who was on SF's payroll, occupied Las Isletas and imposed a pro-government leadership on the cooperative. In May troops and police took control of the SUTRASFCO offices to ensure the victory of the 'Democratic Front' in the union elections, albeit with rather less violence. Earlier in the year reactionary groups had resorted to physical means to overcome the still active progressive current in the *Central General de Trabajadores* (CGT), the small Christian Democrat union federation established in 1970 and based largely on the UNC. The left only clung on to control of SITRATERCO under duress, and by the end of 1977 labour militancy was at its lowest ebb for a decade.

Melgar neither wanted nor was able to conduct a major purge of the reformist faction inside the armed forces. The new year postings and promotions of 1977 broadly favoured the 'apolitical' tendency of the officer corps but the sixth and seventh *tandas* still held important troop commands, were far too young to be pensioned off, and retained strong influence within COSUFA, now consolidated as the centre of military decision-making. Furthermore, as Melgar's *continuista* ambitions strengthened he required broad military support to curb party manoeuvres. These began in earnest in May 1978 once it became apparent to Rodas and Zúñiga that the president was seeking US blessing for his own candidacy in 1980, whilst the officer corps began to court PINU and the PDC, both of which were well thought of in Washington. Melgar, however, was no López Arellano. His style was clumsy – the distribution of 10,000 free records of a song extolling his virtues failed to improve an image that was more vapid than conservative – and despite maintaining a group of advisers from the business sector he lacked strong ties with the ascendant landlord faction.[70] When, in July 1978, the civilian right succeeded in creating a major crisis out of the drugs and murder scandal involving several senior officers ('the Ferrari case'), the students and unions rallied to Melgar's defence since it was clear that his removal was being sought to strengthen the reactionary cause. However, the demonstrations and arrests that followed provided the military rightists with the opportunity to oust the president on the plausible grounds that he could no longer assure public order. He was replaced by General Policarpo Paz, a figure more directly implicated in the scandal and with a reputation sullied by dabbling in the drug and emerald trades, but who, as commander-in-chief, was the ordained successor in hierarchical terms, and, as a close ally of FENAGH, the preferred candidate of the right.

Paz both continued Melgar's containment of popular organization and re-established the military alliance with the PN. This latter policy could no longer be conducted as fully and openly as in the 1960s since many officers possessed little sympathy for the Nationalists, who were fervently pro-military yet associated with the failures of 1971–72 and opposed to the agrarian reform – still an important element in the institution's claim on popular support and legitimacy. Until the death of Rodas in 1979 the PL continued to be seen as liable to anti-militarism and for many middle-ranking officers politicized over the previous decade the most desirable alternative to military government lay with the new parties. However, PINU lacked the resources and appeal to stage a national challenge whilst Zúñiga was able to use his influence with the regime first to speed up the electoral calendar – depriving the PDC of time to organize what might be a dangerous campaign similar to those of its sister parties in the region – and then to have the PN-dominated electoral tribunal deny the Christian Democrats official registration because their international affiliation technically transgressed laws established to proscribe the PCH. With Liberal denunciations of Zúñiga's familiar manipulation of the electoral apparatus, the exclusion of a potential political 'centre', and Paz's clear preference for a Nationalist victory, the scenario appeared remarkably similar to that of 1965. The position was not the same in at least one important respect though, since the elections of April 1980 took place in the wake of the Nicaraguan revolution. This had attracted interest rather than agitation in Honduras, alerting the officer corps to the dangers of a rigid oligarchic alliance and prompting Washington ostentatiously to demand of Paz guarantees for a clean poll once evidence of a planned PN fraud came to light. Furthermore, both political restrictions and the deepening economic crisis had regenerated labour discontent and given the left a rare opportunity to retrieve some ground. Initially this appeared to strengthen the campaign for a boycott of the poll, a move which was favoured by the progressive Liberal tendency ALIPO, centred on San Pedro Sula under Carlos Reina and at odds with the party's *rodista* leadership. However, the Liberal dignitaries managed to contain what had become a serious threat of factionalism following Rodas's death, and the PDC's call for abstention received little support beyond the PCH, the small *Partido Socialista de Honduras* (PASOH; formed from a left-wing split from the PDC after the Olancho massacre of 1975), and the Maoists of the PCH–ML who had left the PCH in 1967 and had some influence amongst the teachers. With none of these forces – formally allied in the *Frente Patriótico Hondureño* – capable of affecting the turnout, US pressure for an open poll, and Paz's support for the PN matched by the military's refusal to veto the PL, the Liberals were able to draw on their diminished association with agrarian reform and the unions to win thirty-five seats in the new constituent assembly (49.4 per cent of the vote) against the PN's thirty-three (42.2 per cent), the balance of power being held by PINU (three seats; 3.5 per cent of the vote), which favoured the PL.

The most interesting feature of the 1980 poll was not the narrow Liberal victory, which counted for very little beyond challenging PN dominion over the spoils system, nor Paz's unbending refusal to step down as president or respect the new protocols, but the very high turnout – 81.3 per cent of an electorate of 1.2 million – which was to be repeated in the 1981 poll. This support for constitutionalism should not be automatically interpreted as evidence of equal enthusiasm for the traditional parties, but even allowing for the exclusion of the PDC and poor showing of PINU it is difficult to dissociate the popularity of the election from the attractions of political organizations that appeared to be thoroughly anachronistic. It is clear that by 1980 military rule was unpopular, even with the conservative interests that it most diligently served. Furthermore, 'the electorate' was in a very real sense a novel category since the people had not been presented with a real choice at the ballot box since 1957 – before many voters in 1980 were born – whilst a significant proportion of voters still cast their vote at the behest of local *caudillos* (landlord, mayor and union boss, all alike) or for the purpose of more direct remuneration. On the other hand, neither party campaigned on a remotely progressive platform or proffered anything beyond traditional assurances of boundless welfare and happiness. Despite the absence of Rodas and the emergence of Zúñiga from his preferred role as *éminence grise*, the parties presented familiar fare without even displacing the military president. If the absence of an electoralist challenge from the left was predictable, the degree of support for the elections was much less so. External factors cannot be excluded – violent chaos in the surrounding states can only have commended the dubious attributes of 'the rule of law' – but it was clear that the relatively untroubled reconstitution of established partisan competition owed more to the weakness of the radical left and the exhaustion of corporatist initiatives. The people voted because this was an alienable right; they voted for continuity because there was no viable alternative either on the ballot paper or, as in El Salvador and Guatemala, absent from and opposed to it.

The twenty months between the poll of 1980 and that of 1981 witnessed renewed conflict that disturbed and occasionally threatened to interrupt the process of 'redemocratization'. On the one hand, the teachers' strike of June and July 1980 included Salvadorean-style occupations of public buildings and attracted a sharp rise in repression, directed particularly against PASOH. On the other, the military's insistence upon retaining four cabinet portfolios gave the four Nationalist ministers a clear advantage over the five Liberals and increased tension with the assembly headed by Rodas's successor, Roberto Suazo Córdoba, whose lack of power encouraged Liberal factionalism beyond the troublesome ALIPO group. Strikes by

TRRC workers and members of the Bajo Aguán co-ops, a large and disorderly demonstration in protest at Honduran involvement in the Rio Sumpul massacre, and discontent within the military at the removal of fifteen officers closely associated with the agrarian reform, sustained an atmosphere of instability through the autumn. The events of early 1981 suggested an even stronger convergence with the regional pattern of conflict as the Paz government – for such it was, despite the existence of the assembly – maintained absolute rigidity in the face of apparently inexorable economic decline, the assembly's continued efforts to obtain a measure of authentic power, and the first signs of guerrillaism on the left. This took the form of the kidnapping of two prominent bankers following the army's arrest and torture of Tomás Nativí, a leader of the *Unión Revolucionaria del Pueblo* (URP), founded late in 1980 by PCH dissidents but soon smashed by the paramilitary police (FUSEP). The kidnap operations were in themselves successful and served to accelerate capital flight, which had reached $350 million over the last eighteen months as inflation rose from 15 to 42 per cent; the prospects for regional peace steadily worsened; and the rural bourgeoisie's long desired treaty with El Salvador failed to boost trade and provoked widespread discontent over joint military actions. By April 1981 the president of the capital's chamber of commerce was urging rapprochement between capital and labour 'before it is too late' whilst sections of the officer corps were manifesting restlessness at collaboration with the Salvadoreans both because of their longstanding enmity and because it threatened to draw guerrilla activity across the highly permeable border.[71]

The failure of the left to exploit this situation must be seen in the context of its complete exclusion from the revived electoralist arena. Deprived of links with reformist currents once the Nationalists opportunistically extended recognition to the PDC in an effort to reduce the Liberal vote, the PCH, which was still formally outlawed, voted to uphold its position of electoral abstentionism and turned its concentration to work inside the unions. PASOH joined the Maoists and a cluster of smaller groups influenced by the experience of Nicaragua and El Salvador in moving towards a strategy of armed struggle. Circumstances favoured neither orientation. Although the PCH was able to gain the collaboration of the Maoists in setting up *Federación Unitaria de Trabajadores de Honduras* (FUTH) as the country's first radical-led union federation, its membership was very small and had little industrial muscle beyond the power workers. Renewed military intervention in Las Isletas, the ousting of the progressive leadership of SITRATERCO, and the failure of the left to make any headway within either ANACH or the UNC combined to make this a particularly inauspicious time at which to stage an offensive within the union movement; the advances made were modest in the extreme. The prospects for a guerrilla strategy appeared slimmer still aside from the refuge available in Nicaragua and northern El Salvador. Yet virtually all the non-Communist left now dedicated itself to forming armed groups, the Maoists establishing the *Frente Morazanista de Liberación National de Honduras* (FMLNH), PASOH forming the kernel of the Honduran wing of the PRTC, whilst student radicals influenced by Nicaragua (but not controlled by the FSLN) set up the *Fuerzas Populares Revolucionarias Lorenzo Zelaya* (FPR) and the *Movimiento Popular de Liberación Cinchonero* (MPL), named after a nineteenth-century rebel against the tithe. With the exception of the FMLNH, which could call upon some support from the teachers, and PASOH, which possessed sympathizers inside the UNC, none of these bodies had a popular base or military experience remotely comparable to that of the guerrillas in the neighbouring countries, and only the MPL and PRTC were ever to engage in serious activity. Within two years this would end in disastrous failure, but when four Cinchoneros hijacked a jet of the national airline SAHSA in April 1981 the threat of a guerrilla campaign seemed very real. This (failed) action prompted the military to undertake more concerted repression of the left, intermittent raids over the following months providing the right with the opportunity to assemble the rudiments of an authoritarian regime behind the facade of constitutionalism.

The prime mover of this strategy, Colonel Gustavo Alvárez, was already engaged in a struggle for power against Colonels Leonardo Torres Arias and Hubert Bodden Cáceres, both from the military centre and 'neutralist' in regional terms, whereas Alvárez espoused a pugnacious policy towards Nicaragua as well as in domestic matters. Long a personal opponent of Zúñiga, Alvárez curried favour with the conservative Suazo leadership of the Liberals that gratefully embraced this unaccustomed military patronage (and the promise of greater US aid that accompanied it) so as to match the fiercely anti-Communist drift of the PN under Zúñiga's candidacy. There can be little doubt that with the outbreak of guerrilla activity inside the country and with frequent fighting along the Salvadorean border the army would in all events have exercised a dominant influence over the incoming administration, widely expected to be formed by the Nationalists.

The last months of Paz's government were clouded by the dismissal of his finance minister, Valentín Mendoza, for an illegal land speculation in which the president himself was reported to be involved. The affair effectively cancelled Paz's authority within the military, which did not bother to oust him but also did not exercise itself to help the PN, which the president had always favoured. Suazo's bureaucratic outmanoeuvring of ALIPO kept the mavericks both silent and within party ranks, thus preventing the emergence of a third 'centrist' civilian force that might have coalesced around ALIPO, PINU and the PDC and driven through the middle of the age-old partisan divide. Separately, these parties had no chance of upsetting the established pattern in the November poll, which was won handsomely by Suazo and the PL (52.3 per cent of the vote; 44 congressional seats) whilst Zúñiga paid the price for his many years of counsel to the colonels in the first full election after seventeen years of military rule (41 per cent of the vote; 34 seats). With PINU winning three seats and the PDC securing a solitary voice in Efraín Díaz Arrivillaga, the new congress contained only a single deputy of clearly progressive views – Díaz was on the left of the region's weakest but most adventurous Christian Democratic formation – and he alone voted against the appointment of Alvárez as the new commander-in-chief. Whereas elsewhere in Central America – even in El Salvador – one could detect some modulation, however temporary and inconsequential, of military behaviour upon the transition to civilian administration, the reverse was true in the case of Honduras. From 1982 the army imposed its stamp upon civil society and extended its operations in an even more emphatic manner than in 1972–75. Fears that the return to constitutionalism would shortly be nullified by renewed military government were misconceived. Expectations that the armed forces would return to a subordinate arbitrational role had even less foundation whilst Alvárez held power.

The Suazo government (1982–85) also differed from its counterparts in El Salvador (Duarte) and Guatemala (Cerezo) in that it did not even pretend to pursue progressive economic reforms, seeking instead to reverse many of the measures introduced by the military and replace them with unqualified neo-liberal policies. Although it was essential to retain INA and even possible to expand the number of titles given to *campesinos* already occupying uncontested property, Suazo broke completely with the policies developed by his party in the halcyon days of the early 1960s. The new strategy for confronting a crisis that had stalled the growth of the 1970s and driven the economy into contraction was directed by Miguel Facusse, who upon his appointment as economic adviser produced a highly controversial memorandum that urged the emulation of the Jamaican model under Seaga with deflation, deregulation, major reductions in public expenditure and full collaboration with the IMF and World Bank. These proposals were heartily endorsed in a document presented to the new government in a less than private fashion by the recently arrived US ambassador, John Negroponte. His experience as a 'political officer' in Saigon and anti-communist zeal commended him for a post that now had less to do with the practice of diplomacy than the running of a local prefecture and covert military operations against Nicaragua.[72] The Liberal leadership possessed no coherent alternative to this orthodox plan, upon which, it was made scrupulously clear, rested the future of international assistance. Accordingly, its adoption and the reduction of public expenditure by 15 per cent in 1982 led to the disbursement of total loans and aid worth $424.4 million in that year (much of this sum being for balance of payments adjustment) whilst US government assistance during the Suazo administration reached $709.5 million.[73] (When, in January 1985, the Honduran government had the temerity to baulk at further deflation and the devaluation demanded by Washington, $147.5 million in USAID funds was stopped and not released until the Liberals in Tegucigalpa resigned themselves to complete sepoy status, which took precisely six weeks.)

The political cost of what soon transpired to be a miserable bargain extended well beyond a surrender of autonomy evocative of the early decades of the century. Price subsidies for basic goods were reduced or annulled, state infrastructure and services scythed back, sales and income taxes of the type successfully opposed by the unions and COHEP in the late 1960s increased or introduced, and virtually all restrictions and tariffs on foreign investment were removed. Inflation was indeed reduced and a balance of trade achieved in 1984, but the economy continued to contract. Real wages fell by 12 per cent in three years, open unemployment rose by 64 per cent, and the foreign debt doubled in the same period (to $2.25 billion); at $314, per capita GDP in 1984 was just one dollar higher than it had been in 1970. Domestic manufacturing took a severe battering at the hands of 'economic discipline', industry falling from 22 to 16 per cent of GDP with 65 bankruptcies in 1982 and a further 440 over the next two years. There was, though, very little evidence that either the capitalist class as a whole or the government was prepared to purge itself with quite the same vigour as demanded, for instance, of the health and education services, where substantial budget reductions provoked major strikes in 1982 and 1983. If the merchants and agro-export lobby represented by Facusse celebrated the influx of Yanqui cash, they had already availed themselves of the advantages of what was a notoriously open economy by exporting at least $1 billion in capital betwen 1980 and 1984. This flight – roughly equivalent to the aid and foreign investment received during the same period – was not unconnected with the bankruptcy of CONADI, which had 'lost' $300 million since 1974 in unrecovered loans to local companies, one of the fifty-eight firms in default being *Mejores Alimentos de Honduras* that owed $49 million and was owned by that disciple of market efficiency Miguel Facusse.[74]

Such a state of affairs could not have greatly surprised the rest of the government, who, if they understood the new economic regime as little more than enforced 'common sense', adopted the same rationale in pursuing entirely traditional policies with respect to milking the state. The potential for this was considerably enhanced by increased foreign aid, very little of which reached its supposed destination. This was evidenced by frequent revelations of cases such as the 900 lbs of donated milk powder from Canada discovered in a private San Pedro Sula bakery, or Señora Olga

Ondina Martínez's positively Thatcherite hoarding of 28 cases of milk, 78 of tinned chicken, 92 of soya oil and 212 of tinned sardines donated by the World Food Program to the poor of Honduras only to end up in her privatized pantry. This, of course, was small fry and always liable to exposure and indignant protest by the authorities, but even at the top of the pile the scramble for pickings was so frantic that little effort was made at concealment, perhaps because Suazo had appointed Abraham Bennaton of 'Bananagate' fame as a government adviser. US officials were soon publicly denouncing the collapse of their aid programme as a result of corruption within the state. It should, however, be recalled that the Liberal Party had not held office for nearly twenty years and had many debts to pay. Thus, if on coming to office Suazo was able to denounce Nationalist patronage of sixty 'phantom' employees at INA costing the state $250,000 a year, his outrage was wholly ritualistic. It little surprised Hondurans that his minister of education should be caught purloining tons of EEC-donated milk powder; that INA should purchase flagrantly overvalued land from the government's friends; that many of Suazo's cheques for public works never reach their destination; or that the road works in his home town of La Paz occupy three-quarters of the country's earth-movers. This was the price – for some the reward – of constitutional government.[75]

The price that had not been anticipated was that exacted by Gustavo Alvárez, who in the space of two years facilitated the massive US military presence in the country, extended full cooperation to the Salvadorean armed forces, launched a fierce campaign against Sandinista Nicaragua, and presided over a process of internal militarization and repression that pushed Honduras towards the pattern of El Salvador and Guatemala. Alvárez had been trained in Argentina, was a friend and admirer of General Videla, relied upon the services of some sixty Argentine military advisers (many of whom stayed after withdrawal from the rest of the region following the Malvinas War). He wasted less breath lauding constitutional government at home than dictatorship abroad although moved to opine that, 'nothing could convince me that any other US president could interpret Central America as well as does Mr Reagan'.[76] Alvárez's virulent anti-Communism and distaste for negotiation when violence would do had been evident in his handling of the Las Isletas occupation of 1977 and his command of FUSEP and the DNI (plain-clothes police) first in San Pedro Sula and then at national level prior to his elevation by Suazo. This was followed in short order by a promotion to the rank of general that contravened all military ordinances but which, once overwhelmingly ratified by congress, permitted Alvárez to exile his challengers Torres Arias and Bodden forthwith. The removal of the leading military advocates of caution in both domestic and foreign policy, fulsome support from Negroponte and the Pentagon, and a grovelling executive and congress enabled the new commander to construct

Table 51: Main Events in Honduran Politics, 1980–85

1980	Mar.	Progressives lose leadership of SITRATERCO; General Paz visits US.
	Apr.	Constituent assembly elections narrowly won by Liberals; Rio Sumpul massacre.
	May	Arrest of PRTC militants.
	Jul.	Teachers' strike; General Paz ratified as provisional president; Partido Nacional and military control cabinet.
	Sept.	*Campesino* strike in Bajo Aguán.
	Oct.	Peace treaty with El Salvador.
1981	Jan.	Kidnap of banker Paul Vinelli; arrest and torture of radical leader Tomás Nativí; military occupy Las Isletas cooperative.
	Apr.	Cinchonero guerrillas hijack SAHSA plane to Panama.
	Oct.	Land scandal involving Minister of Finance Valentín Mendoza.
	Nov.	Liberal Roberto Suazo wins presidential elections; John Negroponte appointed US ambassador.
1982	Jan.	Colonel Alvárez appointed military commander; economic austerity measures.
	Feb.	Washington increases military aid for fiscal year 82/83 by 50%.
	Apr.	Decree 33 outlaws strikes and land occupations; Alvárez promoted general; guerrilla hijack at Tegucigalpa airport.
	Jun.	Joint operations with Salvadorean military; 60 progressive and union leaders arrested.
	Jul.	Bombing of Tegucigalpa power stations in protest at collaboration with Salvadorean military; army captures guerrilla safe house in capital; leading rightists call for paramilitary forces; Suazo and Alvárez visit Washington to request increased aid.
	Aug.	Teachers strike for fortnight; Colonel Torres Arias denounces Alvárez for personalism and seeking a 'national security' state.
	Sept.	Cinchoneros hold 85 hostages in San Pedro Sula Chamber of Commerce; leave for Cuba after a week.
	Nov.	*Newsweek* reveals that Negroponte is in control of Contra operation.
	Dec.	President Reagan visits San Pedro Sula; Ariel Sharon visits Tegucigalpa; Boland amendment passed by US Congress.
1983	Jan.	APROH founded by reactionary and business sectors; Alvárez is appointed its president.
	Feb.	'Big Pine I' joint US–Honduran exercises begin (5,600 troops).
	Mar.	Papal visit; bombing of Guatemalan embassy.

May Alvárez signs agreement in Washington to establish CREM.
Jun. Sixty Salvadorean troops arrive at Puerto Castillo CREM for training.
Jul. Clashes with Nicaraguan gunboats in Gulf of Fonseca.
Aug. 'Big Pine II' exercises begin (5,500 US troops); Liberal Party internal elections denounced as fraudulent; Alvárez requests $300 million in military aid from Washington.
Sept. PRTC column in Olancho destroyed by army; Weinberger visit; APROH talks with Kissinger in Miami.
Oct. Contra/CIA attack on Nicaraguan port of Corinto.
Dec. Government complains at 'meagre' US assistance.

1984 Jan. US helicopter shot down inside Nicaraguan territory; Alvárez announces new constitution for armed forces.
Mar. US Senate forbids further construction of military facilities without congressional approval; kidnap of power workers' leader Rolando Vindel leads to strike and demonstrations; Alvárez overthrown by officer corps and replaced by Colonel Lopez.
Apr. 'Grenadier I' joint exercises on Salvadorean border and 'Ocean Venture' manoeuvres by US fleet in Caribbean; popular demonstrations against US military presence and for trade union rights.
May Labour Day marches attract 100,000 in Tegucigalpa and San Pedro Sula; new military leadership renegotiates CREM agreement; taxes on tobacco and alcoholic beverages withdrawn after popular demonstrations.
Jun. General strike against taxes called off; high command request amendments to 1954 military treaty, $1.3 billion in economic aid, $400 million in military aid, and a dozen advanced F-5E fighters from Washington.
Oct. FBI thwarts Miami plot led by Alvárez loyalist Colonel Bueso Rosa.
Nov. APROH dissolved.
Dec. Army report denies responsibility for the disappeared; Reagan grants $88 million in military aid.

1985 Jan. Miskito Contra chieftain Steadman Fagoth expelled; Robert MacFarlane rejects new military treaty.
Feb. 'Big Pine III' manoeuvres begin; public sector workers occupy Tegucigalpa centre in protest at redundancies.
Mar. Constitutional crisis over congressional appointment of new Supreme Court; Contras formally allowed to stay.

1985 Apr. Political crisis deepens as new judges are arrested by government; Washington declares Honduras has been invaded by Sandinista forces in 'Holy Week crisis'.

May Constitutional crisis finally resolved by military arbitration; pact to allow individual candidacies in November presidential elections but allocating victory by party allegiance accepted by parties and CTH; Suazo and Lopez visit Washington to request $3 billion in aid over four years and a replacement to the 1954 treaty; US offers only minor changes to 1982 annexe to treaty.

Jun. CREM closed; 'Cabañas 85' joint manoeuvres begin.

Aug. Army kills Salvadorean refugees in Colomoncagua camp; strikes in Standard Fruit and hospitals.

Oct. Contras arrested for murder of Major Ricardo Zúñiga; demonstration of coffee farmers from Paraiso against Contra presence; Contra supply plane from New Orleans impounded by military at Tegucigalpa.

Nov. John Ferch replaces Negroponte as US ambassador; Liberal José Azcona del Hoyo wins presidential elections.

---

the vestiges of an autocratic and corporatist state within the shell of constitutional government and behind the shield of the US garrison.

Within two years Alvárez increased the military to 23,000 troops (in 1980 it had been 11,000 strong) and considerably enhanced its arsenal. Purchases made during personal trips to West Germany and Israel as well as the US expanded the armed forces' hardware from 24 armoured vehicles in 1980 to 113 in 1985, the number of fixed-wing aircraft rising from 82 to 109, helicopters from 3 to 15 and ships from 5 to 9. The cost of this was directly subsidized by Washington, US military aid increasing from $2.3 million in 1979 to $8.9 million in 1981 as a result of the Nicaraguan revolution, then rising vertiginously to $31.2 million in 1982 as Alvárez and Reagan took the reins and the offensives, formal and informal, against the Sandinistas got under way. The scale of this support might appear quite modest in comparison to that extended to El Salvador, but in local terms it was a massive increase from previous levels: total US military aid to Honduras between 1946 and 1981 amounted to $32.5 million, only just above the sum disbursed in 1982 alone. At the end of Alvárez's rule the annual figure had reached $78 million, by which time Washington was fully committed to an interventionist strategy that in 1986 provided nearly $90 million for the Honduran military to support the Nicaraguan Contra, which in that year itself officially received the larger sum of $100 million despite much greater difficulty in securing congressional approval.[77] The project of establishing an extensive network of military facilities in Honduras for a substantial rotating US garrison to service counter-insurgency operations in El Salvador and the two-pronged low-intensity campaign against Nicaragua began before Alvárez took charge and continued after he was ousted. Although he greatly assisted and fervently defended this strategy, it was far too large and important to depend upon the brokerage of a single individual, however overbearing he might be. Between 1982 and 1985 US forces either built anew or extended a dozen military installations and bases at a cost of $64 million; ten of these bases were made capable of handling C-130 transport aircraft for a possible invasion of Nicaragua, which was overflown by spy-planes controlled from San Lorenzo, scanned by new radar stations at Tiger Island and Cerro la Mole, and justifiably concerned by military construction of roads in the border region.[78] In 1982 joint US–Honduran manoeuvres were limited to a short operation around the new military base at Durzuna on the border. Over the next four years some 23,000 US land forces were deployed in six major 'manoeuvres' – Big Pine I or Ahuas Tara (February 1983); Big Pine II (August 1983–February 1984); Grenadier I (April–June 1984); Big Pine III (February–May 1985); Cabañas 85 (June–September 1985); Terencio Sierra (March–May 1986) – whilst the four large naval operations conducted between 1982 and 1984 included rehearsals for the blockade of Nicaragua and amphibious landings.

Honduran forces played a minor role in these war games, but it was not just their very low level of training and logistical skill that prompted the Pentagon to insist upon constant participation. Aside from the fact that this was diplomatically desirable in order to maintain the image of equitable collaboration, US law prohibited the retention of a permanent establishment of troops in the country and the treaty of 1954 had been carefully drafted so as not to allow for a US garrison in Honduras. Both of these factors required rotation of US personnel and a higher level of local support than might be expected and – from the Pentagon's viewpoint – desired given the logistical magnitude and political importance of the operation. This was particularly so with regard to the Contra campaign, in which the need for Honduran cooperation and a low official US profile was evident well before it became a diplomatic issue in 1984 and a US domestic controversy in 1986. Similar constraints applied to the much more open North American support for the Salvadorean military, which could not easily be trained in the US and was confronted with the most taxing challenge from the FMLN precisely in the border region. In both cases the Honduran army was required to undertake politically unpopular activity, collaborating with a recent national enemy and supporting a large illegal foreign force that caused disorder, undermined sovereignty on national soil and threatened to provoke an unwanted and unwarranted foreign war when it crossed the border. Alvárez's pugnacious advocacy was, therefore, especially crucial to the initiation of these operations.

Throughout this period the Honduran government stuck to the risible pretence that there were no Contra forces on national territory. Even in November 1985, when the Nicaraguan rebels numbered at least 10,000 and were the object of close and constant international scrutiny, President-elect José Azcona de Hoyo declared, 'I am unaware of the existence of counter-revolutionary camps', displaying a shamelessness peculiar even by the unenviable standards of the Honduran political class in his explanation that this ignorance stemmed from the fact that as a private citizen he had not been able to visit all of the country to check out his suspicions.[79] Alvárez was little concerned to play this game other than in a distinctly half-hearted fashion, and he was far less inhibited than his regional peers in drawing rude conclusions from an equally unsophisticated interpretation of Central America's instability: '[We] would be in agreement with US intervention in Central America because we now confront an armed aggression from the Soviet Union via Cuba'.[80] The general's attitude towards Sandinista Nicaragua left little doubt as to his pro-Contra activities and none whatsoever as to his sympathies: 'Nicaragua has been converted into a base for a war of conquest in the Caribbean Basin . . . [it] is a Soviet base for subversion. How can we defend ourselves against a Soviet base designed for permanent aggression? . . . I don't believe that we can coexist. There's no way it can be done . . . I think that there will soon be a general insurrection in Nicaragua . . . the opposition in Nicaragua will need considerable logistical help; it would be very sad if it didn't receive it.'[81] Indeed, so confident was Alvárez of an overthrow of the FSLN government that in December 1983 he declared that he would spend his next birthday in Managua despite the fact that US commanders had already stopped him from ordering Honduran troops across the border.[82] Such bravado was not shared by many of his subordinates who accepted the windfall gains of Washington's campaign against the Sandinistas yet were loth to get involved in a conflict with the superior army of a country with which they had no historic enmity. In 1980 the far from progressive FUSEP commander Colonel Amilcar Zelaya had succinctly expressed this view in declaring, 'Let's leave the problems of Nicaragua to the Nicaraguans and deal with the problems of Honduras.'[83]

Over the next two years it became impossible to cling on to the luxury of such neutralism. This could now only be fully defended from abroad, as in the case of Torres Arias, who in August 1982 issued from his Mexican exile an uncommonly sharp attack on Alvárez for 'leading Honduras to the abyss of internal destruction and preparing the people for the possibility of war with Nicaragua'.[84] Nonetheless, the antics of the Contra – whose troops were prone to violent pillage around their camps, their leaders to haughty and dissolute behaviour in the capital – increasingly exasperated the officer corps: 'If they are guerrillas why aren't they in the mountains? They are a bunch of dilettantes who spend their lives in the mess. They will never overthrow the Sandinistas.'[85] Although there was no option but to comply with those who proclaimed these people to be 'Freedom Fighters', there were not a few commanders who were inclined to sympathize with the views expressed by López Arellano: 'As of today I have had no information that Nicaragua has a Communist government. It is not that I am partial to the Sandinistas, but rather a friend of those governments that work and struggle for the people . . . [the Nicaraguans] have no desire or reason to invade, attack or fight Honduras.'[86] Alvárez's authority and US largesse were more than a match for such deviant sentiment yet the North Americans appeared oblivious to the possibility that it might have a rational base, historical origins or any significant support, this insensitivity being a direct product of great-power arrogance for which a small but irritating price had subsequently to be paid.

The Salvadorean alliance was always more fragile than that with the Contra, causing sharper and more immediate discontent. From the beginning of his mandate Alvárez had cultivated an increasingly coercive atmosphere within the country, the discovery of unmarked graves near Tegucigalpa in February 1982 confirming popular fears about the existence of death squads. Congress dutifully approved two months later the draconian Decree 33 that imposed twenty years' gaol for 'subversion', understood to include participation in *tomas*, factory occupations or disorderly demonstrations. However, the general's deployment of troops to assist the Salvadorean army in anti-guerrilla operations in July provoked a protest of a very different nature when Tegucigalpa's power station was destroyed by insurgent bombs. This incident was followed by a shoot-out in the suburb of La Florencia in which one rebel was killed, Central America's most placid capital being flooded with troops. As Alvárez's clampdown tightened, the PCH's general secretary Rigoberto Padilla Rush sensibly went underground in fear of his life under conditions in which the right was openly demanding the formation of paramilitary squads whilst twenty foreign nationals, mostly Salvadoreans, were reported to have been 'disappeared', bringing the total for 1982 to over one hundred.[87] In September the Cinchoneros struck back, staging an audacious seizure of the San Pedro Sula Chamber of Commerce, two ministers and the president of the Central Bank being amongst their hostages. This raid was a failure insofar as the guerrillas won none of their demands other than safe conduct to Panama, but the demands themselves – withdrawal from the *Comunidad Democrática Centroamericana*; removal of the anti-terrorist legislation; expulsion of US military advisers; and release of fifty-seven political prisoners including the URP leaders Tomás Nativí and Filadelfio Martínez (both believed dead) – reflected the degree to which Alvárez had drawn the country towards the regional pattern of polarization. Refusing to allow the government to treat with the Cinchoneros, Alvárez stuck to his course. Having signed a confidential amendment to the 1954 treaty in May 1982 so as to allow the presence of US troops, he proceeded to enter into another secret agreement in May 1983 further to alter the treaty and establish a training centre – *Centro Regional de Entrenamiento Militar* (CREM) – on Honduran soil (Puerto Castillo) for Salvadorean troops. Congress was only informed and permitted to debate this illegal tampering with an international treaty in June, when the CREM was opened. It boldly decided by seventy-eight votes against three to approve the measure so long as the Salvadoreans were classified as 'students'. Such a display of 'realism' signalled the complete subjugation of both the traditional parties and the constitutional apparatus as a whole, within which the question of the Contra was not formally discussed over the next three years even after the US Congress had done so in great, not to say embarrassing, detail.

This weakness and lassitude was of only limited value to Alvárez's plans, which could not be realized by military means alone and required more than congressional rubber-stamping. His profound antipathy for organized labour did not preclude an alliance with the compliant leadership of the CTH yet the violent suppression of strikes and unusual withdrawal of official recognition from the properly elected radical officers of the COLPROSUMAH teachers' union complicated matters. It drew forthright opposition from the PDC and ALIPO as well as unsettling a bureaucracy experiencing great difficulty in controlling a membership antagonized by the regime's economic policies, which in March 1983 extended to a freeze of public sector wages. As a result, much less reliance could be placed on co-optation of the labour movement than had been the case in the 1960s. Moreover, Suazo's borrowed economic doctrines had reopened the divisions inside COHEP along sectoral lines and provided the PN with a golden opportunity to attack the government – despite the fact that its policies were little different from those advocated by the Nationalists themselves. In this spirit of sectarianism reborn, the Nationalist president of COHEP, Fernando Landizabal, denounced capital flight, the new taxes, the spate of bankruptcies and the Facusse plan as a whole – 'not worth the paper it's written on'.[88] It thus proved doubly difficult to reconstitute the corporate alliance of 1969–72, and Alvárez was obliged to establish the *Asociación para el Progreso de Honduras* (APROH) in January 1983 as a vehicle for his distinctly authoritarian corporatist project on the basis of only partial representation of the unions (CTH and ANACH), the capitalist class and the political parties. Suazo gave his political and legal blessing to the new body, which had Facusse, who donated $500,000, as its vice president, the ubiquitous Bennaton as its trusted treasurer, and the right-wing rector of UNAH, Oswaldo Ramos Soto, as its secretary (an apt appointment for an organization dedicated to 'fighting Marxism–Leninism with ideas while General Alvárez fights it in other ways').[89] Some members of the government began to temper their enthusiasm when it became clear that APROH's ideas were very largely drawn from the Unification Church ('Moonies'), represented by the highly visible and no less controversial Colonel Bo Hi Pak (a close ally of several dictatorships in South America), that its sympathies lay with paramilitary violence against the left, and its political project was patently neo-Fascist in character. (APROH's much vaunted proposal for 'social forestry cooperatives' envisaged militarized peasant brigades reminiscent of Himmler's prospectus for Prussia although it was the allocation of half the projected $2.3 billion in US aid to 4,400 local landlords that gave the plan real lustre.[90])

None of Alvárez's initiatives was sufficiently controversial in itself to coalesce opposition to his autocratic and personalist rule even though a civilian administration was formally governing the country and the general had come under strong suspicion of corruption – the normal cause of military downfall – following the disappearance of $1 million in an arms transaction. However, when, in March 1984, he presented congress with a bill to reduce the size of COSUFA from forty-five to twenty-one officers, concentrate power in the hands of eight colonels, and establish the minimum age for promotion to general at fifty-five (which he himself had not yet reached), Alvárez succeeded in combining fierce military opposition to a clearly partisan manipulation of institutional norms with broader repudiation of his warmongering, unpopular alliances and unquestioning attendance to Washington's needs. On 31 March he was ousted in a skilfully organized coup d'état directed by officers of the sixth and seventh *tandas*, put on a plane to Costa Rica, and replaced by Colonel Walter López of the airforce who immediately restored COSUFA's authority. On May Day 100,000 people were able to demonstrate and demand the removal of US troops without being molested; in September the Salvadoreans were withdrawn and the CREM closed after surprisingly tough bargaining by the López high command; in November APROH was disbanded; and in December the military deigned to publish a report on human rights that disowned responsibility for the spate of disappearances under Alvárez but also signalled formal opposition to unlawful methods of repression that had in fact been little used since April. Ambassador Negroponte, who was closely associated with Alvárez and shared his boisterous demeanour, was left stranded and eventually replaced in mid 1985 by John Ferch, a career diplomat of almost apologetic character who was averse to dabbling in 'covert' antics and instead dedicated himself to economic matters (for which he received a quite remarkably warm reception in Tegucigalpa and minimal support from Washington). By the end of 1984 it appeared as if the excesses of the Alvárez era had been reversed and the elections slated for November 1985 offered the prospect of a proper revival of constitutionalism.

Such expectations of an unproblematic return to the pre-1982 position were as groundless as had been the conviction – shared by right and left alike – that Alvárez had laid the basis for a stable absolutism. Although both political parties were quick to hitch themselves to the anti-Salvadorean bandwagon – ensuring renewal of the territorial dispute once the 1980 treaty lapsed in December 1985 – it proved much more difficult to renegotiate the terms of US dominion as a whole and the Contra question in particular. In the autumn of 1984 Tegucigalpa made a formal request for $1.7 billion in aid spread over the rest of the decade, but the Reagan administration merely confirmed that it expected to release $88 million for the military budget in 1986. In May 1985 Suazo and López visited Washington to ask for $3 billion over the next four years as well as the transformation of the 1954 treaty into a complete mutual defence pact. Again, the response was negative, which could scarcely have surprised the government although Suazo had at least been finally seen to press for better terms whilst López could claim that he had succeeded in obtaining military aid worth half that given to El Salvador – the smallest differential since 1980.

Despite the shift away from the vehement anti-Sandinismo of the Alvárez period the army was not prepared to adopt a fully neutralist stance towards Nicaragua. One important reason for this was the extraordinarily misconceived decision of the PRTC to send a guerrilla column of some one hundred fighters from Nicaragua into Olancho in August 1983, in the midst of the Big Pine II manoeuvres. Under the leadership of the veteran radical José María Reyes Matta, closely linked to Cuba and often described as a member of Ché Guevara's Bolivian *foco*, this ill-prepared force was surrounded and liquidated within a matter of days, providing the US troops with authentic counter-insurgency experience and the Hondurans with apparent confirmation of Nicaragua's subversive designs.[91] This was the last significant instance of guerrilla activity in the country and the only one clearly to have been launched from Nicaragua. Equally, whilst some officers struck up close and remunerative relations with the Contra military leadership under ex-National Guard Colonel Enrique Bermúdez, whose forces easily outnumbered the Honduran frontier garrisons, the Nicaraguan rebels continued to create as many political and diplomatic problems as they did opportunities for personal and institutional pecuniary advancement. In January 1985 the Miskito Contra leader Steadman Fagoth was expelled for giving a press conference in the capital and undermining at a stroke the basis for Honduran 'deniability'. The Contra was ordered to cease public activity in Tegucigalpa and threatened with collective expulsion although some weeks later the government confirmed that it could stay in the country provided it kept a lower profile.[92] No doubt strenuous US representations lay behind this decision, but it was evident that with Alvárez gone the Hondurans were disposed to barter the terms of their collaboration with some resolution.

In October 1985 tension over the issue rose further still when three Contras were arrested for killing a retired Honduran officer in a private feud whilst coffee growers from El Paraiso raised vigorous complaints that the Nicaraguans prevented them from farming freely. The government responded by declaring that no Contra aid could be channelled through the US embassy whilst the military pointedly detained a supply plane from New Orleans at Toncontín airport and, once Ambassador Ferch disclaimed official US responsibility, sent it back.[93] Fears that Honduran truculence could get completely out of hand led to a visit in November by Lieutenant Colonel Oliver North, who lobbied with some success for restoring cooperation and possibly explained the nature of an operation that remained concealed from the US Congress for at least another year.[94]

Matters became rather more serious in 1986 as the rebels attracted greater international attention and began to undertake major operations inside Nicaragua, provoking 'hot pursuit' retaliatory attacks by the EPS across the border. One such tactical counter-offensive during the Easter holiday was blown up by Washington into an 'invasion' of Honduras and tantamount to a declaration of war. Yet in certain border areas such incursions had been commonplace for some time and, depending upon the Honduran unit concerned, quite often tolerated. In this case the cabinet was notably reluctant to break their seaside vacations and the high command appeared disconcertingly content to allow EPS troops to occupy Honduran soil for several days.[95] A year later a misguided attempt by fleeing Contras to provoke a fight between Honduran and EPS troops by firing on the former only served to attract the ballistic attentions of both forces and once again raise the question of expulsion, for which the Costa Rican government had now provided a precedent, albeit more in word than deed.[96]

The internal problems caused by the presence of the rebels also persisted. In July 1986 paramilitary forces associated with Colonel Roberto Núñez, chief of Honduran military intelligence, attacked the home and arrested the family of PN deputy Rodolfo Zelaya in an apparent effort to wrest from him the lucrative contract for supplying the Contra.[97] That same month the US press accused General López, who had been replaced as commander-in-chief by Colonel Humberto Regalado Hernández in February, of siphoning off at least $450,000 from Contra funds.[98] López's departure had been more directly connected with his attempt to oust some members of the nationalist sixth promotion from their posts against regulations, but the suspicion of corruption and failure to resolve the Contra issue undoubtedly hastened his removal, producing a modest shift further away from automatic collaboration.[99] The revelations of the Irangate scandal gave added impetus to this tendency and suggested that although the Hondurans were in no position to break entirely free from the role assigned them by Washington, they could still pursue the course traditionally adopted by subaltern forces in the hispanic world that is captured in the phrase '*Obedezco pero no cumplo*' (literally, 'I obey but do not comply'). After the removal of Alvárez the managers of Washington's Central American strategy were obliged to treat this problem seriously since the prospect of the Contra campaign collapsing through accumulated incompetence and petty squabbling was just as threatening and far more probable than that of a politically coherent nationalist backlash.

The controversies engendered by Alvárez's stillborn militarist endeavour obscured for at least two years the rapid decomposition of the party system. This was certainly affected by the dominant role adopted by the army but owed just as much to Suazo's economic policies and the inability of both party leaderships to sustain either internal unity or a stable system of competition once the survival of civilian government was no longer reliant upon the balance of domestic forces and enjoyed a measure of protection from Washington. Insofar as elections were now effectively guaranteed and the military had dropped its longstanding allegiance to the PN, inter-party competition was almost bound to increase. However, intra-party feuding and the near implosion of the constitutional concordat in 1985 was also the result of longer-term factors. Most obviously, neither the arbitrational role adopted by the union bureaucracy nor the emergence of PINU and the PDC had compensated for the absence of a centrist party able to provide a programme of moderate reform free from the traditional traits of *caudillismo*, localism and placemanship. Such initiatives came from within the existing structure of the PL, complicating the internal competition that followed Rodas's death. Furthermore, although Zúñiga's faction had won the PN internal elections late in 1982, this victory had only been achieved after a great deal of backroom wheeling and dealing, and it was clear that the defeats of 1980 and 1981 had eroded the *caudillo*'s customary authority. From 1983 the PN was riven by divisions based on both personal ambition and Suazo's offer of a share of the spoils on a bipartisan basis, which was more than a little beguiling now that the PL was pursuing a thoroughly conservative course.

The year preceding the November 1985 elections produced a confusion of alignments and realignments on both sides, combining ideological differences with sheer opportunism. Within the Liberal camp Suazo faced a formidable array of opponents in part simply because he was a president in a period of recession and with only tenuous control over the apparatus of patronage. His clear *continuista* intentions, which should not be considered abnormal in the light of the previous fifty years, alienated his erstwhile ally Efraín Bú Girón, who was, like Suazo, a small town *caudillo* of the *rodista* school and as president of congress harboured more than private designs upon the executive mansion. The president's principal lieutenant in 1980–81, José Azcona de Hoyo, was likewise forced into opposition both by this potential obstacle to his own ambitions and by Suazo's economic programme, which had aggravated the urban middle-class constituency of the PL in which Azcona had his base. The government's imposition of new taxes on tobacco and alcohol in June 1984 was particularly important in this regard since it not only harmed local commercial interests already up in arms over the administration's corruption but also raised the spectre of a CTH-led general strength threatening a complete rupture between the Liberals and the unions. Thus, by early 1985 *rodismo* was itself sundered in three: Suazo's presidential faction shifting between *continuismo* and auctioning off the rights of succession; Bú Girón's personalist challenge based on congress and benefiting from the established antipathy of the legislature for the executive; and Azcona's technocratic wing which had the most solid social base. The picture was further complicated by the division of the longstanding ALIPO faction into two: the brothers Carlos and Jorge Arturo Reina who, leading the new MOLIDER group, adhered to a broadly social democratic line whilst the ALIPO name was retained by those critics of Suazo headed by Jorge Bueso Arias, who enjoyed stronger backing from local business and propounded policies similar to those pursued by Christian Democracy elsewhere in the region and for which the PDCH had shown itself to be an inadequate vehicle.

The position within the Nationalist camp was little better, not least because of Suazo's artful encouragement of a coalitionist tendency led by Juan Pablo Urrutia that favoured a two-year extension of the president's mandate. However, Urrutia's *Movimiento de Unidad y Cambio* enjoyed less support than either of the party's other contenders: Fernando Landizabal, president of FENAGH and holder of the official candidacy but opposed by Zúñiga's clique; and Rafael Callejas, a young, US-educated neo-liberal who headed the *Movimiento Renovador Nacionalista* which promised a radical conservative programme based upon Reagan's 'Caribbean Basin Initiative'. Until the spring of 1985 this unusually wide range of candidacies presented less of a danger to the electoralist system than did the threat of Suazo's *continuismo*, which showed no sign of abating after Alvárez's fall. When the president eventually dropped his pretensions and named the aged minister of justice Oscar Mejía Arellano as his dauphin and the official Liberal candidate the stage was set for a complete free-for-all.[100]

The 'constitutional crisis' of March and April 1985 and the re-emergence of the unions and armed forces as essential power-brokers was immediately provoked by congressional support – by 50 votes to 29 – for Bú Girón's attempt to replace Suazo's appointees to the Supreme Court with men designated by parliament, thereby winning control of the electoral tribunal – whose membership depended in part upon the court – away from the president and opening up the electoral contest, albeit to the particular advantage of Bú Girón himself. In response Suazo ordered the arrest of the congressional appointee to the presidency of the court, which order the police obeyed despite countermanding instructions from parliament. Stalemate prevailed for a fortnight as the military formally upheld the status quo whilst urging the executive to make concessions and reach a rapid solution. When Suazo clearly indicated that he would not countenance negotiation López announced that he was authorized to stage a coup, forcing the president to agree to a compromise cobbled together by the officer corps and the CTH and ratified at a meeting at Toncontín airport. Under its terms the arrested judge was released and his peers required to resign whilst no party was allowed to field an official candidate in the November elections but all factions permitted to stand in their own right. Victory was to be assigned to that party whose various factions had together logged the highest number of votes rather than to the single highest-scoring candidate.[101] This 'Airforce Option' thus provided a short-term resolution to the outburst of sectarianism and underlined the need for direct corporate intervention, but it was far from clear if a formula that encouraged multiple partisanship could provide an enduring basis for stability. Doubts on this score were raised on the eve of the poll by the discovery that 600,000 ballots had been misprinted and then by the result of the election itself, in which discontent with the regime and his agile campaign gave Callejas the single largest number of votes (639,832). However, since the combined total of the PN factions (686,494) was less than that of the Liberals (772,611) victory was assigned to the most successful of the Liberal candidates – Azcona de Hoyo, whose personal tally was only 416,736.[102] The prospects for stability were assisted neither by the fact that the PN held five of the nine seats on the Supreme Court nor by the election of a congress in which the PL's 67 deputies were divided amongst themselves (46 supporting Azcona, 18 Mejía and 3 for Bú Girón) whilst all of the PN's 63 representatives were Callejas loyalists and the minority parties' four deputies (two for the PDCH and two for PINU) held the balance of power.[103] Hence, although Honduras had achieved Central America's first handover from one elected presidency to another (outside Costa Rica) when Guatemala had only just held its first 'open' election and El Salvador had yet to negotiate the travails of a full succession, this had only been effected by forceful extra-constitutional mediation and the propagation of a profusion of cliques and cabals that undermined both the electoralist system and the potential for a secure and coherent administration. The similarities with the 'solutions' of 1902, 1923–24, 1954–57 and 1971–72 were not exact but close enough to puncture confidence about the health of the Honduran polity.

The crisis of civilian government in 1984–85 encouraged union mobilization in a manner resembling that of 1969–72. In April 1984 the UNC staged sixty simultaneous *tomas* that were repulsed but still succeeded in forcing INA to speed up allocation of titles. Early in 1986 the anti-communist bureaucracies united to form the *Consejo Nacional de Obreros y Campesinos de Honduras* (CONOCH), which joined with COHEP to demand that the political parties accept a two-year truce similar in substance to that intended by the 1971 pact.[104] Renewed conflict in the Bajo Aguán from late 1985 led to further military intervention and a strike by the traditionally placid FECORAH. A revival of the FUTH, still under PCH influence, was met with the assassination of one of its leaders, Cristobal Pérez, in April 1986, causing further discontent. According to the human rights organization CODEH, the first six months of 1986 witnessed fifty-eight politically motivated killings as FUSEP became continually occupied in expelling squatters. In July a spate of thirty-five strikes came close to rolling into a national general strike, which was demanded by FUTH and only narrowly evaded by CONOCH.[105] In response to these developments Washington replaced the retiring Ambassador Ferch with the more resourceful Everett Briggs. It is likely that his intervention as well as the historic sectarianism of the unions lay behind the failure of the May 1987 effort to establish a united *campesino* organization on the basis of a nationwide *toma*. Military harassment of the left and preferential treatment of ANACH participants wrecked the initiative within three days, but the fact that it took place at all indicated that the post-1962 methods of control in the countryside were wearing thin.[106]

Far weaker than the Suazo administration in terms of electoral legitimacy and party support, heavily dependent upon the services of the military and a most wary union bureaucracy, unable to escape Washington's economic control or ignore its instructions to impede first Contadora and then the 1987 Arias regional peace proposals, the Azcona government cut a particularly sorry figure by almost any yardstick. The possession of such a dutiful pawn met virtually all of Washington's short-term requirements with respect to its regional strategy. But this was not the only game in progress, and what was treated as a pawn on the shores of the Potomac had to parade at least as a rook in downtown Tegucigalpa. In the real world such castling was far from easy since the US provided the local dominant bloc with minimal space in which to reproduce itself and secure not just a defensible response to the aggregate effects of eight years of 'destabilization' but also a convincing claim to national independence. The post-1979 experience had amply demonstrated that such a structural weakness was by no means automatically conducive to a general crisis of domination. On the other hand, eight years after the Nicaraguan revolution the constituent features of such a breakdown had been rearranged rather than decisively altered. Content to exploit the absence of a 'classic' collapse of control, Washington had not diminished by one jot the possibility of a regionally atypical implosion of the system in which it mistakenly expressed minimal interest and against which it could offer no response bar greater intervention and recourse to autocracy.

Notes

1. Quoted in Víctor Meza, *Historia del Movimiento Obrero Hondureño*, Tegucigalpa 1980, p. 127.

2. Quoted in Daniel Slutzky and Esther Alonso, *Empresas Transnacionales y Agricultura: El Caso del Enclave Bananero en Honduras*, Tegucigalpa 1980, p. 13.

3. *Tiempo*, San Pedro Sula, 19 November 1972, quoted in Mario Posas and Rafael Del Cid, *La Construcción del Sector Público y del Estado Nacional en Honduras, 1876–1979*, Tegucigalpa 1981, p. 187.

4. NYT, 9 August 1981.

5. Quoted in *Washington Times*, 30 January 1981, cited in WOLA, 'Honduras. Democracy in Demise', February 1984.

6. Quoted in *La Tribuna*, San Pedro Sula, 6 August 1982, cited in BIH, Serie Cronologías, no. 2, August 1985, p. 2.

7. Quoted in CAR, 9 August 1985.

8. James Painter and Richard Lapper, *Honduras. State for Sale*, London 1985; Gregorio Selser, *Honduras: República Alquilada*, Mexico 1983; Nancy Peckenham and Annie Street, eds, *Honduras. Portrait of a Captive Nation*, New York 1985; Philip Wheaton, *Inside Honduras, Regional Counter-Insurgency Base*, Washington 1982; Philip Shepherd, 'Six Keys to Honduras', Submission to House Committee on Foreign Relations, April 1984, reprinted in BIH, Serie Especial, no. 20, February 1986.

9. *Tiempo*, 28 July 1983. In August 1985 the new president of COHEP, Jorge Gómez Andino, remarked that Honduras was occupied by its own army, that of the US, that of El Salvador (still holding some disputed territory), the Contra, British and Belizean forces (holding the Zapotillo keys claimed by Honduras) and the unemployed. BIH, no. 53, September 1985.

10. NYT, 20 April 1982.

11. This issue is discussed at length in Durham, *Scarcity and Survival*. In 1950 approximately 48 per cent of land was in private hands, 31 per cent belonged to the state and 17 per cent was in *ejido*.

12. BIH, no. 53, September 1985; LAWR, 22 February 1980.

13. Guillermo Molina Chocano, 'Población, Estructura Productiva y Migraciones Internas en Honduras (1950–1960)', ESC, no. 12, 1975.

14. Ramon Oquelí, 'Gobiernos Hondureños durante el Presente Siglo', *Economía Política*, Tegucigalpa, no. 8, May–October 1984, p. 18. Oquelí's survey of national governments printed at regular intervals in this journal from 1972 provides the fullest chronicle – but no analysis – of public life in the present century.

15. Jiménez, *La Guerra no Fue de Futbol*, p. 24.

16. Posas and Del Cid, *Construcción*, p. 85.

17. Ibid., pp. 85, 90–1.

18. For details, see Filander Díaz, 'Los EEUU en Honduras, 1954–84', BIH, Serie Especial no. 18, March 1985. The establishment of new bases, training centres and large-scale manoeuvres were provided for in an annexe to the 1954 treaty agreed without the approval of the Honduran congress by US Ambassador John D. Negroponte and General Gustavo Alvárez on 6 May 1982.

19. The PL was itself prepared to recognize this, declaring that, 'Gálvez has done more in four and a half years than Carías achieved in sixteen years of fierce and implacable dictatorship.' Oquelí, 'Gobiernos', *Economía Política*, 1972, p. 9.

20. For details of all elections between 1954 and 1981, see James Morris, *Honduras. Caudillo Politics and Military Rulers*, Boulder 1984, p. 37.

21. Oquelí, 'Gobiernos', *Economía Política*, 1973, p. 19.

22. Details of the strike may be found in Meza, *Movimiento Obrero*; Mario Posas, *El Movimiento Obrero Hondureño 1880–1964*, unpublished thesis.

23. Meza, *Movimiento Obrero*, pp. 94–9.

24. Ibid., pp. 115–16; Richard Swedberg, 'The Honduran Trade Union Movement, 1920–1982', CAMINO, Cambridge, Mass. 1983, pp. 15, 21.

25. Swedberg provides a brief survey of the international links of the union leadership but the fullest published account of the struggle for control of the labour movement is Mario Posas, *Lucha Ideológica y Organización Sindical en Honduras (1954–1965)*, Tegucigalpa 1980.

26. Posas and Del Cid, *Construcción* , p. 96; Swedberg, 'Trade Union Movement', p. 16.

27. Slutzky and Alonso, *Empresas Transnacionales*, p. 18.

28. Frank Ellis, *Las Transnacionales del Banano en Centroamérica*, San José 1983.

29. José Roberto López, *La Economía del Banano en Centroamérica*, San José 1986, pp. 17–19, 106; Slutzky and Alonso, *Empresas Transnacionales*, p. 25.

30. Ellis, *Transnacionales*, p. 249.

31. Quoted in Meza, *Movimiento Obrero*, p. 107.

32. Steven C. Ropp, 'The Honduran Army in the Sociopolitical Evolution of the Honduran State', *The Americas*, vol. XXX, April 1974.

33. Oquelí, 'Gobiernos', *Economía Política*, 1984, p. 13.

34. *The Guardian*, London, 12 June 1987.

35. Oquelí, 'Gobiernos', *Economía Política*, 1974, p. 24.

36. Posas and Del Cid, *Construcción*, pp. 119–22.

37. A. Muñoz, 'The People of Honduras and the Fight against Reaction and Imperialism', WMR, vol. 7, no. 6, June 1964.

38. Quoted in *Cuadernos de Ciencias Sociales*, Tegucigalpa, no. 2, 1973, p. 437.

39. Posas, *Lucha Ideológica*, pp. 34–5.

40. *La Guerra Inútil*, pp. 34–5.

41. Mario Posas, *El Movimiento Campesino Hondureño*, Tegucigalpa 1981, pp. 20 ff.; Douglas Kinkaid, 'Rural Politics and Agrarian Reform', in Peckenham and Street, *Captive Nation*.

42. Quoted in Posas and Del Cid, *Construcción*, p. 129.

43. Ibid.

44. Quoted in Meza, *Moviemiento Obrero*, p. 125.

45. Ibid., pp. 130 ff.

46. Antonio Murga Frassinetti, 'Concentratión Industrial en Honduras', *Economía Política*, no. 9, 1974.

47. Ibid.

48. Ibid., p. 48.

49. J. Mark Ruhl, 'Agrarian Structure and Political Stability in Honduras', *Journal of Inter-American Studies*, vol. 26, no. 1, February 1984, p. 40; Neale J. Pearson, 'Peasant Pressure Groups and Agrarian Reform in Honduras, 1962–1977', in William P. Avery et al., eds, *Rural Change and Public Policy. Eastern Europe, Latin America and Australia*, New York 1980, pp. 300–1.

50. Details of rural organization in this period are given in Posas, *Movimiento Campesino*.

51. Ruhl, 'Agrarian Structure', p. 54. According to the Honduran authorities, less than one per cent of Salvadorean immigrants possessed proper documentation. This may well have been a propagandistic claim but was quite possibly accurate simply because until the mid 1960s the Honduran state possessed neither the resources nor the interest in formalizing the status of an immigrant population that had hitherto subsisted without untoward difficulty outside the realm of *tramitación*. Anderson, *War of the Dispossessed*, p. 129.

52. Anderson, *War of the Dispossessed*, pp. 81 ff.

53. The political and diplomatic background and military conduct of the war are surveyed

in Anderson whilst the socio-economic features of the conflict are most fully discussed in *La Guerra Inútil*.

54. *El Tiempo*, 2 May 1972, quoted in Morris, *Caudillo Politics*, p. 44.

55. The Nationalists' manipulation of their victory and the response of COHEP and the CTH are considered in some detail by Posas and Del Cid, *Construcción*, pp. 155–71.

56. In 1973 the PCH declared, 'We did not condemn the military coup since it was clearly directed against the anti-popular "National Unity" regime. It can now be stated definitely that the industrial bourgeoisie of San Pedro Sula was actively involved in the preparations to overthrow the Cruz government.' This support, which was indeed quite evident, must have encouraged the PCH line since it appeared to vindicate the party's identification of a progressive national bourgeoisie whilst the role of the army was explained in perfectly orthodox terms: 'The Armed Forces can temporarily be "above classes", on coming to power can play the role of "arbiter" of social conflicts, and carry through a policy of unity with intermediate social forces.' D.R. Bejarano, 'Something New in Honduras?' WMR, vol. 16, no. 5, May 1973, p. 70.

57. The president's new year speech is reprinted in full in Leticia Salomón, *Militarismo y Reformismo en Honduras*, Tegucigalpa 1982, pp. 199–211.

58. Juan Arancibia, *Honduras. Un Estado Nacional?* Tegucigalpa 1984, pp. 83, 87.

59. LA, 18 January 1974; 8 March 1974.

60. *Crisis en Cifras*, p. 67.

61. Ibid., pp. 47–8.

62. Ibid., p. 69. For the economic organization of the manufacturing bourgeoisie, see Murga Frassinetti, 'Concentración Industrial'; for a brief survey of its political organization and attitudes, see the same author's 'Estado y Burguesía Industrial en Honduras', RMS, vol. XXXIX, no. 2, 1977.

63. At its sixteenth plenum the PCH depicted the López Arellano regime as 'bourgeois reformist, under the influence of a new sector of the governing classes: the reformist bourgeoisie' that required an agrarian reform to increase its domestic market. The party implicitly backed the nationalist tenor of the regime in declaring that 'Honduras has been subsidizing the economic development of the other member countries of the CACM'. *Trabajo*, no. 1, June 1975, pp. 1–6.

64. Details of the events of mid 1975 and shifts in the peasant leadership are given in Posas, *Movimiento Campesino*, pp. 18 ff; Peckenham and Street, *Captive Nation*, pp. 140 ff. This period is unusually well covered by the London-based Latin American Newsletter.

65. LA, 13 June 1975; 18 July 1975.

66. The view of Enrique Astorga, previously an adviser to PROCARRA, quoted in Posas and Del Cid, *Construcción*, p. 218.

67. For details, see Posas, *Movimiento Campesino*, pp. 34 ff.

68. In 1977 radical elements left ANACH and the UNC (since mid 1975 under conservative leadership) to form the *Unión Nacional Campesina Auténtica de Honduras* (UNCAH), a separate division from ANACH producing the *Frente Nacional de Campesinos Independientes de Honduras* (FRENACAINH). In 1979 these groups allied with ANACH, the UNC and FECORAH to set up the *Frente Unitario Nacional Campesino Hondureño* (FUNACAMH) but the larger organizations soon left, alleging that left-wing subversives were manipulating the front; shortly thereafter two more small, *caudillo*-dominated organizations appeared (ACADH and ACAN). In 1980 ANACH's longstanding leader Reyes Rodríguez was defeated in the union's elections and promptly formed ALCONH, which subsequently affiliated itself to the National Party. In 1985 the more progressive bodies united with various cooperative-based organizations to set up the *Central Nacional de Trabajadores del Campo* (CNTC), which proved to be a reasonably stable entity, whilst the main unions remained either under clear right-wing control, as in the case of ANACH (Julín Méndez) and FECORAH (Efraín Díaz Galeas) or split, as in the case of the UNC (whose conservative general secretary Marcial Caballero was under challenge from Marcial Euceda). The attempt to reform a single united *campesino* movement on the basis of a nationwide *toma* in May 1987 collapsed within three days, further postponing consistently coordinated organization in the countryside. For an outline of trade union organizations in the mid 1980s, see BIH, no. 64, August 1986.

69. *Boletín de Estadísticas Laborales*, Tegucigalpa 1978, p. 16, cited in Swedberg, 'Trade

Union Movement', p. 21.

70. Let me tell you about a friend
Who knows how to govern this land;
He's a help to the poor *campesinos*
Though a General so fine and grand.
For he's a simple soldier,
Though the needy know of his fame;
For he listens to all their problems,
General Melgar is his name.
Viva Alberto Melgar . . . Viva!

LAPR, London 21 July 1978. Melgar was a man of humble origin and not without the common touch but lacked both a strategic vision and a stable constituency.

71. TW, 6 April 1981.

72. For these proposals, see Alcides Hernández, *El Neoliberalismo en Honduras*, Tegucigalpa 1983; BIH, no. 15, August 1982. For a concise survey of economic policy under Suazo, see Eugenio Rivera Urrutia, Ana Sojo and José Roberto López, *Centroamérica. Política Economía y Crisis*, San José 1986.

73. Painter and Lapper, *State for Sale*, p. 87.

74. BIH, no. 14, July 1982; no. 62, June 1986.

75. All these examples and a great many more instances of corruption are listed (together with primary source) in 'La Corrupción en Honduras, 1982–5', BIH, Serie Cronologías, no. 3, September 1985.

76. From an interview with *The Miami Herald*, 5 March 1984, quoted in 'Militarismo en Honduras. El Reinado de Gustavo Alvarez, 1982–4', BIH, Serie Cronologías, no. 2, August 1985, p. 8.

77. Full tables of US aid are given in Painter and Lapper, *State for Sale*, pp. 86–7; BIH, no. 64, August 1986.

78. Documentation on US military activity in Honduras is extensive. A brief survey is given in Painter and Lapper, *State for Sale*; greater detail is provided in Wheaton, *Inside Honduras*; Peckenham and Street, *Captive Nation*; INSEH, 'Cambios y Contradicciones en Las FFAA de Honduras', Tegucigalpa 1985; Institute for Policy Studies, 'Background Information on US Security Assistance and Military Operations in Honduras', Background Paper no. 9, May 1984; WOLA, 'Democracy in Demise'. Regular coverage is given in BIH and *Honduras Update*.

79. *FBIS*, 27 November 1985, quoted in *Honduras Update*, January 1986.

80. Quoted in *Barricada*, Managua, 2 April 1982.

81. *La Prensa*, 11 June 1983; *Tiempo*, 16 June 1983; *El Heraldo*, 6 March 1984, all reprinted in BIH, Serie Cronologías, no. 2, August 1985.

82. Painter and Lapper, *State for Sale*, p. 105.

83. *La Tribuna*, 30 May 1980.

84. Torres Arias's full attack is reproduced in BIH, Serie Cronologías, no. 2, August 1985, pp. 18–20.

85. Quoted in Painter and Lapper, *State for Sale*, p. 109.

86. Quoted in CAR, 5 July 1985.

87. LAWR, 24 September 1982. For fuller details, see Committee for the Defence of Human Rights, 'Report on Human Rights in Honduras', Geneva 1984. Each monthly issue of BIH carries information on the state of civil liberties and outstanding cases of their violation. The special issue of October 1986 analyses the position of refugees in the country from 1980 to 1986.

88. LAWR, 2 April 1981; 17 September 1982; 10 December 1982.

89. Quoted in WOLA, 'Democracy in Demise', p. 6.

90. BIH, Serie Especial, no. 7, January 1984; LAWR, 11 March 1983; Painter and Lapper, *State for Sale*, p. 105.

91. The Canadian priest James 'Guadalupe' Carney died in this abortive expedition. For a testimony of his transformation from missionary to guerrilla see *To Be a Revolutionary*, San Francisco 1985; for evidence that he may well have been killed under the direction of US forces, George Black and Anne Nelson in *The Nation*, 4 August 1984.

92. CAR, 11 January 1985; 1 March 1985.

93. Ibid., 4 October 1985; 25 October 1985; NYT, 16 October 1985.

94. BIH, no. 56, December 1985. In the light of the 'Irangate' revelations it is possible that the momentary crisis over the supply plane resulted from the opening of North's operation along channels different from those of the CIA to which the Honduran authorities were accustomed.

95. *Honduras Update*, April and May 1986.

96. *Inforpress*, 11 June 1987; TW, 8 June 1987.

97. BIH, no. 64, August 1986.

98. *Honduras Update*, July 1986.

99. Ibid., March 1986.

100. The various party factions and candidates are outlined in Peckenham and Street, *Captive Nation*, pp. 228–31; BIH, no. 54, October 1985.

101. For details of this labyrinthine process, see Painter and Lapper, *State for Sale*, pp. 114 ff.; CAR, 15 March; 2 April; 3 May 1985. Something of the flavour of the crisis can be captured from one of several interviews given in gaol by the resourceful congressional appointee to the presidency of the Supreme Court, Ramón Valladares Soto, distinguished as much by his candour as by the bright yellow frames of his spectacles: '[When] asked about published reports that he suffers from chronic heart trouble and a bleeding ulcer, Mr Valladares smiled and asserted, "I am in excellent health. That story was put out by a doctor who is a friend of mine and thought that he could help me . . ."' NYT, 2 April 1985.

102. The full result of the poll was:

PINU		23,254
PDC		29,298
PL	Total	772,611
	Azcona	416,736
	Bú Girón	62,031
	Mejía Arellano	247,515
	Reina	42,763
	Unaffiliated	3,566
PN	Total	686,494
	Callejas	639,832
	Landizabal	24,685
	Urrutia	20,031
	Unaffiliated	1,946
Total votes cast		1,512,347

Source: BIH, no. 55, November 1985.

103. Ibid., no. 56, December 1985.

104. Ibid., no. 58, February 1986.

105. Ibid., no. 63, July 1986; no. 64, August 1986.

106. *The Independent*, London, 25 May 1987.

11

Costa Rica: Stability at a Price

The Brazilian *cafetaleros* invest directly in industry; the children of Costa Rican *cafetaleros*, on the other hand, dedicate themselves to running enterprises that don't belong to them.

Samuel Stone, 1975[1]

The Costa Rican citizen is proud that his country has more teachers than soldiers; he abhors militarism; he is a peace-loving, law-abiding citizen, a supporter of constitutional government and an ardent champion of his own rights.

Partido de Vanguardia Popular, 1963[2]

Costa Rica made its choice years ago and is living under an authentic democratic system – and it is no accident that Costa Rica is the least violent society, the nation of the region most free of repression and the one whose relations with the US are most particularly warm.

Kissinger Commission, 1984[3]

The forms of property that should be reserved for the state are those that are so powerful that they cannot be left in private hands without courting great danger.

PLN, *Carta Fundamental*, 1951[4]

One has to recognize that the so-called 'enterprise state' has, for various reasons, been a failure in all of Central America, without exception.

Carlos Manuel Castillo, PLN, 1985[5]

Nicaragua has become a totalitarian dictatorship.

President Luis Alberto Monge, June 1982[6]

The dignity of our people does not require violent or aggressive gestures and attitudes but rather sensitivity and the understanding traditional throughout our history.

Ex-presidents Figueres, Oduber, Trejos and Carazo on foreign policy, August 1985[7]

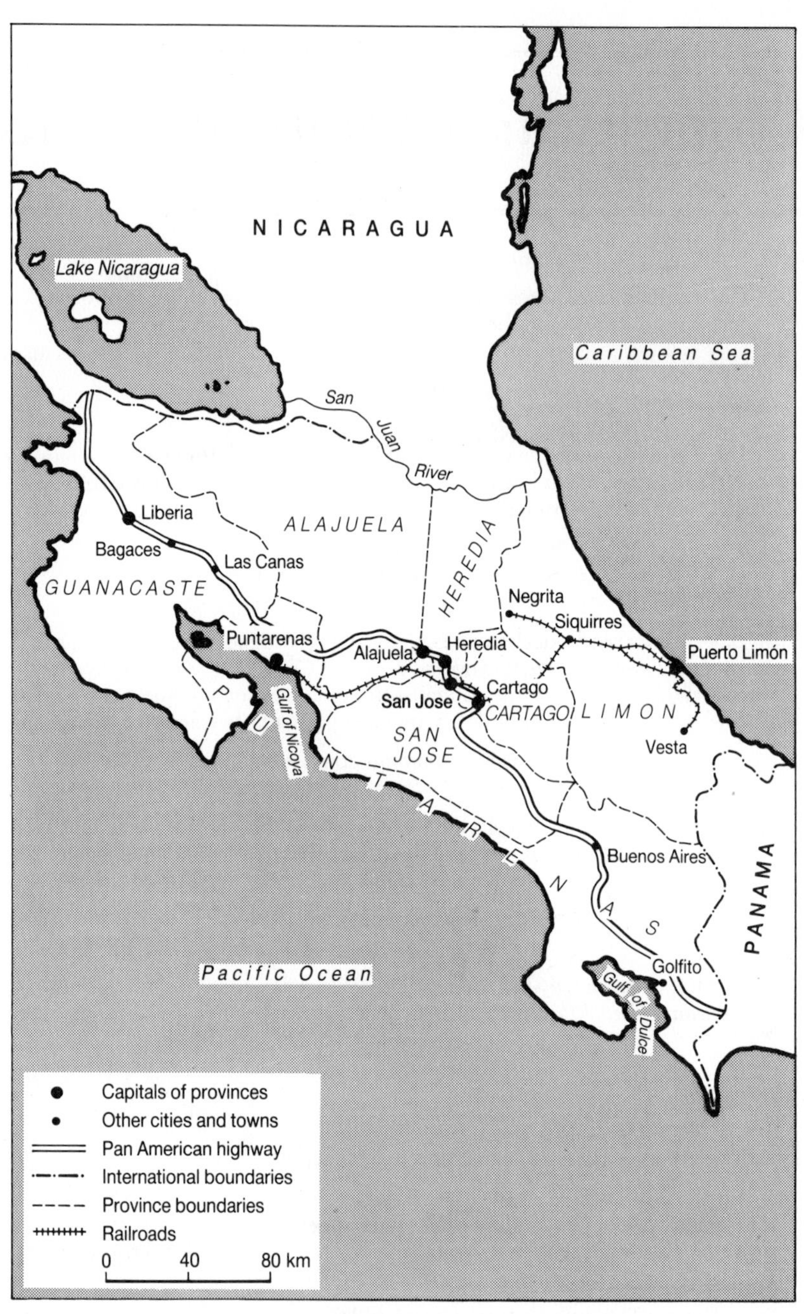
NICARAGUA
Lake Nicaragua
Caribbean Sea
San Juan River
ALAJUELA
HEREDIA
Liberia
Bagaces
Las Canas
GUANACASTE
Negrita
Siquirres
Puntarenas
Alajuela
Heredia
Puerto Limón
Cartago
San Jose
CARTAGO
LIMON
Vesta
SAN JOSE
Gulf of Nicoya
PUNTARENAS
Buenos Aires
PANAMA
Golfito
Gulf of Dulce
Pacific Ocean
Capitals of provinces
Other cities and towns
Pan American highway
International boundaries
Province boundaries
Railroads
0
40
80 km

Costa Rica

There has long been agreement across the ideological spectrum that Costa Rica is different from the rest of Central America, and this continues to be the case despite the considerable pressures caused by the Nicaraguan revolution and the economic crisis of the early 1980s. The stable constitutional government, low level of social violence, significant state intervention in the economy, tangible welfare system and subsidization of middle-class consumption that mark the country's modern history have frequently been depicted with excessive emphasis and further exaggerated through contrast with the rest of the region. Yet the existence of all these features is incontestable, and however flawed the image of a prosperous provincial arcadia packed with a peace-loving yeomanry, Costa Rica is undeniably exceptional.

At the beginning of the 1980s the depth of the economic recession and growing frailty of the 'social democratic' ideology that had prevailed since the early 1950s encouraged some on the left to reach beyond a critique of the weaknesses of the interventionist state and forecast the impending collapse of the entire post-war political system. This failed to occur. It was not, though, an entirely unreasonable expectation insofar as ten years earlier Uruguay, hitherto dubbed 'the Switzerland of Latin America', had been dragged from decades of stable civilian government into political violence and dictatorship by the decay of its relatively advantageous position in the world market and without the kind of external pressure imposed upon Costa Rica after 1979. Within the space of a few years notions of the irreducibly democratic vocation of the Uruguayan character and belief in the resilience of constitutional traditions had to be discarded as the colonels moved in on the back of a right-wing civilian government imposing 'order'. In a rather different manner the Chilean coup of 1973 also put paid to a legion of myths about the cultural foundations of constitutionalism, which in that case could be traced back further still into history, well beyond Uruguay's Batlle y Ordoñez at the turn of the century to the days of Portales and the civilist authoritarianism that followed independence. Given that the celebration of Costa Rica's modern legalism was even more pronounced in its culturist form and had for decades centred on the supposed qualities of the *tico* character, a refusal to accept this intangible guarantee against social disorder and political violence was eminently reasonable in terms of the recent experience of the subcontinent as a whole, let alone the new conditions prevailing in the isthmus. Since there was a broad consensus that, whatever the historical origins and cultural underpinnings of constitutionalism, the modern form of government had become integrally structured around state intervention in the circuits of both production and consumption, the collapse of the coffee price in 1977–78 and rise of that for petrol seemed to herald more than a secular fiscal crisis, threatening the entire basis upon which social equilibrium had been managed for over thirty years.

The analogies with Uruguay and Chile are not, of course, exact. In both cases constitutionalism was liquidated by a powerful national army supported by the US following an open and legal radical challenge for office (successful in the Chilean case) and the appearance of left-wing guerrillas (of formidable strength in Uruguay). Costa Rica neither possessed a significant military apparatus nor had experienced any major domestic radical challenge whilst its political system and both of the two main forces that contest office within it were supported by Washington. Following the Nicaraguan revolution, and in particular since 1982, the US succeeded in cajoling San José into expanding its security apparatus, now four times larger than in 1977 and in logistical terms quite capable of staging a coup. This, together with rudely disguised efforts to support the Contras' southern front, unsettled the country's civilist traditions and weakened its less secure claim to neutrality. On the other hand, whilst insisting upon major reductions in public expenditure and the adoption of free market policies, Washington notably softened the impact of the economic crisis by releasing large amounts of aid so that by 1983 Costa Rica stood second only to Israel in terms of per capita US assistance. In itself this leverage enabled Washington to exact terms that debilitated the post-war model and directly favoured a neo-liberal strategy, but at least in the short term the impoverishment caused amongst the working class and peasantry was sufficiently limited to engender little more than disenchantment with the prevailing system. In the elections of February 1986 a conservative government of the *Partido de Liberación Nacional* (PLN) under Oscar Arias was returned with a clear majority after a high turnout whilst the combined forces of the left – all of which are legal and subscribe to the parliamentary system – amassed less than 6 per cent of the vote in Central America's most open poll. Furthermore, over 45 per cent of the electorate supported the right-wing *Partido de Unidad Social Cristiana* (PUSC), suggesting that if the local traditions of civilism and statism were vulnerable this owed something to the fact that a significant segment of the population favoured their reorganization if not their demise.

The record of the post-1979 conjuncture, which has been far more demanding and disturbing than any period since the civil war of 1948, would seem to refute all the prognostications of the iconoclasts and confirm that the post-war socio-political model has not been deracinated by unprecedented external intervention and a major realignment of the domestic economic structure. As in the case of Honduras, many expectations in this regard were extrapolated from a regional pattern that was endowed with an excessively direct and general logic. Costa Rica is less distinctive than many claim, but it is still sufficiently exceptional to defy any geometrical approach to political economy encouraged by the regional crisis and provoked by cosy projections of democracy as an almost telluric property of the republic. Repeatedly assailed as manifestations of 'false consciousness', such venerable beliefs have acquired popular acceptance, becoming in a sense concrete and part of the equation they seek to explain. Social pacts and political consensus play a far more important role in the Costa Rican system of domination than in those elsewhere. Although constantly subject to material factors, the ideological roots of this system must also be understood in their own terms, as integral to the pattern of social relations rather than mere distortions of the structure of economic power. One may sensibly discount foolish panegyrics about the unique and transcendent affability of national culture but it is clear that the exercise of political power both draws on and replenishes a sense of affinity in civil society which mediates economic antagonisms and class identity to an appreciable degree.

Outside the country at least, the image of a placid social democracy has owed much to Washington's garrulous projections together with slight awareness of domestic developments that have been undermining the post-war model. One should not become too zealous in explaining Costa Rican development in terms different from those elsewhere when a brief glance over the events of the last few years reveals various features. These include: the strengthening of a neo-fascist movement (*Movimiento Costa Rica Libre* – MCRL) that has attacked deputies and peace marchers and encrusted itself in the voluntary militia OPEN (*Organización para Emergencias Nacionales*), from which radicals are specifically excluded; the withdrawal of United Brands (UB) from its Pacific plantations because of falling productivity and union activism; the response to these strikes with state repression in which hundreds have been injured and at least a score killed; the considerable growth of the paramilitary forces and their training in counter-insurgency tactics by the US Green Berets; strong support of sections of the bourgeoisie for the covert operations against Sandinista Nicaragua nurtured by longstanding relations between the political elite and the CIA; the continued practice of corruption and patronage both within the public sector and in its relations with ascendant private capital; the unresolved issue of landlessness and rural poverty and violence that is much less pronounced than in the rest of the isthmus yet still severe in certain regions where *tomas* and *precarismo* (squatting) prevail to a much higher degree than is generally recognized. These and other features show Costa Rica to be very far from the insular idyll that it appears when contrasted with Guatemala or El Salvador.

In more structural and historical terms none of the customary explanations of the peculiarities of the country can in themselves provide a persuasive case. Whether it be the yeoman thesis or the strength of kinship ties in a predominantly 'white' society, the absence of a significant Indian population, mineral wealth or a powerful colonial apparatus of exaction and control, or the early introduction of public education in a relatively small society concentrated in a modest area of temperate land with good communications, the stock answers have increasingly been shown to be either exaggerated or tautological constructions imbricated with a healthy dose of wishful thinking. They should not, however, simply be discounted as rank myth since historical revisionism has yet to deal a wholly decisive coup de grâce on any count.[8] The debate takes on a much more focused character with respect to the developments of the early 1940s, the civil war of 1948 and its aftermath. It is undoubtedly here that one encounters the key to the modern political economy, the decade following the war witnessing consolidation of the contemporary model of economic management, stable constitutional administration and the hegemony of the PLN. For some observers the economic limits of this model have been reached, its capacity to maintain the levels of infrastructure, services and consumption exhausted by the world recession and the fiscal crisis of the state. For others, by no means necessarily on the left, such exhaustion was always imminent in a system where, 'hidden under the slogans of public interest and social welfare, inefficiency and waste are legitimized by pseudo-criticism of the logic of private capital, which is rejected in word but applied in practice'.[9]

If it is difficult to accept that 1948 produced a 'neutralization of class conflict', it is clear that it decisively mediated this conflict, eventually combining the two contending political projects of the day – 'Christian populism' and 'social democratic developmentalism'.[10] The synthesis was unkempt in the extreme, founded upon military victory yet consolidated through the disestablishment of the army, social democratic in character yet initially little less anti-worker than it was anti-Communist, conducted through constitutional channels and parliamentary government yet sustained by a *caudillismo* unmatched in the rest of Central America beyond Nicaragua. These contradictions did, though, mutate into an operable whole, and nowhere else was the resolution of the conflict of the post-war years so complete.

The result was a political 'long wave' of over thirty years which was not markedly distinct from that of the other countries in terms of its duration and frequently echoed tendencies evident elsewhere, albeit in a much more modulated form. Thus, one encounters intra-bourgeois tension over the CACM and industrialization from the 1960s, an upturn in student radicalism and resurgence of anti-Communism in the early 1970s, and, most notably, polarization over Nicaragua and increased social conflict in the early 1980s. If none of these features interrupted the progress of orderly elected administrations or swung the orbit of political activity away from the constitutional arena, they all opened cracks in a system that depended upon both external continuity and internal equilibrium. For this reason conservative advocates of the thesis of an indigenous democratic culture have taken fright, identifying the disturbances of recent years as a product of Sandinista subversion, alien by dint of being both Marxist and Nicaraguan – the two eternal terrors of the Costa Rican bourgeoisie. In the face of this challenge, US aid and the restoration of the military are seen as essential prophylactics whereas from a left-wing standpoint these themselves constitute a far more acute danger for the system, progressively gutting its distributionist powers and liquidating the guarantees against militarism. The continued vitality of this political exchange, which is notable for taking place as much within the PLN as beyond its ranks, is in good measure attributable to the fact that both sides can make strong claims to nationalist sentiment and public tradition. Indeed, despite twenty-five years of formal proscription in the wake of the civil war, the positions of the local Communist Party, the *Partido de Vanguardia Popular* (PVP), had by the early 1980s become almost as conservative as those of the PLN, this attachment to the past playing a major part in the party's division in 1984.

The split in the PVP may be said to have confirmed the end of the first generation of modern Costa Rican politics since it effectively removed the veteran Communist leader Manuel Mora from the political stage. Like José Figueres, Mora had been a central protagonist of the 1940s, and while neither man disappeared from public view and both continued vigorously to hector all and sundry from the sidelines, their authority was no longer integral to political debate and administration. The 1986 election underscored this fact, both the leading candidates being in their early forties (although a sense of historical continuity was lent by the fact that the PUSC leader, Rafael Angel Calderón, was the son of ex-president Calderón). The generational aspect of political life affects the scope of experience and calibre of expectation within a system that has undergone few crises and little change, just as, for instance, those in Mexico or, in a very different mould, Paraguay. The concomitant pattern of political socialization is, therefore, scarcely comparable to that in the rest of the isthmus even if the continuities within civil society are not always so distinctive, as illustrated by the Honduran experience. Such a contrast is manifestly important, but also of limited explanatory value; Costa Rica itself cannot be properly understood within the paradigm of exceptionalism. It is the failure to grasp this and appreciate the intrinsic qualities of the domestic experience that has weakened much radical analysis as well as Washington's policies, based so firmly upon domino theory.

Securing the Constitutional Regime

Few serious accounts of Costa Rica waver from the view that the heart of the country's modern political system was formed in the 1940s, which closed with a far more profound and extensive resolution of the post-war conflicts than achieved elsewhere. In contrast to Nicaragua and El Salvador the liberal democratic impetus of the middle class was not sacrificed to the demands of the Cold War, the anti-authoritarian movement being largely set against rather than parallel to working-class mobilization. This feature also distinguished post-1948 Costa Rica from reformist Guatemala where the political profile of labour and the left increased from the turn of the decade, the developmentalist project being marked by a much lower level of anti-communism which in turn made it exceptionally vulnerable to US attack. The peculiar combination of anti-oligarchic modernism and anti-communist populism in Costa Rica was not, however, the result of a cogent political programme pursued by Figueres and the social democrats so much as the outcome of an impasse between two political blocs neither of which possessed the resource to impose a stable mandate. The experience of the years between 1940 and 1948 had demonstrated that while some state intervention in the economy might be acceptable to the bourgeoisie, it could not last for any length of time on the basis of alliance with the Communist Party, tactical manipulation of the constitution and electoral fraud or the absence of measures to dynamize production as well as to sustain distribution. Much of the character of the Calderón and Picado regimes may be explained in terms of the exceptional conditions prevailing during World War Two, particularly with regard to the opportunities available to the PVP but also with respect to the scope for economic control (the management of German property and limits on coffee and banana markets) and the ideological protection given by support for the Allied cause. On the other hand, the tense and insecure alliance between organized labour, the Church, state employees and a cluster of maverick dignitaries was able to persist for so long only because of the division of the opposition between the oligarchy and the middle-class reformists grouped in the *Centro para el Estudio de Problemas Nacionales*. Once this division was overcome by Figueres's acceptance of Ulate's oligarchic candidacy in the 1948 election as the best means by which to consolidate the democratic and anti-communist movement, the populist regime was destined to suffer a major domestic challenge in addition to losing its wartime comforts.

As has been seen (chapter 4), the pact between the forces of middle-class reform and oligarchic tradition owed much to the reformists' failure to generate an independent popular following, the pact being little less pragmatic than that which upheld the unsteady dominant bloc. Whilst the conservatives lacked a military apparatus and were obliged to yield to Figueres's insurrectionism in the spring of 1948, the *Liberacionista* cause was substantially hamstrung by the fact that arms had been taken up in defence of the claims to electoral victory by a distinctly fairweather friend who threatened to revert to the status quo ante once in office. Thus, in the wake of military victory in the civil war the social democrats found themselves embattled on two fronts. In the short term they were obliged to reconcile their effective control of the repressive apparatus and organs of government with the fact that the political logic by which these had been acquired now required that they be devolved to interests with which they were in barely greater agreement than their overthrown enemies. In the longer term they were confronted with the consequences of having defeated a regime that for all its inefficiency and corruption had remained remarkably popular and pursued many of the policies that the reformists themselves supported and needed to retain if they were to consolidate the immediate gains of their putsch and give them political legitimacy.

This peculiarly fragile balance of forces persisted for several years and was not relieved of its underlying contradictions until the 1953 electoral victory of Figueres and the PLN. The position was most precarious during the months after the civil war when the country was ruled exclusively by the *Junta Fundadora de la Segunda República*; under Figueres's leadership it propagated a highly exaggerated notion of a new democratic era which subsequently waned as the inescapable agreement to call elections for a constituent assembly and hand executive office over to Ulate made itself felt within a regime that lacked support on both left and right. Nonetheless, the social democrats had still won sufficient advantage to delay the surrender of government first for nine and then eighteen months, providing a critical opportunity to introduce pre-emptive measures in the economic field. The most notable of these were the nationalization of the banks and tax on capital which came close to jeopardizing the entire post-bellum truce even though the attempted counter-coup by Cardona was not in itself a very dangerous challenge. Oligarchic condemnation of nationalization was fully in keeping with the tangible loss of economic power that the measure entailed, and it should not be forgotten that in Costa Rica landlord control of finance was particularly tight. On the other hand, the nationalization of the *Banco Nacional de Costa Rica* in 1914 had survived the initial anti-statist backlash fronted by Tinoco, thereby providing something of a link between the era of state monopolies under the colony and the much more limited interventionism witnessed in the 1930s, with the *Instituto de Defensa del Café*, and the 1940s, with the establishment of some provision for social welfare and the expropriation of German property. Furthermore, the 1948 nationalization of three private banks (*Banco de Costa Rica*; *Banco Anglo-Costarricense*; *Banco de Crédito Agrícola de Cartago*) did not itself interrupt the financial control of *ingenio* owners over small coffee producers whilst it did free manufacturing interests from landlord domination of credit. As a result, the measure and the new regime received the full support of the *Cámara de Industrias*, which in 1943 represented only 370 small companies but still constituted an important ally.[11] Once it became apparent that neither the 1949 constituent assembly nor the Ulate administration would reverse the measure, the nationalized banking system ceased to be a major political issue until the early 1980s, when Washington launched a concerted offensive upon it just as Mexico and El Salvador were bringing their financial institutions under state control.

Posterity would ordain the expropriation of the banks to be the junta's central legacy to the post-war system, yet at the time the regime appeared to many to be continuing the questionable fiscal practices of its predecessor. Figueres was quick to secure compensation for the loss of his personal property during the conflict, and the government's approval of Decree 80 – permitting allocation of public funds with virtually no supervision beyond the junta – aroused suspicions that the arrivistes were set on pillaging the treasury before handing over power. Such disquiet scarcely bolstered the social democrats' popularity, which was already weak as a result of their aggressive conduct of the war and doubts about Figueres's commitment to democracy that were little allayed by his overbearing personalism, refusal to honour the treaty with the PVP, and only grudging acceptance of Ulate's claim to office. Matters such as Archbishop Sanabria's intervention to prevent the execution of the PVP leadership were far from unimportant in the traumatized aftermath of the war. Mora and his comrades may not have enjoyed great popularity in the capital but they had neither killed their opponents in cold blood nor mutated in the popular mind into aliens fit only for the firing squad. If the junta was able to rectify the setbacks caused by over-zealous settling of scores by abolishing the army and turning the barracks over to the ministry of education, it could not immediately secure an anti-militarist reputation or instil a sense of popular confidence. This became clear when the social democrats won only four seats in the constituent assembly against the thirty-four held by Ulate's *Partido de Unión Nacional* (PUN) after the elections of December 1948. Acceptance of this defeat, collaboration with congress and Ulate, and the building of the PLN (1951) round a coherent programme that embodied almost all of the social reforms of 1940–44 were, therefore, no less and in some senses more critical to the winning of popular support than had been the *Liberacionista* military campaign and the record of the junta.

The constituent assembly of 1949 codified the new politico-judicial order, and it did so in a notably cautious fashion, resisting social democratic drafts for an entirely new charter that allowed for the administration of an expanded public sector. As a result of the PUN's insistence upon amending the constitution of 1871 the subsequent proliferation of autonomous state bodies created what Figueres called a 'veritable institutional archipelago', for which political as well as economic supervision was exceptionally loose, prompting the (unrealized) proposal for a new constitution in the 1970s.[12]

However, the four deputies (Rodrigo Facio; Rogelio Valverde; Fernando Fournier; Luis Alberto Monge) established an influence out of all proportion to their voting power. In part this was because their colleagues controlled the executive and in part because they entered the assembly with a far more cogent programme than did a conservative majority clear about little beyond refining the mechanisms for elections. Hence, the principle of administrative decentralization, which was directly drawn from the Uruguayan model, was approved along with acceptance of an interventionist state, not least because it soothed fears about the concentration of political power in the executive. Outside the assembly this general proposal, of which Facio was the leading intellectual author, gained popular support with the amalgamation of the US-owned Electric Bond and Share company into the new *Instituto Costarricense de Electricidad* (ICE; 1949), which acquired much prestige by replacing a long unpopular foreign corporation and subsequently maintaining highly subsidized tariffs in an extensively electrified country. (One marked feature of the economic crisis of the 1980s, when ICE controlled 90 per cent of national supply, was the fierce popular resistance to increases in electricity charges; such charges were far less important in the other states where electrical power was either unavailable to the poor or very frequently illegally tapped.) The fact that ICE was constituted under Ulate's conservative presidency on the basis of social democratic proposals and to the detriment of capitalist interests against which the PVP and unions had long inveighed, indicates how far the process of rapprochement had advanced by the end of the decade.

There were, nevertheless, very firm limits to this. One of the central features of the 1949 charter was Article 98 which prohibited 'the formation or the activity of parties that by their ideology, methods of action or international links seek the destruction of democratic organization in Costa Rica'.[13] This clause, which automatically outlawed the PVP, was only amended by the requisite two-thirds majority of congress in 1974 and was central both to the restoration of bourgeois confidence and to support for the PLN, which retained a fiercely anti-communist character well after 1948. Although Rodrigo Facio opposed the clause in the assembly, arguing that democracy could not be imposed by fiat and proscription, few of his colleagues were disposed to insist upon such worthy sentiments against their gut instincts and at the risk of jeopardizing both US support and the truce with the oligarchy. Equally, the PVP, which by the mid 1950s suffered more from bureaucratic obstacles than direct repression, was soon to repent of its uncritical approach to the alliance with Calderón and Picado that condemned it to outlaw status under a regime that its programme required it to support and develop: 'the immediate historical task of the party is to take to its ultimate consequences the bourgeois democratic revolution that corresponds to the present economic and political development of the country'.[14]

It was not until March 1953 that a successor to the banned CTCR union confederation was permitted in the shape of the *Confederación General de Trabajadores Costarricenses* (CGTC), which competed with the *Rerum Novarum* unions organized by Father Benjamin Nuñez and patronized by the social democrats in a less than fruitful effort to establish a mass anti-communist labour organization. By the time it came to office the PLN had ceased to hold the generalized anti-union views that had been so marked in 1948; Monge was seconded to head ORIT in Mexico, and recognition of new plant unions was extended at a moderate pace throughout the 1950s and 1960s. Yet even in 1953 expectations that the PLN could forge a clientelist network within the labour movement along the lines of the PRI in Mexico were shown to be misplaced. Significantly, the level of abstention in the poll of that year was highest in the banana zones where the Calderón and Picado regimes had enjoyed greatest support and the PVP still maintained an important following. In itself the turnout of 68 per cent was somewhat disappointing for the first poll held under universal suffrage despite the fact that voting was not yet obligatory, the levels of abstention of 52 per cent in Puntarenas and 38 per cent in Limón directly reflecting the unpopularity of the PLN's attitude to the left, and these regions subsequently retained a strong anti-*Liberacionista* sentiment.[15]

Whereas all of the Central American charters of the mid twentieth century extended the Liberal codes of the 1870s to include recognition of the 'social function of property' and provision for state intervention as well as stipulating the mechanisms for the division of powers, it was only in Costa Rica that these were realized in a consistent fashion. The 1949 constituent assembly has, therefore, come to be seen as the crucible of modern public life. As vividly illustrated by the dispute over the 1948 poll, the importance of legal protocols to political administration was already established, and in this sphere the constitution did not so much lay out an entirely fresh set of bureaucratic procedures as strengthen those that existed hitherto for the supervision of elections and the division of powers. The most immediately vital aspect in this respect was the role of the overhauled *Tribunal Supremo Electoral* (TSE), which was made fully independent of the executive and legislature, comprised of three magistrates and six deputies appointed by the Supreme Court, and given direct control of the newly established *Guardia Civil* for the period immediately prior to and during elections. The Civil Register section of the TSE was responsible for drawing up the electoral census and providing identification documents whilst the Electoral Department took charge of the administration of polls that by 1958 were conducted as fairly and efficiently as any in Latin America or indeed many in Europe and parts of North America. None of the elections from 1953 was entirely free of dubious actions by the parties and their supporters – the 1982 campaign, for instance, witnessed the tear-gassing of opposition meetings by PLN activists – but the fact that there existed a very low expectation of fraud undoubtedly strengthened confidence in a political system that might easily have decomposed through corruption and inefficiency however strong its social underpinnings.

The constitution introduced female suffrage, which was not in itself a marked innovation – nine Latin American countries had already done so, including El Salvador in 1939, whilst a further seven would do so over the next decade (Guatemala in 1950 and Honduras in 1956, Nicaragua only in 1983). It established a system of proportional representation that yielded at least a couple and sometimes a dozen deputies from minority parties in every subsequent election, and it prohibited the immediate re-election of parliamentarians after a four-year term. This, combined with the fact that the age-limit for deputies was only twenty-one, fuelled a high turnover in the membership of the unicameral congress although its size was only increased from forty-five to fifty-seven seats in 1961. The relative accessibility of parliament was further encouraged by the system of state subsidization of campaign costs, the total being set at a mean of 2 per cent of the budget over the previous three years and distributed to the parties in proportion to their last result, provided this exceeded 10 per cent of the vote.[16]

The 1949 charter increased the authority of congress and diminished that of the presidency to the degree that Costa Rica may legitimately be said to possess an authentic division of powers, if not a parliamentary form of government. In constitutional terms this was secured by making the presidential veto subject to ratification by two-thirds of congress, limiting the scope of direct executive ordinances, and establishing guarantees for employment in the civil service that reduced placemanship even if they did not fully achieve the intended meritocracy. (Employment in the Civil Guard, by contrast, was not protected, leading to a high turnover in personnel.) Until 1969 presidents were restricted to two terms in office, thereafter to only one; in 1970 the post of departmental *jefe político* was replaced by fully elected councillors in the country's provinces. This system of local government (covering 7 departments, 75 cantons and 383 districts) is very weak, depending on San José for some 80 per cent of its budget and lacking the statutory powers to make parochial administration a decisive feature of public life (except, perhaps, for political recruitment and training).

As can be seen from Table 52, parliament has been controlled from 1953 by the PLN although since 1962 this has been with only a modest majority vulnerable to divisions within a heterogeneous and loosely disciplined party. Hence, whilst the freedom of the non-PLN conservative presidents (Echandi; Trejos; Carazo) has been particularly limited, all holders of the office have been required to negotiate in earnest with the legislature. In 1959 parliament passed the *Ley de Fomento Industrial* that favoured manufactur-

Table 52: Costa Rican Elections, 1953–86

Year	*Major Presidential Candidates*	*% Vote*	*PLN Congressional Majority*[1]
1953	José Figueres (PLN)	64.3	15
	Fernando Castro (*Partido Democrático*)	35.3	
1958	Mario Echandi (*Partido de Unión Nacional*)	46.4	15
	Francisco Orlich (PLN)	42.8	
	Jorge Rossi (Partido Independiente)	10.8	
1962	Francisco Orlich (PLN)	50.3	3
	Rafael Angel Calderón (*Partido Republicano*)	35.3	
	Utilio Ulate (PUN)	13.5	
1966	José Joaquín Trejos (*Unificación Nacional*)[2]	50.5	2
	Daniel Oduber (PLN)	49.5	
1970	José Figueres (PLN)	52.5	7
	Mario Echandi (UN)	39.5	
1974	Daniel Oduber (PLN)	44.0	2
	José Joaquín Trejos (*Unidad Nacional*)[3]	30.3	
	Jorge González (PNI)[4]	10.9	
	Rodrigo Carazo (PRD)[5]	9.2	
1978	Rodrigo Carazo (*Unidad Nacional*)	50.5	none[6]
	Luis Alberto Monge (PLN)	43.8	
1982	Luis Alberto Monge (PLN)	58.7	9
	Rafael Angel Calderón Jnr (*Unidad Nacional*)	33.6	
1986	Oscar Arias (PLN)	52.3	1
	Rafael Angel Calderón Jnr (PUSC)[7]	45.8	

Notes:

1. In 1962 the total number of seats in the unicameral congress was raised from 45 to 57. Female suffrage was introduced in 1949; illiterates remain disenfranchised; the voting age was lowered from 20 to 18 in 1974.

2. *Unificación* was an alliance of Calderón's *Partido Republicano* and Ulate's *Partido de Union Nacional*.

3. *Unidad Nacional* did not include the *Partido de Unión*, which effectively collapsed after Ulate's death in 1973.

4. *Partido Nacional Independiente*, a right-wing organization formed for the 1974 elections, in which it gained six congressional seats; the PNI stood in further polls but without gaining any seats.

5. *Partido de Renovación Democrática*.

6. The balance of power lay with the *Partido de Acción Socialista* (PASO), which was effectively an electoral front for the PVP and held three seats, and the social democratic *Frente Popular Costarricense*, which had one; both groups normally supported the PLN.

7. *Partido de Unidad Social Cristiana*, formed in December 1983 to succeed *Unidad Nacional* as the conservative alliance; it includes Calderón's *Partido Republicano*; the *Partido Demócrata Cristiano* (PDC); Carazo's PRD and *Unión Popular*.

ing to a higher degree than desired by Echandi. He did not veto the statute but was able to express landlord aversion to this tendency by withdrawing Costa Rica from discussions to form the CACM so that the country did not join the market until 1963, after the PLN had won back the presidency. In the early 1970s congress insisted that Figueres seek its permission to travel abroad, as stipulated by law, in part simply to curb family trips to Florida by a particularly obstreperous president, but also to restrict his policy of opening relations with the Soviet bloc. In the same vein, Daniel Oduber was stymied in his plans to call a new constituent assembly yet permitted to implement that expansion of the public sector which had initially prompted his call for constitutional revision. Congressional objections thwarted Carazo's introduction of a flexible exchange rate in 1980–81, the Supreme Court upholding the claim that this contravened the constitution, and President Monge experienced considerable difficulty in securing approval for legislation to break the state monopoly in the banking sector (despite the fact that by the early 1980s a secondary banking system had come into existence). In practical terms these and other examples of restraint on the executive have been underpinned by the fact that conservative administrations have been sustained by insecure coalitions whereas the PLN is in itself a very broad alliance. They have also encouraged the predictable criticism that stability has been achieved at the cost of inefficiency and stasis. It would, though, be mistaken to see the system as an effective antidote to personalism. This continues to be a particularly marked trait of national politics, the degree to which the parties are founded upon ideological cohesion and disciplined organization being much less than might be expected given the absence of many of the characteristics evident in the rest of the isthmus.

According to Daniel Oduber, who together with Figueres and Francisco Orlich formed the 'troika' that dominated the party until the end of the 1970s, 'the PLN is something more than an electoral machine and something less than a party'.[17] This seems an ingenuous declaration in view of the fact that the PLN has dominated political life in Costa Rica over the last three decades. Nevertheless, such rhetorical flourishes are something of a *Liberacionista* hallmark, Figueres once stating that, 'Costa Rica is not a country. It is a pilot project. It is an experiment.'[18] The image of process and lack of completion – on occasion almost of insufficiency – is a deliberately fostered motif designed to bolster the open and anti-totalitarian reputation of a party that incarnates officialdom and continuity in a system where a premium is placed upon the exchange of power and rights of opposition. In this respect the PLN is the antithesis of the Mexican PRI, which enforces a direct and total monopoly on the revolutionary heritage and rights to office. The PLN is much less distinct from its Mexican counterpart in the sense that it is associated with the foundations of the political system as a whole as well as competing within it. Hence, there tends to be an elision between national political culture and the ideology of the party. This parallax may be described as hegemony and is frequently termed 'social democratic' since it is in outward form very similar to the beliefs and structures upheld by the European parties of the Second International. The PLN's claim to such status extends well beyond its full membership of the Socialist International (shared in Latin America by the Chilean Radical Party; the PRD of the Dominican Republic; the Ecuadorian *Izquierda Democrática*; the Salvadorean MNR; the PSD in Guatemala; the Paraguayan *Febreristas*; and *Acción Democrática* in Venezuela).[19] Whilst the espousal of a progressive democratic vocation in the party's 1951 *Carta Fundamental* was necessarily subordinate to a new constitution for which the PLN could claim only limited responsibility, economic intervention by the state was far more strongly identified as partisan property, this being at the core of the *Ideario Costarricense* issued by the *Centro para el Estudio de Problemas Nacionales* in 1943:

> The society of tomorrow will have to be cemented . . . by an interventionism on the part of the state that expands on a national scale, and guarantees 'the free citizen within a strong state', or, in other words, which understands how to conciliate in an efficient form the two concepts of authority and liberty . . . this should not involve the elimination of private economic initiative, but state intervention should rather act to guarantee that this initiative has a truly social productivity by means of an intelligent system of checks and balances.[20]

Abstract language of this type belonged to the intellectuals around Rodrigo Facio, but it captured a vision fully shared by Figueres, who understood his impetuous exploits to be directed towards the building of a mixed economy on a Keynesian model and in direct emulation of Roosevelt's 'New Deal'.[21] For Daniel Oduber,

> this position is, in many aspects, a healthy reaction to the cruel excesses of the so-called 'Manchester liberalism' practised in the nineteenth century, which brought, it is certain, prosperity to some nations and at the same time misery for their workers. These excesses also produced Marxism. In short, our political belief is that the modern state can eradicate both these excesses and emancipate the dispossessed masses economically and socially without sacrificing democratic freedoms . . .[22]

Such an outlook and the principal mechanisms adopted to put it into practice were fully in keeping with the international conjuncture in the late 1940s and early 1950s, embodying anti-communism and a developmentalism that sought to compensate for the weakness of local capital in part by direct state appropriation and in part by mediating the role of foreign investment. It combined a strong nationalist element similar to that displayed by APRA (which exercised a significant influence on the PLN in its early days) and, to a lesser extent, by the Venezuelan AD (which, by virtue of Rómulo Betancourt's close ties with Costa Rica, was also a prominent external influence) as well as the examples of the PRI, Peronism and the MNR in Bolivia. At no stage, however, did the party mount a direct challenge to the principal representatives of private foreign capital in Costa Rica – the banana corporations. Here the PLN's policy was undoubtedly affected by its anti-Communism, which put it at loggerheads with the dominant political force within the plantation unions. This was clearly illustrated in Figueres's intervention to split the labour force and defeat the 1955 strike against UFCO as well as in Orlich's use of the Guard to enforce the imposition of a three-year no-strike deal with the company in 1963.[23] Equally, the relatively low pressure for a land reform in the banana zones allied with the comparatively high profile of independent fruit growers entirely reliant upon a market controlled by the corporations reduced the incentive to take the course followed by Arbenz, whose reform was introduced the year before the PLN came to power and whose overthrow occurred one year into Figueres's term. The lessons were crystal clear. However, the party's conduct in this sphere was determined by more than negative and cautionary factors since it never sought the development of a state capitalism so much as a national capitalist circuit in which foreign capital would be fully represented and supported where it could operate most efficiently. This activity was certainly subjected to fiscal obligations that would have made Costa Rican bananas the most expensive to produce in the region had it not been for the particularly high levels of productivity. Yet neither the social wage nor the PLN's partial adjustments of the traditional agro-export model were sufficiently great to prejudice profits or arouse a political backlash until 1974, and even then there was only a temporary hiatus in affable relations until the crisis caused by United Brands' withdrawal a decade later.

The extent to which the PLN fostered private capital as a whole has often been obscured by the formidable expansion of the public sector in the post-war period. This was systematic and it continued, albeit at a slightly slower pace, under non-PLN governments that possessed little control over the autonomous institutions and a central civil service heavily protected by the constitution. Until the mid 1970s growth in the public sector was predominantly service- and employment-based, producing a substantial rise in the labour force of both the central government and the autonomous agencies. In 1927 the civil service employed 8,300 people and in 1949 some 16,000, levels broadly in line with that of the region in general. However, between 1949 and 1958 state employees more than doubled; in 1974 their number exceeded 87,000, and by 1978 it was almost 130,000 – nearly 19 per cent of the economically active population and in receipt of 28 per cent of national income.[24] Between 1950 and 1985 state employment increased eightfold whilst that in the private sector only tripled in size. Much of this expansion was due to the decentralized public agencies, which employed almost half the public workforce in 1974 compared to a quarter in 1954.[25] By 1980 the cost of sustaining the state bureaucracy stood at C8 billion whereas in 1950 it had amounted to C827 million.[26]

The measures enacted by the junta, the 1949 constituent assembly and the Ulate government meant that by the time the PLN came to office in 1953 the autonomous institutions already accounted for nearly 30 per cent of the state budget. In his first term Figueres increased this to 44 per cent, and although the Echandi administration halted expansion, it could only cut the institutional share of the budget by less than two percentage points; Orlich subsequently increased it to nearly 50 per cent whilst Trejos proved unable to do more than hold this level steady.[27] The particularly strong growth of the public sector between 1949 and 1958 should not, of course, be wholly attributed to government policy. This was a period of general economic growth, both Ulate and Figueres enjoying the benefits of a buoyant coffee price with which to fund the expanded budget whilst Echandi was confronted by a short but sharp recession that hardened his determination to reduce expenditure. Nonetheless, after a decade of preparation and strident campaigning, the PLN applied its policies with unusual resolution after 1953. According to the *Oficina de Planificación Nacional y Política Económica* (OFIPLAN), itself an autonomous state agency, there were in 1978 182 decentralized institutions, of which only 76 were established after 1960. In the first phase – before entry into the CACM and the rise of US investment in manufacturing – the bulk of these bodies were dedicated to the provision of services and upkeep of infrastructure. Even in 1975 over 52 per cent of the public labour force was engaged in the tertiary sector and only 18 per cent in industry.[28] This balance was reflected in the rise of secondary school students from 94,000 in 1948 to 191,000 in 1958; the growth of social security coverage from 10 per cent of the labour force in 1944 to 53 per cent in 1975 in the case of accident benefits (4.8 to 47 per cent for pensions); and the considerable investment in road construction in addition to administration of the major railways during Figueres's first term.[29] At the same time it is notable that, despite the 'industrialist' tendency of the PLN, manufacturing remained constant as a proportion of GDP between 1946 and 1954, public investment rising very modestly from 18 to 22 per cent of total capital formation between 1950 and 1958.[30] On the other hand, state intervention during this period was far from exclusively dedicated to securing the general conditions for the reproduction of capital. The expansion in housing under the aegis of INVU (1954) created a boom in construction, and the *Consejo Nacional de Producción* (CNP;

1956) exercised a quite extensive physical and fiscal control over wholesale markets as well as credit to the private sector. Moreover, Figueres pursued markedly more aggressive tax policies than his predecessors, raising the profits tax on banana production to 30 per cent as well as increasing the labour costs and tariffs in the coffee sector as a complement to greater government action over external prices and marketing.[31]

The expansion of the public sector and provision of social services significantly beyond the levels available in the rest of the isthmus can only be understood in terms of the correspondingly higher GDP per capita in Costa Rica in the post-war era (Table 5a, p. 174). In short, a richer economy possessed a greater capacity to sustain a state-sponsored social wage. This was further supported by the minimal expenditure dedicated to the security forces, which even in 1985 received less than 3 per cent of the national budget compared to a regional average of 25 per cent, and the fact that waged labour was much more extensive than elsewhere (in 1950 68.5 per cent of the economically active population against 50.6 per cent for all Central America; in 1970 73.5 against 54.4 per cent), especially in the countryside (where wage-earners already accounted for 61 per cent of the labour force in 1951, rising only modestly to 66 per cent in 1973).[32] Both the high level of salarization and the comparative advantage of Costa Rica's coffee sector – neither of which was a modern phenomenon – remained vital to the maintenance and administration of the welfare state. In purely economic terms this system constituted a major buffer against the degree of impoverishment evident elsewhere and thus, inevitably, against the risk of political conflict. The very low incidence of social disorder cannot be wholly attributed to a consensual heritage given that in 1980 total government expenditure on social security was nearly thirty times that in Honduras, spending on education and housing six times greater, and the health budget 65 per cent higher when the Honduran population was nearly twice as large as that of Costa Rica.[33] Equally, although Table 53 shows that Costa Rica had a significantly higher rate of government revenue and expenditure per capita than the rest of the region in 1975, it also supports the view that until the recession of the early 1980s it proved possible to sustain the welfare state without resorting to extraordinary levels of direct taxation and deficit financing or a ratio between budget and GDP disproportionate to that prevailing in the other countries.

The greater wealth and access to social services enjoyed by the Costa Rican masses is in itself indisputable and a central factor in determining the pattern of regional politics. It cannot, however, be argued that the modern state has been redistributionist, the pattern of income distribution within the country remaining very similar to that of the isthmus as a whole (Table 6, p. 176). Although in 1970 the poorest half of the population received an average income that was twice that of the regional median – 152 against 74

Table 53: Central American Government Finances, 1975

	C. Rica	*El S.*	*Guate.*	*Hon.*	*Nica.*
Population (millions)	1.9	4.1	6.2	3.0	2.3
Central Gov't Expend. ($CA mn)	310	254	363	212	281
Publ. Expend. as % of GDP	15.8	13.9	10.0	20.0	17.7
Publ. Investment as % of GDP	4.9	5.2	2.4	6.2	6.3
Gov't Revenue ($CA mn)	266	231	351	152	189
Gov't Revenue as % of GDP	13.6	12.7	9.7	14.4	11.9
Tax Revenue ($CA mn)	244	217	310	124	164
Direct Tax as % of fiscal revenue	24.8	23.9	15.7	26.7	20.5
Fiscal deficit ($CA mn)	27	23	12	26	90
Fiscal deficit as % of expenditure	8.7	8.9	3.4	12.1	32.1

Source: Crisis en Cifras.

pesos – it accounted for only 18 per cent of national income and the poorest 20 per cent for just 6 per cent, which was less than the proportion received by the same group in Colombia, El Salvador and Brazil. At the same time the richest 5 per cent of the population received 35 per cent of income – a greater share than the corresponding group in the US, El Salvador, Argentina, Colombia and Mexico.[34] There is no reliable statistical basis upon which one can make a comparison with the state of play prior to 1948 but it is exceptionally unlikely that there has been major progress towards more equitable distribution. The figures for 1980 indicate that although the share of the richest fifth of the population fell by 2 per cent over the previous decade, this was to the benefit of middle income earners, the proportion of wealth received by the poorest fifth also declining, from 5.4 to 4.0 per cent.[35] Thus, it would be entirely mistaken to perceive the equilibrium of Costa Rican politics as a result of a progressive redistribution of income by the state. The absence of such a feature normally at the core of a social democratic programme certainly qualifies the reformist claims made by and for the PLN.

The pattern of both foreign investment and industrialization has also been very similar to that elsewhere in Central America notwithstanding the size of the public sector, the comparative advantage of the coffee industry, and the general policy of support for manufacturing since the late 1940s. The size and structure of the manufacturing sector stood closest to that of Nicaragua and Honduras immediately after the war but had developed nearer to that of El Salvador by the end of the 1960s (Table 14, p. 202). Under the CACM the chemical and metal industries acquired a regional strength, comprising nearly half of all exports to the common market in 1971; by the end of the 1970s the Costa Rican manufacturing sector produced the highest proportion of durable and capital goods in Central America. Yet this was only by a slim margin and industry continued to be based upon textiles and food processing, its dependence upon foreign inputs being the greatest in the region. Equally, at the end of the 1970s the industrial labour force remained by far the smallest of the isthmus (Table 17, p. 207). It is notable that after Figueres's first term and the post-war boom in coffee prices, national industry had experienced both the fastest growth rate in Central America and a unique diminution of its share of GDP (from 11.5 to 11.1 per cent between 1950 and 1960); total value added by industry was half the level of that in El Salvador and only marginally greater than that in Honduras. Hence, industry made only a minor contribution to the rising prosperity of the 1950s. Despite the nationalization of the banks, most of the rail system and power supply as well as Figueres's much-vaunted creation of mixed enterprises, the private coffee and banana interests continued to control the commanding heights of the economy and the bulk of national wealth.[36]

It is in this context that one should view what was perhaps the most singular election result of modern times when, in 1958, the conservative coalition secured a clear presidential victory for Mario Echandi on a platform of sobriety in both fiscal and foreign affairs whilst the PLN maintained its large congressional majority, which enabled it to continue with a resolute legislative programme. (Between 1949 and 1970 congress initiated 37 per cent of all laws and the executive 51 per cent, the rest originating either in public agencies or with individuals; under the conservative Trejos administration of 1966–70 parliament sponsored 52 per cent and the presidency only 41 per cent of legislation.[37]) This balance of forces was by no means a simple reflection of vested economic interests and had much to do with Figueres's boisterous management of foreign affairs, where the executive possessed greater independence from parliament. Yet it did produce a nervous balance between the *cafetaleros* and a current that was now taking on the characteristics of a 'state bourgeoisie', dependent upon the economic as well as political rewards of 'big government' and committed to a strategy of state-propelled growth in manufacturing. This balance was not qualitatively different from that which had obtained in more fragile conditions between 1948 and 1953. The manufacturing lobby had certainly been strengthened by high growth and infrastructural development yet it still agitated for the tax concessions and subsidized credit eventually delivered by the *Ley de Fomento Industrial* of 1959. The *cafetaleros* were prepared to concede this measure once it was extended to foreign capital and shorn of markedly protectionist features. It was the prominence of these in the strategy for industrialization incarnated in the establishment of the CACM that drove Echandi and his deeply conservative minister of economy Jorge Borbón to withdraw from the market. Even though the initial import-substitution project drafted by CEPAL was soon marginalized and diversification into manufacturing dominated by US capital, the coffee growers who formed the core of the conservative bloc retained considerable suspicion of any strategy that encroached upon free trade and the hegemony of the export sector.

Their apprehension in this regard was not entirely unfounded since the high level of imported inputs used in Costa Rican manufacturing soon led it to rely heavily upon state support in order to maintain competitiveness. On the other hand, once the country fully entered the CACM in 1964 the profile of US investment rose dramatically: it was nearly fifty times greater in that year than in 1960 and almost three times the level of local investment, whereas four years earlier new Costa Rican capital had been four times greater than that controlled by North Americans.[38] Whilst the banana companies continued to dominate US interests in the country and 44 per cent of new investment between 1960 and 1970 was in textiles, clothing and foodstuffs, both UFCO and R.J. Reynolds diversified considerably (Castle and Cook less so) and by the early 1980s over 200 US companies were running operations in Costa Rica, the level of direct investment being the highest in the region and the labour force of North American corporations the same size as that in Guatemala. Labour and tax costs were also the highest in the isthmus – Costa Rica only adopted the strategy of 'free trade zones' in the late 1970s – but there was full compensation for this in political stability, a relatively tranquil workforce, superior infrastructure, and relations with Washington that were little less consistent than the general pro-US sentiment that prevailed outside the enclave. However much foreign entrepreneurs might decry the inefficiency of the sprawling public sector, they had every cause to exploit the benefits it offered and little, if any, to fear new statist initiatives to curb the operation of capital or threaten private property.

In most respects, then, the post-war pattern of production fitted that of the isthmus as a whole. Traditional agro-exports continued to predominate as the source of foreign exchange – in 1985 coffee and bananas accounted for 56 per cent of export revenue – whilst transnational corporations dominated the fruit trade and a large part of a subordinate manufacturing sector incapable of sustaining the import-substituting project promoted at the end of the 1940s and in the run-up to the CACM. It is, therefore, hard to explain Costa Rica's distinctively large public sector as the product of a powerful national bourgeoisie. Indeed, although Luis Alberto Monge was the first modern president not to be an entrepreneur of standing and despite the fact that before 1977 nearly 70 per cent of the members of the *Cámara de Industrias* supported the PLN, it would seem far more plausible to view the interventionist state as demonstrative of the very weakness of the bourgeoisie.[39] In all events, industry did not receive a disproportionately large degree of credit from the state banking system. Between 1964 and 1980 (that is, between entry into the CACM and the onset of the recession) this rose at a rather higher rate than the mean – 18.9 against 16.6 per cent – but it rarely exceeded a quarter of private sector financing and was usually smaller than that channelled to the beef industry.[40] Furthermore, any identification of the interests of social classes in the form of government must take into account the fact that the high level of employment generated by the interventionist state was crucial to the economy of much of the middle class and a modest but significant portion of the working class. By the time of the Nicaraguan revolution the public sector labour force accounted for 43 per cent of all unionized workers, the level of unionization in the private sector being less than 6 per cent.[41] Some sections of this state workforce, such as the bank employees, enjoyed exceptionally privileged conditions of employment – this is frequently the case for central and nationalized banks in Latin America – and public sector wages as a whole grew marginally faster than did profits, interest rates and national disposable income between 1960 and 1978.[42] Thus, although the emergence of social democratic politics in Costa Rica is peculiar in terms of its initial anti-working-class tendencies – perhaps the only comparison here is that with Germany following World War One – it came to depend upon the support of a substantial part of organized labour.

The PLN's domination of government has not been founded upon direct clientelist control of the union movement, as is the case with similar parties elsewhere in Latin America such as AD in Venezuela or APRA in Peru. While by the mid 1970s the public sector union FENATRAP (*Federación Nacional de Trabajadores Públicos*) contained more than 30 per cent of the unionized labour force, its membership amounted to only a small fraction of an electorate in which the working class as a whole had an exceptionally low profile. Moreover, the union movement remained deeply divided, the left-wing CGT never expanding much beyond the enclave and the *Confederación Costarricense de Trabajadores Democráticos* (CCTD), formed out of *Rerum Novarum* in 1966, organizing no more than a third of all union members under its pro-PLN banner. By 1984, 132,000 Costa Rican workers were grouped in 306 unions but 40 per cent of these bodies belonged to none of the six small and divided confederations, considerably limiting the scope for political organization.[43] The level of unionization in the countryside was exceptionally low, there being only 1,448 members of recognized rural unions outside the enclave in 1963 and less than 14,000 in 1976; this figure more than doubled over the next decade but a still very weak movement remained divided into at least a dozen local bodies with minimal coordination at the national level.[44] Yet it is the countryside that has provided the PLN with its most consistent electoral base, the party never regaining the degree of support it won in San José in 1953 and subsequently achieving a higher percentage of the vote in outlying provinces like Alajuela and Guancaste than in the capital. (It is something of an irony of history that Cartago, the centre of conservatism in the colonial era, has also remained a *Liberacionista* stronghold, and it might not be too fanciful to suggest that this has something to do with the town's enduring dependence upon the fiscal economy.[45]) In 1960 barely a third of the population lived in settlements of more than 2,000, and with over half its people classified as inhabitants of the countryside, Costa Rica remains today a more rural society than either El Salvador or Nicaragua. Thus, it would be mistaken to associate the PLN's brand of modernism with a predominantly urban – still less urbane – politics. All the post-war presidents except Echandi, Monge and Arias have been prominent landlords, both the PLN and the conservative opposition depending upon the traditional motifs of the benevolent rural *caudillo* to drive their election campaigns. This is most marked in the case of Figueres, who prior to the 1970 election visited more than 800 villages, declaring, 'Costa Rica is a country of *campesinos*. I am a *campesino*. And we understand each other instinctively. Our relationship is much more one of affection than of intellect.'[46]

By any standard Figueres has been the outstanding individual of modern public life, upsetting Monge's anti-Sandinista policies with as much vigour and lack of decorum as he had opposed Calderón forty years earlier. Until at least the mid 1970s the PLN was heavily influenced, if not dominated, by *figuerismo*, and 'Don Pepe' had little trouble in being elected president of the party in 1979 despite the very uneven record of a second administration (1970–74) fraught with scandal and disputes over foreign policy. Indeed, Figueres's prominence might alone justify the observation that 'the traditional form of political organization and mobilization in Costa Rica did not rest in clearly defined ideological distinctions. It was, rather, the personalist, *caudillista* element that played a decisive role.'[47] This was certainly the case in terms of internal PLN politics until the late 1970s, disputes between members of the 'troika' corresponding only in part to ideological currents within the party. In 1956 Figueres sponsored a challenge by Jorge Rossi to Orlich's bid for the nomination as presidential candidate. This was ostensibly done on the grounds of promoting internal democracy and debate but in fact it was a spoiling operation, which got badly out of hand when Rossi left the PLN, splitting its vote in the 1958 poll and allowing Echandi to take office.[48] Scarcely less antipathy existed between Figueres and Oduber, who, once he was guaranteed the 1974 nomination, criticized his predecessor's moral and political judgement with disturbing candour. Monge's rise to prominence in the 1970s was very largely due to the fact that he was instrumental in patching up these feuds between the party elders, his skills as a mediator compensating for lack of charisma, a distinctly reactionary bias, and unstable temperament.

The conservative parties, which possessed a much weaker apparatus and less scope for indirect patronage, were correspondingly more dependent upon personalism. For nearly two decades after the *Liberacionistas* first entered office opposition to them revolved around the persons of Utilio Ulate and Rafael Angel Calderón, who returned to lead his *Partido Republicano* in the mid 1950s. Calderón retained an appreciable constituency from the previous decade but although this had been largely gleaned from the reforms of 1940–44, he now reverted to the reactionary, pro-oligarchic positions that had initially commended him as an heir to the Olympian tradition. Rejecting all contact with the PVP, which was seen as the principal element in the collapse of the alliance of 1942–48, Calderón originally resisted an open pact with his old foe Ulate. Yet the Republicans lacked organization and finance, both of which were offered by Ulate's PUN. Moreover, in 1958 the PUN stood the rather colourless Mario Echandi as its candidate, making informal collaboration on the part of Calderón's supporters far more palatable than if Ulate had led the campaign. Echandi's victory was, therefore, peculiar not just by dint of the split in the *Liberacionista* ranks but also because it was based upon a reconstitution of the oligarchic bloc that had been split since 1940.[49] This did not last. By the 1962 election Calderón had regained sufficient popular backing to stage an independent campaign that the PUN refused to support despite the virtually identical nature of their programmes; old animosities re-emerged in Ulate's challenge, which fared very badly and provided Orlich with a particularly comfortable victory. This experience led to a renewal of the oligarchic pact behind Trejos in 1966, the narrow conservative victory and further reduction of the PLN congressional majority to just two votes suggesting that *Liberacionista* hegemony had become distinctly vulnerable to a reactionary alliance. The experience of the following decade revealed expectations in this quarter to have been greatly exaggerated. For the first time the PLN won two consecutive elections (1970 and 1974) whilst that of 1978 was won by the conservative alliance but under the leadership of Rodrigo Carazo, a *Liberacionista* renegade who notably failed to implement its economic programme and supported the Sandinistas far more generously than desired by his allies and, indeed, many in the PLN. By this stage both Calderón and Ulate had died (in 1970 and 1973 respectively), the *Partido de Unión* perishing with its chief whilst the *Partido Republicano* was reduced to little more than one part of an increasingly multi-party conservative bloc, although the old *caudillo*'s son, popularly known as 'Junior', was able to exploit his father's prestige in heading the anti-PLN challenge in the polls of 1982 and 1986.

As we have seen, not even the most programmatically-based of the parties, the PVP, was immune to this personalist trait of national politics. However, the domination of Manuel and Eduardo Mora should also be viewed in the light of a general pattern of tight and prolonged leadership amongst the Communist movement. In practice the party was able to operate in a relatively unhampered manner until it was legalized in 1974, participating in elections through various thinly-veiled front organizations that achieved minimal success despite the emergence of a left-wing *Liberacionista* faction in the late 1950s.[50] The strength of continuism – and hence the Mora leadership – was also a product of its acceptance of 'the peaceful road to socialism' and the parliamentary model, this insulating it from many of the destabilizing influences of the Cuban revolution that were registered in the other parties of the region. Even after the Nicaraguan revolution the PVP adhered firmly to its syndicalist and parliamentarian strategies, both of which had yielded some modest reward; the split of 1984 owed more to differences over how to support the Sandinistas than to disputes over whether the FSLN model was applicable to Costa Rica.[51]

Despite their ideology, which was in any case deviant only in certain respects, the Moras belonged to a political elite that is often identified as the most entrenched of Central America and a critical element in the stability of national political life. The fact that such a stratum exists is as indisputable as the equilibrium of the country's administration, but the explanation of the latter in terms of the former is a precarious intellectual enterprise. It is certainly the case that the particularly tight kinship ties of Spanish and Sephardic families in a very small colonial society produced a genealogical pattern in which many politicians as well as members of the bourgeoisie shared a bloodline. Although Figueres was the son of Galician settlers and the Moras progeny of a family that only acquired prominence in the nineteenth century, some weight should be given to the fact that 33 of the republic's 44 presidents – including Orlich and Oduber – as well as 570 deputies were descended from the conquistador families of Vázquez de Coronado, Acosta and Alvarado. This assuredly bolstered notions of caste and bestowed upon the oligarchy a sense of social superiority to complement its economic power.[52] It is quite a different matter to extrapolate this familial affinity – already very dissipated by the twentieth century – into a dynastic interpretation of modern politics. In purely sociological terms the configuration of the local bourgeoisie has been affected by both high levels of foreign investment and a lesser but not insignificant degree of European immigration – surnames such as Altmann, Brenes, Hine, Beck, Niehaus and Tattenbach being prominent in the contemporary elite. More importantly still, the post-1948 system promoted a process of social mobility and the emergence of a bureaucratic elite, whose characteristics are scarcely oligarchic even if they manifest the consolidation of middle-class privilege. While in the 1920s some two-thirds of deputies were the sons of *finqueros*, by the late 1960s the level was less than a fifth. Between 1948 and 1974 two-thirds of the presidents and over half the deputies had received a university education, but only a fifth of the PLN parliamentarians in this period were the sons of graduates and less than a quarter had fathers who had held a state post.[53] Although we lack corresponding statistics for the civil service, this pattern must be even more marked, reflecting an elitism that is more bureaucratic than property-based and more a product of the modern state than its cause.

The Model Questioned

The 1970s opened with Figueres's second presidency backed by a comfortable *Liberacionista* majority of seven in congress. Despite the damage done to the CACM by the Honduras–El Salvador war, the national political outlook appeared to be one of continued stability and progress. However, Figureres's idiosyncratic management of foreign affairs and his personal business interests, together with the waning capacity of the regulatory state to maintain the diversified economic growth begun in the 1960s, produced a series of disruptions and the emergence of right-wing extremism that were disturbingly unfamiliar. The subsequent administration of Daniel Oduber (1974–78) adopted an altogether more sober political style but it responded to the downturn in the economy and first 'oil shocks' of 1973–74 by enhancing the direct intervention of the public sector in production, greatly alarming the agro-export bourgeoisie. The Carazo government (1978–82) thus came to office with a clear mandate not just to stem this process but also to make sharp cuts in the welfare state under a neo-liberal programme that represented the most radical blueprint yet devised for reversing the public policy of the post-war era. It was never properly applied. Beset by popular pressure, himself only partially committed to the policy, and presiding over an unstable coalition, Carazo ended up accelerating levels of expenditure in all but one year of his term, deploying a series of self-defeating tactical measures to mitigate the effects of the burgeoning economic crisis. The resulting confusion within the conservative alliance was further deepened by the president's emphatic support for the FSLN in the closing stages of the Nicaraguan revolution. This drew Costa Rica firmly into the orbit of regional politics, from which it could not henceforth escape. Both this factor and the impact of a recession that was sharper than that experienced elsewhere made the luxuries of isolation and subsidized stability seem exceptionally vulnerable.

The issue of relations with Nicaragua had always occupied a prominent place in national affairs ever since Somoza's stillborn invasion in the spring of 1948. In December of that year the Nicaraguan dictator patronized an abortive effort by Calderón to stage a counter-revolution against the junta. This prompted the intervention of the OAS, which acted with remarkable celerity because the raid called into question the validity of the Rio treaty for mutual defence signed the previous year as well as threatening an anti-communist civilian regime of the type being promoted by Washington for the hemisphere. However, Figueres did not allow either international treaties or US pressure to interfere with his commitment to a regional anti-dictatorial movement and particularly the overthrow of Somoza. He, alone of all Latin American leaders, refused to attend the tenth Inter-American conference of 1954 because it was held in Caracas and Venezuela was ruled by the dictatorship of General Pérez Jiménez whilst Rómulo Betancourt, leader of the opposition AD, was in exile in Costa Rica. In April 1954 Figueres gave lightly veiled support to a conservative revolt against Somoza that never had much chance of success but could at least be seen as a continuation of the campaign of the Caribbean Legion. In response Somoza staged yet another National Guard incursion into northern Costa Rica in January 1955.

At the time Figueres charged the CIA with connivance in the attack because Washington was indebted to Somoza for assisting in the overthrow of Arbenz and deeply unhappy with Costa Rica's offer of asylum to a broad spectrum of political exiles.[54] It is possible that the president's accusation was not entirely baseless since the Agency had already been caught tapping Figueres's phone and the Eisenhower administration had little reason to applaud his foreign policy, but when Somoza invaded the US moved quickly to support OAS intervention by selling Costa Rica four Mustang fighters at $1 apiece.[55] Moreover, as Figueres himself later freely admitted, both he and the PLN enjoyed quite close relations with the CIA, which was deeply involved behind the scenes at ORIT, headed by Monge, and provided funds for the PLN's *Instituto de Educación Política* and the *Escuela Interamericana de Educación Democrática*, established in Costa Rica under party auspices in 1959 (only to be closed precipitately five years later under mysterious circumstances).[56] Figueres made a celebratory visit to Havana in April 1959 yet his praise for the revolution was so heavily qualified with injunctions to eschew 'divisive' radical policies that Castro immediately declared him a 'bad friend' and a 'bad revolutionary'.[57] Equally, although Figueres, now out of office, patronized a further Nicaraguan revolt in 1959 and convened a meeting in 1961 to plot the overthrow of the Dominican dictator Rafael Trujillo, official foreign policy charted a much more cautious path. Orlich sent a contingent of police to support the US intervention force in the Dominican Republic in 1965, and it was the conservative isolationists who desisted from backing the Bay of Pigs

(Echandi) and withdrew Costa Rica from Condeca (Trejos).

However erratic relations between Figueres and Washington in the 1950s, there is persuasive evidence of CIA involvement in the December 1970 plot against him by the extreme right-wing MCRL led by Guillermo Castro. The conspiracy never got further than the landing on the Osa peninsula of crates believed to contain arms from two ships, one of which was later traced to the CIA.[58] Although Figueres later dismissed this as nothing more than a whisky-smuggling operation, the Civil Guard was put on full alert, automatic weapons were borrowed from the Torrijos regime in Panama, and for a few days in January 1971 San José was in a state of nervous tension. Such precautions were not unjustified since the MCRL was known to be heavily armed and the US embassy dominated by staff extremely hostile to Figueres's policy of opening relations with the Soviet bloc.[59] It was undoubtedly this new turn which antagonized the domestic forces of reaction and sections of the US intelligence services, which were currently confronted with a regional tide of anti-Americanism on the part of governments as well as opposition movements. Figueres, married to his second North American wife and a regular visitor to Disneyland, was by no stretch of the imagination unfriendly to the US; indeed, inside the PLN he was thought to have become excessively accommodating. Nevertheless, the president had come to the view that, 'people everywhere are tired of the Cold War. Russia controls half of Europe and we want to make the Russians drink coffee instead of tea.'[60] This objective of expanding export markets in the wake of the collapse of the CACM had been clearly signalled on Figueres's assumption of office when he declared that the establishment of full relations with the Soviet Union would pave the way for sales of some 300,000 quintals of coffee.[61]

The *cafetaleros* behind the fierce anti-communist campaign of this period were little mollified by such commercial *realpolitik*, which was never realized although the particularly high prices and good markets of 1973–74 more than compensated for both this disappointment and the oil price rise. Once the Soviet ambassador was ensconced in San José in mid 1971 Figueres was able to open relations with Hungary and Romania and even explore the possibilities of doing so with Peking and Tirana, all at comparatively little political risk. This was partly because the especially charged issue of breaking the OAS embargo on Cuba was never taken beyond a war of words with the right and partly because the first months of the Figueres presidency had been exceptionally tense as a result of the conflicts caused by Trejos, who in the dying days of his administration signed a highly controversial contract with the North American Alcoa mining corporation for the exploitation of bauxite at San Isidro. This concession had excited unrest amongst a student population that was registering the influence of radical and anti-imperialist ideas evident elsewhere, the signing of the Alcoa contract less than a fortnight before Trejos left office being the scene of an unprecedented demonstration in which perhaps 45,000 young people effectively stormed the congress and at least 200 were arrested after clashes with the Civil Guard. According to *Radio Reloj*, 'these long-haired youths belong to a phantom movement behind which work supporters of Chinese Communism'.[62] Such orientalist ogres never stalked beyond the hyperventilated imagination of the right, but its apprehension about an upturn in radicalism was not entirely misplaced.

The redoubtable Mora had been returned to congress in the 1970 election and the PVP was enjoying some resurgence of popularity although the left-wing alliance behind PASO had won less than 2 per cent of the vote and orthodox Communism continued to hold little appeal for the youth and workers outside the enclave. It was instead within the PLN that radical ideas began to acquire a wider following. This was particularly so inside the party's youth movement, which in 1966 possessed some 40,000 members organized in 250 groups and, in contrast to the PLN leadership, displayed a marked sympathy for the Cuban revolution.[63] The fact that such a position owed more to generational affinity than to a deep-seated ideological conviction may be seen in the movement's support for Rodrigo Carazo against Figueres in the 1968 contest for the presidential nomination and identification with this current of figures like Fernando Volio, who later entered Monge's cabinet to become one of the most anti-communist and militarist ministers to serve in a Costa Rican administration for forty years. Nonetheless, the left-wing tendency's 1969 'Patio de Agua' manifesto that called for agrarian reform, an extensive programme of nationalization and tough curbs on foreign capital was more than a pubescent flash in the pan, which is perhaps why Figueres described it as 'the work of madmen' and the private enterprise association ANFE (*Asociación Nacional de Fomento Económico*) dubbed it 'Fascist'.[64]

The radical current never achieved enough momentum to stage a split from the PLN or develop an organized tendency within it, but Figueres was clearly seeking to neutralize it with his adventurous *Ostpolitik*, and in 1972 he appointed Padre Benjamin Nuñez, one of the leading leftists, rector of the new National University, which soon acquired a reputation for its progressive management and curriculum. This latter initiative greatly contributed to the restriction of boisterous radicalism to the portals of higher education although the Church hierarchy was not prepared to indulge the political dissidence of priests such as Nuñez and Javier Solis. It prohibited the latter from working as a journalist and pointedly advised the faithful before the 1974 election that they should vote for 'neither Marxist socialism nor liberal capitalism'.[65] If the small group around Nuñez had come to see themselves as pursuing the same social project as Jorge Volio and Archbishops Thiel and Sanabria, the priesthood as a whole remained exceptionally conservative. This was reflected in the weakness of local Christian Democracy, which first contested a national election in 1970 and gained so few votes – at 5,000 only 70 per cent of those won by PASO – that after 1974 it was forced to depend upon alliances with the *calderonistas* and Carazo's PRD.

Whilst the 'higher ground' of political controversy during Figueres's presidency was dominated by relations with the Soviet bloc, the decidedly more murky question of the president's association with the US financier Robert Vesco provoked little less acrimony and threw a suitably sober light upon the activities of 'Don Pepe' and his *argolla* (clique). Lasting more than five years, the Vesco affair spread its tentacles well beyond Figueres and the PLN, but the president's friendship with and protection of this outlaw entrepreneur (alleged to have swindled $224 million through his *Investors Overseas Services* company) continued to be the most publicized feature of a scandal that complicated relations with Washington and demonstrated that Costa Rican public life was far from free of the malfeasance practised elsewhere. The matter of Vesco's presence in the country and generous disbursement of monies in Figueres's direction became a public issue in mid 1983 when the *Wall Street Journal* revealed that the president's New York bank account had received $325,000 from a Vesco subsidiary in the Bahamas. Figueres denied any improper conduct, claiming that these funds were for the establishment of a national symphony orchestra, the development of small businesses, and a loan for his San Cristobal enterprise, and, besides, the electorate knew that he was an entrepreneur when it voted for him.[66] However, the president failed to account for $91,000 on any grounds and his assertion that Vesco's behaviour had been 'exemplary' barely tallied with the detailed charges levelled by the US Department of Justice or mitigated the fact that he himself had gaily channelled supposedly official funds through his private account. Figueres's erratic management of his commercial concerns was well known and would continue to be a matter of official concern – in 1978 his *Unión de Companías Centroamericanas* ran into trouble and required state aid in raising a $6.6 million loan to pay off scores of local creditors and guarantee the jobs of 1,500 workers.[67] All the same, he greatly compounded the consequences of his liaison with Vesco by responding to US demands for the fugitive's extradition with the rapid introduction of a new extradition law that effectively made the financier's removal from the country an impossibility. The PLN-dominated congress failed to block this law in large part, one must surmise, because Vesco had funded the party, but it was such a manifestly unpopular piece of legislation that the PLN presidential candidate Oduber went to great lengths to dissociate himself from it.[68]

In the short term Figueres weathered the storm, sheltering Vesco on one of his ranches, drafting the speculator's speeches in defence of his investments in Costa Rica, winning a libel suit over alleged corruption, and receiving enough support from the judiciary to oblige Washington to suspend its efforts at extradition by the end of the year.[69] Moreover, Vesco's cash had reached enough of the opposition to hold it back from making the affair a central issue in the 1974 election campaign. Still, the president was widely perceived to have abused the country's tradition of asylum that he had done so much to foster whilst Vesco's involvement in Richard Nixon's election campaign, and indirectly in Watergate, did much to reduce the populist potential of the manoeuvre. Gonzalo Facio, Vesco's lawyer who drafted the new extradition bill, blew his chances to be the PLN candidate in 1978. The law itself was repealed in 1976, and although Vesco managed to cling on to his status as a resident of Costa Rica for a further two years, he was harassed by both Oduber and Carazo, refused citizenship, and eventually drummed out of the country to pursue an even more obscure phase of his career under Cuban protection.[70] As Watergate itself had demonstrated, political systems very much larger than that of Costa Rica offered easy prey to powerful and unscrupulous individuals, and one can scarcely evince surprise that an outlaw multi-millionaire might attract such attention in a very small economy. The affair revealed the fragility of local political morality and the squalid side of a system built upon 'understandings' in which the mix of pragmatism, self-interest and propriety was not always as balanced as its advocates claimed. Unlike those of Mexico, Paraguay or Bolivia, the Costa Rican system possessed very limited coercive cover for extra-legal practices. This required both Oduber and Carazo to make a strong display of their repudiation although neither man left office without having attracted charges of corruption.[71]

The Vesco scandal and well supported allegations of PLN malpractice in the 1974 election – in which the forces of the right were unusually split into three serious camps and at least one maverick candidacy – gave rise to fears of an ossification of political life under an increasingly corrupt *Liberacionista* officialdom.[72] However, the Oduber administration responded to the particularly taxing circumstances of the oil crisis, collapse of the CACM, and friction with the fruit companies in a concerted extension of PLN economic policy that rapidly dwarfed more 'political' issues and engendered controversies that were to remain at the forefront of public debate for the next decade.

The formation of UPEB and the clash with the banana companies over export taxes was the most immediate issue, the new tariff of $1 per crate being introduced in mid April 1974 as a result of decisions taken by Figueres. It was clear from the start that this move would spark a crisis, the opposition of Standard Fruit provoking Figueres into threatening expropriation in response to the corporation's bluff of offering to sell its assets to the state. Oduber came to office promising to maintain this hard line, for which there was appreciable support not only from the population at large but also from the country's independent banana producers, who cultivated nearly half of the export crop and thus formed a critical constituency.[73] Nonetheless, the challenge facing the state banana agency ASBANA, which had to contend with three powerful companies, was formidable, and by early July the government had backed down, allowing the tax to follow market rates, which reduced it immediately to a mere 25 cents per crate.[74] Despite the recent scandals there was no question of a 'Honduran scenario' behind this compromise, and since the tax rate underwent a steady rise over the following years relations with the companies continued to be more contentious than elsewhere. Between 1974 and 1983 revenue from this source amounted to nearly half of the Central American total, the corporations responding by cutting back pay (the real plantation wage fell by more than 20 per cent between 1974 and 1980) and reducing direct cultivation (independent growers increased their share of the crop from 47 to 64 per cent between 1974 and 1984). United Brands in particular shifted away from banana production towards that of African palm as part of a strategy that only in the early 1980s came to be seen as threatening complete divestment from the Pacific plantations.[75] The eventual closure of UB operations at Golfito was undoubtedly hastened by the especially bitter strike of July to September 1984, and as late as 1981 production on the company's Costa Rican plantation was twice that of the nearby Armuelles unit in Panama.[76] Equally, over the first five years of the 1980s Costa Rican export tax rates stood at almost twice the level of those prevailing in the neighbouring republic, which fact also prompted the company to withdraw. In response the Monge government reduced taxes so that by early 1986 the rate was virtually the same as that prevailing in July 1974, but it was too little too late to halt a historic reduction of direct foreign investment in the banana trade.

Having proved unable to secure a major alteration of the terms for the operation of foreign capital in the first weeks of his presidency, Oduber proceeded to concentrate upon deepening state intervention in the economy, particularly in the manufacturing sector. The vehicle for this strategy already existed in the shape of the *Corporación Costarricense de Desarrollo SA* (CODESA), established by Figueres late in 1972 as an autonomous agency for the development of mixed enterprises in which the state would contribute two-thirds of investment against one-third from the private sector. Whereas Figueres viewed such an initiative as providing no more than public support and guarantees for new production in the manner of the CNP in the 1950s, Oduber and his advisers saw CODESA as a central element in the construction of a distinct state capitalist circuit.[77] Even so, in its early days CODESA appeared to the bulk of the local manufacturing bourgeoisie less as a costly extension of the public sector replete with burdensome bureaucracy and counterproductive regulations than as a major source of finance and a means by which to somersault over the local limits to accumulation. Thus, in 1975 and 1976, when CODESA invested C999 million in its own projects and funded private initiatives to the tune of C44 million, it enjoyed the full support of the *Cámara de Industrias* and leading entrepreneurs such as Richard Beck, Max Koberg and Alvaro Hernández, who entered into sharp conflict with the traditionalist *Sindicato Nacional de la Empresa Privada* (SINDEP) and landed capital over the new strategy.[78] In purely sectoral terms this produced some reward: between 1970 and 1978 industry's share of private sector finance rose from 20 to 27 per cent whilst that of agriculture fell from 34 to 22 per cent; in the same period the share of GDP attributable to manufacturing rose from 19.9 to 25.5 per cent whilst the proportion of value added in the industrial sector was the highest in Central America throughout the 1970s.[79] However, as noted by Jorge Rovira Mas, CODESA fell far short of providing a basis for stable, internally-orientated growth:

> If the nationalization of the banks in 1948 was the measure that assisted the economic emergence of a new sector linked to the state, CODESA has turned out to be an extremely powerful instrument for bourgeois advancement and quantitative expansion of the normal margins for the accumulation of capital in Costa Rica. However, one major difference deserving of attention lies in the much broader character of the former measure and the more oligarchic nature of the latter, which benefits only a few. This has resulted in contradictions within the dominant bloc and will continue to engender many more.[80]

Indeed, within two years of the establishment of major enterprises under CODESA's management the private sector had jettisoned its early enthusiasm as it became clear that the corporation's operations were being conducted in the interests of the state and a minority of favoured entrepreneurs. CODESA's purchase of shares in *Cementos del Pacífico SA* initially benefited interests close to Figueres and became even more contentious by virtue of the fact that it prejudiced the near monopolistic position of the *Industria Nacional de Cementos* enterprise, the opposition of which was no light matter however desirable the introduction of competition. On the other hand, private capital was excluded from the *Central Azucarera del Tempisque*, which controlled a quarter of sugar production in the Pacific zone and a tenth of the national output under CODESA's management; this was as much a source of discontent amongst local farmers as it was for those investors denied a share of ready returns. Similarly, CODESA was used as a conduit through which to seek full state control of the LACSA airline, the state holding only a third of the shares up to 1976.[81] With many of its members confronted with 'unfair' competition or excluded from the benefits of public investment, the bourgeoisie speedily closed ranks in opposition to the corporation; since by the end of 1976 CODESA's losses amounted to a fifth of its investment this opposition readily took the form of revived assaults on the inefficient and spendthrift character of public enterprise. Undoubtedly some firms drew their lifeblood from CODESA funds and sections of the capitalist class thrived as junior partners of the corporation, but they were a clear minority even within a manufacturing sector that found itself further restricted by the full nationalization of the country's only petrol refining concern (RECOPE) in 1974, precisely at the moment of the first oil shock. In 1975 RECOPE's profits rose nearly threefold to C119 million, much of which was transferred to subsidize state enterprises through the CNP instead of being returned to the consumer, who was charged by far the highest price for gasoline in Central America.[82] It is certainly the case that the boom in coffee exports of 1976–78 offset much of the impact of the oil price rise in the short term, but in view of Oduber's concerted effort to expand the parameters of the public sector it is unsurprising that support for the PLN within the industrial bourgeoisie slumped emphatically in 1976–78 – from 69 to 44 per cent of the membership of the *Cámara de Industrias*, according to one survey.[83]

Oduber's strategy was both a rational extension of established PLN policy and a plausible response to the favourable commercial conditions prevailing through most of his term, real aggregate demand growing by a massive 26 per cent between 1975 and 1977 alone as coffee prices rocketed.[84] This was reflected in accelerated government spending – from 15.1 per cent of GDP in 1970 to 21.8 per cent in 1980 – which was dedicated not only to direct state enterprise but also to the more familiar items of social security provision (extended from 45.3 to 75.2 per cent of the population between 1973 and 1981) and public employment (in 1978 14,000 new jobs were created in the public sector, which by the end of the decade accounted for 74 per cent of all professional and 82 per cent of all technical employees).[85] The 'drive for growth' soon proved to be as vulnerable as that witnessed in the rest of Latin America during the mid 1970s, the transient export boom encouraging increased borrowing facilitated by the global surplus of petro-dollars following the oil price rise of 1973–74. Hence, as government expenditure soared its fiscal revenue failed to keep pace by a very substantial margin and dependence upon foreign borrowing deepened. Moreover, just as the economy was plainly overheating at the end of Oduber's term, the price of coffee plummeted as emphatically as it had risen two years earlier. Within a year the Iranian revolution had provoked a second major oil price rise with the result that in 1979 fuel accounted for 12 per cent of Costa Rica's imports compared with 6.2 per cent in 1973, there being no compensatory movement in any of the country's exports. Although nearly all of the 1977–78 coffee harvest had been sold as futures at relatively favourable prices, the country had acquired a per capita debt that was amongst the highest in the world. There was no apparent means by which to confront the recession other than by engaging in a radical reorganization of the PLN system with the concomitant risk of provoking popular discontent, which, with the exception of a fierce strike in the electricity industry in 1976, had been at a notably low ebb.

The political crisis that many expected in the wake of the recession never arrived. Following the 1978 election the economy continued to decline, popular agitation became more frequent, and the country was subjected to unprecedented external pressure. But there was no substantial breakdown in public order, interruption of the established administrative process or loss of authority on the part of the traditional political formations. On a broad plane this may be explained simply by the low level of state violence, the existence of a system of representative democracy and, eventually, large sums of North American aid. However, it should be recognized that within this general panorama there existed a singular element not normally associated with the maintenance of socio-political equilibrium in Central America – a conservative opposition pledged to the norms of liberal democracy, sufficiently popular to win power through the ballot box, and adroit enough to be identified with its programme rather than the vested interests of a social class (however illusory the distinction, it is the stuff of politics). While it is true that from 1979 onwards the advocates of rearmament and administrative anti-Communism extended well beyond the MCRL and even nestled in the upper echelons of the PLN, the principal forces of the right provided an open alternative to the *Liberacionista* platform within the established political system. This amounted to more than a vindication of the algebra of bourgeois democracy or a product of extended constitutionalist rule; local conservatism possessed a strong populist potential rooted both in the mythical qualities of the Olympian era and in the inherent vulnerability of social democracy to mercantilist 'commonsense'. Furthermore, the parties of the right could plausibly claim to be both the victors and the victims of 1948, the subsequent alliance of Calderón and Ulate considerably weakening the PLN's pretended monopoly upon that history. Since the civil war the organized right had rarely enjoyed formal power, and so was untarnished by *oficialismo*; it had also continued to exercise appreciable influence within the PLN, which, as a predictable consequence of being the 'natural' party of government, attracted all manner of political fauna and possessed a left wing that could happily collaborate with the PVP and a right wing perfectly content to sup with the aspirant gauleiters of the MCRL.

These features came to the fore of political life after the 1978 poll, the right first winning the presidency following the collapse of Oduber's escalated interventionism, then losing the elections of 1982 and 1986 as its own alliance – not dissimilar in essence to that between Calderón and Ulate – pursued inconsistent policies and forced the PLN steadily towards more conservative positions. In short, the heightened tension of the post-1979 period produced a tangible concentration of political positions on the right of the spectrum without sacrificing party identity or suppressing the role of opposition.

The first indications of the ideological convergence that was to produce the hybrid Carazo administration of 1978–82 and the conservative PLN governments of Monge (1982–86) and Arias (1986–) appeared within the PLN in the shape of the '*Acción Patria*' faction. The group had coalesced in 1977 around opposition to Oduber's plans for a constituent assembly principally because this was intended to provide greater leeway for the autonomous agencies and state enterprises that the faction believed to be already out of control and in need of much tighter curbs. Other factors, such as Oduber's final establishment of diplomatic relations with Cuba (after sixteen years and very much in the wake of the momentary rapprochement introduced by the Carter administration), played a part in this intra-party realignment, but the size and management of the public sector was the critical element and even prompted some dissident activists to advocate a vote for Carazo's *Unidad Nacional* coalition in the 1978 poll. Such a position was less deviant than it might appear since Carazo himself was an ex-*Liberacionista* upholding a critique of statism rather than championing a wholesale offensive on the PLN's record. It has been said of the opposition campaign in 1977–78 that it represented the first genuine effort at changing the *Liberacionista* model, the neo-liberals in the conservative coalition such as Rodrigo Altmann (later vice president) and Hernán Sáenz (later minister of economy) proposing a complete suppression of import-substituting policies and the restoration of agro-export hegemony backed by a radical programme of free trade and reduced public expenditure.[86] However, despite the fact that these motifs were prominent in the alliance's platform, providing a sharp and coherent contrast to Oduber's record and the anodyne pronouncements made by Monge, the neo-liberal contingent in *Unidad Nacional* was balanced by an important faction representing manufacturing capital which, led by Rodrigo Madrigal, Richard Beck and Max Koberg, sought a reduction in state intervention rather than its complete elimination. According to Madrigal, the *estado empresario* was manifestly inefficient but it was politically and economically implausible to eradicate the state's role as guarantor of basic infrastructure and the rules of competition.[87] This group based on the refugees from CODESA shared the formal critique of statism sustained by the agrarian and financial factions organized around ANFE and backed by *La Nación*, but in essence it sought to reform rather than to destroy the PLN system, returning to the pre-Oduber period in which local industry received government support but was subjected to limited regulation and little direct competition on the part of the state.

Carazo himself straddled the two constituencies, deriving considerable advantage from the coherence of the neo-liberal attacks on the PLN model and alternatives to it whilst as a former president of the central bank and RECOPE he remained identified with that model and was able to appreciate its political strengths. The potential difficulties of his position were not obvious in the campaign since attacks on inefficiency and corruption in the public sector were standard fare at the hustings and found an echo in an electorate seeking change after two consecutive *Liberacionista* governments. Yet once Carazo had secured a clear victory over Monge his coalition encountered major problems. He resisted the application of the radical fiscal policies of a sizeable contingent of his government whilst pursuing their strategy in the monetary sphere; as he belatedly retrieved his jilted *Liberacionista* persona, Carazo was confronted with the contradiction at the heart of post-1948 conservatism, which required a liberalization of the market and yet could not dismantle enough of the regulatory apparatus to achieve this without courting a division in the ranks of the bourgeoisie. This dilemma was a prime cause of the erraticism of the *Unidad* government but it was far from the only one, many of the administration's problems stemming from the simple fact that between 1977, when the alliance was formed, the economic situation still relatively secure as a result of the coffee boom, and 1979–80, when it was in a position to apply its policies, the world economy underwent a crisis of quite unexpected severity. Undoubtedly, the rise in social discontent and union activism that resulted from this clarified the political costs attendant upon a full application of neo-liberal policies. This threat together with the lack of consensus within the bourgeoisie over how far to roll back the interventionist state lies behind the singular failure to consolidate the defeat of the PLN, which was particularly vulnerable in the wake of the worst election result in its history.

Although disputes over economic policy were to petrify the *Unidad* regime and pave the way for a resurgence of *Liberacionismo*, it was the Nicaraguan revolution that revealed the contradictory character of the conservative alliance most rapidly and emphatically. Carazo's eventual decision to lend full support to the rebel cause was highly popular and fully in keeping with national antipathy towards Somoza – between February and November 1979 the president's popularity rose from a desultory 13 per cent to 61 per cent largely on the basis of his policy on Nicaragua.[88] On the other hand, the major political and logistical backing provided to the Sandinistas – aid that very probably made the difference between victory and defeat in June and July 1979 – transgressed the traditional conservative policy of neutralism, aggravated Washington, weakened the government's anti-radical impetus, and greatly antagonized foreign minister Rafael Angel

Calderón, whose *Partido Republicano* controlled fifteen seats in congress. For these reasons and because the threat of a major counter-strike by the National Guard remained acute until the final weeks of the war, Carazo's policy was widely applauded as an extraordinary and farsighted initiative. The president certainly took a number of tactical and strategic risks that can barely be explained in terms of securing an ephemeral popularity at home – by November his poll rating was down ten points on that of July whilst that of his main opponent Calderón was rising – and although his foreign policy fell short of the 'third worldism' sometimes attributed to it, he maintained relations with the Soviet Union, recognized the PLO (in contrast to the pro-Israeli line of the PLN), and only broke ties with Cuba after concerted pressure.[89] All the same, the Nicaraguan policy was always underpinned by a strong current of opportunism. Popular enthusiasm for the overthrow of Somoza was such that Carazo was able to gain appreciable autonomy from a sceptical and powerful cabinet as well as to steal a march on the PLN. Moreover, he could count on the acquiescence of the Civil Guard, two of whose members had been killed by National Guard troops in December 1978, causing a national outcry and sharpening the traditional dislike for the Nicaraguan force nurtured by its Costa Rican counterpart. (Relations between San José and Sandinista Managua were to reach a similarly low point in May 1985, when several Costa Rican troopers were killed in crossfire between the EPS and Contras.) A number of Civil Guard officers had established close relations with the predominantly *Tercerista* forces operating in the border area, this being a factor in the failure of 'Operation *Jaque Mate*' undertaken early in 1979 with the avowed aim of clearing the guerrillas from the frontier and re-establishing Costa Rican neutralism following the expropriation of Somoza's *Murciélago* hacienda in September 1978.[90]

Efforts such as this to sustain a public evenhandedness were drastically reduced over the spring of 1979 but Carazo was careful not to burn all his bridges. He and Juan José Echeverría, the independently minded minister of security who directed the Nicaraguan operation within the government, granted Washington permission to land two helicopters in the border area in July without informing either their cabinet colleagues or congress, which duly condemned the move as a violation of the constitution, demanded the immediate removal of the craft, and provided the president with a convenient excuse for non-compliance with US manoeuvres to check the advance of the FSLN.[91] Of much greater importance than this was the revelation that Echeverría had secretly organized the supply of large quantities of arms from Cuba not only to the Sandinistas but also to the Salvadorean guerrilla. This operation, which involved at least twenty-one flights and the alleged exchange of considerable sums of money, included a number of senior Civil Guard officers and was undertaken with Carazo's full knowledge.

Echeverría resigned in mid 1980, vigorously defending his actions in terms very similar to those employed by Figueres in the 1940s and 1950s, and the president survived charges that he had received $20 million from the FSLN for his support.[92] There was some irony in the fact that Figueres was at the front of the pack condemning this clandestine operation, but if Carazo's actions were never entirely free of suspicion about underhand practice, it is clear that the PLN badly needed to limit government exploitation of the Nicaraguan question at its expense and was therefore itself not above dubious antics.[93]

Costa Rican support for the overthrow of the Somoza dictatorship cannot be deemed a major historical anomaly in the light of Figueres's own interventionist record, let alone the pattern of the nineteenth century. Furthermore, Carazo was not operating alone or in a purely regional context, receiving general Latin American support and considerable backing from Venezuela and Panama, two states with particularly close ties to Costa Rica. Equally, the subsequent pursuit of a forceful anti-Sandinista policy in San José reflected both the lack of PLN identification with the revolution and the fact that the Costa Rican political elite was no less dismayed by the passage of events in Managua than was the anti-Somoza bourgeoisie of Nicaragua. Within the space of eighteen months it found its most influential neighbour governed not by a fraternal liberal regime but a radical government that both controlled a military apparatus far more powerful than that possessed by Somoza and espoused policies abhorrent to the right and the new leadership of the PLN. In logistical and political terms the situation encouraged the *Liberacionista* mentality to regress to 1948, girding its anti-Communism with a resurgent nationalism that could readily be purveyed as anti-militarist and anti-dictatorial. The response was far more emphatic than that of Figueres to the Cuban revolution since Nicaragua had traditionally been Costa Rica's principal preoccupation in terms of foreign policy and it now posed the unprecedented threat of fortifying domestic forces to the left of the PLN as well as reviving fears of armed incursion. Thus, on the one hand, it proved imperative to return to a 'neutralist' stance but, on the other, there was little resistance to US pressure for an unambiguous anti-FSLN policy so long as this neither entailed direct intervention nor prejudiced domestic control. Obtaining such a balance was to prove exceptionally taxing since although Washington was markedly more sympathetic to the requirements of San José in this regard than it was towards Tegucigalpa, the PLN could not afford to fritter away the considerable political capital it had invested in anti-militarism and ostensible independence from the US simply in order to burnish its anti-communist reputation. The possibilities of reaching such a fragile balance were explored over more than five years, but it is indicative that as early as August 1981 the Carazo government condemned the statement by Jeane

Kirkpatrick that 'the destabilization of Costa Rica has advanced far' at the hands of radicals controlled by Managua. San José declared in response that Costa Rica 'neither needs nor desires military aid' from the US, a policy that would soon be dropped in practice but continued to receive popular support and could not be emphatically reversed, thus limiting the impetus of rearmament.[94]

It was the Monge administration that presided over the expansion of the security apparatus, quietly permitted Edén Pastora's Contra campaign, and levelled the most vituperative attacks against Managua, but Carazo never permitted his patronage of the Sandinista revolt to affect government restrictions on the left within the country, especially as there were indications in the spring of 1981 that Costa Rica was becoming infected by guerrillaism. His government cancelled the licence of *Radio Noticias del Continente*, the anti-dictatorial broadcasts of which had drawn protests from the Argentine military and a bombing attack by ex-Somocistas in November 1980, expelled Soviet diplomats for alleged direction of a strike in the banana enclave (the accused had never visited the relevant plantation), and likewise ejected a number of Central American oppositionists, including the Guatemalan FDCR, which held no insurrectionary brief and would normally have been a prime candidate for succour.[95] At the same time, Carazo sought to meet the charges that he was soft on Castro by breaking relations in May 1981, when misconceived invectives following Cuba's momentary 'open door' policy attracted a spate of troublesome refugees.[96] This rupture followed bomb attacks on a US military jeep and the Honduran embassy by the supposedly pro-Sandinista 'Carlos Aguero Echeverría Commando', these disturbing events prompting both *Unidad* and the PLN to organize a protest march against terrorism that was in turn disrupted by MCRL elements denouncing the president's 'friendship with Cuba'.[97] A month later three policemen were shot by guerrillas apparently belonging to the same radical 'commando', and the threat of a creeping 'Central Americanization' of national life was further raised when one of the dozen detained suspects, Viviana Gallardo, was executed in the offices of the *Organismos de Investigaciones Judiciales* (OIJ).[98] This threat was never realized insofar as the efforts at armed activity by isolated elements on the left were not repeated, and although the Contra was beginning to get underway in the north, the MCRL restricted itself to open thuggery on the streets in a manner that was containable by the Civil Guard and not considered a serious security risk by the government. The incidence of violence during this period was, if anything, more widespread in the sphere of industrial relations than in the purely 'political' field.

The basic features of the recession and attempts to confront it are outlined in Tables 54 and 55. The scale of the crisis may be judged from the fact that whereas in 1978 the state created 14,000 new jobs, in 1981 only

100 were made available; in the private sector the construction industry, which is usually an accurate indicator of the general health of the economy, reduced its activity by over 40 per cent in 1982.[99] As early as 1979 shortage of foreign exchange had obliged RECOPE to seek a barter deal with the Soviet Union, swapping coffee for oil. By the autumn of 1980 the central bank announced that it only had enough dollars to cover half the country's import costs, the National University having already declared that it would be forced to close if it did not receive its grant of $1.8 million, which was being withheld by the government.[100] The following year the *Cámara de Industrias* declared that 400 firms faced bankruptcy, putting some 20,000 jobs at risk.[101] Such examples could be endlessly multiplied – the mark of advanced decline was evident throughout the economy. As has been seen, the Carazo government came to office on an apparently unambiguous deflationary programme yet, as Table 54 shows, it was only in its last year in power that it succeeded in reducing imports, the budget deficit and real wages whilst the external debt rose from $880,000 in 1978 to $3.4 billion in 1982 and inflation soared from 9 to 90 per cent betwen 1979 and 1982. The failure of the *Unidad* administration to apply its avowed policies – or, indeed, any coherent economic programme – was not, however, simply due to internal divisions or the sheer weight of the crisis. In congress the PLN was able to rally the left and independent deputies to defend CODESA from privatization, which was in any case a highly problematic undertaking when so many of its firms were in the red and there was no ready finance for purchases. Equally, the right joined the opposition to Carazo's highly unpopular makeshift solution of a floating exchange rate, which was ruled unconstitutional by the Supreme Court in June 1981, thus restoring not only parliamentary authority but also the position of the *Cámara de Industrias*, whose members had threatened a protest lock-out over the failure to reduce the budget deficit and came close to breaking relations with what was purportedly their own government over the issue of the exchange rate. Beset by such opposition, Carazo resorted to a number of rather desperate ploys ranging from a proposal by ITC to enter into partnership with Disneyland – the Disney phenomenon appears to have exercised a particularly strong attraction upon the Costa Rican elite – to government tours of Asia and the Middle East in search of cash.[102] None of these yielded reward although as the purchasing power of the *colón* withered away thousands of Panamanians flocked across the border to pick up bargains with their dollars and thus provide some pitiful compensation for traders hit by the slump.

Perhaps the most notable feature of the Carazo government's record was its failure to fulfil its accords with the IMF, the administration introducing a series of deflationary measures (in January of 1980, 1981 and 1982) but constantly making recourse to traditional protectionist policies in defiance

Table 54: Costa Rica, Basic Economic Indicators, 1979–85

	1979	*1980*	*1981*	*1982*	*1983*	*1984*	*1985*
Exports (1970 $ mn)	364	342	381	350	358	397	378
Imports (1970 $ mn)	473	441	333	233	251	297	340
GDP (1970 $ mn)	2,202	2,220	2,170	2,012	2,059	2,182	2,217
GDP per cap. (1970 $)	996	974	927	835	834	862	853
Inflation (%)	9.2	18.2	37.0	90.1	32.6	12.0	14.6
Open Unemployment (%)	5.3	6.0	9.1	9.9	8.5	6.6	6.6
Real Wages (1970=100)	151.5	153.5	138.9	131.9	152.7	156.5	152.0
Budget Deficit (% GDP)	6.6	9.6	2.2	2.8	4.0	1.9	2.5
Purchasing Power Colón (1979=1.0)	1.0	0.68	0.50	0.26	0.20	0.18	0.16
External Debt ($ bn)	2.23	3.18	3.36	3.49	3.85	4.11	4.24
Debt per cap. ($)	1,010	1,396	1,436	1,451	1,558	1,626	1,631
Debt service (% exports)	33.0	39.8	43.1	28.0	62.0	47.9	
US Economic Aid ($ mn)	12.7	16.0	15.3	51.7	214.1	178.9	198.2

Sources: Crisis en Cifras; Rivera, Sojo and López, *Centroamérica, Política Economía y Crisis.*

of the Fund's call for free trade (Table 55). It is debatable whether the modifications made to the government's programme could have been averted without compensatory support of the order later tendered by Washington to the PLN regimes since although the union movement as a whole was very weak, it managed under the leadership of the public sector and banana workers to sustain a defence of the real wage until 1981. This modest achievement – unparalleled in Central America – was the result of a series of particularly bitter confrontations that opened with the ten-day stoppage by the stevedores of Limón (FETRAL) in August 1979, when Carazo belied the expectations nurtured by his foreign policy and deployed the Civil Guard both to load fruit and impose what was effectively martial law in the wake of the firing of more than 6,000 strikers. As the Guard infested the town and blackleg labour was shipped in from the interior a major riot broke out, two workers being shot dead and a score wounded by the police, who were themselves subjected to sniper fire. The government attempted to create a 'red scare' by expelling over 150 Latin American political exiles as well as Soviet and Cuban diplomats. Yet the PVP had little influence in FETRAL and only entered the fray through its support for the solidarity strike by plantation workers that followed the initial repression and overlapped with a stoppage by 40,000 teachers, whose action had been independently organized but served to increase tension and the government's sense of embattlement.[103]

The prospect of a complete breakdown of the established norms for industrial relations was further increased by the month-long strike by Standard Fruit workers in January 1980 that divided the cabinet, produced nearly 200 arrests amidst widespread violence, and cost the company over $6 million. Again Carazo charged that the strike had been 'directed by Moscow' with the PVP and CGT deliberately destabilizing democracy.[104] However, the forty-six-day stoppage on United Brands' Pacific plantations in the middle of the year was so patently provoked by company intransigence with respect to wages and redundancies that the regime forbore from red-baiting and felt obliged to mediate – and even administer the plantation on a temporary basis – after a worker had been killed by the police.[105] This initiative reflected government recognition that, with 59 strikes in the first ten months of 1980 compared to 109 over the previous seven years, labour discontent derived directly from the economic crisis and could not be treated exclusively by repression, which was prejudicing public order in the major ports and plantation zones. At the same time, the mobilization of 1980 prompted a rare consolidation of the union movement; the CGT, which included two-thirds of the banana labour force, joined with the public sector organization FENATRAP to form the *Central Unitaria de Trabajadores* (CUT) in October 1980, the new confederation covering 53 unions and 55,000 workers.[106] For a while this convergence seemed to

Table 55: Costa Rica: The Battle for Economic Control, 1980–85

1980	Jan.	Carazo government meets IMF demands for increased consumption taxes (35% on beer; 25% on soft drinks; 20% on tobacco) following the October 1978 reduction of subsidized public credit required by the Fund.
	Mar.	Agreement signed with IMF for one-year $60 million stand-by loan.
	Oct.	Government presents budget for 1981 that raises spending by 8.1%; import restrictions imposed; *colón* allowed to float; the constitutionality of a floating exchange rate is challenged.
	Nov.	IMF loan suspended due to failure to meet quarterly target restrictions.
	Dec.	Congress cuts 1981 budget deficit by 60%.
1981	Jan.	Austerity plan announced; price of fuel rises 85%; electricity 17%; telephone 30%; foreign travel restricted; diplomatic activity reduced.
	Apr.	Petrol price increased by further 27%; Finance Minister Hernán Sáenz resigns when Carazo rejects his planned 43% devaluation.
	May	Government plans to sell gold reserves and extend import restrictions; *colón* devalued from 8.60 to 12.60 to the dollar to meet IMF requirements.
	Jun.	IMF agreement signed for three-year loan of $321 million (terms include: single exchange rate; spending cuts with budget deficit to be 9% in 1981; 7% in 1982; 5% in 1983).
	Oct.	Government introduces new import restrictions and defaults on payment of principal of external debt; IMF suspends loan.
	Dec.	IMF requires increases in water, electricity, gas and telephone rates as prerequisite for new loan; private banks refuse to renegotiate $2.6 billion debt without IMF agreement.
1982	Jan.	Reduction of price subsidies (food prices rise 100%; water by 90%; public sector unions demand 40% wage rise; the government concedes 27%); Carazo attacks IMF for demanding interest rates of 40%; black market rate for *colón* rises to 28.
	Feb.	Monge wins election; first Economic Support Grant (ESF) disbursed by US. USAID declares that after February 1983 funds will depend on changes in Costa Rican law to permit repatriation of foreign funds and funding of private enterprise

without the intervention of the nationalized banking system, challenging state control of dollar allocation within the economy.

Dec. Reagan visits San José; IMF agreement signed for one-year stand-by of $100 million (terms: Public Sector Borrowing Requirement (PSBR) fixed at 4.5% of GDP; further adjustment of exchange rates; interest rates to rise to 24%; scheduled debt repayments).

1983 Jan. AID, using $70 million of Caribbean Basin Initiative funds, sets up *Coalición para Industrias de Desarrollo*, private export promotion lobby.

May Increase in electricity charges provokes broad popular mobilization in towns; government rescinds increase.

Aug. Bill to reform banking law introduced but delayed by strong congressional opposition from within PLN; US financial bodies delay funds.

World Bank makes $80 million structural adjustment loan dependent upon privatization of CODESA companies, curbs in education budget and price subsidies and an increase in interest rates.

Oct. Congress introduces 1% tax on exports and dollar remittances to fund childcare system.

Nov. AID suspends $20 million loan and IMF delays $60 million; congress amends taxes to apply to imports, not exports; AID funds released.

Dec. IMF demands public employment be cut by 3,300, a reduction in higher education spending and increased taxes; Monge warns against IMF 'destabilization of Costa Rican democracy'; black market rate is C70 to $.

1984 Jan. IMF demands budget deficit ceiling of at least 2% of GDP; government rejects this requirement.

Feb. Congress reduces tax on non-traditional exports and increases domestic tax rates; new financial law limits spending, requires autonomous institutions to be liable for central government deficit.

Mar. IMF signs letter of intent; AID makes $190 million appropriated for 1984 dependent upon IMF agreement, freezing $23 million until new banking law passed; Monge secures $50 million emergency loan from Mexico.

Jun. Monge tours Europe in search of economic aid.

Jul. Frozen AID funds secretly released.

Aug. Banking law passed (19th), effectively ending 36 years of state financial control.

Sept. Budget deficit stands at 2.5% of GDP, prejudicing new IMF loan; Fund now demands deficit limit of 1% and devaluation to C50 to $; AID and World Bank, apprehensive at competition from EEC, urge softer terms.

Oct. *Colón* officially devalued to C48 to $; black market rate is C300.

1985 Feb. AID establishes company to supervise privatization of CODESA.

Apr. Costa Rica is first state to be given multi-year rescheduling agreement by Club of Paris.

May IMF 13-month stand-by loan of $55 million agreed on terms of 1.5% PSBR and continued mini-devaluations; reduction of inflation by 5% and a freeze on credit to the public sector.

Jun. AID threatens to withdraw $140 million in ESF if approval is given to congressional bill allocating priority to cooperatives in purchasing CODESA subsidiaries and limiting saleable shares to 40%.

Jul. AID establishes trust to buy CODESA shares if there are insufficient private bidders.

Sept. IMF demands extra budget reductions within six months and the holding of public sector wages beneath inflation; Monge denounces these terms and warns of political unrest; a Costa Rican team flies to Washington to obtain new terms; IMF directors agree to lesser cuts and rises of public sector wages in line with inflation; loan is formally agreed (but eventually suspended in April 1986 when spending targets are again exceeded).

---

promise a shift in labour organization closer to the pattern in the rest of the isthmus, but it soon became clear that this would not be the case, overtures for further unification being rebuffed by the CCTD, the independent teachers (ANEP), and the students, largely on the basis of suspicion of the Communist sympathies of the CUT leadership. This failure to overcome the longstanding ideological differences and physical dispersion of the workers' movement did not bring industrial action to a halt – in 1981 and early 1982 the Standard Fruit plantations in particular were hit by prolonged strikes and renewed violence whilst public sector and transport workers engaged in a series of actions – but it did impede the CUT from staging a general strike and hasten the general retreat that took place under the Monge government. It is true, of course, that neither the level of mass organization nor the repression visited upon it approached the scale witnessed elsewhere in these years, yet both were extraordinary by Costa Rican standards. The outcome was that the unions greatly hampered economic adjustment under Carazo whilst the government's heavy-handed tactics ensured a decisive electoral victory for Monge, who promptly applied the lessons learnt from his predecessor by taking advantage of the disorganization and exhaustion of the labour movement to impose a much more emphatic deflationary programme than was anticipated and was no less an 'ambush' of political expectations than was Carazo's inept and erratic administration.

The Model under Challenge

The relative success of Monge's adjustment policies, which were by far the most rigorous in Central America, must be ascribed in good part to the fact that Carazo had already drawn much of the political fire inherent in such an undertaking. On the other hand, there can be no doubt that the crucial element lay in the preparedness of Washington to subsidize the process. In this regard it should be noted that the PLN government benefited from the emergency of the 'debt crisis' as a major international issue a couple of months into its term. Moreover, Monge's election and the disbursement of the first US Economic Support Funds (ESF) took place at a time when control of the rest of the region was especially tenuous – the guerrilla wars in El Salvador and Guatemala were at their peak and the election campaigns in both countries threatened dangerously embarrassing results – which placed a premium upon securing stability in Washington's one presentable ally in the isthmus. In 1981 Costa Rica received less than 6 per cent of US aid to Central America; the following year this proportion rose to 28.4 per cent and in 1983 to 35 per cent.[107] Over the next two years US assistance accounted for an average 35.7 per cent of the government's budget, the loan component of these funds being phased out completely in 1985, by which time the country was receiving $1.2 million a day from its northern ally.[108] This assistance enabled Monge to restore a good part of the massive cut – from over CA$1 billion to CA$264 million – belatedly made in central government expenditure by Carazo in 1981. Such a degree of financial support came at a high price, as indicated by the passage of events outlined in Table 55. In the first place Costa Rica was required to apply the orthodox deflationary policies of the IMF, which Monge accepted on the understanding that, 'to deal with the IMF is bad, but not to deal with it is catastrophic'.[109] For the public which had just voted overwhelmingly for the PLN this policy was presented in the shape of a 'return to the land', the declaration of 100 days of emergency, and the need to 'establish a social pact that should not imply injustice for anyone although it is possible that all will be asked to make sacrifices'.[110] To support this proposal and mitigate the effects of what was undoubtedly going to be a harsh programme, Monge introduced the *Sector de Economía Laboral* (SEL), which was intended to provide a safety net against unemployment through state assistance for cooperative ventures.[111] For many in the PLN the SEL represented a major adjustment of the party's original Keynesianism to the conditions of recession, reducing the social cost of the crisis and reviving production, particularly of non-traditional exports. In practice the SEL fell far short of such expectations, but it did prove to be critical in transferring management of abandoned plantations and helped to erode the authority of the unions at a time when the popular economy was under exceptional pressure.

The strength of the IMF and US government lay in the high level of the Costa Rican debt, which in 1980 was nearly three times the regional average in per capita terms and even in 1985 twice as large.[112] This provided Washington with the power to demand a return to fiscal sobriety and a strategic reduction in the economic role of the state; the replacement of protectionism with what soon transpired to be equally indiscriminate support for exports; and a freeing of restrictions on foreign capital. This objective of dismantling the post-war model was neither easy nor unchallenged. Within a year of coming to office Monge found himself confronted by an exceptionally powerful and popular campaign against increases in electricity charges, the spontaneous protests in San José obliging the government to withdraw a measure specifically demanded by the IMF.[113] Such flexibility was prompted to a large degree by the fact that the unions played only a minor part in the protest, Monge being unable to denounce it as 'extremist' or part of the 'international Communist campaign against Costa Rica', as he had the seven-week strike in the health service in the wake of his inauguration.[114] All the same, after 1982 mass mobilization was very uneven, and the regime faced greater problems in congress, where deputies like Julio Jurado sustained a trenchant resistance from the majority benches, declaring, 'the United States wants to change laws in effect for thirty years through force, through pressure, through intimidation, by suspending our credit'.[115] Such opposition led the far from diplomatic US Ambassador Curtin Winsor to bemoan the fact that, 'due to their democratic, and therefore inefficient, government they had been unable to put together that [stabilization] program'.[116] Despite this regrettable penchant for open debate in the political system the Monge administration was eventually able to secure the principal changes required by the US as it battled on two fronts in an effort to restrict the political damage of economic aid. The first major capitulation occurred in February 1984 with congressional approval of the *Ley para el Equilibrio Financiero del Sector Público*, which gave the central government extensive powers to regulate the autonomous agencies and eliminate budget shortfalls. No less important was the passing of the banking laws of August 1984 – *Ley de Moneda* and *Ley Orgánica del Banco Central* – that effectively subverted the 1948 nationalization and were only approved after considerable US pressure in the face of resistance by nineteen PLN deputies for whom no amount of foreign cash could justify the removal of the keystone of the modern statist model.[117] Whereas neither the initial deflationary element of Monge's economic programme nor the expansionist element based upon non-traditional exports from 1983 elicited major opposition from within the party, this third phase – described by some as the 'internationalization' of the economy – proved highly contentious.[118] It was, however, a logical consequence of the earlier measures and could not easily be thwarted once the government had come to agreement with the IMF in December 1982, despite the fact that Monge was constantly obliged to dispute the precise terms of the subsequent accords.

The collapse of the central statutory props of the post-war system occurred at the height of the two-month strike in United Brands' Golfito division. This soon transpired to be of little less historical consequence in that it hastened the corporation's decision to cease operations on the Pacific coast. The failure of this prolonged stoppage to halt UB's accelerated decapitalization and reduction of labour costs owed much to the fact that the union (UTG) had lost the support of perhaps 30 per cent of the plantation proletariat over the previous decade. This decline was particularly marked after 1980, when the union was faced with competition from the corporatist current known as *Solidarismo*, under which collective contracts were replaced by local bilateral production agreements with management, these being given pronounced support from a government dedicated to improving the conditions for 'worker cooperatives' and worsening those for traditional syndicalism.[119] By 1983 4,400 workers, or 24 per cent of the banana labour force, were incorporated into this system and structurally divorced from the logic of established trade unionism. The strike was further weakened by the divisions in the CUT that followed the split in the PVP which came to a head in December 1983 with the result that Mora, long the figurehead of banana worker activism, campaigned vehemently against the stoppage. The rupture of Central America's most stable Communist Party had its origins in Mora's rejection of the policy of militant support for the Sandinista revolution. This policy was proposed by the PVP's majority faction led by Arnoldo Ferreto, the patriarch insisting upon limited political sympathy tempered by the considerations of Costa Rican 'national interest' that had for decades subordinated the party's commitment to internationalism. It may well not be coincidental that this dispute broke out in the wake of the US invasion of Grenada and at a time when the Nicaraguan revolution appeared particularly vulnerable, not least to the military and political attacks now being launched openly from Costa Rican territory. Nonetheless, discontent with the prolonged autocratic control of the Mora brothers was also a potent factor, the traditions of the party leadership standing in sharp contrast to the political agility and radicalism of the FSLN, which had captured the imagination of much of Costa Rica's youth. After six months of organizational in-fighting the Mora group was ousted from the PVP at the cost of a debilitating division of the CUT and the decline of the party's power base in the UTG.[120]

The Monge government naturally welcomed these developments within the PLN's ancestral enemy yet within a few months the collapse of the plantation strike presented it with a major challenge as UB announced the ending of its operation a full three years before the termination of the 1930 agreement and with the immediate loss of at least 3,000 jobs. This violation of its contractual obligations – also ignored in the scale of African palm cultivation and degree of decapitalization – should have placed the corporation in a distinctly disadvantageous position in its negotiations with the government. However, the weakness of the state had already been revealed in its purchase of company lands over the previous two years, and the final accord signed in March 1985 (setting a price of $35,000 per hectare) proved no less generous than the original concession half a century earlier. The precise terms of dependence had altered somewhat in the interim, as was demonstrated a few weeks after the UB buy-out when Standard Fruit demanded $200 million in credit from the state, firing 700 workers to show that it was in earnest.[121] Equally, the government was obliged to purchase the abandoned land since the level of redundancies in the Pacific enclave was causing widespread disaffection and prompting a wave of *tomas* in which members of both the union and *Solidarismo* organizations were participating.

In the first eighteen months of the Monge government a total of 185 'rural conflicts' were registered, some being no more than short strikes and isolated protests but others reaching the proportions of a Honduran mass invasion, as in the case of the July 1983 occupation of 3,500 hectares of UB land by the UTG and militants of FENAC, who were only dislodged by the deployment of 600 police. This action prompted the announcement of an 'emergency agrarian plan' designed to give substance to Monge's slogan of 'back to the land' and remedy the manifest insufficiencies of the 1961 'agrarian reform'. Under that act the newly established *Instituto de Tierras y Colonización* (ITCO) directed a colonization programme that succeeded in allocating only 1,222 families to eleven poorly developed settlements up to 1966, whilst the squatter titling programme issued no more than 5,000 deeds between 1966 and 1971, the government itself admitting to the existence of at least 20,000 *precaristas* in its wake.[122] With the boom in cattle ranching the land question began to acquire an importance beyond the department of Guancaste, where the concentration of ownership had long been exaggerated and the source of conflict, the number of *tomas* rising from seventy under Trejos to 500 during the second Figueres and Oduber presidencies whilst the first year of Carazo's government witnessed 120 land invasions.[123] It was the prospect of a Honduran scenario of politicized ex-plantation proletarians with union experience taking to direct action on a mass scale that pushed the Monge administration to make a belated move. This had a high economic cost but produced significant political reward, not least in extending and fortifying *Solidarismo*. Exploiting a populist inheritance more secure than that of any other political formation in the isthmus bar the FSLN, the PLN was able to cull virtue out of an overriding necessity and at least freeze a source of social conflict that was at the heart of the political crises elsewhere.

Such success proved much more elusive in terms of the party's commitment to civilism and neutralism. Monge's erratic resistance to pressure from Washington for rearmament and direct assistance for the anti-Sandinista offensive were the source of considerable controversy within the PLN and caused widespread fears about the decomposition of the consensual political tradition. It is, indeed, hard to credit the notion that Monge's government was an unwilling pawn in Washington's regional strategy when, in April 1985, the Costa Rican president travelled to the US capital precisely as President Reagan was trying to secure congressional approval for aid to the Contras in order to declare that, 'aid for those in arms will be for peace', adding, perhaps a little unnecessarily, '[the Reagan government] has a legitimate interest in having me come to Washington to say this'.[124] On a visit in 1982 Monge had opined that, 'the despotism represented by Marxist–Leninist forces is now mounting an aggressive and expansionist offensive in our region. Our liberty and our peace are threatened as never before', which was scarcely language to discourage the Reagan administration, still less the CIA and the likes of Oliver North, who would shortly be conducting illegal operations in Costa Rican territory without any tangible let or hindrance.[125] Monge and his foreign minister Fernando Volio were undoubtedly trenchant anti-Communists, and the president's background gave every reason to suppose that he was as familiar with the covert aspect as he was opposed to the government in Managua. All the same, the attitude of these individuals was not exceptional within the PLN; as late as October 1985 Oscar Arias, the party's presidential candidate, could declare without a trace of *tristesse* that, 'as long as there are nine *comandantes* in Nicaragua we'll get $200 million a year from Washington'.[126]

Shortly prior to taking office Monge requested OAS supervision of the

Nicaraguan border. This appeared to be a shift towards a more neutralist stance after the rising belligerence of Carazo's final months in power, when US military aid was resumed for the first time in thirteen years. Moreover, the new president immediately reaffirmed Costa Rica's attachment to the Non-Aligned Movement even though one of his earliest actions was to reverse Carazo's pro-Arab policy and remove the country's embassy in Israel to Jerusalem, an especially generous overture to the Israeli government that was repaid by a state visit from Yitzhak Shamir in October.[127] Volio rejected as 'outright lies' rumours that this visit had sealed a military treaty but the minister's outrage appeared less than persuasive in view of the fact that Monge had already petitioned Reagan for military assistance in June, the government receiving $2 million for training and the customary opening batch of 'non-lethal' equipment in November, shortly before the expulsion of seventeen Soviet diplomats and Reagan's much-fêted appearance in San José.[128] In May the government had told Edén Pastora to leave the frontier area, and for a while he had made himself discreetly scarce. Yet before long the renegade Sandinista was back and ARDE was conducting its forays with conspicuous regularity without sign of official impediment. At the same time Alfonso Robelo, Alfredo César and Pedro Joaquín Chamorro junior were permitted to live and undertake political activity in the capital. As press attention turned to this renewal of interventionist policy by proxy and default, the regime resorted to the strangely clumsy ruse of demanding that all journalists be licensed by the *Colegio de Periodistas*, which amounted to a form of censorship.[129] This caused an embarrassing bout of indignation abroad yet failed to stem investigative reporting, which was in any case scarcely necessary to reveal the existence of the Contra forces now engaged in fierce battles with the EPS in the border region. As a result of these the Civil Guard was compelled to stage another bout of 'clearances', that of January 1983 netting a grand total of seven guerrillas.[130] In the same month Jaime Wheelock charged that Costa Rica was participating in joint US–Panamanian military manoeuvres, the Sandinista leader vaulting the psychological barrier that had hitherto limited political exchanges with Managua to testy diplomatic language with his observation that, 'Costa Rica, due to its economic necessities, has been forced to become pro-imperialist and pro-Zionist.' The communiqué issued in response did not stand on ceremony: 'If we don't have an army how are we going to participate in military manoeuvres?'[131]

Costa Rica did not, of course, have an army, but from 1982 it rapidly developed its security apparatus so that within three years it incorporated more personnel – 19,800 men – than were possessed by any Central American force a decade earlier.[132] Even though the Civil Guard lacked heavy weaponry, such expansion was not without regional as well as domestic consequences, and the fact that it was bolstered by $26 million of

US aid did little to quell apprehension. The announcement in November 1983 that a thousand US military engineers were to build bridges in the country was applauded by the bulk of the official opposition but sparked such an outcry within the PLN as well as the left that Monge was eventually obliged to dispense with the services of the hawkish Volio and invite the diplomatic corps along with the leading lights of society to the *Teatro Nacional* to hear a 'Declaration of Perpetual Neutrality'. In this foreign intervention, support for alien rebels, and the re-establishment of the army were all forsworn whilst it was reconfirmed that Costa Rica would maintain her 'ideological alliance' with the US and depend upon the protection afforded by the 1947 Rio treaty.[133] Such a grandiose act momentarily stilled discontent and committed Monge to a policy from which he could only deviate a certain distance without endangering his government. It was the reported opinion of Ambassador Winsor that the declaration amounted to 'bullshit', an interpretation that did not seem entirely erroneous in view of the fact that the pugnacious Volio had been accompanied in his departure from the cabinet by the moderate security minister Angel Edmundo Solano. Solano was replaced by Benjamin Piza, a man who had close ties to the MCRL and was not afraid to announce some eighteen months after the declaration of neutrality that the 'soldiers' of the Civil Guard 'will continue walking the paths of Santa Rosa up to Rivas [Nicaragua] to liberate the isthmus'.[134] Piza presided over the expansion of the *Organización para Emergencias Nacionales* (OPEN), created by Monge immediately upon coming to power, into a 10,000-strong vigilante force that soon lost its apolitical character to become a redoubt of the right protected by its status as the official reserve to the Guard.[135] With developments such as this the calls of the far right Heritage Foundation for greater US aid to an avowedly social democratic government were less anomalous than appeared to be the case.[136]

Ambassador Winsor's assessment of Costa Rican 'neutralism' under Monge was characteristically unrefined. Within a year of his departure from San José in March 1985 it was shown to be founded upon a misplaced confidence in the capacity of the PLN leadership to withstand the pressures caused by collaborating with Washington's anti-Sandinista offensive whilst maintaining the pretence of non-intervention. This contradiction took time to unfold and only became critical once the US escalated its local operations to the point of sending a contingent of Green Berets to train Costa Rican troops for counter-insurgency combat in May 1985. Over the previous two years the staff of the embassy was increased from 35 to 150 – in good measure, one imagines, to support the CIA activities that were to be revealed early in the Irangate scandal; scholarships for Costa Rican students were tripled (to 500); Peace Corps volunteers were expanded to 200; and a *Voice of America* station was set up.[137] Things did not always go smoothly, as was evident in the bombing of a press conference held by Edén Pastora in May 1984 that drew unwanted attention to both the dissident Contra and, later, the possibility that the CIA had been involved in the assassination attempt.[138] Yet if Washington could neither harness nor eliminate Pastora, the southern military campaign against Nicaragua had succeeded in souring relations between the two countries to such a point that by early 1985 – after Managua had issued thirty-six and San José sixty-six formal protests over incursions and border incidents – Sandinista diplomatic representation had been reduced to ten and Monge was being urged to sever all ties by former foreign ministers Niehaus, Facio and Volio. Winsor, therefore, could feel well satisfied with his work as he took leave of 'a beautiful house threatened by the Communist thieves of Nicaragua' to be replaced by Lewis Tambs, an extremist of the right who was associated with the 1980 Santa Fé document that had formed the kernel of Reagan's Latin American policy and who was now charged with supervising the covert operations being set in train by Colonel North and CIA Director Casey.[139]

The impetus towards complete rupture appeared to be uncontainable when, late in May 1985, two members of the Civil Guard were killed in a clash on the frontier. Although a subsequent OAS investigation did not assign responsibility for their deaths to the EPS, this was the version disseminated by the Costa Rican government, which had little difficulty in exploiting the incident to stoke up anti-Sandinista sentiment. The affair provided a particularly propitious atmosphere for the arrival of the US counter-insurgency training team and engineering contingent, which was based at Somoza's old *Murciélago* hacienda. Monge justified this major development of his policy on the basis of the supposed presence of Basque, Palestinian and Italian terrorists in the country.[140] Nonetheless, it was the presence of Northern American troops that excited most concern, attracting open criticism much faster than had been the case in Honduras. In June congress debated a motion of censure against the government for failing to secure its approval for the landing of the C-130 aircraft used to transport the troops, the proceedings being interrupted by an invasion of the chamber by MCRL militants outraged at the impertinence of the deputies. The motion was easily defeated but the administration was damaged by charges that Piza had orchestrated the mob, which moved on to stone a Nicaraguan embassy suspiciously deprived of police protection at the time.[141] These events engendered a distinct nervousness within the hierarchy of the Civil Guard, Colonel Sergio Fernández, the chief of intelligence, revealing in public his ruminations about political foul play at the same time as Piza was alleging that it had been the EPS that had staged the attack as a piece of black propaganda.[142] The government's reputation suffered a further reverse when the US mercenary Steve Carr – captured in April with four French and British colleagues by the openly neutralist Colonel Rigoberto

Badilla – was permitted to publicize from his prison cell the fact that he had been working for the Contras of the FDN on a farm owned by the US citizen John Hall, a member of the Cuban exile 2506 Brigade and closely associated with the CIA. Carr's declaration that, 'Monge pretends to know nothing; it's like when Nixon said he knew nothing about Watergate' was particularly telling because it came from an insider and tallied with popular suspicions that were now finding expression within a PLN leadership anxious about the consequences for the 1986 elections as well as the country's wider strategic interests.[143]

It was Figueres who headed the anti-interventionist reaction to Monge. Since at least mid 1984 Figueres had registered unhappiness at the fact that Costa Rica was 'the meat in the sandwich, caught between the US and Nicaragua'.[144] Whilst he was of the opinion that 'the Sandinistas say and do stupid things', the ex-president recognized that the government was conducting a policy destined to dissolve the very neutralism upon which it was supposedly founded, alienating the country when 'everyone in the world outside this village is with Nicaragua'.[145] Furthermore, regardless of the claims of the administrations in San José and Washington, popular opposition to the offensive against Managua was not limited to those inhabitants of the northern areas that had been disrupted by foraging Contras: 'Only the press and some Costa Ricans who have never held a rifle are ready to fight Nicaragua.'[146] Exploiting his position as 'Ambassador at Large' – an appointment Monge had made to keep Figueres out of the way and from which he subsequently tried to move the meddlesome pensioner – Figueres made a number of much publicized trips to Nicaragua and sponsored the call by all the country's ex-presidents and twenty-two deputies for the dialogue with the Sandinistas that Monge had pronounced 'erased'.[147] The large demonstrations and active press campaign in support of this initiative indicated the risks of further progress down the 'Honduran road', these being forcefully illustrated in mid December when 200 MCRL militants attacked an equal number of local and foreign pacifists intent upon staging a protest march through the isthmus; unsurprisingly, the neo-Fascists inflicted a great many more injuries than they suffered.[148]

The 1986 election campaign proved decisive in shifting the PLN position. Although the party's candidate, Oscar Arias, was on its conservative wing and had hitherto adopted distinctly hawkish positions, the absence of major differences with the PUSC over economic policy and the fact that Calderón was closely identified with rearmament and interventionism presented the PLN with an irresistible opportunity to exploit its retreat from belligerence by converting the poll into a referendum over civilism and neutrality. This manoeuvre was greatly facilitated by Managua's opportune recognition of responsibility for the death of the two Civil Guardsmen in May 1985, an overture that led to the establishment of a joint commission to discuss the border and permitted Monge to flaunt his newfound nationalism: 'Although the commission may not please the US, I am very sorry but this time, as on many other occasions, this deals with a sovereign decision of Costa Rica.'[149] The final election result was sufficiently close – once again the PLN was effectively dependent upon the four independent deputies for a working majority – to suggest that without the change in foreign policy and agile campaign to associate Calderón with the war and instability prevailing in the rest of Central America the party would have been defeated. The threat emanated less from the left, which polled more poorly than in 1982 and continued to reflect the damage caused by the PVP split, than from the fact that the PLN could only sustain its conservative policies on the basis of equivocation which reflected well upon the more forthright and consistent formulations of a similar programme by Calderón and the PUSC.[150] Under such conditions the party stood in greatest danger from abstentionism, which, notwithstanding the easy victory in 1982, could readily have robbed it of office.

It was not only Figueres and the party elders who salvaged the PLN from the consequences of Monge's burgeoning US alliance. On the economic front Arias deviated little from the line adopted by his predecessor; inflation began to rise once again in 1986 but the level remained modest whilst GDP grew by 3 per cent and the fiscal deficit was restricted to 3.4 per cent of GDP – enough to aggravate the IMF yet not to prejudice international credit, which rose by over 16 per cent.[151] This steady improvement, which finally propelled real wages past the level of 1979, served to relieve the government of domestic pressure and fortified the sense that a wider crisis associated with the regional struggles following the overthrow of Somoza was now on the wane. More visibly, Arias was released from many of the risks of the administration's revived neutralism by the Irangate scandal, which dramatically weakened the Contra cause within the US and provided an international climate far more favourable to a diplomatic solution than at any time since Reagan came to office and possibly since July 1979. In February 1987, well before the US Congress had capitalized upon the disorganization of the Reagan administration, Arias presented 'A Time for Peace', a regional peace plan that challenged the entire thrust of US strategy since 1980. This document proposed an amnesty for rebel groups followed by ceasefire and negotiations, the suspension of military aid for insurgent groups from outside the region, and the ending of refuge for rebels fighting in neighbouring states, all of which steps were to be monitored by an international commission. In addition, Arias stipulated the introduction of full press and political freedoms within the space of sixty days and the convening of elections to a Central American parliament. These latter provisions went some way to meet predictable US objections that the proposal was both unenforceable and a gift to Managua, which was required neither to hold new elections nor to sever its Soviet links. At the same time, Arias endeavoured to reduce Nicaraguan wariness by making no requirement for the alteration of foreign funding of governments or the completion of negotiations with the Contra before they lost their support from the surrounding countries. He also sought to meet Sandinista criticism that the plan depended entirely upon US compliance by stressing Washington's own dependence upon its local client states, the political and diplomatic potential of regional autonomy, and the fact that his own government had just declared Contra operations in Costa Rica to be illegal, closing down the principal rebel bases.

The February initiative had the merit of being opportune in terms of the balance of forces in both Central America and the US, and, since it emanated from the only regional regime with a plausible claim to impartiality, none of the affected parties was able to issue a pre-emptive rejection on the basis of the plan's bad faith. It was, however, little less vulnerable to sabotage than had been the myriad of proposals made by the Contadora group over the last four years, as was illustrated by the ease with which Washington pushed the Duarte government into withdrawing from a regional summit planned for June.[152] The sharp condemnation of this move by both Cerezo and Arias, who from the start openly voiced his expectations that Managua could not afford to make the political concessions being demanded, appeared to be no more than the impotent complaint of weakling regimes confronting a task that had already confounded far more resourceful parties. The view that the logistics of the exercise alone constituted an insuperable obstacle prevailed across the political spectrum whilst a large body of progressive opinion renewed its subscription to geographical fatalism. Nevertheless, it was not just members of the US Congress who were being exposed to the scale of the Irangate operation and drawing conclusions as to the prospects for the Reagan government in the wake of the scandal. Its ramifications were similarly studied by all the isthmian regimes, which, as has been seen, confronted differing political and logistical problems but shared the need both to be seen to be seeking domestic peace and to establish greater autonomy from a US administration in decline. Although the substantive impediments to success were formidable, they were qualified to a significant degree by the revival of regional identity as a factor in political discourse. In this Arias played astutely upon the governments' efforts not to be seen as the spoiling party, with the result that each actor was compromised to some degree by an accelerated 'holier than thou' effect. It was a taxing and accomplished diplomatic exercise that exploited the unusually propitious circumstances to the full. The Costa Rican president had little alternative other than to predicate his proposal upon the moral challenge of a 'Central American solution for Central American problems' since only this formulation could address the interventionist fears of both right and left as well as proffering the necessary dose of political pride.

It was the Reagan administration, beleaguered by congressional attacks on several fronts but most vulnerable to a rejection of its plans to renew and increase aid to the Contras, which succeeded in drawing the strength out of the apparent weakness of the Arias proposal. Concerned above all else to maintain military pressure on Managua but no longer able to torpedo diplomatic initiatives at will, Washington sought to outflank Arias by presenting its own proposal. Early in August 1987 Reagan announced a plan that was distinct from the Costa Rican draft in that it required Managua to hold new elections, sever its Soviet links, and effectively accept Washington's stipulations as to what constituted 'democratic pluralism' before aid to the counter-revolutionaries would be halted. This proposal was a new departure inasmuch as it concretized Washington's rhetorical requirements of the past and formally allowed for the possibility of an end to Contra aid. It was also novel in that it derived from an agreement with the new Democratic Speaker of the House, Jim Wright, and thus offered the first prospect in at least three years of a bipartisan policy on Central America.[153] In conceding to the agreement Wright may well have laid a trap for an administration grasping at any straw that would permit it to save face over Contra aid, but it was far from clear that the Democrats themselves were not looking for a compromise. Whatever the case, both sides were primarily interested in exploiting a foreign policy issue for domestic advantage in the run-up to the 1988 election campaign, and if the Democrats had more to gain, neither side appears to have anticipated the consequences of their agreement for the Central American summit held in Guatemala City on 6 and 7 August. This meeting proved to be a diplomatic triumph for Arias and Cerezo insofar as all the heads of state concurred that the timing of the North American announcement – of which none of them had been previously informed despite the fact that it was made forty-eight hours prior to their summit – constituted such a transparent challenge to the authority of their deliberations that it demanded a demonstration of independence. As a result, the meeting took up the gauntlet thrown down by the US and agreed an amended draft of Arias's February proposals.[154] This reaction may have been intended by Wright, whose Democrats now possessed a much stronger hand with which to bargain against Contra aid, but it proved particularly galling to the White House. This was because the Guatemala agreement set a timetable for ceasefires beyond the scheduled vote on renewed finance for the Nicaraguan rebels, which meant that Washington was obliged simultaneously to 'welcome' the Central American accord in public and subvert it in practice if its policy was not to disintegrate entirely. Before too long the 'doubts', objections and discrete acts of non-cooperation began to build up. Nonetheless, Washington had been thrown fully on to the defensive and it was clear that whatever the outcome of the accord an important watershed in regional relations had been reached.

Despite the fact that Costa Rica was the Central American state least directly affected by the stipulations of the treaty – by mid 1987 Honduras was far more substantially tied to both the Contra question and US political aid – the Arias government had committed itself to a policy that brought the country into the centre of regional affairs. The immediate political gains won from its diplomatic initiative at home were more modest than those on the international stage but the pace of destabilization had been reduced and attention diverted to its external causes, thereby reviving the image of Costa Rican exceptionalism. This in itself was a signal achievement given the experience of 1982–85. On the other hand, well before Arias came to office more perspicacious observers had noted that those features that made the country exceptional in terms of the Central American model of political polarization likewise made it quite unexceptional in terms of the broader Latin American experience of economic and social disaggregation. More than five years of economic contraction and radical adjustment had progressively corroded established patterns of public behaviour. The shifts in the structure of the economy that have taken place in the shadow of the crises elsewhere cannot be given a logic of implosion any more persuasively than that of explosion, but they provide a notably poor basis upon which to predict a comfortable passage for smallholder liberalism into the next millenium.

Notes

1. *Dinastía de los Conquistadores*, p. 369.
2. Francisco Espinoza, 'Experience of the Communists of Costa Rica', WMR, vol. 6, no. 7, July 1963, p. 36.
3. *The Report of the President's National Bipartisan Commission on Central America*, New York 1984, p. 13.
4. Quoted in Susanne Jonas, *La Ideología Social Demócrata en Costa Rica*, San José 1984, p. 15.
5. 'La Integración Económica Centroamericana en la Siguiente Etapa: Problemas y Oportunidades', mimeo, San José, November 1985, cited in Rivera, Sojo and López, *Política Economía y Crisis*, p. 61.
6. TW, 28 June 1982.
7. CAR, 23 August 1985.
8. For an example of radical revisionism that courts the danger of wholesale repudiation without providing a coherent alternative, see Jonas, *Ideología Social Demócrata*, which understandably stops short of assembling a material explanation of Costa Rica's development but provides only a partial argument at the superstructural level. For the fullest revisionist account of the pre-coffee era that continues to loom large in explanations of the country's exceptionalism, see Lowell Gudmundson, *Costa Rica before Coffee*, Baton Rouge 1986.

9. Rodolfo Cerdas, 'Costa Rica since 1930', mimeo, San José 1987, p. 63. For a representative critique of the limits of the post-war model, see Juan M. Del Aguila, 'The Limits of Reform Development in Contemporary Costa Rica', *Journal of Inter-American Studies*, vol. 24, no. 3, August 1982.

10. Carmen María Romero, 'Las Transformaciones Recientes del Estado Costarricense y las Politicas Reformistas', ESC, no. 38, San José 1984, p. 42; Jorge Rovira Mas, 'Costa Rica, Economía y Estado. Notas sobre su Evolución Reciente y el Momento Actual', ESC, no. 26, 1980, pp. 38–42. The 'class neutralization' thesis is most cogently argued by Jacobo Schifter, 'La Democracia en Costa Rica como Producto de Neutralización de Clases', in Chester Zelaya, ed., *Democracia en Costa Rica?*, San José 1983. In this same volume Daniel Camacho criticizes Schifter's analysis and lays emphasis upon the fact that the conflict of the 1940s and early 1950s was *within* the bourgeoisie and thus better described as competition between various factions seeking to become the bloc in power. Rodolfo Cerdas provides a more politically pugnacious version of this same criticism, identifying three staple misinterpretations: the 'arcadian' (which suppresses the violence, fraud and inequalities that characterized 1948); the 'Trotsko-anarchist', which devalues those achievements made before and after the civil war; and the 'revisionist', which attacks the model as insufficient but lacks a coherent alternative and fails to perceive the internal logic of these insufficiencies. Ibid., pp. 139–40.

11. 'The *Cámara de Industrias de Costa Rica* declares that it is completely at one with Junta in the present emergency . . . and calls upon all its affiliates and all those who support industry to exercise their greatest efforts to achieve the development of the country's industrial production.' *Diario de Costa Rica*, 16 May 1948, quoted in Flora Oreamuno Boschini, *La Cámara de Industrias de Costa Rica como Grupo de Presión*, San José 1977, pp. 49–53, cited in Ana Sojo, *Estado Empresario y Lucha Política en Costa Rica*, San José 1984, p. 44.

12. Quoted in Cerdas, 'Costa Rica since 1930', p. 52.

13. Quoted in Oscar Aguilar Bulgarelli, *Democracia y Partidos en Costa Rica*, San José 1977, p. 80.

14. PVP 1952 programme, quoted in Alvaro Montero, *Los Socialistas y la Revolución en Costa Rica*, San José 1976, p. 37. Reference to self-criticism over policy in the early 1940s is made in Espinoza, 'Experience of the Communists', p. 37.

15. Aguilar, *Democracia y Partidos*, p. 20.

16. Details of the constitutional system may be found in Charles D. Ameringer, *Democracy in Costa Rica*, New York 1982; Mavis, Richard and Karen Biesanz, *Los Costarricenses*, San José 1979. Studies of elections include John D. Martz, 'Costa Rican Electoral Trends, 1953–1966', *The Western Political Quarterly*, vol. XX, no. 4, December 1967; John Yochelson, 'What Price Political Stability? The 1966 Presidential Campaign in Costa Rica', *Public and International Affairs*, vol. V, no. 1, spring 1967; Henry Wells, 'The 1970 Election in Costa Rica', *World Affairs*, vol. 133, no. 1, June 1970. Detailed information on the background and careers of members of both the legislature and executive is provided in Stone, *Dinastía*, and Oscar Arias Sánchez, *Quien Gobierna en Costa Rica?* San José 1976, which is an orthodox survey of elite formation by one of its members (who became president a decade after his book was published).

17. Quoted in Enrique Benavides, *Nuestro Pensamiento Político en sus Fuentes*, San José 1975, p. 147, cited in Sojo, *Estado Empresario*, p. 68.

18. NYT, 12 January 1982.

19. At the SI's June 1986 congress in Lima the following organizations attended as 'consultative parties': MIR (Bolivia); PDT (Brazil); WPA (Guyana); PRD (Panama); APRA (Peru); PIP (Puerto Rico). Other organizations were invited as 'fraternal guests': UCR (Argentina); MUS (Argentina); PMBD (Brazil); *Alianza Democrática* (Chile); FDR (El Salvador); MOLIDER (Honduras); PRI (Mexico); FSLN (Nicaragua); *Colorados* (Uruguay); PS (Uruguay).

20. *Ideario Costarricense*, San José 1943, pp. 120, 118, quoted in Sojo, *Estado Empresario*, p. 42.

21. José Figueres, *Cartas a un Ciudadano*, San José 1956, pp. 126, 133, cited in Jonas, *Ideología Social Demócrata*, p. 15.

22. Daniel Oduber, *Carta a un Joven Liberacionista*, San José 1965, pp. 10–11, cited in Aguilar, *Democracia y Partidos*, p. 40.

23. Jonas, *Ideología Social Demócrata*, pp. 50–1.

24. Blas Real Espinales, 'Desarrollo, Población y Participación Sindical en los Problemas de Población', ESC, no. 14, May–August 1976, p. 70; Ameringer, *Democracy in Costa Rica*, p. 45.

25. Schifter, 'Neutralización de Clases', in Zelaya, *Democracia?*, p. 224.

26. Ameringer, *Democracy in Costa Rica*, p. 45.

27. Schifter, 'Neutralización de Clases', in Zelaya, *Democracia?*, p. 224. Between 1950 and 1958 central government employment rose by 157 per cent and that in the autonomous institutions by 287 per cent. Romero, 'Transformacions Recientes', p. 44.

28. Sojo, *Estado Empresario*, p. 55. The remaining portion of the public labour force was divided between banking – 14%; transport – 11%; agriculture – 3.2%; and construction – 2.5%.

29. Ibid., p. 49; Manfred Ernst, *Costa Rica – die Schweiz Mittelamerikas: Mythos und Realität*, Bonn 1984, p. 86. Social security coverage accelerated most rapidly after 1960, rising from 27 per cent of the labour force in 1963 to 44 per cent in 1973 and 65 per cent in 1981. Wim Dierkxsens and Paulo Campanario, 'El Papel de la Superpoblación en el Reformismo en Costa Rica', *Revista Centroamericana de Economía*, Tegucigalpa, vol. V, no. 4, 1984, p. 98.

30. Ernst, *Mythos und Realität*, p. 86; Rovira Mas, 'Economía y Estado', p. 42.

31. Rovira Mas, 'Economía y Estado', pp. 45–6.

32. Dierkxsens and Campanario, 'Superpoblación', pp. 91, 94.

33. Ibid., p. 98.

34. Schifter, 'Neutralización de Clases', in Zelaya, *Democracia?*, pp. 226–7.

35. *Crisis en Cifras*, p. 153.

36. It is worth quoting at some length Figueres's presentation of government intervention in the fishing industry in order to illustrate the PLN approach to mixed enterprises: 'The *Plan Pesquero Nacional* was initiated by our Ministry of Agriculture in 1949 and reactivated when we returned to government in 1953. It is a typical case of the mixed economy and functions as follows: a) fishing boats of private entrepreneurs . . . undertake the catch on their own account. b) the state (represented by a flexible autonomous institution, the *Consejo de Producción*) guarantees them a market, buying from them in Puntarenas everything they want to sell at a fixed price. With this alone the major worries of the fishermen are eliminated and they are disposed to accept a modest price. c) the *Consejo* has arrangements with the railway, which is also state-owned, for the transport of the fish in relatively large quantities in suitable rolling stock. d) the trains deliver directly to the refrigerated warehouses of the *Consejo* in San José where the fish can be kept for any length of time without spoiling. This is very important. e) private economic initiative returns to the picture: various small enterprises, some of them butchers, buy the fish at a fixed price at the warehouse and take it to their establishments for sale, at the agreed price. Also, the State banks finance the purchase of the boats at one end and the freezers at the other. When it is necessary, the *Consejo* provides them with guarantees. As can be seen, the state acts as an intermediary, as a stabilizing factor, as a financier, and even as a guarantor without reaping economic gain. Each institution covers only its costs and represents the state in specialized activities as an agent of the national economy.' *Carta a un Ciudadano*, pp. 118–19, quoted in Rovira Mas, 'Economía y Estado', pp. 43–4.

37. Arias, *Quien Gobierna?*, p. 182.

38. Stone, *Dinastía*, p. 348; *Dollars and Dictators*, pp. 208–13; 232.

39. Mylena Vega, *El Estado Costarricense de 1974 a 1978: CODESA y la Fracción Industrial*, San José 1980, p. 92, quoted in Sojo, *Estado Empresario*, p. 110. It should be noted that Monge's declaration that his 'only enterprise has been the PLN' signalled more than a simple difference in class background to the likes of Figueres, Orlich and Oduber; it also carried the strong implication that his predecessors had not always pursued disinterested economic policies. Cerdas, 'Costa Rica since 1930', p. 59. Cerdas interprets the development of the modern system primarily in terms of the weakness of the bourgeoisie: 'The central idea consisted of compensating for the organic weakness of national capital and anticipating the dangers of absorbing foreign capital through a direct intervention of the state in economy and society'. Ibid., p. 48.

40. Sojo, *Estado Empresario*, p. 127; Helio Fallas, *Crisis Económica en Costa Rica. Un Análisis Económico de los Ultimos Veinte Años*, San José 1982, p. 96.

41. Fallas, *Crisis Económica*, p. 55; Santiago Quesedo and Oscar Cuellar, 'Condiciones del Desarrollo Sindical en Costa Rica', *Revista de Ciencias Sociales*, no. 15–16, March–October 1978, p. 96. The overall level of unionization was 10.5 per cent.

42. Fallas, *Crisis Económica*, p. 69. For the bank workers, see Sojo, *Estado Empresario*, p. 59.

43. Manuel Bolaños, 'Movimiento Obrero en Costa Rica', in González Casanova, *Historia del Movimiento Obrero en América Latina*, vol. 2, pp. 277–8; José Manuel Valverde Rojas, Elisa Donato Monje and Sandra Cartín Herrera, 'Movimiento Popular: Problemas Organizativos y Alternativas de Acción', *Costa Rica 1985: Balance de la Situación*, San José 1986, p. 52. The four main bodies at the turn of the 1970s were the CGT, affiliated to the Soviet-controlled WFTU; the CCTD, affiliated to ORIT and the ICFTU; the *Central de Trabajadores Costarricenses* (CTC), formed out of the *Federación de Obreros y Campesinos Cristianos Costarricenses*, affiliated to CLAT; and the *Central Auténtica de Trabajadores Democráticos* (CATD), established in 1978 and without international affiliation.

44. Bolaños, 'Movimiento Obrero', p. 278; Valverde el al., 'Movimiento Popular', pp. 57 ff.

45. Martz, 'Electoral Trends', pp. 901–2.

46. Quoted in Wells, 'The 1970 Election', p. 17.

47. Cerdas, 'Costa Rica since 1930', p. 74.

48. Aguilar, *Democracia y Partidos*, pp. 44 ff. This text is very much a defence of Rossi's position. Aguilar himself supported the *Partido de Renovación Democrática*, a split from the PLN headed by Rodrigo Carazo and eventually part of the conservative PUSC alliance, from which Aguilar again split in the mid 1980s.

49. Ibid., pp. 65 ff.

50. In 1953 the PVP contested the elections in the guise of the *Partido Progresista Independiente*; in 1958 as the *Partido Unión Popular*; and in 1962 as the *Partido Socialista Costarricense*, which subsequently acquired an independent identity. A group of radical *Liberacionistas* which split with the party leadership in 1958 contested the 1962 elections separately as *Acción Democrática Popular* but without success. Ibid., pp. 85–6. The PVP fought the 1970 poll under the banner of the *Partido de Acción Socialista* (PASO), which gained 1.3 per cent of the vote and two seats, one of which was taken by Manuel Mora.

51. The PVP remained consistently faithful to Moscow and paid formal lip-service to Leninism, but Mora stressed that 'revolution is not exported or imported' and that 'all peoples should make their own revolution and wage their own battles'. *Libertad*, 14 November 1971. The PVP 'was born to fight for the economic and social transformation of Costa Rica' and to 'create conditions of real social justice . . . [which] we call a revolution', yet the party also maintained that, 'the social order in Costa Rica [can] be changed through peaceful means'. *La República*, 8 February 1971, quoted in William Ratcliff, ed., *Yearbook on Latin American Communist Affairs*, Stanford 1971, p. 58. The party's thirteenth congress of June 1980 reaffirmed both that 'the strategy of the Costa Rican Communists was aimed at accomplishing an anti-imperialist, agrarian, democratic, people's revolution in order to pave the way for socialism' and that 'the revolution can triumph without recourse to violence'. Eduardo Mora, 'Costa Rica: Conditions for Revolution', WMR, vol. 23, no. 10, October 1980, p. 23. Although the PVP followed the regional pattern of condemning Maoism in the mid 1960s, it was noticeably less forthcoming on the issue of Cuba than its peers. The split of 1983–84 will be considered below.

52. Stone, *Dinastía*, p. 189. Stone adopts an extra criterion for attributing oligarchic status on the basis of membership of social clubs. In 1958 20 per cent of PUN and less than 6 per cent of PLN deputies belonged to the Country Club, membership of which cost C15,000 a year exclusive of corkage and other charges, whereas only 7 per cent of PUN congressmen and 9 per cent of *Liberacionista* parliamentarians belonged to the Tennis Club, the annual charge of which was a paltry C700. Ibid., pp. 198–9.

53. Arias, *Quien Gobierna?*, pp. 62, 99, 116, 232.

54. Ameringer, *Democracy in Costa Rica*, pp. 82–3.

55. Ibid.; *Washington Post*, 9 January 1953; David Wise and Thomas Ross, *The Invisible Government*, New York 1965, p. 127; William Blum, *The CIA. A Forgotten History*, London 1986, pp. 89–91.

56. Jonas, *Ideología Social Demócrata*, pp. 71–2.

57. NYT, 4 April 1959, quoted in Ameringer, *Democracy in Costa Rica*, p. 86.

58. LA, 5 February 1971; *The CIA*, p. 271.

59. According to Yochelson, '1966 Presidential Campaign', p. 304, the MCRL was 'the most heavily armed group in the country' as early as 1966. At this stage the Civil Guard, which numbered no more than 1,500, depended upon handguns and single-shot carbines. The CIA station chief in San José, Earl (Ted) Williamson, was recalled to Washington in February 1971 after the affair although the anti-Figueres ambassador William Plosser retained his post for some time. Blum, *The CIA*, p. 274.

60. NYT, 11 February 1971, quoted in Blum, *The CIA*, p. 271.

61. LA, 29 May 1970.

62. Ibid., 10 April 1970; 1 May 1970.

63. Burt H. English, *Liberación Nacional in Costa Rica. The Development of a Political Party in a Transitional Society*, Gainesville 1971, pp. 70–2.

64. Ibid., p. 54; *La Nación*, 15 February 1970, quoted in Sojo, *Estado Empresario*, p. 70.

65. LA, 18 January 1974; 20 December 1974.

66. Ibid., 1 June 1973.

67. TW, 21 August 1978.

68. According to Oduber, 'the main difference between the President and myself is that I do not believe that it is wise to associate yourself with anyone whilst in office'. LA, 15 June 1973.

69. Ibid., 22 June 1973; 13 July 1973; 27 July 1973; 23 November 1973.

70. Ibid., 29 October 1976; 12 November 1976; 17 February 1977; 21 July 1978. One of the few positive by-products of this saga was the refusal of the Supreme Court to extradite the Chilean revolutionary leader Andrés Pascual Allende under the Figueres law in 1976 although it is unlikely that its decision would have been different under the old legislation. Costa Rica did not subsequently lose its reputation as a haven for criminals as well as refugees. In October 1983 six states filed petitions for the extradition of 62 persons charged with criminal offences, over half of them drug smuggling. TW, 24 October 1983.

71. In 1977 Figueres described the Oduber government as deeply corrupt, charged his successor with receiving large amounts of cash in the 1974 election campaign, and implied that he was in league with the CIA. Oduber subsequently claimed to have paid back donations emanating from Vesco but found it less easy to meet accusations that he had $17 million in an Austrian bank account following bribes from the purchase of a sugar mill and his veto of a bill making it compulsory to bottle the entire output of the state brewing company. Ibid., 3 June 1977. Two years later members of Carazo's cabinet were involved in an apparently lucrative arms smuggling operation in league with the Sandinistas.

72. In the 1974 campaign Trejos was challenged by the extreme conservative PNI of Jorge González and the more modern and populist PRD headed by Carazo, which parties together deprived the PN of enough votes to allow Oduber to take office with the lowest proportion of the poll in the modern era. Although it had little bearing on the final result, the candidacy of Gerardo Wenceslao Villalobos imparted an appropriately desperate air to the right-wing campaign. Villalobos, who liked to be called 'G.W.', took to riding a horse to demonstrate the need to conserve fuel in the wake of the first oil shock and once appeared for a television interview bound and gagged to illustrate the country's plight. Despite having defeated the infamous Central American wrestler '*El Buitre*' and fortified his reputation as a *macho* by arriving at the hustings via parachute, Villalobos failed to politicize his status as a celebrity and remained very much in the mould of European political cranks such as Commander Bill Boakes, Screaming Lord Sutch, and Father Ned Belton. The government later admitted to certain irregularities in the funding of the PLN campaign. LA, 13 September 1974.

73. López, *Economía del Banano*, p. 119; Rovira Mas, 'Economía y Estado', p. 56.

74. López, *Economía del Banano*, p. 50.

75. Ibid., pp. 129; 130–3.

76. Ibid., p. 133.

77. This argument is developed at some length in Sojo, *Estado Empresario*, pp. 68 ff.

78. Ibid., pp. 100 ff.

79. Ibid., p. 127; *Crisis en Cifras*, pp. 69, 71.

80. Rovira Mas, 'Economía y Estado', p. 64.
81. Sojo, *Estado Empresario*, pp. 188 ff., gives full details of these and other cases.
82. Ibid., pp. 86, 179.
83. Vega, *CODESA y la Fracción Industrial*, p. 92, quoted in ibid., p. 110.
84. Claudio González Vega, 'Costa Rica', in D. Schulz and D. Graham, eds, *Revolution and Counter-Revolution in Central America and the Caribbean*, Boulder 1984, p. 361.
85. Dierkxsens and Campanario, 'Superpoblación', p. 104; Morris J. Blachman and Ronald G. Hellman, 'Costa Rica', in Morris J. Blachman, William M. Leogrande and Kenneth Sharpe, eds, *Confronting Revolution. Security through Diplomacy in Central America*, New York 1986, p. 161.
86. Rivera, Sojo and López, *Política Economía y Crisis*, p. 53.
87. Eugenio Rivera Urrutia, *El Fondo Monetario Internacional y Costa Rica, 1978–82*, San José 1982, p. 61.
88. Carlos F. Denton and Olda M. Acuna, *La Elección de un Presidente*, 1978–82, San José 1984, p. 37.
89. Francisco Rojas, 'Costa Rica, 1978–82: Una Política Internacional Tercermundista?' *Foro Internacional*, vol. XXIV, no. 2, October–December 1983. In 1979 the Soviet embassy in San José had a staff of 22 compared with the US legation's complement of 24 diplomats, although it should be added that at that stage this embassy covered Moscow's interests throughout the isthmus.
90. LAPR, 22 September 1978; 27 July 1979. The failure to clear the FSLN from the region must also be explained in terms of the very small contingent of Costa Rican forces available for such a task.
91. Ibid., 27 July 1978; 3 August 1978; TW, 16 July 1979.
92. In July 1980 Colonel Guillermo Martí resigned as chief of the Criminal Intelligence Division along with 35 of his officers after confiscating 18 weapons belonging to Echeverría. The following week Colonel Fernando Muñoz, commander of the Civil Guard, denied all allegations of arms smuggling although congress was already investigating the delivery of 10,000 automatic rifles. In April 1981 five Costa Rican pilots revealed that they had made the flights from Cuba and drew attention to the detention of one of their colleagues by the Salvadorean military. At this point both Carazo and Echeverría admitted to the existence of the operation, Edén Pastora declaring that the FSLN had paid up to $15,000 per flight. Such a sum would have been exceptionally cheap and does not tally with the charge that Carazo received $20 million for his collaboration – a charge made by Fernando Trejos, the Costa Rican father-in-law of FSLN Comandante Humberto Ortega, but with no subsequent vestige of proof. Echeverría resigned in May 1980, his relations with the rest of the cabinet being very badly soured (this was said to be connected with his separation from his wife, the sister of the vice president) but his popularity much enhanced. The ex-minister subsequently moved well to the left, forming the *Partido Radical Demócrata* in 1982.
93. As early as July 1979 Oscar Arias declared, 'the president has managed to hypnotize Costa Rica with Nicaragua's freedom struggle. Now that freedom has been won we're waking up to a disturbing reality – the stagnation of our economy'. TW, 6 August 1979.
94. Ibid., 17 August 1981; 24 August 1981.
95. Ibid., 13 April 1981; LAPR, 24 August 1979; 14 November 1980; 20 February 1981.
96. TW, 11 May 1981; 18 May 1981.
97. LAPR, 3 April 1981.
98. Ibid., 10 June 1981; TW, 6 July 1981.
99. Blachman and Hellman in *Confronting Revolution*, p. 164.
100. TW, 23 June 1980; 6 October 1980.
101. Ibid., 6 November 1981.
102. Ibid., 17 March 1980; 16 June 1980; 21 October 1981; 20 November 1981. Figueres was a great Disney enthusiast and Señora Monge later attempted to revive the project of a 'leisure park' in Costa Rica similar to that planned by the corporation for France, but the first lady's efforts were in vain. The attractions of circus and comic culture should not be consigned to the realm of flippant and cynical explanation, as has been made particularly clear by the work of Ariel Dorfman: *How to Read Donald Duck*, London 1975, and *The Emperor's Old Clothes*, London 1983. Whilst it lags well behind Panama, Costa Rica is the most 'American-

ized' country of the isthmus. It should, though, be noted that the circus is a far from predominantly 'Yanqui' phenomenon and has a long history in Latin American popular culture, acts continuing to tour Guatemala and El Salvador at the height of the guerrilla wars. These days attendance can often be a very costly affair; by the time the 'Dolphins of Miami' ('Flipper' and 'Sysy') big top reached Cochabamba, Bolivia, in August 1987 tickets were priced at $8, but without prejudicing popular support.

103. LAPR, 24 August 1979; 7 September 1979; TW, 20 August 1979; 27 August 1979.

104. LAPR, 1 February 1980; TW, 4 February 1980.

105. LAPR, 18 July 1980; 22 August 1980; 29 August 1980.

106. Ibid., 31 October 1980; TW, 13 November 1980.

107. *Crisis en Cifras*, p. 117.

108. Marc Edelman, 'Back from the Brink', NACLA, vol. XIX, no. 6, November–December 1985, p. 42; Blachman and Hellman in *Confronting Revolution*, p. 168.

109. Quoted in Blachman and Hellman in *Confronting Revolution*, p. 167.

110. LAPR, 14 May 1982; TW, 22 March 1982; *La Prensa Libre*, 8 May 1982, cited in Manuel Rojas, 'Costa Rica: El Final de una Era', in Daniel Camacho and Manuel Rojas, eds, *La Crisis Centroamericana*, San José 1984, p. 144.

111. Maria Eugenia Trejos Paris, 'Un Sector de Economía Laboral en Costa Rica?' ESC, no. 37, 1984.

112. *Debt Per Capita (US$)*

	1980	*1981*	*1982*	*1983*	*1984*	*1985*
Costa Rica	1396	1436	1451	1558	1626	1631
CACM	555	629	684	753	809	842

Source: Crisis en Cifras, p. 124.

113. *Los Hechos*, pp. 148–51.

114. LAPR, 21 May 1982; 18 June 1982; 13 August 1982.

115. Quoted in Blachman and Hellman in *Confronting Revolution*, p. 169.

116. Ibid.

117. *Los Hechos*, pp. 159–62; 175–8.

118. Eugenio Rivera in CEAS, *Costa Rica 1985: Balance de la Situación*, pp. 15–17.

119. Ibid. pp. 51 ff.; López, *Economía del Banano*, p. 134.

120. *Los Hechos*, pp. 155–8.

121. López, *Economía del Banano*, pp. 136–8; CAR, 26 April 1985.

122. LAPR, 30 September 1983; Beatriz Villarreal Montoya, 'Precarismo Rural en Costa Rica (1960–1980)', in Camacho and Rojas, eds, *La Crisis Centroamericana*, p. 429.

123. Villarreal, 'Precarismo Rural', p. 432.

124. CAR, 10 May 1985.

125. TW, 15 November 1982.

126. *Forbes Magazine*, 29 Octoebr 1985. At this time Daniel Ortega charged that the Contra was using estates owned by Daniel Oduber as bases, these being supplied by trucks belonging to ICE. CAR, 4 October 1985.

127. LAPR, 4 June 1982; TW, 11 October 1982.

128. LAPR, 2 July 1982; 19 November 1982; TW, 1 November 1982; 13 December 1982. In January 1983 the government admitted to receiving 'communications equipment' from Israel whilst the following month the *Washington Post* journalist Jack Anderson alleged that Ariel Sharon had offered Costa Rica captured PLO weapons as well as agreeing to construct military defences in the border area. Ibid., 21 January 1983; 21 February 1983. By 1985 it was accepted that the Civil Guard's 'Special Intervention Squad', had been trained by the Israelis and West Germans as well as by the US. CAR, 12 April 1985. For further details, see NACLA, 'The Israeli Connection', vol. XXI, no. 2, 1987.

129. TW, 24 January 1983.

130. LAPR, 21 January 1983.

131. TW, 31 January 1983.

132. *Crisis en Cifras*, p. 244.

133. *Los Hechos*, pp. 151–2.

134. Blachman and Hellman in *Confronting Revolution*, p. 175; CAR, 9 August 1985; *El Día*, Mexico City, 22 June 1986.

135. Blachman and Hellman in *Confronting Revolution*, p. 179; CAR, 12 April 1985.

136. Virginia Polk, 'Why Costa Rica Needs US Help', *Heritage Foundation*, 2 August 1984.

137. Edelman, 'Back from the Brink', p. 46. An outline of CIA activity was provided to the congressional hearings on Irangate by station chief Joe Fernández (alias Tomás Castillo). *The Guardian*, 2 June 1987.

138. CAR, 11 October 1985. Over the following three years both San José and Washington would be embarrassed by the investigation of this matter and its background by the Costa Rican-based journalist Martha Honey, injured in the attack.

139. Ibid., 7 March 1985. It will be recalled that Tambs, an expert on the expansion of the Brazilian frontier in the Amazon at the turn of the century, revealed considerable anger at the lack of loyalty of his political masters at the 1987 Irangate hearings. He had previously been hauled out of academia to serve as a highly controversial ambassador in Bogotá.

140. Ibid., 10 May 1985. In July over 300 Costa Rican troops 'graduated' from the Special Forces' counter-insurgency course in Guanacaste, but by the end of the year at least 100 members of the Guard had 'resigned' from the programme after being made to undergo strenuous training and eat frogs, snakes and monkeys. Ibid., 9 August 1985; 1 November 1985. Although one resists simplistic theses as to the pacifist vocation of certain nations, it may be that this fall-out rate had something in common with the high level of injuries sustained in training by the Icelandic defence force prior to the US–Soviet summit at Reykjavik.

141. Ibid., 14 June 1985.

142. Ibid., 19 July 1985.

143. Ibid. For a critical reflection on the background of the Miami-based brigade, see Joan Didion, 'Miami: La Lucha', *New York Review of Books*, 11 June 1987. The existence of the clandestine military base in Costa Rica was revealed in the report of the Tower Commission (III–23; B, 126–7), issued early in 1987.

144. Quoted in *Los Angeles Times*, 27 May 1984.

145. CAR, 8 November 1985.

146. Ibid. Earlier in the year Jeane Kirkpatrick had used a Gallup survey to claim that 69 per cent of Costa Ricans supported aid to the Contras, but this poll was taken in the wake of the killing of the Civil Guardsmen, and by November a survey taken by the same organization revealed support to have dropped to 39 per cent. WOLA, *Update*, March–April 1986.

147. CAR, 9 August 1985; 23 August 1985.

148. *Inforpress*, 9 January 1986. Fifteen people were injured in the attack, which lasted for two hours and stood in contrast to the firm but non-violent approach taken by the Honduran authorities.

149. *La Nación*, 11 March 1986.

150. Following the PVP split the new leadership withdrew from the *Pueblo Unido* (PU) electoral front and contested the poll as *Alianza Popular* (AP) behind the candidature of Rodrigo Gutiérrez Sáenz, previously the PU candidate (but not a member of the PVP). The new PU included the Mora brothers' faction of the party and a cluster of small progressive and radical organizations – Echeverría's PRD; *Partido Popular Democrático; Movimiento de la Nueva República; Movimiento Social Demócrata* – fighting for the candidacy of Alvaro Montero. Together PU and AP won 5.1 per cent of the vote and two seats; in 1982 the left won 6.4 per cent of the poll. Neither the Ecological nor the Humanist Party was permitted to contest the poll.

151. *Costa Rica 1985: Balance de la Situación*, no. 20, April–May 1987.

152. *The Guardian*, 19 June 1987.

153. Ibid., 5 August 1987.

154. *The Independent*, 8 August 1987.

Afterword

Central American politics have been presented here with an emphasis on two sets of contradictions: unity/diversity and continuity/rupture. Such an approach is obviously open to the objection that it simultaneously complicates life unduly and reduces evident truths to mere platitudes. On the one hand, the harsh extremes of life in the region make the nervous ferreting out of complexity and paradox an exercise in idle scholasticism. On the other, insistence upon the fact that not all things are the same and only some change is a pretty desultory contribution to human knowledge.

As mentioned at the outset, the dangers of succumbing to such silliness were courted in response to the particular condition of isthmian politics some five years after the Nicaraguan revolution. Since then matters have progressed apace, the risks of a book concentrating upon a specific conjuncture and then trying to 'run with history' being made soberingly clear. The week that may be an eternity in the palaces, stock exchanges and barracks of the world is, with some privileged exceptions, a very modest span of time in the university study, publisher's office and on the printshop floor. Writing in the autumn of 1987, when the prospects for a peace plan that might alter the character of Central American politics are still very unclear, one suspects that reflecting upon history is simply taking the safe course and making a virtue out of a necessity. A necessity, nonetheless, it remains.

This account has concentrated on two periods of rupture – the mid 1940s and between 1979 and 1982. Both corresponded to an unusual international situation and abnormal conduct in US foreign policy, albeit of short duration. The 'window of opportunity' between the last stages of World War Two and the Cold War may, upon closer inspection, transpire to have been only partially ajar, yet this aperture was critical to the consolidation of reformism in Guatemala and it fortified the popular bloc in Costa Rica sufficiently to provoke the unprecedented conflict of 1948 that laid the basis of the country's modern political system. If it is plausible to discern a kind of capillary action initiated by the Battle of Stalingrad behind these developments, it is similarly possible to suggest that another, deriving from Inchon, contributed to the staging of the Guatemalan counter-revolution. In all events, since the balance of power in Central America depends so closely upon the US it should be recognized that the shifting position of the US on the world stage works its way through to the isthmus. The importance of this international dimension is vividly underscored by the linkage of events in Iran and Nicaragua in 1979 and 1986–87. What is notable about these rare instances of relaxation in US control is the fact that they have not resulted in a common political response throughout Central America. In the 1940s only Guatemala and Costa Rica were able to scramble through the net. At the end of the 1970s the radical forces in Nicaragua stood alone in their capacity to exploit the confusion of the Carter administration and grasp state power. An explanation of this must assuredly return emphasis to local conditions for although the Salvadorean revolutionaries were clearly stalled by US intervention, both they and their Guatemalan comrades were already confronted with formidable obstacles that were only partly connected with external factors. Equally, the peculiar pattern of Guatemalan and Costa Rican developments in the 1940s owed a great deal to national conditions. In Guatemala the absence of any oligarchic political tradition independent of the military, the relative strength of urban society, and the longstanding weakness of a left impeded by deep racial divisions provided unusual space for the forces of liberal reform. In Costa Rica both the existing socio-economic structure and political tradition compelled the anti-communist project to embrace reform.

By any standard the overthrow of Somoza was a more remarkable product of both local and external factors. While it is entirely possible to explain the Nicaraguan revolution on the basis of general socio-economic factors, these were not markedly distinct from those in countries where the revolutionary offensive was detained or failed to emerge at all. The political condition of the country was, by contrast, quite singular. The historical absence of a strong landed oligarchy was not remedied by the emergence of cotton farming after the war, thereby enabling the Somoza regime to continue into a new epoch. Despite relatively weak economic ties with the US, the political links between Managua and Washington were peculiarly strong, the resulting impetus given to nationalist sentiment greatly compounding the problems of the dynastic order in the 1970s. Central amongst these was the position of the National Guard, which lacked the political independence and logistical capacity of its regional counterparts. Even at the death Washington failed to register the consequences of this, the terms of privileged partnership extended to the Somozas in the 1930s remaining unrevised after the 1972 earthquake and into a period of polarization when Somoza was seen as a puppet yet failed to act like one.

Sandinismo confronted a remarkably vulnerable regime and was presented with a peculiarly propitious set of external circumstances. These, though, were in themselves insufficient to allow the rebels to win the revolution. The particular history that threw up the Somozas also produced Sandino, whose political and military example provided a rich legacy that was realized both before and after July 1979. The FSLN not only derived advantage from the fact that it was seen to be restoring tradition and settling old scores. It also inculcated the importance – signalled if not fully demonstrated by Sandino – of combining social radicalism with patriotism, political democracy and an element of mysticism. It imbricated the new and dangerous with the familiar and reassuring. This, of course, cut little ice with the bourgeoisie which perceived the Sandinistas as Marxists and all the more dangerous for their ambiguities. For the great mass of Nicaraguans, by contrast, the ambiguity was essential. No other radical force in the isthmus possessed such a powerful antecedent in this regard, the level of radical patriotism being appreciably lower in the Salvadorean and Guatemalan rebel movements. On the other hand, the Sandinistas' political inheritance was not exclusively national in scope, the FSLN drawing important lessons from the example of Cuba, where the currents of democratic patriotism and social radicalism were not so much entwined as dominant in successive phases of the revolution. Cuba, of course, had, like Nicaragua, laboured for decades under exceptionally prolonged US tutelage.

All accounts of the Nicaraguan revolution properly stress the enormous political acumen of the FSLN in directing the struggle against Somoza, and it is very tempting to identify the lack of resourcefulness of the revolutionary leadership as the key element in the failure to establish new radical regimes in Guatemala and El Salvador. However, in neither country did matters reach the point at which the left was required to engage in a political war of manoeuvre similar to that waged by the FSLN in 1978–79. The position was perhaps closest in El Salvador between October 1979 and March 1980 yet the differences with Nicaragua even in that period were very substantial. The working class and peasantry were certainly stronger and organized to a higher degree, the left correspondingly more developed in programmatic terms. On the other hand, the popular bloc faced a more formidable oligarchy than existed in Nicaragua, a politically experienced military, and a dangerously influential centrist force in Christian Democracy, to all intents and purposes absent from the Somocista state. In short, both blocs were stronger in El Salvador than in Nicaragua and the balance between them was very narrow. The FMLN's offensive of January 1981 illustrates just how acutely the left perceived the threat of Reagan's assumption of power shifting this balance decisively in favour of the right, and that perception proved to be entirely justified. The subsequent US intervention did not have to be massive in outward form in order to hold the radical challenge at bay. This was the only viable policy in terms of domestic pressures and it was quite achievable in league with the local forces of reaction, which were truculent but appreciably more reliable than those in Nicaragua. From the moment the US resolved to 'hold the line' the context for developing political strategy was completely transformed. Thrown back from an insurrectionary position, the FMLN entered a guerrilla war of attrition in an exceptionally small country. Its ability to maintain this campaign very largely based on local resources over the following six years was quite remarkable and superior to that of any other guerrilla force in the region. The most immediate parallels for this experience were with Venezuela and Colombia, where rural guerrillaism became almost 'socialized' in the 1960s and yet failed to alter the course of national politics. With or without a process of ceasefires and negotiations, the prospect of the Salvadorean rebels enduring as part of the political landscape without being able to change it cannot be discarded. Yet the Salvadorean revolt has persisted in a far smaller and less resourceful political system than that of Colombia, and it continues to be linked to a fluid regional balance of forces. Even with the appalling violence the left in El Salvador retains considerable potential and the greatest experience of both urban and rural struggle of any radical force in Central America.

The reverses suffered by the popular forces in Guatemala were evidently more substantial despite the fact that US intervention after 1979 was really quite modest. Again, it is possible to identify logistical reasons, most notably the over-ambitious rebel offensive of 1981–82. However, behind this untenable salient lay more profound obstacles to the left, particularly the racial question and the strength of the enemy army, both of which were distinct from the rest of the region and deeply embedded in the country's history. Correspondingly, it is of limited value to subject Guatemalan radicalism to a comparison with that in Nicaragua, still less to draw denigratory conclusions from such a comparison. Externally traumatized by the Mexican revolution and internally chastened by the experience of 1944–54, the national forces of reaction have acquired formidable strength and a terrible disposition for slaughter. Together with the deep-rooted cultures of ethnicity this has produced a 'great fear' that is fully evident in a daily conduct so permeated with arrogance and ignorance on the one side and deference and survivalist forgetfulness on the other that Guatemala might legitimately be described as a colonial society. The pustulent old order prevails with a strength that inspires awe even in Latin Americans from other countries which have enjoyed only fleeting periods of democracy. This gordian knot could, quite possibly, be cut through. More likely Guatemalans will have to suffer the consequences of its being frayed away.

Honduras and Costa Rica did not fit into the pattern of crisis that affected these three countries so acutely although, as we have seen, they did not fully escape it. The question as to why a revolutionary situation did not come about is only relevant in the context of the rest of the region and would seem almost bizarre if these two states did not border on to countries in turmoil. It is, therefore, more sensible to explain the real strengths of stability than to engage in contrafactual explorations for an absent revolt. As the particular confusion of 1979–82 grows more distant such a perspective has been progressively jettisoned. Indeed, there is a case for arguing that the sobriety of analysis of Central America in the wake of the revolutionary upsurge has been taken too far and is in danger of mirroring the uncomplicated triumphalism of the early 1980s. If the isthmus is now more stable than at any time in the past decade it is only so through the force of arms. Little or nothing has been done to alleviate the socio-economic factors that lay beneath the revolts of 1979 onwards and have subsequently been worsened by the world recession. In El Salvador and Guatemala exploitation and oppression remain unabated beneath a 're-democratization' built upon fear and death. In Nicaragua the revolution cannot stand still upon its present basis for any length of time. Costa Rica remains dependent upon foreign economic largesse to guarantee its economic model. A reduction in US aid to Honduras would most likely prompt a return to social mobilization and political disaggregation. In no case is it feasible to postulate a repetition of the pattern of events at the turn of the decade. Yet the notion that the Central American revolution has passed definitively into history leaving behind a solitary radical regime is as implausible as that which once held that a single revolt would provoke a general isthmian rebellion.

Select Bibliography

Adams, Richard, *Crucifixion by Power. Essays on Guatemalan Social Structure, 1944–1966*, Austin 1970.

Aguilar, Oscar, *Democracia y Partidos Políticos en Costa Rica*, San José 1981.

Aguilera Peralta, Gabriel, 'Crisis y Alternativa en Guatemala', mimeo, San José 1984.

Albizures, Miguel Angel, 'Struggles and Experiences of the Guatemalan Trade Union Movement, 1976 – July 1978', *Latin American Perspectives*, vol. VIII, nos 2 and 3, 1980.

Alegría, Claribel, and Flakoll, D.J., *La Encrucijada Salvadoreña*, Barcelona 1980.

—— *Nicaragua: la Revolución Sandinista. Una Cronología Política, 1855–1979*, Mexico 1982.

Alphandery, Pierre, and Paga, Federico, 'L'Agriculture Nicaraguayenne à la Recherche d'un Nouvel Équilibre après la Révolution', *Amérique Latine*, no. 11, 1982.

Alvárez Solis, Antonio, et al. (eds), *El Salvador: La Larga Marcha de un Pueblo*, Madrid 1982.

Americas Watch, *Human Rights in Nicaragua, 1985–1986*, Washington 1986.

Ameringer, Charles D., *The Democratic Left in Exile. The Antidictatorial Struggle in the Caribbean, 1945–1959*, Coral Gables 1974.

—— *Don Pepe. A Political Biography of José Figueres of Costa Rica*, Albuquerque 1978.

—— *Democracy in Costa Rica*, New York 1982.

Amnesty International, *Guatemala. A Government Program of Political Murder*, London 1981.

Anderson, Thomas P., *Matanza. El Salvador's Communist Revolt of 1932*, Lincoln, Nebraska 1971.

—— *The War of the Dispossessed. Honduras and El Salvador, 1969*, Lincoln, Nebraska 1981.

—— *Politics in Central America*, New York 1982.

Arancibia, Juan, *Honduras: Un Estado Nacional?*, Tegucigalpa 1985.

Araya Pochet, Carlos, 'La Minería y sus Relaciones con la Acumulación de Capital y la Clase Dirigente de Costa Rica, 1821–1841', ESC, no. 5, 1975.

Arce, Bayardo, 'Speech to the Nicaraguan Socialist Party, May 1984', reproduced in *La Vanguardia*, Barcelona 31 May 1984, translated and distributed by United States Department of State, March 1985.

Arévalo Martinez, Rafael, *Ecce Pericles. La Tiranía de Manuel Estrada Cabrera en Guatemala*, San José 1982.

Arias Gómez, Jorge, *Farabundo Martí. Esbozo Biográfico*, San José 1972.

Arias Sánchez, Oscar, *Quien Gobierna en Costa Rica?*, San José 1976.

Armstrong, Robert, and Shenk, Janet, *El Salvador: The Face of Revolution*, London 1982.

Arnson, Cynthia, *El Salvador: A Revolution Confronts the U.S.*, Washington 1982.

Arrieta Quesada, Santiago, *El Pensamiento Político-Social de Monseñor Sanabria*, San José 1982.

Aybar de Soto, José M., *Dependency and Intervention: The Case of Guatemala in 1954*, Boulder 1978.
Badía, Roberto, 'Consideraciones Básicas para una Política de Población en El Salvador. Aspectos de Salud', ECA, vol. XXXV, 1976.
Baer, Donald E., 'Income and Export Taxation of Agriculture in Costa Rica and Honduras', *The Journal of Developing Areas*, vol. 8., no. 1., 1973.
Bagley, Bruce; Alvarez, Roberto; Hagedorn, Katherine J., *Contadora and the Central American Peace Process. Selected Documents*, Boulder 1985.
Baloyra, Enrique, *El Salvador in Transition*, Chapel Hill 1982.
—— 'Reactionary Despotism in Central America', JLAS, vol. 15, part 2, 1983.
Barry, Tom; Wood, Beth; Preusch, Deb, *Dollars and Dictators. A Guide to Central America*, London 1982.
Bataillon, Claude, and LeBot, Ivon, 'Migración Interna y Empleo Agrícola Temporal en Guatemala', *ESC*, no. 13, 1976.
Batres Jaúregui, Antonio, *Los Indios. Su Historia y Su Civilización*, Guatemala 1894.
Bauer Paiz, Alfonso, *Como Opera en Capital Yanqui en Centroamérica (El Caso de Guatemala)*, Mexico 1956.
Bell, Patrick, *Crisis in Costa Rica. The 1948 Revolution*, Austin 1971.
Berryman, Phillip, *The Religious Roots of Rebellion. Christians in Central American Revolutions*, Maryknoll 1984.
—— *Inside Central America*, New York 1985.
Biderman, Jaime, *Class Structure, the State and Capitalist Development in Nicaraguan Agriculture*, unpublished PhD, University of California, Berkeley 1982.
Bird, Leonard, *Costa Rica. The Unarmed Democracy*, London 1984.
Black, George, *Triumph of the People. The Sandinista Revolution in Nicaragua*, London 1981.
—— *Garrison Guatemala*, London 1984.
Bloque Popular Revolucionario, *El Salvador: The Development of the People's Struggle*, London 1980.
—— *Revolutionary Strategy in El Salvador*, London 1981.
Bonner, Raymond, *Weakness and Deceit. US Policy and El Salvador*, London 1985.
Bonpane, Blase, 'The Church and Revolutionary Struggle in Central America', *Latin American Perspectives*, vol. VII, nos 2 and 3, 1980.
Booth, John, *The End and the Beginning. The Nicaraguan Revolution*, Boulder 1982.
Borge, Tomás, *Los Primeros Pasos. La Revolución Popular Sandinista*, Mexico 1981.
Bossen, Laurel, 'Plantations and Labor Force Discrimination in Guatemala', *Peasant Studies*, vol. VIII, no. 3, 1979.
Bravo, Oscar, 'Modernización, Industrialización y Política en América Central: El Salvador, Guatemala y Honduras', Occasional Paper, Institute of Latin American Studies, Stockholm, August 1980.
Bricker, Victoria, *The Indian Christ, the Indian King. The Historical Substrate of Maya Myth and Ritual*, Austin 1981.
Britnell, G.E., 'Underdeveloped Countries: The Theory and Practice of Technical Assistance. Factors in the Economic Development of Guatemala', *American Economic Review*, vol. XLIII, no. 2, 1953.
Brockett, Charles D., 'Malnutrition, Public Policy and Agrarian Change in Guatemala', *Journal of Inter-American Studies*, vol. 26, no. 4, 1984.
Brockman, James R., *The Word Remains: A Life of Oscar Romero*, Maryknoll 1982.

Browning, David, *El Salvador. Landscape and Society*, Oxford 1971.
—— 'Agrarian Reform in El Salvador', JLAS, vol. 15, part 2, 1983.
Bulmer-Thomas, Victor, *The Political Economy of Central America since 1920*, London 1987.
Bunzel, Ruth, *Chichicastenango. A Guatemalan Village*, Seattle 1952.
Burgess, Paul, *Justo Rufino Barrios*, New York 1926.
Burke, Melvin, 'El Sistema de Plantación y la Proletarización del Trabajo Agrícola en El Salvador', *ECA*, vol. XXXI, 1976.
Burns, E. Bradford, 'The Intellectual Infrastructure of Modernization in El Salvador, 1870–1900', *The Americas*, vol. XLI, no. 3, 1985.
—— 'The Modernization of Underdevelopment: El Salvador, 1858–1931', *The Journal of Developing Areas*, vol. 18, no. 3, 1984.
Busey, James L., 'The Presidents of Costa Rica', *The Americas*, vol. XVIII, no. 1, 1963.
—— *Notes on Costa Rican Democracy*, Boulder 1967.
Cabarrús, Carlos Rafael, *Génesis de una Revolución*, Mexico 1983.
Cable, Vincent, 'The "Football War" and the Central American Common Market', *International Affairs*, vol. XLV, 1969.
Calder, Bruce, 'Crecimiento y Cambio de la Iglesia Católica Guatemalteca, 1944–66', *Estudios Centroamericanos*, no. 6, Guatemala 1970.
Cambranes, Julio C., *Coffee and Peasants in Guatemala. The Origins of the Modern Plantation Economy in Guatemala, 1853–1897*, Stockholm 1985.
Carcanholo, Reinaldo, *Desarrollo del Capitalismo en Costa Rica*, San José 1981.
Cardoso, Ciro F.S., 'Severo Martinez Peláez y el Caracter del Régimen Colonial', ESC, no. 1, 1972.
—— 'La Formación de la Hacienda Cafetalera en Costa Rica (Siglo XIX)', ESC, no. 6, 1973.
Cardoso, Ciro F.S., and Pérez Brignoli, Hector, *Centro América y la Economía Occidental (1520–1930)*, San José 1977.
Cardoza y Aragón, Luis, 'Guatemala en 1960', *Cuadernos Americanos*, vol. CXIII, 1960.
Carías, Marco Virgilio, and Slutzky, Daniel (eds), *La Guerra Inutil. Análisis Socio-Económico del Conflicto entre Honduras y El Salvador*, San José 1971.
Carmack, Robert M., 'Spanish–Indian Relations in Highland Guatemala, 1800–1944', in Murdo Macleod and Robert Wasserstrom (eds), *Spaniards and Indians in Southeastern Mesoamerica. Essays in the History of Ethnic Relations*, Lincoln, Nebraska 1983.
Castillo Rivas, Donald (ed.), *Centroamérica: Mas Allá de la Crisis*, Mexico 1982.
Cazali Avila, Augusto, 'El Desarrollo del Cultivo del Café y su Influencia en el Régimen del Trabajo Agrícola. Epoca de la Reforma Liberal (1871–1885)', *Estudios Centroamericanos*, Guatemala 1976.
Central Sandinista de Trabajadores, *El Papel de los Sindicatos en la Revolución*, Managua 1980.
CEPAL; FAO; OIT, *Tenencia de la Tierra y Desarrollo Rural en Centroamérica*, San José 1980.
Cerdas, Rodolfo, *La Crisis de la Democracia Liberal en Costa Rica*, San José 1972.
—— *Sandino, el APRA y la Internacional Comunista. Antecedentes Históricos de la Nicaragua de Hoy*, San José 1979.
Chamorro, Pedro Joaquín, *Estirpe Sangrienta: Los Somoza*, Mexico 1957.
Chomsky, Noam, *Turning the Tide. US Intervention in Central America and the Struggle for Peace*, London 1986.
Colburn, Forrest D., 'Class, State and Revolution in Rural Nicaragua: the Case of

the Cafetaleros', *The Journal of Developing Areas*, vol. 18, no. 4, 1984.
—— 'Revolutionary Labor and the State in Post-revolutionary Nicaragua', *Latin American Research Review*, vol. XIX, no. 3, 1984.
—— 'La Tenencia de la Tierra en El Salvador', ECA, vol. XXXI, 1976.
Coleman, Kenneth M., and Herring, George C. (eds), *The Central American Crisis. Sources of Conflict and the Failure of US Policy*, Wilmington 1985.
Colindres, Eduardo, *Fondements Économiques de la Bourgeoisie Salvadorienne dans la Période 1950 à 1970*, unpublished thesis, Paris 1975.
—— 'La Tenencia de la Tierra en El Salvador', ECA, vol. XXXI, 1976.
Comisión de Derechos Humanos de Guatemala, 'Informe Preliminar a la ONU sobre la Situación de los Derechos Humanos y Libertades Fundamentales en Guatemala, Julio–Octubre 1983', Mexico 1984.
Concerned Guatemalan Scholars, *Guatemala. Dare to Struggle. Dare to Win*, New York 1982.
Confederación Universitaria Centroamericana, *Estructura Agraria, Dinámica de Población y Desarrollo Capitalista en Centroamérica*, San José 1978.
—— *Estructura Demográfica y Migraciones Internas en Centroamérica*, San José 1978.
Conroy, Michael, 'False Polarization? Alternative Perspectives on the Economic Strategies of Post-Revolutionary Nicaragua', Working Paper no. 26, Kellogg Institute, University of Notre Dame, 1984.
Crain, David A., 'Guatemalan Revolutionaries and Havana's Ideological Offensive of 1966–1968', *Journal of Inter-American Studies*, vol. 17, no. 2, 1975.
Cruz, Vladimir de la, 'El Primer Congreso del Partido Comunista de Costa Rica', ESC, no. 27, 1980.
Dada, Hector, *La Economía de El Salvador y la Integración Centroamericana, 1954–60*, San José 1983.
Dalton, Roque, *Miguel Marmol*, San José 1977.
Danby, Colin, and Swedberg, Richard, *Honduras. Bibliography and Research Guide*, Cambridge, Mass. 1984.
Darenblum, Jaime, *Crisis Internacionales y Economía Nacional. Costa Rica ante las Dos Guerra Mundiales y La Depresión*, San José 1982.
Del Aguila, Juan M., 'The Limits of Reform Development in Contemporary Costa Rica', *Journal of Inter-American Studies*, vol. 24, no. 3, 1982.
De la Selva, Mauricio, 'El Salvador en 1960', *Cuadernos Americanos*, vol. CXIII, no. 6, 1960.
Díaz Chávez, Filander, *Carías. El Ultimo Caudillo Frutero*, Tegucigalpa 1982.
Diederich, Bernard, *Somoza*, London 1982.
Diener, Paul, 'The Tears of St Anthony: Ritual and Revolution in Eastern Guatemala', *Latin American Perspectives*, vol. V, no. 3, 1978.
Dierckxsens, Wim, and Campanario, Paulo, 'El Papel de la Superpoblación en el Reformismo en Costa Rica', *Revista Centroamericana de Economía*, no. 14, 1984.
Di Palma, Guiseppe, and Whitehead, Laurence (eds), *The Central American Impasse*, London 1986.
Diskin, Martin (ed.), *Trouble in Our Backyard. Central America and the United States in the Eighties*, New York 1983.
Dixon, Marlene (ed.), *On Trial. Reagan's War against Nicaragua. Testimony of the Permanent People's Tribunal*, London 1985.
Downing, T.J., 'Agricultural Modernization in El Salvador, Central America', Occasional Paper no. 32, Centre for Latin American Studies, University of Cambridge, 1978.

Durham, W.H., *Scarcity and Survival in Central America*, Stanford 1979.
Durón, Rómulo E., 'Gobernantes de Honduras en el Siglo XIX', *Economía Política*, no. 2, 1972.
Early, John D., 'The Changing Proportion of Maya Indian and Ladino in the Population of Guatemala, 1954–1969', *American Ethnologist*, vol. 2, no. 2, 1975.
Ejército Guerrilero de los Pobres, *Compañero*, 1982—.
Elam, Robert E., *Appeal to Arms: The Army and Politics in El Salvador, 1931–1964*, unpublished PhD thesis, University of New Mexico 1968.
English, Burt H., *Liberación Nacional in Costa Rica. The Development of a Political Party in a Traditional Society*, Gainesville 1971.
Escobar, Francisco Andrés, 'En la Linea de la Muerte', ECA, vol. XXXV, 1980.
Falla, Ricardo, 'Evolución Político-religiosa del Indígena Rural en Guatemala (1945–1965)', ESC, no. 1, 1972.
—— *Quiché Rebelde*, Guatemala 1978.
Fallas, Helio, *Crisis Económica en Costa Rica. Un Análisis de los Ultimos 25 Años*, San José 1981.
Federación de Trabajadores del Campo, *Los Trabajadores del Campo y la Reforma Agraria en El Salvador*, Chilpancingo 1982.
Feinberg, Richard, 'Central America: No Easy Answers', *Foreign Affairs*, summer 1981.
Fernández, Orlando, *Turcios Lima*, Havana 1968.
Fernández Guardia, R. (ed.), *Costa Rica en el Siglo XIX. Antología de Viajeros*, San José 1985.
Finney, Kenneth V., 'Rosario and the Election of 1887: The Political Economy of Mining in Honduras', *Hispanic American Historical Review*, vol. 59, no. 1, 1979.
Fitzgerald, E.V.K., 'Stabilization and Economic Justice: The Case of Nicaragua', Working Paper no. 34, Kellogg Institute, University of Notre Dame, 1984.
Fletcher, Lehman B. et al. (eds), *Guatemala's Economic Development: The Role of Agriculture*, Ames 1970.
Flores Macal, Mario, *Origen, Desarrollo y Crisis de las Formas de Dominación en El Salvador*, San José 1983.
Flores Pinel, Fernando, 'El Golpe de Estado en El Salvador. Un Cambio hacia la Democratización?', RMS, vol. XLII, no. 2, 1980.
Foote, Heather, 'United States Policy toward El Salvador: September 1979 to the Presesnt', mimeo, Washington 1980.
Frente de Acción Popular Unificada, *Polémica Internacional*, 1980—.
Frente Democrático Revolucionario, *El Salvador Libre*, 1981—.
Frente Democrático Revolutionario-Frente Farabundo Martí para la Liberación Nacional, 'Analysis of the New Salvadorean Government in an International Context', mimeo, San Salvador 1984.
Frente Sandinista de Liberación Nacional (Guerra Popular Prolongada), *Lucha Sandinista*, 1978, np.
FSLN Proletario, *Documentos Básicos*, 1978, np.
FSLN, 'The 72-Hour Document', translated and edited by United States Department of State, 1984.
—— *Plan de Lucha del FSLN*, Managua 1984.
Fried, Jonathan et al. (eds), *Guatemala in Rebellion: Unfinished History*, New York 1983.
Galeano, Eduardo, *Guatemala: Occupied Country*, New York 1969.
Gallardo, María Eugenia, and López, José Roberto, *Centroamérica. La Crisis en Cifras*, San José 1986.

García, Graciela, *Páginas de Lucha*, Tegucigalpa 1981.
García Laguardia, Jorge Mario, *El Pensamiento Liberal en Guatemala. Antología*, San José 1977.
Gettleman, Marvin E. et al. (eds), *El Salvador: Central America in the New Cold War*, New York 1981.
Gillin, John, and Silvert, K.H., 'Ambiguities in Guatemala', *Foreign Affairs*, vol. 34, no. 3, 1956.
Gilly, Adolfo, 'Guerrilla, Programa y Partido en Guatemala', *Coyoacán*, no. 3, 1978.
—— *Guerra y Política en El Salvador*, Mexico 1981.
—— 'El Suicidio de Marcial', *Nexos*, no. 76, 1984.
Gollas, Manuel, 'Surplus Labor and Economic Efficiency in the Traditional Sector of a Dual Economy: The Guatemalan Case', *Journal of Development Studies*, vol. 8, no. 4, 1972.
Gonzalez, Vinicio, 'La Insurrección Salvadoreña de 1932 y la Gran Huelga Hondureña de 1954', RMS, vol. XL, no. 2, 1978.
Gonzalez Casanova, Pablo (ed.), *América Latina. Historia de Medio Siglo*, Mexico 1981.
—— *La Hegemonía del Pueblo y la Lucha Centroamericana*, San José 1984.
—— (ed.), *Historia del Movimiento Obrero en América Latina*, vol. 2, Mexico 1985.
Gonzalez García, Yamileth, 'Desintegración de Bienes de Confradías ye de Fondos Pios en Costa Rica, 1805–1845', *Mesoamérica*, no. 8, 1984.
Gordon, Sara, 'La Transformación Agraria en El Salvador. Un Conflicto Interburgués', ESC, no. 36, 1983.
Grabendorrf, Wolf et al. (eds), *Political Change in Central America. Internal and External Dimensions*, Boulder 1985.
Grieb, Kenneth J., 'The United States and the Rise of General Maximiliano Hernandez Martinez', JLAS, vol. 3, no. 2, 1970.
—— *Guatemalan Caudillo. The Regime of Jorge Ubico*, Athens, Ohio 1979.
—— (ed.), *Research Guide to Central America and the Caribbean*, Madison 1985.
Gudmundson, Lowell, 'Peasant Movements and the Transition to Agrarian Capitalism: Freeholding Versus Hacienda Peasantries and Agrarian Reform in Guanacaste, Costa Rica', *Peasant Studies*, vol. X, no. 3, 1983.
—— 'Costa Rica and the 1948 Revolution: Rethinking the Social Democratic Paradigm', *Latin American Research Review*, vol. XIX, no. 1, 1984.
—— *Costa Rica Before Coffee*, Baton Rouge 1986.
Guerra, Tomás (ed.), *El Salvador: Octubre Sangriento*, San José 1979.
Guidos Vejar, Rafael, 'La Crisis Política en El Salvador (1976–1979)', RMS, vol. XLII, no. 1, 1980.
—— *Ascenso del Militarismo en El Salvador*, San José 1982.
Gutiérrez Espeleta, Nelson, 'Notas sobre la Evolución del Estado Costarricense, 1821–1978', ESC, no. 28, 1981.
Guzmán Böckler, Carlos, and Herbert, Jean-Loup, *Guatemala: una Interpretación Histórico-social*, Mexico 1970.
Halperin, Morton (ed.), *Report on Human Rights in El Salvador*, Washington 1982.
Handy, Jim, *Gift of the Devil. A History of Guatemala*, Toronto 1984.
Harris, Richard, and Vilas, Carlos, *Nicaragua. A Revolution under Siege*, London 1985.
Hernandez, Francisco Javier, 'Estado y Sociedad. Crisis Hegemónica y Lucha Ideológica en la Coyuntura de la Transformación Agraria en El Salvador,

1975–1976', RMS, vol. XLI, no. 1, 1979.
Hernandez C., Alcides, *El Neoliberalismo en Honduras*, Tegucigalpa 1983.
—— 'Política Económica y Pensamiento Neoliberal: el Caso de Honduras', ESC, no. 37, 1984.
Herrick, Thomas R., *Desarrollo Económico y Político de Guatemala, 1871–1885*, Guatemala 1974.
Hill, George W., 'The Agrarian Reform in Costa Rica', *Land Economics*, vol. XL, no. 1, 1964.
Hill, George W., and Gollas, Manuel, 'The Minifundia Economy and Society of the Guatemalan Highland Indian', Research Paper no. 30, Land Tenure Center, University of Wisconsin, 1968.
Hodges, Donald C., *Intellectual Origins of the Nicaraguan Revolution*, Austin 1986.
Holleran, Mary P., *Church and State in Guatemala*, New York 1949.
Hoyt, Elizabeth E., 'The Indian Laborer on Guatemalan Coffee Fincas', *Inter-American Economic Affairs*, vol. IX, no. 1, 1955.
Immerman, Richard H., 'Guatemala as Cold War History', *Political Science Quarterly*, vol. 95, no. 4, 1980–81.
—— *The CIA in Guatemala. The Foreign Policy of Intervention*, Austin 1982.
Instituto Centroamericano de Documentación e Investigación Social, *Los Hechos que Formaron la Crisis*, San José 1986.
International Bank for Reconstruction and Development (World Bank), *The Economic Development of Guatemala*, Baltimore 1951.
International Human Rights Law Group and Washington Office on Latin America, *A Political Opening in Nicaragua. Report on the Nicaraguan Elections of November 4 1984*, Washington 1984.
International Monetary Fund and World Bank, 'Confidential IMF and World Bank Reports on El Salvador and Nicaragua', ed. Richard Swedberg, Cambridge, Mass. 1982.
Irvin, George, and Gorostiaga, Xavier (eds), *Towards an Alternative for Central America and the Caribbean*, The Hague 1984.
Jarquin, Edmundo, 'Migraciones Rurales y Estructura Agraria en Nicaragua', ESC, no. 11, 1975.
Johnson, Kenneth F., 'The Guatemalan Presidential Election of March 16, 1966. An Analysis', Institute for the Comparative Study of Politics, Washington 1967.
Jonas Bodenheimer, Susanne, *La Ideología Social Demócrata en Costa Rica*, San José 1984.
Jones, Chester Lloyd, *Costa Rica and Civilization in the Caribbean*, New York 1935.
—— *Guatemala Past and Present*, Minneapolis 1940.
Jones, Clarence F., and Morrison, Paul C., 'Evolution of the Banana Industry in Costa Rica', *Economic Geography*, vol. 28, no. 1, 1952.
Jung, Harald, 'The Fall of Somoza', *New Left Review*, no. 117, 1979.
—— 'Class Struggles in El Salvador', *New Left Review*, no. 122, 1980.
Karush, Gerald E., 'Plantations, Population and Poverty: The Roots of the Demographic Crisis in El Salvador', *Studies in Comparative International Development*, vol. XIII, no. 3, 1978.
Kennedy, Paul P., *The Middle Beat: A Correspondent's View of Mexico, Guatemala and El Salvador*, New York 1971.
Keogh, Dermot, 'The Myth of the Liberal Coup: The United States and the 15 October 1979 Coup in El Salvador', *Millennium*, vol. 13, no. 2, 1984.

—— (ed.), *Central America. Human Rights and US Foreign Policy*, Cork 1985.
Kincaid, A. Douglas, 'Peasants into Rebels. Community and Class in Rural El Salvador', Paper to 28th Annual Convention of the International Studies Association, Washington 1985.
Kissinger, Henry, *The Report of the President's National Bipartisan Commission on Central America*, New York 1984.
Kornbluh, Peter, *Nicaragua. The Price of Intervention. Reagan's War against the Sandinistas*, Washington 1987.
Krehm, William, *Democracies and Tyrannies of the Caribbean*, Westport 1984.
LaBarge, Richard Allen, 'Impact of the United Fruit Company on the Economic Development of Guatemala, 1946–1954', in *Studies in Middle American Economies*, Middle American Research Institute, Tulane University, New Orleans 1968.
LaFeber, Walter, *Inevitable Revolutions. The United States in Central America*, New York 1984.
Lainez, Vilma, and Meza, Víctor, 'El Enclave Bananero en la Historia de Honduras', ESC, no. 5, 1975.
Lapper, Richard, and Painter, James, *Honduras. State for Sale*, London 1985.
Larson, Brooke, and Wasserstrom, Robert, 'Coerced Consumption in Colonial Bolivia and Guatemala', *Radical History Review*, no. 27, 1983.
Latin America Bureau, *El Salvador under General Romero*, London 1979.
Latin American Studies Association, 'Report of the LASA Delegation to Observe the Nicaraguan General Election of November 4, 1984', LASA Bulletin, February 1985.
LeBot, Ivon, 'Tenencia y Renta de la Tierra en el Altiplano Occidental de Guatemala', ESC, no. 13, 1976.
Leiken, Robert (ed.), *Central America: Anatomy of Conflict*, London 1984.
Leonard, Thomas M., *The United States and Central America, 1944–1949*, Birmingham, Alabama 1984.
Lernoux, Penny, *Cry of the People*, London 1982.
Levinson, Jerome, and de Onis, Juan, *The Alliance that Lost its Way. A Critical Report on the Alliance for Progress*, Chicago 1970.
López C., Julio et al. (eds), *La Caida del Somocismo y la Lucha Sandinista en Nicaragua*, San José 1980.
López Vallecillos, Italo, and Orellana, Víctor A., 'La Unidad Popular y el Surgimiento del Frente Democrático Revolucionario', ECA, vol. XXXV, 1980.
Lovell, W. George, 'Surviving Conquest. The Guatemalan Indian in Historical Perspective', Paper to The Institute of British Geographers, Leeds, January 1985.
Löwy, Michael (ed.), *El Marxismo en América Latina*, Mexico 1980.
Luna, David Alejandro, 'Un Heroico y Trágico Suceso de Nuestra Historia', in *El Proceso Político Centroamericano*, San Salvador 1964.
—— 'Análisis de una Dictadura Fascista Latinoamericana. Maximiliano Hernández Martinez, 1931–44', *La Universidad*, San Salvador, September–October 1969.
Macaulay, Neill, *Sandino*, Chicago 1967.
McClintock, Michael, *The American Connection. State Terror and Popular Resistance in El Salvador*, London 1985.
—— *The American Connection. State Terror and Popular Resistance in Guatemala*, London 1985.
McCreery, David, 'Coffee and Class: The Structure of Development in Liberal Guatemala', *Hispanic American Historical Review*, vol. 56, no. 3, 1976.
—— 'Debt Servitude in Rural Guatemala, 1876–1936', *Hispanic American Histor-*

ical Review, vol. 63, no. 4, 1983.
—— *Development and the State in Reforma Guatemala, 1871–1885*, Papers in International Studies, Latin American Series, no. 10, Ohio University, Athens, Ohio 1983.
McDonald, Ronald H., 'Electoral Behaviour and Political Development in El Salvador', *The Journal of Politics*, vol. 31, no. 2, 1969.
Maira Luis (ed.), 'El Impacto Social del Esquema de Desarrollo de la Franja Transversal del Norte sobre los Maya-Kekchi en Guatemala', ESC, no. 29, 1981.
Martin, Percy F., *El Salvador of the Twentieth Century*, London 1911.
Martinez Peláez, Severo, *La Patria del Criollo*, Guatemala 1973.
Martz, John D., *Central America. The Crisis and the Challenge*, Chapel Hill 1959.
—— 'Costa Rican Electoral Trends, 1953–1966', *The Western Political Quarterly*, vol. XX, no. 4, 1967.
Matheson, Kenneth H., 'History of Rosario Mine, Honduras, Central America', *The Mines Magazine*, vol. LI, nos 6 and 7, 1961.
Mecham, J. Lloyd, *Church and State in Latin America. A History of Politico–Ecclesiastical Relations*, Chapel Hill 1966.
Melville, Thomas and Marjorie, *Guatemala: The Politics of Land Ownership*, New York 1971.
Menchú, Rigoberta, *I . . . Rigoberta Menchú*, ed. Elizabeth Burgos-Debray, London 1983.
Menéndez Rodriguez, Mario, *El Salvador: Una Auténtica Guerra Civil*, San José 1980.
Menjívar, Rafael, *Crisis del Desarrollismo. Caso El Salvador*, San José 1977.
—— *Acumulación Originaria y Desarrollo del Capitalismo en El Salvador*, San José 1980.
—— *El Salvador: El Eslabón Mas Pequeño*, San José 1981.
—— *Formación y Lucha del Proletariado Industrial Salvadoreño*, San José 1982.
Meza, Víctor, *Historia del Movimiento Obrero Hondureño*, Tegucigalpa 1980.
Miceli, Keith L., 'Rafael Carrera: Defender and Promoter of Peasant Interest in Guatemala, 1837–1848', *The Americas*, vol. XXXI, no. 1, 1974.
Millett, Richard, *Guardians of the Dynasty. A History of the US-Created Guardia Nacional de Nicaragua and the Somoza Family*, Maryknoll 1977.
Molina Chocano, Guillermo, 'La Formación del Estado y el Origen Minero-mercantil de la Burguesía Hondureña', ESC, no. 25, 1980.
—— 'Estado y Proceso de Acumulación en Centroamérica', ESC, no. 37, 1984.
Monteforte Toledo, Mario, 'La Reforma Agraria en Guatemala', *El Trimestre Económico*, vol. XIX, no. 3, 1952.
—— *Guatemala. Monografía Sociológica*, Mexico 1959.
Montes, Segundo, *El Compadrazgo. Una Estructura de Poder en El Salvador*, San Salvador 1979.
Montgomery, Tommy Sue, *Revolution in El Salvador: Origins and Evolution*, Boulder 1982.
Morris, James A., *Honduras. Caudillo Politics and Military Rulers*, Boulder 1984.
Murga Frassinetti, Antonio, 'Estado y Burguesía Industrial en Honduras', RMS, vol. XXXIX, no. 2, 1977.
Naylor, Robert A., 'Guatemala: Indian Attitudes toward Land Tenure', *Journal of Inter-American Studies*, vol. IX, no. 4, 1967.
Newbold, Stokes (Richard Adams), 'Receptivity to Communist Fomented Agitation in Rural Guatemala', *Economic Development and Cultural Change*, vol. 5, no. 2, 1957.
Newson, Linda, 'Labour in the Colonial Mining Industry of Honduras', *The*

Americas, vol. XXXIX, no. 2, 1982.
Oqueli, R., 'Gobiernos Hondureños Durante el Presente Siglo', *Economía Política*, no. 8, 1984.
Organización del Pueblo en Armas, 'Vivimos para Luchar. Luchamos para Vivir', Guatemala 1979.
Ortega Saavedra, Humberto, *50 Años de Lucha Sandinista*, Mexico 1979.
Ortiz Rosales, Rolando Eliseo, 'Guatemala: Generalidades sobre el Sector Agrícola', *Comercio Exterior*, vol. 34, no. 11, 1984.
Osegueda, Raul, *Operación Centroamericana*, Santiago de Chile 1958.
Palacios, J. Antonio, 'Formas de Redistribución del Ingreso en Guatemala', *El Trimestre Económico*, vol. XIX, no. 3, 1952.
Parker, Franklin D., *The Central American Republics*, London 1964.
Parsons, James J., 'Cotton and Cattle in the Pacific Lowlands of Central America', *Journal of Inter-American Studies*, vol. VII, no. 2, 1965.
Partido Comunista de El Salvador, *Boletín Exterior*, San Salvador 1979—.
Partido Comunista de Honduras, *Trabajo*, Tegucigalpa 1975.
Partido Révolucionario Salvadoreño, *El Salvador: Une Perspective Révolutionnaire*, Algiers 1977.
Payeras, Mario, *Days of the Jungle. The Testimony of a Guatemalan Guerrillero, 1972–1976*, New York 1983.
Pearce, Jenny, *Under the Eagle. US Intervention in Central America and the Caribbean*, London 1981.
—— *Promised Land. Peasant Rebellion in Chalatenango, El Salvador*, London 1986.
Pearson, Neale J., 'Guatemala: The Peasant Union Movement, 1944–1954', in Henry A. Landsberger (ed.), *Latin American Peasant Movements*, Ithaca 1969.
—— 'Peasant Pressure Groups and Agrarian Reform in Honduras, 1962–77', in William P. Avery et al. (eds), *Rural Change and Public Policy. Eastern Europe, Latin America and Australia*, New York 1980.
Pearson, Ross, 'Land Reform. Guatemalan Style', *The American Journal of Economics and Sociology*, vol. 22, no. 2, 1963.
Peckenham, Nancy, 'Land Settlement in the Petén', *Latin American Perspectives*, vol. 7, nos 2 and 3, 1980.
Peckenham, Nancy, and Street, Annie, *Honduras. Portrait of a Captive Nation*, New York 1985.
Pérez Brignoli, Hector, 'Economía y Sociedad en Honduras durante el Siglo XIX. Las Estructuras Demográficas', ESC, no. 6, 1973.
—— 'Growth and Crisis in the Central American Economies, 1950–1980', JLAS, vol. 15, part 2, 1983.
—— 'Reckoning with the Central American Past: Economic Growth and Political Issues', Working Paper no. 160, Latin American Program, Wilson Center, Washington 1984.
Pérez Lopez, Jorge, 'Central America's External Debt in the 1970s and Prospects for the 1980s', Working Paper no. 6, Latin American and Caribbean Center, Florida International University, 1983.
Pike, Frederick B., 'Guatemala, the United States, and Communism in the Americas', *The Review of Politics*, vol. 17, no. 2, 1955.
Pineda, Empar (ed.), *La Revolucion Nicaragüense*, Madrid 1980.
Plant, Roger, *Guatemala: Unnatural Disaster*, London 1978.
Posas, Mario, *El Movimiento Obrero Hondureño (1880–1964)*, mimeo, np, nd.
—— *Lucha Ideológica y Organización Sindical en Honduras (1954–65)*, Tegucigalpa 1980.

—— *El Movimiento Campesino Hondureño*, Tegucigalpa 1981.
Posas, Mario, and del Cid, Rafael, *La Construcción del Sector Público y del Estado Nacional en Honduras, 1876–1979*, Tegucigalpa 1981.
Quirós Guardia, Rodolfo, 'Agricultural Development in Central America: Its Origins and Nature', Research Paper no. 49, Land Tenure Center, University of Wisconsin, Madison 1973.
Ramírez, Ricardo, *Lettres du front guatémaltèque*, Paris 1970.
Ramírez, Sergio, *El Alba de Oro. La Historia Viva de Nicaragua*, Mexico 1983.
Randall, Margaret, *Sandino's Daughters*, London 1982.
Resistencia Nacional, *Por la Causa Proletaria*, San José 1978.
Rey, Julio Adolfo, 'Revolution and Liberation: A Review of Recent Literature on the Guatemalan Situation', *Hispanic American Historical Review*, vol. XXXVIII, no. 2, 1958.
Rincón Gallardo, Gilberto, 'El Asesinato de Ana María', *Nexos*, no. 78, Mexico June 1984.
Rippy, J. Fred, 'Relations of the United States and Guatemala during the Epoch of Justo Rufino Barrios', *Hispanic American Historical Review*, vol. XXII, no. 4, 1942.
Rivera Urrutia, Eugenio, *El Fondo Monetario Internacional y Costa Rica, 1978–82*, San José 1982.
Robinson, William, and Norsworthy, Kent, *David and Goliath. Washington's War against Nicaragua*, London 1987.
Rojas, Aravena Francisco, 'Costa Rica, 1978–1982. Una Política Internacional Tercermundista?', *Foro Internacional*, vol. XXIV, no. 2, 1983.
Romero, Carmen María, 'Las Transformaciones Recientes del Estado Costarricense y las Políticas Reformistas', ESC, no. 38, 1984.
Ropp, Stephen C., *In Search of the New Soldier: Junior Officers and the Prospect of Social Reform in Panama, Honduras and Nicaragua*, unpublished PhD, University of California, Riverside 1971.
—— 'The Honduran Army in the Sociopolitical Evolution of the Honduran State', *The Americas*, vol. XXX, no. 4, 1974.
Rosenberg, Mark B., 'Social Reform in Costa Rica: Social Security and the Presidency of Rafael Angel Calderon', *Hispanic American Historical Review*, vol. LI, no. 2, 1981.
Rosset, Peter, and Vandermeer, John (eds), *The Nicaragua Reader. Documents of a Revolution under Fire*, New York 1983.
Roux, Bernard, 'Expansión del Capitalismo y Desarrollo del Subdesarrollo. La Integración de América Central en el Mercado Mundial de la Carne de Vacuno', ESC, no. 19, 1978.
Rovira Mas, Jorge, 'Costa Rica, Economía y Estado. Notas sobre su Evolución Reciente y el Momento Actual', ESC, no. 26, 1980.
Rowe, J.W.F., *The World's Coffee*, London 1963.
Rubio Sánchez, Manuel, *Historia del Añil o Xiquilite en Centroamérica*, 2 vols, San Salvador 1976.
Ruhl, Arthur, *The Central Americans*, New York 1927.
Ruhl, J. Mark, 'Agrarian Structure and Political Stability in Honduras', *Journal of Inter-American Studies*, vol. 26, no. 1, 1984.
Saint-Lu, André, *Condition Coloniale et Conscience Créole au Guatemala*, Paris 1970.
Samaniego, Carlos, 'Movimiento Campesino o Lucha del Proletariado Rural en El Salvador?', RMS, vol. XLII, no. 2, 1980.
Sarti Castaneda, Carlos, 'La Revolución Guatemalteca de 1944–54 y su Proyección

Actual', ESC, no. 27, 1980.
Schifter, Jacobo, *La Fase Oculta de la Guerra Civil en Costa Rica*, San José 1981.
—— *Costa Rica, 1948. Análisis de Documentos Confidenciales del Departamento del Estado*, San José 1982.
Schlesinger, Stephen, and Kinzer, Stephen, *Bitter Fruit. The Untold Story of the American Coup in Guatemala*, London 1982.
Schmid, Lester, *The Role of Migratory Labor in the Economic Development of Guatemala*, Research Paper no. 22, Land Tenure Center, University of Wisconsin, Madison 1967.
Schneider, Ronald M., *Communism in Guatemala*, New York 1958.
Schulz, Donald, and Graham, Douglas (eds), *Revolution and Counter-Revolution in Central America and the Caribbean*, Boulder 1984.
Seligson, Mitchell A., *Peasants of Costa Rica and the Development of Agrarian Capitalism*, Madison 1980.
Selser, Gregorio, *Sandino*, New York 1981.
—— *Honduras. República Alquilada*, Mexico 1983.
Sepúlveda, Cristian, 'Capitalismo Agreoxportador, Estado y Rentabilidad: el Circuito Cafetalero y Azucarero en Nicaragua', ESC, no. 38, 1984.
Sexton, James D., 'Protestantism and Modernization in Two Guatemalan Towns', *American Ethnologist*, vol. 5, no. 2, 1978.
Sholk, Richard, 'The National Bourgeoisie in Post-Revolutionary Nicaragua', Working Paper no. 123, Latin American Program, Wilson Center, Washington 1982.
Simon, Laurence R., and Stephens, James C., *El Salvador: Land Reform, 1980–1981*, Boston 1981.
Sloan, John W., 'Electoral Frauds and Social Change: The Guatemalan Example', *Science and Society*, vol. XXXIV, no. 1, 1970.
Slutzky, Daniel, *El Caso de Agroindustria de la Carne en Honduras*, Quito 1977.
Slutzky, Daniel, and Alonso, Esther, 'El Salvador: Estructura de la Explotación Cafetalera', ESC, no. 6, 1973.
—— *Empresas Transnacionales y Agricultura: El Caso del Enclave Bananero en Honduras*, Tegucigalpa 1980.
Smith, Carol A., 'Beyond Dependency Theory: National and Regional Patterns of Underdevelopment in Guatemala', *American Ethnologist*, vol. 5, no. 3, 1978.
—— 'El Desarrollo de la Primacia Urbana, la Dependencia en la Explotación y la Formación de Clases en Guatemala', *Mesoamérica*, no. 8, 1984.
—— 'Does a Commodity Economy Enrich the Few while Ruining the Masses? Differentiation among Petty Commodity Producers in Guatemala', *The Journal of Peasant Studies*, vol. 11, no. 3, 1984.
—— 'Indian Class and Class Consciousness in Pre-Revolutionary Guatemala', Working Paper no. 162, Latin American Program, Wilson Center, Washington 1984.
Smith, Robert S., 'Financing the Central American Federation, 1821–1838', *Hispanic American Historical Review*, vol. XLIII, no. 4, 1963.
Sojo, Ana, *Estado Empresario y Lucha Política en Costa Rica*, San José 1984.
Sol, Ricardo (ed.), *El Reto Democrático en Centroamérica*, San José 1983.
Solorzano, Valentín, *Evolución Económica de Guatemala*, Guatemala 1963.
Soto, M. et al., *Guatemala: Desempleo y Subempleo*, San José 1982.
Soto, William R., 'El Caracter de la Crisis Económica en Costa Rica y las Vias de Recuperación', *Revista Centroamericana de Economía*, no. 13, 1984.
Spalding, Rose (ed.), *The Political Economy of Revolutionary Nicaragua*, London 1987.

Squier, E.G., *Nicaragua; its People, Scenery, Monuments and the Proposed Interoceanic Canal*, 2 vols, New York 1852.
—— *Notes on Central America*, New York 1855.
Stansifer, Charles L., 'José Santos Zelaya: A New Look at Nicaragua's "Liberal" Dictator', *Revista Interamericana*, vol. 7, 1977.
Stanford Central American Action Network, *Revolution in Central America*, Boulder 1983.
Stephen, David, and Wearne, Phillip, 'Central America's Indians', Minority Rights Group Report no. 62, London 1984.
Stokes, William S., 'The Land Laws of Honduras', *Agricultural History*, vol. 21, no. 3, 1947.
—— *Honduras. An Area Study in Government*, Madison 1950.
Stone, Samuel, *La Dinastía de los Conquistadores. La Crisis del Poder en la Costa Rica Contemporanea*, San José 1983.
Survival International, *Witness to Genocide. The Present Situation of Indians in Guatemala*, London 1983.
Suslow, Leo A., *Aspects of Social Reform in Guatemala, 1944–1949*, New York 1950.
Torres Rivas, Edelberto, 'Interpretación del Desarrollo Social Centroamericano', CEPAL, Santiago de Chile 1968.
—— *Crisis del Poder en Centroamérica*, San José 1983.
—— 'The Beginning of Industrialization in Central America', Working Paper no. 141, Latin American Program, Wilson Center, Washington 1984.
—— 'Centroamerica: Algunos Rasgos de la Sociedad de Postguerra', Working Paper no. 25, Kellogg Institute, University of Notre Dame 1984.
—— 'Problemas de la Contrarrevolución y Democracia en Guatemala', ESC, no. 38, 1984.
—— *Centroamérica: la Democracia Posible*, San José 1987.
Trejos Paris, María Eugenia, 'Un Sector de Economía Laboral en Costa Rica?' ESC, no. 37, 1984.
Trujillo, Horacio, and Menjívar, Oscar, 'Economía y Política en la Revolución del 1948: Algunos Elementos para su Análisis', ECA, vol. XXXIII, 1978.
Union Revolucionaria Nacional Guatemalteca, 'Proclama Unitaria', Guatemala 1982.
United States of America, Department of State, 'Communist Interference in El Salvador', Washington, March 1981.
—— 'Broken Promises: Sandinista Repression of Human Rights in Nicaragua', Washington, October 1984.
—— 'Aid and U.S. Interests in Latin America and the Caribbean', Washington, March 1985.
—— 'Misconceptions about U.S. Policy toward Nicaragua', Washington, March 1985.
—— 'Sustaining a Consistent Policy in Central America: One Year after the National Bipartisan Commission Report', Washington, April 1985.
United States, Dept State and Dept Defense, 'The Soviet–Cuban Connection in Central America and the Caribbean', Washington, March 1985.
Vargas, Oscar René, 'El Desarrollo del Capitalismo en Nicaragua, 1909–1912', ESC, no. 20, 1978.
Various, *Análisis sobre el conflicto entre Honduras y El Salvador*, Tegucigalpa 1969.
—— *Centro América Hoy*, Mexico 1976.

—— 'Death and Disorder in Guatemala', *Cultural Survival Quarterly*, vol. 17, no. 1, 1983.
—— *El Salvador: Alianzas Políticas y Proceso Político*, Mexico 1968.
—— *Human Rights in Honduras*, Geneva 1984.
—— *La Inversión Extranjera en Centroamérica*, San José 1975.
—— *Listen Compañero. Conversations with Central American Revolutionary Leaders*, San Francisco 1983.
—— *Nicaragua. El Pueblo Vence a la Dinastía*, Madrid 1979.
—— *Nicaragua. The Sandinista People's Revolution. Speeches by Sandinista Leaders*, New York 1985.
—— *Panzós. Testimonio*, Guatemala 1979.
—— *Plataforma Programática del Gobierno Democrático Revolucionario*, San Salvador 1980.
Vega Carballo, José Luis, 'El Nacimiento de un Régimen de Burguesía Dependiente: el Caso de Costa Rica', ESC, no. 6, 1973.
Vilas, Carlos M., 'El Sujeto Social de la Insurrección Popular: la Revolución Sandinista', *Latin American Research Review*, vol. XX, no. 1, 1985.
—— *The Sandinista Revolution. National Liberation and Social Transformation in Central America*, New York 1986.
Walker, Thomas W. (ed.), *Nicaragua in Revolution*, New York 1982.
—— *Nicaragua. The First Five Years*, New York 1985.
Washington Office on Latin America, 'El Salvador. Death Squads as a Political Tool', Washington, February 1984.
Wasserstrom, Robert, 'Revolution in Guatemala: Peasants and Politics under the Arbenz Government', *Comparative Studies in Society and History*, vol. 17, no. 4, 1975.
Weaver, Jerry L., 'Political Style of the Guatemalan Military Elite', in K. Fidel (ed.), *Militarism in Developing Countries*, New Brunswick 1975.
Weber, Henri, *Nicaragua. The Sandinist Revolution*, London 1981.
Webre, Stephan, *José Napoleón Duarte and the Christian Democratic Party in Salvadoran Politics, 1960–1978*, Baton Rouge 1979.
Weeks, John, *The Economies of Central America*, New York 1985.
Wells, Henry, 'The 1970 Election in Costa Rica', *World Affairs*, vol. 133, no. 1, 1970.
Wetzel, Tom, 'Nicaragua: Say Hello to the New Bosses', *No Middle Ground*, New York 1983.
Wheelock, Jaime, *Raices Indígenas de la Lucha Anticolonialista en Nicaragua*, Mexico 1974.
—— *Imperialismo y Dictadura. Crisis de una Formación Social*, Mexico 1975.
Whetten, Nathan L., 'Land Reform in a Modern World', *Rural Sociology*, vol. 19, no. 4, 1954.
—— *Guatemala: the Land and the People*, New York 1961.
White, Alastair, *El Salvador*, London 1973.
—— 'Squatter Settlements, Politics and Class Conflict', Occasional Paper no. 17, Institute of Latin American Studies, University of Glasgow, 1976.
Whitehead, Laurence, 'Explaining Washington's Central American Policies', JLAS, vol. 15, part 2, 1983.
Williams, Robert G., *Export Agriculture and the Crisis in Central America*, Chapel Hill 1986.
Williford, Miriam, *Jeremy Bentham on Spanish America*, Baton Rouge 1980.
Wilson, Everett Alan, *The Crisis of National Integration in El Salvador, 1919–1935*, unpublished PhD, Stanford University, 1970.

Winson, Anthony, 'Class Structure and Agrarian Transition in Central America', *Latin American Perspectives*, vol. V, no. 4, 1978.
Woodward, Ralph Lee, 'Guatemalan Cotton and the American Civil War', *Inter-American Economic Affairs*, vol. XVIII, no. 3, 1964.
—— *Central America: A Nation Divided*, New York 1976.
—— *Privilegio de Clase y Desarrollo Económico. Guatemala 1793–1871*, San José 1981.
—— 'The Rise and Decline of Liberalism in Central America: Historical Perspectives on the Contemporary Crisis', *Journal of Inter-American Studies*, vol. 26, no. 3, 1984.
Wortman, Miles L., *Government and Society in Central America, 1680–1840*, New York 1982.
Yochelson, John, 'What Price Political Stability? The 1966 Presidential Campaign in Costa Rica', *Public and International Affairs*, vol. V, no. 1, 1967.
Zelaya, Chester (ed.), *Democracia en Costa Rica?*, San José 1983.

Index

NOTE: **Bold** numbers refer to illustrations and tables. Numbers with *n* refer to footnotes.